THE PROGRAMMER'S PC SOURCEBOOK

THE PROGRAMMER'S PC SOURCEBOOK

Reference Tables for

IBM® PCs and Compatibles
PS/2® Systems
EISA-based Systems
MS-DOS® Operating System Through Version 5
Microsoft Windows™ Through Version 3

Hundreds of New Charts and Tables!

Thom Hogan

Microsoft PRESS®

SECOND EDITION

PUBLISHED BY
Microsoft Press
A Division of Microsoft Corporation
One Microsoft Way, Redmond, Washington 98052-6399

Library of Congress Cataloging-in-Publication Data
Hogan, Thom, 1952-
The programmer's PC sourcebook / Thom Hogan. -- 2nd ed.
p. cm.
Includes bibliographical references and index.
ISBN 1-55615-321-X
1. IBM microcomputers--Programming. 2. MS-DOS (Computer operating system) 3. IBM Personal System/2 (Computer system) I. Title.
II. Title: Programmer's PC source book.
QA76.8.I1015H64 1991
005.4'469--dc20 91-11237
CIP

Printed and bound in the United States of America.

1 2 3 4 5 6 7 8 9 MLML 6 5 4 3 2 1

Distributed to the book trade in Canada by Macmillan of Canada, a division of Canada Publishing Corporation.

Distributed to the book trade outside the United States and Canada by Penguin Books Ltd.

Penguin Books Ltd., Harmondsworth, Middlesex, England
Penguin Books Australia Ltd., Ringwood, Victoria, Australia
Penguin Books N.Z. Ltd., 182-190 Wairau Road, Auckland 10, New Zealand

British Cataloging-in-Publication Data available.

Acquisitions Editor: Marjorie Schlaikjer
Project Editor: Casey D. Doyle
Technical Editor: Laurie Leber
Production: Online Press Inc.

Contents

PART II: Software

SECTION 2: DOS Commands, Utilities, and Summaries 2-1

Device Driver Functions, Structures, and Supporting Tables

INT 14H — Serial Services

INT 15H — Cassette Services/Miscellaneous Extended Services

INT 16H — Keyboard Services

Extended Memory Functions

VCPI (Virtual Control Program Interface) Functions

Task Switcher API Patch

SECTION 6: Microsoft Windows 6-1

Input Devices

Files

Introduction

The Programmer's PC Sourcebook is a collection of basic hardware and software information about personal computers (PCs). Why is this book necessary and in what ways will you find it useful?

- Suppose you need to pinpoint differences between IBM DOS 3.3 and MS-DOS 5.0. Normally you'd have to consult at least two references to make the comparison. With *The Programmer's PC Sourcebook*, you'll find the information you need in one place.
- Suppose you're tracing execution of a program on a single-step debugger, and your program hits a questionable call to a BIOS video function. You want to know what's going into the 6845 (video controller) chip's registers, what the BIOS function does, and what data the function requires. Again, the answer to all your questions is in this book.

Whatever you need to know about a PC—card sizes, cable connections, ROM BIOS routines, internal registers, DOS functions, and so on—you'll find the basic information here, with pointers to the pages in source references where you can check the finer details if you need to.

What's New in This Edition

The second edition of *The Programmer's PC Sourcebook* includes the latest developments in PC hardware and software. It is nearly 50 percent larger than the first edition, and it draws from a wider variety of sources. New material includes:

MS-DOS 5.0
MS Windows 3.0
CD-ROM Extensions
MS Mouse Driver 8.0 (including the BallPoint Mouse)
LIM 4.0 and new EMS abilities
EISA
Hayes Modem
VCPI
PS/2 Models 80, 90, and 95
80386, 80387, and Weitek 3167
i486 and Weitek 4167

Just like the first edition of *The Programmer's PC Sourcebook*, this edition:

- Acts as a primary source for most information contained in the IBM, Microsoft, and related technical references.
- Provides pointers to further information and to items too detailed for complete inclusion here.
- Organizes the information about personal computers in logical groups and presents the information in consistent ways.

Primary Source of IBM and Microsoft Information

Information in IBM, Microsoft, and other technical references often is spread over several volumes. The IBM personal-computer family has evolved in both hardware and software. Thus, you can find information about a particular BIOS function in as many as four or five places in the IBM references: the XT reference, the AT reference, the PS/2 references, the Options and Adapters reference, and the BIOS reference. And you can find information about similar functions for related products created by independent developers for compatible computers in additional references.

This book distills the important information from these technical and user references. As a result, when you look at a single BIOS-related table in this book, you see information that might have come from eight or nine different manuals. That is why this book is a "primary" source of information—it's the first source you should consult.

Pointers to Further Information

The information in this book always points to the original source data, and the book is fully cross-indexed so that every table also points to related tables elsewhere in the book. These pointers to related information come in the form of *Source* and *See Also* notes at the bottom of each table.

- The *Source* note gives the name and page number(s) of the primary source used in compiling the table.
- The *See Also* note gives the numbers and names of other tables in this book that contain related information you might want to consult.

Every effort has been made to ensure that the page numbers referenced in the *Source* notes are accurate. Technical documentation is updated from time to time, however, and therefore a little "page creep" may find its way into *The Programmer's PC Sourcebook*. Sometimes, developers retain page numbering in new editions (adding a page 1.1 and 1.2 between the original pages 1 and 2, for example); other times, they simply renumber an entire section when they make an update. Thus, the page numbers referenced here are exact if you are using the same edition of the primary source. If you are using a different edition, you'll find yourself in the correct section of the primary source.

Organization

To help you find information easily, as well as to help you see relationships among tables, this book is organized into three main parts:

- Part I includes miscellaneous general information.
- Part II includes software.
- Part III includes hardware.

Each part is further divided into one or more numbered sections, as you can see in the following abbreviated table of contents:

Part I: Miscellaneous Information

Section 1: General Information

Part II: Software

Section 2: DOS Commands, Utilities, and Summaries

Section 3: DOS Function Calls and Support Tables

Section 4: BIOS and DOS Extension Calls and Support Tables

Section 5: Other Interrupts, CD-ROM, Mouse, and EMS Support

Section 6: Microsoft Windows

Part III: General PC Hardware

Section 7: Motherboards, Keyboards, Video Adapters, Peripherals, and Chips

Section 8: Connectors, Buses, and Pinouts

Within each section, all tables are numbered consecutively, and these numbers are used in the *See Also* cross-references.

A word about the overall structure of this book: Programming for the BIOS and for hardware interrupts falls into the software part of the book because you're likely to encounter them while developing software. Physical items such as pins, switches, and registers are found in the hardware part of the book. The organization is based on decisions about ways you are likely to use the information, rather than upon strict hardware/software distinctions.

How Tables Are Presented

Here is a representative sample of a table:

As you can see, at the top of the table is its number and name in boldfaced type. They help you identify the table contents, with the number also serving as the cross-reference used elsewhere in the book.

If a table has been broken into subtables because of differences in implementation (as between the PC-AT and the PS/2), a subtable heading appears in bold italics immediately above each subtable.

Headings down the left side and across the top of a table are in italics to distinguish them from the information within the table. Where headings are grouped (bit numbers, for example, which are usually in groups of eight), a group header appears in bold italics immediately above the group.

Where groups of entries are related, the group appears in a single box with each item on a separate line within the box. Within entries, several abbreviations are consistently used:

MSB	most significant bit or byte
LSB	least significant bit or byte
LO	low order
HO	high order
000	a binary value of zero, zero, zero
010	a binary value of zero, one, zero
0X1	a binary value of zero, don't care, one
1A (26)	the first value is hexadecimal; the parentheses contain the decimal equivalent
string	any group of text characters enclosed in quotes
char	character (a single byte of information)
int	integer number or interrupt
word	two bytes
dbl word	double word (four bytes)

3.010. INT 21H MEMORY MANAGEMENT FUNCTIONS SUMMARY

Function	*Subfunction*	*Function Name*	*Use*
48H		Allocate Memory	Allocates requested amount of memory and returns address of memory block
49H		Free Allocated Memory	Frees memory previously allocated
4AH		Set Memory Block Size	Changes size of memory segment or amount of memory allocated
58H	00H	Get Allocation Strategy	Returns DOS memory allocation method
58H	01H	Set Allocation Strategy	Sets DOS memory allocation method
58H	02H	Get Upper-Memory Link	Specifies whether programs can allocate upper memory
58H	03H	Set Upper-Memory Link	Links or unlinks upper-memory area

Source: Microsoft MS-DOS 5.0 Programmer's Reference, page 206

See Also:
3.121. INT 21H, AH=48H -- Allocate Memory
3.122. INT 21H, AH=49H -- Free Allocated Memory
3.123. INT 21H, AH=4AH -- Set Memory Size Block
3.138. INT 21H, AH=58H, AL=00H -- Get Allocation Strategy
3.139. INT 21H, AH=58H, AL=01H -- Set Allocation Strategy
3.140. INT 21H, AH=58H, AL=02H -- Get Upper-Memory Link
3.141. INT 21H, AH=58H, AL=03H -- Set Upper-Memory Link

R	reserved
O	obsolete
Basic	Basic programming language

A special form of table, like the one shown below, is used for any function or interrupt call that uses registers to pass information.

In such cases, the table shows exact register use. If a register is not used by a function or call, it is blank, and you can assume that it is left unchanged by the function. Destroyed registers are explicitly identified in the tables. Presenting the register use as a consistently formatted table helps you visualize exactly how the function or call uses the registers.

Below each table is a collection of miscellaneous information that can include:

- Footnotes, which give specific information about individual entries in the table.
- *Legend,* which is a key to codes used in some tables.
- *Version,* which tells you about differences in versions or between products.
- *Note,* which gives general information about or exceptions to entries in the table.
- *Source,* which identifies the primary sources of the data in the table.
- *SeeAlso,* which refers you to related tables elsewhere in the book.

The Impact of Evolving Software and Hardware

PC software, and to a lesser extent, hardware, is constantly evolving. To reflect changes that have occurred since publication of the first edition of *The Programmer's PC Sourcebook,* sections have been updated to reflect new software versions. This updating affects Section 3, in particular, where function names have been changed to reflect MS-DOS 5.0 and tables have been organized around MS-DOS 5.0 structures. To the extent possible, however, historical information has been retained throughout this book and equivalent features of earlier software versions have been identified.

3.066. INT 21H, AH=33H, AL=06H -- GET MS-DOS VERSION

Register	Prior to Calling Function: High	Prior to Calling Function: Low	Upon Return from Function: High	Upon Return from Function: Low
AX	33H	06H		
BX			Minor version	Major version
CX				
DX			Version flags§	Revision number†
SP				
BP				
SI				
DI				
IP				
flags				
CS				
DS				
SS				
ES				

†Low three bits only
§08H=DOSINROM, 10H=DOSINHMA.

Version: Applies to all versions of DOS beginning with 5.0

Source: Microsoft MS-DOS 5.0 Programmer's Reference, page 268

See Also: 3.060. INT 21H, AH=30H -- Get Version Number

Section 1

General Information

1.01. HEXADECIMAL TO DECIMAL NUMBER CONVERSION

Byte Values

Most-Significant Digit	Least-Significant Digit 0	1	2	3	4	5	6	7	8	9	A	B	C	D	E	F
0	0	1	2	3	4	5	6	7	8	9	10	11	12	13	14	15
1	16	17	18	19	20	21	22	23	24	25	26	27	28	29	30	31
2	32	33	34	35	36	37	38	39	40	41	42	43	44	45	46	47
3	48	49	50	51	52	53	54	55	56	57	58	59	60	61	62	63
4	64	65	66	67	68	69	70	71	72	73	74	75	76	77	78	79
5	80	81	82	83	84	85	86	87	88	89	90	91	92	93	94	95
6	96	97	98	99	100	101	102	103	104	105	106	107	108	109	110	111
7	112	113	114	115	116	117	118	119	120	121	122	123	124	125	126	127
8	128	129	130	131	132	133	134	135	136	137	138	139	140	141	142	143
9	144	145	146	147	148	149	150	151	152	153	154	155	156	157	158	159
A	160	161	162	163	164	165	166	167	168	169	170	171	172	173	174	175
B	176	177	178	179	180	181	182	183	184	185	186	187	188	189	190	191
C	192	193	194	195	196	197	198	199	200	201	202	203	204	205	206	207
D	208	209	210	211	212	213	214	215	216	217	218	219	220	221	222	223
E	224	225	226	227	228	229	230	231	232	233	234	235	236	237	238	239
F	240	241	242	243	244	245	246	247	248	249	250	251	252	253	254	255

To Use This Table: To convert a one-byte (two-digit) hexadecimal value to decimal, locate the most-significant hex digit in the left-most column. Follow that row across to the right until it intersects with the column that has the least-significant hex digit in its top cell. The value at the intersection is the decimal equivalent of the hex byte. For example, to convert A4 hex to decimal, find the intersection of the row containing A in its leftmost cell with the column containing 4 in its top cell. The decimal value of A4 hex is 164.

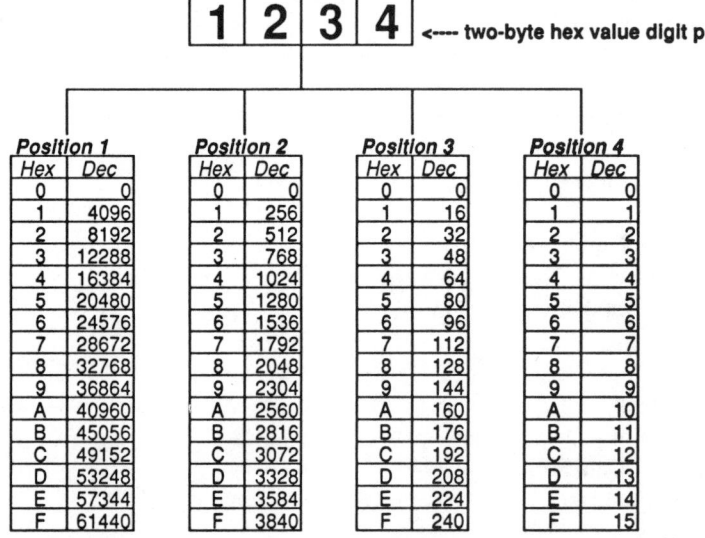

1	2	3	4	<---- two-byte hex value digit positions

Position 1		*Position 2*		*Position 3*		*Position 4*	
Hex	*Dec*	*Hex*	*Dec*	*Hex*	*Dec*	*Hex*	*Dec*
0	0	0	0	0	0	0	0
1	4096	1	256	1	16	1	1
2	8192	2	512	2	32	2	2
3	12288	3	768	3	48	3	3
4	16384	4	1024	4	64	4	4
5	20480	5	1280	5	80	5	5
6	24576	6	1536	6	96	6	6
7	28672	7	1792	7	112	7	7
8	32768	8	2048	8	128	8	8
9	36864	9	2304	9	144	9	9
A	40960	A	2560	A	160	A	10
B	45056	B	2816	B	176	B	11
C	49152	C	3072	C	192	C	12
D	53248	D	3328	D	208	D	13
E	57344	E	3584	E	224	E	14
F	61440	F	3840	F	240	F	15

To Use These Tables: To convert a two-byte (word) hexadecimal value to decimal, find the value associated with each hex digit place in the above table and add the numbers together. For example, the hex value A5D7 would be equal to 40960 (the A value) plus 1280 (the 5 value) plus 208 (the D value) plus 7, or 42455.

See Also:

1.06. Binary Number Conversions
1.09. Octal to Hexadecimal Number Conversion
1.12. Decimal to Hexadecimal Number Conversion

1.02. HEXADECIMAL TO BINARY NUMBER CONVERSION

Nibble Value

Hex	*Binary*	*Hex*	*Binary*
0	0000	8	1000
1	0001	9	1001
2	0010	A	1010
3	0011	B	1011
4	0100	C	1100
5	0101	D	1101
6	0110	E	1110
7	0111	F	1111

To Use This Table: To convert a long hexadecimal value to binary, simply use the table above to substitute for each hexadecimal digit. For example, a hexadecimal value of 9AF2 is 1001 1010 1111 0010 in binary.

See Also:

1.06. Binary Number Conversions
1.10. Octal to Binary Number Conversion
1.11. Decimal to Binary Number Conversion

1.03. HEXADECIMAL TO OCTAL NUMBER CONVERSION

Byte Values

Hex	*Octal*	*Hex*	*Octal*	*Hex*	*Octal*	*Hex*	*Octal*	*Hex*	*Octal*	*Hex*	*Octal*	*Hex*	*Octal*	*Hex*	*Octal*
00	000	20	040	40	100	60	140	80	200	A0	240	C0	300	E0	340
01	001	21	041	41	101	61	141	81	201	A1	241	C1	301	E1	341
02	002	22	042	42	102	62	142	82	202	A2	242	C2	302	E2	342
03	003	23	043	43	103	63	143	83	203	A3	243	C3	303	E3	343
04	004	24	044	44	104	64	144	84	204	A4	244	C4	304	E4	344
05	005	25	045	45	105	65	145	85	205	A5	245	C5	305	E5	345
06	006	26	046	46	106	66	146	86	206	A6	246	C6	306	E6	346
07	007	27	047	47	107	67	147	87	207	A7	247	C7	307	E7	347
08	010	28	050	48	110	68	150	88	210	A8	250	C8	310	E8	350
09	011	29	051	49	111	69	151	89	211	A9	251	C9	311	E9	351
0A	012	2A	052	4A	112	6A	152	8A	212	AA	252	CA	312	EA	352
0B	013	2B	053	4B	113	6B	153	8B	213	AB	253	CB	313	EB	353
0C	014	2C	054	4C	114	6C	154	8C	214	AC	254	CC	314	EC	354
0D	015	2D	055	4D	115	6D	155	8D	215	AD	255	CD	315	ED	355
0E	016	2E	056	4E	116	6E	156	8E	216	AE	256	CE	316	EE	356
0F	017	2F	057	4F	117	6F	157	8F	217	AF	257	CF	317	EF	357
10	020	30	060	50	120	70	160	90	220	B0	260	D0	320	F0	360
11	021	31	061	51	121	71	161	91	221	B1	261	D1	321	F1	361
12	022	32	062	52	122	72	162	92	222	B2	262	D2	322	F2	362
13	023	33	063	53	123	73	163	93	223	B3	263	D3	323	F3	363
14	024	34	064	54	124	74	164	94	224	B4	264	D4	324	F4	364
15	025	35	065	55	125	75	165	95	225	B5	265	D5	325	F5	365
16	026	36	066	56	126	76	166	96	226	B6	266	D6	326	F6	366
17	027	37	067	57	127	77	167	97	227	B7	267	D7	327	F7	367
18	030	38	070	58	130	78	170	98	230	B8	270	D8	330	F8	370
19	031	39	071	59	131	79	171	99	231	B9	271	D9	331	F9	371
1A	032	3A	072	5A	132	7A	172	9A	232	BA	272	DA	332	FA	372
1B	033	3B	073	5B	133	7B	173	9B	233	BB	273	DB	333	FB	373
1C	034	3C	074	5C	134	7C	174	9C	234	BC	274	DC	334	FC	374
1D	035	3D	075	5D	135	7D	175	9D	235	BD	275	DD	335	FD	375
1E	036	3E	076	5E	136	7E	176	9E	236	BE	276	DE	336	FE	376
1F	037	3F	077	5F	137	7F	177	9F	237	BF	277	DF	337	FF	377

To Use This Table: To convert a hexadecimal byte value to octal, find the value in one of the left columns and read the corresponding octal value in the column to the right. For example, a hexadecimal value of 84 results in an octal value of 204.

See Also:

1.08. Octal to Decimal Number Conversion
1.09. Octal to Hexadecimal Number Conversion
1.10. Octal to Binary Number Conversion
1.13. Decimal to Octal Number Conversion

1.04. HEXADECIMAL ADDITION TABLES

Results In Hexadecimal

	0	*1*	*2*	*3*	*4*	*5*	*6*	*7*	*8*	*9*	*A*	*B*	*C*	*D*	*E*	*F*
0	0	1	2	3	4	5	6	7	8	9	A	B	C	D	E	F
1	1	2	3	4	5	6	7	8	9	A	B	C	D	E	F	10
2	2	3	4	5	6	7	8	9	A	B	C	D	E	F	10	11
3	3	4	5	6	7	8	9	A	B	C	D	E	F	10	11	12
4	4	5	6	7	8	9	A	B	C	D	E	F	10	11	12	13
5	5	6	7	8	9	A	B	C	D	E	F	10	11	12	13	14
6	6	7	8	9	A	B	C	D	E	F	10	11	12	13	14	15
7	7	8	9	A	B	C	D	E	F	10	11	12	13	14	15	16
8	8	9	A	B	C	D	E	F	10	11	12	13	14	15	16	17
9	9	A	B	C	D	E	F	10	11	12	13	14	15	16	17	18
A	A	B	C	D	E	F	10	11	12	13	14	15	16	17	18	19
B	B	C	D	E	F	10	11	12	13	14	15	16	17	18	19	1A
C	C	D	E	F	10	11	12	13	14	15	16	17	18	19	1A	1B
D	D	E	F	10	11	12	13	14	15	16	17	18	19	1A	1B	1C
E	E	F	10	11	12	13	14	15	16	17	18	19	1A	1B	1C	1D
F	F	10	11	12	13	14	15	16	17	18	19	1A	1B	1C	1D	1E

Results In Decimal

	0	*1*	*2*	*3*	*4*	*5*	*6*	*7*	*8*	*9*	*A*	*B*	*C*	*D*	*E*	*F*
0	0	1	2	3	4	5	6	7	8	9	10	11	12	13	14	15
1	1	2	3	4	5	6	7	8	9	10	11	12	13	14	15	16
2	2	3	4	5	6	7	8	9	10	11	12	13	14	15	16	17
3	3	4	5	6	7	8	9	10	11	12	13	14	15	16	17	18
4	4	5	6	7	8	9	10	11	12	13	14	15	16	17	18	19
5	5	6	7	8	9	10	11	12	13	14	15	16	17	18	19	20
6	6	7	8	9	10	11	12	13	14	15	16	17	18	19	20	21
7	7	8	9	10	11	12	13	14	15	16	17	18	19	20	21	22
8	8	9	10	11	12	13	14	15	16	17	18	19	20	21	22	23
9	9	10	11	12	13	14	15	16	17	18	19	20	21	22	23	24
A	10	11	12	13	14	15	16	17	18	19	20	21	22	23	24	25
B	11	12	13	14	15	16	17	18	19	20	21	22	23	24	25	26
C	12	13	14	15	16	17	18	19	20	21	22	23	24	25	26	27
D	13	14	15	16	17	18	19	20	21	22	23	24	25	26	27	28
E	14	15	16	17	18	19	20	21	22	23	24	25	26	27	28	29
F	15	16	17	18	19	20	21	22	23	24	25	26	27	28	29	30

To Use These Tables:

To add two hexadecimal nibbles (single digits), locate one of the digits in the leftmost column. Follow its row across to the right until you reach the column containing the other digit in its top cell. The value at the intersection is the sum of the two digits. The top table gives the sum in hexadecimal, the bottom table gives the same number in decimal. For example, the sum of A and 6 hex is 10 hex and 16 decimal.

(Continued)

1.04. Hexadecimal Addition Tables (continued)

Results in Hexadecimal

	10	*20*	*30*	*40*	*50*	*60*	*70*	*80*	*90*	*A0*	*B0*	*C0*	*D0*	*E0*	*F0*
10	20	30	40	50	60	70	80	90	A0	B0	C0	D0	E0	F0	100
20	30	40	50	60	70	80	90	A0	B0	C0	D0	E0	F0	100	110
30	40	50	60	70	80	90	A0	B0	C0	D0	E0	F0	100	110	120
40	50	60	70	80	90	A0	B0	C0	D0	E0	F0	100	110	120	130
50	60	70	80	90	A0	B0	C0	D0	E0	F0	100	110	120	130	140
60	70	80	90	A0	B0	C0	D0	E0	F0	100	110	120	130	140	150
70	80	90	A0	B0	C0	D0	E0	F0	100	110	120	130	140	150	160
80	90	A0	B0	C0	D0	E0	F0	100	110	120	130	140	150	160	170
90	A0	B0	C0	D0	E0	F0	100	110	120	130	140	150	160	170	180
A0	B0	C0	D0	E0	F0	100	110	120	130	140	150	160	170	180	190
B0	C0	D0	E0	F0	100	110	120	130	140	150	160	170	180	190	1A0
C0	D0	E0	F0	100	110	120	130	140	150	160	170	180	190	1A0	1B0
D0	E0	F0	100	110	120	130	140	150	160	170	180	190	1A0	1B0	1C0
E0	F0	100	110	120	130	140	150	160	170	180	190	1A0	1B0	1C0	1D0
F0	100	110	120	130	140	150	160	170	180	190	1A0	1B0	1C0	1D0	1E0

Results in Decimal

	10	*20*	*30*	*40*	*50*	*60*	*70*	*80*	*90*	*A0*	*B0*	*C0*	*D0*	*E0*	*F0*
10	32	48	64	80	96	112	128	144	160	176	192	208	224	240	256
20	48	64	80	96	112	128	144	160	176	192	208	224	240	256	272
30	64	80	96	112	128	144	160	176	192	208	224	240	256	272	288
40	80	96	112	128	144	160	176	192	208	224	240	256	272	288	304
50	96	112	128	144	160	176	192	208	224	240	256	272	288	304	320
60	112	128	144	160	176	192	208	224	240	256	272	288	304	320	336
70	128	144	160	176	192	208	224	240	256	272	288	304	320	336	352
80	144	160	176	192	208	224	240	256	272	288	304	320	336	352	368
90	160	176	192	208	224	240	256	272	288	304	320	336	352	368	384
A0	176	192	208	224	240	256	272	288	304	320	336	352	368	384	400
B0	192	208	224	240	256	272	288	304	320	336	352	368	384	400	416
C0	208	224	240	256	272	288	304	320	336	352	368	384	400	416	432
D0	224	240	256	272	288	304	320	336	352	368	384	400	416	432	448
E0	240	256	272	288	304	320	336	352	368	384	400	416	432	448	464
F0	256	272	288	304	320	336	352	368	384	400	416	432	448	464	480

To Use These Tables:

To add two hexadecimal bytes (double digits), locate the first number of one of the digits in the leftmost column. Follow its row across to the right until you reach the column containing the first number of the other digit in its top cell. The value at the intersection is the sum of the first two digits. The top table gives the sum in hexadecimal, the bottom table gives the same number in decimal. For example, the sum of A0 and 60 hex is 100 hex and 256 decimal. If you are adding hexadecimal bytes that don't end in 0 (e.g., B4 + A6), first look up the result for the least-significant digits (4 + 6 = A hex), then add this value to the result for the most-significant digits (B0 + A0 = 150 hex, so B4 + A6 = 150 + A hex, or 15A). Remember to carry if necessary (B + B = 16, so BB + AB = 166).

See Also:

1.05. Hexadecimal Multiplication Tables

1.05. HEXADECIMAL MULTIPLICATION TABLES

Results In Hexadecimal

	0	*1*	*2*	*3*	*4*	*5*	*6*	*7*	*8*	*9*	*A*	*B*	*C*	*D*	*E*	*F*
0	0	0	0	0	0	0	0	0	0	0	0	0	0	0	0	0
1	0	1	2	3	4	5	6	7	8	9	A	B	C	D	E	F
2	0	2	4	6	8	A	C	E	10	12	14	16	18	1A	1C	1E
3	0	3	6	9	C	F	12	15	18	1B	1E	21	24	27	2A	2D
4	0	4	8	C	10	14	18	1C	20	24	28	2C	30	34	38	3C
5	0	5	A	F	14	19	1E	23	28	2D	32	37	3C	41	46	4B
6	0	6	C	12	18	1E	24	2A	30	36	3C	42	48	4E	54	5A
7	0	7	E	15	1C	23	2A	31	38	3F	46	4D	54	5B	62	69
8	0	8	10	18	20	28	30	38	40	48	50	58	60	68	70	78
9	0	9	12	1B	24	2D	36	3F	48	51	5A	63	6C	75	7E	87
A	0	A	14	1E	28	32	3C	46	50	5A	64	6E	78	82	8C	96
B	0	B	16	21	2C	37	42	4D	58	63	6E	79	84	8F	9A	A5
C	0	C	18	24	30	3C	48	54	60	6C	78	84	90	9C	A8	B4
D	0	D	1A	27	34	41	4E	5B	68	75	82	8F	9C	A9	B6	C3
E	0	E	1C	2A	38	46	54	62	70	7E	8C	9A	A8	B6	C4	D2
F	0	F	1E	2D	3C	4B	5A	69	78	87	96	A5	B4	C3	D2	E1

Results In Decimal

	0	*1*	*2*	*3*	*4*	*5*	*6*	*7*	*8*	*9*	*A*	*B*	*C*	*D*	*E*	*F*
0	0	0	0	0	0	0	0	0	0	0	0	0	0	0	0	0
1	0	1	2	3	4	5	6	7	8	9	10	11	12	13	14	15
2	0	2	4	6	8	10	12	14	16	18	20	22	24	26	28	30
3	0	3	6	9	12	15	18	21	24	27	30	33	36	39	42	45
4	0	4	8	12	16	20	24	28	32	36	40	44	48	52	56	60
5	0	5	10	15	20	25	30	35	40	45	50	55	60	65	70	75
6	0	6	12	18	24	30	36	42	48	54	60	66	72	78	84	90
7	0	7	14	21	28	35	42	49	56	63	70	77	84	91	98	105
8	0	8	16	24	32	40	48	56	64	72	80	88	96	104	112	120
9	0	9	18	27	36	45	54	63	72	81	90	99	108	117	126	135
A	0	10	20	30	40	50	60	70	80	90	100	110	120	130	140	150
B	0	11	22	33	44	55	66	77	88	99	110	121	132	143	154	165
C	0	12	24	36	48	60	72	84	96	108	120	132	144	156	168	180
D	0	13	26	39	52	65	78	91	104	117	130	143	156	169	182	195
E	0	14	28	42	56	70	84	98	112	126	140	154	168	182	196	210
F	0	15	30	45	60	75	90	105	120	135	150	165	180	195	210	225

To Use These Tables: To multiply two hexadecimal nibbles (single digits), locate one of the digits in the leftmost column. Follow its row across to the right until you reach the column containing the other digit in its top cell. The value at the intersection is the product of the two digits. The top table gives the product in hexadecimal, the bottom table gives the same number in decimal. For example, the product of A and 6 hex is 3C hex and 60 decimal.

See Also: 1.04. Hexadecimal Addition Tables

1.06. BINARY NUMBER CONVERSIONS

Binary	*Dec*	*Hex*	*Octal*	*Binary*	*Dec*	*Hex*	*Octal*	*Binary*	*Dec*	*Hex*	*Octal*	*Binary*	*Dec*	*Hex*	*Octal*
0000 0000	0	00	000	0100 0000	64	40	100	1000 0000	128	80	200	1100 0000	192	C0	300
0000 0001	1	01	001	0100 0001	65	41	101	1000 0001	129	81	201	1100 0001	193	C1	301
0000 0010	2	02	002	0100 0010	66	42	102	1000 0010	130	82	202	1100 0010	194	C2	302
0000 0011	3	03	003	0100 0011	67	43	103	1000 0011	131	83	203	1100 0011	195	C3	303
0000 0100	4	04	004	0100 0100	68	44	104	1000 0100	132	84	204	1100 0100	196	C4	304
0000 0101	5	05	005	0100 0101	69	45	105	1000 0101	133	85	205	1100 0101	197	C5	305
0000 0110	6	06	006	0100 0110	70	46	106	1000 0110	134	86	206	1100 0110	198	C6	306
0000 0111	7	07	007	0100 0111	71	47	107	1000 0111	135	87	207	1100 0111	199	C7	307
0000 1000	8	08	010	0100 1000	72	48	110	1000 1000	136	88	210	1100 1000	200	C8	310
0000 1001	9	09	011	0100 1001	73	49	111	1000 1001	137	89	211	1100 1001	201	C9	311
0000 1010	10	0A	012	0100 1010	74	4A	112	1000 1010	138	8A	212	1100 1010	202	CA	312
0000 1011	11	0B	013	0100 1011	75	4B	113	1000 1011	139	8B	213	1100 1011	203	CB	313
0000 1100	12	0C	014	0100 1100	76	4C	114	1000 1100	140	8C	214	1100 1100	204	CC	314
0000 1101	13	0D	015	0100 1101	77	4D	115	1000 1101	141	8D	215	1100 1101	205	CD	315
0000 1110	14	0E	016	0100 1110	78	4E	116	1000 1110	142	8E	216	1100 1110	206	CE	316
0000 1111	15	0F	017	0100 1111	79	4F	117	1000 1111	143	8F	217	1100 1111	207	CF	317
0001 0000	16	10	020	0101 0000	80	50	120	1001 0000	144	90	220	1101 0000	208	D0	320
0001 0001	17	11	021	0101 0001	81	51	121	1001 0001	145	91	221	1101 0001	209	D1	321
0001 0010	18	12	022	0101 0010	82	52	122	1001 0010	146	92	222	1101 0010	210	D2	322
0001 0011	19	13	023	0101 0011	83	53	123	1001 0011	147	93	223	1101 0011	211	D3	323
0001 0100	20	14	024	0101 0100	84	54	124	1001 0100	148	94	224	1101 0100	212	D4	324
0001 0101	21	15	025	0101 0101	85	55	125	1001 0101	149	95	225	1101 0101	213	D5	325
0001 0110	22	16	026	0101 0110	86	56	126	1001 0110	150	96	226	1101 0110	214	D6	326
0001 0111	23	17	027	0101 0111	87	57	127	1001 0111	151	97	227	1101 0111	215	D7	327
0001 1000	24	18	030	0101 1000	88	58	130	1001 1000	152	98	230	1101 1000	216	D8	330
0001 1001	25	19	031	0101 1001	89	59	131	1001 1001	153	99	231	1101 1001	217	D9	331
0001 1010	26	1A	032	0101 1010	90	5A	132	1001 1010	154	9A	232	1101 1010	218	DA	332
0001 1011	27	1B	033	0101 1011	91	5B	133	1001 1011	155	9B	233	1101 1011	219	DB	333
0001 1100	28	1C	034	0101 1100	92	5C	134	1001 1100	156	9C	234	1101 1100	220	DC	334
0001 1101	29	1D	035	0101 1101	93	5D	135	1001 1101	157	9D	235	1101 1101	221	DD	335
0001 1110	30	1E	036	0101 1110	94	5E	136	1001 1110	158	9E	236	1101 1110	222	DE	336
0001 1111	31	1F	037	0101 1111	95	5F	137	1001 1111	159	9F	237	1101 1111	223	DF	337
0010 0000	32	20	040	0110 0000	96	60	140	1010 0000	160	A0	240	1110 0000	224	E0	340
0010 0001	33	21	041	0110 0001	97	61	141	1010 0001	161	A1	241	1110 0001	225	E1	341
0010 0010	34	22	042	0110 0010	98	62	142	1010 0010	162	A2	242	1110 0010	226	E2	342
0010 0011	35	23	043	0110 0011	99	63	143	1010 0011	163	A3	243	1110 0011	227	E3	343
0010 0100	36	24	044	0110 0100	100	64	144	1010 0100	164	A4	244	1110 0100	228	E4	344
0010 0101	37	25	045	0110 0101	101	65	145	1010 0101	165	A5	245	1110 0101	229	E5	345
0010 0110	38	26	046	0110 0110	102	66	146	1010 0110	166	A6	246	1110 0110	230	E6	346
0010 0111	39	27	047	0110 0111	103	67	147	1010 0111	167	A7	247	1110 0111	231	E7	347
0010 1000	40	28	050	0110 1000	104	68	150	1010 1000	168	A8	250	1110 1000	232	E8	350
0010 1001	41	29	051	0110 1001	105	69	151	1010 1001	169	A9	251	1110 1001	233	E9	351
0010 1010	42	2A	052	0110 1010	106	6A	152	1010 1010	170	AA	252	1110 1010	234	EA	352
0010 1011	43	2B	053	0110 1011	107	6B	153	1010 1011	171	AB	253	1110 1011	235	EB	353
0010 1100	44	2C	054	0110 1100	108	6C	154	1010 1100	172	AC	254	1110 1100	236	EC	354
0010 1101	45	2D	055	0110 1101	109	6D	155	1010 1101	173	AD	255	1110 1101	237	ED	355
0010 1110	46	2E	056	0110 1110	110	6E	156	1010 1110	174	AE	256	1110 1110	238	EE	356
0010 1111	47	2F	057	0110 1111	111	6F	157	1010 1111	175	AF	257	1110 1111	239	EF	357
0011 0000	48	30	060	0111 0000	112	70	160	1011 0000	176	B0	260	1111 0000	240	F0	360
0011 0001	49	31	061	0111 0001	113	71	161	1011 0001	177	B1	261	1111 0001	241	F1	361
0011 0010	50	32	062	0111 0010	114	72	162	1011 0010	178	B2	262	1111 0010	242	F2	362
0011 0011	51	33	063	0111 0011	115	73	163	1011 0011	179	B3	263	1111 0011	243	F3	363
0011 0100	52	34	064	0111 0100	116	74	164	1011 0100	180	B4	264	1111 0100	244	F4	364
0011 0101	53	35	065	0111 0101	117	75	165	1011 0101	181	B5	265	1111 0101	245	F5	365
0011 0110	54	36	066	0111 0110	118	76	166	1011 0110	182	B6	266	1111 0110	246	F6	366
0011 0111	55	37	067	0111 0111	119	77	167	1011 0111	183	B7	267	1111 0111	247	F7	367
0011 1000	56	38	070	0111 1000	120	78	170	1011 1000	184	B8	270	1111 1000	248	F8	370
0011 1001	57	39	071	0111 1001	121	79	171	1011 1001	185	B9	271	1111 1001	249	F9	371
0011 1010	58	3A	072	0111 1010	122	7A	172	1011 1010	186	BA	272	1111 1010	250	FA	372
0011 1011	59	3B	073	0111 1011	123	7B	173	1011 1011	187	BB	273	1111 1011	251	FB	373
0011 1100	60	3C	074	0111 1100	124	7C	174	1011 1100	188	BC	274	1111 1100	252	FC	374
0011 1101	61	3D	075	0111 1101	125	7D	175	1011 1101	189	BD	275	1111 1101	253	FD	375
0011 1110	62	3E	076	0111 1110	126	7E	176	1011 1110	190	BE	276	1111 1110	254	FE	376
0011 1111	63	3F	077	0111 1111	127	7F	177	1011 1111	191	BF	277	1111 1111	255	FF	377

To Use This Table: To convert a binary byte to decimal, hex, or octal, find the binary byte in one of the leftmost columns, and read the converted value in the appropriate column in the same row. For example, the octal equivalent of binary 0000 1110 (first column) is 016 (fourth column).

See Also:

1.02. Hexadecimal to Binary Number Conversion
1.10. Octal to Binary Number Conversion
1.11. Decimal to Binary Number Conversion

1.07. BINARY TO SIGNED DECIMAL NUMBER CONVERSION

Binary	*Decimal*	*Binary*	*Decimal*	*Binary*	*Decimal*	*Binary*	*Decimal*
0000 0000	0	0100 0000	64	1000 0000	-128	1100 0000	-64
0000 0001	1	0100 0001	65	1000 0001	-127	1100 0001	-63
0000 0010	2	0100 0010	66	1000 0010	-126	1100 0010	-62
0000 0011	3	0100 0011	67	1000 0011	-125	1100 0011	-61
0000 0100	4	0100 0100	68	1000 0100	-124	1100 0100	-60
0000 0101	5	0100 0101	69	1000 0101	-123	1100 0101	-59
0000 0110	6	0100 0110	70	1000 0110	-122	1100 0110	-58
0000 0111	7	0100 0111	71	1000 0111	-121	1100 0111	-57
0000 1000	8	0100 1000	72	1000 1000	-120	1100 1000	-56
0000 1001	9	0100 1001	73	1000 1001	-119	1100 1001	-55
0000 1010	10	0100 1010	74	1000 1010	-118	1100 1010	-54
0000 1011	11	0100 1011	75	1000 1011	-117	1100 1011	-53
0000 1100	12	0100 1100	76	1000 1100	-116	1100 1100	-52
0000 1101	13	0100 1101	77	1000 1101	-115	1100 1101	-51
0000 1110	14	0100 1110	78	1000 1110	-114	1100 1110	-50
0000 1111	15	0100 1111	79	1000 1111	-113	1100 1111	-49
0001 0000	16	0101 0000	80	1001 0000	-112	1101 0000	-48
0001 0001	17	0101 0001	81	1001 0001	-111	1101 0001	-47
0001 0010	18	0101 0010	82	1001 0010	-110	1101 0010	-46
0001 0011	19	0101 0011	83	1001 0011	-109	1101 0011	-45
0001 0100	20	0101 0100	84	1001 0100	-108	1101 0100	-44
0001 0101	21	0101 0101	85	1001 0101	-107	1101 0101	-43
0001 0110	22	0101 0110	86	1001 0110	-106	1101 0110	-42
0001 0111	23	0101 0111	87	1001 0111	-105	1101 0111	-41
0001 1000	24	0101 1000	88	1001 1000	-104	1101 1000	-40
0001 1001	25	0101 1001	89	1001 1001	-103	1101 1001	-39
0001 1010	26	0101 1010	90	1001 1010	-102	1101 1010	-38
0001 1011	27	0101 1011	91	1001 1011	-101	1101 1011	-37
0001 1100	28	0101 1100	92	1001 1100	-100	1101 1100	-36
0001 1101	29	0101 1101	93	1001 1101	-99	1101 1101	-35
0001 1110	30	0101 1110	94	1001 1110	-98	1101 1110	-34
0001 1111	31	0101 1111	95	1001 1111	-97	1101 1111	-33
0010 0000	32	0110 0000	96	1010 0000	-96	1110 0000	-32
0010 0001	33	0110 0001	97	1010 0001	-95	1110 0001	-31
0010 0010	34	0110 0010	98	1010 0010	-94	1110 0010	-30
0010 0011	35	0110 0011	99	1010 0011	-93	1110 0011	-29
0010 0100	36	0110 0100	100	1010 0100	-92	1110 0100	-28
0010 0101	37	0110 0101	101	1010 0101	-91	1110 0101	-27
0010 0110	38	0110 0110	102	1010 0110	-90	1110 0110	-26
0010 0111	39	0110 0111	103	1010 0111	-89	1110 0111	-25
0010 1000	40	0110 1000	104	1010 1000	-88	1110 1000	-24
0010 1001	41	0110 1001	105	1010 1001	-87	1110 1001	-23
0010 1010	42	0110 1010	106	1010 1010	-86	1110 1010	-22
0010 1011	43	0110 1011	107	1010 1011	-85	1110 1011	-21
0010 1100	44	0110 1100	108	1010 1100	-84	1110 1100	-20
0010 1101	45	0110 1101	109	1010 1101	-83	1110 1101	-19
0010 1110	46	0110 1110	110	1010 1110	-82	1110 1110	-18
0010 1111	47	0110 1111	111	1010 1111	-81	1110 1111	-17
0011 0000	48	0111 0000	112	1011 0000	-80	1111 0000	-16
0011 0001	49	0111 0001	113	1011 0001	-79	1111 0001	-15
0011 0010	50	0111 0010	114	1011 0010	-78	1111 0010	-14
0011 0011	51	0111 0011	115	1011 0011	-77	1111 0011	-13
0011 0100	52	0111 0100	116	1011 0100	-76	1111 0100	-12
0011 0101	53	0111 0101	117	1011 0101	-75	1111 0101	-11
0011 0110	54	0111 0110	118	1011 0110	-74	1111 0110	-10
0011 0111	55	0111 0111	119	1011 0111	-73	1111 0111	-9
0011 1000	56	0111 1000	120	1011 1000	-72	1111 1000	-8
0011 1001	57	0111 1001	121	1011 1001	-71	1111 1001	-7
0011 1010	58	0111 1010	122	1011 1010	-70	1111 1010	-6
0011 1011	59	0111 1011	123	1011 1011	-69	1111 1011	-5
0011 1100	60	0111 1100	124	1011 1100	-68	1111 1100	-4
0011 1101	61	0111 1101	125	1011 1101	-67	1111 1101	-3
0011 1110	62	0111 1110	126	1011 1110	-66	1111 1110	-2
0011 1111	63	0111 1111	127	1011 1111	-65	1111 1111	-1

To Use This Table: To convert a binary value to decimal, find the binary value in one of the left columns and read the corresponding signed decimal value in the column to the right. For example, the signed decimal equivalent of 1111 1000 is -8.

See Also: 1.06. Binary Number Conversions

1.08. OCTAL TO DECIMAL NUMBER CONVERSION

Octal	Dec	Octal	Dec	Octal	Dec	Octal	Dec	Octal	Dec	Octal	Dec	Octal	Dec	Octal	Dec
000	0	020	16	040	32	060	48	100	64	120	80	140	96	160	112
001	1	021	17	041	33	061	49	101	65	121	81	141	97	161	113
002	2	022	18	042	34	062	50	102	66	122	82	142	98	162	114
003	3	023	19	043	35	063	51	103	67	123	83	143	99	163	115
004	4	024	20	044	36	064	52	104	68	124	84	144	100	164	116
005	5	025	21	045	37	065	53	105	69	125	85	145	101	165	117
006	6	026	22	046	38	066	54	106	70	126	86	146	102	166	118
007	7	027	23	047	39	067	55	107	71	127	87	147	103	167	119
010	8	030	24	050	40	070	56	110	72	130	88	150	104	170	120
011	9	031	25	051	41	071	57	111	73	131	89	151	105	171	121
012	10	032	26	052	42	072	58	112	74	132	90	152	106	172	122
013	11	033	27	053	43	073	59	113	75	133	91	153	107	173	123
014	12	034	28	054	44	074	60	114	76	134	92	154	108	174	124
015	13	035	29	055	45	075	61	115	77	135	93	155	109	175	125
016	14	036	30	056	46	076	62	116	78	136	94	156	110	176	126
017	15	037	31	057	47	077	63	117	79	137	95	157	111	177	127

To Use This Table: To convert an octal value to decimal, find the octal value in one of the left columns and read the corresponding decimal value in the column to the right. For example, 067 octal is 55 decimal.

Note: Octal is rarely used for values greater than 128 decimal.

See Also:
1.03. Hexadecimal to Octal Number Conversion
1.06. Binary Number Conversions
1.13. Decimal to Octal Number Conversion

1.09. OCTAL TO HEXADECIMAL NUMBER CONVERSION

Octal	Hex	Octal	Hex	Octal	Hex	Octal	Hex	Octal	Hex	Octal	Hex	Octal	Hex	Octal	Hex
000	00	020	10	040	20	060	30	100	40	120	50	140	60	160	70
001	01	021	11	041	21	061	31	101	41	121	51	141	61	161	71
002	02	022	12	042	22	062	32	102	42	122	52	142	62	162	72
003	03	023	13	043	23	063	33	103	43	123	53	143	63	163	73
004	04	024	14	044	24	064	34	104	44	124	54	144	64	164	74
005	05	025	15	045	25	065	35	105	45	125	55	145	65	165	75
006	06	026	16	046	26	066	36	106	46	126	56	146	66	166	76
007	07	027	17	047	27	067	37	107	47	127	57	147	67	167	77
010	08	030	18	050	28	070	38	110	48	130	58	150	68	170	78
011	09	031	19	051	29	071	39	111	49	131	59	151	69	171	79
012	0A	032	1A	052	2A	072	3A	112	4A	132	5A	152	6A	172	7A
013	0B	033	1B	053	2B	073	3B	113	4B	133	5B	153	6B	173	7B
014	0C	034	1C	054	2C	074	3C	114	4C	134	5C	154	6C	174	7C
015	0D	035	1D	055	2D	075	3D	115	4D	135	5D	155	6D	175	7D
016	0E	036	1E	056	2E	076	3E	116	4E	136	5E	156	6E	176	7E
017	0F	037	1F	057	2F	077	3F	117	4F	137	5F	157	6F	177	7F

To Use This Table: To convert an octal value to hexadecimal, find the octal value in one of the left columns and read the corresponding hexadecimal value in the column to the right. For example, 127 octal is 57 hex.

Note: Octal is rarely used for values greater than 128 decimal.

See Also: 1.03. Hexadecimal to Octal Number Conversion

1.10. OCTAL TO BINARY NUMBER CONVERSION

Octal	Binary	Octal	Binary	Octal	Binary	Octal	Binary
000	0000 0000	040	0010 0000	100	0100 0000	140	0110 0000
001	0000 0001	041	0010 0001	101	0100 0001	141	0110 0001
002	0000 0010	042	0010 0010	102	0100 0010	142	0110 0010
003	0000 0011	043	0010 0011	103	0100 0011	143	0110 0011
004	0000 0100	044	0010 0100	104	0100 0100	144	0110 0100
005	0000 0101	045	0010 0101	105	0100 0101	145	0110 0101
006	0000 0110	046	0010 0110	106	0100 0110	146	0110 0110
007	0000 0111	047	0010 0111	107	0100 0111	147	0110 0111
010	0000 1000	050	0010 1000	110	0100 1000	150	0110 1000
011	0000 1001	051	0010 1001	111	0100 1001	151	0110 1001
012	0000 1010	052	0010 1010	112	0100 1010	152	0110 1010
013	0000 1011	053	0010 1011	113	0100 1011	153	0110 1011
014	0000 1100	054	0010 1100	114	0100 1100	154	0110 1100
015	0000 1101	055	0010 1101	115	0100 1101	155	0110 1101
016	0000 1110	056	0010 1110	116	0100 1110	156	0110 1110
017	0000 1111	057	0010 1111	117	0100 1111	157	0110 1111
020	0001 0000	060	0011 0000	120	0101 0000	160	0111 0000
021	0001 0001	061	0011 0001	121	0101 0001	161	0111 0001
022	0001 0010	062	0011 0010	122	0101 0010	162	0111 0010
023	0001 0011	063	0011 0011	123	0101 0011	163	0111 0011
024	0001 0100	064	0011 0100	124	0101 0100	164	0111 0100
025	0001 0101	065	0011 0101	125	0101 0101	165	0111 0101
026	0001 0110	066	0011 0110	126	0101 0110	166	0111 0110
027	0001 0111	067	0011 0111	127	0101 0111	167	0111 0111
030	0001 1000	070	0011 1000	130	0101 1000	170	0111 1000
031	0001 1001	071	0011 1001	131	0101 1001	171	0111 1001
032	0001 1010	072	0011 1010	132	0101 1010	172	0111 1010
033	0001 1011	073	0011 1011	133	0101 1011	173	0111 1011
034	0001 1100	074	0011 1100	134	0101 1100	174	0111 1100
035	0001 1101	075	0011 1101	135	0101 1101	175	0111 1101
036	0001 1110	076	0011 1110	136	0101 1110	176	0111 1110
037	0001 1111	077	0011 1111	137	0101 1111	177	0111 1111

To Use This Table: To convert an octal value to binary, find the octal value in one of the left columns and read the corresponding binary value in the column to the right. For example 057 octal is 0010 1111 binary.

Note: Octal is rarely used for values greater than 128 decimal.

See Also:

1.06. Binary Number Conversions
1.08. Octal to Decimal Number Conversion
1.09. Octal to Hexadecimal Number Conversion

1.11 DECIMAL TO BINARY NUMBER CONVERSION

Dec	Binary	Dec	Binary	Dec	Binary	Dec	Binary	Dec	Binary	Dec	Binary
0	0000 0000	48	0011 0000	96	0110 0000	144	1001 0000	192	1100 0000	240	1111 0000
1	0000 0001	49	0011 0001	97	0110 0001	145	1001 0001	193	1100 0001	241	1111 0001
2	0000 0010	50	0011 0010	98	0110 0010	146	1001 0010	194	1100 0010	242	1111 0010
3	0000 0011	51	0011 0011	99	0110 0011	147	1001 0011	195	1100 0011	243	1111 0011
4	0000 0100	52	0011 0100	100	0110 0100	148	1001 0100	196	1100 0100	244	1111 0100
5	0000 0101	53	0011 0101	101	0110 0101	149	1001 0101	197	1100 0101	245	1111 0101
6	0000 0110	54	0011 0110	102	0110 0110	150	1001 0110	198	1100 0110	246	1111 0110
7	0000 0111	55	0011 0111	103	0110 0111	151	1001 0111	199	1100 0111	247	1111 0111
8	0000 1000	56	0011 1000	104	0110 1000	152	1001 1000	200	1100 1000	248	1111 1000
9	0000 1001	57	0011 1001	105	0110 1001	153	1001 1001	201	1100 1001	249	1111 1001
10	0000 1010	58	0011 1010	106	0110 1010	154	1001 1010	202	1100 1010	250	1111 1010
11	0000 1011	59	0011 1011	107	0110 1011	155	1001 1011	203	1100 1011	251	1111 1011
12	0000 1100	60	0011 1100	108	0110 1100	156	1001 1100	204	1100 1100	252	1111 1100
13	0000 1101	61	0011 1101	109	0110 1101	157	1001 1101	205	1100 1101	253	1111 1101
14	0000 1110	62	0011 1110	110	0110 1110	158	1001 1110	206	1100 1110	254	1111 1110
15	0000 1111	63	0011 1111	111	0110 1111	159	1001 1111	207	1100 1111	255	1111 1111
16	0001 0000	64	0100 0000	112	0111 0000	160	1010 0000	208	1101 0000		
17	0001 0001	65	0100 0001	113	0111 0001	161	1010 0001	209	1101 0001		
18	0001 0010	66	0100 0010	114	0111 0010	162	1010 0010	210	1101 0010		
19	0001 0011	67	0100 0011	115	0111 0011	163	1010 0011	211	1101 0011		
20	0001 0100	68	0100 0100	116	0111 0100	164	1010 0100	212	1101 0100		
21	0001 0101	69	0100 0101	117	0111 0101	165	1010 0101	213	1101 0101		
22	0001 0110	70	0100 0110	118	0111 0110	166	1010 0110	214	1101 0110		
23	0001 0111	71	0100 0111	119	0111 0111	167	1010 0111	215	1101 0111		
24	0001 1000	72	0100 1000	120	0111 1000	168	1010 1000	216	1101 1000		
25	0001 1001	73	0100 1001	121	0111 1001	169	1010 1001	217	1101 1001		
26	0001 1010	74	0100 1010	122	0111 1010	170	1010 1010	218	1101 1010		
27	0001 1011	75	0100 1011	123	0111 1011	171	1010 1011	219	1101 1011		
28	0001 1100	76	0100 1100	124	0111 1100	172	1010 1100	220	1101 1100		
29	0001 1101	77	0100 1101	125	0111 1101	173	1010 1101	221	1101 1101		
30	0001 1110	78	0100 1110	126	0111 1110	174	1010 1110	222	1101 1110		
31	0001 1111	79	0100 1111	127	0111 1111	175	1010 1111	223	1101 1111		
32	0010 0000	80	0101 0000	128	1000 0000	176	1011 0000	224	1110 0000		
33	0010 0001	81	0101 0001	129	1000 0001	177	1011 0001	225	1110 0001		
34	0010 0010	82	0101 0010	130	1000 0010	178	1011 0010	226	1110 0010		
35	0010 0011	83	0101 0011	131	1000 0011	179	1011 0011	227	1110 0011		
36	0010 0100	84	0101 0100	132	1000 0100	180	1011 0100	228	1110 0100		
37	0010 0101	85	0101 0101	133	1000 0101	181	1011 0101	229	1110 0101		
38	0010 0110	86	0101 0110	134	1000 0110	182	1011 0110	230	1110 0110		
39	0010 0111	87	0101 0111	135	1000 0111	183	1011 0111	231	1110 0111		
40	0010 1000	88	0101 1000	136	1000 1000	184	1011 1000	232	1110 1000		
41	0010 1001	89	0101 1001	137	1000 1001	185	1011 1001	233	1110 1001		
42	0010 1010	90	0101 1010	138	1000 1010	186	1011 1010	234	1110 1010		
43	0010 1011	91	0101 1011	139	1000 1011	187	1011 1011	235	1110 1011		
44	0010 1100	92	0101 1100	140	1000 1100	188	1011 1100	236	1110 1100		
45	0010 1101	93	0101 1101	141	1000 1101	189	1011 1101	237	1110 1101		
46	0010 1110	94	0101 1110	142	1000 1110	190	1011 1110	238	1110 1110		
47	0010 1111	95	0101 1111	143	1000 1111	191	1011 1111	239	1110 1111		

To Use This Table: To convert a decimal byte value, find the decimal byte value in one of the left columns and read the corresponding binary value in the column to the right. For example, 43 decimal is 0010 1011 binary.

See Also:
1.06. Binary Number Conversions
1.10. Octal to Binary Number Conversion

1.12. DECIMAL TO HEXADECIMAL NUMBER CONVERSION

Dec	Hex	Dec	Hex	Dec	Hex	Dec	Hex	Dec	Hex	Dec	Hex	Dec	Hex
1	01	20	14	40	28	60	3C	80	50	100	64	1,000	3E8
2	02	21	15	41	29	61	3D	81	51	200	C8	2,000	7D0
3	03	22	16	42	2A	62	3E	82	52	300	12C	3,000	BB8
4	04	23	17	43	2B	63	3F	83	53	400	190	4,000	FA0
5	05	24	18	44	2C	64	40	84	54	500	1F4	5,000	1388
6	06	25	19	45	2D	65	41	85	55	600	258	6,000	1770
7	07	26	1A	46	2E	66	42	86	56	700	2BC	7,000	1B58
8	08	27	1B	47	2F	67	43	87	57	800	320	8,000	1F40
9	09	28	1C	48	30	68	44	88	58	900	384	9,000	2328
10	0A	29	1D	49	31	69	45	89	59			10,000	2710
11	0B	30	1E	50	32	70	46	90	5A			20,000	4E20
12	0C	31	1F	51	33	71	47	91	5B			30,000	7530
13	0D	32	20	52	34	72	48	92	5C			40,000	9C40
14	0E	33	21	53	35	73	49	93	5D			50,000	C350
15	0F	34	22	54	36	74	4A	94	5E			60,000	EA60
16	10	35	23	55	37	75	4B	95	5F			70,000	11170
17	11	36	24	56	38	76	4C	96	60			80,000	13880
18	12	37	25	57	39	77	4D	97	61			90,000	15F90
19	13	38	26	58	3A	78	4E	98	62			100,000	186A0
		39	27	59	3B	79	4F	99	63				

To Use This Table: To convert a decimal value to hexadecimal, find the decimal value in one of the left columns and read the corresponding hexadecimal value in the column to the right. If you are converting a decimal number larger than 100, you may have to perform several steps, adding the results together. For example, to convert 12345 into hex, first obtain the hex value of decimal 10000 (2710H), then add this to the value for 2000 decimal (7D0H), then add this to the value for 300 decimal (12CH), then add this to the value for 45 decimal (2DH). The result is 3039H. Remember that the numbers you are adding are in hexadecimal.

See Also:
1.01. Hexadecimal to Decimal Number Conversion
1.04. Hexadecimal Addition Tables

1.13. DECIMAL TO OCTAL NUMBER CONVERSION

Dec	Octal	Dec	Octal	Dec	Octal	Dec	Octal	Dec	Octal	Dec	Octal	Dec	Octal
1	001	19	023	39	050	60	074	80	120	100	144	1,000	001750
2	002	20	024	40	051	61	075	81	121	200	310	2,000	003720
3	003	21	025	41	052	62	076	82	122	300	454	3,000	005670
4	004	22	026	42	053	63	077	83	123	400	620	4,000	007640
5	005	23	027	43	054	64	100	84	124	500	764	5,000	011610
6	006	24	030	44	055	65	101	85	125	600	001130	6,000	013560
7	007	25	031	45	056	66	102	86	126	700	001274	7,000	015530
8	010	26	032	46	057	67	103	87	127	800	001440	8,000	017500
9	011	27	034	47	060	68	104	88	130	900	001604	9,000	021450
10	012	28	035	49	061	69	105	89	131			10,000	023420
11	013	29	036	50	062	70	106	90	132			20,000	047040
12	014	30	037	51	063	71	107	91	133			30,000	072460
13	015	31	040	52	064	72	110	92	134			40,000	116100
14	016	32	041	53	065	73	111	93	135			50,000	141520
15	017	33	042	54	066	74	112	94	136			60,000	165140
16	020	34	043	55	067	75	113	95	137			70,000	210560
17	021	35	044	56	070	76	114	96	140			80,000	234200
18	022	36	045	57	071	77	115	97	141			90,000	257620
		37	046	58	072	78	116	98	142			100,000	303240
		38	047	59	073	79	117	99	143				

To Use This Table: To convert a decimal value to octal, find the decimal value in one of the left columns and read the corresponding octal value in the column to the right. If you are converting a decimal number larger than 100, you may have to perform the conversion in steps, adding the results together. For example, to convert 12345 into octal, first obtain the octal value of decimal 10000 (23420), then add this to the value for 2000 decimal (3720), then add this to the value for 300 decimal (454), then add this to the value for 45 decimal (55). The result is 30071. Remember that the numbers you are adding are in octal.

See Also:
1.03. Hexadecimal to Octal Number Conversion
1.06. Binary Number Conversions
1.08. Octal to Decimal Number Conversion

1.14. TWO'S COMPLEMENTS

Binary	*Complement*	*Binary*	*Complement*	*Binary*	*Complement*	*Binary*	*Complement*
1111 1111	0000 0001	1011 1111	0100 0001	0111 1111	1000 0001	0011 1111	1100 0001
1111 1110	0000 0010	1011 1110	0100 0010	0111 1110	1000 0010	0011 1110	1100 0010
1111 1101	0000 0011	1011 1101	0100 0011	0111 1101	1000 0011	0011 1101	1100 0011
1111 1100	0000 0100	1011 1100	0100 0100	0111 1100	1000 0100	0011 1100	1100 0100
1111 1011	0000 0101	1011 1011	0100 0101	0111 1011	1000 0101	0011 1011	1100 0101
1111 1010	0000 0110	1011 1010	0100 0110	0111 1010	1000 0110	0011 1010	1100 0110
1111 1001	0000 0111	1011 1001	0100 0111	0111 1001	1000 0111	0011 1001	1100 0111
1111 1000	0000 1000	1011 1000	0100 1000	0111 1000	1000 1000	0011 1000	1100 1000
1111 0111	0000 1001	1011 0111	0100 1001	0111 0111	1000 1001	0011 0111	1100 1001
1111 0110	0000 1010	1011 0110	0100 1010	0111 0110	1000 1010	0011 0110	1100 1010
1111 0101	0000 1011	1011 0101	0100 1011	0111 0101	1000 1011	0011 0101	1100 1011
1111 0100	0000 1100	1011 0100	0100 1100	0111 0100	1000 1100	0011 0100	1100 1100
1111 0011	0000 1101	1011 0011	0100 1101	0111 0011	1000 1101	0011 0011	1100 1101
1111 0010	0000 1110	1011 0010	0100 1110	0111 0010	1000 1110	0011 0010	1100 1110
1111 0001	0000 1111	1011 0001	0100 1111	0111 0001	1000 1111	0011 0001	1100 1111
1111 0000	0001 0000	1011 0000	0101 0000	0111 0000	1001 0000	0011 0000	1101 0000
1110 1111	0001 0001	1010 1111	0101 0001	0110 1111	1001 0001	0010 1111	1101 0001
1110 1110	0001 0010	1010 1110	0101 0010	0110 1110	1001 0010	0010 1110	1101 0010
1110 1101	0001 0011	1010 1101	0101 0011	0110 1101	1001 0011	0010 1101	1101 0011
1110 1100	0001 0100	1010 1100	0101 0100	0110 1100	1001 0100	0010 1100	1101 0100
1110 1011	0001 0101	1010 1011	0101 0101	0110 1011	1001 0101	0010 1011	1101 0101
1110 1010	0001 0110	1010 1010	0101 0110	0110 1010	1001 0110	0010 1010	1101 0110
1110 1001	0001 0111	1010 1001	0101 0111	0110 1001	1001 0111	0010 1001	1101 0111
1110 1000	0001 1000	1010 1000	0101 1000	0110 1000	1001 1000	0010 1000	1101 1000
1110 0111	0001 1001	1010 0111	0101 1001	0110 0111	1001 1001	0010 0111	1101 1001
1110 0110	0001 1010	1010 0110	0101 1010	0110 0110	1001 1010	0010 0110	1101 1010
1110 0101	0001 1011	1010 0101	0101 1011	0110 0101	1001 1011	0010 0101	1101 1011
1110 0100	0001 1100	1010 0100	0101 1100	0110 0100	1001 1100	0010 0100	1101 1100
1110 0011	0001 1101	1010 0011	0101 1101	0110 0011	1001 1101	0010 0011	1101 1101
1110 0010	0001 1110	1010 0010	0101 1110	0110 0010	1001 1110	0010 0010	1101 1110
1110 0001	0001 1111	1010 0001	0101 1111	0110 0001	1001 1111	0010 0001	1101 1111
1110 0000	0010 0000	1010 0000	0110 0000	0110 0000	1010 0000	0010 0000	1110 0000
1101 1111	0010 0001	1001 1111	0110 0001	0101 1111	1010 0001	0001 1111	1110 0001
1101 1110	0010 0010	1001 1110	0110 0010	0101 1110	1010 0010	0001 1110	1110 0010
1101 1101	0010 0011	1001 1101	0110 0011	0101 1101	1010 0011	0001 1101	1110 0011
1101 1100	0010 0100	1001 1100	0110 0100	0101 1100	1010 0100	0001 1100	1110 0100
1101 1011	0010 0101	1001 1011	0110 0101	0101 1011	1010 0101	0001 1011	1110 0101
1101 1010	0010 0110	1001 1010	0110 0110	0101 1010	1010 0110	0001 1010	1110 0110
1101 1001	0010 0111	1001 1001	0110 0111	0101 1001	1010 0111	0001 1001	1110 0111
1101 1000	0010 1000	1001 1000	0110 1000	0101 1000	1010 1000	0001 1000	1110 1000
1101 0111	0010 1001	1001 0111	0110 1001	0101 0111	1010 1001	0001 0111	1110 1001
1101 0110	0010 1010	1001 0110	0110 1010	0101 0110	1010 1010	0001 0110	1110 1010
1101 0101	0010 1011	1001 0101	0110 1011	0101 0101	1010 1011	0001 0101	1110 1011
1101 0100	0010 1100	1001 0100	0110 1100	0101 0100	1010 1100	0001 0100	1110 1100
1101 0011	0010 1101	1001 0011	0110 1101	0101 0011	1010 1101	0001 0011	1110 1101
1101 0010	0010 1110	1001 0010	0110 1110	0101 0010	1010 1110	0001 0010	1110 1110
1101 0001	0010 1111	1001 0001	0110 1111	0101 0001	1010 1111	0001 0001	1110 1111
1101 0000	0011 0000	1001 0000	0111 0000	0101 0000	1011 0000	0001 0000	1111 0000
1100 1111	0011 0001	1000 1111	0111 0001	0100 1111	1011 0001	0000 1111	1111 0001
1100 1110	0011 0010	1000 1110	0111 0010	0100 1110	1011 0010	0000 1110	1111 0010
1100 1101	0011 0011	1000 1101	0111 0011	0100 1101	1011 0011	0000 1101	1111 0011
1100 1100	0011 0100	1000 1100	0111 0100	0100 1100	1011 0100	0000 1100	1111 0100
1100 1011	0011 0101	1000 1011	0111 0101	0100 1011	1011 0101	0000 1011	1111 0101
1100 1010	0011 0110	1000 1010	0111 0110	0100 1010	1011 0110	0000 1010	1111 0110
1100 1001	0011 0111	1000 1001	0111 0111	0100 1001	1011 0111	0000 1001	1111 0111
1100 1000	0011 1000	1000 1000	0111 1000	0100 1000	1011 1000	0000 1000	1111 1000
1100 0111	0011 1001	1000 0111	0111 1001	0100 0111	1011 1001	0000 0111	1111 1001
1100 0110	0011 1010	1000 0110	0111 1010	0100 0110	1011 1010	0000 0110	1111 1010
1100 0101	0011 1011	1000 0101	0111 1011	0100 0101	1011 1011	0000 0101	1111 1011
1100 0100	0011 1100	1000 0100	0111 1100	0100 0100	1011 1100	0000 0100	1111 1100
1100 0011	0011 1101	1000 0011	0111 1101	0100 0011	1011 1101	0000 0011	1111 1101
1100 0010	0011 1110	1000 0010	0111 1110	0100 0010	1011 1110	0000 0010	1111 1110
1100 0001	0011 1111	1000 0001	0111 1111	0100 0001	1011 1111	0000 0001	1111 1111
1100 0000	0100 0000	1000 0000	1000 0000	0100 0000	1100 0000	0000 0000	0000 0000

To Use This Table: To find the two's complement of a binary value, find the binary value in one of the left columns and read the corresponding two's complement value in the column to the right. For example, the two's complement of 1110 1100 is 0001 0100.

See Also: 1.06. Binary Number Conversions

1.15. COMMON 8086 FAMILY DATA FORMATS

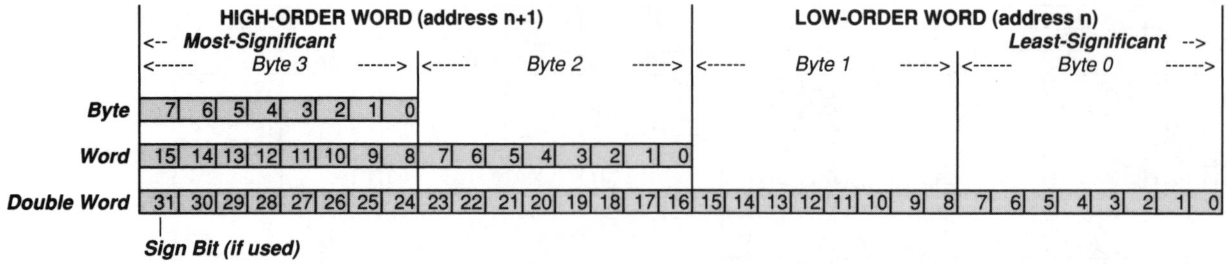
HIGH-ORDER WORD (address n+1)
LOW-ORDER WORD (address n)
<-- Most-Significant
Least-Significant -->
<------ Byte 3 ------>
<------ Byte 2 ------>
<------ Byte 1 ------>
<------ Byte 0 ------>
Byte 7 6 5 4 3 2 1 0
Word 15 14 13 12 11 10 9 8 7 6 5 4 3 2 1 0
Double Word 31 30 29 28 27 26 25 24 23 22 21 20 19 18 17 16 15 14 13 12 11 10 9 8 7 6 5 4 3 2 1 0
Sign Bit (if used)

Note: Numbers in boxes are the bit numbers; note that the bit numbering starts with the least-significant bit labeled zero.

Integer Storage Abilities		*Smallest Integer Value*	*Largest Integer Value*
Nibble	[Binary] bits 3–0	0	15
Byte	[± | Two's complement] bits 7, 6–0	-128	127
Word	[± | Two's complement] bits 15, 14–0	-32,768	32,767
Double Word	[± | Two's complement] bits 31, 30–0	-2,147,483,648	2,147,483,647

Note: Numbers beneath boxes indicate bit numbers (the high number is the most significant).

See Also:
1.14. Two's Complements
1.16. Common Numeric Data Formats
1.17. Common String Formats

1.16. COMMON NUMERIC DATA FORMATS

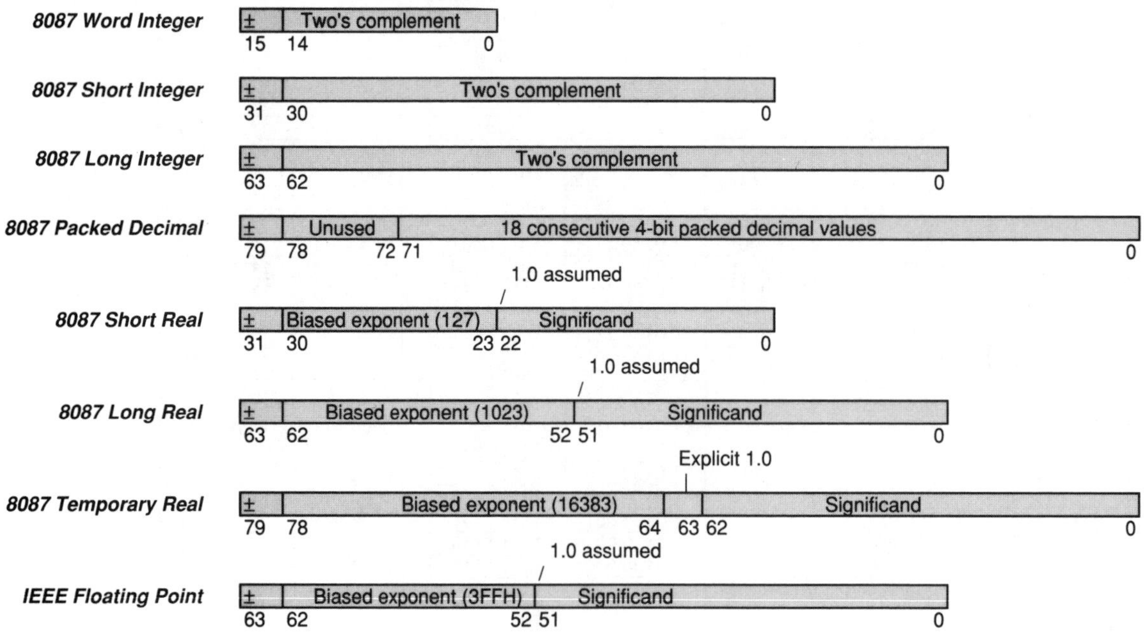
8087 Word Integer
± Two's complement
15 14 0
8087 Short Integer
± Two's complement
31 30 0
8087 Long Integer
± Two's complement
63 62 0
8087 Packed Decimal
± Unused 18 consecutive 4-bit packed decimal values
79 78 72 71 0
1.0 assumed
8087 Short Real
± Biased exponent (127) Significand
31 30 23 22 0
1.0 assumed
8087 Long Real
± Biased exponent (1023) Significand
63 62 52 51 0
Explicit 1.0
8087 Temporary Real
± Biased exponent (16383) Significand
79 78 64 63 62 0
1.0 assumed
IEEE Floating Point
± Biased exponent (3FFH) Significand
63 62 52 51 0

(Continued)

1.16. Common Numeric Data Formats (continued)

MASM Long Real (DQ)

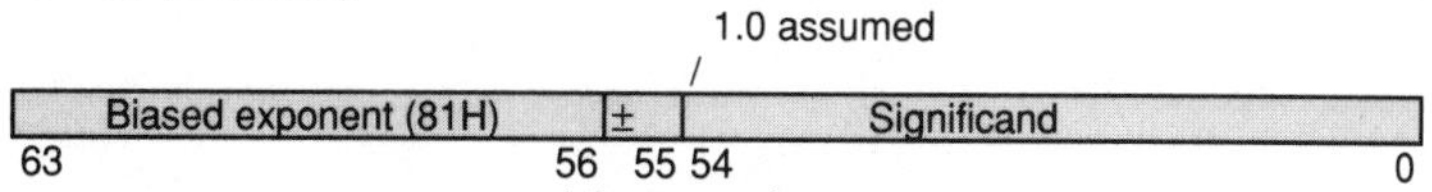
1.0 assumed
Biased exponent (81H)
±
Significand
63
56 55 54
0

MASM Short Real (DD)

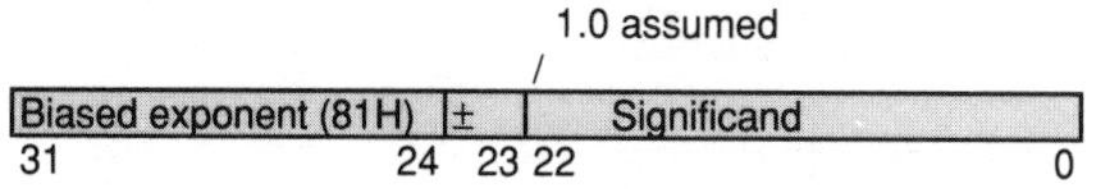
1.0 assumed
Biased exponent (81H)
±
Significand
31
24 23 22
0

Notes:

- Numbers beneath boxes indicate bit numbers (high=most significant).
- A bit value of 1 in the sign position (±) indicates the value is negative.
- Exponent specifies the power of two by which the significand must be raised to obtain the value of a real number.
- Significand specifies a binary value to be raised by the exponent.
- Note that some data formats are "normalized" (i.e., have an assumed leftmost bit of 1). Also, note that the decimal point in real numbers will be to the right of the leftmost digit in the significand.
- The IEEE floating-point format has an assumed high-order bit of 1 (i.e., it is "normalized").
- Note that the exponent for IEEE floating point numbers is "biased" by an implementation-dependent amount. For the 8087, the real exponent = exponent -1023.

Layout of 8087 Data in Memory

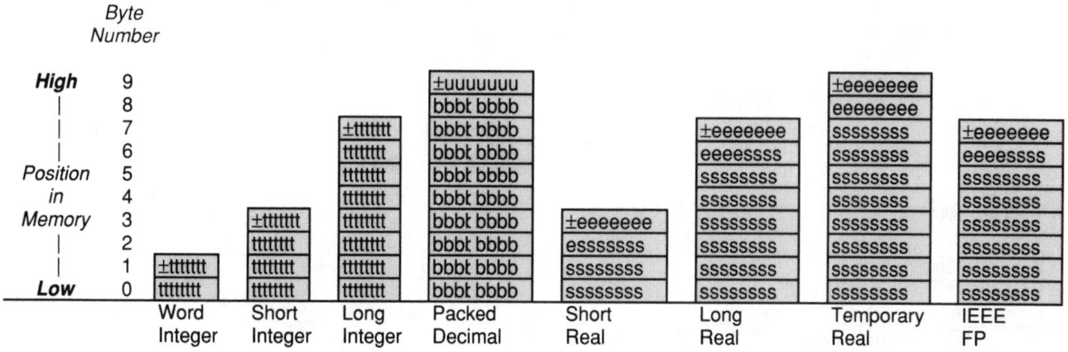
Byte Number
High
Position in Memory
Low
9 8 7 6 5 4 3 2 1 0
±ttttttt
ttttttt
±eeeeeee
eeeessss
eeeeeeee
±uuuuuuu
bbbb bbbb
esssssss
ssssssss
Word Integer
Short Integer
Long Integer
Packed Decimal
Short Real
Long Real
Temporary Real
IEEE FP

Legend:

b=binary digit
e=exponent bit
s=significant bit
t=two's complement
±=sign bit
u=unused bit

To Use This Table: This table shows where each bit position is stored in memory, and what it is used for. Each letter or symbol in the boxes represents one bit (lower right is least significant, upper left is most significant); each row represents one byte in memory.

Numeric Range Acceptable to Data Format

	Range	*Precision*	*Smallest Value Accepted*	*Largest Value Accepted*
8087 Word Integer	10^4	16 bits	-32,768	32,767
8087 Short Integer	10^9	32 bits	-2,147,483,648	2,147,483,647
8087 Long Integer	10^18	64 bits	-9,223,372,036,854,775,808	9,223,372,036,854,775,807
8087 Packed Decimal	10^18	18 digits	-(10^18)-1	(10^18)-1
8087 Short Real	10^±38	24 bits	8.43 x 10^-37	3.37 x 10^38
8087 Long Real	10^±308	53 bits	4.19 x 10^-307	1.67 x 10^308
8087 Temporary Real	10^±4932	64 bits	3.4 x 10^-4932	1.2 x 10^4932
IEEE Floating Point			4.19 x 10^-307	1.67 x 10^308
MASM Long Real			NA	NA
MASM Short Real			NA	NA

Source: Intel 8087 Math Coprocessor Reference

See Also: 1.14. Two's Complements
1.15. Common 8086 Family Data Formats

1.17. COMMON STRING FORMATS

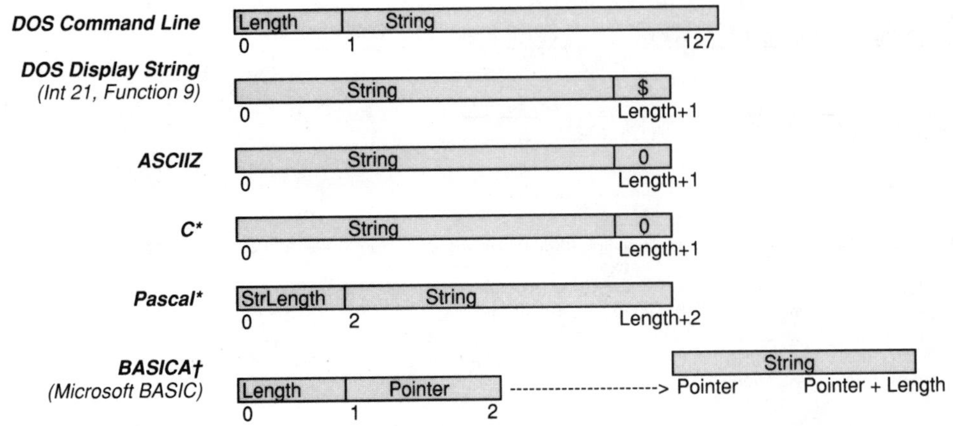
DOS Command Line
Length
String
0
1
127
DOS Display String
(Int 21, Function 9)
String
$
0
Length+1
ASCIIZ
String
0
0
Length+1
C*
String
0
0
Length+1
Pascal*
StrLength
String
0
2
Length+2
BASICA†
(Microsoft BASIC)
Length
Pointer
0
1
2
------------------------> Pointer
String
Pointer + Length

*Not all C and Pascal compilers follow these formats exactly, but these formats are the recognized standard for each compiler.
†Note that for BASICA, the string and the information about it are not stored consecutively in memory.

See Also: 1.15. Common 8086 Family Data Formats
1.16. Common Numeric Data Formats

1.18. COMMON MEMORY AREA TERMINOLOGY

Term	*Bits*	*Possible Values*	*Description*	*Conventional Use*
Bit	1	2	Binary digit - a single digital element	Boolean value
Nibble	4	16	One-half byte	Binary coded digit (0-9) or hex digit (0-F)
Byte	8	256	Standard "cell" of data, especially ASCII characters	ASCII character
Word	16	65536	8086 family of CPUs deal with this amount of data at a time	Short Integer; memory address (not including segment)
Double Word	32	4294967296	Smallest memory area that can handle an 8086 segment:offset address	Long Integers or segment addresses
Paragraph	128	NA	16 consecutive bytes of data	Memory allocation blocks
Page	2048	NA	256 consecutive bytes of data	2 pages = 1 sector of data
Segment	NA	NA	65536 consecutive bytes of data	DS, CS, ES, or SS segment
Kilobyte	NA	NA	1024 bytes	NA
Megabyte	NA	NA	1048576 bytes	NA

See Also: 1.27. Powers of Two

1.19. BINARY CODED DECIMAL NUMBER FORMAT

Nibble (one BCD value)

Decimal	*BCD*
0	0000
1	0001
2	0010
3	0011
4	0100
5	0101
6	0110
7	0111
8	1000
9	1001

Byte (two BCD values)

Decimal	*BCD*	*Decimal*	*BCD*	*Decimal*	*BCD*	*Decimal*	*BCD*
0	0000 0000	25	0010 0101	50	0101 0000	75	0111 0101
1	0000 0001	26	0010 0110	51	0101 0001	76	0111 0110
2	0000 0010	27	0010 0111	52	0101 0010	77	0111 0111
3	0000 0011	28	0010 1000	53	0101 0011	78	0111 1000
4	0000 0100	29	0010 1001	54	0101 0100	79	0111 1001
5	0000 0101	30	0011 0000	55	0101 0101	80	1000 0000
6	0000 0110	31	0011 0001	56	0101 0110	81	1000 0001
7	0000 0111	32	0011 0010	57	0101 0111	82	1000 0010
8	0000 1000	33	0011 0011	58	0101 1000	83	1000 0011
9	0000 1001	34	0011 0100	59	0101 1001	84	1000 0100
10	0001 0000	35	0011 0101	60	0110 0000	85	1000 0101
11	0001 0001	36	0011 0110	61	0110 0001	86	1000 0110
12	0001 0010	37	0011 0111	62	0110 0010	87	1000 0111
13	0001 0011	38	0011 1000	63	0110 0011	88	1000 1000
14	0001 0100	39	0011 1001	64	0110 0100	89	1000 1001
15	0001 0101	40	0100 0000	65	0110 0101	90	1001 0000
16	0001 0110	41	0100 0001	66	0110 0110	91	1001 0001
17	0001 0111	42	0100 0010	67	0110 0111	92	1001 0010
18	0001 1000	43	0100 0011	68	0110 1000	93	1001 0011
19	0001 1001	44	0100 0100	69	0110 1001	94	1001 0100
20	0010 0000	45	0100 0101	70	0111 0000	95	1001 0101
21	0010 0001	46	0100 0110	71	0111 0001	96	1001 0110
22	0010 0010	47	0100 0111	72	0111 0010	97	1001 0111
23	0010 0011	48	0100 1000	73	0111 0011	98	1001 1000
24	0010 0100	49	0100 1001	74	0111 0100	99	1001 1001

Note: Two binary coded digits may be stored in one byte, as shown in the Byte (lower) table.

See Also:

1.11. Decimal to Binary Number Conversion
1.15. Common 8086 Family Data Formats
1.16. Common Numeric Data Formats

1.20. ASCII CONTROL CODES

Dec	Hex	Binary	Mnemonic	Name	Definition
0	00	0000 0000	NUL	Null	Space filler character/used in output timing for some device drivers
1	01	0000 0001	SOH	Start of header	Marks beginning of message header
2	02	0000 0010	STX	Start of text	Marks beginning of data block (text)
3	03	0000 0011	ETX	End of text	Marks end of data block (text)
4	04	0000 0100	EOT	End of transmission	Marks end of transmission session
5	05	0000 0101	ENQ	Inquiry	Request for identification or information
6	06	0000 0110	ACK	Acknowledgment	"Yes" answer to queries or "ready for next transmission"/ used in asynchronous protocols for timing
7	07	0000 0111	BEL	Bell	Rings bell or audible alarm on terminal
8	08	0000 1000	BS	Backspace	Moves cursor position back one character
9	09	0000 1001	HT	Horizontal tab	Moves cursor position to next tab stop on line
10	0A	0000 1010	LF	Line feed	Moves cursor position down one line
11	0B	0000 1011	VT	Vertical tab	Moves cursor position down to next "tab line"
12	0C	0000 1100	FF	Form feed	Moves cursor position to top of next page
13	0D	0000 1101	CR	Carriage return	Moves cursor to left margin
14	0E	0000 1110	SO	Shift out	Next characters do not follow ASCII definitions
15	0F	0000 1111	SI	Shift in	Next characters revert to ASCII meaning
16	10	0001 0000	DLE	Data link escape	Used to control transmissions using "escape sequences"
17	11	0001 0001	DC1	Device control 1	Not defined; normally used for ON controls; usually user defined
18	12	0001 0010	DC2	Device control 2	Not defined; normally used for ON controls; usually user defined
19	13	0001 0011	DC3	Device control 3	Not defined; normally used for OFF controls; usually user defined
20	14	0001 0100	DC4	Device control 4	Not defined; normally used for OFF controls; usually user defined
21	15	0001 0101	NAK	Negative acknowledgment	"No" answer to questions or "errors found, retransmit"/used in asynchronous protocols
22	16	0001 0110	SYN	Synchronous idle	Sent by synchronous devices when idle to insure sync
23	17	0001 0111	ETB	End of transmission block	Marks block boundaries in transmission
24	18	0001 1000	CAN	Cancel	Indicates previous transmission should be disregarded
25	19	0001 1001	EM	End of medium	Marks end of physical media, as in paper tape
26	1A	0001 1010	SUB	Substitute	Used to replace a character known to be wrong
27	1B	0001 1011	ESC	Escape	Marks beginning of an Escape control sequence
28	1C	0001 1100	FS	File separator	Marker for major portion of transmission
29	1D	0001 1101	GS	Group separator	Marker for submajor portion of transmission
30	1E	0001 1110	RS	Record separator	Marker for minor portion of transmission
31	1F	0001 1111	US	Unit separator	Marker for most minor portion of transmission

Note:

- ASCII control codes are sometimes used to "formalize" a communications session between communications devices.
- DC1, DC2, DC3, DC4, FS, GS, RS, and US all have user-defined meanings, and may vary in use between sessions or devices.
- DC4 is often used as a general "stop transmission character."
- Codes used to control cursor position may be used to control print devices, and move the print head accordingly. Not all devices support the full set of positioning codes, however.

See Also: 1.21 ASCII Character Set

1.21. ASCII CHARACTER SET

Dec	*Hex*	*Octal*	*Binary*	*Name*	*Character*
0	00	000	0000 0000	NUL	None
1	01	001	0000 0001	SOH	^A*
2	02	002	0000 0010	STX	^B*
3	03	003	0000 0011	ETX	^C*
4	04	004	0000 0100	EOT	^D*
5	05	005	0000 0101	ENQ	^E*
6	06	006	0000 0110	ACK	^F*
7	07	007	0000 0111	BEL	^G*
8	08	010	0000 1000	BS	^H*
9	09	011	0000 1001	HT	^I*
10	0A	012	0000 1010	LF	^J*
11	0B	013	0000 1011	VT	^K*
12	0C	014	0000 1100	FF	^L*
13	0D	015	0000 1101	CR	^M*
14	0E	016	0000 1110	SO	^N*
15	0F	017	0000 1111	SI	^O*
16	10	020	0001 0000	DLE	^P*
17	11	021	0001 0001	DC1	^Q*
18	12	022	0001 0010	DC2	^R*
19	13	023	0001 0011	DC3	^S*
20	14	024	0001 0100	DC4	^T*
21	15	025	0001 0101	NAK	^U*
22	16	026	0001 0110	SYN	^V*
23	17	027	0001 0111	ETB	^W*
24	18	030	0001 1000	CAN	^X*
25	19	031	0001 1001	EM	^Y*
26	1A	032	0001 1010	SUB	^Z*
27	1B	033	0001 1011	ESC	^[*
28	1C	034	0001 1100	FS	^*
29	1D	035	0001 1101	GS	^]*
30	1E	036	0001 1110	RS	^^*
31	1F	037	0001 1111	US	^ *
32	20	040	0010 0000	space	Space
33	21	041	0010 0001	exclamation point	!
34	22	042	0010 0010	quotation mark	"
35	23	043	0010 0011	number sign	#
36	24	044	0010 0100	dollar sign	$
37	25	045	0010 0101	percent sign	%
38	26	046	0010 0110	ampersand	&
39	27	047	0010 0111	apostrophe	'
40	28	050	0010 1000	opening parenthesis	(
41	29	051	0010 1001	closing parenthesis	)
42	2A	052	0010 1010	asterisk	*
43	2B	053	0010 1011	plus sign	+
44	2C	054	0010 1100	comma	,
45	2D	055	0010 1101	hyphen or minus sign	-
46	2E	056	0010 1110	period	.
47	2F	057	0010 1111	slash	/
48	30	060	0011 0000	zero	0
49	31	061	0011 0001	one	1
50	32	062	0011 0010	two	2
51	33	063	0011 0011	three	3
52	34	064	0011 0100	four	4
53	35	065	0011 0101	five	5
54	36	066	0011 0110	six	6
55	37	067	0011 0111	seven	7
56	38	070	0011 1000	eight	8
57	39	071	0011 1001	nine	9
58	3A	072	0011 1010	colon	:
59	3B	073	0011 1011	semicolon	;
60	3C	074	0011 1100	less than sign	<
61	3D	075	0011 1101	equal sign	=
62	3E	076	0011 1110	greater than sign	>
63	3F	077	0011 1111	question mark	?

Dec	*Hex*	*Octal*	*Binary*	*Name*	*Character*
64	40	100	0100 0000	at sign	@
65	41	101	0100 0001	capital A	A
66	42	102	0100 0010	capital B	B
67	43	103	0100 0011	capital C	C
68	44	104	0100 0100	capital D	D
69	45	105	0100 0101	capital E	E
70	46	106	0100 0110	capital F	F
71	47	107	0100 0111	capital G	G
72	48	110	0100 1000	capital H	H
73	49	111	0100 1001	capital I	I
74	4A	112	0100 1010	capital J	J
75	4B	113	0100 1011	capital K	K
76	4C	114	0100 1100	capital L	L
77	4D	115	0100 1101	capital M	M
78	4E	116	0100 1110	capital N	N
79	4F	117	0100 1111	capital O	O
80	50	120	0101 0000	capital P	P
81	51	121	0101 0001	capital Q	Q
82	52	122	0101 0010	capital R	R
83	53	123	0101 0011	capital S	S
84	54	124	0101 0100	capital T	T
85	55	125	0101 0101	capital U	U
86	56	126	0101 0110	capital V	V
87	57	127	0101 0111	capital W	W
88	58	130	0101 1000	capital X	X
89	59	131	0101 1001	capital Y	Y
90	5A	132	0101 1010	capital Z	Z
91	5B	133	0101 1011	opening bracket	[
92	5C	134	0101 1100	backward slash	\
93	5D	135	0101 1101	closing bracket	]
94	5E	136	0101 1110	caret	^
95	5F	137	0101 1111	underscore	_
96	60	140	0110 0000	grave	`
97	61	141	0110 0001	lowercase A	a
98	62	142	0110 0010	lowercase B	b
99	63	143	0110 0011	lowercase C	c
100	64	144	0110 0100	lowercase D	d
101	65	145	0110 0101	lowercase E	e
102	66	146	0110 0110	lowercase F	f
103	67	147	0110 0111	lowercase G	g
104	68	150	0110 1000	lowercase H	h
105	69	151	0110 1001	lowercase I	i
106	6A	152	0110 1010	lowercase J	j
107	6B	153	0110 1011	lowercase K	k
108	6C	154	0110 1100	lowercase L	l
109	6D	155	0110 1101	lowercase M	m
110	6E	156	0110 1110	lowercase N	n
111	6F	157	0110 1111	lowercase O	o
112	70	160	0111 0000	lowercase P	p
113	71	161	0111 0001	lowercase Q	q
114	72	162	0111 0010	lowercase R	r
115	73	163	0111 0011	lowercase S	s
116	74	164	0111 0100	lowercase T	t
117	75	165	0111 0101	lowercase U	u
118	76	166	0111 0110	lowercase V	v
119	77	167	0111 0111	lowercase W	w
120	78	170	0111 1000	lowercase X	x
121	79	171	0111 1001	lowercase Y	y
122	7A	172	0111 1010	lowercase Z	z
123	7B	173	0111 1011	opening brace	{
124	7C	174	0111 1100	vertical line	|
125	7D	175	0111 1101	closing brace	}
126	7E	176	0111 1110	tilde	~
127	7F	177	0111 1111	DEL	Delete

*ASCII defines characters 0-31 to be control characters (or non-printing characters). On many systems the characters will display as shown and you can use the control sequence shown to enter these values from the keyboard.

Note: IBM does not use the ASCII codes for all characters, using, for example, the lower 32 characters for graphics.

See Also: 1.20. ASCII Control Codes
1.22. IBM ASCII Character Set

1.22. IBM ASCII CHARACTER SET

Dec	Hex	Octal	Binary	Name	Character
0	00	000	0000 0000	blank	
1	01	001	0000 0001	happy face	☺
2	02	002	0000 0010	inverse happy face	☻
3	03	003	0000 0011	heart	♥
4	04	004	0000 0100	diamond	♦
5	05	005	0000 0101	club	♣
6	06	006	0000 0110	spade	♠
7	07	007	0000 0111	bullet	•
8	08	010	0000 1000	inverse bullet	◘
9	09	011	0000 1001	circle	○
10	0A	012	0000 1010	inverse circle	◙
11	0B	013	0000 1011	male sign	♂
12	0C	014	0000 1100	female sign	♀
13	0D	015	0000 1101	single note	♪
14	0E	016	0000 1110	double note	♫
15	0F	017	0000 1111	sun	☼
16	10	020	0001 0000	right triangle	►
17	11	021	0001 0001	left triangle	◄
18	12	022	0001 0010	up/down arrow	↕
19	13	023	0001 0011	double exclamation	‼
20	14	024	0001 0100	paragraph sign	¶
21	15	025	0001 0101	section sign	§
22	16	026	0001 0110	rectangular bullet	▬
23	17	027	0001 0111	up/down to line	↨
24	18	030	0001 1000	up arrow	↑
25	19	031	0001 1001	down arrow	↓
26	1A	032	0001 1010	right arrow	→
27	1B	033	0001 1011	left arrow	←
28	1C	034	0001 1100	lower left box	∟
29	1D	035	0001 1101	left/right arrow	↔
30	1E	036	0001 1110	up triangle	▲
31	1F	037	0001 1111	down triangle	▼
32	20	040	0010 0000	space	Space
33	21	041	0010 0001	exclamation point	!
34	22	042	0010 0010	quotation mark	"
35	23	043	0010 0011	number sign	#
36	24	044	0010 0100	dollar sign	$
37	25	045	0010 0101	percent sign	%
38	26	046	0010 0110	ampersand	&
39	27	047	0010 0111	apostrophe	'
40	28	050	0010 1000	opening parenthesis	(
41	29	051	0010 1001	closing parenthesis	)
42	2A	052	0010 1010	asterisk	*
43	2B	053	0010 1011	plus sign	+
44	2C	054	0010 1100	comma	,
45	2D	055	0010 1101	hyphen or minus sign	-
46	2E	056	0010 1110	period	.
47	2F	057	0010 1111	slash	/
48	30	060	0011 0000	zero	0
49	31	061	0011 0001	one	1
50	32	062	0011 0010	two	2
51	33	063	0011 0011	three	3
52	34	064	0011 0100	four	4
53	35	065	0011 0101	five	5
54	36	066	0011 0110	six	6
55	37	067	0011 0111	seven	7
56	38	070	0011 1000	eight	8
57	39	071	0011 1001	nine	9
58	3A	072	0011 1010	colon	:
59	3B	073	0011 1011	semicolon	;
60	3C	074	0011 1100	less than sign	<
61	3D	075	0011 1101	equal sign	=
62	3E	076	0011 1110	greater than sign	>
63	3F	077	0011 1111	question mark	?

Dec	Hex	Octal	Binary	Name	Character
64	40	100	0100 0000	at sign	@
65	41	101	0100 0001	capital A	A
66	42	102	0100 0010	capital B	B
67	43	103	0100 0011	capital C	C
68	44	104	0100 0100	capital D	D
69	45	105	0100 0101	capital E	E
70	46	106	0100 0110	capital F	F
71	47	107	0100 0111	capital G	G
72	48	110	0100 1000	capital H	H
73	49	111	0100 1001	capital I	I
74	4A	112	0100 1010	capital J	J
75	4B	113	0100 1011	capital K	K
76	4C	114	0100 1100	capital L	L
77	4D	115	0100 1101	capital M	M
78	4E	116	0100 1110	capital N	N
79	4F	117	0100 1111	capital O	O
80	50	120	0101 0000	capital P	P
81	51	121	0101 0001	capital Q	Q
82	52	122	0101 0010	capital R	R
83	53	123	0101 0011	capital S	S
84	54	124	0101 0100	capital T	T
85	55	125	0101 0101	capital U	U
86	56	126	0101 0110	capital V	V
87	57	127	0101 0111	capital W	W
88	58	130	0101 1000	capital X	X
89	59	131	0101 1001	capital Y	Y
90	5A	132	0101 1010	capital Z	Z
91	5B	133	0101 1011	opening bracket	[
92	5C	134	0101 1100	backward slash	\
93	5D	135	0101 1101	closing bracket	]
94	5E	136	0101 1110	caret	^
95	5F	137	0101 1111	underscore	_
96	60	140	0110 0000	grave	`
97	61	141	0110 0001	lowercase A	a
98	62	142	0110 0010	lowercase B	b
99	63	143	0110 0011	lowercase C	c
100	64	144	0110 0100	lowercase D	d
101	65	145	0110 0101	lowercase E	e
102	66	146	0110 0110	lowercase F	f
103	67	147	0110 0111	lowercase G	g
104	68	150	0110 1000	lowercase H	h
105	69	151	0110 1001	lowercase I	i
106	6A	152	0110 1010	lowercase J	j
107	6B	153	0110 1011	lowercase K	k
108	6C	154	0110 1100	lowercase L	l
109	6D	155	0110 1101	lowercase M	m
110	6E	156	0110 1110	lowercase N	n
111	6F	157	0110 1111	lowercase O	o
112	70	160	0111 0000	lowercase P	p
113	71	161	0111 0001	lowercase Q	q
114	72	162	0111 0010	lowercase R	r
115	73	163	0111 0011	lowercase S	s
116	74	164	0111 0100	lowercase T	t
117	75	165	0111 0101	lowercase U	u
118	76	166	0111 0110	lowercase V	v
119	77	167	0111 0111	lowercase W	w
120	78	170	0111 1000	lowercase X	x
121	79	171	0111 1001	lowercase Y	y
122	7A	172	0111 1010	lowercase Z	z
123	7B	173	0111 1011	opening brace	{
124	7C	174	0111 1100	vertical line	|
125	7D	175	0111 1101	closing brace	}
126	7E	176	0111 1110	tilde	~
127	7F	177	0111 1111	small house	⌂

(Continued)

1.22. IBM ASCII Character Set (continued)

Dec	Hex	Octal	Binary	Name	Character
128	80	200	1000 0000	C cedilla	Ç
129	81	201	1000 0001	u umlaut	ü
130	82	202	1000 0010	e acute	é
131	83	203	1000 0011	a circumflex	â
132	84	204	1000 0100	a umlaut	ä
133	85	205	1000 0101	a grave	à
134	86	206	1000 0110	a ring	å
135	87	207	1000 0111	c cedilla	ç
136	88	210	1000 1000	e circumflex	ê
137	89	211	1000 1001	e umlaut	ë
138	8A	212	1000 1010	e grave	è
139	8B	213	1000 1011	i umlaut	ï
140	8C	214	1000 1100	i circumflex	î
141	8D	215	1000 1101	i grave	ì
142	8E	216	1000 1110	A umlaut	Ä
143	8F	217	1000 1111	A ring	Å
144	90	220	1001 0000	E acute	É
145	91	221	1001 0001	ae ligature	æ
146	92	222	1001 0010	AE ligature	Æ
147	93	223	1001 0011	o circumflex	ô
148	94	224	1001 0100	o umlaut	ö
149	95	225	1001 0101	o grave	ò
150	96	226	1001 0110	u circumflex	û
151	97	227	1001 0111	u grave	ù
152	98	230	1001 1000	y umlaut	ÿ
153	99	231	1001 1001	O umlaut	Ö
154	9A	232	1001 1010	U umlaut	Ü
155	9B	233	1001 1011	cent sign	¢
156	9C	234	1001 1100	pound sign	£
157	9D	235	1001 1101	yen sign	¥
158	9E	236	1001 1110	Pt	₧
159	9F	237	1001 1111	function	ƒ
160	A0	240	1010 0000	a acute	á
161	A1	241	1010 0001	i acute	í
162	A2	242	1010 0010	o acute	ó
163	A3	243	1010 0011	u acute	ú
164	A4	244	1010 0100	n tilde	ñ
165	A5	245	1010 0101	N tilde	Ñ
166	A6	246	1010 0110	a macron	ª
167	A7	247	1010 0111	o macron	º
168	A8	250	1010 1000	opening question mark	¿
169	A9	251	1010 1001	upper left box	⌐
170	AA	252	1010 1010	upper right box	¬
171	AB	253	1010 1011	1/2	½
172	AC	254	1010 1100	1/4	¼
173	AD	255	1010 1101	opening exclamation	¡
174	AE	256	1010 1110	opening guillemets	«
175	AF	257	1010 1111	closing guillemets	»
176	B0	260	1011 0000	light block	░
177	B1	261	1011 0001	medium block	▒
178	B2	262	1011 0010	dark block	▓
179	B3	263	1011 0011	single vertical	│
180	B4	264	1011 0100	single right junction	┤
181	B5	265	1011 0101	2 to 1 right junction	╡
182	B6	266	1011 0110	1 to 2 right junction	╢
183	B7	267	1011 0111	1 to 2 upper right	╖
184	B8	270	1011 1000	2 to 1 upper right	╕
185	B9	271	1011 1001	double right junction	╣
186	BA	272	1011 1010	double vertical	║
187	BB	273	1011 1011	double upper right	╗
188	BC	274	1011 1100	double lower right	╝
189	BD	275	1011 1101	1 to 2 lower right	╜
190	BE	276	1011 1110	2 to 1 lower right	╛
191	BF	277	1011 1111	single upper right	┐

Dec	Hex	Octal	Binary	Name	Character
192	C0	300	1100 0000	single lower left	└
193	C1	301	1100 0001	single lower junction	┴
194	C2	302	1100 0010	single upper junction	┬
195	C3	303	1100 0011	single left junction	├
196	C4	304	1100 0100	single horizontal	─
197	C5	305	1100 0101	single intersection	┼
198	C6	306	1100 0110	2 to 1 left junction	╞
199	C7	307	1100 0111	1 to 2 left junction	╟
200	C8	310	1100 1000	double lower left	╚
201	C9	311	1100 1001	double upper left	╔
202	CA	312	1100 1010	double lower junction	╩
203	CB	313	1100 1011	double upper junction	╦
204	CC	314	1100 1100	double left junction	╠
205	CD	315	1100 1101	double horizontal	═
206	CE	316	1100 1110	double intersection	╬
207	CF	317	1100 1111	1 to 2 lower junction	╧
208	D0	320	1101 0000	2 to 1 lower junction	╨
209	D1	321	1101 0001	1 to 2 upper junction	╤
210	D2	322	1101 0010	2 to 1 upper junction	╥
211	D3	323	1101 0011	1 to 2 lower left	╙
212	D4	324	1101 0100	2 to 1 lower left	╘
213	D5	325	1101 0101	2 to 1 upper left	╒
214	D6	326	1101 0110	1 to 2 upper left	╓
215	D7	327	1101 0111	2 to 1 intersection	╫
216	D8	330	1101 1000	1 to 2 intersection	╪
217	D9	331	1101 1001	single lower right	┘
218	DA	332	1101 1010	single upper left	┌
219	DB	333	1101 1011	inverse space	█
220	DC	334	1101 1100	lower inverse	▄
221	DD	335	1101 1101	left inverse	▌
222	DE	336	1101 1110	right inverse	▐
223	DF	337	1101 1111	upper inverse	▀
224	E0	340	1110 0000	alpha	α
225	E1	341	1110 0001	beta	β
226	E2	342	1110 0010	Gamma	Γ
227	E3	343	1110 0011	pi	π
228	E4	344	1110 0100	Sigma	Σ
229	E5	345	1110 0101	sigma	σ
230	E6	346	1110 0110	mu	µ
231	E7	347	1110 0111	tau	τ
232	E8	350	1110 1000	Phi	Φ
233	E9	351	1110 1001	theta	θ
234	EA	352	1110 1010	Omega	Ω
235	EB	353	1110 1011	delta	δ
236	EC	354	1110 1100	infinity	∞
237	ED	355	1110 1101	phi	∅
238	EE	356	1110 1110	epsilon	∈
239	EF	357	1110 1111	intersection of sets	∩
240	F0	360	1111 0000	is identical to	≡
241	F1	361	1111 0001	plus/minus sign	±
242	F2	362	1111 0010	greater/equal sign	≥
243	F3	363	1111 0011	less/equal sign	≤
244	F4	364	1111 0100	top half integral	⌠
245	F5	365	1111 0101	lower half integral	⌡
246	F6	366	1111 0110	divide by sign	÷
247	F7	367	1111 0111	approximately	≈
248	F8	370	1111 1000	degree	°
249	F9	371	1111 1001	filled in degree	•
250	FA	372	1111 1010	small bullet	·
251	FB	373	1111 1011	square root	√
252	FC	374	1111 1100	superscript n	^{n}
253	FD	375	1111 1101	superscript 2	^{2}
254	FE	376	1111 1110	box	■
255	FF	377	1111 1111	phantom space	

(Continued)

1.22. IBM ASCII Character Set (continued)

Note: The line-drawing characters are given arbitrary names in this table in this manner: the leftmost component is named first, followed by the word "to," followed by the rightmost component. Thus, if we were naming the upper-left corner of a single-line box, it would be "1 to 1 upper left ." If the left side of the box were double lined, it would be "2 to 1 upper left."

Source: IBM PC/XT Technical Reference, pages C-12, 13
IBM XT and Portable Technical Reference, pages 7-3 through 7-12.

See Also:
1.21. ASCII Character Set
1.23. IBM Keyboard Extended Function Codes
7.012. PC 83-Key Keyboard Numbers and Scan Codes
7.013. AT 84-Key Keyboard Numbers and Scan Codes
7.014. AT 101/102-Key Keyboard Numbers and Scan Codes
7.015. PS/2 Keyboard Numbers and Scan Codes

1.23. IBM KEYBOARD EXTENDED FUNCTION CODES

Dec	*Hex*	*Octal*	*Binary*	*Actual Keys Pressed*
1	01	001	0000 0001	Alt + Esc
3	03	003	0000 0011	Null character (none)
14	0E	016	0000 1110	Alt + Backspace
15	0F	017	0000 1111	Shift Tab
16	10	020	0001 0000	Alt + Q
17	11	021	0001 0001	Alt + W
18	12	022	0001 0010	Alt + E
19	13	023	0001 0011	Alt + R
20	14	024	0001 0100	Alt + T
21	15	025	0001 0101	Alt + Y
22	16	026	0001 0110	Alt + U
23	17	027	0001 0111	Alt + I
24	18	030	0001 1000	Alt + O
25	19	031	0001 1001	Alt + P
26	1A	032	0001 1010	Alt + [
27	1B	033	0001 1011	Alt +]
28	1C	034	0001 1100	Alt + Enter
30	1E	036	0001 1110	Alt + A
31	1F	037	0001 1111	Alt + S
32	20	040	0010 0000	Alt + D
33	21	041	0010 0001	Alt + F
34	22	042	0010 0010	Alt + G
35	23	043	0010 0011	Alt + H
36	24	044	0010 0100	Alt + J
37	25	045	0010 0101	Alt + K
38	26	046	0010 0110	Alt + L
39	27	047	0010 0111	Alt + ; *
40	28	050	0010 1000	Alt + ; *
41	29	051	0010 1001	Alt + ; *
43	2B	053	0010 1011	Alt + \
44	2C	054	0010 1100	Alt + Z
45	2D	055	0010 1101	Alt + X
46	2E	056	0010 1110	Alt + C
47	2F	057	0010 1111	Alt + V
48	30	060	0011 0000	Alt + B
49	31	061	0011 0001	Alt + N
50	32	062	0011 0010	Alt + M
51	33	063	0011 0011	Alt + ,
52	34	064	0011 0100	Alt + .
53	35	065	0011 0101	Alt + /
55	37	067	0011 0111	Alt + (keypad) asterisk
59	3B	073	0011 1011	F1
60	3C	074	0011 1100	F2
61	3D	075	0011 1101	F3
62	3E	076	0011 1110	F4
63	3F	077	0011 1111	F5
64	40	100	0100 0000	F6
65	41	101	0100 0001	F7
66	42	102	0100 0010	F8
67	43	103	0100 0011	F9
68	44	104	0100 0100	F10

Dec	*Hex*	*Octal*	*Binary*	*Actual Keys Pressed*
71	47	107	0100 0111	Home
72	48	110	0100 1000	Up arrow
73	49	111	0100 1001	Page Up
75	4B	113	0100 1011	Left arrow
76	4C	114	0100 1100	Center cursor
77	4D	115	0100 1101	Right arrow
78	4E	116	0100 1110	Alt + (keypad) plus
79	4F	117	0100 1111	End
80	50	120	0101 0000	Down arrow
81	51	121	0101 0001	Page Down
82	52	122	0101 0010	Insert
83	53	123	0101 0011	Delete
84	54	124	0101 0100	Shift + F1
85	55	125	0101 0101	Shift + F2
86	56	126	0101 0110	Shift + F3
87	57	127	0101 0111	Shift + F4
88	58	130	0101 1000	Shift + F5
89	59	131	0101 1001	Shift + F6
90	5A	132	0101 1010	Shift + F7
91	5B	133	0101 1011	Shift + F8
92	5C	134	0101 1100	Shift + F9
93	5D	135	0101 1101	Shift + F10
94	5E	136	0101 1110	Control + F1
95	5F	137	0101 1111	Control + F2
96	60	140	0110 0000	Control + F3
97	61	141	0110 0001	Control + F4
98	62	142	0110 0010	Control + F5
99	63	143	0110 0011	Control + F6
100	64	144	0110 0100	Control + F7
101	65	145	0110 0101	Control + F8
102	66	146	0110 0110	Control + F9
103	67	147	0110 0111	Control + F10
104	68	150	0110 1000	Alt + F1
105	69	151	0110 1001	Alt + F2
106	6A	152	0110 1010	Alt + F3
107	6B	153	0110 1011	Alt + F4
108	6C	154	0110 1100	Alt + F5
109	6D	155	0110 1101	Alt + F6
110	6E	156	0110 1110	Alt + F7
111	6F	157	0110 1111	Alt + F8
112	70	160	0111 0000	Alt + F9
113	71	161	0111 0001	Alt + F10
114	72	162	0111 0010	Control + PrtSc
115	73	163	0111 0011	Control + Left arrow
116	74	164	0111 0100	Control + Right arrow
117	75	165	0111 0101	Control + End
118	76	166	0111 0110	Control + PgDn
119	77	167	0111 0111	Control + Home
120	78	170	0111 1000	Alt + (upper row) 1
121	79	171	0111 1001	Alt + (upper row) 2
122	7A	172	0111 1010	Alt + (upper row) 3

(Continued)

1.23. IBM Keyboard Extended Function Codes (continued)

Dec	Hex	Octal	Binary	Actual Keys Pressed
123	7B	173	0111 1011	Alt + (upper row) 4
124	7C	174	0111 1100	Alt + (upper row) 5
125	7D	175	0111 1101	Alt + (upper row) 6
126	7E	176	0111 1110	Alt + (upper row) 7
127	7F	177	0111 1111	Alt + (upper row) 8
128	80	200	1000 0000	Alt + (upper row) 9
129	81	201	1000 0001	Alt + (upper row) 0
130	82	202	1000 0010	Alt + - (hyphen)
131	83	203	1000 0011	Alt + = (equals)
132	84	204	1000 0100	Control + PgUp
133	85	205	1000 0101	F11
134	86	206	1000 0110	F12
135	87	207	1000 0111	Shift + F11
136	88	210	1000 1000	Shift + F12
137	89	211	1000 1001	Control + F11
138	8A	212	1000 1010	Control + F12
139	8B	213	1000 1011	Alt + F11
140	8C	214	1000 1100	Alt + F12
141	8D	215	1000 1101	Control + Up/8
142	8E	216	1000 1110	Control + (keypad) -
143	8F	217	1000 1111	Control + (keypad) 5

Dec	Hex	Octal	Binary	Actual Keys Pressed
144	90	220	1001 0000	Control + (keypad) +
145	91	221	1001 0001	Control + Down/2
146	92	222	1001 0010	Control + Ins/0
147	93	223	1001 0011	Control + Del/.
148	94	224	1001 0100	Control + Tab
149	95	225	1001 0101	Control + (keypad) /
150	96	226	1001 0110	Control + (keypad) asterisk
151	97	227	1001 0111	Alt + Home
152	98	230	1001 1000	Alt + Up arrow
153	99	231	1001 1001	Alt + Page Up
155	9B	233	1001 1011	Alt + Left arrow
157	9D	235	1001 1101	Alt + Right arrow
159	9F	237	1001 1111	Alt + End
160	A0	240	1010 0000	Alt + Down arrow
161	A1	241	1010 0001	Alt + Page Down
162	A2	242	1010 0010	Alt + Insert
163	A3	243	1010 0011	Alt + Delete
164	A4	244	1010 0100	Alt + (keypad) /
165	A5	245	1010 0101	Alt + Tab
166	A6	246	1010 0110	Alt + Enter

*Alt + ; is listed only in IBM Technical Reference Personal Computer XT and Portable Personal Computer. The technical reference lists only one function for all three codes.

Note: Extended codes are preceded by a byte of 00H. For example, 00H, 81H means Alt and Zero were held down.

Source: IBM PC/XT Technical Reference, page 2-14
IBM XT and Portable Technical Reference, pages 4-39 through 4-40.

See Also: 1.21. ASCII Character Set
1.22. IBM ASCII Character Set
7.012. PC 83-Key Keyboard Numbers and Scan Codes
7.013. AT 84-Key Keyboard Numbers and Scan Codes
7.014. AT 101/102-Key Keyboard Numbers and Scan Codes
7.015. PS/2 Keyboard Numbers and Scan Codes

1.24. LINE DRAWING CHARACTER SET

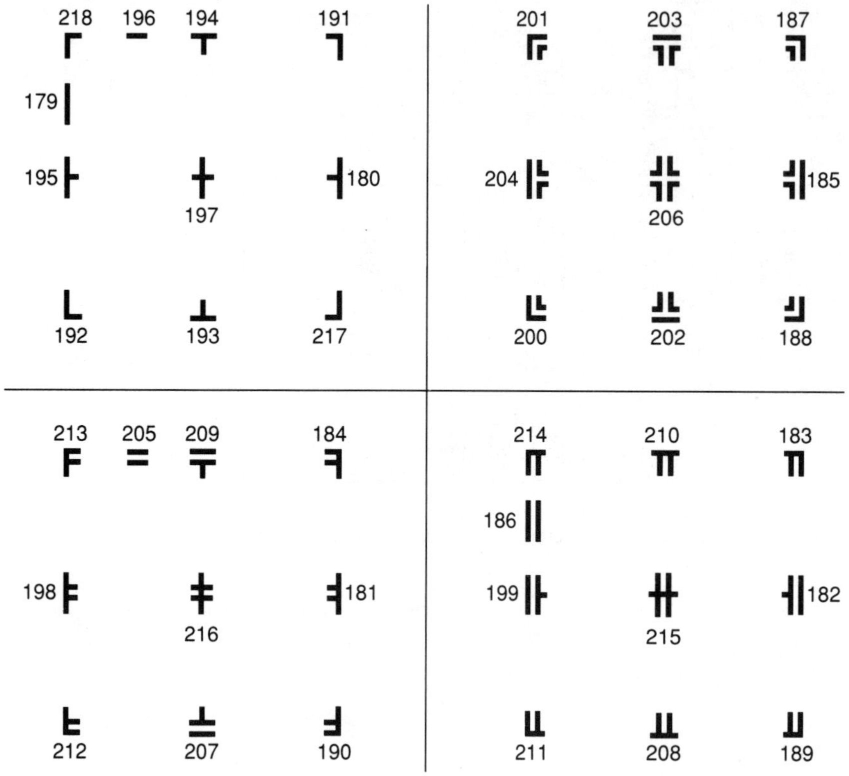
218 196 194 191
179
195 197 180
192 193 217
201 203 187
204 206 185
200 202 188
213 205 209 184
198 216 181
212 207 190
214 210 183
186
199 215 182
211 208 189

Notes: Line characters can be drawn by holding down the Alt key and typing the associated three-digit number on the number pad

Source: IBM PC/XT Technical Reference, page C-13

See Also: 1.22. IBM ASCII Character Set

1.25. EBCDIC CHARACTER SET

Dec	Hex	Octal	Binary	Name	Character
0	00	000	0000 0000	NUL	
1	01	001	0000 0001	SOH	
2	02	002	0000 0010	STX	
3	03	003	0000 0011	ETX	
4	04	004	0000 0100	SEL	
5	05	005	0000 0101	HT	
6	06	006	0000 0110	RNL	
7	07	007	0000 0111	DEL	
8	08	010	0000 1000	GE	
9	09	011	0000 1001	SPS	
10	0A	012	0000 1010	RPT	
11	0B	013	0000 1011	VT	
12	0C	014	0000 1100	FF	
13	0D	015	0000 1101	CR	
14	0E	016	0000 1110	SO	
15	0F	017	0000 1111	SI	
16	10	020	0001 0000	DLE	
17	11	021	0001 0001	DC1	
18	12	022	0001 0010	DC2	
19	13	023	0001 0011	DC3	
20	14	024	0001 0100	RES/ENP	
21	15	025	0001 0101	NL	
22	16	026	0001 0110	BS	
23	17	027	0001 0111	POC	
24	18	030	0001 1000	CAN	
25	19	031	0001 1001	EM	
26	1A	032	0001 1010	UBS	
27	1B	033	0001 1011	CU1	
28	1C	034	0001 1100	IFS	
29	1D	035	0001 1101	IGS	
30	1E	036	0001 1110	IRS	
31	1F	037	0001 1111	IUS/ITB	
32	20	040	0010 0000	DS	
33	21	041	0010 0001	SOS	
34	22	042	0010 0010	FS	
35	23	043	0010 0011	WUS	
36	24	044	0010 0100	BYP/INP	
37	25	045	0010 0101	LF	
38	26	046	0010 0110	ETB	
39	27	047	0010 0111	ESC	
40	28	050	0010 1000	SA	
41	29	051	0010 1001	SFE	
42	2A	052	0010 1010	SM/SW	
43	2B	053	0010 1011	CSP	
44	2C	054	0010 1100	MFA	
45	2D	055	0010 1101	ENQ	
46	2E	056	0010 1110	ACK	
47	2F	057	0010 1111	BEL	
48	30	060	0011 0000		
49	31	061	0011 0001		
50	32	062	0011 0010	SYN	
51	33	063	0011 0011	IR	
52	34	064	0011 0100	PP	
53	35	065	0011 0101	TRN	
54	36	066	0011 0110	NBS	
55	37	067	0011 0111	EOT	
56	38	070	0011 1000	SBS	
57	39	071	0011 1001	IT	
58	3A	072	0011 1010	RFF	
59	3B	073	0011 1011	CU3	
60	3C	074	0011 1100	DC4	
61	3D	075	0011 1101	NAK	
62	3E	076	0011 1110		
63	3F	077	0011 1111	SUB	

Dec	Hex	Octal	Binary	Name	Character
64	40	100	0100 0000	SP	
65	41	101	0100 0001	RSP	
66	42	102	0100 0010		
67	43	103	0100 0011		
68	44	104	0100 0100		
69	45	105	0100 0101		
70	46	106	0100 0110		
71	47	107	0100 0111		
72	48	110	0100 1000		
73	49	111	0100 1001		
74	4A	112	0100 1010		¢
75	4B	113	0100 1011		.
76	4C	114	0100 1100		<
77	4D	115	0100 1101		(
78	4E	116	0100 1110		+
79	4F	117	0100 1111		|
80	50	120	0101 0000		&
81	51	121	0101 0001		
82	52	122	0101 0010		
83	53	123	0101 0011		
84	54	124	0101 0100		
85	55	125	0101 0101		
86	56	126	0101 0110		
87	57	127	0101 0111		
88	58	130	0101 1000		
89	59	131	0101 1001		
90	5A	132	0101 1010		!
91	5B	133	0101 1011		$
92	5C	134	0101 1100		*
93	5D	135	0101 1101		)
94	5E	136	0101 1110		;
95	5F	137	0101 1111		¬
96	60	140	0110 0000		–
97	61	141	0110 0001		/
98	62	142	0110 0010		
99	63	143	0110 0011		
100	64	144	0110 0100		
101	65	145	0110 0101		
102	66	146	0110 0110		
103	67	147	0110 0111		
104	68	150	0110 1000		
105	69	151	0110 1001		
106	6A	152	0110 1010		¦
107	6B	153	0110 1011		,
108	6C	154	0110 1100		%
109	6D	155	0110 1101		_
110	6E	156	0110 1110		>
111	6F	157	0110 1111		?
112	70	160	0111 0000		
113	71	161	0111 0001		
114	72	162	0111 0010		
115	73	163	0111 0011		
116	74	164	0111 0100		
117	75	165	0111 0101		
118	76	166	0111 0110		
119	77	167	0111 0111		
120	78	170	0111 1000		
121	79	171	0111 1001		`
122	7A	172	0111 1010		:
123	7B	173	0111 1011		#
124	7C	174	0111 1100		@
125	7D	175	0111 1101		'
126	7E	176	0111 1110		=
127	7F	177	0111 1111		"

(Continued)

1.25. EBCDIC Character Set (continued)

Dec	Hex	Octal	Binary	Name	Character
128	80	200	1000 0000		
129	81	201	1000 0001		a
130	82	202	1000 0010		b
131	83	203	1000 0011		c
132	84	204	1000 0100		d
133	85	205	1000 0101		e
134	86	206	1000 0110		f
135	87	207	1000 0111		g
136	88	210	1000 1000		h
137	89	211	1000 1001		i
138	8A	212	1000 1010		
139	8B	213	1000 1011		
140	8C	214	1000 1100		
141	8D	215	1000 1101		
142	8E	216	1000 1110		
143	8F	217	1000 1111		
144	90	220	1001 0000		
145	91	221	1001 0001		j
146	92	222	1001 0010		k
147	93	223	1001 0011		l
148	94	224	1001 0100		m
149	95	225	1001 0101		n
150	96	226	1001 0110		o
151	97	227	1001 0111		p
152	98	230	1001 1000		q
153	99	231	1001 1001		r
154	9A	232	1001 1010		
155	9B	233	1001 1011		
156	9C	234	1001 1100		
157	9D	235	1001 1101		
158	9E	236	1001 1110		
159	9F	237	1001 1111		
160	A0	240	1010 0000		
161	A1	241	1010 0001		~
162	A2	242	1010 0010		s
163	A3	243	1010 0011		t
164	A4	244	1010 0100		u
165	A5	245	1010 0101		v
166	A6	246	1010 0110		w
167	A7	247	1010 0111		x
168	A8	250	1010 1000		y
169	A9	251	1010 1001		z
170	AA	252	1010 1010		
171	AB	253	1010 1011		
172	AC	254	1010 1100		
173	AD	255	1010 1101		
174	AE	256	1010 1110		
175	AF	257	1010 1111		
176	B0	260	1011 0000		
177	B1	261	1011 0001		
178	B2	262	1011 0010		
179	B3	263	1011 0011		
180	B4	264	1011 0100		
181	B5	265	1011 0101		
182	B6	266	1011 0110		
183	B7	267	1011 0111		
184	B8	270	1011 1000		
185	B9	271	1011 1001		
186	BA	272	1011 1010		
187	BB	273	1011 1011		
188	BC	274	1011 1100		
189	BD	275	1011 1101		
190	BE	276	1011 1110		
191	BF	277	1011 1111		

Dec	Hex	Octal	Binary	Name	Character
192	C0	300	1100 0000		{
193	C1	301	1100 0001		A
194	C2	302	1100 0010		B
195	C3	303	1100 0011		C
196	C4	304	1100 0100		D
197	C5	305	1100 0101		E
198	C6	306	1100 0110		F
199	C7	307	1100 0111		G
200	C8	310	1100 1000		H
201	C9	311	1100 1001		I
202	CA	312	1100 1010	SHY	
203	CB	313	1100 1011		
204	CC	314	1100 1100		
205	CD	315	1100 1101		
206	CE	316	1100 1110		
207	CF	317	1100 1111		
208	D0	320	1101 0000		}
209	D1	321	1101 0001		J
210	D2	322	1101 0010		K
211	D3	323	1101 0011		L
212	D4	324	1101 0100		M
213	D5	325	1101 0101		N
214	D6	326	1101 0110		O
215	D7	327	1101 0111		P
216	D8	330	1101 1000		Q
217	D9	331	1101 1001		R
218	DA	332	1101 1010		
219	DB	333	1101 1011		
220	DC	334	1101 1100		
221	DD	335	1101 1101		
222	DE	336	1101 1110		
223	DF	337	1101 1111		
224	E0	340	1110 0000		\
225	E1	341	1110 0001	NSP	
226	E2	342	1110 0010		S
227	E3	343	1110 0011		T
228	E4	344	1110 0100		U
229	E5	345	1110 0101		V
230	E6	346	1110 0110		W
231	E7	347	1110 0111		X
232	E8	350	1110 1000		Y
233	E9	351	1110 1001		Z
234	EA	352	1110 1010		
235	EB	353	1110 1011		
236	EC	354	1110 1100		
237	ED	355	1110 1101		
238	EE	356	1110 1110		
239	EF	357	1110 1111		
240	F0	360	1111 0000		0
241	F1	361	1111 0001		1
242	F2	362	1111 0010		2
243	F3	363	1111 0011		3
244	F4	364	1111 0100		4
245	F5	365	1111 0101		5
246	F6	366	1111 0110		6
247	F7	367	1111 0111		7
248	F8	370	1111 1000		8
249	F9	371	1111 1001		9
250	FA	372	1111 1010		
251	FB	373	1111 1011		
252	FC	374	1111 1100		
253	FD	375	1111 1101		
254	FE	376	1111 1110		
255	FF	377	1111 1111	EO	

Source: IBM System/370 Principles of Operation

See Also: 1.21. ASCII Character Set

1.26. DIGIT POSITIONS IN COMMON BASES

Digit Position Value

Base	*Name*	*6th Pos.*	*5th Pos.*	*4th Pos.*	*3rd Pos.*	*2nd Pos.*	*1st Pos.*
2	binary	32	16	8	4	2	1
8	octal	32768	4096	512	64	8	1
10	decimal	100000	10000	1000	100	10	1
16	hexadecimal	1048576	65536	4096	256	16	1

Note: The first digit position is the least significant.

See Also: 1.11. Decimal to Binary Number Conversion
1.12. Decimal to Hexadecimal Number Conversion
1.13. Decimal to Octal Number Conversion

1.27. POWERS OF TWO

Power	*Value*	*Common Definitions and Usage*
2^1	2	(1 bit may have 2 possible values) (2 bytes = word)
2^2	4	(4 bits = nibble, BCD Digit) (4 bytes = double word)
2^3	8	(8 bits = byte, ASCII Character)
2^4	16	(16 bits = word, Near Address) (16 bytes = paragraph)
2^5	32	(32 bits = double word, Far Address)
2^6	64	
2^7	128	
2^8	256	(1 byte may have 256 possible values) (256 bytes = page)
2^9	512	
2^10	1,024	(1,024 bytes = kilobyte)
2^11	2,048	
2^12	4,096	
2^13	8,192	
2^14	16,384	
2^15	32,768	
2^16	65,536	(65,536 bytes = segment)
2^17	131,072	
2^18	262,144	
2^19	524,288	
2^20	1,048,576	(1,048,576 bytes = megabyte)
2^21	2,097,152	
2^22	4,194,304	
2^23	8,388,608	
2^24	16,777,216	
2^25	33,554,432	

Note: 2^15 means 2 raised to the 15th power.

See Also: 1.15. Common 8086 Family Data Formats
1.18. Common Memory Area Terminology

1.28. ASCII AND INTERNATIONAL SORT ORDERING

In ASCII sort ordering, lower numbered ASCII characters appear before higher numbered ones, thus:
- -All uppercase characters appear before lowercase ones.
- -Characters with diacritical marks come after all other letters.

In International sort ordering ASCII sort order is changed as follows:
- -Characters are sorted by alphabetical position: A and a are equal and come before B.
- -Characters with diacritical marks are expanded accordingly: umlauted a becomes ae for sort ordering, ß becomes ss, etc.
- -Lowercase characters are applied first; for example, deJesus appears before Dejesus.
- -Norwegian, Danish, Swedish, and Finnish å, Å, and umlauts are placed at the end of the regular alphabet for those countries.

ASCII sort ordering would treat the alphabet like this:

ASCII Code	*Character*
65	A
66	B
67	C
68	D
69	E
70	F
71	G
72	H
73	I
74	J
75	K
76	L
77	M
78	N
79	O
80	P
81	Q
82	R
83	S
84	T
85	U
86	V
87	W
88	X
89	Y
90	Z
97	a
98	b
99	c
100	d
101	e
102	f
103	g
104	h
105	i
106	j
107	k
108	l
109	m
110	n
111	o
112	p
113	q
114	r
115	s
116	t
117	u
118	v
119	w
120	x
121	y
122	z

ASCII Code	*Character*
128	Ç
129	ü
130	é
131	â
132	ä
133	à
134	å
135	ç
136	ê
137	ë
138	è
139	ï
140	î
141	ì
142	Ä
143	Å
144	É
145	æ
146	Æ
147	ô
148	ö
149	ò
150	û
151	ù
152	ÿ
153	Ö
154	Ü
160	á
161	í
162	ó
163	ú
164	ñ
165	Ñ
224	a
225	b
226	G
227	p
228	S
229	s
230	m
231	t
232	F
233	q
234	W
235	d
236	•
237	ø
238	Œ
239	«
240	X

International sort ordering would treat the alphabet like this:

ASCII Code	*Character*
97	a
132	ä
160	á
133	à
131	â
65	A
142	Ä
98	b
66	B
99	c
135	ç
67	C
128	Ç
100	d
68	D
101	e
137	ë
130	é
138	è
136	ê
69	E
144	É
102	f
70	F
103	g
71	G
104	h
72	H
105	i
139	ï
161	í
141	ì
140	î
73	I
106	j
74	J
107	k
75	K
108	l
76	L
109	m
77	M
110	n
164	ñ
78	N
165	Ñ
111	o
148	ö
162	ó
149	ò
147	ô
79	O

ASCII Code	*Character*
153	Ö
112	p
80	P
113	q
81	Q
114	r
82	R
115	s
225	ß
83	S
116	t
84	T
117	u
129	ü
163	ú
151	ù
150	û
85	U
154	Ü
118	v
86	V
119	w
87	W
120	x
88	X
121	y
152	ÿ
89	Y
122	z
90	Z
134	å
143	Å
145	æ
146	Æ
224	a
226	G
227	p
228	S
229	s
230	m
231	t
232	F
233	q
234	W
235	d
236	•
237	ø
238	Œ
239	«
240	X

Source: Paradox 2.0 User's Guide, pages 519 through 521
Paradox 3.0 User's Guide, pages 276 through 277

See Also: 3.160. INT 21H, AH=65H, AL=06H -- Get Collate Sequence Table

1.29. TRUTH TABLES FOR LOGICAL OPERATIONS

AND

Condition 1	*Condition 2*	*Result*
TRUE	TRUE	TRUE
TRUE	FALSE	FALSE
FALSE	TRUE	FALSE
FALSE	FALSE	FALSE

OR

Condition 1	*Condition 2*	*Result*
TRUE	TRUE	TRUE
TRUE	FALSE	TRUE
FALSE	TRUE	TRUE
FALSE	FALSE	FALSE

NAND

Condition 1	*Condition 2*	*Result*
TRUE	TRUE	FALSE
TRUE	FALSE	TRUE
FALSE	TRUE	TRUE
FALSE	FALSE	TRUE

NOR

Condition 1	*Condition 2*	*Result*
TRUE	TRUE	FALSE
TRUE	FALSE	FALSE
FALSE	TRUE	FALSE
FALSE	FALSE	TRUE

NOT

Condition	*Result*
TRUE	FALSE
FALSE	TRUE

XOR

Condition 1	*Condition 2*	*Result*
TRUE	TRUE	FALSE
TRUE	FALSE	TRUE
FALSE	TRUE	TRUE
FALSE	FALSE	FALSE

To Use This Table: The resulting value is read by finding a row in which the condition or conditions you are looking up are met, and then reading the result in the rightmost column of that row.

Section 2

DOS Commands, Utilities, and Summaries

Other

2.01. DOS COMMAND SUMMARY

Command	*Type*	*Net*	*Function*	*Syntax*
APPEND	ext	Yes	Sets a search path for data files	APPEND [d:]path[;[d:][path]...][/parms] /e -- stores appended dirs in environment /x or /x:on -- extends appending to function 4BH, 11H, 4EH ops /x:off -- turns off extended function operations /path:on -- files having drives or paths will be processed /path:off -- files having drives or paths will not be processed
ASSIGN	ext	Yes	Routes disk I/O from one drive to another drive	ASSIGN [x[:]=y[:] [...]] x -- current drive y -- new drive
ATTRIB	ext	Yes	Sets or displays file attributes	ATTRIB [±r][±a][±s][±h][d:][path]filespec[/s] +r -- sets read-only attribute of file -r -- removes read-only attribute of file +a -- sets archive attribute of file -a -- removes archive attribute of file +s -- sets system file attribute† -s -- removes system file attribute† +h -- sets hidden file attribute† -h -- removes hidden file attribute† /s -- process all subdirectories to path
BACKUP	ext	Yes	Backs up one or more files from one disk to another	BACKUP d1:[path][filespec] d2:[/parms] d1 -- source d2 -- destination /s -- backs up subdirectories /m -- backs up only files that have changed since last backup /a -- adds files to existing backup set /f:size -- formats target disk; size=160,180,320,360,720,1.2,1.44 /d:date -- backs up files created/modified on or after date specified /t:time -- backs up files created/modified on at or after time specified /L[:[d:][path]filespec] -- places backup log in file specified
BREAK	int	Yes	Defines status of control break check	BREAK [ON|OFF]
CHCP*	int	Yes	Displays or changes the code page DOS uses	CHCP [number] number = a valid code page defined by COUNTRY in CONFIG.SYS
CHDIR (CD)	int	Yes	Sets or displays current path	CHDIR [d:][path] CHDIR [..] CD [d:][path] CD [..] .. -- parent directory
CHKDSK	ext	No	Analyzes disk and FAT and produces a disk and memory status report	CHKDSK [d:][[path[filespec][/parms] /f -- fixes errors reported on disk /v -- displays names of all files as disk is checked
CLS	int	Yes	Clears display screen	CLS
COMMAND	ext	Yes	Starts a secondary command processor	COMMAND [[d:]path][ctty-dev][/parms] ctty-dev -- allows you to specify a different device for input and output /e:number -- specifies environment size, in bytes (160 to 32,768) /p -- keeps secondary command processor in memory /c string -- executes commands specified by string, then returns to primary command processor
COMP	ext	Yes	Compares contents of files	COMP [[d:]path][filespec1][[d:]path][filespec2][/parms] /d -- display differences in decimal† /a -- display differences in ASCII characters† /l -- display number of line where difference occurs† /n=number -- compares number of lines specified† /c -- performs comparison regardless of case†
COPY	int	Yes	Copies a file or set of files	COPY [/parms][d:][path]filespec[/parms] [d:][path][filespec][/parms] /v -- verifies that sectors on target disk were written correctly /a -- copies ASCII files up to end-of-file mark /b -- copies binary files using size of file in directory NOTE: first filespec is source, second is target; multiple files may be copied into a single file by specifying multiple sources with + sign
CTTY	int	Yes	Changes device from which you issue commands	CTTY devicename devicename = AUX, COM1, COM2, COM3, COM4, or CON to return to standard I/O
DATE	int	Yes	Sets or displays date	DATE [mm-dd-yy]
DEBUG	ext	No	Starts debug program	DEBUG [[d:][path]filespec [testfile-parms]]
DELOLDOS			Deletes all old versions of DOS from your computer	DELOLDOS
DEL	int	Yes	Deletes specified file or files	DEL [d:][path]filespec[/parm] /p -- prompts prior to deletion

(Continued)

2.01. DOS COMMAND SUMMARY (continued)

Command	Type	Net	Function	Syntax
DIR	int	Yes	Lists directory entries	DIR [d:][path][filespec][/parms] /p -- shows directory page at a time /a[[:]attributes] -- shows files matching attributes† /o[[:]sortorder] -- controls order in which names are sorted† /s -- lists all occurences in current and subdirectories† /b -- lists files one per line† /l -- displays unsorted names in lowercase† /w -- displays directory in wide format
DISKCOMP	ext	No	Compares contents of two disks	DISKCOMP [d1: [d2:]][/parms] /1 -- compares only first side of disk /8 -- compares only first 8 sectors per track
DISKCOPY	ext	No	Copies a disk	DISKCOPY [d1: [d2:]][/parm] d1 -- source d2 -- target /v -- verifies copy is correct† /1 -- copies only first side of disk
DOSKEY†	ext	Yes	Starts resident DOS command editor	DOSKEY [/parms][macroname=[text]] /reinstall -- installs new copy of DOSKEY /bufsize=size -- specifies DOSKEY buffer size (256-512 bytes) /macros -- displays list of DOSKEY macros /history -- displays list of commands stored in memory /insert or /overstrike -- specifies typing mode
DOSSHELL*	ext	Yes	Starts DOS file manager shell in IBM DOS	For syntax, see 2.16 DOSSHELL Program Startup Options
EDIT†	ext	Yes	Starts DOS file editor	EDIT [[d:][path]filespec] [/parms] /b -- displays editor in black and white /g -- uses fast screen updating for CGA monitors /h -- displays maximum lines possible for current monitor /nohi -- enables 8-color monitors to be used
EDLIN	ext	Yes	Starts line-oriented DOS file editor	EDLIN [d:][path]filespec [/b] /b -- ignore end-of-file marker
EMM386†	ext	No	Enables/disables EMS for 386-equipped machines	EMM386 [on|off|auto][w=on|off] [y=path] w -- enables or disables Weitek coprocessor support y -- specifies location of EMM386.EXE file
ERASE	ext	Yes	Deletes specified file or files	ERASE [d:][path]filespec[/parm] /p -- prompts prior to deletion*
EXE2BIN*	ext	Yes	Converts .exe files to binary format	EXE2BIN [d:][path]filespec1 [d:][path][filespec2] filespec1 -- input file filespec2 -- output file
EXIT	int	Yes	Exits COMMAND.COM and returns to previous level, if one exists	EXIT
EXPAND†	ext	Yes	Expands compressed DOS 5.0 file	EXPAND [d:][path]filespec1 [[d:][path]filespec2[...]] destination filespec1 -- first file to expand filespec2 -- second file to expand destination -- drive or filespec for expanded files or file
FASTOPEN	ext	No	Keeps location of opened files on disk or in memory	FASTOPEN d:[=numberfiles]...[/parms] FASTOPEN d:[=(numberfiles,numberextents)]...[/parms] FASTOPEN d:[=([numberfiles],numberextents)]...[/parms] /x -- places file cache in expanded memory
FC*	ext	Yes	Compares two files or sets of files and shows differences	FC [/parms][d:][path]filespec1[d:][path]filespec2 /a -- abbreviates ASCII output comparison /b -- forces binary comparison (precludes other /parms) /c -- ignores case of letters /L -- compares in ASCII mode /Lb number -- sets line buffer to number of lines /n -- displays line number in ASCII comparisons /t -- doesn't expand tabs to spaces /w -- compresses white space in comparison /number -- specifies number of lines that must match after difference
FDISK	ext	No	Creates or changes disk partitions	FDISK
FIND	ext	Yes	Searches for a string of text in a file or set of files	FIND [/parms] "string" [[d:][path]filespec[...]] /c -- displays number of lines that contain a match /i -- specifies search is not case sensitive† /n -- numbers lines /v -- displays all lines not containing string

(Continued)

2.01. DOS COMMAND SUMMARY (continued)

Command	*Type*	*Net*	*Function*	*Syntax*
FORMAT	ext	No	Formats disk for use	FORMAT d:[/parms] /1 -- formats disk as single sided /4 -- formats disk as 5.25", 360K, double-sided in 1.2MB drive /8 -- formats 8 sectors per track /b -- formats disk leaving space for operating system /s -- formats disk and copies operating systems files /q -- deletes FAT and root directory of prev formatted disk† /u -- unconditional format (destroy all old data)† /t:tracks -- formats disk to number of tracks specified /n:sectors -- formats disk to number of sectors specified /v:label -- writes volume label on disk /f:size -- specifies disk size (160,180,320,360,720,1.2,1.44)
GRAFTABL	ext	Yes	Loads special character data into memory	GRAFTABL [number] GRAFTABL /STA[TUS] GRAFTABL [?] number = 437, 850, 860, 863, or 865
GRAPHICS	ext	Yes	Sets system to print graphic displays when using a color or graphics monitor adapter	GRAPHICS type [profile] [/parms] type = COLOR1, COLOR4, COLOR8, GRAPHICS, GRAPHICSWIDE, THERMAL, HPDEFAULT†, DESKJET†, LASERJET†, LASERJETII†, PAINTJET†, QUIETJET†, QUIETJETPLUS†, RUGGEWRITER†, RUGGEDWRITERWIDE†, THINKJET† profile = file containing info on supported printers (graphics.pro) /b -- prints background in color /lcd -- prints using LCD aspect ratio /printbox:id -- selects printbox size; id must match profile /r -- prints black and white
HELP†	ext	Yes	Provides online info about command	HELP [command]
JOIN	ext	No	Logically connects drives	JOIN [d1: [d2:]path] JOIN d: /D (to disconnect a previous JOIN)
KEYB	ext	Yes	Loads replacement keyboard driver if specified, or displays current setting	KEYB[xx[,[yyy][,[d:][path]filespec]]][/parms] xx = keyboard code yyy = code page /e -- specifies enhanced keyboard is installed† number = 437, 850, 860, 863, or 865
LABEL	ext	No	Creates or changes volume label	LABEL [d:][label]
LOADFIX†			Ensures that a program is loaded above the first 64K of conventional memory	LOADFIX [d:][path] filename [program-parameters]
LOADHIGH† (LH)	int	Yes	Loads program in upper memory	LOADHIGH [d:][path]filespec [parameters]
MEM*	ext	Yes	Displays amount of used & free memory	MEM [/PROGRAM] (displays programs loaded in memory) MEM [/CLASSIFY] (displays status of programs in conv and upper mem) MEM [/DEBUG] (displays programming information and program)
MIRROR†	ext	Yes	Starts MIRROR, which records disk info	MIRROR [d:[...]][/1] [/tdrive[-entries][...]] MIRROR [/u] MIRROR [/partn] /tdrive[-entries] -- loads TSR deletion-tracking program /1 -- retains only latest info about disk /u -- unloads deletion-tracking program /partn -- saves partition information
MKDIR (MD)	int	Yes	Creates subdirectory	MKDIR [d:]path
MODE	ext	Yes	Sets printer specifications Reports device status Sets video display mode	MODE LPT#[:][c][,[l][,r]] MODE LPT#[cols=c][lines=l][retry=r] c -- number of characters per line (80 or 132) l -- vertical spacing (6 or 8 lines per inch) # -- printer number r -- retry action (E=error, B=busy, R=ready, none=no retry) MODE [device][/STA[TUS]] MODE display, n MODE [display],shift[,test] MODE con[:][cols=m][lines=n] MODE [n],m[,T] (DOS 3.3 and earlier) n -- number of lines on display (25, 43, or 50) m -- characters per line (40 or 80) shift -- L for shift left or R for shift right (CGA only) display -- 40, 80, BW40, BW80, CO40, CO80, MONO test -- alignment display

(Continued)

2.01. DOS COMMAND SUMMARY (continued)

Command	Type	Net	Function	Syntax
			Sets serial port specifications	MODE COM#[:]b[,[p][,[d][,[s][,r]]]] MODE COM# baud=b[data=d][stop=s][parity=p][retry=r] b -- first two digits of baud rate (IBM source implies all digits required) d -- number of databits (5, 6, 7, or 8) # -- asyncronous port (1, 2, 3 or 4) p -- parity of N (none), O (odd), E (even), M (mark), S (Space) s = number of stop bits (1, 1.5, or 2) r -- retry action (E=error, B=busy, R=ready, none=no retry)
			Redirects parallel printer output	MODE LPT#[:]=COM# # -- port number (1,2,3, or 4)
			Set keyboard typematic rate	MODE con[:] rate=r delay=d d -- auto-repeat delay (1-4, in quarters of second) r -- typematic invertal time (1-32)
			Prepares code pages	MODE device CODEPAGE PREP[ARE]=((cp) [d:][path]filespec)
			Prepares code pages	MODE device CODEPAGE PREP[ARE]=((cplist)[d:][path]filespec)
			Selects or activates code pages	MODE device CODEPAGE SEL[ECT]=cp
			Displays active code page	MODE device CODEPAGE [/STA[TUS]]
			Refreshes a code page	MODE device CODEPAGE REF[RESH] cp -- code page number (437, 850, 860, 863, or 865) cplist -- a list of code page numbers
MORE	ext	Yes	Pipes paged data from stdin to stdout	MORE < source or source | MORE source -- a file or command
NLSFUNC	ext	Yes	Provides extended country support	NLSFUNC [[d:][path]filespec]
PATH	int	Yes	Sets search path for commands	PATH [[d:]path[;[d:]path...]] PATH ; (searches current directory only)
PRINT	ext	Yes	Puts selected files in print queue	PRINT [/parms][[d:][path][filespec]...][/c][/p] /b:size -- size of internal buffer, in bytes (max 1634) /c -- turns on cancel mode, removes filename from queue /d:device -- specifies print device name (LPT1, etc.) /m:number -- clock ticks (1-255) to print a character /p -- turns on print mode, adds filename to queue /q:qsize -- number of files allowed in queue (max 32) /s:number -- clock ticks for print handler (1-255) /t -- deletes all files from queue /u:number -- number of clock ticks PRINT waits for printer (1-255)
PROMPT	int	Yes	Sets new DOS prompt	PROMPT [prompt] see 2.08 PROMPT Special Characters
QBASIC†	ext	Yes	Starts QBasic	QBasic [/parms] [[/run][d:][path]filespec] /b -- displays QBasic in black and white /editor -- invokes MS-DOS editor /g -- provides fast CGA updates /h -- displays maximum number of lines on screen /mbf -- converts built-in functions to new names /nohi -- allows use of computer that doesn't support hi-intensity bit /run -- runs program before displaying it
RECOVER	ext	No	Recovers files from defective disk	RECOVER [d:][path]filespec or RECOVER d:
RENAME (REN)	int	Yes	Renames a file	RENAME [d:][path]filespec1 filespec2 filespec1=old name; filespec2=new name
REPLACE	ext	Yes	Replaces matching files on target	REPLACE [d:][path]filespec1 [d:][path][filespec2][/parms] /a -- adds only new files to target directory /p -- prompts before replacement /r -- replaces read-only files /s -- searches all subdirectories of target directory /u -- replaces only files older than source /w -- waits for disk insertion before searching source files
RESTORE	ext	Yes	Restores files that were backed up using the DOS BACKUP command	RESTORE d1: d2:[path][filespec][/parms] /a:date -- restores files modified on or after date /b:date -- restores files modified on or before date /e:time -- restores files modified at or earlier than time /L:time -- restores files modified at or after time /m -- restores files modified since last backup /d -- displays list of files on backup without restoring them† /n -- restores only files that no longer exist on the target disk (d2) /p -- prompts before restoring files /s -- restores subdirectories
RMDIR (RD)	int	Yes	Deletes a subdirectory from disk	RMDIR [d:]path
SELECT¥	ext	Yes	Installs DOS on new disk	SELECT
SET	int	Yes	Sets one string of characters in the environment equal to another string	SET [string=[string]]

(Continued)

2.01. DOS COMMAND SUMMARY (continued)

Command	Type	Net	Function	Syntax
SETVER†	ext	Yes	Sets version number DOS reports	SETVER [d:path][filespec n.nn] SETVER [d:path][filespec [/delete [/quiet]] SETVER [d:path] filespec -- name to add to version table n.nn -- version number to display /delete -- deletes version entry for specified program /quiet -- hides message displayed during deletion
SHARE	ext	Yes	Loads file sharing and locking support	SHARE [/parms] /f:space -- allocates space for sharing, in bytes /l:locks -- allocates number of locks
SORT	ext	Yes	Sorts stdin data, sends to stdout	[source] | SORT [/parms] SORT [/parms] <source /r -- sorts in descending order /+# -- sorts file using data beginning at column # source -- filename or command producing output
SUBST	ext	No	Creates drive specifier for drive or path	SUBST [d1: d2:path] SUBST d: /d /d -- deletes a virtual drive
SYS	ext	No	Copies DOS onto disk	SYS [d1:][path] d2: d1 -- location of system files d2 -- destination of system files
TIME	int	Yes	Sets, changes, or displays time	TIME [hours:minutes[:seconds[.hundredths]]]
TREE	ext	Yes	Graphically displays directory paths	TREE [d:][/parms] /a -- uses available graphic characters /f -- displays names of all files in directory
TYPE	int	Yes	Displays contents of file on stdout	TYPE [d:][path]filespec
UNDELETE†	ext	No	Restores file previously deleted	UNDELETE [[d:][path]filespec] [/list|/all] [/dos|/dt] /list -- lists deleted files /all -- recovers files without prompt /dos -- recovers only files deleted by DOS /dt -- recovers only files listed as deleted by MIRROR
UNFORMAT†	ext	No	Restores disk erased by FORMAT command or restructured by RECOVER	UNFORMAT d: [/j] UNFORMAT d: [/u] [/l] [/test] [/p] UNFORMAT [/partn] [/l] /j -- verifies file created by MIRROR agrees with system info on disk /u -- unformats a disk without using MIRROR file /l -- lists every file found /test -- shows how unformat will recreate info on disk /p -- sends output messages to printer /partn -- restores corrupted partition table
VER	int	Yes	Displays DOS version number	VER
VERIFY	int	Yes	Sets verify after write status	VERIFY [ON|OFF]
VOL	int	Yes	Displays volume label	VOL [d:]
XCOPY	ext	Yes	Selectively copies groups of files to disk	XCOPY [d:][path]filespec1 [d:][path][filespec2][/parms] XCOPY [d:]path[filespec1] [d:][path][filespec2][/parms] XCOPY d:[path][filespec1] [d:][path][filespec2][/parms] filespec1 = source file(s); filespec2 = destination file(s) /a -- copies source files with archive bit set /d:date -- copies files modified on or after date /e -- copies empty subdirectories (/s must be included) /m -- same as /a, but turns off archive bit in source after copy /p -- prompts at each file /s -- copies all subdirectories in path /v -- verifies each file as it is written /w -- waits before copying files

*Applies to all versions of MS-DOS or PC-DOS beginning with 4.0.
†Applies to all versions of MS-DOS beginning with 5.0.
¥Does not apply to DOS 5.0.

(Continued)

2.01. DOS COMMAND SUMMARY (continued)

Note:

- Some of the above commands may not be in all versions of DOS.
- IBM syntax specifications are followed, except this table uses "file" or "filespec" for "filename[.ext]" and:
  [ ] -- items in square brackets are optional.
  ... -- optional repeats of previous item(s)
  d: -- drive (d1: -- first drive, d2: -- second drive, and so on)
  /parms -- slash parameters (e.g. /a, /b, and so on) described immediately below command syntax
  other items -- represented with short names or mnemonics that should be self-explanatory

Source:

IBM DOS 3.3 Technical Reference, section 7
Microsoft MS-DOS 4.0 User's Guide and Reference, Chapter 3
Using IBM DOS 4.0, Chapters 2, 3, and 6
Microsoft MS-DOS 5.0 User's Guide and Reference, Chapter 14
MIcrosoft MS-DOS 5.0, Getting Started, pages 41 and 53

See Also:

2.05. Editing DOS Command Lines
2.06. Batch File Commands
2.07. CONFIG.SYS Commands and Default Settings
2.08. PROMPT Special Characters
2.16. DOSSHELL Program Startup Options
2.32. Included Command Files Summary

2.02. EXIT CODES RETURNED BY DOS COMMANDS

Command	Exit Codes
BACKUP	0 -- Normal completion 1 -- No files were found to back up 2 -- Some files not backed up due to sharing conflicts 3 -- BACKUP terminated by user 4 -- BACKUP terminated due to error
DISKCOMP	0 -- Compared OK; disks are duplicates 1 -- Did not compare; disks are different 2 -- Compare terminated by Control-C 3 -- Hard error; comparison not completed 4 -- Initialization error; not enough memory, invalid drives or syntax
DISKCOPY	0 -- Copies OK. 1 -- Nonfatal read/write error 2 -- Copy terminated by Control-C 3 -- Fatal hard error; unable to read source or format target 4 -- Initialization error; not enough memory, invalid drives or syntax
FORMAT	0 -- Format OK 3 -- Format terminated by Control-C 4 -- Fatal error 5 -- N response to hard disk format prompt
GRAFTABL	0 -- Command successful; no previous code page loaded 1 -- Table previously loaded replaced by new one 2 -- File error 3 -- Incorrect parameter; no action taken 4 -- Incorrect DOS version; no action taken
KEYB	0 -- Command successful 1 -- Invalid syntax 2 -- Bad or missing keyboard definition file 3 -- Could not create keyboard table in resident memory* 4 -- Error with CON device 5 -- Code page requested not prepared 6 -- Table for selected code page not found in resident keyboard table* 7 -- Incorrect DOS version; no action taken*
REPLACE	0 -- Command successful 2 -- File not found 3 -- Path not found 5 -- Access Denied 8 -- Insufficient memory 11 -- Command line error 15 -- Invalid drive*
RESTORE	0 -- Command successful 1 -- No files found to restore 3 -- Terminated by user 4 -- Terminated due to other error
SETVER	0 -- Command successful 1 -- Invalid command switch 2 -- Invalid filename 3 -- Insufficient system memory to carry out command 4 -- Invalid version-number format 5 -- Entry not found in version table 6 -- SETVER.EXE not found 7 -- Invalid drive 8 -- Too many command line parameters 9 -- Missing command line parameters 10 -- Error while reading SETVER.EXE 11 -- SETVER.EXE is corrupt 12 -- SETVER.EXE does not support version table 13 -- Insufficient space in version table for new entry 14 -- Error while writing SETVER.EXE
XCOPY	0 -- Command successful 1 -- No files found to copy 2 -- Terminated by Control-C 4 -- Initialization error; not enough memory, invalid options 5 -- Int 24 error

*Not in DOS 5.0.

Version: Applies to all versions of DOS beginning with 4.0.

Note:
- Other DOS commands may return values, but are not documented.
- A return of 0 is virtually always indicative of success, non-zero indicates an error.

Source: Microsoft MS-DOS 4.0 User's Guide and Reference, pages 36 through 141
Microsoft MS-DOS 5.0 User's Guide and Reference, pages 370 through 590

See Also: 2.01. DOS Command Summary
2.03. DOS Extended Error Messages
2.04. DOS Parse Error Messages

2.03. DOS EXTENDED ERROR MESSAGES

Number	*Message*
1	Invalid function
2	File not found
3	Path not found
4	Too many open files
5	Access denied
6	Invalid handle
7	Memory control blocks destroyed
8	Insufficient memory
9	Invalid memory block address
10	Invalid environment
11	Invalid format
12	Invalid function parameter
13	Invalid data
15	Invalid drive specification
16	Attempt to remove current directory
17	Not the same device
18	No more files
19	Write protect error
20	Invalid unit
21	Not ready
22	Invalid device request
23	Data error
24	Invalid device request parameters
25	Seek error
26	Invalid media type
27	Sector not found
28	Printer out of paper error
29	Write fault error
30	Read fault error
31	General failure
32	Sharing violation
33	Lock violation
34	Invalid disk change
35	FCB unavailable
36	System resource exhausted
38	Out of input
39	Insufficient disk space
80	File exists
82	Cannot make directory entry
83	Fail on INT 24
84	Too many redirections
85	Duplicate redirection
86	Invalid password
87	Invalid parameter
88	Network data fault
90	Required system component not installed

Note:
- These errors appear when the /MSG parameter is not used for Shell.
- These error numbers appear as "Extended Error x" on display.

Source: Using IBM DOS 4.0, pages 203 through 204
Microsoft MS-DOS 5.0 Programmer's Reference, pages 447 through 449

See Also: 2.01. DOS Command Summary
2.02. Exit Codes Returned by DOS Commands
2.04. DOS Parse Error Messages

2.04. DOS PARSE ERROR MESSAGES

Number	*Message*
1	Too many parameters
2	Required parameter missing
3	Invalid switch
4	Invalid keyword
6	Parameter value not in allowed range
7	Parameter value not allowed
8	Parameter value not allowed
9	Parameter format not correct
10	Invalid parameter
11	Invalid parameter combination

Version: Applies to DOS 4.0 only.

Note:
- These messages appear when the /MSG parameter is not used for Shell.
- These messages appear as "Parse Error x" on display.

Source: Using IBM DOS 4.0, page 204

See Also:
2.01. DOS Command Summary
2.02. Exit Codes Returned by DOS Commands
2.03. DOS Extended Error Messages

2.05. EDITING DOS COMMAND LINES

Key	*Function*
F1	Supplies next character from the command buffer
F2	Supplies all characters from the command buffer up to the next character you type (e.g., [F2][r] is up to r)
F3	Supplies all remaining characters from the command buffer
F4	Skips all characters from the command buffer up to next character typed (e.g., [F4][r] skips to r)
F5	Erases previous command buffer and replaces it with current command line
F6*	Places end-of-file marker (1AH) in the command buffer
Esc	Erases current command line
-->	Supplies next character from the command buffer
<--†	Deletes character before cursor on current command line
Backspace†	Deletes character before cursor on current command line
Ctrl + H	Removes last character from the current command line
Ctrl + J	Inserts a physical end-of-line but does not effect the current command line
Ctrl + X§	Cancels current command line, moves to next line of display
Ins	Inserts a character at current spot in the command buffer
Del	Deletes the character at the current spot in the command buffer

The following keys apply only to DOS 5.0 with DOSKEY resident

Up Arrow	Displays previous command in command list
Down Arrow	Displays next command in command list
F7	Displays list of commands stored by DOSKEY
F8	Cycles through stored commands starting with characters you type (type chars, then F8)
F9	Prompts for the number of a stored command
Page Up	Displays oldest command in command list
Page Down	Displays newest command in command list
Ctrl+T	Separates multiple commands on a single line
Home	Moves cursor to beginning of displayed command
End	Moves cursor to end of displayed command
<--	Moves cursor back one character in displayed command
-->	Moves cursor forward one character in displayed command
Ctrl+<--	Moves cursor back one word in displayed command
Ctrl + -->	Moves cursor forward one word in displayed command
Backspace	Moves cursor back one character by deleting previous character
Del	Deletes current character
Ctrl+End	Deletes all characters from cursor to end of line
Ctrl+Home	Deletes all characters from cursor to start of line
Ins	Toggles between insert and overstrike typing mode
Esc	Clears displayed command from screen

*Applies to all versions of DOS beginning with 4.0.
†Applies to all versions of DOS beginning with 5.0.
§May not work in all versions.

Note: DOS keeps the last command typed in a buffer, and it is available even after the execution of a program, e.g., BASICA "myprog" runs a Basic program named "myprog." After the program has finished, the DOS command line buffer still contains BASICA "myprog."

Source:
IBM DOS 3.3 Technical Reference, page 2-5
Microsoft MS-DOS 4.0 User's Guide and Reference, pages 165 through 171
Using IBM DOS 4.0, pages 12 through 13
Microsoft MS-DOS 5.0 User's Guide and Reference, pages 166 through 174

2.06. BATCH FILE COMMANDS

Command	Function	Syntax	Allowable Settings	Example
:label	Label (destination of a GOTO statement)	:string	Colon followed by any characters or spaces	:ENDOFBATCHFILE
@command*	Does not echo command on display	@command	Any valid DOS or batch command	@ECHO OFF
%number	Substitutes command line parameter	%number	0-9 (0=command name)	DIR %1.%2
%string%	Substitutes environment variable (made with SET)	%string%	Any variable created with SET command	IF %OKAY% == "Y" GOTO YES
BREAK	Sets Control-C interrupt status	BREAK [ON|OFF]	ON, OFF	BREAK ON
CALL	Calls another batch file as a subroutine	CALL filename	Filename may include path	CALL DOINST
ECHO	Sets echo status or displays string	ECHO [ON|OFF] ECHO [string]	ON, OFF, message string	ECHO This is a message.
FOR	Performs a command for a set of files	FOR %%var IN (set) DO command	%%var (can be any characters except 0-9)	FOR %%file IN (DOS,WRITE) DO DEL %%file.DAT
GOTO	Branches execution to new location in batch file	GOTO label	Any valid label	GOTO ENDOFBATCHFILE
IF	Controls execution based upon error level	IF [NOT] ERRORLEVEL # command	# = 0-255	IF ERRORLEVEL 6 GOTO HEK
	Controls execution based upon existence of file	IF [NOT] EXIST filename command	Any DOS filename	IF EXIST %1.%2 ERASE %1.%2
	Controls execution based upon string comparison	IF [NOT] string==string command	Any string or %parameter	IF %1=="hogan" GOTO THOM
PAUSE	Pauses execution until key pressed	PAUSE [string]	Any message string	PAUSE Press a key to continue.
REM	Nonexecutable remark	REM [string]	Any message string	REM Doesn't display if ECHO OFF or @ precedes
SHIFT	Shifts command line parameters down one number	SHIFT	NA	SHIFT

*Command may be any valid DOS command.

Version: @ is available in DOS 3.3 and above.
CALL is available in DOS 3.3 and above.
%string% and SET are not documented in all versions of DOS but appear starting in DOS 2.0.
ECHO and REM should be followed by at least one nonspace character in DOS 3.0 and above.

Source: IBM DOS 3.3 Technical Reference, pages 7-31 through 7-55
Microsoft MS-DOS 4.0 User's Guide and Reference, pages 153 through 163
Using IBM DOS 4.0, pages 117 through 125
Microsoft MS-DOS 5.0 User's Guide and Reference, Chapter 14

2.07. CONFIG.SYS COMMANDS AND DEFAULT SETTINGS

Command	*Allowable Settings*	*Default Settings*	*Example*
AVAILDEV=state	TRUE FALSE	TRUE	AVAILDEV=FALSE
BREAK[=ON|OFF]	ON -- enables Ctrl-C checking OFF -- disables Ctrl-C checking	OFF	BREAK=ON
BUFFERS=n[,m][/x]	n -- # of disk buffers, 1-99 m -- max # of sectors read at once, 1-8 /x -- 10000 buffers (or less if insufficient memory)¥	<128K, 360K disk = 2 <128K, >360K disk = 3 128-255K RAM = 5 256-511K RAM =10 512-640K RAM = 15	BUFFERS=20
COUNTRY=xxx[,[yyy][d:] [path][filespec]	Country code, code page, country info file *Code* *Pages* *Country* 001 437,850 United States 002 863,850 French-Canadian 003 437,850 Latin America 031 437,850 Netherlands 032 437,850 Belgium 033 437,850 France 034 437,850 Spain 036 852,850 Hungary 038 852,850 Yugoslavia 039 437,850 Italy 041 437,850 Switzerland 042 852,850 Czechoslovakia 044 437,850 United Kingdom 045 865,850 Denmark 046 437,850 Sweden 047 865,850 Norway 049 437,850 Germany 055 850,437 Brazil 061 437,850 English (International) 351 860,850 Portugal 358 437,850 Finland 785 437 Arabic 972 437 Israel 081 932,850,437 Japan 082 934,850,437 Korea 086 936,850,437 Republic of China 088 938,850,437 Taiwan	001,437,\country.sys	COUNTRY=044,850,c:\dos\country.sys
DEVICE=[d:][path] filespec[parms]	Any DOS path and filename that references a valid DOS device: display.sys, driver.sys, printer.sys, ramdrive.sys, or ansi.sys, for example	None	DEVICE=DRIVER.SYS
DEVICEHIGH=[d:][path] filespec[parms]§	Any DOS path and filename that references a valid DOS device that you want to load into high memory	None	DEVICEHIGH=DRIVER.SYS
DOS=high|low[,umb|noumb] or DOS=[high,|low,]umb|noumb§	Specifies that DOS should maintain a link to the upper memory area or load itself in high memory	noumb, low	DOS=HIGH
DRIVPARM = /d:# [/c] [/f:#][/h:#][/i][/n][/s:#][/t:#]	/d:# -- physical drive # (0-255) /c -- drive supports change line /f:# -- 0=160/180 or 320/360K disk 1=1.2MB disk 2=720K (3.5") disk 5=hard disk 6=tape drive 7=1.44MB (3.5") disk 8=read/write optical disk 9=2.88MB (3.5") disk /h:# -- number of heads (1-99) /i -- electrically-compatible 3.5" disk /n -- nonremovable block device /s:# -- sectors per track (1-99) /t:# -- tracks per side (1-999)	/F:2 /T:80 /H:2 /S:9	DRIVPARM /D:1 /F:1
FCBS=x,y	x = # of files FCBS can open at one time (≥y) y = # of files opened by FCBS that DOS cannot close automatically¥	4,0	FCBS=20,20
FILES=x	x = number of open files DOS can access (8-255)	8	FILES=20
INSTALL=[d:][path] filespec [commandline]†	Commandline must be FASTOPEN, KEYB, NLSFUNC, or SHARE	None	INSTALL=FASTOPEN.EXE c:50
LASTDRIVE=letter	A-Z	E	LASTDRIVE=H
REM text†	Inserts comment in CONFIG.SYS file	None	REM Add device drivers here:

(Continued)

2.07. CONFIG.SYS COMMANDS AND DEFAULT SETTINGS (continued)

Command	*Allowable Settings*	*Default Settings*	*Example*
SHELL=[d:][path]file [commandline]	Allowable commandline is any command processor program	SHELL=COMMAND.COM	SHELL=C:\DOS\COMMAND.COM
STACKS=n,s	n -- # of stacks (0-64) s -- size of each stack (0-512)	9,128 for AT & newer	STACKS=12,256
SWITCHES=/k§	Forces enhanced keybd to act like standard	None	SWITCHES=/k
SWITCHAR=char	Any character	\	SWITCHAR=/

*For DOS 2.0-3.2. Beginning with DOS 3.3, if RAM ≥128K, BUFFERS=5; if RAM ≥256K, BUFFERS=10; if RAM ≥512K, BUFFERS=15.
†Applies to all versions of DOS beginning with 4.0
§Applies to all versions of DOS beginning with 5.0
¥Not in DOS 5.0

Version: AVAILDEV and SWITCHAR are undocumented and work only in DOS version 2.x.
COUNTRY, FCBS, and LASTDRIVE are available only in DOS 3.0 and later.
STACKS is available only in DOS 3.2 and later.
DRIVPARM is generally only used with DOS 3.2.

Source: IBM DOS 3.3 Technical Reference, pages 4-1 through 4-44
Microsoft MS-DOS 4.0 User's Guide and Reference, pages 277 through 296
Using IBM DOS 4.0, pages 67 through 109
Microsoft MS-DOS 5.0 User's Guide and Reference, pages 249 through 255

See Also: 2.08. PROMPT Special Characters
2.09. PROMPT ANSI Control Strings
2.10. PROMPT ANSI Display Attribute Strings
3.199. Country Codes

2.08. PROMPT SPECIAL CHARACTERS

Character	*Displays As*		*Example*	*Example Displays As*
$b	Pipe (|)	ASCII 124	pb	C:\MYDIR|
$d	Current system date		$d ng	Mon 9-5-1986 C>
$e	Escape character	ASCII 27	See 2.09. PROMPT ANSI Control Strings	
$g	Greater than sign (>)	ASCII 62	pg	C:\MYDIR>
$h	Destructive backspace	ASCII 8	thhh pg	09:30:25 C:\MYDIR>
$l	Less than sign (<)	ASCII 60	ln$g	<C>
$n	Current drive letter		Drive is ng	Drive is C>
$p	Current pathname directory		Path is pg	Path is C:\MYDIR>
$q	Equals sign (=)	ASCII 61	Drive $q ng	Drive = C>
$t	Current system time		Time is $t	Time is 09:30:25.93
$v	DOS version number		$v	IBM Personal Computer DOS Version 3.20
$_	Carriage return/line feed	ASCII 13,10	thhh$_$p$g	9:30:25 C:\MYDIR>
$$	Dollar sign ($)	ASCII 36	Time is $$$g	Time is $>
Any other	Treated as character typed		This is a prompt	This is a prompt

Version: Applies to all versions of DOS beginning with version 2.0.

Note: Examples assume that the current system date is September 5, 1986, the current time is 9:30:25:93, and the current logged drive and directory are C:\MYDIR.

Source: IBM DOS 3.3 Technical Reference, page 7-177
Microsoft MS-DOS 4.0 User's Guide and Reference, pages 111 through 112
Using IBM DOS 4.0, pages 47 through 48
Microsoft MS-DOS 5.0 User's Guide and Reference, pages 545 through 546

See Also: 2.09. PROMPT ANSI Control Strings
2.10. PROMPT ANSI Display Attribute Strings

2.09. PROMPT ANSI CONTROL STRINGS

String	*Function*
$e[#;# f	Moves cursor to row (first #) and column (second #) position
$e[=# h	Sets display mode according to number (#): 0 = 40x25 monochrome 1 = 40x25 color 2 = 80x25 monochrome 3 = 80x25 color 4 = 320x200 color graphics 5 = 320x200 monochrome graphics 6 = 640x200 monochrome graphics 7 = wrap at end of line 14 = 640 x 200 color* 15 = 640 x 350 mono* 16 = 640 x 350 color* 17 = 640 x 480 color* 18 = 640 x 480 color* 19 = 320 x 200 color*
$e[=# l	Resets display mode according to number (#): 0 = 40x25 monochrome 1 = 40x25 color 2 = 80x25 monochrome 3 = 80x25 color 4 = 320x200 color graphics 5 = 320x200 monochrome graphics 6 = 640x200 monochrome graphics 7 = do not wrap at end of line
$e[#;...;#m	Sets display attributes (see 2.10. PROMPT ANSI Display Attribute Strings)
$e[#;# p	Reassigns first key (first #) to second (second #) or remap key (first #) to ASCII string
$e[#,"string";p	Reassigns key (#) to string (in quotes)
$e[s	Saves current cursor position
$e[u	Restores cursor to saved position
$e[#A	Moves cursor up number of rows indicated by # (ignored if cursor on top line)
$e[#B	Moves cursor down number of rows indicated by # (ignored if cursor on bottom line)
$e[#C	Moves cursor right number of columns indicated by # (ignored if cursor in last column)
$e[#D	Moves cursor left number of columns indicated by # (ignored if cursor in first column)
$e[F	Moves cursor to the Home position (row 1, column 1)
$e[#;# F	Moves cursor to row (first #) and column (second #) position
$e[H	Moves cursor to the Home position (row 1, column 1)
$e[#;# H	Moves cursor to row (first #) and column (second #) position
$e[2J	Clears display screen
$e[K	Erases from cursor to end of line, including cursor position
$e[#;# R	Reports cursor position through standard input
$e[6n	Console driver outputs cursor position report sequence (cannot be used as part of prompt)

*First documented in MS-DOS 4.0.

Version: Applies to all versions of DOS beginning with version 2.0.

Note:
- There should be no spaces in the ANSI control strings.
- $e represents the Escape character (ASCII 27).

Source: IBM DOS 3.3 Technical Reference, pages 3-1 through 3-20
Microsoft MS-DOS 4.0 User's Guide and Reference, pages 299 through 308
Microsoft MS-DOS 5.0 User's Guide and Reference, pages 263 through 269

See Also: 1.21. ASCII Character Set
1.23. IBM Keyboard Extended Function Codes
2.08. PROMPT Special Characters
2.10. PROMPT ANSI Display Attribute Strings

2.10. PROMPT ANSI DISPLAY ATTRIBUTE STRINGS

String	Sets Display Attributes to	Video Adapter MDA	CGA	EGA	VGA
$e[0m	Normal	✔	✔	✔	✔
$e[1m	Bright (intensity bit set)	✔	✔	✔	✔
$e[4m	Underscored	✔			
$e[5m	Blinking	✔			
$e[7m	Reversed	✔	✔	✔	✔
$e[8m	Canceled (invisible)	✔			
$e[30m	Black foreground		✔	✔	✔
$e[31m	Red foreground		✔	✔	✔
$e[32m	Green foreground		✔	✔	✔
$e[33m	Yellow foreground		✔	✔	✔
$e[34m	Blue foreground		✔	✔	✔
$e[35m	Magenta foreground		✔	✔	✔
$e[36m	Cyan foreground		✔	✔	✔
$e[37m	White foreground		✔	✔	✔
$e[40m	Black background		✔	✔	✔
$e[41m	Red background		✔	✔	✔
$e[42m	Green background		✔	✔	✔
$e[43m	Yellow background		✔	✔	✔
$e[44m	Blue background		✔	✔	✔
$e[45m	Magenta background		✔	✔	✔
$e[46m	Cyan background		✔	✔	✔
$e[47m	White background		✔	✔	✔

Version: •Applies to all versions of DOS beginning with version 2.0.
•Parameters 30-47 conform to ISO 6429 standard.

Note: • No spaces may appear in the string.
• $e represents the Escape character (ASCII 27).

Source: IBM DOS 3.3 Technical Reference, page 3-15
Microsoft MS-DOS 4.0 User's Guide and Reference, pages 300 through 301
Microsoft MS-DOS 5.0 User's Guide and Reference, pages 269 through 272

See Also: 2.08. PROMPT Special Characters
2.09. PROMPT ANSI Control Strings

2.11 DEVICE DRIVER PARAMETERS

Device Driver	*Syntax*	*Parameters*	*Example*
ANSI.SYS	device=[drive:][path]ansi.sys[/x][/k]	/x remaps extended keys independently on 101-key keyboard /k ignores extended keys on 101-key keyboard	device=ansi.sys /x
DISPLAY.SYS	device=[d:][path]display.sys con[:]= (type[,[codepage][,n,m]])	type -- MONO, CGA, EGA, LCD code page -- 437 United States 850 Multilingual (Latin I) 852 Slavic (Latin II)§ 860 Portugal 863 French-Canadian 865 Norway n -- number of additional code pages m -- number of subfonts/code page	device=display.sys con:=(ega,850,2)
DRIVER.SYS	device=driver.sys /d:#[/c][/f:#] [/h:#][s:#][/t:#]	/d:# -- physical drive # (0-127) /c -- drive supports change line /f:# -- 0=160, 180, 320, or 360K disk 1=1.2MB disk 2=720K (3.5") disk 7=1.44MB (3.5") disk 9=2.88MB (3.5") disk /h:# -- number of heads (1-99) /s:# -- sectors per track (1-99) /t:# -- tracks per side (1-999)	device=driver.sys /d:1/f:2/h:2/s:9/t:80
EMM386.EXE§	device=[d:][path]emm386.exe [on|off|auto][memory][w=on|off] [mx|frame=address|/pmmmm] [pn=address][x=mmmm-nnn] [i=mmmm-nnnn][b=address] [L=minXMS][a=altregs][h=handles] [d=nnn][ram][noems]	on activates driver off suspends driver auto sets driver to auto mode memory amount of memory (16-32768) w=on weitek coprocessor support w=off no weitek support mx x=1-14 and specifies page frame to use (see source) frame specifies page frame location directly (i.e., actual address) /p mmmm is address of frame p n is page number address is segment address x mmmm-nnnn is range of addresses to block i mmmm-nnnn is range of addresses to use b addtress is lowest segment address available for EMS L minXMS is minimum of memory available after load a altregs is number of alt reg sets to allocate (0-254) d nnn is kilobytes of memory to reserve for buffered access (16-256) ram access to both exp memory and upper memory area noems access to upper memory area but not expanded memory h handles is number of handles to use (2-255)	device=emm386.exe frame=d000 x=E000-EC00 h-127 ram
HIMEM.SYS	device=[d:][path]himem.sys [/hmamin=m][/numhandles=n] [/int15=xxxx][/machine:xxxx] [/a20control:on|off] [/shadowram:on|off] [/cpuclock:on|off]	/hmamin amt of memory in K program must use before it can use high memory area (0-63) /num handles max EMB handles that can be used simultaneously (1-128) /int15 xxxx is amout of extended memory in K for INT 15H interface (64-65535) /machine coded value indicating machine A20 handler (see source)	device=himem.sys /machine:ps2

(Continued)

2.11 DEVICE DRIVER PARAMETERS (continued)

Device Driver	Syntax	Parameters	Example
PRINTER.SYS	device=[d:][path]printer.sys lpt#=(type[,codepage[,...]][,n])	type -- 4201, 4208, 5202 code page -- 437 United States 850 Multilingual (Latin I) 852 Slavic (Latin II)§ 860 Portugal 863 French-Canadian 865 Norway n -- number additional code pages	device=printer.sys lpt1=(4201,437,2)
RAMDRIVE.SYS*	device=ramdrive.sys [d][s][e][/e|/a]	d -- disk size in K s -- sector size in bytes (128, 256, 512, or 1024) e -- root dir entries (4-1024) /e -- use extended memory /a -- use expanded memory	device=ramdrive.sys 16 512 64 /e
SMARTDRIVE.SYS†	device=[d:][path]smartdrv.sys [#][/a]	# -- size of cache in K /a -- use expanded memory	device=smartdrv.sys 1024/a

*IBM DOS users should see information on VDISK.SYS (page 84 of Using IBM DOS 4.0).
†Applies to all versions of DOS beginning with 4.0.
§Applies to all versions of DOS beginning with 5.0.

Source: Microsoft MS-DOS 4.0 User's Guide and Reference, pages 297 through 313
Using IBM DOS 4.0, pages 76 through 99
Microsoft MS-DOS 5.0 User's Guide and Reference, pages 591 through 619

See Also: 2.07. CONFIG.SYS Commands and Default Settings

2.12. DEBUG COMMAND SUMMARY

Command Syntax	Function	Example	Example Explanation/Comments
A	Assemble statements into memory immediately following last assembly entry	A	Assemble statements at current pointer Entry continues until ENTER pressed at start of line
A [address]	Assemble statements into memory beginning at address	A100	Assemble statements at 100H Entry continues until ENTER pressed at start of line
C range address	Compare two blocks of memory	C100 L20 200	Compare 32 (20H) bytes at 100H to 32 bytes at 200H
D	Dump (display) contents of memory starting following last position displayed	D	Display memory at current pointer
D [address] ¥	Dump (display) contents of memory starting at address	D208	
D [range]	Dump (display) contents of memory of range specified	D 100 L600	Display 600H bytes of memory, starting at DS:0100
E address	Enter hex bytes of data beginning at address specified	E DS:50	Enter data beginning at 50H in Data Segment Entry continues until ENTER pressed; SPACE skips
E address [list]	Enter list of bytes beginning at address specified	E 100 20 20	Enter two spaces starting at 100 H in current segment
F range list	Fill memory range with sequence of bytes in list	F DS:00 L0F "TEH"	Enter five repetitions of TEH at start of Data Segment Extra items in list beyond end of range are ignored
G	Go (begins execution) at current instruction (CS:IP)	G	Execute instructions at CS:IP
G [=address]	Go (begins execution) at address	G =100	Start execution at 0100H in current CS
G [=address [addresslist]]	Go (begins execution) at address with breakpoints specified in addresslist	G =100 10A 213	Same as above, but break if 10AH or 213H reached
H value1 value2	Hex math performed (add 2 to 1, subtract 2 from 1) on value1 and value2	H 0F 8	Add 8 to 0F, subtract 8 from 0F Results displayed on next line
I portaddress	Input one byte from portaddress	I 2E6	Get input from port 2E6H Results displayed on next line
L	Load file (whose file specification is at CS:80) beginning with length byte	L	Load file whose name and type are at CS:80 File loaded beginning at CS:100
L [address]	Load file (whose file specification is at CS:80) beginning at address	L 506	Load file beginning at 506H in memory COM/EXE files always loaded at CS:100, however
L [address [drive sector 1 sector2]]§	Load sector2 disk sectors from drive, beginning with sector1, into address	L DS:100 2 0 3	Load first three sectors of drive C begining at DS:100
M range address	Move memory from range to new address	M 100 L10 500	Move 16 bytes from 100H to 500H Moves performed w/o loss of memory during transfer
N[filespec]†	Name of file to place at CS:81 and in FCBs	N c:debug.com	Prepare debug.com for use by debugger
O portaddress byte	Send a byte to specified port	O 2E6 FF	Send FFH to port 2E6H

(Continued)

2.12. DEBUG COMMAND SUMMARY (continued)

Command Syntax	*Function*	*Example*	*Example Explanation/Comments*
P	Proceed to end of call, loop, interrupt, or repeat string instruction	P	Execution starts at CS:IP P uses same syntax as T(race)
P [=address]	Proceed from address to end of call, loop, interrupt, or repeat instruction	P =1044	Execution starts at CS:1044 P uses same syntax as T(race)
P [=address] [value]	Proceed from address to end of call, loop, int, or repeat, or for value instructions	P =1044 10	Execution starts at CS:1044 for no more than 16 bytes
Q	Quit DEBUG	Q	DEBUG is terminated immediately Working memory NOT saved by this command
R	Display all registers	R	Display current contents of all registers
R registername*	Display contents of registername and allow entry of new value	R AX	Display AX contents and wait for new value Pressing only ENTER leaves contents unchanged
S range list	Search the range of memory for the contents in list	S 100 L100 "TEH"	Search for pattern "TEH" in 100H bytes starting at CS:100H
T	Trace a single instruction	T	Trace instructions from CS:IP, display registers
T [=address]	Trace a single instruction at address	T CS:106	Trace instructions from CS:106H, display registers
T [=address] [value]	Trace value instructions beginning at address	T 100 10	Trace 16 instructions from CS:100H 0=trace forever (same as G)
U	Unassemble instructions at CS:IP	U	Display disassembly of 20H bytes of instructions at CS:IP
U address	Unassemble instructions at address	U 100	Display disassembly of 20H bytes of instructions at 100H
U range	Unassemble instructions for range bytes	U 100 108	Display disassembly of instructions from 100H to 108H
W	Write file (named at CS:81H) to disk (80H contains number of bytes)	W	Write file in memory to disk BX:CX must contain # of bytes to write
W [address]	Write file (named at CS:80H) to disk beginning with byte at address	W 108	Write file beginning at 108H in memory to disk BX:CX must contain # of bytes to write
W [address [drive: sector1 sector2]]	Write data at address to drive starting with sector1 for sector2 sectors	W 108 2 0 3	Write first three sectors to drive C from memory at 108H
XA [count]¶	Number of 16K pages of EM to allocate	XA 8	Allocate 8 pages of expanded memory
XD [handle]¶	Handle to deallocate	XD 0003	Deallocate handle 0003
XM [lpage][ppage] [handle]¶	Maps logical page of expanded memory to a physical page of memory	XM 5 2 0003	Maps logical page 5 of handle 0003 to physical page 2
XS	Displays expanded memory status	XS	Displays current status

*Valid registers are: AX, BP, BX, CS, CX, DI, DS, DX, ES, F, IP, PC, SI, SP, and SS.
To set flags, use the following two-character mnemonics:

Flag	*Set*	*Clear*
Overflow	OV	NV
Direction	DN (Decrement)	UP (Increment)
Interrupt	EI (Enable)	DI (Disable)
Sign	NG (Negative)	PL (Plus)
Zero	ZR	NZ
Auxiliary Carry	AC	NA
Parity	PE (Even)	PO (Odd)
Carry	CY	NC

†MS-DOS 4.0 allows multiple filenames to be used in the N command.
¶Applies to all versions of DOS beginning with 5.0.
§DOS 5.0 says last number is the number of sectors.
¥Not in DOS 5.0.

Note: Lowercase names in command syntax indicate items you replace with values.

Source: IBM DOS 3.3 Technical Reference, pages 13-15 through 13-58
Microsoft MS-DOS 4.0 User's Guide and Reference, pages 235 through 274
Microsoft MS-DOS 5.0 User's Guide and Reference, pages 399 through 431

See Also: 6.110. Symbolic Debugger (SYMDEB) Command Summary

2.13. EDLIN COMMAND SUMMARY

Command Syntax	Function	Example	Example Explanation/Comments
A	Append lines from file to memory	A	Append lines from file until 75% of memory is full Applies only if file is too large to fit into memory
[#]A	Append # lines from file to memory	5A	Append 5 lines from file
[line] C	Copy current line to line	10C	Copy current line to line 10
[line1],[line2],line3 C	Copy range of line 1 to line 2 to area beginning with line 3	1,2,3C	Copy lines 1 and 2 to lines 3 and 4
[line1],[line2],line3[,count] C	Copy range of line 1 to line 2 count times to area starting at line 3	1,2,3,2C	Copy lines 1 and 2 to lines 3 and 4, 5 and 6
D	Delete current line from memory	D	Delete current line
[line1],[line2] D	Delete range of lines between line 1 and line 2 from memory	1,3D	Delete lines 1 through 3
.	Edit current line		Edit current line
line	Edit line number specified	10	Edit line number 10
E	End EDLIN and save file	E	End EDLIN and saves changes to file Saves original as file.BAK
I	Insert line at current line	I	Insert new line in front of current line
[line] I	Insert line before line specified	10 I	Insert new line in front of line 10
L	List 23 lines (11 before current, current, 11 after current)	L	Show current line in context
[line1][,line2] L	List lines from line 1 to line 2	1,10L	Show lines 1 through 10
[line1],[line2],line3 M	Move range from line 1 to line 2 to area beginning at line 3	1,5,10M	Move lines 1 through 5 to line 10 (through 14)
[line1,]+n,line3M	Move line1 plus the next n lines to area beginning at line 3	5,10,8m	Moves 10 lines beginning at line 5 to line 8
P	List next 23 lines and move current line to last one displayed	P	Page through lines in file
[line1][,line2] P	List lines from line 1 to line 2, move current line to line 2	1,10P	List first 10 lines and makes line 10 the current one
Q	Quit EDLIN without saving changes	Q	Leaves EDLIN User is prompted before leaving EDLIN
R string1^Zstring2*	Replace string 1 with string 2 from line after current line to last line	Rteh^ZTEH	Replace "teh" with "TEH" from next line to EOF
[line1][, line2] R [string1] [^Zstring2]*	Replace string 1 with string 2 in lines from line 1 to line 2	1,7Rmy^zour	Replace "my" with "our" in lines 1 through 7
S string*	Search for string from next line through last line in memory	SIBM	Search for "IBM" in lines starting with next one If no string specified, uses last string searched for
[line1][,line2]S [string]*	Search for string in range of lines from line 1 to line 2	1,10SIBM	Search for "IBM" in lines 1 through 10 If no string specified, uses last string searched for
T filespec	Transfer contents of file into memory starting before current line	TAUTOEXEC.BAT	Transfer contents of AUTOEXEC.BAT to file
[line] T filespec	Transfer contents of file into memory starting before line	10TCONFIG.SYS	Transfer contents of CONFIG.SYS to area before line 10
W	Write lines from memory to file until 75% of memory is available	W	Write lines to file until 75% of memory is free Needed only if file is too large to fit into memory
[#]W	Writes # lines from memory to file	10W	Write 10 lines to file Needed only if file is too large to fit into memory

*In some versions of DOS, a ? before the command letter (R or S) will cause the system to prompt for replacement or search string.

Note:
- EDLIN is considered obsolete in DOS 5.0. Use EDIT instead.
- Lowercase names in command syntax indicate items you replace with values.
- In general, if a line number is omitted from a command, the current line number is used.

Source:
IBM DOS 3.3 Technical Reference, pages 8-11 through 8-36
Microsoft MS-DOS 4.0 User's Guide and Reference, pages 173 through 205
Microsoft MS-DOS 5.0 User's Guide and Reference, pages 460 through 481

2.14. LIB OPERATORS SUMMARY

LIB general command form:
LIB [libfile [pagesize] operators [,[listfile]][,[newlib]][;]]

Operator	Function	Example	Example Explanation
+	Add contents of object or library file to the library	LIB YOUR.LIB+NEW.OBJ	Add NEW.OBJ code to YOUR.LIB library
-	Delete module from the library	LIB YOUR-MINE	Delete module MINE.OBJ from YOUR.LIB library
*	Extract object module from library, place in new file¥	LIB YOUR.LIB*MY.OBJ	Delete module MY.OBJ from YOUR.LIB and place it in file MY.OBJ¥
-+	Delete existing module and replace with new one	LIB YOUR-+MY	Delete module MY.OBJ from YOUR.LIB, then add new MY.OBJ to library
-*	Extract object module from library and delete it	LIB YOUR.LIB-*MINE	Delete module MINE.OBJ from YOUR.LIB and save it in file MINE.OBJ

¥In DOS 4.0, * copies the module from the library to an object file of the same name. The module remains in the library. For example, if you type LIB YOUR.LIB * MY.OBJ from the LIB command line, module MY.OBJ is copied from YOUR.LIB library to fill MY.OBJ. DOS 4.0 allows you to provide input by responding to prompts, using a response file you have created, or entering input at the command line.

Version: Not in DOS 5.0.

Note:
- Operations are performed in this order: 1) erasures and removals, 2) additions.
- Library files have an assumed type of LIB if not explicitly referenced; object files have an assumed type of OBJ.

Source: IBM DOS 3.3 Technical Reference, pages A-3 through A-8
IBM DOS 4.0 Technical Reference, pages 7-3 through 7-4

2.15. LINK PARAMETERS SUMMARY

LINK general command form:
LINK objlist, runffile, mapffile, liblist[parameters]...;
LINK objectfiles [,[executablefile][,[mapfile][,[libraryfile]]]][parms]

Parameter*	Function	Comments
/C[PARMAXALLOC]:# †	Sets max # of paragraphs needed by program	Normally 65,535 (all addressable memory)
/D[SALLOCATION]§	Defines data to be at high end of DGROUP	Default is to load data at the low end of DGROUP
/DO[SEG]†	Links according to DOS segment ordering	CODE, nonDGROUP, DGROUP is DOS ordering
/E[XEPACK]†	Packs executable files	Removes repeated bytes, optimizes load-time relocation table
/HE[LP]†	Shows list of options	
/H[IGH]	Causes run image to be placed as high in memory as possible	Default is to place the file as low in memory as possible
/L[INENUMBERS]¥	Causes line numbers and addresses in input modules to be included in list file	
/M[AP]	Lists all public symbols defined in input modules and their run file locations	The public symbols are listed at end of the list file
/NOD[EFAULTLIBRARYSEARCH]†	Ignores library names found in object file	
/NOI[GNORECASE]†	Treats upper- and lowercase letters differently	
/NOG[ROUPASSOCIATION]†	Ignores group associations when assigning addresses to data and code items	Used only with early versions of FORTRAN or Pascal
/O[VERLAYINTERRUPT]:# †	Sets interrupt # of overlay loading routine	In range of 0 to 255
/P[AUSE]	Directs LINK to pause before creation of EXE file	Message is displayed to change diskettes prior to creating EXE file
/SE[GMENTS]:# †	Process no more than # of segments indicated	In range of 1 to 1024
/ST[ACK]:size´	Overrides stack directive in source	Maximum is 65536; if an odd number, 1 is subtracted for even boundary (hex number format: 0x#)
/X£	Sets number of segments EXE file can contain	Default is 256 segments; limits are 0 to 1024 segments
/O£	Links object modules created by version 1 of Pascal or FORTRAN compilers	

*Portion of parameter in brackets is optional.
†MS-DOS 4.0 is first to document this option; other versions may include some options.
§DOS 3.3 says /D[SALLOCATION] while DOS 4.0 says /D[SALLOCATE] is correct.
¥DOS 3.3 says /L is minimum abbreviation, while DOS 4.0 says /LI is minimum.
´DOS 3.3 says /S is minimum abbreviation, while DOS 4.0 says /ST is minimum.
£Listed only in the DOS 3.3 Technical Reference.

Version: Not in DOS 5.0

Note: Parameters may be added to the four prompts LINK displays when invoked as LINK <Enter>.

Source: IBM DOS 3.3 Technical Reference, pages 12-14 through 12-18
Microsoft MS-DOS 4.0 User's Guide and Reference, pages 207 through 233

2.16. DOSSHELL PROGRAM STARTUP OPTIONS

MS-DOS 4.0 and PC-DOS 4.0 Startup Options

Option	*Function*	*Comments*
[]	Default prompt	
[/T"..."]	Defines title for prompt panel	Put title between quotes (max 40 chars)
[/I"..."]	Defines instructions for prompt panel	Put instruction between quotes (max 40 chars)
[/P"..."]	Defines prompt for entry field in prompt panel	Put prompt between quotes (max 20 chars)
%number	Substitutes number's run time value (as in batch)	
[/D"..."]	Defines default value for entry field in prompt panel	Put default value between quotes (max 40 chars)
[/D"%value"]	Defines default value using run time value	
[/R]	Clears the default value in prompt panel entry field	Clears when any key other than edit key pressed
[/L"number"]	Sets maximum length in prompt panel entry field	Default and maximum is 127 chars
[/M"e"]	Use only existing filenames	
[/C"%value"]	Saves run time value entered in preceding task	Otherwise %# will have no value
[/F"..."]	Checks for existence of file	Up to 76 characters
/#	Substitutes drive from which Shell started	
[%number]*	Defines entry as variable with number as name	Can define up to 10 variables (0-9)
/@	Substitutes path in which SHELL was started	

MS-DOS 5.0 Startup Options

Option	*Function*	*Comments*
:res	Specifies screen resolution	Valid values are l (low), m (medium), and h (high)
n	Specifies screen resolution	Used when there is more than one choice in a category
/t	Text mode	Put instruction between quotes (max 40 chars)
/b	Black and white	Put prompt between quotes (max 20 chars)
g	Graphics mode	

*Described in IBM source only.

Version: MS-DOS 4.0 and PC-DOS 4.0 only.

Note:
- Multiple options may appear within one set of brackets.
- Items shown without brackets must be entered outside the brackets.

Source: Getting Started with IBM DOS 4.0, pages 90 through 95
Microsoft MS-DOS Shell User's Guide, pages 97 through 101
Microsoft MS-DOS 5.0 User's Guide and Reference, pages 454 through 455

2.17. DOSSHELL PROGRAM SPECIAL KEY ASSIGNMENTS

DOS 5.0	*DOS 4.0*	*Function*	*Comments*
*		Display all levels below the selected directory	Directory Tree key
Alt		Select menu bar	
Alt+Esc		Go to next application	When Task Swapper is on
Alt+F4		Quits screen and/or Shell	
Alt+Letter		Carry out shortcut application key that you defined	
Alt+Shift+Esc		Go to previous application	When Task Swapper is on
Alt+Tab		Toggle between applications	When Task Swapper is on
Arrows	Arrows	Moves selection cursor on screen	
Ctrl+*		Display all directories in the tree	Directory Tree key
Ctrl+/		Select all files in the list	
Ctrl+Drive		Move the cursor to the drive and display its directories	Drive selection key
Ctrl+End		Move to end of list	
Ctrl+Esc		Go to Shell from an application	When Task Swapper is on
Ctrl+Home		Move to beginning of list	
Ctrl+Letter		Carry out shortcut application key that you defined	
Ctrl+Shift+Enter		Start a program in the Program List and open a selected file in the File List	
Ctrl+\		Cancel the file selection in the list	
Del		Delete the selected item	
End		Move to end of line or list	
Enter	Enter	Completes a command	
F1	F1	Displays Help information on the topic you pick	
F10	F10	Move selection cursor (select menu bar)	
F2	F2	Saves information typed in text box of dialog box	
F3	F3	Quits screen and/or Shell	
F5		Refresh	Drive selection key
F7		Move selected files from one directory to another	
F8		Copy selected files from one directory to another	
Home		Move to beginning of line or list	
Letter		Scroll to the first item in a list that begins with a particular letter	
Minus (-)		Hide the directories below the selected directory	Directory Tree key
Page Down (PdDn)	Page Down	Scroll to next window of information	
Page Up (PgUp)	Page Up	Scroll to previous window of information	
Plus (+)		Display one level of directories	Directory Tree key
Shift+Down Arrow		Add next file in list to selection	
Shift+Enter		Start a program and add it to the active task list without leaving the Shell	When Task Swapper is on
Shift+F8		Turn ADD mode on or off	
Shift+F9		Save Shell and bring up command prompt	
Shift+Letter		Carry out shortcut application key that you defined	
Shift+Page Down		Add files in the next window's list to the selection	
Shift+Page Up		Add files in the previous window's list to the selection	
Shift+Spacebar		Select files between previously selected files and the cursor	In ADD mode
Shift+Tab	Shift+Tab	Move to previous selection	
Shift+Up Arrow		Add previous file in list to selection	
Spacebar		Add the file at the cursor to the spacebar	In ADD mode
Spacebar		Display the directory on the selected drive	Drive selection key
Tab	Tab	Move to next selection	
	F4	Creates || mark	Indicates separation of commands
	F9	Display key assignments	
	F11	Displays index of all Help topics	
	Alt+F1	Displays index of all Help files	
	Spacebar	Selects one or more files	

Source: Getting Started with IBM DOS 4.0, pages 42 through 43
Microsoft MS-DOS Shell User's Guide, pages 11 through 12
Microsoft MS-DOS 5.0 User's Guide and Reference, pages 27 through 66
Microsoft MS-DOS Help Keys

2.18. DIRECTORY ENTRIES

Offset	*Length*	*Description*	*Format*	*Comments*
0 (0)	8 bytes	Filename	ASCII chars, or special code if first char: 00H = name never used 05H = first character of name is really E5H E5H = file was used, but has been erased 2EH = entry is a directory†	Must be padded with spaces to fill field
8 (8)	3 bytes	File type (extension)	ASCII chars.	Must be padded with spaces to fill field
B (11)	byte	File attribute byte	Bit codes: Bit 0 = read-only Bit 1 = hidden Bit 2 = system Bit 3 = volume label Bit 4 = directory Bit 5 = archive Bit 6 = UNUSED Bit 7 = UNUSED	See 2.19. File Attribute Byte
C (12)	10 bytes	RESERVED		
16 (22)	word	Time file last updated*	Coded word: (unsigned 16-bit integer) Time = Hr*2048+Min*32+Sec÷2	See 2.20. Date/Time Formats
18 (24)	word	Date file last updated*	Coded word: (see above) Date = (Yr-1980)*512+Mon*32+Day	See 2.20. Date/Time Formats
1A (26)	word	Starting cluster number*§	Word binary integer*	See 1.15. Common 8086 Data Formats
1C (28)	dbl word	File size*	Double word binary integer*	See 1.15. Common 8086 Data Formats

*Least significant byte first
†If second byte also 2EH, cluster field contains cluster # of parent directory.
§First cluster for data space on all disks is cluster 002.

Note: There is no period separating the filename and type fields.

Source: IBM DOS 3.3 Technical Reference, pages 5-10 through 5-13
Microsoft MS-DOS 4.0 Programmer's Reference, pages 374 through 376
Microsoft MS-DOS 5.0 Programmer's Reference, pages 38 through 40

See Also: 1.15. Common 8086 Family Data Formats
2.19. File Attribute Byte
2.20. Date/Time Formats
2.35. Allowable Characters in Filenames
2.36. File Separator Characters

2.19. FILE ATTRIBUTE BYTE

Bit Number

7	6	5	4	3	2	1	0	*Meaning if Set to 1*	*Meaning if Set to 0*
							✔	Read-only file	Read/write file
						✔		Hidden file	Visible file
					✔			System file	Regular file
				✔				Volume name	Regular file
			✔					Directory name	Regular file
		✔						File changed since last backup	File unchanged since last backup
✔	✔							RESERVED	RESERVED

Version: DOS 1.x used only bits 0-3.

Note:
- Bits 3 and 4 are mutually exclusive; you may set none, one or the other one, but not both.
- Only one file (in the root directory) may have bit 3 set.
- Function 43H (Get/Set File Attributes) changes only bits 0,1,2,and 5.

Source: IBM DOS 3.3 Technical Reference, pages 5-11 through 5-12
Microsoft MS-DOS 4.0 Programmer's Reference, pages 374 through 375
Microsoft MS-DOS 5.0 Programmer's Reference, pages 46 through 47

See Also: 2.18. Directory Entries
3.082. INT 21H, AH=43H, AL=00H -- Get File Attributes
3.083. INT 21H, AH=43H, AL=01H -- Set File Attributes

2.20. DATE/TIME FORMATS

In DOS Functions 2AH and 2BH, the date is passed using registers, as follows:

Element	*Register*	*Format*	*Allowable Values*
Day of Week	AL	Coded value	0=Sunday 1=Monday 2=Tuesday 3=Wednesday 4=Thursday 5=Friday 6=Saturday
Day	DL	Binary value	1-31 (corresponds to date)
Month	DH	Binary value	1-12 (corresponds to month number)
Year	CX	Binary value	1980-2099 (must be in this range)

In DOS Functions 2CH and 2DH, the time is passed using registers, as follows:

Hundredths	DL	Binary value	0-99 (corresponds to hundredths of a second)
Seconds	DH	Binary value	0-59 (corresponds to seconds)
Minutes	CL	Binary value	0-59 (corresponds to minutes)
Hours	CH	Binary value	0-23 (corresponds to military hours)

In directory entries and function 57H, the date and time are kept as separate 16-bit values (least significant byte first), as follows:*

Element	*Bits Used*	*Format*	*Allowable Values*
Day	0-4	5-bit binary value	1-31 (corresponds to date)
Month	5-8	4-bit binary value	1-12 (corresponds to month number)
Year	9-15	7-bit binary value	0-119 (year biased by 1980)
Seconds	0-4	5-bit binary value	0-29 (multiply by 2 to get seconds)
Minutes	5-10	6-bit binary value	0-59 (corresponds to minutes)
Hours	11-15	5-bit binary value	0-23 (corresponds to military hours)

*In function 57H, the 16-bit time value is set/returned in CX, and the 16-bit date value is set/returned in DX.

Note: Note unusual format of seconds in directory entries.

Source: IBM DOS 3.3 Technical Reference, pages 5-12 through 5-13, 6-98, 6-100 through 6-101, 6-208
Microsoft MS-DOS 4.0 Programmer's Reference, pages 134 through 141, 250, 375 through 376
Microsoft MS-DOS 5.0 Programmer's Reference, pages 256 through 259, and 345 through 346

See Also:
3.013. INT 21H System Management Functions Summary
3.054. INT 21H, AH=2AH -- Get Date
3.055. INT 21H, AH=2BH -- Set Date
3.056. INT 21H, AH=2CH -- Get Time
3.057. INT 21H, AH=2DH -- Set Time
3.136. INT 21H, AH=57H, AL=00H -- Get File Date and Time
3.137. INT 21H, AH=57H, AL=01H -- Set File Date and Time

2.21. FAT LAYOUTS

12-bit FAT Layout

	Entry #	Example Value	Use	
Reserved for DOS {	0	FF8	Disk ID byte	
{	1	FFF	Filler	
From Directory Entry's------> Starting Cluster Number	2	003	Cluster value:	000 = unused cluster
	3	004		002-FEF = next cluster number
	4	005		FF0-FF6 = reserved cluster
	5	FFF		FF7 = cluster marked bad
	6	000		FF8-FFF = last cluster in file

Note: In this example FAT, the first entry indicates that it is a FAT for a hard disk (FF8). The first directory entry in the directory for that disk has a starting cluster of 2, thus pointing to cluster number 2 in this table. The second cluster points to the third, the third to the fourth, the fourth to the fifth. The fifth cluster is the last cluster in the file, and thus has a value of FFFH.

16-bit FAT Layout

	Entry #	Example Value	Use	
Reserved for DOS {	0	FFF8	Disk ID byte	
{	1	FFFF	Filler	
From Directory Entry's------> Starting Cluster Number	2	0003	Cluster value:	0000 = unused cluster
	3	0004		0002-FFEF = next cluster number
	4	0005		FFF0-FFF6 = reserved cluster
	5	FFFF		FFF7 = cluster marked bad
	6	0000		FFF8-FFFF = last cluster in file

Note: In this example FAT, the first entry indicates that it is a FAT for a hard disk (FFF8H). The first directory entry in the directory for that disk has a starting cluster of 2, thus pointing to cluster number 2 in this table. The second cluster points to the third, the third to the fourth, the fourth to the fifth. The fifth cluster is the last cluster in the file, and thus has a value of FFFFH. Remember, words in the FAT are byte swapped (i.e., least significant byte first).

Warning: The sources below agree with the information provided above. However, other reputable books, such as the MS-DOS Encyclopedia, indicate that cluster numbers go from 2 to (F)FF6 and bad clusters are marked with (F)FF7H through (F)FFEH, with the last cluster in the file being only (F)FFFH.

Source: IBM DOS 3.3 Technical Reference, pages 5-5 through 5-9
Microsoft MS-DOS 4.0 Programmer's Reference, pages 376 through 378
Microsoft MS-DOS 5.0 Programmer's Reference, Chapter 3, pages 32 through 33

See Also: 2.22. Disk ID Bytes

2.22. DISK ID BYTES

ID Byte	Tracks/side	Sectors	Sides	Format
FFH	40	8	2	5.25-inch floppy disk
FEH	40	8	1	5.25-inch floppy disk
	77	26,or 8	1	8-inch floppy disk
FDH	40	9	2	5.25-inch floppy disk
	77	26	2	8-inch floppy disk
FCH	40	9	1	5.25-inch floppy disk
	80	9	2	3.5-inch microfloppy disk
	80	9	2	5.25-inch floppy disk
FBH	80	8	2	5.25-inch floppy disk
	80	8	2	3.5-inch microfloppy disk
FAH	80	8	1	5.25-inch floppy disk
	80	8	1	3.5-inch microfloppy disk
F0H	80	18	2	3.5-inch high-density microfloppy disk
F9H	80	9	2	3.5-inch microfloppy disk
	80	9	2	5.25-inch floppy disk
	80	15	2	5.25-inch high-density floppy disk
F8H	-	-	-	Fixed disk

Version: Beginning with DOS 2.x, the usefulness of the disk ID byte in the FAT was reduced, and it is now considered meaningless, since multiple formats may have the same ID. Microsoft recommends that you use the information in the media descriptor table to determine the type of disk being used.

Note:
- The disk ID byte is the low-order byte of the first cluster indicator in the FAT (e.g., a first cluster value of FFF8H yields a disk ID byte of F8H).
- F0H ID bytes may be used for additional media types.

Source: IBM DOS 3.3 Technical Reference, page 5-6
Microsoft MS-DOS 4.0 Programmer's Reference, page 379

See Also: 2.24. Disk Partition Table Layout
3.170. BOOTSECTOR Structure

2.23. DISK BOOT RECORD LAYOUT

DOS 3.3 and 4.0 Boot Record Layout

Offset	*Length*	*Description*	*DOS Version*
0 (0)	3 bytes	JMP to boot code*	DOS 3.3, 4.4 and 5.0 boot sector structure
3 (3)	8 bytes	OEM name and version	
B (11)	word	Bytes per sector	
D (13)	byte	Sectors per cluster (must be a power of 2)	
E (14)	word	Reserved sectors (for Dir, FAT, etc.)	
10 (16)	byte	Number of copies of FAT	
11 (17)	word	Maximum number of root directory entries	
13 (19)	word	Total number of sectors in logical image	
15 (21)	byte	Media descriptor byte	
16 (22)	word	Number of sectors in FAT	
18 (24)	word	Number of sectors per track	
1A (26)	word	Number of heads	
1C (28)	word	Number of hidden sectors§	DOS 3.3 and 4.0 only
1E (30)	word	HO number of hidden sectors†§	
20 (32)	dbl word	Number of logical sectors†§	

DOS 5.0 Boot Sector Structure

Offset	*Length*	*Description*	*DOS Version*
1E (30)	dbl word	Number of hidden sectors	DOS 5.0 boot sector structure
22 (34)	dbl word	Number of sectors if the size of the drive is larger than 32 MB.	
23 (35)	byte	Drive number used internally by DOS	
24 (36)	byte	Reserved	
25 (37)	byte	Boot signature. Always 29h.	
29 (41)	dbl word	Volume ID number	
34 (52)	11 bytes	Volume label	
3C (60)	8 bytes	File-system type	

*For DOS 2.x = 3-byte near jump. For DOS 3.x, 4.x = 2-byte short jump + NOP.
†DOS 4.x: Number of sectors in logical image must be 0.
§Substantial disagreement in meaning exists between the cited sources for these items.

Version: Note that media descriptor bytes are not necessarily valid beginning with DOS 2.x.

Note: OEM name and version are not always present (IBM does not use prior to DOS 4.0).

Source: IBM DOS 3.3 Technical Reference, page 2-31
Microsoft MS-DOS 4.0 Programmer's Reference, pages 337 through 338
Microsoft MS-DOS 5.0 Programmer's Reference, pages 34 through 35

See Also: 1.27. Powers of Two
2.22. Disk ID Bytes

2.24. DISK PARTITION TABLE LAYOUT

A standard Partition Table consists of four records at 01BEH, formatted as follows:¥

Offset	*Length*	*Name*	*Contents*	*Position*
0 (0)	byte	Partition status	00H=nonbootable; 80H=bootable	First Partition
1 (1)	byte	Starting head	Binary value	
2 (2)	word	Starting sector and cylinder	*§	
4 (4)	byte	Partition type	00H=unknown 01H=DOS with 12-bit FAT 04H=DOS with 16-bit FAT 05H=extended DOS partition† 06H=32-bit FAT 07H=OS/2 HPFS§ DBH=concurrent DOS§	
5 (5)	byte	Ending head	Binary value	
6 (6)	word	Ending sector and cylinder	*§	
8 (8)	dbl word	Starting absolute sector	Binary value (least significant word first and byte swapped in each word)	
C (12)	dbl word	Number of sectors	Binary value (least significant word first and byte swapped in each word)	

(Continued)

2.24. DISK PARTITION TABLE LAYOUT (continued)

A standard Partition Table consists of four records at 01BEH, formatted as follows:¥

Offset	Length	Name	Contents	Position
10 (16)	byte	Partition status	00H=nonbootable; 80H=bootable	Second Partition
11 (17)	byte	Starting head	Binary value	
12 (18)	word	Starting sector and cylinder	*	
14 (20)	byte	Partition type	00H=unknown 01H=DOS with 12-bit FAT 04H=DOS with 16-bit FAT 05H=extended DOS partition† 06H=32-bit FAT 07H=OS/2 HPFS DBH=concurrent DOS	
15 (21)	byte	Ending head	Binary value	
16 (22)	word	Ending sector and cylinder	*	
18 (24)	dbl word	Starting absolute sector	Binary value (least significant word first and byte swapped in each word)	
1C (28)	dbl word	Number of sectors	Binary value (least significant word first and byte swapped in each word)	
20 (32)	byte	Partition status	00H=nonbootable; 80H=bootable	Third Partition
21 (33)	byte	Starting head	Binary value	
22 (34)	word	Starting sector and cylinder	*	
24 (36)	byte	Partition type	00H=unknown 01H=DOS with 12-bit FAT 04H=DOS with 16-bit FAT 05H=extended DOS partition† 06H=32-bit FAT 07H=OS/2 HPFS DBH=concurrent DOS	
25 (37)	byte	Ending head	Binary value	
26 (38)	word	Ending sector and cylinder	*	
28 (40)	dbl word	Starting absolute sector	Binary value (least significant word first and byte swapped in each word)	
2C (44)	dbl word	Number of sectors	Binary value (least significant word first and byte swapped in each word)	
30 (48)	byte	Partition status	00H=nonbootable; 80H=bootable	Fourth Partition
31 (49)	byte	Starting head	Binary value	
32 (50)	word	Starting sector and cylinder	*	
34 (52)	byte	Partition type	00H=unknown 01H=DOS with 12-bit FAT 04H=DOS with 16-bit FAT 05H=extended DOS partition† 06H=32-bit FAT 07H=OS/2 HPFS DBH=concurrent DOS	
35 (53)	byte	Ending head	Binary value	
36 (54)	word	Ending sector and cylinder	*	
38 (56)	dbl word	Starting absolute sector	Binary value (least significant word first and byte swapped in each word)	
3C (60)	dbl word	Number of sectors	Binary value (least significant word first and byte swapped in each word)	

In older DOS disk partitions, the partition table is followed by:

40(64)	word	Signature	55AAH (indicates valid boot record)

*Cylinder and sector are stored in bit-position-coded notation. This applies to the starting cylinder and head and the ending cylinder and head. See below.

byte n								byte n+1							
c	c	s	s	s	s	s	s	c	c	c	c	c	c	c	c
msb		msb													lsb

The two most significant bits of byte n precede the eight bits of byte n+1 to form the ten-bit cylinder number. The six least significant bits of byte n form the sector number.

†For each extended partition, an additional partition table is appended to the end of the original.

§Not in DOS 5.0

¥DOS 5.0 supplies a partition table for every drive that can be partitioned. The table consists of one or more PARTENTRY structures. The First Partition in the table above represents one PARTENTRY structure.

Note:
- Some manufacturers allow additional partition types in order to divide large capacity hard disks into several drives.
- The partition tables begin at an offset of 1BEH in the boot record. The actual boot record is defined by the starting head, cylinder, and sector number, and that sector is loaded to location 7C00H.

Source: IBM DOS 3.3 Technical Reference, pages 9-6 through 9-16
"Tutor," PC Magazine, Sept 11, 1990, pages 447 through 450
DOS Programmer's Reference 2nd Edition (Que), pages 215 through 218
Microsoft MS-DOS 5.0 Programmer's Reference, pages 48 through 49

See Also: 2.23. Disk Boot Record Layout

2.25. FLOPPY DISK FORMAT SUMMARY

System That Commonly Uses This Format	Obsolete	PC/XT	AT	Convert.	PS/2
Disk size	5.25	5.25	5.25	3.5	3.5
Disk ID byte (in FAT)*	FC	FD	F9	F9	F0
Number of heads	1	2	2	2	2
Tracks per side	40	40	80	80	80
Sectors per track	9	9	15	9	18
Bytes per sector	512	512	512	512	512
Sectors per cluster	1	2	1	2	1
Number of reserved sectors	1	1	1	1	1
Number of sectors per FAT	2	2	7	3	9
Number of FATs per disk	2	2	2	2	2
Number of root directory sectors	4	7	14	7	14
Maximum number of root directory entries allowed	64	112	224	112	224
Total number of sectors on disk	360	720	2400	1440	2880
Total number of usable sectors on disk	351	708	2371	1426	2847
Total number of usable clusters on disk	351	354	2371	713	2847
Capacity of disk	180 KB	360 KB	1.2 MB	720 KB	1.44MB
Format introduced with DOS version	2	2	3	3.2	3.3

*FAT disk ID bytes are unreliable. Use disk parameter block to determine media type.

Note: Total usable sectors and total usable clusters will change if bad sectors are found during formatting.

Source: Microsoft MS-DOS 3.2 Programmer's Reference, pages 3-9, 3-10
Microsoft MS-DOS 4.0 Programmer's Reference, page 379

See Also: 2.26. Hard Disk Format Summary

2.26. IBM HARD DISK FORMAT SUMMARY

System That Commonly Uses This Format	XT	AT	Model 50	Model 60	Model 80
Disk size	5.25	5.25	3.5	3.5	3.5
Disk ID byte (in FAT)*	F8	F8	F8	F8	F8
Interleave	6 to 1	3 to 1	1 to 1	1 to 1	1 to 1
Heads per disk	4	4			
Cylinders	306	615			
Sectors per track	17	17			
Bytes per sector	512	512	512	512	512
Sectors per cluster	8	4			
Number of reserved sectors	1	1			
Number of sectors per FAT	8	40			
Number of FATs per disk	2	2			
Number of root directory sectors	32	32			
Maximum number of root directory entries allowed	512	512			
Total number of sectors on disk	20808	41820			
Total number of usable sectors on disk	20759	41707			
Total number of usable clusters on disk	2595	10427			
Capacity of disk	10MB	20MB	20MB	44MB	70MB
Format introduced with DOS version	2	2	3.3	3.3	3.3

*FAT disk ID bytes are unreliable. Use disk parameter block to determine media type.

Note: All numbers assume that the entire hard disk is formatted as a DOS partition (i.e., no non-DOS partitions on disk).

Source: IBM PC/XT Technical Reference, pages 1-151 through 1-152.

See Also: 2.25. Floppy Disk Format Summary

2.27. EXE FILE HEADER

Offset	Length	Usual Contents	Description	Comments
0 (0)	word	4D5AH	EXE file signature	
2 (2)	word		Length of file	Modulo 512
4 (4)	word		Size of file, including header	In 512-byte pages
6 (6)	word		Number of relocation table items	
8 (8)	word		Size of header	In 16-byte paragraphs
A (10)	word		Minimum paragraphs needed above program	In 16-byte paragraphs
C (12)	word		Maximum paragraphs desired above program	In 16-byte paragraphs
E (14)	word		Displacement of stack segment in module	Relative to start of program, in paragraphs
10 (16)	word		Contents of SP register at entry	
12 (18)	word		Checksum	Two's complement
14 (20)	word		Contents of IP register at entry	
16 (22)	word		Displacement of code module	Relative to start of program (in paragraphs)
18 (24)	word		Offset to first relocation item in file	Relative to start of file (in bytes)
1A (26)	word		Overlay number	0 for resident part of program
1C (28)*	varies		Variable RESERVED space	
varies*	varies		Relocation table	
varies*	varies		Variable RESERVED space	
varies*	varies		Program and data segments	
varies*	varies		Stack segment	

*Not in DOS 5.0 EXEHEADER structure

Note: EXE files created for use with Microsoft Windows use a different format (See 6.10. Windows EXE File Format).

Source: IBM DOS 3.3 Technical Reference, pages 10-3 through 10-6
Microsoft MS-DOS 4.0 Programmer's Reference, pages 403 through 405
Microsoft MS-DOS 5.0 Programmer's Reference, Chapter 5, pages 81 through 82

See Also: 2.28. COM Program Layout
6.010. Windows EXE File Format

2.28. COM PROGRAM LAYOUT

Offset	Length	Description	Comments
0 (0)	256 bytes	Program segment prefix	Values filled in by DOS
100 (256)	varies	Code and data segment	Only one segment allowed
varies	varies	Stack	Usually at top of segment

Note: The program segment prefix is not usually part of the actual file. It is created and filled in by DOS at program load time. COM files must have code segment ORGed at 100H.

Source: IBM DOS 3.3 Technical Reference, page 7-9
Advanced MS-DOS Programming 2nd Edition (Microsoft Press), pages 22 through 26
Microsoft MS-DOS 5.0 Programmer's Reference, page 75

See Also: 2.27. EXE File Header
2.29. COM Versus EXE File Differences
3.196. PSP Structure

2.29. COM VERSUS EXE FILE DIFFERENCES

Item	COM Programs	EXE Programs
Max. program size	65278*	No limit
Segment use	One segment only	Multiple segments allowed
Entry point	PSP:0100H	Defined by END Segment
CS at entry	PSP	Segment containing module with entry point
IP at entry	0100H	Offset of entry point within its segment
DS at entry	PSP	PSP
ES at entry	PSP	PSP
SS at entry	PSP	Segment with STACK attribute
SP at entry	0FFFEH or top word, whichever is lower	Size of segment defined with STACK attribute
Stack at entry	Zero word on stack	Initialized or uninitialized
Stack size	65536 - (ProgramSize+256)	Defined in segment with STACK attribute (up to 65536 bytes)
Memory allocation	All free memory allocated to program	May be set to allocate portion of memory (offset 0CH in EXE header)
Subroutine calls	NEAR CALLs only	NEAR or FAR CALLS allowed
Size of file	Exact size of program (might not include PSP)	Size of program plus EXE header (multiple of 512 bytes)

*65536 - 256-byte PSP - 2-byte STACK

Source: Advanced MS-DOS Programming 2nd Edition (Microsoft Press), page 36

See Also: 2.27. EXE File Header
2.28. COM Program Layout
3.196. PSP Structure

2.30. FONT FILE (CODE PAGE) LAYOUT

Offset	Length	Description	Contents	DOS 5.0 Structure
0 (0)	8 bytes	File tag	FFH followed by "font," followed by three spaces	FONTFILEHEADER
8 (8)	8 bytes	RESERVED		FONTFILEHEADER
10 (16)	word	Number of pointers in header	1	FONTFILEHEADER
12 (18)	byte	Type of pointer	1	FONTFILEHEADER
13(19)	dbl word*	Offset to info from start of file	Binary value	FONTFILEHEADER
17(23)	word	Number of entries	Binary value	FONT INFO HEADER
19(25)	word	Size of code	Binary value (must be 28 in DOS 5.0)	CPENTRYHEADER
1B(27)	dbl word	Pointer to header of next entry	0000H for last header	CPENTRYHEADER
1F(31)	word	Device type	1=display, 2=printer	CPENTRYHEADER
21(33)	8 bytes	Device name (ID)	ASCII text padded with spaces	CPENTRYHEADER
29(41)	word	Code page ID	437, 850, 852, 860, 863, or 865	CPENTRYHEADER
2B(43)	3 words	RESERVED	Must be zero	CPENTRYHEADER
31(49)	dbl word	Pointer to font info	Binary value	CPENTRYHEADER
35(53)	word	RESERVED	Must be 1	FONTDATAHEADER
37(55)	word	Number of fonts	Binary value	FONTDATAHEADER
39(57)	word	Length of font data	Binary value	FONTDATAHEADER

For Display Font

Offset	Length	Description	Contents	DOS 5.0 Structure
3B(59)	byte	Rows in character box	Binary value	SCREENFONTHEADER
3C(60)	byte	Columns in character box	Binary value	SCREENFONTHEADER
3D(61)	2 bytes	Aspect ratio	Currently not used, = 0,0	SCREENFONTHEADER
3F(63)	word	Number of characters in font	Usually 256	SCREENFONTHEADER
41(65)	varies	Font data	Stored as pixel descriptions	SCREENFONTHEADER

For Printer Font

Offset	Length	Description	Contents	DOS 5.0 Structure
3B(59)	word	Printer selection type	1=4201, 2=5202 or 4208	PRINTFONTHEADER
3D(61)	word	Total bytes in control sequences	Must be < 31	PRINTFONTHEADER
3F(63)	varies	Hardware code page	Maximum length of 31†	
varies	varies	Downloadable code page	Maximum length of 31†	
varies	varies	Downloadable character definitions	See Printer Technical Reference	

*Microsoft MS-DOS 4.0 Programmer's Reference indicates this is a single word.
†Microsoft sources indicate maximum length is less than 31 bytes.

Source: IBM DOS 3.3 Technical Reference, pages 7-17 through 7-20
Microsoft MS-DOS 4.0 Programmer's Reference, pages 391 through 399
Microsoft MS-DOS 5.0 Programmer's Reference, pages 93 through 103

See Also: 3.200. Code Page Assignments

2.31. OPERATING SYSTEM FILES SUMMARY

IBM PC-DOS Version

File	1	1.1	2	2.1	3	3.1	3.2	3.3	4.0	5.0
IBMBIO.COM	1920	1920	4608	4736	8964	9564	16369	22100	32810	†
IBMDOS.COM	6400	6400	17152	17024	27920	27760	28477	30159	35984	†
COMMAND.COM	3231	4959	17664	17792	22042	23210	23791	25307	37637	†
Total file sizes	11551	13279	39424	39552	58926	60534	68637	77566	106453	†

Microsoft MS-DOS Version

File	1	1.1	2	2.1	3	3.1	3.2	3.3	4.0	5.0
IO.SYS	*	*	*	*	*	*	16138	22357	33337	33044
MS-DOS.SYS	*	*	*	*	*	*	28480	30128	37376	37506
COMMAND.COM	*	*	*	*	*	*	23612	25276	37557	46246
Total file sizes	*	*	*	*	*	*	68230	77761	108270	116796

*MS-DOS released only through OEMs, so file sizes vary.
†Not available at time of publication

Note:
- The first total shown is for the entire operating system files only.
- The actual amount of memory used by the operating system is dependent upon the environment size, device drivers that have been loaded, and the settings of the BUFFERS and FILES parameters.
- All sizes are approximate, since minor revisions may have affected actual size.

Source: DOS Disks

See Also: 2.32. Included Command Files Summary
2.34. Typical DOS Memory Usage

2.32. INCLUDED COMMAND FILES SUMMARY*

Included Commands (External)

DOS Version Number

Command File	1	1.1	2	2.1	3	3.1	3.2	3.3	4.0	5.0
APPEND								✔	✔	✔
ASSIGN			✔	✔	✔	✔	✔	✔	✔	✔
ATTRIB					✔	✔	✔	✔	✔	✔
BACKUP			✔	✔	✔	✔	✔	✔	✔	✔
BASIC	✔	✔	✔	✔	✔	✔	✔	✔	✔	
BASICA	✔	✔	✔	✔	✔	✔	✔	✔	✔	
CHKDSK	✔	✔	✔	✔	✔	✔	✔	✔	✔	✔
COMMAND										✔
COMP	✔	✔	✔	✔	✔	✔	✔	✔	✔	✔
DEBUG	✔	✔	✔	✔	✔	✔	✔	✔	✔	✔
DISKCOMP	✔	✔	✔	✔	✔	✔	✔	✔	✔	✔
DISKCOPY	✔	✔	✔	✔	✔	✔	✔	✔	✔	✔
DOSKEY										✔
DOSSHELL									✔	✔
EDIT										✔
EDLIN	✔	✔	✔	✔	✔	✔	✔	✔	✔	✔
EMM386										✔
EXE2BIN			✔	✔	✔	✔	✔	**	**	✔
FASTOPEN								✔	✔	✔
FC									†	†
FDISK			✔	✔	✔	✔	✔	✔	✔	✔
FIND			✔	✔	✔	✔	✔	✔	✔	✔
FORMAT	✔	✔	✔	✔	✔	✔	✔	✔	✔	✔
GRAFTABL			✔	✔	✔	✔	✔	✔	✔	✔
GRAPHICS			✔	✔	✔	✔	✔	✔	✔	✔
HELP										✔
JOIN					✔	✔	✔	✔	✔	✔
KEYB										✔
KEYBFR§					✔	✔	✔	✔	✔	
KEYBGR§					✔	✔	✔	✔	✔	
KEYBIT§					✔	✔	✔	✔	✔	
KEYBSP§					✔	✔	✔	✔	✔	
KEYBUK§					✔	✔	✔	✔	✔	
LABEL					✔	✔	✔	✔	✔	✔
LIB								**	**	
LINK	✔	✔	✔	✔	✔	✔	✔	**	**	
MEM									✔	✔
MIRROR										✔
MODE	✔	✔	✔	✔	✔	✔	✔	✔	✔	✔

(Continued)

2.32. INCLUDED COMMAND FILES SUMMARY (continued)

Included Commands (External)

	DOS Version Number									
Command File	1	1.1	2	2.1	3	3.1	3.2	3.3	4.0	5.0
MORE			✔	✔	✔	✔	✔	✔	✔	✔
NLSFUNC								✔	✔	✔
PRINT			✔	✔	✔	✔	✔	✔	✔	✔
QBASIC										✔
RECOVER			✔	✔	✔	✔	✔	✔	✔	✔
REPLACE					✔	✔	✔	✔	✔	✔
RESTORE			✔	✔	✔	✔	✔	✔	✔	✔
SETVER										✔
SHARE						✔	✔	✔	✔	✔
SORT			✔	✔	✔	✔	✔	✔	✔	✔
SUBST					✔	✔	✔	✔	✔	✔
SYS	✔	✔	✔	✔	✔	✔	✔	✔	✔	✔
TREE			✔	✔	✔	✔	✔	✔	✔	✔
UNDELETE										✔
UNFORMAT										✔
XCOPY						✔	✔	✔	✔	✔

Included Commands (Built-In)

	DOS Version Number									
Command Name	1	1.1	2	2.1	3	3.1	3.2	3.3	4.0	5.0
CD/CHDIR			✔	✔	✔	✔	✔	✔	✔	✔
CHCP									✔	✔
CLS			✔	✔	✔	✔	✔	✔	✔	✔
COPY	✔	✔	✔	✔	✔	✔	✔	✔	✔	✔
CTTY			✔	✔	✔	✔	✔	✔	✔	✔
DATE	✔	✔	✔	✔	✔	✔	✔	✔	✔	✔
DEL/ERASE	✔	✔	✔	✔	✔	✔	✔	✔	✔	✔
DIR	✔	✔	✔	✔	✔	✔	✔	✔	✔	✔
EXIT					✔	✔	✔	✔	✔	✔
EXPAND										✔
LOADHI/LH										✔
MD/MKDIR			✔	✔	✔	✔	✔	✔	✔	✔
PATH			✔	✔	✔	✔	✔	✔	✔	✔
PROMPT			✔	✔	✔	✔	✔	✔	✔	✔
RD/RMDIR			✔	✔	✔	✔	✔	✔	✔	✔
REN/RENAME	✔	✔	✔	✔	✔	✔	✔	✔	✔	✔
SET			✔	✔	✔	✔	✔	✔	✔	✔
TIME	✔	✔	✔	✔	✔	✔	✔	✔	✔	✔
TYPE	✔	✔	✔	✔	✔	✔	✔	✔	✔	✔
VER					✔	✔	✔	✔	✔	✔
VERIFY			✔	✔	✔	✔	✔	✔	✔	✔
VOL			✔	✔	✔	✔	✔	✔	✔	✔

Batch File Commands (Built-In)

	DOS Version Number									
Command	1	1.1	2	2.1	3	3.1	3.2	3.3	4.0	5.0
CALL								✔	✔	✔
ECHO	✔	✔	✔	✔	✔	✔	✔	✔	✔	✔
FOR	✔	✔	✔	✔	✔	✔	✔	✔	✔	✔
GOTO	✔	✔	✔	✔	✔	✔	✔	✔	✔	✔
IF	✔	✔	✔	✔	✔	✔	✔	✔	✔	✔
PAUSE	✔	✔	✔	✔	✔	✔	✔	✔	✔	✔
REM	✔	✔	✔	✔	✔	✔	✔	✔	✔	✔
SHIFT	✔	✔	✔	✔	✔	✔	✔	✔	✔	✔

*These COM and EXE files are from the IBM PC-DOS versions. The MS-DOS versions may differ slightly.
**Supplied with Technical Reference manuals.
†Supplied with MS-DOS only.
§May be supplied only with foreign versions, or derived at installation time. DOS 5.0 uses only KEYB.
¥Not in DOS 5.0

Source: Microsoft MS-DOS 5.0 User's Guide and Reference, pages 359 through 360

See Also: 2.31. Operating System Files Summary

2.33. COMMON FILE TYPES (EXTENSIONS)

File Type	Program	Description
$$$	DOS	A "pipe" file created by using the redirection flag (|) in a DOS command
@@@	CodeViewDisk	Window-oriented debugger
ACT	BITCOM	Communications account data file
ACT	Actor	Source code file for Actor programming language
AIO	APL	APL file transfer format file
AMG	Actor	System image file for Actor programming language
APL	APL	APL work space format file
APP	SQLWindows	Application file
ARF	BASCOM	Automatic response file created by the BM series of compilers; similar to batch files
ARF	FORTRAN	Automatic response file created by the BM series of compilers; similar to batch files
ARF	COBOL	Automatic response file created by the BM series of compilers; similar to batch files
ASC	Many	ASCII text file; may be typed to the screen
ASM	MASM	Assembly language source code file
AUX	Paradox	
BAK	Many	A backup file; contains a previous version of the information in the file
BAS	BASIC	A file containing Basic program code; may not be in ASCII format!
BAS	BASICA	A file containing Basic program code; may not be in ASCII format!
BAS	MS-QuickBasic	A file containing Basic program code; may not be in ASCII format!
BAS	Turbo BASIC	A file containing Basic program code; may not be in ASCII format!
BAT	DOS	Batch file; contains commands to be executed by DOS, in order
BIN	Many	Binary file; often same as an OBJ file; contains 8-bit information (i.e., not ASCII)
BLK	Show Partner	Block file; contains information about a block manipulated by ShowPartner
BMP	MS-Windows	Bitmap file; contains data for a Windows bitmap structure
C	C compilers	Contains C source code
CAL	SuperCalc	Spreadsheet file; contains contents of a spreadsheet
CCL	Intalk	Communication command language file
CFG	Many	A configuration file; contains information about machine and environment
CHK	CHKDSK	Recovered data file; contains data recovered when using the /F option in CHKDSK
CLR	Show Partner	Color palette file
CLS	Actor	Class library file for Actor programming language
CMD	dBASE	Command file; used for file that contains dBASE programs
CMD	CP/M-86	Transient command file (similar to DOS EXE and COM files)
CMP	MS-Word	Compare file; contains dictionary of words to compare for spelling
CNF	Many	A configuration file; contains information about machine environment
COB	COBOL	COBOL program source code
COD	FORTRAN	FORTRAN program compiled code file
COL	MS-Multiplan	Spreadsheet data file; contains contents of a spreadsheet
COM	DOS	Command (program) file
CPL	MS-Windows	Control Panel Applet
CRF	MASM	Cross reference file; listing produced by MASM compiler
CRS	World Tour Golf	Course data file
CTX	Microsoft	Course text file; contains information for on-line tutorials
CUR	MS-Windows	Cursor file; contains data for a Windows cursor
DAT	Many	Data file; usually contains ASCII or specifically formatted data
DB	Paradox	Data file; contains data for a Paradox table
DBD	Norton's DEMO	Demonstration data file
DBF	dBASE	Data file; contains data for a dBASE database
DBS	SQLWindows	Data file; contains data for a SQL Windows database
DBT	dBASE	Data file; contains dBASE textual database information
DBT	SQLWindows	Temporary data file
DCT	SpellStar	Dictionary file; contains spelling dictionary
DEF	MS-Windows	Module definition file
DEF	Access	
DES	Access	
DEV	Many	Device driver file; contains code needed by CONFIG.SYS to install a new device
DFM	Palantir Filer	Data entry form file
DGS	PC-DOS	Diagnostics file
DIB	MS-Windows	Device independent bitmap
DIC	Many	Dictionary file; contains spelling dictionary
DIF	Many	Data interchange format file; used to interchange data between programs
DIR	SideKick	Directory file; used with dialing options
DIS	Q&A	Startup file used by Q&A
DLL	MS-Windows	Dynamic link library
DOC	Many	Document file; may be in ASCII or word processor-specific format
DOC	MS-Word	Document file; contains formatted document in non-ASCII form
DOT	Microsoft	Tutorial file
DRV	Many	Device driver file; contains information to drive a specific device
DTF	Q&A, PFS	Data file; contains data for a PFS or Q&A database
EMU	BITCOM	Terminal emulation file; contains definitions used to emulate a terminal
EPS	PageMaker	Encapsulated PostScript file; contains condensed PostScript printer data
ERR	various	Error log
EXE	DOS	Executable program file
F#	Paradox	Form file; contains form definition information
FLI	Animator	Animation file

(Continued)

2.33. COMMON FILE TYPES (continued)

File Type	Program	Description
FMT	dBASE	Screen format file; contains information about how data is to be displayed on screen
FNT	MS-Windows	Font file; contains description of what a font should look like
FNT	LaserFonts	Font file; contains description of what a font should look like
FNT	PC Paintbrush	Font file; contains description of what a font should look like
FON	MS-Windows	GDI loadable font file
FOR	FORTRAN	FORTRAN source code file
FRM	dBASE	Report form file; contains information about how a dBASE report should be formatted
GIF	various	CompuServe graphic element
GRB	MS-Windows	
GRP	MS-Windows	Group definition
GUI	Guide	Guide document
GX1	Show Partner	Graphics screen capture file
H	C compilers	Header file; contains C source code definitions to be merged with other files
HEX	DEBUG	Hex file; contains ASCII only numbers formatted in Intel HEX format
HIN	Access	
HLP	Many	Help file; contains information to help user understand command or function
ICO	MS-Windows	Icon file; contains bit image of an icon
IDX	Q&A	Index file; contains indexing information for a database
IMG	MS-Windows	Hi-res scanned image file
IMP	Pascal	Implementation file for IBM Pascal
INC	Pascal	Include file for Microsoft Pascal
INC	Turbo BASIC	Include file for Borland Turbo BASIC
INI	MS-Windows	Initialization file; contains information about initial state of system
INI	MS-Word	Printer initialization file
INT	Pascal	Interface file for IBM Pascal
INT	XyWrite	Command file for XyWrite
IT	Intalk	Settings file
JOR	SQLWindows	Journal file
KBD	XyWrite	Keyboard configuration file
LAY	SuperKey	Layout file; contains keyboard reconfiguration information
LBL	dBASE	Label file
LIB	Many	Library file; normally created by a compiler in one of several standard formats
LNK	MS-Windows/C	
LOD	Many	Load file; used by one copy-protection scheme
LST	MASM	Listing file; lists assembled source code
MAC	ProKey	Keyboard macro file; contains instructions to execute when certain keys are pressed
MAC	SuperKey	Keyboard macro file; contains instructions to execute when certain keys are pressed
MAP	LINK	Map file; a list file created by LINK during the linking proces
MDM	Access	Modem file; contains information about modems
ME	Many	Usually a READ.ME file containing information about files on disk
MEM	dBASE	Memory file
MID	MS-Windows	MIDI file
MNU	Access	Menu file; contains menu definition
MOD	MS-Windows	
MSG	MS-Multiplan	Message file
MSG	SideKick	Message file; used with appointment calendar
MSP	MS-Windows	Windows Paint file; contains data for a picture drawn with Windows Paint
NDX	dBASE	Index file; contains indexing information for a database
NET	Paradox	Network configuration file
OBJ	LINK	Object code file; contains result of an assembly or compile in a specified format
OLD	Microsoft	Backup file
OV#	Many	Overlay file; contains part of program to be loaded at a later time
OVD	Paradox	Overlay file
OVL	Many	Overlay file; contains part of program to be loaded at a later time
OVR	Many	Overlay file; contains part of program to be loaded at a later time
PAL	PC Paintbrush	Palette file
PAS	Pascal	Pascal source code file
PCC	PC Paintbrush	Cutout picture file
PCX	PC Paintbrush	Picture file
PFM	MS-Windows	Printer font metric file
PGM	Many	Usually a program overlay file
PHB	Access	
PIC	Many	Picture file
PIF	MS-Windows	Program information file; used by TopView and Windows to load program into memory
PIX	Many	File containing one or more pictures
PJ	SuperProject	Project file; contains information about a scheduling project
PRD	MS-Word	Printer definition file; contains information about how to talk to printer
PRF	VisiCalc	Print format file (spreadsheet printed to disk)
PRG	dBASE	Procedure or program file
PRJ	Harvard TPM	Project data file
PRN	Many	Print format file (print to disk)
PRS	MS-Word	
PUB	PageMaker	Publication file; contains data for page layout

(Continued)

2.33. COMMON FILE TYPES (continued)

File Type	Program	Description
PX	Paradox	Primary Index file
R#	Paradox	Report format file; contains a report definition
RC	MS-Windows	Resource Script file; contains a list of resource definitions used by MS-Windows
REF	CREF	Printable cross-reference file (see CRF)
RTF	Microsoft	Rich text file
SC	Paradox	Script file; contains a PAL script (program)
SCN	Microsoft	Screen file; contains screen displays for on-line tutorials
SCP	BITCOM	Script file; contains a macro script for communications session
SCR	Access	Script file
SET	Paradox	Settings file; contains information about settings for a form or table
SLK	various	Symbolic Link Format for data transfer (SYLK)
SOB	Microsoft	Part of on-line tutorials
SOM	Paradox	Sort information file
SPL	SQLWindows	SQLTALK Spooler file
SPS	Mouse	
SQL	SQLWindows	Data file
STY	MS-Word	Style sheet; contains style formatting information
SYM	MS-Windows	Symbolic debugging definitions
SYN	Word Finder	Synonym file; contains information for thesaurus program
SYS	Many	Device driver file; contains information to create a device driver under CONFIG.SYS
TBK	ToolBook	Book file
TIF	Microsoft	Tagged info file format (see 6.011. Tag Image File Format)
TMP	Many	Temporary file
TPL	Access	
TXT	Many	Text file
VAL	Paradox	Validity check file
VC	VisiCalc	VisiCalc spreadsheet file
WAV	MS-Windows	Sound file
WCM	MS-Works	Works communications files
WDB	MS-Works	Works database file
WK1	Lotus 1-2-3	1-2-3 spreadsheet file (version 2)
WKS	Lotus 1-2-3	1-2-3 spreadsheet file (version 1)
WKS	MS-Works	Works spreadsheet file
WMF	MS-Windows	Metafile picture (see 6.016. MetaFile Format)
WPS	MS-Works	Works word processor file
WRI	MS-Windows	Windows Write document file
X#	Paradox	Index file
XLC	MS-Excel	Chart file
XLS	MS-Excel	Spreadsheet file
Y#	Paradox	Index file
Z#	Paradox	Index file
ZIP	PKZIP	Compressed file

Note:
- A # sign indicates a position held by a digit, 0-9.
- MS-Windows can associate file types with a program. Registration of types is done in the MS-Windows programming SIG on Genie.

2.34. TYPICAL DOS MEMORY USAGE

Address	*Memory Usage*
0000:0000	Interrupt vector table (see 7.004. I/O Port Usage Summary)
0000:0400	ROM BIOS parameter area
0000:0500	DOS parameter area
0000:0700	IBMBIO
0000:0E30	IBMDOS
0000:4DB9	Device drivers (includes ANSI.SYS, BUFFERS=, FILES=, etc.)
0000:53F0	Resident COMMAND.COM
0000:5FD0	Master environment for COMMAND.COM (see 3.198. Environment Blocks)
0000:6080	Environment for program (if any)
0000:60B0	Application program (if any) (see 3.196. PSP Structure) (see 2.29. COM Versus EXE File Differences)
0009:C9E0	Stack (expands towards beginning of memory)
0009:CBE0	Transient COMMAND.COM (error messages, command table, last command)
000A:0000	Hardware RESERVED (video adapters, ROM, ROM expansion) (see 7.003. PC, AT, and PS/2 Memory Usage Summary)
0010:0000	

Version: Memory addresses are for PC-DOS 2.1 only. Other DOS versions will use the same ordering, but the memory addresses may vary. Nonvarying addresses are shown in bold.

Source: IBM DOS 3.3 Technical Reference, pages 7-4 and 7-5

See Also:
2.29. COM Versus EXE File Differences
3.196. PSP Structure
3.198. Environment Blocks
7.003. PC, AT, and PS/2 Memory Usage Summary
7.004. I/O Port Usage Summary

2.35. ALLOWABLE CHARACTERS IN FILENAMES

ASCII Code	*Character(s)*	*Allowed*	*Illegal*
00H-1FH	Control codes		✔
20H	Space		✔
21H	Exclamation point	✔	
22H	Quotation mark		✔
23H-29H	Misc. punctuation	✔	
2AH	Asterisk		✔**
2BH	Plus sign		✔
2CH	Comma		✔
2DH	Hyphen	✔	
2EH	Period		✔**
2FH	Slash		✔
30H-39H	Numbers	✔	
3AH	Colon		✔**
3BH	Semicolon		✔
3CH	Less than sign		✔
3DH	Equals sign		✔
3EH	Greater than sign		✔
3FH	Question mark		✔**
40H	At sign	✔	
41H-5AH	Capital letters	✔	
5BH	Opening bracket		✔
5CH	Backslash		✔**
5DH	Closing bracket		✔
5EH-60H	Misc. punctuation	✔	
61H-7AH	Lowercase letters	✔	
7BH	Opening brace	✔	
7CH	Vertical line		✔
7DH	Closing brace	✔	
7EH	Tilde	✔	
7FH	DEL		✔
80H-FFH	IBM extended ASCII	✔*	

*Cannot necessarily be entered directly from keyboard.
**Has special meaning in filenames.

Note:
- This same table applies to file types, volume, and directory names.
- Filenames cannot be AUX, CLOCK$, COM1, COM2, COM3, COM4, CON, LPT1, LPT2, LPT3, LST, NUL, or PRN, although these names can be used in file extensions.

Source: IBM DOS 3.3 Technical Reference, page 2-4
Using IBM DOS 4.0, page 23
Microsoft MS-DOS 4.0 User's Guide and Reference, pages 16 through 17
Microsoft MS-DOS 5.0 User's Guide and Reference, pages 69 through 70

See Also: 2.36. Filename Separator Characters

2.36. FILENAME SEPARATOR CHARACTERS

ASCII Codes	*Character(s)*	*Separator*	*Terminator*
00H-1FH	Control codes		✔
09H	Tab	✔	✔
20H	Space	✔	✔
22H	Quotation mark	✔	✔
2BH	Plus sign	✔	✔
2CH	Comma	✔	✔
2EH	Period	✔	✔
2FH	Forward slash	✔	✔
3AH	Colon	✔	✔
3BH	Semicolon	✔	✔
3CH	Less than sign	✔	✔
3DH	Equals sign	✔	✔
3EH	Greater than sign	✔	✔
5BH	Opening bracket	✔	✔
5CH	Backslash	✔	✔
5DH	Closing bracket	✔	✔
7CH	Vertical line	✔	✔

Note: Filename separators and terminators are used in parsing filenames.

Source: Microsoft MS-DOS 3.2 Programmer's Reference, page 1-107
Microsoft MS-DOS 4.0 Programmer's Reference, page 132
Microsoft MS-DOS 5.0 Programmer's Reference, page 255

See Also: 2.35. Allowable Characters in Filenames
3.053. INT 21H, AH=29H -- Parse Filename

Section 3

DOS Function Calls and Support Tables

File System Structures and Supporting Tables

Program Management Structures and Supporting Tables

National-Language Support Structures and Supporting Tables

Device Driver Functions, Structures, and Supporting Tables

3.001. INT 21H FUNCTIONS BY DOS VERSION SUMMARY

Function	Subfunction	Minor Code	Function Name	DOS Versions That Support the Function 1	1.1	2	2.1	3	3.1	3.2	3.3	4.0	5.0
00H			Terminate program	✔	✔	O	O	O	O	O	O	O	O
01H			Read keyboard with echo	✔	✔	O	O	O	O	O	O	O	O
02H			Display character	✔	✔	O	O	O	O	O	O	O	O
03H			Auxiliary input	✔	✔	O	O	O	O	O	O	O	O
04H			Auxiliary output	✔	✔	O	O	O	O	O	O	O	O
05H			Print character	✔	✔	O	O	O	O	O	O	O	O
06H			Direct console I/O	✔	✔	✔	✔	✔	✔	✔	✔	✔	✔
07H			Direct console input	✔	✔	✔	✔	✔	✔	✔	✔	✔	✔
08H			Read keyboard without echo	✔	✔	✔	✔	✔	✔	✔	✔	✔	✔
09H			Display string	✔	✔	O	O	O	O	O	O	O	O
0AH			Buffered keyboard input	✔	✔	O	O	O	O	O	O	O	O
0BH			Check keyboard status	✔	✔	✔	✔	✔	✔	✔	✔	✔	✔
0CH			Flush buffer, read keyboard	✔	✔	✔	✔	✔	✔	✔	✔	✔	✔
0DH			Reset drive	✔	✔	✔	✔	✔	✔	✔	✔	✔	✔
0EH			Set default drive	✔	✔	✔	✔	✔	✔	✔	✔	✔	✔
0FH			Open file with FCB	✔	✔	O	O	O	O	O	O	O	O
10H			Close file with FCB	✔	✔	O	O	O	O	O	O	O	O
11H			Find first file with FCB	✔	✔	O	O	O	O	O	O	O	O
12H			Find next file with FCB	✔	✔	O	O	O	O	O	O	O	O
13H			Delete file with FCB	✔	✔	O	O	O	O	O	O	O	O
14H			Sequential read	✔	✔	O	O	O	O	O	O	O	O
15H			Sequential write	✔	✔	O	O	O	O	O	O	O	O
16H			Create file with FCB	✔	✔	O	O	O	O	O	O	O	O
17H			Rename file with FCB	✔	✔	O	O	O	O	O	O	O	O
18H			RESERVED	R	R	R	R	R	R	R	R	R	R
19H			Get default drive	✔	✔	✔	✔	✔	✔	✔	✔	✔	✔
1AH			Set disk transfer address	✔	✔	✔	✔	✔	✔	✔	✔	✔	✔
1BH			Get default drive data			✔	O	O	O	O	O	O	O
1CH			Get drive data			✔	O	O	O	O	O	O	O
1DH			RESERVED	R	R	R	R	R	R	R	R	R	R
1EH			RESERVED	R	R	R	R	R	R	R	R	R	R
1FH			Get default DPB										✔
20H			RESERVED	R	R	R	R	R	R	R	R	R	R
21H			Random read	✔	✔	O	O	O	O	O	O	O	O
22H			Random write	✔	✔	O	O	O	O	O	O	O	O
23H			Get file size	✔	✔	O	O	O	O	O	O	O	O
24H			Set random record number	✔	✔	O	O	O	O	O	O	O	O
25H			Set interrupt vector	✔	✔	✔	✔	✔	✔	✔	✔	✔	✔
26H			Create new PSP	✔	✔	O	O	O	O	O	O	O	O
27H			Random block read	✔	✔	O	O	O	O	O	O	O	O
28H			Random block write	✔	✔	O	O	O	O	O	O	O	O
29H			Parse filename	✔	✔	O	O	O	O	O	O	O	O
2AH			Get date	✔	✔	✔	✔	✔	✔	✔	✔	✔	✔
2BH			Set date	✔	✔	✔	✔	✔	✔	✔	✔	✔	✔
2CH			Get time	✔	✔	✔	✔	✔	✔	✔	✔	✔	✔
2DH			Set time	✔	✔	✔	✔	✔	✔	✔	✔	✔	✔
2EH			Set/reset verify flag	✔	✔	✔	✔	✔	✔	✔	✔	✔	✔
2FH			Get disk transfer address			✔	✔	✔	✔	✔	✔	✔	✔
30H			Get version number			✔	✔	✔	✔	✔	✔	✔	✔
31H			Keep program			✔	✔	✔	✔	✔	✔	✔	✔
32H			Get DPB										✔
33H	00H		Get Ctrl+C check flag			✔	✔	✔	✔	✔	✔	✔	✔
33H	01H		Set Ctrl+C check flag			✔	✔	✔	✔	✔	✔	✔	✔
33H	05H		Get startup drive			✔	✔	✔	✔	✔	✔	✔	✔
33H	06H		Get MS-DOS version										✔
34H			Get InDOS flag address			✔	✔	✔	✔	✔	✔	✔	✔
35H			Get interrupt vector			✔	✔	✔	✔	✔	✔	✔	✔
36H			Get disk free space			✔	✔	✔	✔	✔	✔	✔	✔
37H			RESERVED	R	R	R	R	R	R	R	R	R	R
38H			Get/set country			✔	✔	✔	✔	✔	✔	✔	✔
39H			Create directory			✔	✔	✔	✔	✔	✔	✔	✔
3AH			Remove directory			✔	✔	✔	✔	✔	✔	✔	✔
3BH			Change current directory			✔	✔	✔	✔	✔	✔	✔	✔
3CH			Create file with handle			✔	✔	✔	✔	✔	✔	✔	✔
3DH			Open file with handle			✔	✔	✔	✔	✔	✔	✔	✔
3EH			Close file with handle			✔	✔	✔	✔	✔	✔	✔	✔
3FH			Read file or device			✔	✔	✔	✔	✔	✔	✔	✔

(Continued)

3.001. INT 21H FUNCTIONS BY DOS VERSION SUMMARY (continued)

Function	Subfunction	Minor Code	Function Name	DOS Versions That Support the Function: 1	1.1	2	2.1	3	3.1	3.2	3.3	4.0	5.0
40H			Write file or device			✔	✔	✔	✔	✔	✔	✔	✔
41H			Delete file			✔	✔	✔	✔	✔	✔	✔	✔
42H			Move file pointer			✔	✔	✔	✔	✔	✔	✔	✔
43H	00H		Get file attributes			✔	✔	✔	✔	✔	✔	✔	✔
43H	01H		Set file attributes			✔	✔	✔	✔	✔	✔	✔	✔
44H	00H		Get device data			✔	✔	✔	✔	✔	✔	✔	✔
44H	01H		Set device data			✔	✔	✔	✔	✔	✔	✔	✔
44H	02H		Receive control data from character device			✔	✔	✔	✔	✔	✔	✔	✔
44H	03H		Send control data to character device			✔	✔	✔	✔	✔	✔	✔	✔
44H	04H		Receive control data from block device			✔	✔	✔	✔	✔	✔	✔	✔
44H	05H		Send control data to block device			✔	✔	✔	✔	✔	✔	✔	✔
44H	06H		Check device input status			✔	✔	✔	✔	✔	✔	✔	✔
44H	07H		Check device output status			✔	✔	✔	✔	✔	✔	✔	✔
44H	08H		Does device use removable media					✔	✔	✔	✔	✔	✔
44H	09H		Is drive remote						✔	✔	✔	✔	✔
44H	0AH		Is file or device remote						✔	✔	✔	✔	✔
44H	0BH		Set sharing retry count						✔	✔	✔	✔	✔
44H	0CH	45H	Set iteration count								✔	✔	✔
44H	0CH	4AH	Select code page								✔	✔	✔
44H	0CH	4CH	Start code-page prepare								✔	✔	✔
44H	0CH	4DH	End code-page prepare								✔	✔	✔
44H	0CH	5FH	Set display mode									✔	✔
44H	0CH	65H	Get iteration count								✔	✔	✔
44H	0CH	6AH	Query selected code page								✔	✔	✔
44H	0CH	6BH	Query code-page prepare list								✔	✔	✔
44H	0CH	7FH	Get display mode									✔	✔
44H	0DH	40H	Set device parameters							✔	✔	✔	✔
44H	0DH	41H	Write track on logical drive							✔	✔	✔	✔
44H	0DH	42H	Format track on logical drive							✔	✔	✔	✔
44H	0DH	46H	Set media ID									✔	✔
44H	0DH	60H	Get device parameters							✔	✔	✔	✔
44H	0DH	61H	Read track on logical drive							✔	✔	✔	✔
44H	0DH	62H	Verify track on logical drive							✔	✔	✔	✔
44H	0DH	66H	Get media ID									✔	✔
44H	0DH	68H	Sense media type										✔
44H	0EH		Get logical drive map							✔	✔	✔	✔
44H	0FH		Set logical drive map							✔	✔	✔	✔
44H	10H		Query IOCTL handle										✔
44H	11H		Query IOCTL device										✔
45H			Duplicate file handle			✔	✔	✔	✔	✔	✔	✔	✔
46H			Force duplicate file handle			✔	✔	✔	✔	✔	✔	✔	✔
47H			Get current directory			✔	✔	✔	✔	✔	✔	✔	✔
48H			Allocate memory			✔	✔	✔	✔	✔	✔	✔	✔
49H			Free allocated memory			✔	✔	✔	✔	✔	✔	✔	✔
4AH			Set memory block size			✔	✔	✔	✔	✔	✔	✔	✔
4BH	00H		Load and execute program			✔	✔	✔	✔	✔	✔	✔	✔
4BH	01H		Load program			✔	✔	✔	✔	✔	✔	✔	✔
4BH	03H		Load overlay			✔	✔	✔	✔	✔	✔	✔	✔
4BH	05H		Set execution state										✔
4CH			End program			✔	✔	✔	✔	✔	✔	✔	✔
4DH			Get child program return value			✔	✔	✔	✔	✔	✔	✔	✔
4EH			Find first file			✔	✔	✔	✔	✔	✔	✔	✔
4FH			Find next file			✔	✔	✔	✔	✔	✔	✔	✔
50H			Set PSP address			✔	✔	✔	✔	✔	✔	✔	✔
51H			Get PSP address			✔	✔	✔	✔	✔	✔	✔	✔
52H			RESERVED	R	R	R	R	R	R	R	R	R	R
53H			RESERVED	R	R	R	R	R	R	R	R	R	R

(Continued)

3.001. INT 21H FUNCTIONS BY DOS VERSION SUMMARY (continued)

				DOS Versions That Support the Function									
Function	*Subfunction*	*Minor Code*	*Function Name*	*1*	*1.1*	*2*	*2.1*	*3*	*3.1*	*3.2*	*3.3*	*4.0*	*5.0*
54H			Get verify state			✔	✔	✔	✔	✔	✔	✔	✔
55H			RESERVED	R	R	R	R	R	R	R	R	R	R
56H			Rename file			✔	✔	✔	✔	✔	✔	✔	✔
57H	00H		Get file date and time			✔	✔	✔	✔	✔	✔	✔	✔
57H	01H		Set file date and time			✔	✔	✔	✔	✔	✔	✔	✔
58H	00H		Get allocation strategy					✔	✔	✔	✔	✔	✔
58H	01H		Set allocation strategy					✔	✔	✔	✔	✔	✔
58H	02H		Get upper memory link										✔
58H	03H		Set upper memory link										✔
59H			Get extended error					✔	✔	✔	✔	✔	✔
5AH			Create temporary file					✔	✔	✔	✔	✔	✔
5BH			Create new file					✔	✔	✔	✔	✔	✔
5CH	00H		Lock						✔	✔	✔	✔	✔
5CH	01H		Unlock						✔	✔	✔	✔	✔
5DH	0AH		Set extended error									✔	✔
5EH	00H		Get machine name						✔	✔	✔	✔	✔
5EH	02H		Set printer setup						✔	✔	✔	✔	✔
5EH	03H		Get printer setup						✔	✔	✔	✔	✔
5FH	02H		Get assign-list entry						✔	✔	✔	✔	✔
5FH	03H		Make network connection						✔	✔	✔	✔	✔
5FH	04H		Delete network connection						✔	✔	✔	✔	✔
60H			RESERVED	R	R	R	R	R	R	R	R	R	R
61H			RESERVED	R	R	R	R	R	R	R	R	R	R
62H			Get PSP					✔	✔	✔	✔	✔	✔
63H			Get lead byte table				2.25*						
65H	01H		Get extended country information								✔	✔	✔
65H	02H		Get uppercase table								✔	✔	✔
65H	04H		Get filename uppercase table								✔	✔	✔
65H	05H		Get filename character table								✔	✔	✔
65H	06H		Get collate sequence table								✔	✔	✔
65H	07H		Get double-byte character set								✔	✔	✔
65H	20H		Convert character								✔	✔	✔
65H	21H		Convert string								✔	✔	✔
65H	22H		Convert ASCIIZ string								✔	✔	✔
66H	01H		Get global code page								✔	✔	✔
66H	02H		Set global code page								✔	✔	✔
67H			Set maximum handle count								✔	✔	✔
68H			Commit file								✔	✔	✔
6CH			Extended open/create									✔	✔

*Note that function 63H is available only in DOS 2.25

Legend: √=supported, O=supported but superseded by newer functions, R=reserved

Note: Function column=AH register, subfunction column=AL register, minor code column=CL register

Source: IBM DOS 3.3 Technical Reference, pages 6-6 through 6-7
IBM DOS 4.0 Technical Reference, Appendix B
Microsoft MS-DOS 4.0 Programmer's Reference, pages 5 through 18
Microsoft MS-DOS 5.0 Programmer's Reference, pages 201 through 210

See Also: 3.015. through 3.169. INT 21H function tables

3.002. INT 21H KEYBOARD FUNCTIONS SUMMARY

INT 21H Function #	*Waits for Character*	*Echos Character*	*Interrupt on Ctrl-C*	*Buffer Register Used*
01H*	Yes	Yes	Yes	AL
06H	No	No	No	AL
07H	Yes	No	No	AL
08H	Yes	No	Yes	AL
0AH*	Yes	No	Yes	DS:DX=buffer address
0BH	Keyboard status only			
0CH	Varies upon function requested in AL			
3FH	Yes	No	Yes	DS:DX=buffer address

*Superseded functions

Note: Ctrl-C checking can be turned off completely using function 33H.

Source: IBM DOS 3.3 Technical Reference, pages 6-35, 6-52, 6-57 through 6-60, 6-62 through 6-64, 6-137 through 6-138
IBM DOS 4.0 Technical Reference, pages B13, B-18 through B-20, B-22 through B-24, B-86
Microsoft MS-DOS 4.0 Programmer's Reference, pages 58 through 59,68 through 73, 76 through 81, 178 through 179
Microsoft MS-DOS 5.0 Programmer's Reference, pages 212 through 223 and 282

See Also: 3.019. INT 21H, AH=01H -- Read Keyboard with Echo
3.022. INT 21H, AH=06H -- Direct Console I/O
3.023. INT 21H, AH=07H -- Direct Console Input
3.024. INT 21H, AH=08H -- Read Keyboard Without Echo
3.026. INT 21H, AH=0AH -- Buffered Keyboard Input
3.027. INT 21H, AH=0BH -- Check Keyboard Status
3.028. INT 21H, AH=0CH -- Flush Buffer, Read Keyboard
3.078. INT 21H, AH=3FH -- Read File or Device

3.003. INT 21H FCB-ORIENTED FUNCTIONS SUMMARY

INT 21H Function #	*Function Name*	*Type of FCB Used**	*Replaced by Function*
0FH	Open file with FCB	Unopened FCB	3DH -- open handle
10H	Close file with FCB	Opened FCB	3EH -- close handle
11H	Find first file with FCB	Unopened FCB	4EH -- find first file
12H	Find next file with FCB	Unopened FCB†	4FH -- find next file
13H	Delete file with FCB	Unopened FCB	41H -- delete file
14H	Sequential read	Opened FCB	3FH -- read handle
15H	Sequential write	Opened FCB	40H -- write handle
16H	Create file with FCB	Unopened FCB	3CH -- create handle
17H	Rename file with FCB	Rename FCB	56H -- rename file
21H	Random read	Opened FCB	3FH -- read file or device
22H	Random write	Opened FCB	40H -- write file or device
23H	Get file size	Unopened FCB	42H -- move file pointer
24H	Set random record number	Opened FCB	42H -- move file pointer
27H	Random block read	Opened FCB	3FH -- read file or device, 42H -- move file pointer
28H	Random block write	Opened FCB	40H -- write file or device, 42H -- move file pointer
29H	Parse filename	Opened FCB	

*Opened and unopened FCBs may also be extended if you need to set or are using the file attribute byte.
†Must be unchanged from use of INT 21H, AH=11H -- Find First File with FCB

Source: IBM DOS 3.3 Technical Reference, pages 6-67 through 6-80,6-85 through 6-88, 6-91 through 6-94
IBM DOS 4.0 Technical Reference, pages B-27 through B-39, B-44 through B-49, B-52 through B-55
Microsoft MS-DOS 4.0 Programmer's Reference, pages 85 through 102, 113 through 121, 125 through 130
Microsoft MS-DOS 5.0 Programmer's Reference, pages 203 through 204 and 209 through 210

See Also: 3.031. INT 21H, AH=0FH -- Open File With FCB
3.032. INT 21H, AH=10H -- Close File With FCB
3.033. INT 21H, AH=11H -- Find First File With FCB
3.034. INT 21H, AH=12H -- Find Next File With FCB
3.035. INT 21H, AH=13H -- Delete File With FCB
3.036. INT 21H, AH=14H -- Sequential Read
3.037. INT 21H, AH=15H -- Sequential Write
3.038. INT 21H, AH=16H -- Create File With FCB
3.039. INT 21H, AH=17H -- Rename File With FCB
3.045. INT 21H, AH=21H -- Random Read
3.046. INT 21H, AH=22H -- Random Write
3.047. INT 21H, AH=23H -- Get File Size
3.048. INT 21H, AH=24H -- Set Random Record
3.051. INT 21H, AH=27H -- Random Block Read
3.052. INT 21H, AH=28H -- Random Block Write
3.053. INT 21H, AH=29H -- Parse Filename
3.175. FCB Structure (Opened)
3.176. FCB Structure (Unopened)
3.181. RENAMEFCB Structure
3.185. FCB Error Codes

3.004. INT 21H HANDLE-ORIENTED FUNCTIONS SUMMARY

INT 21H Function #	*Function Name*	*Use*
3CH	Create file with handle	Creates file for subsequent I/O; erases existing file, if any
3DH	Open file with handle	Readies file for I/O; assigns handle number
3EH	Close file with handle	Closes handle; frees handle number
3FH	Read file or device	Reads from file at current pointer location
40H	Write file or device	Writes to file at current pointer location
41H	Delete file	Deletes file
42H	Move file pointer	Moves location of pointer in file
43H	Get/set file attributes	Changes or retrieves attribute byte for file
45H	Duplicate file handle	Assigns additional handle number to existing handle
46H	Force duplicate file handle	Forces existing handle to refer to file that has a different handle
56H	Rename file	Renames file
57H	Get/set file date/time	Changes or retrieves Last Update time and date associated with file
5AH	Create temporary file	Creates file with unique name for subsequent I/O
5BH	Create new file	Creates file for subsequent I/O only if it does not already exist
67H	Set maximum handle count	Allows you to specify more than 20 handles (default)
68H	Commit file	Insures file is written to disk (flushes buffer)
6CH	Extended Open/Create	Combines Open, Create, and Create New functions

Note: The first five handle numbers are preassigned by DOS (See 3.188. Predefined Handles)

Source: IBM DOS 3.3 Technical Reference, pages 6-122 through 6-146, 6-185 through 6-187, 6-206 through 6-209, 6-213 through 6-215, and 6-239 through 6-240
IBM DOS 4.0 Technical Reference, pages B-77 through B-93, B-95 through B-96, B-111 through B-112, B-115 through B-117, B-136 through B-139
Microsoft MS-DOS 4.0 Programmer's Reference, pages 168 through 187, 218 through 221, 248 through 251, 258 through 262, 287 through 288
Microsoft MS-DOS 5.0 Programmer's Reference, pages 201 through 202

See Also:
3.075. INT 21H, AH=3CH -- Create File with Handle
3.076. INT 21H, AH=3DH -- Open File with Handle
3.077. INT 21H, AH=3EH -- Close File with Handle
3.078. INT 21H, AH=3FH -- Read File or Device
3.079. INT 21H, AH=40H -- Write File or Device
3.080. INT 21H, AH=41H -- Delete File
3.081. INT 21H, AH=42H -- Move File Pointer
3.082. INT 21H, AH=43H, AL=00H -- Get File Attributes
3.083. INT 21H, AH=43H, AL=01H -- Set File Attributes
3.118. INT 21H, AH=45H -- Duplicate File Handle
3.119. INT 21H, AH=46H -- Force Duplicate File Handle
3.135. INT 21H, AH=56H -- Rename File
3.136. INT 21H, AH=57H, AL=00H -- Get File Date and Time
3.137. INT 21H, AH=57H, AL=01H -- Set File Date and Time
3.143. INT 21H, AH=5AH -- Create Temporary File
3.144. INT 21H, AH=5BH -- Create New File
3.167. INT 21H, AH=67H -- Set Maximum Handle Count
3.168. INT 21H, AH=68H -- Commit File
3.169. INT 21H, AH=6CH -- Extended Open/Create

3.005. INT 21H IOCTL DEVICE-ORIENTED FUNCTIONS SUMMARY

Function	Subfunction	Minor Code	Function Name	Use
44H	00H		Get device data	Gets the device data word used to control device
44H	01H		Set device data	Sets the device data word used to control device
44H	02H		Receive control data from character device	Receives a string from character-oriented device
44H	03H		Send control data to character device	Sends a string to character-oriented device
44H	04H		Receive control data from block device	Receives a block of data from block-oriented device
44H	05H		Send control data to block device	Sends a block of data to block-oriented device
44H	06H		Check device input status	Checks input device for readiness
44H	07H		Check device output status	Checks output device for readiness
44H	08H		Does device use removable media	Reports whether block device contains removable media
44H	09H		Is drive remote	Reports whether block device is local or remote (network)
44H	0AH		Is file or device remote	Reports whether handle referencing device is local or remote
44H	0BH		Set sharing retry count	Sets number of retries and pause between them for a file-sharing device
44H	0CH		Generic IOCTL for character devices	Sets or gets number of retries for printer devices; prepares code pages
44H	0CH	45H	Set iteration count	
44H	0CH	4AH	Select code page	
44H	0CH	4CH	Start code-page prepare	
44H	0CH	4DH	End code-page prepare	
44H	0CH	5FH	Set display mode	
44H	0CH	65H	Get iteration count	
44H	0CH	6AH	Query selected code page	
44H	0CH	6BH	Query code-page prepare list	
44H	0CH	7FH	Get display mode	
44H	0DH		Generic IOCTL for block devices	Sets/gets block device parameters; writes/reads/formats/verifies tracks
44H	0DH	40H	Set device parameters	
44H	0DH	41H	Write track on logical drive	
44H	0DH	42H	Format track on logical drive	
44H	0DH	46H	Set media ID	
44H	0DH	60H	Get device parameters	
44H	0DH	61H	Read track on logical drive	
44H	0DH	62H	Verify track on logical drive	
44H	0DH	66H	Get media ID	
44H	0DH	68H	Sense media type	
44H	0EH		Get logical drive map	Reports logical drive mapping
44H	0FH		Set logical drive map	Sets logical to physical drive mapping

Note: Function column=AH register, subfunction column=AL register, minor code column=CL register

Source: IBM DOS 3.3 Technical Reference, pages 6-147 through 6-184
IBM DOS 4.0 Technical Reference, Appendix C
Microsoft MS-DOS 4.0 Programmer's Reference, pages 188 through 217
Microsoft MS-DOS 5.0 Programmer's Reference, pages 204 through 205

See Also: 3.084. INT 21H, AH=44H, AL=00H -- Get Device Data
3.085. INT 21H, AH=44H, AL=01H -- Set Device Data
3.086. INT 21H, AH=44H, AL=02H -- Receive Control Data from Character Device
3.087. INT 21H, AH=44H, AL=03H -- Send Control Data to Character Device
3.088. INT 21H, AH=44H, AL=04H -- Receive Control Data from Block Device
3.089. INT 21H, AH=44H, AL=05H -- Send Control Data to Block Device
3.090. INT 21H, AH=44H, AL=06H -- Check Device Input Status
3.091. INT 21H, AH=44H, AL=07H -- Check Device Output Status
3.092. INT 21H, AH=44H, AL=08H -- Does Device Use Removable Media
3.093. INT 21H, AH=44H, AL=09H -- Is Drive Remote
3.094. INT 21H, AH=44H, AL=0AH -- Is File or Device Remote
3.095. INT 21H, AH=44H, AL=0BH -- Set Sharing Retry Count
3.096. through 3.104. INT 21H, AH=44H, AL=0CH, Minor Code tables
3.105. through 3.113. INT 21H, AH=44H, AL=0DH, Minor Code tables
3.114. INT 21H, AH=44H, AL=0EH -- Get Logical Drive Map
3.115. INT 21H, AH=44H, AL=0FH -- Set Logical Drive Map
3.116. INT 21H, AH=44H, AL=10H -- Query IOCTL Handle
3.117. INT 21H, AH=44H, AL=11H -- Query IOCTL Device

3.006. INT 21H DIRECTORY MANAGEMENT FUNCTIONS SUMMARY

Function	Function Name	Use
39H	Create Directory	Creates new directory by using specified path
3AH	Remove Directory	Deletes specified directory
3BH	Change Current Directory	Changes current directory to specified path
41H	Delete File	Deletes specified file
47H	Get Current Directory	Returns path of current directory
4EH	Find First File	Searches directory for first matching file or directory
4FH	Find Next File	Searches directory for next matching file or directory
56H	Rename File	Renames or moves file or directory

Source: Microsoft MS-DOS 5.0 Programmer's Reference, page 202

See Also:
3.072. INT 21H, AH=39H -- Create Directory
3.073. INT 21H, AH=3AH -- Remove Directory
3.074. INT 21H, AH=3BH -- Change Current Directory
3.080. INT 21H, AH=41H -- Delete File
3.120. INT 21H, AH=47H -- Get Current Directory
3.130. INT 21H, AH=4EH -- Find First File
3.131. INT 21H, AH=4FH -- Find Next File
3.135. INT 21H, AH=56H -- Rename File

3.007. INT 21H DRIVE MANAGEMENT FUNCTIONS SUMMARY

Function	Subfunction	Function Name	Use
0DH		Reset Drive	Resets drive. Normally used by Ctrl+C
0EH		Set Default Drive	Sets specified drive to be default drive
19H		Get Default Drive	Returns the number of the default drive
1AH		Set Disk Transfer Address	Sets address of buffer used for file I/O and disk searches
1BH		Get Default Data Drive	Retrieves information about disk in default drive
1CH		Get Drive Data	Retrieves information about disk in specified drive
1FH		Get Default DPB	Retrieves drive parameters for default drive
2FH		Get Disk Transfer Address	Returns segment:offset of current DTA
32H		Get DPB	Retrieves drive parameters for specified drive
33H	05H	Get Startup Drive	Returns drive used to load DOS
36H		Get Disk Free Space	Returns number of clusters available on drive

Source: Microsoft MS-DOS 5.0 Programmer's Reference, page 203

See Also:
3.029. INT 21H, AH=0DH -- Reset Drive
3.030. INT 21H, AH=0EH -- Set Default Drive
3.040. INT 21H, AH=19H -- Get Current Drive
3.041. INT 21H, AH=1AH -- Set Disk Transfer Address
3.042. INT 21H, AH=1BH -- Get Default Drive Data
3.043. INT 21H, AH=1CH -- Get Drive Data
3.044. INT 21H, AH=1FH -- Get Default DPB
3.059. INT 21H, AH=2FH -- Get Disk Transfer Address
3.062. INT 21H, AH=32H -- Get DPB
3.065. INT 21H, AH=33H, AL=05H -- Get Startup Drive
3.069. INT 21H, AH=36H -- Get Disk Free Space

3.008. INT 21H FILE-SHARING FUNCTIONS SUMMARY

Function	Subfunction	Function Name	Use
44H	0BH	Set Sharing Retry Count	Sets number of times DOS retries a file sharing operation
5CH	00H	Lock File	Denies access to specified region in file
5CH	01H	Unlock File	Allow access to specified region in file

Source: Microsoft MS-DOS 5.0 Programmer's Reference, page 203

See Also:
3.095. INT 21H, AH=44H, AL=0BH -- Set Sharing Retry Count
3.145. INT 21H, AH=5CH, AL=00H -- Lock File
3.146. INT 21H, AH=5CH, AL=01H -- Unlock File

3.009. INT 21H CHARACTER I/O FUNCTIONS SUMMARY

Function	Function Name	Use
01H	Read Keyboard with Echo	Reads character from STDIN, writes to STDOUT
02H	Display Character	Displays character on STDOUT
03H	Auxiliary Input	Reads character from AUX. Waits for character
04H	Auxiliary Output	Sends character to auxiliary output device
05H	Print Character	Sends character to printer
06H	Direct Console I/O	Reads character from STDIN or writes to STDOUT
07H	Direct Console Input	Reads character from STDIN. Waits for character
08H	Read Keyboard without Echo	Reads character from STDIN
09H	Display String	Sends string to STDOUT
0AH	Buffered Keyboard Input	Reads string from STDIN, sends to STDOUT buffer
0BH	Check Keyboard Status	Checks availability of character from STDIN
0CH	Flush Buffer, Read Keyboard	Empties STDIN buffer

Source: Microsoft MS-DOS 5.0 Programmer's Reference, pages 205 through 206

See Also:
3.017. INT 21H, AH=01H -- Read Keyboard with Echo
3.018. INT 21H, AH=02H -- Display Character
3.019. INT 21H, AH=03H -- Auxiliary Input
3.020. INT 21H, AH=04H -- Auxiliary Output
3.021. INT 21H, AH=05H -- Print Character
3.022. INT 21H, AH=06H -- Direct Console I/O
3.023. INT 21H, AH=07H -- Direct Console Input
3.024. INT 21H, AH=08H -- Read Keyboard without Echo
3.025. INT 21H, AH=09H -- Display String
3.026. INT 21H, AH=0AH -- Buffered Keyboard Input
3.027. INT 21H, AH=0BH -- Check Keyboard Status
3.028. INT 21H, AH=0CH -- Flush Buffer, Read Keyboard

3.010. INT 21H MEMORY MANAGEMENT FUNCTIONS SUMMARY

Function	Subfunction	Function Name	Use
48H		Allocate Memory	Allocates requested amount of memory and returns address of memory block
49H		Free Allocated Memory	Frees memory previously allocated
4AH		Set Memory Block Size	Changes size of memory segment or amount of memory allocated
58H	00H	Get Allocation Strategy	Returns DOS memory allocation method
58H	01H	Set Allocation Strategy	Sets DOS memory allocation method
58H	02H	Get Upper-Memory Link	Specifies whether programs can allocate upper memory
58H	03H	Set Upper-Memory Link	Links or unlinks upper-memory area

Source: Microsoft MS-DOS 5.0 Programmer's Reference, page 206

See Also:
3.121. INT 21H, AH=48H -- Allocate Memory
3.122. INT 21H, AH=49H -- Free Allocated Memory
3.123. INT 21H, AH=4AH -- Set Memory Size Block
3.138. INT 21H, AH=58H, AL=00H -- Get Allocation Strategy
3.139. INT 21H, AH=58H, AL=01H -- Set Allocation Strategy
3.140. INT 21H, AH=58H, AL=02H -- Get Upper-Memory Link
3.141. INT 21H, AH=58H, AL=03H -- Set Upper-Memory Link

3.011. INT 21H PROGRAM MANAGEMENT FUNCTIONS SUMMARY

Function	Subfunction	Function Name	Use
00H		Terminate Program	Terminates current program. Returns control to parent program
26H		Create New PSP	Creates new Program Segment Prefix
31H		Keep Program	Ends program but leaves it in memory and preserves resources
34H		Get InDOS Flag Address	Returns address of InDOS flag
4BH	00H	Load and Execute Program	Loads program, creates new PSP, transfers control to new program
4BH	01H	Load Program	Loads program and creates new PSP
4BH	03H	Load Overlay	Loads program and overlay
4BH	05H	Set Execution State	Prepares new program for execution
4CH		End Program	Terminates program. Returns control to parent program
4DH		Get Child-Program Return Value	Retrieves return value specified by last child program
50H		Set PSP Address	Sets segment address of current PSP
51H		Get PSP Address	Returns segment address of current PSP
59H		Get Extended Error	Returns extended error information
5DH	0AH	Set Extended Error	Sets error information to return

Source: Microsoft MS-DOS 5.0 Programmer's Reference, pages 206 through 207

See Also:
3.016. INT 21H, AH=00H -- Terminate Program
3.050. INT 21H, AH=26H -- Create New Program Segment Prefix
3.061. INT 21H, AH=31H -- Keep Program
3.067. INT 21H, AH=34H -- Get InDOS Flag Address
3.124. INT 21H, AH=4BH, AL=00H -- Load and Execute Program
3.125. INT 21H, AH=4BH, AL=01H -- Load Program
3.126. INT 21H, AH=4BH, AL=03H -- Load Overlay
3.127. INT 21H, AH=4BH, AL=05H -- Set Execution State
3.128. INT 21H, AH=4CH -- End Program
3.129. INT 21H, AH=4DH -- Get Child-Program Return Value
3.132. INT 21H, AH=50H -- Set PSP Address
3.133. INT 21H, AH=51H -- Get PSP Address
3.142. INT 21H, AH=59H -- Get Extended Error
3.147. INT 21H, AH=5DH, AL=0AH -- Set Extended Error

3.012. INT 21H NATIONAL-LANGUAGE SUPPORT FUNCTIONS SUMMARY

Function	Subfunction	Function Name	Use
38H	00H	Get Country Information	Returns country information
38H	01H	Set Country Information	Sets country information
65H	01H	Get Extended Country Information	Gets country information for screen and keyboard control
65H	02H	Get Uppercase Table	Returns uppercase table for specified code page
65H	04H	Get Filename Uppercase Table	Returns address of filename uppercase table
65H	05H	Get Filename-Character Table	Returns address of filename character table
65H	06H	Get Collate Sequence Table	Returns address of collate sequence table
65H	07H	Get Double-Byte Character Set	Returns address of DBCS lead byte range buffer
65H	20H	Convert Character	Converts specified character to uppercase
65H	21H	Convert String	Converts each character in string to uppercase
65H	22H	Convert ASCIIZ String	Converts each character in string to uppercase
66H	01H	Get Global Code Page	Identifies code page currently used by all programs
66H	02H	Set Global Code Page	Sets code page currently used by all programs

Source: Microsoft MS-DOS 5.0 Programmer's Reference, pages 207 through 208

See Also:
3.070. INT 21H, AH=38H -- Get Country Data
3.071. INT 21H, AH=38H -- Set Country Data
3.156. INT 21H, AH=65H, AL=01H -- Get Extended Country Information
3.157. INT 21H, AH=65H, AL=02H -- Get Uppercase Table
3.158. INT 21H, AH=65H, AL=04H -- Get Filename Uppercase Table
3.159. INT 21H, AH=65H, AL=05H -- Get Filename Character Table
3.160. INT 21H, AH=65H, AL=06H -- Get Collate Sequence Table
3.161. INT 21H, AH=65H, AL=07H -- Get Double-Byte Character Set
3.162. INT 21H, AH=65H, AL=20H -- Convert Character
3.163. INT 21H, AH=65H, AL=21H -- Convert String
3.164. INT 21H, AH=65H, AL=22H -- Convert ASCIIZ String
3.165. INT 21H, AH=66H, AL=01H -- Get Global Code Page
3.166. INT 21H, AH=66H, AL=02H -- Set Global Code Page

3.013. INT 21H SYSTEM MANAGEMENT FUNCTIONS SUMMARY

INT 21H Function #	*Function Name*	*Use*
25H	Set interrupt vector	Replace interrupt vector address in low memory
2AH	Get system date	Retrieve current system date
2BH	Set system date	Store new system date
2CH	Get system time	Retrieve current system time
2DH	Set system time	Store new system time
2EH	Set/reset verify flag	Report or set verify flag state
30H	Get DOS version number	Report DOS version being used
31H	Keep process	End program execution but keep resident
33H	Ctrl+C check	Report or change Ctrl+C check status
35H	Get interrupt vector	Report address associated with Interrupt
54H	Get verify state	Report current verify flag setting

Source: IBM DOS 3.3 Technical Reference, pages 6-35 through 6-37, 6-82, 6-89 through 6-90, 6-98 through 6-121, 6-188 through 6-201, 6-205, 6-210 through 6-212, 6-232 through 6-238
IBM DOS 4.0 Technical Reference, Appendix B
Microsoft MS-DOS 4.0 Programmer's Reference, pages 122 through 152 and 246
Microsoft MS-DOS 5.0 Programmer's Reference, page 208

See Also: 3.049. INT 21H, AH=25H -- Set Interrupt Vector
3.054. INT 21H, AH=2AH -- Get Date
3.055. INT 21H, AH=2BH -- Set Date
3.056. INT 21H, AH=2CH -- Get Time
3.057. INT 21H, AH=2DH -- Set Time
3.058. INT 21H, AH=2EH -- Set/Reset Verify Flag
3.060. INT 21H, AH=30H -- Get Version Number
3.061. INT 21H, AH=31H -- Keep Program
3.063. INT 21H, AH=33H, AL=00H -- Get Ctrl+C Check Flag
3.064. INT 21H, AH=33H, AL=01H -- Set Ctrl+C Check Flag
3.065. INT 21H, AH=33H, AL=05H -- Get Startup Drive Flag
3.066. INT 21H, AH=33H, AL=06H -- Get MS-DOS Version
3.068. INT 21H, AH=35H -- Get Interrupt Vector
3.134. INT 21H, AH=54H -- Get Verify State

3.014. INT 21H NETWORK FUNCTIONS SUMMARY

Function	*Subfunction*	*Function Name*	*Use*
44H	09H	Is drive remote	Reports whether drive letter is local or remote (network)
44H	0AH	Is file or device remote	Reports whether device name is local or remote (network)
5EH	00H	Get machine name	Reports network name of the workstation
5EH	02H	Set printer setup	Defines string of characters to be sent with each file to printer
5EH	03H	Get printer setup	Sent with each file to printer
5FH	02H	Get assign list entry	Reports IDs and names of drives/devices reassigned to network
5FH	03H	Make network connection	Redirects local drive/device to a network directory/device
5FH	04H	Delete network connection	Cancels redirection created with function AH=5FH, AL=03H

Version: Network functions require DOS 3.1 or later

Source: IBM DOS 3.3 Technical Reference, pages 6-155 through 6-156, 6-216 through 6-231
IBM DOS 4.0 Technical Reference, pages B-118 through B-130, C-9 through C-10
Microsoft MS-DOS 4.0 Programmer's Reference, pages 199 through 202, 263 through 280
Microsoft MS-DOS 5.0 Programmer's Reference, page 207

See Also: 3.093. Function 44H, 09H -- Is Drive Remote
3.094. Function 44H, 0AH -- Is File or Device Remote
3.148. Function 5EH, 00H -- Get Machine Name
3.149. Function 5EH, 02H -- Set Printer Setup
3.151. Function 5FH, 02H -- Get Assign-List Entry
3.152. Function 5FH, 03H -- Make Network Connection
3.153. Function 5FH, 04H -- Delete Network Connection

3.015. TYPICAL DOS REGISTER USE

Register	Standard Usage	# Bits	Comments
AX	General purpose accumulator register	16	Passes MS-DOS parameters, returns error
AH	Function request register	8	Contains function number on call (INT 21H)
AL	Error return register	8	Returns error if carry flag set
BX	Data segment base register	16	Also returns data (e.g. handle number)
CX	Loop counter	16	Sometimes used for data passing
DX	General purpose data register	16	Often used as offset to DS for pointer to data
SP	Stack pointer register	16	
IP	Instruction pointer register	16	
BP	Stack segment base register	16	
CS	Code segment of pointer	16	
DS	Data segment of pointer	16	Normally used with DX
ES	Extra segment of pointer	16	
SS	Stack segment of pointer	16	Normally used with BX or CX
SI	Source index in string operations	16	
DI	Destination index in string ops	16	
Flags	Carry flag set=error; carry flag clear=no error	1	Used primarily by DOS 2.1 and later

Source: IBM DOS 3.3 Technical Reference, pages 6-8 through 6-9
IBM DOS 4.0 Technical Reference, pages B-4 through B-6
Microsoft MS-DOS 4.0 Programmer's Reference, pages 23 and 414
Microsoft MS-DOS 5.0 Programmer's Reference

See Also: 3.191. Error Structure and Error Code Values

3.016. INT 21H, AH=00H -- TERMINATE PROGRAM

Prior to Calling Function

	High	Low
AX	00H	
BX		
CX		
DX		
SP		
BP		
SI		
DI		
IP		
flags		
CS	Segment address of PSP*	
DS		
SS		
ES		

*See 3.196. PSP Structure
†DOS versions 2.x and later only

Upon Return from Function

Function does not return.
Function performs the following:
- Flushes file buffers
- Restores termination handler address from PSP:000AH
- Restores Ctrl-C exit address from PSP:000EH
- Restores critical error handler address from PSP:0012H†
- Frees memory owned by the terminating process

Note: Superseded by function 4CH.

Source: IBM DOS 3.3 Technical Reference, page 6-51
IBM DOS 4.0 Technical Reference, page B-12
Microsoft MS-DOS 4.0 Programmer's Reference, pages 56 through 57
Microsoft MS-DOS 5.0 Programmer's Reference, page 211

See Also: 3.061. INT 21H, AH=31H -- Keep Program
3.128. INT 21H, AH=4CH -- End Program
3.196. PSP Structure

3.017. INT 21H, AH=01H -- READ KEYBOARD WITH ECHO

Prior to Calling Function

	High	*Low*
AX	01H	
BX		
CX		
DX		
SP		
BP		
SI		
DI		
IP		
flags		
CS		
DS		
SS		
ES		

Upon Return from Function

	High	*Low*
AX		8-bit char code*
BX		
CX		
DX		
SP		
BP		
SI		
DI		
IP		
flags		
CS		
DS		
SS		
ES		

*Either 8-bit IBM ASCII code, or one of two bytes of an IBM Extended ASCII code

Note:
- Function echoes characters to display; Control-C is enabled; waits for character to be input from standard input device.
- Superseded by function 3FH.

Source:
MS-DOS 3.3 Technical Reference, page 6-52
IBM DOS 4.0 Technical Reference, page B-13
Microsoft MS-DOS 4.0 Programmer's Reference, pages 58 through 59
Microsoft MS-DOS 5.0 Programmer's Reference, page 212

See Also:
1.21. ASCII Character Set
1.22. IBM ASCII Character Set
1.23. IBM Keyboard Extended Function Codes
3.022. INT 21H, AH=06H -- Direct Console I/O
3.023. INT 21H, AH=07H -- Direct Console Input
3.024. INT 21H, AH=08H -- Read Keyboard Without Echo
3.026. INT 21H, AH=0AH -- Buffered Keyboard Input
3.028. INT 21H, AH=0CH -- Flush Buffer, Read Keyboard
3.078. INT 21H, AH=3FH -- Read Using Handle

3.018. INT 21H, AH=02H -- DISPLAY CHARACTER

Prior to Calling Function

Register	High	Low
AX	02H	
BX		
CX		
DX		8-bit char to display
SP		
BP		
SI		
DI		
IP		
flags		
CS		
DS		
SS		
ES		

Upon Return from Function

Function returns no values.

Note:

- Superseded by function 40H.
- Cursor position updated; if character is a backspace (08H), the cursor is moved to the left one position, but the character there is not erased.

Source:

IBM DOS 3.3 Technical Reference, page 6-53
IBM DOS 4.0 Technical Reference, page B-14
Microsoft MS-DOS 4.0 Programmer's Reference, pages 60 through 61
Microsoft MS-DOS 5.0 Programmer's Reference, page 213

See Also:

1.21. ASCII Character Set
1.22. IBM ASCII Character Set
1.23. IBM Extended Keyboard Function Codes
3.022. INT 21H, AH=06H -- Direct Console I/O
3.025. INT 21H, AH=09H -- Display String
3.079. INT 21H, AH=40H -- Write File or Device

3.019. INT 21H, AH=03H -- AUXILIARY INPUT

Prior to Calling Function

	High	Low
AX	03H	
BX		
CX		
DX		

SP	
BP	
SI	
DI	
IP	
flags	
CS	
DS	
SS	
ES	

Upon Return from Function

	High	Low
AX		8-bit char from AUX
BX		
CX		
DX		

SP	
BP	
SI	
DI	
IP	
flags	
CS	
DS	
SS	
ES	

Note:
- This function does not check status of AUX port, buffer input, or return error codes.
- Superseded by function 3FH.
- DOS initializes the standard auxiliary device to 2400 baud, no parity, one stop bit, and 8-bit words.

Source:
IBM DOS 3.3 Technical Reference, page 6-54
IBM DOS 4.0 Technical Reference, page B-15
Microsoft MS-DOS 4.0 Programmer's Reference, pages 62 through 63
Microsoft MS-DOS 5.0 Programmer's Reference, page 214

See Also:
1.21. ASCII Character Set
1.22. IBM ASCII Character Set
3.020. INT 21H, AH=04H -- Auxiliary Output
3.078. INT 21H, AH=3FH -- Read File or Device

3.020. INT 21H, AH=04H -- AUXILIARY OUTPUT

Prior to Calling Function

	High	Low
AX	04H	
BX		
CX		
DX		8-bit char to AUX

SP	
BP	
SI	
DI	
IP	
flags	
CS	
DS	
SS	
ES	

Upon Return from Function

Function returns no values.

Note:
- This function does not check status of AUX port, buffer output, or return error codes.
- Superseded by function 40H.

Source:
IBM DOS 3.3 Technical Reference, page 6-55
IBM DOS 4.0 Technical Reference, page B-16
Microsoft MS-DOS 4.0 Programmer's Reference, pages 64 through 65
Microsoft MS-DOS 5.0 Programmer's Reference, page 215

See Also:
1.21. ASCII Character Set
1.22. IBM ASCII Character Set
3.019. INT 21H, AH=03H -- Auxiliary Input
3.079. INT 21H, AH=40H -- Write File or Device

3.021. INT 21H, AH=05H -- PRINT CHARACTER

Prior to Calling Function

	High	Low
AX	05H	
BX		
CX		
DX		8-bit char to print
SP		
BP		
SI		
DI		
IP		
flags		
CS		
DS		
SS		
ES		

Upon Return from Function

Function returns no values.

Note:
- This function does not check status of printer port, buffer output, or return error codes.
- Superseded by function 40H.

Source:
IBM DOS 3.3 Technical Reference, page 6-56
IBM DOS 4.0 Technical Reference, page B-17
Microsoft MS-DOS 4.0 Programmer's Reference, pages 66 through 67
Microsoft MS-DOS 5.0 Programmer's Reference, page 216

See Also:
3.079. INT 21H, AH=40H -- Write File or Device

3.022. INT 21H, AH=06H -- DIRECT CONSOLE I/O

Prior to Calling Function

	High	Low
AX	06H	
BX		
CX		
DX		IO switch*
SP		
BP		
SI		
DI		
IP		
flags		
CS		
DS		
SS		
ES		

Upon Return from Function

	High	Low
AX		8-bit char or 00H†
BX		
CX		
DX		
SP		
BP		
SI		
DI		
IP		
flags	Zero flag set if no char available	
CS		
DS		
SS		
ES		

*I/O switch: 00H-0FEH=write character to STDOUT; 0FFH=read character from STDIN.
†If input is requested and zero flag is clear, AL contains character from console; otherwise AL = 0.

Note:
- Extended ASCII codes require two function calls.
- No return value if output is requested.

Source:
IBM DOS 3.3 Technical Reference, pages 6-57 through 6-58
IBM DOS 4.0 Technical Reference, page B-18
Microsoft MS-DOS 4.0 Programmer's Reference, pages 68 through 69
Microsoft MS-DOS 5.0 Programmer's Reference, page 217

See Also:
1.21. ASCII Character Set
1.22. IBM ASCII Character Set
3.017. INT 21H, AH=01H -- Read Keyboard with Echo
3.018. INT 21H, AH=02H -- Display Character
3.023. INT 21H, AH=07H -- Direct Console Input
3.024. INT 21H, AH=08H -- Read Keyboard Without Echo
3.025. INT 21H, AH=09H -- Display String
3.026. INT 21H, AH=0AH -- Buffered Keyboard Input
3.028. INT 21H, AH=0CH -- Flush Buffer, Read Keyboard
3.078. INT 21H, AH=3FH -- Read File or Device
3.079. INT 21H, AH=40H -- Write File or Device

3.023. INT 21H, AH=07H -- DIRECT CONSOLE INPUT

Prior to Calling Function

	High	*Low*
AX	07H	
BX		
CX		
DX		

SP	
BP	
SI	
DI	
IP	
flags	
CS	
DS	
SS	
ES	

Upon Return from Function

	High	*Low*
AX		ASCII value of input char
BX		
CX		
DX		

SP	
BP	
SI	
DI	
IP	
flags	
CS	
DS	
SS	
ES	

Note:
- Function does not echo character or check for Ctrl+C.
- Extended ASCII codes require two function calls.

Source:
IBM DOS 3.3 Technical Reference, page 6-59
IBM DOS 4.0 Technical Reference, page B-19
Microsoft MS-DOS 4.0 Programmer's Reference, pages 70 through 71
Microsoft MS-DOS 5.0 Programmer's Reference, page 218

See Also:
3.017. INT 21H, AH=01H -- Read Keyboard with Echo
3.022. INT 21H, AH=06H -- Direct Console I/O
3.024. INT 21H, AH=08H -- Read Keyboard Without Echo
3.026. INT 21H, AH=0AH -- Buffered Keyboard Input
3.028. INT 21H, AH=0CH -- Flush Buffer, Read Keyboard
3.078. INT 21H, AH=3FH -- Read File or Device

3.024. INT 21H, AH=08H -- READ KEYBOARD WITHOUT ECHO

Prior to Calling Function

Register	High	Low
AX	08H	
BX		
CX		
DX		
SP		
BP		
SI		
DI		
IP		
flags		
CS		
DS		
SS		
ES		

Upon Return from Function

Register	High	Low
AX		ASCII value of input char
BX		
CX		
DX		
SP		
BP		
SI		
DI		
IP		
flags		
CS		
DS		
SS		
ES		

Note:
- Function does not echo character.
- Extended ASCII codes require two function calls.

Source:
IBM DOS 3.3 Technical Reference, page 6-60
IBM DOS 4.0 Technical Reference, page B-20
Microsoft MS-DOS 4.0 Programmer's Reference, pages 72 through 73
Microsoft MS-DOS 5.0 Programmer's Reference, page 219

See Also:
3.017. INT 21H, AH=01H -- Read Keyboard with Echo
3.022. INT 21H, AH=06H -- Direct Console I/O
3.023. INT 21H, AH=07H -- Direct Console Input
3.026. INT 21H, AH=0AH -- Buffered Keyboard Input
3.028. INT 21H, AH=0CH -- Flush Buffer, Read Keyboard
3.078. INT 21H, AH=3FH -- Read File or Device

3.025. INT 21H, AH=09H -- DISPLAY STRING

Prior to Calling Function

Register	High	Low
AX	09H	
BX		
CX		
DX	Offset of pointer to $-terminated string	
SP		
BP		
SI		
DI		
IP		
flags		
CS		
DS	Segment of pointer to $-terminated string	
SS		
ES		

Upon Return from Function

Function returns no values.

Note: Superseded by function 40H.

Source:
IBM DOS 3.3 Technical Reference, page 6-61
IBM DOS 4.0 Technical Reference, page B-21
Microsoft MS-DOS 4.0 Programmer's Reference, pages 74 through 75
Microsoft MS-DOS 5.0 Programmer's Reference, page 220

See Also:
1.17. Common String Formats
3.018. INT 21H, AH=02H -- Display Character
3.079. INT 21H, AH=40H -- Write File or Device

3.026. INT 21H, AH=0AH -- BUFFERED KEYBOARD INPUT

Prior to Calling Function

	High	Low
AX	0AH	Max. length of string
BX		
CX		
DX	Offset of pointer to input buffer	
SP		
BP		
SI		
DI		
IP		
flags		
CS		
DS	Segment of pointer to input buffer	
SS		
ES		
Buffer	Max. amount of input	

Upon Return from Function

	High	Low
AX		
BX		
CX		
DX		
SP		
BP		
SI		
DI		
IP		
flags		
CS		
DS		
SS		
ES		
Buffer	Contains max. length, actual length, string typed	

Note: Superseded by function 3FH.

Source:
IBM DOS 3.3 Technical Reference, page 6-62
IBM DOS 4.0 Technical Reference, page B-22
Microsoft MS-DOS 4.0 Programmer's Reference, pages 76 through 77
Microsoft MS-DOS 5.0 Programmer's Reference, page 221

See Also:
3.017. INT 21H, AH=01H -- Read Keyboard with Echo
3.022. INT 21H, AH=06H -- Direct Console I/O
3.023. INT 21H, AH=07H -- Direct Console Input
3.024. INT 21H, AH=08H -- Read Keyboard Without Echo
3.026. INT 21H, AH=0AH -- Buffered Keyboard Input
3.028. INT 21H, AH=0CH -- Flush Buffer, Read Keyboard
3.078. INT 21H, AH=3FH -- Read File or Device

3.027. INT 21H, AH=0BH -- CHECK KEYBOARD STATUS

Prior to Calling Function

	High	Low
AX	0BH	
BX		
CX		
DX		
SP		
BP		
SI		
DI		
IP		
flags		
CS		
DS		
SS		
ES		

Upon Return from Function

	High	Low
AX		Buffer status*
BX		
CX		
DX		
SP		
BP		
SI		
DI		
IP		
flags		
CS		
DS		
SS		
ES		

*00=no character available; FFH=character available in STDIN.

Source:
IBM DOS 3.3 Technical Reference, page 6-63
IBM DOS 4.0 Technical Reference, page B-23
Microsoft MS-DOS 4.0 Programmer's Reference, pages 78 through 79
Microsoft MS-DOS 5.0 Programmer's Reference, page 222

See Also: 3.090. INT 21H, AH=44H, AL=06H -- Check Device Input Status

3.028. INT 21H, AH=0CH -- FLUSH BUFFER, READ KEYBOARD

Prior to Calling Function

	High	Low
AX	0CH	Keyboard function*
BX		
CX		
DX	0FFH¥	
SP		
BP		
SI		
DI		
IP		
flags		
CS		
DS		
SS		
ES		

Upon Return from Function

	High	Low
AX		Varies†
BX		
CX		
DX		
SP		
BP		
SI		
DI		
IP		
flags		
CS		
DS		
SS		
ES		

*1, 6, 7, and 8 are allowable keyboard functions executed after the STDIN buffer is flushed.
†0=buffer was flushed, but no other processing was done. Otherwise, will be the same as for the INT 21H function called by value in AL.
¥If AL=06H

Source: IBM DOS 3.3 Technical Reference, page 6-64
IBM DOS 4.0 Technical Reference, page B-24
Microsoft MS-DOS 4.0 Programmer's Reference, pages 80 through 81
Microsoft MS-DOS 5.0 Programmer's Reference, page 223

See Also: 3.017. INT 21H, AH=01H -- Read Keyboard with Echo
3.022. INT 21H, AH=06H -- Direct Console I/O
3.023. INT 21H, AH=07H -- Direct Console Input
3.024. INT 21H, AH=08H -- Read Keyboard Without Echo
3.026. INT 21H, AH=0AH -- Buffered Keyboard Input
3.078. INT 21H, AH=3FH -- Read File or Device

3.029. INT 21H, AH=0DH -- RESET DRIVE

Prior to Calling Function

	High	Low
AX	0DH	
BX		
CX		
DX		
SP		
BP		
SI		
DI		
IP		
flags		
CS		
DS		
SS		
ES		

Upon Return from Function

Function returns no values.

Note:
- Function flushes all file buffers to disk.
- It is necessary to close all files to update directory.

Source: IBM DOS 3.3 Technical Reference, page 6-65
IBM DOS 4.0 Technical Reference, page B-25
Microsoft MS-DOS 4.0 Programmer's Reference, page 82
Microsoft MS-DOS 5.0 Programmer's Reference, page 224

See Also: 3.032. INT 21H, AH=10H -- Close File with FCB
3.077. INT 21H, AH=3EH -- Close File with Handle

3.030. INT 21H, AH=0EH -- SET DEFAULT DRIVE

Prior to Calling Function

	High	Low
AX	0EH	
BX		
CX		
DX		Drive number*
SP		
BP		
SI		
DI		
IP		
flags		
CS		
DS		
SS		
ES		

Upon Return from Function

	High	Low
AX		# Logical drives†
BX		
CX		
DX		
SP		
BP		
SI		
DI		
IP		
flags		
CS		
DS		
SS		
ES		

*0=A, 1=B, and so on. Note that this is different than logical drive number.
†Same value as LASTDRIVE=in CONFIG.SYS, or total number of devices, whichever is greater.

Note: Note that the value returned in AL does not mean that all of the indicated logical drives are valid drives.

Source:
IBM DOS 3.3 Technical Reference, page 6-66
IBM DOS 4.0 Technical Reference, page B-26
Microsoft MS-DOS 4.0 Programmer's Reference, pages 83 through 84
Microsoft MS-DOS 5.0 Programmer's Reference, page 225

See Also:
3.040. INT 21H, AH=19H -- Get Current Drive
3.184. Logical Drive Numbers

3.031. INT 21H, AH=0FH -- OPEN FILE WITH FCB

Prior to Calling Function

	High	Low
AX	0FH	
BX		
CX		
DX	Offset of pointer to unopened FCB†	
SP		
BP		
SI		
DI		
IP		
flags		
CS		
DS	Segment of pointer to unopened FCB†	
SS		
ES		

Upon Return from Function

	High	Low
AX		Status*
BX		
CX		
DX		
SP		
BP		
SI		
DI		
IP		
flags		
CS		
DS		
SS		
ES		

*00=directory entry found and opened; FFH=directory entry not found.
†See 3.175. FCB Structure (Opened).

Note:
- On networks, file is opened in compatibility mode only.
- Superseded by function 3DH.
- Paths are not supported. You can only open files in the current directory.

Source:
IBM DOS 3.3 Technical Reference, pages 6-67 through 6-68
IBM DOS 4.0 Technical Reference, pages B-27 through B-28
Microsoft MS-DOS 4.0 Programmer's Reference, pages 85 through 86
Microsoft MS-DOS 5.0 Programmer's Reference, page 226

See Also:
3.076. INT 21H, AH=3DH -- Open File with Handle
3.175. FCB Structure (Opened)
3.176. FCB Structure (Unopened)

3.032. INT 21H, AH=10H -- CLOSE FILE WITH FCB

Prior to Calling Function

Register	High	Low
AX	10H	
BX		
CX		
DX	Offset of pointer to opened FCB†	
SP		
BP		
SI		
DI		
IP		
flags		
CS		
DS	Segment of pointer to opened FCB†	
SS		
ES		

Upon Return from Function

Register	High	Low
AX		Status*
BX		
CX		
DX		
SP		
BP		
SI		
DI		
IP		
flags		
CS		
DS		
SS		
ES		

*00=directory entry found and closed; FFH=entry not found.
†See 3.175. FCB Structure (Opened).

Note:
- Superseded by function 3EH.
- Paths are not supported. You can only close files in the current directory.

Source:
IBM DOS 3.3 Technical Reference, page 6-69
IBM DOS 4.0 Technical Reference, page B-29
Microsoft MS-DOS 4.0 Programmer's Reference, pages 87 through 88
Microsoft MS-DOS 5.0 Programmer's Reference, page 227

See Also:
3.077. INT 21H, AH=3EH -- Close File with Handle
3.175. FCB Structure (Opened)

3.033. INT 21H, AH=11H -- FIND FIRST FILE WITH FCB

Prior to Calling Function

Register	High	Low
AX	11H	
BX		
CX		
DX	Offset of pointer to unopened FCB¥	
SP		
BP		
SI		
DI		
IP		
flags		
CS		
DS	Segment of pointer to unopened FCB¥	
SS		
ES		
DTA		

Upon Return from Function

Register	High	Low
AX		Status*
BX		
CX		
DX		
SP		
BP		
SI		
DI		
IP		
flags		
CS		
DS		
SS		
ES		
DTA	Drive # and DIRENTRY structure§	

*00=directory entry found; FFH=entry not found.
¥See 3.176. FCB Structure (Unopened) .
§See 3.172. DIRENTRY Structure.

Note: Superseded by function 4EH.

Source: IBM DOS 3.3 Technical Reference, pages 6-70 through 6-71
IBM DOS 4.0 Technical Reference, pages B-30 through B-31
Microsoft MS-DOS 4.0 Programmer's Reference, pages 89 through 90
Microsoft MS-DOS 5.0 Programmer's Reference, pages 228 through 229

See Also: 3.003. INT 21H FCB-Oriented Functions Summary
3.034. INT 21H, AH=12H -- Find Next File with FCB
3.130. INT 21H, AH=4EH -- Find First File
3.131. INT 21H, AH=4FH -- Find Next File
3.172. DIRENTRY Structure
3.175. FCB Structure (Opened)
3.176. FCB Structure (Unopened)

3.034. INT 21H, AH=12H -- FIND NEXT FILE WITH FCB

Prior to Calling Function

Register	High	Low
AX	12H	
BX		
CX		
DX	Offset of pointer to unopened FCB†	
SP		
BP		
SI		
DI		
IP		
flags		
CS		
DS	Segment of pointer to unopened FCB†	
SS		
ES		
DTA		

Upon Return from Function

Register	High	Low
AX		Status*
BX		
CX		
DX		
SP		
BP		
SI		
DI		
IP		
flags		
CS		
DS		
SS		
ES		
DTA	Drive # and DIRENTRY structure¥	

*00=directory entry found; FFH=entry not found.
†Must be unchanged FCB used previously with function 11H or function 12H. See 3.174. EXTENDEDFCB Structure and EXTHEADER Structure and 3.175. FCB Structure (Opened).
¥See 3.172. DIRENTRY Structure and 3.174. EXTENDEDFCB Structure and EXTHEADER Structure.

Note: Superseded by function 4FH.

Source: IBM DOS 3.3 Technical Reference, pages 6-72 through 6-73
IBM DOS 4.0 Technical Reference, pages B-32 through B-33
Microsoft MS-DOS 4.0 Programmer's Reference, pages 91 through 92
Microsoft MS-DOS 5.0 Programmer's Reference, pages 230 through 231

See Also: 3.033. INT 21H, AH=11H -- Find First File with FCB
3.130. INT 21H, AH=4EH -- Find First File
3.131. INT 21H, AH=4FH -- Find Next File
3.172. DIRENTRY Structure
3.174. EXTENDEDFCB Structure and EXTHEADER Structure
3.175. FCB Structure (Opened)
3.176. FCB Structure (Unopened)

3.035. INT 21H, AH=13H -- DELETE FILE WITH FCB

Prior to Calling Function

Register	High	Low
AX	13H	
BX		
CX		
DX	Offset of pointer to unopened FCB¥	
SP		
BP		
SI		
DI		
IP		
flags		
CS		
DS	Segment of pointer to unopened FCB¥	
SS		
ES		

Upon Return from Function

Register	High	Low
AX		Status*
BX		
CX		
DX		
SP		
BP		
SI		
DI		
IP		
flags		
CS		
DS		
SS		
ES		

*00=at least one matching file found and deleted; FFH=no matching files found.
¥See 3.175. FCB Structure (Opened).

Note:
- Requires delete access rights on networks.
- Superseded by function 41H.

Source:
IBM DOS 3.3 Technical Reference, page 6-74
IBM DOS 4.0 Technical Reference, page B-34
Microsoft MS-DOS 4.0 Programmer's Reference, pages 93 through 94
Microsoft MS-DOS 5.0 Programmer's Reference, page 232

See Also:
3.073. INT 21H, AH=3AH -- Remove Directory
3.080. INT 21H, AH=41H -- Delete File
3.175. FCB Structure (Opened)
3.176. FCB Structure (Unopened)

3.036. INT 21H, AH=14H -- SEQUENTIAL READ

Prior to Calling Function

Register	High	Low
AX	14H	
BX		
CX		
DX	Offset of pointer to opened FCB¥	
SP		
BP		
SI		
DI		
IP		
flags		
CS		
DS	Segment of pointer to opened FCB¥	
SS		
ES		
DTA		

Upon Return from Function

Register	High	Low
AX		Status*
BX		
CX		
DX		
SP		
BP		
SI		
DI		
IP		
flags		
CS		
DS		
SS		
ES		
DTA	One record of data (size=record size)	

*0=successful read; 1=end of file; 2=DTA too small; 3=partial record read.
¥See 3.175. FCB Structure (Opened).

Note:
- Requires read access rights on networks.
- Superseded by function 3FH.

Source:
IBM DOS 3.3 Technical Reference, page 6-75
IBM DOS 4.0 Technical Reference, page B-35
Microsoft MS-DOS 4.0 Programmer's Reference, pages 95 through 96
Microsoft MS-DOS 5.0 Programmer's Reference, page 233

See Also:
3.045. INT 21H, AH=21H -- Random Read
3.051. INT 21H, AH=27H -- Random Block Read
3.078. INT 21H, AH=3FH -- Read File or Device
3.175. FCB Structure (Opened)
3.185. FCB Error Codes

3.037. INT 21H, AH=15H -- SEQUENTIAL WRITE

Prior to Calling Function

	High	Low
AX	15H	
BX		
CX		
DX	Offset of pointer to opened FCB¥	
SP		
BP		
SI		
DI		
IP		
flags		
CS		
DS	Segment of pointer to opened FCB¥	
SS		
ES		
DTA	Record of data (size must match record size)	

Upon Return from Function

	High	Low
AX		Status*
BX		
CX		
DX		
SP		
BP		
SI		
DI		
IP		
flags		
CS		
DS		
SS		
ES		
DTA		

*0=successful write; 1=disk full; 2=DTA too small.
¥See 3.175. FCB Structure (Opened).

Note:
- Requires write access rights on networks.
- Superseded by function 40H.

Source:
IBM DOS 3.3 Technical Reference, page 6-76
IBM DOS 4.0 Technical Reference, page B-36
Microsoft MS-DOS 4.0 Programmer's Reference, pages 97 through 98
Microsoft MS-DOS 5.0 Programmer's Reference, page 234

See Also:
3.046. INT 21H, AH=22H -- Random Write
3.052. INT 21H, AH=28H -- Random Block Write
3.079. INT 21H, AH=40H -- Write File or Device
3.175. FCB Structure (Opened)
3.185. FCB Error Codes

3.038. INT 21H, AH=16H -- CREATE FILE WITH FCB

Prior to Calling Function

Register	High	Low
AX	16H	
BX		
CX		
DX	Offset of pointer to unopened FCB¥	
SP		
BP		
SI		
DI		
IP		
flags		
CS		
DS	Segment of pointer to unopened FCB¥	
SS		
ES		

Upon Return from Function

Register	High	Low
AX		Status*
BX		
CX		
DX		
SP		
BP		
SI		
DI		
IP		
flags		
CS		
DS		
SS		
ES		

*00=file created; 0FFH=unsuccessful.
¥See 3.175. FCB Structure (Opened).

Note:
- Requires create access rights on networks.
- Superseded by function 3CH.

Source:
IBM DOS 3.3 Technical Reference, pages 6-77 through 6-78
IBM DOS 4.0 Technical Reference, page B-37
Microsoft MS-DOS 4.0 Programmer's Reference, pages 99 through 100
Microsoft MS-DOS 5.0 Programmer's Reference, page 235

See Also:
3.031. INT 21H, AH=0FH -- Open File with FCB
3.076. INT 21H, AH=3DH -- Open File with Handle
3.095. INT 21H, AH=3CH -- Create File with Handle
3.143. INT 21H, AH=5AH -- Create Temporary File
3.144. INT 21H, AH=5BH -- Create New File
3.175. FCB Structure (Opened)
3.176. FCB Structure (Unopened)
3.185. FCB Error Codes

3.039. INT 21H, AH=17H -- RENAME FILE WITH FCB

Register	Prior to Calling Function: High	Prior to Calling Function: Low	Upon Return from Function: High	Upon Return from Function: Low
AX	17H			Status*
BX				
CX				
DX	Offset of pointer to rename FCB†			
SP				
BP				
SI				
DI				
IP				
flags				
CS				
DS	Segment of pointer to rename FCB†			
SS				
ES				

*00=at least one file renamed; FFH=no files renamed, or name already exists.
†See 3.181. RENAMEFCB Structure.

Note: Superseded by function 56H.

Source: IBM DOS 3.3 Technical Reference, pages 6-79 through 6-80
IBM DOS 4.0 Technical Reference, pages B-38 through B-39
Microsoft MS-DOS 4.0 Programmer's Reference, pages 101 through 102
Microsoft MS-DOS 5.0 Programmer's Reference, page 236

See Also: 3.135. INT 21H, AH=56H -- Rename File
3.181. RENAMEFCB Structure
3.185. FCB Error Codes

3.040. INT 21H, AH=19H -- GET CURRENT DRIVE

Register	Prior to Calling Function: High	Prior to Calling Function: Low	Upon Return from Function: High	Upon Return from Function: Low
AX	19H			Selected drive*
BX				
CX				
DX				
SP				
BP				
SI				
DI				
IP				
flags				
CS				
DS				
SS				
ES				

*0=A drive, 1=B drive, and so on.

Source: IBM DOS 3.3 Technical Reference, page 6-81
IBM DOS 4.0 Technical Reference, page B-40
Microsoft MS-DOS 4.0 Programmer's Reference, pages 103 through 104
Microsoft MS-DOS 5.0 Programmer's Reference, page 237

3.041. INT 21H, AH=1AH -- SET DISK TRANSFER ADDRESS

Prior to Calling Function

Register	High	Low
AX	1AH	
BX		
CX		
DX	Offset of pointer to disk transfer address	
SP		
BP		
SI		
DI		
IP		
flags		
CS		
DS	Segment of pointer to disk transfer address	
SS		
ES		

Upon Return from Function

Function returns no values.

Note:
- DTA may not cross segment boundaries.
- Default DTA is at 0080H in the PSP.

Source:
IBM DOS 3.3 Technical Reference, page 6-82
IBM DOS 4.0 Technical Reference, B-41
Microsoft MS-DOS 4.0 Programmer's Reference, pages 105 through 106
Microsoft MS-DOS 5.0 Programmer's Reference, page 238

See Also:
3.059. INT 21H, AH=2FH -- Get Disk Transfer Address

3.042. INT 21H, AH=1BH -- GET DEFAULT DRIVE DATA

Prior to Calling Function

Register	High	Low
AX	1BH	
BX		
CX		
DX		
SP		
BP		
SI		
DI		
IP		
flags		
CS		
DS		
SS		
ES		

Upon Return from Function

Register	High	Low
AX		Sectors per cluster*
BX	Offset of pointer to media descriptor	
CX	Number of bytes per sector	
DX	Number of clusters per drive	
SP		
BP		
SI		
DI		
IP		
flags		
CS		
DS	Segment of pointer to media descriptor	
SS		
ES		

*0FFH on error

Note: Superseded by function 36H.

Source:
IBM DOS 3.3 Technical Reference, page 6-83
IBM DOS 4.0 Technical Reference, page B-42
Microsoft MS-DOS 4.0 Programmer's Reference, pages 107 through 109
Microsoft MS-DOS 5.0 Programmer's Reference, pages 239 through 240

See Also:
2.22. Disk ID Bytes
3.043. INT 21H, AH=1CH -- Get Drive Data
3.069. INT 21H, AH=36H -- Get Disk Free Space
3.191. ERROR Structure and Error Code Values

3.043. INT 21H, AH=1CH -- GET DRIVE DATA

Prior to Calling Function

	High	Low
AX	1CH	
BX		
CX		
DX		Logical drive number*
SP		
BP		
SI		
DI		
IP		
flags		
CS		
DS		
SS		
ES		

Upon Return from Function

	High	Low
AX		Sectors per cluster†
BX	Offset of pointer to media descriptor	
CX	Number of bytes per sector	
DX	Number of clusters per drive	
SP		
BP		
SI		
DI		
IP		
flags		
CS		
DS	Segment of pointer to media descriptor	
SS		
ES		

*0=default, 1=A, 2=B, etc.
†0FFH on error

Note: Superseded by function 36H.

Source:
IBM DOS 3.3 Technical Reference, page 6-84
IBM DOS 4.0 Technical Reference, page B-43
Microsoft MS-DOS 4.0 Programmer's Reference, pages 110 through 112
Microsoft MS-DOS 5.0 Programmer's Reference, pages 241 through 242

See Also:
2.22. Disk ID Bytes
3.042. INT 21H, AH=1BH -- Get Default Drive Data
3.069. INT 21H, AH=36H -- Get Disk Free Space
3.184. Logical Drive Numbers

3.044. INT 21H, AH=1FH -- GET DEFAULT DPB

Prior to Calling Function

	High	Low
AX	1FH	
BX		
CX		
DX		
SP		
BP		
SI		
DI		
IP		
flags		
CS		
DS		
SS		
ES		

Upon Return from Function

	High	Low
AX		Status*
BX	Offset of pointer to DPB structure†	
CX		
DX		
SP		
BP		
SI		
DI		
IP		
flags		
CS		
DS	Segement of pointer to DPB structure†	
SS		
ES		

*00H=successful, 0FFH=unsuccessful.
†See 3.171. DEVICEPARAMS Structure.

Source: Microsoft MS-DOS 5.0 Programmer's Reference, page 243

See Also: 3.171. DEVICEPARAMS Structure

3.045. INT 21H, AH=21H -- RANDOM READ

Prior to Calling Function

Register	High	Low
AX	21H	
BX		
CX		
DX	Offset of pointer to opened FCB¥	
SP		
BP		
SI		
DI		
IP		
flags		
CS		
DS	Segment of pointer to opened FCB¥	
SS		
ES		
DTA		

Upon Return from Function

Register	High	Low
AX		Status*
BX		
CX		
DX		
SP		
BP		
SI		
DI		
IP		
flags		
CS		
DS		
SS		
ES		
DTA	One record of data	

*0=successful read; 1=end of file; 2=DTA too small; 3=partial record read.
¥See 3.175. FCB Structure (Opened).

Note:
- Requires read access rights on networks.
- Random record number is usually set by using function 24H.
- Superseded by function 3FH.

Source:
IBM DOS 3.3 Technical Reference, page 6-85
IBM DOS 4.0 Technical Reference, pages B-44 through B-45
Microsoft MS-DOS 4.0 Programmer's Reference, pages 113 through 114
Microsoft MS-DOS 5.0 Programmer's Reference, page 244

See Also:
3.036. INT 21H, AH=14H -- Sequential Read
3.048. INT 21H, AH=24H -- Set Random Record Number
3.051. INT 21H, AH=27H -- Random Block Read
3.078. INT 21H, AH=3FH -- Read File or Device
3.175. FCB Structure (Opened)
3.185. FCB Error Codes

3.046. INT 21H, AH=22H -- RANDOM WRITE

Prior to Calling Function

Register	High	Low
AX	22H	
BX		
CX		
DX	Offset of pointer to opened FCB¥	
SP		
BP		
SI		
DI		
IP		
flags		
CS		
DS	Segment of pointer to opened FCB¥	
SS		
ES		
DTA	One record of data to write to disk	

Upon Return from Function

Register	High	Low
AX		Status*
BX		
CX		
DX		
SP		
BP		
SI		
DI		
IP		
flags		
CS		
DS		
SS		
ES		
DTA	Unchanged data	

*0=successful write; 1=disk full; 2=DTA too small.
¥See 3.175. FCB Structure (Opened).

Note:
- Requires write access rights on networks.
- Random record number is usually set with function 24H.
- Superseded by function 40H.

Source:
IBM DOS 3.3 Technical Reference, page 6-86
IBM DOS 4.0 Technical Reference, pages B-46 through B-47
Microsoft MS-DOS 4.0 Programmer's Reference, pages 115 through 117
Microsoft MS-DOS 5.0 Programmer's Reference, page 245

See Also:
3.037. INT 21H, AH=15H -- Sequential Write
3.048. INT 21H, AH=24H -- Set Random Record Number
3.052. INT 21H, AH=28H -- Random Block Write
3.079. INT 21H, AH=40H -- Write File or Device
3.175. FCB Structure (Opened)
3.185. FCB Error Codes

3.047. INT 21H, AH=23H -- GET FILE SIZE

Prior to Calling Function

	High	*Low*
AX	23H	
BX		
CX		
DX	Offset of pointer to unopened FCB¥	
SP		
BP		
SI		
DI		
IP		
flags		
CS		
DS	Segment of pointer to unopened FCB¥	
SS		
ES		

Upon Return from Function

	High	*Low*
AX		Status*
BX		
CX		
DX		
SP		
BP		
SI		
DI		
IP		
flags		
CS		
DS		
SS		
ES		

*0=file found; 0FFH=file not found.
¥See 3.175. FCB Structure (Opened).

Note: Superseded by function 42H.

Source:
IBM DOS 3.3 Technical Reference, page 6-87
IBM DOS 4.0 Technical Reference, page B-48
Microsoft MS-DOS 4.0 Programmer's Reference, pages 118 through 119
Microsoft MS-DOS 5.0 Programmer's Reference, page 246

See Also:
3.081. INT 21H, AH=42H -- Move File Pointer
3.175. FCB Structure (Opened)
3.176. FCB Structure (Unopened)
3.185. FCB Error Codes

3.048. INT 21H, AH=24H -- SET RANDOM RECORD NUMBER

Prior to Calling Function

Register	High	Low
AX	24H	
BX		
CX		
DX	Offset of pointer to opened FCB¥	
SP		
BP		
SI		
DI		
IP		
flags		
CS		
DS	Segment of pointer to opened FCB¥	
SS		
ES		

Upon Return from Function

Register	High	Low
AX		Always 00H
BX		
CX		
DX		
SP		
BP		
SI		
DI		
IP		
flags		
CS		
DS		
SS		
ES		

¥See 3.175. FCB Structure (Opened).

Note: Superseded by function 42H.

Source:
IBM DOS 3.3 Technical Reference, page 6-88
IBM DOS 4.0 Technical Reference, page B-49
Microsoft MS-DOS 4.0 Programmer's Reference, pages 120 through 121
Microsoft MS-DOS 5.0 Programmer's Reference, page 247

See Also:
3.081. INT 21H, AH=42H -- Move File Pointer
3.175. FCB Structure (Opened)

3.049. INT 21H, AH=25H -- SET INTERRUPT VECTOR

Prior to Calling Function

Register	High	Low
AX	25H	Interrupt number
BX		
CX		
DX	Offset of pointer to interrupt handler routine	
SP		
BP		
SI		
DI		
IP		
flags		
CS		
DS	Segment of pointer to interrupt handler routine	
SS		
ES		

Upon Return from Function

Function returns no values.

Note: The 4-byte address contained in DS:DX is placed at appropriate place in the interrupt vector table.

Source:
IBM DOS 3.3 Technical Reference, page 6-89
IBM DOS 4.0 Technical Reference, page B-50
Microsoft MS-DOS 4.0 Programmer's Reference, pages 122 through 123
Microsoft MS-DOS 5.0 Programmer's Reference, page 248

See Also:
3.068. INT 21H, AH=35H -- Get Interrupt Vector
7.005. PC Interrupt Usage Summary

3.050. INT 21H, AH=26H -- CREATE NEW PROGRAM SEGMENT PREFIX

Prior to Calling Function

	High	Low
AX	26H	
BX		
CX		
DX	Segment address of new program segment	
SP		
BP		
SI		
DI		
IP		
flags		
CS		
DS		
SS		
ES		

Upon Return from Function

Function returns no values.

Note:
- Superseded by function 4BH.
- Only .COM programs should call this function.

Source:
IBM DOS 3.3 Technical Reference, page 6-90
IBM DOS 4.0 Technical Reference, page B-51
Microsoft MS-DOS 4.0 Programmer's Reference, page 124
Microsoft MS-DOS 5.0 Programmer's Reference, page 249

See Also: 3.124. INT 21H, AH=4BH, AL=00H -- Load and Execute Program

3.051. INT 21H, AH=27H -- RANDOM BLOCK READ

Prior to Calling Function

	High	Low
AX	27H	
BX		
CX	Number of records to read	
DX	Offset of pointer to opened FCB†	
SP		
BP		
SI		
DI		
IP		
flags		
CS		
DS	Segment of pointer to opened FCB†	
SS		
ES		
DTA		

Upon Return from Function

	High	Low
AX		Status*
BX		
CX	Number of records actually read	
DX		
SP		
BP		
SI		
DI		
IP		
flags		
CS		
DS		
SS		
ES		
DTA	Data read	

*0=successful read; 1=end of file; 2=DTA too small; 3=partial record read.
†See 3.175. FCB Structure (Opened).

Note:
- Requires read access rights on networks.
- Superseded by functions 3FH and 42H.
- Random record number is usually set by function 24H.

Source:
IBM DOS 3.3 Technical Reference, pages 6-91 through 6-92
IBM DOS 4.0 Technical Reference, pages B-52 through B-53
Microsoft MS-DOS 4.0 Programmer's Reference, pages 125 through 127
Microsoft MS-DOS 5.0 Programmer's Reference, pages 250 through 251

(Continued)

3.051. INT 21H, AH=27H -- RANDOM BLOCK READ (continued)

See Also:
3.036. INT 21H, AH=14H -- Sequential Read
3.045. INT 21H, AH=21H -- Random Read
3.048. INT 21H, AH=24H -- Set Random Record Number
3.052. INT 21H, AH=28H -- Random Block Write
3.078. INT 21H, AH=3FH -- Read File or Device
3.175. FCB Structure (Opened)
3.185. FCB Error Codes

3.052. INT 21H, AH=28H -- RANDOM BLOCK WRITE

Prior to Calling Function

	High	Low
AX	28H	
BX		
CX	Number of records to write	
DX	Offset of pointer to opened FCB†	
SP		
BP		
SI		
DI		
IP		
flags		
CS		
DS	Segment of pointer to opened FCB†	
SS		
ES		
DTA	Data to be written to disk	

Upon Return from Function

	High	Low
AX		Status*
BX		
CX	Number of records actually written	
DX		
SP		
BP		
SI		
DI		
IP		
flags		
CS		
DS		
SS		
ES		
DTA		

*0=successful write; 1=disk full; 2=DTA too small
†See 3.175. FCB Structure (Opened).

Note:
- Requires write access rights on networks.
- Superseded by function 40H.
- If CX=0 prior to call, file size is set to value in random record number field.
- Random record number is usually set with function 24H.

Source:
IBM DOS 3.3 Technical Reference, pages 6-93 through 6-94
IBM DOS 4.0 Technical Reference, pages B-54 through B-55
Microsoft MS-DOS 4.0 Programmer's Reference, pages 128 through 130
Microsoft MS-DOS 5.0 Programmer's Reference, pages 252 through 253

See Also:
3.039. INT 21H, AH=15H -- Sequential Write
3.046. INT 21H, AH=22H -- Random Write
3.048. INT 21H, AH=24H -- Set Random Record Number
3.051. INT 21H, AH=27H -- Random Block Read
3.079. INT 21H, AH=40H -- Write File or Device
3.175. FCB Structure (Opened)
3.185. FCB Error Codes

3.053. INT 21H, AH=29H -- PARSE FILENAME

Prior to Calling Function

	High	Low
AX	29H	Parse control byte
BX		
CX		
DX		
SP		
BP		
SI	Offset of pointer to string to parse	
DI	Offset of pointer to buffer for FCB†	
IP		
flags		
CS		
DS	Segment of pointer to string to parse	
SS		
ES	Segment of pointer to buffer for unopened FCB†	

Upon Return from Function

	High	Low
AX		Status*
BX		
CX		
DX		
SP		
BP		
SI	Offset of pointer 1 byte past parsed string	
DI	Offset of pointer to FCB†	
IP		
flags		
CS		
DS	Segment of pointer 1 byte past parsed string	
SS		
ES	Segment of pointer to FCB†	

*00=FCB created, no wildcard characters; 01=FCB created, wildcard characters used in file name; FFH=drive letter invalid.
†See 3.175. FCB Structure (Opened).

Source: IBM DOS 3.3 Technical Reference, pages 6-95 through 6-97
IBM DOS 4.0 Technical Reference, pages B-56 through B-57
Microsoft MS-DOS 4.0 Programmer's Reference, pages 131 through 133
Microsoft MS-DOS 5.0 Programmer's Reference, pages 254 through 255

See Also: 2.36. Filename Separator Characters
3.175. FCB Structure (Opened)
3.176. FCB Structure (Unopened)
3.186. Parse Control Byte

3.054. INT 21H, AH=2AH -- GET DATE

Prior to Calling Function

	High	Low
AX	2AH	
BX		
CX		
DX		
SP		
BP		
SI		
DI		
IP		
flags		
CS		
DS		
SS		
ES		

Upon Return from Function

	High	Low
AX		Day of week*
BX		
CX	Year	
DX	Month	Day
SP		
BP		
SI		
DI		
IP		
flags		
CS		
DS		
SS		
ES		

*0=Sunday, 1=Monday, etc.

Source: IBM DOS 3.3 Technical Reference, page 6-98
IBM DOS 4.0 Technical Reference, page B-58
Microsoft MS-DOS 4.0 Programmer's Reference, pages 134 through 135
Microsoft MS-DOS 5.0 Programmer's Reference, page 256

See Also: 2.20. Date/Time Formats
3.055. INT 21H, AH=2BH -- Set Date
3.056. INT 21H, AH=2CH -- Get Time

3.055. INT 21H, AH=2BH -- SET DATE

Prior to Calling Function

	High	Low
AX	2BH	
BX		
CX	Year	
DX	Month	Day
SP		
BP		
SI		
DI		
IP		
flags		
CS		
DS		
SS		
ES		

Upon Return from Function

	High	Low
AX		Status*
BX		
CX		
DX		
SP		
BP		
SI		
DI		
IP		
flags		
CS		
DS		
SS		
ES		

*00=valid date supplied; FFH=invalid date supplied.

Source: IBM DOS 3.3 Technical Reference, page 6-99
IBM DOS 4.0 Technical Reference, page B-59
Microsoft MS-DOS 4.0 Programmer's Reference, pages 136 through 137
Microsoft MS-DOS 5.0 Programmer's Reference, page 257

See Also: 2.20. Date/Time Formats
3.054. INT 21H, AH=2AH -- Get Date
3.057. INT 21H, AH=2DH -- Set Time

3.056. INT 21H, AH=2CH -- GET TIME

Prior to Calling Function

	High	Low
AX	2CH	
BX		
CX		
DX		
SP		
BP		
SI		
DI		
IP		
flags		
CS		
DS		
SS		
ES		

Upon Return from Function

	High	Low
AX		
BX		
CX	Hour	Minutes
DX	Seconds	Hundredths
SP		
BP		
SI		
DI		
IP		
flags		
CS		
DS		
SS		
ES		

Note: Hour is in 24-hour clock format.

Source: IBM DOS 3.3 Technical Reference, page 6-100
IBM DOS 4.0 Technical Reference, page B-60
Microsoft MS-DOS 4.0 Programmer's Reference, pages 138 through 139
Microsoft MS-DOS 5.0 Programmer's Reference, page 258

See Also: 2.20. Date/Time Formats
3.054. Function 2AH -- Get Date
3.057. Function 2DH -- Set Time

3.057. INT 21H, AH=2DH -- SET TIME

Prior to Calling Function

	High	Low
AX	2DH	
BX		
CX	Hour	Minutes
DX	Seconds	Hundredths
SP		
BP		
SI		
DI		
IP		
flags		
CS		
DS		
SS		
ES		

Upon Return from Function

	High	Low
AX		Status*
BX		
CX		
DX		
SP		
BP		
SI		
DI		
IP		
flags		
CS		
DS		
SS		
ES		

*00=valid time supplied; FFH=invalid time supplied.

Source: IBM DOS 3.3 Technical Reference, page 6-101
IBM DOS 4.0 Technical Reference, page B-61
Microsoft MS-DOS 4.0 Programmer's Reference, pages 140 through 141
Microsoft MS-DOS 5.0 Programmer's Reference, page 259

See Also: 2.20. Date/Time Formats
3.055. INT 21H, AH=2BH -- Set Date
3.056. INT 21H, AH=2CH -- Get Time

3.058. INT 21H, AH=2EH -- SET/RESET VERIFY FLAG

Prior to Calling Function

	High	Low
AX	2EH	Verify flag*
BX		
CX		
DX		00H†
SP		
BP		
SI		
DI		
IP		
flags		
CS		
DS		
SS		
ES		

Upon Return from Function

Function returns no values.

*00=do not verify after writes; 01=verify after writes.
†DOS 1.x and 2.x only

Version: Verification is not supported for network disk writes in DOS 3.x and later.

Source: IBM DOS 3.3 Technical Reference, page 6-102
IBM DOS 4.0 Technical Reference, page B-62
Microsoft MS-DOS 4.0 Programmer's Reference, pages 142 through 143
Microsoft MS-DOS 5.0 Programmer's Reference, page 260

See Also: 3.066. INT 21H, AH=33H, AL=06H -- Get MS-DOS Version
3.134. INT 21H, AH=54H -- Get Verify State

3.059. INT 21H, AH=2FH -- GET DISK TRANSFER ADDRESS

Prior to Calling Function

	High	Low
AX	2FH	
BX		
CX		
DX		
SP		
BP		
SI		
DI		
IP		
flags		
CS		
DS		
SS		
ES		

Upon Return from Function

	High	Low
AX		
BX	Offset of pointer to disk transfer address	
CX		
DX		
SP		
BP		
SI		
DI		
IP		
flags		
CS		
DS		
SS		
ES	Segment of pointer to disk transfer address	

Version: Applies to all versions of DOS beginning with 2.0.

Note: Default DTA is at 0080H in the PSP.

Source: IBM DOS 3.3 Technical Reference, page 6-103
IBM DOS 4.0 Technical Reference, page B-63
Microsoft MS-DOS 4.0 Programmer's Reference, pages 144 through 145
Microsoft MS-DOS 5.0 Programmer's Reference, page 261

See Also: 3.041. INT 21H, AH=1AH -- Set Disk Transfer Address

3.060. INT 21H, AH=30H -- GET VERSION NUMBER

Prior to Calling Function

	High	Low
AX	30H	
BX		
CX		
DX		
SP		
BP		
SI		
DI		
IP		
flags		
CS		
DS		
SS		
ES		

Upon Return from Function

	High	Low
AX	Minor version #	Major version #
BX	OEM number*	High order serial #
CX	Low order word of 24-bit serial number	
DX		
SP		
BP		
SI		
DI		
IP		
flags		
CS		
DS		
SS		
ES		

*Or version flag

Version: Applies to all versions of DOS beginning with 2.0.

Note:
- OEM and serial numbers may not be present (returns 0000H).
- If AL=0 on return, then version is assumed to be prior to 2.0.

Source: IBM DOS 3.3 Technical Reference, page 6-104
IBM DOS 4.0 Technical Reference, page B-64
Microsoft MS-DOS 4.0 Programmer's Reference, pages 146 through 147
Microsoft MS-DOS 5.0 Programmer's Reference, page 262

See Also: 3.066. INT 21H, AH=33H, AL=06H -- Get MS-DOS Version

3.061. INT 21H, AH=31H -- KEEP PROGRAM

Prior to Calling Function

	High	Low
AX	31H	Return code*
BX		
CX		
DX	# of paragraphs of memory to keep resident	
SP		
BP		
SI		
DI		
IP		
flags		
CS		
DS		
SS		
ES		

Upon Return from Function

Function returns no values.

*You establish return codes. By convention 00=no error.

Version: Applies to all versions of DOS beginning with 2.0.

Note: Open files are not closed by this function.

Source: IBM DOS 3.3 Technical Reference, pages 6-105 through 6-106
IBM DOS 4.0 Technical Reference, page B-65
Microsoft MS-DOS 4.0 Programmer's Reference, pages 148 through 149
Microsoft MS-DOS 5.0 Programmer's Reference, page 263

See Also: 3.124. INT 21H, AH=4BH, AL=00H -- Load and Execute Program
3.128. INT 21H, AH=4CH -- End Program
3.129. INT 21H, AH=4DH -- Get Child-Program Return Value

3.062. INT 21H, AH=32H -- GET DPB

Prior to Calling Function

	High	Low
AX	32H	
BX		
CX		
DX		Drive number*
SP		
BP		
SI		
DI		
IP		
flags		
CS		
DS		
SS		
ES		

Upon Return from Function

	High	Low
AX		Status†
BX	Offset of pointer to DPB structure	
CX		
DX		
SP		
BP		
SI		
DI		
IP		
flags		
CS		
DS	Segment of pointer to DPB structure	
SS		
ES		

0=default, 1=A, 2=B, and so on.
00H=successful, 0FFH=error.

Source: Microsoft MS-DOS 5.0 Programmer's Reference, page 264

See Also: 3.173. DPB Structure

3.063. INT 21H, AH=33H, AL=00H -- GET CTRL+C CHECK FLAG

Prior to Calling Function

Register	High	Low
AX	33H	00H
BX		
CX		
DX		
SP		
BP		
SI		
DI		
IP		
flags		
CS		
DS		
SS		
ES		

Upon Return from Function

Register	High	Low
AX		
BX		
CX		
DX		Break flag*
SP		
BP		
SI		
DI		
IP		
flags		
CS		
DS		
SS		
ES		

*0=checking disabled, 1=checking enabled.

Source: IBM DOS 3.3 Technical Reference, page 6-107
IBM DOS 4.0 Technical Reference, pages B-66 through B-67
Microsoft MS-DOS 4.0 Programmer's Reference, pages 150 through 151
Microsoft MS-DOS 5.0 Programmer's Reference, page 265

See Also: 3.064. INT 21H, AH=33H, AL=01H -- Set Ctrl+C Check Flag

3.064. INT 21H, AH=33H, AL=01H -- SET CTRL+C CHECK FLAG

Prior to Calling Function

Register	High	Low
AX	33H	01H
BX		
CX		
DX		Break flag*
SP		
BP		
SI		
DI		
IP		
flags		
CS		
DS		
SS		
ES		

Upon Return from Function

Function returns no values.

*0=Ctrl+C testing off, 1=Ctrl+C testing on.

Source: IBM DOS 3.3 Technical Reference, page 6-107
IBM DOS 4.0 Technical Reference, pages B-66 through B-67
Microsoft MS-DOS 4.0 Programmer's Reference, pages 150 through 151
Microsoft MS-DOS 5.0 Programmer's Reference, page 266

See Also: 3.063. INT 21H, AH=33H, AL=00H -- Get Ctrl+C Check Flag
3.065. INT 21H, AH=33H, AL=05H -- Get Startup Drive

3.065. INT 21H, AH=33H, AL=05H -- GET STARTUP DRIVE

Prior to Calling Function

	High	Low
AX	33H	05H
BX		
CX		
DX		
SP		
BP		
SI		
DI		
IP		
flags		
CS		
DS		
SS		
ES		

Upon Return from Function

	High	Low
AX		
BX		
CX		
DX		Drive number*
SP		
BP		
SI		
DI		
IP		
flags		
CS		
DS		
SS		
ES		

*1=A, 2=B, and so on.

Source: IBM DOS 3.3 Technical Reference, page 6-107
IBM DOS 4.0 Technical Reference, pages B-66 through B-67
Microsoft MS-DOS 4.0 Programmer's Reference, pages 150 through 151
Microsoft MS-DOS 5.0 Programmer's Reference, page 267

See Also: 3.063. INT 21H, AH=33H, AL=00H -- Get Ctrl+C Check Flag
3.064. INT 21H, AH=33H, AL=01H -- Set Ctrl+C Check Flag

3.066. INT 21H, AH=33H, AL=06H -- GET MS-DOS VERSION

Prior to Calling Function

	High	Low
AX	33H	06H
BX		
CX		
DX		
SP		
BP		
SI		
DI		
IP		
flags		
CS		
DS		
SS		
ES		

Upon Return from Function

	High	Low
AX		
BX	Minor version	Major version
CX		
DX	Version flags§	Revision number†
SP		
BP		
SI		
DI		
IP		
flags		
CS		
DS		
SS		
ES		

†Low three bits only
§08H=DOSINROM, 10H=DOSINHMA.

Version: Applies to all versions of DOS beginning with 5.0

Source: Microsoft MS-DOS 5.0 Programmer's Reference, page 268

See Also: 3.060. INT 21H, AH=30H -- Get Version Number

3.067. INT 21H, AH=34H -- GET INDOS FLAG ADDRESS

Prior to Calling Function

Register	High	Low
AX	34H	
BX		
CX		
DX		
SP		
BP		
SI		
DI		
IP		
flags		
CS		
DS		
SS		
ES		

Upon Return from Function

Register	High	Low
AX		
BX	Offset address of InDOS flag	
CX		
DX		
SP		
BP		
SI		
DI		
IP		
flags		
CS		
DS		
SS		
ES	Segment address of InDOS flag	

Source: Microsoft MS-DOS 5.0 Programmer's Reference, page 269

3.068. INT 21H, AH=35H -- GET INTERRUPT VECTOR

Prior to Calling Function

Register	High	Low
AX	35H	Interrupt number
BX		
CX		
DX		
SP		
BP		
SI		
DI		
IP		
flags		
CS		
DS		
SS		
ES		

Upon Return from Function

Register	High	Low
AX		
BX	Offset of pointer to interrupt routine*	
CX		
DX		
SP		
BP		
SI		
DI		
IP		
flags		
CS		
DS		
SS		
ES	Segment of pointer to interrupt routine*	

*If ES:BX = 0 then no handler is associated with this interrupt.

Version: Applies to all versions of DOS beginning with 2.0.

Source:
IBM DOS 3.3 Technical Reference, page 6-108
IBM DOS 4.0 Technical Reference, page B-68
Microsoft MS-DOS 4.0 Programmer's Reference, pages 152 through 153
Microsoft MS-DOS 5.0 Programmer's Reference, page 270

See Also:
3.049. INT 21H, AH=25H -- Set Interrupt Vector
7.005. PC Interrupt Usage Summary

3.069. INT 21H, AH=36H -- GET DISK FREE SPACE

Prior to Calling Function

	High	Low
AX	36H	
BX		
CX		
DX		Logical drive number†
SP		
BP		
SI		
DI		
IP		
flags		
CS		
DS		
SS		
ES		

Upon Return from Function

	High	Low
AX	Sectors per cluster*	
BX	Number of available clusters	
CX	Number of bytes per sector	
DX	Number of clusters per drive	
SP		
BP		
SI		
DI		
IP		
flags		
CS		
DS		
SS		
ES		

*Or FFFFH if invalid drive was specified in DL.
†0=default, 1=A, and so on.

Version: Applies to all versions of DOS beginning with 2.0.

Source: IBM DOS 3.3 Technical Reference, page 6-109
IBM DOS 4.0 Technical Reference, pages B-69 through B-70
Microsoft MS-DOS 4.0 Programmer's Reference, pages 154 through 155
Microsoft MS-DOS 5.0 Programmer's Reference, page 271

See Also: 3.042. INT 21H, AH=1BH -- Get Default Drive Data
3.043. INT 21H, AH=1CH -- Get Drive Data
3.184. Logical Drive Numbers

3.070. INT 21H, AH=38H -- GET COUNTRY DATA

Prior to Calling Function

	High	Low
AX	38H	Country code or FFH*
BX	Country code if AL=FFH*	
CX		
DX	Offset of pointer to COUNTRYINFO structure	
SP		
BP		
SI		
DI		
IP		
flags		
CS		
DS	Segment of pointer to COUNTRYINFO structure	
SS		
ES		
Buffer	Empty	

Upon Return from Function

	High	Low
AX	Error or country code	
BX	Country code (if carry flag clear)	
CX		
DX		
SP		
BP		
SI		
DI		
IP		
flags		Carry flag†
CS		
DS		
SS		
ES		
Buffer	Country data or COUNTRYINFO structure	

*If country code less than or equal to 254, AL=country code. If country code greater than 254, AL=0FFH and BX=country code.
†Carry flag set if error occurs.

(Continued)

3.070. INT 21H, AH=38H -- GET COUNTRY DATA (continued)

Version: Applies to all versions of DOS beginning with 2.1.

Source:
IBM DOS 3.3 Technical Reference, pages 6-110 through 6-118
IBM DOS 4.0 Technical Reference, pages B-71 through B-73
Microsoft MS-DOS 4.0 Programmer's Reference, pages 156 through 159
Microsoft MS-DOS 5.0 Programmer's Reference, pages 272 through 273

See Also:
3.070. INT 21H, AH=38H -- Set Country Data
3.142. INT 21H, AH=59H -- Get Extended Error
3.191. ERROR Structure and Error Code Values
3.199. Country Codes
3.203. COUNTRYINFO Structure

3.071. INT 21H, AH=38H -- SET COUNTRY DATA

Prior to Calling Function

Register	High	Low
AX	38H	Country code or FFH*
BX	Country code if AL=FFH*	
CX		
DX	FFFFH	
SP		
BP		
SI		
DI		
IP		
flags		
CS		
DS	FFFFH	
SS		
ES		

Upon Return from Function

Register	High	Low
AX	Error code (if carry flag set)	
BX		
CX		
DX		
SP		
BP		
SI		
DI		
IP		
flags		Carry flag†
CS		
DS		
SS		
ES		

*If country code less than or equal to 254, AL=country code. If country code greater than 254, AL=0FFH and BX=country code.
†Carry flag set if error occurs.

Version: Applies to all versions of DOS beginning with 3.0.

Source:
IBM DOS 3.3 Technical Reference, pages 6-110 through 6-118
IBM DOS 4.0 Technical Reference, pages B-71 through B-73
Microsoft MS-DOS 4.0 Programmer's Reference, pages 160 through 161
Microsoft MS-DOS 5.0 Programmer's Reference, pages 272 through 273

See Also:
3.070. INT 21H, AH=38H -- Get Country Data
3.142. INT 21H, AH=59H -- Get Extended Error
3.191. ERROR Structure and Error Code Values
3.199. Country Codes

3.072. INT 21H, AH=39H -- CREATE DIRECTORY

Prior to Calling Function

	High	Low
AX	39H	
BX		
CX		
DX	Offset of pointer to directory name string	
SP		
BP		
SI		
DI		
IP		
flags		
CS		
DS	Segment of pointer to directory name string	
SS		
ES		

Upon Return from Function

	High	Low
AX	Error code (if carry flag set)	
BX		
CX		
DX		
SP		
BP		
SI		
DI		
IP		
flags		Carry flag*
CS		
DS		
SS		
ES		

*Carry flag set if error occurs.

Version: Applies to all versions of DOS beginning with 2.0.

Note:
- Requires create access rights on networks.
- Pathname must be in ASCIIZ form.

Source:
IBM DOS 3.3 Technical Reference, page 6-119
IBM DOS 4.0 Technical Reference, page B-74
Microsoft MS-DOS 4.0 Programmer's Reference, pages 162 through 163
Microsoft MS-DOS 5.0 Programmer's Reference, page 274

See Also:
3.073. INT 21H, AH=3AH -- Remove Directory
3.074. INT 21H, AH=3BH -- Change Current Directory
3.120. INT 21H, AH=47H -- Get Current Directory
3.142. INT 21H, AH=59H -- Get Extended Error
3.191. ERROR Structure and Error Code Values

3.073. INT 21H, AH=3AH -- REMOVE DIRECTORY

Prior to Calling Function

	High	Low
AX	3AH	
BX		
CX		
DX	Offset of pointer to directory name string	
SP		
BP		
SI		
DI		
IP		
flags		
CS		
DS	Segment of pointer to directory name string	
SS		
ES		

Upon Return from Function

	High	Low
AX	Error code (if carry flag set)	
BX		
CX		
DX		
SP		
BP		
SI		
DI		
IP		
flags		Carry flag*
CS		
DS		
SS		
ES		

*Carry flag set if error occurs.

Version: Applies to all versions of DOS beginning with 2.0.

Note:
- Requires create access rights on networks.
- Pathname must be in ASCIIZ form.

Source:
IBM DOS 3.3 Technical Reference, page 6-120
IBM DOS 4.0 Technical Reference, page B-75
Microsoft MS-DOS 4.0 Programmer's Reference, pages 164 through 165
Microsoft MS-DOS 5.0 Programmer's Reference, page 275

See Also:
3.072. INT 21H, AH=39H -- Create Directory
3.074. INT 21H, AH=3BH -- Change Current Directory
3.120. INT 21H, AH=47H -- Get Current Directory
3.142. INT 21H, AH=59H -- Get Extended Error
3.191. ERROR Structure and Error Code Values

3.074. INT 21H, AH=3BH -- CHANGE CURRENT DIRECTORY

Prior to Calling Function

	High	Low
AX	3BH	
BX		
CX		
DX	Offset of pointer to pathname string	
SP		
BP		
SI		
DI		
IP		
flags		
CS		
DS	Segment of pointer to pathname string	
SS		
ES		

Upon Return from Function

	High	Low
AX	Error code (if carry flag set)	
BX		
CX		
DX		
SP		
BP		
SI		
DI		
IP		
flags		Carry flag*
CS		
DS		
SS		
ES		

*Carry flag set if error occurs.

Version: Applies to all versions of DOS beginning with 2.0.

Note:
- Pathname must be in ASCIIZ form.
- Pathname string is limited to 64 characters.

Source:
IBM DOS 3.3 Technical Reference, page 6-121
IBM DOS 4.0 Technical Reference, page B-76
Microsoft MS-DOS 4.0 Programmer's Reference, pages 166 through 167
Microsoft MS-DOS 5.0 Programmer's Reference, page 276

See Also:
3.120. INT 21H, AH=47H -- Get Current Directory
3.142. INT 21H, AH=59H -- Get Extended Error
3.191. ERROR Structure and Error Code Values

3.075. INT 21H, AH=3CH -- CREATE FILE WITH HANDLE

Prior to Calling Function

	High	*Low*
AX	3CH	
BX		
CX	File attribute*	
DX	Offset of pointer to pathname string	
SP		
BP		
SI		
DI		
IP		
flags		
CS		
DS	Segment of pointer to pathname string	
SS		
ES		

Upon Return from Function

	High	*Low*
AX	Handle or error code (if carry flag set)	
BX		
CX		
DX		
SP		
BP		
SI		
DI		
IP		
flags		Carry flag†
CS		
DS		
SS		
ES		

*Attributes:
0000H=Normal (read from or written to)
0001H=Read only
0002H=Hidden
0004H=System File
0008H=Volume
0020H=Archive
†Carry flag set if error occurs.

Version: Applies to all versions of DOS beginning with 2.0.

Note:
- Requires create access rights on networks.
- Pathname must be in ASCIIZ form.
- File is truncated if it already exists.

Source:
IBM DOS 3.3 Technical Reference, pages 6-122 through 6-123
IBM DOS 4.0 Technical Reference, page B-77
Microsoft MS-DOS 4.0 Programmer's Reference, pages 168 through 169
Microsoft MS-DOS 5.0 Programmer's Reference, pages 277 through 278

See Also:
2.19. File Attribute Byte
3.038. INT 21H, AH=16H -- Create File with FCB
3.082. INT 21H, AH=43H, AL=00H -- Get File Attributes
3.083. INT 21H, AH=43H, AL=01H -- Set File Attributes
3.142. INT 21H, AH=59H -- Get Extended Error
3.143. INT 21H, AH=5AH -- Create Temporary File
3.144. INT 21H, AH=5BH -- Create New File
3.169. INT 21H, AH=6CH -- Extended Open/Create
3.191. ERROR Structure and Error Code Values

3.076. INT 21H, AH=3DH -- OPEN FILE WITH HANDLE

Prior to Calling Function

	High	Low
AX	3DH	Access code
BX		
CX		
DX	Offset of pointer to pathname string	
SP		
BP		
SI		
DI		
IP		
flags		
CS		
DS	Segment of pointer to pathname string	
SS		
ES		

Upon Return from Function

	High	Low
AX	Handle or error code (if carry flag set)	
BX		
CX		
DX		
SP		
BP		
SI		
DI		
IP		
flags		Carry flag*
CS		
DS		
SS		
ES		

*Carry flag set if error occurs.

Version: Applies to all versions of DOS beginning with 2.0.

Note: Pathname must be in ASCIIZ form.

Source: IBM DOS 3.3 Technical Reference, pages 6-124 through 6-135
IBM DOS 4.0 Technical Reference, pages B-78 through B-84
Microsoft MS-DOS 4.0 Programmer's Reference, pages 170 through 175
Microsoft MS-DOS 5.0 Programmer's Reference, pages 279 through 280

See Also: 3.031. INT 21H, AH=0FH -- Open File With FCB
3.142. INT 21H, AH=59H -- Get Extended Error
3.169. INT 21H, AH=6CH -- Extended Open/Create
3.187. Handle Access Byte
3.191. ERROR Structure and Error Code Values

3.077. INT 21H, AH=3EH -- CLOSE FILE WITH HANDLE

Prior to Calling Function

	High	Low
AX	3EH	
BX	Handle	
CX		
DX		
SP		
BP		
SI		
DI		
IP		
flags		
CS		
DS		
SS		
ES		

Upon Return from Function

	High	Low
AX	Error code (if carry flag set)	
BX		
CX		
DX		
SP		
BP		
SI		
DI		
IP		
flags		Carry flag*
CS		
DS		
SS		
ES		

*Carry flag set if error occurs.

Version: Applies to all versions of DOS beginning with 2.0.

Source: IBM DOS 3.3 Technical Reference, page 6-136
IBM DOS 4.0 Technical Reference, page B-85
Microsoft MS-DOS 4.0 Programmer's Reference, pages 176 through 177
Microsoft MS-DOS 5.0 Programmer's Reference, page 281

See Also: 3.032. INT 21H, AH=10H -- Close File with FCB
3.142. INT 21H, AH=59H -- Get Extended Error
3.188. Predefined Handles
3.191. ERROR Structure and Error Code Values

3.078. INT 21H, AH=3FH -- READ FILE OR DEVICE

Prior to Calling Function

Register	High	Low
AX	3FH	
BX	Handle	
CX	Maximum number of bytes to read	
DX	Offset of pointer to empty buffer for data	
SP		
BP		
SI		
DI		
IP		
flags		
CS		
DS	Segment of pointer to empty buffer for data	
SS		
ES		
Buffer	Empty	

Upon Return from Function

Register	High	Low
AX	Bytes read or error code (if carry flag set)†	
BX		
CX		
DX		
SP		
BP		
SI		
DI		
IP		
flags		Carry flag*
CS		
DS		
SS		
ES		
Buffer	Data read	

*Carry flag set if error occurs.
†A value of 0 indicates attempt to read at EOF.

Version: Applies to all versions of DOS beginning with 2.0.

Note: Requires read access rights on networks.

Source:
IBM DOS 3.3 Technical Reference, pages 6-137 through 6-138
IBM DOS 4.0 Technical Reference, page B-86
Microsoft MS-DOS 4.0 Programmer's Reference, pages 178 through 179
Microsoft MS-DOS 5.0 Programmer's Reference, page 282

See Also:
3.036. INT 21H, AH=14H -- Sequential Read
3.045. INT 21H, AH=21H -- Random Read
3.051. INT 21H, AH=27H -- Random Block Read
3.142. INT 21H, AH=59H -- Get Extended Error
3.191. ERROR Structure and Error Code Values

3.079. INT 21H, AH=40H -- WRITE FILE OR DEVICE

Prior to Calling Function

	High	Low
AX	40H	
BX	Handle	
CX	Maximum number of bytes to write§	
DX	Offset of pointer to buffer containing data	
SP		
BP		
SI		
DI		
IP		
flags		
CS		
DS	Segment of pointer to buffer containing data	
SS		
ES		
Buffer	Data to write	

Upon Return from Function

	High	Low
AX	Bytes written or error code (if carry flag set)†	
BX		
CX		
DX		
SP		
BP		
SI		
DI		
IP		
flags		Carry flag*
CS		
DS		
SS		
ES		
Buffer	Unchanged data	

*Carry flag set if error occurs.
†If the number of bytes written is less than the number of bytes requested, the destination file or disk is full.
§If 0, file is truncated at the pointer position.

Version: Applies to all versions of DOS beginning with 2.0.

Note: Requires write access rights on networks.

Source: IBM DOS 3.3 Technical Reference, pages 6-139 through 6-140
IBM DOS 4.0 Technical Reference, pages B-87 through B-88
Microsoft MS-DOS 4.0 Programmer's Reference, pages 180 through 181
Microsoft MS-DOS 5.0 Programmer's Reference, page 283

See Also: 3.037. INT 21H, AH=15H -- Sequential Write
3.046. INT 21H, AH=22H -- Random Write
3.052. INT 21H, AH=28H -- Random Block Write
3.142. INT 21H, AH=59H -- Get Extended Error
3.191. ERROR Structure and Error Code Values

3.080. INT 21H, AH=41H -- DELETE FILE

Prior to Calling Function

	High	Low
AX	41H	
BX		
CX		
DX	Offset of pointer to filename string	
SP		
BP		
SI		
DI		
IP		
flags		
CS		
DS	Segment of pointer to filename string	
SS		
ES		

Upon Return from Function

	High	Low
AX	Error code (if carry flag set)	
BX		
CX		
DX		
SP		
BP		
SI		
DI		
IP		
flags		Carry flag*
CS		
DS		
SS		
ES		

*Carry flag set if error occurs.

Version: Applies to all versions of DOS beginning with 2.0.

Note:
- Requires delete access rights on networks.
- Filename must be in ASCIIZ format.

Source:
IBM DOS 3.3 Technical Reference, pages 6-141 through 6-142
IBM DOS 4.0 Technical Reference, page B-89
Microsoft MS-DOS 4.0 Programmer's Reference, pages 182 through 183
Microsoft MS-DOS 5.0 Programmer's Reference, page 284

See Also:
1.17. Common String Formats
3.035. INT 21H, AH=13H -- Delete File with FCB
3.072. INT 21H, AH=3AH -- Remove Directory
3.142. INT 21H, AH=59H -- Get Extended Error
3.191. ERROR Structure and Error Code Values

3.081. INT 21H, AH=42H -- MOVE FILE POINTER

Prior to Calling Function

	High	*Low*
AX	42H	Movement method†
BX	Handle	
CX	High order of offset to move pointer (in bytes)	
DX	Low order of offset to move pointer	
SP		
BP		
SI		
DI		
IP		
flags		
CS		
DS		
SS		
ES		

Upon Return from Function

	High	*Low*
AX	LO position, or error code (if carry flag set)	
BX		
CX		
DX	High order position of pointer in file	
SP		
BP		
SI		
DI		
IP		
flags		Carry flag*
CS		
DS		
SS		
ES		

*Carry flag set if error occurs.
†0=start move at beginning of file; 1=start at current location; 2=start move at end of file.

Version: Applies to all versions of DOS beginning with 2.0.

Note: You can find the size of a file by setting AL=2 and CX:DX=0.

Source:
IBM DOS 3.3 Technical Reference, pages 6-143 through 6-144
IBM DOS 4.0 Technical Reference, pages B-90 through B-91
Microsoft MS-DOS 4.0 Programmer's Reference, pages 184 through 185
Microsoft MS-DOS 5.0 Programmer's Reference, pages 285 through 286

See Also:
3.048. INT 21H, AH=24H -- Set Random Record Number
3.142. INT 21H, AH=59H -- Get Extended Error
3.189. Handle Pointer Movement Methods
3.191. ERROR Structure and Error Code Values

3.082. INT 21H, AH=43H, AL=00H -- GET FILE ATTRIBUTES

Prior to Calling Function

	High	Low
AX	43H	00H
BX		
CX		
DX	Offset of pointer to filename string	
SP		
BP		
SI		
DI		
IP		
flags		
CS		
DS	Segment of pointer to filename string	
SS		
ES		

Upon Return from Function

	High	Low
AX	Error code (if carry flag set)	
BX		
CX		Attributes†
DX		
SP		
BP		
SI		
DI		
IP		
flags		Carry flag*
CS		
DS		
SS		
ES		

*Carry flag set if error occurs.
†Attributes:
0000H=Normal (read from or written to)
0001H=Read-only
0002H=Hidden
0004H=System file
0008H=Volume
0010H=Directory, not file
0020H=Archive

Version: Applies to all versions of DOS beginning with 2.0.

Note: Pathname must be in ASCIIZ format.

Source:
IBM DOS 3.3 Technical Reference, pages 6-145 through 6-146
IBM DOS 4.0 Technical Reference, pages B-92 through B-93
Microsoft MS-DOS 4.0 Programmer's Reference, pages 186 through 187
Microsoft MS-DOS 5.0 Programmer's Reference, page 287

See Also:
1.17. Common String Formats
2.19. File Attribute Byte
3.142. INT 21H, AH=59H -- Get Extended Error
3.191. ERROR Structure and Error Code Values

3.083. INT 21H, AH=43H, AL=01H -- SET FILE ATTRIBUTES

Prior to Calling Function

	High	Low
AX	43H	01H
BX		
CX	0	Attributes†
DX	Offset of pointer to filename string	
SP		
BP		
SI		
DI		
IP		
flags		
CS		
DS	Segment of pointer to filename string	
SS		
ES		

Upon Return from Function

	High	Low
AX	Error code (if carry flag set)	
BX		
CX		
DX		
SP		
BP		
SI		
DI		
IP		
flags		Carry flag*
CS		
DS		
SS		
ES		

*Carry flag set if error occurs.
†Attributes:
0000H=Normal (read from or written to)
0001H=Read-only
0002H=Hidden
0004H=System file
0008H=Volume
0010H=Directory, not file
0020H=Archive

Version: Applies to all versions of DOS beginning with 2.0.

Note:
- Requires create access rights on networks to change any bit other than the archive bit (bit 5).
- Pathname must be in ASCIIZ format.
- You can't change the volume or directory bits of an attribute byte.

Source:
IBM DOS 3.3 Technical Reference, pages 6-145 through 6-146
IBM DOS 4.0 Technical Reference, pages B-92 through B-93
Microsoft MS-DOS 4.0 Programmer's Reference, pages 186 through 187
Microsoft MS-DOS 5.0 Programmer's Reference, page 288

See Also:
1.17. Common String Formats
2.19. File Attribute Byte
3.142. INT 21H, AH=59H -- Get Extended Error
3.191. ERROR Structure and Error Code Values

3.084. INT 21H, AH=44H, AL=00H -- GET DEVICE DATA

Prior to Calling Function

Register	High	Low
AX	44H	00H
BX	Handle	
CX		
DX		
SP		
BP		
SI		
DI		
IP		
flags		
CS		
DS		
SS		
ES		

Upon Return from Function

Register	High	Low
AX	Error code (if carry flag set)	
BX		
CX		
DX	Device data word (if carry flag clear)	
SP		
BP		
SI		
DI		
IP		
flags		Carry flag*
CS		
DS		
SS		
ES		

*Carry flag set if error occurs.

Version: Applies to all versions of DOS beginning with 2.0.

Source: IBM DOS 3.3 Technical Reference, pages 6-148 through 6-150
IBM DOS 4.0 Technical Reference, pages C-3 through C-4
Microsoft MS-DOS 4.0 Programmer's Reference, pages 188 through 190
Microsoft MS-DOS 5.0 Programmer's Reference, page 289

See Also: 3.085. INT 21H, AH=44H, AL=01H -- Set Device Data
3.142. INT 21H, AH=59H -- Get Extended Error
3.191. ERROR Structure and Error Code Values
3.216. Device Data Word

3.085. INT 21H, AH=44H, AL=01H -- SET DEVICE DATA

Prior to Calling Function

Register	High	Low
AX	44H	01H
BX	Handle	
CX		
DX	0	Device data word
SP		
BP		
SI		
DI		
IP		
flags		
CS		
DS		
SS		
ES		

Upon Return from Function

Register	High	Low
AX	Error code (if carry flag set)	
BX		
CX		
DX		
SP		
BP		
SI		
DI		
IP		
flags		Carry flag*
CS		
DS		
SS		
ES		

*Carry flag set if error occurs.

Version: Applies to all versions of DOS beginning with 2.0.

Source: IBM DOS 3.3 Technical Reference, pages 6-148 through 6-150
IBM DOS 4.0 Technical Reference, pages C-3 through C-4
Microsoft MS-DOS 4.0 Programmer's Reference, pages 188 through 190
Microsoft MS-DOS 5.0 Programmer's Reference, page 290

See Also: 3.084. INT 21H, AH=44H, AL=00H -- Get Device Data
3.142. INT 21H, AH=59H -- Get Extended Error
3.191. ERROR Structure and Error Code Values
3.216. Device Data Word

3.086. INT 21H, AH=44H, AL=02H -- RECEIVE CONTROL DATA FROM CHARACTER DEVICE

Prior to Calling Function

Register	High	Low
AX	44H	02H
BX	Handle	
CX	Maximum number of bytes to read	
DX	Offset of pointer to empty buffer	
SP		
BP		
SI		
DI		
IP		
flags		
CS		
DS	Segment of pointer to empty buffer	
SS		
ES		
Buffer	Empty	

Upon Return from Function

Register	High	Low
AX	Bytes read or error code (if carry flag set)	
BX		
CX		
DX		
SP		
BP		
SI		
DI		
IP		
flags		Carry flag*
CS		
DS		
SS		
ES		
Buffer	Data read from device	

*Carry flag set if error occurs.

Version: Applies to all versions of DOS beginning with 2.0.

Source: IBM DOS 3.3 Technical Reference, page 6-151
IBM DOS 4.0 Technical Reference, page C-5
Microsoft MS-DOS 4.0 Programmer's Reference, pages 191 through 192
Microsoft MS-DOS 5.0 Programmer's Reference, page 291

See Also: 3.087. INT 21H, AH=44H, AL=03H -- Send Control Data to Character Device
3.142. INT 21H, AH=59H -- Get Extended Error
3.191. ERROR Structure and Error Code Values

3.087. INT 21H, AH=44H, AL=03H -- SEND CONTROL DATA TO CHARACTER DEVICE

Prior to Calling Function

Register	High	Low
AX	44H	03H
BX	Handle	
CX	Maximum number of bytes to write	
DX	Offset of pointer to buffer of data to write	
SP		
BP		
SI		
DI		
IP		
flags		
CS		
DS	Segment of pointer to buffer of data to write	
SS		
ES		
Buffer	Data to write	

Upon Return from Function

Register	High	Low
AX	Bytes written or error code (if carry flag set)	
BX		
CX		
DX		
SP		
BP		
SI		
DI		
IP		
flags		Carry flag*
CS		
DS		
SS		
ES		
Buffer	Unchanged data	

*Carry flag set if error occurs.

Version: Applies to all versions of DOS beginning with 2.0.

Source: IBM DOS 3.3 Technical Reference, page 6-151
IBM DOS 4.0 Technical Reference, page C-5
Microsoft MS-DOS 4.0 Programmer's Reference, pages 191 through 192
Microsoft MS-DOS 5.0 Programmer's Reference, page 292

See Also: 3.086. INT 21H, AH=44H, AL=02H -- Receive Control Data from Character Device
3.142. INT 21H, AH=59H -- Get Extended Error
3.191. ERROR Structure and Error Code Values

3.088. INT 21H, AH=44H, AL=04H -- RECEIVE CONTROL DATA FROM BLOCK DEVICE

Prior to Calling Function

	High	Low
AX	44H	04H
BX		Logical drive number†
CX	Maximum number of bytes to read	
DX	Offset of pointer to empty buffer	
SP		
BP		
SI		
DI		
IP		
flags		
CS		
DS	Segment of pointer to empty buffer	
SS		
ES		
Buffer	Empty	

Upon Return from Function

	High	Low
AX	Bytes read or error code (if carry flag set)	
BX		
CX		
DX		
SP		
BP		
SI		
DI		
IP		
flags	Carry flag*	
CS		
DS		
SS		
ES		
Buffer	Data read from drive	

*Carry flag set if error occurs.
†Drive 0=default, drive 1=A, and so on.

Version: Applies to all versions of DOS beginning with 2.0.

Source:
IBM DOS 3.3 Technical Reference, page 152
IBM DOS 4.0 Technical Reference, page C-6
Microsoft MS-DOS 4.0 Programmer's Reference, pages 193 through 194
Microsoft MS-DOS 5.0 Programmer's Reference, page 293

See Also:
3.089. INT 21H, AH=44H, AL=05H -- Send Control Data to Block Device
3.142. INT 21H, AH=59H -- Get Extended Error
3.184. Logical Drive Numbers
3.191. ERROR Structure and Error Code Values

3.089. INT 21H, AH=44H, AL=05H -- SEND CONTROL DATA TO BLOCK DEVICE

Prior to Calling Function

	High	Low
AX	44H	05H
BX		Logical drive number†
CX	Number of bytes to write to drive	
DX	Offset of pointer to buffer of data to write	
SP		
BP		
SI		
DI		
IP		
flags		
CS		
DS	Segment of pointer to buffer of data to write	
SS		
ES		
Buffer	Data to write	

Upon Return from Function

	High	Low
AX	Bytes written or error code (if carry flag set)	
BX		
CX		
DX		
SP		
BP		
SI		
DI		
IP		
flags	Carry flag*	
CS		
DS		
SS		
ES		
Buffer	Unchanged data	

*Carry flag set if error occurs.
†Drive 0=default, drive 1=A, and so on.

Version: Applies to all versions of DOS beginning with 2.0.

Source: IBM DOS 3.3 Technical Reference, page 6-152
IBM DOS 4.0 Technical Reference, page C-6
Microsoft MS-DOS 4.0 Programmer's Reference, pages 193 through 194
Microsoft MS-DOS 5.0 Programmer's Reference, page 294

See Also: 3.088. INT 21H, AH=44H, AL=04H -- Receive Control Data from Block Device
3.142. INT 21H, AH=59H -- Get Extended Error
3.184. Logical Drive Numbers
3.191. ERROR Structure and Error Code Values

3.090. INT 21H, AH=44H, AL=06H -- CHECK DEVICE INPUT STATUS

Prior to Calling Function

	High	*Low*
AX	44H	06H
BX	Handle	
CX		
DX		
SP		
BP		
SI		
DI		
IP		
flags		
CS		
DS		
SS		
ES		

Upon Return from Function

	High	*Low*
AX	Error if carry flag set	Status*
BX		
CX		
DX		
SP		
BP		
SI		
DI		
IP		
flags	Carry flag*	
CS		
DS		
SS		
ES		

*For devices: 00=not ready, FF=ready. For files: 00=pointer at EOF, FF=ready.

Version: Applies to all versions of DOS beginning with 2.0.

Source: IBM DOS 3.3 Technical Reference, page 6-153
IBM DOS 4.0 Technical Reference, page C-7
Microsoft MS-DOS 4.0 Programmer's Reference, pages 195 through 196
Microsoft MS-DOS 5.0 Programmer's Reference, page 295

See Also: 3.091. INT 21H, AH=44H, AL=07H -- Check Device Output Status
3.142. INT 21H, AH=59H -- Get Extended Error
3.191. ERROR Structure and Error Code Values

3.091. INT 21H, AH=44H, AL=07H -- CHECK DEVICE OUTPUT STATUS

Prior to Calling Function

Register	High	Low
AX	44H	07H
BX	Handle	
CX		
DX		
SP		
BP		
SI		
DI		
IP		
flags		
CS		
DS		
SS		
ES		

Upon Return from Function

Register	High	Low
AX	Error if carry flag set	Status*
BX		
CX		
DX		
SP		
BP		
SI		
DI		
IP		
flags		Carry flag
CS		
DS		
SS		
ES		

*For devices: 00=not ready, FF=ready. For files: 00=ready, FF=ready.

Version: Applies to all versions of DOS beginning with 2.0.

Source:
IBM DOS 3.3 Technical Reference, page 6-153
IBM DOS 4.0 Technical Reference, page C-7
Microsoft MS-DOS 4.0 Programmer's Reference, pages 195 through 196
Microsoft MS-DOS 5.0 Programmer's Reference, page 296

See Also:
3.090. INT 21H, AH=44H, AL=06H -- Check Device Input Status
3.142. INT 21H, AH=59H -- Get Extended Error
3.191. ERROR Structure and Error Code Values

3.092. INT 21H, AH=44H, AL=08H -- DOES DEVICE USE REMOVABLE MEDIA

Prior to Calling Function

Register	High	Low
AX	44H	08H
BX		Logical drive number¥
CX		
DX		
SP		
BP		
SI		
DI		
IP		
flags		
CS		
DS		
SS		
ES		

Upon Return from Function

Register	High	Low
AX	Status or error code (if carry flag set)†	
BX		
CX		
DX		
SP		
BP		
SI		
DI		
IP		
flags		Carry flag*
CS		
DS		
SS		
ES		

*Carry flag set if error occurs.
†00=removable media; 01=media not removable.
¥00=default, 01=A, and so on.

Version: Applies to all versions of DOS beginning with 3.0.

Source:
IBM DOS 3.3 Technical Reference, page 6-154
IBM DOS 4.0 Technical Reference, page C-8
Microsoft MS-DOS 4.0 Programmer's Reference, pages 197 through 198
Microsoft MS-DOS 5.0 Programmer's Reference, page 297

See Also:
3.142. INT 21H, AH=59H -- Get Extended Error
3.184. Logical Drive Numbers
3.191. ERROR Structure and Error Code Values

3.093. INT 21H, AH=44H, AL=09H -- IS DRIVE REMOTE

Prior to Calling Function

	High	Low
AX	44H	09H
BX		Logical drive number¥
CX		
DX		
SP		
BP		
SI		
DI		
IP		
flags		
CS		
DS		
SS		
ES		

Upon Return from Function

	High	Low
AX	Error code (if carry flag set)	
BX		
CX		
DX	Device attribute code†	
SP		
BP		
SI		
DI		
IP		
flags		Carry flag*
CS		
DS		
SS		
ES		

*Carry flag set if error occurs.
†Bit 12 set=remote device; bit 12 clear=local device.
¥0=default, 1=A, and so on.

Version: Applies to all versions of DOS beginning with 3.1.

Source:
IBM DOS 3.3 Technical Reference, page 6-155
IBM DOS 4.0 Technical Reference, page C-9
Microsoft MS-DOS 4.0 Programmer's Reference, pages 199 through 200
Microsoft MS-DOS 5.0 Programmer's Reference, page 298

See Also:
3.094. INT 21H, AH=44H, AL=0AH -- Is File or Device Remote
3.142. INT 21H, AH=59H -- Get Extended Error
3.184. Logical Drive Numbers
3.191. ERROR Structure and Error Code Values
3.215. Device Attribute Codes

3.094. INT 21H, AH=44H, AL=0AH -- IS FILE OR DEVICE REMOTE

Prior to Calling Function

	High	Low
AX	44H	0AH
BX	Handle	
CX		
DX		
SP		
BP		
SI		
DI		
IP		
flags		
CS		
DS		
SS		
ES		

Upon Return from Function

	High	Low
AX	Error code (if carry flag set)	
BX		
CX		
DX	Device attribute code†	
SP		
BP		
SI		
DI		
IP		
flags		Carry flag*
CS		
DS		
SS		
ES		

*Carry flag set if error occurs.
†Bit 15 set=remote device; bit 15 clear=local device.

Version: Applies to all versions of DOS beginning with 3.1.

Source:
IBM DOS 3.3 Technical Reference, page 6-156
IBM DOS 4.0 Technical Reference, page C-10
Microsoft MS-DOS 4.0 Programmer's Reference, pages 201 through 202
Microsoft MS-DOS 5.0 Programmer's Reference, pages 299 through 300

See Also:
3.093. INT 21H, AH=44H, AL=09H -- Is Drive Remote
3.142. INT 21H, AH=59H -- Get Extended Error
3.184. Logical Drive Numbers
3.191. ERROR Structure and Error Code Values
3.215. Device Attribute Codes

3.095. INT 21H, AH=44H, AL=0BH -- SET SHARING RETRY COUNT

Prior to Calling Function

	High	Low
AX	44H	0BH
BX		
CX	Number of times through pause loop	
DX	Number of times to retry operation	
SP		
BP		
SI		
DI		
IP		
flags		
CS		
DS		
SS		
ES		

Upon Return from Function

	High	Low
AX	Error code (if carry flag set)	
BX		
CX		
DX		
SP		
BP		
SI		
DI		
IP		
flags		Carry flag*
CS		
DS		
SS		
ES		

*Carry flag set if error occurs.

Version: Applies to all versions of DOS beginning with 3.0.

Note:
- Pause time depends on the computer's clock speed.
- Default is 1 loop, 3 retries

Source:
IBM DOS 3.3 Technical Reference, pages 6-157 through 6-158
IBM DOS 4.0 Technical Reference, page C-11
Microsoft MS-DOS 4.0 Programmer's Reference, pages 203 through 204
Microsoft MS-DOS 5.0 Programmer's Reference, page 301

See Also:
3.142. INT 21H, AH=59H -- Get Extended Error
3.191. ERROR Structure and Error Code Values

3.096. INT 21H, AH=44H, AL=0CH, MINOR CODE=45H -- SET ITERATION COUNT

Prior to Calling Function

Register	High	Low
AX	44H	0CH
BX	Handle	
CX	Category†	45H
DX	Offset of pointer to data buffer	
SP		
BP		
SI		
DI		
IP		
flags		
CS		
DS	Segment of pointer to data buffer	
SS		
ES		
Buffer	Iteration count	

Upon Return from Function

Register	High	Low
AX	Error code (if carry flag set)	
BX		
CX		
DX		
SP		
BP		
SI		
DI		
IP		
flags		Carry flag*
CS		
DS		
SS		
ES		
Buffer		

*Carry flag set if error occurs.
†Category is one of:

1 = serial device
3 = display device
5 = parallel printer

Version: Applies to all versions of DOS beginning with 3.3.

Source: IBM DOS 3.3 Technical Reference, pages 6-158 through 6-166
IBM DOS 4.0 Technical Reference, pages C-12 through C-17
Microsoft MS-DOS 4.0 Programmer's Reference, pages 205 through 208
Microsoft MS-DOS 5.0 Programmer's Reference, page 302

See Also: 3.142. INT 21H, AH=59H -- Get Extended Error
3.191. ERROR Structure and Error Code Values
3.201. Code-Page Parameter Blocks
3.229. Device Request Header Status Field and Error Codes

3.097. INT 21H, AH=44H, AL=0CH, MINOR CODE=4AH -- SELECT CODE PAGE

Prior to Calling Function

	High	Low
AX	44H	0CH
BX	Handle	
CX	Category†	4AH
DX	Offset of pointer to data buffer	
SP		
BP		
SI		
DI		
IP		
flags		
CS		
DS	Segment of pointer to data buffer	
SS		
ES		
Buffer	Code page parm block or CODEPAGE structure	

Upon Return from Function

	High	Low
AX		
BX		
CX		
DX		
SP		
BP		
SI		
DI		
IP		
flags		Carry flag*
CS		
DS		
SS		
ES		
Buffer		

*Carry flag set if error occurs.
†Category is one of:

1 = serial device
3 = display device
5 = parallel printer

Version: Applies to all versions of DOS beginning with 3.3.

Source: IBM DOS 3.3 Technical Reference, pages 6-158 through 6-166
IBM DOS 4.0 Technical Reference, pages C-12 through C-17
Microsoft MS-DOS 4.0 Programmer's Reference, pages 205 through 208
Microsoft MS-DOS 5.0 Programmer's Reference, page 303

See Also: 3.142. INT 21H, AH=59H -- Get Extended Error
3.191. ERROR Structure and Error Code Values
3.201. Code-Page Parameter Blocks
3.229. Device Request Header Status Field and Error Codes

3.098. INT 21H, AH=44H, AL=0CH, MINOR CODE=4CH -- START CODE-PAGE PREPARE

Prior to Calling Function

	High	Low
AX	44H	0CH
BX	Handle	
CX	Category†	4CH
DX	Offset of pointer to data buffer	
SP		
BP		
SI		
DI		
IP		
flags		
CS		
DS	Segment of pointer to data buffer	
SS		
ES		
Buffer	Code page parm block or CPPREPARE structure	

Upon Return from Function

	High	Low
AX		
BX		
CX		
DX		
SP		
BP		
SI		
DI		
IP		
flags		Carry flag*
CS		
DS		
SS		
ES		
Buffer		

*Carry flag set if error occurs.
†Category is one of:

1 = serial device
3 = display device
5 = parallel printer

Version: Applies to all versions of DOS beginning with 3.3.

Source:
IBM DOS 3.3 Technical Reference, pages 6-158 through 6-166
IBM DOS 4.0 Technical Reference, pages C-12 through C-17
Microsoft MS-DOS 4.0 Programmer's Reference, pages 205 through 208
Microsoft MS-DOS 5.0 Programmer's Reference, page 304

See Also:
3.142. INT 21H, AH=59H -- Get Extended Error
3.191. ERROR Structure and Error Code Values
3.201. Code-Page Parameter Blocks
3.206. CPPREPARE Structure
3.229. Device Request Header Status Field and Error Codes

3.099. INT 21H, AH=44H, AL=0CH, MINOR CODE=4DH -- END CODE-PAGE PREPARE

Prior to Calling Function

	High	*Low*
AX	44H	0CH
BX	Handle	
CX	Category†	4DH
DX		
SP		
BP		
SI		
DI		
IP		
flags		
CS		
DS		
SS		
ES		
Buffer		

Upon Return from Function

	High	*Low*
AX		
BX		
CX		
DX		
SP		
BP		
SI		
DI		
IP		
flags		Carry flag*
CS		
DS		
SS		
ES		
Buffer		

*Carry flag set if error occurs.
†Category is one of:

1 = serial device
3 = display device
5 = parallel printer

Version: Applies to all versions of DOS beginning with 3.3.

Source:
IBM DOS 3.3 Technical Reference, pages 6-158 through 6-166
IBM DOS 4.0 Technical Reference, pages C-12 through C-17
Microsoft MS-DOS 4.0 Programmer's Reference, pages 205 through 208
Microsoft MS-DOS 5.0 Programmer's Reference, page 305

See Also:
3.142. INT 21H, AH=59H -- Get Extended Error
3.191. ERROR Structure and Error Code Values
3.201. Code-Page Parameter Blocks
3.229. Device Request Header Status Field and Error Codes

3.100. INT 21H, AH=44H, AL=0CH, MINOR CODE=5FH -- SET DISPLAY MODE

Prior to Calling Function

	High	Low
AX	44H	0CH
BX	Handle	
CX	03H	5FH
DX	Offset of pointer to data buffer	
SP		
BP		
SI		
DI		
IP		
flags		
CS		
DS		
SS		
ES		
Buffer	DISPLAYMODE structure	

Upon Return from Function

	High	Low
AX	Error code (if carry flag set)	
BX		
CX		
DX		
SP		
BP		
SI		
DI		
IP		
flags		Carry flag*
CS		
DS		
SS		
ES		
Buffer		

*Carry flag set if error occurs.

Version: Applies to all versions of DOS beginning with 3.3.

Source: IBM DOS 3.3 Technical Reference, pages 6-158 through 6-166
IBM DOS 4.0 Technical Reference, pages C-12 through C-17
Microsoft MS-DOS 4.0 Programmer's Reference, pages 205 through 208
Microsoft MS-DOS 5.0 Programmer's Reference, page 306

See Also: 3.142. INT 21H, AH=59H -- Get Extended Error
3.191. ERROR Structure and Error Code Values
3.201. Code-Page Parameter Blocks
3.229. Device Request Header Status Field and Error Codes

3.101. INT 21H, AH=44H, AL=0CH, MINOR CODE=65H -- GET ITERATION COUNT

Prior to Calling Function

	High	Low
AX	44H	0CH
BX	Handle	
CX	Category†	65H
DX	Offset of pointer to data buffer	
SP		
BP		
SI		
DI		
IP		
flags		
CS		
DS		
SS		
ES		
Buffer		

Upon Return from Function

	High	Low
AX	Error code (if carry flag set)	
BX		
CX		
DX		
SP		
BP		
SI		
DI		
IP		
flags		Carry flag*
CS		
DS		
SS		
ES		
Buffer	Iteration count	

*Carry flag set if error occurs.
†Category is one of:

1 = serial device
3 = display device
5 = parallel printer

Version: Applies to all versions of DOS beginning with 3.3.

Source: IBM DOS 3.3 Technical Reference, pages 6-158 through 6-166
IBM DOS 4.0 Technical Reference, pages C-12 through C-17
Microsoft MS-DOS 4.0 Programmer's Reference, pages 205 through 208
Microsoft MS-DOS 5.0 Programmer's Reference, page 307

See Also: 3.142. INT 21H, AH=59H -- Get Extended Error
3.191. ERROR Structure and Error Code Values
3.201. Code-Page Parameter Blocks
3.229. Device Request Header Status Field and Error Codes

3.102. INT 21H, AH=44H, AL=0CH, MINOR CODE=6AH -- QUERY SELECTED CODE PAGE

Prior to Calling Function

	High	*Low*
AX	44H	0CH
BX	Handle	
CX	Category†	6AH
DX	Offset of pointer to data buffer	
SP		
BP		
SI		
DI		
IP		
flags		
CS		
DS		
SS		
ES		
Buffer	Code page parm block or CODEPAGE structure	

Upon Return from Function

	High	*Low*
AX	Error code (if carry flag set)	
BX		
CX		
DX		
SP		
BP		
SI		
DI		
IP		
flags		Carry flag*
CS		
DS		
SS		
ES		
Buffer	Code page parm block or CODEPAGE structure	

*Carry flag set if error occurs.
†Category is one of:

1 = serial device
3 = display device
5 = parallel printer

Version: Applies to all versions of DOS beginning with 3.3.

Source: IBM DOS 3.3 Technical Reference, pages 6-158 through 6-166
IBM DOS 4.0 Technical Reference, pages C-12 through C-17
Microsoft MS-DOS 4.0 Programmer's Reference, pages 205 through 208
Microsoft MS-DOS 5.0 Programmer's Reference, page 308

See Also: 3.142. INT 21H, AH=59H -- Get Extended Error
3.191. ERROR Structure and Error Code Values
3.201. Code-Page Parameter Blocks
3.202. CODEPAGE Structure
3.229. Device Request Header Status Field and Error Codes

3.103. INT 21H, AH=44H, AL=0CH, MINOR CODE=6BH -- QUERY CODE-PAGE PREPARE LIST

Prior to Calling Function

Register	High	Low
AX	44H	0CH
BX	Handle	
CX	Category†	6BH
DX	Offset of pointer to data buffer	
SP		
BP		
SI		
DI		
IP		
flags		
CS		
DS		
SS		
ES		
Buffer	Code page parm block or CPLIST structure	

Upon Return from Function

Register	High	Low
AX	Error code (if carry flag set)	
BX		
CX		
DX		
SP		
BP		
SI		
DI		
IP		
flags		Carry flag*
CS		
DS		
SS		
ES		
Buffer	Code page parm block or CPLIST structure	

*Carry flag set if error occurs.
†Category is one of:

1 = serial device
3 = display device
5 = parallel printer

Version: Applies to all versions of DOS beginning with 3.3.

Source: IBM DOS 3.3 Technical Reference, pages 6-158 through 6-166
IBM DOS 4.0 Technical Reference, pages C-12 through C-17
Microsoft MS-DOS 4.0 Programmer's Reference, pages 205 through 208
Microsoft MS-DOS 5.0 Programmer's Reference, page 309

See Also: 3.142. INT 21H, AH=59H -- Get Extended Error
3.191. ERROR Structure and Error Code Values
3.201. Code-Page Parameter Blocks
3.205. CPLIST Structure
3.229. Device Request Header Status Field and Error Codes

3.104. INT 21H, AH=44H, AL=0CH, MINOR CODE=7FH -- GET DISPLAY MODE

Prior to Calling Function

Register	High	Low
AX	44H	0CH
BX	Handle	
CX	03H	7FH
DX	Offset of pointer to data buffer	
SP		
BP		
SI		
DI		
IP		
flags		
CS		
DS	Segment of pointer to data buffer	
SS		
ES		
Buffer	DISPLAYMODE structure	

Upon Return from Function

Register	High	Low
AX	Error code (if carry flag set)	
BX		
CX		
DX		
SP		
BP		
SI		
DI		
IP		
flags		Carry flag*
CS		
DS		
SS		
ES		
Buffer	DISPLAYMODE structure	

*Carry flag set if error occurs.

Version: Applies to all versions of DOS beginning with 4.0.

Source: IBM DOS 4.0 Technical Reference, pages C-12 through C-17
Microsoft MS-DOS 4.0 Programmer's Reference, pages 205 through 208
Microsoft MS-DOS 5.0 Programmer's Reference, page 310

See Also: 3.142. INT 21H, AH=59H -- Get Extended Error
3.191. ERROR Structure and Error Code Values
3.201. Code-Page Parameter Blocks
3.229. Device Request Header Status Field and Error Codes

3.105. INT 21H, AH=44H, AL=0DH, MINOR CODE=40H -- SET DEVICE PARAMETERS

Prior to Calling Function

Register	High	Low
AX	44H	0DH
BX	Drive	
CX	08H	40H
DX	Offset of pointer to parameter block	
SP		
BP		
SI		
DI		
IP		
flags		
CS		
DS	Segment of pointer to parameter block	
SS		
ES		
Buffer	DEVICEPARAMS structure	

Upon Return from Function

Register	High	Low
AX	Error code (if carry flag set)	
BX		
CX		
DX		
SP		
BP		
SI		
DI		
IP		
flags	Carry flag*	
CS		
DS		
SS		
ES		
Buffer		

*Carry flag set if error occurs.

Version: Applies to all versions of DOS beginning with 3.3.

Source: IBM DOS 3.3 Technical Reference, pages 6-166 through 6-181
IBM DOS 4.0 Technical Reference, pages C-18 through C-26
Microsoft MS-DOS 4.0 Programmer's Reference, pages 209 through 216
Microsoft MS-DOS 5.0 Programmer's Reference, page 311

See Also: 3.142. INT 21H, AH=59H -- Get Extended Error
3.171. DEVICEPARAMS Structure
3.184. Logical Drive Numbers
3.191. ERROR Structure and Error Code Values

3.106. INT 21H, AH=44H, AL=0DH, MINOR CODE=41H -- WRITE TRACK ON LOGICAL DRIVE

Prior to Calling Function

Register	High	Low
AX	44H	0DH
BX	Drive	
CX	08H	41H
DX	Offset of pointer to parameter block	
SP		
BP		
SI		
DI		
IP		
flags		
CS		
DS	Segment of pointer to parameter block	
SS		
ES		
Buffer	RWBLOCK structure	

Upon Return from Function

Register	High	Low
AX	Error code (if carry flag set)	
BX		
CX		
DX		
SP		
BP		
SI		
DI		
IP		
flags		Carry flag*
CS		
DS		
SS		
ES		
Buffer		

*Carry flag set if error occurs.

Version: Applies to all versions of DOS beginning with 3.3.

Source:
IBM DOS 3.3 Technical Reference, pages 6-166 through 6-181
IBM DOS 4.0 Technical Reference, pages C-18 through C-26
Microsoft MS-DOS 4.0 Programmer's Reference, pages 209 through 216
Microsoft MS-DOS 5.0 Programmer's Reference, page 312

See Also:
3.142. INT 21H, AH=59H -- Get Extended Error
3.171. DEVICEPARAMS Structure
3.182. RWBLOCK Structure
3.184. Logical Drive Numbers
3.191. ERROR Structure and Error Code Values

3.107. INT 21H, AH=44H, AL=0DH, MINOR CODE=42H -- FORMAT TRACK ON LOGICAL DRIVE

Prior to Calling Function

Register	High	Low
AX	44H	0DH
BX	Drive	
CX	08H	42H
DX	Offset of pointer to parameter block	
SP		
BP		
SI		
DI		
IP		
flags		
CS		
DS	Segment of pointer to parameter block	
SS		
ES		
Buffer	Format block or FVBLOCK structure	

Upon Return from Function

Register	High	Low
AX	Error code (if carry flag set)	
BX		
CX		
DX		
SP		
BP		
SI		
DI		
IP		
flags		Carry flag*
CS		
DS		
SS		
ES		
Buffer	Format block or FVBLOCK structure	

*Carry flag set if error occurs.

Version: Applies to all versions of DOS beginning with 3.3.

Source: IBM DOS 3.3 Technical Reference, pages 6-166 through 6-181
IBM DOS 4.0 Technical Reference, pages C-18 through C-26
Microsoft MS-DOS 4.0 Programmer's Reference, pages 209 through 216
Microsoft MS-DOS 5.0 Programmer's Reference, page 313

See Also: 3.142. INT 21H, AH=59H -- Get Extended Error
3.171. DEVICEPARAMS Structure
3.178. FVBLOCK Structure
3.184. Logical Drive Numbers
3.191. ERROR Structure and Error Code Values

3.108. INT 21H, AH=44H, AL=0DH, MINOR CODE=46H -- SET MEDIA ID

Prior to Calling Function

Register	High	Low
AX	44H	0DH
BX	Drive	
CX	08H	46H
DX	Offset of pointer to parameter block	
SP		
BP		
SI		
DI		
IP		
flags		
CS		
DS	Segment of pointer to parameter block	
SS		
ES		
Buffer	Media ID or MID structure	

Upon Return from Function

Register	High	Low
AX	Error code (if carry flag set)	
BX		
CX		
DX		
SP		
BP		
SI		
DI		
IP		
flags		Carry flag*
CS		
DS		
SS		
ES		
Buffer		

*Carry flag set if error occurs.

Version: Applies to all versions of DOS beginning with 4.0.

Source: IBM DOS 4.0 Technical Reference, pages C-18 through C-26
Microsoft MS-DOS 4.0 Programmer's Reference, pages 209 through 216
Microsoft MS-DOS 5.0 Programmer's Reference, page 314

See Also: 3.142. INT 21H, AH=59H -- Get Extended Error
3.171. DEVICEPARAMS Structure
3.179. MID Structure
3.184. Logical Drive Numbers
3.191. ERROR Structure and Error Code Values

3.109. INT 21H, AH=44H, AL=0DH, MINOR CODE=60H -- GET DEVICE PARAMETERS

Prior to Calling Function

	High	Low
AX	44H	0DH
BX	Drive	
CX	08H	60H
DX	Offset of pointer to parameter block	
SP		
BP		
SI		
DI		
IP		
flags		
CS		
DS	Segment of pointer to parameter block	
SS		
ES		
Buffer		

Upon Return from Function

	High	Low
AX	Error code (if carry flag set)	
BX		
CX		
DX		
SP		
BP		
SI		
DI		
IP		
flags		Carry flag*
CS		
DS		
SS		
ES		
Buffer	Device parms or DEVICEPARAMS structure	

*Carry flag set if error occurs.

Version: Applies to all versions of DOS beginning with 3.3.

Source:
IBM DOS 3.3 Technical Reference, pages 6-166 through 6-181
IBM DOS 4.0 Technical Reference, pages C-18 through C-26
Microsoft MS-DOS 4.0 Programmer's Reference, pages 209 through 216
Microsoft MS-DOS 5.0 Programmer's Reference, pages 315 through 316

See Also:
3.142. INT 21H, AH=59H -- Get Extended Error
3.171. DEVICEPARAMS Structure
3.184. Logical Drive Numbers
3.191. ERROR Structure and Error Code Values

3.110. INT 21H, AH=44H, AL=0DH, MINOR CODE=61H -- READ TRACK ON LOGICAL DRIVE

Prior to Calling Function

	High	Low
AX	44H	0DH
BX	Drive	
CX	08H	61H
DX	Offset of pointer to buffer	
SP		
BP		
SI		
DI		
IP		
flags		
CS		
DS	Segment of pointer to buffer	
SS		
ES		
Buffer		

Upon Return from Function

	High	Low
AX	Error code (if carry flag set)	
BX		
CX		
DX		
SP		
BP		
SI		
DI		
IP		
flags		Carry flag*
CS		
DS		
SS		
ES		
Buffer	Read block RWBLOCK structure	

*Carry flag set if error occurs.

Version: Applies to all versions of DOS beginning with 3.2.

Source: IBM DOS 3.3 Technical Reference, pages 6-166 through 6-181
IBM DOS 4.0 Technical Reference, pages C-18 through C-26
Microsoft MS-DOS 4.0 Programmer's Reference, pages 209 through 216
Microsoft MS-DOS 5.0 Programmer's Reference, page 317

See Also: 3.142. INT 21H, AH=59H -- Get Extended Error
3.171. DEVICEPARAMS Structure
3.182. RWBLOCK Structure
3.184. Logical Drive Numbers
3.191. ERROR Structure and Error Code Values

3.111. INT 21H, AH=44H, AL=0DH, MINOR CODE=62H -- VERIFY TRACK ON LOGICAL DRIVE

Prior to Calling Function

	High	*Low*
AX	44H	0DH
BX	Drive	
CX	08H	62H
DX	Offset of pointer to buffer	
SP		
BP		
SI		
DI		
IP		
flags		
CS		
DS	Segment of pointer to buffer	
SS		
ES		
Buffer	FVBLOCK structure	

Upon Return from Function

	High	*Low*
AX	Error code (if carry flag set)	
BX		
CX		
DX		
SP		
BP		
SI		
DI		
IP		
flags		Carry flag*
CS		
DS		
SS		
ES		
Buffer		

*Carry flag set if error occurs.

Version: Applies to all versions of DOS beginning with 3.2.

Source: IBM DOS 3.3 Technical Reference, pages 6-166 through 6-181
IBM DOS 4.0 Technical Reference, pages C-18 through C-26
Microsoft MS-DOS 4.0 Programmer's Reference, pages 209 through 216
Microsoft MS-DOS 5.0 Programmer's Reference, page 318

See Also: 3.142. INT 21H, AH=59H -- Get Extended Error
3.171. DEVICEPARAMS Structure
3.178. FVBLOCK Structure
3.184. Logical Drive Numbers
3.191. ERROR Structure and Error Code Values

3.112. INT 21H, AH=44H, AL=0DH, MINOR CODE=66H -- GET MEDIA ID

Prior to Calling Function

	High	Low
AX	44H	0DH
BX	Drive	
CX	08H	66H
DX	Offset of pointer to buffer	
SP		
BP		
SI		
DI		
IP		
flags		
CS		
DS	Segment of pointer to buffer	
SS		
ES		
Buffer		

Upon Return from Function

	High	Low
AX	Error code (if carry flag set)	
BX		
CX		
DX		
SP		
BP		
SI		
DI		
IP		
flags		Carry flag*
CS		
DS		
SS		
ES		
Buffer	Media ID or MID structure	

*Carry flag set if error occurs.

Version: Applies to all versions of DOS beginning with 4.0.

Source: IBM DOS 4.0 Technical Reference, pages C-18 through C-26
Microsoft MS-DOS 4.0 Programmer's Reference, pages 209 through 216
Microsoft MS-DOS 5.0 Programmer's Reference, page 319

See Also: 3.142. INT 21H, AH=59H -- Get Extended Error
3.171. DEVICEPARAMS Structure
3.179. MID Structure
3.184. Logical Drive Numbers
3.191. ERROR Structure and Error Code Values

3.113. INT 21H, AH=44H, AL=0DH, MINOR CODE=68H -- SENSE MEDIA TYPE

Prior to Calling Function

	High	Low
AX	44H	0DH
BX	Drive	
CX	08H	68H
DX	Offset of pointer to parameter block	
SP		
BP		
SI		
DI		
IP		
flags		
CS		
DS	Segment of pointer to parameter block	
SS		
ES		
Buffer		

Upon Return from Function

	High	Low
AX	Error code (if carry flag set)	
BX		
CX		
DX		
SP		
BP		
SI		
DI		
IP		
flags		Carry flag*
CS		
DS		
SS		
ES		
Buffer	Media type	

*Carry flag set if error occurs.

Version: Applies to all versions of DOS beginning with 5.0.

Source: Microsoft MS-DOS 5.0 Programmer's Reference, page 319

See Also:
3.142. INT 21H, AH=59H -- Get Extended Error
3.171. DEVICEPARAMS Structure
3.184. Logical Drive Numbers
3.191. ERROR Structure and Error Code Values

3.114. INT 21H, AH=44H, AL=0EH -- GET LOGICAL DRIVE MAP

Prior to Calling Function

	High	Low
AX	44H	0EH
BX		Logical drive number¥
CX		
DX		
SP		
BP		
SI		
DI		
IP		
flags		
CS		
DS		
SS		
ES		

Upon Return from Function

	High	Low
AX	Drive or error code (if carry flag set)†	
BX		
CX		
DX		
SP		
BP		
SI		
DI		
IP		
flags		Carry flag*
CS		
DS		
SS		
ES		

*Carry flag set if error occurs.
†AL returns physical drive data; 00=only one drive mapped to logical drive; 1-26(A-Z)=physical drive mapped to logical drive.
¥0=default, 1=A, and so on.

Version: Applies to all versions of DOS beginning with 3.2.

Source:
IBM DOS 3.3 Technical Reference, page 6-182
IBM DOS 4.0 Technical Reference, page C-27
Microsoft MS-DOS 4.0 Programmer's Reference, page 217
Microsoft MS-DOS 5.0 Programmer's Reference, page 321

See Also:
3.115. INT 21H, AH=44H, AL=0FH -- Set Logical Drive Map
3.142. INT 21H, AH=59H -- Get Extended Error
3.184. Logical Drive Numbers
3.191. ERROR Structure and Error Code Values

3.115. INT 21H, AH=44H, AL=0FH -- SET LOGICAL DRIVE MAP

Prior to Calling Function

	High	Low
AX	44H	0FH
BX		Logical drive number¥
CX		
DX		
SP		
BP		
SI		
DI		
IP		
flags		
CS		
DS		
SS		
ES		

Upon Return from Function

	High	Low
AX	Logical drive used or error code (if carry flag set)†	
BX		
CX		
DX		
SP		
BP		
SI		
DI		
IP		
flags		Carry flag*
CS		
DS		
SS		
ES		

*Carry flag set if error occurs.
†AL returns physical drive data; 00=only one drive mapped to logical drive; 1-26(A-Z)=physical drive mapped to logical drive.
¥0=default, 1=A, and so on.

Version: Applies to all versions of DOS beginning with 3.2.

Source:
IBM DOS 3.3 Technical Reference, pages 6-183 through 6-184
IBM DOS 4.0 Technical Reference, pages C-28 through C-29
Microsoft MS-DOS 4.0 Programmer's Reference, page 217
Microsoft MS-DOS 5.0 Programmer's Reference, page 322

See Also:
3.114. INT 21H, AH=44H, AL=0EH -- Get Logical Drive Map
3.142. INT 21H, AH=59H -- Get Extended Error
3.184. Logical Drive Numbers
3.191. ERROR Structure and Error Code Values

3.116. INT 21H, AH=44H, AL=10H -- QUERY IOCTL HANDLE

Prior to Calling Function

	High	Low
AX	44H	10H
BX	Handle	
CX	Category†	Function§
DX		
SP		
BP		
SI		
DI		
IP		
flags		
CS		
DS		
SS		
ES		

Upon Return from Function

	High	Low
AX	Error code (if carry flag set)	
BX		
CX		
DX		
SP		
BP		
SI		
DI		
IP		
flags		Carry flag*
CS		
DS		
SS		
ES		

*Carry flag set if error occurs.
†1=serial, 3=console, 5=parallel printer.
§45H=set iteration count, 65H=get iteration count.

Version: Applies to all versions of DOS beginning with 5.0.

Source: Microsoft MS-DOS 5.0 Programmer's Reference, page 323

See Also: 3.117. INT 21H, AH=44H,AL=11H -- Query IOCTL Device

3.117. INT 21H, AH=44H, AL=11H -- QUERY IOCTL DEVICE

Prior to Calling Function

	High	Low
AX	44H	11H
BX		Drive†
CX	8	Function§
DX		
SP		
BP		
SI		
DI		
IP		
flags		
CS		
DS		
SS		
ES		

Upon Return from Function

	High	Low
AX	Error code (if carry flag set)	
BX		
CX		
DX		
SP		
BP		
SI		
DI		
IP		
flags		Carry flag*
CS		
DS		
SS		
ES		

*Carry flag set if error occurs.
†0=default, 1=A, and so on.
§40H=set device parameters, 41H=write track on logical drive, 42H=format track on logical drive, 46H=set media ID, 60H=get device parameters, 61H=read track on logical drive, 62H=verify track on logical drive, 66H=get media ID, 68H=sense media type.

Version: Applies to all versions of DOS beginning with 5.0.

Source: Microsoft MS-DOS 5.0 Programmer's Reference, page 324

See Also: 3.116. INT 21H, AH=44H, AL=10H -- Query IOCTL Handle

3.118. INT 21H, AH=45H -- DUPLICATE FILE HANDLE

Prior to Calling Function

	High	Low
AX	45H	
BX	Old handle	
CX		
DX		
SP		
BP		
SI		
DI		
IP		
flags		
CS		
DS		
SS		
ES		

Upon Return from Function

	High	Low
AX	New handle or error code (if carry flag set)	
BX		
CX		
DX		
SP		
BP		
SI		
DI		
IP		
flags		Carry flag*
CS		
DS		
SS		
ES		

*Carry flag set if error occurs.

Version: Applies to all versions of DOS beginning with 2.0.

Source:
IBM DOS 3.3 Technical Reference, page 6-185
IBM DOS 4.0 Technical Reference, page B-95
Microsoft MS-DOS 4.0 Programmer's Reference, pages 218 through 219
Microsoft MS-DOS 5.0 Programmer's Reference, page 325

See Also:
3.119. INT 21H, AH=46H -- Force Duplicate File Handle
3.142. INT 21H, AH=59H -- Get Extended Error
3.191. ERROR Structure and Error Code Values

3.119. INT 21H, AH=46H -- FORCE DUPLICATE FILE HANDLE

Prior to Calling Function

Register	High	Low
AX	46H	
BX	Existing handle	
CX	Second handle	
DX		
SP		
BP		
SI		
DI		
IP		
flags		
CS		
DS		
SS		
ES		

Upon Return from Function

Register	High	Low
AX	Error code (if carry flag set)	
BX		
CX		
DX		
SP		
BP		
SI		
DI		
IP		
flags		Carry flag*
CS		
DS		
SS		
ES		

*Carry flag set if error occurs.

Version: Applies to all versions of DOS beginning with 2.0.

Note: Almost always used immediately after INT 21H, AH=45H -- Duplicate File Handle.

Source: IBM DOS 3.3 Technical Reference, pages 6-186 through 6-187
IBM DOS 4.0 Technical Reference, page B-96
Microsoft MS-DOS 4.0 Programmer's Reference, pages 220 through 221
Microsoft MS-DOS 5.0 Programmer's Reference, page 326

See Also: 3.118. INT 21H, AH=45H -- Duplicate File Handle
3.142. INT 21H, AH=59H -- Get Extended Error
3.191. ERROR Structure and Error Code Values

3.120. INT 21H, AH=47H -- GET CURRENT DIRECTORY

Prior to Calling Function

Register	High	Low
AX	47H	
BX		
CX		
DX		Logical drive number†
SP		
BP		
SI	Offset of pointer to 64-byte buffer	
DI		
IP		
flags		
CS		
DS	Segment of pointer to 64-byte buffer	
SS		
ES		
Buffer	Empty	

Upon Return from Function

Register	High	Low
AX	Error code (if carry flag set)	
BX		
CX		
DX		
SP		
BP		
SI		
DI		
IP		
flags		Carry flag*
CS		
DS		
SS		
ES		
Buffer	ASCIIZ pathname (if carry flag clear)	

*Carry flag set if error occurs.
†0=default, 1=A, and so on.

Version: Applies to all versions of DOS beginning with 2.0.

Note: Returned pathname does not begin with a backslash or drive ID.

Source:
IBM DOS 3.3 Technical Reference, pages 6-188 through 6-189
IBM DOS 4.0 Technical Reference, page B-97
Microsoft MS-DOS 4.0 Programmer's Reference, pages 222 through 223
Microsoft MS-DOS 5.0 Programmer's Reference, page 327

See Also:
3.074. INT 21H, AH=3BH -- Change Current Directory
3.142. INT 21H, AH=59H -- Get Extended Error
3.191. ERROR Structure and Error Code Values

3.121. INT 21H, AH=48H -- ALLOCATE MEMORY

Prior to Calling Function

	High	*Low*
AX	48H	
BX	Amount of memory requested	
CX		
DX		
SP		
BP		
SI		
DI		
IP		
flags		
CS		
DS		
SS		
ES		

Upon Return from Function

	High	*Low*
AX	Segment address or error code (if carry flag set)†	
BX	Paragraphs available (if carry flag set)	
CX		
DX		
SP		
BP		
SI		
DI		
IP		
flags		Carry flag*
CS		
DS		
SS		
ES		

*Carry flag set if error occurs.
†Segment address of allocated memory block.

Version: Applies to all versions of DOS beginning with 2.0.

Source:
IBM DOS 3.3 Technical Reference, pages 6-190 through 6-191
IBM DOS 4.0 Technical Reference, page B-98
Microsoft MS-DOS 4.0 Programmer's Reference, pages 224 through 225
Microsoft MS-DOS 5.0 Programmer's Reference, page 328

See Also:
3.122. INT 21H, AH=49H -- Free Allocated Memory
3.123. INT 21H, AH=4AH -- Set Memory Size Block
3.138. INT 21H, AH=58H, AL=00H -- Get Allocation Strategy
3.139. INT 21H, AH=58H, AL=01H -- Set Allocation Strategy
3.142. INT 21H, AH=59H -- Get Extended Error
3.191. ERROR Structure and Error Code Values
3.197. Memory Allocation Strategies

3.122. INT 21H, AH=49H -- FREE ALLOCATED MEMORY

Prior to Calling Function

Register	High	Low
AX	49H	
BX		
CX		
DX		
SP		
BP		
SI		
DI		
IP		
flags		
CS		
DS		
SS		
ES	Segment address of allocated block to free	

Upon Return from Function

Register	High	Low
AX	Error code (if carry flag set)	
BX		
CX		
DX		
SP		
BP		
SI		
DI		
IP		
flags		Carry flag*
CS		
DS		
SS		
ES		

*Carry flag set if error occurs.

Version: Applies to all versions of DOS beginning with 2.0.

Source:
IBM DOS 3.3 Technical Reference, page 6-192
IBM DOS 4.0 Technical Reference, page B-99
Microsoft MS-DOS 4.0 Programmer's Reference, pages 226 through 227
Microsoft MS-DOS 5.0 Programmer's Reference, page 329

See Also:
3.121. INT 21H, AH=48H -- Allocate Memory
3.123. INT 21H, AH=4AH -- Set Memory Size Block
3.138. INT 21H, AH=58H, AL=00H -- Get Allocation Strategy
3.139. INT 21H, AH=58H, AL=01H -- Set Allocation Strategy
3.142. INT 21H, AH=59H -- Get Extended Error
3.191. ERROR Structure and Error Code Values
3.197. Memory Allocation Strategies

3.123. INT 21H, AH=4AH -- SET MEMORY BLOCK SIZE

Prior to Calling Function

Register	High	Low
AX	4AH	
BX	Paragraphs of memory requested	
CX		
DX		
SP		
BP		
SI		
DI		
IP		
flags		
CS		
DS		
SS		
ES	Segment address of memory block to resize	

Upon Return from Function

Register	High	Low
AX	Error code (if carry flag set)	
BX	Paragraphs available (if carry flag set)	
CX		
DX		
SP		
BP		
SI		
DI		
IP		
flags		Carry flag*
CS		
DS		
SS		
ES		

*Carry flag set if error occurs.

Version: Applies to all versions of DOS beginning with 2.0.

Source:
IBM DOS 3.3 Technical Reference, pages 6-193 through 6-194
IBM DOS 4.0 Technical Reference, page B-100
Microsoft MS-DOS 4.0 Programmer's Reference, pages 228 through 229
Microsoft MS-DOS 5.0 Programmer's Reference, page 330

See Also:
3.121. INT 21H, AH=48H -- Allocate Memory
3.122. INT 21H, AH=49H -- Free Allocated Memory
3.138. INT 21H, AH=58H, AL=00H -- Get Allocation Strategy
3.139. INT 21H, AH=58H, AL=01H -- Set Allocation Strategy
3.142. INT 21H, AH=59H -- Get Extended Error
3.191. ERROR Structure and Error Code Values
3.197. Memory Allocation Strategies

3.124. INT 21H, AH=4BH, AL=00H -- LOAD AND EXECUTE PROGRAM

Prior to Calling Function

	High	*Low*
AX	4BH	00H
BX	Offset of pointer to parameter block†	
CX		
DX	Offset of pointer to program name	
SP		
BP		
SI		
DI		
IP		
flags		
CS		
DS	Segment of pointer to program name	
SS		
ES	Segment of pointer to parameter block†	

Upon Return from Function

	High	*Low*
AX	Error code (if carry flag set)	
BX	Destroyed	Destroyed
CX	Destroyed	Destroyed
DX	Destroyed	Destroyed
SP	Destroyed	
BP	Destroyed	
SI	Destroyed	
DI	Destroyed	
IP		
flags		Carry flag*
CS		
DS	Destroyed	
SS	Destroyed	
ES	Destroyed	

*Carry flag set if error occurs.
†In DOS 5.0, points to LOADEXEC structure.

Version: Applies to all versions of DOS beginning with 2.0.

Source:
IBM DOS 3.3 Technical Reference, pages 6-195 through 6-199
IBM DOS 4.0 Technical Reference, pages B-101 through B-104
Microsoft MS-DOS 4.0 Programmer's Reference, pages 230 through 233
Microsoft MS-DOS 5.0 Programmer's Reference, page 331

See Also:
3.061. INT 21H, AH=31H -- Keep Program
3.125. INT 21H, AH=4BH, AL=01H -- Load Program
3.126. INT 21H, AH=4BH, AL=03H -- Load Overlay
3.127. INT 21H, AH=4BH, AL=05H -- Set Execution State
3.142. INT 21H, AH=59H -- Get Extended Error
3.191. ERROR Structure and Error Code Values
3.194. LOADEXEC Structure

3.125. INT 21H, AH=4BH, AL=01H -- LOAD PROGRAM

Prior to Calling Function

Register	High	Low
AX	4BH	01H
BX	Offset of pointer to parameter block†	
CX		
DX	Offset of pointer to program name	
SP		
BP		
SI		
DI		
IP		
flags		
CS		
DS	Segment of pointer to program name	
SS		
ES	Segment of pointer to parameter block†	

Upon Return from Function

Register	High	Low
AX	Error code (if carry flag set)	
BX	Destroyed	Destroyed
CX	Destroyed	Destroyed
DX	Destroyed	Destroyed
SP	Destroyed	
BP	Destroyed	
SI	Destroyed	
DI	Destroyed	
IP		
flags		Carry flag*
CS		
DS	Destroyed	
SS	Destroyed	
ES	Destroyed	

*Carry flag set if error occurs.
†In DOS 5.0, points to LOAD structure.

Version: Applies to all versions of DOS beginning with 2.0.

Source:
IBM DOS 3.3 Technical Reference, pages 6-195 through 6-199
IBM DOS 4.0 Technical Reference, pages B-101 through B-104
Microsoft MS-DOS 4.0 Programmer's Reference, pages 230 through 233
Microsoft MS-DOS 5.0 Programmer's Reference, page 333

See Also:
3.061. INT 21H, AH=31H -- Keep Program
3.124. INT 21H, AH=4BH, AL=00H -- Load and Execute Program
3.126. INT 21H, AH=4BH, AL=03H -- Load Overlay
3.127. INT 21H, AH=4BH, AL=05H -- Set Execution State
3.142. INT 21H, AH=59H -- Get Extended Error
3.191. ERROR Structure and Error Code Values
3.194. LOADEXEC Structure
3.193. LOAD Structure

3.126. INT 21H, AH=4BH, AL=03H -- LOAD OVERLAY

Prior to Calling Function

Register	High	Low
AX	4BH	03H
BX	Offset of pointer to parameter block†	
CX		
DX	Offset of pointer to program name	
SP		
BP		
SI		
DI		
IP		
flags		
CS		
DS	Segment of pointer to program name	
SS		
ES	Segment of pointer to parameter block†	

Upon Return from Function

Register	High	Low
AX	Error code (if carry flag set)	
BX	Destroyed	Destroyed
CX	Destroyed	Destroyed
DX	Destroyed	Destroyed
SP	Destroyed	
BP	Destroyed	
SI	Destroyed	
DI	Destroyed	
IP		
flags		Carry flag*
CS		
DS	Destroyed	
SS	Destroyed	
ES	Destroyed	

*Carry flag set if error occurs.
†In DOS 5.0, points to LOADOVERLAY structure.

Version: Applies to all versions of DOS beginning with 2.0.

Source: IBM DOS 3.3 Technical Reference, pages 6-195 through 6-199
IBM DOS 4.0 Technical Reference, pages B-101 through B-104
Microsoft MS-DOS 4.0 Programmer's Reference, pages 234 through 236
Microsoft MS-DOS 5.0 Programmer's Reference, page 334

See Also: 3.061. INT 21H, AH=31H -- Keep Program
3.124. INT 21H, AH=4BH, AL=00H -- Load and Execute Program
3.125. INT 21H, AH=4BH, AL=01H -- Load Program
3.127. INT 21H, AH=4BH, AL=05H -- Set Execution State
3.142. INT 21H, AH=59H -- Get Extended Error
3.191. ERROR Structure and Error Code Values
3.195. LOADOVERLAY Structure

3.127. INT 21H, AH=4BH, AL=05H -- SET EXECUTION STATE

Prior to Calling Function

	High	Low
AX	4BH	05H
BX		
CX		
DX	Offset of pointer to EXECSTATE structure	
SP		
BP		
SI		
DI		
IP		
flags		
CS		
DS	Segment of pointer to EXECSTATE structure	
SS		
ES		

*Carry flag set if error occurs.

Upon Return from Function

Function returns no values.

Version: Applies to all versions of DOS beginning with 5.0.

Source: Microsoft MS-DOS 5.0 Programmer's Reference, page 335

See Also: 3.061. INT 21H, AH=31H -- Keep Program
3.124. INT 21H, AH=4BH, AL=00H -- Load and Execute Program
3.125. INT 21H, AH=4BH, AL=01H -- Load Program
3.126. INT 21H, AH=4BH, AL=03H -- Load Overlay
3.142. INT 21H, AH=59H -- Get Extended Error
3.191. ERROR Structure and Error Code Values
3.192. EXECSTATE Structure
3.195. LOADOVERLAY Structure

3.128. INT 21H, AH=4CH -- END PROGRAM

Prior to Calling Function

Register	High	Low
AX	4CH	Return code
BX		
CX		
DX		
SP		
BP		
SI		
DI		
IP		
flags		
CS		
DS		
SS		
ES		

Upon Return from Function

Function returns no values.
Functions performs the following:
- Flushes file buffers.
- Restores termination handler address from PSP:000AH.
- Restores Ctrl+C exit address from PSP:000EH.
- Restores critical error handler address from PSP:0012H.
- Frees memory owned by terminating process.

Version: Applies to all versions of DOS beginning with 2.0.

Note:
- All open files are closed by this function.
- You must remove all file-sharing locks issued by process before calling this function.

Source:
IBM DOS 3.3 Technical Reference, page 6-200
IBM DOS 4.0 Technical Reference, page B-105
Microsoft MS-DOS 4.0 Programmer's Reference, pages 237 through 238
Microsoft MS-DOS 5.0 Programmer's Reference, page 336

See Also:
3.061. INT 21H, AH=31H -- Keep Program
3.129. INT 21H, AH=4DH -- Get Child-Program Return Value

3.129. INT 21H, AH=4DH -- GET CHILD-PROGRAM RETURN VALUE

Prior to Calling Function

Register	High	Low
AX	4DH	
BX		
CX		
DX		
SP		
BP		
SI		
DI		
IP		
flags		
CS		
DS		
SS		
ES		

Upon Return from Function

Register	High	Low
AX	Termination method*	Return value
BX		
CX		
DX		
SP		
BP		
SI		
DI		
IP		
flags		
CS		
DS		
SS		
ES		

*0=normal 4CH terminate; 1=Ctrl+C pressed; 2=critical device error; 3=terminated by Keep Program function.

Version: Applies to all versions of DOS beginning with 2.0.

Source:
IBM DOS 3.3 Technical Reference, page 6-201
IBM DOS 4.0 Technical Reference, page B-106
Microsoft MS-DOS 4.0 Programmer's Reference, pages 239 through 240
Microsoft MS-DOS 5.0 Programmer's Reference, page 337

See Also:
3.061. INT 21H, AH=31H -- Keep Program
3.128. INT 21H, AH=4CH -- End Program

3.130. INT 21H, AH=4EH -- FIND FIRST FILE

Prior to Calling Function

	High	Low
AX	4EH	
BX		
CX	0	Attributes¥
DX	Offset of pointer to pathname	
SP		
BP		
SI		
DI		
IP		
flags		
CS		
DS	Segment of pointer to pathname	
SS		
ES		
DTA	Empty	
Pathname	ASCIIZ string†	

Upon Return from Function

	High	Low
AX	Error code (if carry flag set)	
BX		
CX		
DX		
SP		
BP		
SI		
DI		
IP		
flags		Carry flag*
CS		
DS		
SS		
ES		
DTA	File info or FILEINFO structure	
Pathname	Unchanged	

*Carry flag set if error occurs.
¥Attributes:
- 0000H=Normal
- 0001H=Read Only
- 0002H=Hidden
- 0004H=System File
- 0008H=Volume ID
- 0010H=Directory, not file

†Can contain global wildcards; network paths not allowed.

Version: Applies to all versions of DOS beginning with 2.0.

Source:
IBM DOS 3.3 Technical Reference, pages 6-202 through 6-203
IBM DOS 4.0 Technical Reference, pages B-107 through B-108
Microsoft MS-DOS 4.0 Programmer's Reference, pages 241 through 242
Microsoft MS-DOS 5.0 Programmer's Reference, pages 338 through 339

See Also:
2.19. File Attribute Byte
2.20. Date/Time Formats
3.033. INT 21H, AH=11H -- Find First File with FCB
3.034. INT 21H, AH=12H -- Find Next File with FCB
3.131. INT 21H, AH=4FH -- Find Next File
3.142. INT 21H, AH=59H -- Get Extended Error
3.177. FILEINFO Structure
3.191. ERROR Structure and Error Code Values

3.131. INT 21H, AH=4FH -- FIND NEXT FILE

Prior to Calling Function

	High	Low
AX	4FH	
BX		
CX		
DX		
SP		
BP		
SI		
DI		
IP		
flags		
CS		
DS		
SS		
ES		
DTA	Data about previously found file	

Upon Return from Function

	High	Low
AX	Error code (if carry flag set)	
BX		
CX		
DX		
SP		
BP		
SI		
DI		
IP		
flags		Carry flag*
CS		
DS		
SS		
ES		
DTA	FILEINFO structure (if carry flag clear)	

*Carry flag set if error occurs.

Version: Applies to all versions of DOS beginning with 2.0.

Note: This function can be used only after a call to function 4EH.

Source:
IBM DOS 3.3 Technical Reference, page 6-204
IBM DOS 4.0 Technical Reference, page B-109
Microsoft MS-DOS 4.0 Programmer's Reference, pages 244 through 245
Microsoft MS-DOS 5.0 Programmer's Reference, page 340

See Also:
2.19. File Attribute Byte
2.20. Date/Time Formats
3.033. INT 21H, AH=11H -- Find First File with FCB
3.034. INT 21H, AH=12H -- Find Next File with FCB
3.130. INT 21H, AH=4EH -- Find First File
3.142. INT 21H, AH=59H -- Get Extended Error
3.177. FILEINFO Structure
3.191. ERROR Structure and Error Code Values

3.132. INT 21H, AH=50H -- SET PSP ADDRESS

Prior to Calling Function

	High	Low
AX	50H	
BX	Segment address of new PSP	
CX		
DX		
SP		
BP		
SI		
DI		
IP		
flags		
CS		
DS		
SS		
ES		

Upon Return from Function

Function returns no values.

Source: Microsoft MS-DOS 5.0 Programmer's Reference, page 341

See Also: 3.133. INT 21H, AH=51H -- Get PSP Address

3.133. INT 21H, AH=51H -- GET PSP ADDRESS

Prior to Calling Function

	High	Low
AX	51H	
BX		
CX		
DX		
SP		
BP		
SI		
DI		
IP		
flags		
CS		
DS		
SS		
ES		

Upon Return from Function

	High	Low
AX		
BX	Segment address of current PSP	
CX		
DX		
SP		
BP		
SI		
DI		
IP		
flags		
CS		
DS		
SS		
ES		

Note: Functions 51H and 62H are identical. Programs can use either function to get the segment address of the current PSP.

Source: Microsoft MS-DOS 5.0 Programmer's Reference, page 342

See Also: 3.132. INT 21H, AH=50H -- Set PSP Address

3.134. INT 21H, AH=54H -- GET VERIFY STATE

Prior to Calling Function

	High	Low
AX	54H	
BX		
CX		
DX		
SP		
BP		
SI		
DI		
IP		
flags		
CS		
DS		
SS		
ES		

Upon Return from Function

	High	Low
AX		Verify state*
BX		
CX		
DX		
SP		
BP		
SI		
DI		
IP		
flags		
CS		
DS		
SS		
ES		

*0=no verify after write; 01=verify after write.

Version: Applies to all versions of DOS beginning with 2.0.

Source: IBM DOS 3.3 Technical Reference, page 6-205
IBM DOS 4.0 Technical Reference, page B-110
Microsoft MS-DOS 4.0 Programmer's Reference, pages 246 through 247
Microsoft MS-DOS 5.0 Programmer's Reference, page 343

See Also: 3.058. INT 21H, AH=2EH -- Set/Reset Verify Flag

3.135. INT 21H, AH=56H -- RENAME FILE

Prior to Calling Function

Register	High	Low
AX	56H	
BX		
CX		
DX	Offset of pointer to old pathname	
SP		
BP		
SI		
DI	Offset of pointer to new pathname	
IP		
flags		
CS		
DS	Segment of pointer to old pathname	
SS		
ES	Segment of pointer to new pathname	

Upon Return from Function

Register	High	Low
AX	Error code (if carry flag set)	
BX		
CX		
DX		
SP		
BP		
SI		
DI		
IP		
flags		Carry flag*
CS		
DS		
SS		
ES		

*Carry flag set if error occurs.

Version: • Applies to all versions of DOS beginning with 2.0.

Note:
- Requires create and delete access rights on networks.
- Wildcard characters must not be used in the pathname.
- If the directory path is not the same, but the file name and type specified are, the file is "moved" to the new directory.
- You cannot move a file between drives.

Source:
IBM DOS 3.3 Technical Reference, pages 6-206 through 6-207
IBM DOS 4.0 Technical Reference, page B-111
Microsoft MS-DOS 4.0 Programmer's Reference, pages 248 through 249
Microsoft MS-DOS 5.0 Programmer's Reference, page 344

See Also:
3.039. INT 21H, AH=17H -- Rename File with FCB
3.142. INT 21H, AH=59H -- Get Extended Error
3.191. ERROR Structure and Error Code Values

3.136. INT 21H, AH=57H, AL=00H -- GET FILE DATE AND TIME

Prior to Calling Function

Register	High	Low
AX	57H	00H
BX	Handle	
CX		
DX		
SP		
BP		
SI		
DI		
IP		
flags		
CS		
DS		
SS		
ES		

Upon Return from Function

Register	High	Low
AX	Error code (if carry flag set)	
BX		
CX	Time file last changed†	
DX	Date file last changed¥	
SP		
BP		
SI		
DI		
IP		
flags		Carry flag*
CS		
DS		
SS		
ES		

*Carry flag set if error occurs.
†Time format:
Bits 0-4=second divided by 2
Bits 5-10=minute (0-59)
Bits 11-15=hour (0-23)
¥Date format:
Bits 0-4=day of month (1-31)
Bits 5-8=month (1-12)
Bits 9-15=year offset from 1980 (add 1980 to get actual year)

Version: Applies to all versions of DOS beginning with 2.0.

Source: IBM DOS 3.3 Technical Reference, pages 6-208 through 6-209
IBM DOS 4.0 Technical Reference, page B-112
Microsoft MS-DOS 4.0 Programmer's Reference, pages 250 through 251
Microsoft MS-DOS 5.0 Programmer's Reference, page 345

See Also: 2.22. Date/Time Formats
3.142. INT 21H, AH=59H -- Get Extended Error
3.191. ERROR Structure and Error Code Values

3.137. INT 21H, AH=57H, AL=01H -- SET FILE DATE AND TIME

Prior to Calling Function

	High	*Low*
AX	57H	01H
BX	Handle	
CX	Time to be set†	
DX	Date to be set¥	
SP		
BP		
SI		
DI		
IP		
flags		
CS		
DS		
SS		
ES		

Upon Return from Function

	High	*Low*
AX	Error code (if carry flag set)	
BX		
CX		
DX		
SP		
BP		
SI		
DI		
IP		
flags		Carry flag*
CS		
DS		
SS		
ES		

*Carry flag set if error occurs.
†Time format:
Bits 0-4=second divided by 2
Bits 5-10=minute (0-59)
Bits 11-15=hour (0-23)
¥Date format:
Bits 0-4=day of month (1-31)
Bits 5-8=month (1-12)
Bits 9-15=year offset from 1980 (add 1980 to get actual year)

Version: Applies to all versions of DOS beginning with 2.0.

Source: IBM DOS 3.3 Technical Reference, pages 6-208 through 6-209
IBM DOS 4.0 Technical Reference, page B-112
Microsoft MS-DOS 4.0 Programmer's Reference, pages 250 through 251
Microsoft MS-DOS 5.0 Programmer's Reference, page 346

See Also: 2.20. Date/Time Formats
3.142. INT 21H, AH=59H -- Get Extended Error
3.191. ERROR Structure and Error Code Values

3.138. INT 21H, AH=58H, AL=00H -- GET ALLOCATION STRATEGY

Prior to Calling Function

	High	Low
AX	58H	00H
BX		
CX		
DX		
SP		
BP		
SI		
DI		
IP		
flags		
CS		
DS		
SS		
ES		

Upon Return from Function

	High	Low
AX	Strategy or error code (if carry flag set)†	
BX		
CX		
DX		
SP		
BP		
SI		
DI		
IP		
flags		Carry flag*
CS		
DS		
SS		
ES		

*Carry flag set if error occurs.
†Allocation strategy values:
00=first fit low (default)
01=best fit low
02=last fit low
40=first fit high only
41=best fit high only
42=last fit high only
80=first fit high
81=best fit high
82=last fit high

Version: Applies to all versions of DOS beginning with 3.0.

Source: Microsoft MS-DOS 3.2 Programmer's Reference, page 1-214
Microsoft MS-DOS 4.0 Programmer's Reference, pages 252 through 253
Microsoft MS-DOS 5.0 Programmer's Reference, page 347
Not documented in IBM DOS 3.3 or 4.0 Technical References

See Also: 3.121. INT 21H, AH=48H -- Allocate Memory
3.123. INT 21H, AH=4AH -- Set Memory Size Block
3.142. INT 21H, AH=59H -- Get Extended Error
3.191. ERROR Structure and Error Code Values
3.197. Memory Allocation Strategies

3.139. INT 21H, AH=58H, AL=01H -- SET ALLOCATION STRATEGY

Prior to Calling Function

	High	Low
AX	58H	01H
BX	Allocation strategy†	
CX		
DX		
SP		
BP		
SI		
DI		
IP		
flags		
CS		
DS		
SS		
ES		

Upon Return from Function

	High	Low
AX	Error code (if carry flag set)	
BX		
CX		
DX		
SP		
BP		
SI		
DI		
IP		
flags		Carry flag*
CS		
DS		
SS		
ES		

*Carry flag set if error occurs.
†Allocation strategy values:
00=first fit low (default)
01=best fit low
02=last fit low
40=first fit high only
41=best fit high only
42=last fit high only
80=first fit high
81=best fit high
82=last fit high

Version: Applies to all versions of DOS beginning with 3.0.

Source: Microsoft MS-DOS 3.2 Programmer's Reference, page 1-214
Microsoft MS-DOS 4.0 Programmer's Reference, pages 252 through 253
Microsoft MS-DOS 5.0 Programmer's Reference, pages 348 through 349
Not documented in IBM DOS 3.3 or 4.0 Technical Reference

See Also: 3.121. INT 21H, AH=48H -- Allocate Memory
3.123. INT 21H, AH=4AH -- Set Memory Size Block
3.142. INT 21H, AH=59H -- Get Extended Error
3.191. ERROR Structure and Error Code Values
3.197. Memory Allocation Strategies

3.140. INT 21H, AH=58H, AL=02H -- GET UPPER MEMORY LINK

Prior to Calling Function

Register	High	Low
AX	58H	02H
BX		
CX		
DX		
SP		
BP		
SI		
DI		
IP		
flags		
CS		
DS		
SS		
ES		

Upon Return from Function

Register	High	Low
AX		00 or 01†
BX		
CX		
DX		
SP		
BP		
SI		
DI		
IP		
flags	Carry flag*	
CS		
DS		
SS		
ES		

*Carry flag set if error occurs.
†01=upper memory area linked and no error; otherwise 00H.

Version: Applies to all versions of DOS beginning with 5.0.

Source: Microsoft MS-DOS 5.0 Programmer's Reference, page 350

See Also: 3.141. INT 21H, AH=58H, AL=03H -- Set Upper Memory Link

3.141. INT 21H, AH=58H, AL=03H -- SET UPPER MEMORY LINK

Prior to Calling Function

Register	High	Low
AX	58H	03H
BX	Link flag†	
CX		
DX		
SP		
BP		
SI		
DI		
IP		
flags		
CS		
DS		
SS		
ES		

Upon Return from Function

Register	High	Low
AX	Error code (if carry flag set)	
BX		
CX		
DX		
SP		
BP		
SI		
DI		
IP		
flags		Carry flag*
CS		
DS		
SS		
ES		

*Carry flag set if error occurs.
†01=upper memory area linked, 00H=unlinked.

Version: Applies to all versions of DOS beginning with 5.0.

Source: Microsoft MS-DOS 5.0 Programmer's Reference, page 351

See Also: 3.140. INT 21H, AH=58H, AL=02H -- Get Upper Memory Link

3.142. INT 21H, AH=59H -- GET EXTENDED ERROR

Prior to Calling Function

Register	High	Low
AX	59H	
BX		
CX		
DX		
SP		
BP		
SI		
DI		
IP		
flags		
CS		
DS		
SS		
ES		

Upon Return from Function

Register	High	Low
AX	Extended error code (of last error)	
BX	Error class	Suggested action
CX	Location of error	Destroyed*
DX	Destroyed*	Destroyed*
SP		
BP	Destroyed*	
SI	Destroyed*	
DI	Destroyed*	
IP		
flags		
CS		
DS	Destroyed*	
SS		
ES	Destroyed*	

*These registers are not preserved by DOS.

Version: Applies to all versions of DOS beginning with 3.0.

Source: IBM DOS 3.3 Technical Reference, pages 6-210 through 6-212
IBM DOS 4.0 Technical Reference, pages B-113 through B-114
Microsoft MS-DOS 4.0 Programmer's Reference, pages 254 through 255
Microsoft MS-DOS 5.0 Programmer's Reference, pages 352 through 353

See Also: 3.191. ERROR Structure and Error Code Values

3.143. INT 21H, AH=5AH -- CREATE TEMPORARY FILE

Prior to Calling Function

	High	Low
AX	5AH	
BX		
CX	0	Attribute byte¥
DX	Offset of pointer to special pathname†	
SP		
BP		
SI		
DI		
IP		
flags		
CS		
DS	Segment of pointer to special pathname†	
SS		
ES		
Pathname	Pathname	

Upon Return from Function

	High	Low
AX	Handle or error code (if carry flag set)	
BX		
CX		
DX		
SP		
BP		
SI		
DI		
IP		
flags		Carry flag*
CS		
DS		
SS		
ES		
Pathname	Pathname+filename	

*Carry flag set if error occurs.
†Pathname, followed by backslash (\), followed by 14 bytes of 00H
¥Attributes:
0000H=Normal
0001H=Read-only
0002H=Hidden
0003H=System file
0020H=Archive

Version:
- Applies to all versions of DOS beginning with 3.0.
- Requires create access rights on network.

Source:
IBM DOS 3.3 Technical Reference, page 6-213
IBM DOS 4.0 Technical Reference, pages B-115 through B-116
Microsoft MS-DOS 4.0 Programmer's Reference, pages 258 through 260
Microsoft MS-DOS 5.0 Programmer's Reference, page 354

See Also:
2.19. File Attribute Byte
3.038. INT 21H, AH=16H -- Create File with FCB
3.075. INT 21H, AH=3CH -- Create File with Handle
3.142. INT 21H, AH=59H -- Get Extended Error
3.144. INT 21H, AH=5BH -- Create New File
3.191. ERROR Structure and Error Code Values

3.144. INT 21H, AH=5BH -- CREATE NEW FILE

Prior to Calling Function

	High	Low
AX	5BH	
BX		
CX	0	Attribute byte¥
DX	Offset of pointer to pathname	
SP		
BP		
SI		
DI		
IP		
flags		
CS		
DS	Segment of pointer to pathname	
SS		
ES		

Upon Return from Function

	High	Low
AX	Handle or error code (if carry flag set)	
BX		
CX		
DX		
SP		
BP		
SI		
DI		
IP		
flags		Carry flag*
CS		
DS		
SS		
ES		

*Carry flag set if error occurs.
¥Attributes: 0000H=Normal
0000H=Normal
0001H=Read-only
0002H=Hidden
0004H=System file
0020H=Archive

Version:
- Applies to all versions of DOS beginning with 3.0.
- Requires create access rights on networks.

Source:
IBM DOS 3.3 Technical Reference, page 6-215
IBM DOS 4.0 Technical Reference, page B-117
Microsoft MS-DOS 4.0 Programmer's Reference, pages 261 through 262
Microsoft MS-DOS 5.0 Programmer's Reference, page 355

See Also:
2.19. File Attribute Byte
3.038. INT 21H, AH=16H -- Create File with FCB
3.075. INT 21H, AH=3CH -- Create File with Handle
3.142. INT 21H, AH=59H -- Get Extended Error
3.143. INT 21H, AH=5AH -- Create Temporary File
3.191. ERROR Structure and Error Code Values

3.145. INT 21H, AH=5CH, AL=00H -- LOCK FILE

Prior to Calling Function

	High	Low
AX	5CH	00H
BX	Handle	
CX	High order of offset to region in file to lock	
DX	Low order of offset to region in file to lock	
SP		
BP		
SI	High order of length of region in file to lock	
DI	Low order of length of region in file to lock	
IP		
flags		
CS		
DS		
SS		
ES		

Upon Return from Function

	High	Low
AX	Error code (if carry flag set)	
BX		
CX		
DX		
SP		
BP		
SI		
DI		
IP		
flags		Carry flag*
CS		
DS		
SS		
ES		

*Carry flag set if error occurs.

Version: Applies to all versions of DOS beginning with 3.0.

Note: File sharing must be loaded before using lock on a local computer.

Source: IBM DOS 3.3 Technical Reference, pages 6-216 through 6-218
IBM DOS 4.0 Technical Reference, pages B-118 through B-120
Microsoft MS-DOS 4.0 Programmer's Reference, pages 263 through 265
Microsoft MS-DOS 5.0 Programmer's Reference, page 356

See Also: 3.142. INT 21H, AH=59H -- Get Extended Error
3.191. ERROR Structure and Error Code Values

3.146. INT 21H, AH=5CH, AL=01H -- UNLOCK FILE

Prior to Calling Function

	High	*Low*
AX	5CH	01H
BX	Handle	
CX	High order of offset to region in file to unlock	
DX	Low order of offset to region in file to unlock	
SP		
BP		
SI	High order of length of region in file to unlock	
DI	Low order of length of region in file to unlock	
IP		
flags		
CS		
DS		
SS		
ES		

Upon Return from Function

	High	*Low*
AX	Error code (if carry flag set)	
BX		
CX		
DX		
SP		
BP		
SI		
DI		
IP		
flags		Carry flag*
CS		
DS		
SS		
ES		

*Carry flag set if error occurs.

Version: Applies to all versions of DOS beginning with 3.0.

Note: Region must be same as one locked with Function 5CH, 00H.

Source: IBM DOS 3.3 Technical Reference, pages 6-216 through 6-218
IBM DOS 4.0 Technical Reference, pages B-118 through B-120
Microsoft MS-DOS 4.0 Programmer's Reference, pages 266 through 268
Microsoft MS-DOS 5.0 Programmer's Reference, pages 356 through 357

See Also: 3.142. INT 21H, AH=59H -- Get Extended Error
3.145. INT 21H, AH=5CH, AL=00H -- Lock File
3.191. ERROR Structure and Error Code Values

3.147. INT 21H, AH=5DH, AL=0AH -- SET EXTENDED ERROR

Prior to Calling Function

	High	Low
AX	5DH	0AH
BX		
CX		
DX		
SP		
BP		
SI	Offset of pointer to ERROR structure	
DI		
IP		
flags		
CS		
DS		
SS	Segment of pointer to ERROR structure	
ES		

Upon Return from Function

Function returns no values.

Source: Microsoft MS-DOS 5.0 Programmer's Reference, page 358

See Also: 3.142. INT 21H, AH=59H -- Get Extended Error
3.191. ERROR Structure and Error Code Values

3.148. INT 21H, AH=5EH, AL=00H -- GET MACHINE NAME

Prior to Calling Function

	High	Low
AX	5EH	00H
BX		
CX		
DX	Offset of pointer to 16-byte buffer	
SP		
BP		
SI		
DI		
IP		
flags		
CS		
DS	Segment of pointer to 16-byte buffer	
SS		
ES		
Buffer	Empty	

Upon Return from Function

	High	Low
AX	Error code (if carry flag set)	
BX		
CX	Validity†	Netbios # for local
DX	Offset of pointer to 16-byte buffer	
SP		
BP		
SI		
DI		
IP		
flags	Carry flag*	
CS		
DS	Segment of pointer to 16-byte buffer	
SS		
ES		
Buffer	Network name	

*Carry flag set if error occurs.
†0=invalid network device, nonzero=valid.

Version: Applies to all versions of DOS beginning with 3.1.

Source: IBM DOS 3.3 Technical Reference, pages 6-219 through 6-220
IBM DOS 4.0 Technical Reference, page B-121
Microsoft MS-DOS 4.0 Programmer's Reference, pages 269 through 270
Microsoft MS-DOS 5.0 Programmer's Reference, page 359

See Also: 3.142. INT 21H, AH=59H -- Get Extended Error
3.191. ERROR Structure and Error Code Values

3.149. INT 21H, AH=5EH, AL=02H -- SET PRINTER SETUP

Prior to Calling Function

	High	Low
AX	5EH	02H
BX	Assignment list index	
CX	Length of printer setup string	
DX	Offset of pointer to setup string	
SP		
BP		
SI		
DI		
IP		
flags		
CS		
DS	Segment of pointer to setup string	
SS		
ES		
String	Printer setup string	

Upon Return from function

	High	Low
AX	Error code (if carry flag set)	
BX		
CX		
DX		
SP		
BP		
SI		
DI		
IP		
flags		Carry flag*
CS		
DS		
SS		
ES		
Buffer	Unchanged string	

*Carry flag set if error occurs.

Version: Applies to all versions of DOS beginning with 3.1.

Note:
- Printer setup string cannot be longer than 64 bytes.
- Network must be running.

Source:
IBM DOS 3.3 Technical Reference, pages 6-221 through 6-222
IBM DOS 4.0 Technical Reference, page B-122
Microsoft MS-DOS 4.0 Programmer's Reference, pages 271 through 272
Microsoft MS-DOS 5.0 Programmer's Reference, page 360

See Also:
3.142. INT 21H, AH=59H -- Get Extended Error
3.150. INT 21H, AH=5EH, AL=03H -- Get Printer Setup
3.191. ERROR Structure and Error Code Values

3.150. INT 21H, AH=5EH, AL=03H -- GET PRINTER SETUP

Prior to Calling Function

Register	High	Low
AX	5EH	03H
BX	Assignment list index	
CX		
DX		
SP		
BP		
SI		
DI	Offset of pointer to 64-byte buffer	
IP		
flags		
CS		
DS		
SS		
ES	Segment of pointer to 64-byte buffer	
Buffer	Empty	

Upon Return from Function

Register	High	Low
AX	Error code (if carry flag set)	
BX		
CX	Length of printer string	
DX		
SP		
BP		
SI		
DI		
IP		
flags		Carry flag*
CS		
DS		
SS		
ES		
Buffer	Setup string	

*Carry flag set if error occurs.

Version: Applies to all versions of DOS beginning with 3.1.

Note: Network must be running.

Source: IBM DOS 3.3 Technical Reference, pages 6-223 through 6-224
IBM DOS 4.0 Technical Reference, page B-123
Microsoft MS-DOS 4.0 Programmer's Reference, pages 271 through 272
Microsoft MS-DOS 5.0 Programmer's Reference, page 361

See Also: 3.142. INT 21H, AH=59H -- Get Extended Error
3.149. INT 21H, AH=5EH, AL=02H -- Set Printer Setup
3.191. ERROR Structure and Error Code Values

3.151. INT 21H, AH=5FH, AL=02H -- GET ASSIGN-LIST ENTRY

Prior to Calling Function

	High	*Low*
AX	5FH	02H
BX	Assignment list index	
CX		
DX		
SP		
BP		
SI	Offset of pointer to 16-byte local name buffer¥	
DI	Offset of pointer to 128-byte network name buffer	
IP		
flags		
CS		
DS	Segment of pointer to 16-byte local name buffer¥	
SS		
ES	Segment of pointer to 128-byte network name buffer	
16-byte buffer	Empty	
128-byte buffer	Empty	

Upon Return from Function

	High	*Low*
AX	Error code (if carry flag set)	
BX	Status§	Code (if carry flag clear)†
CX	Stored user value	
DX	Destroyed	Destroyed
SP		
BP	Destroyed	
SI		
DI		
IP		
flags		Carry flag*
CS		
DS		
SS		
ES		
16-byte buffer	Local name (ASCIIZ string)	
128-byte buffer	Network name (ASCIIZ string)	

*Carry flag set if error occurs.
†03=printer device; 04=drive device
§0=available network device, 1=temporarily unavailable device
¥IBM sources indicate that this buffer is 128 bytes.

Version: Applies to all versions of DOS beginning with 3.1.

Note: Network must be running.

Source:
IBM DOS 3.3 Technical Reference, pages 6-225 through 6-226
IBM DOS 4.0 Technical Reference, pages B-124 through B-125
Microsoft MS-DOS 3.3 Programmer's Reference, pages 287, 289
Microsoft MS-DOS 4.0 Programmer's Reference, pages 273 through 275
Microsoft MS-DOS 5.0 Programmer's Reference, pages 362 through 363

See Also:
3.142. INT 21H, AH=59H -- Get Extended Error
3.148. INT 21H, AH=5EH, AL=00H -- Get Machine Name
3.191. ERROR Structure and Error Code Values

3.152. INT 21H, AH=5FH, AL=03H -- MAKE NETWORK CONNECTION

Prior to Calling Function

Register	High	Low
AX	5FH	03H
BX		Code†
CX	User value§	
DX		
SP		
BP		
SI	Offset of pointer to 16-byte local name buffer	
DI	Offset of pointer to 128-byte network name buffer	
IP		
flags		
CS		
DS	Segment of pointer to local name buffer	
SS		
ES	Segment of pointer to network name buffer	
Buffer	Local name (ASCIIZ string)	
Buffer	Network name+network password (2 ASCIIZ strings)	

Upon Return from Function

Register	High	Low
AX	Error code (if carry flag set)	
BX		
CX		
DX		
SP		
BP		
SI		
DI		
IP		
flags		Carry flag*
CS		
DS		
SS		
ES		

*Carry flag set if error occurs.
†03=printer device; 04=drive device.
If BL=03, local name buffer must be PRN, LPT1, LPT2, or LPT3.
If BL=04, local name buffer is drive letter followed by a colon or null string.
§Should be zero to retain compatibility with IBM local area networks.

Version: Applies to all versions of DOS beginning with 3.1.

Note: Strings should be in ASCIIZ format.

Source:
IBM DOS 3.3 Technical Reference, pages 6-227 through 6-229
IBM DOS 4.0 Technical Reference, pages B-126 through B-128
Microsoft MS-DOS 4.0 Programmer's Reference, pages 276 through 278
Microsoft MS-DOS 5.0 Programmer's Reference, pages 364 through 365

See Also:
3.142. INT 21H, AH=59H -- Get Extended Error
3.148. INT 21H, AH=5EH, AL=00H -- Get Machine Name
3.191. ERROR Structure and Error Code Values

3.153. INT 21H, AH=5FH, AL=04H -- DELETE NETWORK CONNECTION

Prior to Calling Function

Register	High	Low
AX	5FH	04H
BX		
CX		
DX		
SP		
BP		
SI	Offset of pointer to 16-byte source device name string	
DI		
IP		
flags		
CS		
DS	Segment of pointer to 16-byte source device name string	
SS		
ES		

Upon Return from Function

Register	High	Low
AX	Error code (if carry flag set)	
BX		
CX		
DX		
SP		
BP		
SI		
DI		
IP		
flags		Carry flag*
CS		
DS		
SS		
ES		

*Carry flag set if error occurs.

Version: Applies to all versions of DOS beginning with 3.1.

Note: Strings should be ASCIIZ format.

Source: IBM DOS 3.3 Technical Reference, pages 6-230 through 6-231
IBM DOS 4.0 Technical Reference, pages B-129 through B-130
Microsoft MS-DOS 4.0 Programmer's Reference, pages 279 through 280
Microsoft MS-DOS 5.0 Programmer's Reference, page 366

See Also: 3.142. INT 21H, AH=59H -- Get Extended Error
3.148. INT 21H, AH=5EH, AL=00H -- Get Machine Name
3.191. ERROR Structure and Error Code Values

3.154. INT 21H, AH=62H -- GET PSP ADDRESS

Prior to Calling Function

	High	*Low*
AX	62H	
BX		
CX		
DX		
SP		
BP		
SI		
DI		
IP		
flags		
CS		
DS		
SS		
ES		

Upon Return from Function

	High	*Low*
AX		
BX	Segment address of current PSP	
CX		
DX		
SP		
BP		
SI		
DI		
IP		
flags		
CS		
DS		
SS		
ES		

Version: Applies to all versions of DOS beginning with 3.0.

Note: Functions 51H and 62H are identical. Programs can use either function to get the segment address of the current PSP.

Source: IBM DOS 3.3 Technical Reference, page 6-232
IBM DOS 4.0 Technical Reference, page B-131
Microsoft MS-DOS 4.0 Programmer's Reference, page 281
Microsoft MS-DOS 5.0 Programmer's Reference, page 342

See Also: 3.196. PSP Structure

3.155. INT 21H, AH=63H -- GET LEAD BYTE TABLE

Prior to Calling Function

Register	High	Low
AX	63H	Function*
BX		
CX		
DX		Flag (if AL=1)†
SP		
BP		
SI		
DI		
IP		
flags		
CS		
DS		
SS		
ES		

Upon Return from Function

Register	High	Low
AX		
BX		
CX		
DX		Flag (if AL=2)
SP		
BP		
SI	Offset of pointer to lead byte table¥	
DI		
IP		
flags		
CS		
DS	Segment of pointer to lead byte table¥	
SS		
ES		

*Function is one of:
- 0=to get address of lead byte table
- 1=to set or clear interim console flag
- 2=to obtain interim console flag

†Set/clear flag is one of:
- 0=to clear interim console flag
- 1=to set interim console flag

¥If called with AL=0

Version: Available only in DOS 2.25.

Note: In DOS 4.x and later, use Function 65H.

Source: Advanced MS-DOS 2nd Edition (Microsoft Press), page 385

3.156. INT 21H, AH=65H, AL=01H -- GET EXTENDED COUNTRY INFORMATION

Prior to Calling Function

Register	High	Low
AX	65H	01H
BX	Code-page ID	
CX	Buffer size for country info§	
DX	Country code	
SP		
BP		
SI		
DI	Offset of pointer to country info table	
IP		
flags		
CS		
DS		
SS		
ES	Segment of pointer to country info table	
Table	Empty	

Upon Return from Function

Register	High	Low
AX	Error code (if carry flag set)	
BX		
CX		
DX		
SP		
BP		
SI		
DI		
IP		
flags		Carry flag*
CS		
DS		
SS		
ES		
Table	Country info†	

*Carry flag set if error occurs.
†Single byte followed by EXTCOUNTRYINFO structure in DOS 5.0.
§Must be at least 5.

Version: Applies to all versions of DOS beginning with 3.3.

Source: IBM DOS 3.3 Technical Reference, pages 6-233 through 6-236
IBM DOS 4.0 Technical Reference, pages B-132 through B-134
Microsoft MS-DOS 4.0 Programmer's Reference, pages 282 through 284
Microsoft MS-DOS 5.0 Programmer's Reference, pages 367 through 368

See Also: 3.070. INT 21H, AH=38H -- Get Country Data
3.071. INT 21H, AH=38H -- Set Country Data
3.199. Country Codes
3.203. COUNTRYINFO Structure

3.157. INT 21H, AH=65H, AL=02H -- GET UPPERCASE TABLE

Prior to Calling Function

	High	Low
AX	65H	02H
BX	Code-page ID	
CX	5	
DX	Country code	
SP		
BP		
SI		
DI	Offset of pointer to uppercase country table	
IP		
flags		
CS		
DS		
SS		
ES	Segment of pointer to uppercase country table	
Table	Empty	

Upon Return from Function

	High	Low
AX	Error code (if carry flag set)	
BX		
CX		
DX		
SP		
BP		
SI		
DI		
IP		
flags		Carry flag*
CS		
DS		
SS		
ES		
Table	Pointer to uppercase buffer†	

*Carry flag set if error occurs.
†Points to buffer in which MS-DOS places the 8-bit identifier (02H) of the uppercase table and the 32-bit address (segment:offset) of the table. The buffer must be at least 5 bytes long.

Version: Applies to all versions of DOS beginning with 3.3.

Source: IBM DOS 3.3 Technical Reference, pages 6-233 through 6-236
IBM DOS 4.0 Technical Reference, pages B-132 through B-134
Microsoft MS-DOS 4.0 Programmer's Reference, pages 282 through 284
Microsoft MS-DOS 5.0 Programmer's Reference, pages 369 through 370

See Also: 3.070. INT 21H, AH=38H -- Get Country Data
3.071. INT 21H, AH=38H -- Set Country Data
3.199. Country Codes
3.203. COUNTRYINFO Structure

3.158. INT 21H, AH=65H, AL=04H -- GET FILENAME UPPERCASE TABLE

Prior to Calling Function

Register	High	Low
AX	65H	04H
BX	Code-page ID	
CX	5	
DX	Country code	
SP		
BP		
SI		
DI	Offset of pointer to country info table	
IP		
flags		
CS		
DS		
SS		
ES	Segment of pointer to country info table	
Table	Empty	

Upon Return from Function

Register	High	Low
AX	Error code (if carry flag set)	
BX		
CX		
DX		
SP		
BP		
SI		
DI		
IP		
flags		Carry flag*
CS		
DS		
SS		
ES		
Table	Pointer to filename uppercase buffer†	

*Carry flag set if error occurs.
†Points to a buffer in which MS-DOS places the 8-bit identifier (04H) of the filename uppercase table and the 32-bit address (segment:offset) of the table. The buffer must be at least 5 bytes long.

Version: Applies to all versions of DOS beginning with 3.3.

Source: IBM DOS 3.3 Technical Reference, pages 6-233 through 6-236
IBM DOS 4.0 Technical Reference, pages B-132 through B-134
Microsoft MS-DOS 4.0 Programmer's Reference, pages 282 through 284
Microsoft MS-DOS 5.0 Programmer's Reference, pages 371 through 372

See Also: 3.070. INT 21H, AH=38H -- Get Country Data
3.071. INT 21H, AH=38H -- Set Country Data
3.199. Country Codes
3.203. COUNTRYINFO Structure

3.159. INT 21H, AH=65H, AL=05H -- GET FILENAME CHARACTER TABLE

Prior to Calling Function

Register	High	Low
AX	65H	05H
BX	Code-page ID	
CX	5	
DX	Country code	
SP		
BP		
SI		
DI	Offset of pointer to country info table	
IP		
flags		
CS		
DS		
SS		
ES	Segment of pointer to country info table	
Table	Empty	

Upon Return from Function

Register	High	Low
AX	Error code (if carry flag set)	
BX		
CX		
DX		
SP		
BP		
SI		
DI		
IP		
flags		Carry flag*
CS		
DS		
SS		
ES		
Table	Pointer to filename character buffer†	

*Carry flag set if error occurs.
†Points to a buffer in which MS-DOS places the 8-bit identifier (05H) of the filename character table and the 32-bit address (segment:offset) of the table. The buffer must be at least 5 bytes long.

Version: Applies to all versions of DOS beginning with 3.3.

Source: IBM DOS 3.3 Technical Reference, pages 6-233 through 6-236
IBM DOS 4.0 Technical Reference, pages B-132 through B-134
Microsoft MS-DOS 4.0 Programmer's Reference, pages 282 through 284
Microsoft MS-DOS 5.0 Programmer's Reference, pages 373 through 374

See Also: 3.070. INT 21H, AH=38H -- Get Country Data
3.071. INT 21H, AH=38H -- Set Country Data
3.199. Country Codes
3.203. COUNTRYINFO Structure

3.160. INT 21H, AH=65H, AL=06H -- GET COLLATE SEQUENCE TABLE

Prior to Calling Function

	High	*Low*
AX	65H	06H
BX	Code-page ID	
CX	5	
DX	Country code	
SP		
BP		
SI		
DI	Offset of pointer to country info table	
IP		
flags		
CS		
DS		
SS		
ES	Segment of pointer to country info table	
Table	Empty	

Upon Return from Function

	High	*Low*
AX	Error code (if carry flag set)	
BX		
CX		
DX		
SP		
BP		
SI		
DI		
IP		
flags		Carry flag*
CS		
DS		
SS		
ES		
Table	Pointer to collate sequence buffer†	

*Carry flag set if error occurs.
†Points to a buffer in which MS-DOS places the 8-bit identifier (06H) of the collate sequence table and the 32-bit address (segment:offset) of the table. The buffer must be a least 5 bytes long.

Version: Applies to all versions of DOS beginning with 3.3.

Source: IBM DOS 3.3 Technical Reference, pages 6-233 through 6-236
IBM DOS 4.0 Technical Reference, pages B-132 through B-134
Microsoft MS-DOS 4.0 Programmer's Reference, pages 282 through 284
Microsoft MS-DOS 5.0 Programmer's Reference, pages 375 through 376

See Also: 3.070. INT 21H, AH=38H -- Get Country Data
3.071. INT 21H, AH=38H -- Set Country Data
3.199. Country Codes
3.203. COUNTRYINFO Structure

3.161. INT 21H, AH=65H, AL=07H -- GET DOUBLE-BYTE CHARACTER SET

Prior to Calling Function

	High	Low
AX	65H	07H
BX	Code-page ID	
CX	5	
DX	Country code	
SP		
BP		
SI		
DI	Offset of pointer to country info table	
IP		
flags		
CS		
DS		
SS		
ES	Segment of pointer to country info table	
Table	Empty	

Upon Return from Function

	High	Low
AX	Error code (if carry flag set)	
BX		
CX		
DX		
SP		
BP		
SI		
DI		
IP		
flags		Carry flag*
CS		
DS		
SS		
ES		
Table	Pointer to the DBCS buffer†	

*Carry flag set if error occurs.
†Points to a buffer in which MS-DOS places the 8-bit identifier (07H) of the DBCS values and the 32-bit address (segment:offset) of the table. The buffer must be a least 5 bytes long.

Version: Applies to all versions of DOS beginning with 3.3.

Source: IBM DOS 3.3 Technical Reference, pages 6-233 through 6-236
IBM DOS 4.0 Technical Reference, pages B-132 through B-134
Microsoft MS-DOS 4.0 Programmer's Reference, pages 282 through 284
Microsoft MS-DOS 5.0 Programmer's Reference, pages 377 through 378

See Also: 3.070. INT 21H, AH=38H -- Get Country Data
3.071. INT 21H, AH=38H -- Set Country Data
3.199. Country Codes
3.203. COUNTRYINFO Structure

3.162. INT 21H, AH=65H, AL=20H -- CONVERT CHARACTER

Prior to Calling Function

	High	Low
AX	65H	20H
BX		
CX		
DX		Character
SP		
BP		
SI		
DI		
IP		
flags		
CS		
DS		
SS		
ES		

Upon Return from Function

	High	Low
AX	Error code (if carry flag set)	
BX		
CX		
DX		Uppercase character
SP		
BP		
SI		
DI		
IP		
flags		Carry flag*
CS		
DS		
SS		
ES		

*Carry flag set if error occurs.

Version: Applies to all versions of DOS beginning with 5.0.

Source: Microsoft MS-DOS 5.0 Programmer's Reference, page 379

See Also: 3.070. INT 21H, AH=38H -- Get Country Data
3.071. INT 21H, AH=38H -- Set Country Data
3.199. Country Codes
3.203. COUNTRYINFO Structure

3.163. INT 21H, AH=65H, AL=21H -- CONVERT STRING

Prior to Calling Function

Register	High	Low
AX	65H	21H
BX		
CX		
DX	Offset of pointer to string	
SP		
BP		
SI		
DI		
IP		
flags		
CS		
DS	Segment of pointer to string	
SS		
ES		
String	Lowercase	

Upon Return from Function

Register	High	Low
AX	Error code (if carry flag set)	
BX		
CX		
DX		
SP		
BP		
SI		
DI		
IP		
flags		Carry flag*
CS		
DS		
SS		
ES		
String	Uppercase	

*Carry flag set if error occurs.

Version: Applies to all versions of DOS beginning with 5.0.

Source: Microsoft MS-DOS 5.0 Programmer's Reference, page 380

See Also:
3.070. INT 21H, AH=38H -- Get Country Data
3.071. INT 21H, AH=38H -- Set Country Data
3.199. Country Codes
3.203. COUNTRYINFO Structure

3.164. INT 21H, AH=65H, AL=22H -- CONVERT ASCIIZ STRING

Prior to Calling Function

Register	High	Low
AX	65H	22H
BX		
CX		
DX	Offset of pointer to string	
SP		
BP		
SI		
DI		
IP		
flags		
CS		
DS	Segment of pointer to string	
SS		
ES		
String	ASCIIZ	

Upon Return from Function

Register	High	Low
AX	Error code (if carry flag set)	
BX		
CX		
DX		
SP		
BP		
SI		
DI		
IP		
flags		Carry flag*
CS		
DS		
SS		
ES		
String	Uppercase	

*Carry flag set if error occurs.

Version: Applies to all versions of DOS beginning with 5.0.

Source: Microsoft MS-DOS 5.0 Programmer's Reference, page 381

See Also:
3.070. INT 21H, AH=38H -- Get Country Data
3.071. INT 21H, AH=38H -- Set Country Data
3.199. Country Codes
3.203. COUNTRYINFO Structure

3.165. INT 21H, AH=66H, AL=01H -- GET GLOBAL CODE PAGE

Prior to Calling Function

Register	High	Low
AX	66H	01H
BX		
CX		
DX		
SP		
BP		
SI		
DI		
IP		
flags		
CS		
DS		
SS		
ES		

Upon Return from Function

Register	High	Low
AX	Error code (if carry flag set)	
BX	Active code page (set by user)	
CX		
DX	System code page (boot time)	
SP		
BP		
SI		
DI		
IP		
flags		Carry flag*
CS		
DS		
SS		
ES		

*Carry flag set if error occurs.

Version: Applies to all versions of DOS beginning with 3.3.

Source: IBM DOS 3.3 Technical Reference, pages 6-237 through 6-238
IBM DOS 4.0 Technical Reference, page B-135
Microsoft MS-DOS 4.0 Programmer's Reference, pages 285 through 286
Microsoft MS-DOS 5.0 Programmer's Reference, page 382

See Also: 3.166. INT 21H, AH=66H, AL=02H -- Set Global Code Page
3.191. ERROR Structure and Error Code Values

3.166. INT 21H, AH=66H, AL=02H -- SET GLOBAL CODE PAGE

Prior to Calling Function

Register	High	Low
AX	66H	02H
BX	Active code page	
CX		
DX	System code page†	
SP		
BP		
SI		
DI		
IP		
flags		
CS		
DS		
SS		
ES		

Upon Return from Function

Register	High	Low
AX	Error code (if carry flag set)	
BX		
CX		
DX		
SP		
BP		
SI		
DI		
IP		
flags		Carry flag*
CS		
DS		
SS		
ES		

*Carry flag set if error occurs.
†Not documented in Microsoft references.

Version: Applies to all versions of DOS beginning with 3.3.

Source: IBM DOS 3.3 Technical Reference, pages 6-237 through 6-238
IBM DOS 4.0 Technical Reference, page B-135
Microsoft MS-DOS 4.0 Programmer's Reference, pages 285 through 286
Microsoft MS-DOS 5.0 Programmer's Reference, page 383

See Also: 3.165. INT 21H, AH=66H, AL=01H -- Get Global Code Page
3.191. ERROR Structure and Error Code Values

3.167. INT 21H, AH=67H -- SET MAXIMUM HANDLE COUNT

Prior to Calling Function

Register	High	Low
AX	67H	
BX	Max. number of handles per program	
CX		
DX		
SP		
BP		
SI		
DI		
IP		
flags		
CS		
DS		
SS		
ES		

Upon Return from Function

Register	High	Low
AX	Error code (if carry flag set)	
BX		
CX		
DX		
SP		
BP		
SI		
DI		
IP		
flags		Carry flag*
CS		
DS		
SS		
ES		

*Carry flag set if error occurs.

Version: Applies to all versions of DOS beginning with 3.3.

Note:
- Maximum number of system handles is usually controlled by CONFIG.SYS FILES= setting.
- You must release memory to DOS for the extended handle list.

Source:
IBM DOS 3.3 Technical Reference, page 6-239
IBM DOS 4.0 Technical Reference, page B-136
Microsoft MS-DOS 4.0 Programmer's Reference, page 287
Microsoft MS-DOS 5.0 Programmer's Reference, page 384

See Also:
2.07. CONFIG.SYS Commands and Default Settings
3.191. ERROR Structure and Error Code Values

3.168. INT 21H, AH=68H -- COMMIT FILE

Prior to Calling Function

Register	High	Low
AX	68H	
BX	File handle	
CX		
DX		
SP		
BP		
SI		
DI		
IP		
flags		
CS		
DS		
SS		
ES		

Upon Return from Function

Register	High	Low
AX	Error code (if carry flag set)	
BX		
CX		
DX		
SP		
BP		
SI		
DI		
IP		
flags		Carry flag*
CS		
DS		
SS		
ES		

*Carry flag set if error occurs.

Version: Applies to all versions of DOS beginning with 3.3.

Source:
IBM DOS 3.3 Technical Reference, page 6-240
IBM DOS 4.0 Technical Reference, page B-137
Microsoft MS-DOS 4.0 Programmer's Reference, page 288
Microsoft MS-DOS 5.0 Programmer's Reference, page 385

See Also: 3.191. ERROR Structure and Error Code Values

3.169. INT 21H, AH=6CH -- EXTENDED OPEN/CREATE

Prior to Calling Function

	High	Low
AX	6CH	
BX	Mode†	
CX	0	Attribute byte**
DX	Action§	
SP		
BP		
SI	Offset of pointer to pathname	
DI		
IP		
flags		
CS		
DS	Segment of pointer to pathname	
SS		
ES		

Upon Return from Function

	High	Low
AX	Handle or error code (if carry flag set)	
BX		
CX		
DX		
SP		
BP		
SI		
DI		
IP		
flags		Carry flag*
CS		
DS		
SS		
ES		

*Carry flag set if error occurs.
†Open mode:
0000H=Read-Only
0001H=Write-Only
0002H=Read/Write
0000H=Share Compatibility
0010H=Deny Read/Write
0020H=Deny Write
0030H=Deny Read
0040H=Deny None
0080H=No Inherit
2000H=No Critical Error Handler
4000H=Commits the File
§Action:
0001H=Create New File
0010H=Open File
0020H=Truncate File
**Attributes:
0000H=Normal (read from or written to)
0001H=Read-Only
0002H=Hidden
0004H=System File
0020H=Archive

Version: Applies to MS-DOS beginning with 5.0. A slightly different version of Function 6CH exists in IBM DOS 4.0.

Note: Requires create access rights on networks.

Source: IBM DOS 4.0 Technical Reference, pages B-138 through B-139
Microsoft MS-DOS 5.0 Programmer's Reference, pages 386 through 388

See Also:
2.19. File Attribute Byte
3.038. INT 21H, AH=16H -- Create File with FCB
3.075. INT 21H, AH=3CH -- Create File with Handle
3.142. INT 21H, AH=59H -- Get Extended Error
3.143. INT 21H, AH=5AH -- Create Temporary File
3.144. INT 21H, AH=5BH -- Create New File
3.191. ERROR Structure and Error Code Values

3.170. BOOTSECTOR STRUCTURE

Offset	*Length*	*Name*	*Contents*
0 (0)	3 bytes	bsJump	Jump to boot code
3 (3)	8 bytes	bsOemName	OEM name and version of DOS
B (11)	word	bsBytesPerSec	Bytes per sector
D (13)	byte	bsSecPerClust	Sectors per cluster
E (14)	word	bsResSectors	Number of reserved sectors
10 (16)	byte	bsFATs	Number of file-allocation tables
11 (17)	word	bsRootDirEnts	Number of root-directory entries
13 (19)	word	bsSectors	Total number of sectors; 0=drive > 32MB
15 (21)	byte	bsMedia	Media descriptor
16 (22)	word	bsFATsecs	Number of sectors per FAT
18 (24)	word	bsSecPerTrack	Sectors per track
1A (26)	word	bsHeads	Number of heads
1C (28)	dbl word	bsHiddenSecs	Number of hidden sectors
20 (32)	dbl word	bsHugeSectors	Number of sectors if bsSectors=0
24 (36)	byte	bsDriveNumber	Drive number
25 (37)	byte	bsReserved1	RESERVED
26 (38)	byte	bsBootSignature	Extended boot signature (29H)
27 (39)	dbl word	bsVolumeID	Volume ID number
2B (43)	11 bytes	bsVolumeLabel	Volume label
37 (54)	8 bytes	bsFileSysType	Type of file system; FAT12=12-bit FAT, FAT16=16-bit FAT

Version: DOS 5.0 structure. The layout is identical in previous versions of DOS.

Source: IBM DOS 3.3 Technical Reference, page 2-31
IBM DOS 4.0 Technical Reference, page 11-17
Microsoft MS-DOS 3.3 Programmer's Reference, page 352
Microsoft MS-DOS 4.0 Programmer's Reference, pages 336 through 338
Microsoft MS-DOS 5.0 Programmer's Reference, pages 34 through 35

3.171. DEVICEPARAMS STRUCTURE

For Set Device (CL=40H):

Offset	Length	Name	Bit Number 7	6	5	4	3	2	1	0	Allowable Settings
0 (0)	byte	dpSpecFunc	✔	✔	✔	✔	✔				Must be set to 0
								✔			0=do not use 1=sectors same size
									✔		0=read all fields 1=read only track layout field
										✔	0=build new BPB 1=use device BPB
1 (1)	byte	dpDevType	0	0	0	0	1	0	0	1	9=2.88MB
			0	0	0	0	1	0	0	0	8=read/write optical
			0	0	0	0	0	1	1	1	7=1.44MB floppy
			0	0	0	0	0	1	1	0	6=tape drive
			0	0	0	0	0	1	0	1	5=hard disk
			0	0	0	0	0	1	0	0	4=8" double density floppy
			0	0	0	0	0	0	1	1	3=8" single density floppy
			0	0	0	0	0	0	1	0	2=720K floppy
			0	0	0	0	0	0	0	1	1=1.2MB floppy
			0	0	0	0	0	0	0	0	0=320/360K floppy
2 (2)	word	dpDevAttr	✔	✔	✔	✔	✔	✔			Must be set to 0, RESERVED
									✔		0=disk changeline not supported 1=disk changeline supported
										✔	0=media is removable 1=media not removable
4 (4)	word	dpCylinders									Maximum # cylinders device supports
6 (6)	byte	dpMediaType								✔	0=1.2MB quad density 1=320/360K dbl density
7 (7)	word	dpBytesPerSec									Bytes per sector
9 (9)	byte	dpSecPerClust									Sectors per cluster: must be consecutive, must be power of two
A (10)	word	dpResSectors									Number of reserved sectors. Usually 1
C (12)	byte	dpFATS									Number of FATS
D (13)	word	dpRootDirEnts									Maximum number of entries in root directory
F (15)	word	dpSectors									Number of sectors if drive less than or equal to 32MB. 0=drive greater than 32MB and number of sectors in dpHugeSectors
11 (17)	byte	dpMedia									Media descriptor value*
12 (18)	word	dpFATsecs									Number of sectors occupied by each FAT
14 (20)	word	dpSecsPerTrack									Number of sectors per single track
16 (22)	word	dpHeads									Number of heads per drive
18 (24)	dbl word	dpHiddenSecs									Number of hidden sectors per drive
1C (28)	dbl word	dpHugeSectors									Number of sectors if drive greater than 32MB

*Media descriptor values:

Value	Type of Medium
0F0H	1.44 or 2.88MB 3.5" floppy 1.2MB 5.25" floppy
0F8H	Hard disk, any capacity
0F9H	720 K 3.5" floppy 1.2MB 5.25" floppy
0FAH	320 K 5.25" floppy
0FBH	640 K 3.5" floppy
0FCH	180 K 5.25" floppy
0FDH	360 K 5.25" floppy
0FEH	160 K 5.25" floppy
0FFH	320 K 5.25" floppy

Version: DOS 5.0 structure. The layout through offset 6 is identical in previous versions of DOS.

Source: IBM DOS 3.3 Technical Reference, pages 6-169 through 6-180
IBM DOS 4.0 Technical Reference, pages C-18 through C-26
Microsoft MS-DOS 4.0 Programmer's Reference, pages 209 through 216
Microsoft MS-DOS 5.0 Programmer's Reference, pages 36 through 38, 311, and 315

See Also: 3.105. through 3.113. INT 21H, AH=44H, AL=0DH, Minor Code tables
3.173. DPB Structure

3.172. DIRENTRY STRUCTURE

Offset	*Length*	*Name*	*Contents*
0 (0)	8 bytes	deName	File name
8 (8)	3 bytes	deExtension	File extension
B (11)	byte	deAttributes	File attributes
C (12)	10 bytes	deReserved	RESERVED
16 (22)	word	deTime	Time stamp
18 (24)	word	deDate	Date stamp
1A (26)	word	deStartCluster	Starting cluster number
1C (28)	dbl word	deFileSize	File size

Source: Microsoft MS-DOS 5.0 Programmer's Reference, pages 38 through 40

See Also: 3.033. INT 21H, AH=11 -- Find First File with FCB
3.034. INT 21H, AH=12 -- Find Next File with FCB

3.173. DPB STRUCTURE

Offset	*Length*	*Name*	*Contents*
0 (0)	byte	dpbDrive	Drive number (0=A, 1=B, and so on)
1 (1)	byte	dpbUnit	Unit number for driver
2 (2)	word	dpbSectorSize	Sector size, in bytes
4 (4)	byte	dpbClusterMask	Sectors per cluster -1
5 (5)	byte	dpbClusterShift	Sectors per cluster as powers of 2
6(6)	word	dpbFirstFAT	First sector containing FAT
8 (8)	byte	dpbFATCount	Number of FATs
9 (9)	word	dpbRootEntries	Number of root-directory entries
B (11)	word	dpbFirstSector	First sector of first cluster
D (13)	word	dpbMaxCluster	Number of clusters on drive +1
F (15)	word	dpbFATSize	Number of sectors occupied by FAT
11 (17)	word	dpbDirSector	First sector containing directory
13 (19)	dbl word	dpbDriverAddr	Address of device driver
17 (23)	byte	dpbMedia	Media descriptor
18 (24)	byte	dpbFirstAccess	Access to drive
19 (25)	dbl word	dpbNextDPB	Address of next parameter block
1D (29)	word	dpbNextFree	Last allocated cluster
1F (31)	word	dpbFreeCnt	Number of free clusters

Source: Microsoft MS-DOS 5.0 Programmer's Reference, pages 41 through 42

See Also: 3.044. INT 21H, AH=1F -- Get Default DPB
3.062. INT 21H, AH=32 -- Get DPB

3.174. EXTENDEDFCB STRUCTURE AND EXTHEADER STRUCTURE

Offset	Length	Name	Contents
0 (0)*	byte	extSignature	Always FFH (255)
1 (1)*	5 bytes	extReserved	
6 (6)*	byte	extAttribute	See 2.19. File Attribute Byte
7 (7)	byte	extDriveID	0=default, 1=A, 2=B, and so on
8 (8)	8 bytes	extFileName	ASCII characters, padded with spaces, if necessary
10 (16)	3 bytes	extExtent	ASCII characters, padded with spaces, if necessary
13 (19)	word	extCurBlockNo	Binary value indicating current block (set to 0 on File Open)
15 (21)	word	extRecSize	Number of bytes per record; default=80 (128)
17 (23)	dbl word	extFileSize	Binary value indicating size of file, in bytes
1B (27)	word	extFileDate	Packed word containing file last update date
1D (29)	word	extFileTime	Packed word containing file last update time
1F (31)	8 bytes	extReserved	Used internally by DOS
27 (39)	byte	extCurRecNo	Binary value indicating current record
28 (40)	dbl word	extRandomRecNo	Binary value indicating next random block to read/write

*EXTHEADER structure. Name prefix is eh (ehSignature, ehReserved, ehAttribute).

Version: DOS 5.0 structure. Layout is identical in previous versions of DOS.

Note:
- The EXTHEADER structure consists of offsets 0 through 7.
- A value other than FFH in the first byte of an FCB indicates it is not an Extended FCB (See 3.175. FCB Structure (Opened)).
- In the PSP, an extended FCB starts 7 bytes prior to 5CH.
- In your program (outside the PSP), your FCB pointer probably points directly to the FFH byte of an extended FCB, or to the drive number byte of a normal FCB. Thus, to insure that you address items in an FCB correctly, you must first know if it is extended or not.

Source:
IBM DOS 3.3 Technical Reference, page 7-16
IBM DOS 4.0 Technical Reference, Chapter 4
Microsoft MS-DOS 4.0 Programmer's Reference, pages 19 through 21
Microsoft MS-DOS 5.0 Programmer's Reference, pages 42 through 44

See Also:
2.19. File Attribute Byte
3.175. FCB Structure (Opened)
3.176. FCB Structure (Unopened)
3.181. RENAMEFCB Structure

3.175. FCB STRUCTURE (OPENED)

Offset	Length	Name	Contents
0 (0)	byte	fcbDriveID	Drive number; 0=default, 1=A, 2=B, and so on
1 (1)	8 bytes	fcbFileName	ASCII characters, padded with spaces, if necessary
9 (9)	3 bytes	fcbExtent	ASCII characters, padded with spaces, if necessary
C (12)	word	fcbCurBlockNo	Binary value indicating current block (set to 0 on File Open)
E (14)	word	fcbRecSize	Number of bytes per record (default=128)
10 (16)	dbl word	fcbFileSize	Binary value indicating size of file, in bytes
14 (20)	word	fcbFileDate	Packed word containing file create or last update date
16 (22)	word	fcbFileTime	Packed word containing file create or last update time
18 (24)	8 bytes	fcbReserved	Used internally by DOS
20 (32)	byte	fcbCurRecNo	Binary value indicating current record
21 (33)	dbl word	fcbRandomRecNo	Binary value indicating next random block to read/write

Version: DOS 5.0 structure. Layout is identical in previous versions of DOS.

Note:
- In the PSP, an extended FCB starts 7 bytes prior to 5CH.
- In your program (outside the PSP), your FCB pointer probably points directly to the FFH byte of an extended FCB, or to the drive number byte of a normal FCB. Thus, to insure that you address items in an FCB correctly, you must first know if it is extended or not (See 3.174. EXTENDEDFCB Structure and EXTHEADER Structure).

Source:
IBM DOS 3.3 Technical Reference, pages 7-12 through 7-15
IBM DOS 4.0 Technical Reference, Chapter 4
Microsoft MS-DOS 4.0 Programmer's Reference, pages 19 through 21
Microsoft MS-DOS 5.0 Programmer's Reference, pages 44 through 46

See Also:
2.20. Date/Time Formats
3.174. EXTENDEDFCB Structure and EXTHEADER Structure
3.176. FCB Structure (Unopened)
3.181. RENAMEFCB Structure

3.176. FCB STRUCTURE (UNOPENED)

Offset	Length	Name	Contents
0 (0)	byte	fcbDriveID	Drive number; 0=default, 1=A, 2=B, and so on
1 (1)	8 bytes	fcbFileName	ASCII characters, left justified, padded with spaces (20H), if necessary
9 (9)	3 bytes	fcbExtent	ASCII characters, left justified, padded with spaces (20H), if necessary
C (12)	word	fcbCurBlockNo	0
E (14)	word	fcbRecSize	0
10 (16)	dbl word	fcbFileSize	0
14 (20)	word	fcbFileDate	0
16 (22)	word	fcbFileTime	0
18 (24)	8 bytes	fcbReserved	0
20 (32)	byte	fcbCurRecNo	0
21 (33)	dbl word	fcbRandomRecNo	0

Version: DOS 5.0 structure. Layout is identical in previous versions.

Source: IBM DOS 3.3 Technical Reference, pages 7-12 through 7-15
IBM DOS 4.0 Technical Reference, Chapter 4
Microsoft MS-DOS 4.0 Programmer's Reference, pages 19 through 21
Microsoft MS-DOS 5.0 Programmer's Reference, pages 44 through 46

See Also: 3.003. INT 21H FCB-Oriented Functions Summary
3.174. EXTENDEDFCB Structure and EXTHEADER Structure
3.175. FCB Structure (Opened)
3.181. RENAMEFCB Structure
3.184. Logical Drive Numbers

3.177. FILEINFO STRUCTURE

Offset	Length	Name	Contents
0 (0)	21 bytes	fiReserved	Used by subsequent Search Next functions
15 (21)	byte	fiAttribute	See 2.19. File Attribute Byte
16 (22)	word	fiFileTime	See 2.20. Date/Time Formats
18 (24)	word	fiFileDate	See 2.20. Date/Time Formats
1A (26)	dbl word	fiSize	
1E (30)	13 bytes	fiFileName†	ASCIIZ string

†Filename string includes a period if a file type is present; blanks are removed; terminated by 00H byte.

Version: DOS 5.0 structure. Layout is identical in previous versions of DOS.

Note: Data block is stored in DTA.

Source: IBM DOS 3.3 Technical Reference, page 6-203
IBM DOS 4.0 Technical Reference, pages B-107 through B-109
Microsoft MS-DOS 4.0 Programmer's Reference, page 242
Microsoft MS-DOS 5.0 Programmer's Reference, pages 46 through 47

See Also: 2.19. File Attribute Byte
2.20. Date/Time Formats
3.130. INT 21H, AH=4EH -- Find First File
3.131. INT 21H, AH=4FH -- Find Next File

3.178. FVBLOCK STRUCTURE

For Format/Verify Track (CL=42/62H):

Offset	Length	Name	Contents
0 (0)	byte	fvSpecFunc	Must be zero
1 (1)	word	fvHead	Head number to format/verify
3 (3)	word	fvCylinder	Cylinder number to format/verify

Version: DOS 5.0 structure. The layout is identical in previous versions of DOS.

Source: IBM DOS 3.3 Technical Reference, pages 6-169 through 6-180
IBM DOS 4.0 Technical Reference, pages C-18 through C-26
Microsoft MS-DOS 4.0 Programmer's Reference, pages 209 through 216
Microsoft MS-DOS 5.0 Programmer's Reference, pages 47, 313, and 318

See Also: 3.105. through 3.113. INT 21H, AH=44H, AL=0CH, Minor Code tables
3.173. DPB Structure

3.179. MID STRUCTURE

Offset	Length	Name	Contents
0 (0)	word	midInfoLevel	Information level
2 (2)	dbl word	midSerialNum	Serial number
6 (6)	11 bytes	midVolLabel	ASCII volume label
11 (17)	8 bytes	midFileSysType	File system type

Source: Microsoft MS-DOS 5.0 Programmer's Reference, page 48

See Also: 3.108. INT 21H, AH=44H, AL=0DH, Minor Code=46H -- Set Media ID
3.112. INT 21H, AH=44H, AL=0DH, Minor Code=66H -- Get Media ID

3.180. PARTENTRY STRUCTURE

Offset	Length	Name	Contents
0 (0)	byte	peBootable	Type of partition: 80H=bootable, 00H=nonbootable
1 (1)	byte	peBeginHead	Beginning head
2 (2)	byte	peBeginSector	Beginning sector
3 (3)	byte	peBeginCylinder	Beginning cylinder
4 (4)	byte	peFileSystem	Name of file system: 00=unknown, 01=12-bit FAT, 04=16-bit FAT (partition <32MB), 05H=extended DOS partition, 06H=16-bit FAT (partition >=32MB)
5 (5)	byte	peEndHead	Ending head
6 (6)	byte	peEndSector	Ending sector
7 (7)	byte	peEndCylinder	Ending cylinder
8 (8)	dbl word	peStartSector	Starting sector (relative to beginning of disk)
C (12)	dbl word	peSectors	Number of sectors in the partition

Source: Microsoft MS-DOS 5.0 Programmer's Reference, pages 48 through 49

See Also: 3.106. INT 21H, AH=44H, AL=0DH, Minor Code=41H -- Write Track on Logical Drive
3.110. INT 21H, AH=44H, AL=0DH, Minor Code=61H -- Read Track on Logical Drive

3.181. RENAMEFCB STRUCTURE

Offset	Length	Name	Contents
0 (0)	byte	renDriveID	Drive number; 0=default, 1=A, 2=B, and so on
1 (1)	8 bytes	renOldName	ASCII characters, padded with spaces, if necessary
9 (9)	3 bytes	renOldExtent	ASCII characters, padded with spaces, if necessary
C (12)	5 bytes	renReserved1	
11 (17)	8 bytes	renNewName	ASCII characters, padded with spaces, if necessary
19 (25)	3 bytes	renNewExtent	ASCII characters, padded with spaces, if necessary
1C (28)	9 bytes	renReserved2	Set to zeros

Version: DOS 5.0 structure. Layout is identical in previous versions of DOS.

Note: Both file name and type fields may contain the DOS wildcard character ? (match any character)

Source: IBM DOS 3.3 Technical Reference, page 6-79
IBM DOS 4.0 Technical Reference, pages B-38 through B-39
Microsoft MS-DOS 4.0 Programmer's Reference, pages 101 through 103
Microsoft MS-DOS 5.0 Programmer's Reference, pages 49 through 50

See Also: 3.174. EXTENDEDFCB Structure and EXTHEADER Structure
3.175. FCB Structure (Opened)
3.176. FCB Structure (Unopened)
3.184. Logical Drive Numbers

3.182. RWBLOCK STRUCTURE

Offset	Length	Name	Contents
0 (0)	byte	rwSpecFunc	Must be set to 0
1 (1)	word	rwHead	Head number to read/write
3 (3)	word	rwCylinder	Cylinder number to read/write
5 (5)	word	rwFirstSector	First sector # to read/write
7 (7)	word	rwSectors	Total # of sectors
9 (9)	dbl word	rwBuffer	Segment:Offset of transfer buffer

Version: DOS 5.0 structure. The layout is identical in previous versions of DOS.

Source: IBM DOS 3.3 Technical Reference, pages 6-169 through 6-180
IBM DOS 4.0 Technical Reference, pages C-18 through C-26
Microsoft MS-DOS 4.0 Programmer's Reference, pages 209 through 216
Microsoft MS-DOS 5.0 Programmer's Reference, pages 50, 312, and 317

See Also: 3.105. through 3.113. INT 21H, AH=44H, AL=0DH, Minor Code tables
3.173. DPB Structure

3.183. TRACKLAYOUT STRUCTURE

Offset	Length	Name	Contents
0 (0)	word	tklSectors	Number of sectors in track
2 (2)	dbl word	tklNumSize	Array of sector numbers and sizes

Source: Microsoft MS-DOS 5.0 Programmer's Reference, pages 50 through 51

See Also: 3.105. INT 21H, AH=44H, AL=0DH, Minor Code=40H -- Set Device Parameters

3.184. LOGICAL DRIVE NUMBERS

In FCBs, Functions 1CH, 36H, Some 44H Subfunctions, and 47H

Value	*Drive*
0 (0)	Default
1 (1)	A
2 (2)	B
3 (3)	C
4 (4)	D
5 (5)	E
6 (6)	F
7 (7)	G
8 (8)	H
9 (9)	I
A (10)	J
B (11)	K
C (12)	L
D (13)	M
E (14)	N
F (15)	O
10 (16)	P
11 (17)	Q
12 (18)	R
13 (19)	S
14 (20)	T
15 (21)	U
16 (22)	V
17 (23)	W
18 (24)	X
19 (25)	Y
1A (26)	Z

In Functions 0EH and 19H

Value	*Drive*
0 (0)	A
1 (1)	B
2 (2)	C
3 (3)	D
4 (4)	E
5 (5)	F
6 (6)	G
7 (7)	H
8 (8)	I
9 (9)	J
A (10)	K
B (11)	L
C (12)	M
D (13)	N
E (14)	O
F (15)	P
10 (16)	Q
11 (17)	R
12 (18)	S
13 (19)	T
14 (20)	U
15 (21)	V
16 (22)	W
17 (23)	X
18 (24)	Y
19 (25)	Z

Source: IBM DOS 3.3 Technical Reference, see individual functions
IBM DOS 4.0 Technical Reference, see individual functions
Microsoft MS-DOS 4.0 Programmer's Reference, see individual functions
Microsoft MS-DOS 5.0 Programmer's Reference, see individual functions

See Also: 3.030. INT 21H, AH=0EH -- Set Default Drive
3.040. INT 21H, AH=19H -- Get Current Drive
3.043. INT 21H, AH=1CH -- Get Drive Data
3.069. INT 21H, AH=36H -- Get Disk Free Space
3.084. through 3.117. INT 21H, AH=44H Subfunction tables
3.120. INT 21H, AH=47H -- Get Current Directory

3.185. FCB ERROR CODES

For Read Functions (14H, 21H, and 27H)

Code in AL	*Meaning After Read*
0	Read operation was completed successfully
1	Read attempted at end of file; no data was transferred
2	Not enough room in the DTA for record(s); read canceled
3	Read encountered end of file; partial record read, remainder padded with 0's

For Write Functions (15H, 22H, and 28H)

Code in AL	*Meaning After Write*
0	Write operation was completed successfully
1	Disk full; write canceled
2	DTA does not contain enough data to write record(s); write canceled

Source: IBM DOS 4.0 Technical Reference, pages B-35 through B-36, B-44 through B-47, B-52 through B-55
Microsoft MS-DOS 3.2 Programmer's Reference, pages 1-75 through 1-103
Microsoft MS-DOS 4.0 Programmer's Reference, pages 95 through 98, 113 through 117, 125 through 130
Microsoft MS-DOS 5.0 Programmer's Reference, pages 233 through 234, 244 through 245, 250 through 253

See Also: 3.036. INT 21H, AH=14H -- Sequential Read
3.037. INT 21H, AH=15H -- Sequential Write
3.045. INT 21H, AH=21H -- Random Read
3.046. INT 21H, AH=22H -- Random Write
3.051. INT 21H, AH=27H -- Random Block Read
3.052. INT 21H, AH=28H -- Random Block Write

3.186. PARSE CONTROL BYTE

Bit Number

7	6	5	4	3	2	1	0	*Function*	*Allowable Settings*
							✔	Separator control	0=stop parsing if separator is encountered 1=ignore leading file separators
						✔		Drive # control	0=set FCB drive number to 0 if no drive in string 1=leave FCB drive number unchanged if no drive in string
					✔			File name control	0=set FCB filename to blanks if no name in string 1=leave FCB filename unchanged if no file name in string
				✔				Extension control	0=set FCB file extension to blanks if no type in string 1=leave FCB file extension unchanged if no type in string
✔	✔	✔	✔					UNUSED	Must be 0

Version: DOS version 1.0 also recognizes / " [ ]

Note: Filename separators are : . ; , = + SPACE TAB
Filename terminators are : . ; , = + < > | / " [ ] SPACE TAB and the Control characters (ASCII 01H through 0FH)

Source: IBM DOS 3.3 Technical Reference, pages 6-96 through 6-97
IBM DOS 4.0 Technical Reference, pages B-56 through B-57
Microsoft MS-DOS 4.0 Programmer's Reference, pages 131 through 133
Microsoft MS-DOS 5.0 Programmer's Reference, pages 254 through 255

See Also: 2.36. File Separator Characters
3.053. INT 21H, AH=29H -- Parse Filename

3.187. HANDLE ACCESS BYTE

Bit Number

7	6	5	4	3	2	1	0	*Use*
✔								Inherit bit†
	✔	✔	✔					Sharing mode code†
				✔	✔	✔	✔	Access code*

7	6	5	4	3	2	1	0	*Allowable Values*	*Meaning*
✔								0=child inherits 1=child doesn't inherit	Child program inherits file handle Child program does not inherit file handle
	✔	✔	✔					000=share-compatibility mode 001=share-denyread/write 010=share-denywrite 011=share-denyread 100=share-denynone	Other programs have access to file Other programs can't open file Other programs can't write to file Other programs can't read file Other programs have read or write access but can't open in compatibility mode
				✔	✔	✔	✔	0000=read-only 0001=write-only 0010=read/write	Open file read-only Open file write-only Open file read and write

*Applies to all versions of DOS beginning with 2.0.
†Fully implemented beginning with DOS 3.1.

Version: Normal Access Byte for all non-network workstations would be 02H (inherit, compatibility, read/write).

Source: IBM DOS 3.3 Technical Reference, pages 6-128 through 6-130
IBM DOS 4.0 Technical Reference, pages B-78 through B-80
Microsoft MS-DOS 4.0 Programmer's Reference, pages 170 through 173
Microsoft MS-DOS 5.0 Programmer's Reference, pages 279 through 280

See Also: 3.076. INT 21H, AH=3DH -- Open File with Handle

3.188. PREDEFINED HANDLES

Handle Number	Device Assignment	Default Device	Name
0	Standard input	Keyboard	STDIN
1	Standard output	Display	STDOUT
2	Standard error	Display	STDERR
3	Auxiliary device	COM1:	STDAUX
4	Printer output	LPT1:	STDPRN

Version: Applies to all versions of DOS beginning with 2.0.

Note:
- The auxiliary device handle assumes that the proper parameters have been assigned to COM1: prior to the start of communication.
- Preopened handles may be redirected to devices other than the default by using INT 21H functions 45H and 46H.

Source:
IBM DOS 3.3 Technical Reference, pages 4-8 through 4-9
IBM DOS 4.0 Technical Reference, page 3-3
Microsoft MS-DOS 4.0 Programmer's Reference, page 10
Microsoft MS-DOS 5.0 Programmer's Reference, page 67

See Also:
3.118. INT 21H, AH=45H -- Duplicate File Handle
3.119. INT 21H, AH=46H -- Force Duplicate File Handle
3.231. Reserved Device Names and Chain Order

3.189. HANDLE POINTER MOVEMENT METHODS

Value	Starting Location	Pointer Is Moved to
0	From beginning	Offset bytes (in CX:DX) from beginning of the file
1	From current pointer	Offset bytes (in CX:DX) from current location
2	From end of file	Offset bytes (in CX:DX) from end of file

Version: Applies to all versions of DOS beginning with 2.0.

Note: CX:DX is considered a signed 32-bit integer, allowing offset values from -2,147,483,648 through 2,147,483,647.

Source:
IBM DOS 3.3 Technical Reference, page 6-144
IBM DOS 4.0 Technical Reference, B-91
Microsoft MS-DOS 4.0 Programmer's Reference, page 184
Microsoft MS-DOS 5.0 Programmer's Reference, page 285

See Also: 3.081. INT 21H, AH=42H -- Move File Pointer

3.190. ARENA STRUCTURE (DOS MEMORY CONTROL BLOCKS)

Offset	Length	Name	Description	Contents
0	byte	arenaSignature	Block validity	4DH if not last block; 5AH if last block
1	word	arenaOwner	Owner of memory block	PSP segment address
3	word	arenaSize	Size of block	Number of paragraphs allocated
5	3 bytes	arenaReserved	Reserved	RESERVED
8	8 bytes	arenaName	Owner filename*	ASCII string of program that owns block

*Applies to DOS beginning with version 4.0 only.

Version: DOS 5.0 structure. The layout is identical in previous versions of DOS.

Note: Memory control block and memory controlled are adjacent in memory

Source:
Advanced MS-DOS 2nd Edition (Microsoft Press), page 179
PC Magazine, December 26, 1989, page 261
Microsoft MS-DOS 5.0 Programmer's Reference, pages 70 and 78

See Also: 3.123. INT 21H, AH=4AH -- Set Memory Block Size

3.191. ERROR STRUCTURE AND ERROR CODE VALUES

Offset	*Length*	*Name*	*Contents*
0 (0)	word	errAX	AX register*
2 (2)	word	errBX	BX register†
4 (4)	word	errCX	CX register¥
6 (6)	word	errDX	DX register
8 (8)	word	errSI	SI register
A (10)	word	errDI	DI register
C (12)	word	errDS	DS register
E (14)	word	errES	ES register
10 (16)	word	errReserved	
12 (18)	word	errUID	Computer where error occurred; 0=local computer
14 (20)	word	errPID	Program where error occurred; 0=local program

*Error Code:

Value in AX	*Description*
1 (1)	Invalid function code
2 (2)	File not found
3 (3)	Path not found
4 (4)	Too many open files
5 (5)	Access denied
6 (6)	Invalid handle
7 (7)	Arena trashed
8 (8)	Insufficient memory
9 (9)	Invalid block
A (10)	Invalid environment
B (11)	Invalid format
C (12)	Invalid access code
D (13)	Invalid data
E (14)	RESERVED
F (15)	Invalid drive
10 (16)	Attempt to remove the current directory
11 (17)	Not same device
12 (18)	No more files
13 (19)	Disk is write-protected
14 (20)	Bad disk unit
15 (21)	Drive not ready
16 (22)	Invalid command
17 (23)	CRC error
18 (24)	Bad request structure length
19 (25)	Seek error
1A (26)	Not a DOS disk
1B (27)	Sector not found
1C (28)	Out of paper
1D (29)	Write fault
1E (30)	Read fault
1F (31)	General failure
20 (32)	Sharing violation
21 (33)	Lock violation
22 (34)	Wrong disk
23 (35)	FCB unavailable
24 (36)	Sharing buffer overflow
25 (37)	Error code page mismatched
26 (38)	Handle EOF
27 (39)	Handle disk full
28 (40)	RESERVED
29 (41)	RESERVED
2A (42)	RESERVED
2B (43)	RESERVED
2C (44)	RESERVED
2D (45)	RESERVED
2E (46)	RESERVED
2F (47)	RESERVED
30 (48)	RESERVED
31 (49)	RESERVED
32 (50)	Network request not supported**
33 (51)	Remote computer not listening**
34 (52)	Duplicate name on network**
35 (53)	Network path not found**
36 (54)	Network busy**
37 (55)	Network device no longer exists**
38 (56)	Net BIOS command limit exceeded**
39 (57)	Network adapter hardware error**

(Continued)

3.191. ERROR STRUCTURE AND ERROR CODE VALUES (continued)

*Error Code:

Value in AX	*Description*
3A (58)	Incorrect response from network**
3B (59)	Unexpected network error**
3C (60)	Incompatible remote adapter**
3D (61)	Print queue full**
3E (62)	Not enough space for print file**
3F (63)	Print file was deleted**
40 (64)	Network name was deleted**
41 (65)	Access denied**
42 (66)	Network device type incorrect**
43 (67)	Network name not found**
44 (68)	Network name limit exceeded**
45 (69)	Net BIOS session limit exceeded**
46 (70)	Temporarily paused**
47 (71)	Network request not accepted**
48 (72)	Print or disk redirection is paused**
49 (73)	RESERVED**
4A (74)	RESERVED**
4B (75)	RESERVED**
4C (76)	RESERVED**
4D (77)	RESERVED**
4E (78)	RESERVED**
4F (79)	RESERVED**
50 (80)	File exists
51 (81)	Duplicate FCB
52 (82)	Cannot make directory entry
53 (83)	Interrupt 24H failure
54 (84)	Out of structures
55 (85)	Already assigned
56 (86)	Invalid password**
57 (87)	Invalid parameter
58 (88)	Net write fault**
59 (89)	Function not supported by network**††
5A (90)	Required system component not installed**††

**Applies to network installations only
††Not documented in Microsoft MS-DOS 4.0 Programmer's Reference.

†Error Class:

Value in BH	*Description of Class*	*Example*
1 (1)	Out of a resource	Storage or channels
2 (2)	Temporary situation	Locked region of file
3 (3)	Authorization problem	User doesn't have access rights
4 (4)	Internal error in system software	
5 (5)	Hardware failure	
6 (6)	System software failure	Missing configuration file
7 (7)	Application program failure	
8 (8)	Item not found	File couldn't be found
9 (9)	Invalid format or type	File in wrong format
A (10)	Interlocked item	File is interlocked
B (11)	Media problem	Wrong disk, bad spot on disk
C (12)	Already exists	Declared machine name that exists
D(13)	Unknown	

Suggested Action

Value in BL	*Description of Suggested Action*
1 (1)	Retry, then prompt user
2 (2)	Retry after a brief pause
3 (3)	If user entered item, prompt for it again
4 (4)	Terminate after closing files
5 (5)	Terminate immediately; don't close files
6 (6)	No action; error was informational only
7 (7)	Prompt the user to perform an action (e.g., change disk)

¥Location:

Value in CH	*Probable Location of Error*	*Example*
1(1)	Unknown to DOS	
2(2)	Random access device	Disk drive
3(3)	Network	Network software, hardware
4(4)	Serial device	
5(5)	Memory	RAM

Version:
- DOS 5.0 structure. The layout is identical in previous versions of DOS.
- Error codes apply to all versions of DOS beginning with 2.0.
- Error class, action, and location apply to all versions of DOS beginning with 3.0.

Source: IBM DOS 3.3 Technical Reference, pages 6-40 through 6-46
IBM DOS 4.0 Technical Reference, pages B-6 through B-11
Microsoft MS-DOS 4.0 Programmer's Reference, pages 254 through 257
Microsoft MS-DOS 5.0 Programmer's Reference, pages 78 through 80, 352 through 353, and 447 through 449

See Also: 3.142. INT 21H, AH=59H -- Get Extended Error
3.185. FCB Error Codes

3.192. EXECSTATE STRUCTURE

Offset	Length	Name	Contents
0 (0)	word	esReserved	RESERVED (must be 0)
2 (2)	word	esFlags	Type flags
4 (4)	dbl word	esProgName	Pointer to ASCIIZ program name string
8 (8)	word	esPSP	PSP segment of new program
A (10)	dbl word	esStartAddr	Start CS:IP of new program
E (14)	dbl word	esProgSize	Program size, including PSP

Source: Microsoft MS-DOS 5.0 Programmer's Reference, page 80

See Also: 3.127. INT 21H, AH=4BH, AL=05H -- Set Execution State

3.193. LOAD STRUCTURE

Offset	Length	Name	Contents
0 (0)	word	ldEnvironment	Environment block segment
2 (2)	dbl word	ldCommandTail	Pointer to command tail
6 (6)	dbl word	ldFCB_1	Pointer to default FCB #1
A (10)	dbl word	ldFCB_2	Pointer to default FCB #2
E (14)	dbl word	ldCSIP	Starting code address
12 (16)	dbl word	ldSSSP	Starting stack address

Source: Microsoft MS-DOS 5.0 Programmer's Reference, pages 82 through 83

See Also: 3.125. INT 21H, AH=4BH, AL=10H -- Load Program

3.194. LOADEXEC STRUCTURE

Offset	Length	Name	Contents
0 (0)	word	leEnvironment	Segment address of environment to be passed, or 00H to use parent process's environmen.
2 (2)	dbl word	leCommandTail	Segment:offset address of a command line to be placed at 80H in child process's PSP
6 (6)	dbl word	leFCB_1	Segment:offset address of a FCB to be placed at 5CH of child process's PSP
A (10)	dbl word	leFCB_2	Segment:offset address of a second FCB to be placed at 6CH of child process's PSP

Version: DOS 5.0 structure. The layout is identical in previous versions of DOS.

Source: IBM DOS 3.3 Technical Reference, page 6-197
IBM DOS 4.0 Technical Reference, pages B-101 through B-104
Microsoft MS-DOS 4.0 Programmer's Reference, pages 230 through 233
Microsoft MS-DOS 5.0 Programmer's Reference, pages 83 through 84 and 331

See Also: 3.124. INT 21H, AH=4BH, AL=00H -- Load and Execute Program
3.196. PSP Structure
3.198. Environment Blocks

3.195. LOADOVERLAY STRUCTURE

Offset	*Length*	*Name*	*Contents*
0 (0)	word	loStartSegment	Segment address where overlay is to be loaded
2 (2)	word	loRelocationFactor	Segment:offset where overlay is to be loaded (normally same as load address, but may be increased to overlay only higher portion of a program)

Version: DOS 5.0 structure. The layout is identical in previous versions of DOS.

Source: IBM DOS 3.3 Technical Reference, page 6-197
IBM DOS 4.0 Technical Reference, pages B-101 through B-104
Microsoft MS-DOS 4.0 Programmer's Reference, pages 230 through 233
Microsoft MS-DOS 5.0 Programmer's Reference, page 84

See Also: 3.126. INT 21H, AH=4BH, AL=03H -- Load Overlay
3.194. LOADEXEC Structure

3.196. PSP STRUCTURE

Offset	*Length*	*Name*	*Description*
0 (0)	word	pspInt20	Int 20H instruction
2 (2)	word	pspNextParagraph	End of memory allocation block
4 (4)	byte		RESERVED
5 (5)	5 bytes	pspDispatcher	Far call to DOS function request handler
A (10)	dbl word	pspTerminateVector	Int 22H terminate handler address
E (14)	dbl word	pspControlCVector	Int 23H Ctrl+C handler address
12 (18)	dbl word	pspCritErrorVector	Int 24H Critical Error handler address
16 (22)	11 words		RESERVED
2C (44)	word	pspEnvironment	Segment address of environment block
2E (46)	23 words		RESERVED
48 (72)	16 bytes	pspFCB_1	First 16 bytes of first default FCB
58 (88)	16 bytes	pspFCB_2	First 16 bytes of second default FCB
68 (104)	dbl word		RESERVED
6C (108)	128 bytes	pspCommandTail	Command-line parameters

Version: DOS 5.0 structure. Layout is similar in previous versions of DOS. See sources for more information.

Source: IBM DOS 3.3 Technical Reference, pages 7-10 through 7-11
IBM DOS 4.0 Technical Reference, pages 6-4 through 6-6
Microsoft MS-DOS 4.0 Programmer's Reference, pages 384 through 386
Microsoft MS-DOS 5.0 Programmer's Reference, pages 66 and 84 through 85

See Also: 3.050. INT 21H, AH=26H -- Create New Program Segment Prefix
3.154. INT 21H, AH=62H -- Get PSP Address
3.176. FCB Structure (Unopened)

3.197. MEMORY ALLOCATION STRATEGIES

Prior to DOS 5.0

Value	*Name*	*Description*
0	First fit	Search beginning at lowest available memory and allocate first block large enough to accommodate request (default)
1	Best fit	Search all blocks and allocate smallest block that accommodates request
2	Last fit	Search beginning at highest available memory and allocate first block large enough to accommodate request

DOS 5.0

Value	*Name*	*Description*
0000h	First_fit_low	Search conventional memory for the available block having the lowest address. This is the default strategy.
0001h	Best_fit_low	Search conventional memory for the available block that most closely matches the requested size.
0002h	Last_fit_low	Search conventional memory for the available block at the highest address.
0080h	First_fit_high	Search the upper-memory area for the available block at the lowest address. If no block is found, the search continues in conventional memory.
0081h	Best_fit_high	Search the upper-memory area for the available block that most closely matches the requested size. If no block is found, the search continues in conventional memory.
0082h	Last_fit_high	Search the upper-memory area for the available block at the highest address. If no block is found, the search continues in conventional memory.
0040h	First_fit_highonly	Search the upper-memory area for the available block at the lowest address.
0041h	Best_fit_highonly	Search the upper-memory area for the available block that most closely matches the requested size.
0042h	Last_fit_highonly	Search the upper-memory area for the available block at the highest address.

Version: Applies to all versions of DOS beginning with 3.0 (but undocumented in IBM versions).

Source: Microsoft MS-DOS 3.3 Programmer's Reference, page 262
Microsoft MS-DOS 4.0 Programmer's Reference, pages 252 through 253
Microsoft MS-DOS 5.0 Programmer's Reference, page 347

See Also: 3.121. INT 21H, AH=48H -- Allocate Memory
3.122. INT 21H, AH=49H -- Free Allocated Memory
3.123. INT 21H, AH=4AH -- Set Memory Size Block
3.138. INT 21H, AH=58H, AL=00H -- Get Allocation Strategy
3.139. INT 21H, AH=58H, AL=01H -- Set Allocation Strategy

3.198. ENVIRONMENT BLOCKS

Offset	*Length*	*Name*	*Contents*
0 (0)	varies	Environment string 1	ASCII string in form: PARAMETER=VALUE
varies	byte	String terminator	Must be a 0
varies	varies	Environment string 2	ASCII string in form: PARAMETER=VALUE
varies	byte	String terminator	Must be a 0

and so on, until last string:

varies	varies	Environment string n	ASCII string in form: PARAMETER=VALUE
varies	byte	String terminator	Must be a 0
varies	byte	String terminator	Must be a 0
varies	word	Count	Number of characters following
varies	varies	Initial argument string	ASCIIZ path and file name of current process

Version: Applies to all versions of DOS beginning with 2.0.

Note:
- An environment may have no environment strings, in which case the first two bytes are 00,00.
- PARAMETER value is always in uppercase.

Source: IBM DOS 3.3 Technical Reference, pages 6-198 through 2-199
IBM DOS 4.0 Technical Reference, pages 6-7 through 6-8
Microsoft MS-DOS 5.0 Programmer's Reference, page 66

3.199. COUNTRY CODES

Numerical Order

Code	*Country*	*Keyboard Code*
001	United States	US
002	Canada (French)	CF
003	Latin America	LA
031	Netherlands	NL
032	Belgium	BE
033	France	FR
034	Spain	SP
036	Hungary†	HU
038	Yugoslavia†	YU
039	Italy	IT
041	Switzerland (French)	SF
041	Switzerland (German)	SG
042	Czechoslovakia (Czech)†	CZ
042	Czechoslovakia (Slovak)†	SL
044	United Kingdom	UK
045	Denmark	DK
046	Sweden	SV
047	Norway	NO
048	Poland†	PL
049	Germany	GR
055	Brazil†	BR
061	International English	
081	Japan*	JA
082	Korea*	KO
086	Peoples Republic of China*	CH
088	Taiwan*	TN
351	Portugal	PO
358	Finland	SU
785	Middle East (Arabic)	-
972	Israel (Hebrew)	-

Alphabetical Order

Code	*Country*	*Keyboard Code*
032	Belgium	BE
055	Brazil†	BR
002	Canada (French)	CF
042	Czechoslovakia (Czech)†	CZ
042	Czechoslovakia (Slovak)†	SL
045	Denmark	DK
358	Finland	SU
033	France	FR
049	Germany	GR
036	Hungary†	HU
061	International English	
972	Israel (Hebrew)*	-
039	Italy*	IT
081	Japan*	JA
082	Korea*	KO
003	Latin America	LA
785	Middle East (Arabic)	-
031	Netherlands	NL
047	Norway	NO
086	Peoples Republic of China*	CH
048	Poland†	PL
351	Portugal	PO
034	Spain	SP
046	Sweden	SV
041	Switzerland (French)	SF
041	Switzerland (German)	SG
088	Taiwan*	TN
044	United Kingdom	UK
001	United States	US
038	Yugoslavia†	YU

*DOS 4.0 only
†DOS 5.0 only

Version: Applies to all version of DOS beginning with 2.0

Note: Country codes are usually the international telephone prefix number for the country.

Source: IBM DOS 3.3 Reference, page B-2
IBM Using DOS Version 4.0, page 74
Microsoft MS-DOS 4.0 User's Reference, pages 283 and 328
Microsoft MS-DOS 5.0 User's Guide, pages 334 through 335

See Also: 3.200. Code-Page Assignments
3.203. COUNTRYINFO Structure

3.200. CODE-PAGE ASSIGNMENTS

Country/Region or Language	*Keyboard Code*	*Country Code*	*Default Code Page*	*Alternate Code Page*
Belgium	BE	032	850	437
Brazil†	BR	055	850	437
Canadian-French	CF	002	863	850
Czechoslovakia (Czech)†	CZ	042	852	850
Czechoslovakia (Slovak)†	SL	042	852	850
Denmark	DK	045	850	865
Finland	SU	358	850	437
France	FR	033	850	437
Germany	GR	049	850	437
Hungary	HU	036	852	850
International English		061	437	850
Italy	IT	039	850	437
Japan*	JA			
Korea*	KO			
Latin America	LA	003	850	437
Netherlands	NL	031	850	437
Norway	NO	047	850	865
Peoples Republic of China*	CH			
Poland†	PL	048	852	850
Portugal	PO	351	850	860
Spain	SP	034	854	437
Sweden	SV	046	850	437
Switzerland (French)	SF	041	850	437
Switzerland (German)	SG	041	850	437
Taiwan*	TN			
United Kingdom	UK	044	437	850
United States	US	001	437	850
Yugoslavia†	YU	038	852	850

*DOS 4.0 only
†DOS 5.0 only

Version: Applies to all versions of DOS beginning with 3.3.

Source: IBM DOS 3.3 Reference, pages 9-5 through 9-7
IBM Using DOS Version 4.0, page 74
Microsoft MS-DOS 4.0 User's Reference, pages 283 and 328
Microsoft MS-DOS 5.0 User's Reference, pages 334 through 335

See Also: 3.166. INT 21H, AH=66H, AL=02H -- Set Global Code Page

3.201. SELECT/QUERY CODE-PAGE PARAMETER BLOCKS

Offset	*Length*	*Name*	*Contents*
0	word	Packet length	2+(n+1)*2
2	word	Code-page ID	
4	word	DBCS Vector 1	

and so on, until:

varies	word	DBCS Vector n	

Version: Applies to DOS 3.3 and 4.0 only. DOS 5.0 uses the CODEPAGE structure for these functions.

Source: IBM DOS 3.3 Technical Reference, pages 6-160 through 6-162
IBM DOS 4.0 Technical Reference, pages C-12 through C-17
Microsoft MS-DOS 4.0 Programmer's Reference, pages 392 through 399

See Also: 3.097. INT 21H, AH=44, AL=0CH, Minor Code=4AH -- Select Code Page
3.102. INT 21H, AH=44, AL=0CH, Minor Code=6AH -- Query Selected Code Page
3.166. INT 21H, AH=66H, AL=02H -- Set Global Code Page
3.202. CODEPAGE Structure

3.202. CODEPAGE STRUCTURE

Offset	Length	Name	Contents
0	word	cpLength	Must be 2
2	word	cpId	Code page ID*

*Can be one of the following values:

Value	Meaning
437	U.S.
850	Multilingual (Latin I)
852	Slavic (Latin II)
860	Portuguese
863	Canadian-French
865	Nordic

Version: Applies to all versions of DOS beginning with 3.3.

Source: IBM DOS 3.3 Technical Reference, pages 6-160 through 6-162
IBM DOS 4.0 Technical Reference, pages C-12 through C-17
Microsoft MS-DOS 4.0 Programmer's Reference, pages 392 through 399
Microsoft MS-DOS 5.0 Programmer's Reference, pages 95 and 303

See Also: 3.097. INT 21H, AH=44H, AL=0CH, Minor Code=4AH -- Select Code Page
3.099. INT 21H, AH=44H, AL=0CH, Minor Code=4DH -- End Code-Page Prepare
3.102. INT 21H, AH=44H, AL=0CH, Minor Code=6AH -- Query Selected Code Page
3.166. INT 21H, AH=66H, AL=02H -- Set Global Code Page

3.203. COUNTRYINFO STRUCTURE

Offset	Length	Name	Contents	USA Value
0 (0)	word	ciDateFormat	0 = U.S. (mm/dd/yy) 1 = Europe (dd/mm/yy) 2 = Japan (yy/mm/dd)	0
2 (2)	5 bytes	ciCurrency	ASCIIZ String	$
7 (7)	2 bytes	ciThousands	ASCIIZ String	,
9 (9)	2 bytes	ciDecimal	ASCIIZ String	.
B (11)	2 bytes	ciDateSep	ASCIIZ String	/
D (13)	2 bytes	ciTimeSep	ASCIIZ String	:
F (15)	byte	ciBitField	0 = currency symbol before amount, no spaces between 1 = currency symbol after amount, no spaces between 2 = currency symbol before amount, one space between 3 = currency symbol after amount, one space between 4 = currency symbol replaces decimal separator*	0
10 (16)	byte	ciCurrencyPlaces	Binary value	2
11 (17)	byte	ciTimeFormat	0 = 12-hour clock 1 = 24-hour clock	1
12 (18)	dbl word	ciCaseMap	Segment:offset address of FAR procedure that performs lowercase to uppercase mapping on characters from 80H to FFH	NA
16 (22)	2 bytes	ciDataSep	ASCIIZ String	NA
18 (24)	10 bytes	ciReserved		NA

*Documented in IBM sources only.

Version: DOS 5.0 structure. The layout is identical in previous versions of DOS.

Source: IBM DOS 3.3 Technical Reference, page 6-115
IBM DOS 4.0 Technical Reference, pages B-71 through B-73
Microsoft MS-DOS 4.0 Programmer's Reference, pages 156 through 159
Microsoft MS-DOS 5.0 Programmer's Reference, pages 95 through 96

See Also: 3.070. INT 21H, AH=38 -- Get Country Data
3.199. Country Codes

3.204. CPENTRYHEADER STRUCTURE

Offset	Length	Name	Contents
0 (0)	word	cpeLength	Size of structure in bytes
2 (2)	dbl word	cpeNext	Offset to next CPENTRYHEADER in bytes
6 (6)	word	cpeDevType	1=raster device, 2=printer device
8 (8)	8 bytes	cpeDevSubtype	Name of type of device
10 (16)	word	cpeCodepageID	Code page ID for font
12 (18)	6 bytes	cpeReserved	RESERVED (must be 0)
18 (24)	dbl word	cpeOffset	Offset to font data in bytes

Source: Microsoft MS-DOS 5.0 Programmer's Reference, pages 96 through 97

3.205. CPLIST STRUCTURE

Offset	Length	Name	Contents
0	word	cpLength	Length of remainder of list, in bytes
2	word	cplHIds	Number of hardware code pages
4	word	cplHid	Contains the number of elements specified in cplHIds
varies	word	cplPIds	Number of prepared code pages
varies	word	cplPid	Contains the number of elements specified in cplPids

Version: Applies to all versions of DOS beginning with 3.3.

Source: IBM DOS 3.3 Technical Reference, pages 6-160 through 6-162
IBM DOS 4.0 Technical Reference, pages C-12 through C-17
Microsoft MS-DOS 4.0 Programmer's Reference, pages 392 through 399
Microsoft MS-DOS 5.0 Programmer's Reference, pages 97 and 309

See Also: 3.103. INT 21H, AH=44H, Al=0CH, Minor Code=6BH -- Query Code-Page Prepare List
3.166. INT 21H, AH=66H, AL=02H -- Set Global Code Page

3.206. CPPREPARE STRUCTURE

Offset	Length	Name	Contents
0	word	cppFlags	Device-specific flags
2	word	cppLength	Number of bytes in remainder of structure (n+1)*2
4	word	cppIds	Number of code pages in list (n)
6	word	cppId	Array of code pages. Contains number of elements specified in cppIds.

Version: DOS 5.0 structure. The layout is identical in previous versions of DOS.

Source: IBM DOS 3.3 Technical Reference, pages 6-160 through 6-162
IBM DOS 4.0 Technical Reference, pages C-12 through C-17
Microsoft MS-DOS 4.0 Programmer's Reference, pages 392 through 399
Microsoft MS-DOS 5.0 Programmer's Reference, pages 98 and 304

See Also: 3.098. INT 21H, AH=44H, AL=0CH, Minor Code=4CH -- Start Code-Page Prepare
3.166. INT 21H, AH=66H, AL=02H -- Set Global Code Page

3.207. FILECHARTABLE STRUCTURE

Offset	Length	Name	Contents
0 (0)	byte	fctLength	Length (not including 1st two fields) in bytes
1 (1)	word	fctFirst	Lowest permissible character value
3 (3)	word	fctLast	Highest permissible character value
5 (5)	3 bytes	fctReserved	RESERVED
8 (8)	byte	fctIllegal	Number of illegal characters

Source: Microsoft MS-DOS 5.0 Programmer's Reference, pages 100 through 101

See Also: 3.159. INT 21H, AH=65H, AL=05H -- Get Filename Character Table

3.208. FONTDATAHEADER STRUCTURE

Offset	Length	Name	Contents
0 (0)	word	fdhReserved	RESERVED
2 (2)	word	fdhFonts	Number of fonts
4 (4)	word	fdhLength	Size of font data in bytes

Source: Microsoft MS-DOS 5.0 Programmer's Reference, page 101

3.209. FONTFILEHEADER STRUCTURE

Offset	Length	Name	Contents
0 (0)	8 bytes	ffhFileTag	Font file ID
8 (8)	8 bytes	ffhReserved	RESERVED
10 (16)	word	ffhPointers	Number of pointers
12 (18)	byte	ffhPointerType	Type of pointer
13 (19)	dbl word	ffhOffset	Offset to information header

Source: Microsoft MS-DOS 5.0 Programmer's Reference, pages 101 through 102

3.210. FONTINFOHEADER STRUCTURE

Offset	Length	Name	Contents
0 (0)	word	fihCodePages	Number of code page entries

Source: Microsoft MS-DOS 5.0 Programmer's Reference, page 102

3.211. PRINTERFONTHEADER STRUCTURE

Offset	Length	Name	Contents
0 (0)	word	pfhSelType	Selection type
2 (2)	word	pfhSeqLength	Sequence length

Source: Microsoft MS-DOS 5.0 Programmer's Reference, pages 102 through 103

3.212. SCREENFONTHEADER STRUCTURE

Offset	Length	Name	Contents
0 (0)	byte	sfhHeight	Number of rows character occupies, in pixels
1 (1)	byte	sfhWidth	Number of columns character occupies, in pixels
2 (2)	byte	sfhRelHeight	Relative height (unused, set to 0)
3 (3)	byte	sfhRelWidth	Relative width (unused, set to 0)
4 (4)	word	sfhCharacters	Number of characters defined in bitmap following structure

Source: Microsoft MS-DOS 5.0 Programmer's Reference, page 103

3.213. BUILDBPBREQUEST STRUCTURE

Offset	*Length*	*Name*	*Function*
0 (0)	byte	bbrLength	Number of bytes in request; should be 22
1 (1)	byte	bbrUnit	Subunit (for block devices)
2 (2)	byte	bbrFunction	2 = build BPB
3 (3)	word	bbrStatus	See 3.229. Device Request Header Status Field and Error Codes
5 (5)	8 bytes	bbrReserved	
D (13)	byte	bbrMediaID	See 3.222. MEDIAREQUEST Structure
E (14)	dbl word	bbrFATSector	Segment:offset of buffer address
12 (18)	dbl word	bbrBPBAddress	Segment:offset of BPB structure

Version: DOS 5.0 structure. The layout is identical in previous DOS versions.

Note: • Used in Device Driver Function 02H--Build BPB.

Source: IBM DOS 3.3 Technical Reference, pages 2-29 through 2-30
IBM DOS 4.0 Technical Reference, pages 11-16 through 11-19
Microsoft MS-DOS 4.0 Programmer's Reference, pages 327 through 328
Microsoft MS-DOS 5.0 Programmer's Reference, pages 405 through 406

See Also: 3.215. Device Attribute Codes
3.222. MEDIAREQUEST Structure
3.228. REQUESTHEADER Structure
3.229. Device Request Header Status Field and Error Codes

3.214. DEVICEHEADER STRUCTURE

Offset	*Length*	*Name*	*Contents*
0 (0)	dbl word	dhLink	Segment:offset* address of next device in file, or 0FFFFH if last driver
4 (4)	word	dhAttributes	See 3.215. Device Attribute Codes
6 (6)	word	dhStrategy	Offset address to device strategy routine
8 (8)	word	dhInterrupts	Offset address to device interrupt routine
A (10)	8 bytes	dhNameOrUnits	ASCII device name; for block devices, one byte is optionally the number of units

Note: Segment address must be zero in DOS 5.0.

Version: Applies to all versions of DOS beginning with 2.0.

Source: IBM DOS 3.3 Technical Reference, page 2-6
IBM DOS 4.0 Technical Reference, pages 11-4 through 11-6
Microsoft MS-DOS 4.0 Programmer's Reference, pages 314 through 317
Microsoft MS-DOS 5.0 Programmer's Reference, pages 392 through 394 and 429 through 430

See Also: 3.215. Device Attribute Codes

3.215. DEVICE ATTRIBUTE CODES

For Character-Oriented Devices:

15	14	13	12	11	10	9	8	7	6	5	4	3	2	1	0	Function	Allowable Values
✔																Device type	1=device is character oriented
	✔															Control string support	0=doesn't support control strings 1=supports IOCTL control strings
		✔														Output until busy support	0=doesn't support output until busy 1=supports output until busy
			✔		✔	✔	✔			✔						RESERVED	Must be 0
				✔												Supports open/close	0=doesn't support open/close 1=supports open/close
								✔								Supports IOCTL queries¥	0=doesn't support IOCTL queries 1=supports IOCTL queries
									✔							Supports IOCTL functions and/or logical drive mapping	0=doesn't support mapping functions 1=supports mapping functions
											✔					Supports fast character output¥	0=doesn't support fast character output 1=does support fast character output
												✔				Clock device	0=is not a clock device 1=is a clock device
													✔			Nul device	0=is not a null device 1=is a null device
														✔		Console output device	0=is not standard output device 1=is standard output device
															✔	Console input device	0=is not standard input device 1=is standard input device

For Block-Oriented Devices:

15	14	13	12	11	10	9	8	7	6	5	4	3	2	1	0	Function	Allowable Values
✔																Device type	0=block-oriented device
	✔															Control string support	0=doesn't support control strings 1=supports IOCTL control strings
		✔														Media type determiner	0=doesn't use FAT ID byte 1=uses FAT ID byte to find type*
			✔		✔	✔	✔			✔	✔	✔	✔		✔	RESERVED	Must be 0
				✔												Supports open/close removable media	0=doesn't support open/close 1=supports open/close
								✔								Supports IOCTL queries¥	0=doesn't support IOCTL queries 1=does support IOCTL queries
									✔							Supports IOCTL functions and/or logical drive mapping	0=doesn't support mapping functions 1=supports mapping functions
														✔		32-bit sector addresses†	1=supports; 0=doesn't support

*If FAT ID byte used, the first sector of the FAT must always be in the same physical location.
¥DOS 5.0 only

Version: Applies to all versions of DOS beginning with 2.0.

Source: IBM DOS 3.3 Technical Reference, pages 2-7 through 2-10
IBM DOS 4.0 Technical Reference, pages 11-4 through 11-6
Microsoft MS-DOS 4.0 Programmer's Reference, pages 315 through 317
Microsoft MS-DOS 5.0 Programmer's Reference, pages 392 through 393 and 429 through 430

See Also: 3.214. DEVICEHEADER Structure

3.216. DEVICE DATA WORD

For Devices (Bit 7=1):

Bit Number

15	14	13	12	11	10	9	8	7	6	5	4	3	2	1	0	Function	Allowable Values
✔																Supports character or block device	0=supports block device 1=supports character device
	✔															Supports IOCTL read/write	0=does not support IOCTL read/write 1=supports IOCTL read/write
		✔														Character device: supports output until busy Block device: requires the FAT	0=does not support output until busy 1=supports output until busy 0=does not require the FAT 1=requires the FAT
			✔													RESERVED	
				✔												Character device: supports open/close device Block device: supports open/close/removable media device	0=does not support open/close device 1=supports open/close device 0=does not support open/close/removable media device 1=supports open/close/removable media device
					✔	✔	✔									RESERVED	
								✔								Device type	1=device
									✔							End of File	0=end of file on input 1=not at end of file
										✔						Control Char Check	0=ASCII mode 1=binary mode
											✔					Special device	0=not special device 1=special device
												✔				Clock Device	0=is not a clock device 1=is a clock device
													✔			Null Device	0=is not a null device 1=is a null device
														✔		Console Output Device	0=is not console output device 1=is console output device
															✔	Console Input Device	0=is not console input device 1=is console input device

For Files (Bit 7=0):

Bit Number

15	14	13	12	11	10	9	8	7	6	5	4	3	2	1	0	Function	Allowable Values
✔	✔	✔	✔	✔	✔	✔	✔									RESERVED	Must be 0
								✔								Device type	0=file
									✔							File has been written to	0=file has been written to 1=file has not been written to
										✔	✔	✔	✔	✔	✔	Drive number	000000=A 000001=B and so on

Version: Applies to all versions of DOS beginning with 2.0.

Note: Bit 14 is read only; it cannot be set.

Source: IBM DOS 3.3 Technical Reference, pages 6-149 through 6-150
IBM DOS 4.0 Technical Reference, pages C-3 through C-4
Microsoft MS-DOS 4.0 Programmer's Reference, page 189
Microsoft MS-DOS 5.0 Programmer's Reference, pages 289 and 392 through 393

See Also: 3.084. INT 21H, AH=44H, AL=00H -- Get Device Data
3.085. INT 21H, AH=44H, AL=01H -- Set Device Data
3.214. DEVICEHEADER Structure

3.217. FLUSHREQUEST STRUCTURE

Offset	Length	Name	Contents
0 (0)	byte	frLength	Number of bytes in request; should be 13
1 (1)	byte	frUnit	NOT USED
2 (2)	byte	frFunction	07H(7) = flush input, 0BH(11) = flush output
3 (3)	word	frStatus	See 3.229. Device Request Header Status Field and Error Codes
5 (5)	8 bytes	frReserved	

Version: Applies to all versions of DOS beginning with 2.0.

Note:
- Used in Device Driver Functions 07H -- Input Flush and 0BH -- Output Flush.
- Character devices only; sets the status word.

Source:
IBM DOS 3.3 Technical Reference, page 2-36
IBM DOS 4.0 Technical Reference, page 11-24
Microsoft MS-DOS 4.0 Programmer's Reference, page 334
Microsoft MS-DOS 5.0 Programmer's Reference, pages 412 and 416

See Also:
3.215. Device Attribute Codes
3.228. REQUESTHEADER Structure
3.229. Device Request Header Status Field and Error Codes

3.218. INITREQUEST STRUCTURE

Offset	Length	Name	Contents
0 (0)	byte	irLength	Number of bytes in request; should be 25
1 (1)	byte	irUnit	Subunit (for block devices); not used in DOS 5.0
2 (2)	byte	irFunction	0 = INIT request
3 (3)	word	irStatus	See 3.229. Device Request Header Status Field and Error Codes
5 (5)	8 bytes	irReserved	
D (13)	byte	irUnits	Number of units supported by device
E (14)	dbl word	irEndAddress	Segment:offset of resident portion of driver (returned by Init)
12 (18)	dbl word	irParamAddress	Segment:offset of BPB for block devices. Pointer to BPB structure in DOS 5.0.
16 (22)	byte	irDriveNumber	Logical drive assignment for first unit (0=A, 1=B, etc.)
17 (23)	word	irMessageFlag	Message displays only if driver sets this field to 1 and irStatus indicates error*

*DOS 5.0 only

Version: DOS 5.0 structure. The layout is identical in previous DOS versions.

Note:
- Used in Device Driver Function 00H--Init.
- Note that double words are formatted as offset first, segment second.

Source:
IBM DOS 3.3 Technical Reference, pages 2-21 through 2-22
IBM DOS 4.0 Technical Reference, pages 11-11 through 11-12
Microsoft MS-DOS 4.0 Programmer's Reference, pages 323 through 325
Microsoft MS-DOS 5.0 Programmer's Reference, pages 398 through 402

See Also:
3.228. REQUESTHEADER Structure
3.229. Device Request Header Status Field and Error Codes

3.219. IOCTLREQUEST STRUCTURE

Offset	*Length*	*Name*	*Contents*
0 (0)	byte	giLength	Number of bytes in request; should be 23
1 (1)	byte	giUnit	Subunit (for block devices)
2 (2)	byte	giFunction	13H (19)=generic IOCTL request*; 19H(25)=IOCTL query
3 (3)	word	giStatus	See 3.229. Device Request Header Status Field and Error Codes
5 (5)	8 bytes	giReserved1	
D (13)	byte	giCategory	1=serial device, 3=console (display), 5=parallel printer, 8=disk
E (14)	byte	giMinorCode	Minor code for Int 21H, AX=440CH and AX=440DH†
F (15)	dbl word	giReserved2	
13 (19)	dbl word	giIOCTLData	Segment:offset of pointer to a data buffer

*17 for DOS 3.2 or 3.3

†For character devices:
- 45H=Set Iteration Count
- 4AH=Select Code Page
- 4CH=Start Code-Page Prepare
- 4DH=End Code-Page Prepare
- 65H=Get Iteration Count
- 6AH=Query Selected Code Page
- 6BH=Query Code-Page Prepare List

For block devices:
- 40H=Set Device Parameters
- 41H=Write Track on Logical Drive
- 42H=Format Track on Logical Drive
- 46H=Set Media ID
- 60H=Get Device Parameters
- 61H=Read Track on Logical Drive
- 62H=Verify Track on Logical Drive
- 66H=Get Media ID
- 68H=Sense Media Type

Version: DOS 5.0 structure. The layout is identical in previous versions of DOS.

Note: Used in Device Driver Functions 13H -- Generic IOCTL and 19H -- IOCTL Query.

Source: IBM DOS 3.3 Technical Reference, page 2-40
IBM DOS 4.0 Technical Reference, page11-27
Microsoft MS-DOS 4.0 Programmer's Reference, pages 334 through 335
Microsoft MS-DOS 5.0 Programmer's Reference, pages 422 through 423 and 426

See Also: 3.215. Device Attribute Codes
3.228. REQUESTHEADER Structure
3.229. Device Request Header Status Field and Error Codes

3.220. IOCTLRWREQUEST STRUCTURE

Offset	*Length*	*Name*	*Contents*
0 (0)	byte	irwrLength	Number of bytes in request; should be 20
1 (1)	byte	irwrUnit	Subunit (for block devices)
2 (2)	byte	irwrFunction	3=IOCTL read, 0CH=write
3 (3)	word	irwrStatus	See 3.229. Device Request Header Status Field and Error Codes
5 (5)	8 bytes	irwrReserved	
D (13)	byte	irwrData	
E (14)	dbl word	irwrBuffer	Segment:offset of buffer that receives data from/writes data to device
12 (18)	word	irwrBytes	Number of bytes to read; number of bytes to write

Version: DOS 5.0 structure. The layout is identical in previous DOS versions.

Note: Used in Device Driver Function 03H -- IOCTL Read and 0CH -- IOCTL Write.

Source: IBM DOS 3.3 Technical Reference, pages 2-32 through 2-33
IBM DOS 4.0 Technical Reference, pages 11-20 through 11-21
Microsoft MS-DOS 4.0 Programmer's Reference, pages 329 through 330
Microsoft MS-DOS 5.0 Programmer's Reference, pages 407 and 417

See Also: 3.215. Device Attribute Codes
3.228. REQUESTHEADER Structure
3.229. Device Request Header Status Field and Error Codes

3.221. LOGDEVICEREQUEST STRUCTURE

Offset	Length	Name	Contents
0 (0)	byte	ldrLength	Number of bytes in request; should be 13
1 (1)	byte	ldrUnit	Subunit (for block devices)
2 (2)	byte	ldrFunction	17H(23) = get map, 18H(24) = set map
3 (3)	word	ldrStatus	See 3.229. Device Request Header Status Field and Error Codes
5 (5)	8 bytes	ldrReserved	

*Microsoft MS-DOS 4.0 Technical Reference is confusing: Input or Output byte allowed only.

Version: Applies to all versions of DOS beginning with 3.2

Note: Used in Device Driver Functions 17H--Get Logical Device and 18H--Set Logical Device.

Source: IBM DOS 3.3 Technical Reference, page 2-41
IBM DOS 4.0 Technical Reference, page 11-28
Microsoft MS-DOS 4.0 Programmer's Reference, page 335
Microsoft MS-DOS 5.0 Programmer's Reference, pages 424 and 425

See Also: 3.215. Device Attribute Codes
3.228. REQUESTHEADER Structure
3.229. Device Request Header Status Field and Error Codes

3.222. MEDIAREQUEST STRUCTURE

Offset	Length	Name	Contents
0 (0)	byte	mrLength	Number of bytes in request; should be 19
1 (1)	byte	mrUnit	Subunit (for block devices)
2 (2)	byte	mrFunction	1 = media check
3 (3)	word	mrStatus	Successful=bit 8 set; unsuccessful=bits 8 and 15 set and error value copied to low order byte
5 (5)	8 bytes	RESERVED	
D (13)	byte	mrMediaID	Type of drive†
E (14)	byte	mrReturn	Returned by function 1=not changed, 0=don't know, 0FFH=changed
F (15)	dbl word	mrVolumeID	Previous volume ID returned by function

*Media descriptor values:

Value	Type of Medium
0F0H	1.44 or 2.88MB 3.5" floppy 1.2MB 5.25" floppy
0F8H	Hard disk, any capacity
0F9H	720 K 3.5" floppy 1.2MB 5.25" floppy
0FAH	320 K 5.25" floppy
0FBH	640 K 3.5" floppy
0FCH	180 K 5.25" floppy
0FDH	360 K 5.25" floppy
0FEH	160 K 5.25" floppy
0FFH	320 K 5.25" floppy

Version: DOS 5.0 structure. The layout is identical in previous versions of DOS.

Note:
- Used in Device Driver Function 01H -- Media Check.
- Double words are formatted as offset first, segment second.

Source: IBM DOS 3.3 Technical Reference, pages 2-23 through 2-25
IBM DOS 4.0 Technical Reference, pages 11-13 through 11-15
Microsoft MS-DOS 4.0 Programmer's Reference, pages 325 through 327
Microsoft MS-DOS 5.0 Programmer's Reference, page 403

See Also: 2.22. FAT ID Byte
3.215. Device Attribute Codes
3.228. REQUESTHEADER Structure

3.223. NDREADREQUEST STRUCTURE

Offset	*Length*	*Name*	*Contents*
0 (0)	byte	nrrLength	Number of bytes in request; should be 14
1 (1)	byte	nrrUnit	NOT USED
2 (2)	byte	nrrFunction	5 = non destructive read with no wait function
3 (3)	word	nrrStatus	See 3.229. Device Request Header Status Field and Error Codes
5 (5)	8 bytes	nrrReserved	
D (13)	byte	nrrChar	Returned character from device

Version: DOS 5.0 structure. The layout is identical in previous versions of DOS.

Note: Used in Device Driver Function 05H -- Nondestructive Read.

Source: IBM DOS 3.3 Technical Reference, page 2-34
IBM DOS 4.0 Technical Reference, page 11-22
Microsoft MS-DOS 4.0 Programmer's Reference, page 331
Microsoft MS-DOS 5.0 Programmer's Reference, page 410

See Also: 3.215. Device Attribute Codes
3.228. REQUESTHEADER Structure
3.229. Device Request Header Status Field and Error Codes

3.224. OPENCLOSEREQUEST STRUCTURE

Offset	*Length*	*Name*	*Contents*
0 (0)	byte	ocrLength	Number of bytes in request; should be 13
1 (1)	byte	ocrUnit	Subunit (for block devices)
2 (2)	byte	ocrFunction	0DH(13) = open, 0EH(14) = close
3 (3)	word	ocrStatus	See 3.229. Device Request Header Status Field and Error Codes
5 (5)	8 bytes	ocrReserved	

Version: DOS 5.0 structure. The layout is identical in previous versions of DOS.

Note: Used in Device Driver Functions 0DH -- Open Device and 0EH -- Close Device.

Source: IBM DOS 3.3 Technical Reference, pages 2-37 through 2-38
IBM DOS 4.0 Technical Reference, page 11-25
Microsoft MS-DOS 4.0 Programmer's Reference, page 332
Microsoft MS-DOS 5.0 Programmer's Reference, pages 418 through 419

See Also: 3.215. Device Attribute Codes
3.228. REQUESTHEADER Structure
3.229. Device Request Header Status Field and Error Codes

3.225. OUTPUTREQUEST STRUCTURE

Offset	*Length*	*Name*	*Contents*
0 (0)	byte	orLength	Number of bytes in request; should be 20
1 (1)	byte	orUnit	
2 (2)	byte	orFunction	10H(16)=output until busy
3 (3)	word	orStatus	See 3.229. Device Request Header Status Field and Error Codes
5 (5)	8 bytes	orReserved	
D (13)	byte	orData	
E (14)	dbl word	orBuffer	Segment:offset of buffer to write to device
12 (18)	word	orBytes	Number of bytes to write; number of bytes written

Version: DOS 5.0 structure. The layout is identical in previous versions of DOS.

Note: Used in Device Driver Function 10H -- Output Until Busy.

Source: IBM DOS 3.3 Technical Reference, pages 2-32 through 2-33
IBM DOS 4.0 Technical Reference, pages 11-20 through 11-21
Microsoft MS-DOS 4.0 Programmer's Reference, pages 329 through 330
Microsoft MS-DOS 5.0 Programmer's Reference, page 421

See Also: 3.215. Device Attribute Codes
3.228. REQUESTHEADER Structure
3.229. Device Request HeaderStatus Field and Error Codes

3.226. READWRITEREQUEST STRUCTURE

Offset	Length	Name	Contents
0 (0)	byte	rwrLength	Number of bytes in request; should be 30
1 (1)	byte	rwrUnit	Subunit (for block devices)
2 (2)	byte	rwrFunction	4=read device, 8=write, 9=write w/verify
3 (3)	word	rwrStatus	See 3.229. Device Request Header Status Field and Error Codes
5 (5)	8 bytes	rwrReserved	
D (13)	byte	rwrMediaID	See 3.222. MEDIAREQUEST Structure
E (14)	dbl word	rwrBuffer	Segment offset of buffer to write to device/receive from device
12 (18)	word	rwrBytesSec	Number of bytes (character) or sectors (block) to write/read
14 (20)	word	rwrStartSec	First sector to write (block devices only)/read
16 (22)	dbl word	rwrVolumeID	Returned Offset:segment pointer to volume ID if error 0FH
1A(26)	dbl word	rwrHugeStartSec	Used only if rwrStartSec=0FFFFH

Version: DOS 5.0 structure. The layout is identical in previous versions of DOS.

Note: Used in Device Driver Functions 04H -- Read, 08H -- Write, and 09H -- Write with Verify.

Source: IBM DOS 3.3 Technical Reference, pages 2-32 through 2-33
IBM DOS 4.0 Technical Reference, pages 11-20 through 11-21
Microsoft MS-DOS 4.0 Programmer's Reference, pages 329 through 330
Microsoft MS-DOS 5.0 Programmer's Reference, pages 408 and 413 through 414

See Also: 3.215. Device Attribute Codes
3.222. MEDIAREQUEST Structure
3.228. REQUESTHEADER Structure
3.229. Device Request Header Status Field and Error Codes

3.227. REMOVEMEDIAREQUEST STRUCTURE

Offset	Length	Name	Contents
0 (0)	byte	rmrLength	Number of bytes in request; should be 13
1 (1)	byte	rmrUnit	Checks for removable media
2 (2)	byte	rmrFunction	0FH(15) = removable media
3 (3)	word	rmrStatus	See 3.229. Device Request Header Status Field and Error Codes
5 (5)	8 bytes	rmrReserved	

Version: DOS 5.0 structure. The layout is identical in previous versions of DOS.

Note:
- Used in Device Driver Function 0FH -- Removable Media.
- The open/close/removable media bit must be set in the device attribute code.

Source: IBM DOS 3.3 Technical Reference, page 2-39
IBM DOS 4.0 Technical Reference, pages 11-25 through 11-26
Microsoft MS-DOS 4.0 Programmer's Reference, page 333
Microsoft MS-DOS 5.0 Programmer's Reference, page 420

See Also: 3.215. Device Attribute Codes
3.228. REQUESTHEADER Structure
3.229. Device Request Header Status Field and Error Codes

3.228. REQUESTHEADER STRUCTURE

Offset	*Length*	*Name*	*Contents*
0 (0)	byte	rhLength	Length, in bytes, of the entire request header (including code specific items)
1 (1)	byte	rhUnit	Subunit (minor device within a block device) that request is intended for
2 (2)	byte	rhFunction	00H = init 01H = media check (block devices only) 02H = build BPB (block devices only) 03H = IOCTL input 04H = input (read from device) 05H = non-destructive input, no wait (character devices only) 06H = input status (character devices only) 07H = flush input (character devices only) 08H = output--write to device 09H = output with verify--write to device (block devices only) 0AH = output status (character devices only) 0BH = flush output (character devices only) 0CH = IOCTL output 0DH = open device 0EH = close device 0FH = removable media (block devices only) 10H = output until busy 13H = generic IOCTL request 17H = get drive map (block devices only) 18H = set drive map (block devices only) 19H = IOCTL query*
3 (3)	word	rhStatus	0 before call; set by device routine on return†
5 (5)	8 bytes	rhReserved	RESERVED

*DOS 5.0 only
†See 3.229. Device Request Header Status Field and Error Codes.

Version: DOS 5.0 structure. The layout is identical in previous DOS versions.

Note:
- All unused command codes are reserved
- Many of the command codes require that the appropriate bit be set in the device attribute code

Source:
IBM DOS 3.3 Technical Reference, pages 2-16 through 2-17
IBM DOS 4.0 Technical Reference, pages 11-7 through 11-10
Microsoft MS-DOS 4.0 Programmer's Reference, pages 318 through 320
Microsoft MS-DOS 5.0 Programmer's Reference, pages 431 through 432

See Also:
3.213. BUILDBPBREQUEST Structure
3.215. Device Attribute Codes
3.217. FLUSHREQUEST Structure
3.218. INITREQUEST Structure
3.222. MEDIAREQUEST Structure
3.223. NDREADREQUEST Structure
3.224. OPENCLOSEREQUEST Structure
3.227. REMOVEMEDIAREQUEST Structure
3.229. Device Request Header Status Field and Error Codes
3.230. STATUSREQUEST Structure

3.229. DEVICE REQUEST HEADER STATUS FIELD AND ERROR CODES

Status Field

Bit Number

15	14	13	12	11	10	9	8	7	6	5	4	3	2	1	0	Name	Allowable Values
✔																Error	0=no error 1=error
	✔	✔	✔	✔	✔											RESERVED	
						✔										Busy	0=not busy 1=busy
							✔									Done	0=operation in progress 1=operation complete
								✔	✔	✔	✔	✔	✔	✔	✔	Error code	See table below

Error Codes

Bit Number

15	14	13	12	11	10	9	8	7	6	5	4	3	2	1	0	Error Name
✔																0=write-protect violation
✔															✔	1=unknown unit
✔														✔		2=drive not ready
✔														✔	✔	3=unknown command
✔													✔			4=CRC error
✔													✔		✔	5=bad drive request structure length
✔													✔	✔		6=seek error
✔													✔	✔	✔	7=unknown media
✔												✔				8=sector not found
✔												✔			✔	9=printer out of paper
✔												✔		✔		A=write fault
✔												✔		✔	✔	B=read fault
✔												✔	✔			C=general failure
✔												✔	✔		✔	D=RESERVED
✔												✔	✔	✔		E=RESERVED
✔												✔	✔	✔	✔	F=invalid disk change

Version: Applies to all versions of DOS beginning with 2.0.

Source: IBM DOS 3.3 Technical Reference, pages 2-18 through 2-19
IBM DOS 4.0 Technical Reference, pages 11-7 through 11-9
Microsoft MS-DOS 4.0 Programmer's Reference, 321 through 322
Microsoft MS-DOS 5.0 Programmer's Reference, page 432

See Also: 3.228. REQUESTHEADER Structure

3.230. STATUSREQUEST STRUCTURE

Offset	Length	Name	Contents
0 (0)	byte	srLength	Number of bytes in request; should be 13
1 (1)	byte	srUnit	NOT USED
2 (2)	byte	srFunction	06H(6) = input status, 0AH(10) = output status
3 (3)	word	srStatus	See 3.229. Device Request Header Status Field and Error Codes
5 (5)	8 bytes	srReserved	

Version: Applies to all versions of DOS beginning with 2.0.

Note:
- Used in Device Driver Functions 06H -- Input Status and 0AH -- Output Status.
- Character devices only. Sets status word.

Source: IBM DOS 3.3 Technical Reference, page 2-35
IBM DOS 4.0 Technical Reference, page 11-23
Microsoft MS-DOS 4.0 Programmer's Reference, pages 333 through 334
Microsoft MS-DOS 5.0 Programmer's Reference, pages 411 and 415

See Also: 3.215. Device Attribute Codes
3.228. REQUESTHEADER Structure
3.229. Device Request Header Status Field and Error Codes

3.231. RESERVED DEVICE NAMES AND CHAIN ORDER

Name	*Description*
NUL	Null device
---	Character device drivers, in order encountered in CONFIG.SYS
CON	Console keyboard and display
AUX	Auxiliary device (COM1:)
PRN	Printer device (LPT1:)
CLOCK	Timer device (system clock 18.2 ticks/second)
---	Any other resident block or character devices
---	Installable block device drivers

Version: Applies to all versions of DOS beginning with 2.0.

Note:
- You may substitute your own device drivers for CON, AUX, PRN, and CLOCK (by redirecting their handles), but you may not redirect NUL
- Devices are "chained" in the order presented in the above table (i.e., NUL is the first entry in the device chain, the CONFIG.SYS drivers are next, and so on)

Source: Advanced MS-DOS 2nd Edition (Microsoft Press), page 294

See Also: 3.188. Predefined Handles

3.232. CLOCK DEVICE TABLE LAYOUT

Offset	*Length*	*Name*
0 (0)	word	Days since Jan. 1, 1980 (low byte, high byte)
2 (2)	byte	Minutes
3 (3)	byte	Hours
4 (4)	byte	Hundredths of seconds
5 (5)	byte	Seconds

Version: Not documented for MS-DOS version 5.0. Use INT 21H Functions 2AH through 2DH to set date and time in DOS 5.0.

Source:
IBM DOS 3.3 Technical Reference, page 2-42
IBM DOS 4.0 Technical Reference, page 11-29
Microsoft MS-DOS 4.0 Programmer's Reference, pages 338 through 339
Microsoft MS-DOS 5.0 Programmer's Reference, pages 345 through 346

See Also:
2.20. Date/Time Formats
3.054. INT 21H, AH=2AH -- Get Date
3.055. INT 21H, AH=2BH -- Set Date
3.056. INT 21H, AH=2CH -- Get Time
3.057. INT 21H, AH=2DH -- Set Time

Section 4

BIOS and DOS Extension Calls and Support Tables

4.001. BIOS SERVICES SUMMARY

Interrupt	Func*	Description	Models Supporting Function: PC/XT	PCjr	AT	Conv.	PS/2	PS/1	Comments
0	NA	Divide by zero trap	✔	✔	✔	✔	✔	✔	
1	NA	Single-step (Debug mode)	✔	✔	✔	✔	✔	✔	
2 (NMI)	NA	Parity check routine	✔		✔		✔	✔	
	NA	Coprocessor interrupt direct	✔				✔		
	NA	Coprocessor interrupt via Int 75, IRQ 13			✔		√50+		
	NA	Keyboard interrupt routine		✔		✔			
	NA	I/O channel check				✔	√50+		
	NA	Disk controller power on request				✔			
	NA	System suspend				✔			
	NA	Real time clock (alarm interrupt)				✔			
	NA	System watchdog timer (IRQ0 missed)					√50+		
	NA	Microchannel DMA timer time-out interrupt					√50+		
3	NA	Breakpoint (Debug mode)	✔	✔	✔	✔	✔	✔	
4	NA	Overflow trap	✔	✔	✔	✔	✔	✔	
5	NA	Print screen	✔	✔	✔	✔	✔	✔	Address 50:00H indicates status
6		RESERVED							
7		RESERVED							
8 (IRQ 0)	NA	Timer interrupt handler	✔	✔	✔	✔	✔	✔	18.2 times per second
9 (IRQ 1)	NA	Keyboard interrupt handler	✔	✔	✔	✔	✔	✔	
0AH (IRQ 2)	NA	Invalid task segment state			✔				
0BH (IRQ 3)	NA	COM2 controller interrupt entry	✔	✔	✔	✔			
0CH (IRQ 4)	NA	COM1 controller interrupt entry	✔	✔	✔	✔			
0DH (IRQ 5)	NA	LPT2: controller interrupt entry	✔		✔		✔		Also 80287 entry on AT, hard disk on XT, Model 30, vertical retrace on PCjr
0EH (IRQ 6)	NA	Disk controller interrupt entry	✔	✔	✔	✔	✔	✔	
0FH (IRQ 7)	NA	LPT1: controller interrupt entry	✔	✔	✔	✔	✔		
10H	0	VIDEO set mode	✔	P	✔	✔	✔	✔	
	1	VIDEO set cursor type	✔	✔	✔	✔	✔	✔	
	2	VIDEO set cursor position	✔	✔	✔	✔	✔	✔	
	3	VIDEO read cursor position	✔	✔	✔	✔	✔	✔	
	4	VIDEO read light pen position	✔	✔	✔			✔	PS/1 returns error (not implemented)
	5	VIDEO select display page	✔	P	✔	✔	✔	✔	
	6	VIDEO init window, or scroll contents up	✔	✔	✔	✔	✔	✔	
	7	VIDEO init window, or scroll contents down	✔	✔	✔	✔	✔	✔	
	8	VIDEO read attribute and char at cursor	✔	✔	✔	✔	✔	✔	
	9	VIDEO write attribute and char at cursor	✔	✔	✔	✔	✔	✔	
	0A	VIDEO write character only at cursor	✔	✔	✔	✔	✔	✔	
	0B	VIDEO set color palette	P	P	✔	✔	✔	✔	Only mode 4 CGA, modes 6-8 and 0A on jr
	0C	VIDEO write graphics pixel	✔	✔	✔	✔	✔	✔	Not valid for MDA
	0D	VIDEO read graphics pixel	✔	✔	✔	✔	✔	✔	Not valid for MDA
	0E	VIDEO write text in teletype mode	✔	✔	✔	✔	✔	✔	
	0F	VIDEO get mode	✔	✔	✔	✔	✔	✔	
	10	VIDEO set palette registers		✔			✔	✔	EGA, VGA and PCjr only
	11	VIDEO character generator					✔	✔	EGA only
	12	VIDEO alternate select					✔	✔	EGA and VGA only
	13	VIDEO write character string	P		✔	✔	✔	✔	
	14	VIDEO load LCD char font				✔			
	15	VIDEO return physical parameters				✔			
	16-19	RESERVED							
	1A	VIDEO read/write display combo code					✔	✔	
	1B	VIDEO return state information					✔	✔	
	1C	VIDEO save/restore video state					√50+	✔	
	1D-FF	RESERVED							
11H	-	EQUIPMENT LIST	✔	✔	✔	✔	✔	✔	Returns EQUIP_FLAG for BIOS data area
12H	-	MEMORY SIZE	✔	✔	✔	✔	✔	✔	
13H	0	DISK reset system	✔	✔	✔	✔	✔	✔	
	1	DISK get system status	✔	✔	✔	✔	✔	✔	
	2	DISK read disk	✔	✔	✔	✔	✔	✔	
	3	DISK write disk	✔	✔	✔	✔	✔	✔	
	4	DISK verify disk sectors	✔	✔	✔	✔	✔	✔	
	5	DISK format disk track cylinder	✔	✔	✔	✔	✔	✔	
	6	DISK format cylinder set bad sector flags	√ XT		O		O	O	Considered obsolete except on original XT
	7	DISK format drive starting at cylinder	√ XT		O		O	O	Considered obsolete except on original XT
	8	DISK get current drive parameters			✔		✔	✔	Only Model 319 and 339 ATs
	9	DISK init drive pair characteristics			✔		✔		
	0A	DISK read long			✔				Diagnostics only on Phoenix AT
	0B	DISK write long			✔				Diagnostics only on Phoenix AT

(Continued)

4.001. BIOS Services Summary (continued)

Interrupt	Func*	Description	PC/XT	PCjr	AT	Conv.	PS/2	PS/1	Comments
			Models Supporting Function						
13H	0C	DISK seek to cylinder			✔		✔	✔	
	0D	DISK alternate disk reset			✔		✔	✔	Not on ESDI controllers
	0E	DISK read sector buffer	√ XT						Diagnostics only on Phoenix XT
	0F	DISK write sector buffer	√ XT						Diagnostics only on Phoenix XT
	10	DISK test for drive ready status	√ XT		✔		✔	✔	
	11	DISK recalibrate drive	√ XT		✔		✔	✔	
	12	DISK controller RAM diagnostic	√ XT						
	13	DISK drive diagnostic	√ XT						
	14	DISK controller diagnostics	√ XT						
	15	DISK get disk type	P		✔	✔	✔	✔	Added with XT BIOS dated 1/10/86
	16	FLOPPY DISK change disk status	P		✔	✔	✔	✔	Added with XT BIOS dated 1/10/86
	17	FLOPPY DISK set disk type	P		✔	✔	✔	✔	Added with XT BIOS dated 1/10/86
	18	FLOPPY DISK set media type	P		✔	✔	✔	✔	Added with XT BIOS dated 1/10/86; only ATs after 11/15/85
	19	DISK park heads					✔		ATs after 11/15/85
	1A	DISK format unit					✔		Only on ESDI controllers
	1B-FF	RESERVED							
14H	0	SERIAL init port	✔	✔	✔	✔	✔	✔	2 ports on PCs, 4 ports on PS/2s & PS/1s
	1	SERIAL write character to port	✔	✔	✔	✔	✔	✔	2 ports on PCs, 4 ports on PS/2s & PS/1s
	2	SERIAL read character from port	✔	✔	✔	✔	✔	✔	2 ports on PCs, 4 ports on PS/2s & PS/1s
	3	SERIAL return port status	✔	✔	✔	✔	✔	✔	2 ports on PCs, 4 ports on PS/2s & PS/1s
	4	SERIAL extended initialize					✔	✔	4 ports on PS/2s & PS/1s
	5	SERIAL extended port control					✔	✔	4 ports on PS/2s & PS/1s
	6-FF	RESERVED							
15H	0	CASSETTE motor ON	√PC	✔					Original PC, later models didn't have port
	1	CASSETTE motor OFF	√PC	✔					Original PC, later models didn't have port
	2	CASSETTE read data blocks	√PC	✔					Original PC, later models didn't have port
	3	CASSETTE write data blocks	√PC	✔					Original PC, later models didn't have port
	4-0E	RESERVED							
	0F	DISK format periodic interrupt					√50+		ESDI controllers only
	10-1F	RESERVED							
	20	AL=10 SYSREQ setup; AL=11 SYSREQ completion			✔		√50+		
	21	DEVICE power-on self-test error log					√50+	✔	
	22	RESERVED							
	23	Read/Write DOS 4.00 Flags						✔	
	24-3F	RESERVED							
	40	DEVICE read/modify profiles				✔			
	41	DEVICE wait for external event				✔			
	42	DEVICE request system power OFF				✔			
	43	DEVICE read system status				✔			
	44	DEVICE activate internal modem power				✔			
	45-4E	RESERVED							
	4F	KEYBOARD intercept			✔	✔	✔	✔	ATs after 1/10/84 only
	50-7F	RESERVED							
	80	DEVICE open device			✔	✔	✔		
	81	DEVICE close device			✔	✔	✔		
	82	DEVICE program termination			✔	✔	✔		
	83	DEVICE event wait			✔	✔	✔	✔	
	84	JOYSTICK			✔		✔	✔	
	85	SYSTEM system request key press			✔	✔	✔	✔	
	86	DEVICE wait			✔	✔	✔	✔	
	87	DEVICE move block			✔		√50+	✔	
	88	MEMORY get extended memory size			✔		√50+	✔	
	89	MEMORY switch to protected mode			✔		√50+	✔	
	8A-8F	RESERVED							
	90	DEVICE busy loop			✔	✔	✔	✔	
	91	DEVICE set flag and complete interrupt			✔	✔	✔	✔	
	92-BF	RESERVED							
	C0	DEVICE return system parameters			✔	✔	✔	✔	ATs after 6/10/85 only
	C1	DEVICE return extended BIOS seg.addr.					✔	✔	
	C2	DEVICE pointing device BIOS interface					✔	✔	
	C3	DEVICE enable watchdog time-out					√50+		
	C4	DEVICE programmable option select					√50+		
	C5-FF	RESERVED							

(Continued)

4.001. BIOS Services Summary (continued)

			Models Supporting Function						
Interrupt	*Func**	*Description*	*PC/XT*	*PCjr*	*AT*	*Conv.*	*PS/2*	*PS/1*	*Comments*
16H	0	KEYBOARD read char from keyboard	✔	✔	✔	✔	✔	✔	
	1	KEYBOARD read keyboard status	✔	✔	✔	✔	✔	✔	
	2	KEYBOARD return keyboard flags	✔	✔	✔	✔	✔	✔	
	3	KEYBOARD typematic and delay		✔	✔		✔	✔	ATs after 11/15/85 only
	4	KEYBOARD click ON/OFF		✔		✔		✔	
	5	KEYBOARD write	√XT		✔		✔	✔	XT after 1/10/86, AT after 11/15/85
	6-0F	RESERVED							
	10	KEYBOARD extended keyboard read	√XT		✔		✔	✔	XT after 1/10/86, AT after 11/15/85
	11	KEYBOARD extended keystroke status	√XT		✔		✔	✔	XT after 1/10/86, AT after 11/15/85
	12	KEYBOARD extended shift status	√XT		✔		✔	✔	XT after 1/10/86, AT after 11/15/85
	13-FF	RESERVED							
17H	0	PRINTER write char to printer	✔	✔	✔	✔	✔	✔	3 ports on PCs, 2 on PS/2s & PS/1s
	1	PRINTER init printer port	✔	✔	✔	✔	✔	✔	3 ports on PCs, 2 on PS/2s & PS/1s
	2	PRINTER return printer status	✔	✔	✔	✔	✔	✔	3 ports on PCs, 2 on PS/2s & PS/1s
	3-FF	RESERVED							
18H	-	BASIC load BASIC	✔	✔	✔	✔	✔	✔	
19H	-	BOOTSTRAP loader	✔	✔	✔	✔	✔	✔	PC loads system from disk, PCjr from cartridge or disk, others from any disk
1AH	0	TIME OF DAY read clock count	✔	✔	✔	✔	✔	✔	
	1	TIME OF DAY set clock count	✔	✔	✔	✔	✔	✔	
	2	TIME OF DAY read real time clock			✔	✔	✔	✔	
	3	TIME OF DAY set real time clock			✔	✔	✔	✔	
	4	TIME OF DAY read date from RT clock			✔	✔	✔	✔	
	5	TIME OF DAY set date in RT clock			✔	✔	✔	✔	
	6	TIME OF DAY set alarm			✔	✔	✔	✔	
	7	TIME OF DAY reset alarm			✔	✔	✔	✔	
	8	TIME OF DAY set RTC-activated power ON				✔			
	9	TIME OF DAY read RTC alarm time & status				✔	✔		
	0A	TIME OF DAY read system timer day count	√XT				✔	✔	XT after 1/10/86
	0B	TIME OF DAY set system timer day count	√XT				✔	✔	XT after 1/10/86
	0C-7F	RESERVED							
	80	SOUND set up multiplexer		✔					
	81-FF	RESERVED							

*Usually value in AH register; values in hexadecimal

Legend:
√=supported
√50+=PS/2 Models 50-80, but not Models 20, 25, or 30
√PC=original PC only (not XT)
√XT=XT model only (not original PC)
O=obsolete (implemented but not normally used)
P=partial or peculiar support; see comments and individual tables.
D=diagnostic call only

Source:
IBM PC/XT Technical Reference, BIOS Listings
IBM PC/AT Technical Reference, BIOS Listings
IBM PS/2 and PC BIOS Interface Technical Reference, pages 2-13 through 2-122
BIOS Interface Technical Reference for PS/1 Computer, pages 2-3 through 2-77
System BIOS for IBM PC/XT/AT Computers and Compatibles (Phoenix), pages 113 through 452

See Also:
5.001. DOS Interrupt Usage by Version
5.066. INT 33H, Mouse Functions Summary
5.120. INT 67H, Expanded Memory Manager Functions Summary
7.005. PC Interrupt Usage Summary

4.002. BIOS MEMORY USAGE SUMMARY

Location	*Length*	*Description*	*Bit Number* 7	6	5	4	3	2	1	0	*Comments*
40:00	Word	COM1 base address									
40:02	Word	COM2 base address									
40:04	Word	COM3 base address									Supported only by PS/2, Phoenix BIOS
40:06	Word	COM4 base address									Supported only by PS/2, Phoenix BIOS
40:08	Word	LPT1 base address									
40:0A	Word	LPT2 base address									
40:0C	Word	LPT3 base address									
40:0E	Word	LPT4 base address									PC, XT, AT, Convertible, and Phoenix only
40:10	Byte	Installed hardware 1	✔	✔							Number of floppy drives (0=1 drive, 1=2 drives, etc.)
					✔	✔					Video mode (01=40x25 color, 10=80x25 color, 11=80x25 mono; 00=RESERVED, or EGA/VGA/PGA in Phoenix BIOS)
							✔	✔			RESERVED (old PC and PCjr bits 2-3 indicate memory installed)
								✔			Pointing device installed (PC/XT and later only)
									✔		Math coprocessor installed (not on PCjr, PS/1, or Convertible)
										✔	Floppy drive installed for boot
40:11	Byte	Installed hardware 2	✔	✔							Number of printer adapters
					✔						Internal modem (Convertible only)
						✔					Joystick installed (PS/1 only)
							✔	✔	✔		Number of RS-232 Adapters
										✔	RESERVED (PCjr=DMA device installed)
40:12	Byte	Power-on self test status									Convertible only
40:13	Word	Memory size									In K (0 to 640)
40:15	Word	RESERVED									Manufacturing test port (Phoenix AT only)
40:17	Byte	Keyboard control 1	✔								1=Insert mode active
				✔							1=Caps lock mode active
					✔						1=Num lock mode active
						✔					1=Scroll lock mode active
							✔				1=Alt key held down
								✔			1=Ctrl key held down
									✔		1=Left Shift key held down
										✔	1=Right Shift key held down
40:18	Byte	Keyboard control 2	✔								1=Insert key held down
				✔							1=Caps Lock key held down
					✔						1=Num Lock key held down
						✔					1=Scroll Lock key held down
							✔				1=Pause mode active
								✔			1=System Request key held down
									✔		1=Left Alt key held down
										✔	1=Left Ctrl key held down
40:19	Byte	Alternate keypad entry									
40:1A	Word	Keyboard buffer head pointer									Points to next character in type-ahead buffer
40:1C	Word	Keyboard buffer tail pointer									Points to next available location in type-ahead buffer
40:1E	32 bytes	Keyboard buffer									
40:3E	Byte	Floppy recalibrate status	✔								Interrupt flag
				✔	✔	✔					RESERVED
							✔				Recalibrate drive 3 (not Phoenix, PS/1)
								✔			Recalibrate drive 2 (not Phoenix, PS/1)
									✔		Recalibrate drive 1
										✔	Recalibrate drive 0
40:3F	Byte	Floppy motor status	✔								0=read or verify, 1=write operation
				✔							RESERVED
					✔	✔					Drive selected (binary value equals drive number)
							✔				Drive 3 motor ON status (not Phoenix, PS/1)
								✔			Drive 2 motor ON status (not Phoenix, PS/1)
									✔		Drive 1 motor ON status
										✔	Drive 0 motor ON status
40:40	Byte	Motor off counter									Contains count of time-outs
40:41	Byte	Floppy previous operation status	✔								1=drive not ready
				✔							1=seek operation failed
					✔						1=general controller failure
						✔					1=CRC error on diskette read
							✔				1=DMA overrun on operation
								✔			1=requested sector not found
									✔		1=address mark not found
										✔	1=invalid drive parameter
									✔	✔	00000011=write-protect error
								✔	✔		00000110=disk changed (door opened)
							✔			✔	00001001=DMA attempt across 64K segment boundary
							✔	✔			00001100=media type not found

(Continued)

4.002. BIOS Memory Usage Summary (continued)

Location	Length	Description	Bit 7	Bit 6	Bit 5	Bit 4	Bit 3	Bit 2	Bit 1	Bit 0	Comments
40:42	7 bytes	Floppy controller status bytes									
40:49	Byte	Display mode									
40:4A	Word	Number of columns in display									
40:4C	Word	Length of regen buffer in bytes									(Phoenix: current page size)
40:4E	Word	Address of regen buffer									(Phoenix: address of current page)
40:50	Word	Cursor position page 1									First byte: column, second byte is row
40:52	Word	Cursor position page 2									First byte: column, second byte is row
40:54	Word	Cursor position page 3									First byte: column, second byte is row
40:56	Word	Cursor position page 4									First byte: column, second byte is row
40:58	Word	Cursor position page 5									First byte: column, second byte is row
40:5A	Word	Cursor position page 6									First byte: column, second byte is row
40:5C	Word	Cursor position page 7									First byte: column, second byte is row
40:5E	Word	Cursor position page 8									First byte: column, second byte is row
40:60	Word	Cursor type									HO byte=starting scan line; LO byte=ending scan line
40:62	Byte	Current display page									
40:63	Word	Video controller base address									
40:65	Byte	Current 3x8 register setting									(mode select register)
40:66	Byte	Current 3x9 register setting									(palette value)
40:67	Dbl word	Pointer to reset code									PS/1, PS/2 (except Models 25 and 30), Phoenix only
40:6B	Byte	RESERVED									Phoenix: last unexpected INT
40:6C	Dbl word	Timer counter									Number of ticks since midnight
40:70	Byte	Timer overflow flag									Non-zero means timer passed 24 hours
40:71	Byte	Break key state									If bit 7=1 then Ctrl+Break was pressed
40:72	Word	Reset flag									1234H=bypass mem test; 4321H=preserve mem (PS/1, PS/2); 5678H=system suspended (Convert.); 9ABCH=mfg test (Convert.); ABCDH=system post loop (Convertible only); 64H=burn-in mode (Phoenix only)
40:74	Byte	Fixed disk prev operation status									See 4.051. INT 13H, Disk System Status Byte Layout (not PS/2)
40:75	Byte	Number of fixed drives									
40:76	Byte	Fixed disk drive control									XT and Phoenix only
40:77	Byte	Fixed disk controller port offset									XT and Phoenix only
40:78	Byte	Printer 1 time-out value									
40:79	Byte	Printer 2 time-out value									
40:7A	Byte	Printer 3 time-out value									
40:7B	Byte	Printer 4 time-out value									PC, XT, AT, Phoenix only
40:7C	Byte	COM1 time-out value									
40:7D	Byte	COM2 time-out value									
40:7E	Byte	COM3 time-out value									Not PS/1
40:7F	Byte	COM4 time-out value									Not PS/1
40:80	Word	Kbd buffer start offset pointer									Offset to start of keyboard buffer from segment 40H
40:82	Word	Kbd buffer end offset pointer									Offset to end of keyboard buffer from segment 40H
40:84	Byte	Video rows (minus one)									
40:85	Word	Char height (bytes/char)									
40:87	Byte	Video control states 1	✔								1=clear RAM
				✔	✔						00=64K on adapter; 01=128K; 10=192K; 11=256K
						✔					NOT USED
							✔				0=EGA or VGA compatible adapter
								✔			1=wait for display enable
									✔		0=color monitor; 1=monochrome monitor (EGA/VGA only)
										✔	0=translate cursor modes 0-3; 1=inhibit cursor translation
40:88	Byte	Video control states 2	✔	✔	✔	✔					Feature Connector bits (EGA/VGA)
							✔	✔	✔	✔	Option Switches settings (EGA/VGA)
40:89	Byte	VGA control bits	✔								1=200 lines
				✔	✔						RESERVED
						✔					1=400 lines
							✔				1=no palette load
								✔			1=monochrome monitor
									✔		1=gray scaling on
										✔	RESERVED
40:8A	Byte	Index into VGA DCC Table									Phoenix VGA only
40:8B	Byte	Media control	✔	✔							Last floppy drive data rate*
					✔	✔					Last floppy drive step rate
						✔					Media established (PS/2)
							✔	✔			Start floppy drive transfer rate (Phoenix BIOS)
							✔	✔	✔	✔	RESERVED (PS/1); bits 0-2 RESERVED (PS/2)

(Continued)

4.002. BIOS Memory Usage Summary (continued)

Location	Length	Description	Bit Number 7	6	5	4	3	2	1	0	Comments
40:8C	Byte	Fixed disk controller status									
40:8D	Byte	Fixed disk controller error status									
40:8E	Byte	Fixed disk interrupt control									
40:8F	Byte	Diskette controller info	✔								RESERVED
		(Phoenix only)		✔							1=drive determined for drive 1
					✔						1=drive 1 is multirate
						✔					1=drive 1 supports change line
							✔				RESERVED
								✔			1=driver determined for drive 0
									✔		1=drive 0 is multirate
										✔	1=dirve 0 supports change line
40:90	Byte	Drive 0 media state	✔	✔							Drive data rate*
					✔						Double stepping required
						✔					Media established
							✔				RESERVED
								✔	✔	✔	Drive/media state†
40:91	Byte	Drive 1 media state	✔	✔							Drive data rate*
					✔						Double stepping required
						✔					Media established
							✔				RESERVED
								✔	✔	✔	Drive/media state†
40:92	Word	RESERVED									(diskette drive service work area)(Phoenix)
40:94	Byte	Drive 0 current cylinder									
40:95	Byte	Drive 1 current cylinder									
40:96	Byte	Keyboard mode state, type flags	✔								Read ID in progress
				✔							Last character was first ID character
					✔						Force Num Lock if read ID and KBX
						✔					101/102-key keyboard installed
							✔				Right Alt key held down
								✔			Right Ctrl key held down
									✔		Last code was E0 hidden code
										✔	Last code was E1 hidden code
40:97	Byte	Keyboard LED flags	✔								Keyboard transmit error flag
				✔							Mode indicator update
					✔						Resend receive flag
						✔					Acknowledgment received
							✔				RESERVED (must be 0)
								✔	✔	✔	LED state bits
40:98	Word	User wait complete flag									Offset address
40:9A	Word	User wait complete flag									Segment address
40:9C	Word	User wait count (low word)									In microseconds
40:9E	Word	User wait count (high word)									In microseconds
40:A0	Byte	Wait active flag	✔								Wait time elapsed and POST
				✔	✔	✔	✔	✔	✔		RESERVED
										✔	Int 15H Function 86H (Wait) has occurred
40:A1	7 bytes	RESERVED									
40:A8	Dbl word	Video parameter table pointer									PS/1 and PS/2, Phoenix VGA
40:AC	Dbl word	Dynamic save area pointer									EGA, PS/1, and PS/2, Phoenix VGA
40:B0	Dbl word	Alpha mode aux char gen pointer									EGA, PS/1, and PS/2 only
40:B4	Dbl word	Graph mode aux char gen pointer									EGA, PS/1, and PS/2 only
40:B8	Dbl word	Secondary save pointer									PS/1 and PS/2 only (not Model 25 or 30)
40:BC	8 bytes	RESERVED									Set to zeros only
40:C0	64 bytes	RESERVED									
50:00	Word	Print screen status byte									

*Drive data rates:
00=500 K/second
01=300 K/second
10=250 K/second
11=RESERVED

†Drive media state values are as follows:
000=360K disk/360K drive not established
001=360K disk/1.2MB drive not established
010=1.2MB disk/1.2MB drive not established
011=360K disk/360K drive established
100=360K disk/1.2MB drive established
101=1.2MB disk/1.2MB drive established
110=RESERVED
111=None of the above

Version: PS/2 Extended BIOS uses space at top of memory for an Extended BIOS data area (also PS/1).

Source: IBM PS/2 and PC BIOS Interface Technical Reference, pages 3-3 through 3-17
BIOS Interface Technical Reference for PS/1 Computer, pages 3-3 through 3-14
System BIOS for IBM PC/XT/AT Computers and Compatibles (Phoenix), pages 31 through 37

See Also: 4.003. Extended BIOS Data Area Layout
4.043. Alpha Mode AUX Char Gen Table
4.044. Graphics Mode AUX Char Gen Table
4.045. Save Pointer Data Area and Secondary Save Pointer Data Area
7.003. PC, AT, and PS/2 Memory Usage Summary

4.003. EXTENDED BIOS DATA AREA LAYOUT

Location of the Extended BIOS Data Area is determined as follows:

Location	*Function*
40:13	Kilobytes below 640K limit at which extended BIOS data area begins

Contents of the extended BIOS Data Area are formatted as follows:

Offset	*Function*
0	Single byte containing length of extended BIOS data area in K
1	Beginning of extended BIOS data area

Version: PS/1 and PS/2 only

Source: IBM PS/2 and PC BIOS Interface Technical Reference, page 3-17
BIOS Interface Technical Reference for PS/1 Computer, page 3-15

See Also: 4.109. INT 15H, AH=C0H -- Return System Config Parameters
4.111. INT 15H, AH=C1H -- Return Ext BIOS Segment Address

4.004. CMOS RAM DATA AREA LAYOUT

*Location**	*Size*	*Function*	*Contents*
0 (0)	Byte	Current second	In BCD form
1 (1)	Byte	Alarm second	In BCD form
2 (2)	Byte	Current minute	In BCD form
3 (3)	Byte	Alarm minute	In BCD form
4 (4)	Byte	Current hour	In BCD form
5 (5)	Byte	Alarm hour	In BCD form
6 (6)	Byte	Current day of week	In BCD form
7 (7)	Byte	Current day	In BCD form
8 (8)	Byte	Current month	In BCD form
9 (9)	Byte	Current year	In BCD form
A (10)	Byte	Status Register A	Bit 7 -- 1=update in progress Bits 4-6 -- Divider of time-based frequency Bits 0-3 -- Rate selection bits
B (11)	Byte	Status Register B	Bit 7 -- 1=abort any update cycle in progress; 0=run (update cycle) Bit 6 -- 1=enable periodic interrupt Bit 5 -- 1=enable alarm interrupt Bit 4 -- 1=enable update-ended interrupt Bit 3 -- 1=enable Reg A sqauare wave frequency Bit 2 -- 1=calendar is in binary format; 0=calendar in BCD format Bit 1 -- 1=24-hour clock; 0=12-hour clock Bit 0 -- 1=enable daylight savings time
C (12)	Byte	Status Register C	Bit 7 -- IRQF flag Bit 6 -- PF flag Bit 5 -- AF flag Bit 4 -- UF flag Bits 0-3 -- RESERVED
D (13)	Byte	Status Register D	Bit 7 -- 1=real time clock has power Bits 0-6 -- RESERVED
E (14)	Byte	Diagnostic Status	Bit 7 -- 1=real time clock lost power Bit 6 -- 1=CMOS checksum is bad Bit 5 -- 1=invalid config info found at POST Bit 4 -- 1=memory size compare error at POST Bit 3 -- 1=fixed disk/adapter failed initialization Bit 2 -- 1=CMOS time found invalid Bits 0-1 -- RESERVED

(Continued)

4.004. CMOS RAM Data Area Layout (continued)

Location*	Size	Function	Contents
F (15)	Byte	Shutdown Code	00H=power on or soft reset 01H=memory size pass 02H=memory test pass 03H=memory test fail 04H=POST end; boot system 05H=JMP doubleword pointer with EOI 06H=protected tests pass 07H=protected tests fail 08H=memory size fail 09H=INT 15H block move 0AH=JMP doubleword pointer without EOI 0BH=used by 80386
10 (16)	Byte	Drive Types	Bits 4-7 -- Drive 0 Type: 0000=none; 0001=360K; 0010=1.2MB; 0011=720K; 0100=1.44MB Bits 0-3 -- Drive 1 Type: 0000=none; 0001=360K; 0010=1.2MB; 0011=720K; 0100=1.44MB
11 (17)	Byte	Fixed Disk 0 Type	
12 (18)	Byte	Fixed Disk 1 Type	
13 (19)	Byte	RESERVED	
14 (20)	Byte	Installed Equipment	Bits 6-7 -- Number of diskette drives (0=1; 1=2) Bits 4-5 -- Primary display Bits 2-3 -- RESERVED Bit 1 1=math coprocessor present Bit 0 0=diskette drive present
15 (21)	Byte	Base memory LO byte	In K
16 (22)	Byte	Base memory HO byte	In K
17 (23)	Byte	Expansion memory LO byte	In K
18 (24)	Byte	Expansion memory HO byte	In K
19 (25)	Byte	Fixed Disk 0 Type	
1A (26)	Byte	Fixed Disk 1 Type	
1B (27)	19 bytes	RESERVED	
2E (47)	Byte	HO checksum for 10H-2DH	
2F (48)	Byte	LO checksum for 10H-2DH	
30 (49)	Byte	Actual expansion memory low byte	
31 (50)	Byte	Actual expansion memory high byte	
32 (51)	Byte	Century	In BCD
33 (52)	Byte	Information flag	
34 (53)	12 bytes	RESERVED	

*Actual address undetermined; this is the address written to port 70H during write operation.

Version: Applies to AT BIOS using MC146818A real time clock chip only.

Source: System BIOS for IBM PC/XT/AT Computers and Compatibles (Phoenix), pages 52 through 55

See Also: 1.19 Binary Coded Decimal Number Format

4.005. BIOS ERROR CODES

BIOS Errors generally are indicated by setting the Carry Flag and returning a value in AX.
See individual tables for more details.

See Also: 4.006. Phoenix BIOS Beep Codes
4.051. INT 13H, Disk System Status Byte Layout
4.080. INT 14H, Modem and Line Status Byte
4.120. INT 15H, Mouse Port Status Bytes
4.127. INT 16H, Keyboard Flags Byte
4.133. INT 16H, Extended Keyboard Flags Byte
4.135. INT 17H, Printer Status Byte

4.006. PHOENIX BIOS BEEP CODES

*Code**	*Error Code†*	*Description*
none	01H	CPU register test still in progress
1-1-3	02H	CMOS read/write failure
1-1-4	03H	BIOS checksum failure
1-2-1	04H	Programmable interval timer failure
1-2-2	05H	DMA initialization failure
1-2-3	06H	DMA page register read/write failure
1-3-1	08H	RAM refresh verification failure
none	09H	First 64K RAM test in progress
1-3-3	0AH	First 64K RAM chip or data line failure, multi-bits
1-3-4	0BH	First 64K RAM odd/even logic failure
1-4-1	0CH	First 64K RAM address line failure
1-4-2	0DH	First 64K RAM parity failure
2-1-1	10H	First 64K RAM Bit 0 failure
2-1-2	11H	First 64K RAM Bit 1 failure
2-1-3	12H	First 64K RAM Bit 2 failure
2-1-4	13H	First 64K RAM Bit 3 failure
2-2-1	14H	First 64K RAM Bit 4 failure
2-2-2	15H	First 64K RAM Bit 5 failure
2-2-3	16H	First 64K RAM Bit 6 failure
2-2-4	17H	First 64K RAM Bit 7 failure
2-3-1	18H	First 64K RAM Bit 8 failure
2-3-2	19H	First 64K RAM Bit 9 failure
2-3-3	1AH	First 64K RAM Bit 10 failure
2-3-4	1BH	First 64K RAM Bit 11 failure
2-4-1	1CH	First 64K RAM Bit 12 failure
2-4-2	1DH	First 64K RAM Bit 13 failure
2-4-3	1EH	First 64K RAM Bit 14 failure
2-4-4	1FH	First 64K RAM Bit 15 failure
3-1-1	20H	Slave DMA register failure
3-1-2	21H	Master DMA register failure
3-1-3	22H	Master interrupt mask register failure
3-1-4	23H	Slave interrupt mask register failure
none	25H	Interrupt vector loading in progress
3-2-4	27H	Keyboard controller test failure
none	28H	CMOS power and checksum in progress
none	29H	CMOS configuration validation in progress
3-3-4	2BH	Screen initialization failure
3-4-1	2CH	Screen retrace failure
3-4-2	2DH	Search for video ROM in progress
none	2EH	Screen running with video ROM
none	30H	Screen operable, running with video ROM
none	31H	Monochrome monitor operable
none	32H	Color monitor operable, in 40 column mode
none	33H	Color monitor operable, in 80 column mode

*Numbers indicate beeps; hyphens indicate short silence.
†Error code shows up as contents of port 80H.

Version: Applies to Phoenix BIOS only.

Source: System BIOS for IBM PC/XT/AT Computers and Compatibles (Phoenix), pages 474 through 475

4.007. MODEL NUMBER BYTES

*Model Byte**	*Submodel†*	*Revision†*	*BIOS Version*	*Machine*
FF (255)	NOT USED	NOT USED	All	IBM PC
FE (254)	NOT USED	NOT USED	11/8/82	IBM PC/XT and Portable PC
FD (253)	NOT USED	NOT USED	All	IBM PCjr
FC (252)	NOT USED	NOT USED	1/10/84	IBM PC/AT
	00	01	6/10/85	IBM PC/AT
	01	00	11/15/85	IBM PC/AT
	02	00	All	IBM PC/XT286
	04	00	Initial	IBM PS/2 Model 50
	05	00	Initial	IBM PS/2 Model 60
	0B	00	12/1/89	IBM PS/1
FB (251)	00	01	1/10/86	IBM PC/XT
	00	02	5/9/86	IBM PC/XT
FA (250)	00	00	9/2/86	IBM PS/2 Model 30
F9 (249)	00	00	9/13/85	IBM PC Convertible
F8 (248)	00	00	Initial	IBM PS/2 Model 80
	01	00	Initial	IBM PS/2 Model 80
FE (254)	NOT SUPPORTED	NOT SUPPORTED		Compaq DeskPro
2D (45)	NOT SUPPORTED	NOT SUPPORTED		Compaq Portable
9A (154)	NOT SUPPORTED	NOT SUPPORTED		Compaq Portable Plus

*The model number byte is located at F000:FFFE.
†Submodel and revision numbers are returned by BIOS service INT 15H, AH=C0H (Return System Config Parameters).

Note: Many non-IBM machines use the same Machine ID Byte as the IBM machine they emulate.

Source: IBM PS/2 and PC BIOS Interface Technical Reference, page 4-18
BIOS Interface Technical Reference for PS/1 Computer, page 4-16
System BIOS for IBM PC/XT/AT Computers and Compatibles (Phoenix), pages 60, 384, 414
Manufacturer's information (Compaq, et. al.)

See Also: 4.002. BIOS Memory Usage Summary
4.109. INT 15H, AH=C0H -- Return System Config Parameters

4.008. ADAPTER ROM LAYOUT

*Location**	*Size*	*Description*	*Contents*
0	2 bytes	Adapter ID	55H, AAH
2	Byte	ROM length	In 512K blocks
3	Varies	ROM data	

*Relative to beginning of the Adapter's ROM address

Version: Applies to PS/1 models only.

Source: BIOS Interface Technical Reference for PS/1 Computer, page 4-11

4.009. INT 5H -- PRINT SCREEN SERVICE

Prior to Issuing INT 5H

None

Upon Return from INT 5H

Interrupt returns no values. But RAM Data Area flag will be updated.*

*RAM Data Area 50:00 (40:100) contains status of print screen operation:
00=not called; or, on return, successful
01=print screen in progress
FF= print error encountered

Version: Applies to all PC models.

Source: BIOS Interface Technical Reference for PS/1 Computer, page 2-4
System BIOS for IBM PC/XT/AT Computers and Compatibles (Phoenix), pages 455 through 456

See Also: 4.001. BIOS Services Summary
4.002. BIOS Memory Usage Summary

4.010. INT 9H -- KEYBOARD

Prior to Issuing INT 9H

Varies. Interrupt called upon every make or break of every keystroke.

Upon Return from INT 9H

Interrupt returns no values. But certain keys will cause this interrupt to invoke other routines or to fill in information in the BIOS RAM data area.

Version: Applies to all PC models.

Source: BIOS Interface Technical Reference for PS/1 Computer, page 2-5
System BIOS for IBM PC/XT/AT Computers and Compatibles (Phoenix), pages 131 through 137

See Also: 4.001. BIOS Services Summary
4.002. BIOS Memory Usage Summary

4.011. INT 10H, AH=00H -- SET MODE

Prior to Issuing INT 10H

	High	*Low*
AX	00H	Video mode*
BX		
CX		
DX		
SP		
BP		
SI		
DI		
IP		
flags		
CS		
DS		
SS		
ES		

Upon Return from INT 10H

Interrupt returns no values.†

*See 4.012. INT 10H, Display Modes
†Phoenix BIOS returns video mode to AL, where:
20H=Mode > 7
30H=Mode is from 0-5 or 7
3FH=Mode is 6

Version: Applies to all PC models.

Source: IBM PS/2 and PC BIOS Interface Technical Reference, pages 2-11 through 2-16
BIOS Interface Technical Reference for PS/1 Computer, pages 2-6 through 2-9
System BIOS for IBM PC/XT/AT Computers and Compatibles (Phoenix), page 203

See Also: 4.001. BIOS Services Summary
4.028. INT 10H, AH=0FH -- Get Current Display Mode

4.012. INT 10H, DISPLAY MODES

Mode Number	Type	Max Colors	Text Format	Max Pages	Buffer Start
0 (0)	Text	16	40x25	8	B8000
1 (1)	Text	16	40x25	8	B8000
2 (2)	Text	16	80x25	4* 8†	B8000
3 (3)	Text	16	80x25	4* 8†	B8000
4 (4)	Graphics	4	40x25	1	B8000
5 (5)	Graphics	4	40x25	1	B8000
6 (6)	Graphics	2	80x25	1	B8000
7 (7)	Text	Mono	80x25	1¥ 8´ 4~	B0000
8 (8)	Graphics	16	20x25	1	B0000
9 (9)	Graphics	16	40x25	1	B0000
A (10)	Graphics	4	80x25	1	B0000
B (11)	RESERVED				
C (12)	RESERVED				
D (13)	Graphics	16	40x25	8´	A0000
E (14)	Graphics	16	80x25	4´	A0000
F (15)	Graphics	Mono	80x25	2´	A0000
10 (16)	Graphics	16	80x25	2´	A0000
11 (17)	Graphics	2	80x30	1¥	A0000
12 (18)	Graphics	16	80x30	1¥	A0000
13 (19)	Graphics	256	40x25	1¥	A0000

*CGA, PCjr, Convertible
†EGA, VGA, PS/1, and PS/2
¥MDA
´Convertible
~VGA and PS/2 (except Models 25 and 30)

Source: IBM PS/2 and PC BIOS Interface Technical Reference, pages 2-12 through 2-16
BIOS Interface Technical Reference for PS/1 Computer, pages 2-7 through 2-9
System BIOS for IBM PC/XT/AT Computers and Compatibles (Phoenix), pages 188 through 191

See Also: 4.011. INT 10H, AH=00H -- Set Mode
4.028. INT 10H, AH=0FH -- Get Current Display Mode

4.013. INT 10H, AH=01H -- SET CURSOR TYPE

Prior to Issuing INT 10H

	High	Low
AX	01H	
BX		
CX	Starting scan line	Ending scan line
DX		
SP		
BP		
SI		
DI		
IP		
flags		
CS		
DS		
SS		
ES		

Upon Return from INT 10H

Interrupt returns no values.

Version: Applies to all PC models.

Note:
- CGA allowable scan lines=0-7; MDA = 0-13
- Note that setting bits 5 or 6 in CH may cause erratic behavior (6 and 7 for Phoenix BIOS).
- Phoenix BIOS uses bit 5 of CH for Shut Cursor Off; bits 5-6 of CL for Show Cursor.

Source: IBM PS/2 and PC BIOS Interface Technical Reference, page 2-16
BIOS Interface Technical Reference for PS/1 Computer, page 2-9
System BIOS for IBM PC/XT/AT Computers and Compatibles (Phoenix), pages 204 through 205

See Also: 4.001. BIOS Services Summary
4.014. INT 10H, AH=02H -- Set Cursor Position
4.015. INT 10H, AH=03H -- Read Cursor Position

4.014. INT 10H, AH=02H -- SET CURSOR POSITION

Prior to Issuing INT 10H

	High	Low
AX	02H	
BX	Display page	
CX		
DX	Row	Column
SP		
BP		
SI		
DI		
IP		
flags		
CS		
DS		
SS		
ES		

Upon Return from INT 10H

	High	Low
AX	00*	
BX		
CX		
DX		
SP		
BP		
SI		
DI		
IP		
flags		
CS		
DS		
SS		
ES		

*Return documented by Phoenix BIOS only.

Version: Applies to all PC models.

Note: Page numbers, rows, and columns are 0-based (start counting with 0).

Source: IBM PS/2 and PC BIOS Interface Technical Reference, page 2-16
BIOS Interface Technical Reference for PS/1 Computer, page 2-9
System BIOS for IBM PC/XT/AT Computers and Compatibles (Phoenix), page 206

See Also: 4.001. BIOS Services Summary
4.013. INT 10H, AH=01H -- Set Cursor Type
4.015. INT 10H, AH=03H -- Read Cursor Position

4.015. INT 10H, AH=03H -- READ CURSOR POSITION

Prior to Issuing INT 10H

	High	Low
AX	03H	
BX	Display page	
CX		
DX		
SP		
BP		
SI		
DI		
IP		
flags		
CS		
DS		
SS		
ES		

Upon Return from INT 10H

	High	Low
AX	00*	
BX		
CX	Starting scan line	Ending scan line
DX	Row	Column
SP		
BP		
SI		
DI		
IP		
flags		
CS		
DS		
SS		
ES		

*Return documented in Phoenix BIOS references only.

Version: Applies to all PC models.

Note:
- Page numbers, rows, and columns are 0-based (start with 0).
- CX returns current cursor type.

Source: IBM PS/2 and PC BIOS Interface Technical Reference, page 2-16
BIOS Interface Technical Reference for PS/1 Computer, page 2-9
System BIOS for IBM PC/XT/AT Computers and Compatibles (Phoenix), page 207

See Also: 4.001. BIOS Services Summary
4.013. INT 10H, AH=01H -- Set Cursor Type
4.014. INT 10H, AH=02H -- Set Cursor Position

4.016. INT 10H, AH=04H -- READ LIGHT PEN POSITION

Prior to Issuing INT 10H

	High	Low
AX	04H	
BX		
CX		
DX		
SP		
BP		
SI		
DI		
IP		
flags		
CS		
DS		
SS		
ES		

Upon Return from INT 10H

	High	Low
AX	Pen trigger signal†	
BX	Pixel column	
CX	Pixel row*	
DX	Character row	Character column
SP		
BP		
SI		
DI		
IP		
flags		
CS		
DS		
SS		
ES		

*May be extended to CX for some graphics modes.
†00=pen switch is not active; 01=light pen coordinate values

Version: Light pen is not supported for Convertible, PS/1 or PS/2 models, or VGA Adapters (AH=0).

Source: IBM PS/2 and PC BIOS Interface Technical Reference, page 2-17
BIOS Interface Technical Reference for PS/1 Computer, page 2-9
System BIOS for IBM PC/XT/AT Computers and Compatibles (Phoenix), page 208

See Also: 4.001. BIOS Services Summary

4.017. INT 10H, AH=05H -- SELECT DISPLAY PAGE

Prior to Issuing INT 10H

	High	Low
AX	05H	Page number*
BX	†	†
CX		
DX		
SP		
BP		
SI		
DI		
IP		
flags		
CS		
DS		
SS		
ES		

Upon Return from INT 10H

	High	Low
AX		
BX	CRT†	µProcessor†
CX		
DX		
SP		
BP		
SI		
DI		
IP		
flags		
CS		
DS		
SS		
ES		

*Page numbers are 0-based; PCjr uses AL to set function:
80H=Read CRT/microprocessor page registers
81H=Set microprocessor page register (in BL)
82H=Set CRT page register (in BH)
83H=Set both (CRT in BH, microprocessor in BL)
† Used by PCjr only.

Version: Applies to all PC models.

Sources: IBM PS/2 and PC BIOS Interface Technical Reference, page 2-17
BIOS Interface Technical Reference for PS/1 Computer, page 2-9
System BIOS for IBM PC/XT/AT Computers and Compatibles (Phoenix), page 209

See Also: 4.001. BIOS Services Summary

4.018. INT 10H, AH=06H -- INIT WINDOW, SCROLL WINDOW UP

Prior to Issuing INT 10H

	High	Low
AX	06H	Lines to scroll up*
BX	Blank line attribute	
CX	Upper row	Left column
DX	Lower row	Right column
SP		
BP		
SI		
DI		
IP		
flags		
CS		
DS		
SS		
ES		

*0=blank entire window (Init Window)

Upon Return from INT 10H

Interrupt returns no values.

Version: Applies to all PC models.

Note: BH contains attribute to use for all new blank lines created by function.

Source: IBM PS/2 and PC BIOS Interface Technical Reference, page 2-18
BIOS Interface Technical Reference for PS/1 Computer, page 2-10
System BIOS for IBM PC/XT/AT Computers and Compatibles (Phoenix), page 210

See Also: 4.001. BIOS Services Summary
4.019. INT 10H, AH=07H -- Init Window, Scroll Window Down

4.019. INT 10H, AH=07H -- INIT WINDOW, SCROLL WINDOW DOWN

Prior to Issuing INT 10H

	High	Low
AX	07H	Lines to scroll down*
BX	Blank line attribute	
CX	Upper row	Left column
DX	Lower row	Right column
SP		
BP		
SI		
DI		
IP		
flags		
CS		
DS		
SS		
ES		

*0=blank entire window (Init window)

Upon Return from INT 10H

Interrupt returns no values.

Version: Applies to all PC models.

Note: BH contains attribute to use for all new blank lines created by function.

Source: IBM PS/2 and PC BIOS Interface Technical Reference, page 2-18
BIOS Interface Technical Reference for PS/1 Computer, page 2-10
System BIOS for IBM PC/XT/AT Computers and Compatibles (Phoenix), page 210

See Also: 4.001. BIOS Services Summary
4.018. INT 10H, AH=06H -- Init Window, Scroll Window Up

4.020. INT 10H, AH=08H -- READ CHARACTER AND ATTRIBUTE

Prior to Issuing INT 10H

	High	Low
AX	08H	
BX	Page number	
CX		
DX		
SP		
BP		
SI		
DI		
IP		
flags		
CS		
DS		
SS		
ES		

Upon Return from INT 10H

	High	Low
AX	Attribute*	Character
BX		
CX		
DX		
SP		
BP		
SI		
DI		
IP		
flags		
CS		
DS		
SS		
ES		

*Text modes only

Version: Applies to all PC models.

Source: IBM PS/2 and PC BIOS Interface Technical Reference, page 2-18
BIOS Interface Technical Reference for PS/1 Computer, page 2-10
System BIOS for IBM PC/XT/AT Computers and Compatibles (Phoenix), page 211

See Also: 4.001. BIOS Services Summary
4.021. INT 10H, AH=09H -- Write Character and Attribute
4.022. INT 10H, AH=0AH -- Write Character Only at Cursor
4.026. INT 10H, AH=0DH -- Read Pixel

4.021. INT 10H, AH=09H -- WRITE CHARACTER AND ATTRIBUTE

Prior to Issuing INT 10H

	High	Low
AX	09H	Character
BX	Page number†	Attribute‡
CX	Number of characters to write*	
DX		
SP		
BP		
SI		
DI		
IP		
flags		
CS		
DS		
SS		
ES		

Upon Return from INT 10H

Interrupt returns no values.

*Does not wrap to next line in graphics mode (i.e., characters all on same row, up to limit).
†Background color when in graphics mode
‡Foreground color when in graphics mode

Version:
- Applies to all PC models.
- Bitmap for characters 80H-FFH is pointed to by INT 1FH for some modes and adapters.
- EGA and VGA users can reset normal display fonts with INT 10H, Function 11H.

Source: IBM PS/2 and PC BIOS Interface Technical Reference, pages 2-18 through 2-19
BIOS Interface Technical Reference for PS/1 Computer, pages 2-10 through 2-11
System BIOS for IBM PC/XT/AT Computers and Compatibles (Phoenix), pages 212 through 213

See Also: 4.001. BIOS Services Summary
4.020. INT 10H, AH=08H -- Read Character and Attribute
4.022. INT 10H, AH=0AH -- Write Character Only at Cursor
4.025. INT 10H, AH=0CH -- Write Pixel

4.022. INT 10H, AH=0AH -- WRITE CHARACTER ONLY AT CURSOR

Prior to Issuing INT 10H

	High	Low
AX	0AH	Character
BX	Page number	
CX	Number of characters to write*	
DX		
SP		
BP		
SI		
DI		
IP		
flags		
CS		
DS		
SS		
ES		

Upon Return from INT 10H

Interrupt returns no values.

*Does not wrap to next line in graphics mode (i.e., characters all on same row, up to limit).

Version:
- Applies to all PC models.
- Bitmap for characters 80H-FFH is pointed to by INT 1FH for some modes and adapters.
- EGA and VGA users can reset normal display fonts with INT 10H, Function 11H.

Source:
IBM PS/2 and PC BIOS Interface Technical Reference, page 2-19
BIOS Interface Technical Reference for PS/1 Computer, page 2-11
System BIOS for IBM PC/XT/AT Computers and Compatibles (Phoenix), page 214

See Also:
4.001. BIOS Services Summary
4.020. INT 10H, AH=08H -- Read Character and Attribute
4.021. INT 10H, AH=09H -- Write Character and Attribute
4.025. INT 10H, AH=0CH -- Write Pixel

4.023. INT 10H, AH=0BH -- SET COLOR PALETTE

Prior to Issuing INT 10H

	High	Low
AX	0BH	
BX	Palette ID*	Color ID†
CX		
DX		
SP		
BP		
SI		
DI		
IP		
flags		
CS		
DS		
SS		
ES		

Upon Return from INT 10H

Interrupt returns no values.

*0=red/green/brown, 1=cyan/magenta/white on CGA; 0=set color using value in BL, 1=select palette using value in BL
†See 4.024. INT 10H, Palette and Color Values

Version:
- Applies to all PC models.
- PCjr, EGA, VGA, PS/1, and PS/2 users can manipulate palette more directly with INT 10H, Function 10H.

Source:
IBM PS/2 and PC BIOS Interface Technical Reference, page 2-19
BIOS Interface Technical Reference for PS/1 Computer, page 2-11
System BIOS for IBM PC/XT/AT Computers and Compatibles (Phoenix), page 215

See Also:
4.001. BIOS Services Summary
4.024. INT 10H, Palette and Color Values

4.024. INT 10H, PALETTE AND COLOR VALUES*

If AH=0B and BH=0, then BL register contains the border color as follows:

Value	Color
0 (0)	Black
1 (1)	Blue
2 (2)	Green
3 (3)	Cyan
4 (4)	Red
5 (5)	Magenta
6 (6)	Brown
7 (7)	White
8 (8)	Gray
9 (9)	Light blue
A (10)	Light green
B (11)	Light cyan
C (12)	Light red
D (13)	Light magenta
E (14)	Yellow
F (15)	Bright white

If AH=0BH and BH=1 then BL register contains a palette number, as follows:

Value	Palette
0	Green/red/brown
1	Cyan/magenta/white

*Substantial changes have been made to the definition of the Set Color Palette function with the introduction of EGA.

Version: Information here refers to current (AT and later) implementation, and applies to 320x200 graphics mode only.

Source: IBM Technical Reference Options and Adapters, CGA 8
BIOS Interface Technical Reference for PS/1 Computer, page 2-11
System BIOS for IBM PC/XT/AT Computers and Compatibles (Phoenix), page 215

See Also: 4.023. INT 10H, AH=0BH -- Set Color Palette

4.025. INT 10H, AH=0CH -- WRITE PIXEL

Prior to Issuing INT 10H

	High	Low
AX	0CH	Color*
BX	Page number†	
CX	Pixel column	
DX	Pixel row	
SP		
BP		
SI		
DI		
IP		
flags		
CS		
DS		
SS		
ES		

Upon Return from INT 10H

Interrupt returns no values.

*If bit 7 is set, color value is XORed with current contents (except display mode 13H).
†Only if display mode supports more than one page

Version: Applies to all PC models.

Source: IBM PS/2 and PC BIOS Interface Technical Reference, page 2-20
BIOS Interface Technical Reference for PS/1 Computer, page 2-12
System BIOS for IBM PC/XT/AT Computers and Compatibles (Phoenix), page 216

See Also: 4.001. BIOS Services Summary
4.021. INT 10H, AH=09H -- Write Character and Attribute
4.022. INT 10H, AH=0AH -- Write Character Only at Cursor
4.026. INT 10H, AH=0DH -- Read Pixel

4.026. INT 10H, AH=0DH -- READ PIXEL

Prior to Issuing INT 10H

	High	Low
AX	0DH	
BX	Page number*	
CX	Pixel column	
DX	Pixel row	
SP		
BP		
SI		
DI		
IP		
flags		
CS		
DS		
SS		
ES		

Upon Return from INT 10H

	High	Low
AX		Color
BX		
CX		
DX		
SP		
BP		
SI		
DI		
IP		
flags		
CS		
DS		
SS		
ES		

*Only if display mode supports more than one page

Version: Applies to all PC models.

Source: IBM PS/2 and PC BIOS Interface Technical Reference, page 2-20
BIOS Interface Technical Reference for PS/1 Computer, page 2-12
System BIOS for IBM PC/XT/AT Computers and Compatibles (Phoenix), page 217

See Also: 4.001. BIOS Services Summary
4.020. INT 10H, AH=08H -- Read Character and Attribute
4.025. INT 10H, AH=0CH -- Write Pixel

4.027. INT 10H, AH=0EH -- WRITE TEXT IN TELETYPE MODE

Prior to Issuing INT 10H

	High	Low
AX	0EH	Character†
BX	Page number‡	Foreground color*
CX		
DX		
SP		
BP		
SI		
DI		
IP		
flags		
CS		
DS		
SS		
ES		

Upon Return from INT 10H

Interrupt returns no values.

*If in a graphics display mode
†Carriage Return, Linefeed, Backspace, and Bell are treated as commands, not display chars.
‡PC BIOS dated 4/24/81 and 10/19/81, and Phoenix BIOS must point to active page.

Version: Applies to all PC models.

Source: IBM PS/2 and PC BIOS Interface Technical Reference, page 2-20
BIOS Interface Technical Reference for PS/1 Computer, page 2-12
System BIOS for IBM PC/XT/AT Computers and Compatibles (Phoenix), pages 218 through 219

See Also: 4.001. BIOS Services Summary
4.021. INT 10H, AH=09H -- Write Character and Attribute
4.022. INT 10H, AH=0AH -- Write Character Only at Cursor
4.025. INT 10H, AH=0CH -- Write Pixel

4.028. INT 10H, AH=0FH -- GET CURRENT DISPLAY MODE

Prior to Issuing INT 10H

	High	Low
AX	0FH	
BX		
CX		
DX		
SP		
BP		
SI		
DI		
IP		
flags		
CS		
DS		
SS		
ES		

Upon Return from INT 10H

	High	Low
AX	Columns	Display mode
BX	Active page number	
CX		
DX		
SP		
BP		
SI		
DI		
IP		
flags		
CS		
DS		
SS		
ES		

Version: Applies to all PC models.

Source: IBM PS/2 and PC BIOS Interface Technical Reference, page 2-21
BIOS Interface Technical Reference for PS/1 Computer, page 2-13
System BIOS for IBM PC/XT/AT Computers and Compatibles (Phoenix), page 220

See Also: 4.001. BIOS Services Summary
4.011. INT 10H, AH=00H -- Set Mode
4.012. INT 10H, Display Modes

4.029. INT 10H, AH=10H -- SET PALETTE REGISTERS

Prior to Issuing INT 10H

	High	Low
AX	10H	Command*
BX	Value†	Palette reg†
CX		
DX	Offset of pointer to 17-byte table§	
SP		
BP		
SI		
DI		
IP		
flags		
CS		
DS		
SS		
ES	Segment of pointer to 17-byte table§	

Upon Return from INT 10H

	High	Low
AX		
BX	Value†	
CX		
DX		
SP		
BP		
SI		
DI		
IP		
flags		
CS		
DS		
SS		
ES		

*Sets subfunction to perform, as follows:

AL Value	Other Registers Used
0=set one palette register	BL=register, BH=value
1=set overscan register‡	BH=value
2=set all palette registers and overscan	ES:DX=pointer to 17-byte table
3=toggle intensity/blinking bit	BL=00 enable intensity, 01=enable blinking
7=read one palette register (EGA, VGA)‡	BL=register (returns value in BH)
8=read overscan register (EGA, VGA)‡	(returns value in BH)
9=read all palette registers and overscan (EGA, VGA)‡	ES:DX=pointer to 17-byte buffer for return table values
10H=set one color register (EGA, VGA)‡	BX=color reg, DH=red, CH=green, CL=blue
12H=set block of color registers (EGA, VGA)‡	ES:DX=pointer to color table, BX=1st color reg, CX=number regs to set
13H=select color page (EGA, VGA)‡	BL=subfunction (0=select paging mode, 1=select page)
15H=read single DAC color register (VGA)	BX=color reg (returns DH,CH,CL as RGB value)
17H=read block of color registers (VGA)	BX=start reg, CX=# regs, ES:DX=pointer to 3-byte buffer for return
1AH=read color paging status (VGA)‡	(returns BH=current page, BL=paging mode)
1BH=sum color values to gray shades (VGA)	BX=start reg, CX=count of registers to sum

†See subfunction table above, for exact usage.
‡Does not apply to PS/2 Models 25 and 30.
§Table consists of 16 one-byte palette values, plus one byte overscan value.

Version: Applies to PCjr, EGA (includes PS/1 and PS/2 emulating EGA), and VGA-equipped systems only.

Source: IBM PS/2 and PC BIOS Interface Technical Reference, pages 2-21 through 2-25
BIOS Interface Technical Reference for PS/1 Computer, pages 2-13 through 2-15
System BIOS for IBM PC/XT/AT Computers and Compatibles (Phoenix), pages 221 through 229

See Also: 4.001. BIOS Services Summary

4.030. INT 10H, AH=11H -- CHARACTER GENERATOR

Prior to Issuing INT 10H

	High	Low
AX	11H	Command*
BX	†	†
CX	†	†
DX	†	†
SP		
BP	Offset of pointer to user table†	
SI		
DI		
IP		
flags		
CS		
DS		
SS		
ES	Segment of pointer to user table†	

Upon Return from INT 10H

	High	Low
AX		
BX		
CX	§	§
DX		§
SP		
BP	§	
SI		
DI		
IP		
flags		
CS		
DS		
SS		
ES	§	

*Sets subfunction to perform, as follows:

AL Value	Other Registers Used
00=load user text font	BH=number of bytes per char BL=block CX=number of chars DX=ID of 1st character ES:BP=pointer to table
01=load ROM 8x14 text font‡	BL=block to load
02=load ROM 8x8 text font	BL=block to load
03=set block specifier	BL=select character block
04=load ROM 8x16 text font (VGA)	BL=block to load
10H=load user text font‡	BH=number of bytes per char BL=block CX=number of chars DX=ID of 1st character ES:BP=pointer to table
11H=load ROM 8x14 text font‡	BL=block to load
12H=load ROM 8x8 text font‡	BL=block to load
14H=load ROM 8x16 text font (VGA)	BL=block to load
20H=set user graphics char pointer to INT 1FH	ES:BP=pointer to user graphics font
21H=set user graphics char pointer to INT 43H	BL=rows (coded) CX=bytes per character DL=rows per screen ES:BP=pointer to table
22H=use ROM 8x14 font for graphics‡	BL=rows (coded), DL=rows/screen
23H=use ROM 8x8 font for graphics	BL=rows (coded), DL=rows/screen
24H=use ROM 8x16 font for graphics (VGA)	BL=rows (coded), DL=rows/screen
30H=get font pointer info	BH=font pointer (coded) Returns: CX=bytes per character DL=rows ES:BP=pointer

†See subfunction table above for exact usage.
‡Does not apply to PS/2 Models 25 and 30.
§Applies only to subfunction 30H (see subfunction table above).

Version: Applies to EGA and VGA-equipped systems only (includes PS/1 and PS/2 emulating EGA).

Source: IBM PS/2 and PC BIOS Interface Technical Reference, pages 2-25 through 2-32
BIOS Interface Technical Reference for PS/1 Computer, pages 2-15 through 2-18
System BIOS for IBM PC/XT/AT Computers and Compatibles (Phoenix), pages 230 through 240

See Also: 4.001. BIOS Services Summary

4.031. INT 10H, AH=12H -- ALTERNATE SELECT

Prior to Issuing INT 10H

	High	Low
AX	12H	†
BX	†	Command*
CX	†	†
DX		
SP		
BP		
SI		
DI		
IP		
flags		
CS		
DS		
SS		
ES		

Upon Return from INT 10H

	High	Low
AX		‡
BX	§	§
CX	§	§
DX		
SP		
BP		
SI		
DI		
IP		
flags		
CS		
DS		
SS		
ES		

*Selects subfunction, as follows:

BL Value	Other Registers Used
10H=return config info	(returns BH=color/mono, BL=mem avail, CH=adapter bits, CL=switch settings)
20H=switch to alt print screen rout.	None
30H=select text scan lines (VGA)	AL=scan lines (0=200, 1=350, 2=400)
31H=mode set palette loading (VGA)	AL=0 for disable, 1 for enable palette loading
32H=enable/disable video (VGA)	AL=0 for enable video, 1 for disable
33H=enable/disable gray shades (VGA)	AL=0 for enable summing, 1 for disable
34H=enable/disable cursor scaling (VGA)	AL=0 for enable scaling, 1 for disable
35H=switch display (VGA)	AL=code for switch, ES:DX=pointer to 128-byte save buffer area
36H=video screen ON/OFF (VGA)	AL=0 for ON, 1 for OFF

†Register may be used to pass information to subfunction (see subfunction table above).
‡AL returns 12H if command is supported by VGA, 00 if not supported.
§Register may be used for some return values (see subfunction table above).

Version: Applies to EGA and VGA-equipped systems only (includes PS/1 and PS/2 emulating EGA).

Source: IBM PS/2 and PC BIOS Interface Technical Reference, pages 2-33 through 2-37
BIOS Interface Technical Reference for PS/1 Computer, pages 2-18 through 2-21
System BIOS for IBM PC/XT/AT Computers and Compatibles (Phoenix), pages 241 through 246

See Also: 4.001. BIOS Services Summary
4.030. INT 10H, AH=11H -- Character Generator

4.032. INT 10H, AH=13H -- WRITE STRING

Prior to Issuing INT 10H

	High	Low
AX	13H	Mode*
BX	Page number	Attribute*
CX	Character count	
DX	Start cursor position	
SP		
BP	Offset of pointer to string	
SI		
DI		
IP		
flags		
CS		
DS		
SS		
ES	Segment of pointer to string	

Upon Return from INT 10H

Interrupt returns no values.

*If AL=00 then BL contains attribute, cursor is not moved.
If AL=01 then BL contains attribute, cursor is updated.
If AL=02 then string contains alternating character; attribute and cursor not moved (alpha modes only).
If AL=03 then string contains alternating character; attribute and cursor not moved (alpha modes only).

Version: Applies to all PC models and adapters after 1/08/86.

Note: Carriage Return, Linefeed, Backspace, and Bell are treated as commands, not characters.

Source: IBM PS/2 and PC BIOS Interface Technical Reference, page 2-37
BIOS Interface Technical Reference for PS/1 Computer, page 2-21
System BIOS for IBM PC/XT/AT Computers and Compatibles (Phoenix), page 247

See Also: 4.001. BIOS Services Summary
4.027. INT 10H, AH=0EH -- Write Text in Teletype Mode

4.033. INT 10H, AH=1AH, AL=00H -- READ DISPLAY CODES

Prior to Issuing INT 10H

	High	Low
AX	1AH	00H
BX		
CX		
DX		
SP		
BP		
SI		
DI		
IP		
flags		
CS		
DS		
SS		
ES		

Upon Return from INT 10H

	High	Low
AX		Status*
BX	Alternate disp code†	Active disp code†
CX		
DX		
SP		
BP		
SI		
DI		
IP		
flags		
CS		
DS		
SS		
ES		

*1AH= function was supported (display codes are valid).
†See 4.035. INT 10H, Display Codes.

Version: Applies to PS/1, PS/2, and Phoenix VGA BIOS only.

Source: IBM PS/2 and PC BIOS Interface Technical Reference, page 2-39
BIOS Interface Technical Reference for PS/1 Computer, page 2-22
System BIOS for IBM PC/XT/AT Computers and Compatibles (Phoenix), pages 248 through 249

See Also: 4.001. BIOS Services Summary
4.034. INT 10H, AH=1AH, AL=01H -- Write Display Codes
4.035. INT 10H, Display Codes

4.034. INT 10H, AH=1AH, AL=01H -- WRITE DISPLAY CODES

Prior to Issuing INT 10H

	High	Low
AX	1AH	01H
BX	Alternate disp code†	Active disp code†
CX		
DX		
SP		
BP		
SI		
DI		
IP		
flags		
CS		
DS		
SS		
ES		

Upon Return from INT 10H

	High	Low
AX		Status*
BX		
CX		
DX		
SP		
BP		
SI		
DI		
IP		
flags		
CS		
DS		
SS		
ES		

*1AH= function was supported (display codes were changed).
†See 4.035. INT 10H, Display Codes.

Version: Applies to PS/1, PS/2, and Phoenix VGA BIOS only.

Source: IBM PS/2 and PC BIOS Interface Technical Reference, page 2-39
BIOS Interface Technical Reference for PS/1 Computer, page 2-22
System BIOS for IBM PC/XT/AT Computers and Compatibles (Phoenix), pages 248 through 249

See Also: 4.001. BIOS Services Summary
4.033. INT 10H, AH=1AH, AL=00H -- Read Display Codes
4.035. INT 10H, Display Codes

4.035. INT 10H, DISPLAY CODES

Value	*Function*
0 (0)	No display
1 (1)	Monochrome with 5151 (monochrome) monitor
2 (2)	CGA with 5153/4 (color) monitor
3 (3)	RESERVED
4 (4)	EGA with 5153/4 (color) monitor
5 (5)	EGA with 5151 (monochrome) monitor
6 (6)	PGS with 5175 (color) monitor*
7 (7)	VGA with analog monochrome monitor (except Models 25 and 30)
8 (8)	VGA with analog color monitor (except Models 25 and 30)
9 (9)- A(10)	RESERVED
B (11)	Models 25 and 30 with analog monochrome monitor (MCGA)
C (12)	Models 25 and 30 with analog color monitor (MCGA)
D (13)-FE(254)	RESERVED
FF (255)	Unknown monitor type

*PGS refers to Professional Graphics System.

Source: IBM PS/2 and PC BIOS Interface Technical Reference, page 2-40
BIOS Interface Technical Reference for PS/1 Computer, page 2-22
System BIOS for IBM PC/XT/AT Computers and Compatibles (Phoenix), page 248

See Also: 4.033. INT 10H, AH=1AH, AL=00H -- Read Display Codes
4.034. INT 10H, AH=1AH, AL=01H -- Write Display Codes

4.036. INT 10H, AH=1BH -- RETURN STATE

Register	Prior to Issuing INT 10H: High	Prior to Issuing INT 10H: Low	Upon Return from INT 10H: High	Upon Return from INT 10H: Low
AX	1BH			Status*
BX	Implementation type‡			
CX				
DX				
SP				
BP				
SI				
DI	Offset of pointer to empty buffer		Offset of pointer to video state buffer†	
IP				
flags				
CS				
DS				
SS				
ES	Segment of pointer to empty buffer		Segment of pointer to video state buffer†	

*1BH= function was supported (buffer contains valid info).
†See 4.037. INT 10H, Video State Buffer Layout.
‡Currently only 00 is supported.

Version: Applies to PS/1, PS/2, and Phoenix VGA BIOS only.

Source: IBM PS/2 and PC BIOS Interface Technical Reference, pages 2-41 through 2-44
BIOS Interface Technical Reference for PS/1 Computer, pages 2-23 through 2-26
System BIOS for IBM PC/XT/AT Computers and Compatibles (Phoenix), pages 249 through 253

See Also: 4.001. BIOS Services Summary
4.037. INT 10H, Video State Buffer Layout

4.037. INT 10H, VIDEO STATE BUFFER LAYOUT

Offset	Size	Function	Allowable Values
0 (0)	Word	Offset to static functionality info	See Static Functionality table, below
2 (2)	Word	Segment of static functionality info	See Static Functionality table, below
4 (4)	Byte	Video mode	See 4.012. INT 10H, Display Modes
5 (5)	Word	Character columns in display	
7 (7)	Word	Length of regenerator buffer	In bytes
9 (9)	Word	Start address in regeneration buffer	
B (11)	Word	Cursor position for page 0	Row, column
D (13)	Word	Cursor position for page 1	Row, column
F (15)	Word	Cursor position for page 2	Row, column
11 (17)	Word	Cursor position for page 3	Row, column
13 (19)	Word	Cursor position for page 4	Row, column
15 (21)	Word	Cursor position for page 5	Row, column
17 (23)	Word	Cursor position for page 6	Row, column
19 (25)	Word	Cursor position for page 7	Row, column
1B (27)	Word	Cursor type	Start, end values
1D (29)	Byte	Active display page	
1E (30)	Word	CRT controller address	e.g., 3Bx for monochrome, 3Dx for color
20 (32)	Byte	3x8 register setting	
21 (33)	Byte	3x9 register setting	
22 (34)	Byte	Character rows in display	
23 (35)	Word	Character height	In scan lines per character
25 (37)	Byte	Active display combination code	
26 (38)	Byte	Alternate display combination code	
27 (39)	Word	# colors supported in current mode	
29 (41)	Byte	# pages supported in current mode	
2A (42)	Byte	# scan lines supported in current mode	0=200, 1=350, 2=400, 3=480, 4-255=RESERVED
2B (43)	Byte	Primary character block	0=block 0, 1=block 1, and so on/(RESERVED on PS/2 Model 30)
2C (44)	Byte	Secondary character block	0=block 0, 1=block 1, and so on/(RESERVED on PS/2 Model 30)
2D (45)	Byte	Miscellaneous information	Bits 6,7=RESERVED Bit 5 -- 0=background intensity ON, 1=blinking Bit 4 -- 0=no emulation, 1=cursor emulation ON Bit 3 -- 1=mode set default palette loading DISABLED Bit 2 -- 1=monochrome display attached Bit 1 -- 1=summing is active Bit 0 -- 1=all modes on all displays are active

(Continued)

4.037. INT 10H, Video State Buffer Layout (continued)

Offset	*Size*	*Function*	*Allowable Values*
2E (46)	3 bytes	RESERVED	
31 (49)	Byte	Amount of available video memory	0=64K, 1=128K, 2=192K, 3=256K, 4-255=RESERVED
32 (50)	Byte	Save pointer state information	Bits 6,7=RESERVED Bit 5 -- 1=DCC extension is active Bit 4 -- 1=palette override is active Bit 3 -- 1=graphics font override is active Bit 2 -- 1=alpha font override is active Bit 1 -- 1=dynamic save area is active Bit 1 -- 0=512-character set is active
33 (51)	13 bytes	RESERVED	

Static Functionality Table Layout:

Offset	*Size*	*Description*	*Values*
0	Byte	Supported video modes	Bit 7 -- 1=mode 7 supported Bit 6 -- 1=mode 6 supported Bit 5 -- 1=mode 5 supported Bit 4 -- 1=mode 4 supported Bit 3 -- 1=mode 3 supported Bit 2 -- 1=mode 2 supported Bit 1 -- 1=mode 1 supported Bit 0 -- 1=mode 0 supported
1	Byte	Supported video modes	Bit 7 -- 1=mode 15 supported Bit 6 -- 1=mode 14 supported Bit 5 -- 1=mode 13 supported Bit 4 -- 1=mode 12 supported Bit 3 -- 1=mode 11 supported Bit 2 -- 1=mode 10 supported Bit 1 -- 1=mode 9 supported Bit 0 -- 1=mode 8 supported
2	Byte	Supported video modes	Bits 4-7 RESERVED Bit 3 -- 1=mode 19 supported Bit 2 -- 1=mode 18 supported Bit 1 -- 1=mode 17 supported Bit 1 -- 1=mode 16 supported
3	4 bytes	RESERVED	
7	Byte	Scan line modes available	01H=200, 02H=350, 04H=400
8	Byte	Number of char blocks available	Usually 2 (in Phoenix BIOS only)
9	Byte	Max number of char blocks allowed	
A (10)	Byte	Miscellaneous support	Bit 7 -- 1=color paging supported Bit 6 -- 1=color palette supported Bit 5 -- 1=EGA palette supported Bit 4 -- 1=cursor emulation supported Bit 3 -- 1=default palette loading supported Bit 2 -- 1=character font loading supported Bit 1 -- 1=gray scale summing supported Bit 0 -- 1=all modes on all displays supported
B (11)	Byte	Miscellaneous support	Bits 4-7 RESERVED Bit 3 -- 1=display combination codes supported Bit 2 -- 1=background intensity/blinking control supported Bit 1 -- 1=save/restore supported Bit 0 -- 1=light pen supported
C (12)	Word	RESERVED	
E (14)	Byte	Save pointer functions	Bits 6-7 RESERVED Bit 5 -- 1=DCC extension Bit 4 -- 1=palette override Bit 3 -- 1=graphics font override Bit 2 -- 1=alpha font override Bit 1 -- 1=dynamic save area Bit 0 -- 1=512-character set supported
F (15)	Byte	RESERVED	

Version: Applies to all PC models.

Source: IBM PS/2 and PC BIOS Interface Technical Reference, pages 2-41 through 2-44
BIOS Interface Technical Reference for PS/1 Computer, pages 2-23 through 2-26
System BIOS for IBM PC/XT/AT Computers and Compatibles (Phoenix), pages 250 through 253

See Also: 4.036. INT 10H, AH=1BH -- Return State

4.038. INT 10H, AH=1CH, AL=00H -- RETURN SAVE/RESTORE

Prior to Issuing INT 10H

	High	Low
AX	1CH	00H
BX		
CX	Requested states†	
DX		
SP		
BP		
SI		
DI		
IP		
flags		
CS		
DS		
SS		
ES		

Upon Return from INT 10H

	High	Low
AX		Status*
BX	Number 64-byte blocks for state	
CX		
DX		
SP		
BP		
SI		
DI		
IP		
flags		
CS		
DS		
SS		
ES		

*1CH= function was supported (BX is valid value).
†Bit 0 set = save/restore video hardware state
Bit 1 set = save/restore video BIOS data area
Bit 2 set = save/restore video DAC state and color registers
Bits 3-15 should be set to 0 only.

Version: Applies to PS/2 (except Models 25 and 30), PS/1, and Phoenix VGA BIOS only.

Source: IBM PS/2 and PC BIOS Interface Technical Reference, page 2-45
BIOS Interface Technical Reference for PS/1 Computer, page 2-26
System BIOS for IBM PC/XT/AT Computers and Compatibles (Phoenix), pages 254 through 255

See Also: 4.001. BIOS Services Summary
4.039. INT 10H, AH=1CH, AL=01H -- Save State
4.040. INT 10H, AH=1CH, AL=02H -- Restore State
4.046. Save/Restore Video States

4.039. INT 10H, AH=1CH, AL=01H -- SAVE STATE

Prior to Issuing INT 10H

	High	Low
AX	1CH	01H
BX	Offset of pointer to video state buffer	
CX	Requested states†	
DX		
SP		
BP		
SI		
DI		
IP		
flags		
CS		
DS		
SS		
ES	Segment of pointer to video state buffer	

Upon Return from INT 10H

	High	Low
AX		Status*
BX		
CX		
DX		
SP		
BP		
SI		
DI		
IP		
flags		
CS		
DS		
SS		
ES		

*1CH= function was supported (states were saved).
†Bit 0 set = save/restore video hardware state
Bit 1 set = save/restore video BIOS data area
Bit 2 set = save/restore video DAC state and color registers
Bits 3-15 should be set to 0 only.

Version: Applies to PS/2 (except Models 25 and 30), PS/1, and Phoenix VGA BIOS only.

Source: IBM PS/2 and PC BIOS Interface Technical Reference, page 2-45
BIOS Interface Technical Reference for PS/1 Computer, pages 2-26 through 2-27
System BIOS for IBM PC/XT/AT Computers and Compatibles (Phoenix), page 256

See Also: 4.001. BIOS Services Summary
4.037. INT 10H, Video State Buffer Layout
4.038. INT 10H, AH=1CH, AL=00H -- Return Save/Restore
4.040. INT 10H, AH=1CH, AL=02H -- Restore State
4.046. Save/Restore Video States

4.040. INT 10H, AH=1CH, AL=02H -- RESTORE STATE

Prior to Issuing INT 10H

	High	Low
AX	1CH	02H
BX	Offset of pointer to video state buffer	
CX	Requested states†	
DX		
SP		
BP		
SI		
DI		
IP		
flags		
CS		
DS		
SS		
ES	Segment of pointer to video state buffer	

Upon Return from INT 10H

	High	Low
AX		Status*
BX		
CX		
DX		
SP		
BP		
SI		
DI		
IP		
flags		
CS		
DS		
SS		
ES		

*1CH= function was supported (states were restored).
†Bit 0 set = save/restore video hardware state
Bit 1 set = save/restore video BIOS data area
Bit 2 set = save/restore video DAC state and color registers
Bits 3-15 should be set to 0 only.

Version: Applies to PS/2 (except Models 25 and 30), PS/1, and Phoenix VGA BIOS only.

Source: IBM PS/2 and PC BIOS Interface Technical Reference, page 2-45
BIOS Interface Technical Reference for PS/1 Computer, page 2-27
System BIOS for IBM PC/XT/AT Computers and Compatibles (Phoenix), page 256

See Also:
4.001. BIOS Services Summary
4.037. INT 10H, Video State Buffer Layout
4.038. INT 10H, AH=1CH, AL=00H -- Return Save/Restore
4.039. INT 10H, AH=1CH, AL=01H -- Save State
4.046. Save/Restore Video States

4.041. INT 10H, AH=FEH -- GET VIDEO BUFFER (TOPVIEW)

Prior to Issuing INT 10H

	High	Low
AX	FEH	
BX		
CX		
DX		
SP		
BP		
SI		
DI	Offset of physical video buffer	
IP		
flags		
CS		
DS		
SS		
ES	Segment of physical video buffer	

Upon Return from INT 10H

	High	Low
AX		
BX		
CX		
DX		
SP		
BP		
SI		
DI	Offset of logical video buffer	
IP		
flags		
CS		
DS		
SS		
ES	Segment of logical video buffer	

Note:
- Physical address is B000:0000H for MDA; B800:0000H for CGA and EGA.
- Logical address is memory assigned to video buffer by TopView.
- Function is ignored if TopView is not running.

Source: Advanced MS-DOS Programming 1st Edition (Microsoft Press), pages 418 through 419

See Also:
4.001. BIOS Services Summary
4.042. INT 10H, AH=FFH -- Update Video Buffer (TopView)

4.042. INT 10H, AH=FFH -- UPDATE VIDEO BUFFER (TOPVIEW)

Prior to Calling INT 10H

	High	Low
AX	FFH	
BX		
CX	Number of chars modified*	
DX		
SP		
BP		
SI		
DI	Offset to first char modified	
IP		
FLAGS		
CS		
DS		
SS		
ES	Segment of logical video buffer	

Upon Return from INT 10H

Function returns no values.

*Characters must be in sequence (i.e., contiguous).

Note:
- Logical video buffer is obtained using Function FEH.
- Function is ignored if TopView is not running.

Source: Advanced MS-DOS Programming 1st Edition (Microsoft Press), pages 419 through 420

See Also:
4.001. BIOS Services Summary
4.041. INT 10H, AH=FEH -- Get Video Buffer (TopView)

4.043. ALPHA MODE AUX CHAR GEN TABLE

Offset	Size	Function	Allowable Values
0 (0)	byte	Bytes per character	
1 (1)	byte	Block to load	0=normal operation
2 (2)	word	Count to store	256=normal operation
4 (4)	word	Character offset	0=normal operation
6 (6)	dbl word	Pointer to font table	
A (10)	byte	Displayable rows	FFH=max calculated value should be used instead
B (11)	varies	Mode values allowed for font	FFH byte ends stream of byte-sized mode values

Version: Applies to PS/1 and PS/2 models only.

Source: IBM PS/2 and PC BIOS Interface Technical Reference, pages 3-13 through 3-14
BIOS Interface Technical Reference for PS/1 Computer, page 3-12

See Also: 4.011. INT 10H, AH=00H -- Set Mode

4.044. GRAPHICS MODE AUX CHAR GEN TABLE

Offset	Size	Function	Allowable Values
0 (0)	byte	Displayable Rows	
1 (1)	word	Bytes per Character	
3 (3)	dbl word	Pointer to Font Table	
7 (7)	varies	Mode values allowed for font	FFH byte ends stream of byte-sized mode values

Version: Applies to PS/1 and PS/2 models only.

Source: IBM PS/2 and PC BIOS Interface Technical Reference, page 3-14
BIOS Interface Technical Reference for PS/1 Computer, page 3-12

See Also: 4.011. INT 10H, AH=00H -- Set Mode

4.045. SAVE POINTER DATA AREA AND SECONDARY SAVE POINTER DATA AREA

Save Pointer Data Area

Offset	Size	Function	Allowable Values
0 (0)	dbl word	Video Parameter Table Pointer	initialized to the BIOS video parameter table
4 (4)	dbl word	Dynamic Save Area Pointer	(optional: initialized to 00:00)
8 (8)	dbl word	Alpha Mode AUX Char Gen Pointer	see 4.043. Alpha Mode AUX Char Gen Table
C (12)	dbl word	Graphics Mode AUX Char Gen Pointer	see 4.044. Graphics Mode AUX Char Gen Table
10 (16)	dbl word	Secondary Save Pointer	points to Secondary Save Pointer Area, see below
14 (20)	dbl word	RESERVED	set to 00:00
18 (24)	dbl word	RESERVED	set to 00:00

Secondary Save Pointer Data Area

Offset	Size	Function	Allowable Values
0 (0)	word	Table Length	length, in bytes
2 (2)	dbl word	Display Combo Code Table Pointer	initialized to ROM DCC table
6 (6)	dbl word	2nd Alpha Mode AUX Char Gen Pointer	see 4.043. Alpha Mode AUX Char Gen Table
A (10)	dbl word	User palette profile table pointer	
E (14)	dbl word	RESERVED	set to 00:00
12 (18)	dbl word	RESERVED	set to 00:00
16 (22)	dbl word	RESERVED	set to 00:00

Version: Applies to PS/1 and PS/2 models only.

Source: IBM PS/2 and PC BIOS Interface Technical Reference, pages 3-15 through 3-17
BIOS Interface Technical Reference for PS/1 Computer, pages 3-13 through 3-14

See Also: 4.043. Alpha Mode AUX Char Gen Table
4.044. Graphics Mode AUX Char Gen Table

4.046. SAVE/RESTORE VIDEO STATES

Bit Number

3-15	2	1	0	Description
✔				RESERVED and set to 0
	✔			video DAC state and color registers
		✔		video BIOS data area
			✔	video hardware state

Note: A bit value of 1=save or restore the applicable area.

Source: IBM PS/2 and PC BIOS Interface Technical Reference, page 2-45
BIOS Interface Technical Reference for PS/1 Computer, page 2-27
System BIOS for IBM PC/XT/AT Computers and Compatibles (Phoenix), page 255

See Also: 4.038. INT 10H, AH-1CH, AL=00H -- Return Save/Restore

4.047. INT 11H -- GET EQUIPMENT LIST SERVICE

Register	Prior to Issuing INT 11H: High	Prior to Issuing INT 11H: Low	Upon Return from INT 11H: High	Upon Return from INT 11H: Low
AX			Equipment flag word*	
BX				
CX				
DX				
SP				
BP				
SI				
DI				
IP				
flags				
CS				
DS				
SS				
ES				

*Bit 0 = floppy drive installed
Bit 1 = math coprocessor installed
Bit 2 = pointing device installed (PS/1, PS/2, Phoenix)
Bits 2-3 = 16K blocks RAM installed on system board†
Bits 4-5 = video mode (1=40x25 color, 2=80x25 color, 3=80x25 mono)
Bits 6-7 = number of floppy drives - 1
Bit 8 = DMA present†
Bits 9-11 = number of RS-232 cards attached
Bit 12 = game port adapter attached†
Bit 13 = serial printer attached (PCjr only)
Bit 13 = internal modem installed for all others
Bits 14-15 = number of printers attached
†These bits have different meanings for AT, PS/1, and PS/2.

Source: IBM PS/2 and PC BIOS Interface Technical Reference, page 2-46
BIOS Interface Technical Reference for PS/1 Computer, page 2-28
System BIOS for IBM PC/XT/AT Computers and Compatibles (Phoenix), page 457
DOS Programmer's Reference 2nd Edition (Que), page 892

See Also: 4.001. BIOS Services Summary

4.048. INT 12H -- GET MEMORY SIZE SERVICE

Prior to Issuing INT 12H

	High	Low
AX		
BX		
CX		
DX		
SP		
BP		
SI		
DI		
IP		
flags		
CS		
DS		
SS		
ES		

Upon Return from INT 12H

	High	Low
AX	Memory size*	
BX		
CX		
DX		
SP		
BP		
SI		
DI		
IP		
flags		
CS		
DS		
SS		
ES		

*In 1K bytes

Version: • Applies to all PC models beginning with XT.
• On PS/1 and PS/2, returned value in AX is total memory minus that allocated to Extended BIOS data area.

Note: All memory is assumed to be functional.

Source: IBM PS/2 and PC BIOS Interface Technical Reference, page 2-47
BIOS Interface Technical Reference for PS/1 Computer, page 2-28
System BIOS for IBM PC/XT/AT Computers and Compatibles (Phoenix), page 458

See Also: 4.001. BIOS Services Summary

4.049. INT 13H, AH=00H -- RESET DISK SYSTEM

Prior to Issuing INT 13H

	High	Low
AX	00H	
BX		
CX		
DX		Drive§
SP		
BP		
SI		
DI		
IP		
flags		
CS		
DS		
SS		
ES		

Upon Return from INT 13H

	High	Low
AX	Status†	
BX		
CX		
DX		
SP		
BP		
SI		
DI		
IP		
flags	Carry flag set on error*	
CS		
DS		
SS		
ES		

*On PS/2 only
†On PS/1, PS/2, and Phoenix only; see 4.051. INT 13H, Disk System Status Byte Layout.
§Bit 7=0 for floppy drive, bit 7=1 for fixed drive

Source: IBM PS/2 and PC BIOS Interface Technical Reference, pages 2-48 through 2-49, 2-59
BIOS Interface Technical Reference for PS/1 Computer, pages 2-29 through 2-30, 2-38
System BIOS for IBM PC/XT/AT Computers and Compatibles (Phoenix), page 286

See Also: 4.001. BIOS Services Summary
4.051. INT 13H, Disk System Status Byte Layout

4.050. INT 13H, AH=01H -- GET DISK SYSTEM STATUS

Prior to Issuing INT 13H

	High	Low
AX	01H	
BX		
CX		
DX		Drive§
SP		
BP		
SI		
DI		
IP		
flags		
CS		
DS		
SS		
ES		

Upon Return from INT 13H

	High	Low
AX	Status*	Prev Status¶
BX		
CX		
DX		
SP		
BP		
SI		
DI		
IP		
flags	Carry flag set on error†	
CS		
DS		
SS		
ES		

*See 4.051. INT 13H, Disk System Status Byte Layout.
†Applies to all PC models beginning with XT.
¶Phoenix only (status from previous disk operation)
§Bit 7=0 for floppy drive, bit 7=1 for fixed drive

Source: IBM PS/2 and PC BIOS Interface Technical Reference, page 2-49
BIOS Interface Technical Reference for PS/1 Computer, page 2-30
System BIOS for IBM PC/XT/AT Computers and Compatibles (Phoenix), page 287

See Also: 4.001. BIOS Services Summary
4.051. INT 13H, Disk System Status Byte Layout

4.051. INT 13H, DISK SYSTEM STATUS BYTE LAYOUT

Value	Floppy/Fixed	Description
0 (0)	Both	No error
1 (1)	Both	Invalid diskette parameter (bad command)
2 (2)	Both	Address mark was not found
3 (3)	Both	Attempted write on protected disk
4 (4)	Both	Sector was not found
5 (5)	Fixed	Reset failed
6 (6)	Floppy	Diskette was removed
7 (7)	Fixed	Bad parameter table
8 (8)	Floppy	DMA overrun on previous operation
9 (9)	Both	Attempted to cross 64K segment boundary on DMA operation
A (10)	Fixed	Bad sector flag
B (11)	Fixed	Bad cylinder detected*
C (12)	Floppy	Media type requested was not found*
D (13)	Fixed	Invalid number of sectors in format*
E (14)	Fixed	Control data address mark detected*
F (15)	Fixed	DMA arbitration level out of allowable range*
10 (16)	Both	CRC or ECC error on disk read
11 (17)	Fixed	ECC corrected data error
20 (32)	Both	Controller failed
40 (64)	Both	Seek operation failed
80 (128)	Both	Drive timed out, assumed not ready
AA (170)	Fixed	Drive not ready
BB (187)	Fixed	Undefined error
CC (204)	Fixed	Write fault
EO (224)	Fixed	Status error
FF (255)	Fixed	Sense operation failed*

*Documented for PS/1, PS/2, and Phoenix BIOS only.

Note: Fixed disk status byte applies to all models beginning with the XT; floppy applies to all models of IBM PCs.

Source: IBM PS/2 and PC BIOS Interface Technical Reference, pages 2-49 and 2-59
BIOS Interface Technical Reference for PS/1 Computer, pages 2-30 and 2-38
System BIOS for IBM PC/XT/AT Computers and Compatibles (Phoenix), pages 285 and 326

See Also: 4.049. INT 13H, AH=00H -- Reset Disk System
4.050. INT 13H, AH=01H -- Get Disk System Status

4.052. INT 13H, AH=02H -- READ DISK

Prior to Issuing INT 13H

	High	Low
AX	02H	Number sectors to read
BX	Offset of pointer to read buffer	
CX	Cylinder number	Sector number†
DX	Head number	Drive number§
SP		
BP		
SI		
DI		
IP		
flags		
CS		
DS		
SS		
ES	Segment of pointer to read buffer	

Upon Return from INT 13H

	High	Low
AX	Status*	Number sectors read
BX		
CX		
DX		
SP		
BP		
SI		
DI		
IP		
flags	Carry flag set on error	
CS		
DS		
SS		
ES		

*See 4.051. INT 13H, Disk System Status Byte Layout
†For fixed drives:
CH=cylinder number (low 8 bits of 10-bit cylinder number)
CL=cylinder/sector number
Bits 6,7 = cylinder number (high 2 bits)
Bits 0-5 = sector number
§Bit 7=0 for floppy drive, 1 for fixed drive

Version: Applies to all PC models beginning with XT.

Note: Only value in DL is checked for an appropriate value.

Source: IBM PS/2 and PC BIOS Interface Technical Reference, pages 2-50 and 2-60
BIOS Interface Technical Reference for PS/1 Computer, pages 2-30 through 2-31 and 2-39
System BIOS for IBM PC/XT/AT Computers and Compatibles (Phoenix), page 288 and 329 through 330

See Also: 4.001. BIOS Services Summary
4.051. INT 13H, Disk System Status Byte Layout
4.053. INT 13H, AH=03H -- Write Disk

4.053. INT 13H, AH=03H -- WRITE DISK

Prior to Issuing INT 13H

	High	Low
AX	03H	Number sectors to write
BX	Offset of pointer to buffer with data	
CX	Cylinder number	Sector number†
DX	Head number	Drive number§
SP		
BP		
SI		
DI		
IP		
flags		
CS		
DS		
SS		
ES	Segment of pointer to buffer with data	

Upon Return from INT 13H

	High	Low
AX	Status*	Number sectors written
BX		
CX		
DX		
SP		
BP		
SI		
DI		
IP		
flags	Carry flag set on error	
CS		
DS		
SS		
ES		

*See 4.051. INT 13H, Disk System Status Byte Layout
†For fixed drives:
CH=cylinder number (low 8 bits of 10-bit cylinder number)
CL=cylinder/sector number
Bits 6,7 = cylinder number (high 2 bits)
Bits 0-5 = sector number
§Bit 7=0 for floppy drive, 1 for fixed drive

Version: Applies to all PC models beginning with XT.

Note: Only value in DL is checked for an appropriate value.

Source: IBM PS/2 and PC BIOS Interface Technical Reference, pages 2-50 and 2-61
BIOS Interface Technical Reference for PS/1 Computer, pages 2-31 and 2-39 through 2-40
System BIOS for IBM PC/XT/AT Computers and Compatibles (Phoenix), pages 289 and 331 through 332

See Also: 4.001. BIOS Services Summary
4.051. INT 13H, Disk System Status Byte Layout
4.052. INT 13H, AH=02H -- Read Disk

4.054. INT 13H, AH=04H -- VERIFY SECTORS

Prior to Issuing INT 13H

Register	High	Low
AX	04H	Number sectors to verify
BX	Offset of pointer to data buffer¥	
CX	Cylinder number	Sector number†
DX	Head number	Drive number§
SP		
BP		
SI		
DI		
IP		
flags		
CS		
DS		
SS		
ES	Segment of pointer to buffer with data¥	

Upon Return from INT 13H

Register	High	Low
AX	Status*	Number sectors verified
BX		
CX		
DX		
SP		
BP		
SI		
DI		
IP		
flags	Carry flag set on error	
CS		
DS		
SS		
ES		

*See 4.051. INT 13H, Disk System Status Byte Layout
†For fixed drives:
  CH=cylinder number (low 8 bits of 10-bit cylinder number)
  CL=cylinder/sector number
    Bits 6,7 = cylinder number (high 2 bits)
    Bits 0-5 = sector number
§Bit 7=0 for floppy drive, 1 for fixed drive
¥Not required for AT BIOS after 11/15/85, or for XT286, Convertible, PS/1, or PS/2

Version: Applies to all PC models beginning with XT.

Note: Only value in DL is checked for an appropriate value.

Source: IBM PS/2 and PC BIOS Interface Technical Reference, pages 2-51 and 2-61
BIOS Interface Technical Reference for PS/1 Computer, pages 2-31 through 2-32 and 2-40
System BIOS for IBM PC/XT/AT Computers and Compatibles (Phoenix), page 290 and 333

See Also: 4.001. BIOS Services Summary
4.051. INT 13H, Disk System Status Byte Layout
4.052. INT 13H, AH=02H -- Read Disk

4.055. INT 13H, AH=05H -- FORMAT CYLINDER

Prior to Issuing INT 13H

	High	Low
AX	05H	Number of sectors¶
BX	Offset of pointer to 4-byte address field¥	
CX	Cylinder number	Sector number†
DX	Head number	Drive number§
SP		
BP		
SI		
DI		
IP		
flags		
CS		
DS		
SS		
ES	Segment of pointer to 4-byte address field¥	

Upon Return from INT 13H

	High	Low
AX	Status*	
BX		
CX		
DX		
SP		
BP		
SI		
DI		
IP		
flags	Carry flag set on error	
CS		
DS		
SS		
ES		

*See 4.051. INT 13H, Disk System Status Byte Layout

†For fixed drives:
- CH=cylinder number (low 8 bits of 10-bit cylinder number)
- CL=cylinder/sector number
  - Bits 6,7 = cylinder number (high 2 bits)
  - Bits 0-5 = sector number

§Bit 7=0 for floppy drive, 1 for fixed drive

¥Address field (applies to PC/XT 286, AT, PS/1, and PS/2 only):

Byte	Meaning	Allowable Values
1	Cylinder number	
2	Head number	
3	Sector number	
4	Number bytes/sector	0=128, 1=256, 2=512, 3=1024

¶For floppy drives only; interleave value for PC/XT; not used for other models

Version: Applies to all PC models beginning with XT.

Note: Only value in DL is checked for an appropriate value.

Source: IBM PS/2 and PC BIOS Interface Technical Reference, pages 2-51 through 2-52 and 2-62
BIOS Interface Technical Reference for PS/1 Computer, page 2-32 and 2-40
System BIOS for IBM PC/XT/AT Computers and Compatibles (Phoenix), page 291 through 292 and 334

See Also:
4.001. BIOS Services Summary
4.051. INT 13H, Disk System Status Byte Layout
4.056. INT 13H, AH=06H -- Format Cylinder Set Bad Sector Flags
4.057. INT 13H, AH=07H -- Format Drive Starting at Cylinder

4.056. INT 13H, AH=06H -- FORMAT CYLINDER SET BAD SECTOR FLAGS

Prior to Issuing INT 13H

	High	*Low*
AX	06H	Interleave
BX		
CX	Cylinder number	Sector number†
DX	Head number	Drive number§
SP		
BP		
SI		
DI		
IP		
flags		
CS		
DS		
SS		
ES		

Upon Return from INT 13H

	High	*Low*
AX	Status*	
BX		
CX		
DX		
SP		
BP		
SI		
DI		
IP		
flags	Carry flag set on error	
CS		
DS		
SS		
ES		

*See 4.051. INT 13H, Disk System Status Byte Layout
†For fixed drives:
CH=cylinder number (low 8 bits of 10-bit cylinder number)
CL=cylinder/sector number
Bits 6,7 = cylinder number (high 2 bits)
Bits 0-5 = sector number
§Bit 7=1 for fixed drive

Version: Applies to all PCs with fixed disk drives or ESDI-type devices.

Note: Only value in DL is checked for an appropriate value.

Source: IBM PS/2 and PC BIOS Interface Technical Reference, page 2-63
BIOS Interface Technical Reference for PS/1 Computer, page 2-41
System BIOS for IBM PC/XT/AT Computers and Compatibles (Phoenix), page 336

See Also: 4.001. BIOS Services Summary
4.051. INT 13H, Disk System Status Byte Layout
4.055. INT 13H, AH=05H -- Format Cylinder
4.057. INT 13H, AH=07H -- Format Drive Starting at Cylinder

4.057. INT 13H, AH=07H -- FORMAT DRIVE STARTING AT CYLINDER

Prior to Issuing INT 13H

	High	Low
AX	07H	Interleave
BX		
CX	Cylinder number	Sector number†
DX	Head number	Drive number§
SP		
BP		
SI		
DI		
IP		
flags		
CS		
DS		
SS		
ES		

Upon Return from INT 13H

	High	Low
AX	Status*	
BX		
CX		
DX		
SP		
BP		
SI		
DI		
IP		
flags	Carry flag set on error	
CS		
DS		
SS		
ES		

*See 4.051. INT 13H, Disk System Status Byte Layout
†For fixed drives:
CH=cylinder number (low 8 bits of 10-bit cylinder number)
CL=cylinder/sector number
Bits 6,7 = cylinder number (high 2 bits)
Bits 0-5 = sector number
§Bit 7=1 for fixed drive

Version: Applies to all PC models with hard disks or ESDI-type devices.

Note: Only value in DL is checked for an appropriate value.

Source: IBM PS/2 and PC BIOS Interface Technical Reference, pages 2-63 through 2-64
BIOS Interface Technical Reference for PS/1 Computer, page 2-41
System BIOS for IBM PC/XT/AT Computers and Compatibles (Phoenix), page 337
DOS Programmer's Reference 2nd Edition (Que), page 454

See Also: 4.001. BIOS Services Summary
4.051. INT 13H, Disk System Status Byte Layout
4.055. INT 13H, AH=05H -- Format Cylinder
4.056. INT 13H, AH=06H -- Format Cylinder Set Bad Sector Flags

4.058. INT 13H, AH=08H -- READ DRIVE PARAMETERS

Prior to Issuing INT 13H

	High	Low
AX	08H	
BX		
CX		
DX		Drive number*
SP		
BP		
SI		
DI		
IP		
flags		
CS		
DS		
SS		
ES		

Upon Return from INT 13H

	High	Low
AX	0 (or error)	
BX	0	Drive type†
CX	Max cylinders	Max sectors/track§
DX	Max heads	Number drives
SP		
BP		
SI		
DI	Offset of pointer to 11-byte parm table	
IP		
flags	Carry flag set on error	
CS		
DS		
SS		
ES	Segment of pointer to 11-byte parm table	

*Bit 7=0 for floppy drive, bit 7=1 for fixed drive
†01=360K, 02=1.2Mb, 03=720K, 04=1.44Mb
§Top 2 bits are HO bits of 10-bit max cylinders, bits 0-5 are max sectors per track.

Version: Applies to AT, Phoenix, PS/1, and PS/2 only.

Source: IBM PS/2 and PC BIOS Interface Technical Reference, pages 2-52 through 2-53 and 2-64
BIOS Interface Technical Reference for PS/1 Computer, pages 2-33 through 2-34 and 2-42
System BIOS for IBM PC/XT/AT Computers and Compatibles (Phoenix), pages 293 through 294 and 338 through 339

See Also: 4.001. BIOS Services Summary

4.059. INT 13H, AH=09H -- INIT DRIVE PAIR CHARACTERISTICS

Prior to Issuing INT 13H

	High	Low
AX	09H	
BX		
CX		
DX		Drive number*
SP		
BP		
SI		
DI		
IP		
flags		
CS		
DS		
SS		
ES		

Upon Return from INT 13H

	High	Low
AX	Status†	
BX		
CX		
DX		
SP		
BP		
SI		
DI		
IP		
flags	Carry flag set on error	
CS		
DS		
SS		
ES		

*Bit 7=1 for fixed drive
†See 4.051. INT 13H, Disk System Status Byte Layout

Version: Applies to all PC models beginning with XT.

Source: IBM PS/2 and PC BIOS Interface Technical Reference, pages 2-64 through 2-65
BIOS Interface Technical Reference for PS/1 Computer, page 2-42
System BIOS for IBM PC/XT/AT Computers and Compatibles (Phoenix), page 340

See Also: 4.001. BIOS Services Summary
4.051. INT 13H, Disk System Status Byte Layout

4.060. INT 13H, AH=0AH -- READ LONG SECTORS

Prior to Issuing INT 13H

	High	Low
AX	0AH	Number Sectors
BX	Offset to Disk Transfer Area	
CX	Cylinder Number§	Cylinder Number§
DX	Head Number	Drive number*
SP		
BP		
SI		
DI		
IP		
flags		
CS		
DS		
SS		
ES	Segment of Disk Transfer Area	

Upon Return from INT 13H

	High	Low
AX	Status†	
BX		
CX		
DX		
SP		
BP		
SI		
DI		
IP		
flags	Carry flag set on error	
CS		
DS		
SS		
ES		

*Bit 7=1 for fixed drive
†See 4.051. INT 13H, Disk System Status Byte Layout
§For fixed drives:
CH=cylinder number (low 8 bits of 10-bit cylinder number)
CL=cylinder/sector number
Bits 6,7 = cylinder number (high 2 bits)
Bits 0-5 = sector number

Version: Applies to AT and Phoenix BIOS only.

Source: System BIOS for IBM PC/XT/AT Computers and Compatibles (Phoenix), pages 341 through 342

See Also: 4.001. BIOS Services Summary
4.051. INT 13H, Disk System Status Byte Layout

4.061. INT 13H, AH=0BH -- WRITE LONG SECTORS

Prior to Issuing INT 13H

	High	Low
AX	0BH	Number sectors to read
BX	Offset to Disk Transfer Area	
CX	Cylinder number§	Cylinder number§
DX	Head number	Drive number*
SP		
BP		
SI		
DI		
IP		
flags		
CS		
DS		
SS		
ES	Segment of Disk Transfer Area	

Upon Return from INT 13H

	High	Low
AX	Status†	
BX		
CX		
DX		
SP		
BP		
SI		
DI		
IP		
flags	Carry flag set on error	
CS		
DS		
SS		
ES		

*Bit 7=1 for fixed drive
†See 4.051. INT 13H, Disk System Status Byte Layout
§For fixed drives:
CH=cylinder number (low 8 bits of 10-bit cylinder number)
CL=cylinder/sector number
Bits 6,7 = cylinder number (high 2 bits)
Bits 0-5 = sector number

Version: Applies to AT and Phoenix BIOS only.

Source: System BIOS for IBM PC/XT/AT Computers and Compatibles (Phoenix), pages 343 through 344

See Also: 4.001. BIOS Services Summary
4.051. INT 13H, Disk System Status Byte Layout

4.062. INT 13H, AH=0CH -- SEEK

Prior to Issuing INT 13H

Register	High	Low
AX	0CH	
BX		
CX	Cylinder number§	
DX	Head number	Drive number*
SP		
BP		
SI		
DI		
IP		
flags		
CS		
DS		
SS		
ES		

Upon Return from INT 13H

Register	High	Low
AX	Status†	
BX		
CX		
DX		
SP		
BP		
SI		
DI		
IP		
flags	Carry flag set on error	
CS		
DS		
SS		
ES		

* Bit 7=1 for fixed disk
†See 4.051. INT 13H, Disk System Status Byte Layout
§For fixed drives:
CH=cylinder number (low 8 bits of 10-bit cylinder number)
CL=cylinder/sector number
Bits 6,7 = cylinder number (high 2 bits)
Bits 0-5 = sector number

Version: Applies to all PC models beginning with XT.

Source: IBM PS/2 and PC BIOS Interface Technical Reference, page 2-65
BIOS Interface Technical Reference for PS/1 Computer, pages 2-42 through 2-43
System BIOS for IBM PC/XT/AT Computers and Compatibles (Phoenix), page 345

See Also: 4.001. BIOS Services Summary
4.051. INT 13H, Disk System Status Byte Layout

4.063. INT 13H, AH=0DH -- ALTERNATE DISK RESET

Prior to Issuing INT 13H

Register	High	Low
AX	0DH	
BX		
CX		
DX		Drive number*
SP		
BP		
SI		
DI		
IP		
flags		
CS		
DS		
SS		
ES		

Upon Return from INT 13H

Register	High	Low
AX	Status†	
BX		
CX		
DX		
SP		
BP		
SI		
DI		
IP		
flags	Carry flag set on error	
CS		
DS		
SS		
ES		

*Bit 7=1 for fixed disk
†See 4.051. INT 13H, Disk System Status Byte Layout

Version: Applies to all PC models beginning with XT.

Source: IBM PS/2 and PC BIOS Interface Technical Reference, page 2-66
BIOS Interface Technical Reference for PS/1 Computer, page 2-43
System BIOS for IBM PC/XT/AT Computers and Compatibles (Phoenix), page 346

See Also: 4.001. BIOS Services Summary
4.051. INT 13H, Disk System Status Byte Layout

4.064. INT 13H, AH=0EH -- READ TEST BUFFER

Prior to Issuing INT 13H

	High	Low
AX	0EH	
BX	Offset of Diagnostic Buffer	
CX		
DX		Drive number*
SP		
BP		
SI		
DI		
IP		
flags		
CS		
DS		
SS		
ES	Segment of Diagnostic Buffer	

Upon Return from INT 13H

	High	Low
AX	Status†	
BX		
CX		
DX		
SP		
BP		
SI		
DI		
IP		
flags	Carry flag set on error	
CS		
DS		
SS		
ES		

*Bit 7=1 for fixed drive
†See 4.051. INT 13H, Disk System Status Byte Layout

Version: Applies to XT with 10MB controller and Phoenix XT BIOS only.

Source: System BIOS for IBM PC/XT/AT Computers and Compatibles (Phoenix), page 347

See Also: 4.001. BIOS Services Summary
4.051. INT 13H, Disk System Status Byte Layout

4.065. INT 13H, AH=0FH -- WRITE TEST BUFFER

Prior to Issuing INT 13H

	High	Low
AX	0EH	
BX	Offset of Diagnostic Buffer	
CX		
DX		Drive number*
SP		
BP		
SI		
DI		
IP		
flags		
CS		
DS		
SS		
ES	Segment of Diagnostic Buffer	

Upon Return from INT 13H

	High	Low
AX	Status†	
BX		
CX		
DX		
SP		
BP		
SI		
DI		
IP		
flags	Carry flag set on error	
CS		
DS		
SS		
ES		

*0-based; bit 7=1 for fixed drive
†See 4.051. INT 13H, Disk System Status Byte Layout

Version: Applies to XT with 10MB controller and Phoenix XT BIOS only.

Source: System BIOS for IBM PC/XT/AT Computers and Compatibles (Phoenix), page 348

See Also: 4.001. BIOS Services Summary
4.051. INT 13H, Disk System Status Byte Layout

4.066. INT 13H, AH=10H -- TEST DRIVE READY

Prior to Issuing INT 13H

	High	Low
AX	10H	
BX		
CX		
DX		Drive number*
SP		
BP		
SI		
DI		
IP		
flags		
CS		
DS		
SS		
ES		

Upon Return from INT 13H

	High	Low
AX	Status†	
BX		
CX		
DX		
SP		
BP		
SI		
DI		
IP		
flags	Carry flag set on error	
CS		
DS		
SS		
ES		

*0-based; bit 7=1 for fixed drive
†See 4.051. INT 13H, Disk System Status Byte Layout

Version: Applies to all PC models beginning with the XT.

Source: IBM PS/2 and PC BIOS Interface Technical Reference, page 2-66
BIOS Interface Technical Reference for PS/1 Computer, page 2-43
System BIOS for IBM PC/XT/AT Computers and Compatibles (Phoenix), page 349

See Also: 4.001. BIOS Services Summary
4.051. INT 13H, Disk System Status Byte Layout

4.067. INT 13H, AH=11H -- RECALIBRATE DRIVE

Prior to Issuing INT 13H

	High	Low
AX	11H	
BX		
CX		
DX		Drive number*
SP		
BP		
SI		
DI		
IP		
flags		
CS		
DS		
SS		
ES		

Upon Return from INT 13H

	High	Low
AX	Status†	
BX		
CX		
DX		
SP		
BP		
SI		
DI		
IP		
flags	Carry flag set on error	
CS		
DS		
SS		
ES		

*0-based; bit 7=1 for fixed drive
†See 4.051. INT 13H, Disk System Status Byte Layout

Version: Applies to all PC models beginning with XT.

Source: IBM PS/2 and PC BIOS Interface Technical Reference, page 2-67
BIOS Interface Technical Reference for PS/1 Computer, page 2-43
System BIOS for IBM PC/XT/AT Computers and Compatibles (Phoenix), page 350

See Also: 4.001. BIOS Services Summary
4.051. INT 13H, Disk System Status Byte Layout

4.068. INT 13H, AH=12H -- CONTROLLER RAM DIAGNOSTIC

Prior to Issuing INT 13H

	High	Low
AX	12H	Number of sectors
BX		
CX	Cylinder	Sector
DX	Head	Drive number*
SP		
BP		
SI		
DI		
IP		
flags		
CS		
DS		
SS		
ES		

Upon Return from INT 13H

	High	Low
AX	Status†	00H
BX		
CX		
DX		
SP		
BP		
SI		
DI		
IP		
flags	Carry flag set if status is non-zero	
CS		
DS		
SS		
ES		

*0-based; bit 7=1 for fixed drive
†See 4.051. INT 13H, Disk System Status Byte Layout

Version: Applies to XT with 10MB controller and Phoenix XT BIOS only.

Source: System BIOS for IBM PC/XT/AT Computers and Compatibles (Phoenix), page 351

See Also: 4.001. BIOS Services Summary
4.051. INT 13H, Disk System Status Byte Layout

4.069. INT 13H, AH=13H -- CONTROLLER DRIVE DIAGNOSTIC

Prior to Issuing INT 13H

	High	Low
AX	13H	Number of sectors
BX		
CX	Cylinder	Sector
DX	Head	Drive number*
SP		
BP		
SI		
DI		
IP		
flags		
CS		
DS		
SS		
ES		

Upon Return from INT 13H

	High	Low
AX	Status†	00H
BX		
CX		
DX		
SP		
BP		
SI		
DI		
IP		
flags	Carry flag set on error	
CS		
DS		
SS		
ES		

*0-based; bit 7=1 for fixed drive
†See 4.051. INT 13H, Disk System Status Byte Layout

Version: Applies to XT with 10MB controller and Phoenix XT BIOS only.

Source: System BIOS for IBM PC/XT/AT Computers and Compatibles (Phoenix), page 352

See Also: 4.001. BIOS Services Summary
4.051. INT 13H, Disk System Status Byte Layout

4.070. INT 13H, AH=14H -- CONTROLLER INTERNAL DIAGNOSTIC

Prior to Issuing INT 13H

	High	Low
AX	14H	Number of sectors
BX		
CX	Cylinder	Sector
DX	Head	Drive number*
SP		
BP		
SI		
DI		
IP		
flags		
CS		
DS		
SS		
ES		

Upon Return from INT 13H

	High	Low
AX	Status†	00H
BX		
CX		
DX		
SP		
BP		
SI		
DI		
IP		
flags	Carry flag set on error	
CS		
DS		
SS		
ES		

*0-based; bit 7=1 for fixed drives
†See 4.051. INT 13H, Disk System Status Byte Layout

Version: Applies to XT with 10MB Controller and Phoenix XT and AT BIOS only.

Source: System BIOS for IBM PC/XT/AT Computers and Compatibles (Phoenix), page 353

See Also: 4.001. BIOS Services Summary
4.051. INT 13H, Disk System Status Byte Layout

4.071. INT 13H, AH=15H -- READ DASD TYPE

Prior to Issuing INT 13H

	High	Low
AX	15H	
BX		
CX		
DX		Drive number*
SP		
BP		
SI		
DI		
IP		
flags		
CS		
DS		
SS		
ES		

Upon Return from INT 13H

	High	Low
AX	DASD type†	
BX		
CX	HO word of 512-byte blocks§	
DX	LO word of 512-byte blocks§	
SP		
BP		
SI		
DI		
IP		
flags	Carry flag set on error	
CS		
DS		
SS		
ES		

*0-based; bit 7=1 for fixed drives
†00=drive not present or invalid
01=no change line support
02=change line supported
03=fixed disk
§Fixed disk only returns these values.

Version: Applies to all PC models beginning with XT dated 1/10/86.

Note: DASD (Direct Access Storage Device)

Source: IBM PS/2 and PC BIOS Interface Technical Reference, pages 2-54 and 2-67
BIOS Interface Technical Reference for PS/1 Computer, pages 2-34 and 2-44
System BIOS for IBM PC/XT/AT Computers and Compatibles (Phoenix), pages 295, 354 through 355
DOS Programmer's Reference 2nd Edition (Que), pages 463 through 464

See Also: 4.001. BIOS Services Summary

4.072. INT 13H, AH=16H -- DISKETTE CHANGE LINE STATUS

Prior to Issuing INT 13H

Register	High	Low
AX	16H	
BX		
CX		
DX		Drive number*
SP		
BP		
SI		
DI		
IP		
flags		
CS		
DS		
SS		
ES		

Upon Return from INT 13H

Register	High	Low
AX	Status†	
BX		
CX		
DX		
SP		
BP		
SI		
DI		
IP		
flags	Carry flag set on error	
CS		
DS		
SS		
ES		

*0-based; bit 7=1 for fixed drives
†00=diskette change signal not active
01= invalid diskette parameter
06= diskette change signal active
80H=diskette drive not ready

Version: Applies to all PC models beginning with XT dated 1/10/86.

Source: IBM PS/2 and PC BIOS Interface Technical Reference, page 2-54 and 2-55
BIOS Interface Technical Reference for PS/1 Computer, page 2-34
System BIOS for IBM PC/XT/AT Computers and Compatibles (Phoenix), page 296

See Also: 4.001. BIOS Services Summary

4.073. INT 13H, AH=17H -- SET DASD TYPE FOR FORMAT

Prior to Issuing INT 13H

Register	High	Low
AX	17H	DASD type*
BX		
CX		
DX		Drive number†
SP		
BP		
SI		
DI		
IP		
flags		
CS		
DS		
SS		
ES		

Upon Return from INT 13H

Register	High	Low
AX	Status§	
BX		
CX		
DX		
SP		
BP		
SI		
DI		
IP		
flags	Carry flag set on error	
CS		
DS		
SS		
ES		

*00, 05-FFH=invalid request
01=320/360K diskette in 360K drive
02=360K diskette in 1.2MB drive
03=1.2MB diskette in 1.2MB drive
04=720K disk in 720K drive (only for AT BIOS 6/10/85 and later)
†0-based; bit 7=1 for fixed drives
§See 4.051. INT 13H, Disk System Status Byte Layout

Version: Applies to all PC models beginning with XT dated 1/10/86.

Note: DASD (Direct Access Storage Device)

Source: IBM PS/2 and PC BIOS Interface Technical Reference, pages 2-55 through 2-56
BIOS Interface Technical Reference for PS/1 Computer, pages 2-34 through 2-35
System BIOS for IBM PC/XT/AT Computers and Compatibles (Phoenix), page 297

See Also: 4.001. BIOS Services Summary
4.051. INT 13H, Disk System Status Byte Layout

4.074. INT 13H, AH=18H -- SET MEDIA TYPE FOR FORMAT

Prior to Issuing INT 13H

	High	Low
AX	18H	
BX		
CX	Number of tracks	Number of sectors†
DX		Drive number§
SP		
BP		
SI		
DI		
IP		
flags		
CS		
DS		
SS		
ES		

Upon Return from INT 13H

	High	Low
AX	Status*	
BX		
CX		
DX		
SP		
BP		
SI		
DI	Offset of pointer to 11-byte media parm table¥	
IP		
flags	Carry flag set on error	
CS		
DS		
SS		
ES	Segment of pointer to 11-byte media parm table¥	

*See 4.051. INT 13H, Disk System Status Byte Layout
†For fixed drives:
CH=cylinder number (low 8 bits of 10-bit cylinder number)
CL=cylinder/sector number
Bits 6,7 = cylinder number (high 2 bits)
Bits 0-5 = sector number
§0-based; bit 7=1 for fixed drives
¥See 4.075. INT 13H, Media Descriptor Table

Version: Applies to all PC models beginning with XT dated 1/10/86.

Note: Only value in DL is checked for an appropriate value.

Source: IBM PS/2 and PC BIOS Interface Technical Reference, pages 2-56 through 2-57
BIOS Interface Technical Reference for PS/1 Computer, pages 2-35 through 2-36
System BIOS for IBM PC/XT/AT Computers and Compatibles (Phoenix), pages 298 through 299

See Also: 4.001. BIOS Services Summary
4.051. INT 13H, Disk System Status Byte Layout
4.055. INT 13H, AH=05H -- Format Cylinder
4.056. INT 13H, AH=06H --Format Cylinder Set Bad Sector Flags
4.075. INT 13H, Media Descriptor Table

4.075. INT 13H, MEDIA DESCRIPTOR TABLE

Offset	Length	Description	Allowable Values
0 (0)	Byte	First specify byte	
1 (1)	Byte	Second specify byte	
2 (2)	Byte	Timer ticks to wait until motor OFF	
3 (3)	Byte	Number of bytes/sector	0=128, 1=256, 2=512, 3=1024
4 (4)	Byte	Number of sectors/track	
5 (5)	Byte	Gap length, in bytes	
6 (6)	Byte	Data length, in bytes	
7 (7)	Byte	Gap length for format	
8 (8)	Byte	Fill byte for formatting	
9 (9)	Byte	Head settle time, in milliseconds	
A (10)	Byte	Motor startup time, in 1/8 seconds	

Version: Applies to all PC models beginning with XT dated 1/10/86.

Note: Sometimes referred to as MPT (Media Parameter Table).

Source: IBM PS/2 and PC BIOS Interface Technical Reference, page 3-26
BIOS Interface Technical Reference for PS/1 Computer, page 3-18

See Also: 4.074. INT 13H, AH=18H -- Set Media Type for Format

4.076. INT 13H, AH=19H -- PARK HEADS

Prior to Issuing INT 13H

	High	Low
AX	19H	
BX		
CX		
DX		Drive†
SP		
BP		
SI		
DI		
IP		
flags		
CS		
DS		
SS		
ES		

Upon Return from INT 13H

	High	Low
AX	Status*	
BX		
CX		
DX		
SP		
BP		
SI		
DI		
IP		
flags	Carry flag set on error	
CS		
DS		
SS		
ES		

*See 4.051. INT 13H, Disk System Status Byte Layout
†0-based; bit 7=1 for fixed drive (PS/1 and PS/2 only)

Version: Applies to AT, XT, XT286, PS/1, and PS/2.

Source: IBM PS/2 and PC BIOS Interface Technical Reference, page 2-67
BIOS Interface Technical Reference for PS/1 Computer, page 2-44

See Also: 4.001. BIOS Services Summary
4.051. INT 13H, Disk System Status Byte Layout

4.077. INT 13H, AH=1AH -- FORMAT UNIT

Prior to Issuing INT 13H

	High	Low
AX	1AH	Defect table count*
BX	Offset of pointer to defect table	
CX		Modifier bits†
DX		Drive§
SP		
BP		
SI		
DI		
IP		
flags		
CS		
DS		
SS		
ES	Segment of pointer to defect table	

*0=no defect table used; >0 means use defect table.
†See 4.078. INT 13H, Format Unit Modifier Bits
§0-based; bit 7=1 for fixed drives

Upon Return from INT 13H

Interrupt returns no values.

Version: Applies to all PC models beginning with XT.

Note: Defect table consists of relative block addresses of defective sectors.

Source: IBM PS/2 and PC BIOS Interface Technical Reference, pages 2-67 through 2-68

See Also: 4.001. BIOS Services Summary
4.078. INT 13H, Format Unit Modifier Bits

4.078. INT 13H, FORMAT UNIT MODIFIER BITS

Bit Number	*Function*	*Allowable Values*
5-7	RESERVED	Must be 0
4	Periodic interrupt status	1=ON, 0=OFF
3	Extended surface analysis	1=perform, 0=don't perform
2	Secondary defect map	1=update, 0=don't update
1	Use secondary defect map	1=ignore it, 0=use it
0	Use primary defect map	1=ignore it, 0=use it

Source: IBM PS/2 and PC BIOS Interface Technical Reference, page 2-68

See Also: 4.077. INT 13H, AH=1AH -- Format Unit

4.079. INT 14H, AH=00H -- INIT COMMUNICATIONS PORT

Prior to Issuing INT 14H

	High	Low
AX	00H	Comm parm byte*
BX		
CX		
DX	Comm port number	
SP		
BP		
SI		
DI		
IP		
flags		
CS		
DS		
SS		
ES		

Upon Return from INT 14H

	High	Low
AX	Line status†	Modem status†
BX		
CX		
DX		
SP		
BP		
SI		
DI		
IP		
flags		
CS		
DS		
SS		
ES		

*See 4.081. INT 14H, COM Port Parameter Byte
†See 4.080. INT 14H, Modem and Line Status Byte

Version:
- Applies to all PC models.
- Early PCs and XTs support only 2 ports; later models support 4 ports.

Source:
IBM PS/2 and PC BIOS Interface Technical Reference, pages 2-69 through 2-70
BIOS Interface Technical Reference for PS/1 Computer, pages 2-45 through 2-46
System BIOS for IBM PC/XT/AT Computers and Compatibles (Phoenix), pages 374 through 375

See Also:
4.001. BIOS Services Summary
4.080. INT 14H, Modem and Line Status Byte
4.081. INT 14H, COM Port Parameter Byte

4.080. INT 14H, MODEM AND LINE STATUS BYTE

Modem Status Byte

7	6	5	4	3	2	1	0	Description
✔								Received line signal detect
	✔							Ring indicator
		✔						Data set ready
			✔					Clear to send
				✔				Delta receive line signal detect
					✔			Trailing edge ring detector
						✔		Delta data set ready
							✔	Delta clear to send

Line Status Byte

7	6	5	4	3	2	1	0	Description
✔								Time-out*
	✔							Transmitter shift register empty
		✔						Transmitter holding register empty
			✔					Break detect
				✔				Framing error
					✔			Parity error
						✔		Overrun error
							✔	Data ready

*Unpredictable results in other bits when this bit is set to 1

Version: Applies to all PC models.

Source:
IBM PS/2 and PC BIOS Interface Technical Reference, pages 2-69 through 2-70
BIOS Interface Technical Reference for PS/1 Computer, pages 2-45 through 2-46
System BIOS for IBM PC/XT/AT Computers and Compatibles (Phoenix), pages 374 through 375

See Also:
4.079. INT 14H, AH=00H -- Init Communications Port
4.082. INT 14H, AH=01H -- Write Character
4.083. INT 14H, AH=02H -- Read Character
4.084. INT 14H, AH=03H -- Status Request

4.081. INT 14H, COM PORT PARAMETER BYTE

Bit Number 7	6	5	4	3	2	1	0	Description	Allowable Values
✔	✔	✔						Baud rate	000 = 110 baud 001 = 150 010 = 300 011 = 600 100 = 1200 (default) 101 = 2400 110 = 4800 111 = 9600
			✔	✔				Parity	00 = No parity 01 = Odd parity 10 = No parity 11 = Even parity
					✔			Stop bits	0=1 stop bit, 1=2 stop bits
						✔	✔	Word length	10 = 7 bits 11 = 8 bits

Version: Applies to all PC models.

Note: On PS/2, baud rates higher than 9600 are set using functions 4 and 5.

Source: IBM PS/2 and PC BIOS Interface Technical Reference, pages 2-69 through 2-70
BIOS Interface Technical Reference for PS/1 Computer, pages 2-45 through 2-46
System BIOS for IBM PC/XT/AT Computers and Compatibles (Phoenix), page 374

See Also: 4.079. INT 14H, AH=00H -- Init Communications Port
4.085. INT 14H, AH=04H -- Extended Init
4.087. INT 14H, AH=05, AL=01H -- Write Modem Control Register

4.082. INT 14H, AH=01H -- WRITE CHARACTER

Prior to Issuing INT 14H

	High	Low
AX	01H	Character
BX		
CX		
DX	Comm port number†	
SP		
BP		
SI		
DI		
IP		
flags		
CS		
DS		
SS		
ES		

Upon Return from INT 14H

	High	Low
AX	Line status*	Character
BX		
CX		
DX		
SP		
BP		
SI		
DI		
IP		
flags		
CS		
DS		
SS		
ES		

*See 4.080. INT 14H, Modem and Line Status Byte
†0=COM1, 1=COM2, etc.

Version:
- Applies to all PC models.
- Early PCs and XTs support only 2 ports; later models support 4 ports.

Source: IBM PS/2 and PC BIOS Interface Technical Reference, page 2-70
BIOS Interface Technical Reference for PS/1 Computer, page 2-46
System BIOS for IBM PC/XT/AT Computers and Compatibles (Phoenix), page 376

See Also: 4.001. BIOS Services Summary
4.080. INT 14H, Modem and Line Status Byte
4.081. INT 14H, COM Port Parameter Byte

4.083. INT 14H, AH=02H -- READ CHARACTER

Prior to Issuing INT 14H

	High	Low
AX	02H	
BX		
CX		
DX	Comm port number†	
SP		
BP		
SI		
DI		
IP		
flags		
CS		
DS		
SS		
ES		

Upon Return from INT 14H

	High	Low
AX	Line status*	Character
BX		
CX		
DX		
SP		
BP		
SI		
DI		
IP		
flags		
CS		
DS		
SS		
ES		

*See 4.080. INT 14H, Modem and Line Status Byte
†0=COM1, 1=COM2, etc.

Version:
- Applies to all PC models.
- Early PCs and XTs support only 2 ports; later models support 4 ports.

Source:
IBM PS/2 and PC BIOS Interface Technical Reference, page 2-70
BIOS Interface Technical Reference for PS/1 Computer, page 2-46
System BIOS for IBM PC/XT/AT Computers and Compatibles (Phoenix), page 377

See Also:
4.001. BIOS Services Summary
4.080. INT 14H, Modem and Line Status Byte
4.082. INT 14H, AH=01H -- Write Character

4.084. INT 14H, AH=03H -- STATUS REQUEST

Prior to Issuing INT 14H

	High	Low
AX	03H	
BX		
CX		
DX	Comm port number†	
SP		
BP		
SI		
DI		
IP		
flags		
CS		
DS		
SS		
ES		

Upon Return from INT 14H

	High	Low
AX	Line status*	Modem status*
BX		
CX		
DX		
SP		
BP		
SI		
DI		
IP		
flags		
CS		
DS		
SS		
ES		

*See 4.080. INT 14H, Modem and Line Status Byte
†0=COM1, 1=COM2, etc.

Version:
- Applies to all PC models.
- Early PCs and XTs support only 2 ports; later models support 4 ports.

Source:
IBM PS/2 and PC BIOS Interface Technical Reference, page 2-71
BIOS Interface Technical Reference for PS/1 Computer, page 2-47
System BIOS for IBM PC/XT/AT Computers and Compatibles (Phoenix), page 378

See Also:
4.001. BIOS Services Summary
4.080. INT 14H, Modem and Line Status Byte

4.085. INT 14H, AH=04H -- EXTENDED INIT

Prior to Issuing INT 14H

	High	Low
AX	04H	Break setting *
BX	Parity setting¶	Stop bit setting§
CX	Word length¥	Baud rate‡
DX	Comm port number~	
SP		
BP		
SI		
DI		
IP		
flags		
CS		
DS		
SS		
ES		

Upon Return from INT 14H

	High	Low
AX	Line status†	Modem status†
BX		
CX		
DX		
SP		
BP		
SI		
DI		
IP		
flags		
CS		
DS		
SS		
ES		

*00=no break, 01=break
¶00=no parity, 01=odd parity, 02=even parity, 03=stick parity odd, 04=stick parity even
§00=one, 01=two for 6-, 7-, or 8-bit word lengths (one and a half for 5-bit word lengths)
¥00=5 bits, 01=6 bits, 02=7 bits, 03=8 bits
‡00=110 baud, 01=150 baud, 02=300 baud, 03=600 baud,
04=1200 baud, 05=2400 baud, 06=4800 baud, 07=9600 baud,
08=19,200 baud
~0=COM1, 1=COM2, etc.
†See 4.080. INT 14H, Modem and Line Status Byte

Version: Applies to PS/1 and PS/2 models only.

Source: IBM PS/2 and PC BIOS Interface Technical Reference, page 2-71
BIOS Interface Technical Reference for PS/1 Computer, page 2-47

See Also: 4.001. BIOS Services Summary
4.079. INT 14H, AH=00H -- Init Communications Port
4.080. INT 14H, Modem and Line Status Byte

4.086. INT 14H, AH=05H, AL=00H -- READ MODEM CONTROL REGISTER

Prior to Issuing INT 14H

	High	Low
AX	05H	00H
BX		
CX		
DX	Comm port number†	
SP		
BP		
SI		
DI		
IP		
flags		
CS		
DS		
SS		
ES		

Upon Return from INT 14H

	High	Low
AX		
BX		Modem control reg*
CX		
DX		
SP		
BP		
SI		
DI		
IP		
flags		
CS		
DS		
SS		
ES		

*Modem control register formatted as follows:

Bit	Meaning When Set
5-7	RESERVED
4	Loop
3	Out2
2	Out1
1	Request to send
0	Data terminal ready

†0=COM1, 1=COM2, etc.

Version: Applies to PS/1 and PS/2 models only.

Source: IBM PS/2 and PC BIOS Interface Technical Reference, page 2-72
BIOS Interface Technical Reference for PS/1 Computer, page 2-48

See Also: 4.001. BIOS Services Summary
4.087. INT 14H, AH=05H, AL=01H -- Write Modem Control Register

4.087. INT 14H, AH=05H, AL=01H -- WRITE MODEM CONTROL REGISTER

Prior to Issuing INT 14H

	High	Low
AX	05H	01H
BX		Modem control reg*
CX		
DX	Comm port number†	
SP		
BP		
SI		
DI		
IP		
flags		
CS		
DS		
SS		
ES		

Upon Return from INT 14H

	High	Low
AX	Line status§	Modem status§
BX		
CX		
DX		
SP		
BP		
SI		
DI		
IP		
flags		
CS		
DS		
SS		
ES		

*Modem control register formatted as follows:

Bit	Meaning when set
5-7	RESERVED
4	Loop
3	Out2
2	Out1
1	Request to send
0	Data terminal ready

†0=COM1, 1=COM2, etc.
§See 4.080. INT 14H, Modem and Line Status Byte

Version: Applies to PS/1 and PS/2 models only.

Source: IBM PS/2 and PC BIOS Interface Technical Reference, page 2-72
BIOS Interface Technical Reference for PS/1 Computer, page 2-48

See Also: 4.001. BIOS Services Summary
4.080. INT 14H, Modem and Line Status Byte
4.086. INT 14H, AH=05H, AL=00H -- Read Modem Control Register

4.088. INT 15H, AH=00H -- CASSETTE MOTOR ON (OBSOLETE)

Prior to Issuing INT 15H

	High	Low
AX	00H	
BX		
CX		
DX		
SP		
BP		
SI		
DI		
IP		
flags		
CS		
DS		
SS		
ES		

Upon Return from INT 15H

	High	Low
AX	00H*	
BX		
CX		
DX		
SP		
BP		
SI		
DI		
IP		
flags	Carry clear*	
CS		
DS		
SS		
ES		

*Phoenix BIOS returns status in AH (86H=not present) and sets carry flag if error.

Version: Applies to PC, PCjr, and Phoenix PC BIOS only; all others set carry flag and return 86H in AH.

Note: Obsolete function; no longer supported.

Source: IBM PS/2 and PC BIOS Interface Technical Reference, page 2-74
System BIOS for IBM PC/XT/AT Computers and Compatibles (Phoenix), page 389

See Also: 4.001. BIOS Services Summary
4.089. INT 15H, AH=01H -- Cassette Motor OFF

4.089. INT 15H, AH=01H -- CASSETTE MOTOR OFF (OBSOLETE)

Prior to Issuing INT 15H

	High	Low
AX	01H	
BX		
CX		
DX		
SP		
BP		
SI		
DI		
IP		
flags		
CS		
DS		
SS		
ES		

Upon Return from INT 15H

	High	Low
AX	00H*	
BX		
CX		
DX		
SP		
BP		
SI		
DI		
IP		
flags	Carry clear*	
CS		
DS		
SS		
ES		

*Phoenix BIOS returns status in AH (86H=no cassette) and sets carry flag on error.

Version: Applies to PC, PCjr, and Phoenix PC BIOS only; all others set carry flag and return 86H in AH.

Note: Obsolete function; no longer supported.

Source: IBM PS/2 and PC BIOS Interface Technical Reference, page 2-74
System BIOS for IBM PC/XT/AT Computers and Compatibles (Phoenix), page 390

See Also: 4.001. BIOS Services Summary
4.088. INT 15H, AH=00H -- Cassette Motor ON

4.090. INT 15H, AH=02H -- CASSETTE READ DATA BLOCKS (OBSOLETE)

Prior to Issuing INT 15H

	High	Low
AX	02H	
BX	Offset of pointer to data buffer	
CX	Number of bytes to read	
DX		
SP		
BP		
SI		
DI		
IP		
flags		
CS		
DS		
SS		
ES	Segment of pointer to data buffer	

Upon Return from INT 15H

	High	Low
AX	Error*	
BX	Offset of pointer to last byte read +1	
CX		
DX	Number of bytes to read	
SP		
BP		
SI		
DI		
IP		
flags	Carry flag set on error	
CS		
DS		
SS		
ES	Segment of pointer to last byte read +1	

*1=CRC error, 2=lost data transitions, 4=no data found, 80H=invalid command, 86H=no cassette

Version: PC, Phoenix PC BIOS, and PCjr only; all others set carry flag and return 86H in AH.

Note: Obsolete function; no longer supported.

Source: IBM PS/2 and PC BIOS Interface Technical Reference, pages 2-74 through 2-75
System BIOS for IBM PC/XT/AT Computers and Compatibles (Phoenix), page 391

See Also: 4.001. BIOS Services Summary
4.091. INT 15H, AH=03H -- Cassette Write Data Blocks

4.091. INT 15H, AH=03H -- CASSETTE WRITE DATA BLOCKS (OBSOLETE)

Prior to Issuing INT 15H

Register	High	Low
AX	03H	
BX	Offset of pointer to data buffer	
CX	Number of bytes to write	
DX		
SP		
BP		
SI		
DI		
IP		
flags		
CS		
DS		
SS		
ES	Segment of pointer to data buffer	

Upon Return from INT 15H

Register	High	Low
AX	Status*	
BX	Offset of pointer to last byte written +1	
CX	00H	00H
DX		
SP		
BP		
SI		
DI		
IP		
flags	Carry flag set on error	
CS		
DS		
SS		
ES	Segment of pointer to last byte written +1	

*Phoenix: 00=no error, 80H=invalid command, 86H=no cassette, all others=status

Version: PC, Phoenix PC BIOS, and PCjr only; all others set carry flag and return 86H in AH.

Note: Obsolete function; no longer supported.

Source: IBM PS/2 and PC BIOS Interface Technical Reference, page 2-75
System BIOS for IBM PC/XT/AT Computers and Compatibles (Phoenix), page 392

See Also: 4.001. BIOS Services Summary
4.090. INT 15H, AH=02H -- Cassette Read Data Blocks

4.092. INT 15H, AH=0FH -- FORMAT PERIODIC INTERRUPT

Prior to Issuing INT 15H

Register	High	Low
AX	0FH	Phase code*
BX		
CX		
DX		
SP		
BP		
SI		
DI		
IP		
flags		
CS		
DS		
SS		
ES		

Upon Return from INT 15H

Register	High	Low
AX		
BX		
CX		
DX		
SP		
BP		
SI		
DI		
IP		
flags	Carry set if end formatting or scanning	
CS		
DS		
SS		
ES		

*00=reserved, 01=surface analysis, 02=formatting

Version: Applies only to PS/2 machines using ESDI fixed disk drive adapter.

Source: IBM PS/2 and PC BIOS Interface Technical Reference, pages 2-75 through 2-76

See Also: 4.001. BIOS Services Summary

4.093. INT 15H, AH=21H -- POWER-ON SELF-TEST ERROR LOG

Prior to Issuing INT 15H

Register	High	Low
AX	21H	Read/Write*
BX	Device code§	Device error§
CX		
DX		
SP		
BP		
SI		
DI		
IP		
flags		
CS		
DS		
SS		
ES		

Upon Return from INT 15H

Register	High	Low
AX	Status†	
BX		
CX		
DX		
SP		
BP		
SI		
DI	Offset of pointer to POST error log	
IP		
flags	Carry set if error code full on write, otherwise 0	
CS		
DS		
SS		
ES	Segment of pointer to POST error log	

*0=read, 1=write
†00H=successful, 01H=error code location full
§Write only, AL=01H

Version: Applies only to PS/1 and PS/2 (except Models 25 and 30).

Source: BIOS Interface Technical Reference for PS/1 Computer, pages 2-49 through 2-50
IBM PS/2 and PC BIOS Interface Technical Reference, pages 2-76 through 2-77

See Also: 4.001. BIOS Services Summary

4.094. INT 15H, AH=23H -- READ/WRITE DOS 4.00 FLAGS FOR PS/1

Prior to Issuing INT 15H

Register	High	Low
AX	23H	Read/Write*
BX		
CX	Flag Data† (on write)	
DX		
SP		
BP		
SI		
DI		
IP		
flags		
CS		
DS		
SS		
ES		

Upon Return from INT 15H

Register	High	Low
AX	(Destroyed)	(Destroyed)
BX		
CX	Flag Data† (on read)	
DX		
SP		
BP		
SI		
DI		
IP		
flags		
CS		
DS		
SS		
ES		

*0=read, 1=write
†Flag data formatted as follows:

Bit #	Description	Values
15	RESERVED	
10-14	System Drive	00000=A, 00010=C
8-9	Boot Options	00=ROM, 01=Disk first, 10=Fixed first, 11=invalid
7	Num Lock State	0=ON, 1=OFF
4-6	Application Select	000=ROM shell, 001=Works, 010=Prodigy 011=User's Club, 100=Your Software 101=DOS Shell, 111=DOS Prompt
3	RESERVED	
2	Alt+Sysrq Boot	1=Alt+Sysrq Boot, 0=normal boot
1	Read CONFIG.SYS	0=from ROM, 1=from Sys drive
0	Read AUTOEXEC.BAT	0=from ROM, 1=from Sys drive

Version: Applies only to PS/1 machines.

Source: BIOS Interface Technical Reference for PS/1 Computer, pages 2-50 through 2-51

See Also: 4.001. BIOS Services Summary

4.095. INT 15H, AH=4FH -- KEYBOARD INTERCEPT

Register	Prior to Issuing INT 15H: High	Prior to Issuing INT 15H: Low	Upon Return from INT 15H: High	Upon Return from INT 15H: Low
AX	4FH	Scan code*		Scan code†
BX				
CX				
DX				
SP				
BP				
SI				
DI				
IP				
flags	Carry must be set§		Carry clear if scan code to be ignored	
CS				
DS				
SS				
ES				

*See 7.013. AT 84-Key Keyboard Numbers and Scan Codes
7.014. AT 101/102-Key Keyboard Numbers and Scan Codes
7.015. PS/2 Keyboard Numbers and Scan Codes
†May be changed by interrupt handler.
§Not in Phoenix BIOS

Version: Applies to all PC models after XT dated 11/8/82 and AT dated 1/10/84.

Source: IBM PS/2 and PC BIOS Interface Technical Reference, pages 2-80 through 2-81
BIOS Interface Technical Reference for PS/1 Computer, page 2-51
System BIOS for IBM PC/XT/AT Computers and Compatibles (Phoenix), page 393

See Also: 4.001. BIOS Services Summary
7.013. AT 84-Key Keyboard Numbers and Scan Codes
7.014. AT 101/102-Key Keyboard Numbers and Scan Codes
7.015. PS/2 Keyboard Numbers and Scan Codes

4.096. INT 15H, AH=80H -- OPEN DEVICE

Register	Prior to Issuing INT 15H: High	Prior to Issuing INT 15H: Low	Upon Return from INT 15H: High	Upon Return from INT 15H: Low
AX	80H		00*	80H*
BX	Device ID			
CX	Process ID			
DX				
SP				
BP				
SI				
DI				
IP				
flags	Carry clear*			
CS				
DS				
SS				
ES				

*Phoenix only

Version: Applies to all PC models after XT dated 11/8/82.

Source: IBM PS/2 and PC BIOS Interface Technical Reference, page 2-81
System BIOS for IBM PC/XT/AT Computers and Compatibles (Phoenix), page 394

See Also: 4.001. BIOS Services Summary
4.097. INT 15H, AH=81H -- Close Device

4.097. INT 15H, AH=81H -- CLOSE DEVICE

Prior to Issuing INT 15H

Register	High	Low
AX	81H	
BX	Device ID	
CX	Process ID	
DX		
SP		
BP		
SI		
DI		
IP		
flags	Carry clear*	
CS		
DS		
SS		
ES		

Upon Return from INT 15H

Register	High	Low
AX	00*	81H*
BX		
CX		
DX		
SP		
BP		
SI		
DI		
IP		
flags		
CS		
DS		
SS		
ES		

*Phoenix only

Version: Applies to PC models after XT dated 11/8/82.

Source: IBM PS/2 and PC BIOS Interface Technical Reference, page 2-82
System BIOS for IBM PC/XT/AT Computers and Compatibles (Phoenix), page 395

See Also: 4.001. BIOS Services Summary
4.096. INT 15H, AH=80H -- Open Device

4.098. INT 15H, AH=82H -- PROGRAM TERMINATE

Prior to Issuing INT 15H

Register	High	Low
AX	82H	
BX	Device ID	
CX		
DX		
SP		
BP		
SI		
DI		
IP		
flags	Carry clear*	
CS		
DS		
SS		
ES		

Upon Return from INT 15H

Register	High	Low
AX	00*	82H*
BX		
CX		
DX		
SP		
BP		
SI		
DI		
IP		
flags		
CS		
DS		
SS		
ES		

*Phoenix only

Version: Applies to all PC models after XT dated 11/8/82.

Source: IBM PS/2 and PC BIOS Interface Technical Reference, page 2-82
System BIOS for IBM PC/XT/AT Computers and Compatibles (Phoenix), page 396

See Also: 4.001. BIOS Services Summary

4.099. INT 15H, AH=83H -- EVENT WAIT

Prior to Issuing INT 15H

Register	High	Low
AX	83H	0 or 1*
BX	Offset of pointer to byte	
CX	HO microseconds to posting	
DX	LO microseconds to posting	
SP		
BP		
SI		
DI		
IP		
flags		
CS		
DS		
SS		
ES	Segment of pointer to byte	

Upon Return from INT 15H

Register	High	Low
AX	83H†	00=function busy†
BX		
CX		
DX		
SP		
BP		
SI		
DI		
IP		
flags	Carry flag set on error	
CS		
DS		
SS		
ES		

*0=set interval, 1=cancel set interval (cancel function only on PS/1 and PS/2 models)
†Phoenix only

Version: Applies to AT after 1/10/84, Convertible, Phoenix, PS/1, and PS/2 only.

Note:
- Carry flag always set on PS/2 Models 25 and 30.
- Bit 6 of CMOS RAM location 0BH is set, if successful (Phoenix only).

Source: IBM PS/2 and PC BIOS Interface Technical Reference, pages 2-82 through 2-83
BIOS Interface Technical Reference for PS/1 Computer, pages 2-51 through 2-52
System BIOS for IBM PC/XT/AT Computers and Compatibles (Phoenix), pages 397 through 398

See Also: 4.001. BIOS Services Summary

4.100. INT 15H, AH=84H -- JOYSTICK SUPPORT

Prior to Issuing INT 15H

Register	High	Low
AX	84H	
BX		
CX		
DX	0 or 1†	
SP		
BP		
SI		
DI		
IP		
flags		
CS		
DS		
SS		
ES		

Upon Return from INT 15H

Register	High	Low
AX	A(x) value§	Switch settings*
BX	A(y) value§	
CX	B(x) value§	
DX	B(y) value§	
SP		
BP		
SI		
DI		
IP		
flags	Carry set on error	
CS		
DS		
SS		
ES		

*Bits 7-4 are used to represent switches; returned only if DX was 0 prior to interrupt.
†0=read switch settings, 1=read resistive inputs
§Returned only if DX was 1 prior to interrupt.

Version: Applies to all PC models after XT dated 11/8/82.

Source: IBM PS/2 and PC BIOS Interface Technical Reference, pages 2-83 through 2-84
BIOS Interface Technical Reference for PS/1 Computer, page 2-52
System BIOS for IBM PC/XT/AT Computers and Compatibles (Phoenix), pages 400 through 401

See Also: 4.001. BIOS Services Summary

4.101. INT 15H, AH=85H -- SYSTEM REQUEST KEY PRESSED

Prior to Issuing INT 15H

	High	Low
AX	85H	
BX		
CX		
DX		
SP		
BP		
SI		
DI		
IP		
flags	Carry clear†	
CS		
DS		
SS		
ES		

Upon Return from INT 15H

	High	Low
AX	00H†	Value*
BX		
CX		
DX		
SP		
BP		
SI		
DI		
IP		
flags	Carry set on error†	
CS		
DS		
SS		
ES		

*0=key make, 1=key break (unsupported models return 80H, 85H, or 86H in AL)
†Phoenix only

Version: Applies to AT, Convertible, Phoenix, PS/1, and PS/2 only.

Source: IBM PS/2 and PC BIOS Interface Technical Reference, page 2-84
BIOS Interface Technical Reference for PS/1 Computer, page 2-52
System BIOS for IBM PC/XT/AT Computers and Compatibles (Phoenix), page 402

See Also: 4.001. BIOS Services Summary

4.102. INT 15H, AH=86H -- WAIT

Prior to Issuing INT 15H

	High	Low
AX	86H	
BX		
CX	HO microseconds before return	
DX	LO microseconds before return	
SP		
BP		
SI		
DI		
IP		
flags		
CS		
DS		
SS		
ES		

Upon Return from INT 15H

	High	Low
AX	86H*	Int cont 2 mask*
BX		
CX		
DX		
SP		
BP		
SI		
DI		
IP		
flags	Carry flag set if wait already in progress	
CS		
DS		
SS		
ES		

*Phoenix only; mask written to interrupt controller 2 (if successful)

Version: Applies to AT, Convertible, Phoenix AT BIOS, PS/1, and PS/2 only.

Source: IBM PS/2 and PC BIOS Interface Technical Reference, page 2-85
BIOS Interface Technical Reference for PS/1 Computer, page 2-52
System BIOS for IBM PC/XT/AT Computers and Compatibles (Phoenix), page 403

See Also: 4.001. BIOS Services Summary

4.103. INT 15H, AH=87H -- MOVE BLOCK

Register	Prior to Issuing INT 15H: High	Prior to Issuing INT 15H: Low	Upon Return from INT 15H: High	Upon Return from INT 15H: Low
AX	87H		Status†	
BX				
CX	Word count of block to move*			
DX				
SP				
BP				
SI	Offset of pointer to global desc. table§			
DI				
IP				
flags			Carry, zero flags set on some errors	
CS				
DS				
SS				
ES	Segment of pointer to global desc. table§			

*Maximum of 8000H words (64K bytes)
†00=successful, 01=RAM parity, 02=other exception error, 03=gate address line 20H failed
§Six 8-byte blocks: dummy, GDT location, source GDT, target GDT, BIOS CS, SS

Version: Applies to AT, PC XT 286, Phoenix AT BIOS, PS/1, and PS/2 (except Models 25 and 30) only.

Source: IBM PS/2 and PC BIOS Interface Technical Reference, pages 2-85 through 2-87
BIOS Interface Technical Reference for PS/1 Computer, pages 2-53 through 2-55
System BIOS for IBM PC/XT/AT Computers and Compatibles (Phoenix), pages 404 through 407

See Also: 4.001. BIOS Services Summary
4.106. INT 15H, Global Descriptor Table

4.104. INT 15H, AH=88H -- GET EXTENDED MEMORY SIZE

Register	Prior to Issuing INT 15H: High	Prior to Issuing INT 15H: Low	Upon Return from INT 15H: High	Upon Return from INT 15H: Low
AX	88H		Number of 1K blocks*	
BX				
CX				
DX				
SP				
BP				
SI				
DI				
IP				
flags				
CS				
DS				
SS				
ES				

*Contiguous memory beginning at address 100000H (1MB)

Version: Applies to all PC models beginning with AT, except PS/2 Models 25 and 30, and PC XT 286.

Source: IBM PS/2 and PC BIOS Interface Technical Reference, pages 2-87 through 2-88
BIOS Interface Technical Reference for PS/1 Computer, page 2-55
System BIOS for IBM PC/XT/AT Computers and Compatibles (Phoenix), page 408

See Also: 4.001. BIOS Services Summary

4.105. INT 15H, AH=89H -- SWITCH TO PROTECTED MODE

Prior to Issuing INT 15H

	High	Low
AX	89H	
BX	Index to Int Level 1	Index to Int Level 2
CX		
DX		
SP		
BP		
SI	Offset of pointer to global desc. table*	
DI		
IP		
flags		
CS		
DS		
SS		
ES	Segment of pointer to global desc. table*	

Upon Return from INT 15H

	High	Low
AX	00 if successful,	FFH if unsuccessful
BX	(Destroyed)	
CX	(Destroyed)	
DX	(Destroyed)	
SP	(Destroyed)	
BP	(Destroyed)	
SI	(Destroyed)	
DI	(Destroyed)	
IP	(Destroyed)	
flags	Carry flag set on error (Phoenix)	
CS	(Destroyed)	
DS	(Destroyed)	
SS	(Destroyed)	
ES	(Destroyed)	

*Six 8-byte blocks: dummy, GDT location, source GDT, target GDT, BIOS, CS, SS

Version: Applies to all PC Models beginning with AT, except PS/2 Models 25 and 30, and PC XT 286.

Source: IBM PS/2 and PC BIOS Interface Technical Reference, pages 2-88 through 2-91
BIOS Interface Technical Reference for PS/1 Computer, pages 2-55 through 2-58
System BIOS for IBM PC/XT/AT Computers and Compatibles (Phoenix), pages 409 through 410

See Also: 4.001. BIOS Services Summary
4.106. INT 15H, Global Descriptor Table

4.106. INT 15H, GLOBAL DESCRIPTOR TABLE

Offset	Length	Pointer To
0	8 bytes	Dummy
8	8 bytes	Global descriptor table
10 (16)	8 bytes	Interrupt descriptor table
18 (24)	8 bytes	User data segment
20 (32)	8 bytes	User extra segment
28 (40)	8 bytes	User stack segment
30 (48)	8 bytes	User code segment
38 (56)	8 bytes	Temporary BIOS code segment

Source: IBM PS/2 and PC BIOS Interface Technical Reference, pages 2-89 through 2-90
BIOS Interface Technical Reference for PS/1 Computer, pages 2-56 through 2-57
System BIOS for IBM PC/XT/AT Computers and Compatibles (Phoenix), page 410

See Also: 4.103. INT 15H, AH=87H -- Move Block
4.105. INT 15H, AH=89H -- Switch to Protected Mode

4.107. INT 15H, AH=90H -- DEVICE BUSY

Prior to Issuing INT 15H

	High	Low
AX	90H	Type code*
BX	Offset of pointer to network control block†	
CX		
DX		
SP		
BP		
SI		
DI		
IP		
flags	Carry clear (Phoenix)	
CS		
DS		
SS		
ES	Segment of pointer to network control block†	

Upon Return from INT 15H

	High	Low
AX	Flag§	
BX		
CX		
DX		
SP		
BP		
SI		
DI		
IP		
flags	Carry set if min. wait time satisfied	
CS		
DS		
SS		
ES		

*Type codes are as follows:
00=fixed disk (time out)
01=floppy disk (time out)
02=keyboard (no time out)
03=pointing device (time out)
21H=waiting for keyboard input (Phoenix)
80H=network (no time out)
FCH=fixed disk reset (time out)
FDH=floppy disk drive motor start (time out)
FEH=printer (time-out)
†Only for type code of 80H
§00H if wait time not satisified (Phoenix)

Version: Applies to all PC models beginning with AT, except PC XT 286.

Source: IBM PS/2 and PC BIOS Interface Technical Reference, pages 2-91 through 2-92
BIOS Interface Technical Reference for PS/1 Computer, page 2-58
System BIOS for IBM PC/XT/AT Computers and Compatibles (Phoenix), page 411

See Also: 4.001. BIOS Services Summary

4.108. INT 15H, AH=91H -- INTERRUPT COMPLETE

Prior to Issuing INT 15H

	High	Low
AX	91H	
BX	Offset of pointer to NCB (Phoenix)†	
CX		
DX		
SP		
BP		
SI		
DI		
IP		
flags	Carry clear (Phoenix)	
CS		
DS		
SS		
ES	Segment of pointer to NCB (Phoenix)†	

Upon Return from INT 15H

	High	Low
AX		Type code*
BX		
CX		
DX		
SP		
BP		
SI		
DI		
IP		
flags		
CS		
DS		
SS		
ES		

*Type codes are as follows:
00=fixed disk (time-out)
01=floppy disk (time-out)
02=keyboard (no time-out)
03=pointing device (time-out)
80H=network (no time-out)
FCH=fixed disk reset (time-out)
FDH=floppy disk motor start (time-out)
FEH=printer (time-out)
†Only for type code of 80H

Version: Applies to AT, Convertible, Phoenix AT BIOS, PS/1, and PS/2 only.

Note: Used internally by BIOS; not for application use.

Source: IBM PS/2 and PC BIOS Interface Technical Reference, page 2-92
BIOS Interface Technical Reference for PS/1 Computer, page 2-59
System BIOS for IBM PC/XT/AT Computers and Compatibles (Phoenix), page 412
DOS Programmer's Reference 2nd Edition (Que), pages 488 through 489

See Also: 4.001. BIOS Services Summary

4.109. INT 15H, AH=C0H -- RETURN SYSTEM CONFIG PARAMETERS

Prior to Issuing INT 15H

	High	Low
AX	C0H	
BX		
CX		
DX		
SP		
BP		
SI		
DI		
IP		
flags		
CS		
DS		
SS		
ES		

Upon Return from INT 15H

	High	Low
AX	0†	
BX	Offset of pointer to system descriptor table*	
CX		
DX		
SP		
BP		
SI		
DI		
IP		
flags	Carry clear†	
CS		
DS		
SS		
ES	Segment of pointer to system descriptor table*	

*See 4.110. INT 15H, System Descriptor Table
†Phoenix: if system model could not be determined, AH=86H and carry flag is set.

Version: Applies to AT after 6/10/85, XT after 1/10/86, XT286, Convertible, Phoenix AT BIOS, PS/1, and PS/2 only.

Source: IBM PS/2 and PC BIOS Interface Technical Reference, pages 2-92 through 2-94
BIOS Interface Technical Reference for PS/1 Computer, pages 2-59 through 2-60
System BIOS for IBM PC/XT/AT Computers and Compatibles (Phoenix), pages 413 through 414

See Also: 4.001. BIOS Services Summary
4.110. INT 15H, System Descriptor Table

4.110. INT 15H, SYSTEM DESCRIPTOR TABLE

Offset	*Length*	*Description*	*Allowable Values*
0	Word	Number of bytes in table	Minimum of 8
2	Byte	Model byte	See 4.007. Model Number Bytes
3	Byte	Submodel byte	See 4.007. Model Number Bytes
4	Byte	BIOS revision level	00=first release
5	Byte	Feature information	Bit 7 = fixed disk BIOS use DMA 3 Bit 6 = 2nd interrupt chip present Bit 5 = real-time clock present Bit 4 = keyboard intercept called Bit 3 = wait for ext event supported Bit 2 = extended BIOS area allocated Bit 1 = micro channel-type I/O channel Bit 0 = RESERVED
6	Byte	Feature information RESERVED	Bit 7 = RESERVED Bit 6 1=kbd functionality call supported Bits 0-5 = RESERVED
7	Byte	Feature information RESERVED	
8	Byte	Feature information RESERVED	
9	Byte	Feature information RESERVED	

Version: Applies to AT after 11/15/85, XT after 1/10/86, XT286, PC Convertible, Phoenix AT BIOS, PS/1, and PS/2.

Source: IBM PS/2 and PC BIOS Interface Technical Reference, pages 2-93 through 2-94
BIOS Interface Technical Reference for PS/1 Computer, pages 2-59 through 2-60
System BIOS for IBM PC/XT/AT Computers and Compatibles (Phoenix), page 414

See Also: 4.109. INT 15H, AH=C0H -- Return System Config Parameters

4.111. INT 15H, AH=C1H -- RETURN EXT BIOS SEGMENT ADDRESS

Prior to Issuing INT 15H

Register	*High*	*Low*
AX	C1H	
BX		
CX		
DX		
SP		
BP		
SI		
DI		
IP		
flags		
CS		
DS		
SS		
ES		

Upon Return from INT 15H

Register	*High*	*Low*
AX		
BX		
CX		
DX		
SP		
BP		
SI		
DI		
IP		
flags	Carry flag set on error	
CS		
DS		
SS		
ES	Segment address of extended BIOS data area	

Version: Applies to PS/1 and PS/2 models only.

Note: Used internally by BIOS; not for use by applications.

Source: IBM PS/2 and PC BIOS Interface Technical Reference, pages 2-94 through 2-95
BIOS Interface Technical Reference for PS/1 Computer, page 2-61

See Also: 4.001. BIOS Services Summary
4.003. Extended BIOS Data Area Layout

4.112. INT 15H, AH=C2H, AL=00H -- ENABLE/DISABLE POINTING DEVICE

Prior to Issuing INT 15H

	High	Low
AX	C2H	00H
BX	0=disable, 1=enable	
CX		
DX		
SP		
BP		
SI		
DI		
IP		
flags		
CS		
DS		
SS		
ES		

Upon Return from INT 15H

	High	Low
AX	Mouse status†	
BX		
CX		
DX		
SP		
BP		
SI		
DI		
IP		
flags	Carry flag set on error	
CS		
DS		
SS		
ES		

†See 4.120. INT 15H, Mouse Port Status Bytes

Version: Applies to PS/1 and PS/2 models only.

Source: IBM PS/2 and PC BIOS Interface Technical Reference, pages 2-95 through 2-99
BIOS Interface Technical Reference for PS/1 Computer, pages 2-61 through 2-65

See Also: 4.001. BIOS Services Summary
4.120. INT 15H, Mouse Port Status Bytes

4.113. INT 15H, AH=C2H, AL=01H -- RESET POINTING DEVICE

Prior to Issuing INT 15H

	High	Low
AX	C2H	01H
BX		
CX		
DX		
SP		
BP		
SI		
DI		
IP		
flags		
CS		
DS		
SS		
ES		

Upon Return from INT 15H

	High	Low
AX	Mouse status*	
BX	Device ID†	(Destroyed)
CX		
DX		
SP		
BP		
SI		
DI		
IP		
flags	Carry flag set on error	
CS		
DS		
SS		
ES		

*See 4.120. INT 15H, Mouse Port Status Bytes
†Only if no error occurred; set to 00H

Version: Applies to PS/1 and PS/2 models only.

Note: Pointing device state is set to: disabled, 100 reports/second sample rate, 4 count/mm resolution, 1 to 1 scaling, data package size unmodified.

Source: IBM PS/2 and PC BIOS Interface Technical Reference, page 2-95
BIOS Interface Technical Reference for PS/1 Computer, page 2-61

See Also: 4.001. BIOS Services Summary
4.120. INT 15H, Mouse Port Status Bytes

4.114. INT 15H, AH=C2H, AL=02H -- SET SAMPLE RATE

Prior to Issuing INT 15H

	High	Low
AX	C2H	02H
BX	Sample rate†	
CX		
DX		
SP		
BP		
SI		
DI		
IP		
flags		
CS		
DS		
SS		
ES		

Upon Return from INT 15H

	High	Low
AX	Mouse status*	
BX		
CX		
DX		
SP		
BP		
SI		
DI		
IP		
flags	Carry flag set on error	
CS		
DS		
SS		
ES		

*See 4.120. INT 15H, Mouse Port Status Bytes
†00=10 reports/second, 01=20 rpts/sec, 02=40 rpts/sec, 03=60 rpts/sec, 04=80 rpts/sec, 05=100 rpts/sec (default), 06=200 rpts/sec

Version: Applies to PS/1 and PS/2 models only.

Source: IBM PS/2 and PC BIOS Interface Technical Reference, pages 2-95 through 2-96
BIOS Interface Technical Reference for PS/1 Computer, page 2-62

See Also: 4.001. BIOS Services Summary
4.120. INT 15H, Mouse Port Status Bytes

4.115. INT 15H, AH=C2H, AL=03H -- SET RESOLUTION

Prior to Issuing INT 15H

	High	Low
AX	C2H	03H
BX	Resolution†	
CX		
DX		
SP		
BP		
SI		
DI		
IP		
flags		
CS		
DS		
SS		
ES		

Upon Return from INT 15H

	High	Low
AX	Mouse status*	
BX		
CX		
DX		
SP		
BP		
SI		
DI		
IP		
flags	Carry flag set on error	
CS		
DS		
SS		
ES		

*See 4.120. INT 15H, Mouse Port Status Bytes
†00=1 count/millimeter, 01=2 cnts/mm, 02=4 cnts/mm, 03=8 cnts/mm

Version: Applies to PS/1 and PS/2 models only.

Source: IBM PS/2 and PC BIOS Interface Technical Reference, pages 2-95 through 2-96
BIOS Interface Technical Reference for PS/1 Computer, page 2-62

See Also: 4.001. BIOS Services Summary
4.120. INT 15H, Mouse Port Status Bytes

4.116. INT 15H, AH=C2H, AL=04H -- READ DEVICE TYPE

Prior to Issuing INT 15H

	High	Low
AX	C2H	04H
BX		
CX		
DX		
SP		
BP		
SI		
DI		
IP		
flags		
CS		
DS		
SS		
ES		

Upon Return from INT 15H

	High	Low
AX	Mouse status*	
BX	Device ID†	
CX		
DX		
SP		
BP		
SI		
DI		
IP		
flags	Carry flag set on error	
CS		
DS		
SS		
ES		

*See 4.120. INT 15H, Mouse Port Status Bytes
†Only if operation successful; set to 0

Version: Applies to PS/1 and PS/2 models only.

Source: IBM PS/2 and PC BIOS Interface Technical Reference, page 2-96
BIOS Interface Technical Reference for PS/1 Computer, page 2-62

See Also: 4.001. BIOS Services Summary
4.120. INT 15H, Mouse Port Status Bytes

4.117. INT 15H, AH=C2H, AL=05H -- INITIALIZE POINTING DEVICE

Prior to Issuing INT 15H

	High	Low
AX	C2H	05H
BX	Bytes in data package	
CX		
DX		
SP		
BP		
SI		
DI		
IP		
flags		
CS		
DS		
SS		
ES		

Upon Return from INT 15H

	High	Low
AX	Mouse status*	
BX		
CX		
DX		
SP		
BP		
SI		
DI		
IP		
flags	Carry flag set on error	
CS		
DS		
SS		
ES		

*See 4.120. INT 15H, Mouse Port Status Bytes

Version: Applies to PS/1 and PS/2 models only.

Note: Device is initialized as: disabled state, 100 reports/second sampling rate, 4 count/millimeter resolution, 1 to 1 scaling.

Source: IBM PS/2 and PC BIOS Interface Technical Reference, page 2-97
BIOS Interface Technical Reference for PS/1 Computer, page 2-63

See Also: 4.001. BIOS Services Summary
4.120. INT 15H, Mouse Port Status Bytes

4.118. INT 15H, AH=C2H, AL=06H -- EXTENDED COMMANDS

Prior to Issuing INT 15H

	High	Low
AX	C2H	06H
BX	Command†	
CX		
DX		
SP		
BP		
SI		
DI		
IP		
flags		
CS		
DS		
SS		
ES		

Upon Return from INT 15H

	High	Low
AX	Mouse status*	
BX		Status byte 1§
CX		Status byte 2§
DX		Status byte 3§
SP		
BP		
SI		
DI		
IP		
flags	Carry flag set on error	
CS		
DS		
SS		
ES		

*See 4.120. INT 15H, Mouse Port Status Bytes
†0=get status, 1=set scaling to 1 to 1, 2=set scaling to 2 to 1
§For BH=0 only, successful operation returns:

Status byte 1

Bit	Meaning
7	RESERVED
6	0=stream mode, 1=remote mode
5	0=disable, 1=enable
4	0=1:1 scaling, 1=2:1 scaling
3	RESERVED
2	Left button pressed
1	RESERVED
0	Right button pressed

Status byte 2

Value	Meaning
0	1 count per millimeter
1	2 counts per millimeter
2	4 counts per millimeter
3	8 counts per millimeter

Status byte 3

Value	Meaning
0A	10 reports per second
14	20 reports per second
28	40 reports per second
3C	60 reports per second
50	80 reports per second
64	100 reports per second
C8	200 reports per second

Version: Applies to PS/1 and PS/2 models only.

Source: IBM PS/2 and PC BIOS Interface Technical Reference, pages 2-97 through 2-98
BIOS Interface Technical Reference for PS/1 Computer, pages 2-63 through 2-64

See Also: 4.001. BIOS Services Summary
4.120. INT 15H, Mouse Port Status Bytes

4.119. INT 15H, AH=C2H, AL=07H -- DEVICE DRIVER INIT CALL

Prior to Issuing INT 15H

Register	High	Low
AX	C2H	07H
BX	Offset of pointer to device driver	
CX		
DX		
SP		
BP		
SI		
DI		
IP		
flags		
CS		
DS		
SS		
ES	Segment of pointer to device driver	

Upon Return from INT 15H

Register	High	Low
AX	Mouse status*	
BX		
CX		
DX		
SP		
BP		
SI		
DI		
IP		
flags	Carry flag set on error	
CS		
DS		
SS		
ES		

*See 4.120. INT 15H, Mouse Port Status Bytes

Version: Applies to PS/1 and PS/2 models only.

Source: IBM PS/2 and PC BIOS Interface Technical Reference, page 2-98
BIOS Interface Technical Reference for PS/1 Computer, page 2-64

See Also: 4.001. BIOS Services Summary
4.120. INT 15H, Mouse Port Status Bytes

4.120. INT 15H, MOUSE PORT STATUS BYTES

Value	Meaning
0	No error occurred
1	Invalid function call attempted
2	Invalid input to function call
3	Interface error
4	Resend
5	No far call installed for device

Source: IBM PS/2 and PC BIOS Interface Technical Reference, page 2-95
BIOS Interface Technical Reference for PS/1 Computer, page 2-61

See Also: 4.112. INT 15H, AH=C2H, AL=00H -- Enable/Disable Pointing Device
4.113. INT 15H, AH=C2H, AL=01H -- Reset Pointing Device
4.114. INT 15H, AH=C2H, AL=02H -- Set Sample Rate
4.115. INT 15H, AH=C2H, AL=03H -- Set Resolution
4.116. INT 15H, AH=C2H, AL=04H -- Read Device Type
4.117. INT 15H, AH=C2H, AL=05H -- Initialize Pointing Device
4.118. INT 15H, AH=C2H, AL=06H -- Extended Commands
4.119. INT 15H, AH=C2H, AL=07H -- Device Driver Init Call

4.121. INT 15H, AH=C3H -- WATCHDOG TIMEOUT

Prior to Issuing INT 15H

	High	Low
AX	C3H	1=enable, 0=disable
BX	Watchdog timer count (1-255)	
CX		
DX		
SP		
BP		
SI		
DI		
IP		
flags		
CS		
DS		
SS		
ES		

Upon Return from INT 15H

	High	Low
AX		
BX		
CX		
DX		
SP		
BP		
SI		
DI		
IP		
flags	Carry flag set on error	
CS		
DS		
SS		
ES		

Version: Applies to PS/2 products except Models 25 and 30.

Source: IBM PS/2 and PC BIOS Interface Technical Reference, pages 2-99 through 2-100

See Also: 4.001. BIOS Services Summary

4.122. INT 15H, AH=C4H -- PROG OPTION SELECT

Prior to Issuing INT 15H

	High	Low
AX	C4H	Option*
BX		Slot number†
CX		
DX		
SP		
BP		
SI		
DI		
IP		
flags		
CS		
DS		
SS		
ES		

Upon Return from INT 15H

	High	Low
AX		Option*
BX		Slot number†
CX		
DX	Base POS adapter register address§	
SP		
BP		
SI		
DI		
IP		
flags	Carry flag set on error	
CS		
DS		
SS		
ES		

*0=get base POS adapter register address, 1=enable slot, 2=enable adapter
†Only if AL=1
§Only AL=0

Version: Applies to PS/2 products, except Models 25 and 30.

Source: IBM PS/2 and PC BIOS Interface Technical Reference, pages 2-100 through 2-101

See Also: 4.001. BIOS Services Summary

4.123. INT 16H, AH=00H -- READ CHARACTER

Prior to Issuing INT 16H

	High	Low
AX	00H	
BX		
CX		
DX		
SP		
BP		
SI		
DI		
IP		
flags		
CS		
DS		
SS		
ES		

Upon Return from INT 16H

	High	Low
AX	Scan code	ASCII character
BX		
CX		
DX		
SP		
BP		
SI		
DI		
IP		
flags		
CS		
DS		
SS		
ES		

Version: Applies to all PC models.

Note: Character is extracted from keyboard buffer.

Sources:
IBM PS/2 and PC BIOS Interface Technical Reference, page 2-104
BIOS Interface Technical Reference for PS/1 Computer, pages 2-67 through 2-68
System BIOS for IBM PC/XT/AT Computers and Compatibles (Phoenix), pages 139 through 140

See Also:
1.21. ASCII Character Set
1.22. IBM ASCII Character Set
4.001. BIOS Services Summary
7.012. PC 83-Key Keyboard Numbers and Scan Codes
7.013. AT 84-Key Keyboard Numbers and Scan Codes
7.014. AT 101/102-Key Keyboard Numbers and Scan Codes
7.015. PS/2 Keyboard Numbers and Scan Codes
7.016. PC and XT Type-Ahead Buffer Layout

4.124. INT 16H, AH=01H -- READ STATUS

Prior to Issuing INT 16H

	High	Low
AX	01H	
BX		
CX		
DX		
SP		
BP		
SI		
DI		
IP		
flags		
CS		
DS		
SS		
ES		

Upon Return from INT 16H

	High	Low
AX	Scan code*	ASCII char*
BX		
CX		
DX		
SP		
BP		
SI		
DI		
IP		
flags	Zero flag set if no character available	
CS		
DS		
SS		
ES		

*If zero flag is clear

Version: Applies to all PC models.

Note: Character is not removed from keyboard buffer.

Source: IBM PS/2 and PC BIOS Interface Technical Reference, page 2-104
BIOS Interface Technical Reference for PS/1 Computer, page 2-68
System BIOS for IBM PC/XT/AT Computers and Compatibles (Phoenix), pages 141 through 142

See Also:
1.21. ASCII Character Set
1.22. IBM ASCII Character Set
4.001. BIOS Services Summary
7.012. PC 83-Key Keyboard Numbers and Scan Codes
7.013. AT 84-Key Keyboard Numbers and Scan Codes
7.014. AT 101/102-Key Keyboard Numbers and Scan Codes
7.015. PS/2 Keyboard Numbers and Scan Codes
7.016. PC and XT Type-Ahead Buffer Layout

4.125. INT 16H, AH=02H -- READ FLAGS

Prior to Issuing INT 16H

	High	Low
AX	02H	
BX		
CX		
DX		
SP		
BP		
SI		
DI		
IP		
flags		
CS		
DS		
SS		
ES		

Upon Return from INT 16H

	High	Low
AX	RESERVED	Shift Status Byte*
BX		
CX		
DX		
SP		
BP		
SI		
DI		
IP		
flags		
CS		
DS		
SS		
ES		

*See 4.127. INT 16H, Keyboard Flags Byte

Version: Applies to all PC models.

Source: IBM PS/2 and PC BIOS Interface Technical Reference, page 2-105
BIOS Interface Technical Reference for PS/1 Computer, page 2-68
System BIOS for IBM PC/XT/AT Computers and Compatibles (Phoenix), page 142

See Also:
4.001. BIOS Services Summary
4.127. INT 16H, Keyboard Flags Byte

4.126. INT 16H, AH=03H -- SET TYPEMATIC RATE AND DELAY

Prior to Issuing INT 16H

	High	Low
AX	03H	05H or 06H*
BX	Delay†	Rate†
CX		
DX		
SP		
BP		
SI		
DI		
IP		
flags		
CS		
DS		
SS		
ES		

Upon Return from INT 16H

	High	Low
AX		
BX	Delay§	Rate§
CX		
DX		
SP		
BP		
SI		
DI		
IP		
flags		
CS		
DS		
SS		
ES		

*05H=set rate and delay; 06H=return rate and delay
§No output if AL=05 on call
†Only if AL=05 (set):

Valid Delays:	00H=250 ms	01H=500 ms
	02H=750 ms	03H=1000 ms
Valid Rates:	00h=30 cps	01H=26.7 cps
	02H=24 cps	03H=21.8 cps
	04H=20 cps	05H=18.5 cps
	06H=17.1 cps	07H=16 cps
	08H=15 cps	09H=13.3 cps
	0Ah=12 cps	0BH=10.9 cps
	0CH=10 cps	0DH=9.2 cps
	0EH=8.6 cps	0FH=8 cps
	10H=7.5 cps	11H=6.7 cps
	12H=6 cps	13H=5.5 cps
	14H=5 cps	15H=4.6 cps
	16H=4.3 cps	17H=4 cps
	18H=3.7 cps	19H=3.3 cps
	1AH=3 cps	1BH=2.7 cps
	1CH=2.5 cps	1DH=2.3 cps
	1EH=2.1 cps	1FH=2 cps
	20H-FFH=RESERVED	

Version: Applies to all PC models starting with AT.

Source: IBM PS/2 and PC BIOS Interface Technical Reference, pages 2-105 through 2-106
BIOS Interface Technical Reference for PS/1 Computer, pages 2-68 through 2-69
System BIOS for IBM PC/XT/AT Computers and Compatibles (Phoenix), page 143

See Also: 4.001. BIOS Services Summary

4.127. INT 16H, KEYBOARD FLAGS BYTE

Bit Number

7	6	5	4	3	2	1	0	Description
✔								Insert state locked active
	✔							Caps lock key active
		✔						Num lock key active
			✔					Scroll lock key active
				✔				Alt key held down
					✔			Ctrl key held down
						✔		Left shift key held down
							✔	Right shift key held down

Source: IBM PS/2 and PC BIOS Interface Technical Reference, page 2-107
BIOS Interface Technical Reference for PS/1 Computer, page 2-68
System BIOS for IBM PC/XT/AT Computers and Compatibles (Phoenix), page 142

See Also: 4.125. INT 16H, AH=02H -- Read Flags
4.133. INT 16H, Extended Keyboard Flags Byte

4.128. INT 16H, AH=05H -- KEYBOARD WRITE

Register	Prior to Issuing INT 16H: High	Prior to Issuing INT 16H: Low	Upon Return from INT 16H: High	Upon Return from INT 16H: Low
AX	05H			Status*
BX				
CX	Scan code	ASCII char		
DX				
SP				
BP				
SI				
DI				
IP				
flags				
CS				
DS				
SS				
ES				

*0=successful, 1=buffer full

Version: Applies to AT after 11/15/85, XT after 1/10/86, XT286, Phoenix, PS/1, and PS/2 only.

Note: Function places key in type-ahead buffer as if typed from keyboard.

Source: IBM PS/2 and PC BIOS Interface Technical Reference, pages 2-106 through 2-107
BIOS Interface Technical Reference for PS/1 Computer, page 2-69
System BIOS for IBM PC/XT/AT Computers and Compatibles (Phoenix), page 144

See Also: 4.001. BIOS Services Summary
7.016. PC and XT Type-Ahead Buffer Layout

4.129. INT 16H, AH=09H -- KEYBOARD FUNCTIONALITY DETERMINATION

Register	Prior to Issuing INT 16H: High	Prior to Issuing INT 16H: Low	Upon Return from INT 16H: High	Upon Return from INT 16H: Low
AX	09H			Function code*
BX				
CX				
DX				
SP				
BP				
SI				
DI				
IP				
flags				
CS				
DS				
SS				
ES				

*Bits 4-7=RESERVED
Bit 3 -- 1=get current typematic rate/delay supported
Bit 2 -- 1=set typematic rate/delay supported
Bit 1 -- 1=turn on/off typematic not supported
Bit 0 -- 1=return to default typematic rate/delay supported

Version: Applies to PS/1 and PS/2 only.

Source: IBM PS/2 and PC BIOS Interface Technical Reference, page 2-107
BIOS Interface Technical Reference for PS/1 Computer, page 2-70

See Also: 4.001. BIOS Services Summary

4.130. INT 16H, AH=10H -- EXTENDED KEYBOARD READ

Prior to Issuing INT 16H

	High	Low
AX	10H	
BX		
CX		
DX		
SP		
BP		
SI		
DI		
IP		
flags		
CS		
DS		
SS		
ES		

Upon Return from INT 16H

	High	Low
AX	Scan code	ASCII character
BX		
CX		
DX		
SP		
BP		
SI		
DI		
IP		
flags		
CS		
DS		
SS		
ES		

Version: Applies to AT after 11/15/85, XT after 1/10/86, XT286, Phoenix, PS/1, and PS/2 only.

Note: Key is removed from type-ahead buffer.

Source: IBM PS/2 and PC BIOS Interface Technical Reference, page 2-108
BIOS Interface Technical Reference for PS/1 Computer, page 2-70
System BIOS for IBM PC/XT/AT Computers and Compatibles (Phoenix), page 145

See Also: 4.001. BIOS Services Summary
4.123. INT 16H, AH=00H -- Read Character
7.016. PC and XT Type-Ahead Buffer Layout

4.131. INT 16H, AH=11H -- EXTENDED KEYSTROKE STATUS

Prior to Issuing INT 16H

	High	Low
AX	11H	
BX		
CX		
DX		
SP		
BP		
SI		
DI		
IP		
flags		
CS		
DS		
SS		
ES		

Upon Return from INT 16H

	High	Low
AX	Scan code*	ASCII character*
BX		
CX		
DX		
SP		
BP		
SI		
DI		
IP		
flags	Zero flag set if no character is available	
CS		
DS		
SS		
ES		

*If zero flag is clear

Version: Applies to AT after 11/15/85, XT after 1/10/86, XT286, Phoenix XT & AT BIOS, PS/1, and PS/2 only.

Note: Key is NOT removed from type-ahead buffer.

Source: IBM PS/2 and PC BIOS Interface Technical Reference, page 2-108
BIOS Interface Technical Reference for PS/1 Computer, page 2-70
System BIOS for IBM PC/XT/AT Computers and Compatibles (Phoenix), pages 146 through 147

See Also: 4.001. BIOS Services Summary
4.124. INT 16H, AH=01H -- Read Status
7.016. PC and XT Type-Ahead Buffer Layout

4.132. INT 16H, AH=12H -- EXTENDED SHIFT STATUS

Prior to Issuing INT 16H

	High	Low
AX	12H	
BX		
CX		
DX		
SP		
BP		
SI		
DI		
IP		
flags		
CS		
DS		
SS		
ES		

Upon Return from INT 16H

	High	Low
AX	Ext shift status*	Shift status†
BX		
CX		
DX		
SP		
BP		
SI		
DI		
IP		
flags		
CS		
DS		
SS		
ES		

*See 4.133. INT 16H, Extended Keyboard Flags Byte
†See 4.127. INT 16H, Keyboard Flags Byte

Version: Applies to AT after 11/15/85, XT after 1/10/86, XT286, Phoenix, PS/1, and PS/2 only.

Source: IBM PS/2 and PC BIOS Interface Technical Reference, page 2-109
BIOS Interface Technical Reference for PS/1 Computer, page 2-71
System BIOS for IBM PC/XT/AT Computers and Compatibles (Phoenix), pages 147 through 148

See Also: 4.001. BIOS Services Summary
4.125. INT 16H, AH=02H -- Read Flags
4.127. INT 16H, Keyboard Flags Byte
4.133. INT 16H, Extended Keyboard Flags Byte
7.016. PC and XT Type-Ahead Buffer Layout

4.133. INT 16H, EXTENDED KEYBOARD FLAGS BYTE

Bit Number

7	6	5	4	3	2	1	0	Description
✔								SysRq key held down
	✔							Caps Lock key held down
		✔						Num Lock key held down
			✔					Scroll Lock key held down
				✔				Right Alt key held down
					✔			Right Ctrl key held down
						✔		Left Alt key held down
							✔	Left Ctrl key held down

Source: IBM PS/2 and PC BIOS Interface Technical Reference, page 2-109
BIOS Interface Technical Reference for PS/1 Computer, page 2-71
System BIOS for IBM PC/XT/AT Computers and Compatibles (Phoenix), page 148

See Also: 4.127. INT 16H, Keyboard Flags Byte
4.132. INT 16H, AH=12H -- Extended Shift Status

4.134. INT 17H, AH=00H -- WRITE CHARACTER

Prior to Issuing INT 17H

	High	Low
AX	00H	Character
BX		
CX		
DX	Printer number†	
SP		
BP		
SI		
DI		
IP		
flags		
CS		
DS		
SS		
ES		

Upon Return from INT 17H

	High	Low
AX	Status*	
BX		
CX		
DX		
SP		
BP		
SI		
DI		
IP		
flags		
CS		
DS		
SS		
ES		

*See 4.135. INT 17H, Printer Status Byte
†0=LPT1, 1=LPT2, 2=LPT3; index to port base address (40:08)

Version: Applies to all PC models.

Source: IBM PS/2 and PC BIOS Interface Technical Reference, page 2-110
BIOS Interface Technical Reference for PS/1 Computer, page 2-72
System BIOS for IBM PC/XT/AT Computers and Compatibles (Phoenix), page 424

See Also: 4.135. INT 17H, Printer Status Byte

4.135. INT 17H, PRINTER STATUS BYTE

Bit Number

7	6	5	4	3	2	1	0	*Description*
✔								Not Busy
	✔							Acknowledge
		✔						Out of Paper
			✔					Selected
				✔				I/O Error
					✔			RESERVED
						✔		RESERVED
							✔	Time-Out

Source: IBM PS/2 and PC BIOS Interface Technical Reference, page 2-110
BIOS Interface Technical Reference for PS/1 Computer, page 2-72
System BIOS for IBM PC/XT/AT Computers and Compatibles (Phoenix), page 424

See Also: 4.134. INT 17H, AH=00H -- Write Character
4.136. INT 17H, AH=01H -- Initialize Printer Port
4.137. INT 17H, AH=02H -- Status Request

4.136. INT 17H, AH=01H -- INITIALIZE PRINTER PORT

Register	Prior to Issuing INT 17H: High	Prior to Issuing INT 17H: Low	Upon Return from INT 17H: High	Upon Return from INT 17H: Low
AX	01H		Status*	
BX				
CX				
DX	Printer number†			
SP				
BP				
SI				
DI				
IP				
flags				
CS				
DS				
SS				
ES				

*See 4.135. INT 17H, Printer Status Byte
†0=LPT1, 1=LPT2, 2=LPT3; index into port base address (40:08)

Version: Applies to all PC models.

Source: IBM PS/2 and PC BIOS Interface Technical Reference, page 2-110
BIOS Interface Technical Reference for PS/1 Computer, page 2-72
System BIOS for IBM PC/XT/AT Computers and Compatibles (Phoenix), page 425

See Also: 4.135. INT 17H, Printer Status Byte

4.137. INT 17H, AH=02H -- STATUS REQUEST

Register	Prior to Issuing INT 17H: High	Prior to Issuing INT 17H: Low	Upon Return from INT 17H: High	Upon Return from INT 17H: Low
AX	02H		Status*	
BX				
CX				
DX	Printer number†			
SP				
BP				
SI				
DI				
IP				
flags				
CS				
DS				
SS				
ES				

*See 4.135. INT 17H, Printer Status Byte
†0=LPT1, 1=LPT2, 2=LPT3; index into port base address (40:08)

Version: Applies to all PC models.

Source: IBM PS/2 and PC BIOS Interface Technical Reference, page 2-111
BIOS Interface Technical Reference for PS/1 Computer, page 2-73
System BIOS for IBM PC/XT/AT Computers and Compatibles (Phoenix), page 426

See Also: 4.135. INT 17H, Printer Status Byte

4.138. INT 18H -- BASIC LOADER

Prior to Issuing INT 18H

	High	Low
AX		
BX		
CX		
DX		
SP		
BP		
SI		
DI		
IP		
flags		
CS		
DS		
SS		
ES		

Upon Return from INT 18H

Interrupt does not return.

Version: On XTs and ATs, INT 18H can be vectored to a "no boot device" routine.

Note:
- Interrupt switches control to ROM BASIC.
- Not documented in IBM BIOS reference.
- Invoked if no boot code found by INT 19H.

Source: Programmer's Guide to the IBM PC and PS/2 (Microsoft Press), page 247
System BIOS for IBM PC/XT/AT Computers and Compatibles (Phoenix), page 460

See Also: 4.001. BIOS Services Summary

4.139. INT 19H -- BOOTSTRAP LOADER

Prior to Issuing INT 19H

	High	Low
AX		
BX		
CX		
DX		
SP		
BP		
SI		
DI		
IP		
flags		
CS		
DS		
SS		
ES		

Upon Return from INT 19H

Interrupt does not return.

Note: Interrupt reboots computer by reading cylinder 0, sector 1 into segment 0, offset 7C00H. Control is transferred to that location.

Source: IBM PS/2 and PC BIOS Interface Technical Reference, page 2-113
BIOS Interface Technical Reference for PS/1 Computer, page 2-73
System BIOS for IBM PC/XT/AT Computers and Compatibles (Phoenix), pages 459 through 462

See Also: 4.001. BIOS Services Summary

4.140. INT 1AH, AH=00H -- READ CLOCK COUNT

Register	Prior to Issuing INT 1AH: High	Prior to Issuing INT 1AH: Low	Upon Return from INT 1AH: High	Upon Return from INT 1AH: Low
AX	00H		00H†	24-hour check*
BX				
CX			HO Count	
DX			LO Count	
SP				
BP				
SI				
DI				
IP				
flags			Carry flag set on error†	
CS				
DS				
SS				
ES				

*0=hasn't been 24 hours since power-on; >0=has been 24 hours or more
†Phoenix BIOS only

Version: Applies to all PC models.

Note: Timer overflow flag is reset to 0.

Source: IBM PS/2 and PC BIOS Interface Technical Reference, page 2-114
BIOS Interface Technical Reference for PS/1 Computer, page 2-74
System BIOS for IBM PC/XT/AT Computers and Compatibles (Phoenix), page 438

See Also: 4.001. BIOS Services Summary
4.002. BIOS Memory Usage Summary
4.141. INT 1AH, AH=01H -- Set Clock Count

4.141. INT 1AH, AH=01H -- SET CLOCK COUNT

Register	Prior to Issuing INT 1AH: High	Prior to Issuing INT 1AH: Low	Upon Return from INT 1AH: High	Upon Return from INT 1AH: Low
AX	01H		00H*	
BX				
CX	HO Count			
DX	LO Count			
SP				
BP				
SI				
DI				
IP				
flags			Carry flag set on error*	
CS				
DS				
SS				
ES				

*Phoenix BIOS only

Version: Applies to all PC models.

Note: Timer overflow flag is set to 0.

Source: IBM PS/2 and PC BIOS Interface Technical Reference, page 2-115
BIOS Interface Technical Reference for PS/1 Computer, page 2-74
System BIOS for IBM PC/XT/AT Computers and Compatibles (Phoenix), page 439

See Also: 4.001. BIOS Services Summary
4.002. BIOS Memory Usage Summary
4.140. INT 1AH, AH=00H -- Read Clock Count

4.142. INT 1AH, AH=02H -- READ REAL TIME CLOCK TIME

Prior to Issuing INT 1AH

	High	Low
AX	02H	
BX		
CX		
DX		
SP		
BP		
SI		
DI		
IP		
flags		
CS		
DS		
SS		
ES		

Upon Return from INT 1AH

	High	Low
AX	00H†	BCD Hours†
BX		
CX	BCD Hours	BCD Minutes
DX	BCD Seconds	DST Option*
SP		
BP		
SI		
DI		
IP		
flags	Carry flag set if clock not operating	
CS		
DS		
SS		
ES		

*Daylight savings time option, 0=not used 1=operative
†Phoenix BIOS only

Version: Applies to AT with BIOS dated 6/10/85 and after, XT286, Convertible, Phoenix, PS/1, and PS/2 only.

Source: IBM PS/2 and PC BIOS Interface Technical Reference, page 2-115
BIOS Interface Technical Reference for PS/1 Computer, page 2-75
System BIOS for IBM PC/XT/AT Computers and Compatibles (Phoenix), page 440

See Also: 4.001. BIOS Services Summary
4.143. INT 1AH, AH=03H -- Set Real Time Clock Time
4.144. INT 1AH, AH=04H -- Read Real Time Clock Date

4.143. INT 1AH, AH=03H -- SET REAL TIME CLOCK TIME

Prior to Issuing INT 1AH

	High	Low
AX	03H	
BX		
CX	BCD Hours	BCD Minutes
DX	BCD Seconds	DST Option*
SP		
BP		
SI		
DI		
IP		
flags		
CS		
DS		
SS		
ES		

Upon Return from INT 1AH

	High	Low
AX	00H†	0BH Reg Value†
BX		
CX		
DX		
SP		
BP		
SI		
DI		
IP		
flags	Carry flag set on error†	
CS		
DS		
SS		
ES		

*Daylight savings time option; 0=not used, 1=operative
†Phoenix BIOS only

Version: Applies to AT with BIOS dated 6/10/85 and after, XT286, Phoenix, PS/1, and PS/2 only.

Source: IBM PS/2 and PC BIOS Interface Technical Reference, page 2-116
BIOS Interface Technical Reference for PS/1 Computer, page 2-75
System BIOS for IBM PC/XT/AT Computers and Compatibles (Phoenix), page 441

See Also: 4.001. BIOS Services Summary
4.142. INT 1AH, AH=02H -- Read Real Time Clock Time
4.145. INT 1AH, AH=05H -- Set Real Time Clock Date

4.144. INT 1AH, AH=04H -- READ REAL TIME CLOCK DATE

Prior to Issuing INT 1AH

	High	Low
AX	04H	
BX		
CX		
DX		
SP		
BP		
SI		
DI		
IP		
flags		
CS		
DS		
SS		
ES		

Upon Return from INT 1AH

	High	Low
AX	00H†	
BX		
CX	BCD Century*	BCD Year
DX	BCD Month	BCD Day
SP		
BP		
SI		
DI		
IP		
flags	Carry flag set if clock not operating	
CS		
DS		
SS		
ES		

*Century is binary coded decimal 19 or 20 only.
†Phoenix BIOS only

Version: Applies to all PC models beginning with AT.

Source: IBM PS/2 and PC BIOS Interface Technical Reference, page 2-116
BIOS Interface Technical Reference for PS/1 Computer, page 2-75
System BIOS for IBM PC/XT/AT Computers and Compatibles (Phoenix), page 442

See Also: 4.001. BIOS Services Summary
4.142. INT 1AH, AH=02H -- Read Real Time Clock Time
4.145. INT 1AH, AH=05H -- Set Real Time Clock Date

4.145. INT 1AH, AH=05H -- SET REAL TIME CLOCK DATE

Prior to Issuing INT 1AH

	High	Low
AX	05H	
BX		
CX	BCD Century*	BCD Year
DX	BCD Month	BCD Day
SP		
BP		
SI		
DI		
IP		
flags		
CS		
DS		
SS		
ES		

Upon Return from INT 1AH

	High	Low
AX	00H†	0BH Reg Value†
BX		
CX		
DX		
SP		
BP		
SI		
DI		
IP		
flags	Carry flag set on error†	
CS		
DS		
SS		
ES		

*Century is binary coded decimal 19 or 20 only.
†Phoenix BIOS only

Version: Applies to AT, Convertible, Phoenix, PS/1, and PS/2 only.

Source: IBM PS/2 and PC BIOS Interface Technical Reference, page 2-116
BIOS Interface Technical Reference for PS/1 Computer, page 2-75
System BIOS for IBM PC/XT/AT Computers and Compatibles (Phoenix), page 443

See Also: 4.001. BIOS Services Summary
4.143. INT 1AH, AH=03H -- Set Real Time Clock Time
4.144. INT 1AH, AH=04H -- Read Real Time Clock Date

4.146. INT 1AH, AH=06H -- SET REAL TIME CLOCK ALARM

Prior to Issuing INT 1AH

	High	Low
AX	06H	
BX		
CX	BCD Hours	BCD Minutes
DX	BCD Seconds	
SP		
BP		
SI		
DI		
IP		
flags		
CS		
DS		
SS		
ES		

Upon Return from INT 1AH

	High	Low
AX	00H*	00H*
BX		
CX		
DX		
SP		
BP		
SI		
DI		
IP		
flags	Carry set if alarm already set or no clock	
CS		
DS		
SS		
ES		

*Phoenix BIOS only

Version: Applies to all PC models beginning with AT.

Source: IBM PS/2 and PC BIOS Interface Technical Reference, page 2-117
BIOS Interface Technical Reference for PS/1 Computer, pages 2-75 through 2-76
System BIOS for IBM PC/XT/AT Computers and Compatibles (Phoenix), page 444

See Also: 4.001. BIOS Services Summary
4.147. INT 1AH, AH=07H -- Turn Off Real Time Clock Alarm

4.147. INT 1AH, AH=07H -- TURN OFF REAL TIME CLOCK ALARM

Prior to Issuing INT 1AH

	High	Low
AX	07H	
BX		
CX		
DX		
SP		
BP		
SI		
DI		
IP		
flags		
CS		
DS		
SS		
ES		

Upon Return from INT 1AH

	High	Low
AX	00H†	
BX		
CX		
DX		
SP		
BP		
SI		
DI		
IP		
flags	Carry flag set on error*	
CS		
DS		
SS		
ES		

*Phoenix BIOS only

Version: Applies to all PC models beginning with AT.

Source: IBM PS/2 and PC BIOS Interface Technical Reference, page 2-117
BIOS Interface Technical Reference for PS/1 Computer, page 2-76
System BIOS for IBM PC/XT/AT Computers and Compatibles (Phoenix), page 445

See Also: 4.001. BIOS Services Summary
4.146. INT 1AH, AH=06H -- Set Real Time Clock Alarm

4.148. INT 1AH, AH=09H -- READ REAL TIME CLOCK ALARM

Prior to Issuing INT 1AH

	High	Low
AX	09H	
BX		
CX		
DX		
SP		
BP		
SI		
DI		
IP		
flags		
CS		
DS		
SS		
ES		

Upon Return from INT 1AH

	High	Low
AX		
BX		
CX	BCD Hours	BCD Minutes
DX	BCD Seconds	Alarm Status*
SP		
BP		
SI		
DI		
IP		
flags		
CS		
DS		
SS		
ES		

*0=alarm not enabled; 1=alarm enabled, no power on; 2=alarm enabled, will power on system (Convertible only)

Version: Applies to PS/2 Model 30 and PC Convertible only.

Source: IBM PS/2 and PC BIOS Interface Technical Reference, page 2-118

See Also: 4.001. BIOS Services Summary

4.149. INT 1AH, AH=0AH -- READ SYSTEM TIMER DAY COUNT

Prior to Issuing INT 1AH

	High	Low
AX	0AH	
BX		
CX		
DX		
SP		
BP		
SI		
DI		
IP		
flags		
CS		
DS		
SS		
ES		

Upon Return from INT 1AH

	High	Low
AX		
BX		
CX	Count of days after 1/1/80	
DX		
SP		
BP		
SI		
DI		
IP		
flags		
CS		
DS		
SS		
ES		

Version: Applies to XT after 1/10/86, PS/1, and PS/2 only.

Source: IBM PS/2 and PC BIOS Interface Technical Reference, page 2-119
BIOS Interface Technical Reference for PS/1 Computer, page 2-76

See Also: 4.001. BIOS Services Summary
4.002. BIOS Memory Usage Summary
4.150. INT 1AH, AH=0BH -- Set System Timer Day Count

4.150. INT 1AH, AH=0BH -- SET SYSTEM TIMER DAY COUNT

Prior to Issuing INT 1AH

	High	Low
AX	0BH	
BX		
CX	Count of days after 1/1/80	
DX		
SP		
BP		
SI		
DI		
IP		
flags		
CS		
DS		
SS		
ES		

Upon Return from INT 1AH

Interrupt returns no values.

Version: Applies to XT after 1/10/86, PS/1, and PS/2 only.

Source: IBM PS/2 and PC BIOS Interface Technical Reference, page 2-119
BIOS Interface Technical Reference for PS/1 Computer, page 2-76

See Also: 4.001. BIOS Services Summary
4.002. BIOS Memory Usage Summary
4.149. INT 1AH, AH=0AH -- Read System Timer Day Count

4.151. INT 1AH, AH=80H -- SET SOUND SOURCE

Prior to Issuing INT 1AH

	High	Low
AX	80H	Source*
BX		
CX		
DX		
SP		
BP		
SI		
DI		
IP		
flags		
CS		
DS		
SS		
ES		

Upon Return from INT 1AH

Interrupt returns no values.

*00H=8253 chnl 2, 01H=cassette input, 02H=audio in on I/O channel, 03H=sound gen chip

Version: Applies to PCjr and Phoenix BIOS only.

Source: IBM PS/2 and PC BIOS Interface Technical Reference, page 2-120
System BIOS for IBM PC/XT/AT Computers and Compatibles (Phoenix), page 445

See Also: 4.001. BIOS Services Summary

Section 5

Other Interrupts, CD-ROM, Mouse, and EMS Support

Other Interrupts

Extended Memory Functions

5.001. DOS INTERRUPT USAGE BY DOS VERSION

		DOS Versions that Support Interrupt									
Int. Number	*Interrupt Name*	*1*	*1.1*	*2*	*2.1*	*3*	*3.1*	*3.2*	*3.3*	*4.0*	*5.0*
20 (32)	Program terminate	✔	✔	O	O	O	O	O	O	O	O
21 (33)	Function request	✔	✔	✔	✔	✔	✔	✔	✔	✔	✔
22 (34)	Terminate address	✔	✔	✔	✔	✔	✔	✔	✔	✔	✔
23 (35)	Control-Break exit address	✔	✔	✔	✔	✔	✔	✔	✔	✔	✔
24 (36)	Critical error handler vector	✔	✔	✔	✔	✔	✔	✔	✔	✔	✔
25 (37)	Absolute disk read	✔	✔	✔	✔	✔	✔	✔	✔	✔	O
26 (38)	Absolute disk write	✔	✔	✔	✔	✔	✔	✔	✔	✔	O
27 (39)	Terminate & stay resident	✔	✔	O	O	O	O	O	O	O	O
28 (40)	RESERVED	R	R	R	R	R	R	R	R	R	O
29 (41)	RESERVED	R	R	R	R	R	R	R	R	R	R
2A (42)	MS-Net access						✔	✔	✔	✔	R
2B (43)	RESERVED	R	R	R	R	R	R	R	R	R	R
2C (44)	RESERVED	R	R	R	R	R	R	R	R	R	R
2D (45)	RESERVED	R	R	R	R	R	R	R	R	R	R
2E (46)	Reload transient	R	R	R	R	R	R	R	R	R	R
2F (47)	Printer					✔					
2F (47)	Multiplex						✔	✔	✔	✔	✔
30 (48)	Entry point	R	R	R	R	R	R	R	R	R	R
31 (49)	Entry point	R	R	R	R	R	R	R	R	R	R
32 (50)	RESERVED	R	R	R	R	R	R	R	R	R	R
33 (51)	RESERVED	R	R	R	R	R	R	R	R	R	R
34 (52)	RESERVED	R	R	R	R	R	R	R	R	R	R
35 (53)	RESERVED	R	R	R	R	R	R	R	R	R	R
36 (54)	RESERVED	R	R	R	R	R	R	R	R	R	R
37 (55)	RESERVED	R	R	R	R	R	R	R	R	R	R
38 (56)	RESERVED	R	R	R	R	R	R	R	R	R	R
39 (57)	RESERVED	R	R	R	R	R	R	R	R	R	R
3A (58)	RESERVED	R	R	R	R	R	R	R	R	R	R
3B (59)	RESERVED	R	R	R	R	R	R	R	R	R	R
3C (60)	RESERVED	R	R	R	R	R	R	R	R	R	R
3D (61)	RESERVED	R	R	R	R	R	R	R	R	R	R
3E (62)	RESERVED	R	R	R	R	R	R	R	R	R	R
3F (63)	RESERVED	R	R	R	R	R	R	R	R	R	R

Legend: √=supported
O=supported but considered obsolete
R=reserved for future use

Note: Interrupt 2FH changed name beginning with DOS 3.1.

Source: IBM DOS 3.3 Technical Reference, pages 6-1 through 6-33
Microsoft MS-DOS 4.0 Programmer's Reference, pages 37 through 55
IBM DOS 4.0 Technical Reference, pages A-1 through A-17
Microsoft MS-DOS 5.0 Programmer's Reference, pages 107 through 108

See Also: 3.001. INT 21H Functions by DOS Version Summary
5.002. INT 24H Error Codes
5.003. INT 25H Absolute Disk Read
5.004. INT 26H Absolute Disk Write
5.006. INT 2FH Multiplex for DOS 3.x and 4.x

5.002. INT 24H, ERROR CODES

For Error Codes Returned In AH Register:

Bit Number 7	6	5	4	3	2	1	0	*Name*	*Allowable Values*
							✔	Type of operation	0=read operation; 1=write operation
					✔	✔		Location of error	00 = DOS Area 01 = FAT 10 = directory 11 = data area
				✔				Fail response	0 = fail not allowed, 1 = fail allowed
			✔					Retry response	0 = retry not allowed, 1 = retry allowed
		✔						Ignore response	0 = can't be ignored, 1 = can be ignored
	✔							NOT USED	NOT USED
✔								Device type	0 = disk drive device†, 1 = other device type*

For Error Code Returned In Low Byte of DI Register:

Error Code	*Error Name*	*DOS Version* 1.x	2.x	3.x	4.x	5.x
0 (0)	Write attempt on write-protected media	✔	✔	✔	✔	✔
1 (1)	Unknown unit		✔	✔	✔	✔
2 (2)	Drive not ready	✔	✔	✔	✔	✔
3 (3)	Unknown command		✔	✔	✔	✔
4 (4)	Data error (CRC error)	✔	✔	✔	✔	✔
5 (5)	Bad request structure length		✔	✔	✔	✔
6 (6)	Seek error	✔	✔	✔	✔	✔
7 (7)	Unknown media type		✔	✔	✔	✔
8 (8)	Sector not found	✔	✔	✔	✔	✔
9 (9)	Printer is out of paper		✔	✔	✔	✔
A (10)	Write fault	✔	✔	✔	✔	✔
B (11)	Read fault		✔	✔	✔	✔
C (12)	General failure	✔	✔	✔	✔	✔
D (13)	UNDEFINED	R	R	R	R	R
E (14)	UNDEFINED	R	R	R	R	R
F (15)	Invalid disk change			✔		

†If bit 7=0, then AL contains the failing drive number.

*If bit 7=1, then either the memory image of the FAT is bad, or the error occurred on a character device. To determine the type of error, examine bit 15 of the fifth byte in the device header (attribute bits). If it is 0, the error is a bad memory image of the FAT. Otherwise, bits 0-3 will tell you what character device failed, as follows:

Bit Number 3	2	1	0	*Character Device that Failed*
			✔	Current standard input
		✔		Current standard output
	✔			Current NULL device
✔				Current clock device

Legend: √=supported
R=reserved

Note: These are the same error codes returned by a device driver in its request header.

Source: IBM DOS 3.3 Technical Reference, pages 6-15 through 6-16, 6-19 through 6-23
IBM DOS 4.0 Technical Reference, pages A-3 through A-7
Microsoft MS-DOS 4.0 Programmer's Reference, pages 45 through 47
Microsoft MS-DOS 5.0 Programmer's Reference, pages 122 through 125

See Also: 5.001. DOS Interrupt Usage by Version

5.003. INT 25H, ABSOLUTE DISK READ

Prior to Issuing INT 25H

	High	Low
AX		Drive number*
BX	Offset of transfer address	
CX	Number of sectors to read	
DX	Beginning logical sector #	
SP		
BP		
SI		
DI		
IP		
flags		
CS		
DS	Segment of transfer address	
SS		
ES		

Upon Return from INT 25H

	High	Low
AX	Destroyed	Destroyed †
BX	Destroyed	Destroyed
CX	Destroyed	Destroyed
DX	Destroyed	Destroyed
SP	Destroyed	
BP	Destroyed	
SI	Destroyed	
DI	Destroyed	
IP	Destroyed	
flags	Destroyed; if successful, carry flag is clear †	
CS		
DS		
SS		
ES		

*0=A , 1=B, and so on
†On error, CF=1 and AX contains error data.

Version: Superseded by INT 21H Function 440D Minor Code 61H in DOS 5.0.

Source: IBM DOS 3.3 Technical Reference, pages 6-24 through 6-25
IBM DOS 4.0 Technical Reference, pages A-7 through A-9
Microsoft MS-DOS 4.0 Programmer's Reference, pages 48 through 50
Microsoft MS-DOS 5.0 Programmer's Reference, pages 126 through 127

See Also: 5.004. INT 26H, Absolute Disk Write
5.005. INT 25H and 26H Error Codes

5.004. INT 26H, ABSOLUTE DISK WRITE

Prior to Issuing INT 26H

	High	Low
AX		Drive number*
BX	Offset of transfer address	
CX	Number of sectors to write	
DX	Beginning logical sector #	
SP		
BP		
SI		
DI		
IP		
flags		
CS		
DS	Segment of transfer address	
SS		
ES		

Upon Return from INT 26H

	High	Low
AX	Destroyed	Destroyed †
BX	Destroyed	Destroyed
CX	Destroyed	Destroyed
DX	Destroyed	Destroyed
SP	Destroyed	
BP	Destroyed	
SI	Destroyed	
DI	Destroyed	
IP	Destroyed	
flags	Destroyed; if successful, carry flag is clear †	
CS		
DS		
SS		
ES		

*0=A , 1=B, and so on
†On error, CF=1 and AX contains error data.

Version: Superseded by INT 21H Function 440D Minor Code 41H in DOS 5.0.

Source: IBM DOS 3.3 Technical Reference, page 6-25
IBM DOS 4.0 Technical Reference, pages A-7 through A-9
Microsoft MS-DOS 4.0 Programmer's Reference, pages 51 through 53
Microsoft MS-DOS 5.0 Programmer's Reference, pages 128 through 129

See Also: 5.003. INT 25H, Absolute Disk Read
5.005. INT 25H and 26H Error Codes

5.005. INT 25H AND 26H, ERROR CODES

Prior to DOS 5.0 Error Codes

		DOS Version			
Error Code	*Error Name*	*1.x*	*2.x*	*3.x*	*4.x*
02 (2)	Error (other than those listed below)	✔	✔	✔	✔
03 (3)	Write attempt on write-protected device	✔	✔	✔	✔
04 (4)	Requested sector not found	✔	✔	✔	✔
08 (8)	Bad CRC on disk read	✔	✔	✔	✔
40 (64)	SEEK operation failed	✔	✔	✔	✔
80 (128)	Attachment failed to respond	✔	✔	✔	✔

DOS 5.x Error Codes

Error Code	*Error Name*	
	Device Driver Errors*	IBM Compatible ROM Bios Errors**
00	Write protection violation†	
01	Unknown unit†	Bad command
02	Drive not ready	Address mark not found
03		Write protection fault†
04	Data error (CRC error)	Sector not found
06	Seek error	
07	Unknown media	
08	Sector not found	
0A	Write fault†	
0B	Read fault§	
0C	General failure	
0F	Invalid media change	
10		Data error (CRC error)
20		Controller failure
40		Seek failure
80		No response from drive

*Device Driver Errors are contained in AH
**IBM ROM BIOS Errors are contained in AL
†INT 26H only
§INT 25H only

Legend: √=supported

Source: IBM DOS 3.3 Technical Reference, page 6-25
IBM DOS 4.0 Technical Reference, page A-9
Microsoft MS-DOS 5.0 Programmer's Reference, pages 126 through 129

See Also: 5.003. INT 25H, Absolute Disk Read
5.004. INT 26H, Absolute Disk Write

5.006. INT 2FH, MULTIPLEX FOR DOS 3.X AND 4.X

Prior to Issuing INT 2FH

	High	Low
AX	Process*	Function†
BX		
CX		
DX	Offset of pointer to ASCIIZ string§	
SP		
BP		
SI		
DI		
IP		
flags		
CS		
DS	Segment of pointer to ASCIIZ string§	
SS		
ES		

Upon Return from INT 2FH

	High	Low
AX	Print error codes´	State¥
BX		
CX		
DX	Error count£	
SP		
BP		
SI	Offset of pointer to queue£	
DI		
IP		
flags		
CS		
DS	Segment of pointer to queue£	
SS		
ES		

*Process is one of the following:
1 = resident portion of PRINT
2 = resident portion of ASSIGN
10H = resident portion of SHARE
B7H = resident portion of APPEND
C0H-FFH = reserved for user applications

†Function is one of the following:
0 = get installed state
1 = submit file
2 = cancel file
3 = cancel all files
4 = status
5 = end of status

§Functions 1 and 2 only
¥Function 0 only; one of the following:
0 = not installed, OK to install
1 = not installed, do not install
FFH = installed

£Function 4 only
´Function 5 only (see 5.045. INT 2FH Error Codes)

Version: Interrupt used in DOS 3.x and DOS 4.x. See tables 5.007 through 5.044 for individual INT 2FH functions in DOS 5.0 and later.

Source: IBM DOS 3.3 Technical Reference, pages 6-28 through 6-33
IBM DOS 4.0 Technical Reference, pages A-10 through A-17

See Also: 5.040. INT 2FH Error Codes
5.007 through 5.047 for Individual INT 2FH functions in DOS 5.0 and later

5.007. INT 2FH, AX = 0100H -- GET PRINT.EXE INSTALLED STATE

Register	Prior to Issuing INT 2FH: High	Prior to Issuing INT 2FH: Low	Upon Return from INT 2FH: High	Upon Return from INT 2FH: Low
AX	01	00		Status*
BX				
CX				
DX				
SP				
BP				
SI				
DI				
IP				
flags				
CS				
DS				
SS				
ES				

*00=not loaded, FFH=PRINT loaded

Version: Applies to all versions of DOS beginning with 5.0.

Source: Microsoft MS-DOS 5.0 Programmer's Reference, page 134

5.008. INT 2FH, AX=0101H -- ADD FILE TO QUEUE

Register	Prior to Issuing INT 2FH: High	Prior to Issuing INT 2FH: Low	Upon Return from INT 2FH: High	Upon Return from INT 2FH: Low
AX	01	01	Error number (if carry set)	
BX				
CX				
DX	Offset of pointer to QUEUEPACKET			
SP				
BP				
SI				
DI				
IP				
flags			Carry flag set on error	
CS				
DS	Segment of pointer to QUEUEPACKET			
SS				
ES				

Version: Applies to all versions of DOS beginning with 5.0.

Note: QUEUEPACKET consists of a byte of 00H followed by segment:offset of ASCIIZ pathname.

Source: Microsoft MS-DOS 5.0 Programmer's Reference, page 135

See Also: 5.009. INT 2FH, AX=0102H -- Remove File from Print Queue
5.040. INT 2FH, Error Codes

5.009. INT 2FH, AX=0102H -- REMOVE FILE FROM PRINT QUEUE

Prior to Issuing INT 2FH

	High	Low
AX	01	02
BX		
CX		
DX	Offset of pointer to filename	
SP		
BP		
SI		
DI		
IP		
flags		
CS		
DS	Segment of pointer to filename	
SS		
ES		

Upon Return from INT 2FH

	High	Low
AX	Error number (if carry set)	
BX		
CX		
DX		
SP		
BP		
SI		
DI		
IP		
flags	Carry flag set on error	
CS		
DS		
SS		
ES		

Version: Applies to all versions of DOS beginning with 5.0.

Source: Microsoft MS-DOS 5.0 Programmer's Reference, page 136

See Also: 5.008. INT 2FH, AX=0101H -- Add File to Queue
5.040. INT 2FH, Error Codes

5.010. INT 2FH, AX=0103H -- CANCEL ALL FILES IN PRINT QUEUE

Prior to Issuing INT 2FH

	High	Low
AX	01	03
BX		
CX		
DX		
SP		
BP		
SI		
DI		
IP		
flags		
CS		
DS		
SS		
ES		

Upon Return from INT 2FH

Interrupt returns no values.

Version: Applies to all versions of DOS beginning with 5.0.

Source: Microsoft MS-DOS 5.0 Programmer's Reference, page 137

See Also: 5.009. INT 2FH, AX=0102H -- Remove File from Print Queue

5.011. INT 2FH, AX=0104H -- HOLD PRINT JOBS AND GET STATUS

Prior to Issuing INT 2FH

	High	Low
AX	01	04
BX		
CX		
DX		

SP	
BP	
SI	
DI	
IP	
flags	
CS	
DS	
SS	
ES	

Upon Return from INT 2FH

	High	Low
AX		
BX		
CX		
DX	Error count	

SP	
BP	
SI	Offset of address of print queue
DI	
IP	
flags	
CS	
DS	Segment of address of print queue
SS	
ES	

Version: Applies to all versions of DOS beginning with 5.0.

Source: Microsoft MS-DOS 5.0 Programmer's Reference, page 138

See Also:
5.008. INT 2FH, AX=0101H -- Add File to Queue
5.009. INT 2FH, AX=0102H -- Remove File from Print Queue
5.012. INT 2FH, AX=0105H -- Release Print Jobs
5.040. INT 2FH, Error Codes

5.012. INT 2FH, AX=0105H -- RELEASE PRINT JOBS

Prior to Issuing INT 2FH

	High	Low
AX	01	05
BX		
CX		
DX		

SP	
BP	
SI	
DI	
IP	
flags	
CS	
DS	
SS	
ES	

Upon Return from INT 2FH

Interrupt returns no values.

Version: Applies to all versions of DOS beginning with 5.0.

Source: Microsoft MS-DOS 5.0 Programmer's Reference, page 139

See Also: 5.011. INT 2FH, AX=0104H -- Hold Print Jobs and Get Status

5.013. INT 2FH, AX=0106H -- GET PRINTER DEVICE

Prior to Issuing INT 2FH

Register	High	Low
AX	01	06
BX		
CX		
DX		
SP		
BP		
SI		
DI		
IP		
flags		
CS		
DS		
SS		
ES		

Upon Return from INT 2FH

Register	High	Low
AX	Status or error*	
BX		
CX		
DX		
SP		
BP		
SI	Offset of print device header	
DI		
IP		
flags	Carry flag set on error	
CS		
DS	Segment of print device header	
SS		
ES		

*0000H=Queue is empty, 0008H=Error-Queue is full

Version: Applies to all versions of DOS beginning with 5.0.

Source: Microsoft MS-DOS 5.0 Programmer's Reference, page 140

5.014. INT 2FH, AX=0600H -- GET ASSIGN.COM INSTALLED STATE

Prior to Issuing INT 2FH

Register	High	Low
AX	06	00
BX		
CX		
DX		
SP		
BP		
SI		
DI		
IP		
flags		
CS		
DS		
SS		
ES		

Upon Return from INT 2FH

Register	High	Low
AX		Status*
BX		
CX		
DX		
SP		
BP		
SI		
DI		
IP		
flags		
CS		
DS		
SS		
ES		

*00H=not loaded, FFH=ASSIGN loaded

Version: Applies to all versions of DOS beginning with 5.0.

Source: Microsoft MS-DOS 5.0 Programmer's Reference, page 141

5.015. INT 2FH, AX=1000H -- GET SHARE.EXE INSTALLED STATE

Register	Prior to Issuing INT 2FH: High	Prior to Issuing INT 2FH: Low	Upon Return from INT 2FH: High	Upon Return from INT 2FH: Low
AX	10	00		Status*
BX				
CX				
DX				
SP				
BP				
SI				
DI				
IP				
flags				
CS				
DS				
SS				
ES				

*00H=not loaded, FFH=SHARE loaded

Version: Applies to all versions of DOS beginning with 5.0.

Source: Microsoft MS-DOS 5.0 Programmer's Reference, page 142

5.016. INT 2FH, AX=1100H -- GET NETWORK INSTALLED STATE

Register	Prior to Issuing INT 2FH: High	Prior to Issuing INT 2FH: Low	Upon Return from INT 2FH: High	Upon Return from INT 2FH: Low
AX	11	00		Status*
BX				
CX				
DX				
SP				
BP				
SI				
DI				
IP				
flags				
CS				
DS				
SS				
ES				

*00H=not loaded, FFH=network loaded

Version: Applies to all versions of DOS beginning with 5.0.

Source: Microsoft MS-DOS 5.0 Programmer's Reference, page 143

5.017. INT 2FH, AX=1400H -- GET NLSFUNC.EXE INSTALLED STATE

Register	Prior to Issuing INT 2FH: High	Prior to Issuing INT 2FH: Low	Upon Return from INT 2FH: High	Upon Return from INT 2FH: Low
AX	14	00		Status*
BX				
CX				
DX				
SP				
BP				
SI				
DI				
IP				
flags				
CS				
DS				
SS				
ES				

*00H=not loaded, FFH=NLSFUNC loaded

Version: Applies to all versions of DOS beginning with 5.0.

Source: Microsoft MS-DOS 5.0 Programmer's Reference, page 144

5.018. INT 2FH, AX=1680H -- MS-DOS IDLE CALL

Register	Prior to Issuing INT 2FH: High	Prior to Issuing INT 2FH: Low	Upon Return from INT 2FH: High	Upon Return from INT 2FH: Low
AX	16	80		Status*
BX				
CX				
DX				
SP				
BP				
SI				
DI				
IP				
flags				
CS				
DS				
SS				
ES				

*00H=supports suspension of idle programs; nonzero=idle programs not supported

Version: Applies to all versions of DOS beginning with 5.0.

Source: Microsoft MS-DOS 5.0 Programmer's Reference, page 145

See Also: 3.068. INT 21H, AH=35H -- Get Interrupt Vector

5.019. INT 2FH, AX=1A00H -- GET ANSI.SYS INSTALLED STATE

Prior to Issuing INT 2FH

	High	Low
AX	1A	00
BX		
CX		
DX		
SP		
BP		
SI		
DI		
IP		
flags		
CS		
DS		
SS		
ES		

Upon Return from INT 2FH

	High	Low
AX		Status*
BX		
CX		
DX		
SP		
BP		
SI		
DI		
IP		
flags		
CS		
DS		
SS		
ES		

*00H=not installed; FFH=ANSI.SYS installed

Version: Applies to all versions of DOS beginning with 5.0.

Source: Microsoft MS-DOS 5.0 Programmer's Reference, page 146

5.020. INT 2FH, AX=4300H -- GET HIMEM.SYS INSTALLED STATE

Prior to Issuing INT 2FH

	High	Low
AX	43	00
BX		
CX		
DX		
SP		
BP		
SI		
DI		
IP		
flags		
CS		
DS		
SS		
ES		

Upon Return from INT 2FH

	High	Low
AX		Status*
BX		
CX		
DX		
SP		
BP		
SI		
DI		
IP		
flags		
CS		
DS		
SS		
ES		

*00H=not installed; 80H=HIMEM.SYS installed

Version: Applies to all versions of DOS beginning with 5.0.

Source: Microsoft MS-DOS 5.0 Programmer's Reference, page 147

5.021. INT 2FH, AX=4301H -- GET HIMEM.SYS ENTRY-POINT ADDRESS

Prior to Issuing INT 2FH

	High	Low
AX	43	01
BX		
CX		
DX		
SP		
BP		
SI		
DI		
IP		
flags		
CS		
DS		
SS		
ES		

Upon Return from INT 2FH

	High	Low
AX		
BX	Offset of entry-point address	
CX		
DX		
SP		
BP		
SI		
DI		
IP		
flags		
CS		
DS		
SS		
ES	Segment of entry-point address	

Version: Applies to all versions of DOS beginning with 5.0.

Source: Microsoft MS-DOS 5.0 Programmer's Reference, pages 148 through 149

5.022. INT 2FH, AX=4800H -- GET DOSKEY.COM INSTALLED STATE

Prior to Issuing INT 2FH

	High	Low
AX	48	00
BX		
CX		
DX		
SP		
BP		
SI		
DI		
IP		
flags		
CS		
DS		
SS		
ES		

Upon Return from INT 2FH

	High	Low
AX		Status*
BX		
CX		
DX		
SP		
BP		
SI		
DI		
IP		
flags		
CS		
DS		
SS		
ES		

*00H=not installed; nonzero value=DOSKEY loaded

Version: Applies to all versions of DOS beginning with 5.0.

Source: Microsoft MS-DOS 5.0 Programmer's Reference, page 150

5.023. INT 2FH, AX=4810H -- READ COMMAND LINE

Register	Prior to Issuing INT 2FH: High	Prior to Issuing INT 2FH: Low	Upon Return from INT 2FH: High	Upon Return from INT 2FH: Low
AX	48	10	Status*	
BX				
CX				
DX	Offset of buffer to receive input		Offset to filled in buffer (if AX=0)	
SP				
BP				
SI				
DI				
IP				
flags				
CS				
DS	Segment of buffer to receive input		Segment of filled in buffer (if AX=0)	
SS				
ES				

*00H=successful (buffer not filled in if user typed macro, however)

Version: Applies to all versions of DOS beginning with 5.0.

Source: Microsoft MS-DOS 5.0 Programmer's Reference, page 151

5.024. INT 2FH, AX=4B01H -- BUILD NOTIFICATION CHAIN

Register	Prior to Issuing INT 2FH: High	Prior to Issuing INT 2FH: Low	Upon Return from INT 2FH: High	Upon Return from INT 2FH: Low
AX	4B	01		
BX	00	00	Offset of SWCALLBACKINFO or 0	
CX	Segment of pointer to service function			
DX	Offset of pointer to service function			
SP				
BP				
SI				
DI				
IP				
flags				
CS				
DS				
SS				
ES	00		Segment of SWCALLBACKINFO or 0	

Warning: To make sure that programs in the current session work correctly during the session switch, a client program that adds itself to the notification chain must execute a patch routine each time the Task Switcher calls the client program's Query Suspend. See 5.222. Task Switcher API Patch.

Version: Applies to all versions of DOS beginning with 5.0.

Source: Microsoft MS-DOS 5.0 Programmer's Reference, pages 152 through 153

See Also: 5.044. SWCALLBACKINFO Data Structure
5.222. Task Switcher API Patch

5.025. INT 2FH, AX=4B02H -- DETECT SWITCHER

Prior to Issuing INT 2FH

	High	Low
AX	4B	02
BX	00	00
CX		
DX		
SP		
BP		
SI		
DI	00	
IP		
flags		
CS		
DS		
SS		
ES	00	

Upon Return from INT 2FH

	High	Low
AX	Result*	
BX		
CX		
DX		
SP		
BP		
SI		
DI	Offset of service function handler (if AX=00)	
IP		
flags		
CS		
DS		
SS		
ES	Segment of service function handler (if AX=00)	

*00H=task switcher is loaded and ES:DI contains address

Version: Applies to all versions of DOS beginning with 5.0.

Source: Microsoft MS-DOS 5.0 Programmer's Reference, pages 154 through 155

See Also: 5.041. Service Functions

5.026. INT 2FH, AX=4B03H -- ALLOCATE SWITCHER ID

Prior to Issuing INT 2FH

	High	Low
AX	4B	03
BX	00	00
CX		
DX		
SP		
BP		
SI		
DI	Service function handler address	
IP		
flags		
CS		
DS		
SS		
ES		

Upon Return from INT 2FH

	High	Low
AX	Result*	
BX	Switcher ID (If AX=00)	
CX		
DX		
SP		
BP		
SI		
DI		
IP		
flags		
CS		
DS		
SS		
ES		

*00H=task switcher is loaded and BX contains ID

Version: Applies to all versions of DOS beginning with 5.0.

Source: Microsoft MS-DOS 5.0 Programmer's Reference, page 156

See Also: 5.041. Service Functions

5.027. INT 2FH, AX=4B04H -- FREE SWITCHER ID

Prior to Issuing INT 2FH

Register	High	Low
AX	4B	04
BX	Switcher ID	
CX		
DX		
SP		
BP		
SI		
DI	Address of service function	
IP		
flags		
CS		
DS		
SS		
ES		

Upon Return from INT 2FH

Register	High	Low
AX	Result*	
BX	Result*	
CX		
DX		
SP		
BP		
SI		
DI		
IP		
flags		
CS		
DS		
SS		
ES		

*00H=successful

Version: Applies to all versions of DOS beginning with 5.0.

Source: Microsoft MS-DOS 5.0 Programmer's Reference, page 157

See Also: 5.026. INT 2FH, AX=4B03H -- Allocate Switcher ID

5.028. INT 2FH, AX=4B05H -- IDENTIFY INSTANCE DATA

Prior to Issuing INT 2FH

Register	High	Low
AX	4B	05
BX	00	
CX	Segment of service function address	
DX	Offset of service function address	
SP		
BP		
SI		
DI		
IP		
flags		
CS		
DS		
SS		
ES	00	

Upon Return from INT 2FH

Register	High	Low
AX		
BX	Offset of SWSTARTUPINFO or 0	
CX		
DX		
SP		
BP		
SI		
DI		
IP		
flags		
CS		
DS		
SS		
ES	Segment of SWSTARTUPINFO or 0	

Version: Applies to all versions of DOS beginning with 5.0.

Source: Microsoft MS-DOS 5.0 Programmer's Reference, pages 158 through 159

5.029. INT 2FH, AX=AD80H -- GET KEYB.COM VERSION NUMBER

Prior to Issuing INT 2FH

Register	High	Low
AX	AD	80
BX		
CX		
DX		
SP		
BP		
SI		
DI		
IP		
flags		
CS		
DS		
SS		
ES		

Upon Return from INT 2FH

Register	High	Low
AX		
BX	Version number*	
CX		
DX		
SP		
BP		
SI		
DI		
IP		
flags		
CS		
DS		
SS		
ES		

*BH=major number, BL=minor number; version number returned only if KEYB loaded

Version: Applies to all versions of DOS beginning with 5.0.

Source: Microsoft MS-DOS 5.0 Programmer's Reference, page 160

5.030. INT 2FH, AX=AD81H -- SET KEYB.COM ACTIVE CODE PAGE

Prior to Issuing INT 2FH

Register	High	Low
AX	AD	81
BX	Code page*	
CX		
DX		
SP		
BP		
SI		
DI		
IP		
flags		
CS		
DS		
SS		
ES		

Upon Return from INT 2FH

Register	High	Low
AX	Status†	
BX		
CX		
DX		
SP		
BP		
SI		
DI		
IP		
flags	Carry flag set on error	
CS		
DS		
SS		
ES		

*Code Page ID:

Value	*Meaning*
437	United States
850	Multilingual (Latin I)
852	Slavic (Latin II)
860	Portuguese
863	Canadian-French
865	Nordic

†0000H=no error, 0001H= code page invalid

Version: Applies to all versions of DOS beginning with 5.0.

Source: Microsoft MS-DOS 5.0 Programmer's Reference, page 161

5.031. INT 2FH, AX=AD82H -- SET KEYB.COM COUNTRY FLAG

Prior to Issuing INT 2FH

Register	High	Low
AX	AD	82
BX		Flag*
CX		
DX		
SP		
BP		
SI		
DI		
IP		
flags		
CS		
DS		
SS		
ES		

Upon Return from INT 2FH

Register	High	Low
AX		
BX		
CX		
DX		
SP		
BP		
SI		
DI		
IP		
flags	Carry flag set on error	
CS		
DS		
SS		
ES		

*00H=US keyboard, FFH=foreign keyboard

Version: Applies to all versions of DOS beginning with 5.0.

Source: Microsoft MS-DOS 5.0 Programmer's Reference, page 162

5.032. INT 2FH, AX=AD83H -- GET KEYB.COM COUNTRY FLAG

Prior to Issuing INT 2FH

Register	High	Low
AX	AD	83
BX		
CX		
DX		
SP		
BP		
SI		
DI		
IP		
flags		
CS		
DS		
SS		
ES		

Upon Return from INT 2FH

Register	High	Low
AX		
BX		Flag*
CX		
DX		
SP		
BP		
SI		
DI		
IP		
flags		
CS		
DS		
SS		
ES		

*00H=US keyboard, FFH=foreign keyboard

Version: Applies to all versions of DOS beginning with 5.0.

Source: Microsoft MS-DOS 5.0 Programmer's Reference, page 163

See Also: 5.031. INT 2FH, AX=AD82H -- Set KEYB.COM Country Flag

5.033. INT 2FH, AX=B000H -- GET GRAFTABL.COM INSTALLED STATE

Register	Prior to Issuing INT 2FH: High	Prior to Issuing INT 2FH: Low	Upon Return from INT 2FH: High	Upon Return from INT 2FH: Low
AX	B0	00		Status*
BX				
CX				
DX				
SP				
BP				
SI				
DI				
IP				
flags				
CS				
DS				
SS				
ES				

*00H=not installed; FFH=GRAFTABL loaded

Version: Applies to all versions of DOS beginning with 5.0.

Source: Microsoft MS-DOS 5.0 Programmer's Reference, page 164

5.034. INT 2FH, AX=B700H -- GET APPEND.EXE INSTALLED STATE

Register	Prior to Issuing INT 2FH: High	Prior to Issuing INT 2FH: Low	Upon Return from INT 2FH: High	Upon Return from INT 2FH: Low
AX	B7	00		Status*
BX				
CX				
DX				
SP				
BP				
SI				
DI				
IP				
flags				
CS				
DS				
SS				
ES				

*00H=not installed; FFH=APPEND loaded

Version: Applies to all versions of DOS beginning with 5.0.

Source: Microsoft MS-DOS 5.0 Programmer's Reference, page 165

5.035. INT 2FH, AX=B702H -- GET APPEND.EXE VERSION

Prior to Issuing INT 2FH

	High	Low
AX	B7	02
BX		
CX		
DX		
SP		
BP		
SI		
DI		
IP		
flags		
CS		
DS		
SS		
ES		

Upon Return from INT 2FH

	High	Low
AX	Status*	
BX		
CX		
DX		
SP		
BP		
SI		
DI		
IP		
flags		
CS		
DS		
SS		
ES		

*FFFFH if version is compatible with DOS 5.0

Version: Applies to all versions of DOS beginning with 5.0.

Source: Microsoft MS-DOS 5.0 Programmer's Reference, page 166

5.036. INT 2FH, AX=B704H -- GET APPEND.EXE DIRECTORY LIST ADDRESS

Prior to Issuing INT 2FH

	High	Low
AX	B7	04
BX		
CX		
DX		
SP		
BP		
SI		
DI		
IP		
flags		
CS		
DS		
SS		
ES		

Upon Return from INT 2FH

	High	Low
AX		
BX		
CX		
DX		
SP		
BP		
SI		
DI	Offset of address of appended dirs	
IP		
flags		
CS		
DS		
SS		
ES	Segment of address of appended dirs	

Version: Applies to all versions of DOS beginning with 5.0.

Source: Microsoft MS-DOS 5.0 Programmer's Reference, page 167

5.037. INT 2FH, AX=B706H -- GET APPEND.EXE MODES FLAG

Prior to Issuing INT 2FH

	High	Low
AX	B7	06
BX		
CX		
DX		
SP		
BP		
SI		
DI		
IP		
flags		
CS		
DS		
SS		
ES		

Upon Return from INT 2FH

	High	Low
AX		
BX	Modes*	
CX		
DX		
SP		
BP		
SI		
DI		
IP		
flags		
CS		
DS		
SS		
ES		

Version: Applies to all versions of DOS beginning with 5.0.

Note: Operation modes are as follows:

Bit 15	1=APPEND applies appended directories to functions
Bit 14	1=APPEND stores appended directories in environment variable
Bit 13	1=APPEND applies appended directories to file requests that specify a path
Bit 12	1=APPEND applies appended directories to file requests that specify a drive
Bit 0	1=APPEND is enabled

Source: Microsoft MS-DOS 5.0 Programmer's Reference, page 168

5.038. INT 2FH, AX=B707H -- SET APPEND.EXE MODES FLAG

Prior to Issuing INT 2FH

	High	Low
AX	B7	07
BX	Modes*	
CX		
DX		
SP		
BP		
SI		
DI		
IP		
flags		
CS		
DS		
SS		
ES		

Upon Return from INT 2FH

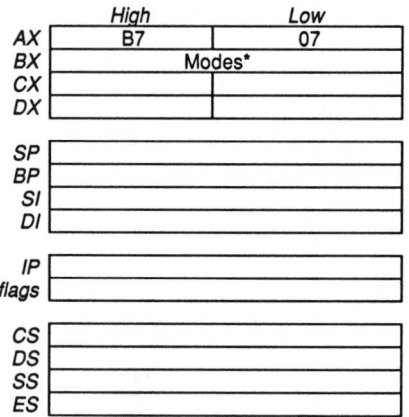

Interrupt returns no values.

Version: Applies to all versions of DOS beginning with 5.0.

Note: Operation modes are as follows:

Bit 15	1=APPEND applies appended directories to functions
Bit 14	1=APPEND stores appended directories in environment variable
Bit 13	1=APPEND applies appended directories to file requests that specify a path
Bit 12	1=APPEND applies appended directories to file requests that specify a drive
Bit 0	1=APPEND is enabled

Source: Microsoft MS-DOS 5.0 Programmer's Reference, page 169

5.039. INT 2FH, AX=B711H -- SET TRUE-NAME FLAG

Prior to Issuing INT 2FH

	High	Low
AX	B7	11
BX		
CX		
DX		
SP		
BP		
SI		
DI		
IP		
flags		
CS		
DS		
SS		
ES		

Upon Return from INT 2FH

Interrupt returns no values.

Version: Applies to all versions of DOS beginning with 5.0.

Source: Microsoft MS-DOS 5.0 Programmer's Reference, page 170

5.040. INT 2FH, ERROR CODES

		DOS Version				
Error Code	*Error Name*	*1.x*	*2.x*	*3.x*	*4.x*	*5.x*
1	Invalid function			✔	✔	✔
2	File not found			✔	✔	✔
3	Path not found			✔	✔	✔
4	Too many open files			✔	✔	✔
5	Access denied			✔	✔	✔
8	Queue full			✔	✔	✔
9	Busy			✔	✔	
12	Name too long/invalid access			✔	✔	✔
15	Invalid drive			✔	✔	✔

Legend: √=supported

Source: IBM DOS 3.3 Technical Reference, pages 6-29 through 6-30
IBM DOS 4.0 Technical Reference, pages A-11 through A-12
Microsoft MS-DOS 5.0 Programmer's Reference, page 135

See Also: 5.006. INT 2FH, Multiplex for DOS 3.x and 4.x
5.008. INT 2FH, AX=0101H -- Add File to Queue
5.009. INT 2FH, AX=0102H -- Remove File from Print Queue
5.011. INT 2FH, AX=0104H -- Hold Print Jobs and Get Status

5.041. SERVICE FUNCTIONS

*Function**	*Name*	*Registers Before Call*	*Registers After Call*
0000	Get Version	None	Carry flag set error AX=0 if no error ES:BX=address of SWVERSION if no error
0001	Test Memory Region	CX=size of buffer in bytes DI=pointer to buffer	Carry flag set on error AX=0 if all of buffer is in global memory AX=1 if buffer is in global and local memory AX=2 if buffer is in local memory
0002	Suspend Switcher	DI=new service function address	Carry flag set on error AX=0 if current switcher suspended ops AX=1 if current switcher didn't suspend ops, new switcher can't start AX=2 if new switcher can start
0003	Resume Switcher	DI=new service function address	Carry flag set on error AX=0 if no error
0004†	Hook Notification Chain	ES:DI=pointer to SWCALLBACKINFO	Carry flag set on error AX=0 if no error
0005	Unhook Notification Chain	ES:DI=pointer to SWCALLBACKINFO	Carry flag set on error AX=0 if no error
0006	Query API Support	BX=API ID	Carry flag set on error AX=00H if no error ES:BX=address of SWAPIINFO if no error

*These functions are used for API task switching.

†WARNING: To make sure that programs work correctly during the session switch, a client program that adds itself to the notification chain must execute a patch routine each time the Task Switcher calls Query Suspend. See 5.222. Task Switcher API Patch.

Version: Applies to all versions of DOS beginning with 5.0.

Note: Function number should be in AX register before call to service function handler.

Source: Microsoft MS-DOS 5.0 Programmer's Reference, pages 182 through 192

See Also: 5.043. SWAPIINFO Data Structure
5.044. SWCALLBACKINFO Data Structure
5.222. Task Switcher API Patch

5.042. NOTIFICATION FUNCTIONS

*Function**	*Name*	*Registers Before Call*	*Registers After Call*
0000	Init Switcher	DI=service function address	AX=non-zero if switcher shouldn't load AX=00H if switcher can load
0001†	Query Suspend	BX=current session ID ES:DI=new service function address	AX=00H if session can be performed safely AX=01H if session cannot be performed safely
0002	Suspend Session	BX=current session ID ES:DI=new service function address	AX=00H if session can be performed safely AX=01H if session cannot be performed safely
0003	Activate Session	BX=session ID CX=session status flags ES:DI=service function handler address	AX=00H
0004	Session Active	BX=session ID CX=session status flags ES:DI=service function handler address	AX=00H
0005	Create Session	BX=session ID ES:DI=service function handler address	AX=00H if session can be created safely AX=01H if client cannot handle new session
0006	Destroy Session	BX=session ID ES:DI=service function handler address	AX=00H
0007	Switcher Exit	BX=flags ES:DI=service function handler address	AX=00H

*These functions are used for API task switching.

†WARNING: To make sure that programs work correctly during the session switch, client programs must execute a patch routine each time the Task Switcher calls Query Suspend. See 5.222. Task Switcher API Patch.

Version: Applies to all versions of DOS beginning with 5.0.

Note: Function number should be in AX register before call to service function handler.

Source: Microsoft MS-DOS 5.0 Programmer's Reference, pages 171 through 181

See Also: 5.222. Task Switcher API Patch

5.043. SWAPIINFO DATA STRUCTURE

Offset	*Length*	*Name*	*Comments*
0 (0)	word	aisLength	size in bytes of structure (10)
2 (2)	word	aisAPI	ID of asynchronous API
4 (4)	word	aisMajor	major version number
6 (6)	word	aisMinor	minor version number
8 (8)	word	aisSupport	support level

Version: Applies to all versions of DOS beginning with 5.0.

Note: This data structure is used for API task switching.

Source: Microsoft MS-DOS 5.0 Programmer's Reference, pages 194 through 195

5.044. SWCALLBACKINFO DATA STRUCTURE

Offset	*Length*	*Name*	*Comments*
0 (0)	dbl word	scbiNext	32-bit address of next structure in notification chain
4 (4)	dbl word	scbiEntryPoint	32-bit address of notification function handler for client program
8 (8)	dbl word	scbiReserved	RESERVED
C (12)	dbl word	scbiAPI	32-bit address to a zero-terminated list of SWAPIINFO

Version: Applies to all versions of DOS beginning with 5.0.

Note: This data structure is used for API task switching.

Source: Microsoft MS-DOS 5.0 Programmer's Reference, page 195

5.045. SWINSTANCEITEM DATA STRUCTURE

Offset	*Length*	*Name*	*Comments*
0 (0)	dbl word	iisPtr	pointer to instance data
4 (4)	word	iisSize	size of instance data in bytes

Version: Applies to all versions of DOS beginning with 5.0.

Note: This data structure is used for API task switching.

Source: Microsoft MS-DOS 5.0 Programmer's Reference, page 196

5.046. SWSTARTUPINFO DATA STRUCTURE

Offset	*Length*	*Name*	*Comments*
0 (0)	word	sisVersion	not used
2 (2)	dbl word	sisNextDev	address of next structure in chain
6 (6)	dbl word	sisVirtDevFile	not used
A (10)	dbl word	sisRefrenceData	not used
E (14)	dbl word	sisInstanceData	address to a list of SWINSTANCEITEM structures

Version: Applies to all versions of DOS beginning with 5.0.

Note: This data structure is used for API task switching.

Source: Microsoft MS-DOS 5.0 Programmer's Reference, page 197

5.047. SWVERSION DATA STRUCTURE

Offset	*Length*	*Name*	*Comments*
0 (0)	word	svsAPIMajor	protocol supported major version
2 (2)	word	svsAPIMinor	protocol supported minor version
4 (4)	word	svsProductMajor	task switcher's major version
6 (6)	word	svsProductMinor	task switcher's minor version
8 (8)	word	svsSwitcherID	task switcher ID
A (10)	word	svsFlags	operation flags
C (12)	dbl word	svsName	pointer to ASCIIZ task switcher name
10 (16)	dbl word	svsPrevSwitcher	previous task switcher's entry address

Version: Applies to all versions of DOS beginning with 5.0.

Note: This data structure is used for API task switching.

Source: Microsoft MS-DOS 5.0 Programmer's Reference, page 197

5.048. INT 2FH, CD-ROM EXTENSION FUNCTIONS SUMMARY

Interrupt	*Function**	*Description*	*Comments*
2FH	00H (0)	Get number of CD-ROM drives	
	01H (1)	Get CD-ROM drive list	
	02H (2)	Get copyright filename	
	03H (3)	Get abstract filename	
	04H (4)	Get bibliographic filename	
	05H (5)	Read volume table of contents	
	06H (6)	RESERVED	Microsoft internal debugging only
	07H (7)	RESERVED	Microsoft internal debugging only
	08H (8)	Absolute disk read	
	09H (9)	Absolute disk write	
	0AH (10)	RESERVED	
	0BH (11)	CD-ROM drive check	
	0CH (12)	Get CD-ROM Extensions version	
	0DH (13)	Get CD-ROM units	
	0EH (14)	Get or set volume descriptor preference	
	0FH (15)	Get directory entry	
	10H (16)	Send device request	

*Value entered in AX register.

Note: Functions 11H-FFH are reserved by Microsoft.

Source: MS-DOS Extensions (Microsoft Press), pages 87 through 88.
Microsoft MS-DOS CD-ROM Extensions 2.20, MSCDEX Function Requests, page 1

See Also: 5.049 through 5.065 for individual functions and data structures

5.049. INT 2FH, AL=00H -- GET NUMBER OF CD-ROM DRIVES

Prior to Issuing INT 2FH

Register	High	Low
AX	15H	00H
BX	00H	00H
CX		
DX		
SP		
BP		
SI		
DI		
IP		
flags		
CS		
DS		
SS		
ES		

Upon Return from INT 2FH

Register	High	Low
AX		
BX	Number of CD-ROM units*	
CX	First CD- ROM unit†	
DX		
SP		
BP		
SI		
DI		
IP		
flags		
CS		
DS		
SS		
ES		

*If 0000H, then driver not installed.
†0=A, 1=B, and so on

Version: Requires hardware device driver in CONFIG.SYS and MSCDEX.EXE in AUTOEXEC.BAT.

Source: MS-DOS Extensions (Microsoft Press), page 88
Microsoft MS-DOS CD-ROM Extensions 2.20, MSCDEX Function Requests, page 2

See Also: 5.048. INT 2FH, CD-ROM Extension Functions Summary
5.050. INT 2FH, AL=01H -- Get CD-ROM Drive List

5.050. INT 2FH, AL=01H -- GET CD-ROM DRIVE LIST

Prior to Issuing INT 2FH

Register	High	Low
AX	15H	01H
BX	Offset of pointer to buffer	
CX		
DX		
SP		
BP		
SI		
DI		
IP		
flags		
CS		
DS		
SS		
ES	Segment of pointer to buffer	

Upon Return from INT 2FH

Interrupt returns no values. Data placed in buffer*.

*Buffer contains the following information:
byte = driver unit code
word = offset of device driver header
word = segment of device driver header

Version: Requires hardware device driver in CONFIG.SYS and MSCDEX.EXE in AUTOEXEC.BAT.

Source: MS-DOS Extensions (Microsoft Press), page 89
Microsoft MS-DOS CD-ROM Extensions 2.20, MSCDEX Function Requests, page 2

See Also: 5.048. INT 2FH, CD-ROM Extension Functions Summary
5.049. INT 2FH, AL=00H -- Get Number of CD-ROM Drives

5.051. INT 2FH, AL=02H -- GET COPYRIGHT FILENAME

Prior to Issuing INT 2FH

Register	High	Low
AX	15H	02H
BX	Offset of pointer to 38-byte buffer	
CX	Drive*	
DX		
SP		
BP		
SI		
DI		
IP		
flags		
CS		
DS		
SS		
ES	Segment of pointer to 38-byte buffer	

Upon Return from INT 2FH

Register	High	Low
AX	Error code†	
BX	Offset of pointer to filled in buffer	
CX		
DX		
SP		
BP		
SI		
DI		
IP		
flags	Carry flag set on error	
CS		
DS		
SS		
ES	Segment of pointer to filled in buffer	

*0=A, 1=B, and so on
†Only if carry flag is set

Version: Requires hardware device driver in CONFIG.SYS and MSCDEX.EXE in AUTOEXEC.BAT.

Note: 38-byte buffer contains 31-character filename, a semicolon, a 5-digit version number, terminated by a NULL.

Source: MS-DOS Extensions (Microsoft Press), pages 89 through 90
Microsoft MS-DOS CD-ROM Extensions 2.20, MSCDEX Function Requests, page 3

See Also: 5.048. INT 2FH, CD-ROM Extension Functions Summary
5.063. INT 2FH, CD-ROM Drive Error Codes

5.052. INT 2FH, AL=03H -- GET ABSTRACT FILENAME

Prior to Issuing INT 2FH

Register	High	Low
AX	15H	03H
BX	Offset of pointer to 38-byte buffer	
CX	Drive*	
DX		
SP		
BP		
SI		
DI		
IP		
flags		
CS		
DS		
SS		
ES	Segment of pointer to 38-byte buffer	

Upon Return from INT 2FH

Register	High	Low
AX	Error code†	
BX	Offset of pointer to filled in buffer	
CX		
DX		
SP		
BP		
SI		
DI		
IP		
flags	Carry flag set on error	
CS		
DS		
SS		
ES	Segment of pointer to filled in buffer	

*0=A, 1=B, and so on
†Only if carry flag is set

Version: Requires hardware device driver in CONFIG.SYS and MSCDEX.EXE in AUTOEXEC.BAT.

Note: 38-byte buffer contains 31-character filename, a semicolon, a 5-digit version number, terminated by a NULL.

Source: MS-DOS Extensions (Microsoft Press), pages 90 through 91
Microsoft MS-DOS CD-ROM Extensions 2.20, MSCDEX Function Requests, page 3

See Also: 5.048. INT 2FH, CD-ROM Extension Functions Summary
5.063. INT 2FH, CD-ROM Drive Error Codes

5.053. INT 2FH, AL=04H -- GET BIBLIOGRAPHIC FILENAME

	Prior to Issuing INT 2FH (High)	Prior to Issuing INT 2FH (Low)	Upon Return from INT 2FH (High)	Upon Return from INT 2FH (Low)
AX	15H	04H	Error code†	
BX	Offset of pointer to 38-byte buffer		Offset of pointer to filled buffer	
CX	Drive*			
DX				
SP				
BP				
SI				
DI				
IP				
flags			Carry flag set on error	
CS				
DS				
SS				
ES	Segment of pointer to 38-byte buffer		Segment of pointer to filled in buffer	

*0=A, 1=B, and so on
†Only if carry flag is set

Version: Requires hardware device driver in CONFIG.SYS and MSCDEX.EXE in AUTOEXEC.BAT.

Note: 38-byte buffer contains 31-character filename, a semicolon, a 5-digit version number, terminated by a NULL.

Source: MS-DOS Extensions (Microsoft Press), page 91
Microsoft MS-DOS CD-ROM Extensions 2.20, MSCDEX Function Requests, page 3

See Also: 5.048. INT 2FH, CD-ROM Extension Functions Summary
5.063. INT 2FH, CD-ROM Drive Error Codes

5.054. INT 2FH, AL=05H -- READ VOLUME TABLE OF CONTENTS

	Prior to Issuing INT 2FH (High)	Prior to Issuing INT 2FH (Low)	Upon Return from INT 2FH (High)	Upon Return from INT 2FH (Low)
AX	15H	05H	Descriptor index†§	
BX	Offset of pointer to 2048-byte buffer		Offset of pointer to filled in buffer	
CX	Drive*			
DX	Descriptor index§			
SP				
BP				
SI				
DI				
IP				
flags			Carry flag set on error	
CS				
DS				
SS				
ES	Segment of pointer to 2048-byte buffer		Segment of pointer to filled in buffer	

*0=A, 1=B, and so on
†AL=error code if carry flag set
§00H=not standard or terminator; 01H=standard descriptor; FFH=descriptor terminator

Version: Requires hardware device driver in CONFIG.SYS and MSCDEX.EXE in AUTOEXEC.BAT.

Source: MS-DOS Extensions (Microsoft Press), page 92
Microsoft MS-DOS CD-ROM Extensions 2.20, MSCDEX Function Requests, page 4

See Also: 5.048. INT 2FH, CD-ROM Extension Functions Summary
5.063. INT 2FH, CD-ROM Drive Error Codes

5.055. INT 2FH, AL=08H -- ABSOLUTE DISK READ

Prior to Issuing INT 2FH

Register	High	Low
AX	15H	08H
BX	Offset of pointer to buffer	
CX	Drive*	
DX	Number of sectors	
SP		
BP		
SI	HO word of starting sector number	
DI	LO word of starting sector number	
IP		
flags		
CS		
DS		
SS		
ES	Segment of pointer to buffer	

Upon Return from INT 2FH

Register	High	Low
AX		Error code†
BX	Offset of pointer to filled in buffer	
CX		
DX		
SP		
BP		
SI		
DI		
IP		
flags	Carry flag set on error	
CS		
DS		
SS		
ES	Segment of pointer to filled in buffer	

*0=A, 1=B, and so on
†AL=error code if carry flag set

Version: Requires hardware device driver in CONFIG.SYS and MSCDEX.EXE in AUTOEXEC.BAT.

Source: MS-DOS Extensions (Microsoft Press), page 93
Microsoft MS-DOS CD-ROM Extensions 2.20, MSCDEX Function Requests, page 5

See Also: 5.048. INT 2FH, CD-ROM Extension Functions Summary
5.056. INT 2FH, AL=09H -- Absolute Disk Write
5.063. INT 2FH, CD-ROM Drive Error Codes

5.056. INT 2FH, AL=09H -- ABSOLUTE DISK WRITE

Prior to Issuing INT 2FH

Register	High	Low
AX	15H	09H
BX	Offset of pointer to buffer	
CX	Drive*	
DX	Number of sectors	
SP		
BP		
SI	HO word of starting sector number	
DI	LO word of starting sector number	
IP		
flags		
CS		
DS		
SS		
ES	Segment of pointer to buffer	

Upon Return from INT 2FH

Register	High	Low
AX	Error code†	
BX		
CX		
DX		
SP		
BP		
SI		
DI		
IP		
flags	Carry flag set on error	
CS		
DS		
SS		
ES		

*0=A, 1=B, and so on
†AL=error code if carry flag set

Version: Requires hardware device driver in CONFIG.SYS and MSCDEX.EXE in AUTOEXEC.BAT.

Source: MS-DOS Extensions (Microsoft Press), pages 93 through 94
Microsoft MS-DOS CD-ROM Extensions 2.20, MSCDEX Function Requests, page 5

See Also: 5.048. INT 2FH, CD-ROM Extension Functions Summary
5.055. INT 2FH, AL=08H -- Absolute Disk Read
5.063. INT 2FH, CD-ROM Drive Error Codes

5.057. INT 2FH, AL=0BH -- CD-ROM DRIVE CHECK

Prior to Issuing INT 2FH

	High	Low
AX	15H	0BH
BX	00H	00H
CX	Drive*	
DX		
SP		
BP		
SI		
DI		
IP		
flags		
CS		
DS		
SS		
ES		

Upon Return from INT 2FH

	High	Low
AX	CD Drive code†	
BX	MSCDEX code§	
CX		
DX		
SP		
BP		
SI		
DI		
IP		
flags		
CS		
DS		
SS		
ES		

*0=A, 1=B, and so on
†0H=not CD-ROM drive; non-zero=CD-ROM drive
§ADADH=MSCDEX installed

Version: Requires hardware device driver in CONFIG.SYS and MSCDEX.EXE in AUTOEXEC.BAT. Added to driver beginning with version 2.0

Source: MS-DOS Extensions (Microsoft Press), pages 94 through 95
Microsoft MS-DOS CD-ROM Extensions 2.20, MSCDEX Function Requests, page 5

See Also: 5.048. INT 2FH, CD-ROM Extension Functions Summary

5.058. INT 2FH, AL=0CH -- GET CD-ROM EXTENSIONS VERSION

Prior to Issuing INT 2FH

	High	Low
AX	15H	0CH
BX	00H	00H
CX		
DX		
SP		
BP		
SI		
DI		
IP		
flags		
CS		
DS		
SS		
ES		

Upon Return from INT 2FH

	High	Low
AX		
BX	Version code*	
CX		
DX		
SP		
BP		
SI		
DI		
IP		
flags		
CS		
DS		
SS		
ES		

*0000H=version 1.0x; otherwise major version in BH, minor version # in BL

Version: Requires hardware device driver in CONFIG.SYS and MSCDEX.EXE in AUTOEXEC.BAT. Added to driver beginning with version 2.0.

Source: MS-DOS Extensions (Microsoft Press), page 95
Microsoft MS-DOS CD-ROM Extensions 2.20, MSCDEX Function Requests, page 6

See Also: 5.048. INT 2FH, CD-ROM Extension Functions Summary

5.059. INT 2FH, AL=0DH -- GET CD-ROM UNITS

Prior to Issuing INT 2FH

	High	Low
AX	15H	0DH
BX	Offset of pointer to buffer	
CX		
DX		
SP		
BP		
SI		
DI		
IP		
flags		
CS		
DS		
SS		
ES	Segment of pointer to buffer	

Upon Return from INT 2FH

Interrupt returns no values.
Buffer contains series of 1-byte entries on return, each representing the logical unit code for a CD-ROM drive (0=A, 1=B, and so on).

Version: Requires hardware device driver in CONFIG.SYS and MSCDEX.EXE in AUTOEXEC.BAT
Added to driver beginning with version 2.0.

Source: MS-DOS Extensions (Microsoft Press), pages 95 through 96
Microsoft MS-DOS CD-ROM Extensions 2.20, MSCDEX Function Requests, page 6

See Also: 5.048. INT 2FH, CD-ROM Extension Functions Summary

5.060. INT 2FH, AL=0EH -- GET OR SET VOLUME DESCRIPTOR PREFERENCE

Prior to Issuing INT 2FH

	High	Low
AX	15H	0EH
BX	00H	Function†
CX	Drive*	
DX	Volume preference¥	Sup. volume pref¥
SP		
BP		
SI		
DI		
IP		
flags		
CS		
DS		
SS		
ES		

Upon Return from INT 2FH

	High	Low
AX	Error code§	
BX		
CX		
DX	Preference settings¥	
SP		
BP		
SI		
DI		
IP		
flags	Carry flag set on error	
CS		
DS		
SS		
ES		

*0=A, 1=B, and so on
†00H=get preferences; 01H=set preferences
§Only if carry flag set
¥Only if get or set preferences function

Version: Requires hardware device driver in CONFIG.SYS and MSCDEX.EXE in AUTOEXEC.BAT.
Added to driver beginning with version 2.0.

Source: MS-DOS Extensions (Microsoft Press), pages 96 through 97
Microsoft MS-DOS CD-ROM Extensions 2.20, MSCDEX Function Requests, page 7

See Also: 5.048. INT 2FH, CD-ROM Extension Functions Summary
5.063. INT 2FH, CD-ROM Drive Error Codes

5.061. INT 2FH, AL=0FH -- GET DIRECTORY ENTRY

Prior to Issuing INT 2FH

	High	Low
AX	15H	0FH
BX	Offset of pointer to ASCIIZ pathname	
CX	Drive*	
DX		
SP		
BP		
SI	Segment of pointer to 255-byte dir buffer	
DI	Offset of pointer to 255-byte dir buffer	
IP		
flags		
CS		
DS		
SS		
ES	Segment of pointer to ASCIIZ pathname	

Upon Return from INT 2FH

	High	Low
AX	Error code†	
BX		
CX		
DX		
SP		
BP		
SI	Segment of pointer to filled in dir buffer	
DI	Offset of pointer to filled in dir buffer	
IP		
flags	Carry flag set on error	
CS		
DS		
SS		
ES		

*0=A, 1=B, and so on
†Error code if carry flag set; otherwise 00H=High Sierra format, 01H=ISO-9660 format

Version: Requires hardware device driver in CONFIG.SYS and MSCDEX.EXE in AUTOEXEC.BAT. Added to driver beginning with version 2.0.

Source: MS-DOS Extensions (Microsoft Press), pages 97 through 98
Microsoft MS-DOS CD-ROM Extensions 2.20, MSCDEX Function Requests, pages 8 through 10

See Also: 5.048. INT 2FH, CD-ROM Extension Functions Summary
5.063. INT 2FH, CD-ROM Drive Error Codes

5.062. INT 2FH, AL=10H -- SEND DEVICE REQUEST

Prior to Issuing INT 2FH

	High	Low
AX	15H	10H
BX	Offset of pointer to device request header	
CX	Drive*	
DX		
SP		
BP		
SI		
DI		
IP		
flags		
CS		
DS		
SS		
ES	Segment of pointer to device request header	

Upon Return from INT 2FH

Interrrupt returns no values.

*0=A, 1=B, and so on

Version: Requires hardware device driver in CONFIG.SYS and MSCDEX.EXE in AUTOEXEC.BAT. Added to driver beginning with version 2.1.

Source: MS-DOS Extensions (Microsoft Press), pages 99 through 100
Microsoft MS-DOS CD-ROM Extensions 2.20, MSCDEX Function Requests, page 11

See Also: 3.228. REQUESTHEADER Structure
5.048. INT 2FH, CD-ROM Extension Functions Summary

5.063. INT 2FH, CD-ROM DRIVE ERROR CODES

Code	*Description*
00H	Write-protect violation
01H	Unknown unit
02H	Drive not ready
03H	Unknown command
04H	CRC error
05H	Bad request header length
06H	Seek error
07H	Unknown media
08H	Sector not found
09H	Printer out of paper
0AH	Write fault
0BH	Read fault
0CH	General failure
0DH	RESERVED
0EH	RESERVED
0FH	Invalid disk change

Note: Error code is a word; bit 15 is set, and code is in LO byte (bits 0 through 7).

Source: MS-DOS Extensions (Microsoft Press), page 100
Microsoft MS-DOS CD-ROM Extensions 2.20, Device Driver Specification, page 6

5.064. HIGH SIERRA CD-ROM DIRECTORY FORMAT

Offset	*Length*	*Description*	*Comments*
0 (0)	byte	length of directory entry	in bytes
1 (1)	byte	length of XAR in LBN	
2 (2)	dbl word	LBN of data	in Intel byte order
6 (6)	dbl word	LBN of data	in Motorola byte order
A (10)	dbl word	length of file	in Intel byte order
E (15)	dbl word	length of data	in Motorola byte order
12 (18)	6 bytes	date and time	
18 (24)	byte	file flags	
19 (25)	byte	RESERVED	
1A (26)	byte	interleave size	
1B (27)	byte	interleave skip factor	
1C (29)	word	volume set sequence number	in Intel byte order
1E (31)	word	volume set sequence number	in Motorola byte order
20 (32)	byte	length of name (n bytes)	
21 (33)	n	filename	n=1-32
21+n (33+n)	0 or 1	optional padding if n is odd	
varies	varies	system-dependent data	

Note: High Sierra and ISO 9660 formats differ slightly:
- Two fields changed position.
- All date and time fields have an extra byte in ISO 9660 to describe the 15-minute offset from GMT.

Source: MS-DOS Extensions (Microsoft Press), page 98
"The Ins and Outs of ISO 9660 and High Sierra," Develop, July 1990

See Also: 5.065. ISO-9660 CD-ROM Directory Format

5.065. ISO-9660 CD-ROM DIRECTORY FORMAT

Offset	*Length*	*Description*	*Comments*
0 (0)	byte	length of directory entry	in bytes
1 (1)	byte	length of XAR in LBN	
2 (2)	dbl word	LBN of data	
6 (6)	dbl word	LBN of data	
A (10)	dbl word	length of file	
E (15)	dbl word	length of data	
12 (18)	7 bytes	date and time	
19 (25)	byte	file flags	
1A (26)	byte	interleave size	
1B (27)	byte	interleave skip factor	
1C (29)	word	volume set sequence number	
1E (31)	word	volume set sequence number	
20 (32)	byte	length of name (n bytes)	
21 (33)	n	filename	n=1-32
21+n (33+n)	0 or 1	optional padding if n is odd	
varies	varies	system-dependent data	

Note: High Sierra and ISO 9660 formats differ slightly:
- Two fields changed position.
- All date and time fields have an extra byte in ISO 9660 to describe the 15-minute offset from GMT.

Source: MS-DOS Extensions (Microsoft Press), page 98
Information Processing -- Volume and File Structure of CD-ROM for Information Interchange (ISO-9660), pages 19 through 21
"The Ins and Outs of ISO 9660 and High Sierra," Develop, July 1990

See Also: 5.064. High Sierra CD-ROM Directory Format

5.066. INT 33H, MOUSE FUNCTIONS SUMMARY

Interrupt	Function*	Description	Comments
33H	00H (00)	Mouse Reset and Status	Also returns number of buttons on mouse
	01H (01)	Show Cursor	
	02H (02)	Hide Cursor	
	03H (03)	Get Button Status and Mouse Position	
	04H (04)	Set Mouse Cursor Position	
	05H (05)	Get Button Press Information	
	06H (06)	Get Button Release Information	
	07H (07)	Set Min/Max Horizontal Cursor Position	Restricts mouse movement to window
	08H (08)	Set Min/Max Vertical Cursor Position	Restricts mouse movement to window
	09H (09)	Set Graphics Cursor Block	
	0AH (10)	Set Text Cursor	
	0BH (11)	Read Mouse Motion Counters	
	0CH (12)	Set Interrupt Subroutine Call Mask & Address	
	0DH (13)	Set Light Pen Emulation On	
	0EH (14)	Set Light Pen Emulation Off	
	0FH (15)	Set Mickey to Pixel Ratio	
	10H (16)	Conditional Off	
	13H (19)	Set Double Speed Threshold	
	14H (20)	Swap Interrupt Subroutines	
	15H (21)	Get Mouse Driver State Storage Requirements	
	16H (22)	Save Mouse Driver State	
	17H (23)	Restore Mouse Driver State	
	18H (24)	Set Alternate Subroutine Call Mask & Address	
	19H (25)	Get User Alternate Interrupt Address	
	1AH (26)	Set Mouse Sensitivity	
	1BH (27)	Get Mouse Sensitivity	
	1CH (28)	Set Mouse Interrupt Rate	
	1DH (29)	Set CRT Page Number	
	1EH (30)	Get CRT Page Number	
	1FH (31)	Disable Mouse Driver	
	20H (32)	Enable Mouse Driver	
	21H (33)	Software Reset	
	22H (34)	Set Language for Messages	
	23H (35)	Get Language Number	
	24H (36)	Get Driver Version, Mouse Type, IRQ Number	
	25H(37)	Get General Driver Information	
	26H(38)	Get Maximum Virtual Coordinates	Also returns mouse disabled flag
	27H(39)	Get Screen/Cursor Masks & Mickey Counts	
	28H(40)	Set Video Mode	Also sets font size
	29H(41)	Enumerate Video Modes	
	30H(42)	Get Cursor Hotspot	Also returns type of mouse
	31H(43)	Load Acceleration Curves	
	32H(44)	Read Acceleration Curves	
	33H(45)	Set/Get Active Acceleration Curve	
	35H(47)	Mouse Hardware Reset	Does not reset software values
	36H(48)	Set/Get Ballpoint Information	
	37H(49)	Get Minimum/Maximum Virtual Coordinates	
	38H(50)	Get Active Advanced Functions	
	39H(51)	Get Switch Settings	
	40H(52)	Get MOUSE.INI Location	Returns pointer to ASCIIZ string

*Value entered in AX register

Source: Microsoft Mouse User's Guide, page 175
Microsoft Mouse Programmer's Reference 2nd Ed. (Microsoft Press), pages 122 through 123

See Also: 5.067 through 5.119 for individual functions and data structures

5.067. INT 33H, AX=00H -- MOUSE RESET AND STATUS

Prior to Issuing INT 33H

Register	High	Low
AX	00H	
BX		
CX		
DX		
SP		
BP		
SI		
DI		
IP		
flags		
CS		
DS		
SS		
ES		

Upon Return from INT 33H

Register	High	Low
AX	Status*	
BX	Buttons†	
CX		
DX		
SP		
BP		
SI		
DI		
IP		
flags		
CS		
DS		
SS		
ES		

*0=mouse not installed; -1=mouse installed and reset
†Number of buttons; always 2 for Microsoft Mouse

Source: Microsoft Mouse User's Guide, pages 176 through 177
Microsoft Mouse Programmer's Reference (Microsoft Press), pages 116 through 121
Microsoft Mouse Programmer's Reference 2nd Ed. (Microsoft Press), pages 124 through 125

See Also: 5.118. INT 33H, Mouse Driver Default Parameters

5.068. INT 33H, AX=01H -- SHOW CURSOR

Prior to Issuing INT 33H

Register	High	Low
AX	01H	
BX		
CX		
DX		
SP		
BP		
SI		
DI		
IP		
flags		
CS		
DS		
SS		
ES		

Upon Return from INT 33H

Interrupt returns no values.

Note: Cursor flag is incremented by this function; cursor is displayed if the cursor flag has a value of 0 (default is -1).

Source: Microsoft Mouse User's Guide, page 178
Microsoft Mouse Programmer's Reference (Microsoft Press), pages 122 through 123
Microsoft Mouse Programmer's Reference 2nd Ed. (Microsoft Press), pages 125 through 126

See Also: 5.118. INT 33H, Mouse Driver Default Parameters

5.069. INT 33H, AX=02H -- HIDE CURSOR

Prior to Issuing INT 33H

Register	High	Low
AX	02H	
BX		
CX		
DX		
SP		
BP		
SI		
DI		
IP		
flags		
CS		
DS		
SS		
ES		

Upon Return from INT 33H

Interrupt returns no values.

Note: Cursor flag is decremented by this function; cursor is removed from screen.

Source: Microsoft Mouse User's Guide, pages 178 through 179
Microsoft Mouse Programmer's Reference (Microsoft Press), pages 124 through 125
Microsoft Mouse Programmer's Reference 2nd Ed. (Microsoft Press), pages TBD

See Also: 5.078. INT 33H, Mouse Driver Default Parameters

5.070. INT 33H, AX=03H -- GET BUTTON STATUS AND MOUSE POSITION

Prior to Issuing INT 33H

Register	High	Low
AX	03H	
BX		
CX		
DX		
SP		
BP		
SI		
DI		
IP		
flags		
CS		
DS		
SS		
ES		

Upon Return from INT 33H

Register	High	Low
AX		
BX	Button status*	
CX	Horizontal position	
DX	Vertical position	
SP		
BP		
SI		
DI		
IP		
flags		
CS		
DS		
SS		
ES		

*Bit 0 represents left button; bit 1 represents right button.

Note: A bit value of 1 represents a button held down (0=button up).

Source: Microsoft Mouse User's Guide, page 179
Microsoft Mouse Programmer's Reference (Microsoft Press), pages 126 through 128
Microsoft Mouse Programmer's Reference 2nd Ed. (Microsoft Press), pages 128 through 130

See Also: 5.071. INT 33H, AX=04H -- Set Mouse Cursor Position
5.072. INT 33H, AX=05H -- Get Button Press Information
5.073. INT 33H, AX=06H -- Get Button Release Information

5.071. INT 33H, AX=04H -- SET MOUSE CURSOR POSITION

Prior to Issuing INT 33H

Register	High / Low
AX	04H
BX	
CX	Horizontal position
DX	Vertical position
SP	
BP	
SI	
DI	
IP	
flags	
CS	
DS	
SS	
ES	

Upon Return from INT 33H

Interrupt returns no values.

Note:

- Position may be rounded to nearest values if screen is not in high resolution mode.
- Position must be within range for current video mode.
- Cursor appears unless one of following is true:
  - Function 1 hasn't yet displayed the cursor.
  - Function 2 hid the cursor.
  - Function 0 or 21H (33) hid the cursor during reset.
  - Cursor would appear in conditional-off region established by Function 10H (16).

Source:

Microsoft Mouse User's Guide, page 180
Microsoft Mouse Programmer's Reference (Microsoft Press), pages 129 through 130
Microsoft Mouse Programmer's Reference 2nd Ed. (Microsoft Press), pages 130 through 132

See Also:

5.070. INT 33H, AX=03H -- Get Button Status and Mouse Postion
5.072. INT 33H, AX=05H -- Get Button Press Information
5.073. INT 33H, AX=06H -- Get Button Release Information

5.072. INT 33H, AX=05H -- GET BUTTON PRESS INFORMATION

Prior to Issuing INT 33H

Register	High / Low
AX	05H
BX	Button*
CX	
DX	
SP	
BP	
SI	
DI	
IP	
flags	
CS	
DS	
SS	
ES	

Upon Return from INT 33H

Register	High / Low
AX	Status†
BX	Count§
CX	Horz position at last press
DX	Vert position at last press
SP	
BP	
SI	
DI	
IP	
flags	
CS	
DS	
SS	
ES	

*0=left button, 1=right button
†Bit 0 represents left button, bit 1 is right button; value of 1=button down, 0=button up.
§Count of button presses, in range of 0 to 65535, set to 0 after call

Source:

Microsoft Mouse User's Guide, page 181
Microsoft Mouse Programmer's Reference (Microsoft Press), pages 131 through 133
Microsoft Mouse Programmer's Reference 2nd Ed. (Microsoft Press), pages 132 through 134

See Also:

5.070. INT 33H, AX=03H -- Get Button Status and Mouse Position
5.071. INT 33H, AX=04H -- Set Mouse Cursor Position
5.073. INT 33H, AX=06H -- Get Button Release Information

5.073. INT 33H, AX=06H -- GET BUTTON RELEASE INFORMATION

Prior to Issuing INT 33H

Register	High / Low
AX	06H
BX	Button*
CX	
DX	
SP	
BP	
SI	
DI	
IP	
flags	
CS	
DS	
SS	
ES	

Upon Return from INT 33H

Register	High / Low
AX	Status†
BX	Count§
CX	Horz position at last release
DX	Vert position at last release
SP	
BP	
SI	
DI	
IP	
flags	
CS	
DS	
SS	
ES	

*0=left button, 1=right button
†Bit 0 represents left button, bit 1 is right button; value of 1=button down, 0=button up.
§Count of button releases, in range of 0 to 65535, set to 0 after call

Source: Microsoft Mouse User's Guide, page 182
Microsoft Mouse Programmer's Reference (Microsoft Press), pages 134 through 136
Microsoft Mouse Programmer's Reference 2nd Ed. (Microsoft Press), pages 134 through 136

See Also: 5.070. INT 33H, AX=03H -- Get Button Status and Mouse Position
5.071. INT 33H, AX=04H -- Set Mouse Cursor Position
5.072. INT 33H, AX=05H -- Get Button Press Information

5.074. INT 33H, AX=07H -- SET MIN/MAX HORIZONTAL CURSOR POSITION

Prior to Issuing INT 33H

Register	High / Low
AX	07H
BX	
CX	Minimum position
DX	Maximum position
SP	
BP	
SI	
DI	
IP	
flags	
CS	
DS	
SS	
ES	

Upon Return from INT 33H

Interrupt returns no values.

Note:
- Function restricts mouse movement to horizontal coordinates specified.
- If min value is greater than max, the two values are swapped.

Source: Microsoft Mouse User's Guide, page 183
Microsoft Mouse Programmer's Reference (Microsoft Press), pages 137 through 138
Microsoft Mouse Programmer's Reference 2nd Ed. (Microsoft Press),pages 136 through 138

See Also: 5.075. INT 33H, AX=08H -- Set Min/Max Vertical Position

5.075. INT 33H, AX=08H -- SET MIN/MAX VERTICAL CURSOR POSITION

Prior to Issuing INT 33H

Register	High / Low
AX	08H
BX	
CX	Minimum position
DX	Maximum position
SP	
BP	
SI	
DI	
IP	
flags	
CS	
DS	
SS	
ES	

Upon Return from INT 33H

Interrupt returns no values.

Note:
- Function restricts mouse movement to vertical coordinates specified.
- If min value is greater than max, the two values are swapped.

Source:
Microsoft Mouse User's Guide, page 184
Microsoft Mouse Programmer's Reference (Microsoft Press), pages 139 through 140
Microsoft Mouse Programmer's Reference 2nd Ed. (Microsoft Press), pages 138 through 140

See Also:
5.074. INT 33H, AX=07H -- Set Min/Max Horizontal Position

5.076. INT 33H, AX=09H -- SET GRAPHICS CURSOR BLOCK

Prior to Issuing INT 33H

Register	High / Low
AX	09H
BX	Horz hot spot
CX	Vert hot spot
DX	Offset of pointer to screen/cursor masks
SP	
BP	
SI	
DI	
IP	
flags	
CS	
DS	
SS	
ES	Segment of pointer to screen/cursor masks

Upon Return from INT 33H

Interrupt returns no values.

Note:
- Hot spot values may be within the range -128 through 127, though are usually 0 through 15.
- Earlier versions required hot spot to be between -16 and 15.

Source:
Microsoft Mouse User's Guide, page 185
Microsoft Mouse Programmer's Reference (Microsoft Press), pages 141 through 146
Microsoft Mouse Programmer's Reference 2nd Ed. (Microsoft Press), pages 140 through 145

See Also:
5.077. INT 33H, AX=0AH -- Set Text Cursor
5.117. INT 33H, Screen and Cursor Masks

5.077. INT 33H, AX=0AH -- SET TEXT CURSOR

Prior to Issuing INT 33H

Register	High / Low
AX	0AH
BX	Cursor type*
CX	Screen mask†
DX	Cursor mask§
SP	
BP	
SI	
DI	
IP	
flags	
CS	
DS	
SS	
ES	

Upon Return from INT 33H

Interrupt returns no values.

*0=software cursor, 1=hardware cursor
†Screen mask if software cursor; otherwise scan line start for hardware cursor
§Cursor mask if software cursor; otherwise scan line end for hardware cursor

Source: Microsoft Mouse User's Guide, page 187
Microsoft Mouse Programmer's Reference (Microsoft Press), pages 147 through 148
Microsoft Mouse Programmer's Reference 2nd Ed. (Microsoft Press), pages 145 through 147

See Also: 5.076. INT 33H, AX=O9H -- Set Graphics Cursor Block
5.117. INT 33H, Screen and Cursor Masks

5.078. INT 33H, AX=0BH -- READ MOUSE MOTION COUNTERS

Register	Prior to Issuing INT 33H (High / Low)	Upon Return from INT 33H (High / Low)
AX	0BH	
BX		
CX		Horizontal count
DX		Vertical count
SP		
BP		
SI		
DI		
IP		
flags		
CS		
DS		
SS		
ES		

Note:
- Count values returned are the number of mickeys moved since last call to function.
- A mickey is 1/200 of an inch for the 200 ppi mouse and 1/400 of an inch for the 400 ppi mouse.
- Count values are in range -32768 through 32767.

Source: Microsoft Mouse User's Guide, page 188
Microsoft Mouse Programmer's Reference (Microsoft Press), pages 149 through 150
Microsoft Mouse Programmer's Reference 2nd Ed. (Microsoft Press), pages 147 through 148

5.079. INT 33H, AX=0CH -- SET INTERRUPT SUBROUTINE CALL MASK AND ADDRESS

Prior to Issuing INT 33H

Register	High	Low
AX	0CH	
BX		
CX	Call mask	
DX	Offset of subroutine	
SP		
BP		
SI		
DI		
IP		
flags		
CS		
DS		
SS		
ES	Segment of subroutine	

Upon Return from INT 33H

Interrupt returns no values.

Note:

• Call mask is an integer defined as follows:

Bit	*Condition*
0	Cursor position changes
1	Left button pressed
2	Left button released
3	Right button pressed
4	Right button released
5-15	NOT USED

• Subroutine is passed information as follows:

Reg	*Information*
AX	Mask with condition bit set that triggered call
BX	Button state (bit 0=left, 1=right)
CX	Horizontal cursor position
DX	Vertical cursor position
SI	Horizontal mouse counts (mickeys)
DI	Vertical mouse counts (mickeys)

Source:

Microsoft Mouse User's Guide, pages 189 through 190
Microsoft Mouse Programmer's Reference (Microsoft Press), pages 151 through 157
Microsoft Mouse Programmer's Reference 2nd Ed. (Microsoft Press), pages 149 through 154

5.080. INT 33H, AX=0DH -- SET LIGHT PEN EMULATION ON

Prior to Issuing INT 33H

Register	High	Low
AX	0DH	
BX		
CX		
DX		
SP		
BP		
SI		
DI		
IP		
flags		
CS		
DS		
SS		
ES		

Upon Return from INT 33H

Interrupt returns no values.

Note: Function causes mouse to emulate light pen, as follows:
- Pen is down when both buttons are down.
- Pen is off screen when both buttons are up.

Source: Microsoft Mouse User's Guide, page 191
Microsoft Mouse Programmer's Reference (Microsoft Press), page 158
Microsoft Mouse Programmer's Reference 2nd Ed. (Microsoft Press), pages 155 through 156

See Also: 5.081. INT 33H, AX=0EH -- Set Light Pen Emulation Off

5.081. INT 33H, AX=0EH -- SET LIGHT PEN EMULATION OFF

Prior to Issuing INT 33H

Register	High	Low
AX	0EH	
BX		
CX		
DX		
SP		
BP		
SI		
DI		
IP		
flags		
CS		
DS		
SS		
ES		

Upon Return from INT 33H

Interrupt returns no values.

Note: Function disables light pen emulation.

Source: Microsoft Mouse User's Guide, page 192
Microsoft Mouse Programmer's Reference (Microsoft Press), page 159
Microsoft Mouse Programmer's Reference 2nd Ed. (Microsoft Press), pages 156 through 157

See Also: 5.080. INT 33H, AX=0DH -- Set Light Pen Emulation On

5.082. INT 33H, AX=0FH -- SET MICKEY/PIXEL RATIO

Prior to Issuing INT 33H

Register	High / Low
AX	0FH
BX	
CX	Horizontal ratio
DX	Vertical ratio
SP	
BP	
SI	
DI	
IP	
flags	
CS	
DS	
SS	
ES	

Upon Return from INT 33H

Interrupt returns no values.

Note:

- Ratio values must be in range 1 through 32767.
- Default horizontal value is 8 mickeys per 8 pixels.
- Default vertical value is 16 mickeys per 8 pixels.
- A mickey is 1/200 of an inch for the 200 ppi mouse and 1/400 for the 400 ppi mouse.

Source:

Microsoft Mouse User's Guide, page 193
Microsoft Mouse Programmer's Reference (Microsoft Press), pages 160 through 161
Microsoft Mouse Programmer's Reference 2nd Ed. (Microsoft Press), pages 157 through 158

5.083. INT 33H, AX=10H -- CONDITIONAL OFF

Prior to Issuing INT 33H

Register	High / Low
AX	10H
BX	
CX	Left x screen coord
DX	Upper y screen coord
SP	
BP	
SI	Right x screen coord
DI	Lower y screen coord
IP	
flags	
CS	
DS	
SS	
ES	

Upon Return from INT 33H

Interrupt returns no values.

Note:

Function defines region for updating; mouse cursor hidden when in this region, and you must use INT 33H, AX=01H to turn it back on.

Source:

Microsoft Mouse User's Guide, page 193
Microsoft Mouse Programmer's Reference (Microsoft Press), pages 162 through 163
Microsoft Mouse Programmer's Reference 2nd Ed. (Microsoft Press), pages 159 through 160

See Also:

5.068. INT 33H, AX=01H -- Show Cursor

5.084. INT 33H, AX=13H -- SET DOUBLE SPEED THRESHOLD

Prior to Issuing INT 33H

Reg	High / Low
AX	13H
BX	
CX	
DX	Threshold speed*
SP	
BP	
SI	
DI	
IP	
flags	
CS	
DS	
SS	
ES	

Upon Return from INT 33H

Interrupt returns no values.

*Speed defined in Mickeys per second; default is 64.

Source: Microsoft Mouse User's Guide, page 194
Microsoft Mouse Programmer's Reference (Microsoft Press), pages 164 through 166
Microsoft Mouse Programmer's Reference 2nd Ed. (Microsoft Press), pages 161 through 162

5.085. INT 33H, AX=14H -- SWAP INTERRUPT SUBROUTINES

Prior to Issuing INT 33H

Reg	High / Low
AX	14H
BX	Segment of new subroutine
CX	New call mask
DX	Offset of new subroutine
SP	
BP	
SI	
DI	
IP	
flags	
CS	
DS	
SS	
ES	

Upon Return from INT 33H

Reg	High / Low
AX	
BX	Segment of old subroutine
CX	Old call mask
DX	Offset of old subroutine
SP	
BP	
SI	
DI	
IP	
flags	
CS	
DS	
SS	
ES	

Note:

• Call mask is an integer defined as follows:

Bit	Condition
0	Cursor position changed
1	Left button pressed
2	Left button released
3	Right button pressed
4	Right button released
5-15	NOT USED

• Subroutine is passed information as follows:

Reg	Information
AX	Mask with condition bit set that triggered call
BX	Button state (bit 0=left, 1=right)
CX	Horizontal cursor position
DX	Vertical cursor position
SI	Horizontal mouse counts (mickeys)
DI	Vertical mouse counts (mickeys)

Source: Microsoft Mouse Programmer's Reference (Microsoft Press), pages 167 through 172
Microsoft Mouse Programmer's Reference 2nd Ed. (Microsoft Press), pages 163 through 168

5.086. INT 33H, AX=15H -- GET MOUSE DRIVER STATE STORAGE REQUIREMENTS

Register	Prior to Issuing INT 33H (High / Low)	Upon Return from INT 33H (High / Low)
AX	15H	
BX		Buffer size required
CX		
DX		
SP		
BP		
SI		
DI		
IP		
flags		
CS		
DS		
SS		
ES		

Note: Buffer size is in bytes.

Source: Microsoft Mouse Programmer's Reference (Microsoft Press), pages 173 through 174
Microsoft Mouse Programmer's Reference 2nd Ed. (Microsoft Press), pages 168 through 169

5.087. INT 33H, AX=16H -- SAVE MOUSE DRIVER STATE

Register	Prior to Issuing INT 33H (High / Low)
AX	16H
BX	
CX	
DX	Offset of buffer
SP	
BP	
SI	
DI	
IP	
flags	
CS	
DS	
SS	
ES	Segment of buffer

Upon Return from INT 33H

Interrupt returns no values.

Note: Determine buffer size needed by calling INT 21H, Function 15H.

Source: Microsoft Mouse Programmer's Reference (Microsoft Press), pages 175 through 176
Microsoft Mouse Programmer's Reference 2nd Ed. (Microsoft Press), pages 169 through 170

See Also: 5.086. INT 33H, AX=15H -- Get Mouse Driver State Storage Requirements
5.088. INT 33H, AX=17H -- Restore Mouse Driver State

5.088. INT 33H, AX=17H -- RESTORE MOUSE DRIVER STATE

Prior to Issuing INT 33H

	High	Low
AX	17H	
BX		
CX		
DX	Offset of buffer	
SP		
BP		
SI		
DI		
IP		
flags		
CS		
DS		
SS		
ES	Segment of buffer	

Upon Return from INT 33H

Interrupt returns no values.

Source: Microsoft Mouse Programmer's Reference (Microsoft Press), pages 177 through 178
Microsoft Mouse Programmer's Reference 2nd Ed. (Microsoft Press), pages 171 through 172

See Also: 5.086. INT 33H, AX=15H -- Get Mouse Driver State Storage Requirements
5.087. INT 33H, AX=16H -- Save Mouse Driver State

5.089. INT 33H, AX=18H -- SET ALTERNATE SUBROUTINE CALL MASK AND ADDRESS

Prior to Issuing INT 33H

	High	Low
AX	18H	
BX		
CX	User interrupt call mask	
DX	Offset of subroutine	
SP		
BP		
SI		
DI		
IP		
flags		
CS		
DS		
SS		
ES	Segment of subroutine	

Upon Return from INT 33H

	High	Low
AX	Status*	
BX		
CX		
DX		
SP		
BP		
SI		
DI		
IP		
flags		
CS		
DS		
SS		
ES		

*-1 if error occurred

Note: • The call mask value describes the mouse and keyboard condition, as follows:

Bit	Condition
0	Cursor position changes
1	Left button pressed
2	Left button released
3	Right button pressed
4	Right button released
5	Shift pressed with button press or release
6	Ctrl pressed with button press or release
7	Alt pressed with button press or release
8-15	NOT USED

(Continued)

5.089. INT 33H, AX=18H -- SET ALTERNATE SUBROUTINE CALL MASK AND ADDRESS (continued)

- Subroutine is passed information as follows:

Reg	Information
AX	Mask with condition bit set that triggered call
BX	Button state (bit 0=left, 1=right)
CX	Horizontal cursor position
DX	Vertical cursor position
SI	Horizontal mouse counts (mickeys)
DI	Vertical mouse counts (mickeys)

Source: Microsoft Mouse Programmer's Reference (Microsoft Press), pages 179 through 184
Microsoft Mouse Programmer's Reference 2nd Ed. (Microsoft Press), pages 172 through 177

5.090. INT 33H, AX=19H -- GET USER ALTERNATE INTERRUPT ADDRESS

Prior to Issuing INT 33H

Reg	High / Low
AX	19H
BX	
CX	User interrupt call mask
DX	
SP	
BP	
SI	
DI	
IP	
flags	
CS	
DS	
SS	
ES	

Upon Return from INT 33H

Reg	High / Low
AX	Status*
BX	Segment of subroutine
CX	User interrupt call mask
DX	Offset of subroutine
SP	
BP	
SI	
DI	
IP	
flags	
CS	
DS	
SS	
ES	

*-1 if no vector/mask, and then BX, CX, DX are 0.

Note:

- The call mask value describes the mouse and keyboard condition, as follows:

Bit	Condition
0	Cursor position changes
1	Left button pressed
2	Left button released
3	Right button pressed
4	Right button released
5	Shift pressed with button press or release
6	Ctrl pressed with button press or release
7	Alt pressed with button press or release
8-15	NOT USED

- Subroutine is passed information as follows:

Reg	Information
AX	Mask with condition bit set that triggered call
BX	Button state (bit 0=left, 1=right)
CX	Horizontal cursor position
DX	Vertical cursor position
SI	Horizontal mouse counts (mickeys)
DI	Vertical mouse counts (mickeys)

Source: Microsoft Mouse Programmer's Reference 2nd Ed. (Microsoft Press), pages 177 through 179

5.091. INT 33H, AX=1AH -- SET MOUSE SENSITIVITY

Prior to Issuing INT 33H

Register	High / Low
AX	1AH
BX	Horizontal mickey sensitivity number
CX	Vertical mickey sensitivity number
DX	Threshold for double speed
SP	
BP	
SI	
DI	
IP	
flags	
CS	
DS	
SS	
ES	

Upon Return from INT 33H

Interrupt returns no values.

Note: A mickey is 1/200 of an inch for the 200 ppi mouse and 1/400 of an inch for the 400 ppi mouse.

Source: Microsoft Mouse Programmer's Reference (Microsoft Press), pages 187 through 188
Microsoft Mouse Programmer's Reference 2nd Ed. (Microsoft Press), pages 179 through 181

5.092. INT 33H, AX=1BH -- GET MOUSE SENSITIVITY

Prior to Issuing INT 33H

Register	High / Low
AX	1BH
BX	
CX	
DX	
SP	
BP	
SI	
DI	
IP	
flags	
CS	
DS	
SS	
ES	

Upon Return from INT 33H

Register	High / Low
AX	
BX	Horizontal mickey sensitivity number
CX	Vertical mickey sensitivity number
DX	Threshold for double speed
SP	
BP	
SI	
DI	
IP	
flags	
CS	
DS	
SS	
ES	

Note: A mickey is 1/200 of an inch for the 200 ppi mouse and 1/400 of an inch for the 400 ppi mouse.

Source: Microsoft Mouse Programmer's Reference (Microsoft Press), pages 188 through 189
Microsoft Mouse Programmer's Reference 2nd Ed. (Microsoft Press), pages 181 through 182

5.093. INT 33H, AX=1CH -- SET MOUSE INTERRUPT RATE

Prior to Issuing INT 33H

Register	High	Low
AX	1CH	
BX	Interrupt rate*	
CX		
DX		
SP		
BP		
SI		
DI		
IP		
flags		
CS		
DS		
SS		
ES		

Upon Return from INT 33H

Interrupt returns no values.

*Maximum number of interrupts per second, defined as follows:

Value	*Interrupt Rate*
0	No interrupts allowed
1	30 interrupts per second
2	50 interrupts per second
3	100 interrupts per second
4	200 interrupts per second
>4	Not Defined (DO NOT USE!)

Source: Microsoft Mouse Programmer's Reference (Microsoft Press), pages 191 through 192
Microsoft Mouse Programmer's Reference 2nd Ed. (Microsoft Press), pages 182 through 183

5.094. INT 33H, AX=1DH -- SET CRT PAGE NUMBER

Prior to Issuing INT 33H

Register	High	Low
AX	1DH	
BX	CRT page number	
CX		
DX		
SP		
BP		
SI		
DI		
IP		
flags		
CS		
DS		
SS		
ES		

Upon Return from INT 33H

Interrupt returns no values.

Source: Microsoft Mouse Programmer's Reference (Microsoft Press), page 193
Microsoft Mouse Programmer's Reference 2nd Ed. (Microsoft Press), page 184

See Also: 5.095. INT 33H, AX=1EH -- Get CRT Page Number
7.022. Video Adapter Memory Usage and Output Specifications

5.095. INT 33H, AX=1EH -- GET CRT PAGE NUMBER

Register	Prior to Issuing INT 33H (High / Low)	Upon Return from INT 33H (High / Low)
AX	1EH	
BX		CRT page number
CX		
DX		
SP		
BP		
SI		
DI		
IP		
flags		
CS		
DS		
SS		
ES		

Source: Microsoft Mouse Programmer's Reference (Microsoft Press), page 193
Microsoft Mouse Programmer's Reference 2nd Ed. (Microsoft Press), page 185

See Also: 5.094. INT 33H, AX=1DH -- Set CRT Page Number
7.022. Video Adapter Memory Usage and Output Specifications

5.096. INT 33H, AX=1FH -- DISABLE MOUSE DRIVER

Register	Prior to Issuing INT 33H (High / Low)	Upon Return from INT 33H (High / Low)
AX	1FH	Status*
BX		Offset of old INT 33H vector
CX		
DX		
SP		
BP		
SI		
DI		
IP		
flags		
CS		
DS		
SS		
ES		Segment of old INT 33H vector

*-1 indicates an error occurred.

Source: Microsoft Mouse Programmer's Reference (Microsoft Press), pages 195 through 196
Microsoft Mouse Programmer's Reference 2nd Ed. (Microsoft Press), pages 186 through 187

See Also: 5.097. INT 33H, AX=20H -- Enable Mouse Driver

5.097. INT 33H, AX=20H -- ENABLE MOUSE DRIVER

Prior to Issuing INT 33H

	High	Low
AX	20H	
BX		
CX		
DX		
SP		
BP		
SI		
DI		
IP		
flags		
CS		
DS		
SS		
ES		

Upon Return from INT 33H

Interrupt returns no values.

Source: Microsoft Mouse Programmer's Reference (Microsoft Press), pages 197 through 198
Microsoft Mouse Programmer's Reference 2nd Ed. (Microsoft Press), pages 187 through 188

See Also: 5.096. INT 33H, AX=1FH -- Disable Mouse Driver

5.098. INT 33H, AX=21H -- SOFTWARE RESET

Prior to Issuing INT 33H

	High	Low
AX	21H	
BX		
CX		
DX		
SP		
BP		
SI		
DI		
IP		
flags		
CS		
DS		
SS		
ES		

Upon Return from INT 33H

	High	Low
AX	Status*	
BX	2†	
CX		
DX		
SP		
BP		
SI		
DI		
IP		
flags		
CS		
DS		
SS		
ES		

*-1 indicates mouse driver installed; 33 (21H) otherwise.
†Only if mouse driver installed (see Status, above)

Source: Microsoft Mouse Programmer's Reference (Microsoft Press), pages 198 through 199
Microsoft Mouse Programmer's Reference 2nd Ed. (Microsoft Press), pages 188 through 190

See Also: 5.118. INT 33H, Mouse Driver Default Parameters

5.099. INT 33H, AX=22H -- SET LANGUAGE FOR MESSAGES

Prior to Issuing INT 33H

Register	High / Low
AX	22H
BX	Language number
CX	
DX	
SP	
BP	
SI	
DI	
IP	
flags	
CS	
DS	
SS	
ES	

*Code value, as follows:

Value	Language
0	English
1	French
2	Dutch
3	German
4	Swedish
5	Finnish
6	Spanish
7	Portuguese
8	Italian

Upon Return from INT 33H

Interrupt returns no values.

Source: Microsoft Mouse Programmer's Reference (Microsoft Press), pages 200 through 201
Microsoft Mouse Programmer's Reference 2nd Ed. (Microsoft Press), pages 190 through 191

See Also: 5.100. INT 33H, AX=23H -- Get Language Number

5.100. INT 33H, AX=23H -- GET LANGUAGE NUMBER

Prior to Issuing INT 33H

Register	High	Low
AX	23H	
BX		
CX		
DX		
SP		
BP		
SI		
DI		
IP		
flags		
CS		
DS		
SS		
ES		

Upon Return from INT 33H

Register	High	Low
AX		
BX	Language number*	
CX		
DX		
SP		
BP		
SI		
DI		
IP		
flags		
CS		
DS		
SS		
ES		

*Code value, as follows:

Value	Language
0	English
1	French
2	Dutch
3	German
4	Swedish
5	Finnish
6	Spanish
7	Portuguese
8	Italian

Source: Microsoft Mouse Programmer's Reference (Microsoft Press), page 202
Microsoft Mouse Programmer's Reference 2nd Ed. (Microsoft Press), pages 191 through 192

See Also: 5.099. INT 33H, AX=22H -- Set Language for Messages

5.101. INT 33H, AX=24H -- GET DRIVER VERSION, MOUSE TYPE, AND IRQ NUMBER

Prior to Issuing INT 33H

Register	High	Low
AX	24H	
BX		
CX		
DX		
SP		
BP		
SI		
DI		
IP		
flags		
CS		
DS		
SS		
ES		

Upon Return from INT 33H

Register	High	Low
AX		
BX	Mouse driver version number	
CX	Mouse type*	IRQ number†
DX		
SP		
BP		
SI		
DI		
IP		
flags		
CS		
DS		
SS		
ES		

*Coded mouse type value, as follows:

Value	Language
1	bus mouse
2	serial mouse
3	InPort mouse
4	PS/2 mouse
5	Hewlett-Packard mouse

†Value of 0 indicates PS/2 model; otherwise values 2 through 5 or 7 are mouse interrupt.

Source: Microsoft Mouse Programmer's Reference (Microsoft Press), pages 203 through 204
Microsoft Mouse Programmer's Reference 2nd Ed. (Microsoft Press), pages 192 through 194

5.102. INT 33H, AX=25H -- GET GENERAL DRIVER INFORMATION

Prior to Issuing INT 33H

Register	High	Low
AX	25H	
BX		
CX		
DX		
SP		
BP		
SI		
DI		
IP		
flags		
CS		
DS		
SS		
ES		

Upon Return from INT 33H

Register	High	Low
AX	Status*	Number of MDDS
BX	fCursor lock	
CX	FinMouse code	
DX	fMouse busy	
SP		
BP		
SI		
DI		
IP		
flags		
CS		
DS		
SS		
ES		

*Status bits:
Bit 7 -- driver type, 1=sys, 0=com
Bit 6 -- 0=non-integrated mouse driver, 1=integrated mouse driver
Bits 4-5 -- cursor type (ver 7.02 or later)
  00=software text cursor
  01=hardware text cursor
  1X=graphics cursor
Bits 0-3 -- Function 28 mouse interrupt rate

Version: Function available in mouse driver version 6.26 or later

Source: Microsoft Mouse Programmer's Reference 2nd Ed. (Microsoft Press), pages 194 through 196

5.103. INT 33H, AX=26H -- GET MAXIMUM VIRTUAL COORDINATES

Prior to Issuing INT 33H

Register	High	Low
AX	26H	
BX		
CX		
DX		
SP		
BP		
SI		
DI		
IP		
flags		
CS		
DS		
SS		
ES		

Upon Return from INT 33H

Register	High	Low
AX		
BX	Mouse disabled flag*	
CX	Absolute virtual X maximum	
DX	Absolute virtual Y maximum	
SP		
BP		
SI		
DI		
IP		
flags		
CS		
DS		
SS		
ES		

*0=enabled, 1=disabled

Version: Function available in mouse driver version 6.26 or later

Source: Microsoft Mouse Programmer's Reference 2nd Ed. (Microsoft Press), pages 196 through 197

See Also: 5.113. INT 33H, Get Minimum/Maximum Virtual Coordinates

5.104. INT 33H, AX=27H -- GET SCREEN/CURSOR MASKS AND MICKEY COUNTS

Register	*Prior to Issuing INT 33H* (High / Low)	*Upon Return from INT 33H* (High / Low)
AX	27H	Screen mask value or scan line start*
BX		Cursor mask value or scan line stop*
CX		Raw horizontal mickey count
DX		Raw vertical mickey count
SP		
BP		
SI		
DI		
IP		
flags		
CS		
DS		
SS		
ES		

*Available in mouse driver 7.02 or later

Version: Function available in mouse driver version 6.26 or later

Source: Microsoft Mouse Programmer's Reference 2nd Ed. (Microsoft Press), pages 197 through 198

See Also: 5.117. INT 33H, Screen and Cursor Masks

5.105. INT 33H, AX=28H -- SET VIDEO MODE

Register	*Prior to Issuing INT 33H* (High / Low)	*Upon Return from INT 33H* (High / Low)
AX	28H	
BX		
CX	Requested video mode	0 if successful; else requested mode
DX	Font size, 0 for default*	
SP		
BP		
SI		
DI		
IP		
flags		
CS		
DS		
SS		
ES		

*High byte=y font size, low byte= x font size

Version: Function available in mouse driver version 7.00 or later

Source: Microsoft Mouse Programmer's Reference 2nd Ed. (Microsoft Press), pages 199 through 200

5.106. INT 33H, AX=29H -- ENUMERATE VIDEO MODES

Register	Prior to Issuing INT 33H (High / Low)	Upon Return from INT 33H (High / Low)
AX	29H	
BX		Segment of named string*
CX	0 for first, <> 0 for next	Video mode number
DX		Offset of named string*
SP		
BP		
SI		
DI		
IP		
flags		
CS		
DS		
SS		
ES		

*Segment:offset=0:0 means no named string returned.

Version: Function available in mouse driver version 7.00 or later

Source: Microsoft Mouse Programmer's Reference 2nd Ed. (Microsoft Press), pages 200 through 201

5.107. INT 33H, AX=30H -- GET CURSOR HOTSPOT

Register	Prior to Issuing INT 33H (High / Low)	Upon Return from INT 33H (High / Low)
AX	30H	fCursor (internal flag)
BX		Horizontal cursor hot spot
CX		Vertical cursor hot spot
DX		Type of mouse*
SP		
BP		
SI		
DI		
IP		
flags		
CS		
DS		
SS		
ES		

*Mouse type, as follows:

Value	Type of mouse
0	none
1	bus
2	serial
3	inport
4	IBM
5	Hewlett Packard

Version: Function available in mouse driver version 7.02 or later

Source: Microsoft Mouse Programmer's Reference 2nd Ed. (Microsoft Press), pages 201 through 203

See Also: 5.076. INT 33H, Set Graphics Cursor Block

5.108. INT 33H, AX=31H -- LOAD ACCELERATION CURVES

Register	Prior to Issuing INT 33H (High / Low)	Upon Return from INT 33H (High / Low)
AX	31H	0 if successful; else -1
BX	Curve number to make active*	
CX		
DX		
SP		
BP		
SI	Offset of curve array	
DI		
IP		
flags		
CS		
DS		
SS		
ES	Segment of curve array	

*Curve number=-1 means restore default curves.

Version: Function available in mouse driver version 7.00 or later

Source: Microsoft Mouse Programmer's Reference 2nd Ed. (Microsoft Press), pages 203 through 205

See Also:
5.109. INT 33H, AX=32H -- Read Acceleration Curves
5.110. INT 33H, AX=33H -- Set/Get Active Acceleration Curves
5.119. INT 33H, Acceleration Curves

5.109. INT 33H, AX=32H -- READ ACCELERATION CURVES

Register	Prior to Issuing INT 33H (High / Low)	Upon Return from INT 33H (High / Low)
AX	32H	0 if successful; else -1
BX		Current active acceleration curve
CX		
DX		
SP		
BP		
SI		Offset of curve array
DI		
IP		
flags		
CS		
DS		
SS		
ES		Segment of curve array

Version: Function available in mouse driver version 7.00 or later

Source: Microsoft Mouse Programmer's Reference 2nd Ed. (Microsoft Press), pages 206 through 207

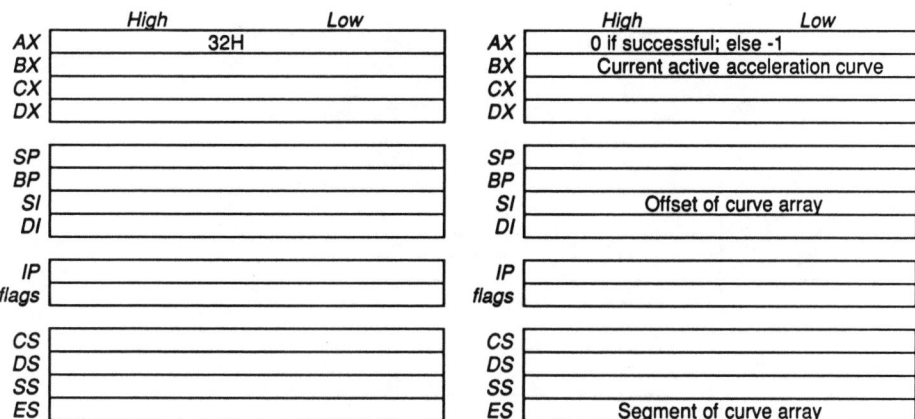

See Also:
5.108. INT 33H, AX=31H -- Load Acceleration Curves
5.110. INT 33H, AX=33H -- Set/Get Active Acceleration Curves
5.119. INT 33H, Acceleration Curves

5.110. INT 33H, AX=33H -- SET/GET ACTIVE ACCELERATION CURVES

Register	Prior to Issuing INT 33H (High / Low)	Upon Return from INT 33H (High / Low)
AX	33H	0 if successful; -2 = bad curve number
BX	Curve number to become active*	Current active acceleration curve
CX		
DX		
SP		
BP		
SI		Offset of 16-byte ASCII string
DI		
IP		
flags		
CS		
DS		
SS		
ES		Segment of 16-byte ASCII string

*-1 to get current active acceleration curve number, a number in the range of 1 through 4 to set the active curve number.

Version: Function available in mouse driver version 7.00 or later

Note: The ASCII string is the name of the current active curve. It is not null terminated.

Source: Microsoft Mouse Programmer's Reference 2nd Ed. (Microsoft Press), pages 207 through 208

See Also:
5.108. INT 33H, AX=31H -- Load Acceleration Curves
5.109. INT 33H, AX=32H -- Read Acceleration Curves
5.119. INT 33H, Acceleration Curves

5.111. INT 33H, AX=35H -- MOUSE HARDWARE RESET

Register	Prior to Issuing INT 33H (High / Low)	Upon Return from INT 33H (High / Low)
AX	35H	0 if error; -1 if successful
BX		
CX		
DX		
SP		
BP		
SI		
DI		
IP		
flags		
CS		
DS		
SS		
ES		

Note: Does NOT reset software values.

Version: Function available in mouse driver version 7.02 or later

Source: Microsoft Mouse Programmer's Reference 2nd Ed. (Microsoft Press), pages 208 through 209

5.112. INT 33H, AX=36H -- SET/GET BALLPOINT INFORMATION

Register	*Prior to Issuing INT 33H*	*Upon Return from INT 33H*
AX	36H	Status§
BX	Rotation angle†	Rotation angle
CX	0 = get, <>0 set†	High: Primary btn mask* / Low: Secondary btn mask*
DX		
SP		
BP		
SI		
DI		
IP		
flags		
CS		
DS		
SS		
ES		

†CX=0 means query, prior value of BX ignored
†CX<>0, BX=rotation angle, CH=primary button mask, CL=secondary button mask
§AX=-1 if Ballpoint not present; otherwise AL=state of buttons
*Button mask=0 0 b1 b3 b2 b4 0 0

Version: Function available in mouse driver version 7.05 or later

Source: Microsoft Mouse Programmer's Reference 2nd Ed. (Microsoft Press), pages 209 through 211

5.113. INT 33H, AX=37H -- GET MINIMUM/MAXIMUM VIRTUAL COORDINATES

Register	*Prior to Issuing INT 33H*	*Upon Return from INT 33H*
AX	37H	Current virtual X minimum
BX		Current virtual Y minimum
CX		Current virtual X maximum
DX		Current virtual Y maximum
SP		
BP		
SI		
DI		
IP		
flags		
CS		
DS		
SS		
ES		

Version: Function available in mouse driver version 7.05 or later

Source: Microsoft Mouse Programmer's Reference 2nd Ed. (Microsoft Press), pages 211 through 212

5.114. INT 33H, AX=38H -- GET ACTIVE ADVANCED FUNCTIONS

Prior to Issuing INT 33H

Register	High / Low
AX	38H
BX	
CX	
DX	
SP	
BP	
SI	
DI	
IP	
flags	
CS	
DS	
SS	
ES	

Upon Return from INT 33H

Register	High / Low
AX	Supported functions*
BX	
CX	
DX	
SP	
BP	
SI	
DI	
IP	
flags	
CS	
DS	
SS	
ES	

*AX is a bit array, msbit for Function 37 ... lsbit for Function 52.

Version: Function available in mouse driver version 7.05 or later

Note: Bit=1 means supported, Bit=0 means not supported.

Source: Microsoft Mouse Programmer's Reference 2nd Ed. (Microsoft Press), pages 212 through 213

5.115. INT 33H, AX=39H -- GET SWITCH SETTINGS

Prior to Issuing INT 33H

Register	High / Low
AX	39H
BX	
CX	Length of buffer
DX	Offset of buffer
SP	
BP	
SI	
DI	
IP	
flags	
CS	
DS	
SS	
ES	Segment of buffer

Upon Return from INT 33H

Register	High / Low
AX	0
BX	
CX	Number of bytes returned
DX	Offset of buffer
SP	
BP	
SI	
DI	
IP	
flags	
CS	
DS	
SS	
ES	Segment of buffer

(Continued)

5.115. INT 33H, AX=39H -- GET SWITCH SETTINGS (continued)

Version: Function available in mouse driver version 7.05 or later

Note: Buffer is formatted as follows:

Offset	Contents	Range
0	mouse type (LO nibble)	0-5
0	mouse port (HO nibble)	0-4
1	language	0-10
2	horizontal sensitivity	0-100
3	vertical sensitivity	0-100
4	double threshold	0-100
5	ballistic curve	1-4
6	interrupt rate	1-4
7	cursor override mask	0-255
8	laptop adjustment	0-255
9	memory type	0-2
10	super VGA support	0-1
11	rotation angle	0-359
13	primary button	1-4
14	secondary button	1-4
15	click lock enabled	0-1
16	acceleration curve data	(bytes 16-339)

Source: Microsoft Mouse Programmer's Reference 2nd Ed. (Microsoft Press), pages 213 through 215

5.116. INT 33H, AX=40H -- GET MOUSE.INI LOCATION

Prior to Issuing INT 33H

Register	High	Low
AX	40H	
BX		
CX		
DX		
SP		
BP		
SI		
DI		
IP		
flags		
CS		
DS		
SS		
ES		

Upon Return from INT 33H

Register	High	Low
AX		
BX		
CX		
DX	Offset of string*	
SP		
BP		
SI		
DI		
IP		
flags		
CS		
DS		
SS		
ES	Segment of string*	

*ASCII null terminated string that is the full path to MOUSE.INI

Version: Function available in mouse driver version 8.00 or later

Source: Microsoft Mouse Programmer's Reference 2nd Ed. (Microsoft Press), pages 215 through 216

5.117. INT 33H, SCREEN AND CURSOR MASKS

Effect of Screen and Cursor Mask Combinations

Screen Mask Bit	*Cursor Mask Bit*	*Resulting Screen Bit*
0	0	0
0	1	1
1	0	Unchanged
1	1	Inverted

Screen Data for Character

*Bit Number**	*Description*	*Comments*
15	Blink control	1=blinking character
12-14	Background color	
11	Intensity control	1=high intensity
8-10	Foreground color	
0-7	Character	ASCII value

*Bytes are stored in reverse order.

Source: Microsoft Mouse User's Guide, pages 165 through 166
Microsoft Mouse Programmer's Reference (Microsoft Press), pages 93 through 98
Microsoft Mouse Programmer's Reference 2nd Ed. (Microsoft Press), pages 91 through 94

See Also: 7.032. CGA Character Attributes

5.118. INT 33H, MOUSE DRIVER DEFAULT PARAMETERS

Parameter	*Value*	*Comments*
Cursor position	Screen center	e.g., 100,320 for CGA in 640x200 mono mode
Internal cursor flag	-1	Cursor hidden
Graphics cursor	-1,-1	Arrow
Text cursor	Reverse video block	Inverting box
Interrupt call mask	All 0	No interrupt subroutine specified
Light pen emulation mode	Enabled	
CRT page number	0	
Mickey/pixel ratio (horz)	8 to 8	
Mickey/pixel ratio (vert)	16 to 8	
Min cursor pos (horz)	0	
Min cursor pos (vert)	0	
Max cursor pos (horz)	Varies	Set to maximum x value of video mode minus 1
Max cursor pos (vert)	Varies	Set to maximum y value of video mode minus 1
Double-speed threshold	64 mickeys/second	

Source: Microsoft Mouse User's Guide, pages 176 through 177
Microsoft Mouse Programmer's Reference (Microsoft Press), page 116
Microsoft Mouse Programmer's Reference 2nd Ed. (Microsoft Press), pages 124 through 125

See Also: 5.067. INT 33H, AX=00H -- Mouse Reset and Status

5.119. INT 33H, ACCELERATION CURVES

Part of Table	*Offset (decimal)*	*Length (in bytes)*	*Description*
Curve Lengths	0	1	Number of counts/factors in first curve†
	1	1	Number of counts/factors in second curve†
	2	1	Number of counts/factors in third curve†
	3	1	Number of counts/factors in fourth curve†
Mouse Counts	4	32	Array of counts for first curve
	36	32	Array of counts for second curve
	68	32	Array of counts for third curve
	100	32	Array of counts for fourth curve
Scale Factors	132	32	Array of scale factors for first curve
	164	32	Array of scale factors for second curve
	196	32	Array of scale factors for third curve
	228	32	Array of scale factors for fourth curve
Curve Names	260	16	ASCII string for first curve*
	276	16	ASCII string for second curve*
	292	16	ASCII string for third curve*
	308	16	ASCII string for fourth curve*

*Not null terminated
†Values should be in range of 1-32.

Version: Function available in mouse driver 7.05 or later

Source: Microsoft Mouse Programmer's Reference 2nd Ed. (Microsoft Press), page 203

5.120. INT 67H, EXPANDED MEMORY MANAGER FUNCTIONS SUMMARY

Interrupt	Function*	Description	Comments
67H	40H (64)	Get status	Original EMS
	41H (65)	Get page frame address	Original EMS
	42H (66)	Get page count	Original EMS
	43H (67)	Allocate pages	Original EMS
	44H (68)	Map memory	Original EMS
	45H (69)	Deallocate pages	Original EMS
	46H (70)	Get version	Original EMS
	47H (71)	Save page map	Original EMS
	48H (72)	Restore page map	Original EMS
	49H (73)	RESERVED	Original EMS
	4AH (74)	RESERVED	Original EMS
	4BH (75)	Get handle count	Original EMS
	4CH (76)	Get page count for a handle	Original EMS
	4DH (77)	Get page counts for all handles	Original EMS
	4EH,0 (78,0)	Get map	Original EMS
	4EH,1 (78,1)	Set map	Original EMS
	4EH,2 (78,2)	Swap map	Original EMS
	4EH,3 (78,3)	Get size	Original EMS
	4FH, 0 (79,0)	Save partial page map	Added with 4.0†
	4FH, 1 (79,1)	Restore partial page map	Added with 4.0†
	4FH, 2 (79,2)	Get size of partial page-map info	Added with 4.0†
	50H, 0 (80,0)	Map multiple pages by number	Added with 4.0†
	50H, 1 (80,1)	Map multiple pages by address	Added with 4.0†
	51H (81)	Reallocate pages for handle	Added with 4.0†
	52H, 0 (82,0)	Get handle attribute	Added with 4.0†
	52H, 1 (82,1)	Set handle attribute	Added with 4.0†
	52H, 2 (82,2)	Get attribute capability	Added with 4.0†
	53H, 0 (83,0)	Get handle name	Added with 4.0†
	53H, 1 (83,1)	Set handle name	Added with 4.0†
	54H, 0 (84,0)	Get all handle names	Added with 4.0†
	54H, 1 (84,1)	Search for handle name	Added with 4.0†
	54H, 2 (84,2)	Get total handles	Added with 4.0†
	55H, 0/1 (85, 0/1)	Map pages and jump	Added with 4.0†
	56H, 0/1 (86, 0/1)	Map pages and call	Added with 4.0†
	56H, 2 (86,2)	Get stack space for map page and call	Added with 4.0†
	57H, 0 (87,0)	Move memory region	Added with 4.0†
	57H, 1 (87,1)	Exchange memory regions	Added with 4.0†
	58H, 0 (88,0)	Get addresses of mappable pages	Added with 4.0†
	58H, 1 (88,1)	Get number of mappable pages	Added with 4.0†
	59H, 0 (89,0)	Get hardware configuration	Added with 4.0†
	59H, 1 (89,1)	Get number of raw pages	Added with 4.0†
	5AH, 0 (90,0)	Allocate handle and standard pages	Added with 4.0†
	5AH, 1 (91,1)	Allocate handle and raw pages	Added with 4.0†
	5BH, 0 (92,0)	Get alternate map registers	Added with 4.0†
	5BH, 1 (92,1)	Set alternate map registers	Added with 4.0†
	5BH, 2 (92,2)	Get size of alt map register save area	Added with 4.0†
	5BH, 3 (92,3)	Allocate alternate map register set	Added with 4.0†
	5BH, 4 (92,4)	Deallocate alternate map register set	Added with 4.0†
	5BH, 5 (92,5)	Allocate DMA register set	Added with 4.0†
	5BH, 6 (92,6)	Enable DMA on alt map register set	Added with 4.0†
	5BH, 7 (92,7)	Disable DMA on alt map register set	Added with 4.0†
	5BH, 8 (92,8)	Deallocate DMA register set	Added with 4.0†
	5CH (93)	Prepare EMM for warm boot	Added with 4.0†
	5DH, 0 (94,0)	Enable EMM OS functions	Added with 4.0†
	5DH, 1 (94,1)	Disable EMM OS functions	Added with 4.0†
	5DH, 2 (94,2)	Release access key	Added with 4.0†
	60H	Get physical window array	EEMS only§
	68H	Get system physical window array	EEMS only§
	69H	Map page into window	EEMS only§
	6AH,0	Get system map	EEMS only§
	6AH,1	Set system map	EEMS only§
	6AH,2	Swap system map	EEMS only§
	6AH,3	Get map size	EEMS only§
	6AH,4	Set standard mapping	EEMS only§
	6AH,5	Set alternate mapping	EEMS only§
	6AH,6	Deallocate initial pages	EEMS only§

*First number is AH value, second number (if any) is AL value.
†In 1987 Microsoft/Intel/Lotus extended EMS to handle many EEMS and additional functions.
§AST's extension of the original EMS, now obsolete

(Continued)

5.120. INT 67H, EXPANDED MEMORY MANAGER FUNCTIONS SUMMARY (continued)

Version: These functions work only if an Expanded Memory Manager (EMM) is active in the system.

Source: Advanced MS-DOS Programming 2nd Ed. (Microsoft Press), pages 614 through 615
AST Rampage Technical Reference
MS-DOS Extensions (Microsoft Press), pages 30 through 31
Expanded Memory Specification Version 4.0 (Intel), pages 3-2 through 3-3

See Also: Individual function tables 5.121 through 5.185

5.121. INT 67H, AH=40H -- GET STATUS

Prior to Issuing INT 67H

	High	Low
AX	40H	
BX		
CX		
DX		
SP		
BP		
SI		
DI		
IP		
flags		
CS		
DS		
SS		
ES		

Upon Return from INT 67H

	High	Low
AX	Status*	
BX		
CX		
DX		
SP		
BP		
SI		
DI		
IP		
flags		
CS		
DS		
SS		
ES		

*00=no error (otherwise see 5.185. INT 67H, Expanded Memory Manager Error Codes)

Source: Advanced MS-DOS Programming 2nd Ed. (Microsoft Press), page 616
MS-DOS Extensions (Microsoft Press), pages 31 through 32
Expanded Memory Specification Version 4.0 (Intel), page 3-4

See Also: 5.120. INT 67H, Expanded Memory Manager Functions Summary
5.185. INT 67H, Expanded Memory Manager Error Codes

5.122. INT 67H, AH=41H -- GET PAGE FRAME ADDRESS

Prior to Issuing INT 67H

	High	Low
AX	41H	
BX		
CX		
DX		
SP		
BP		
SI		
DI		
IP		
flags		
CS		
DS		
SS		
ES		

Upon Return from INT 67H

	High	Low
AX	Status*	
BX	Segment address of page frame (if AH=0)	
CX		
DX		
SP		
BP		
SI		
DI		
IP		
flags		
CS		
DS		
SS		
ES		

*00=no error (otherwise see 5.185. INT 67H, Expanded Memory Manager Error Codes)

Source: Advanced MS-DOS Programming 2nd Ed. (Microsoft Press), page 616
MS-DOS Extensions (Microsoft Press), page 32
Expanded Memory Specification Version 4.0 (Intel), pages 3-5 through 3-6

See Also: 5.120. INT 67H, Expanded Memory Manager Functions Summary
5.185. INT 67H, Expanded Memory Manager Error Codes

5.123. INT 67H, AH=42H -- GET PAGE COUNT

Prior to Issuing INT 67H

	High	Low
AX	42H	
BX		
CX		
DX		
SP		
BP		
SI		
DI		
IP		
flags		
CS		
DS		
SS		
ES		

Upon Return from INT 67H

	High	Low
AX	Status*	
BX	Unallocated pages (if AH=0)	
CX		
DX	Total page count (if AH=0)	
SP		
BP		
SI		
DI		
IP		
flags		
CS		
DS		
SS		
ES		

*00=no error (otherwise see 5.185. INT 67H, Expanded Memory Manager Error Codes)

Source: Advanced MS-DOS Programming 2nd Ed. (Microsoft Press), page 617
MS-DOS Extensions (Microsoft Press), page 33
Expanded Memory Specification Version 4.0 (Intel), pages 3-7 through 3-8

See Also: 5.120. INT 67H, Expanded Memory Manager Functions Summary
5.159. INT 67H, AH=59H, AL=01H -- Get Number of Raw Pages
5.185. INT 67H, Expanded Memory Manager Error Codes

5.124. INT 67H, AH=43H -- ALLOCATE PAGES

Prior to Issuing INT 67H

	High	Low
AX	43H	
BX	Pages to allocate (nonzero)	
CX		
DX		
SP		
BP		
SI		
DI		
IP		
flags		
CS		
DS		
SS		
ES		

Upon Return from INT 67H

	High	Low
AX	Status*	
BX		
CX		
DX	EMM page handle (if AH=0)	
SP		
BP		
SI		
DI		
IP		
flags		
CS		
DS		
SS		
ES		

*00=no error (otherwise see 5.185. INT 67H, Expanded Memory Manager Error Codes)

Source: Advanced MS-DOS Programming 2nd Ed. (Microsoft Press), pages 617 through 618
MS-DOS Extensions (Microsoft Press), pages 33 through 34
Expanded Memory Specification Version 4.0 (Intel), pages 3-9 through 3-11

See Also: 5.120. INT 67H, Expanded Memory Manager Functions Summary
5.160. INT 67H, AH=5AH, AL=00H -- Allocate Handle and Standard Pages
5.161. INT 67H, AH=5AH, AL=01H -- Allocate Handle and Raw Pages
5.185. INT 67H, Expanded Memory Manager Error Codes

5.125. INT 67H, AH=44H -- MAP MEMORY

Register	Prior to Issuing INT 67H: High	Prior to Issuing INT 67H: Low	Upon Return from INT 67H: High	Upon Return from INT 67H: Low
AX	44H	Phys page number†	Status*	
BX	Logical page number			
CX				
DX	EMM page handle			
SP				
BP				
SI				
DI				
IP				
flags				
CS				
DS				
SS				
ES				

*00=no error (otherwise see 5.185. INT 67H, Expanded Memory Manager Error Codes)
†Must be in range 0-3.

Source: Advanced MS-DOS Programming 2nd Ed. (Microsoft Press), pages 618 through 619
MS-DOS Extensions (Microsoft Press), pages 34 through 35
Expanded Memory Specification Version 4.0 (Intel), pages 3-12 through 3-14

See Also: 5.120. INT 67H, Expanded Memory Manager Functions Summary
5.124. INT 67H, AH=43H -- Allocate Pages
5.156. INT 67H, AH=58H, AL=00H -- Get Addresses of Mappable Pages
5.185. INT 67H, Expanded Memory Manager Error Codes

5.126. INT 67H, AH=45H -- DEALLOCATE PAGES

Register	Prior to Issuing INT 67H: High	Prior to Issuing INT 67H: Low	Upon Return from INT 67H: High	Upon Return from INT 67H: Low
AX	45H		Status*	
BX				
CX				
DX	EMM page handle			
SP				
BP				
SI				
DI				
IP				
flags				
CS				
DS				
SS				
ES				

*00=no error (otherwise see 5.185. INT 67H, Expanded Memory Manager Error Codes)

Source: Advanced MS-DOS Programming 2nd Ed. (Microsoft Press), page 619
MS-DOS Extensions (Microsoft Press), page 35
Expanded Memory Specification Version 4.0 (Intel), pages 3-15 through 3-16

See Also: 5.120. INT 67H, Expanded Memory Manager Functions Summary
5.124. INT 67H, AH=43H -- Allocate Pages
5.185. INT 67H, Expanded Memory Manager Error Codes

5.127. INT 67H, AH=46H -- GET EMM VERSION

Prior to Issuing INT 67H

Register	High	Low
AX	46H	
BX		
CX		
DX		
SP		
BP		
SI		
DI		
IP		
flags		
CS		
DS		
SS		
ES		

Upon Return from INT 67H

Register	High	Low
AX	Status*	Version†
BX		
CX		
DX		
SP		
BP		
SI		
DI		
IP		
flags		
CS		
DS		
SS		
ES		

*00=no error (otherwise see 5.185. INT 67H, Expanded Memory Manager Error Codes)
†HO nibble is BCD-coded major version number, LO nibble is BCD-coded minor version number.

Source: Advanced MS-DOS Programming 2nd Ed. (Microsoft Press), pages 619 through 620
MS-DOS Extensions (Microsoft Press), page 36
Expanded Memory Specification Version 4.0 (Intel), pages 317 through 218

See Also: 5.120. INT 67H, Expanded Memory Manager Functions Summary
5.185. INT 67H, Expanded Memory Manager Error Codes

5.128. INT 67H, AH=47H -- SAVE PAGE MAP

Prior to Issuing INT 67H

Register	High	Low
AX	47H	
BX		
CX		
DX	EMM page handle	
SP		
BP		
SI		
DI		
IP		
flags		
CS		
DS		
SS		
ES		

Upon Return from INT 67H

Register	High	Low
AX	Status*	
BX		
CX		
DX		
SP		
BP		
SI		
DI		
IP		
flags		
CS		
DS		
SS		
ES		

*00=no error (otherwise see 5.185. INT 67H, Expanded Memory Manager Error Codes)

Source: Advanced MS-DOS Programming 2nd Ed. (Microsoft Press), page 620
MS-DOS Extensions (Microsoft Press), pages 36 through 37
Expanded Memory Specification Version 4.0 (Intel), pages 3-19 through 3-20

See Also: 5.120. INT 67H, Expanded Memory Manager Functions Summary
5.124. INT 67H, AH=43H -- Allocate Pages
5.185. INT 67H, Expanded Memory Manager Error Codes

5.129. INT 67H, AH=48H -- RESTORE PAGE MAP

Register	Prior to Issuing INT 67H: High	Prior to Issuing INT 67H: Low	Upon Return from INT 67H: High	Upon Return from INT 67H: Low
AX	48H		Status*	
BX				
CX				
DX	EMM page handle			
SP				
BP				
SI				
DI				
IP				
flags				
CS				
DS				
SS				
ES				

*00=no error (otherwise see 5.185. INT 67H, Expanded Memory Manager Error Codes)

Note: Function is used after an INT 67H, AH=47H call.

Source: Advanced MS-DOS Programming 2nd Ed. (Microsoft Press), pages 620 through 621
MS-DOS Extensions (Microsoft Press), page 37
Expanded Memory Specification Version 4.0 (Intel), pages 3-21 through 3-22

See Also: 5.120. INT 67H, Expanded Memory Manager Functions Summary
5.124. INT 67H, AH=43H -- Allocate Pages
5.128. INT 67H, AH=47H -- Save Page Map
5.185. INT 67H, Expanded Memory Manager Error Codes

5.130. INT 67H, AH=4BH -- GET HANDLE COUNT

Register	Prior to Issuing INT 67H: High	Prior to Issuing INT 67H: Low	Upon Return from INT 67H: High	Upon Return from INT 67H: Low
AX	4BH		Status*	
BX			Number of handles†	
CX				
DX				
SP				
BP				
SI				
DI				
IP				
flags				
CS				
DS				
SS				
ES				

*00=no error (otherwise see 5.185. INT 67H, Expanded Memory Manager Error Codes)
†Only if AH=0; If BX = 0, EMM is idle (not in use); never greater than 255.

Source: Advanced MS-DOS Programming 2nd Ed. (Microsoft Press), pages 621 through 622
MS-DOS Extensions (Microsoft Press), page 38
Expanded Memory Specification Version 4.0 (Intel), pages 3-25 through 3-26

See Also: 5.120. INT 67H, Expanded Memory Manager Functions Summary
5.185. INT 67H, Expanded Memory Manager Error Codes

5.131. INT 67H, AH=4CH -- GET PAGE COUNT FOR HANDLE

Prior to Issuing INT 67H

	High	Low
AX	4CH	
BX		
CX		
DX	EMM page handle	
SP		
BP		
SI		
DI		
IP		
flags		
CS		
DS		
SS		
ES		

Upon Return from INT 67H

	High	Low
AX	Status*	
BX	Number of pages†	
CX		
DX		
SP		
BP		
SI		
DI		
IP		
flags		
CS		
DS		
SS		
ES		

*00=no error (otherwise see 5.185. INT 67H, Expanded Memory Manager Error Codes)
†Only if AH=0; logical pages in range of 1 through 512 (version 3), 0 through 2048 (version 4).

Source: Advanced MS-DOS Programming 2nd Ed. (Microsoft Press), page 622
MS-DOS Extensions (Microsoft Press), page 39
Expanded Memory Specification Version 4.0 (Intel), pages 3-27 through 3-28

See Also: 5.120. INT 67H, Expanded Memory Manager Functions Summary
5.185. INT 67H, Expanded Memory Manager Error Codes

5.132. INT 67H, AH=4DH -- GET PAGE COUNTS FOR ALL HANDLES

Prior to Issuing INT 67H

	High	Low
AX	4DH	
BX		
CX		
DX		
SP		
BP		
SI		
DI	Offset of pointer to empty array	
IP		
flags		
CS		
DS		
SS		
ES	Segment of pointer to empty array	

Upon Return from INT 67H

	High	Low
AX	Status*	
BX	Number of handles†	
CX		
DX		
SP		
BP		
SI		
DI	Offset of pointer to filled array (if AH=0)	
IP		
flags		
CS		
DS		
SS		
ES	Segment of pointer to filled array (if AH=0)	

*00=no error (otherwise see 5.185. INT 67H, Expanded Memory Manager Error Codes)
†Only if AH=0; values range between 0 and 255.

Note: Array is a 1024-byte area which will be filled with two words for each handle being used (first word is handle number, second is number of pages associated with it).

Source: Advanced MS-DOS Programming 2nd Ed. (Microsoft Press), page 623
MS-DOS Extensions (Microsoft Press), pages 39 through 40
Expanded Memory Specification Version 4.0 (Intel), pages 3-29 through 3-30

See Also: 5.120. INT 67H, Expanded Memory Manager Functions Summary
5.131. INT 67H, AH=4CH -- Get Page Count for Handle
5.185. INT 67H, Expanded Memory Manager Error Codes

5.133. INT 67H, AH=4EH, AL=00H -- GET PAGE MAP

Register	Prior to Issuing INT 67H (High)	Prior to Issuing INT 67H (Low)	Upon Return from INT 67H (High)	Upon Return from INT 67H (Low)
AX	4EH	00H	Status*	
BX				
CX				
DX				
SP				
BP				
SI				
DI	Offset of pointer to empty array		Offset of pointer to filled array (if AH=0)	
IP				
flags				
CS				
DS				
SS				
ES	Segment of pointer to empty array		Segment of pointer to filled array (if AH=0)	

*00=no error (otherwise see 5.185. INT 67H, Expanded Memory Manager Error Codes)

Version: Added to EMM beginning with version 3.2.

Note:
- Array is a reserved area which will be filled with two words for each handle being used (first word is handle number, second is number of pages associated with it).
- Find size of array by using Function 4EH, AL=03H.

Source:
Advanced MS-DOS Programming 2nd Ed. (Microsoft Press), pages 623 through 624
MS-DOS Extensions (Microsoft Press), page 40
Expanded Memory Specification Version 4.0 (Intel), pages 3-31 through 3-32

See Also:
5.120. INT 67H, Expanded Memory Manager Functions Summary
5.136. INT 67H, AH=4EH, AL=03H -- Get Page Map Array Size
5.185. INT 67H, Expanded Memory Manager Error Codes

5.134. INT 67H, AH=4EH, AL=01H -- SET PAGE MAP

Register	Prior to Issuing INT 67H (High)	Prior to Issuing INT 67H (Low)	Upon Return from INT 67H (High)	Upon Return from INT 67H (Low)
AX	4EH	01H	Status*	
BX				
CX				
DX				
SP				
BP				
SI	Offset of pointer to page map array			
DI				
IP				
flags				
CS				
DS	Segment of pointer to page map array			
SS				
ES				

*00=no error (otherwise see 5.185. INT 67H, Expanded Memory Manager Error Codes)

Version: Added to EMM beginning with version 3.2.

Note: Array is state of mapping registers previously obtained by a call to Function 4EH, 00H or 4EH, 02H.

Source:
Advanced MS-DOS Programming 2nd Ed. (Microsoft Press), page 624
MS-DOS Extensions (Microsoft Press), page 41
Expanded Memory Specification Version 4.0 (Intel), pages 3-33 through 3-34

See Also:
5.120. INT 67H, Expanded Memory Manager Functions Summary
5.133. INT 67H, AH=4EH, AL=00H -- Get Page Map
5.135. INT 67H, AH=4EH, AL=02H -- Swap Page Map
5.185. INT 67H, Expanded Memory Manager Error Codes

5.135. INT 67H, AH=4EH, AL=02H -- SWAP PAGE MAP

Prior to Issuing INT 67H

Register	High	Low
AX	4EH	02H
BX		
CX		
DX		
SP		
BP		
SI	Offset of pointer to new page map array	
DI	Offset of pointer to prev. page map array	
IP		
flags		
CS		
DS	Segment of pointer to new page map array	
SS		
ES	Segment of pointer to prev. page map array	

Upon Return from INT 67H

Register	High	Low
AX	Status*	
BX		
CX		
DX		
SP		
BP		
SI		
DI	Offset of pointer to filled in page map array (if AH=0)	
IP		
flags		
CS		
DS		
SS		
ES	Segment of pointer to filled in page map array (if AH=0)	

*00=no error (otherwise see 5.185. INT 67H, Expanded Memory Manager Error Codes)

Version: Added to EMM beginning with version 3.2.

Note:
- New page map array contains information to swap into the previous page map array.
- Determine size of arrays by using Function 4EH, 03H.

Source:
Advanced MS-DOS Programming 2nd Ed. (Microsoft Press), pages 624 through 625
MS-DOS Extensions (Microsoft Press), pages 41 through 42
Expanded Memory Specification Version 4.0 (Intel), pages 3-35 through 3-36

See Also:
5.120. INT 67H, Expanded Memory Manager Functions Summary
5.136. INT 67H, AH=4EH, AL=03H -- Get Page Map Array Size
5.185. INT 67H, Expanded Memory Manager Error Codes

5.136. INT 67H, AH=4EH, AL=03H -- GET PAGE MAP ARRAY SIZE

Prior to Issuing INT 67H

Register	High	Low
AX	4EH	03H
BX		
CX		
DX		
SP		
BP		
SI		
DI		
IP		
flags		
CS		
DS		
SS		
ES		

Upon Return from INT 67H

Register	High	Low
AX	Status*	Size†
BX		
CX		
DX		
SP		
BP		
SI		
DI		
IP		
flags		
CS		
DS		
SS		
ES		

*00=no error (otherwise see 5.185. INT 67H, Expanded Memory Manager Error Codes)
†Size is in bytes and represents size of current page map array.

Version: Added to EMM beginning with version 3.2.

Source:
Advanced MS-DOS Programming 2nd Ed. (Microsoft Press), page 625
MS-DOS Extensions (Microsoft Press), page 42
Expanded Memory Specification Version 4.0 (Intel), pages 3-37 through 3-38

See Also:
5.120. INT 67H, Expanded Memory Manager Functions Summary
5.185. INT 67H, Expanded Memory Manager Error Codes

5.137. INT 67H, AH=4FH, AL=00H -- SAVE PARTIAL PAGE MAP

Prior to Issuing INT 67H

	High	Low
AX	4FH	00H
BX		
CX		
DX		
SP		
BP		
SI	Offset of pointer to map list	
DI	Offset of pointer to map state buffer	
IP		
flags		
CS		
DS	Segment of pointer to map list	
SS		
ES	Segment of pointer to map state buffer	

Upon Return from INT 67H

	High	Low
AX	Status*	
BX		
CX		
DX		
SP		
BP		
SI		
DI	Offset of pointer to filled in buffer (if AH=0)	
IP		
flags		
CS		
DS		
SS		
ES	Segment of pointer to filled in buffer (if AH=0)	

*00=no error (otherwise see 5.185. INT 67H, Expanded Memory Manager Error Codes)

Version: Added to EMM beginning with version 4.0.

Note: Determine size of map state buffer using Function 4FH, 02H.

Source: Advanced MS-DOS Programming 2nd Ed. (Microsoft Press), pages 625 through 626
MS-DOS Extensions (Microsoft Press), page 43
Expanded Memory Specification Version 4.0 (Intel), pages 3-39 through 3-41

See Also: 5.120. INT 67H, Expanded Memory Manager Functions Summary
5.139. INT 67H, AH=4FH, AL=02H -- Get Size of Partial Page Map Information
5.185. INT 67H, Expanded Memory Manager Error Codes

5.138. INT 67H, AH=4FH, AL=01H -- RESTORE PARTIAL PAGE MAP

Prior to Issuing INT 67H

	High	Low
AX	4FH	01H
BX		
CX		
DX		
SP		
BP		
SI	Offset of pointer to page map buffer	
DI		
IP		
flags		
CS		
DS	Segment of pointer to page map buffer	
SS		
ES		

Upon Return from INT 67H

	High	Low
AX	Status*	
BX		
CX		
DX		
SP		
BP		
SI		
DI		
IP		
flags		
CS		
DS		
SS		
ES		

*00=no error (otherwise see 5.185. INT 67H, Expanded Memory Manager Error Codes)

Version: Added to EMM beginning with version 4.0.

Note: Determine size of map state buffer using Function 4FH, 02H.

Source: Advanced MS-DOS Programming 2nd Ed. (Microsoft Press), page 626
MS-DOS Extensions (Microsoft Press), pages 43 through 44
Expanded Memory Specification Version 4.0 (Intel), pages 3-42 through 3-43

See Also: 5.120. INT 67H, Expanded Memory Manager Functions Summary
5.139. INT 67H, AH=4FH, AL=02H -- Get Size of Partial Page Map Information
5.185. INT 67H, Expanded Memory Manager Error Codes

5.139. INT 67H, AH=4FH, AL=02H -- GET SIZE OF PARTIAL PAGE MAP INFORMATION

Prior to Issuing INT 67H

Register	High	Low
AX	4FH	02H
BX	Number of pages	
CX		
DX		
SP		
BP		
SI		
DI		
IP		
flags		
CS		
DS		
SS		
ES		

Upon Return from INT 67H

Register	High	Low
AX	Status*	Size of array†
BX		
CX		
DX		
SP		
BP		
SI		
DI		
IP		
flags		
CS		
DS		
SS		
ES		

*00=no error (otherwise see 5.185. INT 67H, Expanded Memory Manager Error Codes)
†In bytes

Version: Added to EMM beginning with version 4.0.

Source: Advanced MS-DOS Programming 2nd Ed. (Microsoft Press), pages 626 through 627
MS-DOS Extensions (Microsoft Press), page 44
Expanded Memory Specification Version 4.0 (Intel), pages 3-44 through 3-45

See Also: 5.120. INT 67H, Expanded Memory Manager Functions Summary
5.185. INT 67H, Expanded Memory Manager Error Codes

5.140. INT 67H, AH=50H, AL=00H -- MAP MULTIPLE PAGES BY NUMBER

Prior to Issuing INT 67H

Register	High	Low
AX	50H	00H
BX		
CX	Number of pages	
DX	EMM page handle	
SP		
BP		
SI	Offset of pointer to buffer	
DI		
IP		
flags		
CS		
DS	Segment of pointer to buffer	
SS		
ES		

Upon Return from INT 67H

Register	High	Low
AX	Status*	
BX		
CX		
DX		
SP		
BP		
SI		
DI		
IP		
flags		
CS		
DS		
SS		
ES		

*00=no error (otherwise see 5.185. INT 67H, Expanded Memory Manager Error Codes)

Version: Added to EMM beginning with version 4.0.

Note: Buffer contains dbl word entries for pages to be mapped (first word of each entry is logical EMM page number, second word of each entry is physical page number).

Source: Advanced MS-DOS Programming 2nd Ed. (Microsoft Press), page 627
MS-DOS Extensions (Microsoft Press), pages 44 through 45
Expanded Memory Specification Version 4.0 (Intel), pages 3-48 through 3-50

See Also: 5.120. INT 67H, Expanded Memory Manager Functions Summary
5.185. INT 67H, Expanded Memory Manager Error Codes

5.141. INT 67H, AH=50H, AL=01H -- MAP MULTIPLE PAGES BY ADDRESS

Prior to Issuing INT 67H

Register	High	Low
AX	50H	01H
BX		
CX	Number of pages	
DX	EMM page handle	
SP		
BP		
SI	Offset of pointer to buffer	
DI		
IP		
flags		
CS		
DS	Segment of pointer to buffer	
SS		
ES		

Upon Return from INT 67H

Register	High	Low
AX	Status*	
BX		
CX		
DX		
SP		
BP		
SI		
DI		
IP		
flags		
CS		
DS		
SS		
ES		

*00=no error (otherwise see 5.185. INT 67H, Expanded Memory Manager Error Codes)

Version: Added to EMM beginning with version 4.0.

Note: Buffer contains dbl word entries for pages to be mapped (first word of each entry is logical EMM page number, second word of each entry is physical page number).

Source: Advanced MS-DOS Programming 2nd Ed. (Microsoft Press), pages 627 through 628
MS-DOS Extensions (Microsoft Press), pages 45 through 46
Expanded Memory Specification Version 4.0 (Intel), pages 3-51 through 3-53

See Also: 5.120. INT 67H, Expanded Memory Manager Functions Summary
5.140. INT 67H, AH=50H, AL=00H -- Map Multiple Pages by Number
5.185. INT 67H, Expanded Memory Manager Error Codes

5.142. INT 67H, AH=51H -- REALLOCATE PAGES FOR HANDLE

Prior to Issuing INT 67H

Register	High	Low
AX	51H	
BX	New number of pages	
CX		
DX	EMM page handle	
SP		
BP		
SI		
DI		
IP		
flags		
CS		
DS		
SS		
ES		

Upon Return from INT 67H

Register	High	Low
AX	Status*	
BX	Number of pages	
CX		
DX		
SP		
BP		
SI		
DI		
IP		
flags		
CS		
DS		
SS		
ES		

*00=no error (otherwise see 5.185. INT 67H, Expanded Memory Manager Error Codes)

Version: Added to EMM beginning with version 4.0.

Source: Advanced MS-DOS Programming 2nd Ed. (Microsoft Press), page 628
MS-DOS Extensions (Microsoft Press), page 46
Expanded Memory Specification Version 4.0 (Intel), pages 3-55 through 3-56

See Also: 5.120. INT 67H, Expanded Memory Manager Functions Summary
5.185. INT 67H, Expanded Memory Manager Error Codes

5.143. INT 67H, AH=52H, AL=00H -- GET HANDLE ATTRIBUTE

Prior to Issuing INT 67H

	High	Low
AX	52H	00H
BX		
CX		
DX	EMM page handle	
SP		
BP		
SI		
DI		
IP		
flags		
CS		
DS		
SS		
ES		

Upon Return from INT 67H

	High	Low
AX	Status*	Attribute†
BX		
CX		
DX		
SP		
BP		
SI		
DI		
IP		
flags		
CS		
DS		
SS		
ES		

*00=no error (otherwise see 5.185. INT 67H, Expanded Memory Manager Error Codes)
†00H=volatile, 01H=non-volatile

Version: Added to EMM beginning with version 4.0.

Source: Advanced MS-DOS Programming 2nd Ed. (Microsoft Press), page 629
MS-DOS Extensions (Microsoft Press), page 47
Expanded Memory Specification Version 4.0 (Intel), pages 3-58 through 3-59

See Also: 5.120. INT 67H, Expanded Memory Manager Functions Summary
5.144. INT 67H, AH=52H, AL=01H -- Set Handle Attribute
5.185. INT 67H, Expanded Memory Manager Error Codes

5.144. INT 67H, AH=52H, AL=01H -- SET HANDLE ATTRIBUTE

Prior to Issuing INT 67H

	High	Low
AX	52H	00H
BX		Attribute†
CX		
DX	EMM page handle	
SP		
BP		
SI		
DI		
IP		
flags		
CS		
DS		
SS		
ES		

Upon Return from INT 67H

	High	Low
AX	Status*	
BX		
CX		
DX		
SP		
BP		
SI		
DI		
IP		
flags		
CS		
DS		
SS		
ES		

*00=no error (otherwise see 5.185. INT 67H, Expanded Memory Manager Error Codes)
†00H=volatile, 01H=non-volatile

Note: Use Function 52H, 02H to determine if hardware can support non-volatile pages.

Version: Added to EMM beginning with version 4.0.

Source: Advanced MS-DOS Programming 2nd Ed. (Microsoft Press), page 629
MS-DOS Extensions (Microsoft Press), pages 47 through 48
Expanded Memory Specification Version 4.0 (Intel), pages 3-60 through 3-61

See Also: 5.120. INT 67H, Expanded Memory Manager Functions Summary
5.143. INT 67H, AH=52H, AL=00H -- Get Handle Attribute
5.145. INT 67H, AH=52H, AL=02H -- Get Attribute Capability
5.185. INT 67H, Expanded Memory Manager Error Codes

5.145. INT 67H, AH=52H, AL=02H -- GET ATTRIBUTE CAPABILITY

Prior to Issuing INT 67H

	High	*Low*
AX	52H	02H
BX		
CX		
DX		
SP		
BP		
SI		
DI		
IP		
flags		
CS		
DS		
SS		
ES		

Upon Return from INT 67H

	High	*Low*
AX	Status*	Capability†
BX		
CX		
DX		
SP		
BP		
SI		
DI		
IP		
flags		
CS		
DS		
SS		
ES		

*00=no error (otherwise see 5.185. INT 67H, Expanded Memory Manager Error Codes)
†00H=volatile, 01H=non-volatile

Version: Added to EMM beginning with version 4.0.

Source: Advanced MS-DOS Programming 2nd Ed. (Microsoft Press), page 630
MS-DOS Extensions (Microsoft Press), page 48
Expanded Memory Specification Version 4.0 (Intel), pages 3-62 through 3-63

See Also: 5.120. INT 67H, Expanded Memory Manager Functions Summary
5.143. INT 67H, AH=52H, AL=00H -- Get Handle Attribute
5.144. INT 67H, AH=52H, AL=01H -- Set Handle Attribute
5.185. INT 67H, Expanded Memory Manager Error Codes

5.146. INT 67H, AH=53H, AL=00H -- GET HANDLE NAME

Prior to Issuing INT 67H

	High	*Low*
AX	53H	00H
BX		
CX		
DX	EMM page handle	
SP		
BP		
SI		
DI	Offset of pointer to 8-byte name buffer	
IP		
flags		
CS		
DS		
SS		
ES	Segment of pointer to 8-byte name buffer	

Upon Return from INT 67H

	High	*Low*
AX	Status*	
BX		
CX		
DX		
SP		
BP		
SI		
DI	Offset of filled in name buffer	
IP		
flags		
CS		
DS		
SS		
ES	Segment of filled in name buffer	

*00=no error (otherwise see 5.185. INT 67H, Expanded Memory Manager Error Codes)

Version: Added to EMM beginning with version 4.0.

Source: Advanced MS-DOS Programming 2nd Ed. (Microsoft Press), page 630
MS-DOS Extensions (Microsoft Press), pages 48 through 49
Expanded Memory Specification Version 4.0 (Intel), pages 3-64 through 3-65

See Also: 5.120. INT 67H, Expanded Memory Manager Functions Summary
5.147. INT 67H, AH=53H, AL=01H -- Set Handle Name
5.148. INT 67H, AH=54H, AL=00H -- Get All Handle Names
5.185. INT 67H, Expanded Memory Manager Error Codes

5.147. INT 67H, AH=53H, AL=01H -- SET HANDLE NAME

Prior to Issuing INT 67H

Register	High	Low
AX	53H	01H
BX		
CX		
DX	EMM page handle	
SP		
BP		
SI		
DI	Offset of pointer to 8-byte name buffer	
IP		
flags		
CS		
DS		
SS		
ES	Segment of pointer to 8-byte name buffer	

Upon Return from INT 67H

Register	High	Low
AX	Status*	
BX		
CX		
DX		
SP		
BP		
SI		
DI		
IP		
flags		
CS		
DS		
SS		
ES		

*00=no error (otherwise see 5.185. INT 67H, Expanded Memory Manager Error Codes)

Version: Added to EMM beginning with version 4.0.

Note: Handle name may be any 8 characters other than 8 zeroes (RESERVED).

Source:
Advanced MS-DOS Programming 2nd Ed. (Microsoft Press), page 631
MS-DOS Extensions (Microsoft Press), pages 49 through 50
Expanded Memory Specification Version 4.0 (Intel), pages 3-66 through 3-67

See Also:
5.120. INT 67H, Expanded Memory Manager Functions Summary
5.146. INT 67H, AH=53H, AL=00H -- Get Handle Name
5.148. INT 67H, AH=54H, AL=00H -- Get All Handle Names
5.185. INT 67H, Expanded Memory Manager Error Codes

5.148. INT 67H, AH=54H, AL=00H -- GET ALL HANDLE NAMES

Prior to Issuing INT 67H

Register	High	Low
AX	54H	00H
BX		
CX		
DX		
SP		
BP		
SI		
DI	Offset of pointer to name buffer†	
IP		
flags		
CS		
DS		
SS		
ES	Segment of pointer to name buffer†	

Upon Return from INT 67H

Register	High	Low
AX	Status*	Number active handles
BX		
CX		
DX		
SP		
BP		
SI		
DI	Offset to filled in name buffer (if AH=0)	
IP		
flags		
CS		
DS		
SS		
ES	Segment of filled in name buffer (if AH=0)	

*00=no error (otherwise see 5.185. INT 67H, Expanded Memory Manager Error Codes)
†Name buffer consists of series of 10-byte entries:
First word = EMM handle
Next 8 bytes = handle name

Version: Added to EMM beginning with version 4.0.

Source:
Advanced MS-DOS Programming 2nd Ed. (Microsoft Press), pages 631 through 632
MS-DOS Extensions (Microsoft Press), page 50
Expanded Memory Specification Version 4.0 (Intel), pages 3-68 through 3-70

See Also:
5.120. INT 67H, Expanded Memory Manager Functions Summary
5.146. INT 67H, AH=53H, AL=00H -- Get Handle Name
5.147. INT 67H, AH=53H, AL=01H -- Set Handle Name
5.185. INT 67H, Expanded Memory Manager Error Codes

5.149. INT 67H, AH=54H, AL=01H -- SEARCH FOR HANDLE NAME

Prior to Issuing INT 67H

	High	Low
AX	54H	01H
BX		
CX		
DX		
SP		
BP		
SI		
DI	Offset of pointer to 8-byte name	
IP		
flags		
CS		
DS		
SS		
ES	Segment of pointer to 8-byte name	

Upon Return from INT 67H

	High	Low
AX	Status*	
BX		
CX		
DX	EMM page handle	
SP		
BP		
SI		
DI		
IP		
flags		
CS		
DS		
SS		
ES		

*00=no error (otherwise see 5.185. INT 67H, Expanded Memory Manager Error Codes)

Version: Added to EMM beginning with version 4.0.

Source: Advanced MS-DOS Programming 2nd Ed. (Microsoft Press), page 632
MS-DOS Extensions (Microsoft Press), page 51
Expanded Memory Specification Version 4.0 (Intel), pages 3-71 through 3-72

See Also: 5.120. INT 67H, Expanded Memory Manager Functions Summary
5.185. INT 67H, Expanded Memory Manager Error Codes

5.150. INT 67H, AH=54H, AL=02H -- GET TOTAL HANDLES

Prior to Issuing INT 67H

	High	Low
AX	54H	02H
BX		
CX		
DX		
SP		
BP		
SI		
DI		
IP		
flags		
CS		
DS		
SS		
ES		

Upon Return from INT 67H

	High	Low
AX	Status*	
BX	Number of handles	
CX		
DX		
SP		
BP		
SI		
DI		
IP		
flags		
CS		
DS		
SS		
ES		

*00=no error (otherwise see 5.185. INT 67H, Expanded Memory Manager Error Codes)

Version: Added to EMM beginning with version 4.0.

Source: Advanced MS-DOS Programming 2nd Ed. (Microsoft Press), page 632
MS-DOS Extensions (Microsoft Press), page 51
Expanded Memory Specification Version 4.0 (Intel), pages 3-73 through 3-74

See Also: 5.120. INT 67H, Expanded Memory Manager Functions Summary
5.146. INT 67H, AH=53H, AL=00H -- Get Handle Name
5.147. INT 67H, AH=53H, AL=01H -- Set Handle Name
5.185. INT 67H, Expanded Memory Manager Error Codes

5.151. INT 67H, AH=55H -- MAP PAGES AND JUMP

Prior to Issuing INT 67H

	High	Low
AX	55H	Function†
BX		
CX		
DX	EMM page handle	
SP		
BP		
SI	Offset of pointer to buffer§	
DI		
IP		
flags		
CS		
DS	Segment of pointer to buffer§	
SS		
ES		

Upon Return from INT 67H

	High	Low
AX	Status*	
BX		
CX		
DX		
SP		
BP		
SI		
DI		
IP		
flags		
CS		
DS		
SS		
ES		

*00=no error (otherwise see 5.185. INT 67H, Expanded Memory Manager Error Codes)
†00H=map using page numbers; 01H=map using page segments
§Buffer contains following information:
dbl word=far pointer to jump target
byte=number of pages to map before jump
dbl word=far pointer to map list

Version: Added to EMM beginning with version 4.0.

Source: Advanced MS-DOS Programming 2nd Ed. (Microsoft Press), page 633
MS-DOS Extensions (Microsoft Press), page 52
Expanded Memory Specification Version 4.0 (Intel), pages 3-75 through 3-77

See Also: 5.120. INT 67H, Expanded Memory Manager Functions Summary
5.185. INT 67H, Expanded Memory Manager Error Codes

5.152. INT 67H, AH=56H, AL=00,01H -- MAP PAGES AND CALL

Prior to Issuing INT 67H

	High	Low
AX	56H	Function†
BX		
CX		
DX	EMM page handle	
SP		
BP		
SI	Offset of pointer to buffer§	
DI		
IP		
flags		
CS		
DS	Segment of pointer to buffer§	
SS		
ES		

Upon Return from INT 67H

	High	Low
AX	Status*	
BX		
CX		
DX		
SP		
BP		
SI		
DI		
IP		
flags		
CS		
DS		
SS		
ES		

*00=no error (otherwise see 5.185. INT 67H, Expanded Memory Manager Error Codes)
†00H=map using page numbers; 01H=map using page segments
§Buffer contains following information:
dbl word=far pointer to call target
byte=number of pages to map before call
dbl word=far pointer to list of pages to map before call
byte=number of pages to map before return
dbl word=far pointer to list of pages to map before return
8 bytes=RESERVED (set to 0)

Version: Added to EMM beginning with version 4.0.

Source: Advanced MS-DOS Programming 2nd Ed. (Microsoft Press), pages 633 through 634
MS-DOS Extensions (Microsoft Press), pages 53 through 54
Expanded Memory Specification Version 4.0 (Intel), pages 3-79 through 3-83

See Also: 5.120. INT 67H, Expanded Memory Manager Functions Summary
5.185. INT 67H, Expanded Memory Manager Error Codes

5.153. INT 67H, AH=56H, AL=02H -- GET STACK SPACE FOR MAP PAGE AND CALL

Prior to Issuing INT 67H

	High	Low
AX	56H	02H
BX		
CX		
DX		
SP		
BP		
SI		
DI		
IP		
flags		
CS		
DS		
SS		
ES		

Upon Return from INT 67H

	High	Low
AX	Status*	
BX	Space required†	
CX		
DX		
SP		
BP		
SI		
DI		
IP		
flags		
CS		
DS		
SS		
ES		

*00=no error (otherwise see 5.185. INT 67H, Expanded Memory Manager Error Codes)
†In bytes

Version: Added to EMM beginning with version 4.0.

Source: Advanced MS-DOS Programming 2nd Ed. (Microsoft Press), page 634
MS-DOS Extensions (Microsoft Press), page 54
Expanded Memory Specification Version 4.0 (Intel), pages 3-84 through 3-85

See Also: 5.120. INT 67H, Expanded Memory Manager Functions Summary
5.185. INT 67H, Expanded Memory Manager Error Codes

5.154. INT 67H, AH=57H, AL=00H -- MOVE MEMORY REGION

Prior to Issuing INT 67H

	High	Low
AX	57H	00H
BX		
CX		
DX		
SP		
BP		
SI	Offset of pointer to buffer†	
DI		
IP		
flags		
CS		
DS	Segment of pointer to buffer†	
SS		
ES		

Upon Return from INT 67H

	High	Low
AX	Status*	
BX		
CX		
DX		
SP		
BP		
SI		
DI		
IP		
flags		
CS		
DS		
SS		
ES		

*00=no error (otherwise see 5.185. INT 67H, Expanded Memory Manager Error Codes)
†Buffer formatted as follows:
dbl word=region length in bytes
byte=source memory type (00H for conventional memory, 01H for expanded memory)
word=source memory handle
word=source memory offset
word=source memory segment or logical page number
byte=target memory type (00H for conventional memory, 01H for expanded memory)
word=target memory handle
word=target memory offset
word=target memory segment or logical page number

Version: Added to EMM beginning with version 4.0.

Source: Advanced MS-DOS Programming 2nd Ed. (Microsoft Press), page 635
MS-DOS Extensions (Microsoft Press), pages 54 through 55
Expanded Memory Specification Version 4.0 (Intel), pages 3-86 through 3-91

See Also: 5.120. INT 67H, Expanded Memory Manager Functions Summary
5.185. INT 67H, Expanded Memory Manager Error Codes

5.155. INT 67H, AH=57H, AL=01H -- EXCHANGE MEMORY REGIONS

Prior to Issuing INT 67H

	High	Low
AX	57H	01H
BX		
CX		
DX		
SP		
BP		
SI	Offset of pointer to buffer†	
DI		
IP		
flags		
CS		
DS	Segment of pointer to buffer†	
SS		
ES		

Upon Return from INT 67H

	High	Low
AX	Status*	
BX		
CX		
DX		
SP		
BP		
SI		
DI		
IP		
flags		
CS		
DS		
SS		
ES		

*00=no error (otherwise see 5.185. INT 67H, Expanded Memory Manager Error Codes)
†Buffer formatted as follows:
dbl word=region length in bytes
byte=source memory type (00H for conventional memory, 01H for expanded memory)
word=source memory handle
word=source memory offset
word=source memory segment or logical page number
byte=target memory type (00H for conventional memory, 01H for expanded memory)
word=target memory handle
word=target memory offset
word=target memory segment or logical page number

Version: Added to EMM beginning with version 4.0.

Source: Advanced MS-DOS Programming 2nd Ed. (Microsoft Press), pages 635 through 636
MS-DOS Extensions (Microsoft Press), pages 55 through 56
Expanded Memory Specification Version 4.0 (Intel), pages 3-92 through 3-97

See Also: 5.120. INT 67H, Expanded Memory Manager Functions Summary
5.185. INT 67H, Expanded Memory Manager Error Codes

5.156. INT 67H, AH=58H, AL=00H -- GET ADDRESSES OF MAPPABLE PAGES

Prior to Issuing INT 67H

	High	Low
AX	58H	00H
BX		
CX		
DX		
SP		
BP		
SI		
DI	Offset of pointer to buffer†	
IP		
flags		
CS		
DS		
SS		
ES	Segment of pointer to buffer†	

Upon Return from INT 67H

	High	Low
AX	Status*	
BX		
CX	Number of entries	
DX		
SP		
BP		
SI		
DI	Offset of pointer to filled in buffer	
IP		
flags		
CS		
DS		
SS		
ES	Segment of pointer to filled in buffer	

*00=no error (otherwise see 5.185. INT 67H, Expanded Memory Manager Error Codes)
†Buffer formatted as series of double-word entries:
First dbl word=page's segment base address
Second dbl word=physical page number

Version: Added to EMM beginning with version 4.0.

Source: Advanced MS-DOS Programming 2nd Ed. (Microsoft Press), pages 636 through 637
MS-DOS Extensions (Microsoft Press), pages 56 through 57
Expanded Memory Specification Version 4.0 (Intel), pages 3-98 through 3-100

See Also: 5.120. INT 67H, Expanded Memory Manager Functions Summary
5.185. INT 67H, Expanded Memory Manager Error Codes

5.157. INT 67H, AH=58H, AL=01H -- GET NUMBER OF MAPPABLE PAGES

Prior to Issuing INT 67H

	High	Low
AX	58H	01H
BX		
CX		
DX		
SP		
BP		
SI		
DI		
IP		
flags		
CS		
DS		
SS		
ES		

Upon Return from INT 67H

	High	Low
AX	Status*	
BX		
CX	Number of pages (if AH=0)	
DX		
SP		
BP		
SI		
DI		
IP		
flags		
CS		
DS		
SS		
ES		

*00=no error (otherwise see 5.185. INT 67H, Expanded Memory Manager Error Codes)

Version: Added to EMM beginning with version 4.0.

Source: Advanced MS-DOS Programming 2nd Ed. (Microsoft Press), page 637
MS-DOS Extensions (Microsoft Press), page 57
Expanded Memory Specification Version 4.0 (Intel), pages 3-101 through 3-102

See Also: 5.120. INT 67H, Expanded Memory Manager Functions Summary
5.185. INT 67H, Expanded Memory Manager Error Codes

5.158. INT 67H, AH=59H, AL=00H -- GET HARDWARE CONFIGURATION

Prior to Issuing INT 67H

Register	High	Low
AX	59H	00H
BX		
CX		
DX		
SP		
BP		
SI		
DI	Offset of pointer to buffer†	
IP		
flags		
CS		
DS		
SS		
ES	Segment of pointer to buffer†	

Upon Return from INT 67H

Register	High	Low
AX	Status*	
BX		
CX		
DX		
SP		
BP		
SI		
DI	Offset of pointer to filled in buffer (if AH=0)	
IP		
flags		
CS		
DS		
SS		
ES	Segment of pointer to filled in buffer (if AH=0)	

*00=no error (otherwise see 5.185. INT 67H, Expanded Memory Manager Error Codes)
†Buffer formatted as follows:
word=size of raw EMM pages (in paragraphs)
word=number of alternate register sets
word=size of mapping-context save area (in bytes)
word=number of register sets that can be assigned
word=DMA operation type (0=DMA with alt register sets; 1=only one DMA register set)

Version: Added to EMM beginning with version 4.0.

Source: Advanced MS-DOS Programming 2nd Ed. (Microsoft Press), pages 637 through 638
MS-DOS Extensions (Microsoft Press), pages 57 through 58
Expanded Memory Specification Version 4.0 (Intel), pages 3-103 through 3-106

See Also: 5.120. INT 67H, Expanded Memory Manager Functions Summary
5.185. INT 67H, Expanded Memory Manager Error Codes

5.159. INT 67H, AH=59H, AL=01H -- GET NUMBER OF RAW PAGES

Prior to Issuing INT 67H

Register	High	Low
AX	59H	01H
BX		
CX		
DX		
SP		
BP		
SI		
DI		
IP		
flags		
CS		
DS		
SS		
ES		

Upon Return from INT 67H

Register	High	Low
AX	Status*	
BX	Unallocated raw pages (if AH=0)	
CX	Total raw pages (if AH=0)	
DX		
SP		
BP		
SI		
DI		
IP		
flags		
CS		
DS		
SS		
ES		

*00=no error (otherwise see 5.185. INT 67H, Expanded Memory Manager Error Codes)

Version: Added to EMM beginning with version 4.0.

Source: Advanced MS-DOS Programming 2nd Ed. (Microsoft Press), page 638
MS-DOS Extensions (Microsoft Press), pages 58 through 59
Expanded Memory Specification Version 4.0 (Intel), pages 3-107 through 3-108

See Also: 5.120. INT 67H, Expanded Memory Manager Functions Summary
5.185. INT 67H, Expanded Memory Manager Error Codes

5.160. INT 67H, AH=5AH, AL=00H -- ALLOCATE HANDLE AND STANDARD PAGES

Prior to Issuing INT 67H

	High	Low
AX	5AH	00H
BX	Number of standard pages	
CX		
DX		
SP		
BP		
SI		
DI		
IP		
flags		
CS		
DS		
SS		
ES		

Upon Return from INT 67H

	High	Low
AX	Status*	
BX		
CX		
DX	EMM page handle (if AH=0)	
SP		
BP		
SI		
DI		
IP		
flags		
CS		
DS		
SS		
ES		

*00=no error (otherwise see 5.185. INT 67H, Expanded Memory Manager Error Codes)

Version: Added to EMM beginning with version 4.0.

Source: Advanced MS-DOS Programming 2nd Ed. (Microsoft Press), pages 638 through 639
MS-DOS Extensions (Microsoft Press), page 59
Expanded Memory Specification Version 4.0 (Intel), pages 3-109 through 3-111

See Also: 5.120. INT 67H, Expanded Memory Manager Functions Summary
5.185. INT 67H, Expanded Memory Manager Error Codes

5.161. INT 67H, AH=5AH, AL=01H -- ALLOCATE HANDLE AND RAW PAGES

Prior to Issuing INT 67H

	High	Low
AX	5AH	01H
BX	Number of raw pages	
CX		
DX		
SP		
BP		
SI		
DI		
IP		
flags		
CS		
DS		
SS		
ES		

Upon Return from INT 67H

	High	Low
AX	Status*	
BX		
CX		
DX	EMM page handle (if AH=0)	
SP		
BP		
SI		
DI		
IP		
flags		
CS		
DS		
SS		
ES		

*00=no error (otherwise see 5.185. INT 67H, Expanded Memory Manager Error Codes)

Version: Added to EMM beginning with version 4.0.

Source: Advanced MS-DOS Programming 2nd Ed. (Microsoft Press), page 639
MS-DOS Extensions (Microsoft Press), page 60
Expanded Memory Specification Version 4.0 (Intel), pages 3-109 through 3-111

See Also: 5.120. INT 67H, Expanded Memory Manager Functions Summary
5.185. INT 67H, Expanded Memory Manager Error Codes

5.162. INT 67H, AH=5BH, AL=00H -- GET ALTERNATE MAP REGISTERS

Prior to Issuing INT 67H

Register	High	Low
AX	5BH	00H
BX		
CX		
DX		
SP		
BP		
SI		
DI		
IP		
flags		
CS		
DS		
SS		
ES		

Upon Return from INT 67H

Register	High	Low
AX	Status*	
BX		Current set number or set
CX		
DX		
SP		
BP		
SI		
DI	Offset of pointer to alt map register save area†	
IP		
flags		
CS		
DS		
SS		
ES	Segment of pointer to alt map register save area†	

*00=no error (otherwise see 5.185. INT 67H, Expanded Memory Manager Error Codes)
†Only if BL=0 (alt register set not active)

Version: Added to EMM beginning with version 4.0.

Note: This function is intended for operating system use only.

Source: Advanced MS-DOS Programming 2nd Ed. (Microsoft Press), pages 639 through 640
MS-DOS Extensions (Microsoft Press), pages 60 through 61
Expanded Memory Specification Version 4.0 (Intel), pages 3-114 through 3-116

See Also: 5.120. INT 67H, Expanded Memory Manager Functions Summary
5.185. INT 67H, Expanded Memory Manager Error Codes

5.163. INT 67H, AH=5BH, AL=01H -- SET ALTERNATE MAP REGISTERS

Prior to Issuing INT 67H

Register	High	Low
AX	5BH	01H
BX		Current set number or set
CX		
DX		
SP		
BP		
SI		
DI	Offset of pointer to alt map register save area†	
IP		
flags		
CS		
DS		
SS		
ES	Segment of pointer to alt map register save area†	

Upon Return from INT 67H

Register	High	Low
AX	Status*	
BX		
CX		
DX		
SP		
BP		
SI		
DI		
IP		
flags		
CS		
DS		
SS		
ES		

*00=no error (otherwise see 5.185. INT 67H, Expanded Memory Manager Error Codes)
†Only if BL=0 (alt register set not active)

Version: Added to EMM beginning with version 4.0.

Note: This function is intended for operating system use only.

Source: Advanced MS-DOS Programming 2nd Ed. (Microsoft Press), page 640
MS-DOS Extensions (Microsoft Press), pages 61 through 62
Expanded Memory Specification Version 4.0 (Intel), pages 3-117 through 3-119

See Also: 5.120. INT 67H, Expanded Memory Manager Functions Summary
5.185. INT 67H, Expanded Memory Manager Error Codes

5.164. INT 67H, AH=5BH, AL=02H -- GET SIZE OF ALTERNATE MAP REGISTER SAVE AREA

Prior to Issuing INT 67H

	High	Low
AX	5BH	02H
BX		
CX		
DX		
SP		
BP		
SI		
DI		
IP		
flags		
CS		
DS		
SS		
ES		

Upon Return from INT 67H

	High	Low
AX	Status*	
BX		
CX		
DX	Size of buffer (if AH=0)†	
SP		
BP		
SI		
DI		
IP		
flags		
CS		
DS		
SS		
ES		

*00=no error (otherwise see 5.185. INT 67H, Expanded Memory Manager Error Codes)
†In bytes

Version: Added to EMM beginning with version 4.0.

Note: This function is intended for operating system use only.

Source: Advanced MS-DOS Programming 2nd Ed. (Microsoft Press), page 641
MS-DOS Extensions (Microsoft Press), page 62
Expanded Memory Specification Version 4.0 (Intel), pages 3-120 through 3-121

See Also: 5.120. INT 67H, Expanded Memory Manager Functions Summary
5.185. INT 67H, Expanded Memory Manager Error Codes

5.165. INT 67H, AH=5BH, AL=03H -- ALLOCATE ALTERNATE MAP REGISTER SET

Prior to Issuing INT 67H

	High	Low
AX	5BH	03H
BX		
CX		
DX		
SP		
BP		
SI		
DI		
IP		
flags		
CS		
DS		
SS		
ES		

Upon Return from INT 67H

	High	Low
AX	Status*	
BX		Alt reg set number or 0
CX		
DX		
SP		
BP		
SI		
DI		
IP		
flags		
CS		
DS		
SS		
ES		

*00=no error (otherwise see 5.185. INT 67H, Expanded Memory Manager Error Codes)

Version: Added to EMM beginning with version 4.0.

Note: This function is intended for operating system use only.

Source: Advanced MS-DOS Programming 2nd Ed. (Microsoft Press), page 641
MS-DOS Extensions (Microsoft Press), pages 62 through 63
Expanded Memory Specification Version 4.0 (Intel), pages 3-122 through 3-124

See Also: 5.120. INT 67H, Expanded Memory Manager Functions Summary
5.185. INT 67H, Expanded Memory Manager Error Codes

5.166. INT 67H, AH=5BH, AL=04H -- DEALLOCATE ALTERNATE MAP REGISTER SET

Prior to Issuing INT 67H

	High	Low
AX	5BH	04H
BX		Alt reg set number or 0
CX		
DX		
SP		
BP		
SI		
DI		
IP		
flags		
CS		
DS		
SS		
ES		

Upon Return from INT 67H

	High	Low
AX	Status*	
BX		
CX		
DX		
SP		
BP		
SI		
DI		
IP		
flags		
CS		
DS		
SS		
ES		

*00=no error (otherwise see 5.185. INT 67H, Expanded Memory Manager Error Codes)

Version: Added to EMM beginning with version 4.0.

Note: This function is intended for operating system use only.

Source: Advanced MS-DOS Programming 2nd Ed. (Microsoft Press), page 642
MS-DOS Extensions (Microsoft Press), page 63
Expanded Memory Specification Version 4.0 (Intel), pages 3-125 through 3-126

See Also: 5.120. INT 67H, Expanded Memory Manager Functions Summary
5.185. INT 67H, Expanded Memory Manager Error Codes

5.167. INT 67H, AH=5BH, AL=05H -- ALLOCATE DMA REGISTER SET

Prior to Issuing INT 67H

	High	Low
AX	5BH	05H
BX		
CX		
DX		
SP		
BP		
SI		
DI		
IP		
flags		
CS		
DS		
SS		
ES		

Upon Return from INT 67H

	High	Low
AX	Status*	
BX		DMA set number or 0†
CX		
DX		
SP		
BP		
SI		
DI		
IP		
flags		
CS		
DS		
SS		
ES		

*00=no error (otherwise see 5.185. INT 67H, Expanded Memory Manager Error Codes)
†Only if AH=0 on return

Version: Added to EMM beginning with version 4.0.

Note: This function is intended for operating system use only.

Source: Advanced MS-DOS Programming 2nd Ed. (Microsoft Press), page 642
MS-DOS Extensions (Microsoft Press), page 64
Expanded Memory Specification Version 4.0 (Intel), pages 3-127 through 3-128

See Also: 5.120. INT 67H, Expanded Memory Manager Functions Summary
5.185. INT 67H, Expanded Memory Manager Error Codes

5.168. INT 67H, AH=5BH, AL=06H -- ENABLE DMA ON ALTERNATE MAP REGISTER SET

Prior to Issuing INT 67H

	High	Low
AX	5BH	06H
BX		Alt map register set
CX		
DX		DMA channel
SP		
BP		
SI		
DI		
IP		
flags		
CS		
DS		
SS		
ES		

Upon Return from INT 67H

	High	Low
AX	Status*	
BX		
CX		
DX		
SP		
BP		
SI		
DI		
IP		
flags		
CS		
DS		
SS		
ES		

*00=no error (otherwise see 5.185. INT 67H, Expanded Memory Manager Error Codes)

Version: Added to EMM beginning with version 4.0.

Note: This function is intended for operating system use only.

Source: Advanced MS-DOS Programming 2nd Ed. (Microsoft Press), page 643
MS-DOS Extensions (Microsoft Press), pages 64 through 65
Expanded Memory Specification Version 4.0 (Intel), pages 3-129 through 3-131

See Also: 5.120. INT 67H, Expanded Memory Manager Functions Summary
5.185. INT 67H, Expanded Memory Manager Error Codes

5.169. INT 67H, AH=5BH, AL=07H -- DISABLE DMA ON ALTERNATE MAP REGISTER SET

Prior to Issuing INT 67H

	High	Low
AX	5BH	07H
BX		Alt map register set
CX		
DX		
SP		
BP		
SI		
DI		
IP		
flags		
CS		
DS		
SS		
ES		

Upon Return from INT 67H

	High	Low
AX	Status*	
BX		
CX		
DX		
SP		
BP		
SI		
DI		
IP		
flags		
CS		
DS		
SS		
ES		

*00=no error (otherwise see 5.185. INT 67H, Expanded Memory Manager Error Codes)

Version: Added to EMM beginning with version 4.0.

Note: This function is intended for operating system use only.

Source: Advanced MS-DOS Programming 2nd Ed. (Microsoft Press), pages 643 through 644
MS-DOS Extensions (Microsoft Press), page 65
Expanded Memory Specification Version 4.0 (Intel), pages 3-132 through 3-133

See Also: 5.120. INT 67H, Expanded Memory Manager Functions Summary
5.185. INT 67H, Expanded Memory Manager Error Codes

5.170. INT 67H, AH=5BH, AL=08H -- DEALLOCATE DMA REGISTER SET

Prior to Issuing INT 67H

	High	Low
AX	5BH	08H
BX		DMA register set
CX		
DX		
SP		
BP		
SI		
DI		
IP		
flags		
CS		
DS		
SS		
ES		

Upon Return from INT 67H

	High	Low
AX	Status*	
BX		
CX		
DX		
SP		
BP		
SI		
DI		
IP		
flags		
CS		
DS		
SS		
ES		

*00=no error (otherwise see 5.185. INT 67H, Expanded Memory Manager Error Codes)

Version: Added to EMM beginning with version 4.0.

Note: This function is intended for operating system use only.

Source: Advanced MS-DOS Programming 2nd Ed. (Microsoft Press), page 644
MS-DOS Extensions (Microsoft Press), pages 65 through 66
Expanded Memory Specification Version 4.0 (Intel), pages 3-134 through 3-135

See Also: 5.120. INT 67H, Expanded Memory Manager Functions Summary
5.185. INT 67H, Expanded Memory Manager Error Codes

5.171. INT 67H, AH=5CH -- PREPARE EMM FOR WARM BOOT

Prior to Issuing INT 67H

	High	Low
AX	5CH	
BX		
CX		
DX		
SP		
BP		
SI		
DI		
IP		
flags		
CS		
DS		
SS		
ES		

Upon Return from INT 67H

	High	Low
AX	Status*	
BX		
CX		
DX		
SP		
BP		
SI		
DI		
IP		
flags		
CS		
DS		
SS		
ES		

*00=no error (otherwise see 5.185. INT 67H, Expanded Memory Manager Error Codes)

Version: Added to EMM beginning with version 4.0.

Source: Advanced MS-DOS Programming 2nd Ed. (Microsoft Press), pages 644 through 645
MS-DOS Extensions (Microsoft Press), page 66
Expanded Memory Specification Version 4.0 (Intel), page 3-136

See Also: 5.120. INT 67H, Expanded Memory Manager Functions Summary
5.185. INT 67H, Expanded Memory Manager Error Codes

5.172. INT 67H, AH=5DH, AL=00H -- ENABLE EMM OPERATING SYSTEM FUNCTIONS

Prior to Issuing INT 67H

Register	High	Low
AX	5DH	00H
BX	Access key†	
CX	Access key†	
DX		
SP		
BP		
SI		
DI		
IP		
flags		
CS		
DS		
SS		
ES		

Upon Return from INT 67H

Register	High	Low
AX	Status*	
BX	Access key†	
CX	Access key†	
DX		
SP		
BP		
SI		
DI		
IP		
flags		
CS		
DS		
SS		
ES		

*00=no error (otherwise see 5.185. INT 67H, Expanded Memory Manager Error Codes)
†Access key returned in BX:CX on first call; must be placed in BX:CX prior to subsequent calls to function 5DH.

Version: Added to EMM beginning with version 4.0.

Note: This function is intended for operating system use only.

Source: Advanced MS-DOS Programming 2nd Ed. (Microsoft Press), page 645
MS-DOS Extensions (Microsoft Press), page 67
Expanded Memory Specification Version 4.0 (Intel), pages 3-137 through 3-139

See Also: 5.120. INT 67H, Expanded Memory Manager Functions Summary
5.185. INT 67H, Expanded Memory Manager Error Codes

5.173. INT 67H, AH=5DH, AL=01H -- DISABLE EMM OPERATING SYSTEM FUNCTIONS

Prior to Issuing INT 67H

Register	High	Low
AX	5DH	01H
BX	Access key†	
CX	Access key†	
DX		
SP		
BP		
SI		
DI		
IP		
flags		
CS		
DS		
SS		
ES		

Upon Return from INT 67H

Register	High	Low
AX	Status*	
BX	Access key†	
CX	Access key†	
DX		
SP		
BP		
SI		
DI		
IP		
flags		
CS		
DS		
SS		
ES		

*00=no error (otherwise see 5.185. INT 67H, Expanded Memory Manager Error Codes)
†Access key returned in BX:CX on first call; must be placed in BX:CX prior to subsequent calls to function 5DH.

Version: Added to EMM beginning with version 4.0.

Note: This function is intended for operating system use only.

Source: Advanced MS-DOS Programming 2nd Ed. (Microsoft Press), pages 645 through 646
MS-DOS Extensions (Microsoft Press), pages 67 through 68
Expanded Memory Specification Version 4.0 (Intel), pages 3-140 through 3-142

See Also: 5.120. INT 67H, Expanded Memory Manager Functions Summary
5.185. INT 67H, Expanded Memory Manager Error Codes

5.174. INT 67H, AH=5DH, AL=02H -- RELEASE ACCESS KEY

Register	Prior to Issuing INT 67H: High	Prior to Issuing INT 67H: Low	Upon Return from INT 67H: High	Upon Return from INT 67H: Low
AX	5DH	02H	Status*	
BX	Access key			
CX	Access key			
DX				
SP				
BP				
SI				
DI				
IP				
flags				
CS				
DS				
SS				
ES				

*00=no error (otherwise see 5.185. INT 67H, Expanded Memory Manager Error Codes)

Version: Added to EMM beginning with version 4.0.

Note:
- Access key obtained by previous call to Function 5DH, 00H, or 5DH, 01H.
- This function is intended for operating system use only.

Source: Advanced MS-DOS Programming 2nd Ed. (Microsoft Press), page 646
MS-DOS Extensions (Microsoft Press), page 68
Expanded Memory Specification Version 4.0 (Intel), pages 3-143 through 3-144

See Also: 5.120. INT 67H, Expanded Memory Manager Functions Summary
5.185. INT 67H, Expanded Memory Manager Error Codes

5.175. INT 67H, AH=60H -- GET PHYSICAL WINDOW ARRAY

Register	Prior to Issuing INT 67H: High	Prior to Issuing INT 67H: Low	Upon Return from INT 67H: High	Upon Return from INT 67H: Low
AX	60H		Status*	Number of entries†
BX				
CX				
DX				
SP				
BP				
SI				
DI	Offset of pointer to empty array		Offset of pointer to filled array	
IP				
flags				
CS				
DS				
SS				
ES	Segment of pointer to empty array		Segment of pointer to filled array	

*00=no error (otherwise see 5.185. INT 67H, Expanded Memory Manager Error Codes)
†Size is in entries (four bytes per entry in array).

Version: This function is obsolete; replaced by EMS 4.0.

Source: AST Rampage Technical Reference

See Also: 5.120. INT 67H, Expanded Memory Manager Functions Summary
5.185. INT 67H, Expanded Memory Manager Error Codes

5.176. INT 67H, AH=68H -- GET SYSTEM PHYSICAL WINDOW ARRAY

Prior to Issuing INT 67H

	High	Low
AX	68H	
BX		
CX		
DX		
SP		
BP		
SI		
DI	Offset of pointer to empty array	
IP		
flags		
CS		
DS		
SS		
ES	Segment of pointer to empty array	

Upon Return from INT 67H

	High	Low
AX	Status*	Number of entries†
BX		
CX		
DX		
SP		
BP		
SI		
DI	Offset of pointer to filled array	
IP		
flags		
CS		
DS		
SS		
ES	Segment of pointer to filled array	

*00=no error (otherwise see 5.185. INT 67H, Expanded Memory Manager Error Codes)
†Size is in entries (four bytes per entry in array).

Version: This function is obsolete; replaced by EMS 4.0.

Source: AST Rampage Technical Reference

See Also: 5.120. INT 67H, Expanded Memory Manager Functions Summary
5.185. INT 67H, Expanded Memory Manager Error Codes

5.177. INT 67H, AH=69H -- MAP PAGE TO WINDOW

Prior to Issuing INT 67H

	High	Low
AX	69H	
BX	Page number	
CX		
DX	EMM page handle	
SP		
BP		
SI		
DI		
IP		
flags		
CS		
DS		
SS		
ES		

Upon Return from INT 67H

	High	Low
AX	Status*	
BX		
CX		
DX		
SP		
BP		
SI		
DI		
IP		
flags		
CS		
DS		
SS		
ES		

*00=no error (otherwise see 5.185. INT 67H, Expanded Memory Manager Error Codes)

Version: This function is obsolete; replaced by EMS 4.0.

Source: AST Rampage Technical Reference

See Also: 5.120. INT 67H, Expanded Memory Manager Functions Summary
5.185. INT 67H, Expanded Memory Manager Error Codes

5.178. INT 67H, AH=6AH, AL=00H -- GET SYSTEM MAP

Prior to Issuing INT 67H

Register	High	Low
AX	6AH	00H
BX		
CX	First window	Window count
DX		
SP		
BP		
SI		
DI	Offset of pointer to empty array	
IP		
flags		
CS		
DS		
SS		
ES	Segment of pointer to empty array	

Upon Return from INT 67H

Register	High	Low
AX	Status*	
BX		
CX		
DX		
SP		
BP		
SI		
DI	Offset of pointer to saved page map array	
IP		
flags		
CS		
DS		
SS		
ES	Segment of pointer to saved page map array	

*00=no error (otherwise see 5.185. INT 67H, Expanded Memory Manager Error Codes)

Version: This function is obsolete; replaced by EMS 4.0.

Source: AST Rampage Technical Reference

See Also: 5.120. INT 67H, Expanded Memory Manager Functions Summary
5.185. INT 67H, Expanded Memory Manager Error Codes

5.179. INT 67H, AH=6AH, AL=01H -- SET SYSTEM MAP

Prior to Issuing INT 67H

Register	High	Low
AX	6AH	01H
BX		
CX	1st window	Window count
DX		
SP		
BP		
SI		
DI	Offset of pointer to saved page map array	
IP		
flags		
CS		
DS		
SS		
ES	Segment of pointer to saved page map array	

Upon Return from INT 67H

Register	High	Low
AX	Status*	
BX		
CX		
DX		
SP		
BP		
SI		
DI		
IP		
flags		
CS		
DS		
SS		
ES		

*00=no error (otherwise see 5.185. INT 67H, Expanded Memory Manager Error Codes)

Version: This function is obsolete; replaced by EMS 4.0.

Source: AST Rampage Technical Reference

See Also: 5.120. INT 67H, Expanded Memory Manager Functions Summary
5.185. INT 67H, Expanded Memory Manager Error Codes

5.180. INT 67H, AH=6AH, AL=02H -- SWAP SYSTEM MAP

Prior to Issuing INT 67H

	High	Low
AX	6AH	02H
BX		
CX	1st window	Window count
DX		
SP		
BP		
SI	Offset of pointer to next page map	
DI	Offset of pointer to empty array	
IP		
flags		
CS		
DS	Segment of pointer to next page map	
SS		
ES	Segment of pointer to empty array	

Upon Return from INT 67H

	High	Low
AX	Status*	
BX		
CX		
DX		
SP		
BP		
SI		
DI	Offset of pointer to previous page map	
IP		
flags		
CS		
DS		
SS		
ES	Segment of pointer to previous page map	

*00=no error (otherwise see 5.185. INT 67H, Expanded Memory Manager Error Codes)

Version: This function is obsolete; replaced by EMS 4.0.

Source: AST Rampage Technical Reference

See Also: 5.120. INT 67H, Expanded Memory Manager Functions Summary
5.185. INT 67H, Expanded Memory Manager Error Codes

5.181. INT 67H, AH=6AH, AL=03H -- GET MAP SIZE

Prior to Issuing INT 67H

	High	Low
AX	6AH	03H
BX		
CX	1st window	Window count
DX		
SP		
BP		
SI		
DI		
IP		
flags		
CS		
DS		
SS		
ES		

Upon Return from INT 67H

	High	Low
AX	Status*	Size†
BX		
CX		
DX		
SP		
BP		
SI		
DI		
IP		
flags		
CS		
DS		
SS		
ES		

*00=no error (otherwise see 5.185. INT 67H, Expanded Memory Manager Error Codes)
†Size of page map array in bytes

Version: This function is obsolete; replaced by EMS 4.0.

Source: AST Rampage Technical Reference

See Also: 5.120. INT 67H, Expanded Memory Manager Functions Summary
5.185. INT 67H, Expanded Memory Manager Error Codes

5.182. INT 67H, AH=6AH, AL=04H -- SET STANDARD MAPPING

Prior to Issuing INT 67H

Register	High	Low
AX	6AH	04H
BX		
CX		
DX		
SP		
BP		
SI		
DI		
IP		
flags		
CS		
DS		
SS		
ES		

Upon Return from INT 67H

Register	High	Low
AX	Status*	
BX		
CX		
DX		
SP		
BP		
SI		
DI		
IP		
flags		
CS		
DS		
SS		
ES		

*00=no error (otherwise see 5.185. INT 67H, Expanded Memory Manager Error Codes)

Version: This function is obsolete; replaced by EMS 4.0.

Source: AST Rampage Technical Reference

See Also: 5.120. INT 67H, Expanded Memory Manager Functions Summary
5.185. INT 67H, Expanded Memory Manager Error Codes

5.183. INT 67H, AH=6AH, AL=05H -- SET ALTERNATE MAPPING

Prior to Issuing INT 67H

Register	High	Low
AX	6AH	05H
BX		
CX		
DX		
SP		
BP		
SI		
DI		
IP		
flags		
CS		
DS		
SS		
ES		

Upon Return from INT 67H

Register	High	Low
AX	Status*	
BX		
CX		
DX		
SP		
BP		
SI		
DI		
IP		
flags		
CS		
DS		
SS		
ES		

*00=no error (otherwise see 5.185. INT 67H, Expanded Memory Manager Error Codes)

Version: This function is obsolete; replaced by EMS 4.0.

Source: AST Rampage Technical Reference

See Also: 5.120. INT 67H, Expanded Memory Manager Functions Summary
5.185. INT 67H, Expanded Memory Manager Error Codes

5.184. INT 67H, AH=6AH, AL=06H -- DEALLOCATE INITIAL SYSTEM PAGES

Prior to Issuing INT 67H

	High	Low
AX	6AH	06H
BX		
CX	1st window	Window count
DX		
SP		
BP		
SI		
DI		
IP		
flags		
CS		
DS		
SS		
ES		

Upon Return from INT 67H

	High	Low
AX	Status*	
BX		
CX		
DX		
SP		
BP		
SI		
DI		
IP		
flags		
CS		
DS		
SS		
ES		

*00=no error (otherwise see 5.185. INT 67H, Expanded Memory Manager Error Codes)

Version: This function is obsolete; replaced by EMS 4.0.

Source: AST Rampage Technical Reference

See Also: 5.120. INT 67H, Expanded Memory Manager Functions Summary
5.185. INT 67H, Expanded Memory Manager Error Codes

5.185. INT 67H, EXPANDED MEMORY MANAGER ERROR CODES

Code	Description	Comments
00H	Normal return code	No error occurred
80H	Software error	Might indicate corrupted memory image of driver
81H	Hardware error	
82H	EMM is busy	
83H	Unallocated or invalid handle	
84H	Undefined function code	
85H	Out of handles	
86H	Error in save or restore mapping context	
87H	Page count error	Requested > total physical pages; no pages allocated
88H	Page count error	Requested > total available pages; no pages allocated
89H	Requested zero pages	
8AH	No logical page for this handle	
8BH	Physical page outside valid range	
8CH	Context stack out of memory	
8DH	Handle already has context stack	
8EH	No context stack for that handle	
8FH	Undefined subfunction code	
90H	Subfunction parameter not defined	
91H	Feature not supported	
92H	Source and destination regions overlap	Requested move performed, but part of source region overwritten
93H	Length longer than allocated length	
94H	Conventional and expanded memory regions overlap	
95H	Offset outside of logical page	
96H	Region length greater than 1MB	
97H	Source and destination regions overlap	Exchange was not performed
98H	Memory source and destination types undefined	
99H	UNUSED	
9AH	Alt register set specified does not exist	Alt map or DMA register sets are implicitly supported, however
9BH	Alt register set currently allocated	
9CH	Alt register set specified was not 0	Alt map or DMA register sets are not supported
9DH	Alt register set specified was not defined	
9EH	Dedicated DMA channels not supported	
9FH	Specified DMA channel not supported	DMA channels implicitly supported, however
A0H	Handle for name not found	
A1H	Handle with the same name already exists	
A2H	Memory address wraps	Sum of source or destination base address & length exceeds 1MB
A3H	Invalid pointer	Or contents of source array have been corrupted
A4H	Access to function denied by OS	

Source: MS-DOS Extensions (Microsoft Press), pages 28 through 29

5.186. AH=00H -- GET XMS VERSION

Prior to Issuing Driver

Register	High	Low
AX	00H	
BX		
CX		
DX		
SP		
BP		
SI		
DI		
IP		
flags		
CS		
DS		
SS		
ES		

Upon Return from Driver

Register	High	Low
AX	XMS version number*	
BX	Driver internal revision number*	
CX		
DX	HMA indicator†	
SP		
BP		
SI		
DI		
IP		
flags		
CS		
DS		
SS		
ES		

*BCD coded, AH, BH=major version, AL, BL=minor version
†0000H=no HMA; 0001H=HMA exists

Version: XMS driver 2.0 and later

Source: MS-DOS Extensions (Microsoft Press), pages 73 through 74
Extended Memory Specification Version 2.0 (Microsoft)

See Also: 5.204. XMS Error Codes

5.187. AH=01H --ALLOCATE HMA

Prior to Issuing Driver

Register	High	Low
AX	01H	
BX		
CX		
DX	HMA bytes needed†	
SP		
BP		
SI		
DI		
IP		
flags		
CS		
DS		
SS		
ES		

Upon Return from Driver

Register	High	Low
AX	Status*	
BX		(Error code)
CX		
DX		
SP		
BP		
SI		
DI		
IP		
flags		
CS		
DS		
SS		
ES		

*0001H=no error; 0000H=error (error code in BL -- see 5.204. XMS Error Codes)
†FFFFH if application; otherwise actual bytes needed by driver or operating system

Version: XMS driver 2.0 and later

Note: HMA maximum size=64K – 16 bytes (65,520)

Source: MS-DOS Extensions (Microsoft Press), pages 74 through 75
Extended Memory Specification Version 2.0 (Microsoft)

See Also: 5.204. XMS Error Codes

5.188. AH=02H -- FREE HMA

Register	Prior to Issuing Driver: High	Prior to Issuing Driver: Low	Upon Return from Driver: High	Upon Return from Driver: Low
AX	02H		Status*	
BX				(Error code)
CX				
DX				
SP				
BP				
SI				
DI				
IP				
flags				
CS				
DS				
SS				
ES				

*0001H= no error; 0000H=error (error code in BL -- see 5.204. XMS Error Codes)

Version: XMS driver 2.0 and later

Source: MS-DOS Extensions (Microsoft Press), page 75
Extended Memory Specification Version 2.0 (Microsoft)

See Also: 5.204. XMS Error Codes

5.189. AH=03H -- GLOBAL ENABLE A20 LINE

Register	Prior to Issuing Driver: High	Prior to Issuing Driver: Low	Upon Return from Driver: High	Upon Return from Driver: Low
AX	03H		Status*	
BX				(Error code)
CX				
DX				
SP				
BP				
SI				
DI				
IP				
flags				
CS				
DS				
SS				
ES				

*0001H= no error; 0000H=error (error code in BL -- see 5.204. XMS Error Codes)

Version: XMS driver 2.0 and later

Source: MS-DOS Extensions (Microsoft Press), pages 75 through 76
Extended Memory Specification Version 2.0 (Microsoft)

See Also: 5.204. XMS Error Codes

5.190. AH=04H -- GLOBAL DISABLE A20 LINE

Register	Prior to Issuing Driver: High	Prior to Issuing Driver: Low	Upon Return from Driver: High	Upon Return from Driver: Low
AX	04H		Status*	
BX				(Error code)
CX				
DX				
SP				
BP				
SI				
DI				
IP				
flags				
CS				
DS				
SS				
ES				

*0001H= no error; 0000H=error (error code in BL -- see 5.204. XMS Error Codes)

Version: XMS driver 2.0 and later

Source: MS-DOS Extensions (Microsoft Press), page 76
Extended Memory Specification Version 2.0 (Microsoft)

See Also: 5.204. XMS Error Codes

5.191. AH=05H -- LOCAL ENABLE A20 LINE

Register	Prior to Issuing Driver: High	Prior to Issuing Driver: Low	Upon Return from Driver: High	Upon Return from Driver: Low
AX	05H		Status*	
BX				(Error code)
CX				
DX				
SP				
BP				
SI				
DI				
IP				
flags				
CS				
DS				
SS				
ES				

*0001H= no error; 0000H=error (error code in BL -- see 5.204. XMS Error Codes)

Version: XMS driver 2.0 and later

Source: MS-DOS Extensions (Microsoft Press), pages 76 through 77
Extended Memory Specification Version 2.0 (Microsoft)

See Also: 5.204. XMS Error Codes

5.192. AH=06H -- LOCAL DISABLE A20 LINE

Prior to Issuing Driver

	High	Low
AX	06H	
BX		
CX		
DX		
SP		
BP		
SI		
DI		
IP		
flags		
CS		
DS		
SS		
ES		

Upon Return from Driver

	High	Low
AX	Status*	
BX		(Error code)
CX		
DX		
SP		
BP		
SI		
DI		
IP		
flags		
CS		
DS		
SS		
ES		

*0001H= no error; 0000H=error (error code in BL -- see 5.204. XMS Error Codes)

Version: XMS driver 2.0 and later

Source: MS-DOS Extensions (Microsoft Press), page 77
Extended Memory Specification Version 2.0 (Microsoft)

See Also: 5.204. XMS Error Codes

5.193. AH=07H -- QUERY A20 LINE STATE

Prior to Issuing Driver

	High	Low
AX	07H	
BX		
CX		
DX		
SP		
BP		
SI		
DI		
IP		
flags		
CS		
DS		
SS		
ES		

Upon Return from Driver

	High	Low
AX	Status*	
BX		(Error code)
CX		
DX		
SP		
BP		
SI		
DI		
IP		
flags		
CS		
DS		
SS		
ES		

*0001H= no error and line enabled; 0000H=error or line disabled (value in BL=0 if disabled; otherwise it is an error code)

Version: XMS driver 2.0 and later

Source: MS-DOS Extensions (Microsoft Press), pages 77 through 78
Extended Memory Specification Version 2.0 (Microsoft)

See Also: 5.204. XMS Error Codes

5.194. AH=08H -- QUERY FREE EXTENDED MEMORY

Register	Prior to Issuing Driver: High	Prior to Issuing Driver: Low	Upon Return from Driver: High	Upon Return from Driver: Low
AX	08H		Size of largest free block*†	
BX				(Error code)
CX				
DX			Total free extended memory*	
SP				
BP				
SI				
DI				
IP				
flags				
CS				
DS				
SS				
ES				

*In kilobytes
†0000H=error (see BL for error code)

Version: XMS driver 2.0 and later

Source: MS-DOS Extensions (Microsoft Press), page 78
Extended Memory Specification Version 2.0 (Microsoft)

See Also: 5.204. XMS Error Codes

5.195. AH=09H -- ALLOCATE EXTENDED MEMORY BLOCK

Register	Prior to Issuing Driver: High	Prior to Issuing Driver: Low	Upon Return from Driver: High	Upon Return from Driver: Low
AX	09H		Status†	
BX				(Error code)
CX				
DX	Requested block size*		EMB handle (if AX=0)	
SP				
BP				
SI				
DI				
IP				
flags				
CS				
DS				
SS				
ES				

*In kilobytes
†0000H=error (see BL for error code); 0001H=successful (handle in DX)

Version: XMS driver 2.0 and later

Source: MS-DOS Extensions (Microsoft Press), pages 78 through 79
Extended Memory Specification Version 2.0 (Microsoft)

See Also: 5.204. XMS Error Codes

5.196. AH=0AH -- FREE EXTENDED MEMORY BLOCK

Prior to Issuing Driver

	High	Low
AX	0AH	
BX		
CX		
DX	EMB handle	
SP		
BP		
SI		
DI		
IP		
flags		
CS		
DS		
SS		
ES		

Upon Return from Driver

	High	Low
AX	Status*	
BX		(Error code)
CX		
DX		
SP		
BP		
SI		
DI		
IP		
flags		
CS		
DS		
SS		
ES		

*0001H=no error; 0000H=error (see BL for error code)

Version: XMS driver 2.0 and later

Source: MS-DOS Extensions (Microsoft Press), page 79
Extended Memory Specification Version 2.0 (Microsoft)

See Also: 5.204. XMS Error Codes

5.197. AH=0BH -- MOVE EXTENDED MEMORY BLOCK

Prior to Issuing Driver

	High	Low
AX	0BH	
BX		
CX		
DX		
SP		
BP		
SI	Offset of pointer to parameter block†	
DI		
IP		
flags		
CS		
DS	Segment of pointer to parameter block†	
SS		
ES		

Upon Return from Driver

	High	Low
AX	Status*	
BX		(Error code)
CX		
DX		
SP		
BP		
SI		
DI		
IP		
flags		
CS		
DS		
SS		
ES		

*0001H=no error; 0000H=error (see BL for error code)
†Parameter block formatted as follows:
- dbl word=length of EMB (in bytes; number must be even)
- word=source EMB handle
- dbl word=32-bit offset within source block
- word=destination EMB handle
- dbl word=32-bit offset within destination block

Version: XMS driver 2.0 and later

Source: MS-DOS Extensions (Microsoft Press), page 80
Extended Memory Specification Version 2.0 (Microsoft)

See Also: 5.204. XMS Error Codes

5.198. AH=0CH -- LOCK EXTENDED MEMORY BLOCK

Prior to Issuing Driver

	High	Low
AX	0CH	
BX		
CX		
DX	EMB handle	
SP		
BP		
SI		
DI		
IP		
flags		
CS		
DS		
SS		
ES		

Upon Return from Driver

	High	Low
AX	Status*	
BX	LO word of locked block address† (if AX=0)	
CX		
DX	HO word of locked block address (if AX=0)	
SP		
BP		
SI		
DI		
IP		
flags		
CS		
DS		
SS		
ES		

*0001H=no error; 0000H=error (see BL for error code)
†On error, BL contains error code instead.

Version: XMS driver 2.0 and later

Source: MS-DOS Extensions (Microsoft Press), page 81
Extended Memory Specification Version 2.0 (Microsoft)

See Also: 5.204. XMS Error Codes

5.199. AH=0DH -- UNLOCK EXTENDED MEMORY BLOCK

Prior to Issuing Driver

	High	Low
AX	0DH	
BX		
CX		
DX	EMB handle	
SP		
BP		
SI		
DI		
IP		
flags		
CS		
DS		
SS		
ES		

Upon Return from Driver

	High	Low
AX	Status*	
BX		(Error code)
CX		
DX		
SP		
BP		
SI		
DI		
IP		
flags		
CS		
DS		
SS		
ES		

*0001H=no error; 0000H=error (see BL for error code)

Version: XMS driver 2.0 and later

Source: MS-DOS Extensions (Microsoft Press), pages 81 through 82
Extended Memory Specification Version 2.0 (Microsoft)

See Also: 5.204. XMS Error Codes

5.200. AH=0EH -- GET HANDLE INFORMATION

Prior to Issuing Driver

	High	Low
AX	0EH	
BX		
CX		
DX	EMB handle	
SP		
BP		
SI		
DI		
IP		
flags		
CS		
DS		
SS		
ES		

Upon Return from Driver

	High	Low
AX	Status*	
BX	Lock count	Number handles available†
CX		
DX	Block size (if AX=0)§	
SP		
BP		
SI		
DI		
IP		
flags		
CS		
DS		
SS		
ES		

*0001H=no error; 0000H=error (see BL for error code)
†On error, BL contains error code instead
§In kilobytes

Version: XMS driver 2.0 and later

Source: MS-DOS Extensions (Microsoft Press), page 82
Extended Memory Specification Version 2.0 (Microsoft)

See Also: 5.204. XMS Error Codes

5.201. AH=0FH -- RESIZE EXTENDED MEMORY BLOCK

Prior to Issuing Driver

	High	Low
AX	0FH	
BX	New block size§	
CX		
DX	EMB handle	
SP		
BP		
SI		
DI		
IP		
flags		
CS		
DS		
SS		
ES		

Upon Return from Driver

	High	Low
AX	Status*	
BX		(Error code)
CX		
DX		
SP		
BP		
SI		
DI		
IP		
flags		
CS		
DS		
SS		
ES		

*0001H=no error; 0000H=error (see BL for error code)
§In kilobytes

Version: XMS driver 2.0 and later

Source: MS-DOS Extensions (Microsoft Press), pages 82 through 83
Extended Memory Specification Version 2.0 (Microsoft)

See Also: 5.204. XMS Error Codes

5.202. AH=10H -- ALLOCATE UPPER MEMORY BLOCK

Prior to Issuing Driver

	High	Low
AX	10H	
BX		
CX		
DX	Requested block size§	
SP		
BP		
SI		
DI		
IP		
flags		
CS		
DS		
SS		
ES		

Upon Return from Driver

	High	Low
AX	Status*	
BX	Segment base of allocated block†	
CX		
DX	Actual block size§¥	
SP		
BP		
SI		
DI		
IP		
flags		
CS		
DS		
SS		
ES		

*0001H=no error; 0000H=error (see BL for error code)
†BL=error code if AX=0000H
§In paragraphs
¥DX=size of largest available block if AX=0000H

Version: XMS driver 2.0 and later

Source: MS-DOS Extensions (Microsoft Press), page 83
Extended Memory Specification Version 2.0 (Microsoft)

See Also: 5.204. XMS Error Codes

5.203. AH=11H -- FREE UPPER MEMORY BLOCK

Prior to Issuing Driver

	High	Low
AX	11H	
BX		
CX		
DX	Segment base of block	
SP		
BP		
SI		
DI		
IP		
flags		
CS		
DS		
SS		
ES		

Upon Return from Driver

	High	Low
AX	Status*	
BX		(Error code)
CX		
DX		
SP		
BP		
SI		
DI		
IP		
flags		
CS		
DS		
SS		
ES		

*0001H=no error; 0000H=error (see BL for error code)

Version: XMS driver 2.0 and later

Source: MS-DOS Extensions (Microsoft Press), page 84
Extended Memory Specification Version 2.0 (Microsoft)

See Also: 5.204. XMS Error Codes

5.204. XMS ERROR CODES

Code	Description
80H	Function not implemented
81H	VDISK device driver was detected
82H	A20 error
8EH	General driver error
8FH	Unrecoverable driver error
90H	HMA does not exist
91H	HMA is already in use
92H	DX is less than /HMAMIN=parameter
93H	HMA is not allocated
94H	A20 line is still enabled
A0H	All extended memory is allocated
A1H	EMM handles are exhausted
A2H	Handle is invalid
A3H	Source handle is invalid
A4H	Source offset is invalid
A5H	Destination handle is invalid
A6H	Destination offset is invalid
A7H	Length is invalid
A8H	Overlap in move request is invalid
A9H	Parity error detected
AAH	Block not locked
ABH	Block locked
ACH	Lock count overflowed
ADH	Lock failed
B0H	Smaller UMB is available
B1H	No UMBs are available
B2H	UMB segment number is invalid

Source: MS-DOS Extensions (Microsoft Press), page 72
Extended Memory Specification Version 2.0 (Microsoft)

5.205. INT 67H, AH=DEH, AL=00H -- VCPI PRESENCE DETECTION

Prior to Issuing INT 67H

	High	Low
AX	DEH	00H
BX		
CX		
DX		
SP		
BP		
SI		
DI		
IP		
flags		
CS		
DS		
SS		
ES		

Upon Return from INT 67H

	High	Low
AX	Status*	
BX	Major version number†	Minor version number†
CX		
DX		
SP		
BP		
SI		
DI		
IP		
flags		
CS		
DS		
SS		
ES		

*Nonzero=not present, zero=present; see BX for version number
†Values are in binary; returned only if AH=0.

Version: Applies to all versions of VCPI Driver beginning with 1.0.

Source: "Virtual Control Program Interface Version 1.0," June 12, 1989, page 5

5.206. INT 67H, AH=DEH, AL=01H -- VCPI GET PROTECTED MODE INTERFACE

Prior to Issuing INT 67H

	High	Low
AX	DEH	01H
BX		
CX		
DX		
SP		
BP		
SI	Offset of pointer to client GDT entries	
DI	Offset of pointer to 4K page table buffer	
IP		
flags		
CS		
DS	Segment of pointer to client GDT entries	
SS		
ES	Segment of pointer to 4K page table buffer	

Upon Return from INT 67H

	High	Low
AX	00H	
(E)BX	Offset in CS of protected mode entry point	
CX		
DX		
SP		
BP		
SI		
DI	(Advanced to point to first unused entry in buffer)	
IP		
flags		
CS		
DS		
SS		
ES		

Version: Applies to all versions of VCPI Driver beginning with 1.0.

Source: "Virtual Control Program Interface Version 1.0," June 12, 1989, pages 6 through 7

5.207. INT 67H, AH=DEH, AL=02H -- VCPI GET MAXIMUM PHYSICAL MEMORY ADDRESS

Prior to Issuing INT 67H

	High	Low
AX	DEH	02H
BX		
CX		
DX		
SP		
BP		
SI		
DI		
IP		
flags		
CS		
DS		
SS		
ES		

Upon Return from INT 67H

	High	Low
AX	00H	
BX		
CX		
(E)DX	Physical address of highest 4K memory page	
SP		
BP		
SI		
DI		
IP		
flags		
CS		
DS		
SS		
ES		

Version: Applies to all versions of VCPI Driver beginning with 1.0.

Source: "Virtual Control Program Interface Version 1.0," June 12, 1989, page 7

5.208. INT 67H, AH=DEH, AL=03H -- VCPI GET NUMBER OF FREE 4K PAGES

Prior to Issuing INT 67H

	High	Low
AX	DEH	03H
BX		
CX		
DX		
SP		
BP		
SI		
DI		
IP		
flags		
CS		
DS		
SS		
ES		

Upon Return from INT 67H

	High	Low
AX	00H	
BX		
CX		
(E)DX	Number of free 4K pages	
SP		
BP		
SI		
DI		
IP		
flags		
CS		
DS		
SS		
ES		

Version: Applies to all versions of VCPI Driver beginning with 1.0.

Source: "Virtual Control Program Interface Version 1.0," June 12, 1989, pages 7 through 8

See Also:
5.209. INT 67H, AH=DEH, AL=04H -- VCPI Allocate a 4K Page
5.210. INT 67H, AH=DEH, AL=05H -- VCPI Free a 4K Page
5.211. INT 67H, AH=DEH, AL=06H -- VCPI Get Physical Address of 4K Page in First Megabyte

5.209. INT 67H, AH=DEH, AL=04H -- VCPI ALLOCATE A 4K PAGE

Prior to Issuing INT 67H

	High	Low
AX	DEH	04H
BX		
CX		
DX		
SP		
BP		
SI		
DI		
IP		
flags		
CS		
DS		
SS		
ES		

Upon Return from INT 67H

	High	Low
AX	Status*	
BX		
CX		
(E)DX	Physical address of allocated 4K page	
SP		
BP		
SI		
DI		
IP		
flags		
CS		
DS		
SS		
ES		

*Nonzero (usually 88H)=failure to allocate, EDX modified

Version: Applies to all versions of VCPI Driver beginning with 1.0.

Source: "Virtual Control Program Interface Version 1.0," June 12, 1989, page 8

See Also:
5.208. INT 67H, AH=DEH, AL=03H -- VCPI Get Number of Free 4K Pages
5.210. INT 67H, AH=DEH, AL=05H -- VCPI Free a 4K Page
5.211. INT 67H, AH=DEH, AL=06H -- VCPI Get Physical Address of 4K Page in First Megabyte

5.210. INT 67H, AH=DEH, AL=05H -- VCPI FREE A 4K PAGE

Prior to Issuing INT 67H

	High	Low
AX	DEH	05H
BX		
CX		
(E)DX	Physical address of 4K page to free	
SP		
BP		
SI		
DI		
IP		
flags		
CS		
DS		
SS		
ES		

Upon Return from INT 67H

	High	Low
AX	Status*	
BX		
CX		
DX		
SP		
BP		
SI		
DI		
IP		
flags		
CS		
DS		
SS		
ES		

*Nonzero (usually 8AH)=failure to free

Version: Applies to all versions of VCPI Driver beginning with 1.0.

Source: "Virtual Control Program Interface Version 1.0," June 12, 1989, page 8

See Also: 5.208. INT 67H, AH=DEH, AL=03H -- VCPI Get Number of Free 4K Pages
5.209. INT 67H, AH=DEH, AL=04H -- VCPI Allocate a 4K Page
5.211. INT 67H, AH=DEH, AL=06H -- VCPI Get Physical Address of 4K Page in First Megabyte

5.211. INT 67H, AH=DEH, AL=06H -- VCPI GET PHYSICAL ADDRESS OF 4K PAGE IN FIRST MEGABYTE

Prior to Issuing INT 67H

	High	Low
AX	DEH	06H
BX		
CX	Page number (linear addr of page SHR 12)	
DX		
SP		
BP		
SI		
DI		
IP		
flags		
CS		
DS		
SS		
ES		

Upon Return from INT 67H

	High	Low
AX	Status*	
BX		
CX		
(E)DX	Physical address of 4K page (if AH=0)	
SP		
BP		
SI		
DI		
IP		
flags		
CS		
DS		
SS		
ES		

*Nonzero (usually 8BH)=failure to find

Version: Applies to all versions of VCPI Driver beginning with 1.0.

Source: "Virtual Control Program Interface Version 1.0," June 12, 1989, page 9

See Also: 5.208. INT 67H, AH=DEH, AL=03H -- VCPI Get Number of Free 4K Pages
5.209. INT 67H, AH=DEH, AL=04H -- VCPI Allocate a 4K Page
5.210. INT 67H, AH=DEH, AL=05H -- VCPI Free a 4K Page

5.212. INT 67H, AH=DEH, AL=07H -- VCPI READ CR0

Prior to Issuing INT 67H

	High	Low
AX	DEH	07H
BX		
CX		
DX		
SP		
BP		
SI		
DI		
IP		
flags		
CS		
DS		
SS		
ES		

Upon Return from INT 67H

	High	Low
AX	00H	
(E)BX	CR0 value	
CX		
DX		
SP		
BP		
SI		
DI		
IP		
flags		
CS		
DS		
SS		
ES		

Version: Applies to all versions of VCPI Driver beginning with 1.0.

Source: "Virtual Control Program Interface Version 1.0," June 12, 1989, page 9

5.213. INT 67H, AH=DEH, AL=08H -- VCPI READ DEBUG REGISTERS

Prior to Issuing INT 67H

	High	Low
AX	DEH	08H
BX		
CX		
DX		
SP		
BP		
SI		
DI	Offset of pointer to array of 8 DWORDs	
IP		
flags		
CS		
DS		
SS		
ES	Segment of pointer to array of 8 DWORDs	

Upon Return from INT 67H

	High	Low
AX	00H	
BX		
CX		
DX		
SP		
BP		
SI		
DI		
IP		
flags		
CS		
DS		
SS		
ES		

Version: Applies to all versions of VCPI Driver beginning with 1.0.

Source: "Virtual Control Program Interface Version 1.0," June 12, 1989, page 10

See Also: 5.214. INT 67H, AH=DEH, AL=09H -- VCPI Load Debug Registers

5.214. INT 67H, AH=DEH, AL=09H -- VCPI LOAD DEBUG REGISTERS

Prior to Issuing INT 67H

	High	Low
AX	DEH	08H
BX		
CX		
DX		
SP		
BP		
SI		
DI	Offset of pointer to debug register array	
IP		
flags		
CS		
DS		
SS		
ES	Segment of pointer to debug register array	

Upon Return from INT 67H

	High	Low
AX	00H	
BX		
CX		
DX		
SP		
BP		
SI		
DI		
IP		
flags		
CS		
DS		
SS		
ES		

Version: Applies to all versions of VCPI Driver beginning with 1.0.

Source: "Virtual Control Program Interface Version 1.0," June 12, 1989, page 10

See Also: 5.213. INT 67H, AH=DEH, AL=08H -- VCPI Read Debug Registers

5.215. INT 67H, AH=DEH, AL=0AH -- VCPI GET 8259A INTERRUPT VECTOR MAPPINGS

Prior to Issuing INT 67H

	High	Low
AX	DEH	0AH
BX		
CX		
DX		
SP		
BP		
SI		
DI		
IP		
flags		
CS		
DS		
SS		
ES		

Upon Return from INT 67H

	High	Low
AX	00H	
BX	1st vector mapping (IRQ0-IRQ7)	
CX	2nd vector mapping (IRQ8-IRQ15)	
DX		
SP		
BP		
SI		
DI		
IP		
flags		
CS		
DS		
SS		
ES		

Version: Applies to all versions of VCPI Driver beginning with 1.0.

Source: "Virtual Control Program Interface Version 1.0," June 12, 1989, page 11

See Also: 5.216. INT 67H, AH=DEH, AL=0BH -- VCPI Set 8259A Interrupt Vector Mappings

5.216. INT 67H, AH=DEH, AL=0BH -- VCPI SET 8259A INTERRUPT VECTOR MAPPINGS

Prior to Issuing INT 67H

	High	Low
AX	DEH	0BH
BX	Master vector mapping (IRQ0-IRQ7)	
CX	Slave vector mapping (IRQ8-IRQ15)	
DX		
SP		
BP		
SI		
DI		
IP		
flags		
CS		
DS		
SS		
ES		

Upon Return from INT 67H

	High	Low
AX	00H	
BX		
CX		
DX		
SP		
BP		
SI		
DI		
IP		
flags		
CS		
DS		
SS		
ES		

Version: Applies to all versions of VCPI Driver beginning with 1.0.

Source: "Virtual Control Program Interface Version 1.0," June 12, 1989, page 11

See Also: 5.215. INT 67H, AH=DEH, AL=0AH -- VCPI Get 8259A Interrupt Vector Mappings

5.217. INT 67H, AH=DEH, AL=0CH -- VCPI SWITCH FROM V86 MODE TO PROTECTED MODE

Prior to Issuing INT 67H

	High	Low
AX	DEH	0CH
BX		
CX		
DX		
SP		
BP		
(E)SI	Linear address of system registers to load¥	
DI		
IP		
flags		
CS		
DS		
SS		
ES		
FS		
GS		

Upon Return from INT 67H*

	High	Low
(E)AX	Modified	
BX		
CX		
DX		
(E)SP	†	
BP		
(E)SI	Modified	
DI		
IP		
flags		
CS		
DS	Modified	
SS	†	
ES	Modified	
FS	Modified	
GS	Modified	

*GDTR, IDTR, LDTR, and TR loaded; control transferred to FAR entry point.
†SS:ESP must have at least 16 bytes of space on it.
¥ESI points to data structure:

DWORD	New value to load into CR3
DWORD	Linear address in 1st megabyte of 6-byte GDTR value
DWORD	Linear address in 1st megabyte of 6-byte IDTR value
WORD	Selector value to load into LDTR
WORD	Selector value to load into TR
PWORD	CS:EIP address to transfer control to

Version: Applies to all versions of VCPI Driver beginning with 1.0.

Note: Interrupts must be disabled prior to calling interrupt.

Source: "Virtual Control Program Interface Version 1.0," June 12, 1989, pages 12 through 13

See Also: 5.215. INT 67H, AH=DEH, AL=0AH -- VCPI Get 8259A Interrupt Vector Mappings

5.218. FARCALL AH=DEH, AL=03H -- VCPI PROTECTED MODE GET NUMBER OF FREE 4K PAGES

Prior to FCALL PROT_ENTRY

	High	Low
AX	DEH	03H
BX		
CX		
DX		
SP		
BP		
SI		
DI		
IP		
flags		
CS		
DS		
SS		
ES		

Upon Return from FCALL PROT_ENTRY

	High	Low
AX	00H	
BX		
CX		
(E)DX	Number of free 4K pages	
SP		
BP		
SI		
DI		
IP		
flags		
CS		
DS		
SS		
ES		

Version: Applies to all versions of VCPI Driver beginning with 1.0.

Source: "Virtual Control Program Interface Version 1.0," June 12, 1989, page 13

See Also: 5.208. INT 67H, AH=DEH, AL=03H -- VCPI Get Number of Free 4K Pages
5.219. FARCALL, AH=DEH, AL=04H -- VCPI Protected Mode Allocate a 4K Page
5.220. FARCALL, AH=DEH, AL=05H -- VCPI Protected Mode Free a 4K Page

5.219. FARCALL AH=DEH, AL=04H -- VCPI PROTECTED MODE ALLOCATE A 4K PAGE

Prior to FCALL PROT_ENTRY

	High	Low
AX	DEH	04H
BX		
CX		
DX		
SP		
BP		
SI		
DI		
IP		
flags		
CS		
DS		
SS		
ES		

Upon Return from FCALL PROT_ENTRY

	High	Low
AX	Status*	
BX		
CX		
(E)DX	Physical address of allocated 4K page	
SP		
BP		
SI		
DI		
IP		
flags		
CS		
DS		
SS		
ES		

*Nonzero (usually 88H)=failure to allocate, EDX modified

Version: Applies to all versions of VCPI Driver beginning with 1.0.

Source: "Virtual Control Program Interface Version 1.0," June 12, 1989, page 14

See Also: 5.209. INT 67H, AH=DEH, AL=04H -- VCPI Allocate a 4K Page
5.218. FARCALL, AH=DEH, AL=03H -- VCPI Protected Mode Get Number of Free 4K Pages
5.220. FARCALL, AH=DEH, AL=05H -- VCPI Protected Mode Free a 4K Page

5.220. FARCALL AH=DEH, AL=05H -- VCPI PROTECTED MODE FREE A 4K PAGE

Prior to FCALL PROT_ENTRY

	High	Low
AX	DEH	05H
BX		
CX		
(E)DX	Physical address of 4K page to free	
SP		
BP		
SI		
DI		
IP		
flags		
CS		
DS		
SS		
ES		

Upon Return from FCALL PROT_ENTRY

	High	Low
AX	Status*	
BX		
CX		
DX		
SP		
BP		
SI		
DI		
IP		
flags		
CS		
DS		
SS		
ES		

*Nonzero (usually 8AH)=failure to free

Version: Applies to all versions of VCPI Driver beginning with 1.0.

Source: "Virtual Control Program Interface Version 1.0," June 12, 1989, page 14

See Also: 5.210. INT 67H, AH=DEH, AL=05H -- VCPI Free a 4K Page
5.218. FARCALL, AH=DEH, AL=03H -- VCPI Protected Mode Get Number of Free 4K Pages
5.219. FARCALL, AH=DEH, AL=04H -- VCPI Protected Mode Allocate a 4K Page

5.221. FARCALL AH=DEH, AL=0CH -- VCPI SWITCH FROM PROTECTED MODE TO V86 MODE

Prior to FCALL PROT_ENTRY*

	High	Low
AX	DEH	0CH
BX		
CX		
DX		
(E)SP	(Must be in 1st megabyte of linear memory)	
BP		
SI		
DI		
IP		
flags		
CS		
DS	Segment selector from AH=DEH, AL=01H	
SS	(Must be in 1st megabyte of linear memory)	
ES		
FS		
GS		

Upon Return from FCALL PROT_ENTRY†

	High	Low
(E)AX	Modified	Modified
BX		
CX		
DX		
(E)SP	Loaded from stack	
BP		
SI		
DI		
(E)IP	Loaded from stack	
flags		
CS	Loaded from stack	
DS	Loaded from stack	
SS	Loaded from stack	
ES	Loaded from stack	
FS	Loaded from stack	
GS	Loaded from stack	

†SS:ESP and all segment registers are loaded from values on stack.
*Top of stack must look like this:

QWORD	Return address from FAR call to USE32 Segment
DWORD	EIP value
DWORD	CS value
DWORD	reserved for EFLAGS value
DWORD	ESP value
DWORD	SS value
DWORD	ES value
DWORD	DS value
DWORD	FS value
DWORD	GS value

Version: Applies to all versions of VCPI Driver beginning with 1.0.

Note: Interrupts must be disabled prior to calling interrupt.

Source: "Virtual Control Program Interface Version 1.0," June 12, 1989, page 15

See Also: 5.217. INT 67H, AH=DEH, AL=0CH -- VCPI Switch from V86 to Protected Mode

5.222. TASK SWITCHER API PATCH

Every program that uses Build Notification Chain (INT 2FH, Function 4B01H) or Hook Notification Chain (Service Function 0004H) must check for and install this patch each time the Task Switcher calls Query Suspend (Notification Function 0001H).

Without the patch, the Task Switcher behaves erratically and may lose data. The problem occurs because the Task Switcher inadvertently clears the CX register, which may affect subsequent DOS system functions.

Programs can check for and install the patch by executing the Patch Swapper routine given below. On entry, the client program must make sure the ES:DI registers point to the Task Switcher's service-function address. This is the same address provided by the Task Switcher when it calls Query Suspend.

```
OldCode     db    33h,0C9h,0FBh,0E8h,10h,0,0B8h,1,0
NewCode     db    51h,33h,0C9h,0FBh,0E8h,0Fh,0,59h,90h

PatchSwapper  proc  near

     push  ds
     push  cx
     push  si
     push  di

     cld

     push  cs
     pop   ds

;Check whether the code is the same.

     sub   di,73h            ;offset to the patch area
     mov   cx,9
     lea   si,OldCode        ;old code
     push  cx                ;save size, offset
     push  di
     rep   cmpsb
     or    cx,cx
     pop   di                ;recover
     pop   cx
     jnz   PSDone

;Now patch code with new code.

     lea   si,NewCode
     rep   movsb             ;patch

PSDone:
     pop   di
     pop   si
     pop   cx
     pop   ds
     ret

PatchSwapper   endp
```

Source: Microsoft MS-DOS 5.0 Programmer's Reference

See Also: 5.024. INT 2FH, AX=4B01H -- Build Notification Chain
5.041. Service Functions
5.042. Notification Functions

Section 6

Microsoft Windows

6.001. RESERVED SYSTEM KEYS AND RECOMMENDED KEYBOARD ACTIONS

Key Name	*Windows Action*
Alt+letter	Selects menu from active menu bar
Alt+Shift+Tab	Selects active window from bottom up
Alt+Spacebar	Selects System menu of active window
Alt+Tab	Selects active window from top down
Alt+Backspace§	Undo -- reverses last user action
Alt+Escape†	Selects next application
Alt+F10†	Enlarges window
Alt+F4†	Closes window
Alt+F5†	Restores window
Alt+F6§	Changes active window
Alt+F7†	Moves window
Alt+F8†	Sizes window
Alt+F9†	Shrinks window
Backspace	Deletes selection or deletes character to left of cursor
Ctrl+F6§	Changes active secondary window
Ctrl+End§	Moves cursor to bottom rightmost choice
Ctrl+Escape†	RESERVED
Ctrl+Home§	Moves cursor to top leftmost position in current field
Ctrl+Ins§	Copy -- duplicates selected object/text and copies it to clipboard
Ctrl+Left arrow§	Moves cursor to beginning of word to left of cursor
Ctrl+PgDn§	Scrolls to information to right of currently visible window area
Ctrl+PgUp§	Scrolls to information to left of currently visible window area
Ctrl+Right arrow§	Moves cursor to beginning of word to right of cursor
Ctrl+Shift+Left arrow	Extends selection to beginning of word
Ctrl+Shift+Right arrow	Extends selection to end of word
Del§	Deletes existing selection or character to left of cursor
Down arrow*	Selects command or choice below current one
End	Moves cursor to rightmost choice
Enter	Invokes selected command or action
Escape	Cancels menu or dialog box
F1	Displays information about item or dialog box
F5	Updates contents of windows
F10† or Alt§	Selects system menu or action bar of active window
F6§	Moves cursor in clockwise direction between split windows
Home§	Moves cursor to leftmost choice
Ins§	Toggles between insert and replace mode in field entry
Left arrow*	Selects menu or choice to left of current one
PgDn§	Scrolls to information below currently visible window area
PgUp§	Scrolls to information above currently visible window area
Right arrow*	Selects menu or choice to right of current one
Shift+Down arrow§	Extends selection to line below
Shift+End	Extends selection to end of current line
Shift+Escape†	Selects system menu of active window
Shift+Home	Extends selection to beginning of current line
Shift+Left arrow§	Extends selection one character to left
Shift+Right arrow§	Extends selection one character to right
Shift+Up arrow§	Extends selection to line above
Shift+Tab	Selects active control or field from bottom up
Shift+Del§	Cut -- removes selected object/text and copies it to clipboard
Shift+arrow	Extends selection in that direction
Shift+Ins§	Paste -- copies clipboard contents to selected location
Spacebar	Invokes default action (default push button) or toggles choice§
Tab	Selects active control or field from top down
Up arrow*	Selects command or choice above current one

†Applies to versions of Windows beginning with 2.0 only.
§First defined by IBM's SAA guidelines.
*Any direction key of this type should not be redefined.

Note: On international keyboards, only the left Alt key should be used as an accelerator.

Source: Microsoft Windows 2.0 SDK Application Style Guide, pages 44 through 45
IBM SAA Common User Access Advanced Interface Design Guide, Appendix B

See Also: 1.23. IBM Keyboard Extended Function Codes
6.005. Recommended Mouse Usage
6.027. Common Menu Accelerator Key Definitions

6.002. VIRTUAL KEYS

Sorted by Key Name

Key Name	*Value*	*Description*
VK_0*	30H	0 key
VK_1*	31H	1 key
VK_2*	32H	2 key
VK_3*	33H	3 key
VK_4*	34H	4 key
VK_5*	35H	5 key
VK_6*	36H	6 key
VK_7*	37H	7 key
VK_8*	38H	8 key
VK_9*	39H	9 key
VK_A*	41H	A key
VK_ADD	6BH	Add key
VK_B*	42H	B key
VK_BACK	08H	BACKSPACE key
VK_C*	43H	C key
VK_CANCEL	03H	Cancel key
VK_CAPITAL	14H	CAPITAL (Caps Lock) key
VK_CLEAR	0CH	CLEAR key
VK_CONTROL	11H	CONTROL (Ctrl) key
VK_D*	44H	D key
VK_DECIMAL	6EH	Decimal point key (.)
VK_DELETE	2EH	DELETE (Del) key
VK_DIVIDE	6FH	Divide key
VK_DOWN	28H	DOWN ARROW key
VK_E*	45H	E key
VK_END	23H	END
VK_ESCAPE	1BH	ESCAPE (Esc) key
VK_EXECUTE*	2BH	EXECUTE key
VK_F*	46H	F key
VK_F1	70H	Function key 1
VK_F10	79H	Function key 10
VK_F11	7AH	Function key 11
VK_F12	7BH	Function key 12
VK_F13	7CH	Function key 13
VK_F14	7DH	Function key 14
VK_F15	7EH	Function key 15
VK_F16	7FH	Function key 16
VK_F2	71H	Function key 2
VK_F3	72H	Function key 3
VK_F4	73H	Function key 4
VK_F5	74H	Function key 5
VK_F6	75H	Function key 6
VK_F7	76H	Function key 7
VK_F8	77H	Function key 8
VK_F9	78H	Function key 9
VK_G*	47H	G key
VK_H*	48H	H key
VK_HELP	2FH	HELP key
VK_HOME	24H	HOME key
VK_I*	49H	I key
VK_INSERT	2DH	INSERT (Ins) key
VK_J*	4AH	J key
VK_K*	4BH	K key
VK_L*	4CH	L key
VK_LBUTTON	01H	Left mouse button
VK_LEFT	25H	LEFT ARROW key
VK_M*	4DH	M key
VK_MBUTTON	04H	Middle mouse button
VK_MENU	12H	MENU (Alt) key
VK_MULTIPLY	6AH	Multiply key
VK_N*	4EH	N key
VK_NEXT	22H	PAGE DOWN (PgDn) key
VK_NUMLOCK*	90H	NUM LOCK key
VK_NUMPAD0	60H	Numeric keypad 0 key
VK_NUMPAD1	61H	Numeric keypad 1 key
VK_NUMPAD2	62H	Numeric keypad 2 key

Key Name	*Value*	*Description*
VK_NUMPAD3	63H	Numeric keypad 3 key
VK_NUMPAD4	64H	Numeric keypad 4 key
VK_NUMPAD5	65H	Numeric keypad 5 key
VK_NUMPAD6	66H	Numeric keypad 6 key
VK_NUMPAD7	67H	Numeric keypad 7 key
VK_NUMPAD8	68H	Numeric keypad 8 key
VK_NUMPAD9	69H	Numeric keypad 9 key
VK_O*	4FH	O key
VK_OEM_1*	BAH	Keyboard specific punctuation key
VK_OEM_102*	E2H	<> or \\| on non-USA 102-keyboard
VK_OEM_2*	BFH	Keyboard specific punctuation key
VK_OEM_3*	C0H	Keyboard specific punctuation key
VK_OEM_4*	DBH	Keyboard specific punctuation key
VK_OEM_5*	DCH	Keyboard specific punctuation key
VK_OEM_6*	DDH	Keyboard specific punctuation key
VK_OEM_7*	DEH	Keyboard specific punctuation key
VK_OEM_8*	DFH	Keyboard specific punctuation key
VK_OEM_COMMA*	BCH	Comma key
VK_OEM_MINUS*	BDH	Minus key
VK_OEM_PERIOD*	BEH	Period key
VK_OEM_PLUS*	BBH	Plus key
VK_OEM_SCROLL*	91H	SCROLL LOCK key
VK_P*	50H	P key
VK_PAUSE	13H	PAUSE key
VK_PRIOR	21H	PAGE UP (PgUp) key
VK_Q*	51H	Q key
VK_R*	52H	R key
VK_RBUTTON	02H	Right mouse button
VK_RETURN	0DH	RETURN (Enter) key
VK_RIGHT	27H	RIGHT ARROW key
VK_S*	53H	S key
VK_SELECT	29H	SELECT key
VK_SEPARATER	6CH	Separater key
VK_SHIFT	10H	SHIFT key
VK_SNAPSHOT*	2CH	PRINTSCREEN (PrtSc) key
VK_SPACE	20H	SPACEBAR
VK_SUBTRACT	6DH	Subtract key
VK_T*	54H	T key
VK_TAB	09H	TAB key
VK_U*	55H	U key
VK_UP	26H	UP ARROW key
VK_V*	56H	V key
VK_W*	57H	W key
VK_X*	58H	X key
VK_Y*	59H	Y key
VK_Z*	5AH	Z key
	05H-07H	Unassigned
	0AH-0BH	Unassigned
	0EH-0FH	Unassigned
	15H-19H	Reserved for Kanji
	1AH	Unassigned
	1CH-1FH	Reserved for Kanji
	2AH	OEM specific
	3AH-40H	Unassigned
	5BH-5FH	Unassigned
	80H-87H	OEM specific
	88H-8FH	Unassigned
	92H-B9H	Unassigned
	C1H-DAH	Unassigned
	E0H-E1H	OEM specific
	E3H-E4H	OEM specific
	E5H	Unassigned
	E6H	OEM specific
	E7H-E8H	Unassigned
	E9H-F5H	OEM specific
	F6H-FEH	Unassigned

(Continued)

6.002. VIRTUAL KEYS (continued)

Sorted by Value

Key Name	*Value*	*Description*
VK_LBUTTON	01H	Left mouse button
VK_RBUTTON	02H	Right mouse button
VK_CANCEL	03H	Cancel key
VK_MBUTTON	04H	Middle mouse button
	05H-07H	Unassigned
VK_BACK	08H	BACKSPACE key
VK_TAB	09H	TAB key
	0AH-0BH	Unassigned
VK_CLEAR	0CH	CLEAR key
VK_RETURN	0DH	RETURN (Enter) key
	0EH-0FH	Unassigned
VK_SHIFT	10H	SHIFT key
VK_CONTROL	11H	CONTROL (Ctrl) key
VK_MENU	12H	MENU (Alt) key
VK_PAUSE	13H	PAUSE key
VK_CAPITAL	14H	CAPITAL (Caps Lock) key
	15H-19H	Reserved for Kanji
	1AH	Unassigned
VK_ESCAPE	1BH	ESCAPE (Esc) key
	1CH-1FH	Reserved for Kanji
VK_SPACE	20H	SPACEBAR
VK_PRIOR	21H	PAGE UP (PgUp) key
VK_NEXT	22H	PAGE DOWN (PgDn) key
VK_END	23H	END key
VK_HOME	24H	HOME key
VK_LEFT	25H	LEFT ARROW key
VK_UP	26H	UP ARROW key
VK_RIGHT	27H	RIGHT ARROW key
VK_DOWN	28H	DOWN ARROW key
VK_SELECT	29H	SELECT key
	2AH	OEM specific
VK_EXECUTE*	2BH	EXECUTE key
VK_SNAPSHOT*	2CH	PRINTSCREEN (PrtSc) key
VK_INSERT	2DH	INSERT (Ins) key
VK_DELETE	2EH	DELETE (Del) key
VK_HELP	2FH	HELP key
VK_0*	30H	0 key
VK_1*	31H	1 key
VK_2*	32H	2 key
VK_3*	33H	3 key
VK_4*	34H	4 key
VK_5*	35H	5 key
VK_6*	36H	6 key
VK_7*	37H	7 key
VK_8*	38H	8 key
VK_9*	39H	9 key
	3AH-40H	Unassigned
VK_A*	41H	A key
VK_B*	42H	B key
VK_C*	43H	C key
VK_D*	44H	D key
VK_E*	45H	E key
VK_F*	46H	F key
VK_G*	47H	G key
VK_H*	48H	H key
VK_I*	49H	I key
VK_J*	4AH	J key
VK_K*	4BH	K key
VK_L*	4CH	L key
VK_M*	4DH	M key
VK_N*	4EH	N key
VK_O*	4FH	O key
VK_P*	50H	P key
VK_Q*	51H	Q key
VK_R*	52H	R key
VK_S*	53H	S key
VK_T*	54H	T key
VK_U*	55H	U key
VK_V*	56H	V key
VK_W*	57H	W key
VK_X*	58H	X key
VK_Y*	59H	Y key
VK_Z*	5AH	Z key
	5BH-5FH	Unassigned
VK_NUMPAD0	60H	Numeric keypad 0 key
VK_NUMPAD1	61H	Numeric keypad 1 key
VK_NUMPAD2	62H	Numeric keypad 2 key
VK_NUMPAD3	63H	Numeric keypad 3 key
VK_NUMPAD4	64H	Numeric keypad 4 key
VK_NUMPAD5	65H	Numeric keypad 5 key
VK_NUMPAD6	66H	Numeric keypad 6 key
VK_NUMPAD7	67H	Numeric keypad 7 key
VK_NUMPAD8	68H	Numeric keypad 8 key
VK_NUMPAD9	69H	Numeric keypad 9 key
VK_MULTIPLY	6AH	Multiply key
VK_ADD	6BH	Add key
VK_SEPARATER	6CH	Separater key
VK_SUBTRACT	6DH	Subtract key
VK_DECIMAL	6EH	Decimal point key (.)
VK_DIVIDE	6FH	Divide key
VK_F1	70H	Function key 1
VK_F2	71H	Function key 2
VK_F3	72H	Function key 3
VK_F4	73H	Function key 4
VK_F5	74H	Function key 5
VK_F6	75H	Function key 6
VK_F7	76H	Function key 7
VK_F8	77H	Function key 8
VK_F9	78H	Function key 9
VK_F10	79H	Function key 10
VK_F11	7AH	Function key 11
VK_F12	7BH	Function key 12
VK_F13	7CH	Function key 13
VK_F14	7DH	Function key 14
VK_F15	7EH	Function key 15
VK_F16	7FH	Function key 16
	80H-87H	OEM specific
	88H-8FH	Unassigned
VK_NUMLOCK*	90H	NUM LOCK key
VK_OEM_SCROLL*	91H	SCROLL LOCK key
	92H-B9H	Unassigned
VK_OEM_1*	BAH	Keyboard specific punctuation key
VK_OEM_PLUS*	BBH	Plus key
VK_OEM_COMMA*	BCH	Comma key
VK_OEM_MINUS*	BDH	Minus key
VK_OEM_PERIOD*	BEH	Period key
VK_OEM_2*	BFH	Keyboard specific punctuation key
VK_OEM_3*	C0H	Keyboard specific punctuation key
	C1H-DAH	Unassigned
VK_OEM_4*	DBH	Keyboard specific punctuation key
VK_OEM_5*	DCH	Keyboard specific punctuation key
VK_OEM_6*	DDH	Keyboard specific punctuation key
VK_OEM_7*	DEH	Keyboard specific punctuation key
VK_OEM_8*	DFH	Keyboard specific punctuation key
	E0H-E1H	OEM specific
VK_OEM_102*	E2H	<> or \\| on non-USA 102-keyboard
	E3H-E4H	OEM specific
	E5H	Unassigned
	E6H	OEM specific
	E7H-E8H	Unassigned
	E9H-F5H	OEM specific
	F6H-FEH	Unassigned

*First defined in Windows 3.0 documentation.

Source: Microsoft Windows 2.0 SDK Programmer's Reference, pages 280 through 281
Microsoft Windows 3.0 SDK Programmer's Reference, Appendix A

See Also: 6.001. Reserved System Keys and Recommended Keyboard Actions
6.005. Recommended Mouse Usage

6.003. WINDOWS TERMINAL -- VT52 KEY EMULATIONS

Keyboard Application Mode

ANSI VT52 Key	*Windows Key Equivalent*	*NumLock Status*	*ASCII*	*Hex*
0	Numeric keypad 0	ON	ESC ? p	1B 3F 70
1	Numeric keypad 1	ON	ESC ? q	1B 3F 71
2	Numeric keypad 2	ON	ESC ? r	1B 3F 72
3	Numeric keypad 3	ON	ESC ? s	1B 3F 73
4	Numeric keypad 4	ON	ESC ? t	1B 3F 74
5	Numeric keypad 5	ON	ESC ? u	1B 3F 75
6	Numeric keypad 6	ON	ESC ? v	1B 3F 76
7	Numeric keypad 7	ON	ESC ? w	1B 3F 77
8	Numeric keypad 8	ON	ESC ? x	1B 3F 78
9	Numeric keypad 9	ON	ESC ? y	1B 3F 79
-	Numeric keypad -	ON	ESC ? m	1B 3F 6D
,	Numeric keypad *	ON	ESC ? l	1B 3F 6C
.	Numeric keypad .	ON	ESC ? n	1B 3F 6E
Enter	Numeric keypad plus	ON	ESC ? M	1B 3F 4D
Cursor down	Down arrow	OFF	ESC O B	1B 4F 42
Cursor left	Left arrow	OFF	ESC O D	1B 4F 44
Cursor right	Right arrow	OFF	ESC O C	1B 4F 43
Cursor up	Up arrow	OFF	ESC O A	1B 4F 41
PF1	F1	NA	ESC P	1B 50
PF2	F2	NA	ESC Q	1B 51
PF3	F3	NA	ESC R	1B 52
PF4	F4	NA	ESC S	1B 53

Note: Keys listed are for IBM PC compatible keyboards only.

Source: Microsoft Windows 2.0 Desktop Applications User's Guide, pages 89 through 90
Microsoft Windows 3.0 User's Guide, Appendix C

See Also: 6.001. Reserved System Keys and Recommended Keyboard Actions
6.004. Windows Terminal -- VT100 Key Emulations

6.004. WINDOWS TERMINAL -- VT100 KEY EMULATIONS

Keyboard Application Mode

ANSI VT100 Key	*Windows Key Equivalent*	*NumLock Status*	*ASCII*	*Hex*
0	Numeric keypad 0	ON	ESC O p	1B 4F 70
1	Numeric keypad 1	ON	ESC O q	1B 4F 71
2	Numeric keypad 2	ON	ESC O r	1B 4F 72
3	Numeric keypad 3	ON	ESC O s	1B 4F 73
4	Numeric keypad 4	ON	ESC O t	1B 4F 74
5	Numeric keypad 5	ON	ESC O u	1B 4F 75
6	Numeric keypad 6	ON	ESC O v	1B 4F 76
7	Numeric keypad 7	ON	ESC O w	1B 4F 77
8	Numeric keypad 8	ON	ESC O x	1B 4F 78
9	Numeric keypad 9	ON	ESC O y	1B 4F 79
-	Numeric keypad -	ON	ESC O m	1B 4F 6D
,	Numeric keypad *	ON	ESC O l	1B 4F 6C
.	Numeric keypad .	ON	ESC O n	1B 4F 6E
Enter	Numeric keypad plus	ON	ESC O M	1B 4F 4D
Cursor down	Down arrow	OFF	ESC O B	1B 4F 42
Cursor left	Left arrow	OFF	ESC O D	1B 4F 44
Cursor right	Right arrow	OFF	ESC O C	1B 4F 43
Cursor up	Up arrow	OFF	ESC O A	1B 4F 41

For DEC VT-100

ANSI VT100 Key	*Windows Key Equivalent*	*NumLock Status*	*ASCII*	*Hex*
Cursor down	Down arrow	OFF	ESC [B	1B 5B 42
Cursor left	Left arrow	OFF	ESC [D	1B 5B 44
Cursor right	Right arrow	OFF	ESC [C	1B 5B 43
Cursor up	Up arrow	OFF	ESC [A	1B 5B 41
PF1	F1	NA	ESC O P	1B 4F 50
PF2	F2	NA	ESC O Q	1B 4F 51
PF3	F3	NA	ESC O R	1B 4F 52
PF4	F4	NA	ESC O S	1B 4F 53

Note: Keys listed are for IBM PC compatible keyboards only.

Source: Microsoft Windows 2.0 Desktop Applications User's Guide, pages 89 through 90
Microsoft Windows 3.0 User's Guide, Appendix C

See Also: 6.001. Reserved System Keys and Recommended Keyboard Actions
6.003. Windows Terminal -- VT52 Key Emulations

6.005. RECOMMENDED MOUSE USAGE

Mouse Action	*In Text Selection*	*In Item Selection*
Click	Move insertion point to pointer position	Select item at pointer position
Double-click	Select word at pointer position	Confirm or execute item at pointer position
Drag	Extend selection from pointer to release point	Extend selection from pointer to release point
Shift + drag	Extend current selection to new position	Move left one character
Shift + click	Extend current selection to new release point	Extend current selection to new release point
Shift + double-click	Extend selection to start or end of word	
Control + drag		Allow discontinuous selection; add addition selection
Control + click		Toggle: delete or restore selection

Source: Microsoft Windows 2.0 SDK Application Style Guide, pages 53 through 55
IBM SAA Common User Access Advanced Interface Design Guide, Appendix B

See Also: 1.23. IBM Keyboard Extended Function Codes
6.001. Reserved System Keys and Recommended Keyboard Actions

6.006. WINDOWS OPERATING ENVIRONMENT FILES

Required Core Files

File Name	*Function*	*1.x*	*2.x*	*3.x*
GDI.EXE	Windows code file			✔
KERNEL.EXE	Windows code file			✔
KRNL286.EXE	Windows 286 code file			✔
KRNL386.EXE	Windows 386 code file			✔
MOUSE.COM	Microsoft Mouse driver	✔	✔	✔
SPOOLER.EXE	Print spooler	✔	✔	
SWAPFILE.EXE	Windows swap file			✔
USER.EXE	Windows code file			✔
WIN#.BIN	Windows code file (for 2.0, #=200)	✔	✔	
WIN#.OVL	Windows overlay file (for 2.0, #=200)	✔	✔	
WIN.COM	Windows loader file	✔	✔	✔
WIN.INI	Windows initialization file	✔	✔	✔
WIN386.EXE	Windows 386 code file			✔
WINOA286.MOD	Windows old applications support			✔
WINOA386.MOD	Windows old applications support			✔
WINOLDAP.GRB	Windows old applications support	✔	✔	
WINOLDAP.MOD	Windows old applications support	✔	✔	✔

Optional Files

File Name	*Function*	*1.x*	*2.x*	*3.x*
*.DLL	Dynamically linked library (* is name of application)			✔
*.DRV	Printer driver file (* is printer name)	✔	✔	✔
*.FON†	Font file (* is font name)	✔	✔	✔
*.HLP	Help file (* is application name)			✔
*.PCL	Printer control file (* is port name)	✔	✔	
CALC.EXE	Windows Calculator program	✔	✔	✔
CALENDAR.EXE	Windows Calendar program	✔	✔	✔
CARDFILE.EXE	Windows Cardfile program	✔	✔	✔
CLIPBRD.EXE	Windows Clipboard program	✔	✔	✔
CLOCK.EXE	Windows Clock program	✔	✔	✔
CONTROL.EXE	Windows Control Panel program	✔	✔	✔
EMM386.SYS	Expanded memory device driver			✔
HIMEM.SYS	Device driver for using high memory			✔
MSDOS.EXE	DOS Executive	✔	✔	✔
NOTEPAD.EXE	Windows Notepad program	✔	✔	✔
PAINT.EXE	Windows Paint program	✔	✔	
PBRUSH.EXE	Windows Color Paintbrush program			✔
PIFEDIT.EXE	Windows PIF Editor program	✔	✔	✔
PRINTMAN.EXE	Windows Print Manager program			✔
PROGMAN.EXE	Windows Program Manager program			✔
RAMDRIVE.SYS	RAM drive device driver			✔
RECORDER.EXE	Windows Macro Recorder program			✔
REVERSI.EXE	Windows Reversi program	✔	✔	✔
SETUP.EXE	Windows Setup program			✔
SMARTDRIVE.SYS	Windows RAM drive device driver			✔
SOL.EXE	Windows Solitare program			✔
TASKMAN.EXE	Windows Task Manager program			✔
TERMINAL.EXE	Windows terminal emulation program	✔	✔	✔
TMSR*.FON	Times Roman font file (* is letter)	✔	✔	✔
WINFILE.EXE	Windows File Manager program			✔
WINHELP.EXE	Windows help system			✔
WINVER.EXE	Windows version info			✔
WRITE.EXE	Windows Write program	✔	✔	✔

†At least one font must be installed; additional fonts are optional.

Source: Microsoft Windows 2.03 disks
Microsoft Windows 3.0 disks

See Also: 6.007. Windows C Programming Library and Include Files
6.008. Windows Development Utilities

6.007. WINDOWS C PROGRAMMING LIBRARY AND INCLUDE FILES

File Name	*Function*	*1.x*	*2.x*	*3.x*
ASSERT.H	Defines assert(exp) macro			✔
BIOS.H	Declares constants, structures, functions for BIOS I/O			✔
CDLLCAW.LIB	Alternate math package, compact model, DLL			✔
CDLLCEW.LIB	Emulated math package, compact model, DLL			✔
CLIBC.LIB	Startup library, compact memory model	✔	✔	
CLIBCAW.LIB	Alternate math package, compact model, application			✔
CLIBCEW.LIB	Emulated math package, compact model, application			✔
CLIBW.LIB	Standard library, compact memory model	✔	✔	
CMACROS.INC	Assembler Include File			✔
CNOCRT.LIB				✔
CNOCRTD.LIB				✔
CONIO.H	Function declarations for console & port I/O			✔
CTYPE.H	Defines macros for character classification/conversion			✔
CUSTCNTL.H	Defines custom control library			✔
DDE.H	Defines DDE window messages and structures			✔
DIRECT.H	Function declarations for directory handling			✔
DOS.H	Defines MS-DOS interface routines			✔
DRIVINIT.H	Printer driver initialization routines			✔
ERRNO.H	Defines system-wide error numbers			✔
FCNTL.H	Defines constants for file control options and open()			✔
FLOAT.H	Defines implementation dependent values for math			✔
IO.H	Function declarations for low-level file handling & I/O			✔
LDLLCAW.LIB	Alternate math package, large model, DLL			✔
LDLLCEW.LIB	Emulated math package, large model, DLL			✔
LIB.H				✔
LIBW.LIB				✔
LIMITS.H	Defines implementation dependent values			✔
LLIBC.LIB	Startup library, large memory model	✔	✔	
LLIBCAW.LIB	Alternate math package, large model, application			✔
LLIBCEW.LIB	Emulated math package, large model, application			✔
LLIBW.LIB	Standard library, large memory model	✔	✔	
LOCALE.H	Defines items used by localization routines			✔
LOCKING.H	Defines flags for locking() function			✔
MALLOC.H	Function declarations for memory allocation			✔
MATH.H	Definitions for math subroutine library			✔
MDLLCAW.LIB	Alternate math package, medium model, DLL			✔
MDLLCEW.LIB	Emulated math package, medium model, DLL			✔
MEMORY.H	Function declarations for buffer manipulation			✔
MLIBC.LIB	Startup library, medium memory model	✔	✔	
MLIBCAW.LIB	Alternate math package, medium model, application			✔
MLIBCEW.LIB	Emulated math package, medium model, application			✔
MLIBW.LIB	Standard library, medium memory model	✔	✔	
MNOCRT.LIB				✔
MNOCRTD.LIB				✔
PROCESS.H	Function declarations for process control routines			✔
SDLLCAW.LIB	Alternate math package, small model, DLL			✔
SDLLCEW.LIB	Emulated math package, small model, DLL			✔
SEARCH.H	Declarations for sorting and searching routines			✔
SETJMP.H	Defines machine-dependent setjmp/longjmp buffer			✔
SHARE.H	Defines file sharing modes for sopen()			✔
SIGNAL.H	Defines signal values and functions			✔
SLIBC.LIB	Startup library, small memory model	✔	✔	
SLIBCAW.LIB	Alternate math package, small model, application			✔
SLIBCEW.LIB	Emulated math package, small model, application			✔
SLIBW.LIB	Standard library, small memory model	✔	✔	
STAT.H	Defines structure used by stat() and fstat()			✔
STDARG.H	ANSI-style macros for accessing variable arguments			✔
STDDEF.H	Commonly used constants, types, variables defined			✔
STDIO.H	Defines items used by level 2 I/O routines			✔
STDLIB.H	Miscellaneous function definitions			✔
STRING.H	Defines string manipulation functions			✔
TIME.H	Definitions for time routines			✔
TIMEB.H	Defines ftime() function and uses			✔
TYPES.H	Defines types returned by system level calls			✔
UTIME.H	Defines structure used by utime			✔
VARARGS.H	XENIX-style macros for accessing variable arguments			✔
WIN87EM.LIB	8087, extended memory library		✔	
WINDOWS.H	Windows Include File for C-language applications	✔	✔	✔
WINDOWS.INC	Assembler Include File			✔

Source: Microsoft Windows 2.0 SDK Tools, page 17
Microsoft Windows 3.0 SDK Tools, page 2-12
Microsoft Windows 3.0 SDK distribution disks

See Also: 6.006. Windows Operating Environment Files
6.008. Windows Development Utilities

6.008. WINDOWS DEVELOPMENT UTILITIES

File Name	*Function*	*1.x*	*2.x*	*3.x*
DIALOG.EXE	Creates and edits Windows dialog boxes	X		X
DLGEDIT.EXE	Creates and edits Windows dialog boxes		X	
EXEHDR.EXE	Displays EXE file header information	X		
NEWFON.EXE	Converts version 1.03 fonts to 2.01 or later style		X	
FONTEDIT.EXE	Creates and edits Windows fonts	X	X	X
HEAPWALK.EXE	Displays allocated blocks in Windows global heap	X		X
ICONEDIT.EXE	Creates and edits Windows icons	X	X	
IMPLIB.EXE	Creates linkable, dynamic library files	X		
LIB.EXE	Creates and maintains library files*	X		X
LINK4.EXE	Creates executable Windows applications	X		
MAKE.EXE	Automated file maintenance utility	X		
MAPSYM.EXE	Creates symbol files for symbolic debugger	X		X
RC.EXE	Resource compiler	X	X	X
RCPP.EXE	Preprocessor for resource compiler	X	X	X
SHAKER.EXE	Randomly allocates memory in global heap	X	X	X
WINTOOL.EXE			X	
WIN87EM.EXE	80X87 support		X	
SLAPJR.EXE	Sends screen to file or printer	X		
SYMDEB.EXE	Symbolic debugger for Windows applications	X		
WINSTUB.EXE	Warning message for non-Windows environs	X	X	X

*Not part of Windows 3.0 SDK

Note: Additional utilities are available directly from Microsoft and the Microsoft-supported conference on Genie

Source: Microsoft Windows 2.0 SDK disks
Microsoft Windows 3.0 SDK distribution disks

See Also: 6.006. Windows Operating Environment Files
6.007. Windows C Programming Library and Include Files

6.009. EXTENDED ANSI CHARACTER CODES

Dec	Hex	Octal	Binary	Name	Character
32	20	040	0010 0000	Space	Space
33	21	041	0010 0001	Exclamation point	!
34	22	042	0010 0010	Quotation mark	"
35	23	043	0010 0011	Number sign	#
36	24	044	0010 0100	Dollar sign	$
37	25	045	0010 0101	Percent sign	%
38	26	046	0010 0110	Ampersand	&
39	27	047	0010 0111	Apostrophe	'
40	28	050	0010 1000	Opening parenthesis	(
41	29	051	0010 1001	Closing parenthesis	)
42	2A	052	0010 1010	Asterisk	*
43	2B	053	0010 1011	Plus sign	+
44	2C	054	0010 1100	Comma	,
45	2D	055	0010 1101	Hyphen	-
46	2E	056	0010 1110	Period	.
47	2F	057	0010 1111	Forward slash	/
48	30	060	0011 0000	Zero	0
49	31	061	0011 0001	One	1
50	32	062	0011 0010	Two	2
51	33	063	0011 0011	Three	3
52	34	064	0011 0100	Four	4
53	35	065	0011 0101	Five	5
54	36	066	0011 0110	Six	6
55	37	067	0011 0111	Seven	7
56	38	070	0011 1000	Eight	8
57	39	071	0011 1001	Nine	9
58	3A	072	0011 1010	Colon	:
59	3B	073	0011 1011	Semicolon	;
60	3C	074	0011 1100	Less than sign	<
61	3D	075	0011 1101	Equal sign	=
62	3E	076	0011 1110	Greater than sign	>
63	3F	077	0011 1111	Question mark	?
64	40	100	0100 0000	Commercial at sign	@
65	41	101	0100 0001	Capital A	A
66	42	102	0100 0010	Capital B	B
67	43	103	0100 0011	Capital C	C
68	44	104	0100 0100	Capital D	D
69	45	105	0100 0101	Capital E	E
70	46	106	0100 0110	Capital F	F
71	47	107	0100 0111	Capital G	G
72	48	110	0100 1000	Capital H	H
73	49	111	0100 1001	Capital I	I
74	4A	112	0100 1010	Capital J	J
75	4B	113	0100 1011	Capital K	K
76	4C	114	0100 1100	Capital L	L
77	4D	115	0100 1101	Capital M	M
78	4E	116	0100 1110	Capital N	N
79	4F	117	0100 1111	Capital O	O
80	50	120	0101 0000	Capital P	P
81	51	121	0101 0001	Capital Q	Q
82	52	122	0101 0010	Capital R	R
83	53	123	0101 0011	Capital S	S
84	54	124	0101 0100	Capital T	T
85	55	125	0101 0101	Capital U	U
86	56	126	0101 0110	Capital V	V
87	57	127	0101 0111	Capital W	W
88	58	130	0101 1000	Capital X	X
89	59	131	0101 1001	Capital Y	Y
90	5A	132	0101 1010	Capital Z	Z
91	5B	133	0101 1011	Opening bracket	[
92	5C	134	0101 1100	Backward slash	\
93	5D	135	0101 1101	Closing bracket	]
94	5E	136	0101 1110	Caret (circumflex)	^
95	5F	137	0101 1111	Underscore	_
96	60	140	0110 0000	Grave	`
97	61	141	0110 0001	Lowercase A	a
98	62	142	0110 0010	Lowercase B	b

(Continued)

6.009. EXTENDED ANSI CHARACTER CODES (continued)

Dec	Hex	Octal	Binary	Name	Character
99	63	143	0110 0011	Lowercase C	c
100	64	144	0110 0100	Lowercase D	d
101	65	145	0110 0101	Lowercase E	e
102	66	146	0110 0110	Lowercase F	f
103	67	147	0110 0111	Lowercase G	g
104	68	150	0110 1000	Lowercase H	h
105	69	151	0110 1001	Lowercase I	i
106	6A	152	0110 1010	Lowercase J	j
107	6B	153	0110 1011	Lowercase K	k
108	6C	154	0110 1100	Lowercase L	l
109	6D	155	0110 1101	Lowercase M	m
110	6E	156	0110 1110	Lowercase N	n
111	6F	157	0110 1111	Lowercase O	o
112	70	160	0111 0000	Lowercase P	p
113	71	161	0111 0001	Lowercase Q	q
114	72	162	0111 0010	Lowercase R	r
115	73	163	0111 0011	Lowercase S	s
116	74	164	0111 0100	Lowercase T	t
117	75	165	0111 0101	Lowercase U	u
118	76	166	0111 0110	Lowercase V	v
119	77	167	0111 0111	Lowercase W	w
120	78	170	0111 1000	Lowercase X	x
121	79	171	0111 1001	Lowercase Y	y
122	7A	172	0111 1010	Lowercase Z	z
123	7B	173	0111 1011	Opening brace	{
124	7C	174	0111 1100	Vertical line	|
125	7D	175	0111 1101	Closing brace	}
126	7E	176	0111 1110	Tilde	~
145	91	221	1001 0001	Left single quote	‘
146	92	222	1001 0010	Right single quote	’
160	A0	240	1010 0000	Blank	
161	A1	241	1010 0001	Inverted exclamation	¡
162	A2	242	1010 0010	Cent sign	¢
163	A3	243	1010 0011	Pound sterling sign	£
164	A4	244	1010 0100	General currency sign	¤
165	A5	245	1010 0101	Yen sign	¥
166	A6	246	1010 0110	Pipe symbol	¦
167	A7	247	1010 0111	Section symbol	§
168	A8	250	1010 1000	Diaeresis symbol	¨
169	A9	251	1010 1001	Copyright symbol	©
170	AA	252	1010 1010	Female ordinal	ª
171	AB	253	1010 1011	Left pointing guillemets	«
172	AC	254	1010 1100	Logical not	¬
173	AD	255	1010 1101	Hyphen	-
174	AE	256	1010 1110	Registered symbol	®
175	AF	257	1010 1111	Macron symbol	¯
176	B0	260	1011 0000	Degree symbol	°
177	B1	261	1011 0001	Plus/minus symbol	±
178	B2	262	1011 0010	Superscript 2	2
179	B3	263	1011 0011	Superscript 3	3
180	B4	264	1011 0100	Acute accent	´
181	B5	265	1011 0101	Mu (micro)	µ
182	B6	266	1011 0110	Paragraph symbol	¶
183	B7	267	1011 0111	1 to 2 upper right	·
184	B8	270	1011 1000	Cedilla symbol	¸
185	B9	271	1011 1001	Superscript 1	1
186	BA	272	1011 1010	Superscript 0	º
187	BB	273	1011 1011	Right pointing guillemets	»
188	BC	274	1011 1100	One-quarter	¼
189	BD	275	1011 1101	One-half	½
190	BE	276	1011 1110	Three-quarters	¾
191	BF	277	1011 1111	Inverted question mark	¿
192	C0	300	1100 0000	Grave A	À
193	C1	301	1100 0001	Acute A	Á
194	C2	302	1100 0010	Circumflex A	Â
195	C3	303	1100 0011	Tilde A	Ã
196	C4	304	1100 0100	Umlaut A	Ä

(Continued)

6.009. EXTENDED ANSI CHARACTER CODES (continued)

Dec	Hex	Octal	Binary	Name	Character
197	C5	305	1100 0101	A ring	Å
198	C6	306	1100 0110	Dipthong AE	Æ
199	C7	307	1100 0111	Cedilla C	Ç
200	C8	310	1100 1000	Grave E	È
201	C9	311	1100 1001	Acute E	É
202	CA	312	1100 1010	Circumflex E	Ê
203	CB	313	1100 1011	Umlaut E	Ë
204	CC	314	1100 1100	Grave I	Ì
205	CD	315	1100 1101	Acute I	Í
206	CE	316	1100 1110	Circumflex I	Î
207	CF	317	1100 1111	Umlaut I	Ï
208	D0	320	1101 0000	Uppercase eth	Ð
209	D1	321	1101 0001	Tilde N	Ñ
210	D2	322	1101 0010	Grave O	Ò
211	D3	323	1101 0011	Acute O	Ó
212	D4	324	1101 0100	Circumflex O	Ô
213	D5	325	1101 0101	Tilde O	Õ
214	D6	326	1101 0110	Umlaut O	Ö
215	D7	327	1101 0111	Multiply (times) symbol	x
216	D8	330	1101 1000	Uppercase O oblique	Ø
217	D9	331	1101 1001	Grave U	Ù
218	DA	332	1101 1010	Acute U	Ú
219	DB	333	1101 1011	Circumflex u	Û
220	DC	334	1101 1100	Umlaut U	Ü
221	DD	335	1101 1101	Acute Y	´Y
222	DE	336	1101 1110	Uppercase thorn	Þ
223	DF	337	1101 1111	Lowercase es-zet ligature	ß
224	E0	340	1110 0000	Grave a	à
225	E1	341	1110 0001	Acute a	á
226	E2	342	1110 0010	Circumflex a	â
227	E3	343	1110 0011	Tilde a	ã
228	E4	344	1110 0100	Umlaut a	ä
229	E5	345	1110 0101	a ring	å
230	E6	346	1110 0110	Dipthong ae	æ
231	E7	347	1110 0111	Cedilla c	ç
232	E8	350	1110 1000	Grave e	è
233	E9	351	1110 1001	Acute e	é
234	EA	352	1110 1010	Circumflex e	ê
235	EB	353	1110 1011	Umlaut e	ë
236	EC	354	1110 1100	Grave i	ì
237	ED	355	1110 1101	Acute i	í
238	EE	356	1110 1110	Circumflex i	î
239	EF	357	1110 1111	Umlaut i	ï
240	F0	360	1111 0000	Lowercase eth	ð
241	F1	361	1111 0001	Tilde n	ñ
242	F2	362	1111 0010	Grave o	ò
243	F3	363	1111 0011	Acute o	ó
244	F4	364	1111 0100	Circumflex o	ô
245	F5	365	1111 0101	Tilde o	õ
246	F6	366	1111 0110	Umlaut o	ö
247	F7	367	1111 0111	Divide by	÷
248	F8	370	1111 1000	Lowercase o oblique	ø
249	F9	371	1111 1001	Grave u	ù
250	FA	372	1111 1010	Acute u	ú
251	FB	373	1111 1011	Circumflex u	û
252	FC	374	1111 1100	Umlaut u	ü
253	FD	375	1111 1101	Acute y	´y
254	FE	376	1111 1110	Lowercase thorn	þ
255	FF	377	1111 1111	Umlaut y	ÿ

Source: Microsoft Windows 2.0 SDK Programmer's Reference, page 121
Microsoft Windows 3.0 User's Guide, page 568

See Also: 1.21. ASCII Character Set
1.22. IBM ASCII Character Set

6.010. WINDOWS EXE FILE FORMAT

The overall layout of the file looks like this:

Offset	Size	Function
0 (0)	32 bytes	Old-style EXE header info
20 (32)	29 bytes	RESERVED
3C (60)	4 bytes	New-style offset
40 (64)	Varies	Relocation table for DOS stub program
varies	Varies	New-style EXE information

The layout of the new-style EXE information section looks like this:

Offset	Size	Function	Allowable Values
0 (0)	Word	Signature word	"EN"
2 (2)	Byte	Version number of linker	
3 (3)	Byte	Revision number of linker	
4 (4)	Word	Offset of entry table	(Relative to beginning of this section of header)
6 (6)	Word	Number of bytes in entry table	
8 (8)	Dbl word	32-bit CRC of entire file	
C (12)	Word	Keyword	0000H = NOAUTODATA 0001H = SINGLEDATA (solo) 0002H = MULTIPLEDATA (instance) 2000H = errors detected at link time 8000H = Library module
E (14)	Word	Segment # of automatic data segment	
10 (16)	Word	Initial size of dynamic heap added to DS	(In bytes) 0 = no local allocation
12 (18)	Word	Initial size of stack added to DS	(In bytes) 0 = SS does not equal DS
14 (20)	Dbl word	CS:IP	
18 (24)	Dbl word	SS:SP	
1C (28)	Word	# of entries in segment table	
1E (30)	Word	# of bytes in nonresident-name table	
20 (32)	Word	Offset of segment table	(Relative to beginning of this section of header)
22 (34)	Word	Offset of resource table	(Relative to beginning of this section of header)
24 (36)	Word	Offset of resident-name table	(Relative to beginning of this section of header)
26 (38)	Word	Offset of module-reference table	(Relative to beginning of this section of header)
28 (40)	Word	Offset of imported-names table	(Relative to beginning of this section of header)
2A (42)	Dbl word	Offset of nonresident-name table	(Relative to beginning of file)
2E (46)	Word	# of movable entry points	
30 (48)	Word	Shift count of logical sector alignment	(Log [base 2] of the segment sector size)
32 (50)	Word	# of reserved segments	
34 (52)	10 bytes	RESERVED	Must be 0

Version: Applies to Windows 2.0.

Source: Microsoft Windows 2.0 SDK Programmer's Reference, pages 645 through 648

See Also: 2.27. EXE File Header
2.28. COM Program Layout

6.011. TAG IMAGE FILE FORMAT (TIFF)

Header and Directory Format

Offset	Size	Description	Field Size	Field Description	Comments
0 (0)	8 bytes	Header	Word Word Dbl word	Byte order Version Pointer to first IFD	4949H=least to most; 4D4DH=most to least 2AH (version 42)
A (10)	Varies	Image file directory	Word 12 bytes 12 bytes each Dbl word	Number of directory entries First directory entry Additional directory entries Pointer to next IFD	Must begin on word boundary See below for format
Varies	Varies	Values (tags)			See Tags table below

Directory Entry Format (In Image File Directory)

Offset	Size	Description	Allowable Values, Comments
0 (0)	Word	Tag	See Tags table below
2 (2)	Word	Type	1=bytes 2=ASCIIZ string 3=short (16-bit unsigned integers) 4=long (32-bit unsigned integers) 5=rational (2 longs: first is numerator, second is denominator)
4 (4)	Word	Length	Specified in terms of the data type (1 short=2 bytes)
8 (8)	Dbl word	Pointer to value	If value fits in 4 bytes or less, it is stored here

Tags

Tag	Type	Name	Allowable Values, Comments
FF (255)	Short	Subfile type	1=full resolution image data (requires image width, image length, strip offset) 2=reduced resolution data (requires image width, image length, strip offset)
100 (256)	Short	Image width	Width of image, in pixels
101 (257)	Short	Image length	Length of image, in pixels (rows)
102 (258)	Short	Bits per sample	(default=1)
103 (259)	Short	Compression	1=no compression, but tightly packed (default) 2=CCITT Group 3 compression 3=1-dimensional modified Huffman run length encoding
106 (262)	Short	Photometric interp.	0=min sample value is white, max sample value is black, all other grey 1=min sample value is black, max sample value is white, all other grey 2=RGB; min and max sample values control intensity (planar configuration affects stored order) 3=hue, saturation, brightness
107 (263)	Short	Thresholding	1=bilevel 'line art' scan (default) 2='halftone' or 'dithered' scan (bits per sample must be 1)
108 (264)	Short	Cell width	If thresholding=2, this is width of dithering matrix in 1-bit samples
109 (265)	Short	Cell length	If thresholding=2, this is length of dithering matrix in 1-bit samples
10A (266)	Short	Order of data values	1=most significant bits of byte filled first (default) 2=least significant bits of byte filled first
10D (269)	ASCIIZ	Name of document	
10E (270)	ASCIIZ	Image description	
10F (271)	ASCIIZ	Maker of scanner	
110 (272)	ASCIIZ	Model # of scanner	
111 (273)	Long	Strip offset	For each strip, the byte offset of that strip
112 (274)	Short	Orientation	1=first row at top, first column at left (default) 2=first row at top, first column at right 3=first row at bottom, first column at right 4=first row at bottom, first column at left 5=first row at left, first column at top 6=first row at right, first column at top 7=first row at right, first column at bottom 8=first row at left, first column at bottom
115 (277)	Short	Samples per pixel	1=monochrome (default) 3=color (other values allowed)
116 (278)	Long	Rows per strip	Number of rows per data strip (default=2**32-1)
117 (279)	Long	Strip byte counts	For each strip, the number of bytes it contains
118 (280)	Short	Min sample value	(Default=0)
119 (281)	Short	Max sample value	(Default= 2**(bitspersample)-1)
11A (282)	Rational	Width resolution	Number of pixels per inch
11B (283)	Rational	Length resolution	Number of pixels per inch
11C (284)	Short	Planar configuration	1=samples stored contiguously; single image plane 2=samples stored in separate sample planes
11D (285)	ASCIIZ	Name of page	
11E (286)	Rational	X position	Offset to left side of image on page, in inches
11F (287)	Rational	Y position	Offset to top side of image on page, in inches
120 (288)	Long	Free offsets	For each 'free' block in file, pointer to it, in bytes
121 (289)	Long	Free byte count	For each 'free' block in file, number of bytes in block

Note: • Tags with a value of 8000H (32768) or higher are reserved for user-defined information.
• The entries for image file directories must be sorted in ascending order by value of the tag.

Source: Tag Image File Format Draft (22 October, 1986), pages 2 through 13

See Also: 6.013. Windows Paint File Format

6.012. DYNAMIC DATA EXCHANGE PROTOCOL

Message Type	Purpose	Parameters		
WM_DDE_INITIATE	Request start of conversation	wParam =	identifies sending window	
		lParam =	aApplication	LO
			aTopic	HO
WM_DDE_TERMINATE	End conversation	wParam =	identifies sending window	
		lParam =	RESERVED	
WM_DDE_ACK	Acceptance of prev. message	wparam =	identifies sending window	
		For WM_DDE_INITIATE:		
		lparam =	aApplication (replying app name)	LO
			aTopic (replying topic)	HO
		For WM_DDE_EXECUTE:		
		lparam =	wStatus* (status of response)	LO
			hCommands (handle of command string)	HO
		For all others:		
		lparam =	wStatus* (status of response)	LO
			aItem (data item response is for)	HO
WM_DDE_REQUEST	Request for data item	wParam =	identifies sending window	
		lParam =	cfFormat (clipboard format)	LO
			aItem (data item requested)	HO
WM_DDE_DATA	Publication of data	wParam =	identifies sending window	
		lParam =	hData §	LO
			aItem (data item requested)	HO
WM_DDE_POKE	Place data at destination	wParam =	identifies sending window	
		lParam =	hData§	LO
			aItem	HO
WM_DDE_ADVISE	Request for data	wParam =	identifies sending window	
		lParam =	hOptions† (how data is to be sent)	LO
			aItem (data item requested)	HO
WM_DDE_UNADVISE	Cancel request for data	wParam =	identifies sending window	
		lParam =	aItem	LO
			cfFormat (clipboard format)	HO
WM_DD_EXECUTE	Request to process commands	wParam =	identifies sending window	
		lParam =	RESERVED	LO
			hCommands	HO

*Consists of DDEACK data structure:

Bit 15 -- fAck	1=request accepted; 0=not accepted
Bit 14 -- fBusy	1=busy; 0=not busy
Bits 8-13 -- RESERVED	
Bits 0-7 -- bAppReturnCode	application-defined return codes

†Consists of DDEADVISE data structure:

Word 1, Bit 15 -- fAckReq	1=send WM_DDE_DATA with ACK-requested bit
Word 1, Bit 14 -- fDeferUpd	1=source data has changed
Word 1, Bits 0-13 -- RESERVED	
Word 2 -- cfFormat	standard or registered clipboard format number

§Consists of DDEDATA data structure:

Word 1, Bit 15 -- fAckReq¥	1=send WM_DDE_DATA with ACK-requested bit
	0=don't send WM_DDE_ACK
Word 1, Bit 14 -- RESERVED	
Word 1, Bit 13 -- fRelease	1=client app frees hData object after processing
	0=don't free
Word 1, Bit 12 -- fRequested¥	1=data in response to WM_DDE_REQUEST
	0=in response to WM_DDE_ADVISE
Word 1, Bits 0-11 -- RESERVED	
Word 2 -- cfFormat	standard or registered clipboard format number
Words 3-n -- Value[]	the data (in cfFormat)

¥Not used for WM_DDE_POKE

Source: Microsoft Systems Journal (October 1986), pages 7 through 16
Microsoft Systems Journal (November 1987), page 16
Microsoft Windows 3.0 SDK Programmer's Reference, Chapter 15

6.013. WINDOWS PAINT FILE FORMAT

Offset	*Length*	*Usual Contents*	*Description*
0 (0)	Word	6144H	Key#1 (version of paint program used to create file)
2 (2)	Word	4D6EH	Key#2 (version of paint program used to create file)
4 (4)	Word		Width of bitmap (in pixels)
6 (6)	Word		Height of bitmap (in pixels)
8 (8)	Word		X aspect ratio of bitmap
A (10)	Word		Y aspect ratio of bitmap
C (12)	Word		X aspect ratio of printer at creation time
E (14)	Word		Y aspect ratio of printer at creation time
10 (16)	Word		Width of printer in pixels
12 (18)	Word		Height of printer in pixels
14 (20)	Word		Used for checksum calculations
16 (22)	Word		Used for checksum calculations
18 (24)	Word		Checksum of header
1A (26)	Word		RESERVED
1C (28)	Word		RESERVED
1E (30)	Word		RESERVED
20 (32)	Varies		Bitmap

Version: Paint files in versions of Windows beginning with 2.03 use a different format.

Note:
- A paint file (version 1.01) consists of a 32-byte header, as described above, followed by a bitmap organized as scan lines. The total size of the bitmap will be =WidthOfBitmap x HeightOfBitmap/8
- The third through tenth fields in the header are determined by calling GetDeviceCaps().

Source: Unpublished document from Microsoft University Windows Seminar

See Also:
6.015. Clipboard Formats and Clipboard File Format
6.019. SDKPAINT.DAT File Format
6.069. METAFILEPICT Structure Format

6.014. FONT FILE FORMAT

Field	*Size*	*Description*	*Allowable Values*
dfVersion	Word	Version of the file	Currently must be 100 (256)
dfSize	Dbl word	Total file size (in bytes)	Unsigned 32-bit integer
dfCopyright	60 bytes	Copyright information	ASCIIZ string
dfType	Word	Font file type	LObit0=0 (raster-type file) LObit0=1 (vector-type file) LObit3=1 (bitmap in memory) HO=0 (GDI realized standard font)
dfPoints	Word	Nominal point size for best look	
dfVertRes	Word	Nominal vert resolution dots per inch	Size at which font was digitized
dfHorizRes	Word	Nominal horiz resolution dots per inch	Size at which font was digitized
dfAscent	Word	Dist from top of char to baseline	
dfInternalLeading	Word	Area inside dfPixHeight for accent marks	
dfExternalLeading	Word	Extra leading requested between rows	
dfItalic	Byte	Is font an italic font?	0=no, 1=yes
dfUnderline	Byte	Is font underlined?	0=no, 1=yes
dfStrikeOut	Byte	Is font overstruck?	0=no, 1=yes
dfWeight	Word	Weight of character	Value 1-1000 (200 is normal)
dfCharSet	Byte	Character set used	FF (255)=IBM PC char set
dfPixWidth	Word	Width of grid for vector fonts Width of all chars for raster fonts	Size at which font was digitized 0=variable width
dfPixHeight	Word	Height of grid for vector fonts Height of the char bitmap for raster fonts	Size at which font was digitized
dfPitchAndFamily	Byte	Pitch and family of font	LObit=1 (variable pitch) LObit=0 (fixed pitch) HO4bits=0000 (FF_DONTCARE) HO4bits=0001 (FF_ROMAN) HO4bits=0010 (FF_SWISS) HO4bits=0011 (FF_MODERN) HO4bits=0100 (FF_SCRIPT) HO4bits=0101 (FF_DECORATIVE)
dfAvgWidth	Word	Average width of chars in font	Usually 'X'
dfMaxWidth	Word	Maximum pixel width of any char in font	
dfFirstChar	Byte	Character code of first char defined	
dfLastChar	Byte	Character code of last char defined	
dfDefaultChar	Byte	Character to substitute for missing chars	
dfBreakChar	Byte	Character used to define word breaks	
dfWidthBytes	Word	# of bytes in each row of bitmap	(Raster fonts only)
dfDevice	Dbl word	Offset in file to device name string	0=generic device

(Continued)

6.014. FONT FILE FORMAT (continued)

Field	*Size*	*Description*	*Allowable Values*
dfFace	Dbl word	Offset in file to face name string	
dfBitsPointer	Dbl word	Absolute address of bitmap	(Set by GDI at load time)
dfBitsOffset	Dbl word	Offset in file to beginning of bitmap	
dfCharOffset	Word each 0 bytes Word each Word Word	Offset in bitmap rows to each char in set Not used Offset in bitmap to string for each char in set Offset in bitmap to char strokes for each char Pixel width of the character	For variable-spaced raster fonts For fixed-spaced raster fonts For fixed-spaced vector fonts For variable-spaced vector fonts
(facename)	String	Name of typeface	ASCIIZ string
(devicename)	String	Name of device font was designed for	ASCIIZ string
(bitmap)	Bytes	Bitmap containing font data	Each row must start on word boundary

Version: Applies to all versions of Windows beginning with 2.0.

Source: Microsoft Windows 2.0 SDK Programmer's Reference, pages 639 through 645
Microsoft Windows Device Driver Kit, Device Driver Adaption Guide, pages 13-1 through 13-15

6.015. CLIPBOARD FORMATS AND CLIPBOARD FILE FORMAT

Clipboard Format Names

Format Name	*Description*
CF_BITMAP	Handle to bitmap (HBITMAP)
CF_DIB*	Memory block containing BITMAPINFO data structure and bitmap
CF_DIF	Software Arts Data Interchange Format
CF_DSPBITMAP	Bitmap display associated with a private format
CF_DSPMETAFILEPICT	Metafile picture display associated with a private format
CF_DSPTEXT	Text display associated with a private format
CF_METAFILEPICT	Metafile picture structure (See 6.69. METAFILEPICT Structure Format)
CF_OEMTEXT*	Text containing characters in OEM character set
CF_OWNERDISPLAY	Owner display format (clipboard owner must display and update clipboard)
CF_PALETTE*	Handle to color palette
CF_PRIVATEFIRST	Private format begins with this value
CF_PRIVATELAST	Private format ends with this value
CF_SYLK	Microsoft SYLK data interchange format
CF_TEXT	Text ends with CR-LF-NULL
CF_TIFF*	Tag Image File Format (see 6.011. Tag Image File Format)

Clipboard Format

Offset	*Length*	*Name*	*Description*
0 (0)	Word	FileIdentifier	Must be set to CLP_ID
2 (2)	Word	FormatCount	Number of clipboard formats contained
4 (4)	Word	ClipboardArray	-->

Length	*Name*	*Description*
WORD	FormatID	One of the above clipboard formats
DWORD	LenData	Length of clipboard data, in bytes
DWORD	OffData	Offset, in bytes, to data block
79-bytes	Name	Format name for private clipboard format
Varies	Data	Clipboard data

*Added beginning with Windows 3.0.

Source: Microsoft Windows 2.0 SDK Programmer's Reference, page 423
Microsoft Windows 3.0 SDK Programmer's Reference, pages 4-370 through 4-371, 9-5 through 9-6

See Also: 1.17. Common String Formats
6.011. Tag Image File Format (TIFF)
6.016. MetaFile Format
6.047. BITMAPINFO Structure Format
6.069. METAFILEPICT Structure Format

6.016. METAFILE FORMAT

MetaFile Header

Field	*Size*	*Description*	*Allowable Values*
mtType	WORD	Location indicator	1=in memory, 2=disk file
mtHeaderSize	WORD	Header size	Size in words
mtVersion	WORD	Version number	Current version is 0x300 for Windows 3.0
mtSize	DWORD	MetaFile size	Size in words
mtNoObjects	WORD	Total number of objects	Maximum number of objects
mtMaxRecord	WORD	Size of largest record	Size in words
mtNoParameters	WORD	Number of parameters	Field not currently used

MetaFile GDI Function Records

Field	*Size*	*Description*	*Allowable Values*	
rdSize	DWORD	Size of this record	Size in words	
rdFunction	WORD	Magic number of function	0817H	Arc
			0830H	Chord
			0418H	Ellipse
			0415H	ExcludeClipRect
			0419H	FloodFill
			0416H	IntersectClipRect
			0213H	LineTo
			0214H	MoveTo
			0220H	OffsetClipRgn
			0211H	OffsetViewportOrg
			020FH	OffsetWindowOrg
			061DH	PatBlt
			081AH	Pie
			0035H	RealizePalette (3.0 and later)
			041BH	Rectangle
			0139H	ResizePalette (3.0 and later)
			0127H	RestoreDC
			061CH	RoundRect
			001EH	SaveDC
			0412H	ScaleViewportExt
			0400H	ScaleWindowExt
			0201H	SetBkColor
			0102H	SetBkMode
			0103H	SetMapMode
			0231H	SetMapperFlags
			041FH	SetPixel
			0106H	SetPolyFillMode
			0105H	SetRelAbs
			0104H	SetROP2
			0107H	SetStrectchBltMode
			0108H	SetTextCharExtra
			012EH	SetTextAlign
			0209H	SetTextColor
			020AH	SetTextJustification
			020CH	SetWindowExt
			020BH	SetWindowOrg
			020EH	SetViewportExt
			020DH	SetViewportOrg
rdParm	Varies	Parameter(s) for function	Variable number of words, each containing a parameter	

MetaFile Object-Creation Records*

Field	*Size*	*Description*	*Allowable Values*
rdSize	DWORD	Size of this record	Size in bytes
rdFunction	WORD	Object creation ID	012DH
Index	Varies	Index into table to location of object	

*Not in Windows 3.0

MetaFile AnimatePalette† Records

Field	*Size*	*Description*	*Allowable Values*	
rdSize	DWORD	Size of this record	Size in words	
rdFunction	WORD	AnimatePaletteID	0436H	
rdParm			start	First entry to be animated
			numentries	Number of entries to animate
			entries	PALETTEENTRY blocks

†First defined for Windows 3.0; does not apply to earlier versions.

(Continued)

6.016. METAFILE FORMAT (continued)

MetaFile BitBlt Records

Field	*Size*	*Description*	*Allowable Values*	
rdSize	DWORD	Size of this record	Size in words	
rdFunction	WORD	BitBltID	0922H for 1.0 and 2.0, 0940H for 3.0 and later	
rdParm			rasterop	HO word of raster operation
			SY	y-coordinate of source origin
			SX	x-coordinate of source origin
			DYE	Destination y-extent
			DXE	Destination x-extent
			DY	y-coordinate of destination origin
			DX	x-coordinate of destination origin
			bmWidth¥	Width of bitmap in pixels
			bmHeight¥	Height of bitmap in raster lines
			bmWidthBytes¥	Number of bytes in each raster line
			bmPlanes¥	Number of color planes in bitmap
			bmBitsPixel¥	Number of adjacent color bits
			bits	Actual device-dependent bitmap

¥Replaced in 3.0 with BITMAPINFO structure.

MetaFile CreateBrushIndirect Records

Field	*Size*	*Description*	*Allowable Values*
rdSize	DWORD	Size of this record	Size in words
rdFunction	WORD	CreateBrushIndirectID	02FCH
rdParm		LOGBRUSH structure	See 6.062. LOGBRUSH Structure Format

MetaFile CreateFontIndirect Records

Field	*Size*	*Description*	*Allowable Values*
rdSize	DWORD	Size of this record	Size in words
rdFunction	WORD	CreateFontIndirectID	02FBH
rdParm		LOGFONT structure	See 6.063. LOGFONT Structure Format

MetaFile CreatePalette† Records

Field	*Size*	*Description*	*Allowable Values*
rdSize	DWORD	Size of this record	Size in words
rdFunction	WORD	CreatePaletteID	00F7H
rdParm		LOGPALETTE structure	See 6.064. LOGPALETTE Structure Format

†First defined for Windows 3.0; does not apply to earlier versions.

MetaFile CreatePenIndirect Records

Field	*Size*	*Description*	*Allowable Values*
rdSize	DWORD	Size of this record	5 (size in words)
rdFunction	WORD	CreatePenIndirect ID	02FAH
rdParm		LOGPEN structure	See 6.065. LOGPEN Structure Format

MetaFile CreatePen Records

Field	*Size*	*Description*	*Allowable Values*
rdSize	DWORD	Size of this record	5 (size in words)
rdFunction	WORD	CreatePen ID	0230H
rdParm		LOGPEN structure	See 6.065. LOGPEN Structure Format

MetaFile CreateFont Records

Field	*Size*	*Description*	*Allowable Values*
rdSize	DWORD	Size of this record	28 (size in words)
rdFunction	WORD	CreateFont ID	0231H
rdParm		LOGFONT structure	See 6.063. LOGFONT Structure Format

MetaFile CreateBrush Records

Field	*Size*	*Description*	*Allowable Values*
rdSize	DWORD	Size of this record	7 (size in words)
rdFunction	WORD	CreateBrush ID	0232H
rdParm		LOGBRUSH structure	See 6.062. LOGBRUSH Structure Format

(Continued)

6.016. METAFILE FORMAT (continued)

MetaFile CreatePatternBrush Records

Field	Size	Description	Allowable Values
rdSize	DWORD	Size of this record	Size in words
rdFunction	WORD	CreatePatternBrush ID	012FH for prior to 3.0, 0142H for 3.0
rdParm	Varies	Bitmap	For Windows 1.x & 2.x: bitmap header, 9 unused words, + bmWidth Bitmap width bmHeight Bitmap height bmWidthBytes Bytes per raster line bmPlanes Number of color planes bmBitsPixel Number of adjacent color bits per pixel bmBits Pointer to bit values bits Actual bits of pattern For Windows 3.0 and later: type Bitmap type Usage bmiColors format BITMAPINFO Data structure defining bitmap bits Actual device-dependent bitmap

MetaFile CreateRegion Records

Field	Size	Description	Allowable Values
rdSize	DWORD	Size of this record	Size in words
rdFunction	WORD	CreateRegion ID	06FFH
rdParm		Region	

MetaFile DeleteObject† Records

Field	Size	Description	Allowable Values
rdSize	DWORD	Size of this record	4 (size in words)
rdFunction	WORD	DeleteObject ID	01F0H
rdParm		Index	Handle-table index of object to be deleted

†First defined for Windows 3.0; does not apply to earlier versions.

MetaFile DrawText Records*

Field	Size	Description	Allowable Values
rdSize	DWORD	Size of this record	Size in words
rdFunction	WORD	DrawText ID	062FH
rdParm	Varies	DrawText info	DrawText info consists of: format Method of formatting count Number of bytes in string rectangle Rectangle defining text area string Text array containing string

*Not in Windows 3.0

MetaFile ExtTextOut Records

Field	Size	Description	Allowable Values
rdSize	DWORD	Size of this record	Size in words
rdFunction	WORD	ExtTextOut ID	0A32H
rdParm	Varies	ExtTextOut info	ExtTextOut info consists of: y y-value of string's starting point x x-value of string's starting point count Length of string options Rectangle type rectangle RECT defining text rectangle string Byte array containing string dxarray Word array of intercharacter distances

MetaFile TextOut Records

Field	Size	Description	Allowable Values
rdSize	DWORD	Size of this record	Size in words
rdFunction	WORD	TextOut ID	0521H
rdParm	Varies	TextOut info	TextOut info consists of: count Length of string flstring String flylocation y-value of string's starting point flxlocation x-value of string's starting point

MetaFile Polygon Records

Field	Size	Description	Allowable Values
rdSize	DWORD	Size of this record	Size in words
rdFunction	WORD	Polygon ID	0324H
rdParm	Varies	Polygon info	Polygon info consists of: count Number of points in polygon ptlist List of the individual points

(Continued)

6.016. METAFILE FORMAT (continued)

MetaFile Polyline Records

Field	Size	Description	Allowable Values
rdSize	DWORD	Size of this record	Size in words
rdFunction	WORD	Polyline ID	0325H
rdParm	Varies	Polyline info	Polyline info consists of: count — Number of points in polygon ptlist — List of the individual points

MetaFile PolyPolygon Records

Field	Size	Description	Allowable Values
rdSize	DWORD	Size of this record	Size in words
rdFunction	WORD	PolyPolygon ID	0538H
rdParm	Varies	PolyPolygon info	PolyPolygon info consists of: count — Total number of points list of counts — List of number of points for each polygon list of points — List of individual points

MetaFile Escape Records

Field	Size	Description	Allowable Values
rdSize	DWORD	Size of this record	Size in words
rdFunction	WORD	Escape ID	0626H
rdParm	Varies	Escape info	Escape info consists of: escape# — Number of escape count — Number of bytes of escape data escapedata

MetaFile InvertRegion Records*

Field	Size	Description	Allowable Values
rdSize	DWORD	Size of this record	Size in words
rdFunction	WORD	InvertRegion ID	012AH
rdParm		Region	Index to region in MetaFile table

*Not in Windows 3.0

MetaFile PaintRegion Records*

Field	Size	Description	Allowable Values
rdSize	DWORD	Size of this record	Size in words
rdFunction	WORD	PaintRegion ID	012BH
rdParm		Region	Index to region in MetaFile table

*Not in Windows 3.0

MetaFile FillRegion Records*

Field	Size	Description	Allowable Values
rdSize	DWORD	Size of this record	Size in words
rdFunction	WORD	FillRegion ID	0228H
rdParm		Region	Index to region in MetaFile table

*Not in Windows 3.0

MetaFile FrameRegion Records*

Field	Size	Description	Allowable Values
rdSize	DWORD	Size of this record	Size in words
rdFunction	WORD	FrameRegion ID	0429H
rdParm		Region	Index to region in MetaFile table

*Not in Windows 3.0

MetaFile SelectClipRegion Records

Field	Size	Description	Allowable Values
rdSize	DWORD	Size of this record	Size in words
rdFunction	WORD	SelectClipRegion ID	012CH
rdParm		Region	Index to region in MetaFile table

MetaFile SelectObject Records

Field	Size	Description	Allowable Values
rdSize	DWORD	Size of this record	Size in words
rdFunction	WORD	SelectObject ID	012DH
rdParm		Region	Index to region in MetaFile table

MetaFile SelectPalette† Records

Field	Size	Description	Allowable Values
rdSize	DWORD	Size of this record	Size in words
rdFunction	WORD	SelectPalette ID	0234H
rdParm		Palette	Index to palette in MetaFile table

†First defined for Windows 3.0; does not apply to earlier versions.

(Continued)

6.016. METAFILE FORMAT (continued)

MetaFile SetDIBitsToDevice† Records

Field	Size	Description	Allowable Values	
rdSize	DWORD	Size of this record	Size in words	
rdFunction	WORD	SetDIBitsToDevice ID	0D33H	
rdParm	Varies	SetDLBitsToDevice Info	SetDIBitsToDevice info consists of:	
			wUsage	Color usage flag
			numscans	Number of scanlines in bitmap
			startscan	First scan line in bitmap
			srcY	y-coordinate of origin of source in bitmap
			srcX	x-coordinate of origin of source in bitmap
			extY	Height of source in bitmap
			extX	Width of source in bitmap
			destY	y-coord of origin of destination rectangle
			destX	x-coord of origin of destination rectangle
			BITMAPINFO	Data structure for bitmap
			bits	Actual bitmap

†First defined for Windows 3.0; does not apply to earlier versions.

MetaFile SetPaletteEntries† Records

Field	Size	Description	Allowable Values	
rdSize	DWORD	Size of this record	Size in words	
rdFunction	WORD	SetPaletteEntries ID	0037H	
rdParm	Varies	SetPaletteEntries info	SetPaletteEntries info consists of:	
			start	First entry to be set in palette
			numentries	Number of entries to set in palette
			entries	PALETTEENTRY blocks

†First defined for Windows 3.0; does not apply to earlier versions

MetaFile StretchBlt Records

Field	Size	Description	Allowable Values	
rdSize	DWORD	Size of this record	Size in words	
rdFunction	WORD	StretchBlt ID	0B23H for prior to 3.0, 0F43 for 3.0	
rdParm	Varies	StretchBlt info	StretchBlt info consists of:	
			raster op	LO word of raster operation
			raster op	HO word of raster operation
			SYE	Source y-extent
			SXE	Source x-extent
			SY	y-coordinate of source origin
			SX	x-coordinate of source origin
			DYE	Destination y-extent
			DXE	Destination x-extent
			DY	y-coordinate of the dest origin
			DX	x-coordinate of the dest origin
			bmWidth¥	Width of the bitmap, in pixels
			bmHeight¥	Height of the bitmap, in raster lines
			bmWidthBytes¥	Number of bytes per raster line
			bmPlanes¥	Number of color planes per raster line
			bmBitsPixel¥	Number of adjacent color bits/pixel
			bits	Actual bitmap

¥Replaced in Windows 3.0 with BITMAPINFO structure.

MetaFile StretchDIBits† Records

Field	Size	Description	Allowable Values	
rdSize	DWORD	Size of this record	Size in words	
rdFunction	WORD	StretchDIBits ID	0F43H	
rdParm	Varies	StretchDIBits info	StretchDIBits info consists of:	
			dwRop	Raster operation to be performed
			wUsage	Color usage flag
			srcYExt	Height of source of bitmap
			srcXExt	Width of source of bitmap
			srcY	y-coordinate of origin of source in bitmap
			srcX	x-coordinate of origin of source in bitmap
			dstYExt	Height of destination rectangle
			dstXExt	Width of destination rectangle
			dstY	y-coord of origin of destination rectangle
			dstX	x-coord of origin of destination rectangle
			BITMAPINFO	Data structure defining bitmap
			bits	Actual bitmap

†First defined for Windows 3.0; does not apply to earlier versions.

Note: The actual MetaFile format is comprised of:
-A MetaFile header
-A variable number of MetaFile GDI or other function records
-A table of any objects referenced by function records

Source: Microsoft Windows 2.0 SDK Programmer's Reference, pages 127 through 129
Microsoft Windows 2.0 Beta2 Documentation, pages 646 through 655
Microsoft Windows 3.0 SDK Programmer's Reference, Chapter 9

See Also: 6.062. LOGBRUSH Structure Format
6.063. LOGFONT Structure Format
6.064. LOGPALETTE Structure Format
6.065. LOGPEN Structure Format

6.017. ICON RESOURCE FILE FORMAT

Offset	*Length*	*Name*	*Description*
0 (0)	WORD	icoReserved	RESERVED; must be set to 0
2 (2)	WORD	icoResourceType	Type of resource contained in file; must be 1
4 (4)	WORD	icoResourceCount	Number of arrays (icons) in file
6 (6)	Varies	icoResourceArray	-->

Length	*Name*	*Description*
BYTE	Width	Width, in pixels, of icon image (16,32, or 64)
BYTE	Height	Height, in pixels, of icon (16, 32, or 64)
BYTE	ColorCount	Number of colors in icon (2, 8, or 16)
BYTE	RESERVED	
WORD	RESERVED	
WORD	RESERVED	
DWORD	icoDIBSize	Size of pixel array, in bytes
DWORD	icoDIBOffset	Offset, in bytes, to pixel array

Note: A DIB for a color icon consists of 1) XOR mask bitmap; 2) AND mask (monochrome).

Source: Microsoft Windows 3.0 SDK Programmer's Reference, pages 9-2 through 9-3

See Also: 6.018. Cursor Resource File Format

6.018. CURSOR RESOURCE FILE FORMAT

Offset	*Length*	*Name*	*Description*
0 (0)	WORD	curReserved	RESERVED; must be set to 0
2 (2)	WORD	curResourceType	Type of resource contained in file; must be 2
4 (4)	WORD	curResourceCount	Number of arrays (cursors) in file
6 (6)	Varies	curResourceArray	-->

Length	*Name*	*Description*
BYTE	curWidth	Width, in pixels, of cursor image
BYTE	curHeight	Height, in pixels, of cursor
BYTE	ColorCount	Number of colors in cursor (2, 8, or 16)
BYTE	RESERVED	
WORD	curXHotspot	Horizontal hotspot, in pixels
WORD	curYHotspot	Vertical hotspot, in pixels
DWORD	curDIBSize	Size of pixel array, in bytes
DWORD	curDIBOffset	Offset, in bytes, to pixel array

Note: Cursors consist of 1) XOR mask bitmap; 2) AND mask (both monochrome).

Source: Microsoft Windows 3.0 SDK Programmer's Reference, pages 9-3 through 9-5

See Also: 6.017. Icon Resource File Format

6.019. SDKPAINT.DAT FILE FORMAT

Length	*Name*	*Description*
Up to 10 chars	name	Name of display device
Varies	num-colors	Number of colors of icon/cursor image
Varies	curs-horz-size	Horizontal size of cursor, in pixels
Varies	curs-vert-size	Vertical size of cursor, in pixels
Varies	icon-horz-size	Horizontal size of icon, in pixels
Varies	icon-vert-size	Vertical size of icon, in pixels

Note: File is in ASCII format (i.e., numbers are written out, as in 32, 16, 64); strings are terminated by CR (no null character), one string per display device.

Source: Microsoft Windows 3.0 SDK Tools, pages 4-2 through 4-3

6.020. RESOURCE SCRIPT FILE DIRECTIVES

Directive	*Function*	*Syntax*	*Comments*
#include	Copies contents of file into resource script	#include filename	Filename is a string (e.g., "windows.h")
#define	Assigns a value to a name	#define name value	Name=letters,digits,punc.;value=int,char,string
#undef	Removes definition assigned to name	#undef name	Name=letters,digits,punctuation
#ifdef	Compiles up to #endif if name is defined	#ifdef name	See #endif (see example 1, below)
#ifndef	Compiles up to #endif if name is not defined	#ifndef name	See #endif (see example 1, below)
#if	Compiles up to #endif if constant is non-zero	#if constant	See #endif
#elif	Compiles block within #if- if constant is non-zero	#elif constant	Used within #if, #ifndef, & #ifdef (see example 2)
#else	Optional clause within #if- construct	#else	Used within #if, #ifndef, & #ifdef (see example 3)
#endif	Ends conditional compilation	#endif	Ends #if, #ifndef, #ifdef compilation

Example 1:

```
#ifdef Debug
errbox BITMAP errbox.bmp
#endif
```

Example 2:

```
#if Version<3
errbox BITMAP errbox.bmp
#elif Version<7
errbox BITMAP userbox.bmp
#endif
```

Example 3:

```
#ifdef Debug
errbox BITMAP errbox.bmp
#else
errbox BITMAP userbox.bmp
#endif
```

Source: Microsoft Windows 2.0 SDK Tools, pages 25 through 27
Microsoft Windows 3.0 SDK Programmer's Reference, pages 8-47 through 8-51

See Also:
6.021. Single-line Resource Statements (ICON, CURSOR, BITMAP, FONT)
6.022. RCDATA Resource Script Definitions
6.023. MENU Resource Script Definitions
6.024. DIALOG Resource Script Definitions
6.025. Dialog Box Control Definitions
6.026. ACCELERATORS Resource Script Definitions
6.028. STRINGTABLE Resource Script Definitions

6.021. SINGLE-LINE RESOURCE STATEMENTS (ICON, CURSOR, BITMAP, FONT)

General Single Statement Resource Script Format:
nameID resourcetype [loadoption] [memoryoption] filespec

Item	*Description*	*Allowable Values*
nameID	Name or number used to identify resource	For FONT resource, must be an integer number
resourcetype	Type of resource being defined	One of: CURSOR ICON BITMAP FONT
loadoption	Specifies when resource is to be loaded	One of: PRELOAD (loaded immediately) LOADONCALL (default: loaded only when called)
memoryoption	Determines how resource is treated in memory	One of: FIXED (remains in fixed location) MOVEABLE (may be moved in memory) DISCARDABLE (may be discarded from memory)
filespec	Name and extension of file containing resource	ASCII string, which may contain pathname

Examples: 5 FONT CMMODERN.FNT
cursor CURSOR custom.cur
desk ICON DISCARDABLE desk.ico

Source: Microsoft Windows 2.0 SDK Tools, pages 30 through 31
Microsoft Windows 3.0 SDK Programmer's Reference, pages 8-1 through 8-3

See Also: 6.020. Resource Script File Directives

6.022. RCDATA RESOURCE SCRIPT DEFINITIONS

General RCDATA Resource Script Format:
nameID RCDATA [load-option][mem-option]
BEGIN
raw-data
END

Item	*Description*	*Allowable Values*
nameID	Name or number used to identify resource	
load-option	Specifies when resource is to be loaded	PRELOAD (loaded immediately) LOADONCALL (default: loaded when called)
mem-option	Determines how resource is treated in memory	FIXED (remains in fixed location) MOVEABLE (may be moved to compact memory) DISCARDABLE (may be discarded when not needed)

Version: Applies to all versions of Windows beginning with 3.0.

Source: Microsoft Windows 3.0 SDK Programmer's Reference, pages 8-4 through 8-5

See Also: 6.020. Resource Script File Directives

6.023. MENU RESOURCE SCRIPT DEFINITIONS

General MENU Resource Script Format:
menuID MENU [load-option] [mem-option]
BEGIN
menuitems
END

Item	*Description*	*Allowable Values*
menuID	Name or number used to identify menu resource	
load-option	Specifies when resource is to be loaded	PRELOAD (loaded immediately) LOADONCALL (default: loaded when called)
mem-option	Determines how resource is treated in memory	FIXED (remains in fixed location) MOVEABLE (may be moved to compact memory) DISCARDABLE (may be discarded when not needed)

Allowable MenuItems

MenuItem Name	*Syntax*	*Description*
MENUITEM	MENUITEM text, result, optionlist1	Defines a menu item
POPUP	POPUP text, optionlist2 BEGIN definitions END	Defines a popup menu definition
MENUITEM SEPARATOR	MENUITEM SEPARATOR	Special "dividing" menu item, usually a horiz. bar

optionlist1:	MENUBREAK	Item is immediately preceded by a new line
	MENUBARBREAK	Same as MENUBREAK, but places vertical line between columns
	CHECKED	Item has a checkmark next to it
	INACTIVE	Item is displayed, but cannot be selected
	GRAYED	Item is inactive and displayed "grayed" (disabled)
	HELP	Item has vertical separator to its left
optionlist2:	MENUBREAK	Item is placed in new column
	MENUBARBREAK	Same as MENUBREAK, but places vertical line between columns
	CHECKED	Item has a checkmark next to it
	INACTIVE	Item is displayed, but cannot be selected
	GRAYED	Item is inactive and displayed "grayed" (disabled)

text: ASCII string (in quotes)

result: Integer number of result to return when user selects item

Source: Microsoft Windows 2.0 SDK Tools, pages 36 through 40
Microsoft Windows 3.0 SDK Programmer's Reference, pages 8-8 through 8-13

See Also: 6.020. Resource Script File Directives

6.024. DIALOG RESOURCE SCRIPT DEFINITIONS

General DIALOG Resource Script Format:
nameID DIALOG [loadoption] [memoryoption] x,y,width,height
optionstatements
BEGIN
controlstatements
END

Item	*Description*	*Allowable Values*
nameID	Name or number used to identify dialog	
loadoption	Specifies when resource is to be loaded	PRELOAD (loaded immediately) LOADONCALL (default: loaded when called)
memoryoption	Determines how resource is treated in memory	FIXED (remains in fixed location) MOVEABLE (may be moved to compact memory) DISCARDABLE (may be discarded when not needed)
optionstatements	Define special attributes of dialog box	STYLE (defines style of dialog box) CAPTION text (defines dialog box's title) MENU name (defines dialog box's menu) CLASS class (defines dialog box's class) FONT point size, typeface (defines dialog box's font)
controlstatements	Define attributes of controls within dialog box	See 6.025. Dialog Box Control Definitions

Note: Default STYLE is:
WS_POPUP
WS_BORDER
WS_SYSMENU

Source: Microsoft Windows 2.0 SDK Tools, pages 40 through 46
Microsoft Windows 3.0 SDK Programmer's Reference, pages 8-13 through 8-15

See Also: 6.025. Dialog Box Control Definitions

6.025. DIALOG BOX CONTROL DEFINITIONS

General Resource Script Format:
CONTROLNAME text, id, xposition, yposition, width, height, [style]

Control Name	Class	Appears As	Syntax	Default Style
LTEXT	Static	Left-justified text	LTEXT text,id,x,y,w,h,[style]	SS_LEFT, WS_GROUP
RTEXT	Static	Right-justified text	RTEXT text,id,x,y,w,h,[style]	SS_RIGHT, WS_GROUP
CTEXT	Static	Centered text	CTEXT text,id,x,y,w,h,[style]	SS_CENTER, WS_GROUP
CHECKBOX	Button	Check box with text	CHECKBOX text,id,x,y,w,h,[style]	BS_CHECKBOX, WS_TABSTOP
PUSHBUTTON	Button	Push button with text	PUSHBUTTON text,id,x,y,w,h,[style]	BS_PUSHBUTTON, WS_TABSTOP
LISTBOX	Listbox	Boxed list of strings	LISTBOX id,x,y,w,h,[style]	LBS_NOTIFY,WS_VSCROLL, WS_BORDER
GROUPBOX	Button	Group of buttons	GROUPBOX text,id,x,y,w,h,[style]	BS_GROUPBOX, WS_TABSTOP
DEFPUSHBUTTON	Button	Default push button	DEFPUSHBUTTON text,id,x,y,w,h,[style]	BS_DEFPUSHBUTTON, WS_TABSTOP
RADIOBUTTON	Button	Radio button with text	RADIOBUTTON text,id,x,y,w,h,[style]	BS_RADIOBUTTON, WS_TABSTOP
COMBOBOX†	Combobox	Boxed list with text	COMBOBOX id, x,y,w,h,[style]	WS_TABSTOP, CBS_SIMPLE
SCROLLBAR†	Scrollbar	Scrollbar with thumb	SCROLLBAR id, x,y,w,h,[style]	SBS_HORZ
EDITTEXT	Edit	Boxed text	EDITTEXT id,x,y,w,h,[style]	WS_TABSTOP, ES_LEFT, WS_BORDER
ICON	Static	Icon	ICON text,id,x,y,w,h,[style]	SS_ICON
CONTROL	Varies	User-defined window	CONTROL text,id,class,style,x,y,w,h	none

Control Styles

Style Name	Class	Description
BS_3STATE	Button	Same as BS_CHECKBOX except button can be "grayed"
BS_AUTO3STATE	Button	Same as BS_3STATE except that button automatically toggles state when user clicks on it
BS_AUTOCHECKBOX	Button	Button automatically toggles state when user clicks on it
BS_AUTORADIOBUTTON*	Button	Button checked, application notified, all other radio buttons in group unchecked
BS_CHECKBOX	Button	Same as CHECKBOX
BS_DEFPUSHBUTTON	Button	Same as DEFPUSHBUTTON
BS_GROUPBOX	Button	Same as GROUPBOX
BS_LEFTTEXT*	Button	Causes text to appear to left of button (used with CHECKBOX, 3STATE, or RADIOBUTTON)
BS_OWNERDRAW†	Button	Owner-drawn button handled by parent window
BS_PUSHBOX*	Button	Same as PUSHBUTTON, but no border drawn
BS_PUSHBUTTON	Button	Same as PUSHBUTTON
BS_RADIOBUTTON	Button	Same as RADIOBUTTON
BS_USERBUTTON	Button	User-defined button; parent notified when clicked
DS_LOCALEDIT	Dialog	Edit controls in dialog box will use memory from application's data segment
DS_MODALFRAME	Dialog	Modal dialog box frame
DS_NOIDLEMSG	Dialog	Supress WM_ENTERPRISE messages to dialog box
DS_SYSMODAL	Dialog	Creates a system modal dialog box
ES_AUTOHSCROLL	Edit	Text scrolled 10 chars right at end of line, to 0 when CR pressed
ES_AUTOVSCROLL	Edit	Text scrolled up one "page" when user presses CR on last line
ES_CENTER	Edit	Centered text
ES_LEFT	Edit	Left-justified text
ES_LOWERCASE†	Edit	Lowercase edit control
ES_MULTILINE	Edit	Multiline edit control
ES_NOHIDESEL	Edit	Overrides hiding and inverting of text as focus moves to and from text
ES_OEMCONVERT†	Edit	Text converted from ANSI to OEM character set and back
ES_PASSWORD†	Edit	Displays all characters as asterisk as they are typed
ES_RIGHT	Edit	Right-justified text
ES_UPPERCASE†	Edit	Uppercase edit control
LBS_EXTENDEDSEL†	Listbox	Select multiple items with Shift and/or Control key
LBS_HASSTRINGS†	Listbox	Contains items consisting of strings
LBS_MULTICOLUM†	Listbox	Listbox contains multiple columns
LBS_MULTIPLESEL	Listbox	String selection toggled when user clicks or double clicks
LBS_NOINTEGRALHEIGHT†	Listbox	Size of listbox controlled by application
LBS_NOREDRAW	Listbox	Listbox display not updated when changes are made
LBS_NOTIFY	Listbox	Parent receives message when user clicks or double clicks string
LBS_OWNERDRAWFIXED†	Listbox	Owner of listbox responsible for drawing
LBS_OWNERDRAWVARIABLE†	Listbox	Owner of listbox responsible for drawing; items are variable height
LBS_SORT	Listbox	Strings are listed in box alphabetically
LBS_STANDARD†	Listbox	SORT, NOTIFY, BORDER, VSCROLL
LBS_USETABSTOPS†	Listbox	Listbox expands tab chars when drawing strings

(Continued)

6.025. DIALOG BOX CONTROL DEFINITIONS (continued)

Control Styles (continued)

Style Name	*Class*	*Description*
LBS_WANTKEYBOARDINPUT†	Listbox	Owner of listbox receives WM_VKEYTOITEM or WM_CHARTOITEM messages on keypress
SBS_BOTTOMALIGN	Scrollbar	Used with SBS_HORZ; bottom edge is bottom edge of rectangle
SBS_HORZ	Scrollbar	Horizontal scroll bar
SBS_LEFTALIGN	Scrollbar	Used with SBS_VERT; left edge is left edge of rectangle
SBS_RIGHTALIGN	Scrollbar	Used with SBS_VERT; right edge is right edge of rectangle
SBS_SIZEBOX	Scrollbar	Size box
SBS_SIZEBOXBOTTOMRIGHTALIGN	Scrollbar	Used with SBS_SIZEBOX; aligns sizebox to bottom right corner of rectangle
SBS_SIZEBOXTOPLEFTALIGN	Scrollbar	Used with SBS_SIZEBOX; aligns sizebox to top left corner of rectangle
SBS_TOPALIGN	Scrollbar	Used with SBS_HORZ; top edge is top edge of rectangle
SBS_VERT	Scrollbar	Vertical scroll bar
SS_BLACKFRAME	Static	Box with frame the color of window frame
SS_BLACKRECT	Static	Rectangle filled with color of window frame
SS_CENTER	Static	Same as CENTER
SS_GRAYFRAME	Static	Box with frame the color of desktop
SS_GRAYRECT	Static	Rectangle filled with color of desktop
SS_ICON	Static	Same as ICON
SS_LEFT	Static	Same as LTEXT
SS_LEFTNOWORDWRAP†	Static	Same as LTEXT, but words not wrapped
SS_NOPREFIX†	Static	& characters not intepreted as accelerators
SS_RIGHT	Static	Same as RTEXT
SS_SIMPLE†	Static	Same as LTEXT, but text channot be altered
SS_USERITEM	Static	User-defined static item
SS_WHITEFRAME	Static	Box with frame the color of window background
SS_WHITERECT	Static	Rectangle filled with color of window background
WS_BORDER*	All	Creates window that has a border
WS_CAPTION*	All	Creates window that has a title bar (implies WS_BORDER)
WS_CHILD*	All	Creates child window (cannot be used with WS_POPUP)
WS_CHILDWINDOW*	All	Creates child window with style WS_CHILD
WS_CLIPCHILDREN*	All	Excludes the area occupied by child window when drawing parent window
WS_CLIPSIBLINGS*	All	Clips child windows relative to each other
WS_DISABLED*	All	Creates window that is initially disabled
WS_DLGFRAME*	All	Creates window with a double border but no title
WS_GROUP	All	First control of group in which user may move using cursor keys
WS_HSCROLL*	All	Creates window with horizontal scroll bar
WS_ICONIC*	All	Creates window that is initially iconic (use with WS_TOPLEVEL only)
WS_ICONICPOPUP*§	All	Creates iconic pop-up window
WS_MAXIMIZE*	All	Creates window of maximum size
WS_MAXIMIZEBOX	All	Creates window that has a Maximize box
WS_MINIMIZE	All	Creates window of minimum size
WS_MINIMIZEBOX	All	Creates window that has a Minimize box
WS_OVERLAPPED	All	Creates overlapping window
WS_OVERLAPPEDWINDOW	All	Creates overlapped window with: WS_OVERLAPPED,WS_SYSMENU, WS_CAPTION, WS_SIZEBOX, WS_THICKFRAME, WS_MINIMIZEBOX, WS_MAXIMIZEBOX
WS_POPUP*	All	Creates pop-up window (cannot be used with WS_CHILD)
WS_POPUPWINDOW*	All	Creates pop-up window with: WS_POPUP, WS_BORDER, WS_SYSMENU
WS_SIZEBOX*	All	WS_THICKFRAME
WS_SYSMENU*	All	Creates window that has a system menu box in its title bar
WS_TABSTOP	All	Control in which user may move using Tab key
WS_THICKFRAME†	All	Creates window with thick frame for resizing window
WS_TOPLEVEL*§	All	Creates top-level window
WS_TOPLEVELWINDOW*§	All	Creates window with: WS_TOPLEVEL, WS_CAPTION, WS_SYSMENU, WS_SIZEBOX
WS_VISIBLE*	All	Creates window that is initially visible (applies to toplevel and popup windows)
WS_VSCROLL*	All	Creates window with vertical scroll bar

*First defined in Windows 2.0.
†First defined in Windows 3.0.
§No longer defined in Windows 3.0.

Source: Microsoft Windows 2.0 SDK Tools, pages 44 through 65.
Microsoft Windows 3.0 SDK Programmer's Reference, pages 8-13 through 8-47, 4-66 through 4-68

See Also: 6.020. Resource Script File Directives
6.021. Single-line Resource Statements (ICON, CURSOR, BITMAP, FONT)
6.023. MENU Resource Script Definitions
6.026. ACCELERATORS Resource Script Definitions
6.028. STRINGTABLE Resource Script Definitions

6.026. ACCELERATORS RESOURCE SCRIPT DEFINITIONS

General ACCELERATOR Resource Script Format:
tablename ACCELERATORS
BEGIN
event, idvalue [,type][,NOINVERT][,ALT][,SHIFT][,CONTROL]
END

Item	*Description*	*Allowable Values*
tablename	Name of accelerator table	
event	Keystroke to be used as accelerator	"char" or "^char" (single character, control char) ASCII character code Virtual key character
idvalue	ID of accelerator keystroke	Integer value
type	Defines keytype of accelerator	Not used if using quoted chars (e.g., "^C") ASCII (if ASCII character code) VIRTKEY (if Virtual key character)
NOINVERT	Defines whether top-level menu is highlighted on key	If omitted, top-level menu is highlighted If included, top-level menu is not highlighted
ALT†	Defines if accelerator requres Alt key down	If omitted, Alt key need not be down If included, Alt key must be down
SHIFT	Defines if accelerator requires Shift key down	If omitted, Shift key need not be down If included, Shift key must be down
CONTROL	Defines if accelerator requires Control key down	If omitted, Control key shouldn't be down If included, Control key must also be down

†First defined in Windows 3.0.

Note: More than one key may be defined at once by including additional 'event' statements between the BEGIN and END statements.

Source: Microsoft Windows 2.0 SDK Tools, pages 35 through 36
Microsoft Windows 3.0 SDK Programmer's Reference, pages 8-7 through 8-8

See Also: 6.020. Resource Script File Directives

6.027. COMMON MENU ACCELERATOR KEY DEFINITIONS

Edit Menu in Early Windows Versions

Key Name	*Action Performed in Windows 1*	*Action Performed in Windows 2*
Shift + Escape	Invokes the Edit menu's Undo command	Selects system menu of active window
Alt+Backspace	Not defined	Invokes the Edit menu's Undo command
Delete	Invokes the Edit menu's Cut command	Invokes the Edit menu's Clear command
F2	Invokes the Edit menu's Copy command	Not defined
Insert + Control	Invokes the Edit menu's Paste command	Invokes the Edit menu's Copy command
Shift + Delete	Invokes the Edit menu's Clear command	Invokes the Edit menu's Cut command
Shift + Insert	Not defined	Invokes the Edit menu's Paste command

IBM SAA Menu Definitions

Key Name	*Action*	*Description*
none	File menu	
none	New	Creates new file
none	Open	Opens existing file
none	Save	Saves existing file
none	Save as...	Saves into new file
none	Print	Prints existing file
none	Exit (optional)	Ends active application
none	Edit menu	
Alt+Backspace	Undo	Reverses last action
Shift+Del	Cut	Removes selected object(s), copies to clipboard
Ctrl+Ins	Copy	Copies selected object(s) to clipboard
Shift+Ins	Paste	Pastes object(s) from clipboard
Del (optional)	Clear (optional)	Removes selected object(s), not to clipboard
Del (optional)	Delete (optional)	Removes selected object(s), not to clipboard
none	View menu	
none	Options menu	
none	Window menu	
none	Help menu	
Shift+F10	Help	Describes how to get help
F2	Extended Help	Provides info about tasks application performs
F9	Keys help	Gives listing of all key assignments
F11	Help Index	Gives listing of all help topics
Shift+F2	Tutorial	Provides tutorial for current point of focus
none	About...	Displays application logo and info
Alt+Spacebar	System Menu	
Shift+Esc	System Menu	
none	Restore	Returns primary window to previous size
none	Move	Repositions window on screen
none	Size	Changes dimensions of window
none	Minimize	Removes all windows and replaces with icon
none	Maximize	Enlarges window to largest possible size
Alt+F4, Ctrl+F4	Close	Removes active and associated windows
Ctrl+Esc	Switch to...	Shows dialog of active applications
none	Split (optional)	Shows document in multiple views
F5 (optional)	Refresh	

Source: Microsoft Windows 2.0 SDK Application Style Guide, page 30
IBM SAA Common User Access Advanced Interface Design Guide, Appendix B

See Also: 6.001. Reserved System Keys and Recommended Keyboard Actions
6.026. ACCELERATORS Resource Script Definitions

6.028. STRINGTABLE RESOURCE SCRIPT DEFINITIONS

General STRINGTABLE Resource Script Format:

```
STRINGTABLE [loadoption] [memoryoption]
BEGIN
ID string
END
```

Item	*Description*	*Allowable Values*
loadoption	Specifies when resource is to be loaded	PRELOAD (loaded immediately) LOADONCALL (default: loaded when called)
memoryoption	Determines how resource is treated in memory	FIXED (remains in fixed location) MOVEABLE (may be moved to compact memory) DISCARDABLE (may be discarded when not needed)
ID	Identifier used to name string	Must be an integer value
string	Text comprising string	ASCII string in quotes

Note: Multiple strings may be defined at the same time by including multiple ID string statements between the BEGIN and END statements

Source: Microsoft Windows 2.0 SDK Tools, pages 34 through 35
Microsoft Windows 3.0 SDK Programmer's Reference, pages 8-5 through 8-7

See Also: 6.020. Resource Script File Directives

6.029. WIN.INI EXTENSION SETTINGS

Section Header: [extensions]

Option	*Function*	*Syntax*	*Allowable Values*
Extension setting	Associates extension with application	ext = apname.typ ^.ext	'ext' is the extension to associate with application

Source: Microsoft Windows 2.0 User's Guide, page 207
Running Windows 2nd Edition (Microsoft Press), Chapter 9
WININI.TXT, the read-me file that comes with Windows 3.0

See Also: 6.030. WIN.INI Windows Settings
6.031. WIN.INI Devices Settings
6.032. WIN.INI Colors Settings
6.033. WIN.INI PIF Settings
6.035. WIN.INI Ports Settings
6.036. WIN.INI International Settings
6.037. WIN.INI Fonts Settings

6.030. WIN.INI WINDOWS SETTINGS

Section Header: [windows]

Option	*Function*	*Syntax*	*Example*
Beep	Defines whether system beeps on errors	Beep=boolean	Beep=yes
BorderWidth	Sets area to display outside window	BorderWidth=integer	BorderWidth=5
CursorBlinkRate	Sets system's cursor blink rate	CursorBlinkRate=milliseconds	CursorBlinkRate=817
Device	Defines default output device	Device=name,drivermodule,portname	Device=PCL/LaserJet,HPPCL,LPT1:
DeviceNotSelectedTimeout	Sets device timeout value	DeviceNotSelectedTimeout=seconds	DeviceNotSelectedTimeout=15
Documents	Defines file extensions that are "documents" but not listed in extensions section	Documents=extensions	Documents=bre
DoubleClickSpeed	Sets system's double-click speed	DoubleClickSpeed=milliseconds	DoubleClickSpeed=500
Load	Programs made into icons at startup	Load=list	Load clock notepad
KeyboardSpeed	Defines keyboard repeat speed	KeyboardSpeed=milliseconds	KeyboardSpeed=31
MouseSpeed	Sets mouse acceleration rate	MouseSpeed=integer	MouseSpeed=1
NetWarn	Defines whether a warning message is displayed if network not running	NetWarn=0 or 1	NetWarn=1
NullPort	Defines null port	NullPort=portname	NullPort=none
Programs	Programs listed by MS-DOS Executive	Programs=list	Programs=com exe bat
Run	Programs run at startup	Run=list	Run=excel
Spooler	Defines whether spooler is used	Spooler=boolean	Spooler=yes
SwapMouseButtons†	Allows mouse buttons to be reversed	SwapMouseButtons=boolean	SwapMouseButtons=no
TransmissionRetryTimeout	Sets timeout value for communications	TransmissionRetryTimeout=seconds	TransmissionRetryTimeout=45
xMouseThreshold*	Sets horizontal mouse threshold level	xMouseThreshold=integer	xMouseThreshold=2
yMouseThreshold*	Sets vertical mouse threshold level	yMouseThreshold=integer	yMouseThreshold=2

*In Windows 3.0, xMouseThreshold is MouseThreshold1, and yMouseThreshold is MouseThreshold2.
†Not in Windows 3.0

Note: Values in lists may be separated by commas or white space

Source: Microsoft Windows 2.0 User's Guide, pages 201 to 202
Running Windows 2nd Edition (Microsoft Press), Chapter 9
WININI.TXT, a file that is included in Windows 3.0
WININI2.TXT, a file that is included in Windows 3.0

See Also: 6.029. WIN.INI Extension Settings
6.031. WIN.INI Devices Settings
6.032. WIN.INI Colors Settings
6.033. WIN.INI PIF Settings
6.035. WIN.INI Ports Settings
6.036. WIN.INI International Settings

6.031. WIN.INI DEVICES SETTINGS

Section Header: [devices]

Option	*Function*	*Syntax*	*Allowable values*
devicename	Names output devices and their port	devicename=drivername,portname*	'Portname': See 6.035. WIN.INI Ports Settings

*Additional port names may be specified (separated by commas).

Note: If device not connected, 'portname' should be the NullPort device defined in the Ports section.

Source: Microsoft Windows 2.0 User's Guide, page 214
Running Windows 2nd Edition (Microsoft Press), Chapter 9
WININI.TXT, a file that is included in Windows 3.0
WININI2.TXT, a file that is included in Windows 3.0

See Also: 6.029. WIN.INI Extension Settings
6.030. WIN.INI Windows Settings
6.032. WIN.INI Colors Settings
6.033. WIN.INI PIF Settings
6.035. WIN.INI Ports Settings
6.036. WIN.INI International Settings

6.032. WIN.INI COLORS SETTINGS

Section Header: [colors]

Option	*Function*	*Syntax*	*Allowable values*
Component	Defines Windows background colors	Component = redval greenval blueval	Component is one of: ActiveBorder (active window border) ActiveTitle (active caption bar) AppWorkSpace (application work space) Background (icon area, screen back) ButtonFace (button face) ButtonShadow (button shadow) ButtonText (button text) GrayText (dimmed text) Hilight (background of highlighted text) HighlightText (highlighted text) Inactive Title (inactive caption bar) InactiveBorder (inactive window border) Menu (menu background) MenuText (menu text) Scrollbar (scroll bars) TitleText (title text) Window (Window client area back) WindowFrame (Title back, frame) WindowText (window text) Color vals: 0 (black) to 255 (white)(integer only)

Note: Windows expects a solid color for MenuText, WindowText, TitleText, and Window.

Source: Microsoft Windows 2.0 User's Guide, pages 207 through 208
Running Windows 2nd Edition (Microsoft Press), Chapter 9

See Also: 6.029. WIN.INI Extension Settings
6.030. WIN.INI Windows Settings
6.031. WIN.INI Devices Settings
6.033. WIN.INI PIF Settings
6.035. WIN.INI Ports Settings
6.036. WIN.INI International Settings

6.033. WIN.INI PIF SETTINGS

Section Header: [pif]

Option	*Function*	*Syntax*	*Allowable values*
Program Setting*	Sets memory setting for program	pgmname.typ=value	Value=amount of memory in K
SwapDisk	Sets swap area for applications	SwapDisk=value	Value=? (swap to first fixed disk) Value=letter (swap to that letter drive) Value=0 (do not swap)
SwapSize	Sets amount of memory to swap	SwapSize=value	Value=min amt of memory in K Value=0 (set swap to first app size)

*Multiple Program Settings may appear in [pif] section.

Version: Does not apply to Windows 3.0.

Note: All disk swapping is done to the root directory unless the [environment] section specifies a temporary directory.

Source: Microsoft Windows 2.0 User's Guide, pages 208 through 211
Running Windows 2nd Edition (Microsoft Press), Chapter 9

See Also: 6.029. WIN.INI Extension Settings
6.030. WIN.INI Windows Settings
6.031. WIN.INI Devices Settings
6.034. Default PIF Settings
6.035. WIN.INI Ports Settings
6.036. WIN.INI International Settings
6.037. WIN.INI Fonts Settings

6.034. DEFAULT PIF SETTINGS

Item	*Default Setting*
Program title	Ignored
Initial directory	Ignored
Memory required	52K*, 128K†
Memory desired	640K†
Directly modifies	Nothing
Program switch	Does not prevent program switch
Screen exchange	Text only
Close window on exit	Closes

*For Windows 1.x and 2.x
†For Windows 3.0 and later

Version: Applies to all versions of Windows beginning with 3.0.

Note: These settings are used only if no PIF file exists for the application.

Source: Microsoft Windows 2.0 User's Guide, page 188
Microsoft Windows 3.0 User's Guide, Chapter 12

See Also: 6.033. WIN.INI PIF Settings

6.035. WIN.INI PORTS SETTINGS

Section Header: [ports]

Option	*Function*	*Syntax*	*Allowable values*
Portname	Defines port settings	Portname:=baud,parity,wordlen,stopbits,p	Baud: actual baud rate (e.g., 300) Parity: o, e, n (odd, even, none) Wordlen: # of bits (e.g., 8) Stopbits: # of bits (e.g., 2) p: hardware handshaking

Note:
- 'Portname' must be one of the recognized DOS ports (e.g., COM1), or EPT: or FILE:.
- Alternatively, 'portname' may be a filename, in which case output may be sent directly to a file.

Source:
Microsoft Windows 2.0 User's Guide, pages 212 through 213
Running Windows 2nd Edition (Microsoft Press), Chapter 9
WININI2.TXT, a file that is included in Windows 3.0

See Also:
6.029. WIN.INI Extension Settings
6.030. WIN.INI Windows Settings
6.031. WIN.INI Devices Settings
6.032. WIN.INI Colors Settings
6.033. WIN.INI PIF Settings
6.036. WIN.INI International Settings

6.036. WIN.INI INTERNATIONAL SETTINGS

Section Header: [intl]

Option	*Function*	*Syntax*	*Allowable Values*	*Default*
Country	Sets country code	iCountry=country code	See 3.199. Country Codes	1
Country	Sets country string	sCountry=string		United States
Language	Set language	sLanguage=string	dan=Danish dut=Dutch eng=International English fcf=French Canadian fin=Finnish frn=French ger=German ice=Icelandic itn=Italian nor=Norwegian por=Portuguese spa=Spanish swe=Swedish usa=U.S. English	usa
Date format	Sets format for date	iDate=value	Value of 0=month-day-year Value of 1=day-month-year Value of 2=year-month-day	0
Date format	Sets long date format	sLongDate=string	M=month, 1-12 MM=month, 01-12 MMM=month, Jan-Dec MMMM=month, January-December d=day, 1-31 dd=day, 01-31 ddd=day, Mon-Sun dddd=day, Monday-Sunday yy=year, 00-99 yyyy=year, 1900-2040	dddd,MMMM d,yyyy
Date format	Sets short date format	sShortDate=string	See sLongDate	M/d/yy
Currency format	Sets format for currency	iCurrency=value	Value of 0=currency prefix, no space Value of 1=currency suffix, no space Value of 2=currency prefix, 1 space Value of 3=currency suffix, 1 space	0
Decimal digits	Sets # of decimal digits in currency	iCurrDigits=value	Value=# of significant digits	2
Negative currency	Sets format for negative currency	iNegCurr=value	0=(currency prefix numbers) 1= - currency prefix numbers 2=currency prefix - number 3=currency prefix numbers - 4=(numbers currency prefix) 5= - numbers currency prefix 6=numbers - currency prefix 7=numbers currency prefix -	0
Time format	Sets format for time	iTime=value	Value of 0=12-hour clock Value of 1=24-hour clock	0

(Continued)

6.036. WIN.INI INTERNATIONAL SETTINGS (continued)

Option	*Function*	*Syntax*	*Allowable Values*	*Default*
Digits	Sets # of digits after decimal	iDigits=value		2
Leading zeros	Sets leading zeros in numbers	iLZero=value	0=none, 1=use leading zeros	0
Leading zeros	Sets leading zeros in time	iTLZero	0=none, 1=use leading zeros	0
Measurement	Sets measurement system	iMeasure=value	0=metric, 1=English	1
AM string	Sets trailing string for morning times	s1159=string		AM
PM string	Sets trailing string for afternoon times	s2359=string		PM
Currency symbol	Defines currency symbol	sCurrency=string		$
Thousands separator	Defines thousands separator symbol	sThousand=string		,
Decimal separator	Defines decimal separator symbol	sDecimal=string		.
Date separator	Defines date separator symbol	sDate=string		/
Time separator	Defines time separator symbol	sTime=string		:
List separator	Defines list separator symbol	sList=string sShortDate=		,
Preferences menu	Defines if Country Settings appear	dialog=yes	Always set to yes	yes

Note: The US version of Windows does not require the intl section.

Source: Microsoft Windows 2.0 User's Guide, pages 211 through 212
Running Windows 2nd Edition (Microsoft Press), Chapter 9
WININI2.TXT, a file that is included in Windows 3.0

See Also:
3.199. Country Codes
6.029. WIN.INI Extension Settings
6.030. WIN.INI Windows Settings
6.031. WIN.INI Devices Settings
6.032. WIN.INI Colors Settings
6.033. WIN.INI PIF Settings
6.035. WIN.INI Ports Settings
6.037. WIN.INI Fonts Settings

6.037. WIN.INI FONTS SETTINGS

Section Header: [fonts]

Option	*Function*	*Syntax*	*Allowable values*
Fontname	Names font files to load at startup	Fontname ptsize(s) (set number)=fontfile	Fontname=description font name ptsize=1 or more point sizes to load number=set number fontfile=filename, no extension

Note: Windows 1.xx used the FNT extension for fontfiles, whereas Windows 2.0 and later use the FON extension. The file formats are different.

Source: Microsoft Windows 2.0 User's Guide, page 214
Running Windows 2nd Edition (Microsoft Press), Chapter 9
WININI2.TXT, a file that is included in Windows 3.0

See Also:
6.029. WIN.INI Extension Settings
6.030. WIN.INI Windows Settings
6.031. WIN.INI Devices Settings
6.032. WIN.INI Colors Settings
6.033. WIN.INI PIF Settings
6.035. WIN.INI Ports Settings
6.036. WIN.INI International Settings

6.038. DATA TYPES USED IN WINDOWS ARGUMENT NAMES

Prefix Used	Meaning	Size	Comments
b	Boolean value	WORD	0=false; non-zero=true
c	Character	BYTE	See 6.09. Extended ANSI Character Codes
dw	Long unsigned integer value	DWORD	Unsigned values
f	Bit flag value	WORD	16 individual flags
h	Handle	WORD	Handle is an index into a table
l	Long integer value	DWORD	Signed values
l p	Long pointer	DWORD	Far pointer
n	Short integer value	WORD	Signed values
p	Short pointer	WORD	Near pointer
pt	x,y coordinate point	DWORD	Unsigned, 2-word values
rgb	RGB color value	DWORD	Unsigned
w	Short unsigned integer value	WORD	Unsigned values

Note: The letters in the left column are used as prefixes to an argument name, as in lpMinPos (e.g., MinPos is a long pointer argument).

Source: Microsoft Windows 2.0 SDK Programmer's Reference, page 9
Microsoft Windows 3.0 SDK Programmer's Reference, pages xxii through xxiii

See Also: 1.16. Common Numeric Data Formats
6.009. Extended ANSI Character Codes
6.039. Data Types Available as C Keywords

6.039. DATA TYPES AVAILABLE AS C KEYWORDS

Keyword	Meaning	Size	Signed	Comments
BOOL	Unsigned 16-bit word	WORD	N	0=false, nonzero=true
BYTE	Unsigned byte integer	BYTE	N	
char	ASCII character or signed byte	BYTE	Y	See 6.009. Extended ANSI Character Codes
DWORD	Unsigned 32-bit integer	DWORD	N	May also be Segment:Offset address
FAR	Long pointer	WORD	N	Cast as a long pointer (data in any segment)
FARPROC	Long pointer to function	DWORD	N	Function may be in another segment
GLOBALHANDLE	Global memory handle	WORD	N	
HANDLE	General handle	WORD	N	
HBITMAP	Physical bitmap handle	WORD	N	
HBRUSH	Physical brush handle	WORD	N	
HCURSOR	Cursor resource handle	WORD	N	
HDC	Display context handle	WORD	N	
HFONT	Physical font handle	WORD	N	
HICON	Icon resource handle	WORD	N	
HMENU	Menu resource handle	WORD	N	
HPALETTE*	Logical palette resource handle	WORD	N	
HPEN	Physical pen handle	WORD	N	
HRGN	Physical region handle	WORD	N	
HSTR	String resource handle	WORD	N	
int	Signed 16-bit integer	WORD	Y	
LOCALHANDLE	Local memory handle	WORD	N	
long	Signed 32-bit integer	DWORD	Y	
LONG	Signed 32-bit integer	DWORD	Y	
LPBITMAP*	Long pointer to BITMAP	DWORD	N	See 6.043. BITMAP Structure Format
LPBITMAPCOREHEADER*	Long pointer to BIMPACOREHEADER	DWORD	N	See 6.044. BITMAPCOREHEADER Structure Format
LPBITMAPCOREINFO*	Long pointer to BITMAPCOREINFO	DWORD	N	See 6.045. BITMAPCOREINFO Structure Format
LPBITMAPFILEHEADER*	Long pointer to BITMAPFILEHEADER	DWORD	N	See 6.046. BITMAPFILEHEADER Structure Format
LPBITMAPINFO*	Long pointer to BITMAPINFO	DWORD	N	See 6.047. BITMAPINFO Structure Format
LPBITMAPINFOHEADER*	Long pointer to BITMAPINFOHEADER	DWORD	N	See 6.048. BITMAPINFOHEADER Structure Format
LPCOMPAREITEMSTRUCT*	Long pointer to COMPAREITEMSTRUCT	DWORD	N	See 6.050. COMPAREITEMSTRUCT Structure Format
LPCREATESTRUCT*	Long pointer to CREATESTRUCT	DWORD	N	See 6.052. CREATESTRUCT Structure Format
LPDELETEITEMSTRUCT*	Long pointer to DELETEITEMSTRUCT	DWORD	N	See 6.054. DELETEITEMSTRUCT Structure Format
LPDRAWITEMSTRUCT*	Long pointer to DRAWITEMSTRUCT	DWORD	N	See 6.057. DRAWITEMSTRUCT Structure Format
LPHANDLETABLE*	Long pointer to HANDLETABLE	DWORD	N	See 6.059. HANDLETABLE Structure Format
LPINT	Long pointer to 16-bit integer	DWORD	N	Data may be in another segment
LPLOGBRUSH	Long pointer to LOGBRUSH	DWORD	N	See 6.062. LOGBRUSH Structure Format
LPLOGFONT	Long pointer to LOGFONT	DWORD	N	See 6.063. LOGFONT Structure Format
LPLOGPALETTE*	Long pointer to LOGPALETTE	DWORD	N	See 6.064. LOGPALETTE Structure Format
LPLOGPEN	Long pointer to LOGPEN	DWORD	N	See 6.065. LOGPEN Structure Format
LPMEASUREITEMSTRUCT	Long pointer to MEASUREITEMSTRUCT	DWORD	N	See 6.067. MEASUREITEMSTRUCT Structure Format
LPMETAFILEPICT	Long pointer to METAFILEPICT	DWORD	N	See 6.069. METAFILEPICT Structure Format

(Continued)

6.039. DATA TYPES AVAILABLE AS C KEYWORDS (continued)

Keyword	*Meaning*	*Size*	*Signed*	*Comments*
LPMSG	Long pointer to MSG struct.	DWORD	N	Data may be in another segment
LPOFSTRUCT	Long pointer to OFSTRUCT	DWORD	N	See 6.072. OFSTRUCT Structure Format
LPPAINTSTRUCT	Long pointer to PAINTSTRUCT	DWORD	N	See 6.073. PAINTSTRUCT Structure Format
LPPALETTEENTRY*	Long pointer to PALETTEENTRY	DWORD	N	See 6.074. PALETTEENTRY Structure Format
LPPOINT	Long pointer to POINT struct.	DWORD	N	See 6.075. POINT Structure Format
LPRECT	Long pointer to RECT struct.	DWORD	N	Data may be in another segment
LPRESOURCELIST	Long pointer to RESOURCELIST	DWORD	N	
LPSTR	Long pointer to char string	DWORD	N	Data may be in another segment
LPTEXTMETRIC	Long pointer to TEXTMETRIC	DWORD	N	See 6.080. TEXTMETRIC Structure Format
LPVOID	Long pointer to undefined data type	DWORD	N	
LPWNDCLASS	Long pointer to WNDCLASS	DWORD	N	See 6.081. WNDCLASS Structure Format
NEAR	Short pointer	WORD	N	Cast as a short pointer (data in current segment)
NPSTR	Near pointer to character string	WORD	N	
PINT	Pointer to 16-bit integer	WORD	N	Data is assumed within current segment
PSTR	Pointer to character string	WORD	N	Data is assumed within current segment
PWORD	Pointer to unsigned 16-bit integer	WORD	N	
short	Signed word integer	WORD	Y	
void	Empty value		N	
WORD	Unsigned word integer	WORD	N	

*First defined in Windows 3.0.

Source: Microsoft Windows 2.0 SDK Programmer's Reference, pages 607 through 608
Microsoft Windows 3.0 SDK Programmer's Reference, pages 7-1 through 7-5

See Also: 1.16. Common Numeric Data Formats
6.009. Extended ANSI Character Codes
6.038. Data Types Used in Windows Argument Names

6.040. WINDOWS HANDLE AND POINTER TYPES

Name	*Function*
FAR	Data type attribute that can be used to create a long pointer
FARPROC	Long pointer to a function
GLOBALHANDLE	Global memory handle; index to memory block in system's global heap
HANDLE	General handle; index to table entry identifying program data
HBITMAP	Physical bitmap handle; index to GDI's physical drawing objects
HBRUSH	Physical brush handle; index to GDI's physical drawing objects
HCURSOR	Cursor resource handle; index to a resource table entry
HDC	Display context handle; index to GDI's display context tables
HFONT	Physical font handle; index to GDI's physical drawing objects
HICON	Icon resource handle; index to a resource table entry
HMENU	Menu resource handle; index to a resource table entry
HPEN	Physical pen handle; index to GDI's physical drawing objects
HRGN	Physical region handle; index to GDI's physical drawing objects
HSTR	String resource handle; index to a resource table entry
LOCALHANDLE	Local memory handle; index to memory block in application's local heap
LPINT	Long pointer to a signed 16-bit integer
LPMSG	Long pointer to MSG data structure
LPRECT	Long pointer to RECT data structure
LPSTR	Long pointer to a character string
NEAR	Data type attribute that can be used to create a short pointer
PINT	Pointer to a signed 16-bit integer
PSTR	Pointer to a character string

Note: All handles are 16-bit values.

Source: Microsoft Windows 2.0 SDK Programmer's Reference, pages 607 through 608
Microsoft Windows 3.0 SDK Programmer's Reference, pages 7-1 through 7-5

See Also: 6.038. Data Types Used in Windows Argument Names
6.039. Data Types Available as C Keywords

6.041. INCLUDE FILE CONSTANTS DEFINITIONS BY NAME

Defined Name	Used As	Hex Value	Decimal Value	Comments
ABORTDOC	GDI escape	2	2	
ABSOLUTE	GDI coordinate mode	1	1	
ALTERNATE	Polyfill mode	1	1	
ANSI_CHARSET	Logical font constant	0	0	
ANSI_FIXED_FONT	Stock logical object	B	11	
ANSI_VAR_FONT	Stock logical object	C	12	
ASPECTX	GetDeviceCaps device parameter	28	40	
ASPECTXY	GetDeviceCaps device parameter	2C	44	
ASPECTY	GetDeviceCaps device parameter	2A	42	
ASPECT_FILTERING		1	1	
BANDINFO*	GDI escape code	18	24	
BEGIN_PATH†	GDI escape	1000	4096	
BITSPIXEL	GetDeviceCaps device parameter	C	12	
BI_RBG†	biCompression constant	0	0	
BI_RLE4†	biCompression constant	2	2	
BI_RLE8†	biCompression constant	1	1	
BLACKNESS	Ternary raster op	0000 0042H	66	Dest = BLACK
BLACKONWHITE	StretchBlt mode	1	1	
BLACK_BRUSH	Stock logical object	4	4	
BLACK_PEN	Stock logical object	7	7	
BM_GETCHECK*	Control message	400	1024	WM_USER+0
BM_GETSTATE*	Control message	402	1026	WM_USER+2
BM_SETCHECK*	Control message	401	1025	WM_USER+1
BM_SETSTATE*	Control message	403	1027	WM_USER+3
BM_SETSTYLE*	Control message	404	1208	WM_USER+4
BN_CLICKED	User button notification code	0	0	
BN_DISABLE	User button notification code	4	4	
BN_DOUBLECLICKED*	Control message	5	5	
BN_HILITE	User button notification code	2	2	
BN_PAINT	User button notification code	1	1	
BN_UNHILITE	User button notification code	3	3	
BS_3STATE	Button control style	5	5	
BS_AUTO3STATE	Button control style	6	6	
BS_AUTOCHECKBOX	Button control style	3	3	
BS_AUTORADIOBUTTON*	Button style	9	9	
BS_CHECKBOX	Button control style	2	2	
BS_DEFPUSHBUTTON	Button control style	1	1	
BS_DIBPATTERN†	Brush style	5	5	
BS_GROUPBOX	Button control style	7	7	
BS_HATCHED	Brush style	2	2	
BS_HOLLOW	Brush style			Defined as BS_NULL
BS_INDEXED*	Button control style	4	4	
BS_LEFTTEXT*	Button style	20	32	
BS_NULL	Brush style	1	1	
BS_OWNERDRAW†	Button style	B	11	
BS_PATTERN	Brush style	3	3	
BS_PUSHBOX*	Button style	A	10	
BS_PUSHBUTTON	Button control style	0	0	
BS_RADIOBUTTON	Button control style	4	4	
BS_SOLID	Brush style	0	0	
BS_USERBUTTON	Button control style	8	8	
CBM_INIT†	DIBitmap constant	4	4	
CBN_DBLCLK†	Combobox notification code	2	2	
CBN_DROPDOWN†	Combobox notification code	7	7	
CBN_EDITCHANGE†	Combobox notification code	5	5	
CBN_EDITUPDATE†	Combobox notification code	6	6	
CBN_ERRSPACE†	Combobox notification code		-1	
CBN_KILLFOCUS†	Combobox notification code	4	4	
CBN_SELCHANGE†	Combobox notification code	1	1	
CBN_SETFOCUS†	Combobox notification code	3	3	
CBS_AUTOHSCROLL†	Combobox styles	40	64	
CBS_DROPDOWNLIST†	Combobox styles	3	3	
CBS_DROPDOWN†	Combobox styles	2	2	
CBS_HASSTRINGS†	Combobox styles	200	512	
CBS_NOINTEGRALHEIGHT†	Combobox styles	400	1024	
CBS_OEMCONVERT†	Combobox styles	80	128	
CBS_OWNERDRAWFIXED†	Combobox styles	10	16	
CBS_OWNERDRAWVARIABLE†	Combobox styles	20	32	
CBS_SIMPLE†	Combobox styles	1	1	
CBS_SORT†	Combobox styles	100	256	
CB_ADDSTRING†	Combobox message	403	1027	WM_USER+3
CB_DELETESTRING†	Combobox message	404	1028	WM_USER+4
CB_DIR†	Combobox message	405	1029	WM_USER+5
CB_ERRSPACE†	Combobox values		-2	
CB_ERR†	Combobox values		-1	

(Continued)

6.041. INCLUDE FILE CONSTANTS DEFINITIONS BY NAME (continued)

Defined Name	*Used As*	*Hex Value*	*Decimal Value*	*Comments*
CB_FINDSTRING†	Combobox message	40C	1036	WM_USER+12
CB_GETCOUNT†	Combobox message	406	1030	WM_USER+6
CB_GETCURSEL†	Combobox message	407	1031	WM_USER+7
CB_GETDROPPEDCONTROLRECT†	Combobox message	412	1042	WM_USER+18
CB_GETEDITSEL†	Combobox message	400	1024	WM_USER+0
CB_GETIITEMDATA†	Combobox message	410	1040	WM_USER+16
CB_GETLBTEXTLEN†	Combobox message	409	1033	WM_USER+9
CB_GETLBTEXT†	Combobox message	408	1032	WM_USER+8
CB_INSERTSTRING†	Combobox message	40A	1034	WM_USER+10
CB_LIMITTEXT†	Combobox message	401	1025	WM_USER+1
CB_MSGMAX†	Combobox message	413	1043	WM_USER+19
CB_OKAY†	Combobox values	0	0	
CB_RESETCONTENT†	Combobox message	40B	1035	WM_USER+11
CB_SELECTSTRING†	Combobox message	40D	1037	WM_USER+13
CB_SETCURSEL†	Combobox message	40E	1038	WM_USER+14
CB_SETEDITSEL†	Combobox message	402	1026	WM_USER+2
CB_SETITEMDATA†	Combobox message	411	1041	WM_USER+17
CB_SHOWDROPDOWN†	Combobox message	40F	1039	WM_USER+15
CC_CHORD	Device capability mask	4	4	
CC_CIRCLES	Device capability mask	1	1	
CC_ELLIPSES	Device capability mask	8	8	
CC_INTERIORS	Device capability mask	80	128	
CC_NONE	Device capability mask	0	0	
CC_PIE	Device capability mask	2	2	
CC_STYLED	Device capability mask	20	32	
CC_WIDE	Device capability mask	10	16	
CC_WIDESTYLED	Device capability mask	40	64	
CE_BREAK	Comm device driver error	10	16	
CE_CTSTO	Comm device driver error	20	32	
CE_DNS	Comm device driver error	800	2048	
CE_DSRTO	Comm device driver error	40	64	
CE_FRAME	Comm device driver error	8	8	
CE_IOE	Comm device driver error	400	1024	
CE_MODE	Comm device driver error	8000	32768	
CE_OOP	Comm device driver error	1000	4096	
CE_OVERRUN	Comm device driver error	2	2	
CE_PTO	Comm device driver error	200	512	
CE_RLSDTO	Comm device driver error	80	128	
CE_RXOVER	Comm device driver error	1	1	
CE_RXPARITY	Comm device driver error	4	4	
CE_TXFULL	Comm device driver error	100	256	
CF_BITMAP	Clipboard format	2	2	
CF_DIB†	Clipboard format	8	8	
CF_DIF	Clipboard format	5	5	
CF_DSPBITMAP	Clipboard format	82	130	
CF_DSPMETAFILEPICT	Clipboard format	83	131	
CF_DSPTEXT	Clipboard format	81	129	
CF_GDIOBJFIRST	Clipboard format	300	768	
CF_GDIOBJLAST	Clipboard format	3FF	1023	
CF_METAFILEPICT	Clipboard format	3	3	
CF_OEMTEXT*	Clipboard format	7	7	
CF_OWNERDISPLAY	Clipboard format	80	128	
CF_PALETTE†	Clipboard format	9	9	
CF_PRIVATEFIRST	Clipboard format	200	512	
CF_PRIVATELAST	Clipboard format	2FF	767	
CF_SYLK	Clipboard format	4	4	
CF_TEXT	Clipboard format	1	1	
CF_TIFF*	Clipboard format	6	6	
CLIPCAPS	GetDeviceCaps device parameter	24	36	
CLIP_CHARACTER_PRECIS	Logical font constant	1	1	
CLIP_DEFAULT_PRECIS	Logical font constant	0	0	
CLIP_STROKE_PRECIS	Logical font constant	2	2	
CLIP_TO_PATH†	GDI escape	1001	4097	
CLRDTR	Comm escape function	6	6	
CLRRTS	Comm escape function	4	4	
COLORES†	GetDeviceCaps device parameter	6C	108	
COLORONCOLOR	StretchBlt mode	3	3	
COLOR_ACTIVEBORDER*	Color type index	A	10	
COLOR_ACTIVECAPTION	Color type index	2	2	
COLOR_APPWORKSPACE*	Color type index	C	12	
COLOR_BACKGROUND	Color type index	1	1	
COLOR_BTNFACE†	Color type index	F	15	
COLOR_BTNSHADOW†	Color type index	10	16	
COLOR_BTNTEXT†	Color type index	12	18	
COLOR_CAPTIONTEXT	Color type index	9	9	

(Continued)

6.041. INCLUDE FILE CONSTANTS DEFINITIONS BY NAME (continued)

Defined Name	*Used As*	*Hex Value*	*Decimal Value*	*Comments*
COLOR_ENDCOLORS†	Color type index			COLOR_BTNTEXT
COLOR_GRAYTEXT†	Color type index	11	17	
COLOR_HIGHLIGHTTEXT†	Color type index	E	14	
COLOR_HIGHLIGHT†	Color type index	D	13	
COLOR_INACTIVEBORDER*	Color type index	B	11	
COLOR_INACTIVECAPTION	Color type index	3	3	
COLOR_MENU	Color type index	4	4	
COLOR_MENUTEXT	Color type index	7	7	
COLOR_SCROLLBAR	Color type index	0	0	
COLOR_WINDOW	Color type index	5	5	
COLOR_WINDOWFRAME	Color type index	6	6	
COLOR_WINDOWTEXT	Color type index	8	8	
COMPLEXREGION	Region flag	3	3	
CP_DIRECT‡	Device capability mode	2	2	
CP_GETBEEP‡	Control panel info	1	1	
CP_GETBORDER‡	Control panel info	5	5	
CP_GETMOUSE‡	Control panel info	3	3	
CP_HWND*	Device capability mode	0	0	
CP_KANJIMENU‡	Control panel info	8	8	
CP_NONE	Device capability mask	0	0	
CP_OPEN*	Device capability mode	1	1	
CP_RECTANGLE	Device capability mask	1	1	
CP_SETBEEP‡	Control panel info	2	2	
CP_SETBORDER‡	Control panel info	6	6	
CP_SETMOUSE‡	Control panel info	4	4	
CP_TIMEOUTS‡	Control panel info	7	7	
CS_BYTEALIGNCLIENT*	Class style	1000	4096	
CS_BYTEALIGNWINDOW*	Class style	2000	8192	
CS_CLASSDC	Class style	40	64	
CS_DBLCLKS	Class style	8	8	
CS_GLOBALCLASS†	Class style	4000	16384	
CS_HREDRAW	Class style	2	2	
CS_KEYCVTWINDOW	Class style	4	4	
CS_MENUPOPUP‡	Class style	80	128	
CS_NOCLOSE*	Class style	200	512	
CS_NOKEYCVT	Class style	100	512	
CS_OEMCHARS‡	Class style	10	16	
CS_OWNDC	Class style	20	32	
CS_PARENTDC*	Class style	80	128	
CS_SAVEBITS*	Class style	800	2048	
CS_VREDRAW	Class style	1	1	
CTLCOLOR_BTN	Color type index	3	3	
CTLCOLOR_DLG	Color type index	4	4	
CTLCOLOR_EDIT	Color type index	1	1	
CTLCOLOR_LISTBOX	Color type index	2	2	
CTLCOLOR_MAX	Color type index	8	8	
CTLCOLOR_MSGBOX	Color type index	0	0	
CTLCOLOR_SCROLLBAR	Color type index	5	5	
CTLCOLOR_STATIC	Color type index	6	6	
CURVECAPS	GetDeviceCaps device parameter	1C	28	
CW_USEDEFAULT†	lopen flag	(int)8000	32768	
DC_HASDEFID		0x534B	21323	
DEFAULT_PALETTE		F	15	
DEFAULT_PITCH	Logical font constant	0	0	
DEFAULT_QUALITY	Logical font constant	0	0	
DEVICEDATA	MetaFile comment esc.	13	19	
DEVICEDEFAULT_FONT	Stock logical object	E	14	
DEVICE_FONTTYPE	EnumFonts mask	2	2	
DF_ACTIVEBORDER‡	DrawFrame index			COLOR_ACTIVEBORDER+1<<3
DF_ACTIVECAPTION‡	DrawFrame index			COLOR_ACTIVECAPTION+1<<3
DF_APPWORKSPACE‡	DrawFrame index			COLOR_APPWORKSPACE+1<<3
DF_BACKGROUND‡	DrawFrame index			COLOR_BACKGROUND+1<<3
DF_CAPTIONTEXT‡	DrawFrame index			COLOR_CAPTIONTEXT+1<<3
DF_GRAY‡	DrawFrame index			COLOR_APPWORKSPACE+(1<<3)
DF_INACTIVEBORDER‡	DrawFrame index			COLOR_INACTIVEBORDER+1<<3
DF_INACTIVECAPTION‡	DrawFrame index			COLOR_INACTIVECAPTION+1<<3
DF_MENU‡	DrawFrame index			COLOR_MENU+1<<3
DF_MENUTEXT‡	DrawFrame index			COLOR_MENUTEXT+1<<3
DF_PATCOPY‡	DrawFrame index	0	0	
DF_PATINVERT‡	DrawFrame index	4	4	
DF_SCROLLBAR‡	DrawFrame index			COLOR_SCROLLBAR+1<<3
DF_SHIFT0‡	DrawFrame index	0	0	
DF_SHIFT1‡	DrawFrame index	1	1	
DF_SHIFT2‡	DrawFrame index	2	2	
DF_SHIFT3‡	DrawFrame index	3	3	

(Continued)

6.041. INCLUDE FILE CONSTANTS DEFINITIONS BY NAME (continued)

Defined Name	*Used As*	*Hex Value*	*Decimal Value*	*Comments*
DF_WINDOW‡	DrawFrame index			COLOR_WINDOW+1<<3
DF_WINDOWFRAME‡	DrawFrame index			COLOR_WINDOWFRAME+1<<3
DF_WINDOWTEXT‡	DrawFrame index			COLOR_WINDOWTEXT+1<<3
DIB_PAL_COLORS†	DIB color table ID	1	1	
DIB_RGB_COLORS†	DIB color table ID	0	0	
DKGRAY_BRUSH	Stock logical object	3	3	
DLGC_BUTTON*	Dialog code	2000	8192	
DLGC_DEFPUSHBUTTON*	Dialog code	10	16	
DLGC_HASSETSEL	Dialog code	8	8	
DLGC_RADIOBUTTON*	Dialog code	40	64	
DLGC_STATIC*	Dialog code	100	256	
DLGC_UNDEFPUSHBUTTON*	Dialog code	20	32	
DLGC_WANTALLKEYS	Dialog code	4	4	
DLGC_WANTARROWS	Dialog code	1	1	
DLGC_WANTCHARS*	Dialog code	80	128	
DLGC_WANTMESSAGE*	Dialog code	4	4	
DLGC_WANTTAB	Dialog code	2	2	
DLGWINDOWEXTRA		1E	30	
DM_GETDEFID	Dialog style bits	400	1024	WM_USER+0
DM_HASDEFID‡	Dialog style bits	534B	21323	
DM_SETDEFID	Dialog style bits	401	1025	WM_USER+1
DRAFTMODE	GDI escape	7	7	
DRAFT_QUALITY	Logical font constant	1	1	
DRAWPATTERNRECT*	GDI escape code	19	25	
DRIVERVERSION	GetDeviceCaps device parameter	0	0	
DRIVE_FIXED†	GetDriveType value	3	3	
DRIVE_REMOTE†	GetDriveType value	4	4	
DRIVE_REMOVABLE†	GetDriveType value	2	2	
DSTINVERT	Ternary raster op	0055 0009H	5570569	Dest = (not dest)
DS_ABSALIGN	Dialog style	1	1	
DS_LOCALEDIT*	Dialog style	20	32	
DS_MODALFRAME†	Dialog style	80	128	
DS_NOIDLEMSG†	Dialog style	100	256	
DS_SETFONT†	Dialog style	40	64	
DS_SYSMODAL	Dialog style	2	2	
DT_BOTTOM	DrawText format flag	8	8	
DT_CALCRECT*	DrawText format flag	400	1024	
DT_CENTER	DrawText format flag	1	1	
DT_CHARSTREAM	Device capability mask	4	4	
DT_DISPFILE	Device capability mask	6	6	
DT_EXPANDTABS	DrawText format flag	40	64	
DT_EXTERNALLEADING	DrawText format flag	200	512	
DT_INTERNAL	DrawText format flag	1000	4096	
DT_LEFT	DrawText format flag	0	0	
DT_METAFILE	Device capability mask	5	5	
DT_NOCLIP	DrawText format flag	100	256	
DT_NOPREFIX*	DrawText format flag	800	2048	
DT_PLOTTER	Device capability mask	0	0	
DT_RASCAMERA	Device capability mask	3	3	
DT_RASDISPLAY	Device capability mask	1	1	
DT_RASPRINTER	Device capability mask	2	2	
DT_RIGHT	DrawText format flag	2	2	
DT_SINGLELINE	DrawText format flag	20	32	
DT_TABSTOP	DrawText format flag	80	128	
DT_TOP	DrawText format flag	0	0	
DT_VCENTER	DrawText format flag	4	4	
DT_WORDBREAK	DrawText format flag	10	16	
EM_CANUNDO†	Edit control message	416	1046	WM_USER+22
EM_EMPTYUNDOBUFFER†	Edit control message	41D	1053	WM_USER+29
EM_FMTLINES†	Edit control message	418	1048	WM_USER+24
EM_GETHANDLE†	Edit control message	40D	1039	WM_USER+13
EM_GETLINE†	Edit control message	414	1044	WM_USER+20
EM_GETLINECOUNT†	Edit control message	40A	1034	WM_USER+10
EM_GETMODIFY†	Edit control message	408	1031	WM_USER+8
EM_GETRECT*	Edit control message	402	1026	WM_USER+2
EM_GETSEL*	Edit control message	400	1024	WM_USER+0
EM_GETTHUMB†	Edit control message	40E	1038	WM_USER+14
EM_LIMITTEXT†	Edit control message	415	1043	WM_USER+21
EM_LINEFROMCHAR†	Edit control message	419	1069	WM_USER+25
EM_LINEINDEX†	Edit control message	40B	1035	WM_USER+11
EM_LINELENGTH†	Edit control message	411	1051	WM_USER+17
EM_LINESCROLL*	Edit control message	406	1030	WM_USER+6
EM_MSGMAX†	Edit control message	41E	1054	WM_USER+30
EM_REPLACESEL†	Edit control message	412	1042	WM_USER+18
EM_SCROLL*	Edit control message	405	1029	WM_USER+5

(Continued)

6.041. INCLUDE FILE CONSTANTS DEFINITIONS BY NAME (continued)

Defined Name	Used As	Hex Value	Decimal Value	Comments
EM_SETFONT†	Edit control message	413	1043	WM_USER+19
EM_SETHANDLE†	Edit control message	40C	1036	WM_USER+12
EM_SETMODIFY†	Edit control message	409	1033	WM_USER+9
EM_SETPASSWORDCHAR†	Edit control message	41C	1052	WM_USER+28
EM_SETRECT*	Edit control message	403	1027	WM_USER+3
EM_SETRECTNP*	Edit control message	404	1028	WM_USER+4
EM_SETSEL*	Edit control message	401	1025	WM_USER+1
EM_SETTABSTOPS†	Edit control message	41B	1071	WM_USER+27
EM_SETWORDBREAK†	Edit control message	41A	1070	WM_USER+26
EM_UNDO†	Edit control message	417	1067	WM_USER+23
ENABLEDUPLEX*	GDI escape code	1C	28	
ENABLEMANUALFEED*	GDI escape code	1D	29	
ENABLEPAIRKERNING*	GDI escape code	301	769	
ENABLERELATIVEWIDTHS*	GDI escape code	300	768	
ENDDOC	GDI escape	B	11	
END_PATH†	GDI escape	1002	4098	
ENUMPAPERBINS†	GDI escape	1F	31	
ENUMPAPERMETRICS†	GDI escape	22	34	
EN_CHANGE	Edit control notification code	300	768	
EN_ERRSPACE	Edit control notification code	501	1281	
EN_HSCROLL	Edit control notification code	601	1537	
EN_KILLFOCUS	Edit control notification code	200	512	
EN_MAXTEXT†	Edit control notification code	501	1281	
EN_SETFOCUS	Edit control notification code	100	256	
EN_UPDATE*	Edit control notification code	400	1024	
EN_VSCROLL	Edit control notification code	602	1538	
EPSPRINTING†	GDI escape	21	33	
ERROR	Region flag	0	0	
ES_AUTOHSCROLL	Edit control style	80	128	
ES_AUTOVSCROLL	Edit control style	400	1024	
ES_CENTER	Edit control style	1	1	
ES_LEFT	Edit control style	0	0	
ES_LOWERCASE†	Edit control style	10	16	
ES_MULTILINE	Edit control style	4	4	
ES_NOHIDESEL	Edit control style	100	256	
ES_OEMCONVERT†	Edit control style	400	1024	
ES_PASSWORD†	Edit control style	20	32	
ES_RIGHT	Edit control style	2	2	
ES_UPPERCASE†	Edit control style	8	8	
ETO_CLIPPED*	Edit text option	4	4	
ETO_GRAYED*	Edit text option	1	1	
ETO_OPAQUE*	Edit text option	2	2	
EVENPARITY	Dcb field definition	2	2	
EV_BREAK	Comm event definition	40	64	
EV_CTS	Comm event definition	8	8	
EV_DSR	Comm event definition	10	16	
EV_ERR	Comm event definition	80	128	
EV_PERR	Comm event definition	200	512	
EV_RING	Comm event definition	100	256	
EV_RLSD	Comm event definition	20	32	
EV_RXCHAR	Comm event definition	1	1	
EV_RXFLAG	Comm event definition	2	2	
EV_TXEMPTY	Comm event definition	4	4	
EXTTEXTOUT*	GDI escape code	200	512	
EXT_DEVICE_CAPS†	GDI escape	1003	4099	
FALSE	Standard definitions	0	0	
FF_DECORATIVE†	Font family ID	50	80	
FF_DONTCARE†	Font family ID	00	0	
FF_MODERN†	Font family ID	30	48	
FF_ROMAN†	Font family ID	10	16	
FF_SCRIPT†	Font family ID	40	64	
FF_SWISS†	Font family ID	20	32	
FIXED_PITCH	Logical font constant	1	1	
FLOODFILLBORDER†	ExtFloodFill style flag	0	0	
FLOOFILLSURFACE†	ExtFloodFill style flag	1	1	
FLUSHOUTPUT	GDI escape	6	6	
FW_BLACK	Font weight constant	384	900	Defined as FW_HEAVY
FW_BOLD	Font weight constant	26C	700	
FW_DEMIBOLD	Font weight constant	258	600	Defined as FW_SEMIBOLD
FW_DONTCARE	Font weight constant	0	0	
FW_EXTRABOLD	Font weight constant	320	800	
FW_EXTRALIGHT	Font weight constant	C8	200	
FW_HEAVY	Font weight constant	384	900	
FW_LIGHT	Font weight constant	12C	300	
FW_MEDIUM	Font weight constant	1F4	500	

(Continued)

6.041. INCLUDE FILE CONSTANTS DEFINITIONS BY NAME (continued)

Defined Name	Used As	Hex Value	Decimal Value	Comments
FW_NORMAL	Font weight constant	190	400	
FW_REGULAR*	Font weight constant	190	400	FW_NORMAL
FW_SEMIBOLD	Font weight constant	258	600	
FW_THIN	Font weight constant	64	100	
FW_ULTRABOLD	Font weight constant	320	800	Defined as FW_EXTRABOLD
FW_ULTRALIGHT	Font weight constant	C8	200	Defined as FW_EXTRALIGHT
GCL_MENUNAME	Class field offset		-8	
GCL_WNDPROC	Class field offset		-24	
GCW_CBCLSEXTRA†	Class field offset		-20	
GCW_CBWNDEXTRA†	Class field offset		-18	
GCW_HBRBACKGROUND	Class field offset		-10	
GCW_HCURSOR	Class field offset		-12	
GCW_HICON	Class field offset		-14	
GCW_HMODULE	Class field offset		-16	
GCW_STYLE	Class field offset		-26	
GETCOLORTABLE	GDI escape	5	5	
GETEXTENDEDTEXTMETRICS*	GDI escape code	100	256	
GETEXTENTTABLE*	GDI escape code	101	257	
GETPAIRKERNTABLE*	GDI escape code	102	258	
GETPENWIDTH*	GDI escape code	10	16	
GETPHYSPAGESIZE	GDI escape	C	12	
GETPRINTINGOFFSET	GDI escape	D	13	
GETSCALINGFACTOR	GDI escape	E	14	
GETSETPAPERBINS†	GDI escape	1D	29	
GETSETPAPERMETRICS†	GDI escape	23	35	
GETSETPRINTORIENT†	GDI escape	1E	30	
GETTECHNOLOGY*	GDI escape code	14	20	
GETTRACKKERNTABLE*	GDI escape code	103	259	
GETVECTORBRUSHSIZE*	GDI escape code	1B	27	
GETVECTORPENSIZE*	GDI escape code	1A	26	
GHND*	Global memory management	42	66	GMEM_MOVEABLE | GMEM_ZEROINIT
GMEM_DDESHARE*	Global memory management	2000	8192	
GMEM_DISCARDABLE†	Global memory management	100	256	
GMEM_DISCARDED	GlobalFlag flag	4000	16384	
GMEM_FIXED	Global memory management	0	0	
GMEM_LOCKCOUNT	GlobalFlag flag	FF	255	
GMEM_LOWER*	Global memory management	1000	4096	GMEM_NOT_BANKED
GMEM_MODIFY	Global memory management	80	128	
GMEM_MOVEABLE	Global memory management	2	2	
GMEM_NOCOMPACT	Global memory management	10	16	
GMEM_NODISCARD	Global memory management	20	32	
GMEM_NOTBANKED*	Global memory management	1000	4096	
GMEM_NOTIFY*	Global memory management	4000	16384	
GMEM_SHARE*	Global memory management	2000	8196	
GMEM_SWAPPED‡	GlobalFlag flag	8000	32768	
GMEM_ZEROINIT	Global memory management	40	64	
GPTR*	Global memory management	2	2	GMEM_FIXED | GMEM_ZEROINIT
GRAY_BRUSH	Stock logical object	2	2	
GWL_EXSTYLE†	Window field offset		-20	
GWL_STYLE	Window field offset		-16	
GWL_WNDPROC	Window field offset		-4	
GWW_HINSTANCE	Window field offset		-6	
GWW_HWNDPARENT	Window field offset		-8	
GWW_HWNDTEXT‡	Window field offset		-10	
GWW_ID	Window field offset		-12	
GW_CHILD*	GetWindow constant	5	5	
GW_HWNDFIRST*	GetWindow constant	0	0	
GW_HWNDLAST*	GetWindow constant	1	1	
GW_HWNDNEXT*	GetWindow constant	2	2	
GW_HWNDPREV*	GetWindow constant	3	3	
GW_OWNER*	GetWindow constant	4	4	
HCBT_MINMAX*	Hook code	1	1	
HCBT_MOVESIZE*	Hook code	0	0	
HCBT_QS	Hook code	2	2	
HC_ACTION*	Hook code	0	0	
HC_GETNEXT*	Hook code	1	1	
HC_LPFNNEXT*	Hook code		-1	
HC_LPLPFNNEXT*	Hook code		-2	
HC_NOREM*	Hook code	3	3	
HC_NOREMOVE†	Hook code	3	3	
HC_SKIP*	Hook code	2	2	
HC_SYSMODALOFF†	Hook code	5	5	
HC_SYSMODALON†	Hook code	4	4	
HELP_CONTENT†	WinHelp command	1	1	
HELP_HELPONHELP†	WinHelp command	4	4	

(Continued)

6.041. INCLUDE FILE CONSTANTS DEFINITIONS BY NAME (continued)

Defined Name	Used As	Hex Value	Decimal Value	Comments
HELP_INDEX†	WinHelp command	3	3	
HELP_KEY†	WinHelp command	101	257	
HELP_MULTIKEY†	WinHelp command	201	513	
HELP_QUIT†	WinHelp command	2	2	
HELP_SETINDEX†	WinHelp command	5	5	
HIDE_WINDOW	ShowWindow command	0	0	
HOLLOW_BRUSH	Stock logical object	5	5	Defined as NULL_BRUSH
HORZRES	GetDeviceCaps device parameter	8	8	
HORZSIZE	GetDeviceCaps device parameter	4	4	
HS_BDIAGONAL	Hatch style	3	3	
HS_CROSS	Hatch style	4	4	
HS_DIAGCROSS	Hatch style	5	5	
HS_FDIAGONAL	Hatch style	2	2	
HS_HORIZONTAL	Hatch style	0	0	
HS_VERTICAL	Hatch style	1	1	
HTBOTTOM*	WinWhere area code	F	15	
HTBOTTOMLEFT*	WinWhere area code	10	16	
HTBOTTOMRIGHT*	WinWhere area code	11	17	
HTCAPTION	WinWhere area code	2	2	
HTCLIENT	WinWhere area code	1	1	
HTERROR	WinWhere area code		-2	
HTGROWBOX	WinWhere area code	4	4	
HTHSCROLL	WinWhere area code	6	6	
HTLEFT*	WinWhere area code	A	10	
HTMENU	WinWhere area code	5	5	
HTNOWHERE	WinWhere area code	0	0	
HTREDUCE*	WinWhere area code	8	8	
HTRIGHT*	WinWhere area code	B	11	
HTSIZE*	WinWhere area code	4	4	HTGROWBOX
HTSIZEFIRST*	WinWhere area code	A	10	HTLEFT
HTSIZELAST*	WinWhere area code	11	17	HTBOTTOMRIGHT
HTSYSMENU	WinWhere area code	3	3	
HTTOP*	WinWhere area code	C	12	
HTTOPLEFT*	WinWhere area code	D	13	
HTTOPRIGHT*	WinWhere area code	E	14	
HTTRANSPARENT	WinWhere area code		-1	
HTVSCROLL	WinWhere area code	7	7	
HTZOOM*	WinWhere area code	9	9	
IDABORT	Dialog/message box command ID	3	3	
IDCANCEL	Dialog/message box command ID	2	2	
IDC_ARROW	Standard cursor ID	7F00	32512	MAKEINTRESOURCE(32512)
IDC_CROSS	Standard cursor ID	7F03	32515	MAKEINTRESOURCE(32515)
IDC_IBEAM	Standard cursor ID	7F01	32513	MAKEINTRESOURCE(32513)
IDC_ICON	Standard cursor ID	7F81	32641	MAKEINTRESOURCE(32641)
IDC_SIZE	Standard cursor ID	7F80	32640	MAKEINTRESOURCE(32640)
IDC_SIZENESW	Standard cursor ID	7F83	32643	MAKEINTRESOURCE(32643)
IDC_SIZENS	Standard cursor ID	7F85	32645	MAKEINTRESOURCE(32645)
IDC_SIZENWSE	Standard cursor ID	7F82	32642	MAKEINTRESOURCE(32642)
IDC_SIZEWE	Standard cursor ID	7F84	32644	MAKEINTRESOURCE(32644)
IDC_UPARROW	Standard cursor ID	7F04	32516	MAKEINTRESOURCE(32516)
IDC_WAIT	Standard cursor ID	7F02	32514	MAKEINTRESOURCE(32514)
IDIGNORE	Dialog/message box command ID	5	5	
IDI_APPLICATION	Standard icon ID	7F00	32512	MAKEINTRESOURCE(32512)
IDI_ASTERISK	Standard icon ID	7F04	32516	MAKEINTRESOURCE(32516)
IDI_EXCLAMATION	Standard icon ID	7F03	32515	MAKEINTRESOURCE(32515)
IDI_HAND	Standard icon ID	7F01	32513	MAKEINTRESOURCE(32513)
IDI_QUESTION	Standard icon ID	7F02	32514	MAKEINTRESOURCE(32514)
IDNO	Dialog/message box command ID	7	7	
IDOK	Dialog/message box command ID	1	1	
IDRETRY	Dialog/message box command ID	4	4	
IDYES	Dialog/message box command ID	6	6	
IE_BADID	Comm init error		-1	
IE_BAUDRATE	Comm init error		-12	
IE_BYTESIZE	Comm init error		-11	
IE_DEFAULT	Comm init error		-5	
IE_HARDWARE	Comm init error		-10	
IE_MEMORY	Comm init error		-4	
IE_NOPEN	Comm init error		-3	
IE_OPEN	Comm init error		-2	
IGNORE	Dcb field definition	0	0	
INFINITE	Dcb field definition	FFFF	-1	
KNJ_ACCEPT	Conversion function	24	36	
KNJ_CHANGE_UDIC	Conversion function	33	51	
KNJ_CODECONVERT	Conversion function	20	32	
KNJ_CONVERT	Conversion function	21	33	

(Continued)

6.041. INCLUDE FILE CONSTANTS DEFINITIONS BY NAME (continued)

Defined Name	*Used As*	*Hex Value*	*Decimal Value*	*Comments*
KNJ_CVT_DEFAULT	Conversion function	7	7	
KNJ_CVT_HIRAGANA	Conversion function	4	4	
KNJ_CVT_JIS1‡	Conversion function	5	5	
KNJ_CVT_JIS2‡	Conversion function	6	6	
KNJ_CVT_KATAKANA	Conversion function	3	3	
KNJ_CVT_NEXT	Conversion function	1	1	
KNJ_CVT_PREV	Conversion function	2	2	
KNJ_CVT_SJIS2	Conversion function	6	6	
KNJ_CVT_TYPED	Conversion function	8	8	
KNJ_END	Conversion function	2	2	
KNJ_GETMODE	Conversion function	11	17	
KNJ_JIS1 to DEFAULT	Conversion function	10	16	
KNJ_JIS1 to JIS1 KATAKANA	Conversion function	14	20	
KNJ_JIS1 to JIS2	Conversion function	13	19	
KNJ_JIS1 to JIS2 HIRAGANA	Conversion function	15	21	
KNJ_JIS1 to JIS2 KATAKANA	Conversion function	16	22	
KNJ_JIS1 to JIS2 OEM	Conversion function	1F	31	
KNJ_JIS2 to JIS2	Conversion function	23	35	
KNJ_LEARN	Conversion function	30	48	
KNJ_LEARN_MODE	Conversion function	10	16	
KNJ_MD_ALPHA	Conversion function	1	1	
KNJ_MD_HALF	Conversion function	4	4	
KNJ_MD_HIRAGANA	Conversion function	2	2	
KNJ_MD_JIS	Conversion function	8	8	
KNJ_MD_SPECIAL	Conversion function	10	16	
KNJ_NEXT	Conversion function	22	34	
KNJ_PREVIOUS	Conversion function	23	35	
KNJ_QUERY	Conversion function	3	3	
KNJ_REGISTER	Conversion function	31	49	
KNJ_REMOVE	Conversion function	32	50	
KNJ_SETMODE	Conversion function	12	18	
KNJ_SJIS2 to JIS2	Conversion function	32	50	
KNJ_START	Conversion function	1	1	
LBN_DBLCLK	Listbox notification code	2	2	
LBN_ERRSPACE	Listbox notification code		-2	
LBN_KILLFOCUS†	Listbox notification code	5	5	
LBN_SELCANCEL†	Listbox notification code	3	3	
LBN_SELCHANGE	Listbox notification code	1	1	
LBN_SETFOCUS†	Listbox notification code	4	4	
LBS_EXTENDEDSEL†	Listbox style	800	2048	
LBS_HASSTRINGS†	Listbox style	40	64	
LBS_MULTICOLUMN†	Listbox style	200	512	
LBS_MULTIPLESEL	Listbox style	8	8	
LBS_NOINTEGRALHEIGHT†	Listbox style	100	256	
LBS_NOREDRAW	Listbox style	4	4	
LBS_NOTIFY	Listbox style	1	1	
LBS_OWNERDRAWFIXED†	Listbox style	10	16	
LBS_OWNERDRAWVARIABLE†	Listbox style	20	32	
LBS_SORT	Listbox style	2	2	
LBS_STANDARD*	Listbox style	F	15	LBS_NOTIFY | LBS_SORT**
LBS_USETABSTOPS†	Listbox style	80	128	
LBS_WANTKEYBOARDINPUT†	Listbox style	400	1024	
LB_ADDSTRING*	Listbox message	401	1025	WM_USER+1
LB_CTLCODE	Listbox control	0	0	
LB_DELETESTRING*	Listbox message	403	1027	WM_USER+3
LB_DIR*	Listbox message	40E	1038	WM_USER+14
LB_ERR	Listbox control		-1	
LB_ERRSPACE	Listbox control		-2	
LB_FINDSTRING†	Listbox notification code	410	1040	WM_USER+16
LB_GETCOUNT*	Listbox message	40C	1036	WM_USER+12
LB_GETCURSEL†	Listbox message	409	1033	WM_USER+9
LB_GETHORIZONTALEXTENT†	Listbox notification code	414	1044	WM_USER+20
LB_GETITEMDATA†	Listbox notification code	41A	1050	WM_USER+26
LB_GETITEMRECT†	Listbox notification code	419	1049	WM_USER+25
LB_GETSEL†	Listbox message	408	1032	WM_USER+8
LB_GETSELCOUNT†	Listbox notification code	411	1041	WM_USER+17
LB_GETSELITEMS†	Listbox notification code	412	1042	WM_USER+18
LB_GETTEXT†	Listbox message	40A	1034	WM_USER+10
LB_GETTEXTLEN*	Listbox message	40B	1035	WM_USER+11
LB_GETTOPINDEX†	Listbox message	40F	1039	WM_USER+15
LB_INSERTSTRING*	Listbox message	402	1026	WM_USER+2
LB_MSGMAX†	Listbox notification code	421	1057	WM_USER+33
LB_OKAY	Listbox control	0	0	
LB_RESETCONTENT*	Listbox message	405	1029	WM_USER+5
LB_SELECTSTRING*	Listbox message	40D	1037	WM_USER+13

(Continued)

6.041. INCLUDE FILE CONSTANTS DEFINITIONS BY NAME (continued)

Defined Name	Used As	Hex Value	Decimal Value	Comments
LB_SELITEMRANGE†	Listbox notification code	41C	1052	WM_USER+28
LB_SETCOLUMNWIDTH†	Listbox notification code	416	1046	WM_USER+22
LB_SETCURSEL*	Listbox message	407	1031	WM_USER+7
LB_SETHORIZONTALEXTENT†	Listbox notification code	415	1045	WM_USER+21
LB_SETITEMDATA†	Listbox notification code	41B	1051	WM_USER+27
LB_SETSEL*	Listbox message	406	1030	WM_USER+6
LB_SETTABSTOPS†	Listbox notification code	413	1043	WM_USER+19
LB_SETTOPINDEX†	Listbox notification code	418	1048	WM_USER+24
LC_INTERIORS	Device capability mask	80	128	
LC_MARKER	Device capability mask	4	4	
LC_NONE	Device capability mask	0	0	
LC_POLYLINE	Device capability mask	2	2	
LC_POLYMARKER	Device capability mask	8	8	
LC_STYLED	Device capability mask	20	32	
LC_WIDE	Device capability mask	10	16	
LC_WIDESTYLED	Device capability mask	40	64	
LF_FACESIZE	Logical font constant	20	32	
LHND*	Global memory management	42	66	LMEM_MOVEABLE††
LINECAPS	GetDeviceCaps device parameter	1E	30	
LMEM_DISCARDABLE	Local memory management	F00	3840	
LMEM_DISCARDED*	Local memory management	4000	16384	
LMEM_FIXED	Local memory management	0	0	
LMEM_LOCKCOUNT	Local memory management	FF	255	
LMEM_MODIFY	Local memory management	80	128	
LMEM_MOVEABLE	Local memory management	2	2	
LMEM_NOCOMPACT	Local memory management	10	16	
LMEM_NODISCARD	Local memory management	20	32	
LMEM_ZEROINIT	Local memory management	40	64	
LNOTIFY_DISCARD	Local memory management	2	2	
LNOTIFY_MOVE	Local memory management	1	1	
LNOTIFY_OUTOFMEM	Local memory management	0	0	
LOGPIXELSX	GetDeviceCaps device parameter	58	88	
LOGPIXELSY	GetDeviceCaps device parameter	5A	90	
LPTR*	Global memory management	2	2	LMEM_FIXED††
LPTx*	Device description	80	128	
LTGRAY_BRUSH	Stock logical object	1	1	
MARKPARITY	Dcb field definition	3	3	
MA_ACTIVATE*	Mouse activate return code	1	1	
MA_ACTIVATEANDEAT*	Mouse activate return code	2	2	
MA_NOACTIVATE*	Mouse activate return code	3	3	
MB_ABORTRETRYIGNORE	MessageBox type flag	2	2	
MB_APPLMODAL	MessageBox type flag	0	0	
MB_DEFBUTTON1	MessageBox type flag	0	0	
MB_DEFBUTTON2	MessageBox type flag	100	256	
MB_DEFBUTTON3	MessageBox type flag	200	512	
MB_DEFMASK	MessageBox type flag	F00	3840	
MB_ICONASTERISK	MessageBox type flag	40	64	
MB_ICONEXCLAMATION	MessageBox type flag	30	48	
MB_ICONHAND	MessageBox type flag	10	16	
MB_ICONINFORMATION†	MessageBox type flag	40	64	MB_ICONASTERISK
MB_ICONMASK	MessageBox type flag	F0	240	
MB_ICONQUESTION	MessageBox type flag	20	32	
MB_ICONSTOP†	MessageBox type flag	10	16	MB_ICONHAND
MB_MISCMASK	MessageBox type flag	C000	49152	
MB_MODEMASK	MessageBox type flag	3000	12288	
MB_NOFOCUS	MessageBox type flag	8000	32768	
MB_OK	MessageBox type flag	0	0	
MB_OKCANCEL	MessageBox type flag	1	1	
MB_RETRYCANCEL	MessageBox type flag	5	5	
MB_SYSTEMMODAL	MessageBox type flag	1000	4096	
MB_TASKMODAL†	MessageBox type flag	2000	8192	
MB_TYPEMASK	MessageBox type flag	F	15	
MB_YESNO	MessageBox type flag	4	4	
MB_YESNOCANCEL	MessageBox type flag	3	3	
MERGECOPY	Ternary raster op	00C0 00CA	12583114	Dest = (source AND pattern)
MERGEPAINT	Ternary raster op	00BB 0226	12255782	Dest = (not source) OR dest
META_ANIMATEPALETTE†	MetaFile function	436	1078	
META_ARC*	MetaFile function	817	2071	
META_BITBLT*	MetaFile function	922	2338	
META_CHORD†	MetaFile function	830	2096	
META_CREATEBITMAP*	MetaFile function	6FE	1790	
META_CREATEBITMAPINDIRECT*	MetaFile function	2FD	765	
META_CREATEBRUSH*	MetaFile function	F8	248	
META_CREATEBRUSHINDIRECT*	MetaFile function	2FC	764	
META_CREATEFONTINDIRECT*	MetaFile function	2FB	763	

(Continued)

6.041. INCLUDE FILE CONSTANTS DEFINITIONS BY NAME (continued)

Defined Name	*Used As*	*Hex Value*	*Decimal Value*	*Comments*
META_CREATEPALETTE†	MetaFile function	F7	247	
META_CREATEPATTERNBRUSH*	MetaFile function	1F9	505	
META_CREATEPENDIRECT*	MetaFile function	2FA	762	
META_CREATEREGION*	MetaFile function	6FF	1791	
META_DELETEOBJECT†	MetaFile function	1F0	496	
META_DIBBITBLT†	MetaFile function	940	2368	
META_DIBCREATEPATTERNBRUSH†	MetaFile function	142	322	
META_DIBSTRETCHBLT†	MetaFile function	B41	2881	
META_DRAWTEXT*	MetaFile function	62F	1583	
META_ELLIPSE*	MetaFile function	418	1048	
META_ESCAPE*	MetaFile function	626	1574	
META_EXCLUDECLIPRECT*	MetaFile function	415	1045	
META_EXTTEXTOUT†	MetaFile function	A32	2610	
META_FILLREGION*	MetaFile function	228	552	
META_FLOODFILL*	MetaFile function	419	1049	
META_FRAMEREGION*	MetaFile function	429	1065	
META_INTERSECTCLIPRECT*	MetaFile function	416	1046	
META_INVERTREGION*	MetaFile function	12A	298	
META_LINETO*	MetaFile function	213	531	
META_MOVETO*	MetaFile function	214	532	
META_OFFSETCLIPRGN*	MetaFile function	220	544	
META_OFFSETVIEWPORTORG*	MetaFile function	211	529	
META_OFFSETWINDOWORG*	MetaFile function	20F	527	
META_PAINTREGION*	MetaFile function	12B	299	
META_PATBLT*	MetaFile function	61D	1565	
META_PIE*	MetaFile function	81A	2074	
META_POLYGON*	MetaFile function	324	804	
META_POLYLINE*	MetaFile function	325	805	
META_POLYPOLYGON†	MetaFile function	538	1336	
META_REALIZEPALETTE†	MetaFile function	35	53	
META_RECTANGLE*	MetaFile function	41B	1051	
META_RESIZEPALETTE†	MetaFile function	139	313	
META_RESTOREDC*	MetaFile function	127	295	
META_ROUNDRECT*	MetaFile function	61C	1564	
META_SAVEDC*	MetaFile function	1E	30	
META_SCALEVIEWPORTEXT*	MetaFile function	412	1042	
META_SCALEWINDOWEXT*	MetaFile function	400	1024	
META_SELECTCLIPREGION*	MetaFile function	12C	300	
META_SELECTOBJECT*	MetaFile function	12D	301	
META_SELECTPALETTE†	MetaFile function	234	564	
META_SETBKCOLOR*	MetaFile function	201	513	
META_SETBKMODE*	MetaFile function	102	258	
META_SETDIBTODEV†	MetaFile function	D33	3379	
META_SETMAPMODE*	MetaFile function	103	259	
META_SETMAPPERFLAGS†	MetaFile function	231	561	
META_SETPALENTRIES†	MetaFile function	37	55	
META_SETPIXEL*	MetaFile function	41F	1055	
META_SETPOLYFILLMODE*	MetaFile function	106	262	
META_SETRELABS*	MetaFile function	105	261	
META_SETROP2*	MetaFile function	104	260	
META_SETSTRECTCHBLTMODE*	MetaFile function	107	263	
META_SETTEXTALIGN*	MetaFile function	12E	302	
META_SETTEXTCHAREXTRA*	MetaFile function	108	264	
META_SETTEXTCOLOR*	MetaFile function	209	521	
META_SETTEXTJUSTIFICATION*	MetaFile function	20A	522	
META_SETVIEWPORTEXT*	MetaFile function	20E	526	
META_SETVIEWPORTORG*	MetaFile function	20D	525	
META_SETWINDOWEXT*	MetaFile function	20C	524	
META_SETWINDOWORG*	MetaFile function	20B	523	
META_STRETCHBLT*	MetaFile function	B23	2851	
META_STRETCHDIB†	MetaFile function	F43	3907	
META_TEXTOUT*	MetaFile function	521	1313	
MFCOMMENT*	GDI escape code	F	15	
MF_APPEND	MenuItem menu flag	100	256	
MF_BITMAP	MenuItem menu flag	4	4	
MF_BYCOMMAND	MenuItem menu flag	0	0	
MF_BYPOSITION	MenuItem menu flag	400	1024	
MF_CHANGE	MenuItem menu flag	80	128	
MF_CHECKED	MenuItem menu flag	8	8	
MF_DELETE	MenuItem menu flag	200	512	
MF_DISABLED	MenuItem menu flag	2	2	
MF_ENABLED	MenuItem menu flag	0	0	
MF_END†	MenuItem menu flag	80	128	
MF_GRAYED	MenuItem menu flag	1	1	
MF_HELP*	MenuItem menu flag	4000	16384	

(Continued)

6.041. INCLUDE FILE CONSTANTS DEFINITIONS BY NAME (continued)

Defined Name	Used As	Hex Value	Decimal Value	Comments
MF_HILITE	MenuItem menu flag	80	128	
MF_INSERT	MenuItem menu flag	0	0	
MF_MENUBARBREAK	MenuItem menu flag	20	32	
MF_MENUBREAK	MenuItem menu flag	40	64	
MF_MOUSESELECT*	MenuItem menu flag	8000	32768	
MF_OWNERDRAW†	MenuItem menu flag	100	256	
MF_POPUP	MenuItem menu flag	10	16	
MF_REMOVE*	MenuItem menu flag	1000	4096	
MF_SEPARATOR	MenuItem menu flag	800	2048	
MF_STRING	MenuItem menu flag	0	0	
MF_SYSMENU*	MenuItem menu flag	2000	8192	
MF_UNCHECKED	MenuItem menu flag	0	0	
MF_UNHILITE	MenuItem menu flag	0	0	
MF_USECHECKBITMAPS†	MenuItem menu flag	200	512	
MK_CONTROL	Key state mask f/mouse msg.	8	8	
MK_LBUTTON	Key state mask f/mouse msg.	1	1	
MK_MBUTTON	Key state mask f/mouse msg.	10	16	
MK_RBUTTON	Key state mask f/mouse msg.	2	2	
MK_SHIFT	Key state mask f/mouse msg.	4	4	
MM_ANISOTROPIC	GDI map mode	8	8	
MM_HIENGLISH	GDI map mode	5	5	
MM_HIMETRIC	GDI map mode	3	3	
MM_ISOTROPIC	GDI map mode	7	7	
MM_LOENGLISH	GDI map mode	4	4	
MM_LOMETRIC	GDI map mode	2	2	
MM_TEXT	GDI map mode	1	1	
MM_TWIPS	GDI map mode	6	6	
MSGF_DIALOGBOX	Filter procedure code	0	0	
MSGF_MENU	Filter procedure code	2	2	
MSGF_MESSAGEBOX	Filter procedure code	1	1	
MSGF_MOVE*	Filter procedure code	3	3	
MSGF_NEXTWINDOW*	Filter procedure code	6	6	
MSGF_SCROLLBAR*	Filter procedure code	5	5	
MSGF_SIZE*	Filter procedure code	4	4	
NEWFRAME	GDI escape	1	1	
NEXTBAND	GDI escape	3	3	
NONZEROLHND*	Global memory management	2	2	LMEM_MOVEABLE
NONZEROLPTR*	Global memory management	0	0	LMEM_FIXED
NOPARITY	Dcb field definition	0	0	
NOTSRCCOPY	Ternary raster op	0033 0008	3342344	Dest = (not source)
NOTSRCERASE	Ternary raster op	0011 00A6	1114278	Dest = (not source) AND (not dest)
NULL	Standard definitions	0	0	
NULLREGION	Region flag	1	1	
NULL_BRUSH	Stock logical object	5	5	
NULL_PEN	Stock logical object	8	8	
NUMBRUSHES	GetDeviceCaps device parameter	10	16	
NUMCOLORS	GetDeviceCaps device parameter	18	24	
NUMFONTS	GetDeviceCaps device parameter	16	22	
NUMMARKERS	GetDeviceCaps device parameter	14	20	
NUMPENS	GetDeviceCaps device parameter	12	18	
NUMRESERVED†	GetDeviceCaps device parameter	6A	106	
OBJ_BRUSH	Object definition	2	2	
OBJ_PEN	Object definition	1	1	
OBM_BTNCORNERS	OEM definition	7FF6	32758	
OBM_BTSIZE	OEM definition	7FF9	32761	
OBM_CHECK	OEM definition	7FF8	32760	
OBM_CHECKBOXES	OEM definition	7FF7	32759	
OBM_CLOSE§	OEM definition	7FF2	32754	
OBM_COMBO†	OEM definition	7FE2	32738	
OBM_DNARROWD†	OEM definition	7FE6	32742	
OBM_DNARROW§	OEM definition	7FF0	32752	
OBM_LFARROWD†	OEM definition	7FE4	32740	
OBM_LFARROW§	OEM definition	7FEE	32750	
OBM_MNARROW†	OEM definition	7FE3	32739	
OBM_OLD_CLOSE	OEM definition	7FFF	32767	
OBM_OLD_DNARROW	OEM definition	7FFC	32764	
OBM_OLD_LFARROW	OEM definition	7FFA	32762	
OBM_OLD_REDUCE*	OEM definition	7FF5	32757	
OBM_OLD_RESTORE*	OEM definition	7FF3	32755	
OBM_OLD_RGARROW	OEM definition	7FFB	32763	
OBM_OLD_UPARROW	OEM definition	7FFD	32765	
OBM_OLD_ZOOM*	OEM definition	7FF4	32756	
OBM_REDUCED†	OEM definition	7FEA	32746	
OBM_REDUCE§	OEM definition	7FED	32749	
OBM_RESTORE	OEM definition	7FEB	32747	

(Continued)

6.041. INCLUDE FILE CONSTANTS DEFINITIONS BY NAME (continued)

Defined Name	Used As	Hex Value	Decimal Value	Comments
OBM_RESTOREDt	OEM definition	7FE8	32744	
OBM_RGARROWDt	OEM definition	7FE5	32741	
OBM_RGARROW§	OEM definition	7FEF	32751	
OBM_SIZE	OEM definition	7FFE	32766	
OBM_UPARROWDt	OEM definition	7FE7	32743	
OBM_UPARROW§	OEM definition	7FF1	32753	
OBM_ZOOMDt	OEM definition	7FE9	32745	
OBM_ZOOM§	OEM definition	7FEC	32748	
OCR_CROSS	OEM definition	7F03	32515	
OCR_IBEAM	OEM definition	7F01	32513	
OCR_ICOCURt	OEM definition	7F87	32647	
OCR_ICON	OEM definition	7F81	32641	
OCR_NORMAL	OEM definition	7F00	32512	
OCR_SIZE	OEM definition	7F80	32640	
OCR_SIZEALL*	OEM definition	7F86	32646	
OCR_SIZENESW*	OEM definition	7F83	32643	
OCR_SIZENS*	OEM definition	7F85	32645	
OCR_SIZENWSE*	OEM definition	7F82	32642	
OCR_SIZEWE*	OEM definition	7F84	32644	
OCR_UP	OEM definition	7F04	32516	
OCR_WAIT	OEM definition	7F02	32514	
ODA_DRAWENTIREt	Owner draw action	1	1	
ODA_FOCUSt	Owner draw action	4	4	
ODA_SELECTt	Owner draw action	2	2	
ODDPARITY	Dcb field definition	1	1	
ODS_CHECKEDt	Owner draw style	8	8	
ODS_DISABLEDt	Owner draw style	4	4	
ODS_FOCUSt	Owner draw style	10	16	
ODS_GRAYEDt	Owner draw style	2	2	
ODS_SELECTEDt	Owner draw style	1	1	
ODT_BUTTONt	Owner draw control	4	4	
ODT_COMBOBOXt	Owner draw control	3	3	
ODT_LISTBOXt	Owner draw control	2	2	
ODT_MENUt	Owner draw control	1	1	
OEM_CHARSET	Logical font constant	FF	255	
OEM_FIXED_FONT	Stock logical object	A	10	
OF_CANCEL	OpenFile flag	800	2048	
OF_CREATE	OpenFile flag	1000	4096	
OF_DELETE	OpenFile flag	200	512	
OF_EXIST	OpenFile flag	4000	16384	
OF_PARSE	OpenFile flag	100	256	
OF_PROMPT	OpenFile flag	2000	8192	
OF_READ	OpenFile flag	0	0	
OF_READWRITE	OpenFile flag	2	2	
OF_REOPEN	OpenFile flag	8000	32768	
OF_SHARE_COMPATt	OpenFile flag	0x0000	0	
OF_SHARE_DENY_NONEt	OpenFile flag	0x0040	64	
OF_SHARE_DENY_READt	OpenFile flag	0x0030	48	
OF_SHARE_DENY_WRITEt	OpenFile flag	0x0020	32	
OF_SHARE_EXCLUSIVEt	OpenFile flag	0x0010	16	
OF_VERIFY	OpenFile flag	400	1024	
OF_WRITE	OpenFile flag	1	1	
OIC_BANGt	OEM definition	7F03	32515	
OIC_HANDt	OEM definition	7F01	32513	
OIC_NOTEt	OEM definition	7F04	32516	
OIC_QUESt	OEM definition	7F02	32514	
OIC_SAMPLEt	OEM definition	7F00	32512	
ONE5STOPBITS	Dcb field definition	1	1	
ONESTOPBIT	Dcb field definition	0	0	
OPAQUE	GDI background mode	2	2	
ORD_LANDDRIVERt	Language driver	1	1	
OUT_CHARACTER_PRECIS	Logical font constant	2	2	
OUT_DEFAULT_PRECIS	Logical font constant	0	0	
OUT_STRING_PRECIS	Logical font constant	1	1	
OUT_STROKE_PRECIS	Logical font constant	3	3	
PASSTHROUGH*	GDI escape code	13	19	
PATCOPY	Ternary raster op	00F0 0021	15728673	Dest = pattern
PATINVERT	Ternary raster op	005A 0049	5898313	Dest = pattern XOR dest
PATPAINT	Ternary raster op	00FB 0A09	16452105	Dest = DPSnoo
PC_EXPLICITt	Palette entry flag	2	2	
PC_INTERIORS	Device capability mask	80	128	
PC_NOCOLLAPSEt	Palette entry flag	4	4	
PC_NONE	Device capability mask	0	0	
PC_POLYGON	Device capability mask	1	1	
PC_RECTANGLE	Device capability mask	2	2	

(Continued)

6.041. INCLUDE FILE CONSTANTS DEFINITIONS BY NAME (continued)

Defined Name	Used As	Hex Value	Decimal Value	Comments
PC_RESERVED†	Palette entry flag	1	1	
PC_SCANLINE	Device capability mask	8	8	
PC_STYLED	Device capability mask	20	32	
PC_TRAPEZOID	Device capability mask	4	4	
PC_WIDE	Device capability mask	10	16	
PC_WIDESTYLED	Device capability mask	40	64	
PC_WINDPOLYGON†	Device capability mask	4	4	
PDEVICESIZE	GetDeviceCaps device parameter	1A	26	
PLANES	GetDeviceCaps device parameter	E	14	
PM_NOREMOVE*	Peekmessage options	0	0	
PM_NOYIELD*	Peekmessage options	2	2	
PM_REMOVE*	Peekmessage options	1	1	
POLYGONALCAPS	GetDeviceCaps device parameter	20	32	
POSTSCRIPT_DATA†	GDI escape	25	37	
POSTSCRIPT_IGNORE†	GDI escape	26	38	
PROOF_QUALITY	Logical font constant	2	2	
PR_JOBSTATUS	Spooler wparm class	0	0	
PS_DASH	Pen style	1	1	
PS_DASHDOT	Pen style	3	3	
PS_DASHDOTDOT	Pen style	4	4	
PS_DOT	Pen style	2	2	
PS_INSIDEFRAME†	Pen style	6	6	
PS_NULL	Pen style	5	5	
PS_SOLID	Pen style	0	0	
QUERYESCSUPPORT	GDI escape	8	8	
R2_BLACK	Binary raster op	1	1	O
R2_COPYPEN	Binary raster op	13	13	P
R2_MASKNOTPEN	Binary raster op	3	3	DPna
R2_MASKPEN	Binary raster op	9	9	DPa
R2_MASKPENNOT	Binary raster op	5	5	PDna
R2_MERGENOTPEN	Binary raster op	12	12	DPno
R2_MERGEPEN	Binary raster op	15	15	DPo
R2_MERGEPENNOT	Binary raster op	14	14	PDno
R2_NOP	Binary raster op	11	11	D
R2_NOT	Binary raster op	6	6	Dn
R2_NOTCOPYPEN	Binary raster op	4	4	PN
R2_NOTMASKPEN	Binary raster op	8	8	DPan
R2_NOTMERGEPEN	Binary raster op	2	2	DPon
R2_NOTXORPEN	Binary raster op	10	10	DPxn
R2_WHITE	Binary raster op	16	16	1
R2_XORPEN	Binary raster op	7	7	DPx
RASTERCAPS	GetDeviceCaps device parameter	26	38	
RASTER_FONTTYPE	EnumFonts mask	1	1	
RC_BANDING	Device capability mask	2	2	
RC_BIGFONT†	Device capability mask	400	1024	
RC_BITBLT	Device capability mask	1	1	
RC_BITMAP64*	Device capability mask	8	8	
RC_DIBTODEV†	Device capability mask	200	512	
RC_DI_BITMAP	Device capability mask	80	128	
RC_FLOODFILL†	Device capability mask	1000	4096	
RC_GDIZO_OUTPUT†	Device capability mask	10	16	
RC_PALETTE†	Device capability mask	100	256	
RC_SCALING	Device capability mask	4	4	
RC_STRETCHBLT†	Device capability mask	800	2048	
RC_STRETCHDIB†	Device capability mask	2000	8192	
READ_WRITE†	lopen flag	2	2	
READ†	lopen flag	0	0	
RELATIVE	GDI coordinate mode	2	2	
RESETDEV	Comm escape function	7	7	
RESTORE_CTM†	GDI escape	1004	4100	
RGN_AND	Combinergn style	1	1	
RGN_COPY	Combinergn style	5	5	
RGN_DIFF	Combinergn style	4	4	
RGN_OR	Combinergn style	2	2	
RGN_XOR	Combinergn style	3	3	
RT_ACCELERATOR	Predefined resource type	9	9	MAKEINTRESOURCE (9)
RT_BITMAP	Predefined resource type	2	2	MAKEINTRESOURCE (2)
RT_CURSOR	Predefined resource type	1	1	MAKEINTRESOURCE (1)
RT_DIALOG	Predefined resource type	5	5	MAKEINTRESOURCE (5)
RT_FONT	Predefined resource type	8	8	MAKEINTRESOURCE (8)
RT_FONTDIR	Predefined resource type	7	7	MAKEINTRESOURCE (7)
RT_ICON	Predefined resource type	3	3	MAKEINTRESOURCE (3)
RT_MENU	Predefined resource type	4	4	MAKEINTRESOURCE (4)
RT_RCDATA*	Predefined resource type	A	10	MAKEINTRESOURCE(10)
RT_STRING	Predefined resource type	6	6	MAKEINTRESOURCE (6)

(Continued)

6.041. INCLUDE FILE CONSTANTS DEFINITIONS BY NAME (continued)

Defined Name	*Used As*	*Hex Value*	*Decimal Value*	*Comments*
SAVE_CTM†	GDI escape	1005	4101	
SBS_BOTTOMALIGN*	Scrollbar style	4	4	
SBS_HORZ*	Scrollbar style	0	0	
SBS_LEFTALIGN*	Scrollbar style	2	2	
SBS_RIGHTALIGN*	Scrollbar style	4	4	
SBS_SIZEBOX*	Scrollbar style	8	8	
SBS_SIZEBOXBOTTOMRIGHTALIGN*	Scrollbar style	4	4	
SBS_SIZEBOXTOPLEFTALIGN*	Scrollbar style	2	2	
SBS_TOPALIGN*	Scrollbar style	2	2	
SBS_VERT*	Scrollbar style	1	1	
SB_BOTH*	Scrollbar constant	3	3	
SB_BOTTOM	Scrollbar constant	7	7	
SB_CTL	Scrollbar constant	2	2	
SB_ENDSCROLL	Scrollbar constant	8	8	
SB_HORZ	Scrollbar constant	0	0	
SB_LINEDOWN	Scrollbar constant	1	1	
SB_LINEUP	Scrollbar constant	0	0	
SB_PAGEDOWN	Scrollbar constant	3	3	
SB_PAGEUP	Scrollbar constant	2	2	
SB_THUMBPOSITION	Scrollbar constant	4	4	
SB_THUMBTRACK	Scrollbar constant	5	5	
SB_TOP	Scrollbar constant	6	6	
SB_VERT	Scrollbar constant	1	1	
SC_ARRANGE*	System menu command	F110	61712	
SC_CLOSE	System menu command	F060	61536	
SC_HSCROLL	System menu command	F080	61568	
SC_ICON	System menu command	F020	61472	SC_MINIMIZE
SC_KEYMENU	System menu command	F100	61696	
SC_MAXIMIZE*	System menu command	F030	61488	
SC_MINIMIZE*	System menu command	F020	61472	
SC_MOUSEMENU	System menu command	F090	61584	
SC_MOVE	System menu command	F010	61456	
SC_NEXTWINDOW	System menu command	F040	61504	
SC_PREVWINDOW	System menu command	F050	61520	
SC_RESTORE*	System menu command	F120	61728	
SC_SIZE	System menu command	F000	61440	
SC_TASKLIST†	System menu command	F130	61744	
SC_VSCROLL	System menu command	F070	61552	
SC_ZOOM	System menu command	F030	61488	SC_MAXIMIZE
SELECTPAPERSOURCE*	GDI escape code	12	18	
SETABORTPROC	GDI escape	9	9	
SETALLJUSTVALUES†	GDI escape	303	771	
SETCHARSET†	GDI escape	304	772	
SETCOLORTABLE	GDI escape	4	4	
SETCOPYCOUNT*	GDI escape code	11	17	
SETDIBSCALING†	GDI escape	20	32	
SETDTR	Comm escape function	5	5	
SETENDCAP	MetaFile comment esc.	15	21	
SETKERNTRACK*	GDI escape code	302	770	
SETLINEJOIN*	GDI escape code	16	22	
SETMITERLIMIT*	GDI escape code	17	23	
SETRTS	Comm escape function	3	3	
SETXOFF	Comm escape function	1	1	
SETXON	Comm escape function	2	2	
SET_ARC_DIRECTION†	GDI escape	1006	4102	
SET_BACKGROUND_COLOR†	GDI escape	1007	4103	
SET_BOUNDS†	GDI escape	1013	4109	
SET_CLIP_BOX†	GDI escape	1012	4108	
SET_MIRROR_MODE†	GDI escape	1014	4110	
SET_POLY_MODE†	GDI escape	1008	4104	
SET_SCREEN_ANGLE†	GDI escape	1009	4105	
SET_SPREAD†	GDI escape	1010	4106	
SHIFTJIS_CHARSET*	Logical font constant	80	128	
SHOW_FULLSCREEN	ShowWindow command	3	3	
SHOW_ICONWINDOW	ShowWindow command	2	2	
SHOW_OPENNOACTIVATE	ShowWindow command	4	4	
SHOW_OPENWINDOW	ShowWindow command	1	1	
SIMPLEREGION	Region flag	2	2	
SIZEFULLSCREEN	Size message command	2	2	
SIZEICONIC	Size message command	1	1	
SIZENORMAL	Size message command	0	0	
SIZEPALETTE†	GetDeviceCaps device parameter	68	104	
SIZEZOOMHIDE	Size message command	4	4	
SIZEZOOMSHOW	Size message command	3	3	
SM_CMETRICS†	GetSystemMetrics code	24	36	

(Continued)

6.041. INCLUDE FILE CONSTANTS DEFINITIONS BY NAME (continued)

Defined Name	*Used As*	*Hex Value*	*Decimal Value*	*Comments*
SM_CXBORDER	GetSystemMetrics code	5	5	
SM_CXCURSOR	GetSystemMetrics code	D	13	
SM_CXDLGFRAME	GetSystemMetrics code	7	7	
SM_CXFRAME*	GetSystemMetrics code	20	32	
SM_CXFULLSCREEN	GetSystemMetrics code	10	16	
SM_CXHSCROLL	GetSystemMetrics code	15	21	
SM_CXHTHUMB	GetSystemMetrics code	A	10	
SM_CXICON	GetSystemMetrics code	B	11	
SM_CXMIN*	GetSystemMetrics code	1C	28	
SM_CXMINTRACK*	GetSystemMetrics code	22	34	
SM_CXSCREEN	GetSystemMetrics code	0	0	
SM_CXSIZE*	GetSystemMetrics code	1E	30	
SM_CXVSCROLL	GetSystemMetrics code	2	2	
SM_CYBORDER	GetSystemMetrics code	6	6	
SM_CYCAPTION	GetSystemMetrics code	4	4	
SM_CYCURSOR†	GetSystemMetrics code	E	14	
SM_CYDLGFRAME	GetSystemMetrics code	8	8	
SM_CYFRAME*	GetSystemMetrics code	21	33	
SM_CYFULLSCREEN	GetSystemMetrics code	11	17	
SM_CYHSCROLL	GetSystemMetrics code	3	3	
SM_CYICON	GetSystemMetrics code	C	12	
SM_CYICONSLOT‡	GetSystemMetrics code	1B	27	
SM_CYKANJIWINDOW	GetSystemMetrics code	12	18	
SM_CYMENU	GetSystemMetrics code	F	15	
SM_CYMIN*	GetSystemMetrics code	1D	29	
SM_CYMINTRACK*	GetSystemMetrics code	23	35	
SM_CYSCREEN	GetSystemMetrics code	1	1	
SM_CYSIZE*	GetSystemMetrics code	1F	31	
SM_CYVSCROLL	GetSystemMetrics code	14	20	
SM_CYVTHUMB	GetSystemMetrics code	9	9	
SM_DEBUG	GetSystemMetrics code	16	22	
SM_FULLSCREEN‡	GetSystemMetrics code	18	24	
SM_MOUSEPRESENT	GetSystemMetrics code	13	19	
SM_RESERVED1†	GetSystemMetrics code	18	24	
SM_RESERVED2†	GetSystemMetrics code	19	25	
SM_RESERVED3†	GetSystemMetrics code	1A	26	
SM_RESERVED4†	GetSystemMetrics code	1B	27	
SM_SWAPBUTTON	GetSystemMetrics code	17	23	
SPACEPARITY	Dcb field definition	4	4	
SP_APPABORT	Spooler error code		-2	
SP_ERROR	Spooler error code		-1	
SP_NOTREPORTED	Spooler error code	4000	16384	
SP_OUTOFDISK	Spooler error code		-4	
SP_OUTOFMEMORY	Spooler error code		-5	
SP_USERABORT	Spooler error code		-3	
SRCAND	Ternary raster op	0088 00C6	8913094	Dest = source AND dest
SRCCOPY	Ternary raster op	00CC 0020	13369376	Dest = source
SRCERASE	Ternary raster op	0044 0328	4457256	Dest = source AND (not dest)
SRCINVERT	Ternary raster op	0066 0046	6684742	Dest = source XOR dest
SRCPAINT	Ternary raster op	00EE 0086	15597702	Dest = source OR dest
SS_BLACKFRAME	Static control constant	7	7	
SS_BLACKRECT	Static control constant	4	4	
SS_CENTER	Static control constant	1	1	
SS_GRAYFRAME	Static control constant	8	8	
SS_GRAYRECT	Static control constant	5	5	
SS_ICON	Static control constant	3	3	
SS_LEFT	Static control constant	0	0	
SS_LEFTNOWORDWRAP†	Static control constant	C	12	
SS_NOPREFIX*	Static control constant	80	128	
SS_RIGHT	Static control constant	2	2	
SS_SIMPLE*	Static control constant	B	11	
SS_USERITEM	Static control constant	A	10	
SS_WHITEFRAME	Static control constant	9	9	
SS_WHITERECT	Static control constant	6	6	
STARTDOC	GDI escape	A	10	
STRETCHBLT*	GDI escape code	800	2048	
ST_BEGINSWP*		0	0	
ST_ENDSWP*		1	1	
SWP_DRAWFRAME*	SetWindow position flag	20	32	
SWP_HIDEWINDOW*	SetWindow position flag	80	128	
SWP_NOACTIVATE*	SetWindow position flag	10	16	
SWP_NOCOPYBITS*	SetWindow position flag	100	256	
SWP_NOMOVE*	SetWindow position flag	2	2	
SWP_NOREDRAW*	SetWindow position flag	8	8	
SWP_NOREPOSITION*	SetWindow position flag	200	512	

(Continued)

6.041. INCLUDE FILE CONSTANTS DEFINITIONS BY NAME (continued)

Defined Name	Used As	Hex Value	Decimal Value	Comments
SWP_NOSIZE*	SetWindow position flag	1	1	
SWP_NOZORDER*	SetWindow position flag	4	4	
SWP_SHOWWINDOW*	SetWindow position flag	40	64	
SW_HIDE*	ShowWindow message ID	0	0	
SW_MAXIMIZE*	ShowWindow message ID	3	3	
SW_MINIMIZE*	ShowWindow message ID	6	6	
SW_NORMAL*	ShowWindow message ID	1	1	
SW_OTHERUNZOOM	ShowWindow message ID	4	4	
SW_OTHERZOOM	ShowWindow message ID	2	2	
SW_PARENTCLOSING	ShowWindow message ID	1	1	
SW_PARENTOPENING	ShowWindow message ID	3	3	
SW_RESTORE†	ShowWindow message ID	9	9	
SW_SHOW*	ShowWindow message ID	5	5	
SW_SHOWMAXIMIZED*	ShowWindow message ID	3	3	
SW_SHOWMINIMIZED*	ShowWindow message ID	2	2	
SW_SHOWMINNOACTIVE*	ShowWindow message ID	7	7	
SW_SHOWNA*	ShowWindow message ID	8	8	
SW_SHOWNOACTIVE*	ShowWindow message ID	4	4	
SW_SHOWNORMAL*	ShowWindow message ID	1	1	
SYMBOL_CHARSET†	Logical font constant	2	2	
SYSPAL_NOSTATIC2†	System palette use constant	2	2	
SYSPAL_STATIC1†	System palette use constant	1	1	
SYSTEM_FIXED_FONT	Stock logical object	10	16	
SYSTEM_FONT	Stock logical object	D	13	
S_ALLTHRESHOLD*	WaitSoundState constant	2	2	
S_LEGATO	Accent mode constant	1	1	
S_NORMAL	Accent mode constant	0	0	
S_PERIOD1024	SetSoundNoise source	1	1	
S_PERIOD2048	SetSoundNoise source	2	2	
S_PERIOD512	SetSoundNoise source	0	0	
S_PERIODVOICE	SetSoundNoise source	3	3	
S_QUEUEEMPTY	WaitSoundState constant	0	0	
S_SERBDNT	SetSoundNoise source		-5	
S_SERDCC	SetSoundNoise source		-7	
S_SERDDR	SetSoundNoise source		-14	
S_SERDFQ	SetSoundNoise source		-13	
S_SERDLN	SetSoundNoise source		-6	
S_SERDMD	SetSoundNoise source		-10	
S_SERDPT	SetSoundNoise source		-12	
S_SERDSH	SetSoundNoise source		-11	
S_SERDSR	SetSoundNoise source		-15	
S_SERDST	SetSoundNoise source		-16	
S_SERDTP	SetSoundNoise source		-8	
S_SERDVL	SetSoundNoise source		-9	
S_SERDVNA	SetSoundNoise source		-1	
S_SERMACT	SetSoundNoise source		-3	
S_SEROFM	SetSoundNoise source		-2	
S_SERQFUL	SetSoundNoise source		-4	
S_STACCATO	Accent mode constant	2	2	
S_THRESHOLD	WaitSoundState constant	1	1	
S_WHITE1024	SetSoundNoise source	5	5	
S_WHITE2048	SetSoundNoise source	6	6	
S_WHITE512	SetSoundNoise source	4	4	
S_WHITEVOICE	SetSoundNoise source	7	7	
TA_BASELINE*	Text alignment option	18	24	
TA_BOTTOM*	Text alignment option	8	8	
TA_CENTER*	Text alignment option	6	6	
TA_LEFT*	Text alignment option	0	0	
TA_NOUPDATECP*	Text alignment option	0	0	
TA_RIGHT*	Text alignment option	2	2	
TA_TOP*	Text alignment option	0	0	
TA_UPDATECP*	Text alignment option	1	1	
TC_CP_STROKE	Device capability mask	4	4	
TC_CR_90	Device capability mask	8	8	
TC_CR_ANY	Device capability mask	10	16	
TC_EA_DOUBLE	Device capability mask	200	512	
TC_IA_ABLE	Device capability mask	400	1024	
TC_OP_CHARACTER	Device capability mask	1	1	
TC_OP_STROKE	Device capability mask	2	2	
TC_RA_ABLE	Device capability mask	2000	8192	
TC_RESERVED	Device capability mask	8000	32768	
TC_SA_CONTIN	Device capability mask	100	256	
TC_SA_DOUBLE	Device capability mask	40	64	
TC_SA_INTEGER	Device capability mask	80	128	
TC_SF_X_YINDEP	Device capability mask	20	32	

(Continued)

6.041. INCLUDE FILE CONSTANTS DEFINITIONS BY NAME (continued)

Defined Name	Used As	Hex Value	Decimal Value	Comments
TC_SO_ABLE	Device capability mask	1000	4096	
TC_UA_ABLE	Device capability mask	800	2048	
TC_VA_ABLE	Device capability mask	4000	16384	
TECHNOLOGY	GetDeviceCaps device parameter	2	2	
TEXTCAPS	GetDeviceCaps device parameter	22	34	
TF_FORCEDRIVE†	GetTempFileName flag	0x80	128	
TRANSFORM_CTM†	GDI escape	1011	4107	
TRANSPARENT	GDI background mode	1	1	
TRUE	Standard definitions	1	1	
TWOSTOPBITS	Dcb field definition	2	2	
VARIABLE_PITCH	Logical font constant	2	2	
VERTRES	GetDeviceCaps device parameter	A	10	
VERTSIZE	GetDeviceCaps device parameter	6	6	
VK_ACCEPT*	Virtual key	1E	30	
VK_ADD	Standard set virtual key	6B	107	
VK_BACK	Standard set virtual key	8	8	
VK_CANCEL	Standard set virtual key	3	3	
VK_CAPITAL	Standard set virtual key	14	20	
VK_CLEAR	Standard set virtual key	C	12	
VK_CONTROL	Standard set virtual key	11	17	
VK_CONVERT*	Virtual key	1C	28	
VK_COPY‡	Standard set virtual key	2C	44	Not used by keyboards
VK_DECIMAL	Standard set virtual key	6E	110	
VK_DELETE	Standard set virtual key	2E	46	
VK_DIVIDE	Standard set virtual key	6F	111	
VK_DOWN	Standard set virtual key	28	40	
VK_END	Standard set virtual key	23	35	
VK_ESCAPE	Standard set virtual key	1B	27	
VK_EXECUTE	Standard set virtual key	2B	43	
VK_F1	Standard set virtual key	70	112	
VK_F10	Standard set virtual key	79	121	
VK_F11	Standard set virtual key	7A	122	
VK_F12	Standard set virtual key	7B	123	
VK_F13	Standard set virtual key	7C	124	
VK_F14	Standard set virtual key	7D	125	
VK_F15	Standard set virtual key	7E	126	
VK_F16	Standard set virtual key	7F	127	
VK_F2	Standard set virtual key	71	113	
VK_F3	Standard set virtual key	72	114	
VK_F4	Standard set virtual key	73	115	
VK_F5	Standard set virtual key	74	116	
VK_F6	Standard set virtual key	75	117	
VK_F7	Standard set virtual key	76	118	
VK_F8	Standard set virtual key	77	119	
VK_F9	Standard set virtual key	78	120	
VK_HELP	Standard set virtual key	2F	47	
VK_HIRAGANA*	Virtual key	18	24	
VK_HOME	Standard set virtual key	24	36	
VK_INSERT	Standard set virtual key	2D	45	
VK_KANA*	Virtual key	15	21	
VK_KANJI*	Virtual key	19	25	
VK_LBUTTON	Standard set virtual key	1	1	
VK_LEFT	Standard set virtual key	25	37	
VK_MBUTTON	Standard set virtual key	4	4	
VK_MENU	Standard set virtual key	12	18	
VK_MODECHANGE*	Virtual key	1F	31	
VK_MULTIPLY	Standard set virtual key	6A	106	
VK_NEXT	Standard set virtual key	22	34	
VK_NONCONVERT*	Virtual key	1D	29	
VK_NUMLOCK	Standard set virtual key	90	144	
VK_NUMPAD0	Standard set virtual key	60	96	
VK_NUMPAD1	Standard set virtual key	61	97	
VK_NUMPAD2	Standard set virtual key	62	98	
VK_NUMPAD3	Standard set virtual key	63	99	
VK_NUMPAD4	Standard set virtual key	64	100	
VK_NUMPAD5	Standard set virtual key	65	101	
VK_NUMPAD6	Standard set virtual key	66	102	
VK_NUMPAD7	Standard set virtual key	67	103	
VK_NUMPAD8	Standard set virtual key	68	104	
VK_NUMPAD9	Standard set virtual key	69	105	
VK_PAUSE	Standard set virtual key	13	19	
VK_PRINT	Standard set virtual key	2A	42	
VK_PRIOR	Standard set virtual key	21	33	
VK_RBUTTON	Standard set virtual key	2	2	
VK_RETURN	Standard set virtual key	D	13	

(Continued)

6.041. INCLUDE FILE CONSTANTS DEFINITIONS BY NAME (continued)

Defined Name	*Used As*	*Hex Value*	*Decimal Value*	*Comments*
VK_RIGHT	Standard set virtual key	27	39	
VK_ROMAJI*	Virtual key	16	22	
VK_SELECT	Standard set virtual key	29	41	
VK_SEPARATOR	Standard set virtual key	6C	108	
VK_SHIFT	Standard set virtual key	10	16	
VK_SNAPSHOT†	Standard set virtual key	2C	44	
VK_SPACE	Standard set virtual key	20	32	
VK_SUBTRACT	Standard set virtual key	6D	109	
VK_TAB	Standard set virtual key	9	9	
VK_UP	Standard set virtual key	26	38	
VK_ZENKAKU*	Virtual key	17	23	
WC_DEFWINDOWPROC*	Window manager hook code	3	3	
WC_DRAWCAPTION*	Window manager hook code	7	7	
WC_INIT*	Window manager hook code	1	1	
WC_MINMAX*	Window manager hook code	4	4	
WC_MOVE*	Window manager hook code	5	5	
WC_SIZE*	Window manager hook code	6	6	
WC_SWP*	Window manager hook code	2	2	
WEP_FREE_DLL	System exit flags	0	0	
WEP_SYSTEM_EXIT	System exit flags	1	1	
WF_80x87†	GetWinFlags	400	1024	
WF_CPU086†	GetWinFlags	40	64	
WF_CPU186†	GetWinFlags	80	128	
WF_CPU286†	GetWinFlags	2	2	
WF_CPU386†	GetWinFlags	4	4	
WF_CPU486†	GetWinFlags	8	8	
WF_ENHANCED†	GetWinFlags	20	32	
WF_LARGEFRAME†	GetWinFlags	100	256	
WF_PMODE†	GetWinFlags	1	1	
WF_SMALLFRAME†	GetWinFlags	200	512	
WF_STANDARD†	GetWinFlags	10	16	
WF_WIN286†	GetWinFlags	10	16	
WF_WIN386†	GetWinFlags	20	32	
WHITENESS	Ternary raster op	00FF 0062	16711778	Dest = WHITE
WHITEONBLACK	StretchBlt mode	2	2	
WHITE_BRUSH	Stock logical object	0	0	
WHITE_PEN	Stock logical object	6	6	
WH_CALLWNDPROC	SetWindowsHook code	4	4	
WH_CBT*	Window hook	5	5	
WH_GETMESSAGE	SetWindowsHook code	3	3	
WH_JOURNALPLAYBACK	SetWindowsHook code	1	1	
WH_JOURNALRECORD	SetWindowsHook code	0	0	
WH_KEYBOARD	SetWindowsHook code	2	2	
WH_MSGFILTER	SetWindowsHook code		-1	
WH_SYSMSGFILTER*	Window hook	6	6	
WH_WINDOWMGR*	Window hook	7	7	
WINDING	Polyfill mode	2	2	
WM_ACTIVATE	Window procedure message ID	6	6	
WM_ACTIVATEAPP	Window procedure message ID	1C	28	
WM_ASKCBFORMATNAME	Window procedure message ID	30C	780	
WM_CANCELMODE	Window procedure message ID	1F	31	
WM_CHANGECBCHAIN	Window procedure message ID	30D	781	
WM_CHAR	Window procedure message ID	102	258	
WM_CHARTOITEM†	Window procedure message ID	2F	47	
WM_CHILDACTIVATE*	Window procedure message ID	22	34	
WM_CLEAR	Window procedure message ID	303	771	
WM_CLOSE	Window procedure message ID	10	16	
WM_COMMAND	Window procedure message ID	111	273	
WM_COMPACTING†	Window procedure message ID	41	65	
WM_COMPAREITEM†	Window procedure message ID	39	57	
WM_CONVERTREQUEST	Window procedure message ID	10A	266	
WM_CONVERTRESULT	Window procedure message ID	10B	267	
WM_COPY	Window procedure message ID	301	769	
WM_CREATE	Window procedure message ID	1	1	
WM_CTLCOLOR	Window procedure message ID	19	25	
WM_CUT	Window procedure message ID	300	768	
WM_DEADCHAR	Window procedure message ID	103	259	
WM_DELETEITEM†	Window procedure message ID	2D	45	
WM_DESTROY	Window procedure message ID	2	2	
WM_DESTROYCLIPBOARD	Window procedure message ID	307	775	
WM_DEVMODECHANGE	Window procedure message ID	1B	27	
WM_DRAWCLIPBOARD	Window procedure message ID	308	776	
WM_DRAWITEM†	Window procedure message ID	2B	43	
WM_ENABLE	Window procedure message ID	0A	10	
WM_ENDSESSION	Window procedure message ID	16	22	

(Continued)

6.041. INCLUDE FILE CONSTANTS DEFINITIONS BY NAME (continued)

Defined Name	Used As	Hex Value	Decimal Value	Comments
WM_ENTERIDLE	Window procedure message ID	121	289	
WM_ERASEBKGND	Window procedure message ID	14	20	
WM_FONTCHANGE	Window procedure message ID	1D	29	
WM_GETDLGCODE	Window procedure message ID	87	135	
WM_GETFONT†	Window procedure message ID	31	49	
WM_GETMINMAXINFO*	Window procedure message ID	24	36	
WM_GETTEXT	Window procedure message ID	D	13	
WM_GETTEXTLENGTH	Window procedure message ID	E	14	
WM_HSCROLL	Window procedure message ID	114	276	
WM_HSCROLLCLIPBOARD	Window procedure message ID	30E	782	
WM_ICONERASEBKGND*	Window procedure message ID	27	39	
WM_INITDIALOG	Window procedure message ID	110	272	
WM_INITMENU	Window procedure message ID	116	278	
WM_INITMENUPOPUP	Window procedure message ID	117	279	
WM_KANJIFIRST‡	Window procedure message ID	280	640	
WM_KANJILAST‡	Window procedure message ID	29F	671	
WM_KEYDOWN	Window procedure message ID	100	256	
WM_KEYFIRST	Window procedure message ID	100	256	
WM_KEYLAST†	Window procedure message ID	108	264	
WM_KEYUP	Window procedure message ID	101	257	
WM_KILLFOCUS	Window procedure message ID	8	8	
WM_LBUTTONDBLCLK	Window procedure message ID	203	515	
WM_LBUTTONDOWN	Window procedure message ID	201	513	
WM_LBUTTONUP	Window procedure message ID	202	514	
WM_MBUTTONDBLCLK	Window procedure message ID	209	521	
WM_MBUTTONDOWN	Window procedure message ID	207	519	
WM_MBUTTONUP	Window procedure message ID	208	520	
WM_MDIACTIVATE†	Window procedure message ID	222	546	
WM_MDICASCADE†	Window procedure message ID	227	551	
WM_MDICREATE†	Window procedure message ID	220	544	
WM_MDIDESTROY†	Window procedure message ID	221	545	
WM_MDIGETACTIVE†	Window procedure message ID	229	553	
WM_MDIICONARRANGE†	Window procedure message ID	228	552	
WM_MDIMAXIMIZE†	Window procedure message ID	225	549	
WM_MDINEXT†	Window procedure message ID	224	548	
WM_MDIRESTORE†	Window procedure message ID	223	547	
WM_MDISETMENU†	Window procedure message ID	230	560	
WM_MDITILE†	Window procedure message ID	226	550	
WM_MEASUREITEM†	Window procedure message ID	2C	44	
WM_MENUCHAR*	Window procedure message ID	120	45	
WM_MENUSELECT*	Window procedure message ID	11F	46	
WM_MOUSEACTIVATE*	Window procedure message ID	21	33	
WM_MOUSEFIRST	Window procedure message ID	200	512	
WM_MOUSELAST	Window procedure message ID	209	521	
WM_MOUSEMOVE	Window procedure message ID	200	512	
WM_MOVE	Window procedure message ID	3	3	
WM_NCACTIVATE	Window procedure message ID	86	134	
WM_NCCALCSIZE	Window procedure message ID	83	131	
WM_NCCREATE	Window procedure message ID	81	129	
WM_NCDESTROY	Window procedure message ID	82	130	
WM_NCHITTEST	Window procedure message ID	84	132	
WM_NCLBUTTONDBLCLK	Window procedure message ID	A3	163	
WM_NCLBUTTONDOWN	Window procedure message ID	A1	161	
WM_NCLBUTTONUP	Window procedure message ID	A2	162	
WM_NCMBUTTONDBLCLK	Window procedure message ID	A9	169	
WM_NCMBUTTONDOWN	Window procedure message ID	A7	167	
WM_NCMBUTTONUP	Window procedure message ID	A8	168	
WM_NCMOUSEMOVE	Window procedure message ID	A0	160	
WM_NCPAINT	Window procedure message ID	85	133	
WM_NCRBUTTONDBLCLK	Window procedure message ID	A6	166	
WM_NCRBUTTONDOWN	Window procedure message ID	A4	164	
WM_NCRBUTTONUP	Window procedure message ID	A5	165	
WM_NEXTDLGCTL*	Window procedure message ID	28	40	
WM_NULL	Window procedure message ID	0	0	
WM_PAINT	Window procedure message ID	F	15	
WM_PAINTCLIPBOARD	Window procedure message ID	309	777	
WM_PAINTICON*	Window procedure message ID	26	38	
WM_PALETTECHANGED†	Window procedure message ID	311	785	
WM_PALETTEISCHANGING†	Window procedure message ID	310	784	
WM_PARENTNOTIFY†	Window procedure message ID	210	528	
WM_PASTE	Window procedure message ID	302	770	
WM_QUERYDRAGICON†	Window procedure message ID	37	55	
WM_QUERYENDSESSION	Window procedure message ID	11	17	
WM_QUERYNEWPALETTE†	Window procedure message ID	30F	783	
WM_QUERYOPEN	Window procedure message ID	13	19	

(Continued)

6.041. INCLUDE FILE CONSTANTS DEFINITIONS BY NAME (continued)

Defined Name	*Used As*	*Hex Value*	*Decimal Value*	*Comments*
WM_QUEUESYNC*	Window procedure message ID	23	35	
WM_QUIT	Window procedure message ID	12	18	
WM_RBUTTONDBLCKL	Window procedure message ID	206	518	
WM_RBUTTONDOWN	Window procedure message ID	204	516	
WM_RBUTTONUP	Window procedure message ID	205	517	
WM_RENDERALLFORMATS	Window procedure message ID	306	774	
WM_RENDERFORMAT	Window procedure message ID	305	773	
WM_SETCURSOR*	Window procedure message ID	20	32	
WM_SETFOCUS	Window procedure message ID	7	7	
WM_SETFONT†	Window procedure message ID	30	48	
WM_SETREDRAW	Window procedure message ID	B	11	
WM_SETTEXT	Window procedure message ID	C	12	
WM_SETVISIBLE‡	Window procedure message ID	9	9	
WM_SHOWWINDOW	Window procedure message ID	18	24	
WM_SIZE	Window procedure message ID	5	5	
WM_SIZECLIPBOARD	Window procedure message ID	30B	779	
WM_SIZEWAIT‡	Window procedure message ID	4	4	
WM_SPOOLERSTATUS	Window procedure message ID	2A	42	
WM_SYNCPAINT‡	Window procedure message ID	88	136	
WM_SYNCTASK‡	Window procedure message ID	89	137	
WM_SYSCHAR	Window procedure message ID	106	262	
WM_SYSCOLORCHANGE	Window procedure message ID	15	21	
WM_SYSCOMMAND	Window procedure message ID	112	274	
WM_SYSDEADCHAR	Window procedure message ID	107	263	
WM_SYSKEYDOWN	Window procedure message ID	104	260	
WM_SYSKEYUP	Window procedure message ID	105	261	
WM_SYSTEMERROR‡	Window procedure message ID	17	23	
WM_SYSTIMER‡	Window procedure message ID	118	280	
WM_TIMECHANGE	Window procedure message ID	1E	30	
WM_TIMER	Window procedure message ID	113	275	
WM_UNDO	Window procedure message ID	304	772	
WM_USER	Window procedure message ID	400	1024	First application window message
WM_VKEYTOITEM†	Window procedure message ID	2E	46	
WM_VSCROLL	Window procedure message ID	115	277	
WM_VSCROLLCLIPBOARD	Window procedure message ID	30A	778	
WM_WININICHANGE	Window procedure message ID	1A	26	
WM_YOMICHAR‡	Window procedure message ID	108	264	
WRITE†	lopen flag	1	1	
WS_BORDER	Window style	0080 0000	8388608	
WS_CAPTION	Window style	00C0 0000	12582912	
WS_CHILD	Window style	4000 0000	1073741824	
WS_CHILDWINDOW*	Window style	4000 0000	1073741824	WS_CHILD
WS_CLIPCHILDREN	Window style	0200 0000	33554432	
WS_CLIPSIBLINGS	Window style	0400 0000	67108864	
WS_DISABLED	Window style	0800 0000	134217728	
WS_DLGFRAME	Window style	0040 0000	4194304	
WS_EX_DLGMODALFRAME†	Window style	1	1	
WS_EX_NOPARENTNOTIFY†	Window style	4	4	
WS_GROUP	Window style	0002 0000	131072	
WS_HSCROLL	Window style	0010 0000	1048576	
WS_ICONIC	Window style	2000 0000	536870912	Defined as WS_MINIMIZE
WS_ICONICPOPUP‡	Window style	C000 0000	3221225472	
WS_MAXIMIZE*	Window style	0100 0000	16777216	
WS_MAXIMIZEBOX*	Window style	0001 0000	65536	
WS_MINIMIZE	Window style	2000 0000	536870912	
WS_MINIMIZEBOX*	Window style	0002 0000	131072	
WS_OVERLAPPED*	Window style	0	0	
WS_OVERLAPPEDWINDOW*	Window style	00CC 0000	13369344	WS_OVERLAPPED¥¥
WS_POPUP	Window style	8000 0000	-2147483648	
WS_POPUPWINDOW*	Window style	8088 0000	2156396544	WS_POPUP | WS_BORDER§§
WS_SIZEBOX	Window style	0004 0000	262144	WS_THICKFRAME
WS_SYSMENU	Window style	0008 0000	524288	
WS_TABSTOP	Window style	0001 0000	65536	
WS_THICKFRAME*	Window style	0004 0000	262144	
WS_TILED	Window style	0	0	WS_OVERLAPPED
WS_TILEDWINDOW*	Window style	00CC 0000	13369344	WS_OVERLAPPEDWINDOW
WS_VISIBLE	Window style	1000 0000	268435456	
WS_VSCROLL	Window style	0020 0000	2097152	

(Continued)

6.041. INCLUDE FILE CONSTANTS DEFINITIONS BY NAME (continued)

*Applies to all versions of Windows beginning with 2.0.
†Applies to all versions of Windows beginning with 3.0.
§Pre-3.0 versions of these calls have had OLD added to name (e.g., OBM_OLD_CLOSE).
‡Not in Windows 3.0
**And WS_VSCROLL | WS_BORDER
††And LMEM_ZEROINIT
§§And WS_SYSMENU
¥¥And WS_CAPTION | WS_SYSMENU | WS_THICKFRAME | WS_MINIMIZEBOX | WS_MAXIMIZEBOX

Source: WINDOWS.H file in development kit

See Also: 6.042. Include File Constants Definitions by Use

6.042. INCLUDE FILE CONSTANTS DEFINITIONS BY USE

Defined Name	*Used As*	*Hex Value*	*Decimal Value*	*Comments*
S_LEGATO	Accent mode constant	1	1	
S_NORMAL	Accent mode constant	0	0	
S_STACCATO	Accent mode constant	2	2	
BI_RBG†	biCompression constant	0	0	
BI_RLE4†	biCompression constant	2	2	
BI_RLE8†	biCompression constant	1	1	
R2_BLACK	Binary raster op	1	1	0
R2_COPYPEN	Binary raster op	13	13	P
R2_MASKNOTPEN	Binary raster op	3	3	DPna
R2_MASKPEN	Binary raster op	9	9	DPa
R2_MASKPENNOT	Binary raster op	5	5	PDna
R2_MERGENOTPEN	Binary raster op	12	12	DPno
R2_MERGEPEN	Binary raster op	15	15	DPo
R2_MERGEPENNOT	Binary raster op	14	14	PDno
R2_NOP	Binary raster op	11	11	D
R2_NOT	Binary raster op	6	6	Dn
R2_NOTCOPYPEN	Binary raster op	4	4	PN
R2_NOTMASKPEN	Binary raster op	8	8	DPan
R2_NOTMERGEPEN	Binary raster op	2	2	DPon
R2_NOTXORPEN	Binary raster op	10	10	DPxn
R2_WHITE	Binary raster op	16	16	1
R2_XORPEN	Binary raster op	7	7	DPx
BS_DIBPATTERN†	Brush style	5	5	
BS_HATCHED	Brush style	2	2	
BS_HOLLOW	Brush style			Defined as BS_NULL
BS_NULL	Brush style	1	1	
BS_PATTERN	Brush style	3	3	
BS_SOLID	Brush style	0	0	
BS_3STATE	Button control style	5	5	
BS_AUTO3STATE	Button control style	6	6	
BS_AUTOCHECKBOX	Button control style	3	3	
BS_CHECKBOX	Button control style	2	2	
BS_DEFPUSHBUTTON	Button control style	1	1	
BS_GROUPBOX	Button control style	7	7	
BS_INDEXED*	Button control style	4	4	
BS_PUSHBUTTON	Button control style	0	0	
BS_RADIOBUTTON	Button control style	4	4	
BS_USERBUTTON	Button control style	8	8	
BS_AUTORADIOBUTTON*	Button style	9	9	
BS_LEFTTEXT*	Button style	20	32	
BS_OWNERDRAW†	Button style	B	11	
BS_PUSHBOX*	Button style	A	10	
GCL_MENUNAME	Class field offset		-8	
GCL_WNDPROC	Class field offset		-24	
GCW_CBCLSEXTRA†	Class field offset		-20	
GCW_CBWNDEXTRA†	Class field offset		-18	
GCW_HBRBACKGROUND	Class field offset		-10	
GCW_HCURSOR	Class field offset		-12	
GCW_HICON	Class field offset		-14	
GCW_HMODULE	Class field offset		-16	
GCW_STYLE	Class field offset		-26	
CS_BYTEALIGNCLIENT*	Class style	1000	4096	
CS_BYTEALIGNWINDOW*	Class style	2000	8192	
CS_CLASSDC	Class style	40	64	
CS_DBLCLKS	Class style	8	8	

(Continued)

6.042. INCLUDE FILE CONSTANTS DEFINITIONS BY USE (continued)

Defined Name	Used As	Hex Value	Decimal Value	Comments
CS_GLOBALCLASS†	Class style	4000	16384	
CS_HREDRAW	Class style	2	2	
CS_KEYCVTWINDOW	Class style	4	4	
CS_MENUPOPUP‡	Class style	80	128	
CS_NOCLOSE*	Class style	200	512	
CS_NOKEYCVT	Class style	100	512	
CS_OEMCHARS‡	Class style	10	16	
CS_OWNDC	Class style	20	32	
CS_PARENTDC*	Class style	80	128	
CS_SAVEBITS*	Class style	800	2048	
CS_VREDRAW	Class style	1	1	
CF_BITMAP	Clipboard format	2	2	
CF_DIB†	Clipboard format	8	8	
CF_DIF	Clipboard format	5	5	
CF_DSPBITMAP	Clipboard format	82	130	
CF_DSPMETAFILEPICT	Clipboard format	83	131	
CF_DSPTEXT	Clipboard format	81	129	
CF_GDIOBJFIRST	Clipboard format	300	768	
CF_GDIOBJLAST	Clipboard format	3FF	1023	
CF_METAFILEPICT	Clipboard format	3	3	
CF_OEMTEXT*	Clipboard format	7	7	
CF_OWNERDISPLAY	Clipboard format	80	128	
CF_PALETTE†	Clipboard format	9	9	
CF_PRIVATEFIRST	Clipboard format	200	512	
CF_PRIVATELAST	Clipboard format	2FF	767	
CF_SYLK	Clipboard format	4	4	
CF_TEXT	Clipboard format	1	1	
CF_TIFF*	Clipboard format	6	6	
COLOR_ACTIVEBORDER*	Color type index	A	10	
COLOR_ACTIVECAPTION	Color type index	2	2	
COLOR_APPWORKSPACE*	Color type index	C	12	
COLOR_BACKGROUND	Color type index	1	1	
COLOR_BTNFACE†	Color type index	F	15	
COLOR_BTNSHADOW†	Color type index	10	16	
COLOR_BTNTEXT†	Color type index	12	18	
COLOR_CAPTIONTEXT	Color type index	9	9	
COLOR_ENDCOLORS†	Color type index			COLOR_BTNTEXT
COLOR_GRAYTEXT†	Color type index	11	17	
COLOR_HIGHLIGHTTEXT†	Color type index	E	14	
COLOR_HIGHLIGHT†	Color type index	D	13	
COLOR_INACTIVEBORDER*	Color type index	B	11	
COLOR_INACTIVECAPTION	Color type index	3	3	
COLOR_MENU	Color type index	4	4	
COLOR_MENUTEXT	Color type index	7	7	
COLOR_SCROLLBAR	Color type index	0	0	
COLOR_WINDOW	Color type index	5	5	
COLOR_WINDOWFRAME	Color type index	6	6	
COLOR_WINDOWTEXT	Color type index	8	8	
CTLCOLOR_BTN	Color type index	3	3	
CTLCOLOR_DLG	Color type index	4	4	
CTLCOLOR_EDIT	Color type index	1	1	
CTLCOLOR_LISTBOX	Color type index	2	2	
CTLCOLOR_MAX	Color type index	8	8	
CTLCOLOR_MSGBOX	Color type index	0	0	
CTLCOLOR_SCROLLBAR	Color type index	5	5	
CTLCOLOR_STATIC	Color type index	6	6	
RGN_AND	CombineRgn style	1	1	
RGN_COPY	CombineRgn style	5	5	
RGN_DIFF	CombineRgn style	4	4	
RGN_OR	CombineRgn style	2	2	
RGN_XOR	CombineRgn style	3	3	
CB_ADDSTRING†	Combobox message	403	1027	WM_USER+3
CB_DELETESTRING†	Combobox message	404	1028	WM_USER+4
CB_DIR†	Combobox message	405	1029	WM_USER+5
CB_FINDSTRING†	Combobox message	40C	1036	WM_USER+12
CB_GETCOUNT†	Combobox message	406	1030	WM_USER+6
CB_GETCURSEL†	Combobox message	407	1031	WM_USER+7
CB_GETDROPPEDCONTROLRECT†	Combobox message	412	1042	WM_USER+18
CB_GETEDITSEL†	Combobox message	400	1024	WM_USER+0
CB_GETIITEMDATA†	Combobox message	410	1040	WM_USER+16
CB_GETLBTEXTLEN†	Combobox message	409	1033	WM_USER+9
CB_GETLBTEXT†	Combobox message	408	1032	WM_USER+8
CB_INSERTSTRING†	Combobox message	40A	1034	WM_USER+10
CB_LIMITTEXT†	Combobox message	401	1025	WM_USER+1
CB_MSGMAX†	Combobox message	413	1043	WM_USER+19

(Continued)

6.042. INCLUDE FILE CONSTANTS DEFINITIONS BY USE (continued)

Defined Name	*Used As*	*Hex Value*	*Decimal Value*	*Comments*
CB_RESETCONTENT†	Combobox message	40B	1035	WM_USER+11
CB_SELECTSTRING†	Combobox message	40D	1037	WM_USER+13
CB_SETCURSEL†	Combobox message	40E	1038	WM_USER+14
CB_SETEDITSEL†	Combobox message	402	1026	WM_USER+2
CB_SETITEMDATA†	Combobox message	411	1041	WM_USER+17
CB_SHOWDROPDOWN†	Combobox message	40F	1039	WM_USER+15
CBN_DBLCLK†	Combobox notification code	2	2	
CBN_DROPDOWN†	Combobox notification code	7	7	
CBN_EDITCHANGE†	Combobox notification code	5	5	
CBN_EDITUPDATE†	Combobox notification code	6	6	
CBN_ERRSPACE†	Combobox notification code		-1	
CBN_KILLFOCUS†	Combobox notification code	4	4	
CBN_SELCHANGE†	Combobox notification code	1	1	
CBN_SETFOCUS†	Combobox notification code	3	3	
CBS_AUTOHSCROLL†	Combobox styles	40	64	
CBS_DROPDOWNLIST†	Combobox styles	3	3	
CBS_DROPDOWN†	Combobox styles	2	2	
CBS_HASSTRINGS†	Combobox styles	200	512	
CBS_NOINTEGRALHEIGHT†	Combobox styles	400	1024	
CBS_OEMCONVERT†	Combobox styles	80	128	
CBS_OWNERDRAWFIXED†	Combobox styles	10	16	
CBS_OWNERDRAWVARIABLE†	Combobox styles	20	32	
CBS_SIMPLE†	Combobox styles	1	1	
CBS_SORT†	Combobox styles	100	256	
CB_ERRSPACE†	Combobox values		-2	
CB_ERR†	Combobox values		-1	
CB_OKAY†	Combobox values	0	0	
CE_BREAK	Comm device driver error	10	16	
CE_CTSTO	Comm device driver error	20	32	
CE_DNS	Comm device driver error	800	2048	
CE_DSRTO	Comm device driver error	40	64	
CE_FRAME	Comm device driver error	8	8	
CE_IOE	Comm device driver error	400	1024	
CE_MODE	Comm device driver error	8000	32768	
CE_OOP	Comm device driver error	1000	4096	
CE_OVERRUN	Comm device driver error	2	2	
CE_PTO	Comm device driver error	200	512	
CE_RLSDTO	Comm device driver error	80	128	
CE_RXOVER	Comm device driver error	1	1	
CE_RXPARITY	Comm device driver error	4	4	
CE_TXFULL	Comm device driver error	100	256	
CLRDTR	Comm escape function	6	6	
CLRRTS	Comm escape function	4	4	
RESETDEV	Comm escape function	7	7	
SETDTR	Comm escape function	5	5	
SETRTS	Comm escape function	3	3	
SETXOFF	Comm escape function	1	1	
SETXON	Comm escape function	2	2	
EV_BREAK	Comm event definition	40	64	
EV_CTS	Comm event definition	8	8	
EV_DSR	Comm event definition	10	16	
EV_ERR	Comm event definition	80	128	
EV_PERR	Comm event definition	200	512	
EV_RING	Comm event definition	100	256	
EV_RLSD	Comm event definition	20	32	
EV_RXCHAR	Comm event definition	1	1	
EV_RXFLAG	Comm event definition	2	2	
EV_TXEMPTY	Comm event definition	4	4	
IE_BADID	Comm init error		-1	
IE_BAUDRATE	Comm init error		-12	
IE_BYTESIZE	Comm init error		-11	
IE_DEFAULT	Comm init error		-5	
IE_HARDWARE	Comm init error		-10	
IE_MEMORY	Comm init error		-4	
IE_NOPEN	Comm init error		-3	
IE_OPEN	Comm init error		-2	
BM_GETCHECK*	Control message	400	1024	WM_USER+0
BM_GETSTATE*	Control message	402	1026	WM_USER+2
BM_SETCHECK*	Control message	401	1025	WM_USER+1
BM_SETSTATE*	Control message	403	1027	WM_USER+3
BM_SETSTYLE*	Control message	404	1208	WM_USER+4
BN_DOUBLECLICKED*	Control message	5	5	
CP_GETBEEP‡	Control panel info	1	1	
CP_GETBORDER‡	Control panel info	5	5	
CP_GETMOUSE‡	Control panel info	3	3	

(Continued)

6.042. INCLUDE FILE CONSTANTS DEFINITIONS BY USE (continued)

Defined Name	*Used As*	*Hex Value*	*Decimal Value*	*Comments*
CP_KANJIMENU‡	Control panel info	8	8	
CP_SETBEEP‡	Control panel info	2	2	
CP_SETBORDER‡	Control panel info	6	6	
CP_SETMOUSE‡	Control panel info	4	4	
CP_TIMEOUTS‡	Control panel info	7	7	
KNJ_ACCEPT	Conversion function	24	36	
KNJ_CHANGE_UDIC	Conversion function	33	51	
KNJ_CODECONVERT	Conversion function	20	32	
KNJ_CONVERT	Conversion function	21	33	
KNJ_CVT_DEFAULT	Conversion function	7	7	
KNJ_CVT_HIRAGANA	Conversion function	4	4	
KNJ_CVT_JIS1‡	Conversion function	5	5	
KNJ_CVT_JIS2‡	Conversion function	6	6	
KNJ_CVT_KATAKANA	Conversion function	3	3	
KNJ_CVT_NEXT	Conversion function	1	1	
KNJ_CVT_PREV	Conversion function	2	2	
KNJ_CVT_SJIS2	Conversion function	6	6	
KNJ_CVT_TYPED	Conversion function	8	8	
KNJ_END	Conversion function	2	2	
KNJ_GETMODE	Conversion function	11	17	
KNJ_JIS1 to DEFAULT	Conversion function	10	16	
KNJ_JIS1 to JIS1 KATAKANA	Conversion function	14	20	
KNJ_JIS1 to JIS2	Conversion function	13	19	
KNJ_JIS1 to JIS2 HIRAGANA	Conversion function	15	21	
KNJ_JIS1 to JIS2 KATAKANA	Conversion function	16	22	
KNJ_JIS1 to JIS2 OEM	Conversion function	1F	31	
KNJ_JIS2 to JIS2	Conversion function	23	35	
KNJ_LEARN	Conversion function	30	48	
KNJ_LEARN_MODE	Conversion function	10	16	
KNJ_MD_ALPHA	Conversion function	1	1	
KNJ_MD_HALF	Conversion function	4	4	
KNJ_MD_HIRAGANA	Conversion function	2	2	
KNJ_MD_JIS	Conversion function	8	8	
KNJ_MD_SPECIAL	Conversion function	10	16	
KNJ_NEXT	Conversion function	22	34	
KNJ_PREVIOUS	Conversion function	23	35	
KNJ_QUERY	Conversion function	3	3	
KNJ_REGISTER	Conversion function	31	49	
KNJ_REMOVE	Conversion function	32	50	
KNJ_SETMODE	Conversion function	12	18	
KNJ_SJIS2 to JIS2	Conversion function	32	50	
KNJ_START	Conversion function	1	1	
EVENPARITY	Dcb field definition	2	2	
IGNORE	Dcb field definition	0	0	
INFINITE	Dcb field definition	FFFF	-1	
MARKPARITY	Dcb field definition	3	3	
NOPARITY	Dcb field definition	0	0	
ODDPARITY	Dcb field definition	1	1	
ONE5STOPBITS	Dcb field definition	1	1	
ONESTOPBIT	Dcb field definition	0	0	
SPACEPARITY	Dcb field definition	4	4	
TWOSTOPBITS	Dcb field definition	2	2	
CC_CHORD	Device capability mask	4	4	
CC_CIRCLES	Device capability mask	1	1	
CC_ELLIPSES	Device capability mask	8	8	
CC_INTERIORS	Device capability mask	80	128	
CC_NONE	Device capability mask	0	0	
CC_PIE	Device capability mask	2	2	
CC_STYLED	Device capability mask	20	32	
CC_WIDE	Device capability mask	10	16	
CC_WIDESTYLED	Device capability mask	40	64	
CP_NONE	Device capability mask	0	0	
CP_RECTANGLE	Device capability mask	1	1	
DT_CHARSTREAM	Device capability mask	4	4	
DT_DISPFILE	Device capability mask	6	6	
DT_METAFILE	Device capability mask	5	5	
DT_PLOTTER	Device capability mask	0	0	
DT_RASCAMERA	Device capability mask	3	3	
DT_RASDISPLAY	Device capability mask	1	1	
DT_RASPRINTER	Device capability mask	2	2	
LC_INTERIORS	Device capability mask	80	128	
LC_MARKER	Device capability mask	4	4	
LC_NONE	Device capability mask	0	0	
LC_POLYLINE	Device capability mask	2	2	
LC_POLYMARKER	Device capability mask	8	8	

(Continued)

6.042. INCLUDE FILE CONSTANTS DEFINITIONS BY USE (continued)

Defined Name	Used As	Hex Value	Decimal Value	Comments
LC_STYLED	Device capability mask	20	32	
LC_WIDE	Device capability mask	10	16	
LC_WIDESTYLED	Device capability mask	40	64	
PC_INTERIORS	Device capability mask	80	128	
PC_NONE	Device capability mask	0	0	
PC_POLYGON	Device capability mask	1	1	
PC_RECTANGLE	Device capability mask	2	2	
PC_SCANLINE	Device capability mask	8	8	
PC_STYLED	Device capability mask	20	32	
PC_TRAPEZOID	Device capability mask	4	4	
PC_WIDE	Device capability mask	10	16	
PC_WIDESTYLED	Device capability mask	40	64	
PC_WINDPOLYGON†	Device capability mask	4	4	
RC_BANDING	Device capability mask	2	2	
RC_BIGFONT†	Device capability mask	400	1024	
RC_BITBLT	Device capability mask	1	1	
RC_BITMAP64*	Device capability mask	8	8	
RC_DIBTODEV†	Device capability mask	200	512	
RC_DI_BITMAP	Device capability mask	80	128	
RC_FLOODFILL†	Device capability mask	1000	4096	
RC_GDIZO_OUTPUT†	Device capability mask	10	16	
RC_PALETTE†	Device capability mask	100	256	
RC_SCALING	Device capability mask	4	4	
RC_STRETCHBLT†	Device capability mask	800	2048	
RC_STRETCHDIB†	Device capability mask	2000	8192	
TC_CP_STROKE	Device capability mask	4	4	
TC_CR_90	Device capability mask	8	8	
TC_CR_ANY	Device capability mask	10	16	
TC_EA_DOUBLE	Device capability mask	200	512	
TC_IA_ABLE	Device capability mask	400	1024	
TC_OP_CHARACTER	Device capability mask	1	1	
TC_OP_STROKE	Device capability mask	2	2	
TC_RA_ABLE	Device capability mask	2000	8192	
TC_RESERVED	Device capability mask	8000	32768	
TC_SA_CONTIN	Device capability mask	100	256	
TC_SA_DOUBLE	Device capability mask	40	64	
TC_SA_INTEGER	Device capability mask	80	128	
TC_SF_X_YINDEP	Device capability mask	20	32	
TC_SO_ABLE	Device capability mask	1000	4096	
TC_UA_ABLE	Device capability mask	800	2048	
TC_VA_ABLE	Device capability mask	4000	16384	
CP_DIRECT‡	Device capability mode	2	2	
CP_HWND*	Device capability mode	0	0	
CP_OPEN*	Device capability mode	1	1	
LPTx*	Device description	80	128	
DLGC_BUTTON*	Dialog code	2000	8192	
DLGC_DEFPUSHBUTTON*	Dialog code	10	16	
DLGC_HASSETSEL	Dialog code	8	8	
DLGC_RADIOBUTTON*	Dialog code	40	64	
DLGC_STATIC*	Dialog code	100	256	
DLGC_UNDEFPUSHBUTTON*	Dialog code	20	32	
DLGC_WANTALLKEYS	Dialog code	4	4	
DLGC_WANTARROWS	Dialog code	1	1	
DLGC_WANTCHARS*	Dialog code	80	128	
DLGC_WANTMESSAGE*	Dialog code	4	4	
DLGC_WANTTAB	Dialog code	2	2	
DS_ABSALIGN	Dialog style	1	1	
DS_LOCALEDIT*	Dialog style	20	32	
DS_MODALFRAME†	Dialog style	80	128	
DS_NOIDLEMSG†	Dialog style	100	256	
DS_SETFONT†	Dialog style	40	64	
DS_SYSMODAL	Dialog style	2	2	
DM_GETDEFID	Dialog style bits	400	1024	WM_USER+0
DM_HASDEFID‡	Dialog style bits	534B	21323	
DM_SETDEFID	Dialog style bits	401	1025	WM_USER+1
IDABORT	Dialog/MessageBox command ID	3	3	
IDCANCEL	Dialog/MessageBox command ID	2	2	
IDIGNORE	Dialog/MessageBox command ID	5	5	
IDNO	Dialog/MessageBox command ID	7	7	
IDOK	Dialog/MessageBox command ID	1	1	
IDRETRY	Dialog/MessageBox command ID	4	4	
IDYES	Dialog/MessageBox command ID	6	6	
DIB_PAL_COLORS†	DIB color table ID	1	1	
DIB_RGB_COLORS†	DIB color table ID	0	0	
CBM_INIT†	DIBitmap constant	4	4	

(Continued)

6.042. INCLUDE FILE CONSTANTS DEFINITIONS BY USE (continued)

Defined Name	*Used As*	*Hex Value*	*Decimal Value*	*Comments*
DF_ACTIVEBORDER‡	DrawFrame index			COLOR_ACTIVEBORDER+1<<3
DF_ACTIVECAPTION‡	DrawFrame index			COLOR_ACTIVECAPTION+1<<3
DF_APPWORKSPACE‡	DrawFrame index			COLOR_APPWORKSPACE+1<<3
DF_BACKGROUND‡	DrawFrame index			COLOR_BACKGROUND+1<<3
DF_CAPTIONTEXT‡	DrawFrame index			COLOR_CAPTIONTEXT+1<<3
DF_GRAY‡	DrawFrame index			COLOR_APPWORKSPACE+(1<<3)
DF_INACTIVEBORDER‡	DrawFrame index			COLOR_INACTIVEBORDER+1<<3
DF_INACTIVECAPTION‡	DrawFrame index			COLOR_INACTIVECAPTION+1<<3
DF_MENUTEXT‡	DrawFrame index			COLOR_MENUTEXT+1<<3
DF_MENU‡	DrawFrame index			COLOR_MENU+1<<3
DF_PATCOPY‡	DrawFrame index	0	0	
DF_PATINVERT‡	DrawFrame index	4	4	
DF_SCROLLBAR‡	DrawFrame index			COLOR_SCROLLBAR+1<<3
DF_SHIFT0‡	DrawFrame index	0	0	
DF_SHIFT1‡	DrawFrame index	1	1	
DF_SHIFT2‡	DrawFrame index	2	2	
DF_SHIFT3‡	DrawFrame index	3	3	
DF_WINDOWFRAME‡	DrawFrame index			COLOR_WINDOWFRAME+1<<3
DF_WINDOWTEXT‡	DrawFrame index			COLOR_WINDOWTEXT+1<<3
DF_WINDOW‡	DrawFrame index			COLOR_WINDOW+1<<3
DT_BOTTOM	DrawText format flag	8	8	
DT_CALCRECT*	DrawText format flag	400	1024	
DT_CENTER	DrawText format flag	1	1	
DT_EXPANDTABS	DrawText format flag	40	64	
DT_EXTERNALLEADING	DrawText format flag	200	512	
DT_INTERNAL	DrawText format flag	1000	4096	
DT_LEFT	DrawText format flag	0	0	
DT_NOCLIP	DrawText format flag	100	256	
DT_NOPREFIX*	DrawText format flag	800	2048	
DT_RIGHT	DrawText format flag	2	2	
DT_SINGLELINE	DrawText format flag	20	32	
DT_TABSTOP	DrawText format flag	80	128	
DT_TOP	DrawText format flag	0	0	
DT_VCENTER	DrawText format flag	4	4	
DT_WORDBREAK	DrawText format flag	10	16	
EM_CANUNDO†	Edit control message	416	1046	WM_USER+22
EM_EMPTYUNDOBUFFER†	Edit control message	41D	1053	WM_USER+29
EM_FMTLINES†	Edit control message	418	1048	WM_USER+24
EM_GETHANDLE†	Edit control message	40D	1039	WM_USER+13
EM_GETLINECOUNT†	Edit control message	40A	1034	WM_USER+10
EM_GETLINE†	Edit control message	414	1044	WM_USER+20
EM_GETMODIFY†	Edit control message	408	1031	WM_USER+8
EM_GETRECT*	Edit control message	402	1026	WM_USER+2
EM_GETSEL*	Edit control message	400	1024	WM_USER+0
EM_GETTHUMB†	Edit control message	40E	1038	WM_USER+14
EM_LIMITTEXT†	Edit control message	415	1043	WM_USER+21
EM_LINEFROMCHAR†	Edit control message	419	1069	WM_USER+25
EM_LINEINDEX†	Edit control message	40B	1035	WM_USER+11
EM_LINELENGTH†	Edit control message	411	1051	WM_USER+17
EM_LINESCROLL*	Edit control message	406	1030	WM_USER+6
EM_MSGMAX†	Edit control message	41E	1054	WM_USER+30
EM_REPLACESEL†	Edit control message	412	1042	WM_USER+18
EM_SCROLL*	Edit control message	405	1029	WM_USER+5
EM_SETFONT†	Edit control message	413	1043	WM_USER+19
EM_SETHANDLE†	Edit control message	40C	1036	WM_USER+12
EM_SETMODIFY†	Edit control message	409	1033	WM_USER+9
EM_SETPASSWORDCHAR†	Edit control message	41C	1052	WM_USER+28
EM_SETRECT*	Edit control message	403	1027	WM_USER+3
EM_SETRECTNP*	Edit control message	404	1028	WM_USER+4
EM_SETSEL*	Edit control message	401	1025	WM_USER+1
EM_SETTABSTOPS†	Edit control message	41B	1071	WM_USER+27
EM_SETWORDBREAK†	Edit control message	41A	1070	WM_USER+26
EM_UNDO†	Edit control message	417	1067	WM_USER+23
EN_CHANGE	Edit control notification code	300	768	
EN_ERRSPACE	Edit control notification code	501	1281	
EN_HSCROLL	Edit control notification code	601	1537	
EN_KILLFOCUS	Edit control notification code	200	512	
EN_MAXTEXT†	Edit control notification code	501	1281	
EN_SETFOCUS	Edit control notification code	100	256	
EN_UPDATE*	Edit control notification code	400	1024	
EN_VSCROLL	Edit control notification code	602	1538	
ES_AUTOHSCROLL	Edit control style	80	128	
ES_AUTOVSCROLL	Edit control style	400	1024	
ES_CENTER	Edit control style	1	1	
ES_LEFT	Edit control style	0	0	

(Continued)

6.042. INCLUDE FILE CONSTANTS DEFINITIONS BY USE (continued)

Defined Name	Used As	Hex Value	Decimal Value	Comments
ES_LOWERCASE†	Edit control style	10	16	
ES_MULTILINE	Edit control style	4	4	
ES_NOHIDESEL	Edit control style	100	256	
ES_OEMCONVERT†	Edit control style	400	1024	
ES_PASSWORD†	Edit control style	20	32	
ES_RIGHT	Edit control style	2	2	
ES_UPPERCASE†	Edit control style	8	8	
ETO_CLIPPED*	Edit text option	4	4	
ETO_GRAYED*	Edit text option	1	1	
ETO_OPAQUE*	Edit text option	2	2	
DEVICE_FONTTYPE	EnumFonts mask	2	2	
RASTER_FONTTYPE	EnumFonts mask	1	1	
FLOODFILLBORDER†	ExtFloodFill style flag	0	0	
FLOOFILLSURFACE†	ExtFloodFill style flag	1	1	
MSGF_DIALOGBOX	Filter procedure code	0	0	
MSGF_MENU	Filter procedure code	2	2	
MSGF_MESSAGEBOX	Filter procedure code	1	1	
MSGF_MOVE*	Filter procedure code	3	3	
MSGF_NEXTWINDOW*	Filter procedure code	6	6	
MSGF_SCROLLBAR*	Filter procedure code	5	5	
MSGF_SIZE*	Filter procedure code	4	4	
FF_DECORATIVE†	Font family ID	50	80	
FF_DONTCARE†	Font family ID	00	0	
FF_MODERN†	Font family ID	30	48	
FF_ROMAN†	Font family ID	10	16	
FF_SCRIPT†	Font family ID	40	64	
FF_SWISS†	Font family ID	20	32	
FW_BLACK	Font weight constant	384	900	Defined as FW_HEAVY
FW_BOLD	Font weight constant	26C	700	
FW_DEMIBOLD	Font weight constant	258	600	Defined as FW_SEMIBOLD
FW_DONTCARE	Font weight constant	0	0	
FW_EXTRABOLD	Font weight constant	320	800	
FW_EXTRALIGHT	Font weight constant	C8	200	
FW_HEAVY	Font weight constant	384	900	
FW_LIGHT	Font weight constant	12C	300	
FW_MEDIUM	Font weight constant	1F4	500	
FW_NORMAL	Font weight constant	190	400	
FW_REGULAR*	Font weight constant	190	400	FW_NORMAL
FW_SEMIBOLD	Font weight constant	258	600	
FW_THIN	Font weight constant	64	100	
FW_ULTRABOLD	Font weight constant	320	800	Defined as FW_EXTRABOLD
FW_ULTRALIGHT	Font weight constant	C8	200	Defined as FW_EXTRALIGHT
OPAQUE	GDI background mode	2	2	
TRANSPARENT	GDI background mode	1	1	
ABSOLUTE	GDI coordinate mode	1	1	
RELATIVE	GDI coordinate mode	2	2	
ABORTDOC	GDI escape	2	2	
BEGIN_PATH†	GDI escape	1000	4096	
CLIP_TO_PATH†	GDI escape	1001	4097	
DRAFTMODE	GDI escape	7	7	
ENDDOC	GDI escape	B	11	
END_PATH†	GDI escape	1002	4098	
ENUMPAPERBINS†	GDI escape	1F	31	
ENUMPAPERMETRICS†	GDI escape	22	34	
EPSPRINTING†	GDI escape	21	33	
EXT_DEVICE_CAPS†	GDI escape	1003	4099	
FLUSHOUTPUT	GDI escape	6	6	
GETCOLORTABLE	GDI escape	5	5	
GETPHYSPAGESIZE	GDI escape	C	12	
GETPRINTINGOFFSET	GDI escape	D	13	
GETSCALINGFACTOR	GDI escape	E	14	
GETSETPAPERBINS†	GDI escape	1D	29	
GETSETPAPERMETRICS†	GDI escape	23	35	
GETSETPRINTORIENT†	GDI escape	1E	30	
NEWFRAME	GDI escape	1	1	
NEXTBAND	GDI escape	3	3	
POSTSCRIPT_DATA†	GDI escape	25	37	
POSTSCRIPT_IGNORE†	GDI escape	26	38	
QUERYESCSUPPORT	GDI escape	8	8	
RESTORE_CTM†	GDI escape	1004	4100	
SAVE_CTM†	GDI escape	1005	4101	
SETABORTPROC	GDI escape	9	9	
SETALLJUSTVALUES†	GDI escape	303	771	
SETCHARSET†	GDI escape	304	772	
SETCOLORTABLE	GDI escape	4	4	

(Continued)

6.042. INCLUDE FILE CONSTANTS DEFINITIONS BY USE (continued)

Defined Name	*Used As*	*Hex Value*	*Decimal Value*	*Comments*
SETDIBSCALING†	GDI escape	20	32	
SET_ARC_DIRECTION†	GDI escape	1006	4102	
SET_BACKGROUND_COLOR†	GDI escape	1007	4103	
SET_BOUNDS†	GDI escape	1013	4109	
SET_CLIP_BOX†	GDI escape	1012	4108	
SET_MIRROR_MODE†	GDI escape	1014	4110	
SET_POLY_MODE†	GDI escape	1008	4104	
SET_SCREEN_ANGLE†	GDI escape	1009	4105	
SET_SPREAD†	GDI escape	1010	4106	
STARTDOC	GDI escape	A	10	
TRANSFORM_CTM†	GDI escape	1011	4107	
BANDINFO*	GDI escape code	18	24	
DRAWPATTERNRECT*	GDI escape code	19	25	
ENABLEDUPLEX*	GDI escape code	1C	28	
ENABLEMANUALFEED*	GDI escape code	1D	29	
ENABLEPAIRKERNING*	GDI escape code	301	769	
ENABLERELATIVEWIDTHS*	GDI escape code	300	768	
EXTTEXTOUT*	GDI escape code	200	512	
GETEXTENDEDTEXTMETRICS*	GDI escape code	100	256	
GETEXTENTTABLE*	GDI escape code	101	257	
GETPAIRKERNTABLE*	GDI escape code	102	258	
GETPENWIDTH*	GDI escape code	10	16	
GETTECHNOLOGY*	GDI escape code	14	20	
GETTRACKKERNTABLE*	GDI escape code	103	259	
GETVECTORBRUSHSIZE*	GDI escape code	1B	27	
GETVECTORPENSIZE*	GDI escape code	1A	26	
MFCOMMENT*	GDI escape code	F	15	
PASSTHROUGH*	GDI escape code	13	19	
SELECTPAPERSOURCE*	GDI escape code	12	18	
SETCOPYCOUNT*	GDI escape code	11	17	
SETKERNTRACK*	GDI escape code	302	770	
SETLINEJOIN*	GDI escape code	16	22	
SETMITERLIMIT*	GDI escape code	17	23	
STRETCHBLT*	GDI escape code	800	2048	
MM_ANISOTROPIC	GDI map mode	8	8	
MM_HIENGLISH	GDI map mode	5	5	
MM_HIMETRIC	GDI map mode	3	3	
MM_ISOTROPIC	GDI map mode	7	7	
MM_LOENGLISH	GDI map mode	4	4	
MM_LOMETRIC	GDI map mode	2	2	
MM_TEXT	GDI map mode	1	1	
MM_TWIPS	GDI map mode	6	6	
ASPECTX	GetDeviceCaps device parameter	28	40	
ASPECTXY	GetDeviceCaps device parameter	2C	44	
ASPECTY	GetDeviceCaps device parameter	2A	42	
BITSPIXEL	GetDeviceCaps device parameter	C	12	
CLIPCAPS	GetDeviceCaps device parameter	24	36	
COLORES†	GetDeviceCaps device parameter	6C	108	
CURVECAPS	GetDeviceCaps device parameter	1C	28	
DRIVERVERSION	GetDeviceCaps device parameter	0	0	
HORZRES	GetDeviceCaps device parameter	8	8	
HORZSIZE	GetDeviceCaps device parameter	4	4	
LINECAPS	GetDeviceCaps device parameter	1E	30	
LOGPIXELSX	GetDeviceCaps device parameter	58	88	
LOGPIXELSY	GetDeviceCaps device parameter	5A	90	
NUMBRUSHES	GetDeviceCaps device parameter	10	16	
NUMCOLORS	GetDeviceCaps device parameter	18	24	
NUMFONTS	GetDeviceCaps device parameter	16	22	
NUMMARKERS	GetDeviceCaps device parameter	14	20	
NUMPENS	GetDeviceCaps device parameter	12	18	
NUMRESERVED†	GetDeviceCaps device parameter	6A	106	
PDEVICESIZE	GetDeviceCaps device parameter	1A	26	
PLANES	GetDeviceCaps device parameter	E	14	
POLYGONALCAPS	GetDeviceCaps device parameter	20	32	
RASTERCAPS	GetDeviceCaps device parameter	26	38	
SIZEPALETTE†	GetDeviceCaps device parameter	68	104	
TECHNOLOGY	GetDeviceCaps device parameter	2	2	
TEXTCAPS	GetDeviceCaps device parameter	22	34	
VERTRES	GetDeviceCaps device parameter	A	10	
VERTSIZE	GetDeviceCaps device parameter	6	6	
DRIVE_FIXED†	GetDriveType value	3	3	
DRIVE_REMOTE†	GetDriveType value	4	4	
DRIVE_REMOVABLE†	GetDriveType value	2	2	
SM_CMETRICS†	GetSystemMetrics code	24	36	
SM_CXBORDER	GetSystemMetrics code	5	5	

(Continued)

6.042. INCLUDE FILE CONSTANTS DEFINITIONS BY USE (continued)

Defined Name	Used As	Hex Value	Decimal Value	Comments
SM_CXCURSOR	GetSystemMetrics code	D	13	
SM_CXDLGFRAME	GetSystemMetrics code	7	7	
SM_CXFRAME*	GetSystemMetrics code	20	32	
SM_CXFULLSCREEN	GetSystemMetrics code	10	16	
SM_CXHSCROLL	GetSystemMetrics code	15	21	
SM_CXHTHUMB	GetSystemMetrics code	A	10	
SM_CXICON	GetSystemMetrics code	B	11	
SM_CXMIN*	GetSystemMetrics code	1C	28	
SM_CXMINTRACK*	GetSystemMetrics code	22	34	
SM_CXSCREEN	GetSystemMetrics code	0	0	
SM_CXSIZE*	GetSystemMetrics code	1E	30	
SM_CXVSCROLL	GetSystemMetrics code	2	2	
SM_CYBORDER	GetSystemMetrics code	6	6	
SM_CYCAPTION	GetSystemMetrics code	4	4	
SM_CYCURSOR†	GetSystemMetrics code	E	14	
SM_CYDLGFRAME	GetSystemMetrics code	8	8	
SM_CYFRAME*	GetSystemMetrics code	21	33	
SM_CYFULLSCREEN	GetSystemMetrics code	11	17	
SM_CYHSCROLL	GetSystemMetrics code	3	3	
SM_CYICON	GetSystemMetrics code	C	12	
SM_CYICONSLOT‡	GetSystemMetrics code	1B	27	
SM_CYKANJIWINDOW	GetSystemMetrics code	12	18	
SM_CYMENU	GetSystemMetrics code	F	15	
SM_CYMIN*	GetSystemMetrics code	1D	29	
SM_CYMINTRACK*	GetSystemMetrics code	23	35	
SM_CYSCREEN	GetSystemMetrics code	1	1	
SM_CYSIZE*	GetSystemMetrics code	1F	31	
SM_CYVSCROLL	GetSystemMetrics code	14	20	
SM_CYVTHUMB	GetSystemMetrics code	9	9	
SM_DEBUG	GetSystemMetrics code	16	22	
SM_FULLSCREEN‡	GetSystemMetrics code	18	24	
SM_MOUSEPRESENT	GetSystemMetrics code	13	19	
SM_RESERVED1†	GetSystemMetrics code	18	24	
SM_RESERVED2†	GetSystemMetrics code	19	25	
SM_RESERVED3†	GetSystemMetrics code	1A	26	
SM_RESERVED4†	GetSystemMetrics code	1B	27	
SM_SWAPBUTTON	GetSystemMetrics code	17	23	
TF_FORCEDRIVE†	GetTempFileName flag	0x80	128	
GW_CHILD*	GetWindow constant	5	5	
GW_HWNDFIRST*	GetWindow constant	0	0	
GW_HWNDLAST*	GetWindow constant	1	1	
GW_HWNDNEXT*	GetWindow constant	2	2	
GW_HWNDPREV*	GetWindow constant	3	3	
GW_OWNER*	GetWindow constant	4	4	
WF_80x87†	GetWinFlags	400	1024	
WF_CPU086†	GetWinFlags	40	64	
WF_CPU186†	GetWinFlags	80	128	
WF_CPU286†	GetWinFlags	2	2	
WF_CPU386†	GetWinFlags	4	4	
WF_CPU486†	GetWinFlags	8	8	
WF_ENHANCED†	GetWinFlags	20	32	
WF_LARGEFRAME†	GetWinFlags	100	256	
WF_PMODE†	GetWinFlags	1	1	
WF_SMALLFRAME†	GetWinFlags	200	512	
WF_STANDARD†	GetWinFlags	10	16	
WF_WIN286†	GetWinFlags	10	16	
WF_WIN386†	GetWinFlags	20	32	
GHND*	Global memory management	42	66	GMEM_MOVEABLE | GMEM_ZEROINIT
GMEM_DDESHARE*	Global memory management	2000	8192	
GMEM_DISCARDABLE†	Global memory management	100	256	
GMEM_FIXED	Global memory management	0	0	
GMEM_LOWER*	Global memory management	1000	4096	GMEM_NOT_BANKED
GMEM_MODIFY	Global memory management	80	128	
GMEM_MOVEABLE	Global memory management	2	2	
GMEM_NOCOMPACT	Global memory management	10	16	
GMEM_NODISCARD	Global memory management	20	32	
GMEM_NOTBANKED*	Global memory management	1000	4096	
GMEM_NOTIFY*	Global memory management	4000	16384	
GMEM_SHARE*	Global memory management	2000	8196	
GMEM_ZEROINIT	Global memory management	40	64	
GPTR*	Global memory management	2	2	GMEM_FIXED | GMEM_ZEROINIT
LHND*	Global memory management	42	66	LMEM_MOVEABLE††
LPTR*	Global memory management	2	2	LMEM_FIXED††
NONZEROLHND*	Global memory management	2	2	LMEM_MOVEABLE
NONZEROLPTR*	Global memory management	0	0	LMEM_FIXED

(Continued)

6.042. INCLUDE FILE CONSTANTS DEFINITIONS BY USE (continued)

Defined Name	*Used As*	*Hex Value*	*Decimal Value*	*Comments*
GMEM_DISCARDED	GlobalFlag flag	4000	16384	
GMEM_LOCKCOUNT	GlobalFlag flag	FF	255	
GMEM_SWAPPED‡	GlobalFlag flag	8000	32768	
HS_BDIAGONAL	Hatch style	3	3	
HS_CROSS	Hatch style	4	4	
HS_DIAGCROSS	Hatch style	5	5	
HS_FDIAGONAL	Hatch style	2	2	
HS_HORIZONTAL	Hatch style	0	0	
HS_VERTICAL	Hatch style	1	1	
HCBT_MINMAX*	Hook code	1	1	
HCBT_MOVESIZE*	Hook code	0	0	
HCBT_QS	Hook code	2	2	
HC_ACTION*	Hook code	0	0	
HC_GETNEXT*	Hook code	1	1	
HC_LPFNNEXT*	Hook code		-1	
HC_LPLPFNNEXT*	Hook code		-2	
HC_NOREM*	Hook code	3	3	
HC_NOREMOVE†	Hook code	3	3	
HC_SKIP*	Hook code	2	2	
HC_SYSMODALOFF†	Hook code	5	5	
HC_SYSMODALON†	Hook code	4	4	
MK_CONTROL	Key state mask f/mouse msg.	8	8	
MK_LBUTTON	Key state mask f/mouse msg.	1	1	
MK_MBUTTON	Key state mask f/mouse msg.	10	16	
MK_RBUTTON	Key state mask f/mouse msg.	2	2	
MK_SHIFT	Key state mask f/mouse msg.	4	4	
ORD_LANDDRIVER†	Language driver	1	1	
LBN_KILLFOCUS†	Listbox notification code	5	5	
LBN_SELCANCEL†	Listbox notification code	3	3	
LBN_SETFOCUS†	Listbox notification code	4	4	
LB_FINDSTRING†	Listbox notification code	410	1040	WM_USER+16
LB_GETHORIZONTALEXTENT†	Listbox notification code	414	1044	WM_USER+20
LB_GETITEMDATA†	Listbox notification code	41A	1050	WM_USER+26
LB_GETITEMRECT†	Listbox notification code	419	1049	WM_USER+25
LB_GETSELCOUNT†	Listbox notification code	411	1041	WM_USER+17
LB_GETSELITEMS†	Listbox notification code	412	1042	WM_USER+18
LB_MSGMAX†	Listbox notification code	421	1057	WM_USER+33
LB_SELITEMRANGE†	Listbox notification code	41C	1052	WM_USER+28
LB_SETCOLUMNWIDTH†	Listbox notification code	416	1046	WM_USER+22
LB_SETHORIZONTALEXTENT†	Listbox notification code	415	1045	WM_USER+21
LB_SETITEMDATA†	Listbox notification code	41B	1051	WM_USER+27
LB_SETTABSTOPS†	Listbox notification code	413	1043	WM_USER+19
LB_SETTOPINDEX†	Listbox notification code	418	1048	WM_USER+24
LBS_EXTENDEDSEL†	Listbox style	800	2048	
LBS_HASSTRINGS†	Listbox style	40	64	
LBS_MULTICOLUMN†	Listbox style	200	512	
LBS_NOINTEGRALHEIGHT†	Listbox style	100	256	
LBS_OWNERDRAWFIXED†	Listbox style	10	16	
LBS_OWNERDRAWVARIABLE†	Listbox style	20	32	
LBS_USETABSTOPS†	Listbox style	80	128	
LBS_WANTKEYBOARDINPUT†	Listbox style	400	1024	
LB_CTLCODE	Listbox control	0	0	
LB_ERR	Listbox control		-1	
LB_ERRSPACE	Listbox control		-2	
LB_OKAY	Listbox control	0	0	
LB_ADDSTRING*	Listbox message	401	1025	WM_USER+1
LB_DELETESTRING*	Listbox message	403	1027	WM_USER+3
LB_DIR*	Listbox message	40E	1038	WM_USER+14
LB_GETCOUNT*	Listbox message	40C	1036	WM_USER+12
LB_GETCURSEL†	Listbox message	409	1033	WM_USER+9
LB_GETSEL†	Listbox message	408	1032	WM_USER+8
LB_GETTEXTLEN*	Listbox message	40B	1035	WM_USER+11
LB_GETTEXT†	Listbox message	40A	1034	WM_USER+10
LB_GETTOPINDEX†	Listbox message	40F	1039	WM_USER+15
LB_INSERTSTRING*	Listbox message	402	1026	WM_USER+2
LB_RESETCONTENT*	Listbox message	405	1029	WM_USER+5
LB_SELECTSTRING*	Listbox message	40D	1037	WM_USER+13
LB_SETCURSEL*	Listbox message	407	1031	WM_USER+7
LB_SETSEL*	Listbox message	406	1030	WM_USER+6
LBN_DBLCLK	Listbox notification code	2	2	
LBN_ERRSPACE	Listbox notification code		-2	
LBN_SELCHANGE	Listbox notification code	1	1	
LBS_MULTIPLESEL	Listbox style	8	8	
LBS_NOREDRAW	Listbox style	4	4	

(Continued)

6.042. INCLUDE FILE CONSTANTS DEFINITIONS BY USE (continued)

Defined Name	Used As	Hex Value	Decimal Value	Comments
LBS_NOTIFY	Listbox style	1	1	
LBS_SORT	Listbox style	2	2	
LBS_STANDARD*	Listbox style	F	15	LBS_NOTIFY | LBS_SORT**
LMEM_DISCARDABLE	Local memory management	F00	3840	
LMEM_DISCARDED*	Local memory management	4000	16384	
LMEM_FIXED	Local memory management	0	0	
LMEM_LOCKCOUNT	Local memory management	FF	255	
LMEM_MODIFY	Local memory management	80	128	
LMEM_MOVEABLE	Local memory management	2	2	
LMEM_NOCOMPACT	Local memory management	10	16	
LMEM_NODISCARD	Local memory management	20	32	
LMEM_ZEROINIT	Local memory management	40	64	
LNOTIFY_DISCARD	Local memory management	2	2	
LNOTIFY_MOVE	Local memory management	1	1	
LNOTIFY_OUTOFMEM	Local memory management	0	0	
ANSI_CHARSET	Logical font constant	0	0	
CLIP_CHARACTER_PRECIS	Logical font constant	1	1	
CLIP_DEFAULT_PRECIS	Logical font constant	0	0	
CLIP_STROKE_PRECIS	Logical font constant	2	2	
DEFAULT_PITCH	Logical font constant	0	0	
DEFAULT_QUALITY	Logical font constant	0	0	
DRAFT_QUALITY	Logical font constant	1	1	
FIXED_PITCH	Logical font constant	1	1	
LF_FACESIZE	Logical font constant	20	32	
OEM_CHARSET	Logical font constant	FF	255	
OUT_CHARACTER_PRECIS	Logical font constant	2	2	
OUT_DEFAULT_PRECIS	Logical font constant	0	0	
OUT_STRING_PRECIS	Logical font constant	1	1	
OUT_STROKE_PRECIS	Logical font constant	3	3	
PROOF_QUALITY	Logical font constant	2	2	
SHIFTJIS_CHARSET*	Logical font constant	80	128	
SYMBOL_CHARSET†	Logical font constant	2	2	
VARIABLE_PITCH	Logical font constant	2	2	
CW_USEDEFAULT†	lopen flag	(int)8000	32768	
READ_WRITE†	lopen flag	2	2	
READ†	lopen flag	0	0	
WRITE†	lopen flag	1	1	
MF_APPEND	MenuItem menu flag	100	256	
MF_BITMAP	MenuItem menu flag	4	4	
MF_BYCOMMAND	MenuItem menu flag	0	0	
MF_BYPOSITION	MenuItem menu flag	400	1024	
MF_CHANGE	MenuItem menu flag	80	128	
MF_CHECKED	MenuItem menu flag	8	8	
MF_DELETE	MenuItem menu flag	200	512	
MF_DISABLED	MenuItem menu flag	2	2	
MF_ENABLED	MenuItem menu flag	0	0	
MF_END†	MenuItem menu flag	80	128	
MF_GRAYED	MenuItem menu flag	1	1	
MF_HELP*	MenuItem menu flag	4000	16384	
MF_HILITE	MenuItem menu flag	80	128	
MF_INSERT	MenuItem menu flag	0	0	
MF_MENUBARBREAK	MenuItem menu flag	20	32	
MF_MENUBREAK	MenuItem menu flag	40	64	
MF_MOUSESELECT*	MenuItem menu flag	8000	32768	
MF_OWNERDRAW†	MenuItem menu flag	100	256	
MF_POPUP	MenuItem menu flag	10	16	
MF_REMOVE*	MenuItem menu flag	1000	4096	
MF_SEPARATOR	MenuItem menu flag	800	2048	
MF_STRING	MenuItem menu flag	0	0	
MF_SYSMENU*	MenuItem menu flag	2000	8192	
MF_UNCHECKED	MenuItem menu flag	0	0	
MF_UNHILITE	MenuItem menu flag	0	0	
MF_USECHECKBITMAPS†	MenuItem menu flag	200	512	
MB_ICONINFORMATION†	MessageBox type flag	40	64	MB_ICONASTERISK
MB_ICONSTOP†	MessageBox type flag	10	16	MB_ICONHAND
MB_TASKMODAL†	MessageBox type flag	2000	8192	
MB_ABORTRETRYIGNORE	MessageBox type flag	2	2	
MB_APPLMODAL	MessageBox type flag	0	0	
MB_DEFBUTTON1	MessageBox type flag	0	0	
MB_DEFBUTTON2	MessageBox type flag	100	256	
MB_DEFBUTTON3	MessageBox type flag	200	512	
MB_DEFMASK	MessageBox type flag	F00	3840	
MB_ICONASTERISK	MessageBox type flag	40	64	
MB_ICONEXCLAMATION	MessageBox type flag	30	48	

(Continued)

6.042. INCLUDE FILE CONSTANTS DEFINITIONS BY USE (continued)

Defined Name	Used As	Hex Value	Decimal Value	Comments
MB_ICONHAND	MessageBox type flag	10	16	
MB_ICONMASK	MessageBox type flag	F0	240	
MB_ICONQUESTION	MessageBox type flag	20	32	
MB_MISCMASK	MessageBox type flag	C000	49152	
MB_MODEMASK	MessageBox type flag	3000	12288	
MB_NOFOCUS	MessageBox type flag	8000	32768	
MB_OK	MessageBox type flag	0	0	
MB_OKCANCEL	MessageBox type flag	1	1	
MB_RETRYCANCEL	MessageBox type flag	5	5	
MB_SYSTEMMODAL	MessageBox type flag	1000	4096	
MB_TYPEMASK	MessageBox type flag	F	15	
MB_YESNO	MessageBox type flag	4	4	
MB_YESNOCANCEL	MessageBox type flag	3	3	
DEVICEDATA	MetaFile comment esc.	13	19	
SETENDCAP	MetaFile comment esc.	15	21	
META_ANIMATEPALETTE†	MetaFile function	436	1078	
META_ARC*	MetaFile function	817	2071	
META_BITBLT*	MetaFile function	922	2338	
META_CHORD†	MetaFile function	830	2096	
META_CREATEBITMAP*	MetaFile function	6FE	1790	
META_CREATEBITMAPINDIRECT*	MetaFile function	2FD	765	
META_CREATEBRUSH*	MetaFile function	F8	248	
META_CREATEBRUSHINDIRECT*	MetaFile function	2FC	764	
META_CREATEFONTINDIRECT*	MetaFile function	2FB	763	
META_CREATEPALETTE†	MetaFile function	F7	247	
META_CREATEPATTERNBRUSH*	MetaFile function	1F9	505	
META_CREATEPENDIRECT*	MetaFile function	2FA	762	
META_CREATEREGION*	MetaFile function	6FF	1791	
META_DELETEOBJECT†	MetaFile function	1F0	496	
META_DIBBITBLT†	MetaFile function	940	2368	
META_DIBCREATEPATTERNBRUSH†	MetaFile function	142	322	
META_DIBSTRETCHBLT†	MetaFile function	B41	2881	
META_DRAWTEXT*	MetaFile function	62F	1583	
META_ELLIPSE*	MetaFile function	418	1048	
META_ESCAPE*	MetaFile function	626	1574	
META_EXCLUDECLIPRECT*	MetaFile function	415	1045	
META_EXTTEXTOUT†	MetaFile function	A32	2610	
META_FILLREGION*	MetaFile function	228	552	
META_FLOODFILL*	MetaFile function	419	1049	
META_FRAMEREGION*	MetaFile function	429	1065	
META_INTERSECTCLIPRECT*	MetaFile function	416	1046	
META_INVERTREGION*	MetaFile function	12A	298	
META_LINETO*	MetaFile function	213	531	
META_MOVETO*	MetaFile function	214	532	
META_OFFSETCLIPRGN*	MetaFile function	220	544	
META_OFFSETVIEWPORTORG*	MetaFile function	211	529	
META_OFFSETWINDOWORG*	MetaFile function	20F	527	
META_PAINTREGION*	MetaFile function	12B	299	
META_PATBLT*	MetaFile function	61D	1565	
META_PIE*	MetaFile function	81A	2074	
META_POLYGON*	MetaFile function	324	804	
META_POLYLINE*	MetaFile function	325	805	
META_POLYPOLYGON†	MetaFile function	538	1336	
META_REALIZEPALETTE†	MetaFile function	35	53	
META_RECTANGLE*	MetaFile function	41B	1051	
META_RESIZEPALETTE†	MetaFile function	139	313	
META_RESTOREDC*	MetaFile function	127	295	
META_ROUNDRECT*	MetaFile function	61C	1564	
META_SAVEDC*	MetaFile function	1E	30	
META_SCALEVIEWPORTEXT*	MetaFile function	412	1042	
META_SCALEWINDOWEXT*	MetaFile function	400	1024	
META_SELECTCLIPREGION*	MetaFile function	12C	300	
META_SELECTOBJECT*	MetaFile function	12D	301	
META_SELECTPALETTE†	MetaFile function	234	564	
META_SETBKCOLOR*	MetaFile function	201	513	
META_SETBKMODE*	MetaFile function	102	258	
META_SETDIBTODEV†	MetaFile function	D33	3379	
META_SETMAPMODE*	MetaFile function	103	259	
META_SETMAPPERFLAGS†	MetaFile function	231	561	
META_SETPALENTRIES†	MetaFile function	37	55	
META_SETPIXEL*	MetaFile function	41F	1055	
META_SETPOLYFILLMODE*	MetaFile function	106	262	
META_SETRELABS*	MetaFile function	105	261	
META_SETROP2*	MetaFile function	104	260	

(Continued)

6.042. INCLUDE FILE CONSTANTS DEFINITIONS BY USE (continued)

Defined Name	Used As	Hex Value	Decimal Value	Comments
META_SETSTRECTCHBLTMODE*	MetaFile function	107	263	
META_SETTEXTALIGN*	MetaFile function	12E	302	
META_SETTEXTCHAREXTRA*	MetaFile function	108	264	
META_SETTEXTCOLOR*	MetaFile function	209	521	
META_SETTEXTJUSTIFICATION*	MetaFile function	20A	522	
META_SETVIEWPORTEXT*	MetaFile function	20E	526	
META_SETVIEWPORTORG*	MetaFile function	20D	525	
META_SETWINDOWEXT*	MetaFile function	20C	524	
META_SETWINDOWORG*	MetaFile function	20B	523	
META_STRETCHBLT*	MetaFile function	B23	2851	
META_STRETCHDIB†	MetaFile function	F43	3907	
META_TEXTOUT*	MetaFile function	521	1313	
MA_ACTIVATE*	Mouse activate return code	1	1	
MA_ACTIVATEANDEAT*	Mouse activate return code	2	2	
MA_NOACTIVATE*	Mouse activate return code	3	3	
OBJ_BRUSH	Object definition	2	2	
OBJ_PEN	Object definition	1	1	
OBM_BTNCORNERS	OEM definition	7FF6	32758	
OBM_BTSIZE	OEM definition	7FF9	32761	
OBM_CHECK	OEM definition	7FF8	32760	
OBM_CHECKBOXES	OEM definition	7FF7	32759	
OBM_CLOSE§	OEM definition	7FF2	32754	
OBM_COMBO†	OEM definition	7FE2	32738	
OBM_DNARROWD†	OEM definition	7FE6	32742	
OBM_DNARROW§	OEM definition	7FF0	32752	
OBM_LFARROWD†	OEM definition	7FE4	32740	
OBM_LFARROW§	OEM definition	7FEE	32750	
OBM_MNARROW†	OEM definition	7FE3	32739	
OBM_OLD_CLOSE	OEM definition	7FFF	32767	
OBM_OLD_DNARROW	OEM definition	7FFC	32764	
OBM_OLD_LFARROW	OEM definition	7FFA	32762	
OBM_OLD_REDUCE*	OEM definition	7FF5	32757	
OBM_OLD_RESTORE*	OEM definition	7FF3	32755	
OBM_OLD_RGARROW	OEM definition	7FFB	32763	
OBM_OLD_UPARROW	OEM definition	7FFD	32765	
OBM_OLD_ZOOM*	OEM definition	7FF4	32756	
OBM_REDUCED†	OEM definition	7FEA	32746	
OBM_REDUCE§	OEM definition	7FED	32749	
OBM_RESTORE	OEM definition	7FEB	32747	
OBM_RESTORED†	OEM definition	7FE8	32744	
OBM_RGARROWD†	OEM definition	7FE5	32741	
OBM_RGARROW§	OEM definition	7FEF	32751	
OBM_SIZE	OEM definition	7FFE	32766	
OBM_UPARROWD†	OEM definition	7FE7	32743	
OBM_UPARROW§	OEM definition	7FF1	32753	
OBM_ZOOMD†	OEM definition	7FE9	32745	
OBM_ZOOM§	OEM definition	7FEC	32748	
OCR_CROSS	OEM definition	7F03	32515	
OCR_IBEAM	OEM definition	7F01	32513	
OCR_ICOCUR†	OEM definition	7F87	32647	
OCR_ICON	OEM definition	7F81	32641	
OCR_NORMAL	OEM definition	7F00	32512	
OCR_SIZE	OEM definition	7F80	32640	
OCR_SIZEALL*	OEM definition	7F86	32646	
OCR_SIZENESW*	OEM definition	7F83	32643	
OCR_SIZENS*	OEM definition	7F85	32645	
OCR_SIZENWSE*	OEM definition	7F82	32642	
OCR_SIZEWE*	OEM definition	7F84	32644	
OCR_UP	OEM definition	7F04	32516	
OCR_WAIT	OEM definition	7F02	32514	
OIC_BANG†	OEM definition	7F03	32515	
OIC_HAND†	OEM definition	7F01	32513	
OIC_NOTE†	OEM definition	7F04	32516	
OIC_QUES†	OEM definition	7F02	32514	
OIC_SAMPLE†	OEM definition	7F00	32512	
OF_CANCEL	OpenFile flag	800	2048	
OF_CREATE	OpenFile flag	1000	4096	
OF_DELETE	OpenFile flag	200	512	
OF_EXIST	OpenFile flag	4000	16384	
OF_PARSE	OpenFile flag	100	256	
OF_PROMPT	OpenFile flag	2000	8192	
OF_READ	OpenFile flag	0	0	
OF_READWRITE	OpenFile flag	2	2	
OF_REOPEN	OpenFile flag	8000	32768	

(Continued)

6.042. INCLUDE FILE CONSTANTS DEFINITIONS BY USE (continued)

Defined Name	Used As	Hex Value	Decimal Value	Comments
OF_SHARE_COMPAT†	OpenFile flag	0x0000	0	
OF_SHARE_DENY_NONE†	OpenFile flag	0x0040	64	
OF_SHARE_DENY_READ†	OpenFile flag	0x0030	48	
OF_SHARE_DENY_WRITE†	OpenFile flag	0x0020	32	
OF_SHARE_EXCLUSIVE†	OpenFile flag	0x0010	16	
OF_VERIFY	OpenFile flag	400	1024	
OF_WRITE	OpenFile flag	1	1	
ODA_DRAWENTIRE†	Owner draw action	1	1	
ODA_FOCUS†	Owner draw action	4	4	
ODA_SELECT†	Owner draw action	2	2	
ODT_BUTTON†	Owner draw control	4	4	
ODT_COMBOBOX†	Owner draw control	3	3	
ODT_LISTBOX†	Owner draw control	2	2	
ODT_MENU†	Owner draw control	1	1	
ODS_CHECKED†	Owner draw style	8	8	
ODS_DISABLED†	Owner draw style	4	4	
ODS_FOCUS†	Owner draw style	10	16	
ODS_GRAYED†	Owner draw style	2	2	
ODS_SELECTED†	Owner draw style	1	1	
PC_EXPLICIT†	Palette entry flag	2	2	
PC_NOCOLLAPSE†	Palette entry flag	4	4	
PC_RESERVED†	Palette entry flag	1	1	
PM_NOREMOVE*	PeekMessage options	0	0	
PM_NOYIELD*	PeekMessage options	2	2	
PM_REMOVE*	PeekMessage options	1	1	
PS_DASH	Pen style	1	1	
PS_DASHDOT	Pen style	3	3	
PS_DASHDOTDOT	Pen style	4	4	
PS_DOT	Pen style	2	2	
PS_INSIDEFRAME†	Pen style	6	6	
PS_NULL	Pen style	5	5	
PS_SOLID	Pen style	0	0	
ALTERNATE	Polyfill mode	1	1	
WINDING	Polyfill mode	2	2	
RT_ACCELERATOR	Predefined resource type	9	9	MAKEINTRESOURCE (9)
RT_BITMAP	Predefined resource type	2	2	MAKEINTRESOURCE (2)
RT_CURSOR	Predefined resource type	1	1	MAKEINTRESOURCE (1)
RT_DIALOG	Predefined resource type	5	5	MAKEINTRESOURCE (5)
RT_FONT	Predefined resource type	8	8	MAKEINTRESOURCE (8)
RT_FONTDIR	Predefined resource type	7	7	MAKEINTRESOURCE (7)
RT_ICON	Predefined resource type	3	3	MAKEINTRESOURCE (3)
RT_MENU	Predefined resource type	4	4	MAKEINTRESOURCE (4)
RT_RCDATA*	Predefined resource type	A	10	MAKEINTRESOURCE(10)
RT_STRING	Predefined resource type	6	6	MAKEINTRESOURCE (6)
COMPLEXREGION	Region flag	3	3	
ERROR	Region flag	0	0	
NULLREGION	Region flag	1	1	
SIMPLEREGION	Region flag	2	2	
SB_BOTH*	Scrollbar constant	3	3	
SB_BOTTOM	Scrollbar constant	7	7	
SB_CTL	Scrollbar constant	2	2	
SB_ENDSCROLL	Scrollbar constant	8	8	
SB_HORZ	Scrollbar constant	0	0	
SB_LINEDOWN	Scrollbar constant	1	1	
SB_LINEUP	Scrollbar constant	0	0	
SB_PAGEDOWN	Scrollbar constant	3	3	
SB_PAGEUP	Scrollbar constant	2	2	
SB_THUMBPOSITION	Scrollbar constant	4	4	
SB_THUMBTRACK	Scrollbar constant	5	5	
SB_TOP	Scrollbar constant	6	6	
SB_VERT	Scrollbar constant	1	1	
SBS_BOTTOMALIGN*	Scrollbar style	4	4	
SBS_HORZ*	Scrollbar style	0	0	
SBS_LEFTALIGN*	Scrollbar style	2	2	
SBS_RIGHTALIGN*	Scrollbar style	4	4	
SBS_SIZEBOX*	Scrollbar style	8	8	
SBS_SIZEBOXBOTTOMRIGHTALIGN*	Scrollbar style	4	4	
SBS_SIZEBOXTOPLEFTALIGN*	Scrollbar style	2	2	
SBS_TOPALIGN*	Scrollbar style	2	2	
SBS_VERT*	Scrollbar style	1	1	
S_PERIOD1024	SetSoundNoise source	1	1	
S_PERIOD2048	SetSoundNoise source	2	2	
S_PERIOD512	SetSoundNoise source	0	0	
S_PERIODVOICE	SetSoundNoise source	3	3	

(Continued)

6.042. INCLUDE FILE CONSTANTS DEFINITIONS BY USE (continued)

Defined Name	Used As	Hex Value	Decimal Value	Comments
S_SERBDNT	SetSoundNoise source		-5	
S_SERDCC	SetSoundNoise source		-7	
S_SERDDR	SetSoundNoise source		-14	
S_SERDFQ	SetSoundNoise source		-13	
S_SERDLN	SetSoundNoise source		-6	
S_SERDMD	SetSoundNoise source		-10	
S_SERDPT	SetSoundNoise source		-12	
S_SERDSH	SetSoundNoise source		-11	
S_SERDSR	SetSoundNoise source		-15	
S_SERDST	SetSoundNoise source		-16	
S_SERDTP	SetSoundNoise source		-8	
S_SERDVL	SetSoundNoise source		-9	
S_SERDVNA	SetSoundNoise source		-1	
S_SERMACT	SetSoundNoise source		-3	
S_SEROFM	SetSoundNoise source		-2	
S_SERQFUL	SetSoundNoise source		-4	
S_WHITE1024	SetSoundNoise source	5	5	
S_WHITE2048	SetSoundNoise source	6	6	
S_WHITE512	SetSoundNoise source	4	4	
S_WHITEVOICE	SetSoundNoise source	7	7	
SWP_DRAWFRAME*	SetWindow position flag	20	32	
SWP_HIDEWINDOW*	SetWindow position flag	80	128	
SWP_NOACTIVATE*	SetWindow position flag	10	16	
SWP_NOCOPYBITS*	SetWindow position flag	100	256	
SWP_NOMOVE*	SetWindow position flag	2	2	
SWP_NOREDRAW*	SetWindow position flag	8	8	
SWP_NOREPOSITION*	SetWindow position flag	200	512	
SWP_NOSIZE*	SetWindow position flag	1	1	
SWP_NOZORDER*	SetWindow position flag	4	4	
SWP_SHOWWINDOW*	SetWindow position flag	40	64	
WH_CALLWNDPROC	SetWindowsHook code	4	4	
WH_GETMESSAGE	SetWindowsHook code	3	3	
WH_JOURNALPLAYBACK	SetWindowsHook code	1	1	
WH_JOURNALRECORD	SetWindowsHook code	0	0	
WH_KEYBOARD	SetWindowsHook code	2	2	
WH_MSGFILTER	SetWindowsHook code		-1	
HIDE_WINDOW	ShowWindow command	0	0	
SHOW_FULLSCREEN	ShowWindow command	3	3	
SHOW_ICONWINDOW	ShowWindow command	2	2	
SHOW_OPENNOACTIVATE	ShowWindow command	4	4	
SHOW_OPENWINDOW	ShowWindow command	1	1	
SW_HIDE*	ShowWindow message ID	0	0	
SW_MAXIMIZE*	ShowWindow message ID	3	3	
SW_MINIMIZE*	ShowWindow message ID	6	6	
SW_NORMAL*	ShowWindow message ID	1	1	
SW_OTHERUNZOOM	ShowWindow message ID	4	4	
SW_OTHERZOOM	ShowWindow message ID	2	2	
SW_PARENTCLOSING	ShowWindow message ID	1	1	
SW_PARENTOPENING	ShowWindow message ID	3	3	
SW_RESTORE†	ShowWindow message ID	9	9	
SW_SHOW*	ShowWindow message ID	5	5	
SW_SHOWMAXIMIZED*	ShowWindow message ID	3	3	
SW_SHOWMINIMIZED*	ShowWindow message ID	2	2	
SW_SHOWMINNOACTIVE*	ShowWindow message ID	7	7	
SW_SHOWNA*	ShowWindow message ID	8	8	
SW_SHOWNOACTIVE*	ShowWindow message ID	4	4	
SW_SHOWNORMAL*	ShowWindow message ID	1	1	
SIZEFULLSCREEN	Size message command	2	2	
SIZEICONIC	Size message command	1	1	
SIZENORMAL	Size message command	0	0	
SIZEZOOMHIDE	Size message command	4	4	
SIZEZOOMSHOW	Size message command	3	3	
SP_APPABORT	Spooler error code		-2	
SP_ERROR	Spooler error code		-1	
SP_NOTREPORTED	Spooler error code	4000	16384	
SP_OUTOFDISK	Spooler error code		-4	
SP_OUTOFMEMORY	Spooler error code		-5	
SP_USERABORT	Spooler error code		-3	
PR_JOBSTATUS	Spooler wparm class	0	0	
IDC_ARROW	Standard cursor ID	7F00	32512	MAKEINTRESOURCE(32512)
IDC_CROSS	Standard cursor ID	7F03	32515	MAKEINTRESOURCE(32515)
IDC_IBEAM	Standard cursor ID	7F01	32513	MAKEINTRESOURCE(32513)
IDC_ICON	Standard cursor ID	7F81	32641	MAKEINTRESOURCE(32641)
IDC_SIZE	Standard cursor ID	7F80	32640	MAKEINTRESOURCE(32640)
IDC_SIZENESW	Standard cursor ID	7F83	32643	MAKEINTRESOURCE(32643)

(Continued)

6.042. INCLUDE FILE CONSTANTS DEFINITIONS BY USE (continued)

Defined Name	*Used As*	*Hex Value*	*Decimal Value*	*Comments*
IDC_SIZENS	Standard cursor ID	7F85	32645	MAKEINTRESOURCE(32645)
IDC_SIZENWSE	Standard cursor ID	7F82	32642	MAKEINTRESOURCE(32642)
IDC_SIZEWE	Standard cursor ID	7F84	32644	MAKEINTRESOURCE(32644)
IDC_UPARROW	Standard cursor ID	7F04	32516	MAKEINTRESOURCE(32516)
IDC_WAIT	Standard cursor ID	7F02	32514	MAKEINTRESOURCE(32514)
FALSE	Standard definitions	0	0	
NULL	Standard definitions	0	0	
TRUE	Standard definitions	1	1	
IDI_APPLICATION	Standard icon ID	7F00	32512	MAKEINTRESOURCE(32512)
IDI_ASTERISK	Standard icon ID	7F04	32516	MAKEINTRESOURCE(32516)
IDI_EXCLAMATION	Standard icon ID	7F03	32515	MAKEINTRESOURCE(32515)
IDI_HAND	Standard icon ID	7F01	32513	MAKEINTRESOURCE(32513)
IDI_QUESTION	Standard icon ID	7F02	32514	MAKEINTRESOURCE(32514)
VK_ADD	Standard set virtual key	6B	107	
VK_BACK	Standard set virtual key	8	8	
VK_CANCEL	Standard set virtual key	3	3	
VK_CAPITAL	Standard set virtual key	14	20	
VK_CLEAR	Standard set virtual key	C	12	
VK_CONTROL	Standard set virtual key	11	17	
VK_COPY‡	Standard set virtual key	2C	44	Not used by keyboards
VK_DECIMAL	Standard set virtual key	6E	110	
VK_DELETE	Standard set virtual key	2E	46	
VK_DIVIDE	Standard set virtual key	6F	111	
VK_DOWN	Standard set virtual key	28	40	
VK_END	Standard set virtual key	23	35	
VK_ESCAPE	Standard set virtual key	1B	27	
VK_EXECUTE	Standard set virtual key	2B	43	
VK_F1	Standard set virtual key	70	112	
VK_F10	Standard set virtual key	79	121	
VK_F11	Standard set virtual key	7A	122	
VK_F12	Standard set virtual key	7B	123	
VK_F13	Standard set virtual key	7C	124	
VK_F14	Standard set virtual key	7D	125	
VK_F15	Standard set virtual key	7E	126	
VK_F16	Standard set virtual key	7F	127	
VK_F2	Standard set virtual key	71	113	
VK_F3	Standard set virtual key	72	114	
VK_F4	Standard set virtual key	73	115	
VK_F5	Standard set virtual key	74	116	
VK_F6	Standard set virtual key	75	117	
VK_F7	Standard set virtual key	76	118	
VK_F8	Standard set virtual key	77	119	
VK_F9	Standard set virtual key	78	120	
VK_HELP	Standard set virtual key	2F	47	
VK_HOME	Standard set virtual key	24	36	
VK_INSERT	Standard set virtual key	2D	45	
VK_LBUTTON	Standard set virtual key	1	1	
VK_LEFT	Standard set virtual key	25	37	
VK_MBUTTON	Standard set virtual key	4	4	
VK_MENU	Standard set virtual key	12	18	
VK_MULTIPLY	Standard set virtual key	6A	106	
VK_NEXT	Standard set virtual key	22	34	
VK_NUMLOCK	Standard set virtual key	90	144	
VK_NUMPAD0	Standard set virtual key	60	96	
VK_NUMPAD1	Standard set virtual key	61	97	
VK_NUMPAD2	Standard set virtual key	62	98	
VK_NUMPAD3	Standard set virtual key	63	99	
VK_NUMPAD4	Standard set virtual key	64	100	
VK_NUMPAD5	Standard set virtual key	65	101	
VK_NUMPAD6	Standard set virtual key	66	102	
VK_NUMPAD7	Standard set virtual key	67	103	
VK_NUMPAD8	Standard set virtual key	68	104	
VK_NUMPAD9	Standard set virtual key	69	105	
VK_PAUSE	Standard set virtual key	13	19	
VK_PRINT	Standard set virtual key	2A	42	
VK_PRIOR	Standard set virtual key	21	33	
VK_RBUTTON	Standard set virtual key	2	2	
VK_RETURN	Standard set virtual key	D	13	
VK_RIGHT	Standard set virtual key	27	39	
VK_SELECT	Standard set virtual key	29	41	
VK_SEPARATOR	Standard set virtual key	6C	108	
VK_SHIFT	Standard set virtual key	10	16	
VK_SNAPSHOT†	Standard set virtual key	2C	44	
VK_SPACE	Standard set virtual key	20	32	
VK_SUBTRACT	Standard set virtual key	6D	109	

(Continued)

6.042. INCLUDE FILE CONSTANTS DEFINITIONS BY USE (continued)

Defined Name	Used As	Hex Value	Decimal Value	Comments
VK_TAB	Standard set virtual key	9	9	
VK_UP	Standard set virtual key	26	38	
SS_BLACKFRAME	Static control constant	7	7	
SS_BLACKRECT	Static control constant	4	4	
SS_CENTER	Static control constant	1	1	
SS_GRAYFRAME	Static control constant	8	8	
SS_GRAYRECT	Static control constant	5	5	
SS_ICON	Static control constant	3	3	
SS_LEFT	Static control constant	0	0	
SS_LEFTNOWORDWRAP†	Static control constant	C	12	
SS_NOPREFIX*	Static control constant	80	128	
SS_RIGHT	Static control constant	2	2	
SS_SIMPLE*	Static control constant	B	11	
SS_USERITEM	Static control constant	A	10	
SS_WHITEFRAME	Static control constant	9	9	
SS_WHITERECT	Static control constant	6	6	
ANSI_FIXED_FONT	Stock logical object	B	11	
ANSI_VAR_FONT	Stock logical object	C	12	
BLACK_BRUSH	Stock logical object	4	4	
BLACK_PEN	Stock logical object	7	7	
DEVICEDEFAULT_FONT	Stock logical object	E	14	
DKGRAY_BRUSH	Stock logical object	3	3	
GRAY_BRUSH	Stock logical object	2	2	
HOLLOW_BRUSH	Stock logical object	5	5	Defined as NULL_BRUSH
LTGRAY_BRUSH	Stock logical object	1	1	
NULL_BRUSH	Stock logical object	5	5	
NULL_PEN	Stock logical object	8	8	
OEM_FIXED_FONT	Stock logical object	A	10	
SYSTEM_FIXED_FONT	Stock logical object	10	16	
SYSTEM_FONT	Stock logical object	D	13	
WHITE_BRUSH	Stock logical object	0	0	
WHITE_PEN	Stock logical object	6	6	
BLACKONWHITE	StretchBlt mode	1	1	
COLORONCOLOR	StretchBlt mode	3	3	
WHITEONBLACK	StretchBlt mode	2	2	
WEP_FREE_DLL	System exit flags	0	0	
WEP_SYSTEM_EXIT	System exit flags	1	1	
SC_ARRANGE*	System menu command	F110	61712	
SC_CLOSE	System menu command	F060	61536	
SC_HSCROLL	System menu command	F080	61568	
SC_ICON	System menu command	F020	61472	SC_MINIMIZE
SC_KEYMENU	System menu command	F100	61696	
SC_MAXIMIZE*	System menu command	F030	61488	
SC_MINIMIZE*	System menu command	F020	61472	
SC_MOUSEMENU	System menu command	F090	61584	
SC_MOVE	System menu command	F010	61456	
SC_NEXTWINDOW	System menu command	F040	61504	
SC_PREVWINDOW	System menu command	F050	61520	
SC_RESTORE*	System menu command	F120	61728	
SC_SIZE	System menu command	F000	61440	
SC_TASKLIST†	System menu command	F130	61744	
SC_VSCROLL	System menu command	F070	61552	
SC_ZOOM	System menu command	F030	61488	SC_MAXIMIZE
SYSPAL_NOSTATIC2†	System palette use constant	2	2	
SYSPAL_STATIC1†	System palette use constant	1	1	
BLACKNESS	Ternary raster op	0000 0042H	66	Dest = BLACK
DSTINVERT	Ternary raster op	0055 0009H	5570569	Dest = (not dest)
MERGECOPY	Ternary raster op	00C0 00CA	12583114	Dest = (source AND pattern)
MERGEPAINT	Ternary raster op	00BB 0226	12255782	Dest = (not source) OR dest
NOTSRCCOPY	Ternary raster op	0033 0008	3342344	Dest = (not source)
NOTSRCERASE	Ternary raster op	0011 00A6	1114278	Dest = (not source) AND (not dest)
PATCOPY	Ternary raster op	00F0 0021	15728673	Dest = pattern
PATINVERT	Ternary raster op	005A 0049	5898313	Dest = pattern XOR dest
PATPAINT	Ternary raster op	00FB 0A09	16452105	Dest = DPSnoo
SRCAND	Ternary raster op	0088 00C6	8913094	Dest = source AND dest
SRCCOPY	Ternary raster op	00CC 0020	13369376	Dest = source
SRCERASE	Ternary raster op	0044 0328	4457256	Dest = source AND (not dest)
SRCINVERT	Ternary raster op	0066 0046	6684742	Dest = source XOR dest
SRCPAINT	Ternary raster op	00EE 0086	15597702	Dest = source OR dest
WHITENESS	Ternary raster op	00FF 0062	16711778	Dest = WHITE
TA_BASELINE*	Text alignment option	18	24	
TA_BOTTOM*	Text alignment option	8	8	
TA_CENTER*	Text alignment option	6	6	
TA_LEFT*	Text alignment option	0	0	
TA_NOUPDATECP*	Text alignment option	0	0	

(Continued)

6.042. INCLUDE FILE CONSTANTS DEFINITIONS BY USE (continued)

Defined Name	Used As	Hex Value	Decimal Value	Comments
TA_RIGHT*	Text alignment option	2	2	
TA_TOP*	Text alignment option	0	0	
TA_UPDATECP*	Text alignment option	1	1	
BN_CLICKED	User button notification code	0	0	
BN_DISABLE	User button notification code	4	4	
BN_HILITE	User button notification code	2	2	
BN_PAINT	User button notification code	1	1	
BN_UNHILITE	User button notification code	3	3	
VK_ACCEPT*	Virtual key	1E	30	
VK_CONVERT*	Virtual key	1C	28	
VK_HIRAGANA*	Virtual key	18	24	
VK_KANA*	Virtual key	15	21	
VK_KANJI*	Virtual key	19	25	
VK_MODECHANGE*	Virtual key	1F	31	
VK_NONCONVERT*	Virtual key	1D	29	
VK_ROMAJI*	Virtual key	16	22	
VK_ZENKAKU*	Virtual key	17	23	
S_ALLTHRESHOLD*	WaitSoundState constant	2	2	
S_QUEUEEMPTY	WaitSoundState constant	0	0	
S_THRESHOLD	WaitSoundState constant	1	1	
GWL_EXSTYLE†	Window field offset		-20	
GWL_STYLE	Window field offset		-16	
GWL_WNDPROC	Window field offset		-4	
GWW_HINSTANCE	Window field offset		-6	
GWW_HWNDPARENT	Window field offset		-8	
GWW_HWNDTEXT‡	Window field offset		-10	
GWW_ID	Window field offset		-12	
WH_CBT*	Window hook	5	5	
WH_SYSMSGFILTER*	Window hook	6	6	
WH_WINDOWMGR*	Window hook	7	7	
WC_DEFWINDOWPROC*	Window manager hook code	3	3	
WC_DRAWCAPTION*	Window manager hook code	7	7	
WC_INIT*	Window manager hook code	1	1	
WC_MINMAX*	Window manager hook code	4	4	
WC_MOVE*	Window manager hook code	5	5	
WC_SIZE*	Window manager hook code	6	6	
WC_SWP*	Window manager hook code	2	2	
WM_ACTIVATE	Window procedure message ID	6	6	
WM_ACTIVATEAPP	Window procedure message ID	1C	28	
WM_ASKCBFORMATNAME	Window procedure message ID	30C	780	
WM_CANCELMODE	Window procedure message ID	1F	31	
WM_CHANGECBCHAIN	Window procedure message ID	30D	781	
WM_CHAR	Window procedure message ID	102	258	
WM_CHARTOITEM†	Window procedure message ID	2F	47	
WM_CHILDACTIVATE*	Window procedure message ID	22	34	
WM_CLEAR	Window procedure message ID	303	771	
WM_CLOSE	Window procedure message ID	10	16	
WM_COMMAND	Window procedure message ID	111	273	
WM_COMPACTING†	Window procedure message ID	41	65	
WM_COMPAREITEM†	Window procedure message ID	39	57	
WM_CONVERTREQUEST	Window procedure message ID	10A	266	
WM_CONVERTRESULT	Window procedure message ID	10B	267	
WM_COPY	Window procedure message ID	301	769	
WM_CREATE	Window procedure message ID	1	1	
WM_CTLCOLOR	Window procedure message ID	19	25	
WM_CUT	Window procedure message ID	300	768	
WM_DEADCHAR	Window procedure message ID	103	259	
WM_DELETEITEM†	Window procedure message ID	2D	45	
WM_DESTROY	Window procedure message ID	2	2	
WM_DESTROYCLIPBOARD	Window procedure message ID	307	775	
WM_DEVMODECHANGE	Window procedure message ID	1B	27	
WM_DRAWCLIPBOARD	Window procedure message ID	308	776	
WM_DRAWITEM†	Window procedure message ID	2B	43	
WM_ENABLE	Window procedure message ID	0A	10	
WM_ENDSESSION	Window procedure message ID	16	22	
WM_ENTERIDLE	Window procedure message ID	121	289	
WM_ERASEBKGND	Window procedure message ID	14	20	
WM_FONTCHANGE	Window procedure message ID	1D	29	
WM_GETDLGCODE	Window procedure message ID	87	135	
WM_GETFONT†	Window procedure message ID	31	49	
WM_GETMINMAXINFO*	Window procedure message ID	24	36	
WM_GETTEXT	Window procedure message ID	D	13	
WM_GETTEXTLENGTH	Window procedure message ID	E	14	
WM_HSCROLL	Window procedure message ID	114	276	
WM_HSCROLLCLIPBOARD	Window procedure message ID	30E	782	

(Continued)

6.042. INCLUDE FILE CONSTANTS DEFINITIONS BY USE (continued)

Defined Name	Used As	Hex Value	Decimal Value	Comments
WM_ICONERASEBKGND*	Window procedure message ID	27	39	
WM_INITDIALOG	Window procedure message ID	110	272	
WM_INITMENU	Window procedure message ID	116	278	
WM_INITMENUPOPUP	Window procedure message ID	117	279	
WM_KANJIFIRST‡	Window procedure message ID	280	640	
WM_KANJILAST‡	Window procedure message ID	29F	671	
WM_KEYDOWN	Window procedure message ID	100	256	
WM_KEYFIRST	Window procedure message ID	100	256	
WM_KEYLAST†	Window procedure message ID	108	264	
WM_KEYUP	Window procedure message ID	101	257	
WM_KILLFOCUS	Window procedure message ID	8	8	
WM_LBUTTONDBLCLK	Window procedure message ID	203	515	
WM_LBUTTONDOWN	Window procedure message ID	201	513	
WM_LBUTTONUP	Window procedure message ID	202	514	
WM_MBUTTONDBLCLK	Window procedure message ID	209	521	
WM_MBUTTONDOWN	Window procedure message ID	207	519	
WM_MBUTTONUP	Window procedure message ID	208	520	
WM_MDIACTIVATE†	Window procedure message ID	222	546	
WM_MDICASCADE†	Window procedure message ID	227	551	
WM_MDICREATE†	Window procedure message ID	220	544	
WM_MDIDESTROY†	Window procedure message ID	221	545	
WM_MDIGETACTIVE†	Window procedure message ID	229	553	
WM_MDIICONARRANGE†	Window procedure message ID	228	552	
WM_MDIMAXIMIZE†	Window procedure message ID	225	549	
WM_MDINEXT†	Window procedure message ID	224	548	
WM_MDIRESTORE†	Window procedure message ID	223	547	
WM_MDISETMENU†	Window procedure message ID	230	560	
WM_MDITILE†	Window procedure message ID	226	550	
WM_MEASUREITEM†	Window procedure message ID	2C	44	
WM_MENUCHAR*	Window procedure message ID	120	45	
WM_MENUSELECT*	Window procedure message ID	11F	46	
WM_MOUSEACTIVATE*	Window procedure message ID	21	33	
WM_MOUSEFIRST	Window procedure message ID	200	512	
WM_MOUSELAST	Window procedure message ID	209	521	
WM_MOUSEMOVE	Window procedure message ID	200	512	
WM_MOVE	Window procedure message ID	3	3	
WM_NCACTIVATE	Window procedure message ID	86	134	
WM_NCCALCSIZE	Window procedure message ID	83	131	
WM_NCCREATE	Window procedure message ID	81	129	
WM_NCDESTROY	Window procedure message ID	82	130	
WM_NCHITTEST	Window procedure message ID	84	132	
WM_NCLBUTTONDBLCLK	Window procedure message ID	A3	163	
WM_NCLBUTTONDOWN	Window procedure message ID	A1	161	
WM_NCLBUTTONUP	Window procedure message ID	A2	162	
WM_NCMBUTTONDBLCLK	Window procedure message ID	A9	169	
WM_NCMBUTTONDOWN	Window procedure message ID	A7	167	
WM_NCMBUTTONUP	Window procedure message ID	A8	168	
WM_NCMOUSEMOVE	Window procedure message ID	A0	160	
WM_NCPAINT	Window procedure message ID	85	133	
WM_NCRBUTTONDBLCLK	Window procedure message ID	A6	166	
WM_NCRBUTTONDOWN	Window procedure message ID	A4	164	
WM_NCRBUTTONUP	Window procedure message ID	A5	165	
WM_NEXTDLGCTL*	Window procedure message ID	28	40	
WM_NULL	Window procedure message ID	0	0	
WM_PAINT	Window procedure message ID	F	15	
WM_PAINTCLIPBOARD	Window procedure message ID	309	777	
WM_PAINTICON*	Window procedure message ID	26	38	
WM_PALETTECHANGED†	Window procedure message ID	311	785	
WM_PALETTEISCHANGING†	Window procedure message ID	310	784	
WM_PARENTNOTIFY†	Window procedure message ID	210	528	
WM_PASTE	Window procedure message ID	302	770	
WM_QUERYDRAGICON†	Window procedure message ID	37	55	
WM_QUERYENDSESSION	Window procedure message ID	11	17	
WM_QUERYNEWPALETTE†	Window procedure message ID	30F	783	
WM_QUERYOPEN	Window procedure message ID	13	19	
WM_QUEUESYNC*	Window procedure message ID	23	35	
WM_QUIT	Window procedure message ID	12	18	
WM_RBUTTONDBLCKL	Window procedure message ID	206	518	
WM_RBUTTONDOWN	Window procedure message ID	204	516	
WM_RBUTTONUP	Window procedure message ID	205	517	
WM_RENDERALLFORMATS	Window procedure message ID	306	774	
WM_RENDERFORMAT	Window procedure message ID	305	773	
WM_SETCURSOR*	Window procedure message ID	20	32	
WM_SETFOCUS	Window procedure message ID	7	7	
WM_SETFONT†	Window procedure message ID	30	48	

(Continued)

6.042. INCLUDE FILE CONSTANTS DEFINITIONS BY USE (continued)

Defined Name	*Used As*	*Hex Value*	*Decimal Value*	*Comments*
WM_SETREDRAW	Window procedure message ID	B	11	
WM_SETTEXT	Window procedure message ID	C	12	
WM_SETVISIBLE‡	Window procedure message ID	9	9	
WM_SHOWWINDOW	Window procedure message ID	18	24	
WM_SIZE	Window procedure message ID	5	5	
WM_SIZECLIPBOARD	Window procedure message ID	30B	779	
WM_SIZEWAIT‡	Window procedure message ID	4	4	
WM_SPOOLERSTATUS	Window procedure message ID	2A	42	
WM_SYNCPAINT‡	Window procedure message ID	88	136	
WM_SYNCTASK‡	Window procedure message ID	89	137	
WM_SYSCHAR	Window procedure message ID	106	262	
WM_SYSCOLORCHANGE	Window procedure message ID	15	21	
WM_SYSCOMMAND	Window procedure message ID	112	274	
WM_SYSDEADCHAR	Window procedure message ID	107	263	
WM_SYSKEYDOWN	Window procedure message ID	104	260	
WM_SYSKEYUP	Window procedure message ID	105	261	
WM_SYSTEMERROR‡	Window procedure message ID	17	23	
WM_SYSTIMER‡	Window procedure message ID	118	280	
WM_TIMECHANGE	Window procedure message ID	1E	30	
WM_TIMER	Window procedure message ID	113	275	
WM_UNDO	Window procedure message ID	304	772	
WM_USER	Window procedure message ID	400	1024	First application window message
WM_VKEYTOITEM†	Window procedure message ID	2E	46	
WM_VSCROLL	Window procedure message ID	115	277	
WM_VSCROLLCLIPBOARD	Window procedure message ID	30A	778	
WM_WININICHANGE	Window procedure message ID	1A	26	
WM_YOMICHAR‡	Window procedure message ID	108	264	
WS_BORDER	Window style	0080 0000	8388608	
WS_CAPTION	Window style	00C0 0000	12582912	
WS_CHILD	Window style	4000 0000	1073741824	
WS_CHILDWINDOW*	Window style	4000 0000	1073741824	WS_CHILD
WS_CLIPCHILDREN	Window style	0200 0000	33554432	
WS_CLIPSIBLINGS	Window style	0400 0000	67108864	
WS_DISABLED	Window style	0800 0000	134217728	
WS_DLGFRAME	Window style	0040 0000	4194304	
WS_EX_DLGMODALFRAME†	Window style	1	1	
WS_EX_NOPARENTNOTIFY†	Window style	4	4	
WS_GROUP	Window style	0002 0000	131072	
WS_HSCROLL	Window style	0010 0000	1048576	
WS_ICONIC	Window style	2000 0000	536870912	Defined as WS_MINIMIZE
WS_ICONICPOPUP‡	Window style	C000 0000	3221225472	
WS_MAXIMIZE*	Window style	0100 0000	16777216	
WS_MAXIMIZEBOX*	Window style	0001 0000	65536	
WS_MINIMIZE	Window style	2000 0000	536870912	
WS_MINIMIZEBOX*	Window style	0002 0000	131072	
WS_OVERLAPPED*	Window style	0	0	
WS_OVERLAPPEDWINDOW*	Window style	00CC 0000	13369344	WS_OVERLAPPED§§
WS_POPUP	Window style	8000 0000	-2147483648	
WS_POPUPWINDOW*	Window style	8088 0000	2156396544	WS_POPUP | WS_BORDER¥¥
WS_SIZEBOX	Window style	0004 0000	262144	WS_THICKFRAME
WS_SYSMENU	Window style	0008 0000	524288	
WS_TABSTOP	Window style	0001 0000	65536	
WS_THICKFRAME*	Window style	0004 0000	262144	
WS_TILED	Window style	0	0	WS_OVERLAPPED
WS_TILEDWINDOW*	Window style	00CC 0000	13369344	WS_OVERLAPPEDWINDOW
WS_VISIBLE	Window style	1000 0000	268435456	
WS_VSCROLL	Window style	0020 0000	2097152	
HELP_CONTENT†	WinHelp command	1	1	
HELP_HELPONHELP†	WinHelp command	4	4	
HELP_INDEX†	WinHelp command	3	3	
HELP_KEY†	WinHelp command	101	257	
HELP_MULTIKEY†	WinHelp command	201	513	
HELP_QUIT†	WinHelp command	2	2	
HELP_SETINDEX†	WinHelp command	5	5	
HTBOTTOM*	WinWhere area code	F	15	
HTBOTTOMLEFT*	WinWhere area code	10	16	
HTBOTTOMRIGHT*	WinWhere area code	11	17	
HTCAPTION	WinWhere area code	2	2	
HTCLIENT	WinWhere area code	1	1	
HTERROR	WinWhere area code		-2	
HTGROWBOX	WinWhere area code	4	4	
HTHSCROLL	WinWhere area code	6	6	
HTLEFT*	WinWhere area code	A	10	
HTMENU	WinWhere area code	5	5	
HTNOWHERE	WinWhere area code	0	0	

(Continued)

6.042. INCLUDE FILE CONSTANTS DEFINITIONS BY USE (continued)

Defined Name	Used As	Hex Value	Decimal Value	Comments
HTREDUCE*	WinWhere area code	8	8	
HTRIGHT*	WinWhere area code	B	11	
HTSIZE*	WinWhere area code	4	4	HTGROWBOX
HTSIZEFIRST*	WinWhere area code	A	10	HTLEFT
HTSIZELAST*	WinWhere area code	11	17	HTBOTTOMRIGHT
HTSYSMENU	WinWhere area code	3	3	
HTTOP*	WinWhere area code	C	12	
HTTOPLEFT*	WinWhere area code	D	13	
HTTOPRIGHT*	WinWhere area code	E	14	
HTTRANSPARENT	WinWhere area code		-1	
HTVSCROLL	WinWhere area code	7	7	
HTZOOM*	WinWhere area code	9	9	
ASPECT_FILTERING		1	1	
DC_HASDEFID		0x534B	21323	
DEFAULT_PALETTE		F	15	
DLGWINDOWEXTRA		1E	30	
ST_BEGINSWP*		0	0	
ST_ENDSWP*		1	1	

*Applies to all versions of Windows beginning with 2.0.
†Applies to all versions of Windows beginning with 3.0.
§Pre-3.0 versions of these calls have had OLD added to name (e.g., OBM_OLD_CLOSE).
‡Not in Windows 3.0
**And WS_VSCROLL | WS_BORDER
††And LMEM_ZEROINIT
§§And WS_SYSMENU
¥¥And WS_CAPTION | WS_SYSMENU | WS_THICKFRAME | WS_MINIMIZEBOX | WS_MAXIMIZEBOX

Source: WINDOWS.H file in development kit

See Also: 6.041. Include File Constants Definitions by Name

6.043. BITMAP STRUCTURE FORMAT

Field Type	Argument Type	Description	Restrictions on Allowable Values
Short	bmType	Bitmap type	Must be 0 for logical bitmaps
Short	bmWidth	Width of bitmap in pixels	Must be greater than 0
Short	bmHeight	Height of bitmap in raster lines	Must be greater than 0
Short	bmWidthBytes	Number of bytes per raster line	Must be an even number
BYTE	bmPlanes	Points to number of color planes in bitmap	
BYTE	bmBitsPixel	Points to number of adjacent color bits on each plane	
LPSTR	bmBits	Points to bitmap	Pointer to array of BYTE values comprising bitmap

Note: In monochrome bitmap, a one-bit, one-plane format is used; bit=1 means pixel is white (on).

Source: Microsoft Windows 2.0 SDK Programmer's Reference, pages 609 through 611
Microsoft Windows 3.0 SDK Programmer's Reference, pages 7-6 through 7-7

See Also: 1.17. Common String Formats
6.039. Data Types Available as C Keywords
6.040. Windows Handle and Pointer Types

6.044. BITMAPCOREHEADER STRUCTURE FORMAT

Field Type	*Argument Type*	*Description*	*Restrictions on Allowable Values*
DWORD	bcSize	Number of bytes in structure	
WORD	bcWidth	Width of bitmap in pixels	
WORD	bcHeight	Height of bitmap in pixels	
WORD	bcPlanes	Number of planes for target device	Must be set to 1
WORD	bcBitCount	Number of bits per pixel	Must be 1, 4, 8, or 24

Version: Applies to all versions of Windows beginning with 3.0.

Note: Device-independent bitmap is compatible with OS/2 Presentation Manager version 1.1 and 1.2 bitmaps.

Source: Microsoft Windows 3.0 SDK Programmer's Reference, pages 7-7 through 7-8

See Also: 1.17. Common String Formats
6.039. Data Types Available as C Keywords
6.040. Windows Handle and Pointer Types

6.045. BITMAPCOREINFO STRUCTURE FORMAT

Field Type	*Argument Type*	*Description*	*Restrictions on Allowable Values*
BITMAPCOREHEADER	bmciHeader[]	Dimensions and color format of bitmap	See 6.044. BITMAPCOREHEADER Structure Format
RGBTRIPLE	bmciColors[]	Array of color data structures	Colors should appear in order of importance

Version: Applies to all versions of Windows beginning with 3.0.

Note: Device-independent bitmap is compatible with OS/2 Presentation Manager version 1.1 and 1.2 bitmaps.

Source: Microsoft Windows 3.0 SDK Programmer's Reference, pages 7-8 through 7-9

See Also: 1.17. Common String Formats
6.039. Data Types Available as C Keywords
6.040. Windows Handle and Pointer Types
6.044. BITMAPCOREHEADER Structure Format
6.079. RGBTRIPLE Structure Format

6.046. BITMAPFILEHEADER STRUCTURE FORMAT

Field Type	*Argument Type*	*Description*	*Restrictions on Allowable Values*
WORD	bfType	Type of file	Must be BM
DWORD	bfSize	Size of file	Specified in DWORDs
WORD	bfReserved1	RESERVED	Must be set to 0
WORD	bfReserved2	RESERVED	Must be set to 0
DWORD	bfOffBits	Offset to beginning of bitmap	Specified in bytes

Version: Applies to all versions of Windows beginning with 3.0.

Note: A BITMAPINFO or BITMAPCOREINFO data structure immediately follows this structure in a DIB file.

Source: Microsoft Windows 3.0 SDK Programmer's Reference, page 7-10

See Also: 1.17. Common String Formats
6.039. Data Types Available as C Keywords
6.040. Windows Handle and Pointer Types
6.047. BITMAPINFO Structure Format
6.045. BITMAPCOREINFO Structure Format

6.047. BITMAPINFO STRUCTURE FORMAT

Field Type	Argument Type	Description	Restrictions on Allowable Values
BITMAPINFOHEADER	bmiHeader	Dimensions and color format of bitmap	See 6.048. BITMAPINFOHEADER Structure Format
RGBQUAD	bmiColors[1]	Array of color data structures	Colors should appear in order of importance

Version: Applies to all versions of Windows beginning with 3.0.

Source: Microsoft Windows 3.0 SDK Programmer's Reference, pages 7-10 through 7-12

See Also:
1.17. Common String Formats
6.039. Data Types Available as C Keywords
6.040. Windows Handle and Pointer Types
6.048. BITMAPINFOHEADER Structure Format
6.078. RGBQUAD Structure Format

6.048. BITMAPINFOHEADER STRUCTURE FORMAT

Field Type	Argument Type	Description	Restrictions on Allowable Values
DWORD	biSize	Number of bytes required by BITMAPINFOHEADER	
DWORD	biWidth	Width of bitmap in pixels	
DWORD	biHeight	Height of bitmap in pixels	
WORD	biPlanes	Number of planes for target device	Must be set to 1
WORD	biBitCount	Number of bits per pixel	Must be 1, 4, 8, or 24
DWORD	biCompression	Specifies type of compression to use	BI_RGB=not compressed BI_RLE8=run length encoded, 8 bits/pixel BI_RLE4=run length encoded, 4 bits/pixel
DWORD	biSizeImage	Size of image, in bytes	
DWORD	biXPelsPerMeter	Horizontal resolution of target device	In pixels per meter
DWORD	biYPelsPerMeter	Vertical resolution of target device	In pixels per meter
DWORD	biClrUsed	Number of color indexes in color table	0=maximum (i.e., biBitCount)
DWORD	biClrImportant	Number of color indexes important to display bitmap	0=all colors are important

Version: Applies to all versions of Windows beginning with 3.0.

Source: Microsoft Windows 3.0 SDK Programmer's Reference, pages 7-12 through 7-16

See Also:
1.17. Common String Formats
6.039. Data Types Available as C Keywords
6.040. Windows Handle and Pointer Types
6.047. BITMAPINFO Structure Format

6.049. CLIENTCREATESTRUCT STRUCTURE FORMAT

Field Type	Argument Type	Description
HMENU	hWindowMenu	Handle of application's Window menu
WORD	idFirstChild	First child window ID created

Version: Applies to all versions of Windows beginning with 3.0.

Source: Microsoft Windows 3.0 SDK Programmer's Reference, pages 7-16 through 7-17

See Also:
1.17. Common String Formats
6.039. Data Types Available as C Keywords
6.040. Windows Handle and Pointer Types

6.050. COMPAREITEMSTRUCT STRUCTURE FORMAT

Field Type	Argument Type	Description	Restrictions on Allowable Values
WORD	CtlType	Type of box to be drawn	ODT_LISTBOX or ODT_COMBOBOX
WORD	CtlID	Control ID for box	
HWND	hwndItem	Window handle of the control	
WORD	itemID1	Index of first item in box	
DWORD	itemData1	Application-supplied data for first item	
WORD	itemID2	Index of second item in box	
DWORD	itemData2	Application-supplied data for second item	

Version: Applies to all versions of Windows beginning with 3.0.

Source: Microsoft Windows 3.0 SDK Programmer's Reference, pages 7-19 through 7-20

See Also: 1.17. Common String Formats
6.039. Data Types Available as C Keywords
6.040. Windows Handle and Pointer Types

6.051. COMSTAT STRUCTURE FORMAT

Field Type	Argument Type	Description
BYTE:1	fCtsHold	Waiting for CTS?
BYTE:1	fDsrHold	Waiting for DSR?
BYTE:1	fRlsdHold	Waiting for received signal detect?
BYTE:1	fXoffHold	Waiting due to received XOFF?
BYTE:1	fXoffSent	Waiting due to sent XOFF?
BYTE:1	fEof	Has EOF been received?
BYTE:1	fTxim	Character waiting for xmit?
WORD	cbInQue	Number of characters in receive queue
WORD	cbOutQue	Number of characters in transmit queue

Version: Applies to all versions of Windows beginning with 2.0.

Source: Microsoft Windows 2.0 SDK Programmer's Reference, pages 611 through 612
Microsoft Windows 3.0 SDK Programmer's Reference, pages 7-20 through 7-21

See Also: 6.039. Data Types Available as C Keywords

6.052. CREATESTRUCT STRUCTURE FORMAT

Field Type	Argument Type	Description	Restrictions on Allowable Values
LPSTR	lpCreateParams	Pointer to data for window creation	
HANDLE	hInstance	Module instance handle of module owning new window	
HANDLE	hMenu	Handle of menu to be used by new window	
HWND	hwndParent	Window handle of window opening the new window	NULL=top-level window
int	cy	Height of new window	
int	cx	Width of new window	
int	y	y coordinate of upper-left corner of new window	Relative to parent (if new is child)
int	x	x coordinate of upper-left corner of new window	Relative to parent (if new is child)
long	style	New window's style	
LPSTR	lpszName	New window's name	Pointer to ASCIIZ string
LPSTR	lpszClass	New window's class name	Pointer to ASCIIZ string
long	ExStyle*	Extended style for new window	

*Argument added with Windows 3.0.

Version: Applies to all versions of Windows beginning with 2.0.

Source: Microsoft Windows 2.0 SDK Programmer's Reference, pages 612 through 613
Microsoft Windows 3.0 SDK Programmer's Reference, pages 7-21 through 7-22

See Also: 1.17. Common String Formats
6.039. Data Types Available as C Keywords

6.053. DCB STRUCTURE FORMAT

Field Type	Argument Type	Description	Restrictions on Allowable Values
BYTE	Id	Communication device ID	Set by device driver; sig. bit set=parallel device
WORD	BaudRate	Baud rate	
BYTE	ByteSize	Number of bits in transmitted char	Must in range 4 to 8
BYTE	Parity	Parity scheme to use	Must be one of: NOPARITY (0) ODDPARITY (1) EVENPARITY (2) MARKPARITY (3) SPACEPARITY (4)
BYTE	StopBits	Number of stop bits in transmitted char	Must be one of: ONESTOPBIT (0) ONE5STOPBITS (1) TWOSTOPBITS (2)
WORD	RlsTimeout	Milliseconds to wait for CD to go high	
WORD	CtsTimeout	Milliseconds to wait for CTS to go high	
WORD	DsrTimeout	Milliseconds to wait for DSR to go high	
BYTE	Bit 7:fBinary Bit 6:fRtsDisable Bit 5:fParity Bit 4:fOutxCtsFlow Bit 3:fOutxDsrFlow Bits 1-2: fDummy Bit 0:fDtrDisable	Is binary mode? Is RTS disabled? Is parity checking enabled? Monitor CTS for output flow control? Monitor DSR for output flow control? Place holder only Is DTR enabled?	0=ASCII mode; 1=binary mode 0=RTS enabled; 1=RTS disabled 0=parity not checked; 1=parity enabled 0=don't monitor CTS; 1=monitor CTS 0=don't monitor DSR; 1=monitor DSR 0=DTR enabled; 1=DTR not enabled
BYTE	Bit 7:fOutX Bit 6:fInX Bit 5:fPeChar Bit 4:fNull Bit 3:fChEvt Bit 2:fDtrFlow Bit 1:fRtsFlow Bit 0:fDummy2	Use XON/XOFF during transmission? Use XON/XOFF during reception? Replace parity chars with PeChar? Discard NULL characters? Flag EvtChar as an event? Monitor DTR for input flow control? Monitor RTS for input flow control? Place holder only	0=don't use; 1=use XON/XOFF 0=don't use; 1=use XON/XOFF 0=don't replace; 1=replace chars with parity error 0=don't discard; 1=discard NULL characters 0=don't flag; 1=EvtChar indicates event 0=don't monitor DTR; 1=monitor DTR 0=don't monitor RTS; 1=monitor RTS
char	XonChar	XON character for transmit & receive	ASCII value
char	XoffChar	XOFF character for transmit & receive	ASCII value
WORD	XonLim	Min. chars in receive queue before XON	
WORD	XoffLim	Max. chars in receive queue before XOFF	
char	PeChar	Character that replaces parity errors	ASCII value
char	EofChar	Character that signals an event	ASCII value
char	EvtChar	Character that signals end-of-data	ASCII value
WORD	TxDelay	Min. milliseconds between transmissions	

Version: Applies to all versions of Windows beginning with 2.0.

Note: Numbers in parentheses show actual values.

Source: Microsoft Windows 2.0 SDK Programmer's Reference, pages 613 through 617
Microsoft Windows 3.0 SDK Programmer's Reference, pages 7-22 through 7-26

See Also: 1.17. Common String Formats

6.054. DELETEITEMSTRUCT STRUCTURE FORMAT

Field Type	Argument Type	Description	Restrictions on Allowable Values
WORD	CtlType	Type of control	ODT_LISTBOX or ODT_COMBOBOX
WORD	CtlID	Control ID for box	
WORD	itemID	Index of item being removed	
HWND	hwndItem	Window handle of control	
DWORD	itemData	Value passed to control in lParam	

Version: Applies to all versions of Windows beginning with 3.0.

Source: Microsoft Windows 3.0 SDK Programmer's Reference, pages 7-26 through 7-27

6.055. DEVMODE STRUCTURE FORMAT

Field Type	*Argument Type*	*Description*	*Restrictions on Allowable Values*
char	dmDeviceName[32]	Name of the device driver supports	
WORD	dmSpecVersion	Version number of init data of structure	0x300
WORD	dmDriverVersion	Printer driver version number	
WORD	dmSize	Size of DEVMODE structure	In bytes
WORD	dmDriverExtra	Size of dmDriverData field	
DWORD	dmFields	Specifies which fields in DEVMODE have been initialized	
short	dmOrientation	Paper orientation	DMORIENT_PORTRAIT or DMORIENT_LANDSCAPE
short	dmPaperSize	Size of paper to print on	DMPAPER_LETTER = 8.5 x 11" DMPAPER_LEGAL = 8.5 x 14" DMPAPER_A4 = 210 x 297 mm DMPAPER_CSHEET = 17 x 22" DMPAPER_DSHEET = 22 x 34" DMPAPER_ESHEET = 34 x 44" DMPAPER_ENV_9 = #9 envelope DMPAPER_ENV_10 = #10 envelope DMPAPER_ENV_11 = #11 envelope DMPAPER_ENV_12 = #12 envelope DMPAPER_ENV_14 = #14 envelope
short	dmPaperLength	Override for paper length, if necessary	In tenths of a millimeter
short	dmPaperWidth	Override for paper width, if necessary	In tenths of a millimeter
short	dmScale	Scaling factor	
short	dmCopies	Number of copies to print	
short	dmDefaultSource	Paper bin	DMBIN_DEFAULT DMBIN_UPPER DMBIN_LOWER DMBIN_MANUAL DMBIN_TRACTOR DMBIN_ENVELOPE
short	dmPrintQuality	Printer resolution	DMRES_HIGH (-4) DMRES_MEDIUM (-3) DMRES_LOW (-2) DMRES_DRAFT (-1)
short	dmColor	Monochrome or color output	DMCOLOR_COLOR (1) DMCOLOR_MONOCHROME (2)
short	dmDuplex	Duplex printing	DMDUP_SIMPLEX (1) DMDUP_HORIZONTAL (2) DMDUP_VERTICAL (3)
BYTE	dmDriverData[]	Device-specific data	Defined by device driver

Version: Applies to all versions of Windows beginning with 3.0.

Note: Numbers in parentheses are actual values.

Source: Microsoft Windows 3.0 SDK Programmer's Reference, pages 7-27 through 7-30

6.056. DLGTEMPLATE STRUCTURE FORMAT

DLGTEMPLATE Header

Field Type	*Argument Type*	*Description*	*Restrictions on Allowable Values*
long	dtStyle	Style of dialog box	DS_LOCALEDIT DS_SYSMODAL DS_MODALFRAME DS_ABSALIGN DS_SETFONT DS_NOIDLEMSG
BYTE	dtItemCount	Number of items in dialog box (controls)	Max 255
int	dtX	x-coordinate of upper-left corner of box	In units of 1/4 base width unit
int	dtY	y-coordinate of upper-left corner of box	In units of 1/8 base height unit
int	dtCX	x-extent of the dialog box	In units of 1/4 base width unit
int	dtCY	y-extent of the dialog box	In units of 1/8 base height unit
char	dtMenuName[]	Name of dialog box's menu	ASCIIZ string
char	dtClassName[]	Dialog's class name	ASCIIZ string
char	dtCaptionText[]	Caption string for dialog box	ASCIIZ string

Font Information Data Structure (optional) follows header, as follows:

Field Type	*Argument Type*	*Description*	*Restrictions on Allowable Values*
short int	PointSize	Size of dialog's typeface	In points
char	szTypeFace[]	Name of typeface	ASCIIZ string

Item List (of Controls) follows font information, with each item containing:

Field Type	*Argument Type*	*Description*	*Restrictions on Allowable Values*
int	dtilX	x-coordinate of upper-left corner of item	(Relative to origin of box) In units of 1/4 base width unit
int	dtilY	y-coordinate of upper-left corner of item	(Relative to origin of box) In units of 1/8 base height unit
int	dtilCX	x-extent of item	In units of 1/4 base width unit
int	dtilCY	y-extent of item	In units of 1/8 base height unit
int	dtilID	Dialog item ID number	
long	dtilStyle	Style of the dialog item	
char	dtilClass[]*	Control's class	ASCIIZ string; one of: BUTTON, EDIT, STATIC, LISTBOX, SCROLLBAR, COMBOBOX
char	dtilText	Text for the item (if any)	ASCIIZ string
BYTE	dtilInfo	Number of bytes to next item in structure	
PTR	dtilData*	Pointer to additional data for CreateWindow	

*Added in Windows 3.0.

Version: Applies to all versions of Windows beginning with 2.0.

Note: dtMenuName was dtResourceName in Windows 2.x.

Source: Microsoft Windows 2.0 SDK Programmer's Reference, pages 617 through 618
Microsoft Windows 3.0 SDK Programmer's Reference, pages 7-31 through 7-35

6.057. DRAWITEMSTRUCT STRUCTURE FORMAT

Field Type	*Argument Type*	*Description*	*Restrictions on Allowable Values*
WORD	CtlType	Type of control	ODT_BUTTON ODT_COMBOBOX ODT_LISTBOX ODT_MENU
WORD	CtlID	ID for control	
WORD	itemID	ID for menu, or index of item in list/combo box	-1 for empty list or combo box allowed
WORD	itemAction	Drawing action required	ODA_DRAWENTIRE ODA_FOCUS ODA_SELECT
WORD	itemState	Visual state of item after drawing	ODS_CHECKED ODS_DISABLED ODS_FOCUS ODS_GRAYED ODS_SELECTED
HWND	hwndItem	Window handle of control, or menu handle	
HDC	hDC	Device context for drawing	
RECT	rcItem	Boundaries of control to be drawn	
DWORD	itemData	lParam parameter for list/combo box, lpNewItem parameter for menus	

Version: Applies to all versions of Windows beginning with 3.0.

Source: Microsoft Windows 3.0 SDK Programmer's Reference, pages 7-36 through 7-38

6.058. EXTTEXTMETRIC STRUCTURE FORMAT

Field Type	*Argument Type*	*Description*	*Restrictions on Allowable Values*
Short	etmsize	Size of EXTTEXTMETRIC structure	
Short	etmPointSize	Font's point size in twips	
Short	etmOrientation	Font orientation	1=portrait, 2=landscape, 0=either
Short	etmMasterHeight	Font height in device units	
Short	etmMinScale	Mmin range of device units for font	
Short	etmMaxScale	Mmax range of device units for font	
Short	etmMasterUnits	Number of units per em	
Short	etmCapHeight	Height of uppercase letters	In font units, typically height of 'H'
Short	etmXHeight	Height of lowercase letters	In font units, typically height of 'x'
Short	etmLowerCaseAscent	Distance ascenders above baseline	In font units, typically ascent of 'd'
Short	etmUpperCaseDescent	Distance descenders below baseline	In font units, typically descent of 'p'
Short	etmSlant	Angle counterclockwise from vert.	In degrees
Short	etmSuperScript	Distance above baseline	Specified as negative offset
Short	etmSubScript	Distance below baseline	Specified as positive offset
Short	etmSuperScriptSize	Recommended size of superscripts	
Short	etmSubScriptSize	Recommended size of subscripts	
Short	etmUnderlineOffset	Distance below baseline to top of line	
Short	etmUnderlineWidth	Thickness of underline	
Short	etmDoubleUpperUnderlineOffset	Distance below baseline to top of line	
Short	etmDoubleLowerUnderlineOffset	Distance below baseline to top of line	
Short	etmDoubleUpperUnderlineWidth	Thickness of underline	
Short	etmDoubleLowerUnderlineWidth	Thickness of underline	
Short	etmStrikeOutOffset	Distance above baseline to strikeout	
Short	etmStrikeOutWidth	Thickness of strikeout line	
Short	etmNKernPairs	Number of kerned pairs in font	
Short	etmNKernTracks	Number of kerning tracks defined for font	

Version: Applies to Windows 1.0 only.

Source: Microsoft Windows 1.0 Reference Update, pages 46 through 48

6.059. HANDLETABLE STRUCTURE FORMAT

DLGTEMPLATE Header

Field Type	*Argument Type*	*Description*	*Restrictions on Allowable Values*
HANDLE	objectHandle[1]	Array of handles	(Each handle contains address and description of GDI object)

Version: Applies to all versions of Windows beginning with 2.0.

Source: Microsoft Windows 2.0 SDK Programmer's Reference, page 619
Microsoft Windows 3.0 SDK Programmer's Reference, page 7-38

6.060. KERNPAIR STRUCTURE FORMAT

Field Type	*Argument Type*	*Description*	*Restrictions on Allowable Values*
BYTE*	letter1	First letter of kerning pair	ASCII character code
BYTE*	letter2	Second letter of kerning pair	ASCII character code
short	kernAmount	Amount that pair will be kerned	Generally a negative value

*Note that the first two bytes of KERNPAIR are defined as a union, which may contain either two individual bytes, as shown here, or a single WORD, in which case letters are reversed in byte order.

Version: Applies to Windows 1.0 only.

Source: Microsoft Windows 1.0 Reference Update, page 49

See Also: 1.21. ASCII Character Set

6.061. KERNTRACK STRUCTURE FORMAT

Field Type	Argument Type	Description	Restrictions on Allowable Values
Short	degree	Controls amount of track kerning	Increasing negative increases track kerning
Short	minSize	Minimum font size to apply track kerning	
Short	minAmount	Amount of track kerning to apply to fonts smaller than min size	
Short	maxSize	Maximum font size to apply track kerning	
Short	maxAmount	Amount of track kerning to apply to fonts larger than max size	

Version: Applies to Windows 1.0 only.

Source: Microsoft Windows 1.0 Reference Update, pages 50 through 51

See Also: 1.17. Common String Formats

6.062. LOGBRUSH STRUCTURE FORMAT

Field Type	Argument Type	Description	Restrictions on Allowable Values
WORD	lbStyle	Brush style	Must be one of following: BS_SOLID BS_HOLLOW BS_HATCHED BS_PATTERN BS_DIBPATTERN
COLORREF*	lbColor	Brush color	If lbStyle=BS_HOLLOW or BS_PATTERN, lbHatch is ignored If lbStyle=BS_DIBPATTERN: DIB_PAL_COLORS DIB_RBG_COLORS
Short int	lbHatch	Brush hatch style	If lbStyle=BS_SOLID or BS_HOLLOW, lbHatch is ignored If lbStyle=BS_HATCHED: HS_HORIZONTAL ----- HS_VERTICAL ||||| HS_FDIAGONAL ///// HS_BDIAGONAL \\\\\\\\\\ HS_CROSS +++++ HS_DIAGCROSS xxxxx If lbStyle=BS_PATTERN, must be handle to pattern bitmap If lbStyle=BS_DIBPATTERN, must be handle to packed DIB

*Windows 2.0 defines this as a field type of DWORD.

Source: Microsoft Windows 2.0 SDK Programmer's Reference, pages 619 through 620
Microsoft Windows 3.0 SDK Programmer's Reference, pages 7-39 through 7-40

See Also: 1.17. Common String Formats
6.077. RGB and COLORREF Structure Format

6.063. LOGFONT STRUCTURE FORMAT

Field Type	*Argument Type*	*Description*	*Restrictions on Allowable Values*
short int	lfHeight	Font height in user units	0=use reasonable size; <0 transform to device units
short int	lfWidth	Font width in device units	0=match aspect ratio against digitization aspect ratio
short int	lfEscapement	Angle between line origins and x-axis	In tenths of degree; measured counterclockwise from x-axis
short int	lfOrientation	Angle between char baseline and x-axis	In tenths of degree; measured counterclockwise from x-axis
short int	lfWeight	Font weight in inked pixels per 1000	400=normal, 700=bold, 0=use default weight, 1000=max
BYTE	lfItalic	Is font italic?	0=not italic; nonzero = italic
BYTE	lfUnderline	Is font underlined?	0=not underlined; nonzero = underlined
BYTE	lfStrikeOut	Is font struck out?	0=not stricken; nonzero = struck out
BYTE	lfCharSet	Character set to use for font	Must be ANSI-CHARSET, OEM_CHARSET or SYMBOL_CHARSET
BYTE	lfOutPrecision	Font's output precision	Default is OUT_DEFAULT_PRECIS
BYTE	lfClipPrecision	Font's clipping precision	Default is CLIP_DEFAULT_PRECIS
BYTE	lfQuality	Font's output quality	Must be one of: PROOF_QUALITY DRAFT_QUALITY DEFAULT_QUALITY
BYTE	lfPitchAndFamily	Font's pitch and family type	Pitch is indicated by low-order two bits Pitch must be one of: DEFAULT_PITCH FIXED_PITCH VARIABLE_PITCH Font family is indicated by high-order four bits Family must be one of: FF_DONTCARE FF_ROMAN FF_SWISS FF_MODERN FF_SCRIPT FF_DECORATIVE
BYTE	lfFaceName[LF_FACESIZE]	Font's typeface name	ASCIIZ string; if NULL, uses default typeface

Version: Applies to all versions of Windows beginning with 2.0.

Source: Microsoft Windows 2.0 SDK Programmer's Reference, pages 620 through 624
Microsoft Windows 3.0 SDK Programmer's Reference, pages 7-40 through 7-45

6.064. LOGPALETTE STRUCTURE FORMAT

Field Type	*Argument Type*	*Description*	*Restrictions on Allowable Values*
WORD	palVersion	Windows version number of structure	0x300
WORD	palNumEntries	Number of palette entries	
PALETTEENTRY	palPalEntry[]	Array of PALETTEENTRY structures	See 6.074. PALETTEENTRY Structure Format

Version: Applies to all versions of Windows beginning with 3.0.

Source: Microsoft Windows 3.0 SDK Programmer's Reference, page 7-45

See Also: 6.074. PALETTEENTRY Structure Format

6.065. LOGPEN STRUCTURE FORMAT

Field Type	*Argument Type*	*Description*	*Restrictions on Allowable Values*
WORD	lopnStyle	Pen type	Must be one of following: PS_SOLID PS_DASHED PS_DOT PS_DASHDOT PS_DASHDOTDOT PS_NULL PS_INSIDEFRAME *
POINT	lopnWidth	Pen width	In logical units; 0=one pixel on raster devices
COLORREF	lopnColor	Pen color	Must be RGB color value†

*Added in Windows 3.0.
†Windows 2.0 specifies field type as DWORD.

Source: Microsoft Windows 2.0 SDK Programmer's Reference, page 624
Microsoft Windows 3.0 SDK Programmer's Reference, pages 7-45 through 7-46

See Also: 6.077. RGB and COLORREF Structure Format

6.066. MDICREATESTRUCT STRUCTURE FORMAT

Field Type	Argument Type	Description	Restrictions on Allowable Values
LPSTR	szClass	Pointer to app-defined class of MDI child window	
LPSTR	szTitle	Pointer to window title of MDI child window	
HANDLE	hOwner	Instance handle of app creating MDI child window	
int	x	Initial left side of MDI child window	=CW_USEDEFAULT, use default position
int	y	Initial top edge of MDI child window	=CW_USEDEFAULT, use default position
int	cx	Initial width of MDI child window	=CW_USEDEFAULT, use default width
int	cy	Initial height of MDI child window	=CW_USEDEFAULT, use default height
LONG	style	Additional styles for child window	May be: WS_MINIMIZE WS_MAXIMIZE WS_HSCROLL WS_VSCROLL
LONG	lParam	Application-defined value	

Version: Applies to all versions of Windows beginning with 3.0.

Source: Microsoft Windows 3.0 SDK Programmer's Reference, pages 7-47 through 7-48

6.067. MEASUREITEMSTRUCT STRUCTURE FORMAT

Field Type	Argument Type	Description	Restrictions on Allowable Values
WORD	CtlType	Control type	One of: ODT_BUTTON ODT_COMBOBOX ODT_LISTBOX ODT_MENU
WORD	CtlID	Control ID	Not used for menu controls
WORD	itemID	Menu-item ID or list-box item ID	Not used for combo/list boxes or buttons
WORD	itemWidth	Width of menu item	
WORD	itemHeight	Height of item in list box or menu	
DWORD	itemData	Value passed to combo/list box via lParam	One of: CB_ADDSTRING CB_INSERTSTRING LB_ADDSTRING LB_INSERTSTRING

Version: Applies to all versions of Windows beginning with 3.0.

Source: Microsoft Windows 3.0 SDK Programmer's Reference, pages 7-48 through 7-50

6.068. MENUITEMTEMPLATE STRUCTURE FORMAT

Menu-Template Header

Field Type	Argument Type	Description	Restrictions on Allowable Values
WORD	versionNumber	Version number	Should be 0
WORD	offset	Offset to menu-item list	In bytes

Menu-Item List

Field Type	Argument Type	Description	Restrictions on Allowable Values
WORD*	mtOption	Predefined menu option	One of the following options: MF_CHECKED MF_END MF_GRAYED MF_HELP MF_MENUBARBREAK MF_MENUBREAK MF_OWNERDRAW MF_POPUP
WORD	mtID	ID code for menu item	(Must be non-popup menu item)
LPSTR	mtString	Name of menu item	ASCIIZ string

*Windows 2.0 defines this field as a BYTE.

Version: Applies to all versions of Windows beginning with 2.0.

Source: Microsoft Windows 2.0 SDK Programmer's Reference, pages 625 through 626
Microsoft Windows 3.0 SDK Programmer's Reference, pages 7-50 through 7-51

6.069. METAFILEPICT STRUCTURE FORMAT

Field Type	*Argument Type*	*Description*
Int	mm	Mapping mode picture was drawn in
Int	xExt	x width of rectangle for picture*
Int	yExt	y height of rectangle for picture*
HANDLE	hMF	Memory metafile handle

*Except MM_ISOTROPIC and MM_ANISOTROPIC mapping modes

Note:
- xExt and yExt are 0 or suggested size for MM_ANISOTROPIC.
- xExt and yExt are negative values representing aspect ratio for MM_ISOTROPIC (only ratio, not actual values, are used).

Source: Microsoft Windows 2.0 SDK Programmer's Reference, pages 626 through 627
Microsoft Windows 3.0 SDK Programmer's Reference, page 7-52

See Also: 6.016. MetaFile Format

6.070. MSG STRUCTURE FORMAT

Field Type	*Argument Type*	*Description*	*Restrictions on Allowable Values*
HWND	hwnd	Handle to window receiving message	
WORD	message	Message number	
WORD	wParam	Additional info about the message	Exact value depends on message value
LONG	lParam	Additional info about the message	Exact value depends on message value
DWORD	time	Time message posted	
POINT	pt	Position of mouse when message posted	In screen coordinates

Source: Microsoft Windows 2.0 SDK Programmer's Reference, page 627
Microsoft Windows 3.0 SDK Programmer's Reference, page 7-53

6.071. MULTIKEYHELP STRUCTURE FORMAT

Field Type	*Argument Type*	*Description*	*Restrictions on Allowable Values*
WORD	mkSize	Length of the structure	In bytes
BYTE	mkKeylist	Character that identifies key-word table	
BYTE	szKeyphrase[]	Key word to be located	ASCIIZ string

Version: Applies to all versions of Windows beginning with 3.0.

Source: Microsoft Windows 3.0 SDK Programmer's Reference, pages 7-53 through 7-54

6.072. OFSTRUCT STRUCTURE FORMAT

Field Type	*Argument Type*	*Description*	*Restrictions on Allowable Values*
BYTE	cBytes	Length of OFSTRUCT	In bytes
BYTE	fFixedDisk	Is file on fixed disk?	0=not fixed; nonzero=on fixed disk
WORD	nErrCode	DOS error code if open failed	-1
BYTE	RESERVED [4]	RESERVED	
BYTE	szPathName [120]*	File pathname	ASCIIZ string

*Windows 2.0 defines as 128 bytes.

Source: Microsoft Windows 2.0 SDK Programmer's Reference, page 628
Microsoft Windows 3.0 SDK Programmer's Reference, page 7-54

See Also: 1.17. Common String Formats

6.073. PAINTSTRUCT STRUCTURE FORMAT

Field Type	*Argument Type*	*Description*	*Restrictions on Allowable Values*
HDC	hdc	Display context for painting	
BOOL	fErase	Has background been drawn	0=no; nonzero=yes
RECT	rcPaint	Upper-left, lower-right corners of rectangle to paint	
BOOL	fRestore	USED INTERNALLY BY WINDOWS	
BOOL	fIncUpdate	USED INTERNALLY BY WINDOWS	
BYTE	rgbReserved[16]	Block of memory reserved for use by Windows	

Source: Microsoft Windows 2.0 SDK Programmer's Reference, pages 628 through 629
Microsoft Windows 3.0 SDK Programmer's Reference, page 7-55

6.074. PALETTEENTRY STRUCTURE FORMAT

Field Type	*Argument Type*	*Description*	*Restrictions on Allowable Values*
BYTE	peRed	Intensity of red	
BYTE	peGreen	Intensity of green	
BYTE	peBlue	Intensity of blue	
BYTE	peFlags	How palette entry will be used	One of: NULL PC_EXPLICIT PC_NOCOLLAPSE PC_RESERVED

Version: Applies to all versions of Windows beginning with 3.0.

Source: Microsoft Windows 3.0 SDK Programmer's Reference, pages 7-55 through 7-56

6.075. POINT STRUCTURE FORMAT

Field Type	*Argument Type*	*Description*
int	x	x-coordinate value of a point
int	y	y-coordinate value of a point

Source: Microsoft Windows 2.0 SDK Programmer's Reference, page 629
Microsoft Windows 3.0 SDK Programmer's Reference, pages 7-56 through 7-57

6.076. RECT STRUCTURE FORMAT

Field Type	*Argument Type*	*Description*
int	Left	x-coordinate of upper-left corner of rectangle
int	Top	y-coordinate of upper-left corner of rectangle
int	Right	x-coordinate of lower-right corner of rectangle
int	Bottom	y-coordinate of lower-right corner of rectangle

Note: The width of a rectangle (right-left) must not exceed 32,768 units.

Source: Microsoft Windows 2.0 SDK Programmer's Reference, page 630
Microsoft Windows 3.0 SDK Programmer's Reference, page 7-57

6.077. RGB AND COLORREF STRUCTURE FORMAT

Format of the long integer that constitutes a RGB or COLORREF depends upon use, as follows:

RGB Structure Format

Byte 3	2	1	0	*Description*	*Allowable Values*
X				NOT USED	Must be 00H
	X			Blue intensity of color	0=no blue; 0FFH=maximum blue
		X		Green intensity of color	0=no green; 0FFH=maximum green
			X	Red intensity of color	0=no red; 0FFH=maximum red

Palette Index Structure Format

Byte 3	2	1	0	*Description*	*Allowable Values*
X				Index identifier	Must be 01
	X			UNUSED	Must be 00
		X	X	Index into logical palette	

Palette-Relative RGB Structure Format

Byte 3	2	1	0	*Description*	*Allowable Values*
X				Identifier	Must be 02H
	X			Blue intensity to match	
		X		Green intensity to match	
			X	Red intensity to match	

Version: •RGB applies to Windows versions 1.0 and 2.0.
•COLORREF applies to Windows 3.0 and later.

Note: Black is defined as 0000 0000H; white is defined as 00FF FFFFH; medium gray is defined as 0080 8080H.

Source: Microsoft Windows 2.0 SDK Programmer's Reference, page 630
Microsoft Windows 3.0 SDK Programmer's Reference, pages 7-17 through 7-19

6.078. RGBQUAD STRUCTURE FORMAT

Field Type	*Argument Type*	*Description*
BYTE	rgbBlue	Blue intensity of color
BYTE	rgbGreen	Green intensity of color
BYTE	rgbRed	Red intensity of color
BYTE	rgbReserved	RESERVED, must be 0

Version: Applies to all versions of Windows beginning with 3.0.

Source: Microsoft Windows 3.0 SDK Programmer's Reference, page 7-58

See Also: 6.077. RGB and COLORREF Structure Format
6.079. RGBTRIPLE Structure Format

6.079. RGBTRIPLE STRUCTURE FORMAT

Field Type	*Argument Type*	*Description*
BYTE	rgbBlue	Blue intensity of color
BYTE	rgbGreen	Green intensity of color
BYTE	rgbRed	Red intensity of color

Version: Applies to all versions of Windows beginning with 3.0.

Source: Microsoft Windows 3.0 SDK Programmer's Reference, page 7-58 through 7-59

See Also: 6.077. RGB and COLORREF Structure Format
6.078. RGBQUAD Structure Format

6.080. TEXTMETRIC STRUCTURE FORMAT

Field Type	Argument Type	Description	Restrictions on Allowable Values
short int	tmHeight	Height of characters (ascent+descent)	
short int	tmAscent	Ascent of characters above baseline	
short int	tmDescent	Descent of characters below baseline	
short int	tmInternalLeading	Amount of leading within tmHeight	
short int	tmExternalLeading	Amount of leading outside char box	
short int	tmAveCharWidth	Average width of characters	Usually width of X character
short int	tmMaxCharWidth	Maximum width of characters	Must be actual maximum width
short int	tmWeight	Font weight	0=default weight; 400=normal; 700=bold
BYTE	tmItalic	Is font italic?	0=not italic; nonzero=italic
BYTE	tmUnderlined	Is font underlined?	0=not underlined; nonzero=underlined
BYTE	tmStruckOut	Is font struck out?	0=not stricken; nonzero=struck out
BYTE	tmFirstChar	Value of first character defined in font	
BYTE	tmLastChar	Value of last character defined in font	
BYTE	tmDefaultChar	Value of character substituted for missing chars	
BYTE	tmBreakChar	Value of character used for word breaks	Usually 20H
BYTE	tmPitchAndFamily	Font's pitch and family type	See 6.063. LOGFONT Structure Format, lfPitchAndFamily
BYTE	tmCharSet	Character set to use for font	
short int	tmOverhang	Extra width per string to add	Assumed to be top of char skew for italic fonts
short int	tmDigitizedAspectX	x aspect ratio of device font was designed for	
short int	tmDigitizedAspectY	y aspect ratio of device font was designed for	

Source: Microsoft Windows 2.0 SDK Programmer's Reference, pages 631 through 633
Microsoft Windows 3.0 SDK Programmer's Reference, pages 7-59 through 7-61

See Also: 6.063. LOGFONT Structure Format

6.081. WNDCLASS STRUCTURE FORMAT

Field Type	Argument Type	Description	Restrictions on Allowable Values
WORD	style	Class style	Must be one of: CS_VREDRAW CS_HREDRAW CS_DBLCKS CS_OEMCHARS ¥ CS_OWNDC CS_CLASSDC CS_BYTEALIGNCLIENT * CS_BYTEALIGNWINDOW * CS_PARENTDC * CS_GLOBALCLASS† CS_SAVEBITS * CS_NOCLOSE *
long	lpfnWndProc	Window function	
int	cbClsExtra	# bytes to allocate after window class structure	
int	cbWndExtra	# bytes to allocate after window instance	
HANDLE	hInstance	Class module	Must not be NULL
HICON	hIcon	Class icon	If NULL, application must draw icon on close
HCURSOR	hCursor	Class cursor	If NULL, application must set cursor shape
HBRUSH	hbrBackground	Class background brush	Handle of physical brush; NULL, or one of: COLOR_SCROLLBAR+1 COLOR_BACKGROUND+1 COLOR_ACTIVECAPTION+1 COLOR_INACTIVECAPTION+1 COLOR_MENU+1 COLOR_WINDOW+1 COLOR_WINDOWFRAME+1 COLOR_MENUTEXT+1 COLOR_WINDOWTEXT+1 COLOR_CAPTIONTEXT+1 COLOR_ACTIVEBORDER+1* COLOR_BTNFACE+1† COLOR_BTNSHADOW+1† COLOR_BTNTEXT+1† COLOR_GRAYTEXT+1† COLOR_HIGHLIGHT+1† COLOR_HIGHLIGHTTEXT+1† COLOR_SCROLLBAR+1† COLOR_APPWORKSPACE+1* COLOR_INACTIVEBORDER+1*
LPSTR	lpszMenuName	Resource name of class menu	Points to ASCIIZ string; if NULL, no default menu
LPSTR	lpszClassName	Name of window class	Points to ASCIIZ string

*Applies only to version 2.0 and later.
†Applies only to version 3.0 and later.
¥No longer appears in Windows 3.0 documentation.

Source: Microsoft Windows 2.0 SDK Programmer's Reference, pages 634 through 636
Microsoft Windows 3.0 SDK Programmer's Reference, pages 7-62 through 7-66

6.082. FORMAT OF A WINDOWS MESSAGE

Offset	*Size*	*Name*	*Function*
0	WORD	-	Message identifier (message number)
2	WORD	wParam	Word parameter (set to 0 if not used)
4	DWORD	lParam	Long parameter (set to 0 if not used)

Source: Microsoft Windows 2.0 SDK Programmer's Reference, page 517
Microsoft Windows 3.0 SDK Programmer's Reference, page 5-21

See Also: 6.083. Windows General Message Numbering

6.083. WINDOWS GENERAL MESSAGE NUMBERING

Number	*Function*
0 to (WM_USER-1)	RESERVED for use by Windows
WM_USER to 7FFFH	"Integer" messages for use within an application
8000 to BFFFH	RESERVED for future use by Windows
C000 to FFFFH	"String" messages for use by applications

Source: Microsoft Windows 2.0 SDK Programmer's Reference, page 517
Microsoft Windows 3.0 SDK Programmer's Reference, pages 5-21 through 5-22

See Also: 6.082. Format of a Windows Message

6.084. WINDOW MANAGEMENT MESSAGES

Message Name	*Purpose*	*wParam*	*lParam*	*Return*
WM_ACTIVATE	Occurs when window becomes active or inactive	State of window: 0=inactive 1=active (not via mouse click) 2=active (via mouse click)	HO=nonzero if minimized, otherwise 0 LO: wParam=0, handle to activated win wParam≠0, handle to inactivated win	None
WM_ACTIVATEAPP	Sent when window activation is another app	0=window going inactive Nonzero=window becoming active	If wParam=0, LO=task handle of prev app owning window If wParam≠0, LO is task handle of app owning window	None
WM_CANCELMODE†	Sent to cancel any mode System is in	Not used	Not used	None
WM_CHILDACTIVE*	Occurs when child window has moved	Not used	Not used	None
WM_CLOSE	Occurs when a window is closed	Not used	Not used	None
WM_CREATE	Occurs when CreateWindow called	Not used	Long pointer to CREATESTRUCT	None
WM_CTLCOLOR	Sent to parent of control just before drawing it	Handle of display context for child window	LO=handle to child window HO is one of: CTLCOLOR_BTN CTLCOLOR_DLG CTLCOLOR_EDIT CTLCOLOR_LISTBOX CTLCOLOR_MSGBOX CTLCOLOR_SCROLLBAR CTLCOLOR_STATIC	Handle to the brush used for painting control background
WM_DESTROY	Sent on call to DestroyWindow, after removal	Not used	Not used	None
WM_ENABLE	Occurs after window enabled or disabled	0=disabled, nonzero=enabled	Not used	None
WM_ENDSESSION	Sent when application responds nonzero to WM_QUERYENDSESSION	0=not end of session Nonzero=session ending	Not used	None
WM_ENTERIDLE†	Sent when modal dialog or menu is entering idle state	Why idle: MSGF_DIALOGBOX MSGF_MENU	HO: not used LO: handle of dialog box or window containing displayed menu	None
WM_ERASEBKGND	Occurs when background needs erasing	Handle of display context	Not used	Nonzero if erased
WM_GETMINMAXINFO*	Sent to determine size of window	Not used	lp to 5 pt array of min and max sizes	None

(Continued)

6.084. WINDOW MANAGEMENT MESSAGES (continued)

Message Name	Purpose	wParam	lParam	Return
WM_ICONERASEBKGND†	Sent when background of icon must be filled before painting	Handle of icon's device context	Not used	None
WM_KILLFOCUS	Sent before window loses input focus	Handle of window receiving focus	Not used	None
WM_MENUSELECT†	Occurs when user selects a menu item	Item selected	LO contains combination of menu flags: MF_BITMAP MF_CHECKED MF_DISABLED MF_GRAYED MF_MOUSESELECT MF_OWNERDRAW MF_POPUP MF_SYSMENU	None
WM_MOVE	Sent when a window is moved	Not used	New upper-left client area location	None
WM_PAINT	Occurs when request to repaint window occurs	Not used	Not used¶	None
WM_PAINTICON†	Sent when icon is to be painted	Not used	Not used	None
WM_PARENTNOTIFY†	Sent to parent window when child created, destroyed, or mouse active in	Why parent notified: WM_CREATE WM_DESTROY WM_LBUTTONDOWN WM_MBUTTONDOWN WM_RBUTTONDOWN	LO=window handle of child window HO=child window ID If WM_CREATE or WM_DESTROY, LOB is x-coordinate HOB is y-corrdinate	None
WM_QUERYDRAGICON†	Sent to minimized window that is about to be dragged (no class icon)	Not used	Not used	LO=cursor handle or NULL
WM_QUERYENDSESSION	Occurs when user invokes End Session command	Not used	Not used	≠0 if shutdown
WM_QUERYNEWPALETTE†	Sent to window about to receive input focus	Not used	Not used	TRUE=realized, else FALSE
WM_QUERYOPEN	Sent to icon when user requests it be opened	Not used	Not used	Nonzero=openable
WM_QUIT	Indicates a request to terminate an application	Exit code in PostQuitMessage call	Not used	None
WM_SETFONT†	Specifies font dialog box control is to use when drawing text	Handle of font (NULL=default)	TRUE=control to redraw FALSE=don't redraw	None
WM_SETFOCUS	Sent after a window gets the input focus	Handle of window losing focus	Not used	None
WM_SETREDRAW	Sets or clears the redraw flag	If nonzero, redraw flag is set	Not used	None
WM_SETTEXT	Used to set the text of a window	Not used	Lp to ASCIIZ string of window text	May be error msg
WM_SETVISIBLE§	Sent before a window is made visible or hidden	Nonzero if window visible	Not used	None
WM_SHOWWINDOW	Sent when a window is hidden or shown	Nonzero if window being shown Zero if being hidden	0 if message sent due to ShowWindow Otherwise one of: SW_PARENTCLOSING SW_PARENTOPENING	None
WM_SIZE	Occurs after size of window has been changed	One of: SIZEICONIC SIZEFULLSCREEN SIZENORMAL SIZEZOOMSHOW SIZEZOOMHIDE	New width and height of client area (width=LO, height=HO)	None

*Message available beginning with Windows 2.0
†Message available beginning with Windows 3.0
§Message omitted beginning with Windows 3.0
¶Previously documented as long pointer to PAINTSTRUCT

Source: Microsoft Windows 2.0 SDK Programmer's Reference, pages 501 through 502 and 549 through 594
Microsoft Windows 3.0 SDK Programmer's Reference, pages 6-47 through 6-102

See Also:
6.082. Format of a Windows Message
6.083. Windows General Message Numbering
6.085. Initialization Messages
6.086. Input Messages
6.087. System and System Information Messages
6.088. Clipboard Messages
6.089. Control Messages
6.090. Notification Messages
6.091. Nonclient Area Messages
6.092. Scroll-Bar Messages
6.093. Multiple Document Interface Messages
6.094. DDE Messages

6.085. INITIALIZATION MESSAGES

Message Name	*Purpose*	*wParam*	*lParam*	*Return*
WM_INITDIALOG	Sent before dialog box displayed	Handle to first control item that can take input focus	Not used Same as value passed by dwInitParam if dialog box created by Create Dialog Indirect Param Create Dialog Param Dialog Box Indirect Param Dialog Box Param	If ≠ 0, the focus set to item in wParam
WM_INITMENU	Request to initialize a menu	Handle of the menu to be initialized	Not used	None
WM_INITMENUPOPUP	Sent before popup menu is displayed	Handle of the popup menu	HO=nonzero if popup is system menu LO=index of popup menu in the main menu	

Source: Microsoft Windows 2.0 SDK Programmer's Reference, pages 503 and 565 through 567
Microsoft Windows 3.0 SDK Programmer's Reference, pages 6-67 through 6-68

See Also: 6.082. Format of a Windows Message
6.083. Windows General Message Numbering
6.084. Window Management Messages
6.086. Input Messages
6.087. System and System Information Messages
6.088. Clipboard Messages
6.089. Control Messages
6.090. Notification Messages
6.091. Nonclient Area Messages
6.092. Scroll-Bar Messages
6.093. Multiple Document Interface Messages
6.094. DDE Messages

6.086. INPUT MESSAGES

Message Name	*Purpose*	*wParam*	*lParam*	*Return*
WM_CHAR	Result of translated WM_KEYUP or WM_KEYDOWN	ASCII value of key	Key info¥	None
WM_CHARTOITEM*	Sent by list box in response to a WM_CHAR message	ASCII value of key	LO=window handle of list box HO=current caret position	Action†
WM_COMMAND	Menu item selected, control passed message to Parent, or accelerator key translated	Either menu item, control ID, or accelerator ID	0=message f/menu or HO=1 if f/accel otherwise HO=notification code and LO=window handle of control	None
WM_DEADCHAR	Result of translated WM_KEYUP or WM_KEYDOWN	Character value of dead key	Key info¥	None
WM_GETDLGCODE	Sent by Windows dialog manager to control	Not used	Not used	DLGC value‡
WM_GETTEXT	Used to copy text corresponding to a window	Number of bytes to be copied (including ending NULL)	Long pointer to buffer to receive text	Number of bytes copied
WM_GETTEXTLENGTH	Used to find length of text associated with a window	Not used	Not used	Length of text
WM_HSCROLL	Occurs when user clicks mouse in scroll bar	One of following scroll-bar codes: SB_LINEUP (scroll one line up) SB_LINEDOWN (scroll one line down) SB_PAGEUP (scroll one page up) SB_PAGEDOWN (scroll one page down) SB_THUMBPOSITION (to position) SB_THUMBTRACK (thumb dragged) SB_TOP (scroll to upper left) SB_BOTTOM (scroll to lower right) SB_ENDSCROLL (end of scroll)	HO=window handle of scroll-bar control LO=current position of thumb LO=current position of thumb	None
WM_KEYDOWN	Sent when nonsystem key pressed	Virtual key code of the key pressed	Key info¥	None
WM_KEYUP	Sent when nonsystem key released	Virtual key code of the key released	Key info¥	None
WM_LBUTTONDBLCLK	Sent when user double clicks left mouse button	One of the following: MK_RBUTTON (right button down) MK_MBUTTON (middle button down) MK_LBUTTON (left button down) MK_SHIFT (Shift key down) MK_CONTROL (Control key down)	LO=x coordinate of mouse cursor HO=y coordinate of mouse cursor (Coordinates relative to top left corner of window)	None
WM_LBUTTONDOWN	Sent when left mouse button pressed	One of the following: MK_RBUTTON (right button down) MK_MBUTTON (middle button down) MK_SHIFT (Shift key down) MK_CONTROL (Control key down)	LO=x coordinate of mouse cursor HO=y coordinate of mouse cursor (Coordinates relative to top left corner of window)	None

(Continued)

6.086. INPUT MESSAGES (continued)

Message Name	Purpose	wParam	lParam	Return
WM_LBUTTONUP	Sent when left mouse button released	One of the following: MK_RBUTTON (right button down) MK_MBUTTON (middle button down) MK_SHIFT (Shift key down) MK_CONTROL (Control key down)	LO=x coordinate of mouse cursor HO=y coordinate of mouse cursor (Coordinates relative to top left corner of window)	None
WM_MBUTTONDBLCLK	Sent when user double clicks middle mouse button	One of the following: MK_RBUTTON (right button down) MK_MBUTTON (middle button down) MK_LBUTTON (left button down) MK_SHIFT (Shift key down) MK_CONTROL (Control key down)	LO=x coordinate of mouse cursor HO=y coordinate of mouse cursor (Coordinates relative to top left corner of window)	None
WM_MBUTTONDOWN	Sent when middle mouse button pressed	One of the following: MK_RBUTTON (right button down) MK_LBUTTON (left button down) MK_SHIFT (Shift key down) MK_CONTROL (Control key down)	LO=x coordinate of mouse cursor HO=y coordinate of mouse cursor (Coordinates relative to top left corner of window)	None
WM_MBUTTONUP	Sent when middle mouse button released	One of the following: MK_RBUTTON (right button down) MK_LBUTTON (left button down) MK_SHIFT (Shift key down) MK_CONTROL (Control key down)	LO=x coordinate of mouse cursor HO=y coordinate of mouse cursor (Coordinates relative to top left corner of window)	None
WM_MENUCHAR§	Sent when user presses mnemonic char not matching those predefined	ASCII char user pressed	HO=handle of menu LO=MF_POPUP or MF_SYSMENU Upon return, HO of return value should contain: 0=discard character and beep 1=close current menu 2=LO has selected menu item-number	<--see lParam
WM_MOUSEACTIVATE*	Sent when cursor in inactive window with mouse down	Handle to topmost parent window of activated window	LO=hit-test area code HO=mouse message number	**
WM_MOUSEMOVE	Sent when mouse is moved	One of the following: MK_RBUTTON (right button down) MK_MBUTTON (middle button down) MK_LBUTTON (left button down) MK_SHIFT (Shift key down) MK_CONTROL (Control key down)	LO=x coordinate of mouse cursor HO=y coordinate of mouse cursor (Coordinates relative to top left corner of window)	None
WM_RBUTTONDBLCKL	Sent when right mouse button is doubled clicked	One of the following: MK_RBUTTON (right button down) MK_MBUTTON (middle button down) MK_LBUTTON (left button down) MK_SHIFT (Shift key down) MK_CONTROL (Control key down)	LO=x coordinate of mouse cursor HO=y coordinate of mouse cursor (Coordinates relative to top left corner of window)	None
WM_RBUTTONDOWN	Sent when right mouse button is pressed	One of the following: MK_MBUTTON (middle button down) MK_LBUTTON (left button down) MK_SHIFT (Shift key down) MK_CONTROL (Control key down)	LO=x coordinate of mouse cursor HO=y coordinate of mouse cursor (Coordinates relative to top left corner of window)	None
WM_RBUTTONUP	Sent when right mouse button is released	One of the following: MK_MBUTTON (middle button down) MK_LBUTTON (left button down) MK_SHIFT (Shift key down) MK_CONTROL (Control key down)	LO=x coordinate of mouse cursor HO=y coordinate of mouse cursor (Coordinates relative to top left corner of window)	None
WM_SETCURSOR*	Occurs if mouse input not captured and mouse moves	Handle to window containing cursor	LO=hit-test area code HO=mouse message number	None
WM_TIMER	Sent when time limit for timer is elapsed	Timer ID	Lp to function passed to SetTimer	None
WM_VKEYTOITEM*	Sent by list box in response to WM_KEYDOWN	Virtual-key code user pressed	LO=window handle of list box HO=current caret position	Action†
WM_VSCROLL	Sent when user clicks mouse in vert scroll bar	One of following scroll-bar codes: SB_LINEUP (scroll up one line) SB_LINEDOWN (scroll down one line) SB_PAGEUP (scroll up one page) SB_PAGEDOWN (scroll down one page) SB_THUMBPOSITION (to position) SB_THUMBTRACK (thumb dragged) SB_TOP (scroll to top) SB_BOTTOM (scroll to bottom) SB_ENDSCROLL (end of scroll)	If sent by scroll-bar control, HO=handle of control LO= current position of thumb LO= current position of thumb	None

*Applies to all versions of Windows beginning with 3.0.
†Action defined as one of following:
= -2, application handled selection, no further action needed.
= -1, list box should perform default action.
= 0 or larger, index of list box item on which default action for keystroke should be made
¥Key information coded as follows:

Bits and Meaning	*Allowable Values*
Bit 31 = transition state	1=released, 0=pressed
Bit 30 = previous key state	1=down, 0=up
Bit 29 = context code	1=Alt down, 0=Alt up
Bits 27-28 = used by Windows	
Bits 25-26 = not used	
Bit 24 = extended key status	1=extended key, 0=no
Bits 16-23 = scan code	OEM dependent value
Bits 0-15 = repeat count	

‡One of the following:
DLGC_DEFPUSHBUTTON
DLGC_HASSETSEL
DLGC_PUSHBUTTON
DLGC_RADIOBUTTON
DLGC_WANTALLKEYS
DLGC_WANTARROWS
DLGC_WANTCHARS
DLGC_WANTMESSAGE
DLGC_WANTTAB
§Message available beginning with Windows 3.0
**MA_ACTIVATE | MA_NOACTIVATE | MA_ACTIVATEANDEAT

Source: Microsoft Windows 2.0 SDK Programmer's Reference, pages 503 through 504, 551 through 602
Microsoft Windows 3.0 SDK Programmer's Reference, pages 6-49 through 6-112

See Also:
6.082. Format of a Windows Message
6.083. Windows General Message Numbering
6.084. Window Management Messages
6.085. Initialization Messages
6.087. System and System Information Messages
6.088. Clipboard Messages
6.089. Control Messages
6.090. Notification Messages
6.091. Nonclient Area Messages
6.092. Scroll-Bar Messages
6.093. Multiple Document Interface Messages
6.094. DDE Messages

6.087. SYSTEM AND SYSTEM INFORMATION MESSAGES

Message Name	*Purpose*	*wParam*	*lParam*
WM_COMPACTING*	Sent to top-level windows if >12.5% time spent performing memory compaction	Ratio of CPU time compacting	Not used
WM_DEVMODECHANGE	Sent to top-level windows when device mode settings change	Not used	Long pointer to WIN.INI device name
WM_FONTCHANGE	Sent to top-level windows when pool of font resources changes	Not used	Not used
WM_PALETTECHANGED*	Informs all windows that system palette is changed	Handle of window causing change	Not used
WM_SPOOLERSTATUS*	Sent whenever Print Manager adds or removes a job in queue	SP_JOBSTATUS	LO=number of jobs remaining; HO=not used
WM_SYSCHAR	Sent when WM_SYSKEYUP or WM_SYSKEYDOWN translated	ASCII-code of System-menu key	Key info†
WM_SYSCOLORCHANGE	Sent to top-level windows when system color setting changes	Not used	Not used
WM_SYSCOMMAND	Sent when user selects command from System menu or when user selects maximize or minimize box	Type of system command	If mouse used, LO=x-coordinate, HO=y-coordinate; otherwise not used
WM_SYSDEADCHAR	Sent when WM_SYSKEYUP or WM_SYSKEYDOWN translated	Dead-key character value	LO=repeat count, HO=auto repeat count
WM_SYSKEYDOWN	Sent when user holds down Alt key and another key	Virtual-key code	Key info†
WM_SYSKEYUP	Sent when user releases Alt key and another key	Virtual-key code	Key info†
WM_SYSTEMERROR‡	Sent to top-level windows when out-of-memory error occurs	8=out of memory error code	Not used
WM_TIMECHANGE	Sent to top-level windows when application changes system time	Not used	Not used
WM_WININICHANGE	Sent to top-level windows when WIN.INI is changed	Not used	Long pointer to string specifying section that changed; 0 if more than one change

*Applies to all versions of Windows beginning with 3.0.
†Key information coded as follows:

Bits and Meaning	*Allowable Values*
Bit 31 = transition state	1=released, 0=pressed
Bit 30 = previous key state	1=down, 0=up
Bit 29 = context code	1=Alt down, 0=Alt up
Bits 27-28 = used internally by Windows	
Bits 25-26 = not used	
Bit 24 = extended key status	1=extended key, 0=no
Bits 16-23 = scan code	OEM dependent value
Bits 0-15 = repeat count	

‡Not in Windows 3.0

Source: Microsoft Windows 2.0 SDK Programmer's Reference, pages 507 and 558 through 604
Microsoft Windows 3.0 SDK Programmer's Reference, pages 6-52 through 6-114

See Also:
6.082. Format of a Windows Message
6.083. Windows General Message Numbering
6.084. Window Management Messages
6.085. Initialization Messages
6.086. Input Messages
6.088. Clipboard Messages
6.089. Control Messages
6.090. Notification Messages
6.091. Nonclient Area Messages
6.092. Scroll-Bar Messages
6.093. Multiple Document Interface Messages
6.094. DDE Messages

6.088. CLIPBOARD MESSAGES

Message Name	*Purpose*	*wParam*	*lParam*
WM_ASKCBFORMATNAME	Sent when clipboard needs handle for CF_OWNERDISPLAY format	Integer number of bytes to copy	Long pointer to buffer where copy of format name is to be stored
WM_CHANGECBCHAIN	Sent to first window in viewer chain when window is removed from chain	Handle of window being removed	LO=handle of window following one being removed (next window)
WM_DESTROYCLIPBOARD	Sent to clipboard owner when clipboard is emptied by EmptyClipboard	Not used	Not used
WM_DRAWCLIPBOARD	Sent to first window in viewer chain when contents are changed	Not used	Not used
WM_HSCROLLCLIPBOARD	Sent when clipboard is CF_OWNERDISPLAY and horizontal scroll event occurs	Handle to clipboard application window	LO contains one of these scroll bar codes: SB_LINEUP (scroll one line up) SB_LINEDOWN (scroll one line down) SB_PAGEUP (scroll one page up) SB_PAGEDOWN (scroll one page down) SB_THUMBPOSITION (scroll to position) SB_TOP (scroll to upper left) SB_BOTTOM (scroll to lower right) SB_ENDSCROLL (end of scroll) HO contains thumb position if LO=SB_THUMBPOSITION
WM_PAINTCLIPBOARD	Sent when clipboard is CF_OWNERDISPLAY and clipboard app's client area needs repainting	Handle to clipboard application window	Long pointer to PAINTSTRUCT
WM_RENDERALLFORMATS	Sent to application that owns clipboard when application is being destroyed	Not used	Not used
WM_RENDERFORMAT	Sent to request clipboard owner format data in specified format	Data format to render	Not used
WM_SIZECLIPBOARD	Sent when clipboard is CF_OWNERDISPLAY and clipboard app window has changed size	Handle to clipboard application window	LO=pointer to RECT
WM_VSCROLLCLIPBOARD	Sent when clipboard is CF_OWNERDISPLAY and vertical scroll event occurs	Handle to clipboard application window	LO contains one of these scroll bar codes: SB_LINEUP (scroll one line up) SB_LINEDOWN (scroll one line down) SB_PAGEUP (scroll one page up) SB_PAGEDOWN (scroll one page down) SB_THUMBPOSITION (scroll to position) SB_TOP (scroll to upper left) SB_BOTTOM (scroll to lower right) SB_ENDSCROLL (end of scroll) HO contains thumb position if LO=SB_THUMBPOSITION

Source: Microsoft Windows 2.0 SDK Programmer's Reference, pages 506 through 507, 550 through 603
Microsoft Windows 3.0 SDK Programmer's Reference, pages 6-48 through 6-113

See Also:
6.015. Clipboard Formats and Clipboard File Format
6.082. Format of a Windows Message
6.083. Windows General Message Numbering
6.084. Window Management Messages
6.085. Initialization Messages
6.086. Input Messages
6.087. System and System Information Messages
6.089. Control Messages
6.090. Notification Messages
6.091. Nonclient Area Messages
6.092. Scroll-Bar Messages
6.093. Multiple Document Interface Messages
6.094. DDE Messages

6.089. CONTROL MESSAGES

Message Name	*Purpose*	*wParam*	*lParam*	*Return*
BM_GETCHECK	Sent to determine status of check box or radio button	Not used	Not used	≠0 if checked, 0 for PUSHBUTTON
BM_GETSTATE	Sent to determine if pushbutton highlighted or mouse button pressed or SPACEBAR pressed when button has focus or user presses mouse button when cursor over button	Not used	Not used	≠0 under some states
BM_SETCHECK	Sent to radio button or check box	0=remove check Nonzero=place check	Not used	None
BM_SETSTATE	Sent to highlight button or check box	0=highlight removed Nonzero=highlighted	Not used	None
BM_SETSTYLE*	Sent to alter button style	One of following style values: BS_AUTOCHECKBOX BS_AUTORADIOBUTTON BS_AUTO3STATE BS_CHECKBOX BS_DEFPUSHBUTTON BS_GROUPBOX BS_LEFTTEXT BS_OWNERDRAW BS_PUSHBUTTON BS_RADIOBUTTON BS_3STATE	0=not redrawn Nonzero=redrawn	None
CB_ADDSTRING†	Adds string to list box of combo box	Not used	Lp to ASCIIZ string	Index to string or CB_ERR or CB_ERRSPACE
CB_DELETESTRING†	Deletes string from list box	Index to string	Not used	String count remaining
CB_DIR†	Adds list of files to list box	DOS attribute value	File specification string	Item count or error
CB_FINDSTRING†	Finds first matching string in list box	Index of item before search start or -1	Lp to ASCIIZ prefix string	Index of match or error
CB_GETCOUNT†	Returns count of items in list box	Not used	Not used	Item count
CB_GETCURSEL†	Returns currently selected item	Not used	Not used	Index of item or CB_ERR
CB_GETEDITSEL†	Returns position of selected text	Not used	Not used	Position¥
CB_GETITEMDATA†	Retrieves application-supplied value	Index to item	Not used	32-bit value or CB_ERR
CB_GETLBTEXT†	Copies string from list box to buffer	Index to string	Lp to buffer	Length in bytes or CB_ERR
CB_GETLBTEXTLEN†	Returns length of string in list box	Index of string	Not used	Length in bytes or CB_ERR
CB_INSERTSTRING†	Inserts string into list box	Index to string position or -1	Lp to ASCIIZ string to insert	Index of string or error
CB_LIMITTEXT†	Limits length of text user may enter	Max number of bytes	Not used	TRUE=success
CB_RESETCONTENT†	Removes all strings from list box	Not used	Not used	None
CB_SELECTSTRING†	Selects first matching string	Index of item before search start or -1	Lp to ASCIIZ prefix string	Index of match or CB_ERR
CB_SETCURSEL†	Selects string and scrolls into view	Index of string or -1	Not used	May be CB_ERR
CB_SETEDITSEL†	Selects chars in edit control	Not used	LO=start position HO=end position	TRUE=success or error
CB_SETITEMDATA†	Sets value for item	Index of item	New value for item	May be CB_ERR
CB_SHOWDROPDOWN†	Shows or hides drop-down list box	TRUE=display if not visible FALSE=hide if visible	Not used	None
DM_GETDEFID	Retrieves ID of default push-button control for dialog box	Not used	Not used	LO=ID HO=DC_HASDEFID or NULL
DM_SETDEFID	Sets default push-button control for dialog box	ID of new default control	Not used	None
EM_CANUNDO	Sent to determine if edit control can undo last edit	Not used	Not used	Nonzero if control accepts EM_UNDO
EM_EMPTYUNDOBUFFER†	Directs control to empty undo buffer	Not used	Not used	None
EM_FMTLINES	Sent to add or remove EOL char from text lines	0=remove EOL Nonzero=add CR CR LF to lines	Not used	Nonzero if any formatting occurs
EM_GETHANDLE	Sent to determine handle of buffer holding control window contents	Not used	Not used	Data handle of edit control buffer
EM_GETLINE	Sent to copy a line from the edit control	Line number	Far pointer to buffer to store line (first word=max length allowed)	Number of bytes copied
EM_GETLINECOUNT	Sent to determine number of lines of text in edit control	Not used	Not used	Number of lines in control
EM_GETMODIFY	Returns current value of modify flag	Not used	Not used	Modify flag

(Continued)

6.089. CONTROL MESSAGES (continued)

Message Name	Purpose	wParam	lParam	Return
EM_GETRECT	Sent to determine formatting rectangle of control	Not used	Long pointer to RECT	None
EM_GETSEL	Sent to determine start and end positions of selection	Not used	Not used	LO=start position HO=first non-select
EM_LIMITTEXT	Sent to limit length of text the user may enter	Maximum bytes	Not used	None
EM_LINEFROMCHAR*	Sent to determine which line contains a specific character	Index to character or -1	Not used	Line number
EM_LINEINDEX	Sent to determine number of char positions before first char on line	Line number or -1 for current line	Not used	Char positions that precede first char
EM_LINELENGTH	Sent to determine length of line in edit control's text buffer	Line number or -1 for current line	Not used	Line length
EM_LINESCROLL	Sent to scroll context of control by a number of lines	Not used	LO=number of vert. lines HO=number of horiz. char positions	None
EM_REPLACESEL	Sent to replace selection with new text	Not used	Far pointer to ASCIIZ string of replacement text	None
EM_SCROLL¶	Sent to direct edit control to scroll window vertically	One of the following values: SB_LINEUP SB_LINEDOWN SB_PAGEUP SB_PAGEDOWN SB_THUMBPOSITION EM_GETTHUMB	Not used	None
EM_SETFONT¶	Sent to set edit control font being used	Font ID (must be fixed pitch)	Not used	None
EM_SETHANDLE	Sent to establish text buffer used to hold control window contents	Handle to buffer in application's data segment	Not used	None
EM_SETMODIFY	Sets modify flag for control	New modify flag value	Not used	None
EM_SETPASSWORDCHAR†	Sets char displayed in control created with ES_PASSWORD	Char to display or NULL	Not used	None
EM_SETRECT	Sent to set formatting rectangle of control	Not used	Lp to RECT specifying new rectangle	None
EM_SETRECTNP	Sent to set formatting rect of control with no repainting	Not used	Lp to RECT specifying new rectangle	None
EM_SETSEL	Sent to select chars between start and end position	Not used	LO=start position HO=ending position	None
EM_SETTABSTOPS†	Sets tab stop positions for multiline control	Number of tabs	Lp to array of integers describing tab stops	TRUE=all tabs set
EM_SETWORDBREAK*	Sent to set word break for multiline edit controls	Not used	Lp to application-supplied word break function	None
EM_UNDO	Sent to undo last edit to edit control	Not used	Not used	Nonzero=success
LB_ADDSTRING	Sent to add string to list box	Not used	Lp to ASCIIZ string to add	Index to string or error
LB_DELETESTRING	Sent to delete string from list box	Index to string to delete	Not used	Strings remaining or error
LB_DIR	Sent to add list of files in current directory to list box	DOS attribute value	Lp to file specification string (may include * and ?)	Item count or error
LB_FINDSTRING†	Finds first string matching prefix	Index of item preceding start	Pointer to ASCIIZ string	Index of match or error
LB_GETCOUNT	Sent to get count of number of items in list box	Not used	Not used	Item count or error
LB_GETCURSEL	Sent to return index of current selection, if any	Not used	Not used	Index of selection or error
LB_GETHORIZONTALEXTENT†	Retrieves width in pixels box can scroll	Not used	Not used	Width, in pixels
LB_GETITEMDATA†	Retrieves value associated with item	Index to item	Not used	32-bit value
LB_GETITEMRECT†	Retrieves rectangle bounding item	Index to item	Lp to RECT	May be LB_ERR
LB_GETSEL	Sent to return selection state of an item	Index to the item	Not used	>0 if item selected or 0 or LB_ERR
LB_GETSELCOUNT†	Returns number of selected items	Not used	Not used	Item count, LB_ERR
LB_GETSELITEMS†	Fills buffer with selected item numbers	Max number of selected items	Lp to buffer	May be LB_ERR or number of items
LB_GETTEXT	Sent to copy string from list into buffer	Index to string to copy into buffer	Lp of buffer to receive string copy	Length of string in bytes or error
LB_GETTEXTLEN	Sent to determine length of string in list box	Index to the string	Not used	Length of string in bytes or error
LB_GETTOPINDEX†	Returns index of first visible item	Not used	Not used	Index of item
LB_INSERTSTRING	Sent to insert string into list box	Index to position for string, or -1 for end of list	Lp to ASCIIZ string to insert	Index of insertion or error
LB_RESETCONTENT	Sent to remove all strings from box	Not used	Not used	None

(Continued)

6.089. CONTROL MESSAGES (continued)

Message Name	Purpose	wParam	lParam	Return
LB_SELECTSTRING	Sent to change selection to first string matching prefix	Index of start point for search, -1=search all strings	Lp to ASCIIZ prefix string	Index of selected item or LB_ERR
LB_SELITEMRANGE†	Selects one or more items	0=deselect, nonzero=select	LO=index of first HO=index of last	May be LB_ERR
LB_SETCOLUMNWIDTH†	Sets width in pixels of all columns	Width, in pixels	Not used	None
LB_SETCURSEL	Sent to select string and scroll it into view, if necessary	Index to string to select or -1		May be LB_ERR
LB_SETHORIZONTALEXTENT†	Sets width list box can be scrolled	Pixels list box can scroll horz.	Not used	None
LB_SETITEMDATA†	Sets value associated with item	Index to item	New value of item	May be LB_ERR
LB_SETSEL	Sent to set selection state of a string	0=unhighlight; ≠0=highlight	LO=index to string or -1 for all	May be LB_ERR
LB_SETTABSTOPS†	Sets tab stop positions in list box	Number of tab stops	Lp to integer array of tab positions	TRUE=all tabs set
LB_SETTOPINDEX†	Sets first visible item in list box	Index of item	Not used	May be LB_ERR
WM_CLEAR	Sent to delete current selection	Not used	Not used	Not used
WM_COMPAREITEM†	Determines relative position of item	Not used	Lp to COMPAREITEMSTRUCT	Value§
WM_COPY	Sent to copy current selection to clipboard in CF_TEXT format	Not used	Not used	None
WM_CUT	Sent to perform WM_COPY and WM_CLEAR, in that order	Not used	Not used	None
WM_DELETEITEM†	Indicates list box item was removed	Not used	Lp to DELETEITEMSTRUCT	None
WM_DRAWITEM†	Sent when visual aspect changed	Not used	Lp to DRAWITEMSTRUCT	None
WM_GETFONT†	Gets current control's font	Not used	Not used	Font handle or NULL
WM_PASTE	Sent to copy clipboard data to current window at current cursor pos	Not used	Not used	None
WM_MEASUREITEM†	Sent when control is created	Not used	Lp to MEASUREITEMSTRUCT	None
WM_NEXTDLGCTL	Sent to alter control focus	Control receiving focus	Control flag	None
WM_SETFONT†	Specifies font to draw text in	Font handle or NULL (default)	TRUE=redraw itself	None
WM_UNDO	Undoes last operation	Not used	Not used	None

*Applies to all versions of Windows beginning with version 2.0.
†Applies to all versions of Windows beginning with version 3.0.
¶No longer documented beginning with Windows 3.0
¥LO word=start position, HO word=end position
§-1=item 1 sorts before item 2
0=item 1 and 2 sort the same
1=item 1 sorts after item 2

Source: Microsoft Windows 2.0 SDK Programmer's Reference, pages 508-510, 519 through 586
Microsoft Windows 3.0 SDK Programmer's Reference, pages 5-2 through 6-114

See Also:
6.082. Format of a Windows Message
6.083. Windows General Message Numbering
6.084. Window Management Messages
6.085. Initialization Messages
6.086. Input Messages
6.087. System and System Information Messages
6.088. Clipboard Messages
6.090. Notification Messages
6.091. Nonclient Area Messages
6.092. Scroll-Bar Messages
6.093. Multiple Document Interface Messages
6.094. DDE Messages

6.090. NOTIFICATION MESSAGES

Message	Meaning	wParam	lParam
BN_CLICKED	Button has been clicked	Control ID	LO=control handle HO=BN_CLICKED
BN_DISABLE§	Button should be drawn as disabled	Control ID	LO=control handle HO=BN_DISABLED
BN_DOUBLECLICKED*	User has double clicked a mouse button	Control ID	LO=control handle HO=BN_DOUBLECLICKED
BN_HILITE§	Button requires highlighting	Control ID	LO=control handle HO=BN_HILITE
BN_PAINT§	Button requires repainting	Control ID	LO=control handle HO=BN_PAINT
BN_UNHILITE§	Button requires unhighlighting	Control ID	LO=control handle HO=BN_UNHILITE

(Continued)

6.090. NOTIFICATION MESSAGES (continued)

Message	*Meaning*	*wParam*	*lParam*
CBN_DBLCLK†	User has double clicked in a list box	Control ID	LO=control handle HO=CBN_DBLCLK
CBN_DROPDOWN†	List box of a combo box will be dropped down	Control ID	LO=control handle HO=CBN_DROPDOWN
CBN_EDITCHANGE†	User has taken action that may have altered the text in an edit control	Control ID	LO=control handle HO=CBN_EDITCHANGE
CBN_EDITUPDATE†	Combo box of an edit control will display altered text	Control ID	LO=control handle HO=CBN_EDITUPDATE
CBN_ERRSPACE†	List box control cannot allocate enough memory	Control ID	LO=control handle HO=CBN_ERRSPACE
CBN_KILLFOCUS†	Combo box has lost input focus	Control ID	LO=control handle HO=CBN_KILLFOCUS
CBN_SELCHANGE†	Selection in list box has changed	Control ID	LO=control handle HO=CBN_SELCHANGE
CBN_SETFOCUS†	Combo box has received input focus	Control ID	LO=control handle HO=CBN_SETFOCUS
EN_CHANGE	User has taken an action that may have changed the content of the text	Control ID and wParam parm of WM_COMMAND	LO=control handle HO=EN_CHANGE
EN_ERRSPACE	Edit control is out of space	Control ID and wParam parm of WM_COMMAND	LO=control handle HO=EN_ERRSPACE
EN_HSCROLL	User has clicked on the edit control's horiz scroll bar	Control ID and wParam parm of WM_COMMAND	LO=control handle HO=EN_HSCROLL
EN_KILLFOCUS	Edit control has lost the input focus	Control ID and wParam parm of WM_COMMAND	LO=control handle HO=EN_KILLFOCUS
EN_MAXTEXT†	Current insertion exceded the specified number of chars for the edit control	Control ID and wParam parm of WM_COMMAND	LO=control handle HO=EN_MAXTEXT
EN_SETFOCUS	Edit control has obtained the input focus	Control ID and wParam parm of WM_COMMAND	LO=control handle HO=EN_SETFOCUS
EN_UPDATE*	Edit control will display altered text	Control ID and wParam parm of WM_COMMAND	LO=control handle HO=EN_UPDATE
EN_VSCROLL	User has clicked on the edit control's vert scroll bar	Control ID and wParam parm of WM_COMMAND	LO=control handle HO=EN_VSCROLL
LBN_DBLCLK	User has double clicked the mouse button over a string	Control ID and wParam parm of WM_COMMAND	LO=window handle HO=LBN_DBLCLK
LBN_ERRSPACE	Out of memory	Control ID and wParam parm of WM_COMMAND	LO=window handle HO=LBN_ERRSPACE
LBN_KILLFOCUS†	List box has lost input focus	Control ID and wParam parm of WM_COMMAND	LO=window handle HO=LBN_KILLFOCUS
LBN_SELCHANGE	Selection has been changed	Control ID and wParam parm of WM_COMMAND	LO=window handle HO=LBN_SELCHANGE
LBN_SETFOCUS†	List box has received input focus	Control ID and wParam parm of WM_COMMAND	LO=window handle HO=LBN_SETFOCUS

*Applies to versions of Windows beginning with 2.0.
†Applies to versions of Windows beginning with 3.0.
§No longer documented beginning with Windows 3.0

Source: Microsoft Windows 2.0 SDK Programmer's Reference, pages 511 through 512, 522 through 548
Microsoft Windows 3.0 SDK Programmer's Reference, pages 6-7 through 6-46

See Also:
6.082. Format of a Windows Message
6.083. Windows General Message Numbering
6.084. Window Management Messages
6.085. Initialization Messages
6.086. Input Messages
6.087. System and System Information Messages
6.088. Clipboard Messages
6.089. Control Messages
6.091. Nonclient Area Messages
6.092. Scroll-Bar Messages
6.093. Multiple Document Interface Messages
6.094. DDE Messages

6.091. NONCLIENT AREA MESSAGES

Message Name	*Purpose*	*wParam*	*lParam*
WM_NCACTIVATE	Sent to window when its nonclient area needs to be changed	0=make active; nonzero=make inactive	Not used
WM_NCCALCSIZE	Sent when size of client area needs to be calculated	Not used	Long pointer to RECT
WM_NCCREATE	Sent before WM_CREATE message when window created	Handle to window being created	Lp to CREATESTRUCT for window
WM_NCDESTROY	Sent after WM_DESTROY message	Not used	Not used
WM_NCHITTEST	Sent each time mouse moved	Not used	LO=x coord of mouse HO=y coord of mouse
WM_NCLBUTTONDBLCLK	Sent when left mouse button double clicked in nonclient area	Code returned by WM_NCHITTEST*	LO=x coord of mouse HO=y coord of mouse
WM_NCLBUTTONDOWN	Sent when left mouse button is pressed in nonclient area	Code returned by WM_NCHITTEST*	LO=x coord of mouse HO=y coord of mouse
WM_NCLBUTTONUP	Sent when left mouse button released in nonclient area	Code returned by WM_NCHITTEST*	LO=x coord of mouse HO=y coord of mouse
WM_NCMBUTTONDBLCLK	Sent when middle mouse button double clicked in nonclient area	Code returned by WM_NCHITTEST*	LO=x coord of mouse HO=y coord of mouse
WM_NCMBUTTONDOWN	Sent when middle mouse button is pressed in nonclient area	Code returned by WM_NCHITTEST*	LO=x coord of mouse HO=y coord of mouse
WM_NCMBUTTONUP	Sent when middle mouse button released in nonclient area	Code returned by WM_NCHITTEST*	LO=x coord of mouse HO=y coord of mouse
WM_NCMOUSEMOVE	Sent when mouse is moved in nonclient area of window	Code returned by WM_NCHITTEST*	LO=x coord of mouse HO=y coord of mouse
WM_NCPAINT	Sent to window when frame needs repainting	Not used	Not used Not used
WM_NCRBUTTONDBLCLK	Sent when right mouse button double clicked in nonclient area	Code returned by WM_NCHITTEST*	LO=x coord of mouse HO=y coord of mouse
WM_NCRBUTTONDOWN	Sent when right mouse button pressed in nonclient area	Code returned by WM_NCHITTEST*	LO=x coord of mouse HO=y coord of mouse
WM_NCRBUTTONUP	Sent when right mouse button released in nonclient area	Code returned by WM_NCHITTEST*	LO=x coord of mouse HO=y coord of mouse

*One of the following hit-text codes:

HTBOTTOM
HTBOTTOMLEFT
HTBOTTOMRIGHT
HTCAPTION
HTCLIENT
HTERROR
HTGROWBOX
HTHSCROLL
HTLEFT
HTMENU
HTNOWHERE
HTREDUCE
HTRIGHT
HTSIZE
HTSYSMENU
HTTOP
HTTOPLEFT
HTTOPRIGHT
HTTRANSPARENT
HTVSCROLL
HTZOOM

Source: Microsoft Windows 2.0 SDK Programmer's Reference, pages 513 through 514 and 576 through 584
Microsoft Windows 3.0 SDK Programmer's Reference, pages 6-83 through 6-90

See Also:
6.082. Format of a Windows Message
6.083. Windows General Message Numbering
6.084. Window Management Messages
6.085. Initialization Messages
6.086. Input Messages
6.087. System and System Information Messages
6.088. Clipboard Messages
6.089. Control Messages
6.090. Notification Messages
6.092. Scroll-Bar Messages
6.093. Multiple Document Interface Messages
6.094. DDE Messages

6.092. SCROLL-BAR MESSAGES

Message Name	*Purpose*	*wParam*	*lParam*
WM_HSCROLL	Sent when user clicks in horz scroll bar	Scroll bar code: SB_BOTTOM SB_ENDSCROLL SB_LINEDOWN SB_LINEUP SB_PAGEDOWN SB_PAGEUP SB_THUMBPOSITION SB_THUMBTRACK SB_TOP	HO=window handle of control, unless sent by pop-up window scroll bar
WM_VSCROLL	Sent when user clicks in vertical scroll bar	Scroll bar code: SB_BOTTOM SB_ENDSCROLL SB_LINEDOWN SB_LINEUP SB_PAGEDOWN SB_PAGEUP SB_THUMBPOSITION SB_THUMBTRACK SB_TOP	HO=window handle of control, unless sent by pop-up window scroll bar

Source: Microsoft Windows 3.0 SDK Programmer's Reference, pages 6-65 and 6-112

See Also:
6.082. Format of a Windows Message
6.083. Windows General Message Numbering
6.084. Window Management Messages
6.085. Initialization Messages
6.086. Input Messages
6.087. System and System Information Messages
6.088. Clipboard Messages
6.089. Control Messages
6.090. Notification Messages
6.091. Nonclient Area Messages
6.093. Multiple Document Interface Messages
6.094. DDE Messages

6.093. MULTIPLE DOCUMENT INTERFACE MESSAGES

Message Name	Purpose	wParam	lParam	Return
WM_DIACTIVATE*	Sent to client to activate a different MDI child window	Window handle of child window	LO=window handle of child activated† HO=window handle of child deactivated†	None
WM_MDICASCADE*	Arranges child windows in cascade format	Not used	Not used	None
WM_MDICREATE*	Sent to MDI client to create a child window	Not used	Lp to MDICREATESTRUCT	LO=wind ID HO=zero
WM_MDIDESTROY*	Sent to MDI client to close a child window	Window handle of child window	Not used	None
WM_MDIGETACTIVE*	Returns current active MDI child window	Not used	Not used	LO=wind ID HO=(1=max)
WM_MDIICONARRANGE*	Sent to MDI client to arrange minimized child windows	Not used	Not used	None
WM_MDIMAXIMIZE*	Sent to MDI client to maximize child window	Window ID of child window	Not used	None
WM_MDINEXT*	Activates next MDI child window and places previous active window behind all others	Not used	Not used	None
WM_MDIRESTORE*	Restores MDI child window from maximized or minimized size	Window ID of child window	Not used	None
WM_MDISETMENU*	Replaces menu of MDI frame window, the window pop-up menu, or both	Not used	LO=menu handle of new frame-wind menu HO=menu handle of new pop-up menu§	Handle of menu replaced
WM_MDITILE*	Sent to cause MDI client to arrange all child windows in tiled format	Not used	Not used	None

*Applies to all versions of Windows beginning with 3.0.
§If either LO or HO value is zero, that menu is not replaced.

Source: Microsoft Windows 3.0 SDK Programmer's Reference, pages 6-75 through 6-79

See Also:
6.082. Format of a Windows Message
6.083. Windows General Message Numbering
6.084. Window Management Messages
6.085. Initialization Messages
6.086. Input Messages
6.087. System and System Information Messages
6.088. Clipboard Messages
6.089. Control Messages
6.090. Notification Messages
6.091. Nonclient Area Messages
6.092. Scroll-Bar Messages
6.094. DDE Messages

6.094. DDE MESSAGES

Message Name	*Purpose*	*wParam*	*lParam*
WM_DDE_ACK (reply to INITIATE)	Notifies application of receipt and processing of WM_DDE_INITIATE	Sending window ID	LO=aApplication HO=aTopic
WM_DDE_ACK (reply to EXECUTE)	Notifies application of receipt and processing of WM_DDE_ACK	Sending window ID	LO=wStatus HO=hCommands
WM_DDE_ACK (reply to other messages)	Notifies application of receipt and processing of all other WM_DDE messages	Sending window ID	LO=wStatus (DDEACK structure) HO=altem
WM_DDE_ADVISE	Requests server application to supply update for data item	Sending window ID	LO=handle to DDEADVISE structure HO=altem
WM_DDE_DATA	Sends data item value to client application	Sending window ID	LO=handle to DDEDATA structure HO=altem
WM_DDE_EXECUTE	Sends command string to server application	Sending window ID	LO=RESERVED HO=handle to Commands
WM_DDE_INITIATE	Initiates conversation with applications responding to application and topic names	Sending window ID	LO=aApplication HO=aTopic
WM_DDE_POKE	Requests server application to accept unsolicted data item value	Sending window ID	LO=handle to DDEPOKE structure HO=altem
WM_DDE_REQUEST	Requests server application to provide value of a data item	Sending window ID	LO=cfFormat HO=altem
WM_DDE_TERMINATE	Sent to terminate a DDE conversation	Sending window ID	RESERVED
WM_DDE__UNADVISE	Sent to server application to indicate item should no longer be updated	Sending window ID	LO=cfFormat HO=altem

Note:

• DDEACK structure:
bit 15 - fAck
bit 14 - fBusy
bit 13-8 - reserved
bit 7-0 - bAppReturnCode

• DDEADVISE structure:
word 1, bit 15 - fAckReq
word 1, bit 14 - fDeferUpd
word 1, bits 13-0 - reserved
word 2, cfFormat

• DDEDATA structure:
word 1, bit 15 - fAckReq
word 1, bit 14 - reserved
word 1, bit 13 - fRelease
word 1, bit 12 - fRequested
word 1, bits 11-0 - reserved
word 2 - cfFormat
word 3-n - value[]

• DDEPOKE structure:
word 1, bits 15-14 - reserved
word 1, bit 13 - fRelease
word 1, bits 12-0 - reserved
word 2 - cfFormat
word 3-n - value[]

Source: Microsoft Windows 3.0 SDK Programmer's Reference, pages 15-6 through 15-18

See Also:

6.012. Dynamic Data Exchange Protocol
6.082. Format of a Windows Message
6.083. Windows General Message Numbering
6.084. Window Management Messages
6.085. Initialization Messages
6.086. Input Messages
6.087. System and System Information Messages
6.088. Clipboard Messages
6.089. Control Messages
6.090. Notification Messages
6.091. Nonclient Area Messages
6.092. Scroll-Bar Messages
6.093. Multiple Document Interface Messages

6.095. WINDOWS FUNCTION SUMMARY BY VERSION

Function Name	*1.x*	*2.x*	*3.x*
AccessResource	✔	✔	✔
AddAtom	✔	✔	✔
AddFontResource	✔	✔	✔
AdjustWindowRect	✔	✔	✔
AdjustWindowRectEx			✔
AllocDStoCSAlias			✔
AllocResource	✔	✔	✔
AllocSelector			✔
AnimatePalette			✔
AnsiLower	✔	✔	✔
AnsiLowerBuff			✔
AnsiNext	✔	✔	✔
AnsiPrev	✔	✔	✔
AnsiToOEM	✔	✔	✔
AnsiToOEMBuff			✔
AnsiUpper	✔	✔	✔
AnsiUpperBuff			✔
AnyPopup	✔	✔	✔
AppendMenu			✔
Arc	✔	✔	✔
ArrangeIconicWindows			✔
BeginDeferWindowPos			✔
BeginPaint	✔	✔	✔
BitBlt	✔	✔	✔
BringWindowToTop	✔	✔	✔
BuildCommDCB	✔	✔	✔
CallMsgFilter	✔	✔	✔
CallWindowProc	✔	✔	✔
Catch	✔	✔	✔
ChangeClipboardChain	✔	✔	✔
ChangeMenu	✔	✔	✔
ChangeSelector			✔
CheckDlgButton	✔	✔	✔
CheckMenuItem	✔	✔	✔
CheckRadioButton	✔	✔	✔
ChildWindowFromPoint	✔	✔	✔
Chord		✔	✔
ClearCommBreak	✔	✔	✔
ClientToScreen	✔	✔	✔
ClipCursor	✔	✔	✔
CloseClipboard	✔	✔	✔
CloseComm	✔	✔	✔
CloseMetaFile	✔	✔	✔
CloseSound	✔	✔	✔
CloseWindow	✔	✔	✔
CombineRgn	✔	✔	✔
CopyMetaFile	✔	✔	✔
CopyRect	✔	✔	✔
CountClipboardFormats	✔	✔	✔
CountVoiceNotes	✔	✔	✔
CreateBitmap	✔	✔	✔
CreateBitmapIndirect	✔	✔	✔
CreateBrushIndirect	✔	✔	✔
CreateCaret	✔	✔	✔
CreateCompatibleBitmap	✔	✔	✔
CreateCompatibleDC	✔	✔	✔
CreateCursor			✔
CreateDC	✔	✔	✔
CreateDialog	✔	✔	✔
CreateDialogIndirect		✔	✔
CreateDialogIndirectParam			✔
CreateDialogParam			✔
CreateDLBitmap			✔
CreateDLBPatternBrush			✔
CreateDiscardableBitmap	✔	✔	✔
CreateEllipticRgn	✔	✔	✔
CreateEllipticRgnIndirect	✔	✔	✔

Function Name	*1.x*	*2.x*	*3.x*
CreateFont	✔	✔	✔
CreateFontIndirect	✔	✔	✔
CreateHatchBrush	✔	✔	✔
CreateIC	✔	✔	✔
CreateIcon			✔
CreateMenu	✔	✔	✔
CreateMetaFile	✔	✔	✔
CreatePalette			✔
CreatePatternBrush	✔	✔	✔
CreatePen	✔	✔	✔
CreatePenIndirect	✔	✔	✔
CreatePolygonRgn	✔	✔	✔
CreatePolyPolygonRgn			✔
CreatePopupMenu			✔
CreateRectRgn	✔	✔	✔
CreateRectRgnIndirect	✔	✔	✔
CreateRoundRectRegion			✔
CreateSolidBrush	✔	✔	✔
CreateWindow	✔	✔	✔
CreateWindowEx			✔
DebugBreak			✔
DefDlgProc			✔
DeferWindowPos			✔
DefFrameProc			✔
DefHookProc		✔	✔
DefineHandleTable			✔
DefMDIChildProc			✔
DefWindowProc	✔	✔	✔
DeleteAtom	✔	✔	✔
DeleteDC	✔	✔	✔
DeleteMenu			✔
DeleteMetaFile	✔	✔	✔
DeleteObject	✔	✔	✔
Destroy Caret	✔	✔	✔
DestroyCursor			✔
DestroyIcon			✔
DestroyMenu	✔	✔	✔
DestroyWindow	✔	✔	✔
DeviceCapabilities			✔
DeviceMode	✔		
DialogBox	✔	✔	✔
DialogBoxIndirect		✔	✔
DialogBoxIndirectParam			✔
DialogBoxParam			✔
DispatchMessage	✔	✔	✔
DlgDirList	✔	✔	✔
DlgDirListComboBox			✔
DlgDirSelect	✔	✔	✔
DlgDirSelectComboBox			✔
DOS3Call			✔
DPtoLP	✔	✔	✔
DrawFocusRect			✔
DrawIcon	✔	✔	✔
DrawMenuBar	✔	✔	✔
DrawText	✔	✔	✔
Ellipse	✔	✔	✔
EmptyClipboard	✔	✔	✔
EnableHardwareInput		✔	✔
EnableMenuItem	✔	✔	✔
EnableWindow	✔	✔	✔
EndDeferWindowPos			✔
EndDialog	✔	✔	✔
EndPaint	✔	✔	✔
EnumChildWindows	✔	✔	✔
EnumClipboardFormats	✔	✔	✔
EnumFonts	✔	✔	✔
EnumMetaFile		✔	✔

(Continued)

6.095. WINDOWS FUNCTION SUMMARY BY VERSION (continued)

Function Name	*1.x*	*2.x*	*3.x*
EnumObjects	✔	✔	✔
EnumProps	✔	✔	✔
EnumTaskWindows		✔	✔
EnumWindows	✔	✔	✔
EqualRect		✔	✔
EqualRgn	✔	✔	✔
Escape (ABORTDOC)	✔	✔	✔
Escape (BANDINFO)		✔	✔
Escape (BEGIN_PATH)		✔	
Escape (CLIP_TO_PATH)		✔	
Escape (DEVICEDATA)	✔	✔	✔
Escape (DRAFTMODE)	✔	✔	✔
Escape (DRAWPATTERNRECT)		✔	✔
Escape (ENABLEDUPLEX)		✔	✔
Escape (ENABLEMANUALFEED)	✔	✔	
Escape (ENABLEPAIRKERNING)	✔	✔	✔
Escape (ENABLERELATIVEWIDTHS)	✔	✔	✔
Escape (ENDDOC)	✔	✔	✔
Escape (END_PATH)			✔
Escape (ENUMPAPERBINS)			✔
Escape (ENUMPAPERMETRICS)			✔
Escape (EPSPRINTING)			✔
Escape (EXT_DEVICE_CAPS)			✔
Escape (EXTTEXTOUT)	✔	✔	✔
Escape (FLUSHOUTPUT)	✔	✔	✔
Escape (GETCOLORTABLE)	✔	✔	✔
Escape (GETEXTENDEDTEXTMETRICS)	✔	✔	✔
Escape (GETEXTENTTABLE)	✔	✔	✔
Escape (GETFACENAME)			✔
Escape (GETPAIRKERNTABLE)	✔	✔	✔
Escape (GETPHYSPAGESIZE)	✔	✔	✔
Escape (GETPRINTINGOFFSET)	✔	✔	✔
Escape (GETSCALINGFACTOR)	✔	✔	✔
Escape (GETSETPAPERBINS)			✔
Escape (GETSETPAPERMETRICS)			✔
Escape (GETSETPAPERORIENT)			✔
Escape (GETSETSCREENPARAMS)			✔
Escape (GETTECHNOLOGY)	✔	✔	✔
Escape (GETTRACKKERNTABLE)	✔	✔	✔
Escape (GETVECTORBRUSHSIZE)			✔
Escape (GETVECTORPENSIZE)			✔
Escape (MFCOMMENT)		✔	✔
Escape (NEWFRAME)	✔	✔	✔
Escape (NEXTBAND)	✔	✔	✔
Escape (PASSTHROUGH)			✔
Escape (QUERYESCSUPPORT)	✔	✔	✔
Escape (RESTORE_CTM)			✔
Escape (SAVE_CTM)			✔
Escape (SELECTPAPERSOURCE)	✔	✔	✔
Escape (SETABORTPROC)	✔	✔	✔
Escape (SETALLJUSTVALUES)		✔	✔
Escape (SET_ARC_DIRECTION)			✔
Escape (SET_BACKGROUND_COLOR)			✔
Escape (SET_BOUNDS)			✔
Escape (SETCHARSET)	✔	✔	
Escape (SETCOLORTABLE)	✔	✔	✔
Escape (SETCOPYCOUNT)	✔	✔	✔
Escape (SETKERNTRACK)	✔	✔	✔
Escape (SETLINECAP)		✔	✔
Escape (SETLINEJOIN)		✔	✔
Escape (TRANSORM_CTM)			✔
EscapeCommFunction	✔	✔	✔
ExcludeClipRect	✔	✔	✔
ExcludeUpdateRgn		✔	✔
ExitWindows			✔
ExtDevMode			✔
ExtFloodFill			✔

Function Name	*1.x*	*2.x*	*3.x*
ExtTextOut		✔	✔
FatalAppExit			✔
FatalExit	✔	✔	✔
FillRect	✔	✔	✔
FillRgn	✔	✔	✔
FindAtom	✔	✔	✔
FindResource	✔	✔	✔
FindWindow	✔	✔	✔
FlashWindow	✔	✔	✔
FloodFill	✔	✔	✔
FlushComm	✔	✔	✔
FrameRect	✔	✔	✔
FrameRgn	✔	✔	✔
FreeLibrary	✔	✔	✔
FreeModule			✔
FreeProcInstance	✔	✔	✔
FreeResource	✔	✔	✔
FreeSelector			✔
GetActiveWindow	✔	✔	✔
GetAspectRatioFilter		✔	✔
GetAsyncKeyState		✔	✔
GetAtomHandle	✔	✔	✔
GetAtomName	✔	✔	✔
GetBitmapBits	✔	✔	✔
GetBitmapDimension	✔	✔	✔
GetBkColor	✔	✔	✔
GetBkMode	✔	✔	✔
GetBrushOrg	✔	✔	✔
GetBValue	✔	✔	✔
GetCapture		✔	✔
GetCaretBlinkTime	✔	✔	✔
GetCaretPos		✔	✔
GetCharWidth		✔	✔
GetClassInfo			✔
GetClassLong	✔	✔	✔
GetClassName	✔	✔	✔
GetClassWord	✔	✔	✔
GetClientRect	✔	✔	✔
GetClipboardData	✔	✔	✔
GetClipboardFormatName	✔	✔	✔
GetClipboardOwner	✔	✔	✔
GetClipboardViewer	✔	✔	✔
GetClipBox	✔	✔	✔
GetCodeHandle	✔	✔	✔
GetCodeInfo			✔
GetCommError	✔	✔	✔
GetCommEventMask	✔	✔	✔
GetCommState	✔	✔	✔
GetCurrentPDB			✔
GetCurrentPosition	✔	✔	✔
GetCurrentTask	✔	✔	✔
GetCurrentTime	✔	✔	✔
GetCursorPos	✔	✔	✔
GetDC	✔	✔	✔
GetDCOrg		✔	✔
GetDesktopWindow			✔
GetDeviceCaps	✔	✔	✔
GetDialogBaseUnits			✔
GetDLBits			✔
GetDlgCtrlID			✔
GetDlgItem	✔	✔	✔
GetFocus	✔	✔	✔
GetFreeSpace			✔
GetGValue	✔	✔	✔
GetInputState		✔	✔
GetInstanceData	✔	✔	✔
GetKBCodePage			✔

(Continued)

6.095. WINDOWS FUNCTION SUMMARY BY VERSION (continued)

Function Name	1.x	2.x	3.x
GetKeyboardState		✔	✔
GetKeyboardType			✔
GetKeyNameText			✔
GetKeyState	✔	✔	✔
GetLastActivePopup			✔
GetMapMode	✔	✔	✔
GetMenu	✔	✔	✔
GetMenuCheckMarkDimensions			✔
GetMenuItemCount		✔	✔
GetMenuItemID		✔	✔
GetMenuState		✔	✔
GetMenuString	✔	✔	✔
GetMessage	✔	✔	✔
GetMessagePos	✔	✔	✔
GetMessageTime	✔	✔	✔
GetMetaFile	✔	✔	✔
GetMetaFileBits	✔	✔	✔
GetModuleFileName	✔	✔	✔
GetModuleHandle	✔	✔	✔
GetModuleUsage	✔	✔	✔
GetNearestColor	✔	✔	✔
GetNearestPaletteIndex			✔
GetNextDlgGroupItem		✔	✔
GetNextDlgTabItem		✔	✔
GetNextWindow		✔	✔
GetNumTasks		✔	✔
GetObject	✔	✔	✔
GetPaletteEntries			✔
GetParent	✔	✔	✔
GetPixel	✔	✔	✔
GetPolyFillMode	✔	✔	✔
GetPriorityClipboardFormat			✔
GetPrivateProfileInt			✔
GetPrivateProfileString			✔
GetProcAddress	✔	✔	✔
GetProfileInt	✔	✔	✔
GetProfileString	✔	✔	✔
GetProp	✔	✔	✔
GetRgnBox			✔
GetRelAbs	✔	✔	
GetROP2	✔	✔	✔
GetRValue	✔	✔	✔
GetScrollPos	✔	✔	✔
GetScrollRange	✔	✔	✔
GetStockObject	✔	✔	✔
GetStretchBltMode	✔	✔	✔
GetSubMenu	✔	✔	✔
GetSysColor	✔	✔	✔
GetSysModalWindow	✔	✔	✔
GetSystemDirectory			✔
GetSystemMenu	✔	✔	✔
GetSystemMetrics	✔	✔	✔
GetSystemPaletteEntries			✔
GetSystemPaletteUse			✔
GetTabbedTextExtent			✔
GetTempDrive	✔	✔	✔
GetTempFileName	✔	✔	✔
GetTextAlign		✔	✔
GetTextCharacterExtra	✔	✔	✔
GetTextColor	✔	✔	✔
GetTextExtent	✔	✔	✔
GetTextFace	✔	✔	✔
GetTextMetrics	✔	✔	✔
GetThresholdEvent	✔	✔	✔
GetThresholdStatus	✔	✔	✔
GetTickCount		✔	✔
GetTopWindow		✔	✔

Function Name	1.x	2.x	3.x
GetUpdateRect	✔	✔	✔
GetUpdateRgn		✔	✔
GetVersion	✔	✔	✔
GetViewportExt	✔	✔	✔
GetViewportOrg	✔	✔	✔
GetWindow		✔	✔
GetWindowDC	✔	✔	✔
GetWindowExt	✔	✔	✔
GetWindowLong	✔	✔	✔
GetWindowOrg	✔	✔	✔
GetWindowRect	✔	✔	✔
GetWindowsDirectory			✔
GetWindowTask		✔	✔
GetWindowText	✔	✔	✔
GetWindowTextLength	✔	✔	✔
GetWindowWord	✔	✔	✔
GetWinFlags			✔
GlobalAddAtom		✔	✔
GlobalAlloc	✔	✔	✔
GlobalCompact	✔	✔	✔
GlobalDeleteAtom		✔	✔
GlobalDiscard	✔	✔	✔
GlobalDosAlloc			✔
GlobalDosFree			✔
GlobalFindAtom		✔	✔
GlobalFix			✔
GlobalFlags	✔	✔	✔
GlobalFree	✔	✔	✔
GlobalGetAtomName		✔	✔
GlobalHandle	✔	✔	✔
GlobalLock	✔	✔	✔
GlobalLRUNewest			✔
GlobalLRUOldest			✔
GlobalNotify			✔
GlobalPageLock			✔
GlobalPageUnlock			✔
GlobalReAlloc	✔	✔	✔
GlobalSize	✔	✔	✔
GlobalUnfix			✔
GlobalUnlock	✔	✔	✔
GlobalUnwire		✔	✔
GlobalWire		✔	✔
GrayString	✔	✔	✔
HIBYTE	✔	✔	✔
HideCaret	✔	✔	✔
HiliteMenuItem	✔	✔	✔
HIWORD	✔	✔	✔
InflateRect	✔	✔	✔
InitAtomTable	✔	✔	✔
InSendMessage	✔	✔	✔
InsertMenu			✔
IntersectClipRect	✔	✔	✔
IntersectRect	✔	✔	✔
InvalidateRect	✔	✔	✔
InvalidateRgn	✔	✔	✔
InvertRect	✔	✔	✔
InvertRgn	✔	✔	✔
IsCharAlpha			✔
IsCharNumeric			✔
IsCharLower			✔
IsCharUpper			✔
IsChild	✔	✔	✔
IsClipboardFormatAvailable	✔	✔	✔
IsDialogMessage	✔	✔	✔
IsDlgButtonChecked	✔	✔	✔
IsIconic	✔	✔	✔
IsRectEmpty	✔	✔	✔

(Continued)

6.095. WINDOWS FUNCTION SUMMARY BY VERSION (continued)

Function Name	*1.x*	*2.x*	*3.x*
IsWindow	✔	✔	✔
IsWindowEnabled	✔	✔	✔
IsWindowVisible	✔	✔	✔
IsZoomed		✔	✔
KillTimer	✔	✔	✔
_lclose			✔
_lcreat			✔
LimitEmsPages			✔
LineDDA	✔	✔	✔
LineTo	✔	✔	✔
_llseek			✔
LoadAccelerators	✔	✔	✔
LoadBitmap	✔	✔	✔
LoadCursor	✔	✔	✔
LoadIcon	✔	✔	✔
LoadLibrary	✔	✔	✔
LoadMenu	✔	✔	✔
LoadMenuIndirect		✔	✔
LoadModule			✔
LoadResource	✔	✔	✔
LoadString	✔	✔	✔
LOBYTE	✔	✔	✔
LocalAlloc	✔	✔	✔
LocalCompact	✔	✔	✔
LocalData	✔	✔	
LocalDiscard	✔	✔	✔
LocalFlags	✔	✔	✔
LocalFree	✔	✔	✔
LocalFreeze	✔	✔	
LocalHandle	✔	✔	✔
LocalHandleDelta	✔	✔	
LocalInit	✔	✔	✔
LocalLock	✔	✔	✔
LocalMelt	✔	✔	
LocalNotify	✔	✔	
LocalReAlloc	✔	✔	✔
LocalShrink		✔	✔
LocalSize	✔	✔	✔
LocalUnlock	✔	✔	✔
LockData			✔
LockResource	✔	✔	✔
LockSegment	✔	✔	✔
_lopen			✔
LOWORD	✔	✔	✔
LPtoDP	✔	✔	✔
_lread			✔
lstrcat			✔
lstrcmp			✔
lstrcmpi			✔
lstrcpy			✔
lstrlen			✔
_lwrite			✔
MAKEINTATOM	✔	✔	✔
MAKEINTRESOURCE	✔	✔	✔
MAKELONG	✔	✔	✔
MAKEPOINT	✔	✔	✔
MakeProcInstance	✔	✔	✔
MapDialogRect	✔	✔	✔
MapVirtualKey			✔
max	✔	✔	✔
MessageBeep	✔	✔	✔
MessageBox	✔	✔	✔
min	✔	✔	✔
ModifyMenu			✔
MoveConvertWindow		✔	
MoveTo	✔	✔	✔
MoveWindow	✔	✔	✔
MulDiv			✔
NetBIOSCall			✔
OemKeyScan			✔
OemToAnsi	✔	✔	✔
OemToAnsiBuff			✔
OffsetClipRgn	✔	✔	✔
OffsetRect	✔	✔	✔
OffsetRgn	✔	✔	✔
OffsetViewportOrg		✔	✔
OffsetWindowOrg		✔	✔
OpenClipboard	✔	✔	✔
OpenComm	✔	✔	✔
OpenFile	✔	✔	✔
OpenIcon	✔	✔	✔
OpenSound	✔	✔	✔
OpenDebugString			✔
PaintRgn	✔	✔	✔
PALETTEINDEX			✔
PALETTERGB			✔
PatBlt	✔	✔	✔
PeekMessage	✔	✔	✔
Pie	✔	✔	✔
PlayMetaFile	✔	✔	✔
PlayMetaFileRecord		✔	✔
Polygon	✔	✔	✔
Polyline	✔	✔	✔
PolyPolygon			✔
PostAppMessage	✔	✔	✔
PostMessage	✔	✔	✔
PostQuitMessage	✔	✔	✔
ProfClear			✔
ProfFinish			✔
ProfFlush			✔
ProfInsChk			✔
ProfSampRate			✔
ProfSetup			✔
ProfStart			✔
ProfStop			✔
PtInRect	✔	✔	✔
PtInRegion	✔	✔	✔
PtVisible	✔	✔	✔
ReadComm	✔	✔	✔
RealizePalette			✔
Rectangle	✔	✔	✔
RectInRegion			✔
RectVisible	✔	✔	✔
RegisterClass	✔	✔	✔
RegisterClipboardFormat	✔	✔	✔
RegisterWindowDestroy		✔	
RegisterWindowMessage	✔	✔	✔
ReleaseCapture	✔	✔	✔
ReleaseDC	✔	✔	✔
RemoveFontResource	✔	✔	✔
RemoveMenu			✔
RemoveProp	✔	✔	✔
ReplyMessage	✔	✔	✔
ResizePalette			✔
RestoreDC	✔	✔	✔
RGB	✔	✔	✔
RoundRect	✔	✔	✔
SaveDC	✔	✔	✔
ScaleViewportExt		✔	✔
ScaleWindowExt		✔	✔
ScreenToClient	✔	✔	✔
ScrollDC		✔	✔
ScrollWindow	✔	✔	✔
SelectClipRgn	✔	✔	✔

(Continued)

6.095. WINDOWS FUNCTION SUMMARY BY VERSION (continued)

Function Name	*1.x*	*2.x*	*3.x*
SelectObject	✔	✔	✔
SelectPalette			✔
SendDlgItemMessage	✔	✔	✔
SendMessage	✔	✔	✔
SetActiveWindow	✔	✔	✔
SetBitmapBits	✔	✔	✔
SetBitmapDimension	✔	✔	✔
SetBkColor	✔	✔	✔
SetBkMode	✔	✔	✔
SetBrushOrg	✔	✔	✔
SetCapture	✔	✔	✔
SetCaretBlinkTime	✔	✔	✔
SetCaretPos	✔	✔	✔
SetClassLong	✔	✔	✔
SetClassWord	✔	✔	✔
SetClipboardData	✔	✔	✔
SetClipboardViewer	✔	✔	✔
SetCommBreak	✔	✔	✔
SetCommEventMask	✔	✔	✔
SetCommState	✔	✔	✔
SetConvertHook		✔	
SetConvertParms		✔	
SetConvertWindowHeight		✔	
SetCursor	✔	✔	✔
SetCursorPos	✔	✔	✔
SetDIBits			✔
SetDLBitsToDevice			✔
SetDlgItemInt	✔	✔	✔
SetDlgItemText	✔	✔	✔
SetDoubleClickTime		✔	✔
SetEnvironment	✔	✔	✔
SetErrorMode			✔
SetFocus	✔	✔	✔
SetHandleCount			✔
SetKeyboardState		✔	✔
SetMapMode	✔	✔	✔
SetMapperFlags		✔	✔
SetMenu	✔	✔	✔
SetMenuItemBitmaps			✔
SetMessageQueue		✔	✔
SetMetaFileBits	✔	✔	✔
SetPaletteEntries			✔
SetParent		✔	✔
SetPixel	✔	✔	✔
SetPolyFillMode	✔	✔	✔
SetPriority	✔	✔	
SetProp	✔	✔	✔
SetRect	✔	✔	✔
SetRectEmpty	✔	✔	✔
SetRectRgn		✔	✔
SetRelAbs	✔	✔	
SetResourceHandler	✔	✔	✔
SetROP2	✔	✔	✔
SetScrollPos	✔	✔	✔
SetScrollRange	✔	✔	✔
SetSoundNoise	✔	✔	✔
SetStretchBltMode	✔	✔	✔
SetSwapAreaSize		✔	✔
SetSysColors	✔	✔	✔
SetSysModalWindow	✔	✔	✔
SetSystemPaletteUse			✔
SetTextAlign		✔	✔
SetTextCharacterExtra	✔	✔	✔
SetTextColor	✔	✔	✔
SetTextJustification	✔	✔	✔
SetTimer	✔	✔	✔
SetViewportExt	✔	✔	✔

Function Name	*1.x*	*2.x*	*3.x*
SetViewportOrg	✔	✔	✔
SetVoiceAccent	✔	✔	✔
SetVoiceEnvelope	✔	✔	✔
SetVoiceNote	✔	✔	✔
SetVoiceQueueSize	✔	✔	✔
SetVoiceSound	✔	✔	✔
SetVoiceThreshold	✔	✔	✔
SetWindowExt	✔	✔	✔
SetWindowLong	✔	✔	✔
SetWindowOrg	✔	✔	✔
SetWindowPos		✔	✔
SetWindowsHook	✔	✔	✔
SetWindowText	✔	✔	✔
SetWindowWord	✔	✔	✔
ShowCaret	✔	✔	✔
ShowCursor	✔	✔	✔
ShowOwnedPopups		✔	✔
ShowScrollBar		✔	✔
ShowWindow	✔	✔	✔
SizeofResource	✔	✔	✔
StartSound	✔	✔	✔
StopSound	✔	✔	✔
StretchBlt	✔	✔	✔
StretchDIBits			✔
SwapMouseButton	✔	✔	✔
SwapRecording			✔
SwitchStackBack			✔
SwitchStackTo			✔
SyncAllVoices	✔	✔	✔
TabbedTextOut			✔
TextOut	✔	✔	✔
Throw	✔	✔	✔
ToAscii			✔
TrackPopupMenu			✔
TranslateAccelerator	✔	✔	✔
TranslateMDISysAccel			✔
TranslateMessage	✔	✔	✔
TransmitCommChar	✔	✔	
UngetCommChar	✔	✔	✔
UnhookWindowsHook		✔	✔
UnionRect	✔	✔	✔
UnlockData	✔	✔	✔
UnlockResource		✔	✔
UnlockSegment	✔	✔	✔
UnrealizeObject	✔	✔	✔
UnregisterClass			✔
UpdateColors			✔
UpdateWindow	✔	✔	✔
ValidateCodeSegments			✔
ValidateFreeSpaces		✔	✔
ValidateRect	✔	✔	✔
ValidateRgn	✔	✔	✔
VkKeyScan			✔
WaitMessage	✔	✔	✔
WaitSoundState	✔	✔	✔
WindowFromPoint	✔	✔	✔
WinExec			✔
WinHelp			✔
WinMain	✔	✔	
WndProc	✔	✔	
WriteComm	✔	✔	✔
WritePrivateProfileString			✔
WriteProfileString	✔	✔	✔
wsprintf			✔
wvsprintf			✔
Yield	✔	✔	✔

Source: Microsoft Windows 3.0 SDK Programmer's Reference, pages 4-1 through 4-469

6.096. WINDOWS FUNCTION SUMMARY BY NAME

Function Name	Type	Parameters*	Parm Type	Parameter Definition	Return Value	Pg§
AccessResource	int	hInstance hResInfo	HANDLE HANDLE	IDs instance of module containing resource IDs desired resource	DOS file handle or -1 if none	2
AddAtom	ATOM	lpstring	LPSTR	Points to char string to add to table	ATOM or NULL	2
AddFontResource	int	lpFilename	LPSTR	Points to char string containing font res file or contains handle to loaded module	Number of fonts added or 0	3
AdjustWindowRect	void	lpRect dwStyle bMenu	LPRECT DWORD BOOL	Points to RECT structure of client rectangle Specifies window styles Specifies whether window has menu	None	3
AdjustWindowRectEx†	void	lpRect dwStyle bMenu dwExStyle	LPRECT DWORD BOOL DWORD	Points to RECT of client rectangle Specifies window styles of window to convert Specifies whether window has a menu Specifies extended style of window	None	4
AllocDStoCSAlias†	WORD	wSelector	WORD	Specifies data-segment selector	CS selector or 0 if error	5
AllocResource	HANDLE	hInstance hResInfo dwSize	HANDLE HANDLE DWORD	ID of module containing resource ID of resource Specifies override size in bytes (0=ignore)	Global memory block allocated for resource	5
AllocSelector†	WORD	wSelector	WORD	Specifies selector to be copied or NULL if new, uninitialized sector desired	Selector, or 0 if error	6
AnimatePalette†	void	hPalette wStartIndex wNumEntries lpPaletteColors	HPALETTE WORD WORD LPPALETTEENTRY	ID of logical palette First entry of palette to be animated Number of entries to be animated Points to first entry of replacement structs	None	7
AnsiLower	LPSTR	lpString	LPSTR	Points to ASCIIZ string, or if HO=0 then LO byte contains character	Ptr to converted string, or char in LO	7
AnsiLowerBuff†	WORD	lpString nLength	LPSTR WORD	Points to buffer containing 1 or more chars Number of chars in buffer (0=65,536)	Length of converted string	8
AnsiNext	LPSTR	lpCurrentChar	LPSTR	Points to char in ASCIIZ string	Next char in string	8
AnsiPrev	LPSTR	lpStart lpCurrentChar	LPSTR LPSTR	Points to beginning of string Points to char in ASCIIZ string	Prev char in string	9
AnsiToOem	int	lpAnsiStr lpOemStr	LPSTR LPSTR	Points to ASCIIZ string (in ANSI set) Points to location to put translated string	Always -1	9
AnsiToOemBuff†	void	lpAnsiStr lpOemStr nLength	LPSTR LPSTR WORD	Points to buffer containing ANSI chars Points to location to put translated string Number of chars in buffer (0=65,536)	None	10
AnsiUpper	LPSTR	lpString	LPSTR	Points to ASCIIZ string, or if HO=0 then LO byte contains character	Ptr to converted string, or char in LO	10
AnsiUpperBuff†	WORD	lpString nLength	LPSTR WORD	Points to buffer containing ANSI chars Number of chars in buffer (0=65,536)	Length of converted string	11
AnyPopup	BOOL	none			≠0=popup exists	11
AppendMenu†	BOOL	hMenu wFlags wIDNewItem lpNewItem	HMENU WORD WORD LPSTR	ID of menu to change Specifies state of new menu item to add Command ID of new item, or menu handle of popup Content of new menu item	TRUE=success	11
Arc	BOOL	hDC X1 Y1 X2 Y2 X3 Y3 X4 Y4	HDC int int int int int int int int	ID of device context x-coord of upper-left corner of bounding rect y-coord of upper-left corner of bounding rect x-coord of lower-right corner of bounding rect y-coord of lower-right corner of bounding rect x-coord of arc's start point y-coord of arc's start point x-coord of arc's end point y-coord of arc's end point	≠0 if arc drawn	14
ArrangeIconicWindows†	WORD	hWnd	HWND	ID of window	Height of icons or 0	15
BeginDeferWindowPos†	HANDLE	nNumWindows	int	Number of windows	ID of data struct or NULL	16
BeginPaint	HDC	hWnd lpPaint	HWND LPPAINTSTRUCT	ID of window Data structure to receive painting info	DC of window	16
BitBlt	BOOL	hDestDC X Y nWidth nHeight hSrcDC XSrc YSrc dwRop	HDC int int int int HDC int int DWORD	ID of device context to receive bitmap x-coord of upper-left corner of dest rect y-coord of upper-left corner of dest rect Width of bitmap in logical units Height of bitmap in logical units ID of device context to receive bitmap x-coord of upper-left corner of source bitmap y-coord of upper-left corner of source bitmap Raster operation to perform	≠0 if bitmap drawn	17
BringWindowToTop	void	hWnd	HWND	ID of window to bring to top	None	20
BuildCommDCB	int	lpDef lpDCB	LPSTR DCB FAR *	Points to ASCIIZ string with device-control info Points to DCB structure to receive string	0 if success <0 if error	20
CallMsgFilter	BOOL	lpMsg nCode	LPMSG int	Points to MSG structure to be filtered Code used by filter function to process message	FALSE=message should be processed	21

(Continued)

6.096. WINDOWS FUNCTION SUMMARY BY NAME (continued)

Function Name	Type	Parameters*	Parm Type	Parameter Definition	Return Value	Pg§
CallWindowProc	LONG	lpPrevWndFunc hWnd wMsg wParam lParam	FARPROC HWND WORD WORD DWORD	Address of previous window function ID of window receiving message Message number Message-dependent information Message-dependent information	Depends upon message sent	22
Catch	int	lpCatchBuf	LPCATCHBUF	Points to CATCHBUF structure	0=environment copied to buffer	22
ChangeClipboardChain	BOOL	hWnd hWndNext	HWND HWND	ID of window to be removed from chain ID of window following hWnd in chain	≠0 if window found and removed	23
ChangeMenu	No longer supported by 3.0 (replaced by AppendMenu, DeleteMenu, InsertMenu, ModifyMenu, and RemoveMenu)					23
ChangeSelector†	WORD	wDestSelector wSourceSelector	WORD WORD	Selector to receives the converted selector Selector to be converted	Selector copied and converted 0 if failure	24
CheckDlgButton	void	hDlg nIDButton wCheck	HWND int WORD	ID of dialog box containing button Button control to be modified Action to take	none	24
CheckMenuItem	BOOL	hMenu wIDCheckItem wCheck	HMENU WORD WORD	ID of menu Menu item to be checked Method to check menu item	Previous state of item or -1 if menu item doesn't exist	25
CheckRadioButton	void	hDlg nIDFirstButton nIDLastButton nIDCheckButton	HWND int int int	ID of dialog box Integer ID of first radio button in group Integer ID of last radio button in group Integer ID of radio button to be checked	None	26
ChildWindowFromPoint	HWND	hWndParent Point	HWND POINT	ID of parent window Client coordinates of point to be tested	ID of child window containing point or NULL	26
Chord	BOOL	hDC X1 Y1 X2 Y2 X3 Y3 X4 Y4	HDC int int int int int int int int	ID of device context chord to appear in x-coord of bounding rects upper-left corner y-coord of bounding rects upper-left corner x-coord of bounding rects lower-right corner y-ccord of bounding rects lower-right corner x-coord of one end of line segment y-coord of one end of line segment x-coord of one end of line segment y-coord of one end of line segment	≠0 if arc drawn	27
ClearCommBreak	int	nCid	int	Communication device to be restored	0=success <0 if invalid device	28
ClientToScreen	void	hWnd lpPoint	HWND LPPOINT	ID of window whose client area will be used for conv. Points to POINT structure with coords to convert	None	28
ClipCursor	void	lpRect	LPRECT	Points to RECT structure with confining rectangle	None	29
CloseClipboard	BOOL				≠0 clipboard closed	29
CloseComm	int	nCid	int	Communication device to be closed	0=success	30
CloseMetaFile	HANDLE	hDC	HANDLE	ID of metafile DC to close	≠0 file closed else NULL	30
CloseSound	void				None	30
CloseWindow	void	hWnd	HWND	ID of window to minimize	None	30
CombineRgn	int	hDestRgn hSrcRgn1 hSrcRgn2 nCombineMode	HRGN HRGN HRGN int	ID of existing region to be replaced ID of first region to combine ID of second region to combine Type of operation to perform on regions	Type of resulting region	31
CopyMetaFile	HANDLE	hSrcMetaFile lpFilename	HANDLE LPSTR	ID of source metafile Points to ASCIIZ string of file to recieve metafile	ID of new metafile	32
CopyRect	int	lpDestRect lpSourceRect	LPRECT LPRECT	Points to destination RECT data structure Points to source RECT data structure	Not used (has no meaning)	32
CountClipboardFormats	int				Number of formats	33
CountVoiceNotes	int	nVoice	int	Voice queue to be counted	Number of notes	33
CreateBitmap	HBITMAP	nWidth nHeight nPlanes nBitCount lpBits	int int BYTE BYTE LPSTR	Width of bitmap in pixels Height of bitmap in pixels Number of color planes in bitmap Number of color bits per display Points to array of initial bitmap bit values	ID of bitmap if successful, or NULL	33
CreateBitmapIndirect	HBITMAP	lpBitmap	BITMAP FAR *	Points to BITMAP struct	ID of bitmap if successful, or NULL	34
CreateBrushIndirect	HBRUSH	lpLogBrush	LOGBRUSH FAR *	Points to LOGBRUSH struct	ID of logbrush if successful, or NULL	35
CreateCaret	void	hWnd hBitmap nWidth nHeight	HWND HBITMAP int int	ID of window owning caret ID of bitmap defining shape Width of caret in logical units Height of caret in logical units	None	35
CreateCompatibleBitmap	HBITMAP	hDC nWidth nHeight	HDC int int	ID of device context Width of bitmap in bits Height of bitmap in bits	ID of bitmap if successful, or NULL	36

(Continued)

6.096. WINDOWS FUNCTION SUMMARY BY NAME (continued)

Function Name	*Type*	*Parameters**	*Parm Type*	*Parameter Definition*	*Return Value*	*Pg§*
CreateCompatibleDC	HDC	hDC	HDC	ID of device context or NULL	ID of DC if successful, or NULL	37
CreateCursor†	HCURSOR	hInstance	HANDLE	ID of module creating cursor	ID of cursor if successful, or NULL	38
		nXhotspot	int	Horz position of cursor hotspot		
		nYhotspot	int	Vert position of cursor hotspot		
		nWidth	int	Width of cursor in pixels		
		nHeight	int	Height of cursor in pixels		
		lpANDbitPlane	LPSTR	Points to array containing bit values for AND mask		
		lpXORbitPlane	LPSTR	Points to array containing bit values for XOR mask		
CreateDC	HDC	lpDriverName	LPSTR	Points to ASCIIZ string containing DOS filename	ID of device context or NULL	39
		lpDeviceName	LPSTR	Points to ASCIIZ string of name of device		
		lpOutput	LPSTR	Points to ASCIIZ string of DOS file or device		
		lpInitData	LPDEVMODE	Points to DEVMODE struct of initialization data		
CreateDialog	HWND	hInstance	HANDLE	ID of file containing dialog-box template	Window handle of dialog box or NULL	39
		lpTemplateName	LPSTR	Points to character string naming template		
		hWndParent	HWND	ID of window owning dialog box		
		lpDialogFunc	FARPROC	Address of dialog function		
CreateDialogIndirect	HWND	hInstance	HANDLE	ID of file containing dialog-box template	Window handle of dialog box or NULL	41
		lpDialogTemplate	LPSTR	Points to DLGTEMPLATE structure		
		hWndParent	HWND	ID of window owning dialog box		
		lpDialogFunc	FARPROC	Address of dialog function		
CreateDialogIndirectParam†	HWND	hInstance	HANDLE	ID of file containing dialog-box template	Window handle of dialog box or NULL	43
		lpDialogTemplate	LPSTR	Points to DLGTEMPLATE structure		
		hWndParent	HWND	ID of window owning dialog box		
		lpDialogFunc	FARPROC	Address of dialog function		
		dwInitParam	DWORD	32-bit value to pass to dialog function		
CreateDialogParam†	HWND	hInstance	HANDLE	ID of file containing dialog-box template	Window handle of dialog box or -1 if unable to create	44
		lpTemplateName	LPSTR	Points to char string naming dialog-box template		
		hWndParent	HWND	ID of window owning dialog box		
		lpDialogFunc	FARPROC	Address of dialog function		
		dwInitParam	DWORD	32-bit value to pass to dialog function		
CreateDIBitmap†	HBITMAP	hDC	HDC	ID of device context	ID of bitmap or NULL	44
		lpInfoHeader	LPBITMAPINFORHEADER	Points to BITMAPINFOHEADER structure		
		dwUsage	DWORD	Indicates whether bitmap is to be initialized		
		lpInitBits	LPSTR	Points to array of bitmap values		
		lpInitInfo	LPBITMAPINFO	Points to BITMAPINFO structure		
		wUsage	WORD	Specifies whether bmiColors is PAL or RGB		
CreateDIBPatternBrush†	HBRUSH	hPackedDIB	GLOBALHANDLE	ID of object containing packed bitmap	ID of logical brush or NULL	46
		wUsage	WORD	Specifies whether bmiColors is PAL or RGB		
CreateDiscardableBitmap	HBITMAP	hDC	HDC	ID of device context	ID of bitmap or NULL	46
		nWidth	int	Width of bitmap in bits		
		nHeight	int	Height of bitmap in bits		
CreateEllipticRgn	HRGN	X1	int	x-coord of upper-left corner of bounding rect	ID of new region or NULL	47
		Y1	int	y-coord of upper-left corner of bounding rect		
		X2	int	x-coord of lower-right corner of bounding rect		
		Y2	int	y-coord of lower-right corner of bounding rect		
CreateEllipticRgnIndirect	HRGN	lpRect	LPRECT	Points to RECT structure	ID of new region or NULL	48
CreateFont	HFONT	nHeight	int	Height of font in logical units	ID of logical font or NULL	48
		nWidth	int	Average width of font in logical units		
		nEscapement	int	Angle of each line of text in tenths of degrees		
		nOrientation	int	Angle of baseline in tenths of degrees		
		nWeight	int	Weight of font, in units 0-1000		
		cItalic	BYTE	Specifies whether font is italic		
		cUnderline	BYTE	Specifies whether font is underlined		
		cStrikeOut	BYTE	Specifies whether characters in font are struck out		
		cCharSet	BYTE	Specifies desired character set		
		cOutputPrecision	BYTE	Specifies desired output precision		
		cClipPrecision	BYTE	Specifies desired clipping precision		
		cQuality	BYTE	Specifies desired output quality		
		cPitchAndFamily	BYTE	Specifies pitch and family of font		
		lpFacename	LPSTR	Points to ASCIIZ string containing name of font		
CreateFontIndirect	HFONT	lpLogFont	LOGFONT FAR *	Points to LOGFONT structure	ID of logical font or NULL	51
CreateHatchBrush	HBRUSH	nIndex	int	Hatch style of brush	ID of logical brush or NULL	51
		crColor	COLORREF	Foreground color of brush		
CreateIC	HDC	lpDriverName	LPSTR	Points to ASCIIZ string of DOS filename	ID of information context for device or NULL	52
		lpDeviceName	LPSTR	Points to ASCIIZ string of device to be supported		
		lpOutput	LPSTR	Points to ASCIIZ string of DOS file or device name		
		lpInitData	LPSTR	Points to device-specific initialization data		

(Continued)

6.096. WINDOWS FUNCTION SUMMARY BY NAME (continued)

Function Name	Type	Parameters*	Parm Type	Parameter Definition	Return Value	Pg§
CreateIcon†	HICON	hInstance	HANDLE	ID of module creating icon	ID of icon or NULL	53
		nWidth	int	Width of icon in pixels		
		nHeight	int	Height of icon in pixels		
		nPlanes	BYTE	Number of planes in XOR mask of icon		
		nBitsPixel	BYTE	Bits per pixel in XOR mask of icon		
		lpANDbits	LPSTR	Points to array of bytes containing AND mask		
		lpXORbits	LPSTR	Points to array of bytes containing XOR mask		
CreateMenu	HMENU				ID of menu or NULL	54
CreateMetaFile	HANDLE	lpFilename	LPSTR	Points to ASCIIZ string containing name of file	ID of metafile device context or NULL	54
CreatePalette†	HPALETTE	lpLogPalette	LPLOGPALETTE	Points to LOGPALETTE structure	ID of logical palette or NULL	55
CreatePatternBrush	HBRUSH	hBitmap	HBITMAP	ID of bitmap	ID of logical brush or NULL	55
CreatePen	HPEN	nPenStyle	int	Pen style	ID of logical pen or NULL	56
		nWidth	int	Width of pen in logical units		
		crColor	COLORREF	Color of pen		
CreatePenIndirect	HPEN	lpLogPen	LOGPEN FAR *	Points to LOGPEN structure	ID of logical pen or NULL	57
CreatePolygonRgn	HRGN	lpPoints	LPPOINT	Points to array of POINT structures	ID of new region or NULL	57
		nCount	int	Number of points in array		
		nPolyFillMode	int	Polygon-filling mode to use in filling region		
CreatePolyPolygonRgn†	HRGN	lpPoints	LPPOINT	Points to array of POINT structures	ID of region or NULL	58
		lpPolyCounts	LPINT	Points to array of numbers of points in each polygon		
		nCount	int	Number of points in array		
		nPolyFillMode	int	Polygon-filling mode to use in filling region		
CreatePopupMenu†	HMENU				ID of menu or NULL	59
CreateRectRgn	HRGN	X1	int	x-coord of upper-left corner of region	ID of new region or NULL	59
		Y1	int	y-coord of upper-left corner of region		
		X2	int	x-coord of lower-right corner of region		
		Y2	int	y-coord of lower-right corner of region		
CreateRectRgnIndirect	HRGN	lpRect	LPRECT	Points to RECT structure	ID of new region or NULL	60
CreateRoundRectRegion†	HRGN	X1	int	x-coord of upper-left corner of region	ID of new region or NULL	60
		Y1	int	y-coord of upper-left corner of region		
		X2	int	x-coord of lower-right corner of region		
		Y2	int	y-coord of lower-right corner of region		
		X3	int	Width of ellipse used to create rounded corners		
		Y3	int	Height of ellipse used to create rounded corners		
CreateSolidBrush	HBRUSH	crColor	COLORREF	Color of brush	ID of logical brush or NULL	61
CreateWindow	HWND	lpClassName	LPSTR	Points to ASCIIZ string naming window class	ID of new window or NULL	61
		lpWindowName	LPSTR	Points to ASCIIZ string of window name		
		dwStyle	DWORD	Style of window to create		
		X	int	Initial x-position of window		
		Y	int	Initial y-position of window		
		nWidth	int	Width of window in device units		
		nHeight	int	Height of window in device units		
		hWndParent	HWND	Parent or owner window ID		
		hMenu	HMENU	Menu or child-window ID		
		hInstance	HANDLE	ID of module to be associated with window		
		lpParam	LPSTR	Points to value to pass to window		
CreateWindowEx†	HWND	dwExStyle	DWORD	Extended style of window	ID of new window or NULL	76
		lpClassName	LPSTR	Points to ASCIIZ string naming window class		
		lpWindowName	LPSTR	Points to ASCIIZ string of window name		
		dwStyle	DWORD	Style of window to create		
		X	int	Initial x-position of window		
		Y	int	Initial y-position of window		
		nWidth	int	Width of window in device units		
		nHeight	int	Height of window in device units		
		hWndParent	HWND	Parent or owner window ID		
		hMenu	HMENU	Menu or child-window ID		
		hInstance	HANDLE	ID of module to be associated with window		
		lpParam	LPSTR	Points to value to pass to window		
DebugBreak†	void				None	78
DefDlgProc†	LONG	hDlg	HWND	ID of dialog box	Result of message processing	78
		wMsg	WORD	Message number		
		wParam	WORD	Message-dependent information		
		lParam	DWORD	Message-dependent information		

(Continued)

6.096. WINDOWS FUNCTION SUMMARY BY NAME (continued)

Function Name	Type	Parameters*	Parm Type	Parameter Definition	Return Value	Pg§
DeferWindowPos†	HANDLE	hWinPosInfo	HANDLE	ID of multiwindow position data structure	ID updated multi	79
		hWnd	HWND	ID of window to update information about	window structure	
		hWndInsertAfter	HWND	ID of window following one to update	or NULL	
		x	int	x-coord of window's upper-left corner		
		y	int	y-coord of window's upper-left corner		
		cx	int	Window's new width		
		cy	int	Window's new height		
		wFlags	WORD	Size and position of window flags		
DefFrameProc†	LONG	hWnd	HWND	ID of MDI frame window	Result of message	81
		hWndMDIClient	HWND	ID of MDI client window	processing	
		wMsg	WORD	Message number		
		wParam	WORD	Message-dependent information		
		lParam	DWORD	Message-dependent information		
DefHookProc	DWORD	code	int	Code used by hook function to process function	Value related to	82
		wParam	WORD	Message-dependent information	code parameter	
		lParam	DWORD	Message-dependent information		
		lplpfnNextHook	FARPROC FAR *	Points to FARPROC structure		
DefineHandleTable†	BOOL	wOffset	WORD	Offset from beginning of DS to private table	≠0 if successful	83
DefMDIChildProc†	LONG	hWnd	HWND	ID of MDI child window	Result of message	84
		wMsg	WORD	Message number	processing	
		wParam	WORD	Message-dependent information		
		lParam	DWORD	Message-dependent information		
DefWindowProc	LONG	hWnd	HWND	ID of window passing message	Result of message	85
		wMsg	WORD	Message number	processing	
		wParam	WORD	Message-dependent information		
		lParam	DWORD	Message-dependent information		
DeleteAtom	ATOM	nAtom	ATOM	ID of atom and char string to delete	NULL=success	86
DeleteDC	BOOL	hDC	HDC	ID of device context to delete	≠0 if successful	86
DeleteMenu†	BOOL	hMenu	HMENU	ID of menu to be changed	TRUE=success	87
		nPosition	WORD	Menu item to be deleted		
		wFlags	WORD	Interpretation of nPostition parameter		
DeleteMetaFile	BOOL	hMF	HANDLE	ID of metafile to delete	≠0 if successful	87
DeleteObject	BOOL	hObject	HANDLE	ID of handle to object	≠0 if successful	88
DestroyCaret	void				None	88
DestroyCursor†	BOOL	hCursor	HCURSOR	ID of cursor to destroy	≠0 if successful	89
DestroyIcon†	BOOL	hIcon	HICON	ID of icon to destroy	≠0 if successful	89
DestroyMenu	BOOL	hMenu	HMENU	ID of menu to destroy	≠0 if successful	90
DestroyWindow	BOOL	hWnd	HWND	ID of window to destroy	≠0 if successful	90
DeviceCapabilities†	DWORD	lpDeviceName	LPSTR	Points to ASCIIZ string naming printer device	Depends on setting	91
		lpPort	LPSTR	Points to ASCIIZ string naming DOS port	nIndex value	
		nIndex	WORD	Capabilities to query		
		lpOutput	LPSTR	Points to array of bytes to receive query results		
		lpDevMode	DEVMODE FAR *	Points to DEVMODE structure		
DeviceMode	void	hWnd	HWND	ID of window to own dialog box	None	94
		hModule	HANDLE	ID of printer-driver module		
		lpDeviceName	LPSTR	Points to ASCIIZ string of device supported		
		lpOutput	LPSTR	Points to ASCIIZ string naming DOS file or device		
DialogBox	int	hInstance	HANDLE	ID of file containing dialog-box template	Value of nResult	95
		lpTemplateName	LPSTR	Points to ASCIIZ string naming dialog-box template	parameter used to	
		hWndParent	HWND	ID of window owning dialog box	terminate box	
		lpDialogFunc	FARPROC	Address of dialog function	or -1	
DialogBoxIndirect	int	hInstance	HANDLE	ID of file containing dialog-box template	Value of wResult	96
		hDialogTemplate	HANDLE	ID of block of memory containing DLGTEMPLATE	parameter used to	
		hWndParent	HWND	ID of window owning dialog box	terminate box	
		lpDialogFunc	FARPROC	Address of dialog function	or -1	
DialogBoxIndirectParam†	int	hInstance	HANDLE	ID of file containing dialog-box template	Value of wResult	98
		hDialogTemplate	HANDLE	ID of block of memory containing DLGTEMPLATE	parameter used to	
		hWndParent	HWND	ID of window owning dialog box	terminate box	
		lpDialogFunc	FARPROC	Address of dialog function	or -1	
		dwInitParam	DWORD	32-bit value passed to dialog function		
DialogBoxParam†	int	hInstance	HANDLE	ID of file containing dialog-box template	Value of nResult	99
		lpTemplateName	LPSTR	Points to ASCIIZ string of name of template	parameter used to	
		hWndParent	HWND	ID of window owning dialog box	terminate box	
		lpDialogFunc	FARPROC	Address of dialog function	or -1	
		dwInitParam	DWORD	32-bit value passed to dialog function		
DispatchMessage	LONG	lpMsg	LPMSG	Points to MSG structure	Value returned by window function	99
DlgDirList	int	hDlg	HWND	ID of dialog box containing list box	≠0 if listing made	100
		lpPathSpec	LPSTR	Pointer to ASCIIZ pathname string		
		nIDListBox	int	ID of list-box control		
		nIDStaticPath	int	ID of static-text control of current drive/directory		
		wFiletype	WORD	DOS file attributes of files to display		

(Continued)

6.096. WINDOWS FUNCTION SUMMARY BY NAME (continued)

Function Name	Type	Parameters*	Parm Type	Parameter Definition	Return Value	Pg§
DlgDirListComboBox†	int	hDlg lpPathSpec nIDComboBox nIDStaticPath wFiletype	HWND LPSTR int int WORD	ID of dialog containing combo box Points to ASCIIZ pathname string ID of combo-box control in dialog box ID of static-text control of current drive/directory DOS file attributes of files to display	≠0 if listing made	102
DlgDirSelect	BOOL	hDlg lpString nIDListBox	HWND LPSTR int	ID of dialog box containing list box Points to buffer to receive pathname ID of list-box control in dialog box	≠0 if directory name	103
DlgDirSelectComboBox†	BOOL	hDlg lpString nIDComboBox	HWND LPSTR int	ID of dialog box containing combo box Pointer to buffer to receive pathname ID of combo-box control in dialog box	≠0 if directory name	104
DOS3Call†	Special call: set registers as for corresponding INT 21H				Varies	104
DPtoLP	BOOL	hDC lpPoints nCount	HDC LPPOINT int	ID of device context Pointer to array of POINT structures Number of points in array	≠0 if converted	105
DrawFocusRect†	void	hDC lpRect	HDC LPRECT	ID of device context Pointer to RECT structure to draw	None	106
DrawIcon	BOOL	hDC X Y hIcon	HDC int int HICON	ID of device context for window x-coord of upper-left corner of icon y-coord of upper-left corner of icon Icon to draw	≠0 if successful	106
DrawMenuBar	void	hWnd	HWND	ID of window whose menu needs redrawing	None	107
DrawText	int	hDC lpString nCount lpRect wFormat	HDC LPSTR int LPSTR LPSTR	ID of device context Pointer to string to draw Bytes in string, or -1 if string is ASCIIZ Pointer to RECT structure in which to draw text Method of formatting text	Height of text	107
Ellipse	BOOL	hDC X1 Y1 X2 Y2	HDC int int int int	ID of device context x-coord of upper-left corner of bounding rectangle y-coord of upper-left corner of bounding rectangle x-coord of lower-right corner of bounding rectangle y-coord of lower-right corner of bounding rectangle	≠0 if ellipse drawn	110
EmptyClipboard	BOOL				≠0 if emptied	110
EnableHardwareInput	BOOL	bEnableInput	BOOL	Nonzero if function should save input	≠0 if input previous enabled	111
EnableMenuItem	BOOL	hMenu wIDEnableItem wEnable	HMENU WORD WORD	Menu Menu item to be checked Action to take	Previous state of menu or -1 if it does not exist	111
EnableWindow	BOOL	hWnd bEnable	HWND BOOL	ID of window Nonzero if function should enable input	≠0 if successful	112
EndDeferWindowPos†	void	hWinPosInfo	HANDLE	ID of multiwindow positition structure	None	113
EndDialog	void	hDlg nResult	HWND int	ID of dialog box to destroy Value to be returned to function that created it	None	113
EndPaint	void	hWnd lpPaint	HWND LPPAINTSTRUCT	ID of window to repaint Pointer to PAINTSTRUCT	None	114
EnumChildWindows	BOOL	hWndParent lpEnumFunc lParam	HWND FARPROC DWORD	ID of parent window Address of callback function Value to be passed to callback function	≠0 if all child windows enumerated	115
EnumClipboardFormats	WORD	wFormat	WORD	Format	Next known format or 0	116
EnumFonts	int	hDC lpFacename lpFontFunc lpData	HDC LPSTR FARPROC LPSTR	ID of device context Pointer to ASCIIZ string of typeface name Address of callback function Pointer to application-supplied data	Last value returned by callback function	117
EnumbMetaFile	BOOL	hDC hMF lpCallbackFunc lpClientData	HDC LOCALHANDLE FARPROC BYTE FAR *	ID of device context ID of metafile Address of callback function Pointer to callback-function data	≠0 if callback enumerates all GDI calls in metafile	118
EnumObjects	int	hDC nObjectType lpObjectFunc lpData	HDC int FARPROC LPSTR	ID of device context Object type Address of callback function Application-supplied data for callback function	Last value returned by callback function	120
EnumProps	int	hWnd lpEnumFunc	HWND FARPROC	ID of window to enumerate Address of callback function	Last value returned by callback function or -1	121
EnumTaskWindows	BOOL	hTask lpEnumFunc lParam	HANDLE FARPROC DWORD	ID of task Address of window's callback function 32-bit value for callback function	≠0 if all windows enumerated	123
EnumWindows	BOOL	lpEnumFunc lParam	FARPROC DWORD	Address of callback function Value to pass to callback function	≠0 if all windows enumerated	125

(Continued)

6.096. WINDOWS FUNCTION SUMMARY BY NAME (continued)

Function Name	Type	Parameters*	Parm Type	Parameter Definition	Return Value	Pg§
EqualRect	BOOL	lpRect1	LPRECT	Pointer to RECT of first rectangle	≠0 if rectangles are identical	126
		lpRect2	LPRECT	Pointer to RECT of second rectangle		
EqualRgn	BOOL	hSrcRgn1	HRGN	ID of first region	≠0 if regions are equal	126
		hSrcRgn2	HRGN	ID of second region		
Escape	See 6.097. Windows Escape Functions by Name					126
EscapeCommFunction	int	nCid	int	Communication device to carry out function	0=successful	127
		nFunc	int	Function code		
ExcludeClipRect	int	hDC	HDC	ID of device context	New clipping Region's type	128
		X1	int	x-coord of upper-left corner of rectangle		
		Y1	int	y-coord of upper-left corner of rectangle		
		X2	int	x-coord of lower-right corner of rectangle		
		Y2	int	y-coord of lower-right corner of rectangle		
ExcludeUpdateRgn	int	hDC	HANDLE	ID of device context	Type of resultant region	129
		hWnd	HWND	ID of window to update		
ExitWindows†	BOOL	dwReserved	DWORD	RESERVED--set to 0	FALSE if any application refused to terminate	130
		wReturnCode	WORD	Return value to pass to DOS		
ExtDeviceMode†	int	hWnd	HWND	ID of window	<0 if function fails or size of the DEVMODE struct	130
		hDriver	HANDLE	ID of device-driver module		
		lpDevModeOutput	DEVMODE FAR *	Pointer to DEVMODE structure		
		lpDeviceName	LPSTR	Pointer to ASCIIZ string with name of printer dev.		
		lpPort	LPSTR	Pointer to ASCIIZ string with name of DOS port		
		lpDevModeInput	DEVMODE FAR *	Pointer to DEVMODE structure		
		lpProfile	LPSTR	Pointer to ASCIIZ string with name of init file		
		wMode	WORD	Mask of values to determine operations		
ExtFloodFill†	BOOL	hDC	HDC	ID of device context	≠0 if successful	133
		X	int	x-coord of point where filling begins		
		Y	int	y-coord of point where filling begins		
		crColor	COLORREF	Color of boundary or area to be filled		
		wFillType	WORD	Type of flood fill to perform		
ExtTextOut	BOOL	hDC	HDC	ID of device context	≠0 if string drawn	134
		X	int	x-coord of origin of char cell for first character		
		Y	int	y-coord of origin of char cell for first character		
		wOptions	WORD	Rectangle type		
		lpRect	LPRECT	Pointer to RECT structure or NULL		
		lpString	LPSTR	Pointer to character string		
		nCount	int	Number of characters in string		
		lpDx	LPINT	Pointer to array of inter char cells widths		
FatalAppExit†	void	wAction	WORD	RESERVED--must be set to 0	None	136
		lpMessageText	LPSTR	Pointer to string to display in msg box		
FatalExit	void	Code	int	Error code to display	None	136
FillRect	int	hDC	HDC	ID of device context	Not used and has no meaning	137
		lpRect	LPRECT	Pointer to RECT to be filled		
		hBrush	HBRUSH	ID of brush to use in fill		
FillRgn	BOOL	hDC	HDC	ID of device context	≠0 if successful	138
		hRgn	HRGN	ID of region to fill		
		hBrush	HBRUSH	ID of brush to use in fill		
FindAtom	ATOM	lpString	LPSTR	Pointer to ASCIIZ string to search for	Atom associated with string or NULL	138
FindResource	HANDLE	hInstance	HANDLE	ID of file containing resource	ID of resource or NULL	139
		lpName	LPSTR	Pointer to ASCIIZ string naming resource		
		lpType	LPSTR	Pointer to ASCIIZ string giving resource type		
FindWindow	HWND	lpClassName	LPSTR	Pointer to ASCIIZ string giving window's class	ID of window or NULL	140
		lpWindowName	LPSTR	Pointer to ASCIIZ string naming window		
FlashWindow	BOOL	hWnd	HWND	ID of window to flash	State before call	141
		bInvert	BOOL	Flash or return to original state flag		
FloodFill	BOOL	hDC	HDC	ID of device context	≠0 if successful <0 if invalid device	141
		X	int	x-coord of point where filling begins		
		Y	int	y-coord of point where filling begins		
		crColor	COLORREF	Color of boundary		
FlushComm	int	nCid	int	Communication device to flush	0 if successful	142
		nQueue	int	Queue to flush (0=transmit, 1=receive)		
FrameRect	int	hDC	HDC	ID of device context	Has no meaning	143
		lpRect	LPRECT	Pointer to RECT to frame		
		hBrush	HBRUSH	ID of brush to use in frame		
FrameRgn	BOOL	hDC	HDC	ID of device context	≠0 if successful	143
		hRgn	HANDLE	ID of region to be enclosed in border		
		hBrush	HBRUSH	ID of brush to use in border draw		
		nWidth	int	Width of vertical brush strokes in logical units		
		nHeight	int	Height of horizontal brush strokes in logical units		

(Continued)

6.096. WINDOWS FUNCTION SUMMARY BY NAME (continued)

Function Name	*Type*	*Parameters**	*Parm Type*	*Parameter Definition*	*Return Value*	*Pg§*
FreeLibrary	void	hLibModule	HANDLE	ID of loaded library module	None	144
FreeModule†	void	hModule	HANDLE	ID of loaded module	None	144
FreeProcInstance	void	lpProc	FARPROC	Address of function to be freed	None	145
FreeResource	BOOL	hResData	HANDLE	ID of data associated with resource	0 if successful	145
FreeSelector†	WORD	wSelector	WORD	Selector to be freed	NULL if successful	146
GetActiveWindow	HWND				ID of active window	147
GetAspectRatioFilter	DWORD	hDC	HDC	ID of device context containing aspect ratio	LO=y-coord HO=x-coord	147
GetAsyncKeyState	int	vKey	int	Virtual-key code value	Key state MSB=current down LSB=prev down	147
GetAtomHandle	HMEM	wAtom	WORD	ID of atom	ID of atom's string or 0	148
GetAtomName	WORD	nAtom lpBuffer nSize	ATOM LPSTR int	ID of string to retrieve Pointer to buffer to receive string Maximum size of buffer in bytes	Actual bytes copied to buffer or 0	148
GetBitmapBits	DWORD	hBitmap dwCount lpBits	HBITMAP DWORD LPSTR	ID of bitmap Number of bytes to copy Pointer to buffer to receive bitmap	Actual bytes copied to buffer or 0	149
GetBitmapDimension	DWORD	hBitmap	HBITMAP	ID of bitmap	LO=width of bitmap HO=height of bitmap or 0	149
GetBkColor	DWORD	hDC	HDC	ID of device context	RGB color value	150
GetBkMode	int	hDC	HDC	ID of device context	Current bkgnd mode	150
GetBrushOrg	DWORD	hDC	HDC	ID of device context	Current origin of brush	150
GetBValue	BYTE	rgbColor	DWORD	Color specification	Blue value	151
GetCapture	HWND				ID of window or NULL if none	151
GetCaretBlinkTime	WORD				Blink rate (in ms)	151
GetCaretPos	void	lpPoint	LPPOINT	Pointer to POINT to receive caret coords	None	152
GetCharWidth	BOOL	hDC wFirstChar wLastChar lpBuffer	HDC WORD WORD LPINT	ID of device context First char of consecutive group of characters Last char of consecutive group of characters Pointer to buffer to receive width values	≠0 if successful	152
GetClassInfo†	BOOL	hInstance lpClassName lpWndClass	HANDLE LPSTR LPWNDCLASS	ID of application that created class Pointer to ASCIIZ string naming class to find Pointer to WNDCLASS structure to receive data	TRUE if successful	153
GetClassLong	LONG	hWnd nIndex	HWND int	ID of window Byte offset of value to retrieve	Value retrieved	153
GetClassName	int	hWnd lpClassName nMaxCount	HWND LPSTR int	ID of window whose class name to retrieve Pointer to buffer to receive class name Maximum size of buffer	Number of chars copied to buffer or 0	154
GetClassWord	WORD	hWnd nIndex	HWND int	ID of window Byte offset to retrieve	Value retrieved	155
GetClientRect	void	hWnd lpRect	HWND LPRECT	ID of window associated with client area Pointer to RECT	None	156
GetClipboardData	HANDLE	wFormat	WORD	Data format	ID of memory block containing data or NULL	156
GetClipboardFormatName	int	wFormat lpFormatName nMaxCount	WORD LPSTR int	Type of format to retrieve Pointer to buffer to receive format name Maximum size of buffer	Actual length of string copied or 0	157
GetClipboardOwner	HWND				ID of window owning clipboard or NULL	157
GetClipboardViewer	HWND				ID of window resp for displaying clipboard or NULL	158
GetClipBox	int	hDC lpRect	HDC LPRECT	ID of device context Pointer to RECT to receive dimensions	Clipping region's type	158
GetCodeHandle	HANDLE	lpProc	FARPROC	Address of procedure instance	CS containing function	159
GetCodeInfo†	void	lpProc lpSegInfo	FARPROC LPVOID	Address of function to retrieve info for Pointer to array of four 32-bit values to fill	None	159
GetCommError	int	nCid lpStat	int COMSTAT FAR *	Communication device to examine Pointer to COMSTAT to receive status	Error code of most recent comm function	161
GetCommErrMask	WORD	nCid nEvtMask	int int	Communication device to examine Events to enable	Current event-mask value	162
GetCommState	int	nCid lpDCB	int DCB FAR *	Device to examine Pointer to DCB to receive data	0 if successful <0 if error	162

(Continued)

6.096. WINDOWS FUNCTION SUMMARY BY NAME (continued)

Function Name	*Type*	*Parameters**	*Parm Type*	*Parameter Definition*	*Return Value*	*Pg§*
GetCurrentPDB†	WORD				Current PDB address or selector	163
GetCurrentPosition	DWORD	hDC	HDC	ID of device context	LO=x-coord HO=y coord	163
GetCurrentTask	HANDLE				Task ID or NULL	164
GetCurrentTime	DWORD				Current time (in ms)	164
GetCursorPos	void	lpPoint	LPPOINT	Pointer to POINT to receive cursor position	None	164
GetDC	HDC	hWnd	HWND	ID of window to retrieve context for	Display context or NULL	165
GetDCOrg	HDC	hDC	HDC	ID of device context to retrieve origin for	LO=x-coord HO=y-coord	165
GetDesktopWindow†	HWND				ID of desktop wind	166
GetDeviceCaps	int	hDC nIndex	HDC int	ID of device context Item to return	Value of item	166
GetDialogBaseUnits†	LONG				Dialog base units	170
GetDLBits†	int	hDC hBitmap nStartScan nNumScans lpBits lpBitsInfo wUsage	HDC HBITMAP WORD WORD LPSTR LPBITMAPINFO WORD	ID of device context ID of bitmap First scan line to set in lpBits Number of lines to copy Pointer to buffer to receive bitmap bits Pointer to BITMAPINFO specifying color and dim RGB or PAL colors for bmiColors	Number of scan lines copied or 0	171
GetDlgCtrlID†	int	hWnd	HWND	ID of child window	ID of child window or NULL	172
GetDlgItem	HWND	hDlg nIDDlgItem	HWND int	ID of dialog box containing control ID of item to retrieve	ID of control or NULL	173
GetDlgItemInt	WORD	hDlg nIDDlgItem lpTranslated bSigned	HWND int BOOL FAR * BOOL	ID of dialog box ID of dialog-box item to translate Variable to receive translated flag Specifies signed or unsigned value	Translated value	174
GetDlgItemText	int	hDlg nIDDlgItem lpString nMaxCount	HWND int LPSTR int	ID of dialog box containing control ID of dialog-box item to retrieve caption or text for Pointer to buffer to receive text Maximum length of buffer	Actual number of chars copied to buffer or 0	174
GetDOSEnvironment†	LPSTR				Far pointer to environment string	175
GetDoubleClickTime	WORD				Dbl click time (in ms)	175
GetDriveType†	WORD	nDrive	int	Drive to get type for (A=0, B=1, and so on)	Drive type or 0	175
GetEnvironment	int	lpPortName lpEnviron nMaxCount	LPSTR LPSTR WORD	Pointer to ASCIIZ string naming port Pointer to buffer to receive environment Maximum number of bytes in buffer	Number of bytes copied to buffer or 0	176
GetFocus	HWND				ID of window with focus, or NULL	177
GetFreeSpace†	DWORD	wFlags	WORD	Flag specifying where to scan heap	Amount of avail memory in bytes	177
GetGValue	BYTE	rgbColor	DWORD	Color specification	Green value of color	178
GetInputState	BOOL				Input state or 0	178
GetInstanceData	int	hInstance pData nCount	HANDLE NPSTR int	ID of previous call of application Pointer to buffer in current instance Number of bytes to copy	Number of bytes actually copied	178
GetKBCodePage†	int				Code page	179
GetKeyboardState	void	lpKeyState	BYTE FAR *	Pointer to 256-byte buffer of virtual-key codes	None	180
GetKeyboardType†	int	nTypeFlag	int	Type or subtype flag	Type or subtype	181
GetKeyNameText†	int	lParam lpBuffer nSize	DWORD LPSTR WORD	32-bit parameter of keyboard message Buffer to receive key name Maximum length of name int bytes	Actual length of string copied	182
GetKeyState	int	nVirtKey	int	Virtual key	State of key	183
GetLastActivePopup†	HWND	hwndOwner	HWND	ID of owner window	ID of most recent popup	183
GetMapMode	int	hDC	HDC	ID of device context	Mapping mode	184
GetMenu	HMENU	hWnd	HWND	ID of window with menu to examine	ID of menu or NULL	184
GetMenuCheckMark Dimensions†	DWORD				LO=width HO=height	184
GetMenuItemCount	WORD	hMenu	HMENU	ID of menu handle to examine	Number of items in menu or -1	185
GetMenuItemID	WORD	hMenu nPos	HMENU int	ID of handle to popup menu containing item Position of menu item to retreive ID for	Item ID or -1	185
GetMenuState	WORD	hMenu wID wFlags	HMENU WORD WORD	ID of menu Menu item ID Nature of wID parameter	Doesn't exist=-1 or mask of values	186

(Continued)

6.096. WINDOWS FUNCTION SUMMARY BY NAME (continued)

Function Name	Type	Parameters*	Parm Type	Parameter Definition	Return Value	Pg§
GetMenuString	int	hMenu wIDItem lpString nMaxCount wFlag	HMENU WORD LPSTR int WORD	ID of menu Menu item ID Pointer to buffer to receive label Maximum length of label Nature of wID parameter	Actual bytes copied to buffer	187
GetMessage	BOOL	lpMsg hWnd wMsgFilterMin wMsgFilterMax	LPMSG HWND WORD WORD	Pointer to MSG struct ID of window or NULL Integer value of lowest message value to retrieve Integer value of highest message value to retrieve	≠0 if message other than WM_QUIT, or 0	188
GetMessagePos	DWORD				LO=x-coord HO=y-coord	189
GetMessageTime	DWORD				Message time	189
GetMetaFile	HANDLE	lpFilename	LPSTR	Pointer to ASCIIZ string of DOS metafile name	Metafile ID or NULL	190
GetMetaFileBits	HANDLE	hMF	HANDLE	ID of metafile in memory	Memory block that contains metafile or NULL	190
GetModuleFileName	int	hModule lpFilename nSize	HANDLE LPSTR int	ID of module Pointer to buffer to receive filename Maximum size of buffer	Actual length of string copied	190
GetModuleHandle	HANDLE	lpModuleName	LPSTR	Pointer to ASCIIZ string specifying module	ID of module or NULL	191
GetModuleUsage	int	hModule	HANDLE	ID of module	Reference count of module	191
GetNearestColor	DWORD	hDC crColor	HDC COLORREF	ID of device context Color to be matched	RGB value	192
GetNearestPaletteIndex†	WORD	hPalette crColor	HPALETTE COLORREF	ID of logical palette Color to be matched	Index to palette	192
GetNextDlgGroupItem	HWND	hDlg hCtl bPrevious	HWND HWND BOOL	ID of dialog box to search ID of control in dialog box to start search How function is to search dialog box	Next or previous control in group	193
GetNextDlgTabItem	HWND	hDlg hCtl bPrevious	HWND HWND BOOL	ID of dialog box to search ID of control in dialog box to start search How function is to search dialog box	Next or previous control having tab style	193
GetNextWindow	HWND	hWnd wFlag	HWND WORD	ID of current window Handle of next or previous window flag	Next or previous window	194
GetNumTasks	int				Number of tasks	194
GetObject	int	hObject nCount lpObject	HANDLE int LPSTR	ID of object Number of bytes to copy to buffer Pointer to buffer to receive data	Actual number of bytes retrieved or 0	195
GetPaletteEntries†	WORD	hPalette wStartIndex wNumEntries lpPaletteEntries	HPALETTE WORD WORD LPPALETTEENTRY	ID of logical palette First entry in palette to retrieve Number of entries to retrieve Pointer to array of structs to receive entries	Number of entries retrieved, or 0	195
GetParent	HWND	hWnd	HWND	ID of window to retrieve parent window ID for	ID of parent window or NULL	196
GetPixel	DWORD	hDC X Y	HDC int int	ID of device context x-coord of point to examine y-coord of point to examine	RGB color or -1 if not in clip region	196
GetPolyFillMode	int	hDC	HDC	ID of device context	Polygon filling mode	197
GetPriorityClipboard Format†	int	lpPriorityList nCount	WORD FAR * int	Pointer to array of clipboard formats Number of clipboard formats in list	Highest clipboard format, NULL, or -1 data not in list	197
GetPrivateProfileInt†	WORD	lpApplicationName lpKeyName nDefault lpFileName	LPSTR LPSTR int LPSTR	Pointer to name of application Pointer to key name Default value for given key if not in file Pointer to string naming initialization file	0 if value not int or negative, or numeric value	198
GetPrivateProfileString†	int	lpApplicationName lpKeyName lpDefault lpReturnedString nSize lpFileName	LPSTR LPSTR LPSTR LPSTR int LPSTR	Pointer to name of application Pointer to key name Default value for key if not in file Pointer to buffer to receive char string Maximum number of characters in buffer Pointer to string naming initialization file	Number of chars copied or NULL	199
GetProcAddress	FARPROC	hModule lpProcName	HANDLE LPSTR	ID of library module containing function Pointer to function name or ordinal value of function	Pointer to entry point, or NULL	200
GetProfileInt	WORD	lpAppName lpKeyName nDefault	LPSTR LPSTR int	Pointer to application name Pointer to key name Default value for key if not found in file	0 if value not int or negative, or numeric value	201

(Continued)

6.096. WINDOWS FUNCTION SUMMARY BY NAME (continued)

Function Name	Type	Parameters*	Parm Type	Parameter Definition	Return Value	Pg§
GetProfileString	int	lpAppName lpKeyName lpDefault lpReturnedString nSize	LPSTR LPSTR LPSTR LPSTR int	Pointer to ASCIIZ string naming application Pointer to ASCIIZ string naming key Default value for key if not found in file Pointer to buffer to receive string Number of characters in buffer	Number of chars copied or NULL	202
GetProp	HANDLE	hWnd lpString	HWND LPSTR	ID of window with property list to search Pointer to ASCIIZ string or atom ID of string	ID of handle or NULL	203
GetRgnBox†	int	hRgn lpRect	HRGN LPRECT	ID of region Pointer to RECT to receive coordinates	Region type	203
GetROP2	int	hDC	HDC	ID of device context for raster device	Drawing mode	204
GetRValue	BYTE	rgbColor	DWORD	RGB color	Red value	204
GetScrollPos	int	hWnd nBar	HWND int	ID of window Type of scroll bar	Current thumb position	205
GetScrollRange	void	hWnd nBar lpMinPos lpMaxPos	HWND int LPINT LPINT	ID of window Which scroll bar Pointer to int receiving minimum position Pointer to int receiving maximum position	None	205
GetStockObject	HANDLE	nIndex	int	Type of object desired	ID of object or NULL	208
GetStretchBltMode	int	hDC	HDC	ID of device context	Current stretching mode	208
GetSubMenu	HMENU	hMenu nPos	HMENU int	ID of menu Position of menu	ID of popup or NULL	209
GetSysColor	DWORD	nIndex	int	Display element	RGB color	209
GetSysModalWindow	HWND				ID of window, or NULL	210
GetSystemDirectory†	WORD	lpBuffer nSize	LPSTR int	Pointer to buffer to receive ASCIIZ pathname Maximum size of buffer in bytes	Length of string copied to buffer or 0	210
GetSystemMenu	HMENU	hWnd bRevert	HWND BOOL	ID of window to own System menu Action to take	ID of system menu or NULL if system menu not modified and bRevert≠0	211
GetSystemMetrics	int	nIndex	int	Measurement to retreive	System metric measurement	212
GetSystemPaletteEntries†	WORD	hDC wStartIndex wNumEntries lpPaletteEntries	HDC WORD WORD LPPALETTEENTRY	ID of device context First entry to retrieve Number of entries to retrieve Pointer to array to receive entries	Number of entries retrieved or 0	213
GetSystemPaletteUse†	WORD	hDC	HDC	ID of device context	Current use	214
GetTabbedTextExtent†	DWORD	hDC lpString nCount nTabPositions lpnTabStopPositions	HDC LPSTR int int LPINT	ID of device context Pointer to text string Number of characters in text string Number of tab-stop positions in array Pointer to tab-stop position array	LO=width HO=height of string	215
GetTempDrive	BYTE	cDriveLetter	BYTE	Disk drive letter	Optimal drive for temp files	216
GetTempFileName	int	cDriveLetter lpPrefixString wUnique lpTempFileName	BYTE LPSTR WORD LPSTR	Suggested drive for temp file Pointer to ASCIIZ temp filename prefix string Unsigned short integer Pointer to buffer to receive temp filename	Unique numeric value used in temp filename	216
GetTextAlign	WORD	hDC	HDC	ID of device context	Status of text alignment flags	217
GetTextCharacterExtra	int	hDC	HDC	ID of device context	Current interchar spacing	219
GetTextColor	DWORD	hDC	HDC	ID of device context	RGB value	219
GetTextExtent	DWORD	hDC lpString nCount	HDC LPSTR int	ID of device context Pointer to text string Number of characters in text string	LO=width HO=height of text string	220
GetTextFace	int	hDC nCount lpFacename	HDC int LPSTR	ID of device context Size of buffer in bytes Pointer to buffer to receive typeface name	Actual number of bytes copied to buffer or 0	220
GetTextMetrics	BOOL	hDC lpMetrics	HDC LPTEXTMETRIC	ID of device context Pointer to TEXTMETRIC struct	≠0 if successful	221
GetThresholdEvent	LPINT				Pointer to integer threshold event	221
GetThresholdStatus	int				Status flags of threshold event	222

(Continued)

6.096. WINDOWS FUNCTION SUMMARY BY NAME (continued)

Function Name	Type	Parameters*	Parm Type	Parameter Definition	Return Value	Pg§
GetTickCount	DWORD				Ms since system was started	222
GetTopWindow	HWND	hWnd	HWND	ID of parent window	ID of top-level child window or NULL	222
GetUpdateRect	BOOL	hWnd lpRect bErase	HWND LPRECT BOOL	ID of window to retrieve update region from Pointer to RECT to receive coords Should background be erased flag	≠0 if not empty	223
GetUpdateRgn	int	hWnd hRgn fErase	HWND HRGN BOOL	ID of window with region to update ID of update region Should background be erased flag	Type of resulting region	223
GetVersion	WORD				LO=major vers # HO=minor vers #	224
GetViewportExt	DWORD	hDC	HDC	ID of device context	LO=x-extent HO=y-extent	225
GetViewportOrg	DWORD	hDC	HDC	ID of device context	LO=x-coord HO=y-coord	225
GetWindow	HWND	hWnd wCmd	HWND WORD	ID of original window Relationship of original and returned window	ID of window or NULL	225
GetWindowDC	HDC	hWnd	HWND	ID of window to retrieve display context from	ID of display context or NULL	226
GetWindowExt	DWORD	hDC	HDC	ID of device context	LO=x-extent HO=y-extent	227
GetWindowLong	LONG	hWnd nIndex	HWND int	ID of window Byte offset of value to retrieve	Window info	228
GetWindowOrg	DWORD	hDC	HDC	ID of device context	LO=x-extent HO=y-extent	228
GetWindowRect	void	hWnd lpRect	HWND LPRECT	ID of window Pointer to RECT to receive coords	None	229
GetWindowsDirectory†	WORD	lpBuffer nSize	LPSTR int	Pointer to buffer to receive ASCIIZ pathname Maximum size of buffer (minimum 144 bytes)	Length of string copied to buffer or 0	229
GetWindowTask	HANDLE	hWnd	HWND	ID of window	Task ID	230
GetWindowText	int	hWnd lpString nMaxCount	HWND LPSTR int	ID of window Pointer to buffer to receive string Maximum number of chars in buffer	Length of copied string or 0	230
GetWindowTextLength	int	hWnd	HWND	ID of window or control	Text length or 0	231
GetWindowWord	WORD	hWnd nIndex	HWND int	ID of window Offset of value to retrieve	Window info	231
GetWinFlags†	DWORD				Flags	232
GlobalAddAtom	ATOM	lpString	LPSTR	Pointer to string to add to table	ID of atom or NULL	233
GlobalAlloc	HANDLE	wFlags dwBytes	WORD DWORD	Allocation flags Number of bytes to allocate	ID of global memory or NULL	233
GlobalCompact	DWORD	dwMinFree	DWORD	Number of free bytes desired	Number of bytes in largest free block	235
GlobalDeleteAtom	ATOM	nAtom	ATOM	ID of atom and string to delete	NULL if successful	235
GlobalDiscard	HANDLE	hMem	HANDLE	ID of global memory block to discard	ID of block or 0	236
GlobalDosAlloc†	DWORD	dwBytes	DWORD	Number of bytes to allocate	LO=selector HO=¶ seg value	236
GlobalDosFree†	WORD	wSelector	WORD	Selector of memory to free	NULL if successful	237
GlobalFindAtom	ATOM	lpString	LPSTR	Pointer of string to search for	Atom with string or NULL	237
GlobalFix†	void	hMem	HANDLE	ID of global memory block	None	238
GlobalFlags	WORD	hMem	HANDLE	ID of global memory block	LO=lock count HO=mem alloc flag	238
GlobalFree	HANDLE	hMem	HANDLE	ID of global memory block	NULL if successful	239
GlobalGetAtomName	WORD	nAtom lpBuffer nSize	ATOM LPSTR int	ID of string to retrieve Pointer to buffer to receive string Maximum size of buffer in bytes	Actual number of bytes copied to buffer or 0	240
GlobalHandle	DWORD	wMem	WORD	Segment address or selector of memory object	LO=handle HO=segment add or selector or NULL	240
GlobalLock	LPSTR	hMem	HANDLE	ID of global memory block to lock	First byte of mem in block or NULL	241
GlobalLRUNewest	HANDLE	hMem	HANDLE	ID of global memory block to move	NULL if error	241
GlobalLRUOldest	HANDLE	hMem	HANDLE	ID of global memory object to move	NULL if error	242
GlobalNotify	void	lpNotifyProc	FARPROC	Address of task's notification procedure	None	242
GlobalPageLock†	WORD	wSelector	WORD	Selector of memory to page-lock	Page lock count or 0	243
GlobalPageUnlock†	WORD	wSelector	WORD	Selector of memory to page-unlock	Page lock count or 0	244

(Continued)

6.096. WINDOWS FUNCTION SUMMARY BY NAME (continued)

Function Name	Type	Parameters*	Parm Type	Parameter Definition	Return Value	Pg§
GlobalReAlloc	HANDLE	hMem dwBytes wFlags	HANDLE DWORD WORD	ID of global memory block to reallocate New size of block How to reallocate block	ID of block or NULL	245
GlobalSize	DWORD	hMem	HANDLE	ID of global memory block	Actual size of block in bytes or 0	246
GlobalUnfix†	BOOL	hMem	HANDLE	ID of global memory block	Block's lock count or 0	247
GlobalUnlock	BOOL	hMem	HANDLE	ID of global memory block	0 if lock count decreased to 0	247
GlobalUnWire	BOOL	hMem	HANDLE	ID of segment to unlock	TRUE if successful	248
GlobalWire	LPSTR	hMem	HANDLE	ID of segment to move and lock	New segment location or NULL	248
GrayString	BOOL	hDC hBrush lpOutputFunc lpData nCount X Y nWidth nHeight	HDC HBRUSH FARPROC DWORD int int int int int	ID of device context ID of brush to gray with Address of function to draw string Pointer to data to pass to output function Number of character to output x-coord of starting rect position y-coord of starting rect position Width of rect in logical units Height of rect in logical units	≠0 if string drawn	249
HIBYTE	BYTE	nInteger	int	Value to convert	HO byte of value	252
HideCaret	void	hWnd	HWND	ID of window owning caret or NULL	None	252
HiliteMenuItem	BOOL	hWnd hMenu wIDHiliteItem wHilite	HWND HMENU WORD WORD	ID of window containing menu ID of top-level menu with item to highlight ID of menu item or offset of menu item Hilight type	≠0 if highlighted	253
HIWORD	WORD	dwInteger	DWORD	Value to convert	HO word of value	254
InflateRect	void	lpRect X Y	LPRECT int int	Pointer to RECT to be modified Amount to increase or decrease width Amount to increase or decrease height	None	255
InitAtomTable	BOOL	nSize	int	Size in entries of atom hash table	≠0 if successful	255
InSendMessage	BOOL				TRUE if processing message through SendMessage	256
InsertMenu†	BOOL	hMenu nPosition wFlags wIDNewItem lpNewItem	HMENU WORD WORD WORD LPSTR	ID of menu to change Menu item before insertion point How nPosition is to be interpreted Command ID of new menu item or popup handle Content of new menu item	TRUE if successful	256
IntersectClipRect	int	hDC X1 Y1 X2 Y2	HDC int int int int	ID of device context x-coord of upper-left corner of rectangle y-coord of upper-left corner of rectangle x-coord of lower-right corner of rectangle y-coord of lower-right corner of rectangle	Clipping region type	259
IntersectRect	int	lpDestRect lpSrc1Rect lpSrc2Rect	LPRECT LPRECT LPRECT	Pointer to RECT to receive intersection Pointer to first RECT to intersect Pointer to second RECT to intersect	≠0 if not empty	260
InvalidateRect	void	hWnd lpRect bErase	HWND LPRECT BOOL	ID of window with region to modify Pointer to RECT to add to update region Whether background should be erased flag	None	261
InvalidateRgn	void	hWnd hRgn bErase	HWND HRGN BOOL	ID of window with region to modify ID of region to add to update region Whether background should be erased flag	None	261
InvertRect	void	hDC lpRect	HDC LPRECT	ID of device context Pointer to RECT to invert	None	262
InvertRgn	BOOL	hDC hRgn	HDC HRGN	ID of device context ID of region to fill	≠0 if successful	263
IsCharAlpha†	BOOL	cChar	char	Character to test	TRUE if alphabetic	263
IsCharAlphaNumeric†	BOOL	cChar	char	Character to test	TRUE if alphanumeric	264
IsCharLower†	BOOL	cChar	char	Character to test	TRUE if lowercase	264
IsCharUpper†	BOOL	cChar	char	Character to test	TRUE if uppercase	264
IsChild	BOOL	hWndParent hWnd	HWND HWND	ID of window ID of window to check	TRUE if hWnd is child of hWndParent	265
IsClipboardFormatAvailable	BOOL	wFormat	WORD	Format to check	TRUE if data with format is present	265
IsDialogMessage	BOOL	hDlg lpMsg	HWND LPMSG	ID of dialog box Pointer to MSG struct with message to check	≠0 if message processed	266
IsDlgButtonChecked	WORD	hDlg nIDButton	HWND int	ID of dialog box with control to check ID of button control	2=grayed 1=checked 0=otherwise	267

(Continued)

6.096. WINDOWS FUNCTION SUMMARY BY NAME (continued)

Function Name	Type	Parameters*	Parm Type	Parameter Definition	Return Value	Pg§
IsIconic	BOOL	hWnd	HWND	ID of window	≠0 if window minimized	267
IsRectEmpty	BOOL	lpRect	LPRECT	Pointer to RECT	≠0 if rect empty	267
IsWindow	BOOL	hWnd	HWND	ID of window	≠0 if valid window	268
IsWindowEnabled	BOOL	hWnd	HWND	ID of window	≠0 if wind enabled	268
IsWindowVisible	BOOL	hWnd	HWND	ID of window	≠0 if wind exists	269
IsZoomed	BOOL	hWnd	HWND	ID of window	≠0 if window is maximized	269
KillTimer	BOOL	hWnd nIDEvent	HWND int	ID of window associated with timer event Timer event to kill	≠0 if timer killed	270
_lclose	int	hFile	int	MS-DOS file handle to close	0 if closed, -1 if fails	271
_lcreat	int	lpPathName iAttribute	LPSTR int	Pointer to ASCIIZ string of name of file to open File attributes	File handle or -1	271
LimitEmsPages	void	dwKbytes	DWORD	Kilobytes of expanded memory to access	None	272
LineDDA	void	X1 Y1 X2 Y2 lpLineFunc lpData	int int int int FARPROC LPSTR	x-coord of start point y-coord of start point x-coord of end point y-coord of end point Address of application-supplied function Pointer to application-supplied data	None	272
LineTo	BOOL	hDC X Y	HDC int int	ID of device context x-coord of end point y-coord of end point	≠0 if line drawn	273
_llseek	LONG	hFile lOffset iOrigin	int LONG int	MS-DOS file handle Number of bytes pointer should move Starting position and direction of pointer	New offset of pointer or -1	274
LoadAccelerators	HANDLE	hInstance lpTableName	HANDLE LPSTR	ID of file containing accelerator table Pointer to string naming accelerator table	ID of accelerator or NULL	275
LoadBitmap	HBITMAP	hInstance lpBitmapName	HANDLE LPSTR	ID of file containing bitmap Pointer to ASCIIZ string naming bitmap	ID of bitmap or NULL	275
LoadCursor	HCURSOR	hInstance lpCursorName	HANDLE LPSTR	ID of file containing cursor Pointer to ASCIIZ string naming cursor	ID of cursor or NULL	277
LoadIcon	HICON	hInstance lpIconName	HANDLE LPSTR	ID of file containing icon Pointer to ASCIIZ string naming icon	ID of icon or NULL	278
LoadLibrary	HANDLE	lpLibFileName	LPSTR	Pointer to ASCIIZ string naming library file	ID of library module or <32 = error	279
LoadMenu	HMENU	hInstance lpMenuName	HANDLE LPSTR	ID of file containing menu Pointer to ASCIIZ string naming menu	ID of menu or NULL	280
LoadMenuIndirect	HMENU	lpMenuTemplate	LPSTR	Pointer to menu template	ID of menu or NULL	281
LoadModule†	HANDLE	lpModuleName lpParameterBlock	LPSTR LPVOID	Pointer to ASCIIZ string of filename to run Pointer to data structure for parameter block	ID of module or <32 if error	281
LoadResource	HANDLE	hInstance hResInfo	HANDLE HANDLE	ID of file containing resource ID of resource	ID of memory block or NULL	283
LoadString	int	hInstance wID lpBuffer nBufferMax	HANDLE WORD LPSTR int	ID of file containing string ID of string to load Pointer to buffer to receive string Maximum number of characters in buffer	Number of chars copied to buffer or 0	284
LOBYTE	BYTE	nInteger	int	Value to convert	LO byte of value	285
LocalAlloc	HANDLE	wFlags wBytes	WORD WORD	How to allocate memory Total bytes to allocate	ID of memory block or NULL	285
LocalCompact	WORD	wMinFree	WORD	Number of free bytes desired	Number of bytes in largest free block	286
LocalDiscard	HANDLE	hMem	HANDLE	ID of local memory block to discard	NULL if successful	287
LocalFlags	WORD	hMem	HANDLE	ID of local memory block	LO=ref count HO=mem alloc flag	287
LocalFree	HANDLE	hMem	HANDLE	ID of local memory block to free	NULL if successful	288
LocalHandle	HANDLE	wMem	WORD	Address of local memory object	ID of local object	288
LocalInit	BOOL	wSegment pStart pEnd	WORD PSTR PSTR	Segment address of segment to get local heap Address of start of local heap Address of end of local heap	≠0 if initialized	288
LocalLock	PSTR	hMem	HANDLE	ID of local memory block to free	First byte in local block if successful or NULL	289
LocalReAlloc	HANDLE	hMem wBytes wFlags	HANDLE WORD WORD	ID of local memory block to reallocate New size of memory block How to reallocate block	ID of reallocated block or NULL	290
LocalShrink	WORD	hSeg wSize	HANDLE WORD	ID of segment containing local heap Size desired for local heap after shrinking	Size of local heap	291
LocalSize	WORD	hMem	HANDLE	ID of local memory block	Size of block or NULL	292

(Continued)

6.096. WINDOWS FUNCTION SUMMARY BY NAME (continued)

Function Name	*Type*	*Parameters**	*Parm Type*	*Parameter Definition*	*Return Value*	*Pg§*
LocalUnlock	BOOL	hMem	HANDLE	ID of local memory block	0 if ref count is 0	292
LockData	HANDLE	Dummy	int	Not used--set to 0	ID of locked data segment or NULL	293
LockResource	LPSTR	hResData	HANDLE	ID of resource	First byte of loaded resource or NULL	293
LockSegment	HANDLE	wSegment	WORD	Segment address of segment to lock	ID of segment or NULL	294
_lopen	int	lpPathName iReadWrite	LPSTR int	Pointer to ASCIIZ string naming file to open File access method	MS-DOS file handle or -1	295
LOWORD	WORD	dwInteger	DWORD	Value to convert	LO word of value	296
LPtoDP	BOOL	hDC lpPoints nCount	HANDLE LPPOINT int	ID of device context Pointer to array of pointers Number of points in array	≠0 if all converted	296
_lread	int	hFile lpBuffer wBytes	int LPSTR WORD	MS-DOS file handle to read Pointer to buffer to receive data Number of bytes to read from file	Number of bytes read or -1	297
lstrcat	LPSTR	lpString1 lpString2	LPSTR LPSTR	Pointer to ASCIIZ string to add to Pointer to ASCIIZ string to append	Pointer to lpString1 or 0	297
lstrcmp†	int	lpString1 lpString2	LPSTR LPSTR	Pointer to ASCIIZ string to compare Pointer to ASCIIZ string to compare	Less than, equal to, or greater than 0	298
lstrcmpi†	int	lpString1 lpString2	LPSTR LPSTR	Pointer to ASCIIZ string to compare Pointer to ASCIIZ string to compare	Less than, equal to, or greater than 0	299
lstrcpy	int	lpString1 lpString2	LPSTR LPSTR	Pointer to ASCIIZ string to receive copy Pointer to ASCIIZ string to copy	Pointer to lpString1 or 0	299
lstrlen	int	lpString	LPSTR	Pointer to ASCIIZ string	Length of string	300
_lwrite	int	hFile lpBuffer wBytes	int LPSTR WORD	MS-DOS file handle of file to write Pointer to buffer of data to write Number of bytes to write	Number of bytes written, or -1	300
MAKEINTATOM	LPSTR	wInteger	WORD	Numeric value of atom's string	Pointer to atom created	302
MAKEINTRESOURCE	LPSTR	nInteger	int	Integer value to convert	Pointer to string	302
MAKELONG	DWORD	wLow wHigh	WORD WORD	LO word of new long value HO word of new long value	Unsigned long	302
MAKEPOINT	POINT	dwInteger	DWORD	x- and y-coords of point	POINT struct	303
MakeProcInstance	FARPROC	lpProc hInstance	FARPROC HANDLE	Procedure-instance address ID of instance associated with DS	Pointer to function or NULL	303
MapDialogRect	void	hDlg lpRect	HWND LPRECT	ID of dialog box Pointer to RECT with coordinates to convert	None	304
MapVirtualKey†	WORD	wCode wMapType	WORD WORD	Virtual-key code or scan code for key Type of mapping to perform	Varies depending upon input	305
max	int	value1 value2	int int	First value Second value	Greater of the two values	305
MessageBeep	void	wType	WORD	Not used--set to 0	None	306
MessageBox	int	hWndParent lpText lpCaption wType	HWND LPSTR LPSTR WORD	ID of window owning message box Pointer to ASCIIZ string with message to display Pointer to ASCIIZ string with dialog-box caption Contents of dialog box	Menu-item value or 0	306
min	int	value1 value2	int int	First value Second value	Lessor of the two values	309
ModifyMenu†	BOOL	hMenu nPosition wFlags wIDNewItem lpNewItem	HMENU WORD WORD WORD LPSTR	ID of menu to change Menu item to change Interpretation of nPosition parameter Command ID of menu item or menu handle of popup Content of changed menu item	TRUE if successful	309
MoveTo	DWORD	hDC X Y	HDC int int	ID of device context x-coord of new position y-coord of new position	LO=old x-coord HO=old y-coord	312
MoveWindow	void	hWnd X Y nWidth nHeight bRepaint	HWND int int int int BOOL	ID of popup or child window New x-coord of upper-left corner New y-coord of upper-left corner New width of window New height of window Whether window is repainted after moving	None	313
MulDiv†	int	nNumber nNumerator nDenominator	int int int	Number to be multiplied by nNumerator Number to be multiplied by nNumber Number to divide result of nNumber*nNumerator by	Result or 32,767 or -32767 if error	314
NetBIOSCall†	Set all registers as for an actual INT 5CH call				None	315
OemKeyScan†	DWORD	wOemChar	WORD	ASCII value of OEM character	LO=OEM scan ID HO=shift state	316

(Continued)

6.096. WINDOWS FUNCTION SUMMARY BY NAME (continued)

Function Name	Type	Parameters*	Parm Type	Parameter Definition	Return Value	Pg§
OemToAnsi	int	lpOemStr	LPSTR	Pointer to ASCIIZ string from OEM char set	Always -1	316
		lpAnsiStr	LPSTR	Pointer to location for translated string		
OemToAnsiBuff	void	lpOemStr	LPSTR	Pointer to buffer containing OEM char set	None	317
		lpAnsiStr	LPSTR	Pointer to location for translated string		
		nLength	WORD	Number of characters in OEM char set buffer		
OffsetClipRgn	int	hDC	HDC	ID of device context	New region type	317
		X	int	Logical units to move left or right		
		Y	int	Logical units to move up or down		
OffsetRect	void	lpRect	LPRECT	Pointer to RECT to be moved	None	318
		X	int	Amount to move left or right		
		Y	int	Amount to move up or down		
OffsetRgn	int	hRgn	HRGN	ID of region to move	New region type	319
		X	int	Units to move left or right		
		Y	int	Units to move up or down		
OffsetViewportOrg	DWORD	hDC	HDC	ID of device context	LO=prev x-coord	319
		X	int	Device units to add to current x-coord	HO=prev y-coord	
		Y	int	Device units to add to current y-coord		
OffsetWindowOrg	DWORD	hDC	HDC	ID of device context	LO=prev x-coord	320
		X	int	Logical units to add to current x-coord	HO=prev y-coord	
		Y	int	Logical units to add to current y-coord		
OpenClipboard	BOOL	hWnd	HWND	ID of window associated with open clipboard	≠0 if clipboard opened	321
OpenComm	int	lpComName	LPSTR	Pointer to COMn or LPTn string	ID of comm device	321
		wInQueue	WORD	Size of receive queue	or negative for	
		wOutQueue	WORD	Size of transmit queue	error	
OpenFile	int	lpFileName	LPSTR	Pointer to ASCIIZ string naming file to open	DOS file handle	322
		lpReOpenBuff	LPOFSTRUCT	Pointer to OFSTRUCT to receive file info	or -1	
		wStyle	WORD	Action to take		
OpenIcon	BOOL	hWnd	HWND	ID of window	≠0 if successful	325
OpenSound	int				Number of voices	326
OutputDebugString†	void	lpOutputString	LPSTR	Pointer to ASCIIZ string to output	None	326
PaintRgn	BOOL	hDC	HDC	ID of device context	≠0 if successful	327
		hRgn	HRGN	ID of region to fill		
PALETTEINDEX†	COLORREF	nPaletteIndex	int	Index to palette entry	Logical palette index specifier	327
PALETTERGB†	COLORREF	cRed	BYTE	Intensity of red	Palette-relative	327
		cGreen	BYTE	Intensity of green	RGB value	
		cBlue	BYTE	Intensity of blue		
PatBlt	BOOL	HDC	HDC	ID of device context	≠0 if pattern	328
		X	int	x-coord of upper-left corner of rectangle	drawn	
		Y	int	y-coord of upper-left corner of rectangle		
		nWidth	int	Width of rectangle		
		nHeight	int	Height of rectangle		
		dwRop	DWORD	Raster operation code		
PeekMessage	BOOL	lpMsg	LPMSG	Pointer to MSG struct	≠0 if message	329
		hWnd	HWND	ID of window to examine messages for	available	
		wMsgFilterMin	WORD	Value of lowest message position to examine		
		wMsgFilterMax	WORD	Value of highest message position to examine		
		wRemoveMsg	WORD	Flag indicating what to do with message		
Pie	BOOL	hDC	HDC	ID of device context	≠0 if pie drawn	331
		X1	int	x-coord of upper-left corner of bounding rect		
		Y1	int	y-coord of upper-left corner of bounding rect		
		X2	int	x-coord of lower-right corner of bounding rect		
		Y2	int	y-coord of lower-right corner of bounding rect		
		X3	int	x-coord of arc's start point		
		Y3	int	y-coord of arc's start point		
		X4	int	x-coord of arc's end point		
		Y4	int	y-coord of arc's end point		
PlayMetaFile	BOOL	hDC	HDC	ID of device context	≠0 if successful	332
		hMF	HANDLE	ID of metafile		
PlayMetaFileRecord	void	hDC	HDC	ID of device context	None	332
		lpHandletable	LPHANDLETABLE	Pointer to object handle table for playback		
		lpMetaRecord	LPMETARECORD	Poitner to metafile to play		
		nHandles	WORD	Number of handles in handle table		
Polygon	BOOL	hDC	HDC	ID of device context	≠0 if successful	333
		lpPoints	LPPOINT	Pointer to array specifying vertices of polygon		
		nCount	int	Number of vertices in array		
Polyline	BOOL	hDC	HDC	ID of device context	≠0 if lines drawn	334
		lpPoints	LPPOINT	Pointer to array of points to connect		
		nCount	int	Number of points in array		

(Continued)

6.096. WINDOWS FUNCTION SUMMARY BY NAME (continued)

Function Name	Type	Parameters*	Parm Type	Parameter Definition	Return Value	Pg§
PolyPolygon†	BOOL	hDC lpPoints lpPolyCounts nCount	HDC LPPOINT LPINT int	ID of device context Pointer to array defining vertices of polygons Pointer to array defining points in each polygon Total number points in lpPolyCounts	≠0 if polygons drawn	334
PostAppMessage	BOOL	hTask wMsg wParam lParam	HANDLE WORD WORD DWORD	ID of task to receive message Type of message to post Message-dependent information Message-dependent information	≠0 if message posted	335
PostMessage	BOOL	hWnd wMsg wParam lParam	HWND WORD WORD DWORD	ID of window to receive message Type of message to post Message-dependent information Message-dependent information	≠0 if message posted	335
PostQuitMessage	void	nExitCode	int	Application exit code	None	336
ProfClear†	void				None	337
ProfFinish†	void				None	337
ProfFlush†	void				None	337
ProfInsChk†	int				0=not installed 1=installed, not enhanced mode 2=installed in enhanced mode	338
ProfSampRate†	void	nRate286 nRate386	int int	Sampling rate for profiler in nonenhanced 386 mode Sampling rate for profiler in enhanced 386 mode	None	338
ProfSetup†	void	nBufferSize nSamples	int int	Size of output buffer in K How much sampling data to write to disk	None	339
ProfStart†	void				None	340
ProfStop†	void				None	340
PtInRect	BOOL	lpRect Point	LPRECT POINT	Pointer to RECT Pointer to POINT	≠0 if point in RECT	340
PtInRegion	BOOL	hRgn X Y	HRGN int int	ID of region to examine x-coord of point y-coord of point	≠0 if point in RGN	341
PtVisible	BOOL	hDC X Y	HDC int int	ID of device context x-coord of point y-coord of point	≠0 if point in clipping region	341
ReadComm	int	nCid lpBuf nSize	int LPSTR int	Communication device to read Pointer to buffer to receive characters read Number of characters to read	Number chars actually read or 0	343
RealizePalette†	int	hDC	HDC	ID of device context	Number of entries mapped	343
Rectangle	BOOL	hDC X1 Y1 X2 Y2	HDC int int int int	ID of device context x-coord of upper-left corner y-coord of upper-left corner x-coord of lower-right corner y-coord of lower-right corner	≠0 if rectangle drawn	344
RectInRegion†	BOOL	hRegion lpRect	HRGN LPRECT	ID of region ID of rectangle	TRUE if part of RECT inside RGN	345
RectVisible	BOOL	hDC lpRect	HDC LPRECT	ID of device context Pointer to RECT	≠0 if part of RECT inside clip region	345
RegisterClass	BOOL	lpWndClass	LPWNDCLASS	Pointer to WNDCLASS	≠0 if class is registered	345
RegisterClipboardFormat	WORD	lpFormatName	LPSTR	Pointer to ASCIIZ string naming format	Registered format or 0	346
RegisterWindowMessage	WORD	lpString	LPSTR	Pointer to message string to register	C000-FFFFH if registered, or 0	347
ReleaseCapture	void				None	348
ReleaseDC	int	hWnd hDC	HWND HDC	ID of window with device context to release ID of device context to release	1 if released	348
RemoveFontResource	BOOL	lpFilename	LPSTR	Pointer to ASCIIZ string naming font-resource file or handle to loaded module	≠0 if successful	348
RemoveMenu†	BOOL	hMenu nPosition wFlags	HMENU WORD WORD	ID of menu to change Menu item to remove How nPosition should be interpreted	TRUE if successful	349
RemoveProp	HANDLE	hWnd lpString	HWND LPSTR	ID of window with property list to change Pointer to ASCIIZ string or atom ID of string	ID of string or NULL	350
ReplyMessage	void	lReply	LONG	Result of message processing	None	351
ResizePalette†	BOOL	hPalette nNumEntries	HPALETTE int	ID of palette Number of entries in resized palette	TRUE if resized	351
RestoreDC	BOOL	hDC nSavedDC	HDC int	ID of device context Device context to be restored	TRUE if restored	352

(Continued)

6.096. WINDOWS FUNCTION SUMMARY BY NAME (continued)

Function Name	*Type*	*Parameters**	*Parm Type*	*Parameter Definition*	*Return Value*	*Pg§*
RGB	COLORREF	cRed	BYTE	Intensity of red	RGB color	352
		cGreen	BYTE	Intensity of green		
		cBlue	BYTE	Intensity of blue		
RoundRect	BOOL	hDC	HDC	ID of device context	≠0 if rect drawn	353
		X1	int	x-coord of upper-left corner of rect		
		Y1	int	y-coord of upper-left corner of rect		
		X2	int	x-coord of lower-right corner of rect		
		Y2	int	y-coord of lower-right corner of rect		
		X3	int	Width of ellipse to draw rounded corners		
		Y3	int	Height of ellipse to draw rounded corners		
SaveDC	int	hDC	HDC	ID of device context to save	Saved device context or 0	355
ScaleViewportExt	DWORD	hDC	HDC	ID of device context	LO=prev x-extent HO=prev y-extent	355
		Xnum	int	Amount to multiply current x-extent		
		Xdenom	int	Amount to divide current x-extent		
		Ynum	int	Amount to multiply current y-extent		
		Ydenom	int	Amount to divide current y-extent		
ScaleWindowExt	DWORD	hDC	HDC	ID of device context	LO=prev x-extent HO=prev y-extent	356
		Xnum	int	Amount to multiply current x-extent		
		Xdenom	int	Amount to divide current x-extent		
		Ynum	int	Amount to multiply current y-extent		
		Ydenom	int	Amount to divide current y-extent		
ScreenToClient	void	hWnd	HWND	ID of window with client area to convert	None	356
		lpPoint	LPPOINT	Pointer to POINT struct with points to convert		
ScrollDC	BOOL	hDC	HDC	ID of device context	≠0 if scrolled	357
		dx	int	Number of horizontal scroll units		
		dy	int	Number of vertical scroll units		
		lprcScroll	LPRECT	Pointer to RECT containing coords of scroll rect		
		lprcClip	LPRECT	Pointer to RECT containing coords of clip rect		
		hrgnUpdate	HGRN	ID of region uncovered by scroll		
		lprcUpdate	LPRECT	Pointer to RECT to contain scroll update region		
ScrollWindow	void	hWnd	HWND	ID of window to scroll client area	None	358
		XAmount	int	Amount to scroll in x-direction		
		YAmount	int	Amount to scroll in y-direction		
		lpRect	LPRECT	Pointer to RECT of client area to scroll		
		lpClipRect	LPRECT	Pointer to RECT of clip area to scroll		
SelectClipRegion	int	hDC	HDC	ID of device context	Region type	359
		hRgn	HRGN	ID of region to select		
SelectObject	HANDLE	hDC	HDC	ID of device context	ID of object or NULL	360
		hObject	HANDLE	ID of object to select		
SelectPalette†	HPALETTE	hDC	HDC	ID of device context	ID of logical palette replaced or NULL	361
		hPalette	HPALETTE	ID of logical palette to select		
		bForceBackground	BOOL	Whether logical palette is forced to be background		
SendDlgItemMessage	DWORD	hDlg	HWND	ID of dialog box containing control	Value returned by control's window function or 0	362
		nIDDlgItem	int	ID of dialog item		
		wMsg	WORD	Message value		
		wParam	WORD	Message-dependent information		
		lParam	DWORD	Message-dependent information		
SendMessage	DWORD	hWnd	HWND	ID of window to receive message	Value returned by window function receiving message	362
		wMsg	WORD	Message to be sent		
		wParam	WORD	Message-dependent information		
		lParam	DWORD	Message-dependent information		
SetActiveWindow	HWND	hWnd	HWND	Top-level window to activate	ID of prev active window	363
SetBitmapBits	LONG	hBitmap	HBITMAP	ID of bitmap to set	Number of bytes used in setting bitmaps or 0	363
		dwCount	DWORD	Number of bytes pointer to by lpBits		
		lpBits	LPSTR	Pointer to bitmap bits		
SetBitmapDimension	DWORD	hBitmap	HANDLE	ID of bitmap	LO=prev width HO=prev height	364
		X	int	Width of bitmap in .1 mm units		
		Y	int	Height of bitmap in .1 mm units		
SetBkColor	DWORD	hDC	HDC	ID of device context	Prev background color or 80000000H	364
		crColor	COLORREF	New background color		
SetBkMode	int	hDC	HDC	ID of device context	Previous bkground mode	365
		nBkMode	int	Background mode		
SetBrushOrg	DWORD	hDC	HDC	ID of device context	LO=prev x-origin HO=prev y-origin	365
		X	int	x-coord of new origin		
		Y	int	y-coord of new origin		
SetCapture	HWND	hWnd	HWND	ID of window to receive mouse input	Prev window receiving input or NULL	366
SetCaretBlinkTime	void	wMSeconds	WORD	New blink rate in ms	None	367

(Continued)

6.096. WINDOWS FUNCTION SUMMARY BY NAME (continued)

Function Name	Type	Parameters*	Parm Type	Parameter Definition	Return Value	Pg§
SetCaretPos	void	X Y	int int	New x-coord for caret New y-coord for caret	None	367
SetClassLong	LONG	hWnd nIndex dwNewLong	HWND int DWORD	ID of window Byte offset of word to change Replacement value	Prev value of integer	367
SetClassWord	WORD	hWnd nIndex wNewWord	HWND int WORD	ID of window Byte offset of word to change Replacement value	Prev value of word	368
SetClipboardData	HANDLE	wFormat hMem	WORD HANDLE	Data format ID of global memory block containing data	ID of data	369
SetClipboardViewer	HWND	hWnd	HWND	ID of window to receive chain messages	Next window in clipboard viewer chain	372
SetCommBreak	int	nCid	int	Comm device to suspend	0 if successful	372
SetCommEventMask	WORD FAR *	nCid nEvtMask	int int	Comm device to enable Events to enable	Pointer to event mask	373
SetCommState	int	lpDCB	DCB FAR *	Pointer to DCB containing comm settings	0 if successful	374
SetCursor	HCURSOR	hCursor	HCURSOR	ID of cursor resource	ID of prev cursor resource or NULL	374
SetCursorPos	void	X Y	int int	New x-coord for cursor New y-coord for cursor	None	375
SetDIBits†	int	hDC hBitmap nStartScan nNumScans lpBits lpBitsInfo wUsage	HDC HBITMAP WORD WORD LPSTR LPBITMAPINFO WORD	ID of device context ID of bitmap Scan number of first scan line in lpBits buffer Scan lines in lpBits buffer Pointer to DIB bits Pointer to BITMAPINFO with DIB info Whether bmiColors is RGB or PAL	Number of scan lines copied or 0	375
SetDIBitsToDevice†	WORD	hDC DestX DestY nWidth nHeight SrcX SrcY nStartScan nNumScans lpBits lpBitsInfo wUsage	HDC WORD WORD WORD WORD WORD WORD WORD WORD LPSTR LPBITMAPINFO WORD	ID of device context x-coord of origin of dest rectangle y-coord of origin of dest rectangle x-extent of rectangle in DIB y-extent of rectangle in DIB x-coord of source in DIB y-coord of source in DIB Scan number of first scan line in lpBits buffer Scan lines in lpBits buffer Pointer to DIB bits Pointer to BITMAPINFO with DIB info Whether bmiColors is RGB or PAL	Number of scan lines copied	377
SetDlgItemInt	void	hDlg nIDDlgItem wValue bSigned	HWND int WORD BOOL	ID of dialog box containing control Control to modify Value to set Whether or not integer value is signed	None	378
SetDlgItemText	void	hDlg nIDDlgItem lpString	HWND int LPSTR	ID of dialog box containing control Control whose text should be set Pointer to ASCIIZ string to copy to control	None	379
SetDoubleClickTime	void	wCount	WORD	Number of ms that can occur between dbl clicks	None	379
SetEnvironment	int	lpPortName lpEnviron nCount	LPSTR LPSTR WORD	Pointer to ASCIIZ string naming port Pointer to buffer containing new environment Number of byes to copy	Actual number of bytes copied, 0, or -1 if environment deleted	380
SetErrorMode	WORD	wMode	WORD	Error mode flag	Prev error mode flag	380
SetFocus	HWND	hWnd	HWND	ID of window to receive keyboard input	ID of prev window getting input or NULL	381
SetHandleCount†	WORD	wNumber	WORD	Number of file handles needed by app (max=255)	Number of handles available to app	382
SetKeyboardState	void	lpKeyState	BYTE FAR *	Pointer to 256-byte array of key states	None	382
SetMapMode	int	hDC nMapMode	HDC int	ID of device context New mapping mode	Prev mapping mode	383
SetMapperFlags	DWORD	hDC dwFlag	HDC DWORD	ID of device context Whether mapper matches aspects with device	Prev value of font-mapper flag	384
SetMenu	BOOL	hWnd hMenu	HWND HMENU	ID of window to change ID of new menu	≠0 if changed	385
SetMenuItemBitmaps†	BOOL	hMenu nPosition wFlags hBitmapUnchecked hBitmapChecked	HMENU WORD WORD HBITMAP HBITMAP	ID of menu to change Menu item to change How nPosition should be interpreted ID of bitmap to display when not checked ID of bitmap to display when checked	TRUE if successful	385

(Continued)

6.096. WINDOWS FUNCTION SUMMARY BY NAME (continued)

Function Name	*Type*	*Parameters**	*Parm Type*	*Parameter Definition*	*Return Value*	*Pg§*
SetMessageQueue	BOOL	cMsg	int	Maximum number of messages in new queue	≠0 if queue created	386
SetMetaFileBits	HANDLE	hMem	HANDLE	ID of global memory block with metafile data	ID of metafile or NULL	387
SetPaletteEntries†	WORD	hPalette wStartIndex wNumEntries lpPaletteEntries	HPALETTE WORD WORD LPPALETTEENTRY	ID of logical palette First entry in logical palette to set Number of entries to set Pointer to first memory of PALETTEENTRY array	Number of entries set or 0	387
SetParent	HWND	hWndChild hWndNewParent	HWND HWND	ID of child window ID of new parent window	Prev parent window ID	388
SetPixel	DWORD	hDC X Y crColor	HDC int int COLORREF	ID of device context x-coord of point to set y-coord of point to set Color to paint the point	RGB value actually painted, or -1	388
SetPolyFillMode	int	hDC nPolyFillMode	HDC int	ID of device context New filling mode	Prev filling mode or 0	389
SetProp	BOOL	hWnd lpString hData	HWND LPSTR HANDLE	ID of window to receive new entry Pointer to ASCIIZ string or atom IDing string ID of handle to be copied to property list	≠0 if string added	390
SetRect	void	lpRect X1 Y1 X2 Y2	LPRECT int int int int	Pointer to RECT to receive new coords x-coord of upper-left corner y-coord of upper-left corner x-coord of lower-right corner y-coord of lower-right corner	None	390
SetRectEmpty	void	lpRect	LPRECT	Pointer to RECT to receive empty rectangle	None	391
SetRectRgn	void	hRgn X1 Y1 X2 Y2	HANDLE int int int int	ID of region x-coord of upper-left corner of rect region y-coord of upper-left corner of rect region x-coord of lower-right corner of rect region y-coord of lower-right corner of rect region	None	391
SetResourceHandler	FARPROC	hInstance lpType lpLoadFunc	HANDLE LPSTR FARPROC	ID of file containing resource Pointer to short int specifying resource type Address of application-supplied callback function	Pointer to app-supplied function	392
SetROP2	int	hDC nDrawMode	HDC int	ID of device context New drawing mode	Prev drawing mode	394
SetScrollPos	int	hWnd nBar nPos bRedraw	HWND int int BOOL	ID of window with scroll bar to set Scroll bar to set New position Whether scroll bar should be redrawn	Prev position of scroll bar thumb	396
SetScrollRange	void	hWnd nBar nMinPos nMaxPos bRedraw	HWND int int int BOOL	ID of window or scroll bar control Scroll bar to set Minimum scrolling position Maximum scrolling position Whether scroll bar should be redrawn	None	397
SetSoundNoise	int	nSource nDuration	int int	Noise source Duration in noise in noise ticks	0 if successful	398
SetStretchBltMode	int	hDC nStretchMode	HDC int	ID of device context New stretching mode	Prev stretching mode	398
SetSwapAreaSize	LONG	rsSize	WORD	Number of 16-byte paragraphs requested for CS	LO=# ¶s obtained HO=max available	399
SetSysColors	void	nChanges lpSysColor lpColorValues	int LPINT DWORD FAR *	Number of system colors to change Pointer to array of indexes to elements to change Pointer to array of RGB color values	None	400
SetSysModalWindow	HWND	hWnd	HWND	ID of window to be made system modal	Prev window	401
SetSystemPaletteUse†	WORD	hDC wUsage	HDC WORD	ID of device context New use of system palette	Prev use	402
SetTextAlign	WORD	hDC wFlags	HDC WORD	ID of device or display for text output Mask of alignment values	LO=horz align HO=vert align	403
SetTextCharacterExtra	int	hDC nCharExtra	HDC int	ID of device context Amount of extra space to add to characters	Prev spacing	405
SetTextColor	DWORD	hDC crColor	HDC COLORREF	ID of device context Color of text	Prev RGB value	405
SetTextJustification	int	hDC nBreakExtra nBreakCount	HDC int int	ID of device context Total extra space to add to text Number of break characters in line	1 if successful	406
SetTimer	WORD	hWnd nIDEvent wElapse lpTimerFunc	HWND int WORD FARPROC	ID of window to associate with menu Nonzero timer-event ID (if hWnd not 0) Elapsed time between timer events in ms Address of function to be notified	ID of new timer event or 0	407
SetViewportExt	DWORD	hDC X Y	HDC int int	ID of device context x-extent of viewport in device units y-extent of viewport in device units	LO=prev x-extent HO=prev y-extent or 0	408

(Continued)

6.096. WINDOWS FUNCTION SUMMARY BY NAME (continued)

Function Name	*Type*	*Parameters**	*Parm Type*	*Parameter Definition*	*Return Value*	*Pg§*
SetViewportOrg	DWORD	hDC	HDC	ID of device context	LO=prev x-extent	409
		X	int	x-coord of origin of viewport in device units	HO=prev y-extent	
		Y	int	y-coord of origin of viewport in device units		
SetVoiceAccent	int	nVoice	int	Voice queue	0 if successful	410
		nTempo	int	Number of quarter notes played per minute		
		nVolume	int	Volume level		
		nMode	int	How notes are played		
		nPitch	int	Pitch of notes to be played		
SetVoiceEnvelope	int	nVoice	int	Voice queue to receive envelope	0 if successful	411
		nShape	int	Index to OEM wave-shape table		
		nRepeat	int	Number of repetitions of wave shape during note		
SetVoiceNote	int	nVoice	int	Voice queue to receive note	0 if successful	412
		nValue	int	Note value (0=rest)		
		nLength	int	Reciprocal of duration of note		
		nCdots	int	Duration of note in dots		
SetVoiceQueueSize	int	nVoice	int	Voice queue	0 if successful	413
		nBytes	int	Number of bytes in queue		
SetVoiceSound	int	nVoice	int	Voice queue	0 if successful	413
		lFrequency	long	Frequency		
		nDuration	int	Duration of sound in clock ticks		
SetVoiceThreshold	int	nVoice	int	Voice queue	0 if successful	414
		nNotes	int	Number of notes in threshold level		
SetWindowExt	DWORD	hDC	HDC	ID of device context	LO=prev x-extent	414
		X	int	x-extent of window in logical units	HO=prev y-extent	
		Y	int	y-extent of window in logical units	or 0	
SetWindowLong	LONG	hWnd	HWND	ID of window	Prev value	415
		nIndex	int	Byte offset of attribute to change		
		dwNewLong	DWORD	Replacement value		
SetWindowOrg	DWORD	hDC	HDC	ID of device context	LO=prev x-coord	416
		X	int	x-coord of new origin of window	HO=prev y-coord	
		Y	int	y-coord of new origin of window		
SetWindowPos	void	hWnd	HWND	ID of window to position	None	417
		hWndInsertAfter	HWND	ID of window preceding positioned window		
		X	int	x-coord of window's upper-left corner		
		Y	int	y-coord of window's upper-left corner		
		cx	int	New window's width		
		cy	int	New window's height		
		wFlags	WORD	Size and positioning flags		
SetWindowsHook	FARPROC	nFilterType	int	System hook to install	Prev filter address	419
		lpFilterFunc	FARPROC	Address of filter function to install	or NULL	
SetWindowText	void	hWnd	HWND	ID of window or control to change text for	None	427
		lpString	LPSTR	Pointer to ASCIIZ string		
SetWindowWord	WORD	hWnd	HWND	ID of window to modify	Prev value of word	428
		nIndex	int	Byte offset of word to change		
		wNewWord	WORD	Replacement value		
ShowCaret	void	hWnd	HWND	ID of window owning caret or NULL	None	429
ShowCursor	int	bShow	BOOL	Whether display count should be increased/decreased	New display count	429
ShowOwnedPopups	void	hWnd	HWND	ID of window owning popups	None	430
		fShow	BOOL	Whether popups are hidden		
ShowScrollBar	void	hWnd	HWND	ID of window containing scroll bar, or control	None	430
		wBar	WORD	Whether scroll bar in nonclient area		
		bShow	BOOL	Whether scroll bar should be hidden		
ShowWindow	BOOL	hWnd	HWND	ID of window	Prev window state	431
		nCmdShow	int	How window is shown		
SizeofResource	WORD	hInstance	HANDLE	ID of file containing resource	Number of bytes	432
		hResInfo	HANDLE	ID of resource	in resource or 0	
StartSound	int				Should be ignored	433
StopSound	int				Should be ignored	433
StretchBlt	BOOL	hDestDC	HDC	ID of device context to receive bitmap	≠0 if drawn	433
		X	int	x-coord of upper-left corner of dest rectangle		
		Y	int	y-coord of upper-left corner of dest rectangle		
		nWidth	int	Width of destination rectangle		
		nHeight	int	Height of destination rectangle		
		hSrcDC	HDC	ID of device context containing source bitmap		
		XSrc	int	x-coord of upper-left corner of source rectangle		
		YSrc	int	y-coord of upper-left corner of source rectangle		
		nSrcWidth	int	Width of source rectangle		
		nSrcHeight	int	Height of source rectangle		
		dwRop	DWORD	Raster operation to perform		

(Continued)

6.096. WINDOWS FUNCTION SUMMARY BY NAME (continued)

Function Name	*Type*	*Parameters**	*Parm Type*	*Parameter Definition*	*Return Value*	*Pg§*
StretchDIBits†	WORD	hDC	HDC	ID of device context to receive bitmap	Number of scan lines copied	435
		DestX	WORD	x-coord of upper-left corner of dest rectangle		
		DestY	WORD	y-coord of upper-left corner of dest rectangle		
		wDestWidth	WORD	Width of destination rectangle		
		wDestHeight	WORD	Height of destination rectangle		
		SrcX	WORD	x-coord of upper-left corner of source rectangle		
		SrcY	WORD	y-coord of upper-left corner of source rectangle		
		wSrcWidth	WORD	Width of source rectangle		
		wSrcHeight	WORD	Height of source rectangle		
		lpBits	LPSTR	Pointer to DIB bits		
		lpBitsInfo	LPBITMAPINFO	Pointer to BITMAPINFO		
		wUsage	WORD	Whether bmiColors are RGB or PAL		
		dwRop	DWORD	Raster operation to perform		
SwapMouseButton	BOOL	bSwap	BOOL	Whether button meanings are reversed or restored	TRUE if reversed	437
SwapRecording†	void	wFlag	WORD	Swap behavior flag	None	438
SwitchStackBack†	void				None	438
SwitchStackTo†	void	wStackSegment	WORD	DS to contain stack	None	438
		wStackPointer	WORD	Offset of beginning of stack in DS		
		wStackTop	WORD	Offset of top of stack from beginning		
SyncAllVoices	int				0 if successful	439
TabbedTextOut†	long	hDC	HDC	ID of device context	LO=width HO=height	440
		X	int	x-coord of starting point of string		
		Y	int	y-coord of starting point of string		
		lpString	LPSTR	Pointer to string to draw		
		nCount	int	Number of characters in string		
		nTabPositions	int	Number of tab-stop positions in string		
		lpnTabStopPositions	LPINT	Pointer to array of tab stop positions in pixels		
		nTabOrigin	int	Logical x-coord of starting position		
TextOut	BOOL	hDC	HDC	ID of device context	≠0 if string drawn	441
		X	int	x-coord of starting point of string		
		Y	int	y-coord of starting point of string		
		lpString	LPSTR	Pointer to string to draw		
		nCount	int	Number of characters in string		
Throw	void	lpCatchBuf	LPCATCHBUF	Pointer to array containing execution environment	None	441
		nThrowBack	int	Value to return		
ToAscii†	int	wVirtKey	WORD	Virtual-key code to translate	Number of chars copied to buffer or negative if dead key	442
		wScanCode	WORD	Hardware raw scan code of key to translate		
		lpKeyState	LPSTR	Pointer to 256-byte key state array		
		lpChar	LPVOID	Pointer to 32-bit buffer for translated chars		
		wFlags	WORD	Bit 0--flag's menu display		
TrackPopupMenu†	BOOL	hMenu	HMENU	ID of popup menu to display	TRUE if successful	443
		wFlags	WORD	NOT USED--set to 0		
		x	int	Horizontal position of left side of menu		
		y	int	Vertical position of left side of menu		
		nReserved	int	RESERVED--must be 0		
		hWnd	HWND	ID of window owning popup		
		lpReserved	LPVOID	RESERVED--must be NULL		
TranslateAccelerator	int	hWnd	HWND	ID of window whose messages to translate	≠0 if translated	444
		hAccTable	HANDLE	ID of accelerator table		
		lpMsg	LPMSG	Pointer to message		
TranslateMDISysAccel†	BOOL	hWndClient	HWND	ID of parent MDI client window	TRUE if translated	445
		lpMsg	LPMSG	Pointer to message		
TranslateMessage	BOOL	lpMsg	LPMSG	Pointer to message	≠0 if translated	446
TransmitCommChar	int	nCid	int	Comm device to receive character	0 if successful	446
		cChar	char	Character to transmit		
UngetCommChar	int	nCid	int	Comm device to receive character	0 if successful	448
		cChar	char	Character to place in receive queue		
UnhookWindowsHook	BOOL	nHook	int	Hook function type	≠0 if removed	448
		lpfnHook	FARPROC	Address of hook function		
UnionRect	int	lpDestRect	LPRECT	Pointer to RECT to receive union	≠0 if union not empty	449
		lpSrc1Rect	LPRECT	Pointer to first source RECT		
		lpSrc2Rect	LPRECT	Pointer to second source RECT		
UnlockData	HANDLE	Dummy	int	NOT USED--can set to 0	None	449
UnlockResource	BOOL	hResData	HANDLE	ID of global memory block to unlock	0 if ref count 0	450
UnlockSegment	BOOL	wSegment	WORD	Segment address to unlock or -1 for current	0 if lock count 0	450
UnrealizeObject	BOOL	hObject	HANDLE	ID of object to reset	≠0 if successful	451
UnregisterClass†	BOOL	lpClassName	LPSTR	Pointer to ASCIIZ string of class name	TRUE if successful	452
		hInstance	HANDLE	ID of module creating class		

(Continued)

6.096. WINDOWS FUNCTION SUMMARY BY NAME (continued)

Function Name	Type	Parameters*	Parm Type	Parameter Definition	Return Value	Pg§
UpdateColors†	int	hDC	HDC	ID of device context	Not used	452
UpdateWindow	void	hWnd	HWND	ID of window to update	None	453
ValidateCodeSegments†	void				None	454
ValidateFreeSpaces	LPSTR				None	454
ValidateRect	void	hWnd lpRect	HWND LPRECT	ID of window to modify Pointer to RECT to remove from update region	None	455
ValidateRgn	void	hWnd hRgn	HWND HRGN	ID of window to modify ID of region to remove from update region	None	455
VkKeyScan	int	cChar	char	Character to find virtual key for	LO=virt key code HO=shift state or -1	456
WaitMessage	void				None	457
WaitSoundState	int	nState	int	State of voice queues	0 if successful	457
WindowFromPoint	HWND	Point	POINT	POINT struct defining point to check	ID of window with point or NULL	458
WinExec†	WORD	lpCmdLine nCmdShow	LPSTR int	Pointer to ASCIIZ string containing command line How window is to be shown	>32 if successful	459
WinHelp†	BOOL	hWnd lpHelpFile wCommand dwData	HWND LPSTR WORD DWORD	ID of window requesting help Pointer to ASCIIZ string of help file Type of help requested Context or key word of help requested	TRUE if successful	460
WriteComm	int	nCid lpBuf nSize	int LPSTR int	Device to receive characters Pointer to buffer of characters to write Number of characters to write	Number of chars actually written or 0	462
WritePrivateProfile Sting†	BOOL	lpApplicationName lpKeyName lpString lpFileName	LPSTR LPSTR LPSTR LPSTR	Pointer to application heading in init file Pointer to key name Pointer to string containing new key value Pointer to ASCIIZ string naming init file	≠0 if successful	462
WriteProfileString	BOOL	lpApplicationName lpKeyName lpString	LPSTR LPSTR LPSTR	Pointer to application heading in WIN.INI Pointer to key name Pointer to string containing new key value	≠0 if successful	464
wsprintf†	int	lpOutput lpFormat [argument(s)]	LPSTR LPSTR varies	Pointer to ASCIIZ string to receive output Pointer to ASCIIZ string containing format control Varies	Number of chars in lpOutput	465
wvsprintf†	int	lpOutput lpFormat lpArglist	LPSTR LPSTR LPSTR	Pointer to ASCIIZ string to receive output Pointer to ASCIIZ string containing format control Pointer to array of words containing arguments	Number of chars in lpOutput	467
Yield	void				None	469

†Applies to all versions of Windows beginning with 3.0.
*Parameters are listed in required order.
§Page numbers apply to Chapter 4 of the Microsoft Windows 3.0 SDK Programmer's Reference, e.g., a page number of 52 refers to page 4-52.

Source: Microsoft Windows 2.0 SDK Programmer's Reference
Microsoft Windows 3.0 SDK Programmer's Reference, Chapters 4 and 12

See Also: 6.095. Windows Function Summary by Version
6.097. Windows Escape Function Summary by Name
6.098. Windows Function Summary by Type

6.097. WINDOWS ESCAPE FUNCTION SUMMARY BY NAME

Function Name	Parameters*	Parm Type	Parameter Definition	Return Value	Pg¥
ABORTDOC	hDC	HDC	ID of device context	Positive if	2
	ABORTDOC	int	Command	successful	
	NULL	int			
	NULL	LPSTR			
	NULL	LPSTR			
BANDINFO	hDC	HDC	ID of device context	1 if successful	2
	BANDINFO	int	Command		
	sizeof(BANDINFOSTRUCT)	int			
	lpInData	BANDINFOSTRUCT FAR *	Pointer to BANDINFOSTRUCT		
	lpOutData	BANDINFOSTRUCT FAR *	Pointer to BANDINFOSTRUCT		
BEGIN_PATH	hDC	HDC	ID of device context	Number of	5
	BEGIN_PATH	int	Command	BEGIN_PATH	
	NULL	int		calls without	
	NULL	LPSTR		END_PATH	
	NULL	LPSTR			
CLIP_TO_PATH	hDC	HDC	ID of device context	≠0 if successful	6
	CLIP_TO_PATH	int	Command		
	sizeof(int)	int			
	lpClipMode	LPINT	Pointer to clipping mode type		
	NULL	LPSTR			
DEVICEDATA	hDC	HDC	ID of device context	Number of bytes	7
	DEVICEDATA	int	Command	transferred	
	nCount	int	Number of bytes in lpInData		
	lpInData	LPSTR	Data		
	lpOutData	LPSTR	Data		
DRAFTMODE	hDC	HDC	ID of device context	Positive if	7
	DRAFTMODE	int	Command	successful	
	sizeof(int)	int			
	lpDraftMode	LPINT	Pointer to draft mode type		
	NULL	LPSTR			
DRAWPATTERNRECT	hDC	HDC	ID of device context	1 if successful	8
	DRAWPATTERNRECT	int	Command		
	sizeof(PRECTSTRUCT)	int			
	lpInData	PRECT_STRUCT FAR *	Pointer to PRECT_STRUCT		
	NULL	LPSTR			
ENABLEDUPLEX	hDC	HDC	ID of device context	1 if successful	9
	ENABLEDUPLEX	int	Command		
	sizeof(WORD)	int			
	lpInData	WORD FAR *	Pointer to printing duplex type		
	NULL	LPSTR			
ENABLEPAIRKERNING	hDC	HDC	ID of device context	1 if successful	10
	ENABLEPAIRKERNING	int	Command		
	sizeof(int)	int			
	lpNewKernFlag	LPINT	Pointer to enable/disable flag		
	lpOldKernFlag	LPINT	Pointer to old flag holder		
ENABLERELATIVEWIDTHS	hDC	HDC	ID of device context	1 if successful	11
	ENABLERELATIVEWIDTHS	int	Command		
	sizeof(int)	int			
	lpNewWidthFlag	LPINT	Pointer to relative width flag		
	lpOldWidthFlag	LPINT	Pointer to old flag holder		
ENDDOC	hDC	HDC	ID of device context	Positive if	12
	ENDDOC	int	Command	successful	
	NULL	int			
	NULL	LPSTR			
	NULL	LPSTR			
END_PATH	hDC	HDC	ID of device context	Number of	12
	END_PATH	int	Command	BEGIN_PATH	
	sizeof(PATH_INFO)	int		calls without	
	lpInData	PATH_INFO FAR *	Pointer to PATH_INFO struct	END_PATH	
	NULL	LPSTR		or -1	
ENUMPAPERBINS	hDC	HDC	ID of device context	1 if successful	15
	ENUMPAPERBINS	int	Command		
	sizeof(int)	int			
	lpNumBins	LPINT	Pointer to number of bins		
	lpOutData	LPSTR	Pointer to struct for bin data		

(Continued)

6.097. WINDOWS ESCAPE FUNCTION SUMMARY BY NAME (continued)

Function Name	*Parameters**	*Parm Type*	*Parameter Definition*	*Return Value*	*Pg#*
ENUMPAPERMETRICS	hDC	HDC	ID of device context	Positive if	16
	ENUMPAPERMETRICS	int	Command	successful, 0 if	
	sizeof(int)	int		not implemented,	
	lpMode	LPINT	Pointer to escape mode type	negative for	
	lpOutData	LPRECT	Pointer to array of RECT structs	error	
EPSPRINTING	hDC	HDC	ID of device context	Positive if	16
	EPSPRINTING	int	Command	successful, 0 if	
	sizeof(BOOL)	int		not implemented,	
	lpBool	BOOL FAR *	Pointer to download enable/disable flag	negative for	
	NULL	LPSTR		error	
EXT_DEVICE_CAPS	hDC	HDC	ID of device context	Nonzero if	17
	EXT_DEVICE_CAPS	int	Command	supported	
	sizeof(int)	int			
	lpIndex	LPINT	Pointer to capability type		
	lpCaps	DWORD FAR *	Pointer to 32-bit for capability		
EXTTEXTOUT	hDC	HDC	ID of device context	1 if successful	19
	EXTTEXTOUT	int	Command		
	sizeof(EXTTEXT_STRUCT)	int			
	lpInData	EXTTEXT_STRUCT FAR *	Pointer to EXTTEXT_STRUCT		
	NULL	LPSTR			
FLUSHOUTPUT	hDC	HDC	ID of device context	Positive if	21
	FLUSHOUTPUT	int	Command	successful	
	NULL	int			
	NULL	LPSTR			
	NULL	LPSTR			
GETCOLORTABLE	hDC	HDC	ID of device context	Positive if	21
	GETCOLORTABLE	int	Command	successful	
	sizeof(int)	int			
	lpIndex	LPINT	Pointer to index of color-table entry		
	lpColor	DWORD FAR *	Pointer to RGB value holder		
GETEXTENDEDTEXTMETRICS	hDC	HDC	ID of device context	Number of bytes	21
	GETEXTENDEDTEXTMETRICS	int	Command	copied or 0	
	sizeof(WORD)	int			
	lpInData	WORD FAR *	Pointer to number of lpOutData bytes		
	lpOutData	EXTTEXTMETRIC FAR *	Pointer to EXTTEXTMETRIC		
GETEXTENTTABLE	hDC	HDC	ID of device context	1 if successful	26
	GETEXTENTTABLE	int	Command		
	sizeof(CHAR_RANGE_STRUCT)	int			
	lpInData	LPSTR	Pointer to CHAR_RANGE_STRUCT		
	lpOutData	LPINT	Pointer to char width array		
GETFACENAME	hDC	HDC	ID of device context	Positive if	27
	GETFACENAME	int	Command	successful, 0 if	
	NULL	int		not implemented,	
	NULL	LPSTR	Pointer to 60-byte buffer for name	or negative for	
	lpFaceName	LPSTR		error	
GETPAIRKERNTABLE	hDC	HDC	ID of device context	Number of	27
	GETPAIRKERNTABLE	int	Command	KERNPAIR	
	NULL	int		structs copied,	
	NULL	LPSTR		or 0	
	lpOutData	KERNPAIR FAR *	Pointer to array of KERNPAIR		
GETPHYSPAGESIZE	hDC	HDC	ID of device context	Positive if	29
	GETPHYSPAGESIZE	int	Command	successful	
	NULL	int			
	NULL	LPSTR			
	lpDimensions	LPPOINT	Pointer to POINT for page size		
GETPRINTINGOFFSET	hDC	HDC	ID of device context	Positive if	29
	GETPRINTINGOFFSET	int	Command	successful	
	NULL	int			
	NULL	LPSTR			
	lpOffset	LPPOINT	Pointer to POINT for offset		
GETSCALINGFACTOR	hDC	HDC	ID of device context	Positive if	30
	GETSCALINGFACTOR	int	Command	successful	
	NULL	int			
	NULL	LPSTR			
	lpFactors	LPPOINT	Pointer to POINT for scaling factor		

(Continued)

6.097. WINDOWS ESCAPE FUNCTION SUMMARY BY NAME (continued)

Function Name	Parameters*	Parm Type	Parameter Definition	Return Value	Pg¥
GETSETPAPERBINS	hDC	HDC	ID of device context	None	30
	GETSETPAPERBINS	int	Command		
	nCount	int	Number of bytes in lpInData		
	lpInData	BinInfo FAR *	Pointer to BinInfo structure		
	lpOutData	BinInfo FAR *	Pointer to BinInfo structure		
GETSETPAPERMETRICS	hDC	HDC	ID of device context	Positive if successful	32
	GETSETPAPERMETRICS	int	Command		
	sizeof(RECT)	int			
	lpNewPaper	LPRECT	Pointer to RECT of new image area		
	lpPrevPaper	LPRECT	Pointer to RECT for old image area		
GETSETPAPERORIENT	hDC	HDC	ID of device context	Current or previous orientation, or -1 if fails	32
	GETSETPAPERORIENT	int	Command		
	nCount	int	Number of bytes in lpInData		
	lpInData	ORIENT FAR *	Pointer to ORIENT structure		
	NULL	LPPOINT			
GETSETSCREENPARAMS	hDC	HDC	ID of device context	Positive if successful	33
	GETSETSCREENPARAMS	int	Command		
	sizeof(SCREENPARAMS)	int			
	lpInData	SCREENPARAMS FAR *	Pointer to SCREENPARAMS for new		
	lpOutData	SCREENPARAMS FAR *	Pointer to SCREENPARAMS for prev		
GETTECHNOLOGY	hDC	HDC	ID of device context	1 if successful	35
	GETTECHNOLOGY	int	Command		
	NULL	int			
	NULL	LPSTR			
	lpTechnology	LPSTR	Pointer to buffer for ASCIIZ string		
GETTRACKKERNTABLE	hDC	HDC	ID of device context	Number of KERNTRACK structs copied to buffer, or 0 if fails	35
	GETTRACKKERNTABLE	int	Command		
	NULL	int			
	NULL	LPSTR			
	lpOutData	KERNTRACK FAR *	Pointer to array of KERNTRACK		
GETVECTORBRUSHSIZE	hDC	HDC	ID of device context	1 if successful	37
	GETVECTORBRUSHSIZE	int	Command		
	sizeof(LOGBRUSH)	int			
	lpInData	LOGBRUSH FAR *	Pointer to LOGBRUSH to return data on		
	lpOutData	LPPOINT	Pointer to POINT with width of pen		
GETVECTORPENSIZE	hDC	HDC	ID of device context	1 if successful	37
	GETVECTORPENSIZE	int	Command		
	sizeof(LOGPEN)	int			
	lpInData	LOGPEN FAR *	Pointer to LOGPEN to return data on		
	lpOutData	LPPOINT	Pointer to POINT with width of pen		
MFCOMMENT	hDC	HDC	ID of device context	Positive if successful	38
	MFCOMMENT	int	Command		
	nCount	short	Number of chars in string		
	lpComment	LPSTR	ASCIIZ string containing comment		
	NULL	LPSTR			
NEWFRAME	hDC	HDC	ID of device context	Positive if successful	38
	NEWFRAME	int	Command		
	NULL	int			
	NULL	LPSTR			
	NULL	LPSTR			
NEXTBAND	hDC	HDC	ID of device context	Positive if successful	39
	NEXTBAND	int	Command		
	NULL	int			
	NULL	LPSTR			
	lpBandRect	LPRECT	Pointer to RECT to receive band coords		
PASSTHROUGH	hDC	HDC	ID of device context	Number of bytes if successful, or 0 if not successful, or negative if fails	40
	PASSTHROUGH	int	Command		
	nCount	short	Number of bytes in lpInData		
	lpInData	LPSTR	Pointer to data buffer		
	NULL	LPSTR			
QUERYESCSUPPORT	hDC	HDC	ID of device context	0 if feature is implmented	41
	QUERYESCSUPPORT	int	Command		
	sizeof(int)	int			
	lpEscNum	LPINT	Pointer to function to check		
	NULL	LPSTR			

(Continued)

6.097. WINDOWS ESCAPE FUNCTION SUMMARY BY NAME (continued)

Function Name	*Parameters**	*Parm Type*	*Parameter Definition*	*Return Value*	*Pg#*
RESTORE_CTM	hDC	HDC	ID of device context	Number of	42
	RESTORE_CTM	int	Command	SAVE_CTM	
	NULL	int		calls without	
	NULL	LPSTR		RESTORE_CTM	
	NULL	LPSTR		or negative	
SAVE_CTM	hDC	HDC	ID of device context	Number of	42
	SAVE_CTM	int	Command	SAVE_CTM	
	NULL	int		calls without	
	NULL	LPSTR		RESTORE_CTM	
	NULL	LPSTR		or negative	
SELECTPAPERSOURCE	Superseded by GETSETPAPERBINS				43
SETABORTPROC	hDC	HDC	ID of device context	Positive if	43
	SETABORTPROC	int	Command	successful	
	NULL	int			
	lpAbortFunc	FARPROC	Pointer to abort function		
	NULL	LPSTR			
SETALLJUSTVALUES	hDC	HDC	ID of device context	1 if successful	44
	SETALLJUSTVALUES	int	Command		
	sizeof(JUST_VALUE_STRUCT)	int			
	lpInData	JUST_VALUE_STRUCT FAR *	Pointer to JUST_VALUE_STRUCT		
	NULL	LPSTR			
SET_ARC_DIRECTION	hDC	HDC	ID of device context	Previous arc	45
	SET_ARC_DIRECTION	int	Command	direction	
	sizeof(int)	int			
	lpDirection	LPINT	Pointer to arc direction indicator		
	NULL	LPSTR			
SET_BACKGROUND_COLOR	hDC	HDC	ID of device context	TRUE if	46
	SET_BACKGROUND_COLOR	int	Command	successful	
	nCount	int	Number of bytes in lpNewColor		
	lpNewColor	DWORD FAR *	Pointer to 32-bit background color		
	lpOldColor	DWORD FAR *	Pointer to 32-bit prev background color		
SET_BOUNDS	hDC	HDC	ID of device context	TRUE if	47
	SET_BOUNDS	int	Command	successful	
	sizeof(RECT)	int			
	lpInData	LPRECT	Pointer to RECT of image output		
	NULL	LPSTR			
SETCOLORTABLE	hDC	HDC	ID of device context	Positive if	48
	SETCOLORTABLE	int	Command	successful	
	sizeof(COLORTABLE_STRUCT)	int			
	lpInData	COLORTABLE_STRUCT FAR *	Pointer to COLORTABLE_STRUCT		
	lpColor	DWORD FAR *	Pointer to value to receive RGB color		
SETCOPYCOUNT	hDC	HDC	ID of device context	1 if	49
	SETCOPYCOUNT	int	Command	successful	
	sizeof(int)	int			
	lpNumCopies	LPINT	Pointer to copies requested		
	lpActualCopies	LPINT	Pointer to receive actual copies		
SETKERNTRACK	hDC	HDC	ID of device context	1 if	50
	SETKERNTRACK	int	Command	successful	
	sizeof(int)	int			
	lpNewTrack	LPINT	Pointer to kerning track or 0		
	lpOldTrack	LPINT	Pointer to receiver of prev kern track		
SETLINECAP	hDC	HDC	ID of device context	Positive if	51
	SETLINECAP	int	Command	successful	
	sizeof(int)	int			
	lpNewCap	LPINT	Pointer to end-cap type		
	lpOldCap	LPINT	Pointer to receiver of prev end-cap type		
SETLINEJOIN	hDC	HDC	ID of device context	Positive if	52
	SETLINEJOIN	int	Command	successful	
	sizeof(int)	int			
	lpNewJoin	LPINT	Pointer to intersection type		
	lpOldJoin	LPINT	Pointer to receiveer of prev intersection		
SETMITERLIMIT	hDC	HDC	ID of device context	Positive if	53
	SETMITERLIMIT	int	Command	successful	
	nCount	short	Number of bytes in lpNewMiter		
	lpNewMiter	LPINT	Pointer to miter limit		
	lpOldMiter	LPINT	Pointer to receiver of prev miter limit		

(Continued)

6.097. WINDOWS ESCAPE FUNCTION SUMMARY BY NAME (continued)

Function Name	Parameters*	Parm Type	Parameter Definition	Return Value	Pg¥
SET_POLY_MODE	hDC SET_POLY_MODE sizeof(int) lpMode NULL	HDC int int LPINT LPSTR	ID of device context Command Pointer to poly mode	0 if driver didn't handle request	53
SET_SCREEN_ANGLE	hDC SET_SCREEN_ANGLE sizeof(int) lpAngle NULL	HDC int int LPINT LPSTR	ID of device context Command Pointer to screen angle	Previous screen angle	55
SET_SPREAD	hDC SET_SPREAD sizeof(int) lpSpread NULL	HDC int int LPINT LPSTR	ID of device context Command Pointer to spread value in pixels	Previous spread value	56
STARTDOC	hDC STARTDOC nCount lpDocName NULL	HDC int short LPSTR LPSTR	ID of device context Command Number of chars in lpDocName Pointer to ASCIIZ string w/ name of doc	Positive if successful	57
TRANSFORM_CTM	hDC TRANSFORM_CTM 36 lpMatrix NULL	HDC int int LPSTR LPSTR	ID of device context Command Pointer to 3x3 array of 32-bit values	TRUE if successful	58

†Applies to all versions of Windows beginning with 3.0.
*Parameters are listed in required order.
¥Page numbers apply to Chapter 12 of the Microsoft Windows 3.0 SDK Programmer's Reference, e.g., a page number of 12 refers to page 12-12.

Source: Microsoft Windows 2.0 SDK Programmer's Reference
Microsoft Windows 3.0 SDK Programmer's Reference, Chapters 4 and 12

See Also: 6.095. Windows Function Summary by Version
6.096. Windows Function Summary by Name
6.098. Windows Function Summary by Type

6.098. WINDOWS FUNCTION SUMMARY BY TYPE

Function Name	*Description*	*Type*
LoadModule†	Loads and executes a Windows program	Application-execution
WinExec†	Executes application	Application-execution
WinHelp†	Invokes Windows Help application	Application-execution
AddAtom	Creates atom for character string lpString	Atom manager
DeleteAtom	Deletes nAtom if its reference count is zero	Atom manager
FindAtom	Retrieves atom associated with lpString	Atom manager
GetAtomHandle	Returns handle of atom string	Atom manager
GetAtomName	Copies nSize chars of string of atom to lpBuffer	Atom manager
GlobalAddAtom*	Adds global atom to the atom table	Atom manager
GlobalDeleteAtom*	Deletes global atom from the atom table	Atom manager
GlobalFindAtom*	Finds character string within atom table	Atom manager
GlobalGetAtomName	Returns copy of string associated with an atom	Atom manager
InitAtomTable	Initializes atom hash table	Atom manager
BuildCommDCB	Fills device control block with control codes	Communications
ClearCommBreak	Clears comm break state for nCid device	Communications
CloseComm	Closes comm device nCid (first transmits buffer)	Communications
EscapeCommFunction	Executes escape function nFunct for device nCid	Communications
FlushComm	Flushes characters from queue of device nCid	Communications
GetCommError	Fills lpStat buffer with status of nCid device	Communications
GetCommEventMask	Retrieves, then clears, the event mask for nCid	Communications
GetCommState	Fills lpDCB buffer with DCB of nCid device	Communications
OpenComm	Opens device named by lpCommName for comm use	Communications
ReadComm	Reads up to nSize bytes from nCid into lpBuf	Communications
SetCommBreak	Sets break state of device nCid and suspends transmission	Communications
SetCommEventMask	Sets event mask of device nCid	Communications
SetCommState	Sets device to state specified in lpDCB	Communications
TransmitCommChar	Places character cChar at head of transmit queue	Communications
UngetCommChar	Makes character cChar next character to be read from queue	Communications
WriteComm	Writes nSize bytes from buffer to device nCid	Communications
DebugBreak†	Forces a break to the debugger	Debugging
FatalAppExit†	Displays message in lpMessageText and terminates app	Debugging
FatalExit	Halts Windows and prompts through AUX	Debugging
OutputDebugString†	Sends debugging message to debugger, if present	Debugging
ValidateCodeSegments†	Outputs debugging information to terminal if CS altered	Debugging
ValidateFreeSpaces	Checks free segments in memory for valid contents§	Debugging
ValidateFreeSpaces*	Determines whether free segments contain valid contents	Debugging
GetDriveType†	Determines whether a disk drive is removeable, fixed, or remote	File I/O
GetSystemDirectory†	Returns pathname of Windows system subdirectory	File I/O
GetTempDrive	Returns optimal drive letter for temp file	File I/O
GetTempFileName	Creates temporary file name	File I/O
GetWindowsDirectory†	Returns pathname of Windows directory	File I/O
OpenFile	Creates, opens, reopens, or deletes file named by lpFileName	File I/O
SetHandleCount†	Changes number of file handles available to task	File I/O
_lclose	Closes file specified by hFile	File I/O
_lcreat	Opens a file with name specified by lpPathName	File I/O
_llseek	Repositions pointer in previously opened file	File I/O
_lopen	Opens file specified by lpPathName	File I/O
_lread	Reads data from file indentified by hFile	File I/O
_lwrite	Writes data to file specified by hFile	File I/O
BitBlt	Moves bitmap from src device to dest device	GDI bitmap
CreateBitmap	Creates bitmap of specified height, width, pattern	GDI bitmap
CreateBitmapIndirect	Creates bitmap from existing bitmap	GDI bitmap
CreateCompatibleBitmap	Creates bitmap compatible with device hDC	GDI bitmap
CreateDiscardableBitmap	Creates discardable bitmap	GDI bitmap
ExtFloodFill†	Fills display surface within a border	GDI bitmap
FloodFill	Fills area with current brush starting at X,Y	GDI bitmap
GetBitmapBits	Copies lCount bits of bitmap to lpBits buffer	GDI bitmap
GetBitmapDimension	Returns width and height of bitmap	GDI bitmap
GetPixel	Retrieves RGB color of pixel at X,Y	GDI bitmap
SetBitmapBits	Sets bitmap bits to values given at lpBits	GDI bitmap
SetBitmapDimension	Associates width and height with a bitmap (in .1 mm)	GDI bitmap
SetPixel	Sets pixel at X,Y to device color closest to rgbColor	GDI bitmap
StretchBlt	Moves bitmap from source rect to destination rect	GDI bitmap
IntersectClipRect	Forms new clipping region from intersection	GDI clipping
OffsetClipRgn	Moves clipping region X units horiz and Y units vertically	GDI clipping
RectVisible	Determines if any part of lpRect lies within clipping rgn	GDI clipping
SelectClipRgn	Selects hRgn as current clipping region for disp context	GDI clipping
ExcludeClipRect	Creates new clipping region for rectangle	GDI clipping
GetClipBox	Copies clipping rect boundary to lpRect	GDI clipping
Escape	Accesses device facilities not available through GDI	GDI control
Escape (ABORTDOC)	Aborts current job	GDI control
Escape (BANDINFO)*	Copies banding capability info to lpIndata structure	GDI control
Escape (DEVICEDATA)	Send data directly to printer	GDI control
Escape (DRAFTMODE)	Turns draft mode ON or OFF	GDI control
Escape (DRAWPATTERNRECT)*	Creates pattern using rules for PCL printers	GDI control

(Continued)

6.098. WINDOWS FUNCTION SUMMARY BY TYPE (continued)

Function Name	Description	Type
Escape (ENABLEDUPLEX)*	Enables duplex printing capabilities	GDI control
Escape (ENABLEPAIRKERNING)	Enables or disables kerning ability of device	GDI control
Escape (ENABLERELATIVEWIDTHS)	Enables or disables relative character widths on device	GDI control
Escape (ENDDOC)	Ends print job started by EscapeSTARTDOC	GDI control
Escape (EXTTEXTOUT)	More efficient TextOut for justification and kerning	GDI control
Escape (FLUSHOUTPUT)	Flushes output in device buffer	GDI control
Escape (GETCOLORTABLE)	Copies RGB color table to lpOutData	GDI control
Escape (GETEXTENDEDTEXTMETRICS)	Fills buffer with extended text metrics for font	GDI control
Escape (GETEXTENTTABLE)	Returns width of individual group of consec chars	GDI control
Escape (GETPAIRKERNTABLE)	Fills buffer at lpOutData with kerning-pair table for font	GDI control
Escape (GETPHYSPAGESIZE)	Copies physical page size to lpOutData POINT structure	GDI control
Escape (GETPRINTINGOFFSET)	Copies printing offset to lpOutData POINT structure	GDI control
Escape (GETSCALINGFACTOR)	Returns scaling factors for x and y axes of printer	GDI control
Escape (GETTRACKKERNTABLE)	Fills buffer at lpOutData with track-kerning table for font	GDI control
Escape (MFCOMMENT)*	Adds comment to metafile	GDI control
Escape (NEWFRAME)	Ends writing to a page	GDI control
Escape (NEXTBAND)	Ends writing to a band	GDI control
Escape (QUERYESCSUPPORT)	Tests whether device supports Escape	GDI control
Escape (SELECTPAPERSOURCE)	Determines and selects available paper sources	GDI control
Escape (SETABORTPROC)	Sets abort function for print task	GDI control
Escape (SETALLJUSTVALUES)	Sets text justification values	GDI control
Escape (SETCOLORTABLE)	Sets RGB color table entry	GDI control
Escape (SETCOPYCOUNT)	Specifies number of copies per page to print (uncollated)	GDI control
Escape (SETKERNTRACK)	Specifies which kerning track to use	GDI control
Escape (SETLINECAP)	Sets line end cap	GDI control
Escape (SETLINEJOIN)	Sets how line segments joined	GDI control
Escape (SETMITERLIMIT)	Sets miter limit for a device	GDI control
Escape (STARTDOC)	Starts print task	GDI control
Escape (STRETCHBLT)	Implements StretchBlt on driver level	GDI control
GetNearestColor	Returns device color closest to rgbColor	GDI conversion
ClientToScreen	Converts client coords to equiv screen coords	GDI coordinate
DPtoLP	Converts device points into logical points	GDI coordinate
LPtoDP	Converts logical points to device points	GDI coordinate
ScreenToClient	Converts screen coords at lpPoint to client coords	GDI coordinate
CreateCompatibleDC	Creates memory display context compat with hDC	GDI device context
CreateDC	Creates display context for specified device	GDI device context
CreateIC	Creates information context for device	GDI device context
DeleteDC	Deletes specified display context	GDI device context
GetDCOrg*	Returns origin for display context	GDI device context
RestoreDC	Restores display context to previous state	GDI device context
SaveDC	Saves current state of display context	GDI device context
CreateDIBitmap	Creates device-specific bitmap from DIB	GDI DIB
GetDIBits†	Returns bits for device-specific bitmap	GDI DIB
SetDIBitsToDevice	Sets bits on a device surface directly from a dIB	GDI DIB
SetDIBits†	Sets memory bitmap's bits from a DIB	GDI DIB
StretchDIBits†	Moves DIB from source rect to dest rect	GDI DIB
GetRelAbs‡	Returns the relabs flag	GDI display context
SetRelAbs‡	Sets the relabs flag	GDI display context
CreateBrushIndirect	Creates logical brush from existing brush	GDI drawing
CreateDIBPatternBrush†	Creates logical brush from pattern defined by DIB	GDI drawing
CreateHatchBrush	Creates logical brush with hatched pattern	GDI drawing
CreatePatternBrush	Creates logical brush with hBitmap pattern	GDI drawing
CreatePen	Creates logical pen	GDI drawing
CreatePenIndirect	Creates logical pen like lpLogPen	GDI drawing
CreateSolidBrush	Creates logical brush of a solid color	GDI drawing
DeleteObject	Deletes object by freeing system storage	GDI drawing
EnumObjects	Enumerates objects available on device	GDI drawing
GetBkColor	Returns current background color of device	GDI drawing
GetBkMode	Returns background mode of device	GDI drawing
GetBrushOrg	Returns current brush origin	GDI drawing
GetObject	Copies nCount bytes of hObject data to lpObject	GDI drawing
GetPolyFillMode	Returns current polygon filling mode	GDI drawing
GetROP2	Returns current drawing mode	GDI drawing
GetStretchBltMode	Returns current stretching mode	GDI drawing
GetTextColor	Returns current text color	GDI drawing
SelectObject	Selects hObject as current object	GDI drawing
SetBkColor	Sets background color to closest to rgbColor	GDI drawing
SetBkMode	Sets background mode	GDI drawing
SetBrushOrg	Sets origin of all brushes into hDC display context	GDI drawing
SetPolyFillMode	Sets polygon filling mode for hDC	GDI drawing
SetROP2	Sets drawing mode	GDI drawing
SetStretchBltMode	Sets stretching mode for StretchBlt function	GDI drawing
SetTextColor	Sets text color to device color closest to rgbColor	GDI drawing
UnrealizeObject	Directs GDI to reset origin of brush when it is selected	GDI drawing
GetStockObject	Returns handle to predefined object	GDI drawing

(Continued)

6.098. WINDOWS FUNCTION SUMMARY BY TYPE (continued)

Function Name	Description	Type
GetEnvironment	Copies device environment to lpEnviron	GDI environment
SetEnvironment	Copies data at lpEnviron to device at lpPortName	GDI environment
AddFontResource	Adds resource in lpFilename to system font table	GDI font
CreateFont	Creates logical font	GDI font
CreateFontIndirect	Creates logical font like lpLogFont	GDI font
EnumFonts	Enumerates fonts available on device	GDI font
GetAspectRatioFilter	Get setting of current aspect-ratio filter	GDI font
GetCharWidth*	Retrieves width of a character	GDI font
RemoveFontResource	Removes font from font table	GDI font
SetMapperFlags*	Alters algorithm used by font mapper	GDI font
GetDeviceCaps	Returns device-specific info	GDI information
Arc	Draws arc from X3,Y3 to X4,Y4	GDI line output
LineDDA	Computes successive points in line X1,Y1 X2,Y2	GDI line output
LineTo	Draws line from current pos up to X,Y (but not X,Y)	GDI line output
MoveTo	Moves current position to point X,Y	GDI line output
Polyline	Draws set of line segments	GDI line output
GetMapMode	Returns current mapping mode	GDI mapping
GetViewportExt	Returns x-/y-extents of display context's viewport	GDI mapping
GetViewportOrg	Returns x-/y-coords of display context viewport org.	GDI mapping
GetWindowExt	Returns x-/y-extents of display context's window	GDI mapping
GetWindowOrg	Returns x-/y-coords of display context window origin	GDI mapping
OffsetViewportOrg*	Modifes viewport origin relative to current values	GDI mapping
OffsetWindowOrg*	Modifies window origin relative to current values	GDI mapping
ScaleViewportExt*	Modifies viewport extents relative to current values	GDI mapping
ScaleWindowExt*	Modifies window extents relative to current values	GDI mapping
SetMapMode	Sets mapping mode of hDC	GDI mapping
SetViewportExt	Sets x-/y-extents of viewport for hDC	GDI mapping
SetViewportOrg	Sets viewport origin for hDC	GDI mapping
SetWindowExt	Sets x-/y-extents of window of hDC	GDI mapping
SetWindowOrg	Sets window origin of hDC	GDI mapping
CloseMetaFile	Closes metafile and creates handle	GDI metafile
CopyMetaFile	Copies metafile to lpFilename and returns new hMF	GDI metafile
CreateMetaFile	Creates metafile display context	GDI metafile
DeleteMetaFile	Deletes access to metafile; frees system resources	GDI metafile
EnumMetaFile*	Enumerates GDI calls in a metafile	GDI metafile
GetMetaFile	Creates handle for metafile named by lpFilename	GDI metafile
GetMetaFileBits	Stores metafile bits in global memory block	GDI metafile
PlayMetaFile	Plays contents of metafile on device context hDC	GDI metafile
PlayMetaFileRecord*	Plays metafile record by executing GDI calls	GDI metafile
SetMetaFileBits	Creates memory metafile from data in memory block	GDI metafile
Chord*	Draws a chord (ellipse intersection with line segment)	GDI output
Ellipse	Draws ellipse with center in X1,Y1 X2,Y2 rect	GDI output
GetCurrentPosition	Returns logical coords of current position	GDI output
Pie	Draws arc and connects two end points to center	GDI output
Polygon	Draws polygon	GDI output
PolyPolygon†	Draws a series of closed polygons	GDI output
Rectangle	Draws rectangle	GDI output
RoundRect	Draws rounded rectangle	GDI output
AnimatePalette†	Replaces entries in logical palette	GDI palette
CreatePalette†	Creates logical palette	GDI palette
GetNearestPaletteIndex†	Returns index of logical palette entry closest to RGB color	GDI palette
GetPaletteEntries†	Returns entries from logical palette	GDI palette
GetSystemPaletteEntries†	Returns range of entries from system palette	GDI palette
GetSystemPaletteUse†	Determines if application has full access to system palette	GDI palette
RealizePalette†	Maps entries in logical palette to system palette	GDI palette
SelectPalette†	Selects logical palette into device context	GDI palette
SetPaletteEntries†	Sets new palette entries in a logical palette	GDI palette
SetSystemPaletteUse†	Allows application to use full system palette	GDI palette
UpdateColors†	Performs pixel-by-pixel translation to system palette colors	GDI palette
CombineRgn	Combines two existing regions into new region	GDI region
CreateEllipticRgn	Creates elliptical region bounded by rect X1,Y1 X2,Y2	GDI region
CreateEllipticRgnIndirect*	Creates elliptical region bounded by lpRect	GDI region
CreatePolygonRgn	Creates polygonal region	GDI region
CreatePolyPolygonRgn†	Creates region of a series of closed polygons	GDI region
CreateRectRgn	Creates rectangular region	GDI region
CreateRectRgnIndirect	Creates rectangular region sized like lpRect	GDI region
CreateRoundRectRegion†	Creates rounded rectangular region	GDI region
EqualRgn	Determines if two regions are identical	GDI region
FillRgn	Fills region with specified brush	GDI region
FrameRgn	Draws border for region	GDI region
GetRgnBox†	Returns coordinates of bounding region	GDI region
InvertRgn	Inverts colors in hRgn	GDI region
OffsetRgn	Moves region X unit horiz and Y units vertically	GDI region
PaintRgn	Fills hRgn with current brush	GDI region
PtInRegion	Determines whether X,Y is within hRgn	GDI region

(Continued)

6.098. WINDOWS FUNCTION SUMMARY BY TYPE (continued)

Function Name	*Description*	*Type*
PtVisible	Determines whether X,Y is in clipping region of hDC	GDI region
RectInRegion	Tests whether any part of rectangle is in region	GDI region
SetRectRgn*	Creates rectangular region	GDI region
ExtTextOut*	Writes character string within rect region on display	GDI text
GetTabbedTextExtent†	Computes width and height of line of text with tabs	GDI text
GetTextAlign*	Returns status of text alignment flag	GDI text
GetTextExtent	Computes width and height of text line in lpString	GDI text
GetTextFace	Copies current font facename to lpFacename	GDI text
GetTextMetrics	Fills buffer with metrics for current font	GDI text
SetTextAlign*	Sets text alignment flag	GDI text
SetTextJustification	Prepares GDI to justify text line	GDI text
TabbedTextOut†	Writes character string with expanded tabs in current font	GDI text
TextOut	Writes character string at X,Y	GDI text
GetTextCharacterExtra	Returns current intercharacter spacing	GDI text justify
SetTextCharacterExtra	Sets amount of intercharacter spacing	GDI text justify
DefineHandleTable†	Creates private handle table in default data segment	Memory manager
GetFreeSpace†	Returns number of bytes of memory available in global heap	Memory manager
GetWinFlags†	Returns 32-bit value specifying memory configuration	Memory manager
GlobalAlloc	Allocates dwBytes of memory from global heap	Memory manager
GlobalCompact	Compacts global memory to free dwMinFree bytes	Memory manager
GlobalDiscard	Discards global memory block if ref count is zero	Memory manager
GlobalDosAlloc†	Allocates global memory which can be accessed by DOS	Memory manager
GlobalDosFree†	Frees global memory block	Memory manager
GlobalFlags	Returns memory type of global memory block	Memory manager
GlobalFree	Removes global memory block if ref count is zero	Memory manager
GlobalHandle	Returns handle of global memory object	Memory manager
GlobalLock	Returns address of block, locks it in mem, increases ref count	Memory manager
GlobalLRUNewest†	Moves global memory object to newest LRU position	Memory manager
GlobalLRUOldest†	Moves global memory object to oldest LRU position	Memory manager
GlobalNotify	Installs notification procedure for current task	Memory manager
GlobalReAlloc	Reallocates global memory block to dwBytes	Memory manager
GlobalSize	Returns the size of global memory block, in bytes	Memory manager
GlobalUnlock	Unlocks block, decreases reference count	Memory manager
GlobalUnwire*	Unlocks memory segment	Memory manager
GlobalWire*	Moves segment to low memory and locks it	Memory manager
LimitEMSPages	Limits EMS memory Windows assigns to application	Memory manager
LocalAlloc	Allocates wBytes of memory from local heap	Memory manager
LocalCompact	Compacts local memory to generate wMinFree free bytes	Memory manager
LocalDiscard	Discards local memory block hMem if ref count is zero	Memory manager
LocalFlags	Returns memory type of block hMem	Memory manager
LocalFree	Frees local memory block hMem if ref count is zero	Memory manager
LocalFreeze‡	Prevents compaction of local heap	Memory manager
LocalHandle	Returns handle of local memory object at wMem	Memory manager
LocalHandleDelta	Sets entry count for each new handle table in local heap	Memory manager
LocalInit	Initializes the local heap	Memory manager
LocalLock	Returns address of block, locks block, increases ref count by 1	Memory manager
LocalMelt‡	Permits compaction of local heap	Memory manager
LocalNotify‡	Sets callback function for handling notification messages	Memory manager
LocalReAlloc	Reallocates local memory block hMem to wBytes	Memory manager
LocalShrink‡	Shrinks specified memory heap	Memory manager
LocalSize	Returns the size of local block hMem, in bytes	Memory manager
LocalUnlock	Unlocks local memory block, decreases ref count by 1	Memory manager
LockData	Locks data segment in memory	Memory manager
LockSegment	Locks segment at address wSegment	Memory manager
SetSwapAreaSize*	Changes amount of memory used by code segment	Memory manager
SwitchStackBack†	Returns stack of current task to task's DS	Memory manager
SwitchStackTo†	Changes stack of current task to segment IDed by wStackSegment	Memory manager
UnlockData	Unlocks data segment	Memory manager
UnlockSegment	Unlocks wSegment	Memory manager
FreeLibrary	Removes library module if reference count is zero	Module manager
FreeModule†	Decreases reference count of loaded module by 1	Module manager
FreeProcInstance	Removes function instance at address lpProc	Module manager
GetCodeHandle	Returns handle of code segment containing function	Module manager
GetCodeHandle	Determines which code segment contains function in lpProc	Module manager
GetInstanceData	Copies nCount bytes from hInstance to current Instance	Module manager
GetModuleFileName	Copies module filename to lpFilename	Module manager
GetModuleHandle	Returns module handle	Module manager
GetModuleUsage	Returns reference count of module hModule	Module manager
GetProcAddress	Returns address of lpProcName function	Module manager
GetVersion	Returns Windows version number	Module manager
LoadIcon	Loads icon named by lpIconName	Module manager
MakeProcInstance	Returns address for lpProc	Module manager
ProfClear†	Discards all samples in sampling buffer if Profiler running	Optimizing
ProfFinish†	Stops sampling and flushes buffer to disk if Profiler running	Optimizing
ProfFlush†	Flushes sampling buffer to disk if Profiler running	Optimizing

(Continued)

6.098. WINDOWS FUNCTION SUMMARY BY TYPE (continued)

Function Name	*Description*	*Type*
ProfInsChk†	Determines whether Profiler installed	Optimizing
ProfSampRate†	Sets rate of code sampling if Profiler running	Optimizing
ProfSetup†	Specifies size of output buffer if Profiler running in 386 enhanced	Optimizing
ProfStart†	Starts sampling if Profiler running	Optimizing
ProfStop†	Stops sampling if Profiler running	Optimizing
SwapRecording†	Begins or ends analyzing swapping behavior if Swap running	Optimizing
DOS3Call†	Issues a DOS 21H interrupt function request	OS interrupt
NetBIOSCall†	Issues a NETBIOS 5CH interrupt	OS interrupt
DeviceCapabilities	Gets printer driver capabilities	Printer control
ExtDeviceMode	Gets or changes driver initialization	Printer control
SetPriority‡	Sets task priority	Printer control
AccessResource	Sets file pointer for read access to hRefInfo	Resource manager
AllocResource	Allocates dwSize bytes of memory for hResInfo	Resource manager
FindResource	Locates resource lpName of type lpType	Resource manager
FreeResource	Removes resource from memory if ref count is zero	Resource manager
LoadAccelerators	Loads accelerator table named by lpTableName	Resource manager
LoadBitmap	Loads bitmap named by lpBitmapName	Resource manager
LoadCursor	Loads cursor named by lpCursorName	Resource manager
LoadLibrary	Loads library module named by lpLibFileName	Resource manager
LoadMenu	Loads menu named by lpMenuName	Resource manager
LoadResource	Loads the resource named by hResInfo	Resource manager
LoadString	Loads string wID into buffer lpBuffer	Resource manager
LockResource	Returns address of hResInfo, locks it, increases ref count by 1	Resource manager
PatBlt	Combines bit pattern with one already on device	Resource manager
SetResourceHandler	Sets function address of resource handler	Resource manager
SizeofResource	Returns size of resource hResInfo, in bytes	Resource manager
UnlockResource*	Unlocks resource, decrements reference count	Resource manager
AllocDStoCSAlias†	Returns a CS selector to execute code in DS	Segment
AllocSelector†	Allocates a new selector	Segment
ChangeSelector†	Generates a code selector that corresponds to a data selector	Segment
FreeSelector†	Frees selector allocated by AllocSelector	Segment
GetCodeInfo†	Returns pointer to array containing CS information for lpProc	Segment
GlobalFix†	Prevents global memory block from moving in linear memory	Segment
GlobalPageLock†	Increments page lock count of memory selector	Segment
GlobalPageUnlock†	Decrements page lock count of memory selector	Segment
GlobalUnfix†	Unlocks global memory block	Segment
CloseSound	Closes play device (first flushes voice queues)	Sound
CountVoiceNotes	Returns number of notes in voice queue	Sound
GetThresholdEvent	Returns pointer to threshold flag	Sound
GetThresholdStatus	Returns bit mask containing threshold event status	Sound
OpenSound	Opens play device for exclusive use	Sound
SetSoundNoise	Sets source and duration of noise from play device	Sound
SetVoiceAccent	Places an accent in voice queue	Sound
SetVoiceEnvelope	Places envelope in voice queue	Sound
SetVoiceNote	Places note in voice queue	Sound
SetVoiceQueueSize	Allocates nBytes of memory for voice queue	Sound
SetVoiceSound	Places frequency and duration in voice queue	Sound
SetVoiceThreshold	Sets threshold level for voice queue	Sound
StartSound	Starts play in each voice queue	Sound
StopSound	Stops playing all voices	Sound
SyncAllVoices	Places sync mark in each voice queue	Sound
WaitSoundState	Waits until play driver enters nState	Sound
AnsiLower	Converts string lpStr to lowercase	String translation
AnsiLowerBuff†	Converts string in buffer to lowercase	String translation
AnsiNext	Points to next character in string lpCurrentChar	String translation
AnsiPrev	Points to prev character in string lpStart	String translation
ANSIToOEM	Converts ANSI string to OEM char string	String translation
AnsiToOemBuff†	Converts ANSI string in buffer to OEM char string	String translation
AnsiUpper	Converts string lpStr to uppercase	String translation
AnsiUpperBuff†	Converts string in buffer to uppercase	String translation
IsCharAlphaNumeric†	Determines whether character is an alphabetical or numeric char	String translation
IsCharAlpha†	Determines whether character is an alphabetical character	String translation
IsCharLower†	Determines whether character is a lowercase character	String translation
IsCharUpper†	Determines whether character is an uppercase character	String translation
lstrcat	Concatenates lpString2 to string specified by lpString1	String translation
lstrcmpi†	Compares two strings and returns value indicating relationship	String translation
lstrcmp†	Compares two strings and returns value indicating relationship	String translation
lstrcpy†	Copies lpString2 to lpString1	String translation
lstrlen†	Returns length of lpString in bytes	String translation
OemToAnsi	Translates lpOemStr to OEM-defined char set	String translation
OemToAnsiBuff	Translates string in buffer to OEM-defined char set	String translation
ToAscii†	Translates virtual-key code and current keyboard state	String translation
wsprintf†	Formats and stores series of chars in buffer	String translation
wvsprintf†	Formats and stores series of chars in buffer	String translation
Catch	Copies current exec environ to buffer lpCatchBuf	Task

(Continued)

6.098. WINDOWS FUNCTION SUMMARY BY TYPE (continued)

Function Name	*Description*	*Type*
ExitWindows†	Initiates standard Windows shutdown procedure	Task
GetCurrentPDB†	Returns paragraph address of selector of DOS PSP	Task
GetCurrentTask	Returns handle of current task	Task
GetDOSEnvironment†	Returns far pointer to environment string of current task	Task
GetNumTasks*	Returns number of tasks in system	Task
SetErrorMode	Controls whether Windows or application handles DOS 24H errors	Task
Throw	Restores execution environment to values in lpCatchBuf	Task
Yield	Halts current task and starts any waiting task	Task
DeviceMode	Displays dialog box for setting printer modes	Utility
GetBValue	Returns blue component of rgbColor	Utility
GetGValue	Returns green component of rgbColor	Utility
GetRValue	Returns red component of rgbColor	Utility
HIBYTE	Returns hi-order byte of nInteger	Utility
HIWORD	Returns hi-order word of lInteger	Utility
LOBYTE	Returns lo-order byte of nInteger	Utility
LOWORD	Returns lo-order word of lInteger	Utility
MAKEINTATOM	Casts integer as argument for AddAtom	Utility
MAKEINTRESOURCE	Casts integer as argument for AddAtom	Utility
MAKELONG	Creates unsigned long integer	Utility
MAKEPOINT	Converts long value into a POINT structure	Utility
max	Returns maximum value of A and B	Utility
min	Returns minimum value of A and B	Utility
MulDiv†	Multiplies two words and divides result by a third word	Utility
PALETTEINDEX†	Returns value of palette entry in LO bytes	Utility
PALETTERGB†	Returns value of palette entry in LO bytes	Utility
RGB	Creates RGB color from individual color values	Utility
WndProc‡	Processes messages sent to it	Window
GetSysModalWindow	Returns handle of system modal window, if present	Window attribute
CreateCaret	Creates caret for hWnd using hBitmap	Window caret
DestroyCaret	Destroys current caret and memory it occupies	Window caret
GetCaretBlinkTime	Returns current caret flash rate	Window caret
GetCaretPos*	Returns current caret position	Window caret
HideCaret	Removes system caret from window	Window caret
SetCaretBlinkTime	Establishes caret flash rate	Window caret
SetCaretPos	Moves caret to X,Y position	Window caret
ShowCaret	Displays new caret or redisplays hidden caret	Window caret
CallWindowProc	Passes message info to lpPrevWndFunc function	Window class
ChangeClipboardChain	Removes hWnd from clipboard viewer chain	Window clipboard
CloseClipboard	Closes the clipboard	Window clipboard
CountClipboardFormats	Counts number of formats clipboard can render	Window clipboard
EmptyClipboard	Empties clipboard, frees data handles	Window clipboard
EnumClipboardFormats	Enumerates available clipboard formats	Window clipboard
GetClipboardData	Returns data from clipboard in specified format	Window clipboard
GetClipboardFormatName	Copies nMaxCount chars of format to lpFormatName	Window clipboard
GetClipboardOwner	Returns window handle of clipboard owner	Window clipboard
GetClipboardViewer	Returns window handle of 1st window in viewer chn	Window clipboard
GetPriorityClipboardFormat†	Returns data from clipboard in prioritized format	Window clipboard
IsClipboardFormatAvailable	Returns True if data is available in wFormat	Window clipboard
OpenClipboard	Open clipboard (prevents other apps from modifying)	Window clipboard
RegisterClipboardFormat	Registers new clipboard format	Window clipboard
SetClipboardData	Copies hMem into clipboard	Window clipboard
SetClipboardViewer	Adds hWnd to clipboard viewer chain	Window clipboard
AdjustWindowRect	Converts client rectangle to a window rectangle	Window creation
AdjustWindowRectEx	Computes size of window with extended style to fit client area	Window creation
CreateWindow	Creates tiled, popup, or child window	Window creation
CreateWindowEx†	Creates overlapped, popup, or child window w/ ext style	Window creation
DefDlgProc†	Provides default processing for dialog-box messages	Window creation
DefFrameProc†	Provides default processing for MDI frame-window msgs	Window creation
DefMDIChildProc†	Provides default processing for MDI child-window msgs	Window creation
DefWindowProc	Does default processing of messages that are ignored	Window creation
DestroyWindow	Sends WM_DESTROY message; frees memory	Window creation
GetClassInfo†	Returns info about specified class	Window creation
GetClassLong	Returns info at nIndex in WNDCLASS structure	Window creation
GetClassName	Copies nMaxCount chars of hWnd's class name	Window creation
GetClassWord	Returns info at nIndex in WNDCLASS structure	Window creation
GetLastActivePopup†	Determines which popup window was most recently active	Window creation
GetWindowLong	Returns information about window	Window creation
GetWindowWord	Returns information about window	Window creation
RegisterClass	Registers a window class	Window creation
SetClassLong	Replaces long value at nIndex in WNDCLASS struct	Window creation
SetClassWord	Replaces word at nIndex in WNDCLASS struct	Window creation
SetWindowLong	Changes window attribute identified by nIndex	Window creation
SetWindowWord	Changes window attribute specified by nIndex	Window creation
UnregisterClass†	Removes window class from window-class table	Window creation
ClipCursor	Restricts mouse cursor to given rectangle on screen	Window cursor

(Continued)

6.098. WINDOWS FUNCTION SUMMARY BY TYPE (continued)

Function Name	*Description*	*Type*
CreateCursor	Creates cursor from two bit masks	Window cursor
DestroyCursor	Destroys cursor	Window cursor
GetCursorPos	Stores cursor position in POINT structure	Window cursor
SetCursor	Sets cursor shape to hCursor; removes if hCursor=Null	Window cursor
SetCursorPos	Sets mouse cursor to screen coords X,Y	Window cursor
ShowCursor	Adds 1 to cursor display count if nonzero; otherwise -1	Window cursor
CheckDlgButton	Changes state of button	Window dialog box
CheckRadioButton	Changes checkmark to wIDCheckButton in group	Window dialog box
CreateDialog	Creates modeless dialog box	Window dialog box
CreateDialogIndirect*	Creates modeless dialog box like one in lpDialogTemplate	Window dialog box
CreateDialogIndirectParam†	Creates modeless dialog box from template and passes data	Window dialog box
CreateDialogParam†	Creates modeless dialog box and passes data to it	Window dialog box
DialogBox	Creates modal dialog box	Window dialog box
DialogBoxIndirect*	Creates modal dialog box like hDTemplate	Window dialog box
DialogBoxIndirectParam†	Creates modal dialog box like template and passes data to it	Window dialog box
DialogBoxParam†	Creates modal dialog box and passes dialog to it	Window dialog box
DlgDirList	Fills nIDListBox with files matching lpPathSpec	Window dialog box
DlgDirListComboBox†	Fills combo box with names of files matching path	Window dialog box
DlgDirSelect	Copies selection from nIDListBox to lpString	Window dialog box
DlgDirSelectComboBox†	Copies current selection from combo box to string	Window dialog box
EndDialog	Frees resources and destroys windows of dialog box	Window dialog box
GetDialogBaseUnits†	Returns base dialog units	Window dialog box
GetDialogCtrlID†	Returns ID value of a control window	Window dialog box
GetDlgItem	Returns dialog control handle	Window dialog box
GetDlgItemInt	Translates text of nIDDlgItem to integer value	Window dialog box
GetDlgItemText	Copies nMaxCount chars of control text to lpString	Window dialog box
GetNextDlgGroupItem*	Searches for next control in group of dialog controls	Window dialog box
GetNextDlgTabItem*	Obtains handle for first control preceding another	Window dialog box
IsDialogMessage	Determines whether lpMsg is intended for modeless dialog	Window dialog box
IsDlgButtonChecked	Returns state of nIDButton	Window dialog box
MapDialogRect	Converts dialog-box coords to client coords	Window dialog box
SendDlgItemMessage	Sends message to nIDDlgItem within dialog box hDlg	Window dialog box
SetDlgItemInt	Sets text of nIDDlgItem to string representing wValue	Window dialog box
SetDlgItemText	Sets caption or text of nIDDlgItem to String	Window dialog box
ArrangeIconicWindows†	Arranges iconic child windows	Window display
BeginDeferWindowPos†	Initializes memory used by DeferWindowPos function	Window display
BringWindowToTop	Makes popup or child window the top window	Window display
CloseWindow	Closes specified window	Window display
DeferWindowPos†	Records positioning info for window to be moved or resized	Window display
EndDeferWindowPos†	Positions or sizes several windows simultaneously	Window display
GetClientRect	Copies window client area coords to lpRect	Window display
GetWindowRect	Copies dimensions of entire window to lpRect	Window display
GetWindowText	Copies window's caption into lpString	Window display
GetWindowTextLength	Returns length of window's caption or text	Window display
IsIconic	Returns status of window (iconic or open)	Window display
IsWindowVisible	Determines whether hWnd is visible	Window display
IsZoomed*	Determines whether window is at maximum size	Window display
MoveWindow	Causes WM_SIZE message to be sent to hWnd	Window display
OpenIcon	Opens specified window	Window display
SetWindowPos*	Changes size, position, ordering of window	Window display
SetWindowText	Sets window caption or text to lpString	Window display
ShowOwnedPopups*	Displays or hides all popup windows	Window display
ShowWindow	Displays or removes window as specified by nCmdShow	Window display
FlashWindow	Flashes window once	Window error
MessageBeep	Generates a beep when message box displayed	Window error
MessageBox	Creates message-box window	Window error
EnableHardwareInput*	Enables/disables mouse and keyboard	Window hardware
GetAsyncKeyState*	Determines whether key is up or down	Window hardware
GetInputState*	Determines whether there are input events in queue	Window hardware
GetKBCodePage†	Determines which OEM/ANSI tables are loaded	Window hardware
GetKeyboardState*	Copies status of virtual keys to a buffer	Window hardware
GetKeyNamText†	Retrieves string containing name of key from driver	Window hardware
GetKeyState	Returns state of virtual key	Window hardware
MapVirtualKey†	Accepts virtual-key or scan code and returns vice versa	Window hardware
OemKeyScan†	Maps OEM ASCII codes 0-FFH to OEM scan codes	Window hardware
SetKeyboardState*	Copies buffer to keyboard state table	Window hardware
VkKeyState†	Translates ANSI char to virtual-key code	Window hardware
CallMsgFilter	Passes message and code to message filter funct	Window hook
DefHookProc*	Provides default hook processing of WM messages	Window hook
SetWindowHook	Installs system or application hook	Window hook
UnhookWindowHook*	Removes filter function from hook chain	Window hook
AnyPopup	Indicates whether any popup window is visible	Window information
ChildWindowFromPoint	Determines which child window contains Point	Window information
EnumChildWindows	Enumerates child windows of hWndParent	Window information
EnumTaskWindows*	Enumerates all windows associated with a task	Window information

(Continued)

6.098. WINDOWS FUNCTION SUMMARY BY TYPE (continued)

Function Name	Description	Type
EnumWindows	Enumerates windows on screen	Window information
FindWindow	Returns handle of window	Window information
GetNextWindow*	Searches for next window handle	Window Information
GetParent	Retrieves window handle of window's parent (if any)	Window information
GetTopWindow*	Returns handle to top-level child window	Window information
GetWindow*	Searches for window in window manager's list	Window information
GetWindowTask*	Returns task handle	Window information
IsChild	Returns True if window is child of hParentWnd	Window information
IsWindow	Determines whether hWnd is a valid, existing window	Window information
SetParent*	Changes parent window of child window	Window information
WindowFromPoint	Identifies window containing Point (in screen coords)	Window information
EnableWindow	Enables or disables mouse, keybd input to hWnd	Window input
GetActiveWindow	Returns handle to active window	Window input
GetCapture*	Determines which window is receiving mouse input	Window input
GetCurrentTime	Returns elapsed time since boot	Window input
GetDoubleClickTime	Returns double-click time for mouse	Window input
GetFocus	Returns handle of window with input focus	Window input
GetTickCount*	Returns time since system started	Window input
IsWindowEnabled	Returns state of hWnd input from mouse and keyboard	Window input
KillTimer	Kills timer event identified by hWnd and nIDEvent	Window input
ReleaseCapture	Release mouse input, restores normal processing	Window input
SetActiveWindow	Makes tiled or popup window the active window	Window input
SetCapture	Causes mouse input to be sent to hWnd	Window input
SetDoubleClickTime*	Sets mouse double-click time	Window input
SetFocus	Assigns input focus to hWnd	Window input
SetSysModalWindow	Makes window a system modal window	Window input
SetTimer	Creates system timer event	Window input
SwapMouseButton	Swaps meaning of left/right mouse buttons if bSwap=True	Window input
WinMain	Entry point for Windows application execution	Window main
RegisterWindowDestroy‡	Locks windows from destruction by other tasks	Window manager
AppendMenu†	Appends menu item to menu	Window menu
ChangeMenu‡	Changes menu item in hMenu	Window menu
CheckMenuItem	Changes checkmark status of menu item	Window menu
CreateMenu	Creates empty menu	Window menu
CreatePopupMenu†	Creates empty popup menu	Window menu
DeleteMenu†	Removes menu item and destroys associated popup menus	Window menu
DestroyMenu	Destroys hMenu and frees memory it occupied	Window menu
DrawMenuBar	Redraws menu bar	Window menu
EnableMenuItem	Enables, disables, or grays menu item	Window menu
GetMenu	Returns handle to window's menu	Window menu
GetMenuCheckMarkDimensions†	Returns dimensions of checkmark bitmap	Window menu
GetMenuItemCount*	Determines how many items are in hMenu	Window menu
GetMenuItemID*	Obtains identifier for a menu item	Window menu
GetMenuState*	Identifies top-level menu	Window menu
GetMenuString	Copies nMaxCount chars of menu label to lpString	Window menu
GetSubMenu	Returns menu handle of popup menu	Window menu
GetSystemMenu	Allows access to system menu	Window menu
HiliteMenuItem	Hilites or unHilites top-level menu item	Window menu
InsertMenu†	Inserts menu item in menu	Window menu
LoadMenuIndirect*	Loads menu from lpMenuTemplate	Window menu
ModifyMenu†	Changes menu item	Window menu
RemoveMenu†	Removes item from a menu	Window menu
SetMenu	Sets window menu to hMenu; removes if hMenu=Null	Window menu
SetMenuItemBitmaps†	Associates bitmaps with menu item	Window menu
TrackPopupMenu	Displays popup menu and tracks user interaction	Window menu
DispatchMessage	Passes message to window function in MSG structure	Window message
GetMessage	Retrieves message	Window message
GetMessagePos	Returns mouse position scrn coords at last message	Window message
GetMessageTime	Returns time of last message	Window message
InSendMessage	Returns True if function is processing SendMessage	Window message
PeekMessage	Places message (if any) at lpMsg	Window message
PostAppMessage	Posts message to application	Window message
PostMessage	Posts message in application queue	Window message
PostQuitMessage	Posts WM_QUIT message to application	Window message
RegisterWindowMessage	Defines new, unique window message	Window message
ReplyMessage	Replies to message without returning control	Window message
SendMessage	Sends message to window or windows	Window message
SetMessageQueue*	Creates new message queue	Window message
TranslateAccelerator	Processes keyboard accelerators for menu commands	Window message
TranslateMDISysAccel	Process MDI child-window command accelerators	Window message
TranslateMessage	Translates virtual keystrokes into char messages	Window message
WaitMessage	Yields control to other application	Window message
BeginPaint	Prepares window for painting	Window painting
DrawFocusRect†	Draws rect in style used to indicate focus	Window painting
DrawIcon	Draws icon with upper-left corner at X,Y	Window painting

(Continued)

6.098. WINDOWS FUNCTION SUMMARY BY TYPE (continued)

Function Name	*Description*	*Type*
DrawText	Draws nCount chars of lpString clipped in lpRect	Window painting
EndPaint	Marks end of window repainting	Window painting
ExcludeUpdateRgn*	Excludes a region in window from clipping region for window	Window painting
FillRect	Fills rectangle using specified brush	Window painting
FrameRect	Draws border for rectangle	Window painting
GetDC	Returns display context of client area for window	Window painting
GetUpdateRect	Copies dim of rect that needs updating to lpRect	Window painting
GetUpdateRgn*	Copies window's update region to specified region	Window painting
GetWindowDC	Returns display context for entire window	Window painting
GrayString	Writes nCount chars of String using hBrush to gray	Window painting
InvalidateRect	Marks lpRect for repainting	Window painting
InvalidateRgn	Marks hRgn for repainting	Window painting
InvertRect	Inverts display bits of lpRect	Window painting
ReleaseDC	Release display context	Window painting
UpdateWindow	Notifies application when window needs redrawing	Window painting
ValidateRect	Releases rectangle lpRect from repainting	Window painting
ValidateRgn	Releases hRgn from repainting	Window painting
EnumProps	Passes each property of hWnd to lpEnumFunc	Window property
GetProp	Returns handle associated with lpString	Window property
RemoveProp	Removes lpString from property list	Window property
SetProp	Copies string and data handle to property list of hWnd	Window property
CopyRect	Copies an existing rectangle	Window rectangle
EqualRect*	Determines whether two rectangles are equal	Window rectangle
InflateRect	Resizes lpRect by X units horiz and Y units vertically	Window rectangle
IntersectRect	Finds intersection of two rects, copies to lpDestRect	Window rectangle
IsRectEmpty	Determines whether lpRect is empty	Window rectangle
OffsetRect	Moves rectangle X units horiz and Y units vertically	Window rectangle
PtInRect	Determines whether point lies within lpRect	Window rectangle
SetRect	Fills RECT struct at lpRect with given coords	Window rectangle
SetRectEmpty	Sets lpRect to empty rectangle (all coords zero)	Window rectangle
UnionRect	Stores union of two rectangles	Window rectangle
GetScrollPos	Returns current position of scroll bar	Window scrolling
GetScrollRange	Copies min/max scroll-bar positions	Window scrolling
ScrollDC*	Scrolls rectangle of bits in display context	Window scrolling
ScrollWindow	Moves contents of client area by X-amount,Y-amount	Window scrolling
SetScrollPos	Sets scroll-bar elevator to nPos; redraws if nonzero	Window scrolling
SetScrollRange	Sets min/max scroll-bar positions for scroll bar	Window scrolling
ShowScrollBar*	Displays or hides scroll bar	Window scrolling
GetSysColor	Returns system color identified by nIndex	Window system info
GetSystemMetrics	Returns information about system metrics	Window system info
SetSysColors	Changes one or more system colors	Window system info
GetPrivateProfileInt†	Returns value of integer key from initialization file	Windows init file
GetPrivateProfileString†	Copies a character string from initialization file to buffer	Windows init file
GetProfileInt	Returns integer info from WIN.INI file	Windows init file
GetProfileString	Returns string info from WIN.INI file	Windows init file
WritePrivateProfileString†	Copies character string into specified initialization file	Windows init file
WriteProfileString	Copies lpString to WIN.INI file	Windows init file

*Applies to versions of Windows beginning with 2.0.
†Applies to versions of Windows beginning with 3.0.
§Debugging version of Windows only
‡Not in Windows 3.0

Source: Microsoft Windows 2.0 SDK Programmer's Reference
Microsoft Windows 3.0 SDK Programmer's Reference, Chapters 1 through 4

See Also: 6.095. Windows Function Summary by Version
6.096. Windows Function Summary by Name

6.099. WINDOWS WINMEM32.DLL LIBRARY FUNCTIONS

Function Name	Type	Parameters (in order)	Parm Type	Parameter Definition	Return Value
GetWinMem32Version	WORD	None			LO=minor version HO=major version
Global16PointerAlloc	WORD	wSelector dwOffset lpBuffer dwSize wFlags	WORD DWORD LpDWORD DWORD WORD	Selector of object for alias to be created Offset from first byte to alias to be created Pointer to 4-byte location for pointer alias Addressable size in bytes of region RESERVED (must be 0)	0=success*
Global16PointerFree	WORD	wSelector dwAlias wFlags	WORD DWORD WORD	Selector of object for alias to be freed Pointer of alias to be freed RESERVED (must be 0)	0=success*
Global32Alloc	WORD	dwSize lpSelector dwMaxSize wFlags	DWORD LPWORD DWORD WORD	Initial size in bytes of block to allocate Pointer to word to receive selector Maximum size in bytes object will reach RESERVED (must be 0)	0=success*
Global32CodeAlias	WORD	wSelector lpAlias wFlags	WORD LPWORD WORD	Selector of object for alias to be created Pointer to word to receive CS selector RESERVED (must be 0)	0=success*
Global32CodeAliasFree	WORD	wSelector wAlias wFlags	WORD WORD WORD	Selector of object for alias to be freed USE32 code selector alias to be freed RESERVED (must be 0)	0=success*
Global32Free	WORD	wSelector wFlags	WORD WORD	Selector of object to be freed RESERVED (must be 0)	0=success*
Global32Realloc	WORD	wSelector dwNewSize wFlags	WORD DWORD WORD	Selector of object to be changed New size of object in bytes RESERVED (must be 0)	0=success*

*Otherwise may be one of the following error codes:

1	Invalid function
2	Invalid flags
3	Invalid parameter
4	Selector not available
5	Insufficient memory

Version: Applies to all versions of Windows beginning with 3.0.

Source: Microsoft Windows 3.0 SDK Programmer's Reference, Appendix E, pages E-10 through E-15

6.100. DIAGNOSTIC AND FATAL ERROR CODES

Value	*Message*
1 (1)	Insufficient memory for allocation
2 (2)	Error reallocating memory
3 (3)	Memory cannot be freed
4 (4)	Memory cannot be locked
5 (5)	Memory cannot be unlocked
6 (6)	Invalid handle passed to a GDI function
7 (7)	Window handle not valid
8 (8)	Cached display contexts are busy
9 (9)	DefWindowProc function not found in application
A (10)	Clipboard already open
B (11)	Application attempted to destroy a window while using DC
C (12)	Keyboard driver not initialized correctly
D (13)	Mouse driver not initialized correctly
E (14)	Display driver not initialized correctly
F (15)	Unlocked segment should be locked
10 (16)	Clipboard already open
13 (19)	Mouse module not valid
14 (20)	Display module not valid
15 (21)	Unlocked data segment should be locked
16 (22)	Invalid lock on system queue
16 (22)	Class counter exceeded limit of 32, 767
17 (23)	Class counter became negative number
18 (24)	Class counter not zero when class destroyed
19 (25)	Message-box function was called during DLL's init routine
100 (256)	Local memory errors
103 (259)	LocalReAlloc -- invalid local heap
140 (320)	Local heap is busy
143 (323)	Invalid local heap
14B (331)	Invalid local heap
15B (347)	Invalid local heap
180 (384)	Invalid local handle
1C0 (448)	LocalLock count overflow
1F0 (496)	LocalUnlock count underflow
200 (512)	Global memory errors
240 (576)	Critical section problems
280 (640)	Invalid global handle
2C0 (704)	GlobalLock count overflow
2F0 (752)	GlobalUnlock count underflow
300 (768)	Task schedule errors
301 (769)	Invalid task ID
302 (770)	Invalid exit system call
303 (771)	Invalid BP register chain
400 (1024)	Dynamic loader/linker errors
401 (1025)	Error during boot process
402 (1026)	Error loading a module
403 (1027)	Invalid ordinal reference
404 (1028)	Invalid entry name reference
405 (1029)	Invalid start procedure
406 (1030)	Invalid module handle
407 (1031)	Invalid relocation record
408 (1032)	Error saving forward reference
409 (1033)	Error reading segment contents
410 (1034)	Error reading segment contents
411 (1035)	Insert disk for specified file
412 (1036)	Error reading nonresident table
4FF (1279)	INT 3F handler unable to load segment
500 (1280)	Resource manager/user profile errors
501 (1281)	Missing resource table
502 (1282)	Bad resource type
503 (1283)	Bad resource name
504 (1284)	Bad resource file
505 (1285)	Error reading resource
506 (1286)	Default value in get profile string was NULL
600 (1536)	Atom manager errors
700 (1792)	Input/Output package errors
FFEE (65518)	Divide by zero

Source: Microsoft Windows 2.0 SDK Tools, pages 247 through 248
Microsoft Windows 1.0 Reference Manual, page 225.
Microsoft Windows 3.0 Programmer's Reference, Vol. 2, Appendix C, pages C-1 through C-11
Internal Microsoft Memo

6.101. WINDOWS LOGICAL COORDINATE MAPPING

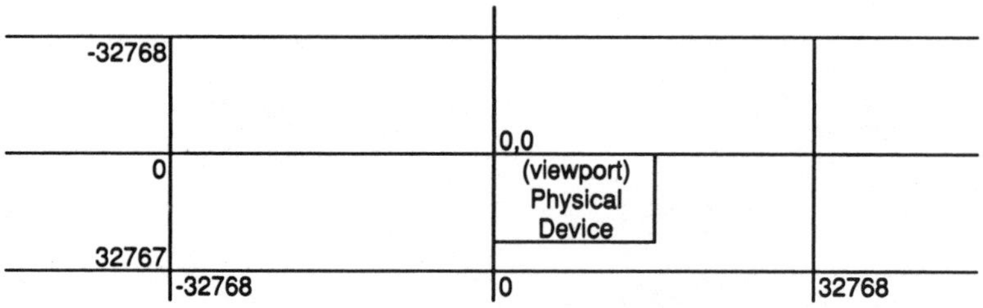
-32768
0
32767
0,0
(viewport)
Physical
Device
-32768
0
32768

Coordinate System Transformation Equations

Variable	*Meaning*
xWO	The x coordinate of the window origin
yWO	The y coordinate of the window origin
xWE	The x component of the window extent
yWE	The y component of the window extent
xVO	The x coordinate of the viewport origin
yVO	The y coordinate of the viewport origin
xYE	The x component of the viewport extent
yVE	The y component of the viewport extent
Lx	The x coordinate in the logical coordinate system
Ly	The y coordinate in the logical coordinate system
Dx	The x coordinate in the physical coordinate system
Dy	The y coordinate in the physical coordinate system

Thus:

$$Dx = (Lx - xWO) * xVE/xWE + xVO$$
$$Dy = (Ly - yWO) * yVE/yWE + yVO$$
$$Lx = (Dx - xVO) * (xWE/xVE) + xWO$$
$$Ly = (Dy - yVO) * yWE/yVE + yWO$$

Note: •The viewport generally, but not always, is the same as the physical device.
•Width and height of the viewport must be >-1 and <32768.

Source: Microsoft Windows 2.0 SDK Programmer's Reference, pages 88 through 90
Microsoft Windows 3.0 SDK Guide to Programming, page 3-4

6.102. WINDOW STYLES

Style Name	*Description*	*Restrictions*
DS_LOCALEDIT§	Controls in dialog box use application's data segment memory	
DS_MODALFRAME§	Dialog box with modal dialog-box frame	Can be used with title bar and system menu
DS_NOIDLEMSG§	Suppresses WM_ENTERIDLE messages	
DS_SYSMODAL§	System-modal dialog box	
WS_BORDER	Window with a border	
WS_CAPTION	Window with a caption bar	Implies WS_BORDER
WS_CHILD	Child window	Cannot be used with WS_POPUP
WS_CHILDWINDOW	Child window	Style WS_CHILD
WS_CLIPCHILDREN	Exclude area occupied by child windows when drawing within parent	Used when creating parent window
WS_CLIPSIBLINGS	Clip child windows relative to one another	Used with WS_CHILD only
WS_DISABLED	Window is initially disabled	
WS_DLGFRAME	Window with double border, no caption	
WS_GROUP†	Defines a group of controls	Group applies until next WS_GROUP
WS_HSCROLL	Window with horizontal scroll bar	
WS_ICONIC	Window is initially iconic	For use with WS_OVERLAPPED only
WS_MAXIMIZE†	Window is maximum size possible	
WS_MAXIMIZEBOX†	Window contains maximize box	
WS_MINIMIZE†	Window is minimum size possible	
WS_MINIMIZEBOX†	Window contains minimize box	
WS_OVERLAPPED†	Overlapping window	
WS_OVERLAPPEDWINDOW†	Window with WS_OVERLAPPED, WS_CAPTION, WS_SYSMENU, WS_THICKFRAME, WS_MINIMIZE_BOX, WS_MAXIMIZE_BOX	
WS_POPUP	Popup window	Cannot be used with WS_CHILD
WS_POPUPWINDOW	Window with styles WS_POPUP, WS_BORDER, WS_SYSMENU	
WS_SIZEBOX*	Window with a size box	Used with windows w/caption or scroll bars only
WS_SYSMENU	Window with system menu box in caption bar	Used with windows w/ caption bars only
WS_TABSTOP†	Defines controls that can be moved to by tabbing	Tabbing applies until next WS_TABSTOP
WS_THICKFRAME†	Window with thick frame, which can be used to size window	
WS_TILED*	Tiled window	
WS_TILEDWINDOW*	Window with WS_TILED, WS_CAPTION, WS_SYSMENU, WS_SIZEBOX	
WS_VISIBLE	Window is initially visible	
WS_VSCROLL	Window with vertical scroll bar	

*Applies to Windows 1.0 only.
†Applies to all versions of Windows beginning with 2.0.
§Applies to all versions of Windows beginning with 3.0.

Source: Microsoft Windows 1.0 SDK Programmer's Reference, pages 28 through 29
Microsoft Windows 2.0 SDK Programmer's Reference, pages 199 through 200
Microsoft Windows 3.0 SDK Programmer's Reference, pages 8-16 through 8-18

See Also:
6.041. Include File Constants Definitions by Name
6.042. Include File Constants Definitions by Use
6.096. Windows Function Summary by Name
6.097. Windows Escape Function Summary by Name
6.098. Windows Function Summary by Type

6.103. WINDOWS FILE TYPES

Bit Is wFiletype	*Meaning*	*Use*
0 (0)	Normal file	Find all "normal" files
1 (1)	Read-only file	Find all read-only files
2 (2)	Hidden file	Find all hidden files
3 (3)	System file	Find all System files
10 (16)	Directory file*	Find all Directories
20 (32)	Archive file*	Find all files with "archive" bit set
2000 (8192)	LB_DIR flag*	If set, Windows puts message in apps queue
4000 (16384)	Drive bit*	
8000 (32768)	Exclusive bit*	Find only files of the type listed (don't include normal files)

*No longer documented in Windows 3.0

Note: wFiletype is determined by ANDing together the bits for the file types you want to match.

Source: Microsoft Windows 2.0 SDK Programmer's Reference, page 216
Microsoft Windows 3.0 SDK Programmer's Reference, page 4-271

See Also: 6.096. Windows Function Summary by Name
6.097. Windows Escape Function Summary by Name
6.098. Windows Function Summary by Type

6.104. DISPLAY CONTEXT DEFAULT SETTINGS

Attribute	*Default Setting*
Background Color	White
Background Mode	OPAQUE
Bitmap	No default
Brush	WHITE_BRUSH
Brush Origin	(0,0)
Clipping Region	The whole display surface
Color Palette*	DEFAULT_PALETTE
Current Pen Position	(0,0)
Device Origin*	Upper-left corner of client area
Drawing Mode	R2_COPYPEN
Font	SYSTEM_FONT (or SYSTEM_FIXED_FONT)
Intercharacter spacing	0
Mapping Mode	MM_TEXT
Pen	BLACK_PEN
Polygon Filling Mode	ALTERNATE
Relative-Absolute Flag	ABSOLUTE
Stretching Mode	BLACKONWHITE
Text Color	Black
Viewport Extents	(1,1)
Viewport Orgin	(0,0)
Window Extents	(1,1)
Window Origin	(0,0)

*Applies to all versions of Windows beginning with 3.0.

Source: Microsoft Windows 2.0 SDK Programmer's Reference, pages 92 through 93
Microsoft Windows 3.0 SDK Programmer's Reference, pages 1-33 through 1-34

See Also: 6.041. Include File Constants Definitions by Name
6.042. Include File Constants Definitions by Use

6.105. BINARY RASTER OPERATION CODES (ROP2)

Operation	*Boolean Op**	*Function*
R2_BLACK	0	Pixel is always black
R2_COPYPEN	P	Pixel is the pen color
R2_MASKNOTPEN	DPna	Pixel is combination of colors common to the display and inverse of pen
R2_MASKPEN	DPa	Pixel is combination of colors common to the pen and the display
R2_MASKPENNOT	PDna	Pixel is combination of colors common to the pen and inverse of display
R2_MERGENOTPEN	DPno	Pixel is a combination of display color and inverse of the pen color
R2_MERGEPEN	DPo	Pixel is a combination of pen color and the display color
R2_MERGEPENNOT	PDno	Pixel is a combination of pen color and the inverse of the display color
R2_NOP	D	Pixel remains unchanged
R2_NOT	Dn	Pixel is inverse of the display color
R2_NOTCOPYPEN	Pn	Pixel is inverse of pen color
R2_NOTMASKPEN	Dpan	Pixel is inverse of R2_MASKPEN
R2_NOTMERGEPEN	DPon	Pixel is inverse of R2_MERGEPEN color
R2_NOTXORPEN	DPxn	Pixel is inverse of R2_XORPEN color
R2_WHITE	1	Pixel is always white
R2_XORPEN	DPx	Pixel is combination of colors in pen and display, but not in both

*Boolean operation is coded as follows:

- D destination bitmap
- P selected pen
- a bitwise AND
- n bitwise NOT (inverse)
- o bitwise OR
- x bitwise exclusive OR (XOR)

Source: Microsoft Windows 2.0 SDK Programmer's Reference, page 443
Microsoft Windows 3.0 SDK Programmer's Reference, pages 11-1 through 11-4

See Also: 6.041. Include File Constants Definitions by Name
6.042. Include File Constants Definitions by Use

6.106. TERNARY RASTER OPERATION CODES

Name (if any)	ROP Value (in hex)	Boolean Function (in hex)	Boolean Function (in Reverse Polish)*
BLACKNESS†	00000042	00	0
†	00010289	01	DPSoon
†	00020C89	02	SPSona
†	000300AA	03	PSon
†	00040C88	04	SDPona
†	000500A9	05	DPon
†	00060865	06	DPSxnon
†	000702C5	07	PDSaon
†	00080F08	08	SDPnaa
†	00090245	09	PDSxon
†	000A0329	0A	DPna
†	000B0B2A	0B	PSDnaon
†	000C0324	0C	SPna
†	000D0B25	0D	PDSnaon
†	000E08A5	0E	PDSonon
†	000F0001	0F	Pn
†	00100C85	10	PDSona
NOTSRCERASE	001100A6	11	DSon
†	00120868	12	SDPxnon
†	001302C8	13	SDPaon
†	00140869	14	DPSxnon
†	001502C9	15	DPSaon
†	00165CCA	16	PSDPSanaxx
†	00171D54	17	SSPxDSxaxn
†	00180D59	18	SPxPDxa
†	00191CC8	19	SDPSanaxn
†	001A06C5	1A	PDSPaox
†	001B0768	1B	SDPSxaxn
†	001C06CA	1C	PSDPaox
†	001D0766	1D	DSPDxaxn
†	001E01A5	1E	PDSox
†	001F0385	1F	PDSoan
†	00200F09	20	DPSnaa
†	00210248	21	SDPxon
†	00220326	22	DSna
†	00230B24	23	SPDnaon
†	00240D55	24	SPxDSxa
†	00251CC5	25	PDSPanaxn
†	002606C8	26	SDPSaox
†	00271868	27	SDPSxnox
†	00280369	28	DPSxa
†	002916CA	29	PSDPSaoxxn
†	002A0CC9	2A	DPSana
†	002B1D58	2B	SSPxPDxaxn
†	002C0784	2C	SPDSoax
†	002D060A	2D	PSDnox
†	002E064A	2E	PSDPxox
†	002F0E2A	2F	PSDnoan
†	0030032A	30	PSna
†	00310B28	31	SDPnaon
†	00320688	32	SDPSoox
NOTSRCCOPY	00330008	33	Sn
†	003406C4	34	SPDSaox
†	00351864	35	SPDSxnox
†	003601A8	36	SDPox
†	00370388	37	SDPoan
†	0038078A	38	PSDPoax
†	00390604	39	SPDnox
†	003A0644	3A	SPDSxox
†	003B0E24	3B	SPDnoan
†	003C004A	3C	PSx
†	003D18A4	3D	SPDSonox
†	003E1B24	3E	SPDSnaox
†	003F00EA	3F	PSan
†	00400F0A	40	PSDnaa
†	00410249	41	DPSxon
†	00420D5D	42	DSxPDxa
†	00431CC4	43	SPDSanaxn
SRCERASE	00440328	44	SDna
†	00450B29	45	DPSnaon
†	004606C6	46	DSPDaox
†	0047076A	47	PSDPxaxn
†	00480368	48	SDPxa
†	004916C5	49	PDSPDaoxxn
†	004A0789	4A	DPSDoax

(Continued)

6.106. TERNARY RASTER OPERATION CODES (continued)

Name (if any)	*ROP Value (in hex)*	*Boolean Function (in hex)*	*Boolean Function (in Reverse Polish)**
†	004B0605	4B	PDSnox
†	004C0CC8	4C	SDPana
†	004D1954	4D	SSPxDSxoxn
†	004E0645	4E	PDSPxox
†	004F0E25	4F	PDSnoan
†	00500325	50	PDna
†	00510B26	51	DSPnaon
†	005206C9	52	DPSDaox
†	00530764	53	SPDSxaxn
†	005408A9	54	DPSonon
DSTINVERT	00550009	55	Dn
†	005601A9	56	DPSox
†	00570389	57	DPSoan
†	00580785	58	PDSPoax
†	00590609	59	DPSnox
PATINVERT	005A0049	5A	DPx
†	005B18A9	5B	DPSDonox
†	005C0649	5C	DPSDxox
†	005D0E29	5D	DPSnoan
†	005E1B29	5E	DPSDnaox
†	005F00E9	5F	DPan
†	00600365	60	PDSxa
†	006116C6	61	DSPDSaoxxn
†	00620786	62	DSPDoax
†	00630608	63	SDPnox
†	00640788	64	SDPSoax
†	00650606	65	DSPnox
SRCINVERT	00660046	66	DSx
†	006718A8	67	SDPSonox
†	006858A6	68	DSPDSonoxxn
†	00690145	69	PDSxxn
†	006A01E9	6A	DPSax
†	006B178A	6B	PSDPSoaxxn
†	006C01E8	6C	SDPax
†	006D1785	6D	PDSPDoaxxn
†	006E1E28	6E	SDPSnoax
†	006F0C65	6F	PDSxnan
†	00700CC5	70	PDSana
†	00711D5C	71	SSDxPDxaxn
†	00720648	72	SDPSxox
†	00730E28	73	SDPnoan
†	00740646	74	DSPDxox
†	00750E26	75	DSPnoan
†	00761B28	76	SDPSnaox
†	007700E6	77	DSan
†	007801E5	78	PDSax
†	00791786	79	DSPDSoaxxn
†	007A1E29	7A	DPSDnoax
†	007B0C68	7B	SDPxnan
†	007C1E24	7C	SPDSnoax
†	007D0C69	7D	DPSxnan
†	007E0955	7E	SPxDSxo
†	007F03C9	7F	DPSaan
†	008003E9	80	DPSaa
†	00810975	81	SPxDSxon
†	00820C49	82	DPSxna
†	00831E04	83	SPDSnoaxn
†	00840C48	84	SDPxna
†	00851E05	85	PDSPnoaxn
†	008617A6	86	DSPDSoaxx
†	008701C5	87	PDSaxn
SRCAND	008800C6	88	DSa
†	00891B08	89	SDPSnaoxn
†	008A0E06	8A	DSPnoa
†	008B0666	8B	DSPDxoxn
†	008C0E08	8C	SDPnoa
†	008D0668	8D	SDPSxoxn
†	008E1D7C	8E	SSDxPDxax
†	008F0CE5	8F	PDSanan
†	00900C45	90	PDSxna
†	00911E08	91	SDPSnoaxn
†	009217A9	92	DPSDPoaxx
†	009301C4	93	SPDaxn
†	009417AA	94	PSDPSoaxx
†	009501C9	95	DPSaxn

(Continued)

6.106. TERNARY RASTER OPERATION CODES (continued)

Name (if any)	ROP Value (in hex)	Boolean Function (in hex)	Boolean Function (in Reverse Polish)*
†	00960169	96	DPSxx
†	0097588A	97	PSDPSonoxx
†	00981888	98	SDPSonoxn
†	00990066	99	DSxn
†	009A0709	9A	DPSnax
†	009B07A8	9B	SDPSoaxn
†	009C0704	9C	SPDnax
†	009D07A6	9D	DSPDoaxn
†	009E16E6	9E	DSPDSaoxx
†	009F0345	9F	PDSxan
†	00A000C9	A0	DPa
†	00A11B05	A1	PDSPnaoxn
†	00A20E09	A2	DPSnoa
†	00A30669	A3	DPSDxoxn
†	00A41855	A4	PDSPonoxn
†	00A50065	A5	PDxn
†	00A60706	A6	DSPnax
†	00A707A5	A7	PDSPoaxn
†	00A803A9	A8	DPSoa
†	00A90189	A9	DPSoxn
†	00AA0029	AA	D
†	00AB0889	AB	DPSono
†	00AC0744	AC	SPDSxax
†	00AD06E9	AD	DPSDaoxn
†	00AE0B06	AE	DSPnao
†	00AF0229	AF	DPno
†	00B00E05	B0	PDSnoa
†	00B10665	B1	PDSPxoxn
†	00B21974	B2	SSPxDSxox
†	00B30CE8	B3	SDPanan
†	00B4070A	B4	PSDnax
†	00B507A9	B5	DPSDoaxn
†	00B616E9	B6	DPSDPaoxx
†	00B70348	B7	SDPxan
†	00B8074A	B8	PSDPxax
†	00B906E6	B9	DSPDaoxn
†	00BA0B09	BA	DPSnao
MERGEPAINT	00BB0226	BB	DSno
†	00BC1CE4	BC	SPDSanax
†	00BD0D7D	BD	SDxPDxan
†	00BE0269	BE	DPSxo
†	00BF08C9	BF	DPSano
MERGECOPY	00C000CA	C0	PSa
†	00C11B04	C1	SPDSnaoxn
†	00C21884	C2	SPDSonoxn
†	00C3006A	C3	PSxn
†	00C40E04	C4	SPDnoa
†	00C50664	C5	SPDSxoxn
†	00C60708	C6	SDPnax
†	00C707AA	C7	PSDPoaxn
†	00C803A8	C8	SDPoa
†	00C90184	C9	SPDoxn
†	00CA0749	CA	DPSDxax
†	00CB06E4	CB	SPDSaoxn
SRCCOPY	00CC0020	CC	S
†	00CD0888	CD	SDPono
†	00CE0B08	CE	SDPnao
†	00CF0224	CF	SPno
†	00D00E0A	D0	PSDnoa
†	00D1066A	D1	PSDPxoxn
†	00D20705	D2	PDSnax
†	00D307A4	D3	SPDSoaxn
†	00D41D78	D4	SSPxPDxax
†	00D50CE9	D5	DPSanan
†	00D616EA	D6	PSDPSaoxx
†	00D70349	D7	DPSxan
†	00D80745	D8	PDSPxax
†	00D906E8	D9	SDPSaoxn
†	00DA1CE9	DA	DPSDanax
†	00DB0D75	DB	SPxDSxan
†	00DC0B04	DC	SPDnao
†	00DD0228	DD	SDno
†	00DE0268	DE	SDPxo
†	00DF08C8	DF	SDPano
†	00E003A5	E0	PDSoa

(Continued)

6.106. TERNARY RASTER OPERATION CODES (continued)

Name (if any)	*ROP Value (in hex)*	*Boolean Function (in hex)*	*Boolean Function (in Reverse Polish)**
†	00E10185	E1	PDSoxn
†	00E20746	E2	DSPDxax
†	00E306EA	E3	PSDPaoxn
†	00E40748	E4	SDPSxax
†	00E506E5	E5	PDSPaoxn
†	00E61CE8	E6	SDPSanax
†	00E70D79	E7	SPxPDxan
†	00E81D74	E8	SSPxDSxax
†	00E95CE6	E9	DSPDSanaxxn
†	00EA02E9	EA	DPSao
†	00EB0849	EB	DPSxno
†	00EC02E8	EC	SDPao
†	00ED0848	ED	SDPxno
SRCPAINT	00EE0086	EE	DSo
†	00EF0A08	EF	SDPnoo
PATCOPY	00F00021	F0	P
†	00F10885	F1	PDSono
†	00F20B05	F2	PDSnao
†	00F3022A	F3	PSno
†	00F40B0A	F4	PSDnao
†	00F50225	F5	PDno
†	00F60265	F6	PDSxo
†	00F708C5	F7	PDSano
†	00F802E5	F8	PDSao
†	00F90845	F9	PDSxno
†	00FA0089	FA	DPo
PATPAINT	00FB0A09	FB	DSPnoo
†	00FC008A	FC	PSo
†	00FD0A0A	FD	PSDnoo
†	00FE02A9	FE	DPSoo
WHITENESS	00FF0062	FF	1

†Applies to all versions of Windows beginning with 3.0 (unnamed ROPs).
*Boolean function is coded as follows:

- D destination bitmap
- P selected brush (pattern)
- S source bitmap
- a bitwise AND
- n bitwise NOT (inverse)
- o bitwise OR
- x bitwise exclusive OR (XOR)

Source: Microsoft Windows 2.0 SDK Programmer's Reference, pages 670 through 677
Microsoft Windows 3.0 SDK Programmer's Reference, pages 11-4 through 11-13

See Also: 6.041. Include File Constants Definitions by Name
6.042. Include File Constants Definitions by Use

6.107. GDI INFORMATION INDEX DATA

Index Name	*Description*	*Allowable Values*
DRIVERVERSION	GDI version number	
TECHNOLOGY	Device technology used	DT_PLOTTER=vector plotter DT_RASDISPLAY=raster display DT_RASPRINTER=raster printer DT_RASCAMERA=raster camera DT_CHARSTREAM=character stream, PLP DT_METAFILE=metafile, VDM DT_DISPFILE=display file
HORZSIZE	Width of physical display	In millimeters
VERTSIZE	Height of physical display	In millimeters
HORZRES	Width of display	In pixels
VERTRES	Height of display	In raster lines
LOGPIXELSX*	Number pixels along display width	In pixels per logical inch
LOGPIXELSY*	Number pixels along display height	In pixels per logical inch
BITSPIXEL	Number of adjacent color bits per pixel	
PLANES	Number of color planes	
NUMBRUSHES	Number of device-specific brushes	
NUMPENS	Number of device-specific pens	
NUMFONTS	Number of device-specific fonts	
NUMCOLORS	Number of entries in device's color table	
ASPECTX	Relative width of device pixel used for lines	
ASPECTY	Relative height of device pixel used for lines	
ASPECTXY	Diagonal width of device pixel used for lines	
PDEVICESIZE	Size of internal data structure PDEVICE	In bytes
SIZEPALETTE†	Number of entries in system palette	
NUMRESERVED†	Reserved entries in system palette	
COLORRES†	Color resolution in bits per pixel	
CLIPCAPS	Clipping capabilities of device	0=cannot clip, 1=can clip rectangle
RASTERCAPS	Raster capabilities of device	RC_BITBLT (can transfer bitmap) RC_BANDING (requires banding support) RC_DI_BITMAP (supports DIBs)† RC_DIBTODEV (supports DITBitsToDevice)† RC_FLOODFILL (supports flood fills)† RC_PALETTE (palette-based device)† RC_STRETCHBLT (supports StretchBlt)† RC_STRETCHDIB (supports StretchDIBits)† RC_GDI20_OUTPUT (supports 2.0 features) RC_BITMAP64 (supports bitmaps >64K) RC_SCALING (capable of scaling)
CURVECAPS	Curve creation capabilities of device	Bit 0=can do circles Bit 1=can do pie wedges Bit 2=can do chord arcs Bit 3=can do ellipses Bit 4=can do wide borders Bit 5=can do styled borders Bit 6=can do wide and styled borders Bit 7=can do interiors Bits 8-15=zero
LINECAPS	Line creation capabilities of device	Bit 0=RESERVED Bit 1=can do polyline Bits 2-3=RESERVED Bit 4=can do wide lines Bit 5=can do styled lines Bit 6=can do wide and styled lines Bit 7=can do interiors Bits 8-15=zero
POLYGONALCAPS	Polygonal creation capabilities of device	Bit 0=can do alternate fill polygon Bit 1=can do rectangle Bit 2=can do winding number fill polygon Bit 3=can do scanline Bit 4=can do wide borders Bit 5=can do styled borders Bit 6=can do both wide and styled borders Bit 7=can do interiors Bits 8-15=zero

(Continued)

6.107. GDI INFORMATION INDEX DATA (continued)

Index Name	Description	Allowable Values
TEXTCAPS	Text creation capabilities of device	Bit 0=can do character output precision Bit 1=can do stroke output precision Bit 2=can do stroke clip precision Bit 3=can do 90-degree character rotations Bit 4=can do any character rotation Bit 5=can do scaling independent of X and Y Bit 6=can do doubled character for scaling Bit 7=can do integer multiples for scaling Bit 8=can do any multiples for exact scaling Bit 9=can do double weight characters Bit 10=can do italics Bit 11=can do underlining Bit 12=can do strikeouts Bit 13=can do raster fonts Bit 14=can do vector fonts Bit 15=RESERVED, must be 0

*First defined in Windows 2.0.
†Applies to all versions of Windows beginning with 3.0.

Source: Microsoft Windows 2.0 SDK Programmer's Reference, pages 270 through 273
Microsoft Windows 3.0 SDK Programmer's Reference, pages 4-167 through 4-170

6.108. DEVELOPMENT TOOLS COMMAND SYNTAX

Command	Syntax	Function
IMPLIB	IMPLIB imp-lib-name mod-def-file	
LINK	LINK [options] object-files, [exe-file],[map-file],[lib-files],def-file	
EXEHDR	EXEHDR exe-filename	
RC	RC -R [options] script-file RC [options] script-file [executable-file] RC [options] dll-file RC [options] res-file.RES [executable-file]	Compile resources separately Compile an .RC file and add to executable Compile 3.0 of DLL without .RES file Add compiled resource file to executable

Version: Applies to all versions of Windows beginning with 3.0.

Source: Microsoft Windows 3.0 SDK Tools, pages 2-6, 2-7, 2-13, 3-5

See Also: 6.109. Common Windows C Compiler Options Summary
6.110. Symbolic Debugger (SYMDEB) Command Summary
6.111. LINK Module Definition Statements Command Summary
6.112. WDEB386 Debugger Command Summary

6.109. COMMON WINDOWS C COMPILER OPTIONS SUMMARY

Command Line Options

Option	Function
-AC	Compiles application for compact memory model
-AL	Compiles application for large memory model
-AM	Compiles application for medium memory model
-AS	Compiles application for small memory model
Aw	Ensures pointers receive proper segment address when cast to 32-bit addresses
-c	Compiles only
-Gs	Removes stack probes to improve performance
-Gw	Adds Windows prolog and epilog to all functions
-GW	Substitutes a reduced Windows prolog and epilog to functions that are far calls within app
-Os	Optimizes for code size instead of speed
-Ow	Relaxes alias checking within constraints imposed by Windows*
-Zd	Creates object file for use with SYMDEB or WDEB386
-Zi	Creates object file for use with CodeView for Windows
-Zp	Packs structures on single-byte boundaries

*C 6.0 and later only

Version: Applies to Microsoft C 5.1 or later.

Source: Microsoft Windows 3.0 SDK Tools, pages 1-1 through 1-3

6.110. SYMBOLIC DEBUGGER (SYMDEB) COMMAND SUMMARY

Command Line Options

Option	*Function*	*Allowable Values*
/m	Redirects output to secondary mono monitor	
/x	Disables the 'more' feature	
/w#	Sets memory allocation reporting level to #	0=no reporting 1=allocation messages only (default) 2=movement messages only 3=both allocation & movement msgs
/@filename	Loads macro definitions from named file	
/n	Permits use of nonmaskable interrupts	
/i[bm]	Use features available on IBM compatibles	
/ffilename	Prevents named symbol file being used with executable file	
/"cmdlist"	Causes commands in list to be executed	Commands separated by semicolon

SYMDEB Commands

Command	*Function*
a[address]	Assemble
ba mode size address [value][cmdstring]	Set 80386 address breakpoint(s)
bc idlist	Clear breakpoint(s)
bd idlist	Disable breakpoint(s)
be idlist	Enable breakpoint(s)
bl	List breakpoint(s)
bp[id]address [value][cmdstring]	Set breakpoint(s)
c range address	Compare
d [range]	Dump memory using previous type
da [range]	Dump memory in ASCII format
db [range]	Dump memory in bytes
dd [range]	Dump memory in double words
df*	Display list of global free blocks
dg	Display global memory heap
dh	Display local memory heap for current DS
dl [range]	Dump memory as long floating point
dm*	Display list of loaded modules
dq	Display task queue
ds [range]	Dump memory as short floating point
dt [range]	Dump memory in 10-byte real numbers
du*	Display LRU list
dw [range]	Dump memory in words
e address [list]	Enter values using previous type
ea address [list]	Enter ASCII values
eb address [list]	Enter bytes
ed address [list]	Enter double words
el address [list]	Enter long floating-point values
es address [list]	Enter short floating-point values
et address [list]	Enter 10-byte real values
ew address [list]	Enter words
f range list	Fill
g [=address][address]...	Go
h value value	Add hexadecimal values
i value	Input from port
k [value]	Backtrace stack
kt pdb [value]	Backtrace task
kv [value]*	Annotate stack frame with frame pointer value
l [address[drive record count]]	Load
m range address	Move
m id[=cmdstring]	Define or execute macro
n [filename][arguments]	Set name of file
o value byte	Output byte to port
p [=address][value]	Trace program instruction
q	Quit
r [register][[=]value]	Set register
s range list	Search for match
s-	Set machine debugging only
s&	Set machine and source debugging
s+	Set source debugging only
t [=address][value]	Trace program instruction
u [range]	Display unassembled instructions
v range	View source code lines
w [address[drive record count]]	Write to disk
x [*|?] symbol	Examine symbols
xo [symbol!]	Open map or segment
z symbol value	Set symbol to value
?*	Display list of SYMDEB commands and operators

(Continued)

6.110. SYMBOLIC DEBUGGER (SYMDEB) COMMAND SUMMARY (continued)

SYMDEB Commands

? expression	Compute and display expression
.	Display current source code line
<filename	Redirect SYMDEB input to file
>filename	Redirect SYMDEB output to file
==filename	Redirect SYMDEB input and output
{filename	Redirect program input to file
}filename	Redirect program output to file
~filename	Redirect program input and output
![doscommand]	Execute DOS shell or command and return
* string	Comment

*Applies to all versions of Windows beginning with 3.0.

Note: • Options may be preceded by a hyphen instead of a forward slash.
• Options may be identified with upper- or lowercase letters.

Source: Microsoft Windows 2.0 SDK Tools, pages 100 through 102, 110 through 138
Microsoft Windows 3.0 SDK Tools, pages 8-15 through 8-41

6.111. LINK MODULE DEFINITION STATEMENTS COMMAND SUMMARY

Statement	*Syntax*	*Function*
CODE	CODE options*	Defines code-segment attributes
DATA	DATA options*	Defines data-segment attributes
DESCRIPTION	DESCRIPTION 'string'	Describes the module
EXETYPE	EXETYPE WINDOWS	Tells LINK what type of .EXE header to use
EXPORTS	EXPORTS functionlist	Lists functions in module called by others
HEAPSIZE	HEAPSIZE bytes	Specifies default local heap size
IMPORTS	IMPORTS functionlist	Lists other functions called by the app
LIBRARY	LIBRARY name	Specifies module name of dynamic link lib
NAME	NAME name	Specifies module name of application
SEGMENTS	SEGMENTS options	Specifies attributes of added code or data segs
STACKSIZE	STACKSIZE bytes	Determines default size of local stack
STUB	STUB name	Specifies applications old-style executable file

*Options include MOVEABLE, MULTIPLE, DISCARDABLE, and SINGLE.

Version: Applies to all versions of Windows beginning with 3.0.

Source: Microsoft Windows 3.0 SDK Tools, pages 2-2 through 2-3

6.112. WDEB386 DEBUGGER COMMAND SUMMARY

Command Line Options

Option	Function
/v[p]	Enable verbose mode (p parm used for applications only)
/c:{1 | 2 | 3 | 4}	Specifies COM port for debugger output
/s:symfilespec	Specifies symbol file to load

WDEB386 Commands

Command	Function
? expr | "string"	Display expression
?	Display help
.?	Display external commands
.b baudrate [port]	Set COM port baud rate
.df	Display global free list
.dg [object]	Display global heap
.dh	Display local heap
.dm	Display global module list
.dq	Dump task queue
.du	Display global LRU list
.reboot	Reboot target system
bc {list | *}	Clear breakpoints
bd {list | *}	Disable breakpoints
be {list | *}	Enable breakpoints
bl	List breakpoints
bp[n] addr [passcnt] ["cmds"]	Set breakpoints
c range addr	Compare memory
d [range]	Display memory
db [range]	Display bytes
dd [range]	Display double words
dg [a] [range]	Display GDT
di [a] [range]	Display IDT
dl [a | p | s | h] [range]	Display LDT
dt [addr]	Display TSS
dw [range]	Display words
e addr [list]	Enter byte
f range list	Fill memory
g [=addr [addr...]]	Go
h word word	Hexadecimal arithmetic
i word	Input byte
j expr ["cmds"]	Conditional execute
k [ss:bp] [cs:ip]	Backtrace stack
ka value	Set backtrace arguments
kt [tdb]	Backtrace task stack
kv	Verbose backtrace stack
la	List absolute symbols
lg	List groups
lm	List map
ln [addr]	List near
ls {group-name | name-chars | *}	List symbols
m range addr	Move memory
o word byte	Output to port
p [N] [=addr] [count]	Program trace
r reg=word	Display registers
s range {list | "string"}	Search bytes
t [N] [=addr] [word]	Trace instructions
u range	Unassemble bytes
v [1 | 3]	Set interrupt vector trapping
vl	Display interrupt trapping information
w [mapname]	Change map
y [? | 386env | dislwr | regterse | codebytes | symaddres]	Debugger configuration options
z	Zap embedded INT1 and INT3 instructions
zd	Execute default command string
zl	Display default command string
zs "string"	Change default command string

Version: Applies to all versions of Windows beginning with 3.0.

Source: Microsoft Windows 3.0 SDK Tools, pages 9-9 through 9-47

Section 7

Motherboards, Keyboards, Video Adapters, Peripherals, and Chips

Peripheral Support Chips

7.001. MACHINE SUMMARY AND HISTORY

		PC Class Machines					AT Class Machines	
		PC	PC/XT	PCJr	Portable	Convertible	PC/AT	PC/XT 286
System	Processor speed	5 Mhz 8088	5 Mhz 8088	5 Mhz 8088	5 Mhz 8088	5 Mhz 8088	6,8 Mhz§ 80286	6 Mhz 80286
	Processor type	8088	8088	8088	8088	8088	80286	80286
	Math coprocessor	Optional	Optional	No	Optional	No	Optional	Optional
	RAM on motherboard	64K∞	256K∞	128K	256K	256K	512K	640K
	Maximum RAM allowed	512K∞	640K	512K	640K	640K	640K,16MB	640K, 16MB
	ROM on motherboard	40K	40K	64K	40K		64K	64K
	Power supply	63.5-watt	130-watt	33-watt	130-watt		450VA	130-watt
Slots	8-bit PC slots	5	8	0	8	0	2	2
	16-bit AT slots	0	0	0	0	0	6	
	16-bit PS/2 slots	0	0	0	0	0	0	0
	32-bit PS/2 slots	0	0	0	0	0	0	0
Drives	Drive slots ¶	4	4	1	2	2	3	3
	Supplied floppy drive(s)	1 180K Δ	1 360K 5.25"	None	2 360K 5.25"	2 720K 3.5"	1 1.2MB 5.25"	1 360K 5.25"
	Supplied hard drive	None	10 MB	None	None	None	20 MB	20 MB
	Optional hard drive	None	20 MB	None	None	None	40 MB	None
	Cassette	Supported	No	Supported	No	No	No	No
I/O	Parallel ports	Optional	Optional	Optional	Optional	Optional	Optional	Optional
	Serial ports	Optional	Optional	Optional	Optional	Optional	Optional	Optional
	Mouse ports	Optional	Optional	Optional	Optional	No	Optional	Optional
	Supplied video adapter	None	None	Built-in PCJr	Special	CGA emulation	Optional	Optional
	Optional video adapter	MDA,CGA	MDA,CGA,EGA	None	None	None	MDA,CGA,EGA	MDA,CGA,EGA
	Keyboard	83-key	83-key	"Chiclet"	83-key	78-key	84-key, 101-key	84-key, 101-key
Size*	Height	5.5"	5.5"	3.8"	8"	2.7"	5.6	5.5
	Width	19.6"	19.6"	13.9"	20"	12.8"	21.2	19.6
	Depth	16.1"	16.1"	11.4"	17"	14.7"	16.9	16.1
	Weight	29 lbs	32 lbs	8 lbs 4 oz	30 lbs	12.7 lbs	43 lbs	32 lbs
Software	Cassette BIOS support	Yes	Yes	Yes	No	No	No	No
	EGA BIOS support	No ∂	Yes	No	No	No	Yes	Yes
	Serial BIOS support	Yes-2 ports	Yes-2 ports	Yes	Yes-2 ports	Yes-2 ports	Yes-2 ports	Yes-2 ports
	Parallel BIOS support	Yes-2 ports	Yes-2 ports	Yes	Yes-2 ports	Yes-2 ports	Yes-2 ports	Yes-2 ports
	Hard-disk BIOS support	No	Yes	No	No	No	Yes	Yes
	Recommended DOS version†	1.0	2.0	2.0	2.0	3.2	2.1	3.2
History	Introduction	Aug-81	Mar-83	Oct-83	Mar-84	Apr-86	Aug-84	Sep-86
	Updated		Jul-85			Jun-87	Apr-86	
	Dropped		Jul-87				Jul-87	

		PS/2 Machines							
		Model 25	Model 30	30-286	Model 50	Model 60	Model 65XS	Model 70	Model 80
System	Processor speed	8 Mhz	8 Mhz	10 Mhz	10 Mhz	10 Mhz	16 Mhz	16, 20, 25 Mhz	16, 20, 25 Mhz
	Processor type	8086	8086	80286	80286	80286	80386sx	80386	80386
	Math coprocessor	Optional	Optional	Optional	Optional	Optional	Optional	Optional	Optional
	RAM on motherboard	512K	640K	640K	1MB	1MB	1MB	1MB	1MB
	Maximum RAM allowed	640K	2MB	16MB	16MB	16MB	16MB	16MB	16MB
	ROM on motherboard	64K	64K	128K	128K	128K		128K	128K
	Power supply	90,115-watt	70-watt	90-watt	94-watt		250-watt	132-watt	250-watt
Slots	8-bit PC slots	2	3	0	0	0	0	0	0
	16-bit AT slots	0	0	3	0	0	0	0	0
	16-bit PS/2 slots	0	0	0	4	8	8	1	5
	32-bit PS/2 slots	0	0	0	0	0	0	2	3
Drives	Drive slots †	2	2	2	3	4	4	3	4
	Supplied floppy drive(s)	1 720K 3.5"	1 720K 3.5"	1 1.4MB 3.5"	1 1.4MB 3.5"	1 1.4MB 3.5"	1 1.4MB 3.5"	1 1.4MB 3.5"	1 1.4MB 3.5"
	Supplied hard drive	None	20 MB	20 MB	20 MB	44 MB	60 MB	60 MB	44 MB
	Optional hard drive	20 MB	None	30 MB	30, 60 MB	70 MB	120 MB	120 MB	60, 120, 320 MB
	Cassette	No	No	No	No	No	No	No	No
I/O	Parallel ports	Yes, 1	Yes, 1	Yes, 1	Yes, 1	Yes, 1	Yes, 1	Yes, 1	Yes, 1
	Serial ports	Yes, 1	Yes, 1	Yes, 1	Yes, 1	Yes, 1	Yes, 1	Yes, 1	Yes, 1
	Mouse ports	Yes	Yes	Yes	Yes	Yes	Yes	Yes	Yes
	Supplied video adapter	MCGA¥	MCGA	VGA	VGA	VGA	VGA	VGA	VGA
	Optional video adapter	None	VGA	None	8514/A, XGA	8514/A, XGA	8514/A, XGA	8514/A, XGA	8514/A, XGA
	Keyboard	84/101-key	101-key	101-key	101-key	101-key	101-key	101-key	101-key
Size*	Height		4	4	5.5	23.5	23.5	5.5	23.5
	Width		16	16	14.1	6.5	6.5	14.1	6.5
	Depth		15.6	15.6	16.5	19	19	16.5	19
	Weight		15.7 lbs		21 lbs	44 lbs		21 lbs	44 lbs

(Continued)

7.001. MACHINE SUMMARY AND HISTORY (continued)

PS/2 Machines (continued)

		Model 25	Model 30	30-286	Model 50	Model 60	Model 65XS	Model 70	Model 80
Software	Cassette BIOS support	No	No	No	No	No	No	No	No
	EGA BIOS support	Yes	Yes	Yes	Yes	Yes	Yes	Yes	Yes
	Serial BIOS support	Yes-4 ports	Yes-4 ports	Yes-4 ports	Yes-4 ports	Yes-4 ports	Yes-4 ports	Yes-4 ports	Yes-4 ports
	Parallel BIOS support	Yes-3 ports	Yes-3 ports	Yes-3 ports	Yes-3 ports	Yes-3 ports	Yes-3 ports	Yes-3 ports	Yes-3 ports
	Hard-disk BIOS support	Yes	Yes	Yes	Yes	Yes	Yes	Yes	Yes
	Rec DOS version	3.2	3.2	3.2	3.3	3.3	4.x	3.3	3.3
History	Introduction		Apr-87	89	Apr-87	Apr-87	Apr-90	Jun-88	Jul-87
	Updated				6/88 (50Z)	Jul-87			Apr-90
	Dropped								

PS/2 Machines

		Model 90	Model 95
System	Processor speed	25, 33 Mhz	25, 33 Mhz
	Processor type	80486	80486
	Math coprocessor	Optional	Optional
	RAM on motherboard	4MB	4MB
	Maximum RAM allowed	15MB	15MB
	ROM on motherboard	128K	128K
	Power supply		
Slots	8-bit PC slots	0	0
	16-bit AT slots	0	0
	16-bit PS/2 slots	0	0
	32-bit PS/2 slots	4	6
Drives	Drive slots †	3	7
	Supplied floppy drive(s)	2 1.4MB 3.5"	1 1.4MB 3.5", 5.25"
	Supplied hard drive	80 MB	80 MB
	Optional hard drive	160, 320 MB	160, 320 MB
	Cassette	No	No
I/O	Parallel ports	Yes, 1	Yes, 1
	Serial ports	Yes, 2	Yes, 1
	Mouse ports	Yes	Yes
	Supplied video adapter	XGA	XGA
	Optional video adapter	None	None
	Keyboard	101-key	101-key
Size*	Height	17.3	20.5
	Width	5.5	8
	Depth	17	19.5
	Weight	26 lbs	50 lbs
Software	Cassette BIOS support	No	No
	EGA BIOS support	Yes	Yes
	Serial BIOS support	Yes-4 ports	Yes-4 ports
	Parallel BIOS support	Yes-3 ports	Yes-3 ports
	Hard-disk BIOS support	Yes	Yes
	Rec DOS version	3.3	3.3
History	Introduction	Oct-90	Oct-90
	Updated		
	Dropped		

*Case housing motherboard
†At time of introduction
§Originally 6; upgraded to 8
∞Eventually upgraded to 640K
¶For half-height drives
ΔOther drives and sizes available
∂Eventually upgraded to Yes

Source:
Byte, June 1987
Byte, August 1987
PC Magazine, May 26, 1987
PC Magazine, July 21, 1987
PCjr Technical Reference, pages 2-19, 2-135, and D-1
PC Magazine, January 15, 1991
PC Magazine, May 29, 1990
IBM PS/2 Hardware Interface Technical Reference, System Specific Information

7.002 IBM PC MODEL NUMBERS AND CONFIGURATIONS

Line	Model Number	Stand. RAM	Stand. Floppy	Stand. Hard Disk	Opt. Hard Disk	Other
PC	5150 Model 166	256K	360K	-	-	
	5150 Model 176	256K	2 - 360K	-	-	
	5155 Portable	256K	360K	-	-	half-height drives
	5140 Convertible	256K	2 - 720K	-	-	laptop
XT	5160 Model 087	128K	360K	10MB	-	
	5160 Model 086	256K	360K	10MB	-	
	5160 Model 068	256K	360K	10MB	-	
	5160 Model 078	256K	2 - 360K	10MB	-	
	5160 Model 267/268	256K	360K	20MB		half-height drives
	5160 Model 277/278	256K	2 - 360K	20MB		half-height drives
	5160 Model 089	256K	360K	20MB		
	XT 370	640K+	360K	20MB		runs VM/PC
	5162 Model XT 286	640K	1.2MB	20MB	-	AT in XT skin
AT	5170 Model 068	256K	1.2MB	-	-	
	5170 Model 099	256K	1.2MB	20MB	-	
	5170 Model 239	256K	1.2MB	30MB	-	only 6Mhz clock allowed
	5170 Model 319	512K	1.2MB	30MB	-	8 Mhz
	5170 Model 339	512K	1.2MB	30MB	-	8 Mhz, new keyboard
	AT 370	640K+	1.2MB	20MB	-	runs VM/PC
PS/2	Model 25	512K	720K	-	20MB	
	Model 30-002	640K	2 - 720K	-	20MB	
	Model 30-021	640K	720K	20MB	-	
	Model 30-E01	512K	1.4MB	-	20MB	286 processor Model 30
	Model 30-E21	512K	1.4MB	20MB	-	286 processor Model 30
	Model 50-021	1MB	1.4MB	20MB	60MB	
	Model 50-031	1MB	1.4MB	30MB	60MB	
	Model 50-061	1MB	1.4MB	60MB	-	
	Model 50Z-031	1MB	1.4MB	30MB	-	
	Model 50Z-061	1MB	1.4MB	60MB	-	
	Model 60-041	1MB	1.4MB	44MB	-	
	Model 60-071	1MB	1.4MB	70MB	115MB	
	Model 65SX-121	1MB	1.4MB	120MB	-	
	Model 65SX-061	1MB	1.4MB	60MB	-	
	Model 70-E21	1MB	1.4MB	60MB	-	
	Model 70-121	2MB	1.4MB	120MB	-	
	Model 70-A21	2MB	1.4MB	120MB	-	
	Model P70-061	1MB	1.4MB	60MB	-	
	Model P70-121	1MB	1.4MB	120MB	-	
	Model P75 486	8MB	1.4MB	160MB	-	
	Model 80-041	1MB	1.4MB	44MB	-	
	Model 80-071	2MB	1.4MB	70MB	115, 314MB	
	Model 80-121	4MB	1.4MB	120MB	320MB	
	Model 80-131	4MB	1.4MB	320MB	-	
	Model 80-A31	4MB	1.4MB	320MB	-	
	Model 90 XP 486	4MB	1.4MB	80MB	160, 320MB	
	Model 95 XP 486	4MB	1.4MB	80MB	160, 320MB	

Source: IBM Microcomputers, A Programmer's Handbook (McGraw-Hill), page 364
Upgrading and Repairing PCs (Que), Chapters 3 and 4
PC Magazine, May 29, 1990, pages 33 through 35
PC Magazine, January 29, 1991, pages 33 through 35

7.003. PC, AT, AND PS/2 MEMORY USAGE SUMMARY

Address	Used By	Comments
00000 - 9FFFF	640K on system board	May be 64K to 640K depending upon model
A0000 - BFFFF	Display adapter reserved	EGA and VGA use all of this; CGA and MDA use portion
C0000 - DFFFF	Reserved for ROM expansion	Used for I/O channel BIOS (as in XT disk controller) C0000-C3FFF EGA BIOS C6000-C63FF PGA communications area C8000-CBFFF hard-disk BIOS D0000-D7FFF cluster adapter BIOS D0000-DFFFF PCjr expansion cartridges
E0000 - EFFFF	Expansion of system ROM	As in AT, PS/2 (standard cartridges in PCjr)
F0000 - FFFFF	System ROM	May be duplicate of ROM in higher memory
100000 - 15FFFF	384K on system board	Model 50, 60, and 80 only
160000 - FDFFFF	Memory expansion	AT and PS/2 only
FE0000 - FEFFFF	RESERVED	AT and PS/2 only
FF0000 - FFFFFF	64K ROM BIOS	AT and PS/2 only

Source: IBM PS/2 Model 80 Technical Reference, pages 2-40 through 2-43
IBM PS/2 Model 50 and 60 Technical Reference, page 4-181
IBM PS/2 Model 30 Technical Reference, page 1-5
IBM PC/AT Technical Reference, page 1-8
IBM PC/XT Technical Reference, pages 1-8 and 1-9

See Also: 4.002. BIOS Memory Usage Summary

7.004. I/O PORT USAGE SUMMARY

Hex Range	XT Use	AT Use (ISA and EISA)	PS/2 Use	Comments
0-F	DMA controller (8237A-5)	DMA controller 1 (8237A-5)	DMA controller	
10-1F	UNDOCUMENTED	DMA Controller 1 (8237A-5)	DMA controller	
20-2F	Interrupt controller (8259A)	Interrupt controller 1 (8259A)	Interrupt controller 1 (8259A)	Only ports 20, 21 actually used
30-3F	UNDOCUMENTED	Interrupt controller 1 (8259A)	UNDOCUMENTED	
40-4F	Timer (8253-5)	Timer (8254-2)	System timers	XT uses 40-43; PS/2 uses 40,42-44, 47; EISA uses 48, 4A-4B
50-5F		Timer (8254-2)	UNDOCUMENTED	
60-6F	Parallel port (8255A-5)	Keyboard (8042)	Keyboard	XT uses 60-63; PS/2 uses 60-61, 64
70-7F	UNDOCUMENTED	RTC, NMI mask	RTC, NMI mask	PS/2 uses 70-71 only, reserves 74-76
80-8F	DMA page registers	DMA page registers (74LS612)	DMA page registers	XT uses 80-83; AT and PS/2 use 81-83, 87, 89-8B, 8F
90-9F	DMA page registers	DMA page registers (74LS612)	I/O channel	PS/2 uses 90-94, 96-97 only
A0-AF	NMI mask register	Interrupt controller 2 (8259A)	Interrupt controller 2 (8259A)	PS/2 uses A0-A1 only
BO-BF	UNDOCUMENTED	Interrupt controller 2 (8259A)	UNDOCUMENTED	
CO-CF	UNDOCUMENTED	DMA controller 2 (8237A-5)	DMA controller	
D0-DF	UNDOCUMENTED	DMA controller 2 (8237A-5)	DMA controller	
E0-EF	UNDOCUMENTED	UNDOCUMENTED	Split address register, memory encoding register	PS/2 Model 80 only
F0-FF	UNDOCUMENTED	Math coprocessor (80287)	Math coprocessor (80x87)	AT uses F0-F1, F8-FF only
100-10F	UNDOCUMENTED	UNDOCUMENTED	Programmable option select	PS/2 uses 100-107 only
110-1EF	UNDOCUMENTED	UNDOCUMENTED	UNDOCUMENTED	
1F0-1FF	UNDOCUMENTED	Fixed disk	UNDOCUMENTED	AT and ISA use IF0-IF8 only
200-20F	Game I/O adapter	Game I/O adapter	UNDOCUMENTED	Game I/O uses 200-207 only
210-21F	Expansion unit	UNDOCUMENTED	UNDOCUMENTED	XT uses 210-217 only
220-24F	UNDOCUMENTED	UNDOCUMENTED	UNDOCUMENTED	
250-25F	UNDOCUMENTED	UNDOCUMENTED	UNDOCUMENTED	
260-26F	UNDOCUMENTED	UNDOCUMENTED	UNDOCUMENTED	
270-27F	Parallel printer 2	Parallel printer port 2	Parallel port 3	All use 278-27F, except PS/2 uses 278-27B
280-28F	UNDOCUMENTED	UNDOCUMENTED	UNDOCUMENTED	
290-29F	UNDOCUMENTED	UNDOCUMENTED	UNDOCUMENTED	
2A0-2AF	UNDOCUMENTED	UNDOCUMENTED	UNDOCUMENTED	
2B0-2BF	Alternate EGA	Alternate EGA	UNDOCUMENTED	

(Continued)

7.004. I/O PORT USAGE SUMMARY (continued)

Hex Range	*XT Use*	*AT Use (ISA and EISA)*	*PS/2 Use*	*Comments*
2C0-2CF	Alternate EGA	Alternate EGA	UNDOCUMENTED	
2D0-2DF	Alternate EGA (3270 also uses)	Alternate EGA	UNDOCUMENTED	
2E0-2EF	GAB 0, Data aquisition 0	GPIB 0, data acquisition 0	UNDOCUMENTED	XT and AT use 2E1, 2E2-2E3 only
2F0-2FF	Serial port 2	Serial port 2	Serial port 2 (RS-232-C)	All use 2F8-2FF only
300-30F	Prototype card	Prototype card	UNDOCUMENTED	
310-31F	Prototype card	Prototype card	UNDOCUMENTED	
320-32F	Fixed disk adapter	UNDOCUMENTED	UNDOCUMENTED	
330-33F	UNDOCUMENTED	UNDOCUMENTED	UNDOCUMENTED	
340-34F	DCA 3278	UNDOCUMENTED	UNDOCUMENTED	XT uses 348-34F only
350-35F	DCA 3278	UNDOCUMENTED	UNDOCUMENTED	XT uses 350-357 only
360-36F	PC network	RESERVED	UNDOCUMENTED	XT uses 360-367 only
370-37F	Parallel printer	Parallel printer 1	Parallel port 2	All use 378-37F, except PS/2 uses 378-37B
380-38F	SDLC or second bisync controller	SDLC or second bisync controller	UNDOCUMENTED	
390-39F	Cluster adapter	Cluster adapter	UNDOCUMENTED	XT uses 390-393 only
3A0-3AF	First bisync controller	First bisync controller	UNDOCUMENTED	
3B0-3BF	Monochrome display and printer adapter	Monochrome display and printer adapter	Video subsystem, parallel 1	All use 3BC-3BF for parallel port
3C0-3CF	Enhanced graphics adapter	Enhanced graphics adapter	Video subsystem	
3D0-3DF	Color graphics adapter	Color graphics adapter	Video subsystem	
3E0-3EF	UNDOCUMENTED	UNDOCUMENTED	UNDOCUMENTED	ISA uses 3E8-3EF only
3F0-3FF	Floppy disk adapter, serial 1	Floppy disk adapter, serial 1	Diskette drive controller, serial 1	3F0-3F7 for disk, 3F8-3FF for async comm
400-4FF	UNUSED*	EISA: DMA	UNUSED	
500-7FF	UNUSED*	EISA: Alias of 100-3FF	UNUSED	
800-8FF	UNUSED*	EISA: CMOS RAM	UNUSED	
900-BFF	UNUSED*	EISA: Alias of 100-3FF	UNUSED	
C00-FFF	UNUSED*	EISA: Misc. Ports, RESERVED	UNUSED	
1000-1FFF	UNUSED*	EISA: Slot 1 and alias of 100-3FF	Parallel 1, 4†	Alternates: 100H of slot, 200H of alias
2000-2FFF	UNUSED*	EISA: Slot 2 and alias of 100-3FF	Video subsystem†	Alternates: 100H of slot, 200H of alias
3000-3FFF	UNUSED*	EISA: Slot 3 and alias of 100-3FF	Serial 3, 4†	Alternates: 100H of slot, 200H of alias
4000-4FFF	UNUSED*	EISA: Slot 4 and alias of 100-3FF	Serial 5, 6†	Alternates: 100H of slot, 200H of alias
5000-5FFF	UNUSED*	EISA: Slot 5 and alias of 100-3FF	Serial 7, 8†	Alternates: 100H of slot, 200H of alias
6000-6FFF	UNUSED*	EISA: Slot 6 and alias of 100-3FF	UNUSED	Alternates: 100H of slot, 200H of alias
7000-7FFF	UNUSED*	EISA: Slot 7 and alias of 100-3FF	UNUSED	Alternates: 100H of slot, 200H of alias
8000-8FFF	UNUSED*	EISA: Slot 8 and alias of 100-3FF	Serial 1, 2 DMA mode†	Alternates: 100H of slot, 200H of alias
9FFF-FFFF	UNUSED*	EISA: Undefined	Serial 3-8 DMA mode†	

†PS/2 Model 90

Note: The AT also uses additional ports in the range 6E2-E2E1 for GPIB, Cluster, and Data Acquisition adapters

Source: IBM PC/XT and Portable PC Technical Reference, pages 1-24 and 1-25
IBM PC/AT Technical Reference, pages 1-37 and 1-38
IBM PS/2 Model 50 and 60 Technical Reference, page 1-9
IBM PS/2 Model 80 Technical Reference, page 1-7
IBM PS/2 Hardware Interface Technical Reference, System Specific Information, pages Model 90 1-4 and Model 95 1-4
Inside the EISA Computers (Addison-Wesley), pages 74 through 81

7.005. PC INTERRUPT USAGE SUMMARY

Int Number	*Vector Addr*	*Interrupt Name*	*Type*	*BIOS Entry Label*	*Comments*
0H	00-03	Divide-by-zero exception	System	D11	
1H	04-07	Single step	System	D11	
2H	08-0B	Nonmaskable	System	NMI_INT	
3H	0C-0F	Breakpoint	System	D11	
4H	10-13	Overflow	System	D11	
5H	14-17	Print screen	BIOS	PRINT_SCREEN	See 4.001. BIOS Services Summary
6H	18-1B	RESERVED		D11	
7H	1C-1F	RESERVED		D11	
8H	20-23	Time of day service	Hardware	TIMER_INT	IRQ0 timer 0
9H	24-27	Keyboard service	Hardware	KB_INT	IRQ1 keyboard
AH	28-2B	RESERVED		D11	IRQ2 AT slave 8259
BH	2C-2F	Communications service COM1:	Hardware	D11	IRQ3 COM1:
CH	30-33	Communications service COM2:	Hardware	D11	IRQ4 COM1:
DH	34-37	Disk service/alt. printer service	Hardware	D11	IRQ5 PC: fixed disk adapter AT: LPT2
EH	38-3B	Diskette service	Hardware	DISK_INT	IRQ6 floppy disk adapter
FH	3C-3F	Printer service	Hardware	D11	IRQ7 LPT1:
10H	40-43	Video I/O	BIOS	VIDEO_IO	See 4.001. BIOS Services Summary
11H	44-47	Equipment check	BIOS	EQUIPMENT	See 4.001. BIOS Services Summary
12H	48-4B	Memory size	BIOS	MEMORY_SIZE_DETERMINE	See 4.001. BIOS Services Summary
13H	4C-4F	Disk I/O	BIOS	DISKETTE_IO	See 4.001. BIOS Services Summary
14H	50-53	Communications	BIOS	RS232_IO	See 4.001. BIOS Services Summary
15H	54-57	PC: cassette AT: extended services	BIOS	CASSETTE_IO	See 4.001. BIOS Services Summary
16H	58-5B	Keyboard I/O	BIOS	KEYBOARD_IO	See 4.001. BIOS Services Summary
17H	5C-5F	Printer	BIOS	PRINTER_IO	See 4.001. BIOS Services Summary
18H	60-63	Resident BASIC	BIOS	F600:0000	See 4.001. BIOS Services Summary
19H	64-67	Bootstrap	BIOS	BOOT_STRAP	See 4.001. BIOS Services Summary
1AH	68-6B	Time of day	BIOS	TIME_OF_DAY	See 4.001. BIOS Services Summary
1BH	6C-6F	Keyboard break	BIOS	DUMMY_RETURN	Ctrl-Break exit
1CH	70-73	Timer tick	BIOS	DUMMY_RETURN	18.2 ticks/second
1DH	74-77	Video parameters	BIOS	VIDEO_PARMS	Table address of video parameters
1EH	78-7B	Disk parameters	BIOS	DISK_BASE	Table address of disk parameters
1FH	7C-7F	Video graphics	BIOS		Table address of graphics characters
20H	80-83	Program termination	DOS		Obsolete
21H	84-87	General function services	DOS		All DOS services available through this int
22H	88-8B	Terminate address	DOS		
23H	8C-8F	Ctrl-C exit address	DOS		
24H	90-93	Critical-error-handler address	DOS		
25H	94-97	Absolute disk read	DOS		Read logical sector(s)
26H	98-9B	Absolute disk write	DOS		Write logical sector(s)
27H	9C-9F	Terminate/stay resident	DOS		Obsolete
28H	A0-A3	Idle handler	DOS		Obsolete
29H	A4-A7	RESERVED	DOS		TTY output
2AH	A8-AB	RESERVED	DOS		Network critical section
2BH	AC-AF	RESERVED	DOS		
2CH	B0-B3	RESERVED	DOS		
2DH	B4-B7	RESERVED	DOS		
2EH	B8-BB	RESERVED	DOS		
2FH	BC-BF	Multiplex	DOS		
30H	C0-C3	RESERVED	DOS		Entry point
31H	C4-C7	RESERVED	DOS		Entry point
32H	C8-CB	RESERVED	DOS		
33H	CC-CF	RESERVED	DOS		
34H	D0-D3	RESERVED	DOS		
35H	D4-D7	RESERVED	DOS		
36H	D8-DB	RESERVED	DOS		
37H	DC-DF	RESERVED	DOS		
38H	E0-E3	RESERVED	DOS		
39H	E4-E7	RESERVED	DOS		
3AH	E8-EB	RESERVED	DOS		
3BH	EC-EF	RESERVED	DOS		
3CH	F0-F3	RESERVED	DOS		
3DH	F4-F7	RESERVED	DOS		
3EH	F8-FB	RESERVED	DOS		
3FH	FC-FF	RESERVED	DOS		
40H	100-103	RESERVED	BIOS		Revectored disk I/O (Int 13)
41H	104-107	RESERVED	BIOS		Fixed disk 0 parameter table address
42H	108-10B	RESERVED	BIOS		EGA revectored video (Int 10)
43H	10C-10F	RESERVED	BIOS		EGA video parameters table address
44H	110-113	RESERVED	BIOS		EGA/PCjr 1st 128 chars table address
45H	114-117	RESERVED	BIOS		
46H	118-11B	RESERVED	BIOS		Fixed disk 1 parameter table address

(Continued)

7.005. PC INTERRUPT USAGE SUMMARY (continued)

Int Number	Vector Addr	Interrupt Name	Type	BIOS Entry Label	Comments
47H	11C-11F	RESERVED	BIOS		
48H	120-123	RESERVED	BIOS		PCjr translate from 62-key keyboard
49H	124-127	RESERVED	BIOS		PCjr scan code translate table address
4AH	128-12B	ROM BIOS alarm handler	BIOS		Address of user-installed alarm
4BH	12C-12F	RESERVED	BIOS		
4CH	130-133	RESERVED	BIOS		
4DH	134-137	RESERVED	BIOS		
4EH	138-13B	RESERVED	BIOS		
4FH	13C-13F	RESERVED	BIOS		
50H	140-143	AT alarm interrupt	BIOS		
51H	144-147	RESERVED	BIOS		
52H	148-14B	RESERVED	BIOS		
53H	14C-14F	RESERVED	BIOS		
54H	150-153	RESERVED	BIOS		
55H	154-157	RESERVED	BIOS		
56H	158-15B	RESERVED	BIOS		
57H	15C-15F	RESERVED	BIOS		
58H	160-163	RESERVED	BIOS		
59H	164-167	RESERVED	BIOS		
5AH	168-16B	Functions	PC Cluster		
5BH	16C-16F	Revectored in 19H	PC Cluster		
5CH	170-173	Network use	PC Cluster		NETBIOS entry point
5DH	174-177	RESERVED	BIOS		
5EH	178-17B	RESERVED	BIOS		
5FH	17C-17F	RESERVED	BIOS		
60H	180-183	RESERVED	PROGS		
61H	184-187	RESERVED	PROGS		
62H	188-18B	RESERVED	PROGS		
63H	18C-18F	RESERVED	PROGS		
64H	190-193	RESERVED	PROGS		
65H	194-197	RESERVED	PROGS		
66H	198-19B	RESERVED	PROGS		
67H	19C-19F	Functions	LIM EMS		See 5.120. Expanded Memory Manager Functions Summary
68H	1A0-1A3	UNUSED	-		
69H	1A4-1A7	UNUSED	-		
6AH	1A8-1AB	UNUSED	-		
6BH	1AC-1AF	UNUSED	-		
6CH	1B0-1B3	UNUSED	-		Also resume system vector
6DH	1B4-1B7	UNUSED	-		
6EH	1B8-1BB	UNUSED	-		
6FH	1BC-1BF	UNUSED	-		
70H	1C0-1C3	PC: RESERVED AT/PS2:IRQ8 real time clock	AT BIOS	RTC_INT	IRQ8
71H	1C4-1C7	PC:RESERVED AT/PS2:IRQ9 redirected to IRQ2	AT BIOS	RE_DIRECT	IRQ9
72H	1C8-1CB	PC:RESERVED AT/PS2:IRQ10	AT BIOS	D11	IRQ10
73H	1CC-1CF	PC:RESERVED AT/PS2:IRQ11	AT BIOS	D11	IRQ11
74H	1D0-1D3	PC:RESERVED AT/PS2:IRQ12	AT BIOS	D11	IRQ12
75H	1D4-1D7	PC:RESERVED AT/PS2:IRQ13, 80287	AT BIOS	INT_287	IRQ13
76H	1D8-1DB	PC:RESERVED AT/PS2: fixed disk controller	AT BIOS	D11	IRQ14
77H	1DC-1DF	PC:RESERVED AT/PS2:IRQ15	AT BIOS	D11	IRQ15
78H-7FH	1E0-1FF	NOT USED			
80H-85H	200-217	RESERVED FOR BASIC			
86H-F0H	218-3C3	Used by BASIC			
F1H-FFH	3C4-3FF	NOT USED			

Source: IBM PC/XT Technical Reference, Section 2 (see BIOS listings or page 2-4 of old XT manual for summary)
IBM PC/AT Technical Reference, Section 5 (see pages 5-5 and 5-6 for summary)
IBM DOS 3.3 Technical Reference, pages 6-13 through 6-33
IBM PS/2 and PC BIOS Interface Technical Reference, page 2-3
Microsoft MS-DOS 5.0 Programmer's Reference, pages 107 through 109

See Also: 4.001. BIOS Services Summary
5.001. DOS Interrupt Usage by Version
5.066. INT 33H, Mouse Functions Summary
5.120. INT 67H, Expanded Memory Manager Functions Summary

7.006. PC POST (DIAGNOSTICS) ERROR CODES

Code	*Location of Error/Description*	*Comments*
01x	Undetermined	
02x	Power supply	
1xx	System board	
2xx	Memory (RAM)	*
3xx	Keyboard	
4xx	Monochrome adapter or display	Parallel port on PS/2
5xx	Color graphics adapter or display	
6xx	Floppy drive or adapter	
7xx	Math coprocessor	
9xx	Parallel printer adapter	
10xx	Alternate parallel printer adapter	
11xx	Async comm adapter	System board async port on PS/2
12xx	Alternate async comm adapter	Dual async adapter on PS/2
13xx	Game control adapter	
14xx	Matrix or graphics printer	
15xx	Syncrhonous data link control adapter	
16xx	Display emulation (327x, 5520, 525x)	
17xx	Fixed disk or adapter	
18xx	I/O expansion unit	
19xx	3270 PC attachment card	
20xx	Binary synchronous comm adapter	
21xx	Alternate binary synchronous comm adapter	
22xx	Cluster adapter	
24xx	Enhanced graphics adapter	System board VGA on PS/2
25xx	Alternate enhanced graphics adapter	
26xx	XT/370	
27xx	AT/370	
28xx	3278/79 emulation adapter	
29xx	Color/graphics printer	
30xx	Primary PC network adapter	
31xx	Secondary PC network adapter	
33xx	Compact printer	
36xx	GPIB adapter, IEEE 488 Adapter	
38xx	Data acquisition adapter	
39xx	Professional graphics controller	
48xx	Internal modem	
49xx	Alternate internal modem	
71xx	Voice communications adapter	
73xx	External 3.5" disk drive	
74xx	VGA display adapter	
84xx	PS/2 speech option	
85xx	Expanded memory adapter	
86xx	Mouse	
89xx	Music feature card	
100xx	Multiprotocol adapter	
104xx	ESDI fixed disk	
ROM ERROR	Checksum error in ROM memory	
PARITY CHECK 1	System board parity error	Error location indicated
PARITY CHECK 2	Memory board parity error	Error location indicated
CC0000 ROM	PC network adapter	
I/O ROM CC0000	PC network adapter	
110	System board parity check	PS/2 only
111	Memory adapter parity check	PS/2 only

*See 7.007. PC POST Memory Error Codes

Source: Upgrading and Repairing PCs (Que), pages 557 through 558
PC Configuration Handbook, 2nd Edition (Bantam), pages 68 through 69

7.007. PC POST MEMORY ERROR CODES

Error Code as It Appears for Machine

PC1*	PC2*	XT*	AT†	Failed Chip Is Located in
00xx	0xxx	0xxxx	00xxxx-03xxxx	System board, bank 0
04xx	1xxx	1xxxx	04xxxx-07xxxx	System board, bank 1
08xx	2xxx	2xxxx		System board, bank 2
0Cxx	3xxx	3xxxx		System board, bank 3
10xx-84xx	40xx-94xx	40xxx-94xxx		Memory expansion option board
			08xxxx-09xxxx	128K expansion option
			10xxxx-17xxxx	512K expansion option 1
			18xxxx-1Fxxxx	512K expansion option 2
			20xxxx-27xxxx	512K expansion option 3
			28xxxx-2Fxxxx	512K expansion option 4
			30xxxx-37xxxx	512K expansion option 5

*xx=00 for leftmost chip, then 01, 02, 04, 08, 10, 20, 40, and 80 proceeding to the right.
†xxxx=0100 for leftmost chip, then 0200, 0400, 0800, 1000, 2000, 4000, 8000, 0000 for banks 0 and 2.
xxxx=0001 for leftmost chip, then 0002, 0004, 0008, 0010, 0020, 0040, 0080, 0200 for banks 1 and 3.

Note: Bank 0 is the topmost looking down from the front; bank 3 is the bottommost.

Source: PC Configuration Handbook, 2nd Edition (Bantam), pages 266 through 267

7.008. PC SYSTEM BOARD SWITCH SETTINGS

For Switch 1

Switch Number	Function	Settings
1	Number of drives	ON=drives installed; OFF=no drives (see switch 7/8)
2	Not used (PC1)	Must be ON (PC1)
3 & 4	Memory on system board	ON ON = 16K (PC1) or 64K (PC2) OFF ON = 32K (PC1) or 128K (PC2) ON OFF = 48K (PC1) or 192K (PC2) OFF OFF = 64K (PC1) or 256K (PC2)
5 & 6	Display adapter	ON ON = no adapter OFF ON = CGA, 40-columns ON OFF = CGA, 80 columns OFF OFF = MDA, or more than one adapter
7 & 8	Floppy drives	ON ON = 1 drive OFF ON = 2 drives ON OFF = 3 drives OFF OFF = 4 drives

For Switch 2

Switch Number	Function	Settings
1 through 5	Memory Installed	ON ON ON ON ON = 16-64K* OFF ON ON ON ON = 96K† ON OFF ON ON ON = 128K† OFF OFF ON ON ON = 160K† ON ON OFF ON ON = 192K† OFF ON OFF ON ON = 224K† ON OFF OFF ON ON = 256K† OFF OFF OFF ON ON = 288K† ON ON ON OFF ON = 320K† OFF ON ON OFF ON = 352K† ON OFF ON OFF ON = 384K† OFF OFF ON OFF ON = 416K† ON ON OFF OFF ON = 448K† OFF ON OFF OFF ON = 480K† ON OFF OFF OFF ON = 512K† OFF OFF OFF OFF ON = 544K† ON ON ON ON OFF = 576K† OFF ON ON ON OFF = 608K† ON OFF ON ON OFF = 640K†
6 - 8	NOT USED	Must be OFF (switch 7 reserved for 8087 on PC2)

*SW1 switches 3 & 4 control total memory.
†SW1 switches 3 & 4 should be OFF.

Source: IBM PC Guide to Operations, pages Options 6 through 24

See Also: 7.009. XT System Board Switch Settings

7.009. XT SYSTEM BOARD SWITCH SETTINGS

Switch Number	Function	Settings
1	Test	ON=loops on POST routine; OFF=normal operation
2	Coprocessor	ON=8087 installed; OFF=no 8087
3 & 4	System board RAM*	ON ON = 64K (64/256K) or 256K (256/640K) OFF ON = 128K (64/256K) or 512K (256/640K) ON OFF = 192K (64/256K) or 576K (256/640K) OFF OFF = 256K (64/256K) or 640K (256/640K)
5 & 6	Display adapter	ON ON = no adapter OFF ON = CGA, 40-columns ON OFF = CGA, 80 columns OFF OFF = MDA, or more than one adapter
7 & 8	Floppy drives	ON ON = 1 drive OFF ON = 2 drives ON OFF = 3 drives OFF OFF = 4 drives

*There are two types of system boards: 64/256K and 256/640K.

Note: Normal switch setting would be OFF OFF OFF OFF OFF OFF ON ON (256K, 1 floppy, MDA).

Source: IBM PC/XT and Portable PC Technical Reference, page 1-28

7.010. AT J18 RAM JUMPER

Pin Number	Signal Name
1	No connection
2	-RAM SEL
3	Ground

Note:
- Connector is a 3-pin keyed Berg-strip connector (keyed on pin 3).
- To enable 2nd 256K on system board, jumper pins 1 and 2.
- To disable 2nd 256K on system board, jumper pins 2 and 3.

Source: IBM PC/AT Technical Reference, pages 1-40 through 1-41

7.011. AT DISPLAY SWITCH (SW1)

Switch Number	Function	Settings
1	Display type	ON=CGA, EGA, or PGA is primary display OFF=MDA or EGA is primary display

Note: ON is toward front of the machine.

Source: IBM PC/AT Technical Reference, page 1-41

7.012. PC 83-KEY KEYBOARD NUMBERS AND SCAN CODES

Key Number	Hex Scan Code	Base Case	Uppercase	With Ctrl	With Alt
1	01	Esc	Esc	Suppressed	Suppressed
2	02	1	!	Suppressed	Extended
3	03	2	@	Nul (Extended)	Extended
4	04	3	#	Suppressed	Extended
5	05	4	$	Suppressed	Extended
6	06	5	%	Suppressed	Extended
7	07	6	^	RS (30)	Extended
8	08	7	&	Suppressed	Extended
9	09	8	*	Suppressed	Extended
10	0A	9	(	Suppressed	Extended
11	0B	0	)	Suppressed	Extended
12	0C	-		US (31)	Extended
13	0D	=	+	Suppressed	Extended
14	0E	Backspace (8)	Backspace (8)	Del (127)	Suppressed
15	0F	Tab (9)	Back Tab (Extended)	Suppressed	Suppressed
16	10	q	Q	DC1 (17)	Extended
17	11	w	W	ETB (23)	Extended
18	12	e	E	ENQ (5)	Extended

(Continued)

7.012. PC 83-KEY KEYBOARD NUMBERS AND SCAN CODES (continued)

Key Number	*Hex Scan Code*	*Base Case*	*Uppercase*	*With Ctrl*	*With Alt*
19	13	r	R	DC2 (18)	Extended
20	14	t	T	DC4 (20)	Extended
21	15	y	Y	EM (25)	Extended
22	16	u	U	NAK (21)	Extended
23	17	i	I	HT (9)	Extended
24	18	o	O	SI (15)	Extended
25	19	p	P	DLE (16)	Extended
26	1A	[	{	Esc (27)	Extended
27	1B	]	}	GS (29)	Suppressed
28	1C	Enter	Enter	LF (10)	Suppressed
29	1D	Ctrl	Suppressed	Suppressed	Suppressed
30	1E	a	A	SOH (1)	Extended
31	1F	s	S	DC3 (19)	Extended
32	20	d	D	EOT (4)	Extended
33	21	f	F	ACK (6)	Extended
34	22	g	G	BEL (7)	Extended
35	23	h	H	BS (8)	Extended
36	24	j	J	LF (10)	Extended
37	25	k	K	VT (11)	Extended
38	26	l	L	FF (12)	Extended
39	27	;	:	Suppressed	Suppressed
40	28	'	"	Suppressed	Suppressed
41	29	`	~	FS (28)	Suppressed
42	2A	Left Shift	Suppressed	Suppressed	Suppressed
43	2B	\	|	FS (28)	Suppressed
44	2C	z	Z	SUB (26)	Extended
45	2D	x	X	CAN (24)	Extended
46	2E	c	C	ETX (3)	Extended
47	2F	v	V	SYN (22)	Extended
48	30	b	B	STX (2)	Extended
49	31	n	N	SO (14)	Extended
50	32	m	M	CR (13)	Extended
51	33	,	<	Suppressed	Suppressed
52	34	.	>	Suppressed	Suppressed
53	35	/	?	Suppressed	Suppressed
54	36	Right Shift	Suppressed	Suppressed	Suppressed
55	37	*	Print Screen	Undefined	Undefined
56	38	Alt	Suppressed	Suppressed	Suppressed
57	39	Spacebar	Spacebar	Spacebar	Spacebar
58	3A	Caps Lock	Suppressed	Suppressed	Suppressed
59	3B	F1	Extended	Extended	Extended
60	3C	F2	Extended	Extended	Extended
61	3D	F3	Extended	Extended	Extended
62	3E	F4	Extended	Extended	Extended
63	3F	F5	Extended	Extended	Extended
64	40	F6	Extended	Extended	Extended
65	41	F7	Extended	Extended	Extended
66	42	F8	Extended	Extended	Extended
67	43	F9	Extended	Extended	Extended
68	44	F10	Extended	Extended	Extended
69	45	Num Lock	Suppressed	Pause	Suppressed
70	46	Scroll Lock	Suppressed	Break	Suppressed
71	47	Home	NA	Clear Screen	Suppressed
72	48	Up Arrow	NA	Suppressed	Suppressed
73	49	PgUp	NA	Top of Text	Suppressed
74	4A	Keypad -	NA	Suppressed	Suppressed
75	4B	Left Arrow	NA	Extended	Suppressed
76	4C	Keypad 5	NA	Suppressed	Suppressed
77	4D	Right Arrow	NA	Extended	Suppressed
78	4E	Keypad +	NA	Suppressed	Suppressed
79	4F	End	NA	Extended	Suppressed
80	50	Down Arrow	NA	Suppressed	Suppressed
81	51	PgDn	NA	Extended	Suppressed
82	52	Ins	NA	Suppressed	Suppressed
83	53	Del	NA	Reset the system	

Note: • Extended means the first scan code returned is 00, followed by an extended ASCII code.
• Suppressed indicates the key combination is not passed by the keyboard routine in BIOS.

Source: IBM PC/XT and Portable PC Technical Reference, pages 4-7 through 4-8, and 4-18

See Also: 1.21. ASCII Character Set
1.23. IBM Keyboard Extended Function Codes

7.013. AT 84-KEY KEYBOARD NUMBERS AND SCAN CODES

Key Number	Hex Scan Code	Base Case	Uppercase
1	29	`	~
2	02	1	!
3	03	2	@
4	04	3	#
5	05	4	$
6	06	5	%
7	07	6	^
8	08	7	&
9	09	8	*
10	0A	9	(
11	0B	0	)
12	0C	-	_
13	0D	=	+
14	2B	\	|
15	0E	Backspace	Backspace
16	0F	Tab	Back Tab
17	10	q	Q
18	11	w	W
19	12	e	E
20	13	r	R
21	14	t	T
22	15	y	Y
23	16	u	U
24	17	i	I
25	18	o	O
26	19	p	P
27	1A	[	{
28	1B	]	}
30	1D	Ctrl (suppressed)	Suppressed
31	1E	a	A
32	1F	s	S
33	20	d	D
34	21	f	F
35	22	g	G
36	23	h	H
37	24	j	J
38	25	k	K
39	26	l	L
40	27	;	:
41	28	'	"
43	1C	Enter	Enter
44	2A	Left Shift (suppressed)	Suppressed
46	2C	z	Z
47	2D	x	X
48	2E	c	C
49	2F	v	V
50	30	b	B
51	31	n	N
52	32	m	M
53	33	,	<
54	34	.	>
55	35	/	?
57	36	Right Shift (suppressed)	Suppressed
58	38	Alt (suppressed)	Suppressed
61	39	Spacebar	Spacebar
64	3A	Caps Lock (suppressed)	Suppressed
65	3C	F2	
66	3E	F4	
67	40	F6	
68	42	F8	
69	44	F10	
70	3B	F1	
71	3D	F3	
72	3F	F5	
73	41	F7	
74	43	F9	
90	01	Esc	Esc
91	47	Keypad 7	Home

(Continued)

7.013. AT 84-KEY KEYBOARD NUMBERS AND SCAN CODES (continued)

Key Number	Hex Scan Code	Base Case	Uppercase
92	4B	Keypad 4	Left Arrow
93	4F	Keypad 1	End
95	45	Num Lock (suppressed)	Suppressed
96	48	Keypad 8	Up Arrow
97	4C	Keypad 5	Suppressed
98	50	Keypad 2	Down Arrow
99	52	-	Ins
100	46	Scroll Lock (suppressed)	Suppressed
101	49	Keypad 9	Page Up
102	4D	Keypad 6	Right Arrow
103	51	Keypad 3	Page Down
104	53	Keypad .	Delete
105¥	54	Sys Req	
106¥	Not documented	Keypad *	Prt Sc
107¥	4A	Keypad -	
108¥	4E	Keypad +	

¥The base case and uppercase of keys 105 through 108 differ in the source. The base case and uppercase used in this table are shown on the U.S. English keyboard diagram (page 4-33).

Note:
- Some key numbers and scan-code numbers are missing because they are reserved by IBM.
- Suppressed indicates the key combination is not passed by the keyboard routine in BIOS.

Source: IBM PC/AT Technical Reference, pages 1-44 through 1-46.4, 4-18 through 4-20, and 4-33

See Also:
1.21. ASCII Character Set
1.23. IBM Keyboard Extended Function Codes
7.012. PC 83-Key Keyboard Numbers and Scan Codes
7.014. AT 101/102-Key Keyboard Numbers and Scan Codes

7.014. AT 101/102-KEY KEYBOARD NUMBERS AND SCAN CODES

Key Number	*Hex Scan Code*	*Base Case*	*Uppercase*
1	29	`	~
2	02	1	!
3	03	2	@
4	04	3	#
5	05	4	$
6	06	5	%
7	07	6	^
8	08	7	&
9	09	8	*
10	0A	9	(
11	0B	0	)
12	0C	-	
13	0D	=	+
15	0E	Backspace	Backspace
16	0F	Tab	Back Tab
17	10	q	Q
18	11	w	W
19	12	e	E
20	13	r	R
21	14	t	T
22	15	y	Y
23	16	u	U
24	17	i	I
25	18	o	O
26	19	p	P
27	1A	[	{
28	1B	]	}
29	2B	\	|
30	3A	Caps Lock (suppressed)	Suppressed
31	1E	a	A
32	1F	s	S
33	20	d	D
34	21	f	F
35	22	g	G
36	23	h	H
37	24	j	J
38	25	k	K
39	26	l	L
40	27	;	:
41	28	'	"
42†	2B	#	~
43	1C	Enter	Enter
44	2A	Left Shift (suppressed)	Suppressed
45†	D5	\	|
46	2C	z	Z
47	2D	x	X
48	2E	c	C
49	2F	v	V
50	30	b	B
51	31	n	N
52	32	m	M
53	33	,	<
54	34	.	>
55	35	/	?
57	36	Right Shift (suppressed)	Suppressed
58	1D	Left Ctrl (suppressed)	Suppressed
60	38	Left Alt (suppressed)	Suppressed
61	39	Spacebar	Spacebar
62	E0,38	Right Alt (suppressed)	Suppressed
64	E0,1D	Right Ctrl (suppressed)	Suppressed
75	E0,52	Insert	
76	E0,53	Delete	
79	E0,4B	Left Arrow	
80	E0,47	Home	
81	EO,4F	End	

(Continued)

7.014. AT 101/102-KEY KEYBOARD NUMBERS AND SCAN CODES (continued)

Key Number	Hex Scan Code	Base Case	Uppercase
83	E0,48	Up Arrow	
84	E0,50	Down Arrow	
85	EO,49	PgUp	
86	E0,51	PgDn	
89	E0,4D	Right Arrow	
90	45,C5	Num Lock (suppressed)	Suppressed
91	47	Keypad 7	Home
92	4B	Keypad 4	Left Arrow
93	4F	Keypad 1	End
95	EO,35	Keypad /	Keypad /
96	48	Keypad 8	Up Arrow
97	4C	Keypad 5	
98	50	Keypad 2	Down Arrow
99	52	Keypad 0	Ins
100	E0,37	Keypad *	Keypad *
101	49	Keypad 9	Page Up
102	4D	Keypad 6	Right Arrow
103	51	Keypad 3	Page Down
104	53	Keypad .	Delete
105	4A	Keypad -	Keypad -
106	4E	Keypad +	Keypad +
108	E0,1C	Keypad Enter	Keypad Enter
110	01	Esc	Esc
112	3B	F1	
113	3C	F2	
114	3D	F3	
115	3E	F4	
116	3F	F5	
117	40	F6	
118	41	F7	
119	42	F8	
120	43	F9	
121	44	F10	
122	D9	F11	
123	DA	F12	
124	2A,37	Print Screen	
125	46	Scroll Lock	
126	1D,E0,45,E0,C5,9D	Pause	

†Only applicable to non-U.S. keyboards. Actual characters vary depending on the country of the keyboard.

Note:
- Some key numbers and scan-code numbers are missing because they are reserved by IBM.
- Suppressed indicates the key combination is not passed by the keyboard routine in BIOS.

Source: IBM PC/AT Technical Reference, pages 1-45 through 1-46.4, and 4-65 through 4-68

See Also:
1.21. ASCII Character Set
1.22. IBM ASCII Character Set
7.012. PC 83-Key Keyboard Numbers and Scan Codes
7.013. AT 84-Key Keyboard Numbers and Scan Codes
7.015. PS/2 Keyboard Numbers and Scan Codes

7.015. PS/2 KEYBOARD NUMBERS AND SCAN CODES

Key Number	*Set 1 Make/Break*	*Set 2 Make/Break*	*Set 3 Make/Break*	*Base Case*	*Uppercase*
1	29 / A9	0E / F0 0E	0E / F0 0E	'	~
2	02 / 82	16 / F0 16	16 / F0 16	1	!
3	03 / 83	1E / F0 1E	1E / F0 1E	2	@
4	04 / 84	26 / F0 26	26 / F0 26	3	#
5	05 / 85	25 / F0 25	25 / F0 25	4	$
6	06 / 86	2E / F0 2E	2E / F0 2E	5	%
7	07 / 87	36 / F0 36	36 / F0 36	6	^
8	08 / 88	3D / F0 3D	3D / F0 3D	7	&
9	09 / 89	3E / F0 3E	3E / F0 3E	8	*
10	0A / 8A	46 / F0 46	46 / F0 46	9	(
11	0B / 8B	45 / F0 45	45 / F0 45	0	)
12	0C / 8C	4E / F0 4E	4E / F0 4E	-	
13	0D / 8D	55 / F0 55	55 / F0 55	=	+
15	0E / 8E	66 / F0 66	66 / F0 66	Backspace	Backspace
16	0F / 8F	0D / F0 0D	0D / F0 0D	Tab	Back Tab
17	10 / 90	15 / F0 15	15 / F0 15	q	Q
18	11 / 91	1D / F0 1D	1D / F0 1D	w	W
19	12 / 92	24 / F0 24	24 / F0 24	e	E
20	13 / 93	2D / F0 2D	2D / F0 2D	r	R
21	14 / 94	2C / F0 2C	2C / F0 2C	t	T
22	15 / 95	35 / F0 35	35 / F0 35	y	Y
23	16 / 96	3C / F0 3C	3C / F0 3C	u	U
24	17 / 97	43 / F0 43	43 / F0 43	i	I
25	18 / 98	44 / F0 44	44 / F0 44	o	O
26	19 / 99	4D / F0 4D	4D / F0 4D	p	P
27	1A / 9A	54 / F0 54	54 / F0 54	[	{
28	1B / 9B	5B / F0 5B	5B / F0 5B	]	}
29†	2B/AB	5D / F0 5D	5C / F0 5C	\	|
30	3A / BA	58 / F0 58	14 / F0 14	Caps Lock	
31	1E / 9E	1C / F0 1C	1C / F0 1C	a	A
32	1F / 9F	1B / F0 1B	1B / F0 1B	s	S
33	20 / A0	23 / F0 23	23 / F0 23	d	D
34	21 / A1	2B / F0 2B	2B / F0 2B	f	F
35	22 / A2	34 / F0 34	34 / F0 34	g	G
36	23 / A3	33 / F0 33	33 / F0 33	h	H
37	24 / A4	3B / F0 3B	3B / F0 3B	j	J
38	25 / A5	42 / F0 42	42 / F0 42	k	K
39	26 / A6	4B / F0 4B	4B / F0 4B	l	L
40	27 / A7	4C / F0 4C	4C / F0 4C	;	:
41	28 / A8	52 / F0 52	52 / F0 52	'	"
42¥	2B/AB	5D / F0 5D	53 / F0 53		
43	1C / 9C	5A / F0 5A	5A / F0 5A	Enter	Enter
44	2A / AA	12 / F0 12	12 / F0 12	Left Shift	
45¥	56/D6	61 / F0 61	13 / F0 13		
46	2C / AC	1A / F0 1A	1A / F0 1A	z	Z
47	2D / AD	22 / F0 22	22 / F0 22	x	X
48	2E /AE	21 / F0 21	21 / F0 21	c	C
49	2F / AF	2A / F0 2A	2A / F0 2A	v	V
50	30 / B0	32 / F0 32	32 / F0 32	b	B
51	31 / B1	31 / F0 31	31 / F0 31	n	N
52	32 / B2	3A / F0 3A	3A / F0 3A	m	M
53	33 / B3	41 / F0 41	41 / F0 41	,	<
54	34 / B4	49 / F0 49	49 / F0 49	.	>
55	35 / B5	4A / F0 4A	4A / F0 4A	/	?
57	36 / B6	59 / F0 59	59 / F0 59	Right Shift	
58	1D / 9D	14 / F0 14	11 / F0 11	Left Ctrl	
60	38 / B8	11 / F0 11	19 / F0 19	Left Alt	
61	39 / B9	29 / F0 29	29 / F0 29	Spacebar	Spacebar
62	E0 38 / E0 B8	E0 11 / E0 F0 11	39 / F0 39	Right Alt	
64	E0 1D / E0 9D	E0 14 / E0 F0 14	58 / F0 58	Right Ctrl	
75	E0 52 / E0 D2 (base)	E0 70 / E0 F0 70 (base)	67 / F0 67	Insert	
76	E0 53 / E0 D3 (base)	E0 71 / E0 F0 71 (base)	64 / F0 64	Delete	
79	E0 4B / E0 CB (base)	E0 6B / E0 F0 6B (base)	61 / F0 61	Left Arrow	
80	E0 47 / E0 C7 (base)	E0 6C / E0 F0 6C (base)	6E / F0 6E	Home	
81	E0 4F / E0 CF (base)	E0 69 / E0 F0 69 (base)	65 / F0 65	End	
83	E0 48 / E0 C8 (base)	E0 75 / E0 F0 75 (base)	63 / F0 63	Up Arrow	
84	E0 50 / E0 D0 (base)	E0 72 / E0 F0 72 (base)	60 / F0 60	Down Arrow	
85	E0 49 / E0 C9 (base)	E0 7D / E0 F0 7D (base)	6F / F0 6F	PgUp	
86	E0 51 / E0 D1 (base)	E0 7A / E0 F0 7A (base)	6D / F0 6D	PgDn	
89	E0 4D / E0 CD (base)	E0 74 / E0 F0 74 (base)	6A / F0 6A	Right Arrow	
90	45 / C5	77 / F0 77	76 / F0 76	NumLock	
91	47 / C7	6C / F0 6C	6C / F0 6C	Keypad 7	Home

(Continued)

7.015. PS/2 KEYBOARD NUMBERS AND SCAN CODES (continued)

Key Number	*Set 1 Make/Break*	*Set 2 Make/Break*	*Set 3 Make/Break*	*Base Case*	*Uppercase*
92	4B / CB	6B / F0 6B	6B / F0 6B	Keypad 4	Left Arrow
93	4F / CF	69 / F0 69	69 / F0 69	Keypad 1	End
95	E0 35 / E0 B5 (base)	E0 4A / E0 F0 4A (base)	77 / F0 77	Keypad /	/
96	48 / C8	75 / F0 75	75 / F0 75	Keypad 8	Up Arrow
97	4C / CC	73 / F0 73	73 / F0 73	Keypad 5	
98	50 / D0	72 / F0 72	72 / F0 72	Keypad 2	Down Arrow
99	52 / D2	70 / F0 70	70 / F0 70	Keypad 0	Ins
100	37 / B7	7C / F0 7C	7E / F0 7E	Keypad *	*
101	49 / C9	7D / F0 7D	7D / F0 7D	Keypad 9	Page Up
102	4D / CD	74 / F0 74	74 / F0 74	Keypad 6	Right Arrow
103	51 / D1	7A / F0 7A	7A / F0 7A	Keypad 3	Page Down
104	53 / D3	71 / F0 71	71 / F0 71	Keypad .	Del
105	4A / CA	7B / F0 7B	84 / F0 84	Keypad -	-
106	4E / CE	79 / F0 79	7C / F0 7C	Keypad +	+
108	E0 1C / E0 9C	E0 5A / E0 F0 5A	79 / F0 79	Keypad Enter	Keypad Enter
110	01 / 81	76 / F0 76	08 / F0 08	Esc	Esc
112	3B / BB	05 / F0 05	07 / F0 07	F1	
113	3C / BC	06 / F0 06	0F / F0 0F	F2	
114	3D / BD	04 / F0 04	17 / F0 17	F3	
115	3E / BE	0C / F0 0C	1F / F0 1F	F4	
116	3F / BF	03 / F0 03	27 / F0 27	F5	
117	40 / C0	0B / F0 0B	2F / F0 2F	F6	
118	41 / C1	83 / F0 83	37 / F0 37	F7	
119	42 / C2	0A / F0 0A	3F / F0 3F	F8	
120	43 / C3	01 / F0 01	47 / F0 47	F9	
121	44 / C4	09 / F0 09	4F / F0 4F	F10	
122	57 / D7	78 / F0 78	56 / F0 56	F11	
123	58 / D8	07 / F0 07	5E / F0 5E	F12	
124	E0 2A E0 37 / E0 B7 E0 AA	E0 12 E0 7C /E0 F0 7C E0 FO 12	57 / F0 57	Print Screen	
125	46 / C6	7E / F0 7E	5F / F0 5F	Scroll Lock	
126	E1 1D 45 E1 9D C5	E1 14 77 E1 F0 14 F0 77	62 / F0 62	Pause Break	

†101-key keyboard only
¥102-key keyboard only

Note:
- Some key numbers and scan-code numbers are missing because they are reserved by IBM.
- In set 1, Shift case adds an E0 AA preceding the make code and an E0 2A following the break code (for applicable keys only).
- In set 1, Num Lock case adds an E0 2A preceding the make code and an E0 AA following the break code (for applicable keys only).
- In set 2, Shift case adds an E0 F0 12 preceding the make code and an E0 12 following the break code (for applicable keys only).
- In set 2, Num Lock case adds an E0 12 preceding the make code and an E0 F0 12 following the break code (for applicable keys only).
- Set 2 is the default set.

Source: IBM PS/2 Model 50 and 60 Technical Reference, pages 6-30 through 6-46
IBM PS/2 Model 80 Technical Reference, pages 6-30 through 6-46

See Also:
1.21. ASCII Character Set
1.23. IBM Keyboard Extended Function Codes
7.012. PC 83-Key Keyboard Numbers and Scan Codes
7.013. AT 84-Key Keyboard Numbers and Scan Codes
7.014. AT 101/102-Key Keyboard Numbers and Scan Codes

7.016. PC AND XT TYPE-AHEAD BUFFER LAYOUT

Offset	Length	Name	Description
0 (0)	word	Buffer_Head	Points to next character in buffer
2 (2)	word	Buffer_Tail	Points to next blank space in buffer
4 (4)	32 bytes	Buffer_Area	Area used to store keystroke data

Note:
- If Buffer_Head = Buffer_Tail, the buffer is empty.
- Two bytes are necessary to store each keystroke, because the IBM extended keys (F1-F10, for example) consist of 2-byte codes. If the first byte for a keystroke is nonzero, then it represents the ASCII key, and the second byte is zero. If the first byte is zero, then it represents an extended key, and the second byte indicates the actual key pressed.
- Two low-memory words store the location of the buffer start (at 0040:0080) and one byte past its end (at 0040:0082).
- On a standard PC, the keyboard buffer is usually located at 0040:001A.

Source: IBM PC/XT Technical Reference, BIOS Listing, page A-3 (original manuals only)
IBM PS/2 and PC BIOS Interface Technical Reference, pages 3-5 and 3-10

See Also: 4.002. BIOS Memory Usage Summary

7.017. AT KEYBOARD STATUS REGISTER

Bit Number

7	6	5	4	3	2	1	0	Name	Allowable Values
✔								Parity error	0=odd parity (no error), 1=even parity
	✔							Receive time out	0=no error, 1=keyboard did not finish
		✔						Transmit time out	0=no error, 1=keyboard did not finish
			✔					Inhibit switch	0=keyboard inhibited, 1=not inhibited
				✔				Command/data	0=addressed as port 60H, 1=port 64H
					✔			System flag	0=reset by power ON, 1=self test OK
						✔		Input buffer full	0=empty, 1=full
							✔	Output buffer full	0=empty, 1=full

Note: The status register is at I/O address 64H.

Source: IBM PC/AT Technical Reference, pages 1-49 through 1-50

See Also: 7.018. AT Keyboard I/O Command Summary
7.019. AT Keyboard Input Port Bit Definitions
7.020. AT Keyboard Output Port Bit Definitions

7.018. AT KEYBOARD I/O COMMAND SUMMARY

			Bit Number							
Command Value	*Command Name*	*Comments*	*7*	*6*	*5*	*4*	*3*	*2*	*1*	*0*
20H	Read keyboard controller									
60H	Write keyboard controller	Writes command byte--see bitmap at right								
		RESERVED--always 0	0							
		IBM PC compatibility mode		✔						
		IBM PC mode			✔					
		Disable keyboard				✔				
		Inhibit override					✔			
		System flag						✔		
		RESERVED--always 0							0	
		Enable output-buffer-full interrupt								✔
AAH	Self test	55H placed in output buffer if successful								
ABH	Interface test	Returns code in output buffer as follows:								
		No error detected	0	0	0	0	0	0	0	0
		Keyboard clock line is stuck low	0	0	0	0	0	0	0	1
		Keyboard clock line is stuck high	0	0	0	0	0	0	1	0
		Keyboard data line is stuck low	0	0	0	0	0	0	1	1
		Keyboard data line is stuck high	0	0	0	0	0	1	0	0
ACH	Diagnostic dump	Sends 16 bytes of controller's RAM								
ADH	Disable keyboard feature	Sets bit 4 of controller's command byte								
AEH	Enable keyboard interface	Clears bit 4 of controller's command byte								
C0H	Read input port	Reads input port, data put in output buffer								
D0H	Read output port	Reads output port, data put in output buffer								
D1H	Write output port	Next byte placed in controller's output port								
E0H	Read test inputs	T0 and T1 inputs placed in output buffer								
F0-FFH	Pulse output port	Bits 0-3 of command determine bits to pulse								

Source: IBM PC/AT Technical Reference, pages 1-51 through 1-54

7.019. AT KEYBOARD INPUT PORT BIT DEFINITIONS

Bit Number									
7	*6*	*5*	*4*	*3*	*2*	*1*	*0*	*Function*	*Allowable Values*
✔								Keyboard inhibit switch	0=inhibited, 1=not inhibited
	✔							Display switch	0=CGA, 1=MDA
		✔						Manufacturing jumper status	0=jumper installed, 1=not installed
			✔					System RAM	0=512K, 1=256K
				✔	✔	✔	✔	RESERVED	

Source: IBM PC/AT Technical Reference, page 1-55

See Also: 7.018. AT Keyboard I/O Command Summary

7.020. AT KEYBOARD OUTPUT PORT BIT DEFINITIONS

Bit Number									
7	*6*	*5*	*4*	*3*	*2*	*1*	*0*	*Function*	*Allowable Values*
✔								Keyboard data output	
	✔							Keyboard clock output	
		✔						Input buffer empty	0=buffer full, 1=buffer empty
			✔					Output buffer full	0=buffer empty, 1=buffer full
				✔	✔			RESERVED	
						✔		Gate A20	
							✔	System reset	

Source: IBM PC/AT Technical Reference, page 1-55

See Also: 7.018. AT Keyboard I/O Command Summary

7.021. AT KEYBOARD TYPEMATIC RATE DEFINITIONS

Bit Number

7	*6*	*5*	*4*	*3*	*2*	*1*	*0*	*Typematic Rate (±20%)*
0	*	*	0	0	0	0	0	30.0
0	*	*	0	0	0	0	1	26.7
0	*	*	0	0	0	1	0	24.0
0	*	*	0	0	0	1	1	21.8
0	*	*	0	0	1	0	0	20.0
0	*	*	0	0	1	0	1	18.5
0	*	*	0	0	1	1	0	17.1
0	*	*	0	0	1	1	1	16.0
0	*	*	0	1	0	0	0	15.0
0	*	*	0	1	0	0	1	13.3
0	*	*	0	1	0	1	0	12.0
0	*	*	0	1	0	1	1	10.9
0	*	*	0	1	1	0	0	10.0
0	*	*	0	1	1	0	1	9.2
0	*	*	0	1	1	1	0	8.6
0	*	*	0	1	1	1	1	8.0
0	*	*	1	0	0	0	0	7.5
0	*	*	1	0	0	0	1	6.7
0	*	*	1	0	0	1	0	6.0
0	*	*	1	0	0	1	1	5.5
0	*	*	1	0	1	0	0	5.0
0	*	*	1	0	1	0	1	4.6
0	*	*	1	0	1	1	0	4.3
0	*	*	1	0	1	1	1	4.0
0	*	*	1	1	0	0	0	3.7
0	*	*	1	1	0	0	1	3.3
0	*	*	1	1	0	1	0	3.0
0	*	*	1	1	0	1	1	2.7
0	*	*	1	1	1	0	0	2.5
0	*	*	1	1	1	0	1	2.3
0	*	*	1	1	1	1	0	2.1
0	*	*	1	1	1	1	1	2.0

*Used to set delay (1 plus binary value * 250 milliseconds)

Source: IBM PC/AT Technical Reference, pages 4-10 and 4-45

See Also: 7.018. AT Keyboard I/O Command Summary

7.022. VIDEO ADAPTER MEMORY USAGE AND OUTPUT SPECIFICATIONS

		MDA	CGA	EGA	VGA	XGA
Memory Use	Buffer Address	B0000	B8000	*	*	*
	Buffer Size	4 K	16 K	64 K - 256 K	256 K	512K-1MB
	Pages in Buffer	1	4 to 8	Max of 8	Max of 8	varies
	I/O Ports Used	3B0-3BF	3D0-3DF	3B0-3DF	3B0-3DF	3B0-3DF
Output	Bandwidth	16.257 MHz†	14.30 MHz	14.3 to 16.3 MHz	28 MHz	44.9, 25.9 MHz
	Horiz. Sweep Rate	18.432 KHz†	15.75 KHz	15.7 to 21.8 KHz	31.5 KHz	35.5, 31.5 KHz
	Vert. Sweep Rate	50 Hz†	60 Hz	60 Hz	50 to 70 Hz	43.5, 59.9 Hz
	Max. Horiz. Pixels	720	640	*	720	1024
	Max. Vert. Pixels	350	200	350	480	768
	Character Box Size	9x14	8x8	9x14 or 8x8	9x16	8x14 to 1x23
	Actual Character Size	7x9	7x7 or 5x7	7x9 or 7x7	7x9	varies
System	Accesses CPU	When not refreshing	Anytime	Anytime	Anytime	Anytime
	Data Transfer Rate	1.8 M/sec	1.5 M/sec			
Features	Light Pen	NO	YES	YES	NO	NO
	Composite Out	NO	YES	NO	NO	NO
	Digital RGB Out	NO	YES	YES	NO	NO
	Analog RGB Out	NO	NO	NO	YES	YES
	Direct Video Out	YES	YES	YES	NO	NO
	Color Palette	NONE	16 colors	64 colors	256 K colors	256 K colors
	Feature Connector	NO	NO	YES	NO	NO
	Modulator Connector	NO	YES	NO	NO	NO

*B0000 for 32 K, or B8000 for 32 K, or A0000 for 64 K, or A0000 for 128 K. Also for the EGA, a 16 K BIOS EGA extension module is mapped to processor address C0000.
†When used with IBM Monochrome Display

Source: IBM Options and Adapters Technical Reference, Vol. 2, pages Monochrome Adapter 1 through 7 and Color Graphics Monitor Adapter 1 through 13
IBM PS/2 Model 50 and 60 Technical Reference, pages 4-19 through 4-29
IBM PS/2 XGA Adapter Interface Technical Reference, pages 1-1 through 1-4
IBM PS/2 Model 80 Technical Reference, pages 4-19 through 4-29
IBM PS/2 Display Adapter 8514/A Technical Reference, page 1-4
"XGA Standard is Good, But It's Not For Everyone--Yet," PC/Computing, January 1991, page 39

See Also:
7.026. MDA Memory Map
7.029. MDA I/O Port Usage
7.030. CGA Memory Map
7.033. CGA I/O Port Usage
7.034. EGA Memory Map
7.037. EGA I/O Port Usage
7.038. VGA Memory Map
7.041. VGA I/O Port Usage

7.023. VIDEO MODES SUMMARY

BIOS Mode Details

Mode # (Hex #)	*Type*	*Rows*	*Cols*	*Resolution*	*Colors*
0 (0)	Char	25	40	320x200	16
1 (1)	Char	25	40	320x200	16
2 (2)	Char	25	80	640x200	16
3 (3)	Char	25	80	640x200	16
4 (4)	Graph	25	40	320x200	4
5 (5)	Graph	25	40	320x300	4
6 (6)	Graph	25	80	640x200	2
7 (7)	Char	25	80	720x350*	Mono
13 (D)	Graph	25	40	320x200	16
14 (E)	Graph	25	80	640x200	16
15 (F)	Graph	25	80	640x350	Mono
16 (10)	Graph	25	80	640x350	16
17 (11)	Graph	30	80	640x480	2
18 (12)	Graph	30	80	640x480	16
19 (13)	Graph	25	40	320x200	256
20 (14)†	Char	43, 50, or 60	132		

Adapter Support

MDA	*CGA*	*EGA*	*MCGA*	*VGA*	*XGA¥*
	✔	✔	✔	✔	✔
	✔	✔	✔	✔	✔
	✔	✔	✔	✔	✔
	✔	✔	✔	✔	✔
	✔	✔	✔	✔	✔
	✔	✔	✔	✔	✔
	✔	✔	✔	✔	✔
✔		✔		✔	✔
		✔		✔	✔
		✔		✔	✔
		✔		✔	✔
		✔		✔	✔
			✔	✔	✔
				✔	✔
			✔	✔	
					✔

*720x400 on VGA
†Virtual resolution is 1056 by 200, 350, or 400 scan lines. Each character is 8 pixels wide.
Character height depends on font used.
¥XGA supports all VGA modes, but only works on 386 or 486 machines.

Note:

- EGA figures assume it has a full 256K of RAM.
- Modes 8-12 are used by PCjr only.
- The default XGA mode is VGA. XGA also supports special non-BIOS modes via the HSMODE function, with the following new modes available:

Mode	*Screen Size*	*Cell Size*	*Rows*	*Cols*
0	1024x768	12x20	38	85
1	640x480	8x14	34	80
2	1024x768	8x14	54	128
3	1024x768	7x15	51	146

Source:

IBM PS/2 Model 30 Technical Reference, page 1-39
IBM PS/2 Model 50 and 60 Technical Reference, page 4-27
IBM PS/2 XGA Adapter Interface Technical Reference, page 3-35
IBM PS/2 Model 80 Technical Reference, page 4-27
XGA Video Subsystem Hardware Users Guide, pages 1, 126, and 134
"XGA: A New Graphics Standard," Byte, February 1991, pages 285 through 290

7.024. VIDEO CHARACTER FONT SIZES

BIOS Mode

Mode #	*Rows*	*Cols*	*Colors*
0	25	40	16
1	25	40	16
2	25	80	16
3	25	80	16
7	25	80	Mono
20 (14)*	43, 50, or 60	132	

Character Box Size

MDA	*CGA*	*EGA*	*MCGA*	*VGA*
	8x8	8x14	8x16	9x16
	8x8	8x14	8x16	9x16
	8x8	8x14	8x16	9x16
	8x8	8x14	8x16	9x16
9x14		9x14		9x16

*Mode 20 (14H) is a VGA extension.

Version: Applies to text modes 0-3 and 7 only.

Note: XGA emulates VGA for text modes or uses 132-column text mode (a VGA extension) for higher resolution.

Source:

IBM PS/2 Model 50 and 60 Technical Reference, page 4-27
IBM PS/2 Model 80 Technical Reference, page 4-27
IBM PS/2 and PC BIOS Interface Technical Reference, page 2-13
IBM PS/2 XGA Adapter Interface Technical Reference, page 1-1
XGA Video Subsystem Hardware Users Guide, pages 1, 126, and 134
"XGA: A New Graphics Standard," Byte, February 1991, pages 285 through 290

See Also:

7.027. MDA Character Box
7.031. CGA Character Box
7.035. EGA Character Box
7.039. VGA Character Box
7.042. XGA Character Boxes

7.025. VIDEO MONITOR USAGE SUMMARY

	MDA	*CGA*	*EGA*	*MCGA*	*VGA*	*XGA*
Can Use B/W TV	NO	MARGINAL	NO	NO	NO	NO
Can Use B/W Composite Monitor	NO	YES	NO	NO	NO	NO
Can Use IBM Monochrome Monitor	OPTIMUM	NO	YES	NO	NO	NO
Can Use Color TV	NO	MARGINAL	NO	NO	NO	NO
Can Use Composite Color Monitor	NO	MARGINAL	NO	NO	NO	NO
Can Use Digital RGB Monitor	NO	OPTIMUM	OPTIMUM	NO	NO	NO
Can Use Analog RGB Monitor	NO	NO	NO	OPTIMUM	OPTIMUM	OPTIMUM

Note:
- **Optimum indicates monitor for which display adapter was designed.**
- **Marginal indicates monitor will work, but results will not be high-quality.**

7.026. MDA MEMORY MAP

For Alphanumeric Text Display (Mode 7):

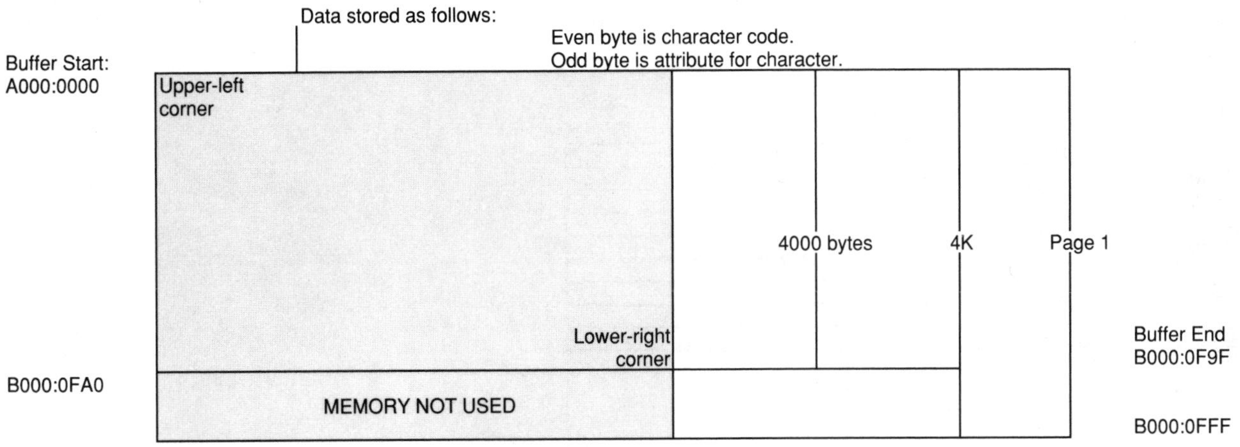
Data stored as follows:
Even byte is character code.
Odd byte is attribute for character.
Buffer Start:
A000:0000
Upper-left corner
4000 bytes
4K
Page 1
Lower-right corner
Buffer End
B000:0F9F
B000:0FA0
MEMORY NOT USED
B000:0FFF

Up to seven additional pages follow sequentially, using memory through B000:7FFF.

Source: IBM Options and Adapters Technical Reference, Vol. 2, page Monochrome Adapter 6

See Also:
7.022. Video Adapter Memory Usage and Output Specifications
7.023. Video Modes Summary
7.028. MDA Character Attributes

7.027. MDA CHARACTER BOX

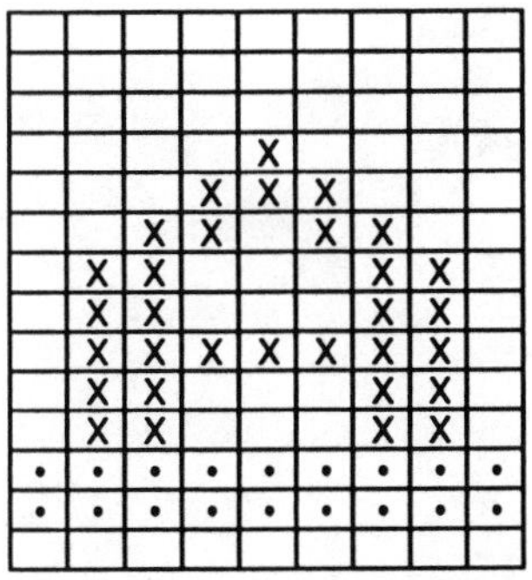

Character is a 7x9 pixel area in a 9x14 pixel box.

X = pixels set for a typical character "A"
• = pixels set for default cursor

Source: **IBM Options and Adapters Technical Reference, Vol. 2, page Monochrome Adapter 2**

See Also: **7.024. Video Character Font Sizes**

7.028. MDA CHARACTER ATTRIBUTES

Bit Number

7	6	5	4	3	2	1	0	Function	Allowable Values
✔								Blink	0=no blink, 1=blink
	✔	✔	✔					Background	000=black background 111=white background
				✔				Intensity	0=normal, 1=high intensity
					✔	✔	✔	Foreground	000=black character 001=underline 111=white character

Note: Invisible characters are created by placing a character on a background of the same color (e.g., white on white).

Source: IBM Options and Adapters Technical Reference, Vol. 2, page Monochrome Adapter 6

See Also: 7.032. CGA Character Attributes
7.036. EGA Character Attributes
7.040. VGA Character Attributes
7.043. XGA Character Attributes

7.029. MDA I/O PORT USAGE

Port	Function	Comment
3B0H	NOT USED	
3B1H	NOT USED	
3B2H	NOT USED	
3B3H	NOT USED	
3B4H	6845 index register	
3B5H	6845 data register	
3B6H	NOT USED	
3B7H	NOT USED	
3B8H	CRT control port 1	Bit 0 = +high resolution mode Bit 1 = NOT USED Bit 2 = NOT USED Bit 3 = +video enable Bit 4 = NOT USED Bit 5 = +enable blink Bit 6 = NOT USED Bit 7 = NOT USED
3B9H	RESERVED	
3BAH	CRT status Port	Bit 0 = +horizontal drive Bit 1 = RESERVED Bit 2 = RESERVED Bit 3 = +black/white video
3BBH	RESERVED	
3BCH	Parallel data port	*
3BDH	Parallel status port	*
3BEH	Parallel control port	*
3BFH	NOT USED	

*See 7.086. Printer Adapter I/O Port Usage.

Source: IBM Options and Adapters Technical Reference, Vol. 2, pages Monochrome Adapter 7 and 8

See Also: 7.033. CGA I/O Port Usage
7.037. EGA I/O Port Usage
7.086. Printer Adapter I/O Port Usage

7.030. CGA MEMORY MAP

For Alphanumeric Text Display (modes 0-3):

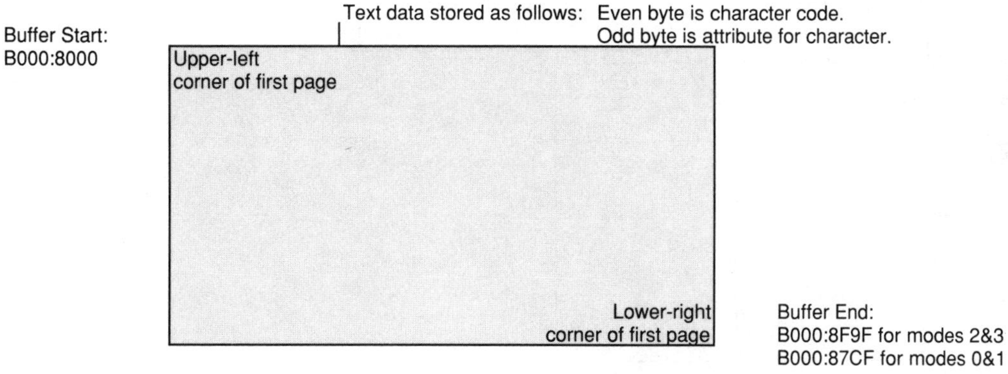
Text data stored as follows:
Even byte is character code.
Odd byte is attribute for character.
Buffer Start:
B000:8000
Upper-left
corner of first page
Lower-right
corner of first page
Buffer End:
B000:8F9F for modes 2&3
B000:87CF for modes 0&1

Up to eight consecutive pages in modes 0 and 1, four consecutive pages in modes 2 and 3

For Medium Resolution Graphics Display (320x200 all points addressable, modes 4 and 5):

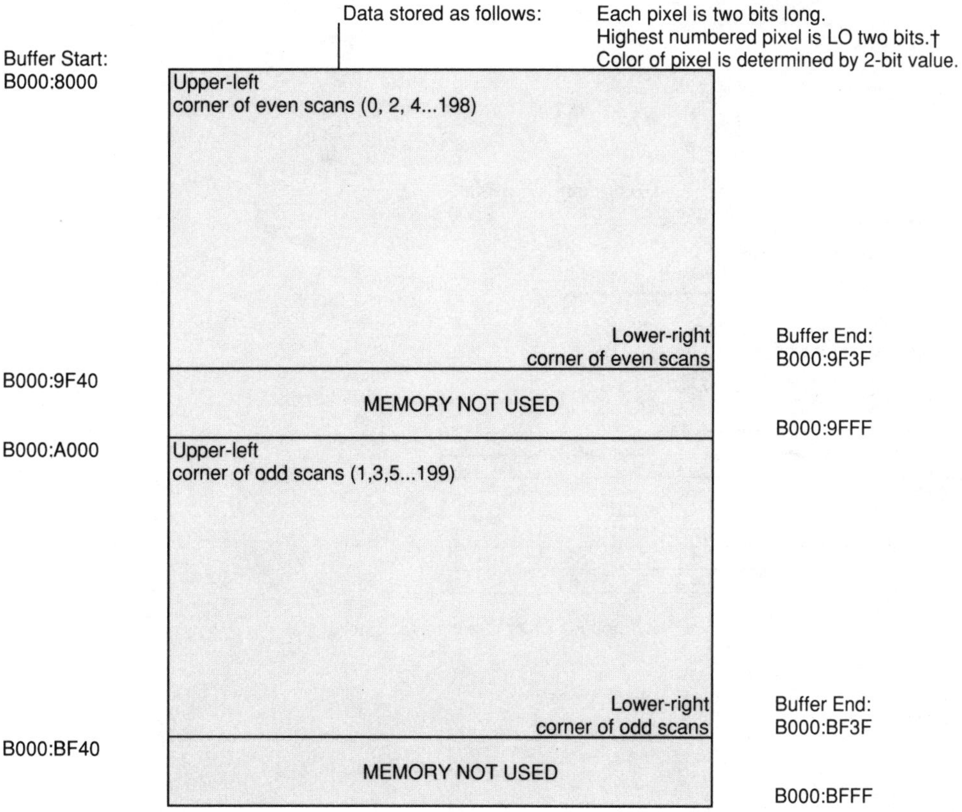
Data stored as follows:
Each pixel is two bits long.
Highest numbered pixel is LO two bits.†
Color of pixel is determined by 2-bit value.
Buffer Start:
B000:8000
Upper-left
corner of even scans (0, 2, 4...198)
Lower-right
corner of even scans
Buffer End:
B000:9F3F
B000:9F40
MEMORY NOT USED
B000:9FFF
B000:A000
Upper-left
corner of odd scans (1,3,5...199)
Lower-right
corner of odd scans
Buffer End:
B000:BF3F
B000:BF40
MEMORY NOT USED
B000:BFFF

(Continued)

7.030. CGA MEMORY MAP (continued)

For High Resolution Graphics Display (640x200 all points addressable, mode 6):

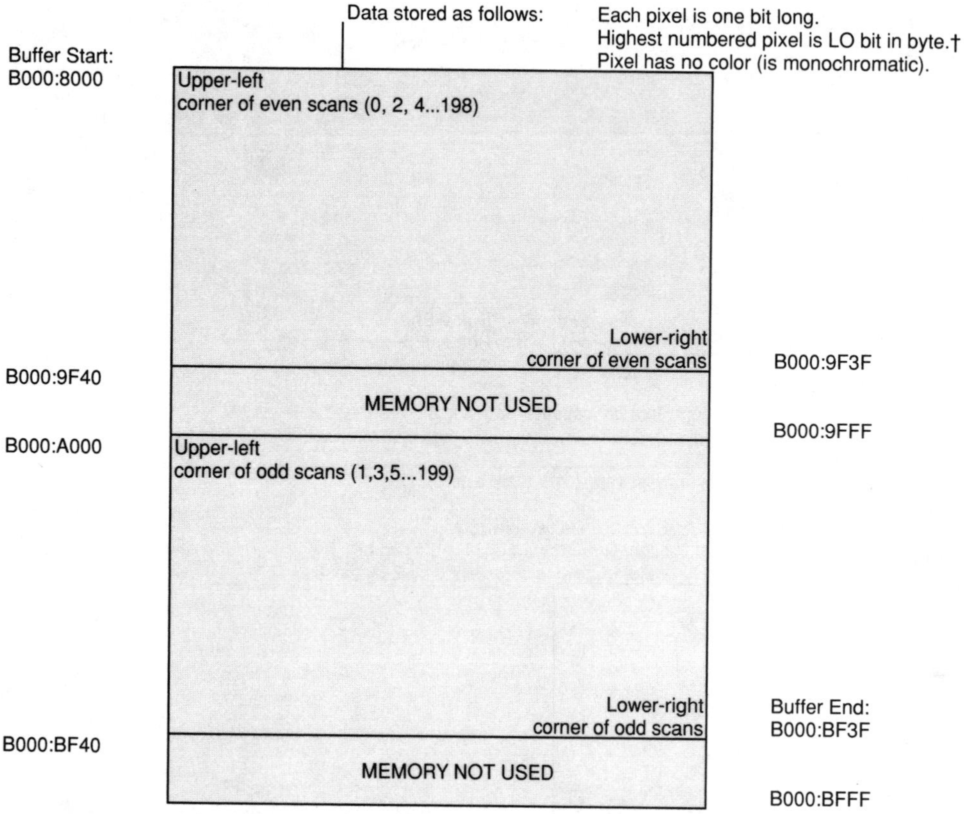
Data stored as follows:
Each pixel is one bit long.
Highest numbered pixel is LO bit in byte.†
Pixel has no color (is monochromatic).
Buffer Start:
B000:8000
Upper-left
corner of even scans (0, 2, 4...198)
Lower-right
corner of even scans
B000:9F3F
B000:9F40
MEMORY NOT USED
B000:9FFF
B000:A000
Upper-left
corner of odd scans (1,3,5...199)
Lower-right
corner of odd scans
Buffer End:
B000:BF3F
B000:BF40
MEMORY NOT USED
B000:BFFF

†In other words, the highest numbered pixel goes into the lowest bit (or bits), and the lowest numbered pixel goes into the highest bit (or bits).
For example:
-The first byte in medium resolution:

Bit Number	7	6	5	4	3	2	1	0
Pixel Number	1		2		3		4	

-The first byte in high resolution:

Bit Number	7	6	5	4	3	2	1	0
Pixel Number	1	2	3	4	5	6	7	8

Source: IBM Options and Adapters Technical Reference, Vol. 2, pages Color/Graphics Monitor Adapter 1 through 11

See Also: 7.022. Video Adapter Memory Usage and Output Specifications
7.032. CGA Character Attributes

7.031. CGA CHARACTER BOX

			X	X	X		
		X	X		X	X	
	X	X				X	X
	X	X				X	X
	X	X	X	X	X	X	X
	X	X				X	X
	X	X				X	X
•	•	•	•	•	•	•	•

Character is a 7x7 pixel area in an 8x8 pixel box.*

X = pixels set for a typical character "A"
• = pixels set for default cursor

*Optionally, if jumper P3 inserted, character is 5x7 pixel area in 8x8 box.

Source: IBM Options and Adapters Technical Reference Vol. 2, pages Color/Graphics Monitor Adapter 5 through 8

See Also: 7.024. Video Character Font Sizes

7.032. CGA CHARACTER ATTRIBUTES

Bit Number

7	*6*	*5*	*4*	*3*	*2*	*1*	*0*	*Function*	*Allowable Values*	
✔								Blink	0=no blink, 1=blink	
	✔	✔	✔					Background	000=black 001=blue 010=green 011=cyan 100=red 101=magenta 110=brown 111=white	
				✔				Intensity	0=normal, 1=high intensity	
					✔	✔	✔	Foreground	000=black 001=blue 010=green 011=cyan 100=red 101=magenta 110=brown 111=white	gray with intensity on light blue with intensity on light green with intensity on light cyan with intensity on light red with intensity on light magenta with intensity on yellow with intensity on bright white with intensity on

Note: Invisible characters are created by placing a character on a background of the same color (e.g., white on white).

Source: IBM Options and Adapters Technical Reference, Vol. 2, pages Color/Graphics Monitor Adapter 6 through 8

See Also: 7.028. MDA Character Attributes
7.036. EGA Character Attributes
7.040. VGA Character Attributes
7.043. XGA Character Attributes

7.033. CGA I/O PORT USAGE

Port	Function	Bit 7	Bit 6	Bit 5	Bit 4	Bit 3	Bit 2	Bit 1	Bit 0	Allowable Values
3D0	RESERVED									
3D1	RESERVED									
3D2	RESERVED									
3D3	RESERVED									
3D4	6845 index register									*
3D5	6845 data register									*
3D6	RESERVED									
3D7	RESERVED									
3D8	Mode control register (D0)	✔	✔							NOT USED
				✔						0=blink disabled, 1=blink enabled
					✔					1=640x200 graphics mode
						✔				0=video signal disabled, 1=video signal enabled
							✔			0=color enabled, 1=monochrome (black and white) signal
								✔		0=text mode, 1=320x200 graphics mode
									✔	0=40x25 text mode, 1=80x25 text mode
3D9	Color select register (D0)	✔	✔							NOT USED
				✔						Active color set: 0=red/green/brown, 1=cyan/magenta/white
					✔					Intense colors in graphics, background colors in text mode
						✔				Intense border in 40x25 text, background in 320x200 graphics, foreground in 640x200 graphics
							✔			Red border in 40x25 text, background in 320x200 graphics, foreground in 640x200 graphics
								✔		Green border in 40x25 text, background in 320x200 graphics, foreground in 640x200 graphics
									✔	Blue border in 40x25 text, background in 320x200 graphics, foreground in 640x200 graphics
3DA	Status register (D1)	✔	✔	✔	✔					NOT USED
						✔				0=not in retrace, 1=in vertical retrace mode
							✔			0=light pen switch is ON, 1=light pen switch is OFF
								✔		0=no trigger, 1=positive-going edge from light pen has set trigger
									✔	0=do not use memory, 1=memory may be accessed without interfering with display
3DB	Clear light pen latch									
3DC	Preset light pen latch									
3DD	RESERVED									
3DE	RESERVED									
3DF	RESERVED									

*See 7.114. 6845 Registers.

Source: IBM Options and Adapters Technical Reference Vol. 2, pages Color/Graphics Monitor Adapter 15 through 21

See Also: 7.029. MDA I/O Port Usage
7.037. EGA I/O Port Usage

7.034. EGA MEMORY MAP

For Alphanumeric Text Display (modes 0-3):

Text data stored as follows: Even byte is character code.
Odd byte is attribute for character.

Buffer Start:
B000:8000

Upper-left
corner of first page
Lower-right
corner of first page

Buffer End:
B000:8F9F for modes 2&3
B000:87CF for modes 0&1

Up to eight consecutive pages in modes 0 and 1, four consecutive pages in modes 2 and 3

(Continued)

7.034. EGA MEMORY MAP (continued)

For Medium Resolution Graphics Display (320x200 all points addressable, modes 4 and 5):

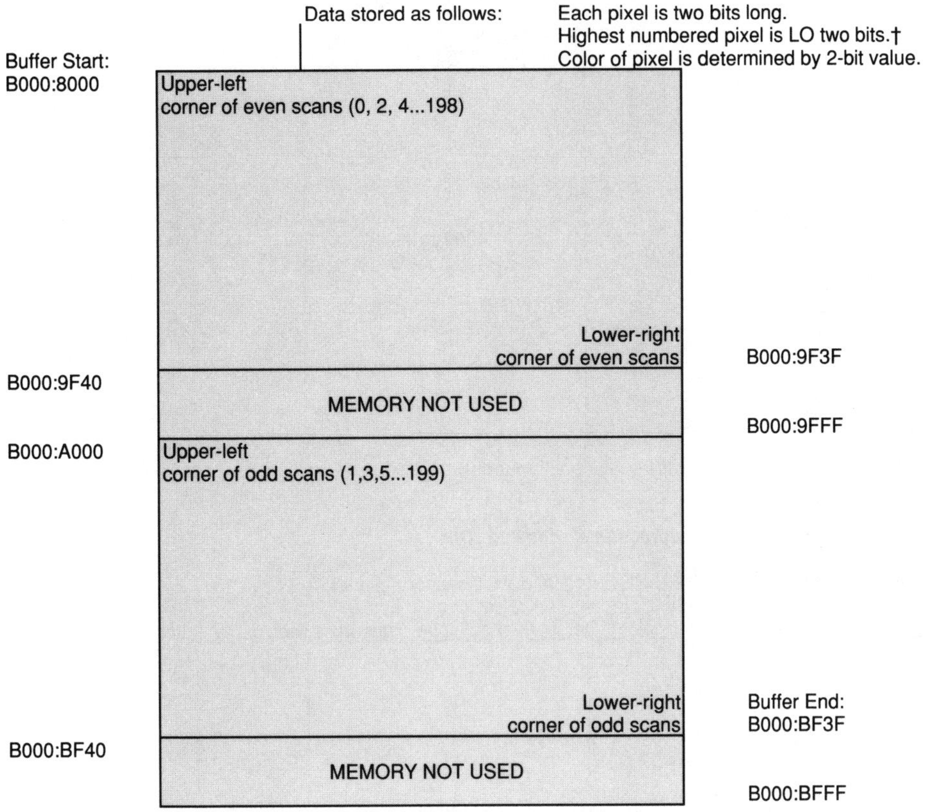
Data stored as follows:
Each pixel is two bits long.
Highest numbered pixel is LO two bits.†
Color of pixel is determined by 2-bit value.
Buffer Start:
B000:8000
Upper-left
corner of even scans (0, 2, 4...198)
Lower-right
corner of even scans
B000:9F3F
B000:9F40
MEMORY NOT USED
B000:9FFF
B000:A000
Upper-left
corner of odd scans (1,3,5...199)
Lower-right
corner of odd scans
Buffer End:
B000:BF3F
B000:BF40
MEMORY NOT USED
B000:BFFF

For High Resolution Graphics Display (640x200 all points addressable, mode 6):

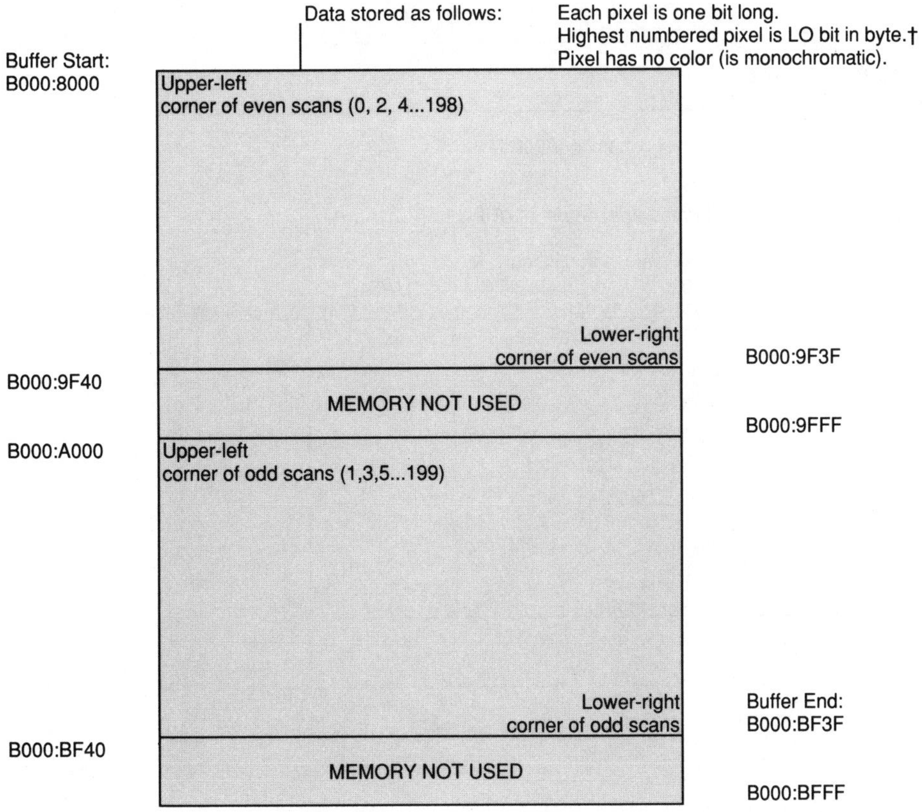
Data stored as follows:
Each pixel is one bit long.
Highest numbered pixel is LO bit in byte.†
Pixel has no color (is monochromatic).
Buffer Start:
B000:8000
Upper-left
corner of even scans (0, 2, 4...198)
Lower-right
corner of even scans
B000:9F3F
B000:9F40
MEMORY NOT USED
B000:9FFF
B000:A000
Upper-left
corner of odd scans (1,3,5...199)
Lower-right
corner of odd scans
Buffer End:
B000:BF3F
B000:BF40
MEMORY NOT USED
B000:BFFF

(Continued)

7.034. EGA MEMORY MAP (continued)

For Alphanumeric Text Display (mode 7):

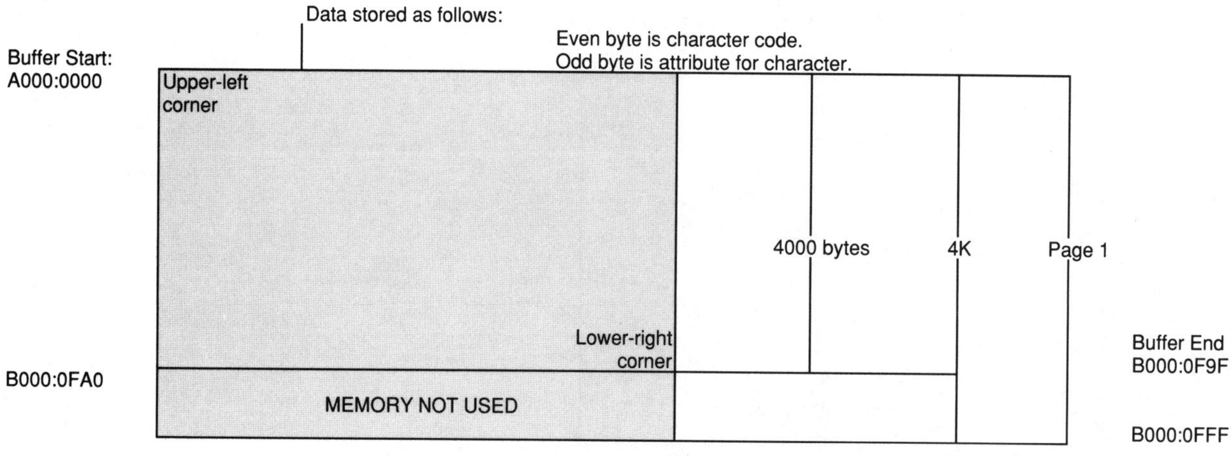
Data stored as follows:
Even byte is character code.
Odd byte is attribute for character.
Buffer Start:
A000:0000
Upper-left corner
Lower-right corner
4000 bytes
4K
Page 1
Buffer End
B000:0F9F
B000:0FA0
MEMORY NOT USED
B000:0FFF

Up to seven additional pages follow sequentially, using memory through B000:7FFF.

For Medium Resolution Graphics Display (320x200 all points addressable, mode 13 (D)):

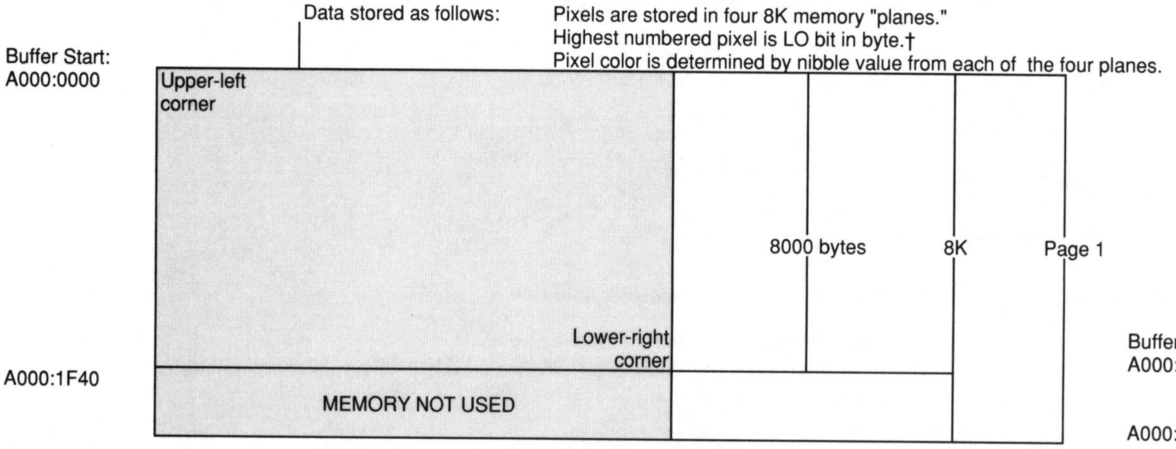
Data stored as follows:
Pixels are stored in four 8K memory "planes."
Highest numbered pixel is LO bit in byte.†
Pixel color is determined by nibble value from each of the four planes.
Buffer Start:
A000:0000
Upper-left corner
Lower-right corner
8000 bytes
8K
Page 1
Buffer End
A000:1F3F
A000:1F40
MEMORY NOT USED
A000:2000

Up to three additional tables follow sequentially, using memory A000:7FFF.

For High Resolution Graphics Display (640x200 all points addressable, mode 14 (E)):

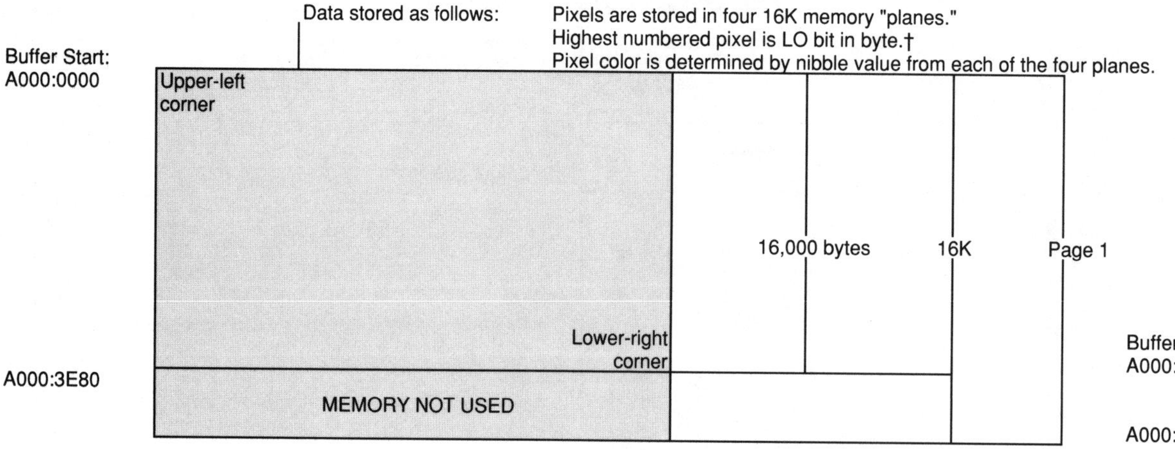
Data stored as follows:
Pixels are stored in four 16K memory "planes."
Highest numbered pixel is LO bit in byte.†
Pixel color is determined by nibble value from each of the four planes.
Buffer Start:
A000:0000
Upper-left corner
Lower-right corner
16,000 bytes
16K
Page 1
Buffer End
A000:3E7F
A000:3E80
MEMORY NOT USED
A000:4000

Up to three additional tables follow sequentially, using memory through A000:FFFF.

(Continued)

7.034. EGA MEMORY MAP (continued)

For High Resolution Graphics Display (640x350 all points addressable, mode 15 (F)):

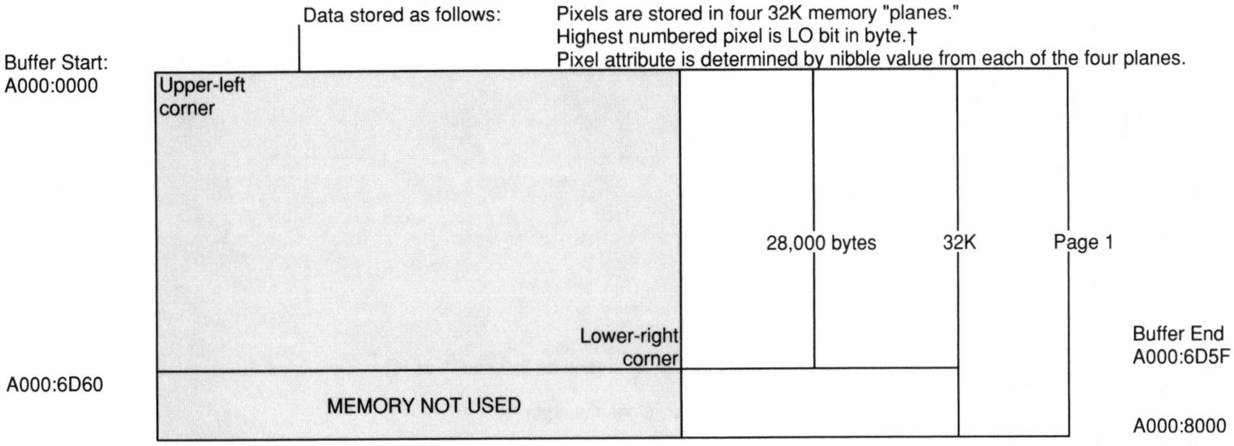
Data stored as follows:
Pixels are stored in four 32K memory "planes."
Highest numbered pixel is LO bit in byte.†
Pixel attribute is determined by nibble value from each of the four planes.
Buffer Start:
A000:0000
Upper-left corner
28,000 bytes
32K
Page 1
Lower-right corner
Buffer End
A000:6D5F
A000:6D60
MEMORY NOT USED
A000:8000

Up to one additional page follows, using memory through A000:FFFF.

For High Resolution Graphics Display (640x350 all points addressable, mode 16 (10)):

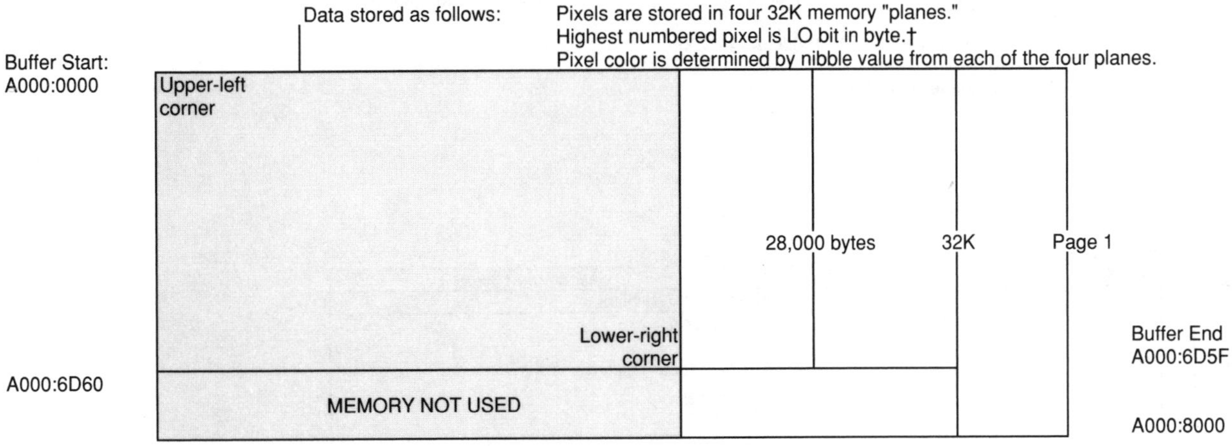
Data stored as follows:
Pixels are stored in four 32K memory "planes."
Highest numbered pixel is LO bit in byte.†
Pixel color is determined by nibble value from each of the four planes.
Buffer Start:
A000:0000
Upper-left corner
28,000 bytes
32K
Page 1
Lower-right corner
Buffer End
A000:6D5F
A000:6D60
MEMORY NOT USED
A000:8000

Up to one additional page follows, using memory through A000:FFFF.

†In other words, the highest numbered pixel goes into the lowest bit (or bits), and the lowest numbered pixel goes into the highest bit (or bits).
For example:
-The first byte in medium resolution:

Bit Number	7	6	5	4	3	2	1	0
Pixel Number	1		2		3		4	

-The first byte in high resolution:

Bit Number	7	6	5	4	3	2	1	0
Pixel Number	1	2	3	4	5	6	7	8

Note: When in purely EGA modes, memory organization is four planes of either 16K or 64K, and the use and definition of "pages" is up to the programmer.

Source: IBM Options and Adapters Technical Reference, Vol. 2, pages Color/Graphics Monitor Adapter, pages 1 through 34
IBM PS/2 Model 80 Technical Reference, pages 4-34 through 4-55

See Also: 7.022. Video Adapter Memory Usage and Output Specifications
7.036. EGA Character Attributes

7.035. EGA CHARACTER BOX

For modes 7 and 15:

				X				
			X	X	X			
		X	X		X	X		
	X	X				X	X	
	X	X				X	X	
	X	X	X	X	X	X	X	
	X	X				X	X	
	X	X				X	X	
•	•	•	•	•	•	•	•	•
•	•	•	•	•	•	•	•	•

Character is a 7x9 pixel area in a 9x14 pixel box.

X = pixels set for a typical character "A"
• = pixels set for default cursor

For modes 0-3:

			X	X	X		
		X	X		X	X	
	X	X				X	X
	X	X				X	X
	X	X	X	X	X	X	X
	X	X				X	X
	X	X				X	X
•	•	•	•	•	•	•	•

Character is a 7x7 pixel area in an 8x8 pixel box.

X = pixels set for a typical character "A"
• = pixels set for default cursor

Source: IBM Options and Adapters Technical Reference, Vol. 2, page Color/Graphics Monitor Adapter, pages 7 through 8
IBM PS/2 Model 80 Technical Reference, page 4-27

See Also: 7.024. Video Character Font Sizes

7.036. EGA CHARACTER ATTRIBUTES

For Text (modes 0-3):

7	*6*	*5*	*4*	*3*	*2*	*1*	*0*	*Function*	*Allowable Values*
✔								Blink	0=no blink, 1=blink
	✔	✔	✔					Background	000=black 001=blue 010=green 011=cyan 100=red 101=magenta 110=brown 111=white
				✔				Intensity	0=normal, 1=high intensity
					✔	✔	✔	Foreground	000=black gray with intensity on 001=blue light blue with intensity on 010=green light green with intensity on 011=cyan light cyan with intensity on 100=red light red with intensity on 101=magenta light magenta with intensity on 110=brown yellow with intensity on 111=white bright white with intensity on

For Text (mode 7):

7	*6*	*5*	*4*	*3*	*2*	*1*	*0*	*Function*	*Allowable Values*
✔								Blink	0=no blink, 1=blink
	✔	✔	✔					Background	000=black 111=white
				✔				Intensity	0=normal, 1=high intensity
					✔	✔	✔	Foreground	000=black gray with intensity on 001=underline 111=white bright white with intensity on

(Continued)

7.036. EGA CHARACTER ATTRIBUTES (continued)

For mode 15:

Pixel Plane 3	2	1	0	Function
	0		0	Black character
	0		1	White character
	1		0	Blinking white character
	1		1	Intense white character

For modes 13,14, and 16:

Pixel Plane 3	2	1	0	Function
			X	Blue pixel component
		X		Green pixel component
	X			Red pixel component
X				Intensity pixel component

Note: Invisible characters in modes 0-3 and 7 are created by placing a character on a background of the same color (e.g., white on white).

Source: IBM PS/2 Model 50 and 60 Technical Reference, pages 4-30 through 4-33 and 4-38
IBM PS/2 Model 80 Technical Reference, pages 4-30 through 4-33 and 4-38

See Also: 7.028. MDA Character Attributes
7.032. CGA Character Attributes
7.040. VGA Character Attributes

7.037. EGA I/O PORT USAGE

Register Name	Register Type	R/W	I/O Port Used: Mono	Color	Either
Miscellaneous output	General	W			3C2H
Miscellaneous output	General	R			3CCH
Input status register 0	General	R			3C2H
Input status register 1	General	R	3BAH	3DAH	
Feature control register	General	W	3BAH	3DAH	
Feature control register	General	R			3CAH
Video subsystem enable	General	RW			3C3H
Address register	Attribute	RW			3C0H
Other attribute register	Attribute	W			3C0H
Other attribute register	Attribute	R			3C1H
Index register	CRT controller	RW	3B4H	3D4H	
Other CRT controller registers	CRT controller	RW	3B5H	3D5H	
Address register	Sequencer	RW			3C4H
Other sequencer register	Sequencer	RW			3C5H
Address register	Graphics	RW			3CEH
Other graphics register	Graphics	RW			3CFH

Source: IBM PS/2 Model 50 and 60 Technical Reference, pages 4-58 through 4-59

See Also: 7.041. VGA I/O Port Usage

7.038. VGA MEMORY MAP

For Alphanumeric Text Display (modes 0-3):

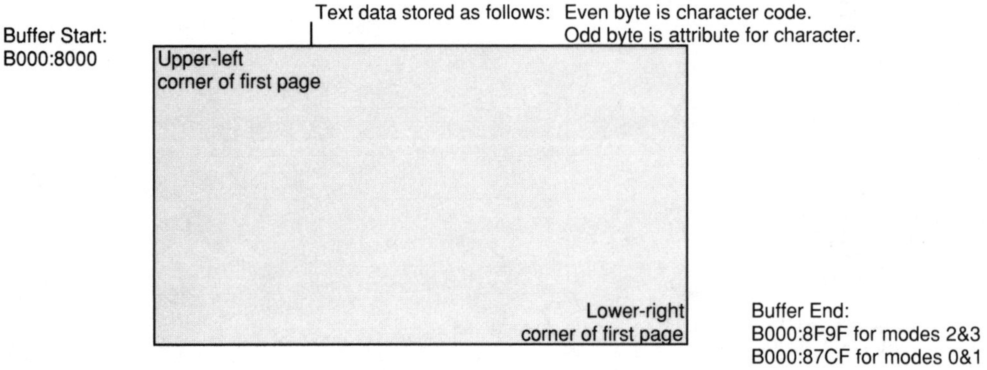
Text data stored as follows:
Even byte is character code.
Odd byte is attribute for character.
Buffer Start:
B000:8000
Upper-left
corner of first page
Lower-right
corner of first page
Buffer End:
B000:8F9F for modes 2&3
B000:87CF for modes 0&1

Up to eight consecutive pages in modes 0 and 1; four consecutive pages in modes 2 and 3

For Medium Resolution Graphics Display (320x200 all points addressable, modes 4 and 5):

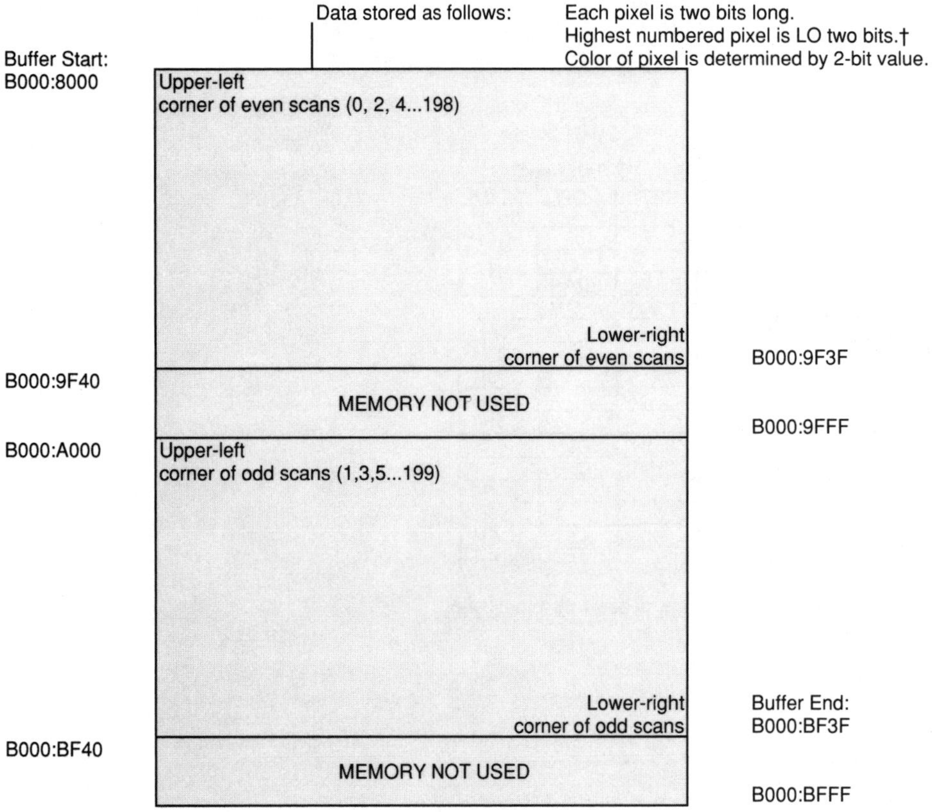
Data stored as follows:
Each pixel is two bits long.
Highest numbered pixel is LO two bits.†
Color of pixel is determined by 2-bit value.
Buffer Start:
B000:8000
Upper-left
corner of even scans (0, 2, 4...198)
Lower-right
corner of even scans
B000:9F3F
B000:9F40
MEMORY NOT USED
B000:9FFF
B000:A000
Upper-left
corner of odd scans (1,3,5...199)
Lower-right
corner of odd scans
Buffer End:
B000:BF3F
B000:BF40
MEMORY NOT USED
B000:BFFF

(Continued)

7.038. VGA MEMORY MAP (continued)

For High Resolution Graphics Display (640x200 all points addressable, mode 6):

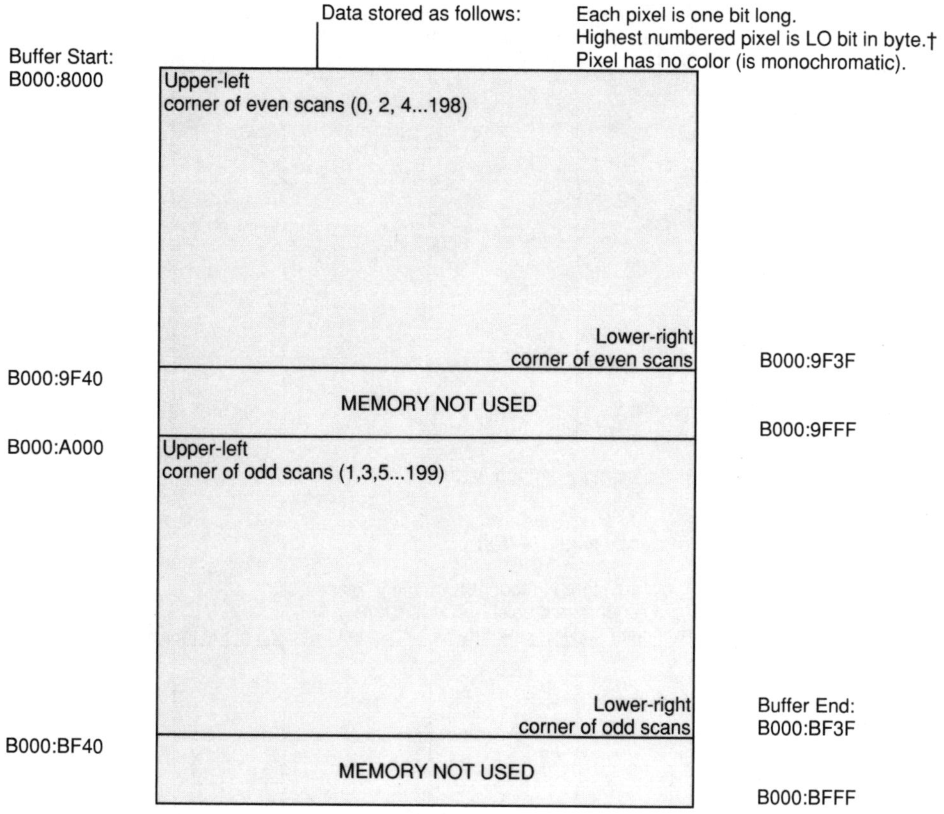
Data stored as follows:
Each pixel is one bit long.
Highest numbered pixel is LO bit in byte.†
Pixel has no color (is monochromatic).
Buffer Start:
B000:8000
Upper-left
corner of even scans (0, 2, 4...198)
Lower-right
corner of even scans
B000:9F3F
B000:9F40
MEMORY NOT USED
B000:9FFF
B000:A000
Upper-left
corner of odd scans (1,3,5...199)
Lower-right
corner of odd scans
Buffer End:
B000:BF3F
B000:BF40
MEMORY NOT USED
B000:BFFF

For Alphanumeric Text Display (mode 7):

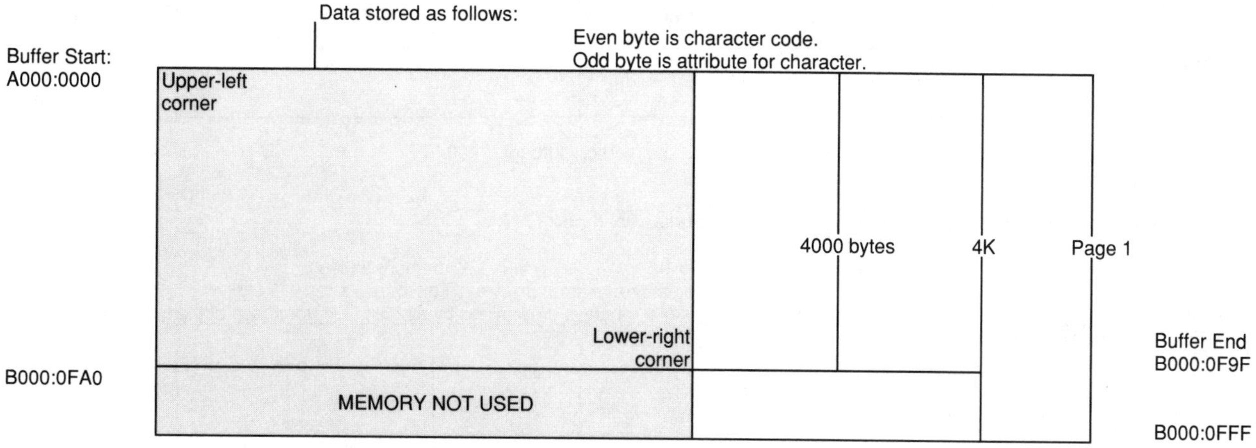
Data stored as follows:
Even byte is character code.
Odd byte is attribute for character.
Buffer Start:
A000:0000
Upper-left
corner
4000 bytes
4K
Page 1
Lower-right
corner
Buffer End
B000:0F9F
B000:0FA0
MEMORY NOT USED
B000:0FFF

Up to seven additional pages follow sequentially, using memory through B000:7FFF.

(Continued)

7.038. VGA MEMORY MAP (continued)

For Medium Resolution Graphics Display (320x200 all points addressable, mode 13 (D)):

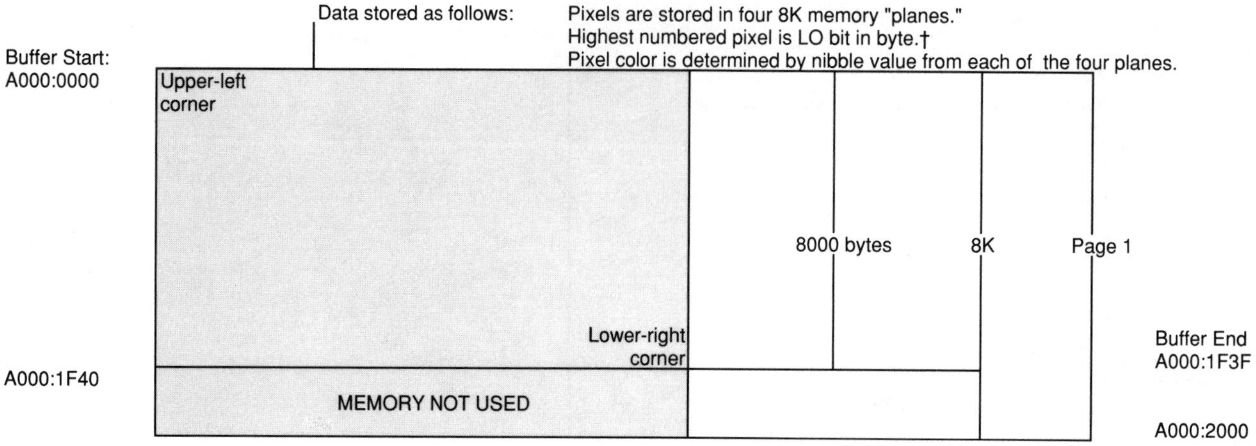
Data stored as follows:
Pixels are stored in four 8K memory "planes."
Highest numbered pixel is LO bit in byte.†
Pixel color is determined by nibble value from each of the four planes.
Buffer Start:
A000:0000
Upper-left corner
8000 bytes
8K
Page 1
Lower-right corner
Buffer End
A000:1F3F
A000:1F40
MEMORY NOT USED
A000:2000

Up to three additional tables follow sequentially, using memory through A000:7FFF.

For High Resolution Graphics Display (640x200 all points addressable, mode 14 (E)):

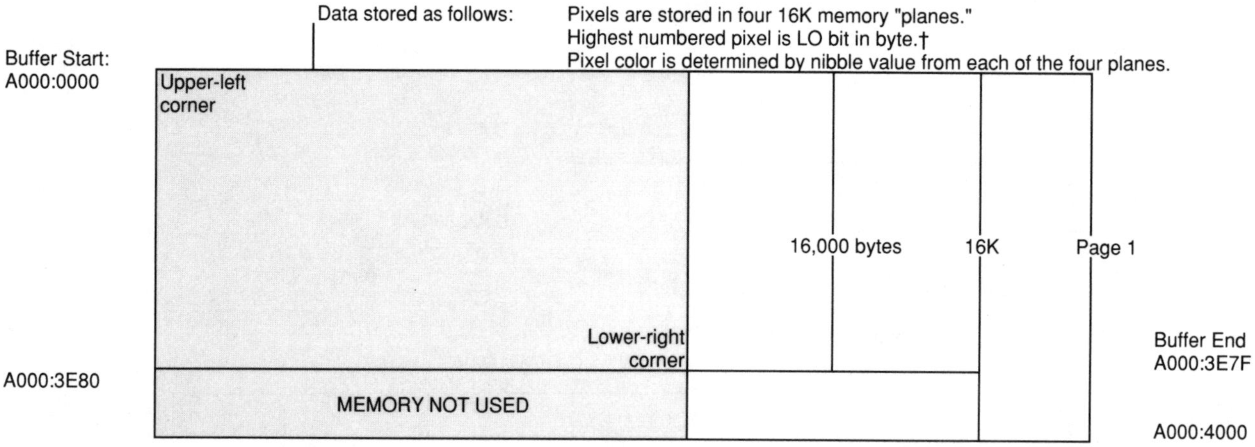
Data stored as follows:
Pixels are stored in four 16K memory "planes."
Highest numbered pixel is LO bit in byte.†
Pixel color is determined by nibble value from each of the four planes.
Buffer Start:
A000:0000
Upper-left corner
16,000 bytes
16K
Page 1
Lower-right corner
Buffer End
A000:3E7F
A000:3E80
MEMORY NOT USED
A000:4000

Up to three additional tables follow sequentially, using memory through A000:FFFF.

For High Resolution Graphics Display (640x350 all points addressable, mode 15 (F)):

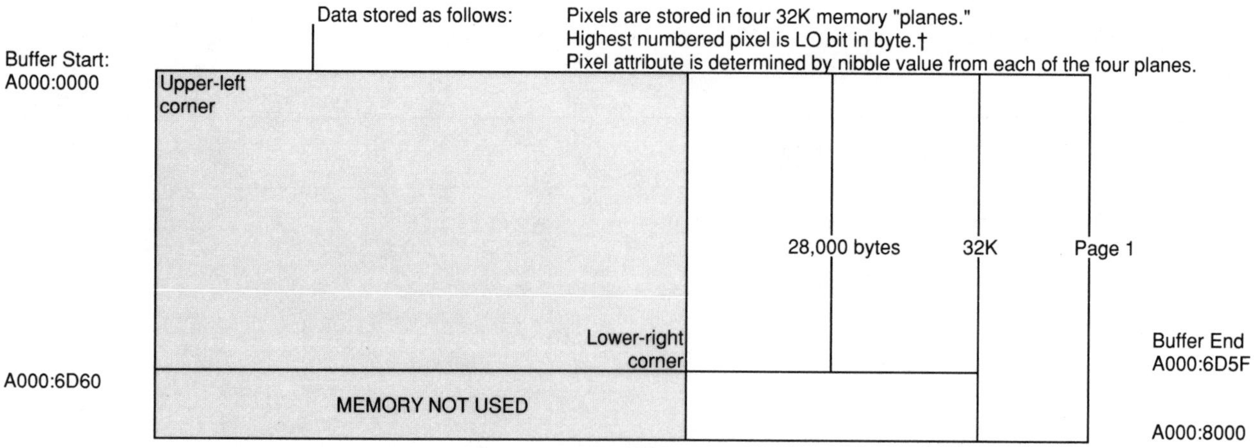
Data stored as follows:
Pixels are stored in four 32K memory "planes."
Highest numbered pixel is LO bit in byte.†
Pixel attribute is determined by nibble value from each of the four planes.
Buffer Start:
A000:0000
Upper-left corner
28,000 bytes
32K
Page 1
Lower-right corner
Buffer End
A000:6D5F
A000:6D60
MEMORY NOT USED
A000:8000

Up to one additional table follows, using memory through A000:FFFF.

(Continued)

7.038. VGA MEMORY MAP (continued)

For High Resolution Graphics Display (640x350 all points addressable, mode 16 (10)):

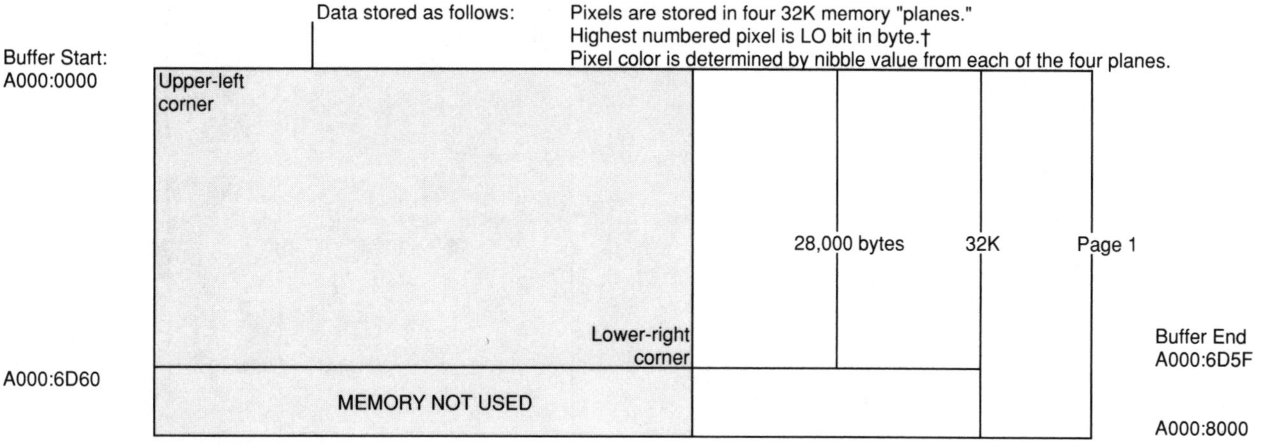
Data stored as follows:
Pixels are stored in four 32K memory "planes."
Highest numbered pixel is LO bit in byte.†
Pixel color is determined by nibble value from each of the four planes.
Buffer Start:
A000:0000
Upper-left corner
28,000 bytes
32K
Page 1
Lower-right corner
Buffer End
A000:6D5F
A000:6D60
MEMORY NOT USED
A000:8000

Up to one additional table follows, using memory through A000:FFFF.

For High Resolution Graphics Display (640x480 all points addressable, mode 17 (11)):

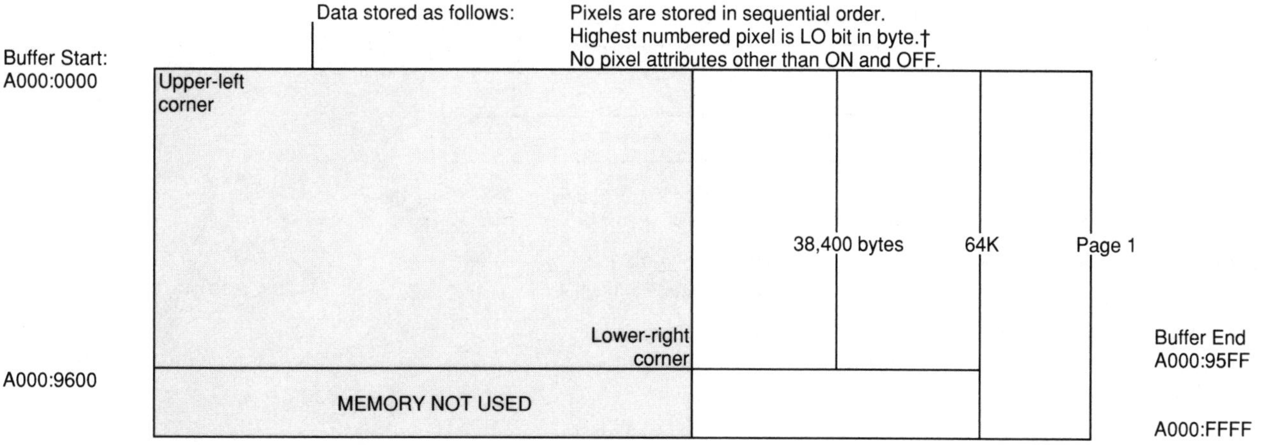
Data stored as follows:
Pixels are stored in sequential order.
Highest numbered pixel is LO bit in byte.†
No pixel attributes other than ON and OFF.
Buffer Start:
A000:0000
Upper-left corner
38,400 bytes
64K
Page 1
Lower-right corner
Buffer End
A000:95FF
A000:9600
MEMORY NOT USED
A000:FFFF

For High Resolution Graphics Display (640x480 all points addressable, mode 18 (12)):

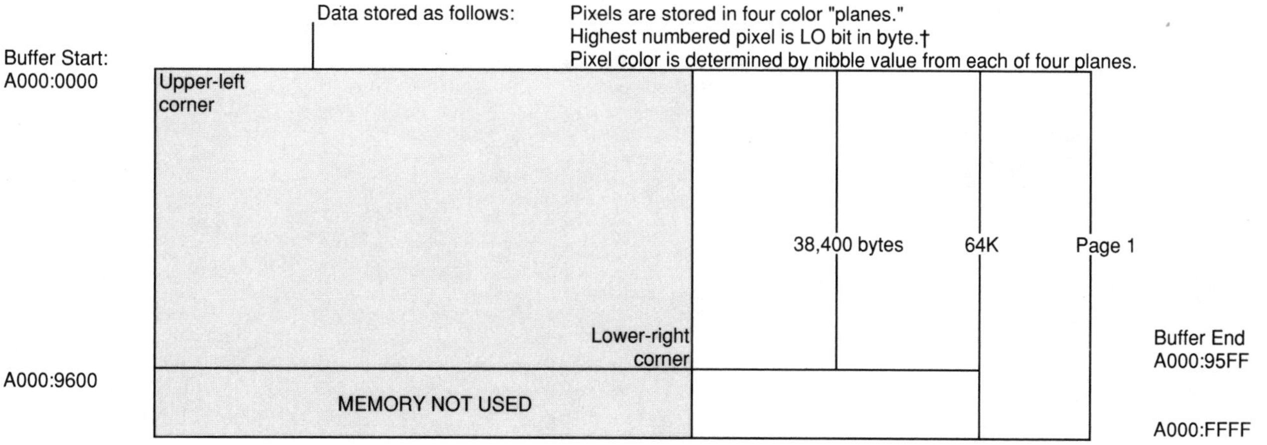
Data stored as follows:
Pixels are stored in four color "planes."
Highest numbered pixel is LO bit in byte.†
Pixel color is determined by nibble value from each of four planes.
Buffer Start:
A000:0000
Upper-left corner
38,400 bytes
64K
Page 1
Lower-right corner
Buffer End
A000:95FF
A000:9600
MEMORY NOT USED
A000:FFFF

(Continued)

7.038. VGA MEMORY MAP (continued)

For Medium Resolution Graphics Display (320x200 all points addressable, mode 19 (13)):

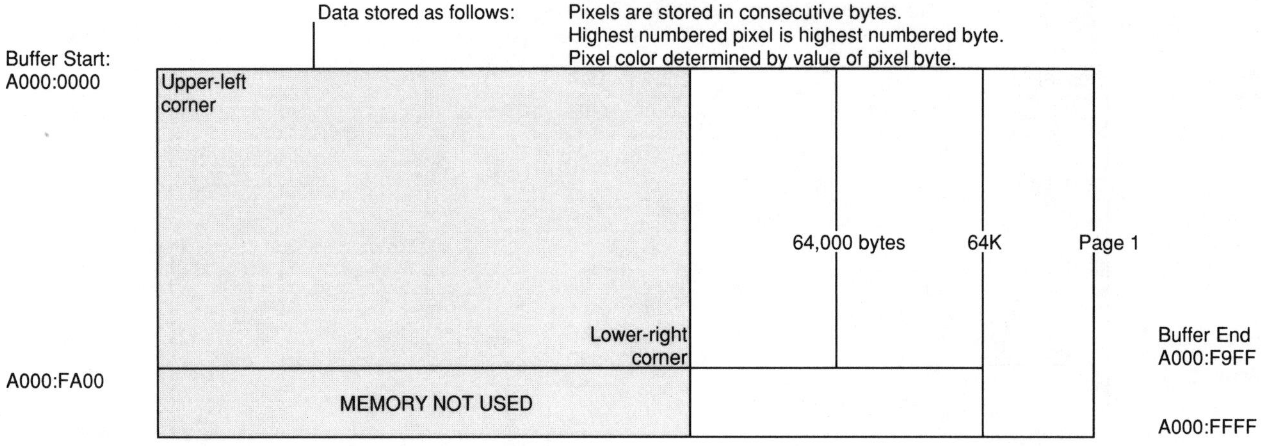
Data stored as follows:
Pixels are stored in consecutive bytes.
Highest numbered pixel is highest numbered byte.
Pixel color determined by value of pixel byte.
Buffer Start:
A000:0000
Upper-left corner
64,000 bytes
64K
Page 1
Lower-right corner
Buffer End
A000:F9FF
A000:FA00
MEMORY NOT USED
A000:FFFF

†In other words, the highest numbered pixel goes into the lowest bit (or bits), and the lowest numbered pixel goes into the highest bit (or bits).
For example:
-The first byte in medium resolution:

Bit Number	7	6	5	4	3	2	1	0
Pixel Number	1		2		3		4	

-The first byte in high resolution:

Bit Number	7	6	5	4	3	2	1	0
Pixel Number	1	2	3	4	5	6	7	8

Note: When in purely VGA modes, memory organization is four planes of either 16K or 64K, and the use and definition of "pages" is up to the programmer.

Source: IBM PS/2 Model 50 and 60 Technical Reference, pages 4-34 through 4-55
IBM PS/2 Model 80 Technical Reference, pages 4-34 through 4-55

See Also: 7.022. Video Adapter Memory Usage and Output Specifications
7.040. VGA Character Attributes

7.039. VGA CHARACTER BOX

For modes 7 and 15:

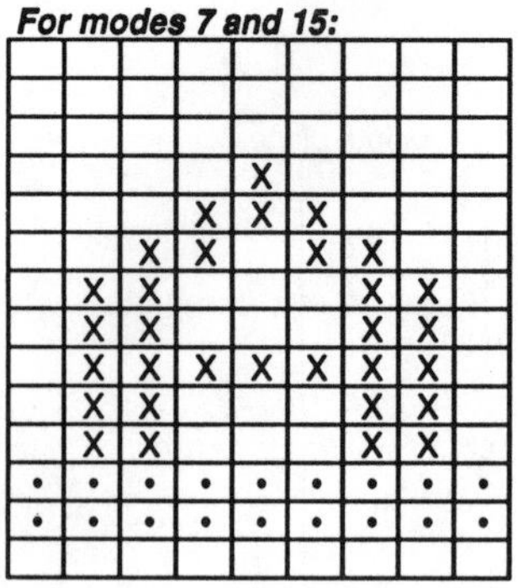

Character is a 7x9 pixel area in an 8x14, 9x14, or 9x16 pixel box.

X = pixels set for a typical character "A"
• = pixels set for default cursor

(Continued)

7.039. VGA CHARACTER BOX (continued)

For modes 0-3:

			X	X	X		
		X	X		X	X	
	X	X				X	X
	X	X				X	X
	X	X	X	X	X	X	X
	X	X				X	X
	X	X				X	X
•	•	•	•	•	•	•	•

Character is a 7x7 pixel area in an 8x8, 8x14, or 9x16 pixel box.

X = pixels set for a typical character "A"
• = pixels set for default cursor

Source: IBM PS/2 Model 50 and 60 Technical Reference, pages 4-27 through 4-28
IBM PS/2 Model 80 Technical Reference, pages 4-27 through 4-28

See Also: 7.024. Video Character Font Sizes

7.040. VGA CHARACTER ATTRIBUTES

For Text (modes 0-3):

7	*6*	*5*	*4*	*3*	*2*	*1*	*0*	*Function*	*Allowable Values*
✔								Blink	0=no blink, 1=blink
	✔	✔	✔					Background	000=black 001=blue 010=green 011=cyan 100=red 101=magenta 110=brown 111=white
				✔				Intensity	0=normal, 1=high intensity
					✔	✔	✔	Foreground	000=black gray with intensity on 001=blue light blue with intensity on 010=green light green with intensity on 011=cyan light cyan with intensity on 100=red light red with intensity on 101=magenta light magenta with intensity on 110=brown yellow with intensity on 111=white bright white with intensity on

For Text (mode 7):

7	*6*	*5*	*4*	*3*	*2*	*1*	*0*	*Function*	*Allowable Values*
✔								Blink	0=no blink, 1=blink
	✔	✔	✔					Background	000=black 111=white
				✔				Intensity	0=normal, 1=high intensity
					✔	✔	✔	Foreground	000=black gray with intensity on 001=underline 111=white bright white with intensity on

For modes 15 and 18:

Pixel Plane

3	*2*	*1*	*0*	*Function*
	0		0	Black character
	0		1	White character
	1		0	Blinking white character
	1		1	Intense white character

For modes 13, 14, and 16:

Pixel Plane

	Function
C0	Blue pixel component
C1	Green pixel component
C2	Red pixel component
C3	Intensity pixel component

Note: Invisible characters in modes 0-3 and 7 are created by placing a character on a background of the same color (e.g., white on white).

Source: IBM PS/2 Model 50 and 60 Technical Reference, pages 4-30 through 4-39
IBM PS/2 Model 80 Technical Reference, pages 4-30 through 4-39

See Also: 7.028. MDA Character Attributes
7.032. CGA Character Attributes
7.036. EGA Character Attributes
7.043. XGA Character Attributes

7.041. VGA I/O PORT USAGE

			I/O Port Used		
Register Name	*Register Type*	*R/W*	*Mono*	*Color*	*Either*
Miscellaneous output	General	W			3C2H
Miscellaneous output	General	R			3CCH
Input status register 0	General	R			3C2H
Input status register 1	General	R	3BAH	3DAH	
Feature control register	General	W	3BAH	3DAH	
Feature control register	General	R			3CAH
Video subsystem enable	General	RW			3C3H
Address register	Attribute	RW			3C0H
Other attribute register	Attribute	W			3C0H
Other attribute register	Attribute	R			3C1H
Index register	CRT controller	RW	3B4H	3D4H	
Other CRT controller registers	CRT controller	RW	3B5H	3D5H	
Address register	Sequencer	RW			3C4H
Other sequencer register	Sequencer	RW			3C5H
Address register	Graphics	RW			3CEH
Other graphics register	Graphics	RW			3CFH
PEL address write mode	Video DAC	RW			3C8H
PEL address read mode	Video DAC	W			3C7H
DAC state register	Video DAC	R			3C7H
PEL data register	Video DAC	RW			3C9H
PEL mask register	Video DAC	RW			3C6H

Source: IBM PS/2 Model 50 and 60 Technical Reference, pages 4-58 through 4-59
IBM PS/2 Model 80 Technical Reference, pages 4-58 through 4-59

See Also: 7.029. MDA I/O Port Usage
7.033. CGA I/O Port Usage
7.037. EGA I/O Port Usage

7.042. XGA CHARACTER BOXES

12x23 cell size

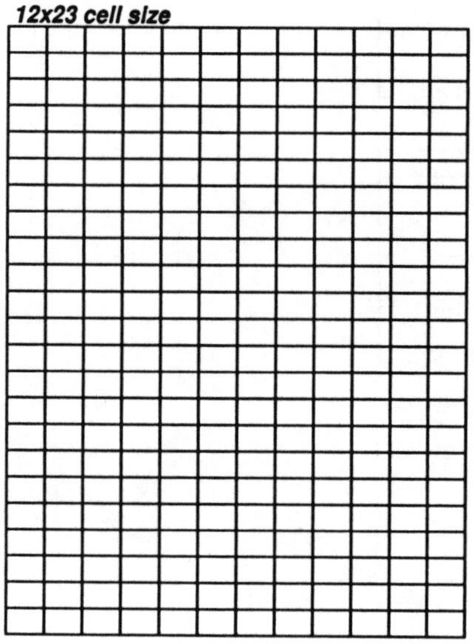

(Continued)

7.042. XGA CHARACTER BOXES (continued)

12x20 cell size

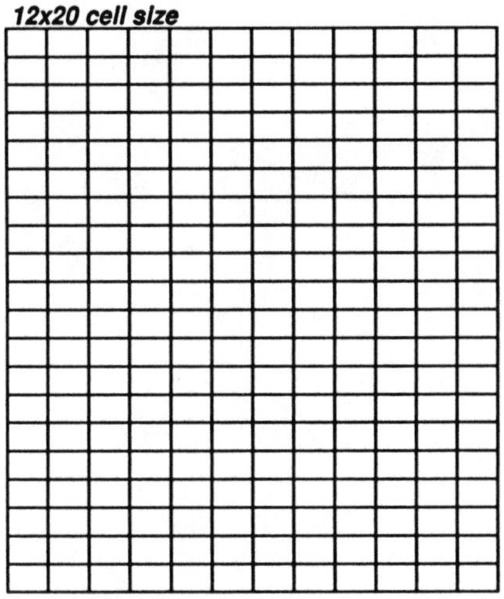

7x15 cell size

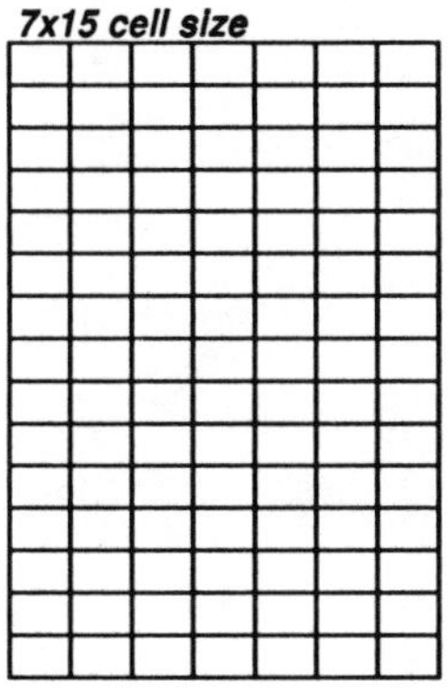

8x14 cell size

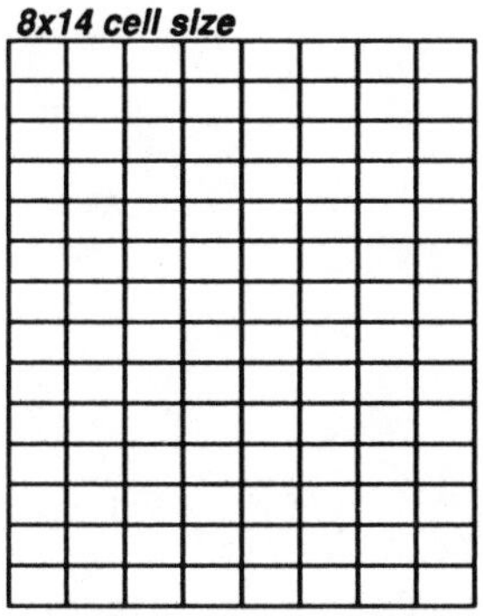

Source: IBM PS/2 XGA Adapter Interface Technical Reference, page 1-4

See Also: 7.024. Video Character Font Sizes

7.043. XGA ATTRIBUTES/MODES

Mode	*Contents*
VGA	Default
132 column text	Currently a VGA extension. Will be video mode 14H.
Extended graphics	High Resolution: 1024x768, 256 colors; 640x480, 64 K colors
	Direct Color: 16-bit pixels in video memory define color, not the palette§
	256 K Color Palette: 1-, 2-, 4-, or 8-bit pixels used as index to color table (palette)
	Sprite: 64x64 pixel image used as cursor. Overlays screen without affecting video memory†.
	Coprocessor Drawing-Assist Functions¶ Pixel block or bit block transfers Line draw. Uses Bresenham line drawing algorithm. Area fill Mixing (raster operations)¥ Map masking. Used for clipping windows environments. Scissoring x-, y-axis addressing

*Modes available:

	512 K Video Memory		*1 MB Video Memory*	
Display ID in XGA Reg. 52H	*Maximum Number of Colors Displayed*	*Resolution*	*Maximum Number of Colors Displayed*	*Resolution*
1111b		None		None
1101b	64 grays	640x480	64 grays	640x480
1110b	256	640x480	256	640x480
			64 K	640x480
1011b	256	640x480	256	640x480
	16	1024x768	64 K	640x480
			16	1024x768
			256	1024x768
1001b	64 grays	640x480	64 grays	640x480
	16 grays	1024x768	16 grays	1024x768
			64 grays	1024x768
1010b	256	640x480	256	640x480
	16	1024x768	64 K	640x480
			16	1024x768
			256	1024x768

§16-bit pixel layout:

Bit	*15 14 13 12 11*	*10 9 8 7 6 5*	*4 3 2 1 0*
Color	Red	Green	Blue

Color shades per pixel: 32 red, 64 green, 32 blue

†Sprite appearance (determined by 2-bit pixel):
00=Sprite color 0
01=Sprite color 1
10=Transparent
11=Complement

¶Supports 1, 2, 4, or 8 bits per pixel

¥Mixes and colors (raster operations):

Code	*Function*
0	zeros
1	source AND destination
2	source AND NOT destination
3	source
4	NOT source AND destination
5	destination
6	source XOR destination
7	source OR destination
8	NOT source AND NOT destination
9	source XOR NOT destination
A	NOT destination
B	source OR NOT destination
C	NOT source
D	NOT source OR destination
E	NOT source OR NOT destination

(Continued)

7.043. XGA ATTRIBUTES/MODES (continued)

Code	Function
F	ones
10	maximum
11	minimum
12	add with saturate
13	subtract (destination-source) with saturate
14	subtract (source-destination) with saturate
15	average

Source: XGA Video Subsystem Hardware Users Guide
"XGA: A New Graphics Standard," Byte, February 1991, pages 285 through 290

See Also: 7.040. VGA Character Attributes
7.042. XGA Character Boxes
7.044. XGA Function Set
7.045. XGA Extended Function Set

7.044. XGA FUNCTION SET

Function	Function Description	Byte	Type	Parameter Meaning
HLINE	Line at Given Position: defines zero or more connected straight lines as absolute coordinates	0	WORD	length of following data (≥p)
		2	P0	coordinate data of line start
		2+p	P1	coordinate data of first line end
		2+np	Pn	coordinate data of nth line end
HCLINE	Line at Current Position: defines zero or more connected straight lines as absolute coordinates	0	WORD	length of following data (≥0)
		2	P1	coordinate data of first line end
		2+p	P2	coordinate data of second line end
		2+(n-1)p	Pn	coordinate data of nth line end
HRLINE	Relative Line at Given Position: defines zero or more connected straight lines as offsets from start of line	0	WORD	length of following data (≥p)
		2	P0	coordinate data of line start
		2+p	OFF1	offset data of first line end
		2+p+r	OFF2	offset data of second line end
		2+p+(n-1)r	OFFn	offset data of nth line end
HCRLINE	Relative Line at Current Position: defines zero or more connected straight lines as offsets from start of line	0	WORD	length of following data (≥0)
		2	OFF1	offset data of first line end
		2+r	OFF2	offset data of second line end
		2+(n-1)r	OFFn	offset data of nth line end
HBAR	Begin Area: turns on area drawing mode	-	-	
HEAR	End Area: identifies the end of an area definition	0	WORD	length of following data
		2	BYTE	flags
HRECT	Fill Rectangle: performs rectangular fill at one or more positions	0	WORD	length of following data (4+p)
		2	COORD	top-left corner of first rectangle
		2+p	WORD	width of first rectangle
		4+p	WORD	height of first rectangle
		6+p	COORD	top-left corner of second rectangle
		6+2p	WORD	width of second rectangle
		8+2p	WORD	height of second rectangle
		(4n-2)+(n-1)p	COORD	top-left corner of nth rectangle
		(4n-2)+np	WORD	width of nth rectangle
		4n+np	WORD	height of nth rectangle
HMRK	Marker at Given Position: draws current marker symbol at one or more positions	0	WORD	length of following data (≥p)
		2	P0	coordinate data of first marker
		2+p	P1	coordinate data of second marker
		2+np	Pn	coordinate data of nth marker
HCMRK	Marker at Current Position: draws current marker symbol at one or more positions	0	WORD	length of following data (≥0)
		2	P1	coordinate data of second marker
		2+p	P2	coordinate data of third marker
		2+(n-1)p	Pn	coordinate data of nth marker

(Continued)

7.044. XGA FUNCTION SET (continued)

Function	Function Description	Byte	Type	Parameter Meaning
HBBW	BITBLT Write Image Data: identifies start of block of data to be written to current bitmap	0	WORD	length of following data (≥6+p)
		2	WORD	format of BITBLT data
		4	WORD	width of BITBLT data
		6	WORD	height of BITBLT data
		8	P0	coordinates of position
		8+p	WORD	left margin in pels
		10+p	WORD	top margin in pels
		12+p	WORD	width of subrectangle
		14+p	WORD	height of subrectangle
HCBBW	BITBLT Write Image Data at Current Position: identifies start of block of data to be written to current bitmap	0	WORD	length of following data (≥6)
		2	WORD	format of BITBLT data
		4	WORD	width of BITBLT data
		6	WORD	height of BITBLT data
		8	WORD	left margin in pels
		10	WORD	top margin in pels
		12	WORD	width of subrectangle
		14	WORD	height of subrectangle
HBBR	BITBLT Read Image Area: identifies start of block of data to be copied from current bitmap	0	WORD	length of following data (≥8+p)
		2	WORD	format of BITBLT data
		4	WORD	width of BITBLT data
		6	WORD	height of BITBLT data
		8	BYTE	source bit plane
		9	BYTE	RESERVED
		10	P0	coordinates of position to read
		10+p	WORD	left margin in pels
		12+p	WORD	top margin in pels
		14+p	WORD	width of rectangle
		16+p	WORD	height of rectangle
HBBCHN	BITBLT Changed Data: holds image for BITBLT orders HBBR and HBBW	0	WORD	length of following data (6)
		2	DWORD	address of data in controlling system
		6	WORD	length of data in controlling system
HBBC	BITBLT Copy: copies BITBLT block within bit planes	0	WORD	length of following data (8+2p)
		2	WORD	format of BITBLT data
		4	WORD	width of BITBLT data
		6	WORD	height of BITBLT data
		8	BYTE	source bit plane
		9	BYTE	RESERVED
		10	P0	coordinates of source data
		10+p	P1	coordinates of destination
HSCP	Set Current Position: sets current position	0	WORD	length of following data
		2	P0	coordinate data
HOPEN	Open Adapter: initializes adapter interface	0	WORD	length of following data (3)
		2	BYTE	flags
		3	BYTE	mode
		4	BYTE	return flags
HCLOSE	Close Adapter: swtiches adapter out of adapter interface mode	0	WORD	length of following data (1)
		2	BYTE	RESERVED (must be 0)
HQCP	Query Current Position; returns current position coordinates	0	WORD	length of following data (p)
		2	P0	coordinate data
HQDFPAL	Query Default Palette: returns first 16 color index values	0	WORD	length of following data (64)
		2-62	16 DWORDS	16 palette entries
HINIT	Initialize State: sets task-dependent data to initial state	0	WORD	length of following data (2)
		2	WORD	address of task state buffer
HSYNC	Synchronize Adapter: synchronizes adapter hardware with given task state	0	WORD	length of following data (2)
		2	WORD	address of task state buffer
HINT	Interrupt: synchronizes with a hardware event or interrupt	0	WORD	length of following data (4)
		2	DWORD	interrupt or event ID
HSMODE	Set Mode: sets adapter mode	0	WORD	length of following data (1 or 2)
		2	BYTE	mode byte
		3	BYTE	flags

(Continued)

7.044. XGA FUNCTION SET (continued)

Function	Function Description	Byte	Type	Parameter Meaning
HQMODE	Query Current Mode: returns data specifying adapter mode and configuration	0	WORD	length of following data (≥18)
		2	BYTE	mode number
		3	WORD	driver code level
		5	BYTE	adapter type
		6	BYTE	display type (RESERVED)
		7	BYTE	alpha cell width in pels
		8	BYTE	alpha cell height in pels
		9	BYTE	number of bit planes
		10	WORD	screen width in pels
		12	WORD	screen height in pels
		14	WORD	pels/inch horizontal
		16	WORD	pels/inch vertical
		18	BYTE	monochrome or color flag
		19	BYTE	intensity levels
		20	BYTE	software area fill plane required
		21	BYTE	VGA mode
HQMODES	Query Adapter Modes: returns data specifying modes available at the interface	0	WORD	length of following data (33)
		2	BYTE	adapter type
		3	DATA	modes
HEGS	Erase Graphics Screen: causes screen to clear	-	-	
HSGQ	Set Graphics Quality: sets miscellaneous drawing attributes	0	WORD	length of following data (2)
		2	WORD	flag settings
HSHS	Set Scissor: causes drawing process scissor rectangle to be set	0	WORD	length of following data (0, 8, or 13)
		2	WORD	left limit of rectangle
		4	WORD	right limit of rectangle
		6	WORD	bottom limit of rectangle
		8	WORD	top limit of rectangle
		10	ADDRESS	pointer to Z buffer map
		14	BYTE	flag settings
HLDPAL	Load Palette: loads palette into color lookup tables	0	WORD	length of following data (≥1)
		2	BYTE	palette ID
		3	BYTE	RESERVED
		4	WORD	number of first entry to be loaded
		6	WORD	number of entries to load
		8	DWORD	address of palette entries in storage
HSPAL	Save Palette: saves contents of color palette and display mask	0	WORD	length of following data
		2	DATA	buffer
HRPAL	Restore Palette: restores contents of color palette and display mask	0	WORD	length of following data
		2	DATA	buffer
HSLPC	Save Line Pattern Count: saves current line pattern count	0	WORD	length of following data (0 or 2)
		2	WORD	area in which line pattern count is saved
HRLPC	Restore Line Pattern Count: restores saved line pattern count	0	WORD	length of following data (0 or 2)
		2	WORD	area in which line pattern count is saved
HSBP	Set Bit Plane Controls: selects bit planes and controls the use of the palette	0	WORD	length of following data (12 or 26)
		2	DWORD	planes selected for update bit mask (graphics or text)
		6	DWORD	planes selected for update bit mask (alphanumeric)
		10	DWORD	planes enabled for display bit mask
		14	BYTE	flags
		15	BYTE	RESERVED
		16	DWORD	green bits mask
		20	DWORD	red bits mask
		24	DWORD	blue bits mask
HQCOORD	Query Coordinate Types: verifies support for a coordinate type	0	WORD	length of following data (4)
		2	BYTE	format of each coordinate
		3	BYTE	format of each relative coordinate
		4	BYTE	number of dimensions (2)
		5	BYTE	return flags
HSCOORD	Set Coordinate Types: no effect on adapter	-	-	
HESC	Stop Processing (Esc): no effect on adapter	-	-	
HSAFP	Set Area Fill Plane: specifies address to be used as area fill plane	0	WORD	length of following data (5)
		2	DWORD	address of area fill buffer
		6	BYTE	flags

(Continued)

7.044. XGA FUNCTION SET (continued)

Function	Function Description	Byte	Type	Parameter Meaning
HQDPS	Query Drawing Process State Size: returns size of elements in drawing process	0	WORD	length of following data (6 or 14)
		2	WORD	buffer size in bytes
		4	WORD	stack usage in bytes
		6	WORD	save palette buffer size in bytes
		8	DWORD	size of installed direct access storage
		12	DWORD	size of area fill plane required
HSMARK	Set Marker Shape: defines shape of current marker symbol	0	WORD	length of following data (≥0)
		2	BYTE	cell width in pels
		3	BYTE	cell height in pels
		4	BYTE	flags
		5	BYTE	RESERVED (must be 0)
		6	WORD	length of image definition in bytes
		8	DWORD	address of marker image definition
		12	DWORD	address of marker color definition
HSPATT	Set Pattern Shape: defines shape of current area fill pattern symbol	0	WORD	length of following data (≥0)
		2	BYTE	cell width in pels
		3	BYTE	cell height in pels
		4	BYTE	flags
		5	BYTE	RESERVED (must be 0)
		6	WORD	length of image definition in bytes
		8	DWORD	address of pattern image definition
		12	DWORD	address of pattern color definition
HSPATTO	Set Pattern Reference Point: sets reference point or origin for area fill pattern symbols	0	WORD	length of following data (p)
		2	P0	pattern reference point
HSLT	Set Line Type: sets current line type to the value specified	0	WORD	length of following data (≥1)
		2	BYTE	line type value
		3	BYTE	RESERVED
		4	DWORD	address of user line type definition
HSLW	Set Line Width: sets current line width value	0	WORD	length of following data (1)
		2	BYTE	line width value
HSCOL	Set Color: sets foreground color index to the value specified	0	WORD	length of following data (4)
		2	DWORD	color index
HSBCOL	Set Background Color: sets background color index to the value specified	0	WORD	length of following data
		2	DWORD	color index
HSMX	Set Mix: sets value of color comparison register	0	WORD	length of following data (2)
		2	BYTE	foreground mix value
		3	BYTE	background mix value
HSCMP	Set Color Comparison Register: sets value of color comparison register	0	WORD	length of following data (5)
		2	DWORD	comparison color index
		6	BYTE	logic function
HSCS	Set Character Set: sets current character set	0	WORD	length of following data(4)
		2	DWORD	address of character set definition block
HCHST	Character Set at Given Point: draws a character string at a given position	0	WORD	length of following data (≥p+s)
		2	P0	coordinate of point at which the bottom left corner of string is placed
		2+p	STRING	list of code points in string
HCCHST	Character String at Current Position: draws character string at current position	0	WORD	length of following data (≥0)
		2	STRING	list of code points in string
HXLATE	Assign Multiplane Text Color Index Table: provides color index translate table for use with multiplane text orders	0	WORD	length of following data (32)
		2-30	8 DWORDS	8 translate table entries
ABLOCKMFI	Write Character Block: writes block of characters to bit planes in MFI (mainframe interactive) mode	0	WORD	length of following data (10)
		2	BYTE	start column
		3	BYTE	start row
		4	BYTE	number of char cells across
		5	BYTE	number of char cells down
		6	DWORD	start address of character block
		10	BYTE	width of character buffer
		11	BYTE	RESERVED (must be 0)
ABLOCKCGA	Write Character Block (CGA): writes block of characters to bit planes in MFI mode. Supports 2-byte character attribute sequence for color graphics adapter (CGA) operation	0	WORD	length of following data (10)
		2	BYTE	start column
		3	BYTE	start row
		4	BYTE	number of char cells across
		5	BYTE	number of char cells down
		6	DWORD	start address of character block
		10	BYTE	width of character buffer
		11	BYTE	highlight attribute for block
ASCELL	Set Alpha Cell Size: sets cell size for alpha-numeric operations	0	WORD	length of following data (2)
		2	BYTE	cell width in pels
		3	BYTE	cell height in pels

(Continued)

7.044. XGA FUNCTION SET (continued)

Function	Function Description	Byte	Type	Parameter Meaning
AERASE	Erase Rectangle: sets rectangle of character cells to a background color	0	WORD	length of following data (5)
		2	BYTE	starting column
		3	BYTE	starting row
		4	BYTE	number of char cells in horz axis across
		5	BYTE	number of char cells in vert axis down
		6	BYTE	color
ASCROLL	Scroll Rectangle: copies rectangle of character cells on screen	0	WORD	length of following data (6)
		2	BYTE	starting column of source
		3	BYTE	starting row of source
		4	BYTE	number of char cells across
		5	BYTE	number of char cells down
		6	BYTE	starting column of destination
		7	BYTE	starting row of destination
ACURSOR	Set Cursor Position: sets alphanumeric cursor position	0	WORD	length of following data (2)
		2	BYTE	cursor position, column
		3	BYTE	cursor position, row
ASCUR	Set Cursor Shape: sets alphanumeric cursor shape	0	WORD	length of following data (3)
		2	BYTE	cursor start line
		3	BYTE	cursor stop line
		4	BYTE	attribute
ASFONT	Select Character Set: selects one of four alphanumeric character sets	0	WORD	length of following data (6)
		2	BYTE	font number
		3	BYTE	RESERVED
		4	DWORD	address of character set definition block
AXLATE	Assign Alpha Attribute Color Index Table: provides attribute to color index translate table	0	WORD	length of following data
		2-62	16 DWORDS	foreground translate table entries
		66-126	16 DWORDS	background translate table entries

Source: IBM PS/2 XGA Adapter Interface Technical Reference, pages 3-1 through 3-90

7.045. XGA EXTENDED FUNCTION SET

Function	Function Description	Byte	Type	Parameter Meaning
HDLINE	Disjoint Line: defines zero or more disconnected straight lines	0	WORD	length of following data (≥p)
		2	COORD	coordinate data of first line start
		2+p	COORD	coordinate data of first line end
		2+np	COORD	coordinate data of nth line end
HQDEVICE	Query Device Specific: no effect on adapter	-	-	
ASGO	Set Alpha Grid Origin: changes cell grid for alphanumeric operations	0	WORD	length of following data (4)
		2	WORD	horizontal cell offset in pels
		4	WORD	vertical cell offset in pels
HPEL	Write Pel String: writes a string of pels from left to right horizontally	0	WORD	length of following data (≥2+p)
		2	P0	coordinate data of first pel
		2+p	WORD	pel count
		2+n(p+2)	Pn	coordinate data of first pel of pel run n
		(n+1)(p+2)	WORD	pel count of pel run n
HRPEL	Read Pel String: reads a string of pels from left to right horizontally, starting at given position	0	WORD	length of following data (6+p)
		2	DWORD	address of buffer for data read
		6	P0	coordinate data of first pel
		6+p	WORD	pel count
HPSTEP	Plot and Step: defines series of adjacent pel runs starting at given position	0	WORD	length of following data (4+p or 8+p)
		2	P0	coordinate data of first pel
		2+p	DWORD	address of plot and step definition buffer
		6+p	DWORD	address of source data buffer
HCPSTEP	Plot and Step at Current Position: defines series of adjacent pel runs starting at current position	0	WORD	length of following data (4 or 8)
		2	DWORD	address of plot and step definition buffer
		6	DWORD	address of source data buffer
HRSTEP	Read and Step: read series of adjacent pel runs	0	WORD	length of following data (8+p)
		2	P0	coordinate data of first pel
		2+p	DWORD	address of read and step definition buffer
		6+p	DWORD	address of target data buffer
HRWVEC	Read or Write Vector: read or write vector drawing with color data	0	WORD	length of following data [6+(np)]
		2	BYTE	flags (bit 7=1 for write, 0 for read)
		3	BYTE	RESERVED (must be 0)
		4	DWORD	address of data buffer
		8	P0	coordinate line start
		8+p	P1	coordinate of first line end
		8+np	Pn	coordinate of nth line end

(Continued)

7.045. XGA EXTENDED FUNCTION SET (continued)

Function	Function Description	Byte	Type	Parameter Meaning
HSFPAL	Save Full Palette: saves contents of color palette and display mask	0	WORD	length of following data (8)
		2	WORD	format (=8)
		4	DATA	buffer
HRFPAL	Restore Full Palette: restores contents of color palette and display mask	0	WORD	length of following data (varies)
		2	WORD	format (=8)
		4	DATA	buffer
HSBMAP	Set Bitmap Attributes: sets current bitmap and makes it the destination for subsequent drawing primatives	0	WORD	length of following data (10)
		2	BYTE	flags
		3	BYTE	format (bits per pel)
		4	DWORD	address of bitmaps
		8	WORD	width of bitmaps in pels
		10	WORD	height of bitmaps in pels
HQBMAP	Query Bitmap Attributes: returns attributes of current bitmap	0	WORD	length of following data (10 or 14+p)
		2	BYTE	flags
		3	BYTE	format (bits per pel)
		4	DWORD	address of bitmap
		8	WORD	width of bitmap in pels
		10	WORD	height of bitmap in pels
		12	P0	coordinate of display window origin
		12+p	WORD	display window width
		14+p	WORD	display window height
HBMC	Bitmap copy: copies a block within current bitmap, or from bitmap to bitmap	0	WORD	length of following data (=36+3p)
		2	WORD	flags
		4	WORD	width of block in pels
		6	WORD	height of block in pels
		8	BYTE	format of destination bitmap
		9	BYTE	RESERVED
		10	ADDR	pointer to destination bitmap
		14	WORD	width of destination bitmap
		16	WORD	height of destination bitmap
		18	P0	coordinate of destination data
		18+p	BYTE	format of source bitmap
		19+p	BYTE	RESERVED
		20+p	ADDR	pointer to source bitmap
		24+p	WORD	width of source bitmap
		26+p	WORD	height of source bitmap
		28+p	P1	coordinate of source data
		28+2p	BYTE	format of pattern bitmap
		29+2p	BYTE	RESERVED
		30+2p	ADDR	pointer to pattern bitmap
		34+2p	WORD	width of pattern bitmap
		36+2p	WORD	height of pattern bitmap
		38+2p	P2	coordinate of pattern data
HSDW	Set Window Display: sets display window within screen bitmap in display direct access storage	0	WORD	length of following data (4+p)
		2	P0	coordinate of display window origin
		2+p	WORD	window width
		4+p	WORD	window height
HSPRITE	Sprite at Given Position: draws current Sprite shape at position	0	WORD	length of following data (p)
		2	P0	coordinate data of Sprite
HSSPRITE	Set Sprite Shape: defines shape of Sprite	0	WORD	length of following data (24 or 1)
		2	BYTE	flags
		3	BYTE	RESERVED (must be 0)
		4	BYTE	hot point x offset
		5	BYTE	hot point y offset
		6	DWORD	Sprite image definition address
		10	WORD	Sprite image width
		12	WORD	Sprite image height
		14	WORD	color 1 green value
		16	WORD	color 1 red value
		18	WORD	color 1 blue value
		20	WORD	color 2 green value
		22	WORD	color 2 red value
		24	WORD	color 2 blue value

Source: IBM PS/2 XGA Adapter Interface Technical Reference, pages 4-1 through 4-27

See Also: 7.044. XGA Function Set

7.046. 8514/A I/O PORT USAGE

Type	*Port*	*Function*	*Comment*
Setup	100H	setup mode ID 1	read
	101H	setup mode ID 2	read
	102H	setup option mode select	read/write
Lookup	2EAH	DAC mask	read/write
	2EBH	DAC read index	write
	2ECH	DAC write index	write
	2EDH	DAC data	read/write
CRT Control	2E8H	read: display status; write: horizontal total	read/write
	6E8H	horizontal displayed	write
	AE8H	horizontal sync start	write
	EE8H	horizontal sync width	write
	12E8H	vertical total	write
	16E8H	vertical displayed	write
	1AE8H	vertical sync start	write
	1EE8H	vertical sync width	write
	22E8H	display control	write
	4AE8H	advanced function control	write
Misc. Control	42E8H	read: subsystem status; write: subsystem control	read/write
	46E8H	ROM page select	write
Drawing Control	82E8H	current Y position	read/write
	86E8H	current X position	read/write
	8AE8H	destination Y position/axial step constant	write
	8EE8H	destination X position/diagonal step constant	write
	92E8H	error term	read/write
	96E8H	major axis pixel count	write
	9AE8H	read: graphics processor status; write: command	read/write
	9EE8H	short stroke vector transfer	write
	A2E8H	background color	write
	A6E8H	foreground color	write
	AAE8H	write mask	write
	AEE8H	read mask	write
	B2E8H	color compare	write
	B6E8H	background mix	write
	BAE8H	foreground mix	write
	BEE8H	multifunction control	write
	E2E8H	pixel data transfer	read/write

Source: "Harnessing the 8514/A," MIPS, January 1990, page 88

See Also: 7.029. MDA I/O Port Usage
7.033. CGA I/O Port Usage
7.037. EGA I/O Port Usage
7.041. VGA I/O Port Usage

7.047. 8514/A STATUS REGISTER

Bit Number

15	*14*	*13*	*12*	*11*	*10*	*9*	*8*	*7*	*6*	*5*	*4*	*3*	*2*	*1*	*0*	*Description*	*Allowable Values*
✔	✔	✔	✔	✔	✔											RESERVED	
						✔										Busy	0=idle; 1=busy
							✔									Data RDY	0=no data; 1=data waiting to be read
								✔	✔	✔	✔	✔	✔	✔	✔	Queue State	each bit represents a queue position: 0=empty; 1=filled

Source: "Harnessing the 8514/A," MIPS, January 1990, page 91

See Also: 7.048. 8514/A Command Register

7.048. 8514/A COMMAND REGISTER

Bit Number 15	14	13	12	11	10	9	8	7	6	5	4	3	2	1	0	*Description*	*Allowable Values*
✔	✔	✔														Command	000=no operation 001=line draw 010=fast fill rectangle 011=fill rectangle vertically#1 100=fill rectangle vertically#2 (4 pixels) 101=line draw, one pixel per scan line 110=copy rectangle 111=RESERVED
			✔													BYTSEQ	0=high byte first; 1=high byte last
				✔	✔											RESERVED	
						✔										16 BIT	0=disable 16-bit writes; 1=enable
							✔									PCDATA	0=use 8514/A data; 1=pixel data trans reg
								✔								INC_Y	0=draw lines up; 1=draw lines down
									✔							YMAJAXIS	0=x is major axis; 1=y is major axis
										✔						INC_X	0=draw lines left; 1=draw lines right
											✔					DRAW	0=do move only; 1=draw and move
												✔				LINETYPE	0=Bresenham line draw; 1=directional vector
													✔			LASTPIX	0=draw last pixel; 1=don't draw last pixel
														✔		PLANAR	0=access one pixel at a time; 1=4 pixels
															✔	RD/WR	0=read from display memory; 1=write data

Source: "Harnessing the 8514/A," MIPS, January 1990, page 91

See Also: 7.047. 8514/A Status Register

7.049. PC AND XT FLOPPY DISK CONTROLLER COMMAND SUMMARY

Command Name	*Command Sequence*	*Direction*	*Comments*	Bit Number 7	6	5	4	3	2	1	0
Read Data	Command code byte 1	Write	See bit mask at right	MT	MF	SK	0	0	1	1	0
	Command code byte 2	Write	See bit mask at right	*	*	*	*	*	HD	US1	US0
	Start cylinder	Write									
	Start head	Write									
	Start sector number	Write									
	Number bytes/sector	Write									
	Last sector on cylinder	Write									
	Gap length	Write	Length of gap 3								
	Data length	Write	Used if number/bytes sector is 0								
	Status register 0	Read	See 7.050. FDC Status Register 0								
	Status register 1	Read	See 7.051. FDC Status Register 1								
	Status register 2	Read	See 7.052. FDC Status Register 2								
	Current cylinder	Read	Location after read								
	Current head	Read	Location after read								
	Current sector number	Read	Location after read								
	Number bytes/sector	Read									
Read Deleted Data	Command code byte 1	Write	See bit mask at right	MT	MF	SK	0	1	1	0	0
	Command code byte 2	Write	See bit mask at right	*	*	*	*	*	HD	US1	US0
	Start cylinder	Write									
	Start head	Write									
	Start sector number	Write									
	Number bytes/sector	Write									
	Last sector on cylinder	Write									
	Gap length	Write	Length of gap 3								
	Data length	Write	Used if number/bytes sector is 0								
	Status register 0	Read	See 7.050. FDC Status Register 0								
	Status register 1	Read	See 7.051. FDC Status Register 1								
	Status register 2	Read	See 7.052. FDC Status Register 2								
	Current cylinder	Read	Location after read								
	Current head	Read	Location after read								
	Current sector number	Read	Location after read								
	Number bytes/sector	Read									

(Continued)

7.049. PC AND XT FLOPPY DISK CONTROLLER COMMAND SUMMARY (continued)

Command Name	Command Sequence	Direction	Comments	Bit Number 7	6	5	4	3	2	1	0
Write Data	Command code byte 1	Write	See bit mask at right	MT	MF	0	0	0	1	0	1
	Command code byte 2	Write	See bit mask at right	*	*	*	*	*	HD	US1	US0
	Start cylinder	Write									
	Start head	Write									
	Start sector number	Write									
	Number bytes/sector	Write									
	Last sector on cylinder	Write									
	Gap length	Write	Length of gap 3								
	Data length	Write	Used if number/bytes sector is 0								
	Status register 0	Read	See 7.050. FDC Status Register 0								
	Status register 1	Read	See 7.051. FDC Status Register 1								
	Status register 2	Read	See 7.052. FDC Status Register 2								
	Current cylinder	Read	Location after write								
	Current head	Read	Location after write								
	Current sector number	Read	Location after write								
	Number bytes/sector	Read									
Write Deleted Data	Command code byte 1	Write	See bit mask at right	MT	MF	0	0	1	0	0	1
	Command code byte 2	Write	See bit mask at right	*	*	*	*	*	HD	US1	US0
	Start cylinder	Write									
	Start head	Write									
	Start sector number	Write									
	Number bytes/sector	Write									
	Last sector on cylinder	Write									
	Gap length	Write	Length of gap 3								
	Data length	Write	Used if number/bytes sector is 0								
	Status register 0	Read	See 7.050. FDC Status Register 0								
	Status register 1	Read	See 7.051. FDC Status Register 1								
	Status register 2	Read	See 7.052. FDC Status Register 2								
	Current cylinder	Read	Location after write								
	Current head	Read	Location after write								
	Current sector number	Read	Location after write								
	Number bytes/sector	Read									
Read Track	Command code byte 1	Write	See bit mask at right	0	MF	SK	0	0	0	1	0
	Command code byte 2	Write	See bit mask at right	*	*	*	*	*	HD	US1	US0
	Start cylinder	Write									
	Start head	Write									
	Start sector number	Write									
	Number bytes/sector	Write									
	Last sector on cylinder	Write									
	Gap length	Write	Length of gap 3								
	Data length	Write	Used if number/bytes sector is 0								
	Status register 0	Read	See 7.050. FDC Status Register 0								
	Status register 1	Read	See 7.051. FDC Status Register 1								
	Status register 2	Read	See 7.052. FDC Status Register 2								
	Current cylinder	Read	Location after read								
	Current head	Read	Location after read								
	Current sector number	Read	Location after read								
	Number bytes/sector	Read									
Read ID	Command code byte 1	Write	See bit mask at right	0	MF	0	0	1	0	1	0
	Command code byte 2	Write	See bit mask at right	*	*	*	*	*	HD	US1	US0
	Status register 0	Read	See 7.050. FDC Status Register 0								
	Status register 1	Read	See 7.051. FDC Status Register 1								
	Status register 2	Read	See 7.052. FDC Status Register 2								
	Current cylinder	Read	Location after read								
	Current head	Read	Location after read								
	Current sector number	Read	Location after read								
	Number bytes/sector	Read									
Format Track	Command code byte 1	Write	See bit mask at right	0	MF	0	0	1	1	0	0
	Command code byte 2	Write	See bit mask at right	*	*	*	*	*	HD	US1	US0
	Number bytes/sector	Write									
	Sectors per cylinder	Write									
	Gap length	Write	Length of gap 3								
	Filler byte	Write	Data pattern to initialize sectors								
	Status register 0	Read	See 7.050. FDC Status Register 0								
	Status register 1	Read	See 7.051. FDC Status Register 1								
	Status register 2	Read	See 7.052. FDC Status Register 2								
	Current cylinder	Read	No meaning in this context								
	Current head	Read	No meaning in this context								
	Current sector number	Read	No meaning in this context								
	Number bytes/sector	Read	No meaning in this context								

(Continued)

7.049. PC AND XT FLOPPY DISK CONTROLLER COMMAND SUMMARY (continued)

Command Name	Command Sequence	Direction	Comments	Bit Number 7	6	5	4	3	2	1	0
Scan Equal	Command code byte 1	Write	See bit mask at right	MT	MF	SK	1	0	0	0	1
	Command code byte 2	Write	See bit mask at right	*	*	*	*	*	HD	US1	US0
	Start cylinder	Write									
	Start head	Write									
	Start sector number	Write									
	Number bytes/sector	Write									
	Last sector on cylinder	Write									
	Gap length	Write	Length of gap 3								
	Scan test code	Write	1=compare contiguous, 2=compare alt								
	Status register 0	Read	See 7.050. FDC Status Register 0								
	Status register 1	Read	See 7.051. FDC Status Register 1								
	Status register 2	Read	See 7.052. FDC Status Register 2								
	Current cylinder	Read	Location after scan								
	Current head	Read	Location after scan								
	Current sector number	Read	Location after scan								
	Number bytes/sector	Read									
Scan Low or Equal	Command code byte 1	Write	See bit mask at right	MT	MF	SK	1	1	0	0	1
	Command code byte 2	Write	See bit mask at right	*	*	*	*	*	HD	US1	US0
	Start cylinder	Write									
	Start head	Write									
	Start sector number	Write									
	Number bytes/sector	Write									
	Last sector on cylinder	Write									
	Gap length	Write	Length of gap 3								
	Scan test code	Write	1=compare contiguous, 2=compare alt								
	Status register 0	Read	See 7.050. FDC Status Register 0								
	Status register 1	Read	See 7.051. FDC Status Register 1								
	Status register 2	Read	See 7.052. FDC Status Register 2								
	Current cylinder	Read	Location after scan								
	Current head	Read	Location after scan								
	Current sector number	Read	Location after scan								
	Number bytes/sector	Read									
Scan High or Equal	Command code byte 1	Write	See bit mask at right	MT	MF	SK	1	1	1	0	1
	Command code byte 2	Write	See bit mask at right	*	*	*	*	*	HD	US1	US0
	Start cylinder	Write									
	Start head	Write									
	Start sector number	Write									
	Number bytes/sector	Write									
	Last sector on cylinder	Write									
	Gap length	Write	Length of gap 3								
	Scan test code	Write	1=compare contiguous, 2=compare alt								
	Status register 0	Read	See 7.050. FDC Status Register 0								
	Status register 1	Read	See 7.051. FDC Status Register 1								
	Status register 2	Read	See 7.052. FDC Status Register 2								
	Current cylinder	Read	Location after scan								
	Current head	Read	Location after scan								
	Current sector number	Read	Location after scan								
	Number bytes/sector	Read									
Recalibrate	Command code byte 1	Write	See bit mask at right	0	0	0	0	0	1	1	1
	Command code byte 2	Write	See bit mask at right	*	*	*	*	*	0	US1	US0
Sense Interrupt Status	Command code byte 1	Write	See bit mask at right	0	0	0	0	1	0	0	0
	Status register 0	Read	See 7.050. FDC Status Register 0								
	Present cylinder number	Read									
Specify	Command code byte 1	Write	See bit mask at right	0	0	0	0	0	0	1	1
	Command code byte 2	Write	HO=Step Rate Time, LO=Head Unload Time	SRT	SRT	SRT	SRT	HUT	HUT	HUT	HUT
	Command code byte 3	Write	Bits 1-7=Head Load Time, Bit 0=non-DMA	HLT	HLT	HLT	HLT	HLT	HLT	HLT	ND
Sense Drive Status	Command code byte 1	Write	See bit mask at right	0	0	0	0	0	1	0	0
	Command code byte 2	Write	See bit mask at right	*	*	*	*	*	HD	US1	US0
	Status register 3	Read	See 7.053. FDC Status Register 3								
Seek	Command code byte 1	Write	See bit mask at right	0	0	0	0	1	1	1	1
	Command code byte 2	Write	See bit mask at right	*	*	*	*	*	HD	US1	US0
	Cylinder to seek	Write									
Invalid	Any invalid code	Write									
	Status register 0	Read	See 7.050. FDC Status Register 0								

* = value ignored, may be 1 or 0

Legend: MT = multitrack operation (high=TRUE)
MF = FM mode (high=MFM, low=FM)
SK = skip deleted data address mark
HD = head number
US0 = unit select zero
US1 = unit select one

Note: The terms "track" and "cylinder" are used interchangeably in the IBM documentation.

Source: IBM PC/XT Technical Reference, pages 1-112 through 1-119

See Also: 7.050. PC and XT Floppy Disk Controller Status Register 0
7.051. PC and XT Floppy Disk Controller Status Register 1
7.052. PC and XT Floppy Disk Controller Status Register 2
7.053. PC and XT Floppy Disk Controller Status Register 3
7.055. XT Fixed Disk Controller Command Summary

7.050. PC AND XT FLOPPY DISK CONTROLLER STATUS REGISTER 0

Bit Number

7	*6*	*5*	*4*	*3*	*2*	*1*	*0*	*Name*	*Function*	*Allowable Values*
✔	✔							Interrupt code	Reports status due to last command	00=normal termination 01=abnormal termination 10=invalid command issued 11=abnormal termination, change in ready state
		✔						Seek end	Reports completion of seek op.	1=seek operation completed
			✔					Equipment check	Set when fault received from FDD	(Also set when recalibrate fails to find track 0)
				✔				Not ready	Reports FDD is not in ready state	1=not ready
					✔			Head address	Reports state of head at interrupt	0=0 head, 1=1 head
						✔	✔	Unit select	Reports selected unit at interrupt	Bit 0=unit select 2, bit 1=unit select 1

Source: IBM PC/XT Technical Reference, page 1-120

See Also: 7.049. PC and XT Floppy Disk Controller Command Summary
7.051. PC and XT Floppy Disk Controller Status Register 1
7.052. PC and XT Floppy Disk Controller Status Register 2
7.053. PC and XT Floppy Disk Controller Status Register 3
7.055. XT Fixed Disk Controller Command Summary

7.051. PC AND XT FLOPPY DISK CONTROLLER STATUS REGISTER 1

Bit Number

7	*6*	*5*	*4*	*3*	*2*	*1*	*0*	*Name*	*Function*	*Allowable Values*
✔								End of cylinder	Reports movement past last track	1=FDC tried to access beyond final sector
	✔							NOT USED		Always 0
		✔						Data error	Reports CRC error in ID or data field	1=error, 0=no error
			✔					Overrun	Reports FDC not serviced	1=FDC not serviced within time limit
				✔				NOT USED		Always 0
					✔			No data	Reports cannot find sector or ID	1=error, 0=no error
						✔		Not writable	Reports write-protect signal from FDD	1=write protect during write op., 0=no error
							✔	Missing address mark	Reports FDC didn't find address mark	1=missing address mark, 0=no error

Source: IBM PC/XT Technical Reference, page 1-121

See Also: 7.049. PC and XT Floppy Disk Controller Command Summary
7.050. PC and XT Floppy Disk Controller Status Register 0
7.052. PC and XT Floppy Disk Controller Status Register 2
7.053. PC and XT Floppy Disk Controller Status Register 3
7.055. XT Fixed Disk Controller Command Summary

7.052. PC AND XT FLOPPY DISK CONTROLLER STATUS REGISTER 2

Bit Number

7	*6*	*5*	*4*	*3*	*2*	*1*	*0*	*Name*	*Function*	*Allowable Values*
✔								NOT USED		Always 0
	✔							Control mark	Reports deleted data address mark	1=deleted mark detected 0=no error
		✔						Data error in data field	Reports CRC error in data	1=CRC error in data field, 0=no error
			✔					Wrong cylinder	Track contents don't match track ID	1=error, 0=no error
				✔				Scan equal hit	Reports scan found equal condition	1=scan equal, 0=scan not equal
					✔			Scan not satisified	Reports scan not satisified condition	1=scan not satisifed, 0=scan satisfied
						✔		Bad cylinder	Track contents: no match, FFH found	1=error, 0=no error
							✔	Missing address in data field	Reports FDC couldn't find mark	1=couldn't find address mark, 0=no error

Source: IBM PC/XT Technical Reference, page 1-122

See Also:
7.049. PC and XT Floppy Disk Controller Command Summary
7.050. PC and XT Floppy Disk Controller Status Register 0
7.051. PC and XT Floppy Disk Controller Status Register 1
7.053. PC and XT Floppy Disk Controller Status Register 3
7.055. XT Fixed Disk Controller Command Summary

7.053. PC AND XT FLOPPY DISK CONTROLLER STATUS REGISTER 3

Bit Number

7	*6*	*5*	*4*	*3*	*2*	*1*	*0*	*Name*	*Function*	*Allowable Values*
✔								Fault	FDD fault signal status	1=FDD fault, 0=no fault
	✔							Write protected	FDD write-protected status	1=write-protected, 0=not protected
		✔						Ready	FDD ready status	1=disk drive ready, 0=not ready
			✔					Track 0	FDD at track zero signal	1=FDD is at track 0, 0=not at track 0
				✔				Two sided	FDD two-sided media signal	1=two-sided media, 0=one-sided media
					✔			Head address	FDD head selected	1=head 1, 0=head 0
						✔		Unit select 1	FDD unit select 1 status	
							✔	Unit select 0	FDD unit select 0 status	

Source: IBM PC/XT Technical Reference, page 1-123

See Also:
7.049. PC and XT Floppy Disk Controller Command Summary
7.050. PC and XT Floppy Disk Controller Status Register 0
7.051. PC and XT Floppy Disk Controller Status Register 1
7.052. PC and XT Floppy Disk Controller Status Register 2
7.055. XT Fixed Disk Controller Command Summary

7.054. PC AND XT FDC DISK PROGRAM CONTROL REGISTERS

Register Name	*I/O Address*
Data register	3F5H
Main status register	3F4H
Digital output register	3F2H

Digital Output Register

Bit Number

7	*6*	*5*	*4*	*3*	*2*	*1*	*0*	*Name*	*Allowable Values*
						✔	✔	Drive select	00=A, 01=B, 10=C, 11=D
					✔			Not FDC reset	
				✔				Enable INT & DMA requests	
			✔					Drive A motor enable	1=motor on, 0=motor off
		✔						Drive B motor enable	1=motor on, 0=motor off
	✔							Drive C motor enable	1=motor on, 0=motor off
✔								Drive D motor enable	1=motor on, 0=motor off

Source: IBM PC/XT Technical Reference, page 1-123

See Also:
7.049. PC and XT Floppy Disk Controller Command Summary
7.055. XT Fixed Disk Controller Command Summary

7.055. XT FIXED DISK CONTROLLER COMMAND SUMMARY

Command Name	Command Sequence	Direction	Bit Number 7	6	5	4	3	2	1	0
Test drive ready	Command code byte 1	Write	0	0	0	0	0	0	0	0
	Command code byte 2	Write	0	0	DR	*	*	*	*	*
	Don't care	Write	*	*	*	*	*	*	*	*
	Don't care	Write	*	*	*	*	*	*	*	*
	Don't care	Write	*	*	*	*	*	*	*	*
	Don't care	Write	*	*	*	*	*	*	*	*
Recalibrate	Command code byte 1	Write	0	0	0	0	0	0	0	1
	Command code byte 2	Write	0	0	DR	*	*	*	*	*
	Don't care	Write	*	*	*	*	*	*	*	*
	Don't care	Write	*	*	*	*	*	*	*	*
	Don't care	Write	*	*	*	*	*	*	*	*
	Command code byte 6	Write	RT	0	0	0	0	Step option		
Request sense status	Command code byte 1	Write	0	0	0	0	0	0	1	1
	Command code byte 2	Write	0	0	DR	*	*	*	*	*
	Don't care	Write	*	*	*	*	*	*	*	*
	Don't care	Write	*	*	*	*	*	*	*	*
	Don't care	Write	*	*	*	*	*	*	*	*
	Don't care	Write	*	*	*	*	*	*	*	*
Format drive	Command code byte 1	Write	0	0	0	0	0	1	0	0
	Command code byte 2	Write	0	0	DR	Head number				
	Command code byte 3	Write	Hi cylinder		0	0	0	0	0	0
	Command code byte 4	Write	Lo cylinder (cylinder=10 bit value)							
	Command code byte 5	Write	0	0	0	Interleave factor (1-16)				
	Command code byte 6	Write	RT	0	0	0	0	Step option		
Ready verify	Command code byte 1	Write	0	0	0	0	0	1	0	1
	Command code byte 2	Write	0	0	DR	Head number				
	Command code byte 3	Write	Hi cylinder		Sector number					
	Command code byte 4	Write	Lo cylinder (cylinder=10 bit value)							
	Command code byte 5	Write	Block count							
	Command code byte 6	Write	RT	RTO	0	0	0	Step option		
Format track	Command code byte 1	Write	0	0	0	0	0	1	1	0
	Command code byte 2	Write	0	0	DR	Head number				
	Command code byte 3	Write	Hi cylinder		0	0	0	0	0	0
	Command code byte 4	Write	Lo cylinder (cylinder=10 bit value)							
	Command code byte 5	Write	0	0	0	Interleave factor (1-16)				
	Command code byte 6	Write	RT	0	0	0	0	Step option		
Format bad track	Command code byte 1	Write	0	0	0	0	0	1	1	1
	Command code byte 2	Write	0	0	DR	Head number				
	Command code byte 3	Write	Hi cylinder		0	0	0	0	0	0
	Command code byte 4	Write	Lo cylinder (cylinder=10 bit value)							
	Command code byte 5	Write	0	0	0	Interleave factor (1-16)				
	Command code byte 6	Write	RT	0	0	0	0	Step option		
Read	Command code byte 1	Write	0	0	0	0	1	0	0	0
	Command code byte 2	Write	0	0	DR	Head number				
	Command code byte 3	Write	Hi cylinder		Sector number					
	Command code byte 4	Write	Lo cylinder (cylinder=10 bit value)							
	Don't care	Write	*	*	*	*	*	*	*	*
	Command code byte 6	Write	RT	RTO	0	0	0	Step option		
Write	Command code byte 1	Write	0	0	0	0	1	0	1	0
	Command code byte 2	Write	0	0	DR	Head number				
	Command code byte 3	Write	Hi cylinder		Sector number					
	Command code byte 4	Write	Lo cylinder (cylinder=10 bit value)							
	Command code byte 5	Write	Block count							
	Command code byte 6	Write	RT	0	0	0	0	Step option		
Seek	Command code byte 1	Write	0	0	0	0	1	0	1	1
	Command code byte 2	Write	0	0	DR	Head number				
	Command code byte 3	Write	Hi cylinder		0	0	0	0	0	0
	Command code byte 4	Write	Lo cylinder (cylinder=10 bit value)							
	Command code byte 5	Write	*	*	*	*	*	*	*	*
	Command code byte 6	Write	RT	0	0	0	0	Step option		
Init drive characteristics	Command code byte 1	Write	0	0	0	0	1	1	0	0
	Don't care	Write	*	*	*	*	*	*	*	*
	Don't care	Write	*	*	*	*	*	*	*	*
	Don't care	Write	*	*	*	*	*	*	*	*
	Don't care	Write	*	*	*	*	*	*	*	*
	Don't care	Write	*	*	*	*	*	*	*	*
	HO max number of cylinders	Write								
	LO max number of cylinders	Write								
	Max number of heads	Write								
	HO reduced write cylinder	Write								
	LO reduced write cylinder	Write								
	HO write precomp cylinder	Write								
	LO write precomp cylinder	Write								
	Max ECC data burst length	Write								

(Continued)

7.055. XT FIXED DISK CONTROLLER COMMAND SUMMARY (continued)

Command Name	Command Sequence	Direction	Bit Number 7	6	5	4	3	2	1	0
Read ECC burst	Command code byte 1	Write	0	0	0	0	1	1	0	1
	Don't care	Write	*	*	*	*	*	*	*	*
	Don't care	Write	*	*	*	*	*	*	*	*
	Don't care	Write	*	*	*	*	*	*	*	*
	Don't care	Write	*	*	*	*	*	*	*	*
	Don't care	Write	*	*	*	*	*	*	*	*
Read data from sector buffer	Command code byte 1	Write	0	0	0	0	1	1	1	0
	Don't care	Write	*	*	*	*	*	*	*	*
	Don't care	Write	*	*	*	*	*	*	*	*
	Don't care	Write	*	*	*	*	*	*	*	*
	Don't care	Write	*	*	*	*	*	*	*	*
	Don't care	Write	*	*	*	*	*	*	*	*
Write data to sector buffer	Command code byte 1	Write	0	0	0	0	1	1	1	1
	Don't care	Write	*	*	*	*	*	*	*	*
	Don't care	Write	*	*	*	*	*	*	*	*
	Don't care	Write	*	*	*	*	*	*	*	*
	Don't care	Write	*	*	*	*	*	*	*	*
	Don't care	Write	*	*	*	*	*	*	*	*
RAM diagnostic	Command code byte 1	Write	1	1	1	0	0	0	0	0
	Don't care	Write	*	*	*	*	*	*	*	*
	Don't care	Write	*	*	*	*	*	*	*	*
	Don't care	Write	*	*	*	*	*	*	*	*
	Don't care	Write	*	*	*	*	*	*	*	*
	Don't care	Write	*	*	*	*	*	*	*	*
Drive diagnostic	Command code byte 1	Write	1	1	1	0	0	0	1	1
	Command code byte 2	Write	0	0	DR	*	*	*	*	*
	Command code byte 3	Write	*	*	*	*	*	*	*	*
	Command code byte 4	Write	*	*	*	*	*	*	*	*
	Command code byte 5	Write	*	*	*	*	*	*	*	*
	Command code byte 6	Write	RT	0	0	0	0	Step option		
Controller internal diagnostics	Command code byte 1	Write	1	1	1	0	0	1	0	0
	Don't care	Write	*	*	*	*	*	*	*	*
	Don't care	Write	*	*	*	*	*	*	*	*
	Don't care	Write	*	*	*	*	*	*	*	*
	Don't care	Write	*	*	*	*	*	*	*	*
	Don't care	Write	*	*	*	*	*	*	*	*
Read long (sector plus 4 bytes of ECC data)	Command code byte 1	Write	1	1	1	0	0	1	0	1
	Command code byte 2	Write	0	0	DR	Head number				
	Command code byte 3	Write	Hi cylinder		Sector number					
	Command code byte 4	Write	Lo cylinder (cylinder = 10 bits)							
	Command code byte 5	Write	Block count							
	Command code byte 6	Write	RT	0	0	0	0	Step option		
Write long (sector plus 4 bytes of ECC data)	Command code byte 1	Write	1	1	1	0	0	1	1	0
	Command code byte 2	Write	0	0	DR	Head number				
	Command code byte 3	Write	Hi cylinder		Sector number					
	Command code byte 4	Write	Lo cylinder (cylinder = 10 bits)							
	Command code byte 5	Write	Block count							
	Command code byte 6	Write	RT	0	0	0	0	Step option		

Legend:
DR = drive (0 or 1)
RT = retries
RTO = retry option on data ECC

Note: The terms "track" and "cylinder" are used interchangeably in the IBM documentation.

Source: IBM PC/XT Technical Reference, pages 1-143 through 1-146

See Also: 7.049. PC and XT Floppy Disk Controller Command Summary

7.056. XT FIXED DISK CONTROLLER PORT USAGE

Port	*Direction*	*Function*
320H	Controller to system	Read data
320H	System to controller	Write data
321H	Controller to system	Read controller hardware status
321H	System to controller	Reset controller
322H	Controller to system	RESERVED
322H	System to controller	Generate controller-select pulse
323H	Controller to system	NOT USED
323H	System to controller	Write pattern to DMA and INT mask register

Source: IBM PC/XT Technical Reference, page 1-147

See Also: 7.004. I/O Port Usage Summary

7.057. XT FIXED DISK CONTROLLER DEVICE CONTROL BLOCK

Bit Number

Byte	*7*	*6*	*5*	*4*	*3*	*2*	*1*	*0*	*Name*	*Allowable Values*
Byte 0	✔	✔	✔						Command class	000 and 111 are only values used
				✔	✔	✔	✔	✔	Command opcode	00000=test drive ready 00001=recalibrate 00010=RESERVED 00011=request sense status 00100=format drive 00101=ready verify 00110=format track 00111=format bad track 01000=read 01001=RESERVED 01010=write 01011=seek 01100=initialize drive 01101=read ECC burst error length 01110=read data from sector buffer 01111=write data to sector buffer
Byte 1	0	0							Always zero	
			✔						Drive number	
				✔	✔	✔	✔	✔	Head number	
Byte 2	✔	✔							Hi order 2 bits of cylinder number	
			✔	✔	✔	✔	✔	✔	Sector number	
Byte 3	✔	✔	✔	✔	✔	✔	✔	✔	Lo order 8 bits of cylinder number	
Byte 4	✔	✔	✔	✔	✔	✔	✔	✔	Interleave or block count	Interleave must be 0-16
Byte 5	✔								Retries	1=disables 4 retries by controller during ops
		✔							Retry option on data ECC error	1=no rereads; 0=reread attempted
			0	0	0				Always zero	
						✔	✔	✔	Step option	000=3 milliseconds per step 001=NOT USED 010=NOT USED 011=NOT USED 100=200 microseconds per step 101=70 microseconds per step (BIOS setting) 110=3 milliseconds per step 111=3 milliseconds per step

Source: IBM PC/XT Technical Reference, pages 1-141 through 1-146

See Also: 7.055. XT Fixed Disk Controller Command Summary

7.058. XT FIXED DISK CONTROLLER STATUS REGISTER

Bit Number

7	6	5	4	3	2	1	0	Name	Allowable Values
0	0							Always zero	
		✔						Logical unit number	0 or 1
			0	0	0			Always zero	
						✔		Error status	0=no error, 1=error occurred
							0	Always zero	

Source: IBM PC/XT Technical Reference, page 1-137

See Also: 7.059. XT Fixed Disk Controller Sense Bytes
7.060. XT Fixed Disk Controller Error Codes

7.059. XT FIXED DISK CONTROLLER SENSE BYTES

Bit Number

Byte	7	6	5	4	3	2	1	0	Name	Allowable Values
Byte 0	✔								Address valid	1=address is valid
		0							Always zero	
			✔	✔					Error type	*
					✔	✔	✔	✔	Error code	*
Byte 1	0	0							Always zero	
			✔						Drive number	0 or 1
				✔	✔	✔	✔	✔	Head number	
Byte 2	✔	✔	✔						HO 3 bits of cylinder number	
				✔	✔	✔	✔	✔	Sector number	
Byte 3	✔	✔	✔	✔	✔	✔	✔	✔	LO 8 bits of cylinder number	

*See 7.060. XT Fixed Disk Controller Error Codes

Source: IBM PC/XT Technical Reference, page 1-137

See Also: 7.058. XT Fixed Disk Controller Status Register
7.060. XT Fixed Disk Controller Error Codes

7.060. XT FIXED DISK CONTROLLER ERROR CODES

Bit Number

5	4	3	2	1	0	Value	Error Description
0	0	0	0	0	0	0 (0)	No error during previous operation
0	0	0	0	0	1	1 (1)	No index signal detected from drive
0	0	0	0	1	0	2 (2)	No seek complete signal detected from drive after seek requested
0	0	0	0	1	1	3 (3)	Write fault detected from drive during previous operation
0	0	0	1	0	0	4 (4)	Drive did not respond with ready signal after being selected
0	0	0	1	0	1	5 (5)	NOT USED
0	0	0	1	1	0	6 (6)	No Track 00 signal detected from drive when it was expected
0	0	0	1	1	1	7 (7)	NOT USED
0	0	1	0	0	0	8 (8)	Drive still seeking
0	1	0	0	0	0	10 (16)	ECC error in target ID field on the disk
0	1	0	0	0	1	11 (17)	Uncorrectable ECC error in target sector during read
0	1	0	0	1	0	12 (18)	No target address mark detected on the disk
0	1	0	0	1	1	13 (19)	NOT USED
0	1	0	1	0	0	14 (20)	Sector not found (cylinder and head found correctly)
0	1	0	1	0	1	15 (21)	Seek compare error (may be cylinder and/or head address)
0	1	0	1	1	0	16 (22)	NOT USED
0	1	0	1	1	1	17 (23)	NOT USED
0	1	1	0	0	0	18 (24)	Correctable ECC error in the target field detected
0	1	1	0	0	1	19 (25)	Bad track detected during previous operation

Source: IBM PC/XT Technical Reference, pages 1-138 through 1-139

See Also: 7.059. XT Fixed Disk Controller Sense Bytes

7.061. AT FIXED DISK DRIVE TYPES

Type	*Cylinders*	*Heads*	*Write PreComp*	*Landing Zone*	*Defect Map*
0	No hard disk drive installed				
1	306	4	128	305	No
2	615	4	300	615	No
3	615	6	300	615	No
4	940	8	512	940	No
5	940	6	512	940	No
6	615	4	None	615	No
7	462	8	256	511	No
8	733	5	None	733	No
9	900	15	None	901	No
10	820	3	None	820	No
11	855	5	None	855	No
12	855	7	None	855	No
13	306	8	128	319	No
14	733	7	None	733	No
15	Extended				
16	612	4	All	663	No
17	977	5	300	977	No
18	977	7	None	977	No
19	1024	7	512	1023	No
20	733	5	300	732	No
21	733	7	300	732	No
22	733	5	300	733	No
23	306	4	All	336	No
24	612	4	305	663	No
25	306	4	None	340	No
26	612	4	None	670	No
27	698	7	300	732	Yes
28	976	5	488	977	Yes
29	306	4	All	340	No
30	611	4	306	663	Yes
31	732	7	300	732	Yes
32	1023	5	None	1023	Yes
33-255	RESERVED				

Note:
- IBM AT supports types 1 through 15.
- IBM XT Model 286 supports types 1 through 24.
- IBM PS/1 and PS/2 support types 1 through 32.
- Other manufacturers may deviate in definitions above type 15.

Source: IBM PC/AT Technical Reference, pages 1-63 and 1-66
IBM Microcomputers, A Programmer's Handbook (McGraw-Hill), pages 365 through 366
The Winn Rosch Hardware Bible (Brady), pages 575 through 582

See Also: 7.095. AT Real Time Clock Status Register A

7.062. IDE REGISTERS

Port	*Write Function*	*Read Function*	*Comment*
1F0H	data register	data register	hard disk only
1F1H	write precomp	error register	hard disk only
1F2H	sector count	sector count	hard disk only
1F3H	sector number	sector number	hard disk only
1F4H	cylinder low	cylinder low	hard disk only
1F5H	cylinder high	cylinder high	hard disk only
1F6H	drive/head	drive/head	hard disk only
1F7H	command register	status register	hard disk only
3F2H	digital output	-	floppy disk only
3F4H	main status	main status	floppy disk only
3F5H	diskette data	diskette data	floppy disk only
3F6H	fixed disk	-	hard disk only
3F7H	diskette control	digital input	hard or floppy disk

Source: "IDE Hard Disk Drive Interface," Byte, March 1991, page 321

See Also: 7.063. IDE Commands

7.063. IDE COMMANDS

Code	*Command*	*Class*	*Optional?*
20	Read sector(s) with retry	1	
21	Read sector(s) without retry	1	
22	Read long with retry	1	
23	Read long without retry	1	
30	Write sector(s) with retry	2	
31	Write sector(s) without retry	2	
32	Write sector(s) with retry	2	
33	Write sector(s) without retry	2	
40	Read verify sector(s) with retry	1	
41	Read verify sector(s) without retry	1	
50	Format track	2	
90	Execute drive diagnostic	1	
91	Initialize drive parameters	1	
1x	Recalibrate	1	
3C	Write verify	3	✔
7x	Seek	1	
8x	Vendor unique 3		
94 E0	Standby immediate	1	✔
95 E1	Idle immediate	1	✔
96 E2	Standby	1	✔
97 E3	Idle	1	✔
98 E5	Check power mode	1	✔
99 E6	Set sleep mode	1	✔
9A	Vendor unique 1		
C0-C3	Vendor unique 2		
C4	Read multiple	1	✔
C5	Write multiple	3	✔
C6	Set multiple mode	1	✔
C8	Read DMA with retry	1	✔
C9	Read DMA without retry	1	✔
CA	Write DMA with retry	3	✔
CB	Write DMA without retry	3	✔
E4	Read buffer	1	✔
E8	Write buffer	2	✔
E9	Write same	3	✔
EC	Identify drive	1	✔
EF	Set features	1	✔
F5-FF	Vendor unique 4		

Source: "IDE Hard Disk Drive Interface," Byte, March 1991, page 322

See Also: 7.062. IDE Registers

7.064. PS/2 POS I/O ADDRESS SPACE

Address	*Function*	*Comments/Bit Meanings*
94 (148)	System board enable/setup register	Bit 7 set=enable functions, zero=setup functions Bit 5 set=enables VGA, zero=setup VGA
95 (149)	RESERVED	
96 (150)	Adapter enable/setup register	Bit 3 set=setup adapters, zero=enable registers
97 (151)	RESERVED	
100 (256)	POS register 0 -- LO adapter ID byte	Read only
101 (257)	POS register 1 -- HO adapter ID byte	Read only
102 (258)	POS register 2 -- option select data byte 1	Read/write if implemented (bit 0=card enable)
103 (259)	POS register 3 -- option select data byte 2	Read/write if implemented
104 (260)	POS register 4 -- option select data byte 3	Read/write if implemented
105 (261)	POS register 5 -- option select data byte 4	Read/write if implemented (bit 7=channel active, bit 6=channel status)
106 (262)	POS register 6 -- LO subaddress extension	
107 (263)	POS register 7 -- HO subaddress extension	

Version: Applies to Models 50, 60, and 80 only.

Source: IBM PS/2 Model 50 and 60 Technical Reference, pages 2-21 through 2-28
IBM PS/2 Model 80 Technical Reference, pages 2-29 through 2-47

See Also: 7.065. PS/2 POS Descriptor File Format
7.066. PS/2 POS ID Assignments

7.065. PS/2 POS DESCRIPTOR FILE FORMAT

Command Syntax	Function	Example*	Example Explanation
ADAPTER ID number	Defines card's ID number	AdapterId 0DEAFh	Card's ID is 0DEAF hex
ADAPTER NAME string	Defines card's name	AdapterName "Thom's Hearing Aid"	Card's name is "Thom's Hearing Aid"
NUMBYTES number	Number of POS bytes used	NumBytes 2	Card uses 2 POS bytes
FIXED RESOURCES pos_setting resource_setting	Defines resources required by card	FixedResources POS[1]="XXXXXX01" int 3	Card uses first POS byte, LO 2 bits
NAMED ITEM prompt {choice...} help	Defines choices for a resource	Named_Item Prompt "Communications Port to Use:" choice "COM1" pos[0]=XXXXXX01b io 03f8h-03ffh int 4 choice "COM2" pos[0]=XXXXXX10b io 02f8h-02ffh int 3 Help "select 1 of the two serial ports listed"	Names an item in pos[0] used to store the user's choice of serial ports
PROMPT string	Defines a string	See Named Item, above	
CHOICE choice_name pos_setting resource_setting	Defines a named choice	See Named Item, above	
HELP string	Defines a help string	See Named Item, above	
POS[number]=bitlist	Defines 1 or more POS byte settings	Pos[0]=XX1XX0XXb	X=ignored, 1=set bit, 0=clear bit
IO {range...}	Defines 1 or more I/O address ranges	io 03f8h-03ffh	
INT {number...}	Defines 1 or more interrupts used	int 4	
ARB {number...}	Defines 1 or more arbitration levels	ARB 1	Sets arbitration level 1
MEM {range...}	Defines 1 or more memory ranges	MEM 0C0000h-0CFFFFh	Card uses mem from 0C0000-CFFFFh

*Keywords are not case-sensitive. The case is preserved in text strings. Blanks, tabs, and new lines are ignored except in text strings. Lines beginning with semicolons are ignored.

Version: Does not apply to Model 25 or 30.

Note:
- IO, INT, ARB, and MEM are resource_settings.
- POS is a pos_setting.
- File must contain at least one Card_ID, one Card_Name, and NumBytes; all else is optional.

Source: IBM PS/2 Model 50 and 60 Technical Reference, pages 2-38 through 2-46
IBM PS/2 Model 80 Technical Reference, pages 2-55 through 2-63

See Also: 7.066. PS/2 POS ID Assignments

7.066. PS/2 POS ID ASSIGNMENTS

ID	IBM Definition
0000	RESERVED
0001-0FFF	Bus master
5000-5FFF	Direct memory access devices
6000-6FFF	Direct program control (includes memory-mapped I/O devices)
7000-7FFF	Storage or multiple function devices
8000-80FF	Video devices
FFFF	Device not attached

Note: These IDs are IBM guidelines only; manufacturers are free to determine their own IDs, although to do so may cause conflicts.

Source: IBM PS/2 Model 50 and 60 Technical Reference, page 2-108
IBM PS/2 Model 80 Technical Reference, page 2-134

See Also: 7.064. PS/2 POS I/O Address Space

7.067. PS/2 MODEL 50/60/70/80 DMA I/O ADDRESS MAP

Address	*Function*
0 (0)	Channel 0 memory address register
1 (1)	Channel 0 transfer count register
2 (2)	Channel 1 memory address register
3 (3)	Channel 1 transfer count register
4 (4)	Channel 2 memory address register
5 (5)	Channel 2 transfer count register
6 (6)	Channel 3 memory address register
7 (7)	Channel 3 transfer count register
8 (8)	Status register for channels 0-3
A (10)	Mask register (set/reset) for channels 0-3
B (11)	Mode register (write) for channels 0-3
C (12)	Clear byte pointer
D (13)	Master clear
E (14)	Clear mask register for channels 0-3
F (15)	Write mask register for channels 0-3
18 (24)	Extended function register
1A (26)	Extended function execute
81 (129)	Channel 2 page table address register (upper byte)
82 (130)	Channel 3 page table address register (upper byte)
83 (131)	Channel 1 page table address register (upper byte)
87 (135)	Channel 0 page table address register (upper byte)
89 (137)	Channel 6 page table address register (upper byte)
8A (138)	Channel 7 page table address register (upper byte)
8B (139)	Channel 5 page table address register (upper byte)
8F (143)	Channel 4 page table address register (upper byte)
C0 (192)	Channel 4 memory address register
C2 (194)	Channel 4 transfer count register
C4 (196)	Channel 5 memory address register
C6 (198)	Channel 5 transfer count register
C8 (200)	Channel 6 memory address register
CA (202)	Channel 6 transfer count register
CC (204)	Channel 7 memory address register
CE (206)	Channel 7 transfer count register
D0 (208)	Status register for channels 4-7
D4 (212)	Mask register for channels 4-7
D6 (214)	Mode register for channels 4-7
D8 (216)	Clear byte pointer
DA (218)	Master clear
DC (220)	Clear mask register for channels 4-7
DE (222)	Write mask register for channels 4-7

Note:
- Channels 0-3 follow PC/AT guidelines.
- Models 25 and 30 follow XT DMA guidelines.

Source: IBM PS/2 Model 50 and 60 Technical Reference, page 3-13
IBM PS/2 Model 80 Technical Reference, page 3-19

See Also: 7.068. PS/2 DMA Registers

7.068. PS/2 DMA REGISTERS

Register	*Size*	*Comments*	*7*	*6*	*5*	*4*	*3*	*2*	*1*	*0*	*Allowable Values*
			Bit Number								
Memory address	24 bits	1 per channel									
I/O address	16 bits	1 per channel									
Transfer count	16 bits	1 per channel									Always one more than the number of DMA transfers
Temporary holding	16 bits	All channels									
Mask	4 bits	1 for channels 0-3	✔	✔	✔	✔	✔				RESERVED
		1 for channels 4-7						✔			Mask bit (0=clear, 1=set)
									✔	✔	Channel select (00=0 or 4, 01=1 or 5, 10=2 or 6, 11=3 or 7)
Arbus	4 bits	1 for channel 0	✔	✔	✔	✔					RESERVED
		1 for channel 4					✔	✔	✔	✔	Arbitration level (4-bit binary value)
Mode	8 bits	1 per channel	✔	✔	✔	✔					RESERVED (bit 5 must be set to 0)
							✔	✔			00=verify op, 01=write op, 10=read op, 11=reserved
									✔	✔	00=select channel 0 or 4, 01=1 or 5, 10=2 or 6, 11=3 or 7
Status	8 bits	1 for channels 0-3	✔								Channel 3 or 7 request
		1 for channels 4-7		✔							Channel 2 or 6 request
					✔						Channel 1 or 5 request
						✔					Channel 0 or 4 request
							✔				Terminal count on channel 3 or 7
								✔			Terminal count on channel 2 or 6
									✔		Terminal count on channel 1 or 5
										✔	Terminal count on channel 0 or 4
Function	8 bits	1 for all channels*									When operating as function register:
			✔	✔	✔	✔					program command
							✔				RESERVED
								✔	✔	✔	channel number
											When operating as extended mode register:
			✔		✔	✔			✔		RESERVED (bit 4 must be 0)
				✔							0=8 bit transfer, 1=16-bit transfer
							✔				0=read memory transfer, 1=write to memory transfer
								✔			0=verify, 1=transfer data
										✔	0=I/O address equals 0000H, 1=use programmed I/O addr.
Refresh	9 bits	Independent of DMA									

*See note in source on DMA Extended Operations, page 3-18 of the IBM PS/2 Model 50 and 60 Technical Reference or page 3-24 of the IBM PS/2 Model 80 Technical Reference.

Version: Does not apply to Model 25 or 30.

Source: IBM PS/2 Model 50 and 60 Technical Reference, pages 3-14 through 3-20
IBM PS/2 Model 80 Technical Reference, pages 3-20 through 3-27

See Also: 7.067. PS/2 Model 50/60/80 DMA I/O Address Map

7.069. PS/2 COUNTER REGISTERS

Register	Address	Comments	7	6	5	4	3	2	1	0	Allowable Values
Read/write counter 0	40 (64)										
Read/write counter 2	42 (66)										
Write control byte	43 (67)	For counter 0 and 2	✔	✔							SC1 and SC0: 00=counter 0, 10=counter 2 (others reserved)
					✔	✔					RW1 and RW0: 00=counter latch command 01=read/write counter bits 0-7 only 10=read/write counter bits 8-15 only 11=read/write counter bits 0=7, then 8-15
							✔	✔	✔		M2, M1, and M0: 000=mode 0, 001=mode 1 010=mode 2, 011=mode 3 100=mode 4, 101=mode 5
										✔	BCD: 0=16 bit binary counter 1=BCD decimal counter
Read/write counter 3	44 (68)										
Write control byte	47 (71)	For counter 3	✔	✔							SC1 and SC0: 00=counter 3 (others reserved)
					✔	✔					RW1 and RW0: 00=counter latch select counter 0 01=read/write counter bits 0-7 only 10=reserved 11=reserved
							✔	✔	✔	✔	Must be 0

Version: Does not apply to Model 25 or 30.

Source: IBM PS/2 Model 50 and 60 Technical Reference, pages 3-29 through 3-31
IBM PS/2 Model 80 Technical Reference, pages 3-35 through 3-37

7.070. PS/2 SYSTEM CONTROL PORT A (92H)

7	6	5	4	3	2	1	0	Function	Allowable Values
✔	✔							Disk activity light	Any bit set to 1 turns activity light on
		✔			✔			RESERVED	
			✔					Watchdog timer status*	0=no timeout, 1=timeout occurred
				✔				RT/CMOS security lock	0=unlocked, 1=locked (done by POST)
						✔		A20 active indicator	0=A20 line is inactive, 1=A20 is active
							✔	Alternate CPU reset	0=system reset or write, 1=pulse alt reset pin

*The Watchdog timer status is read only. All others are read/write.

Version: Does not apply to Model 25 or 30.

Source: IBM PS/2 Model 50 and 60 Technical Reference, pages 4-194 through 4-195
IBM PS/2 Model 80 Technical Reference, pages 4-195 through 4-196

See Also: 7.071. PS/2 System Control Port B (61H)

7.071. PS/2 SYSTEM CONTROL PORT B (61H)

7	6	5	4	3	2	1	0	Function for Write Operations	Function for Read Operations
✔								Reset timer 0 output latch (1=IRQ 0 reset)	Parity check state (1=parity check occurred)
	✔							RESERVED	Channel check state (1=channel check occurred)
		✔						RESERVED	Mirrors timer 2 output condition
			✔					RESERVED	Toggles on each refresh request
				✔				Enable channel check (0=disable)	Channel check status
					✔			Enable parity check (0=disable)	Parity check status
						✔		Enable speaker data (0=disable)	Speaker data status
							✔	Enable timer 2 gate (0=disable)	Timer 2 gate status

Version: Does not apply to Model 25 or 30.

Source: IBM PS/2 Model 50 and 60 Technical Reference, pages 4-192 through 4-194
IBM PS/2 Model 80 Technical Reference, pages 4-193 through 4-194

See Also: 7.070. PS/2 System Control Port A (92H)

7.072. PS/2 RT/CMOS AND NMI MASK (70H)

Bit Number

7	6	5	4	3	2	1	0	Function	Allowable Values
✔								Non-maskable interrupt (NMI)	*
	✔							RESERVED	
		✔	✔	✔	✔	✔	✔	RT/CMOS RAM address	(Used with port 71H to write to that address)

*The sources disagree on setting the NMI:
PS/2 Model 50 and 60 Technical Reference: 0=NMI masked, 1=NMI enabled
PS/2 Model 80 Technical Reference: 1=NMI masked, 0=NMI enabled

Version: Does not apply to Model 25 or 30.

Source: IBM PS/2 Model 50 and 60 Technical Reference, pages 4-183 through 4-184 and 4-194
IBM PS/2 Model 80 Technical Reference, pages 4-183 through 4-184 and 4-194

7.073. PS/2 MODEL 70/80 MEMORY ENCODING REGISTERS

Model 70 Memory Encoding Register 1

Bit Number

7	6	5	4	3	2	1	0	Function	Allowable Values
✔								-Card 2 EN2	0=enables second 1MB block in connector 2
	✔							-Card 2 EN1	0=enables first 1MB block in connector 2
		✔						-Card 1 EN2	0=enables second 1MB block in connector 1
			✔					-Card 1 EN1	0=enables first 1MB block in connector 1
				✔				-ENSPLIT	0=split block enabled
					✔			-640	0=640K mapped to 1st MB; 1=512K mapped to 1st MB
						✔		ROMEN	0=ROM disabled during read; 1=ROM disabled during write
							✔	-ENPLRPCH	0=enables parity checking

Model 70 Memory Encoding Register 2

Bit Number

7	6	5	4	3	2	1	0	Function	Allowable Values
✔	✔							RESERVED	set to 1
		✔						-Card 3 EN2	0=enables second 1MB block in connector 3
			✔					-Card 3 EN1	0=enables first 1MB block in connector 3
				✔				SPA23	address 23 of split memory block
					✔			SPA22	address 22 of split memory block
						✔		SPA21	address 21 of split memory block
							✔	SPA20	address 20 of split memory block

Model 80 Memory Encoding Register Type 1

Bit Number

7	6	5	4	3	2	1	0	Function	Allowable Values
✔	✔							EN3, EN4	10=1MB card enabled in connector 2; 11=card disabled in connector 2
		✔	✔					EN1, EN2	10=1MB card enabled in connector 1; 11=card disabled in connector 1
				✔				-ENSPLIT	0=split block enabled
					✔			-640	0=640K mapped to 1st MB; 1=512K mapped to 1st MB
						✔		ROMEN	0=ROM disabled during read; 1=ROM disabled during write
							✔	-ENPLRPCH	0=enables parity checking

Model 80 Split Address Register Type 1

Bit Number

7	6	5	4	3	2	1	0	Function	Allowable Values
✔	✔	✔	✔					RESERVED	set to 0
				✔				SPA23	address 23 of split memory block
					✔			SPA22	address 22 of split memory block
						✔		SPA21	address 21 of split memory block
							✔	SPA20	address 20 of split memory block

Model 80 Memory Encoding Register 1 Type 2

Bit Number

7	6	5	4	3	2	1	0	Function	Allowable Values
✔	✔							RESERVED	set to 1
		✔	✔					EN1, EN2	00=2MB card in conn.1; 01=1st MB disabled ; 10=2nd MB disabled; 11=invalid
				✔				-ENSPLIT	0=split block enabled
					✔			-640	0=640K mapped to 1st MB; 1=512K mapped to 1st MB
						✔		ROMEN	0=ROM disabled during read; 1=ROM disabled during write
							✔	-ENPLRPCH	0=enables parity checking

(Continued)

7.073. PS/2 MODEL 70/80 MEMORY ENCODING REGISTERS (continued)

Model 80 Memory Encoding Register 2 Type 2

7	6	5	4	3	2	1	0	Function	Allowable Values
✔	✔							RESERVED	set to 1
		✔	✔					EN1, EN2	00=2MB card in conn.2; 01=1st MB disabled; 10=2nd MB disabled; 11=disabled
				✔				SPA23	address 23 of split memory block
					✔			SPA22	address 22 of split memory block
						✔		SPA21	address 21 of split memory block
							✔	SPA20	address 20 of split memory block

Models 90 and 95 Split Address Register

7	6	5	4	3	2	1	0	Function	Allowable Values
✔								SPA27	split address bit 27
	✔							SPA26	split address bit 26
		✔						SPA25	split address bit 25
			✔					SPA24	split address bit 24
				✔				SPA23	split address bit 23
					✔			SPA22	split address bit 22
						✔		SPA21	split address bit 21
							✔	SPA20	split address bit 20

Models 90 and 95 Memory Encoding Register

7	6	5	4	3	2	1	0	Function	Allowable Values
✔								-System bus enable	0=disabled, 1=enabled
	✔							RESERVED	
		✔						Disable ROM space decode	0=disabled, 1=enabled
			✔					Lock	0=enabled, 1=disabled
				✔				Enable split	0=enabled, 1=disabled
					✔			640	0=640, 1=512K
						✔		ROM enable	0=disabled, 1=enabled
							✔	Enable planar parity check	0=enabled, 1=disabled

Source: IBM PS/2 Hardware Interface Technical Reference, pages Model 70 System Board 3-14 through 3-16, Model 80 System Board 3-20 through 3-26
IBM PS/2 Hardware Interface Technical Reference, System Specific Information, Model 90 pages 4-15 through 4-16 and Model 95 pages 4-15 through 4-16

7.074. PS/2 MICROCHANNEL ARBITRATION BUS PRIORITY ASSIGNMENTS

ARB level	Assignment
-2	Memory refresh
-1	NMI
0	DMA channel 0
1	DMA channel 1
2	DMA channel 2
3	DMA channel 3
4	DMA channel 4
5	DMA channel 5
6	DMA channel 6
7	DMA channel 7
8-E	Available
F	System microprocessor

Source: IBM PS/2 Hardware Interface Technical Reference, page Microchannel Arbitration 31 and under Central Arbiter in the chapters on the individual models

7.075. ASYNC ADAPTER I/O PORT USAGE

I/O Port

*Primary**	*Secondary†*	*Used for*	*Comments*
3F8H	2F8H	TX buffer	If bit 7 of line control register is 0
3F8H	2F8H	RX buffer	If bit 7 of line control register is 0
3F8H	2F8H	Divisor latch LO byte	If bit 7 of line control register is 1
3F9H	2F9H	Divisor latch HO byte	If bit 7 of line control register is 1
3F9H	2F9H	Interrupt enable register	
3FAH	2FAH	Interrupt identification registers	
3FBH	2FBH	Line control register	
3FCH	2FCH	Modem control register	
3FDH	2FDH	Line status register	
3FEH	2FEH	Modem status register	

*Primary asynchronous adapter is mapped to COM1 by MS-DOS.
†Secondary asynchronous adapter is mapped to COM2 by MS-DOS.

Source: IBM Options and Adapters Technical Reference, Vol. 2, page Async 3

See Also: 7.076. Async Line Control Register
7.077. Async Divisor Latch Register
7.078. Async Line Status Register
7.079. Async Interrupt Identification Register
7.080. Async Interrupt Enable Register
7.081. Async Modem Control Register
7.082. Async Modem Status Register

7.076. ASYNC LINE CONTROL REGISTER

Bit Number

7	*6*	*5*	*4*	*3*	*2*	*1*	*0*	*Function*	*State on Reset*	*Allowable Values*
✔								Divisor latch access bit	0	1=access baud rate divisor latch
	✔							Set break control	0	0=disabled, 1=enabled
		✔						Stick parity	0	
			✔					Even parity select	0	0=odd parity, 1=even parity
				✔				Parity enable	0	0=disabled, 1=enabled
					✔			Stop bits	0	0=1 stop bit, 1=1.5 (if bits 0/1=00) or 2
						✔	✔	Word length	00	00=5 bits 01=6 bits 10=7 bits 11=8 bits

Note: Bits 4 and 5 affect parity only if bit 3 is enabled.

Source: IBM Options and Adapters Technical Reference, Vol. 2, pages Async 5 through 7

See Also: 7.075. Async Adapter I/O Port Usage

7.077. ASYNC DIVISOR LATCH REGISTER

Bit Number HO byte (3F9H)								Bit Number LO byte (3F8H)										
7	6	5	4	3	2	1	0	7	6	5	4	3	2	1	0	Hex Value	Baud Rate Selected	Comments
				✔			✔									900	50	
					✔	✔										600	75	
					✔						✔		✔	✔	✔	417	110	.026 percent error
						✔	✔		✔		✔	✔			✔	359	134.5	.058 percent error
						✔	✔									300	150	
							✔	✔								180	300	
								✔	✔							C0	600	
									✔	✔						60	1200	
									✔							40	1800	
										✔	✔	✔		✔		3A	2000	.69 percent error
										✔	✔					30	2400	
										✔						20	3600	
											✔	✔				18	4800	
											✔					10	7200	
												✔	✔			C	9600	

Note: Assumes baud-rate generator with a frequency of 1.8432 Mhz.

Source: IBM Options and Adapters Technical Reference, Vol. 2, pages Async 7 through 9

See Also: 7.075. Async Adapter I/O Port Usage

7.078. ASYNC LINE STATUS REGISTER

Bit Number										
7	6	5	4	3	2	1	0	Function	State on Reset	Allowable Values
✔								Always zero	0	No function
	✔							Trans-shift-register empty	1	0=data transfer; 1=transmitter idle
		✔						Trans-hold-register empty	1	0=ready; 1=transferring character
			✔					Break interrupt indicator	0	0=normal receive; 1=break received
				✔				Framing error indicator	0	0=normal receive; 1=framing error
					✔			Parity error indicator	0	0=normal receive; 1=parity error
						✔		Overrun error indicator	0	0=normal receive; 1=overrun error
							✔	Receiver data ready	0	0=no data received; 1=data received

Note: Bit 6 is read only.

Source: IBM Options and Adapters Technical Reference, Vol. 2, pages Async 10 through 11

See Also: 7.075. Async Adapter I/O Port Usage

7.079. ASYNC INTERRUPT IDENTIFICATION REGISTER

Bit Number										
7	6	5	4	3	2	1	0	Function	State on Reset	Allowable Values
✔	✔	✔	✔	✔				Always zero	00000	No function
					✔	✔		Interrupt ID	00	11=receiver line status interrupt 10=received data available interrupt 01=transmitter holding register empty interrupt 00=modem status interrupt
							✔	Interrupt pending	1	0=interrupt pending; 1=no interrupt pending

Source: IBM Options and Adapters Technical Reference, Vol. 2, pages Async 12 through 13

See Also: 7.075. Async Adapter I/O Port Usage

7.080. ASYNC INTERRUPT ENABLE REGISTER

7	6	5	4	3	2	1	0	Function	State on Reset	Allowable Values
✔	✔	✔	✔					Always zero	0000	No function
				✔				Enable modem status Int	0	1=enable modem status interrupt; 0=disabled
					✔			Receiver line status Int	0	1=enable receiver line status interrupt; 0=disabled
						✔		Transmitter holding reg empty	0	1=enable trans. holding reg. empty int; 0=disabled
							✔	Received data available Int	0	1=enable received data avail. interrupt; 0=disabled

Source: IBM Options and Adapters Technical Reference, Vol. 2, pages Async 14 through 15

See Also: 7.075. Async Adapter I/O Port Usage

7.081. ASYNC MODEM CONTROL REGISTER

7	6	5	4	3	2	1	0	Function	State on Reset	Allowable Values
✔	✔	✔						Always zero	000	No function
			✔					Loopback test mode	0	0=disabled; 1=enabled
				✔				-OUT2 signal	0	0=-OUT2 forced high; 1=-OUT2 forced low
					✔			-OUT1 signal	0	0=-OUT1 forced high; 1=-OUT1 forced low
						✔		-RTS output	0	0=-RTS forced high; 1=-RTS forced low
							✔	-DTR output	0	0=-DTR forced high; 1=-DTR forced low

Source: IBM Options and Adapters Technical Reference, Vol. 2, pages Async 15 through 16

See Also: 7.075. Async Adapter I/O Port Usage

7.082. ASYNC MODEM STATUS REGISTER

7	6	5	4	3	2	1	0	Function	State on Reset	Allowable Values
✔								-RLSD complement	Input signal	
	✔							-RI complement	Input signal	
		✔						-DSR complement	Input signal	
			✔					-CTS complement	Input signal	
				✔				Delta RLSD	0	0=no change; 1=-RLSD has changed state
					✔			Trailing edge ring indicator	0	0=no TE RI; 1=-RI has changed to OFF
						✔		Delta DSR indicator	0	0=no change; 1=-DSR has changed state
							✔	Delta CTS indicator	0	0=no change; 1=-CTS has changed state

Source: IBM Options and Adapters Technical Reference, Vol. 2, pages Async 16 through 18

See Also: 7.075. Async Adapter I/O Port Usage

7.083. GAME ADAPTER I/O PORT USAGE

Port	Direction	Function
201H	Write	Fire joysticks four one-shots
	Read	Read joystick position and status

Note: Resistive inputs are read by first outputting to port 201H, then noting the amount of time they remain high by inputting continuously from port 201H.

Source: IBM Options and Adapters Technical Reference, Vol. 2, pages Game Control Adapter 3 through 6

See Also: 7.084. Game Adapter AB Joystick Data Byte
7.085. Game Adapter ABCD Paddle Data Byte

7.084. GAME ADAPTER AB JOYSTICK DATA BYTE

Bit Number								
7	6	5	4	3	2	1	0	Function
✔								Status of B joystick button 2
	✔							Status of B joystick button 1
		✔						Status of A joystick button 2
			✔					Status of A joystick button 1
				✔				B joystick Y coordinate*
					✔			B joystick X coordinate*
						✔		A joystick Y coordinate*
							✔	A joystick X coordinate*

*Coordinates are determined by the length of time the bit is held high.

Source: IBM Options and Adapters Technical Reference, Vol. 2, pages Game Control Adapter 5 through 6

See Also: 7.083. Game Adapter I/O Port Usage
7.085. Game Adapter ABCD Paddle Data Byte

7.085. GAME ADAPTER ABCD PADDLE DATA BYTE

Bit Number								
7	6	5	4	3	2	1	0	Function
✔								Status of D paddle button
	✔							Status of C paddle button
		✔						Status of B paddle button
			✔					Status of A paddle button
				✔				D paddle coordinate*
					✔			C paddle coordinate*
						✔		B paddle coordinate*
							✔	A paddle coordinate*

*Coordinates are determined by the length of time the bit is held high.

Source: IBM Options and Adapters Technical Reference, Vol. 2, pages Game Control Adapter 5 through 6

See Also: 7.083. Game Adapter I/O Port Usage
7.084. Game Adapter AB Joystick Data Byte

7.086. PRINTER ADAPTER I/O PORT USAGE

	Bit Number										
Port	*7*	*6*	*5*	*4*	*3*	*2*	*1*	*0*	*Adapter*	*Direction*	*Function*
378	✔								Printer	Output	Controls pin 9 (data bit 7)
		✔							Printer	Output	Controls pin 8 (data bit 6)
			✔						Printer	Output	Controls pin 7 (data bit 5)
				✔					Printer	Output	Controls pin 6 (data bit 4)
					✔				Printer	Output	Controls pin 5 (data bit 3)
						✔			Printer	Output	Controls pin 4 (data bit 2)
							✔		Printer	Output	Controls pin 3 (data bit 1)
								✔	Printer	Output	Controls pin 2 (data bit 0)
379	✔								Printer	Input	Status of pin 11 (busy)
		✔							Printer	Input	Status of pin 10 (acknowledge)
			✔						Printer	Input	Status of pin 12 (out of paper)
				✔					Printer	Input	Status of pin 13 (select)
					✔				Printer	Input	Status of pin 15 (error)
						✔	✔	✔	Printer	Input	NOT USED
37A	✔	✔	✔						Printer	Input	NOT USED
				✔					Printer	Input	Status of IRQ Enable
					✔				Printer	Input	Inverted status of pin 17 (select input)
						✔			Printer	Input	Status of pin 16 (initialize printer)
							✔		Printer	Input	Inverted status of pin 14 (auto feed)
								✔	Printer	Input	Inverted status of pin 1 (strobe)
	✔	✔	✔	✔					Printer	Output	NOT USED
					✔				Printer	Output	Inverted status of pin 17 (select input)
						✔			Printer	Output	Status of pin 16 (initialize printer)
							✔		Printer	Output	Inverted status of pin 14 (auto feed)
								✔	Printer	Output	Inverted status of pin 1 (strobe)
3BC	✔								MDA	Output	Controls pin 9 (data bit 7)
		✔							MDA	Output	Controls pin 8 (data bit 6)
			✔						MDA	Output	Controls pin 7 (data bit 5)
				✔					MDA	Output	Controls pin 6 (data bit 4)
					✔				MDA	Output	Controls pin 5 (data bit 3)
						✔			MDA	Output	Controls pin 4 (data bit 2)
							✔		MDA	Output	Controls pin 3 (data bit 1)
								✔	MDA	Output	Controls pin 2 (data bit 0)
3BD	✔								MDA	Input	Status of pin 11 (busy)
		✔							MDA	Input	Status of pin 10 (acknowledge)
			✔						MDA	Input	Status of pin 12 (out of paper)
				✔					MDA	Input	Status of pin 13 (select)
					✔				MDA	Input	Status of pin 15 (error)
						✔	✔	✔	MDA	Input	NOT USED
3BE	✔	✔	✔						MDA	Input	NOT USED
				✔					MDA	Input	Status of IRQ enable
					✔				MDA	Input	Inverted status of pin 17 (select input)
						✔			MDA	Input	Status of pin 16 (initialize printer)
							✔		MDA	Input	Inverted status of pin 14 (auto feed)
								✔	MDA	Input	Inverted status of pin 1 (strobe)
	✔	✔	✔	✔					MDA	Output	NOT USED
					✔				MDA	Output	Inverted status of pin 17 (select input)
						✔			MDA	Output	Status of pin 16 (initialize printer)
							✔		MDA	Output	Inverted status of pin 14 (auto feed)
								✔	MDA	Output	Inverted status of pin 1 (strobe)

Note:
- Although the printer adapter and MDA printer ports work identically, they appear at different port addresses.
- The source contains incomplete material.

Source: IBM Options and Adapters Technical Reference, Vol. 2, pages Printer Adapter 3 through 7 and Monochrome Adapter 13 through 17

7.087. IBM PRINTER CONTROL CODES SUMMARY

Function Type	Function	Code	ASCII	Hex	Printer Type* Graphics	Color	Compact
Character Style	Select char set 1	<ESC>7	55	1B 37	✔	✔	
	Select char set 2	<ESC>6	54	1B 36	✔	✔	
	10 characters per inch (Compressed OFF) spacing	<DC2>	18	12	✔	✔	✔
	17.1 characters per inch (Compressed ON) spacing	<SI>	15	0F	✔	✔	✔
	Doublestrike ON	<ESC>G	71	1B 47	✔	✔	
	Doublestrike OFF	<ESC>H	72	1B 48	✔	✔	
	Doublewidth ON (lines)	<ESC>W<SOH>	87	1B 57 01	✔	✔	✔
	Doublewidth OFF (lines)	<ESC>W<NUL>	87	1B 57 00	✔	✔	✔
	Doublewidth by line ON	<SO>	14	0E	✔	✔	✔
				1B 0E		✔	
	Doublewidth by line OFF	<DC4>	20	14	✔	✔	✔
	Emphasized printing ON	<ESC>E	69	1B 45	✔	✔	
	Emphasized printing OFF	<ESC>F	70	1B 46	✔	✔	
	Subscript ON	<ESC>S<SOH>	83	1B 53 01	✔	✔	
	Superscript ON	<ESC>S<NUL>	83	1B 53 00	✔	✔	
	Subscript/superscript OFF	<ESC>T	84	1B 54	✔	✔	
	Set draft quality print	<ESC>I<SOH>	73	1B 49 01		✔	
	Set text quality print	<ESC>I<STX>	73	1B 49 02		✔	
	Set letter quality print	<ESC>I<ETX>	73	1B 49 03		✔	
	Proportional spacing ON	<ESC>P<SOH>	80	1B 50 01		✔	
	Proportional spacing OFF	<ESC>P<NUL>	80	1B 50 00		✔	
	12 characters per inch spacing	<ESC>:	58	1B 3A		✔	
	Print all characters†	<ESC>##	92	1B 5C##		✔	
	Print next character	<ESC>^	94	1B 5E		✔	
	Underline ON	<ESC>-<SOH>	45	1B 2D 01	✔	✔	✔
	Underline OFF	<ESC>-<NUL>	45	1B 2D 00	✔	✔	✔
Page Settings	Ignore paper end ON	<ESC>8	56	1B 38	✔		
	Ignore paper end OFF	<ESC>8	56	1B 38	✔		
	Set length of page in lines (1-127)	<ESC>C#	67	1B 43#	✔	✔	✔
	Set length of page in inches (1-22)	<ESC>C<SOH>#	67	1B 43 00#	✔	✔	
	Automatic line justification ON	<ESC>M<SOH>	77	1B 4D 01		✔	
	Automatic line justification OFF	<ESC>M<NUL>	77	1B 4D 00		✔	
	Perforation skip ON (1-127)	<ESC>N#	78	1B 4E#	✔	✔	✔
	Perforation skip OFF	<ESC>O	79	1B 4F	✔	✔	✔
	Set top of page (form)	<ESC>4	52	1B 34		✔	
	Set left and right margins	<ESC>X##	88	1B 58##		✔	
	Clear tabs (set tabs to power-on defaults)	<ESC>R	82	1B 52		✔	✔
	Set horizontal tab stops	<ESC>D#...#<NUL>	68	1B 44#...# 00	✔	✔	✔
	Set vertical tab stops	<ESC>B#...#<NUL>	66	1B 42#...# 00		✔	✔
Line Settings	Carriage return	<CR>	13	0D	✔	✔	✔
	Line feed	<LF>	10	0A	✔	✔	✔
	Set variable line feed to #/72 inch (1-85)	<ESC>A#	65	1B 41#	✔	✔	
	Set variable line feed to #/216 inch (1-255)	<ESC>J#	74	1B 4A#	✔	#/144"	
	Set 1/8 inch line feed	<ESC>0	48	1B 30	✔	✔	✔
Line Settings	Set 7/72 inch line feed	<ESC>1	49	1B 31	✔	6/72"	6/72"
	Start variable line feed (used after EscA)	<ESC>2	50	1B 32	✔	✔	✔
	Set #/216 inch line feed (1-255)	<ESC>3#	51	1B 33#	✔	#/144"	
	Vertical tab	<VT>	11	0B		✔	✔
	Reverse line feed	<ESC>]	93	1B 5D		✔	
	Automatic line feed ON	<ESC>5<SOH>	53	1B 35 01		✔	✔
	Automatic line feed OFF	<ESC>5<NUL>	53	1B 35 00		✔	✔

(Continued)

7.087. IBM PRINTER CONTROL CODES SUMMARY (continued)

Function Type	Function	Code	ASCII	Hex	Printer Type*: Graphics	Color	Compact
Printer Control	Escape (command start)	<ESC>	27	1B	✔	✔	✔
	Null (command end)	<NUL>	0	0	✔	✔	✔
	Ring bell	<BELL>	7	7	✔	✔	
	Cancel (clear printer buffer)	<CAN>	24	18	✔	✔	✔
	Select printer	<DC1>	17	11		✔	
	Deselect color printer	<ESC>Q<STX>	81	1B 51 02		✔	
	Deselect printer	<DC3>	19	13		✔	
	Automatic ribbon band shift	<ESC>a	97	1B 61		✔	
	Select ribbon band 4 (black)	<ESC>b	98	1B 62		✔	
	Select ribbon band 3	<ESC>c	99	1B 63		✔	
	Space #/120 forward to next character	<ESC>d##	100	1B 64##		✔	
	Space #/120 backward to next character	<ESC>e##	101	1B 65##		✔	
	Select ribbon band 2	<ESC>m	109	1B 6D		✔	
	Set aspect ratio to 1:1	<ESC>n<SOH>	110	1B 6E 01		✔	
	Set aspect ratio to 5:6	<ESC>n<NUL>	110	1B 6E 00		✔	
	Select ribbon band 1	<ESC>y	121	1B 79		✔	
	Initialize function ON	<ESC>?<SOH>	63	1B 3F 01		✔	
	Initialize function OFF	<ESC>?<NUL>	63	1B 3F 00		✔	
	Unidirectional printing ON	<ESC>U<SOH>	85	1B 55 01	✔	✔	
	Unidirectional printing OFF	<ESC>U<NUL>	85	1B 55 00	✔	✔	
	Home print head	<ESC><	60	1B 3C	✔	✔	✔
	Form feed	<FF>	12	0C	✔	✔	✔
	Horizontal tab	<HT>	9	9	✔	✔	✔
	Select control-value data type	<ESC>@#	64	1B 40#		✔	
	Backspace	<BS>	8	8		✔	
Graphics	Set to 480 bit image graphics mode	<ESC>K## [data]	75	1B 4B##	✔	1108	560
	Set to 960 bit image graphics mode, half speed	<ESC>L## [data]	76	1B 4C##	✔	2216	
	Set to 960 bit image graphics mode, normal speed	<ESC>Y## [data]	89	1B 59##	✔	2216	
	Set to 1920 bit image graphics mode	<ESC>Z## [data]	90	1B 5A##	✔	4432	

*Refers to IBM Graphics Printer, IBM Color Printer, and IBM Compact Printer, respectively.
†Number of characters to print

Note:
- Characters enclosed in brackets are ASCII code names, as in <ESC>.
- # should be replaced by the relevant numeric value in this chart.
- [data] indicates a bitstream of appropriately formatted data.
- Numbers in "bit image graphics modes" indicate number of data bytes that follow.

Source: IBM Options and Adapters Technical Reference, Vol. 1, pages Graphics Printer 4 through 6, Color Printer 9 through 35, and Compact Printer 3 through 10

See Also:
1.20. ASCII Control Codes
7.088. Qume Sprint 11/Diablo 630 Printer Control Codes Summary
7.089. Epson Printer Control Codes Summary
7.090. HP Laserjet Printer Control Codes Summary

7.088. QUME SPRINT II/DIABLO 630 PRINTER CONTROL CODES SUMMARY

Function Type	*Function*	*Code*	*ASCII*	*Hex*	*Diablo 630*
Carriage Movement	Backspace 1/120 inch	<ESC><BS>	8	1B 08	✔
	Backward (negative) line feed	<ESC><LF>	10	1B 0A	✔
	Define vertical spacing increment as #-1	<ESC><RS>#	30	1B 1E#	✔
	Set horizontal space increment to #-1	<ESC><US>#	31	1B 1F#	✔
	Absolute vertical tab to line #-1	<ESC><VT>#	11	1B 0B#	✔
	Absolute vertical to line #	<ESC>P#	80	1B 50#	
	Absolute horizontal tab to column #-1	<ESC><HT>	9	1B 09	✔
	Absolute horizontal tab to column #	<ESC>C##	67	1B 43##	
	Backward (negative) half line feed	<ESC>D	68	1B 44	✔
	Half-line feed	<ESC>U	85	1B 55	✔
Printer Control	Shift to primary mode	<ESC><SO>	14	1B 0E	
	Return to normal mode	<ESC><SI>	15	1B 0F	
	Initialize printer	<ESC><SUB>I	26	1B 1A 49	
	Terminal self-test	<ESC><SUB><SO>	26	1B 1A 0E	
	Initialize printer	<ESC><CR>P	13	1B 0D	
	Enter user test mode	<ESC>@ T	64	1B 40 54	
	Enter secondary mode	<ESC>#	35	1B 23	
	Sheet feeder page eject	<ESC>e	101	1B 65	
	Sheet feeder insert page from tray one	<ESC>i	105	1B 69	
Print Special Characters	Print special character position 004	<ESC><SP>	32	1B 20H	
	Print special character position 002	<ESC>/	47	1B 2F	
Printer Settings	Set right margin	<ESC>0	48	1B 30	✔
	Set horizontal tab stop	<ESC>1	49	1B 31	✔
	Clear all horizontal tab stops	<ESC>2	50	1B 32	✔
	Graphics on 1/60 inch	<ESC>3	51	1B 33	✔
	Graphics off	<ESC>4	52	1B 34	✔
	Forward print	<ESC>5	53	1B 35	✔
	Backward print	<ESC>6	54	1B 36	✔
	Clear horizontal tab stop	<ESC>8	56	1B 38	✔
	Set left margin	<ESC>9	57	1B 39	✔
	Auto line feed on	<ESC>.	46	1B 2E	
	Auto line feed off	<ESC>,	44	1B 2C	
	Auto bi-directional printing on	<ESC><	60	1B 3C	
	Auto bi-directional printing off	<ESC>>	62	1B 3E	
	Set top margin	<ESC>+	43	1B 2B	
	Set bottom margin	<ESC>-	45	1B 2D	
	Proportional printwheel on	<ESC>$	36	1B 24	✔
	Proportional printwheel off	<ESC>%	37	1B 25	✔
	Set tabs at #	<ESC>(#	40	1B 28#	
	Clear tabs at #	<ESC>)#	41	1B 29#	
	Define horizontal space increments	<ESC>E##	69	1B 45##	
	Set form length	<ESC>F##	70	1B 46##	
	Graphics on 1/120 inch	<ESC>G	71	1B 47	✔
	Relative horizontal motion	<ESC>H###	72	1B 48###	
	Underline on	<ESC>I	73	1B 49	
	Underline off	<ESC>J	74	1B 4A	
	Bold overprint on	<ESC>K#	75	1B 4B#	
	Define vertical spacing increment	<ESC>L##	76	1B 4C##	
	Bold overprint off	<ESC>M#	77	1B 4D#	
	No carriage movement on next character	<ESC>N	78	1B 4E	
	Right margin control on	<ESC>O	79	1B 4F	
	Shadow print on	<ESC>Q	81	1B 51	
	Shadow print off	<ESC>R	82	1B 52	
	No print on	<ESC>S	83	1B 53	
	No print off	<ESC>T	84	1B 54	
	Auto carriage return/line feed on	<ESC>W	87	1B 57	
	Relative vertical paper motion	<ESC>V###	86	1B 56###	
	Force execution	<ESC>X	88	1B 58	
	Right margin control off	<ESC>Y	89	1B 59	
	Auto carriage return/line feed off	<ESC>Z	90	1B 5A	
	Force execution	<ESC>x	120	1B 78	

Note:

- Characters enclosed in brackets are ASCII code names, as in <ESC>.
- # should be replaced by the relevant numeric value in this chart.
- Printers also recognize the following ASCII control sequences:

Function	*ASCII Control Code*	*ASCII*	*Diablo 630*
Perform user test continuously	SOH	1	
Perform user test once	STX	2	
Halt continuous user test	ENQ	5	
Sound bell	BEL	7	
Backspace	BS	8	✔
Horizontal tab	HT	9	✔
Line feed	LF	10	✔
Vertical tab	VT	11	✔
Form feed	FF	12	✔
Carriage return	CR	13	✔
Escape (return to normal)	ESC	27	
Program mode carriage motion	US	31	
No operation	DEL	127	✔

Source: The Winn Rosch Hardware Bible (Brady), pages 400 through 401

See Also:
1.20. ASCII Control Codes
7.087. IBM Printer Control Codes Summary
7.089. Epson Printer Control Codes Summary
7.090. HP LaserJet Printer Control Codes Summary

7.089. EPSON PRINTER CONTROL CODES SUMMARY

Function Type	*Function*	*Code*	*ASCII*	*Hex*
Character Style	Deactivate high-order control codes	<ESC>6	54	1B 36
	Turn alternate character (italics) ON	<ESC>4	52	1B 34
	10 characters per inch (Compressed OFF) spacing	<DC2>	18	12
	17.1 characters per inch (Compressed ON) spacing	<SI>	15	0F
	Doublestrike ON	<ESC>G	71	1B 47
	Doublestrike OFF	<ESC>H	72	1B 48
	Doublewidth ON (lines)	<ESC>W<SOH>	87	1B 57 01
	Doublewidth OFF (lines)	<ESC>W<NUL>	87	1B 57 00
	Enlarged print mode ON	<SO>	14	0E
	Enlarged print mode OFF	<DC4>	20	14
	Emphasized printing ON	<ESC>E	69	1B 45
	Emphasized printing OFF	<ESC>F	70	1B 46
	Turn alternate character (italics) ON	<ESC>4	52	1B 34
	Turn alternate character (italics) OFF	<ESC>5	53	1B 35
	Elite mode ON (Pica mode OFF)	<ESC>M	77	1B 4D
	Select family of type styles	<ESC>k	107	1B 6B
	Proportional printing OFF	<ESC>p<NUL>	112	1B 70 00
	Proportional printing ON	<ESC>p<SOH>	112	1B 70 01
	Select letter or draft quality printing	<ESC>z	122	1B 7A
	Subscript ON	<ESC>S<SOH>	83	1B 53 01
	Superscript ON	<ESC>S<NUL>	83	1B 53 00
	Subscript/superscript OFF	<ESC>T	84	1B 54
	Control code select	<ESC>I	73	1B 49
	Elite mode OFF (Pica mode ON)	<ESC>P	80	1B 50
	Nine-pin graphics mode	<ESC>^	94	1B 5E
	Underline ON	<ESC>-<SOH>	45	1B 2D 01
	Underline OFF	<ESC>-<NUL>	45	1B 2D 00
Page Settings	Ignore paper end ON	<ESC>8	56	1B 38
	Ignore paper end OFF	<ESC>9	57	1B 39
	Set length of page in lines (1-127)	<ESC>C#	67	1B 43#
	Set length of page in inches (1-22)	<ESC>C<NUL>#	67	1B 43 00#
	Set absolute tab	<ESC>$	36	1B 24
	Set vertical tab	<ESC>/	47	1B 2F
	Set vertical tab	<ESC>b	98	1B 62
	Set horizontal tab unit	<ESC>e<NUL>	101	1B 65 00
	Set vertical tab unit	<ESC>e<SOH>	101	1B 65 01
	Set horizontal skip position	<ESC>f<NUL>	102	1B 66 00
	Set vertical skip position	<ESC>f<SOH>	102	1B 66 01
	Perforation skip ON (1-127)	<ESC>N#	78	1B 4E#
	Perforation skip OFF	<ESC>O	79	1B 4F
	Set horizontal tab stop	<ESC>D	68	1B 44
	Set vertical tab stop	<ESC>B	66	1B 42

(Continued)

7.089. EPSON PRINTER CONTROL CODES SUMMARY (continued)

Function Type	*Function*	*Code*	*ASCII*	*Hex*
Line Settings	Carriage return	<CR>	13	0D
	Line feed	<LF>	10	0A
	Set variable line feed to #/72 inch (1-85)	<ESC>A#	65	1B 41#
	Set variable line feed to #/216 inch	<ESC>J#	74	1B 4A#
	Set spacing at 1/8 inch	<ESC>0	48	1B 30
	Set spacing at 7/72 inch	<ESC>1	49	1B 31
	Set line spacing at 1/6 inch	<ESC>2	50	1B 32
	Set #/216 inch line feed (0-255)	<ESC>3#	51	1B 33#
	Vertical tab	<VT>	11	0B
Printer Control	Ring bell	<BELL>	7	7
	Clear line	<CAN>	24	18
	Select printer	<DC1>	17	11
	Deselect printer	<DC3>	19	13
	Set justification	<ESC>a	97	1B 61
	Cut sheet feeder control	<ESC>EM	25	1B 19
	Select character space	<ESC>SP	32	1B 20
	Select mode combinations	<ESC>!	33	1B 21
	Select active character set	<ESC>%	37	1B 25
	Copies ROM to user RAM	<ESC>:	58	1B 3A
	Defines user characters	<ESC>&	38	1B 26
	Set MSB=0	<ESC>>	62	1B 3E
	Set MSB=1	<ESC>=	61	1B 3D
	Select international character set	<ESC>R#*	114	1B 72#
	Select 15 width	<ESC>g	103	1B 67
	Select immediate print (typewriter mode)	<ESC>i	105	1B 69
	Half-speed printing OFF	<ESC>s<NUL>	115	1B 73 00
	Half-speed printing ON	<ESC>s<SOH>	115	1B 73 01
	Set horizontal tab unit	<ESC>e<NUL>	101	1B 65 00
	Set vertical tab unit	<ESC>e<SOH>	102	1B 6D 01
	Special character generator selection (control codes accepted)	<ESC>m<NUL>	109	1B 6D 00
	Special character generator selection (graphics chars accepted	<ESC>m<SOH>	109	1B 6D 01
	Unidirectional printing ON	<ESC>U<SOH>	85	1B 55 01
	Unidirectional printing OFF	<ESC>U<NUL>	85	1B 55 00
	Turn unidirectional (left-to-right) ON	<ESC><	60	1B 3C
	Form feed	<FF>	12	0C
	Horizontal tab	<HT>	9	9
	Initialize printer	<ESC>@	64	1B 40
	Backspace	<BS>	8	8
Graphics	Normal-density bit image follows	<ESC>K	75	1B 4B##
	Dual-density bit image follows	<ESC>L	76	1B 4C##
	Double-speed, dual-density bit image follows	<ESC>Y	89	1B 59##
	Quadruple-density bit image follows	<ESC>Z	90	1B 5A##

*International character set:
0=U.S.
1=France
2=Germany
3=England
4=Denmark
5=Sweden
6=Italy
7=Spain
8=Japan
9=Norway
10=Denmark II

Note:
- Characters enclosed in brackets are ASCII code names, as in <ESC>.
- # should be replaced by the relevant numeric value in this chart.
- [data] indicates a bitstream of appropriately formatted data.
- Numbers in "bit image graphics modes" indicate number of data bytes that follow.

Source: The Winn Rosch Hardware Bible (Brady), pages 402 through 405

See Also:
1.20. ASCII Control Codes
7.088. Qume Sprint II/Diablo 630 Printer Control Codes Summary
7.087. IBM Printer Control Codes Summary
7.090. HP LaserJet Printer Control Codes Summary

7.090. HP LASERJET PRINTER CONTROL CODES SUMMARY

Function Type	*Function*	*Code Sequence in ASCII Chars*	*Code Sequence in Hex Bytes*
Orientation	Portrait mode	<ESC>&l0O	1B 26 6C 30 4F
	Landscape mode	<ESC>&l1O	1B 26 6C 31 4F
Font Symbol Set	Roman-8	<ESC>(8U	1B 28 38 55
	USASCII	<ESC>(0U	1B 28 30 55
	Danish/Norwegian	<ESC>(0D	1B 28 30 44
	British (U.K.)	<ESC>(1E	1B 28 31 45
	French	<ESC>(1F	1B 28 31 46
	German	<ESC>(7G	1B 28 31 47
	Italian	<ESC>(0I	1B 28 30 49
	Swedish/Finnish	<ESC>(0S	1B 28 30 53
	Spanish	<ESC>(2S	1B 28 32 53
	Legal	<ESC>(1U	1B 28 31 55
	Linedraw	<ESC>(0B	1B 28 30 42
	Math8	<ESC>(8M	1B 28 38 4D
	Math7	<ESC>(0A	1B 28 30 41
	PiFont	<ESC>(15U	1B 28 31 35 55
Character Spacing	Proportional	<ESC>(s1P	1B 28 73 31 50
	Fixed	<ESC>(s0P	1B 28 73 30 50
Character Pitch	10 chars per inch	<ESC>(s10H	1B 28 73 31 30 48
	12 chars per inch	<ESC>(s12H	1B 28 73 31 32 48
	16.6 chars per inch	<ESC>(s16.6H	1B 28 73 31 36 2E 36 48
	Standard pitch (10 cpi)	<ESC>&k0S	1B 26 6B 30 53
	Compressed pitch (16.6 cpi)	<ESC>&k2S	1B 26 6B 32 53
	Elite (12.0)	<ESC>&k4s	1B 26 6B 34 53
Character Point Size	7 point	<ESC>(s7V	1B 28 73 37 56
	8 point	<ESC>(s8V	1B 28 73 38 56
	8.5 point	<ESC>(s8.5V	1B 28 73 38 2E 35 56
	10 point	<ESC>(s10V	1B 28 73 31 30 56
	12 point	<ESC>(s12V	1B 28 73 31 32 56
	14.4 point	<ESC>(s14.4V	1B 28 73 31 34 2E 34 56
Character Style	Upright	<ESC>(s0S	1B 28 73 30 53
	Italic	<ESC>(s1S	1B 28 73 31 53
Character Weight	Light stroke	<ESC>(s-3B	1B 28 73 -33 42
	Medium stroke	<ESC>(s0B	1B 28 73 30 42
	Bold (heavy) stroke	<ESC>(s3B	1B 28 73 33 42
Character Typeface	Courier	<ESC>(s3T	1B 28 73 33 54
	Line Printer	<ESC>(s0T	1B 28 73 30 54
	Helv	<ESC>(s4T	1B 28 73 34 54
	TMS RMN	<ESC>(s5T	1B 28 73 35 54
	Prestige Elite	<ESC>(s8T	1B 28 73 38 54
	Gothic	<ESC>(s6T	1B 28 73 36 54
Page Settings	Page length	<ESC>&l#P	1B 26 6C # 50
	Top margin	<ESC>&l#E	1B 26 6C # 45
	Text length	<ESC>&l#F	1B 26 6C # 46
	Clear left/right margin	<ESC>9	1B 39
	Set left margin	<ESC>&a#L	1B 26 61 # 4C
	Set right margin	<ESC>&a#M	1B 26 61 # 4D
	Perforation skip enable	<ESC>&l1L	1B 26 6C 31 4C
	Perforation skip disable	<ESC>&l0L	1B 26 6C 30 4C
Line Spacing	Vertical motion index	<ESC>&l#C	1B 26 6C # 43
	1 line/inch	<ESC>&l1D	1B 26 6C 31 44
	2 lines/inch	<ESC>&l2D	1B 26 6C 32 44
	3 lines/inch	<ESC>&l3D	1B 26 6C 33 44
	4 lines/inch	<ESC>&l4D	1B 26 6C 34 44
	6 lines/inch	<ESC>&l6D	1B 26 6C 36 44
	8 lines/inch	<ESC>&l8D	1B 26 6C 38 44
	12 lines/inch	<ESC>&l12D	1B 26 6C 31 32 44
	16 lines/inch	<ESC>&l16D	1B 26 6C 31 36 44
	24 lines/inch	<ESC>&l24D	1B 26 6C 32 34 44
	Half line feed	<ESC>=	1B 3D
Raster Graphics	75 dpi resolution	<ESC>*t75R	1B 2A 74 37 35 52
	100 dpi resolution	<ESC>*t100R	1B 2A 74 31 30 30 52
	150 dpi resolution	<ESC>*t150R	1B 2A 74 31 35 30 52
	300 dpi resolution	<ESC>*t300R	1B 2A 74 33 30 30 52
	Start at leftmost pos.	<ESC>*r0A	1B 2A 72 30 41
	Start at current cursor	<ESC>*r1A	1B 2A 72 31 41
Raster Graphics	Transfer graphic rows	<ESC>*b#W [data]	1B 2A 62 # 57
	End graphics	<ESC>*rB	1B 2A 72 42
Printer Control	Reset printer	<ESC>E	1B 45
	Self test mode	<ESC>z	1B 7A
Cursor Positioning	Move to row	<ESC>&a#R	1B 26 61 # 52
	Move to column	<ESC>&a#C	1B 26 61 # 43
	Horizontal movement	<ESC>&a#H	1B 26 61 # 48
	Vertical movement	<ESC>&a#V	1B 26 61 # 56

(Continued)

7.090. HP LASERJET PRINTER CONTROL CODES SUMMARY (continued)

Function Type	*Function*	*Code Sequence in ASCII Chars*	*Code Sequence in Hex Bytes*
Underlining	Underline ON	<ESC>&d#D	1B 26 64 # 44
	Underline OFF	<ESC>&d@	1B 26 64 40
Miscellaneous Control	Display functions ON	<ESC>Y	1B 59
	Display functions OFF	<ESC>Z	1B 5A
	Transparent print data	<ESC>&p#X [data]	1B 26 70 # 58
	Horizontal motion index	<ESC>&k#H	1B 26 6B # 48
	Carriage return=CR	<ESC>&k0G	1B 26 6B 30 47
	Carriage return=CR+LF	<ESC>&k1G	1B 26 6B 31 47
	LF=CR+LF, FF=CR+FF, CR=CR	<ESC>&k2G	1B 26 6B 32 47
	Add CR to LF and FF, CR=CR+LF	<ESC>&k3G	1B 26 6B 33 47
	Enable end of line wrap	<ESC>&s0C	1B 26 73 30 43
	Disable end of line wrap	<ESC>&s1C	1B 26 73 31 43
	Number of copies	<ESC>&l#X	1B 26 6C # 58
	Eject page	<ESC>&l0H	1B 26 6C 30 48
	Feed from tray	<ESC>&l1H	1B 26 6C 31 48
	Manual feed	<ESC>&l2H	1B 26 6C 32 48
	Envelope feed	<ESC>&l3H	1B 26 6C 33 48
Laserjet +/500+ Extensions	Graphics horz cursor position	<ESC>*p#X	1B 2A 70 # 58
	Graphics vert cursor position	<ESC>*p#Y	1B 2A 70 # 59
	Font ID number	<ESC>*c#D	1B 2A 63 # 44
	ASCII char code number	<ESC>*c#E	1B 2A 63 # 45
	Create font	<ESC>)s#W [data]	1B 29 73 # 57
	Download character	<ESC>(s#W [data]	1B 28 73 # 57
	Primary font ID number	<ESC>(#X	1B 28 # 58
	Secondary font ID number	<ESC>)#X	1B 29 # 58
	Delete all fonts	<ESC>*c0F	1B 2A 63 30 46
	Delete all temp fonts	<ESC>*c1F	1B 2A 63 31 46
	Delete last font ID specified	<ESC>*c2F	1B 2A 63 32 46
	Delete last font ID & char code	<ESC>*c3F	1B 2A 63 33 46
	Make temporary font	<ESC>*c4F	1B 2A 63 34 46
	Make permanent font	<ESC>*c5F	1B 2A 63 35 46
	Copy/assign font	<ESC>*c6F	1B 2A 63 36 46
	Primary font default	<ESC>(3@	1B 28 30 40
	Secondary font default	<ESC>)3@	1B 29 30 40
	Macro ID	<ESC>&f#Y	1B 26 66 # 59
	Start macro	<ESC>&f0X	1B 26 66 30 58
	Stop macro	<ESC>&f1X	1B 26 66 31 58
	Execute macro	<ESC>&f2X	1B 26 66 32 58
	Call macro	<ESC>&f3X	1B 26 66 33 58
	Enable overlay	<ESC>&f4X	1B 26 66 34 58
	Disable overlay	<ESC>&f5X	1B 26 66 35 58
	Delete macros	<ESC>&f6X	1B 26 66 36 58
	Delete all temporary macros	<ESC>&f7X	1B 26 66 37 58
	Delete macro ID	<ESC>&f8X	1B 26 66 38 58
	Make macro temporary	<ESC>&f9X	1B 26 66 39 58
	Make macro permanent	<ESC>&f10X	1B 26 66 31 30 58
	Push position	<ESC>&f0S	1B 26 66 30 53
	Pop position	<ESC>&f1S	1B 26 66 31 53
	Horz # dots in pattern	<ESC>*c#A	1B 2A 63 # 41
	Horz # decipoints in pattern	<ESC>*c#H	1B 2A 63 # 48
	Vert # dots in pattern	<ESC>*c#B	1B 2A 63 # 42
	Vert # decipoints in pattern	<ESC>*c#V	1B 2A 63 # 56
	Print solid black	<ESC>*c0P	1B 2A 63 30 50
	Print shaded fill	<ESC>*c2P	1B 2A 63 32 50
	Print cross-hatched fill	<ESC>*c3P	1B 2A 63 33 50
Laserjet+/500+ Extensions	Print 2% gray scale	<ESC>*c2G	1B 2A 63 32 47
	Print 10% gray scale	<ESC>*c10G	1B 2A 63 31 30 47
	Print 15% gray scale	<ESC>*c15G	1B 2A 63 31 35 47
	Print 30% gray scale	<ESC>*c30G	1B 2A 63 33 30 47
	Print 45% gray scale	<ESC>*c45G	1B 2A 63 34 35 47
	Print 70% gray scale	<ESC>*c70G	1B 2A 63 37 30 47
	Print 90% gray scale	<ESC>*c90G	1B 2A 63 39 30 47
	Print 100% gray scale	<ESC>*c100G	1B 2A 63 31 30 30 47
	HP Pattern 1 horz lines	<ESC>*c1G	1B 2A 63 31 47
	HP Pattern 2 vert lines	<ESC>*c2G	1B 2A 63 32 47
	HP pattern 3 diagonal lines	<ESC>*c3G	1B 2A 63 33 47
	HP pattern 4 diagonal lines	<ESC>*c4G	1B 2A 63 34 47
	HP pattern 5 grid	<ESC>*c5G	1B 2A 63 35 47
	HP pattern 6 diagonal grid	<ESC>*c6G	1B 2A 63 36 47

(Continued)

7.090. HP LASERJET PRINTER CONTROL CODES SUMMARY (continued)

Function Type	*Function*	*Code Sequence in ASCII Chars*	*Code Sequence in Hex Bytes*
Laserjet 500+ Extensions	Default stacking position	<ESC>&l0T	1B 26 6C 30 54
	Toggle stacking position	<ESC>&l1T	1B 26 6C 31 54
	Eject page	<ESC>&l0H	1B 26 6C 30 48
	Paper tray auto feed	<ESC>&l1H	1B 26 6C 31 48
	Manual feed	<ESC>&l2H	1B 26 6C 32 48
	Envelope feed	<ESC>&l3H	1B 26 6C 33 48
	Feed from lower cassette	<ESC>&l4H	1B 26 6C 34 48

Note:
- # should be replaced by the relevant numeric value in this chart.
- [data] indicates a bitstream of appropriately formatted data.

Source: HP LaserJet Printer Family Technical Reference, pages A1 through A6
HP LaserJet III Technical Reference, pages B-2 through B-9

See Also: 7.087. IBM Printer Control Codes Summary
7.088. Qume Sprint II/Diablo 630 Printer Control Codes Summary
7.089. Epson Printer Control Codes Summary

7.091. HAYES MODEM COMMAND SET

Command	*Function*	*Allowable Values/Comments*
AT	Attention	Starts all commands
ATI#	Request product code and ROM checksum	#=0 -- modem sends its 3-digit product code #=1 -- request numeric checksum of firmware ROM #=2 -- request OK or ERROR state of ROM checksum
A/	Repeat last command	Not AT or Return commands
A	Answer without waiting for ring	
B#	Bell 1200 bps protocol mode	#=0 -- CCITT v.22/v.22bis #=1 -- Bell 212A
C#	Carrier state	#=0 -- off #=1 -- on
D#	Dial telephone number	#=telephone number (may include / or - chars)
E#	Echo modem commands	#=0 -- no #=1 -- yes
F#	Set duplex	#=0 -- set half duplex #=1 -- set full duplex
H#	Set hook status	#=0 -- on hook (hang up) #=1 -- off hook
L#	Set speaker volume	#=0 or 1 -- low #=2 -- medium #=3 -- high
M#	Set speaker mode	#=0 -- off #=1 -- on #=2 -- always on #=3 -- disable speaker when carrier received
O#	Set on-line state	#=0 -- modem returns to on-line state #=1 -- modem returns on-line and retrains equalizer*
P	Set pulse dialing mode	
Q#	Set quiet command state	#=0 -- commands are sent #=1 -- commands are not sent
R	Reserve mode	Use answer frequencies when originating call
S	Dial stored number	
S#=value	Set S-register	#=S-register number; value=value to set register to
S#?	Display S-register value	#=S-register number
T	Set tone dialing mode	
V#	Set verbose mode	#=0 -- use digits #=1 -- use words
W	Wait for second dial or access tone	
X#	Enable extended result code & mode setting	#=0 -- basic (300 bps) #=1 -- extended (no dialtone or busy signal detect) #=2 -- extended (detects dialtone but not busy signals) #=3 -- extended (no dialtone detect but detects busy signal) #=4 -- extended (detects both dialtones and busy signals)
Y#	Long space disconnect	#=0 -- disabled #=1 -- enabled (disconnects after receiving 1.6 sec break)
Z	Fetch configuration profile from nonvolatile memory	
@	Wait for quiet answer	
,	Pause	Delay in dialing sequence
!	Flash	On-hook for 1/2 second
;	Return to command mode after dialing	

(Continued)

7.091. HAYES MODEM COMMAND SET (continued)

Command	*Function*	*Allowable Values/Comments*
&C#	Set data carrier detect handling	#=0 -- modem keeps DCD on #=1 -- DCD tracks data carrier detect
&D#	Set DTR handling	#=0 -- modem ignores DTR #=1 -- modem assumes command state when DTR triggered #=2 -- DTR off switches modem off hook #=3 -- DTR off initializes modem
&F	Fetch factory configuration profile from ROM	
&G#	Set guard tone selection	#=0 -- no guard tones #=1 -- 550 Hz guard tone #=2 -- 1800 guard tone
&J#	Set telephone jack selection	#=0 -- RJ11, RJ41S, or RJ45S #=1 -- RJ12 or RJ13
&L#	Set leased line or dialup line selection	#=0 -- dialup operation #=1 -- leased line operation
&M#	Set async/sync mode selection	#=0 -- asynchronous #=1 -- synchronous mode 1 (async dialing, then sync comm) #=2 -- synchronous mode 2 (stored number dialing) #=3 -- synchronous mode 3 (manual dialing)
&P#	Set pulse dial and length	#=0 -- 39% make, 61% break (US, Canadian standard) #=1 -- 33% make, 67% break
&R#	Set RTS and CTS handling	#=0 -- CTS tracks RTS #=1 -- modem ignores RTS, CTS turned on to recieve sync data
&S#	Set DSR handling	#=0 -- modem forces DSR when modem turned on #=1 -- DSR operates according to EIA specifications
&T#	Set test mode	#=0 -- terminate any test in progress (when last command on line) #=1 -- initiate local analog loopback test #=3 -- initiate local digital loopback test #=4 -- conditions modem to perform remote digital loopback #=5 -- prohibits remote digital loopback #=6 -- initiates remote digital loopback with another modem #=7 or 8 -- intiates remote digital loopback with self-test
&W	Write active configuration to memory	
&X#	Select sync transmit clock source (in sync mode)	#=0 -- modem generates and sends through pin 15 #=1 -- host computer sends through pin 24, modem routes to pin 15 #=2 -- modem derives timing from incomng signal, sends to pin 15
&Z#	Store telephone number	# is telephone number compatible with Dial command

*2400-baud mode only

Source: The Winn Rosch Hardware Bible (Brady), pages 455 through 457

See Also: 7.092. Hayes Modem S-Register Definitions
7.093. Hayes Modem Response Codes

7.092. HAYES MODEM S-REGISTER DEFINITIONS

Register	*Function*	*Allowable Range*	*Units*	*Default Value*
SO	Answer on ring number	0-255	rings	0
S1	Count number of rings	0-255	rings	0
S2	Escape code	0-127	ASCII	43
S3	Character used as return	0-127	ASCII	13
S4	Character used as line feed	0-127	ASCII	10
S5	Character used as backspace	0-32, 127	ASCII	8
S6	Time to wait for dial tone	2-255	seconds	2
S7	Time to wait for carrier	1-255	seconds	30
S8	Length of comma pause	0-255	seconds	2
S9	Response time for carrier detect	1-255	tenths of sec	6
S10	Delay before hang up	1-255	tenths of sec	7
S11	RESERVED			
S12	Escape code dead time	20-255	2/100ths sec	50
S13	RESERVED			

(Continued)

7.092. HAYES MODEM S-REGISTER DEFINITIONS (continued)

Register	*Function*	*Allowable Range*	*Units*	*Default Value*
S14	Modem options	One of following:		
		Bit 0	RESERVED	
		Bit 1	Cmd echo	1=echo
		Bit 2	result codes	1=disabled
		Bit 3	verbose mode	1=verbose on
		Bit 4	dumb mode	1=dumb on
		Bit 5	dial method	1=pulse
		Bit 6	RESERVED	
		Bit 7	orig/answer mode	1=originate
S15	RESERVED			
S16	Modem test options	One of following:		
		Bit 0	local analog loop	1=enabled
		Bit 1	RESERVED	
		Bit 2	local digital loop	1=enabled
		Bit 3	status bit	1=loopback in progress
		Bit 4	remote digital loop	1=enabled
		Bit 5	remote dig w/ test	1=enabled
		Bit 6	local analog w/ test	1=enabled
		Bit 7	RESERVED	1=originate
S17	RESERVED			
S18	Test timer	0-255	seconds	0
S19	RESERVED			
S20	RESERVED			
S21	Modem options	One of following:		
		Bit 0	telco jack	1=RJ12/RJ13, 0=RJ11/RJ41S/RJ45S
		Bit 1	RESERVED	
		Bit 2	RTS/CTS handling	1=CTS always on, 0=RTS follows CTS
		Bits 3, 4	DTR handling	00=ignored, 01=cmd, 10=hang up, 11=init
		Bit 5	DCD handling	1=DCD follows carrier
		Bit 6	DSR handling	1=modem off-hook and in data mode
		Bit 7	long space disc.	1=enabled
S22	Modem option register	One of following:		
		Bits 0, 1	speaker vol	00=low, 01=low, 10=medium, 11=high
		Bits 2, 3	speaker control	00=disabled, 01=to CD, 10=on, 11=on from dial to CD
		Bits 4, 5, 6	result code option	000=300 baud codes, 100=no dial tone or busy, 101=dialtone only, 110=busy only, 111=dialtone and busy
		Bit 7	make/break	0=39% make, 61% break; 1=33, 67
S23	Modem option register	One of following:		
		Bit 0	remote digital loop	1=enabled
		Bits 1, 2	comm rate	00=0-300 bps, 01=RESERVED, 10=1200 bps, 11=2400 bps
		Bit 3	RESERVED	
		Bits 4, 5	parity option	00=even, 01=space, 10=odd, 11=mark/none
		Bits 6, 7	guard tone	00=disabled, 01=550 Hz, 10=1800 Hz, 11=RESERVED
S24	RESERVED			
S25	Delay to DTR	0-255	1/100 second	5
S26	RTS to CTS delay	0-255	1/100 second	1
S27	Modem option register	One of following:		
		Bits 0, 1	transmission mode	00=async, 01=sync with async call placement, 10=sync f/ stored number, 11=manual sync
		Bit 2	line type	0=dial up, 1=leased line
		Bit 3	RESERVED	
		Bits 4, 5	sync clock source	00=local modem, 01=host computer, 10=derived, 11=RESERVED
		Bit 6	operation type	0=CCITT, 1=Bell 212A
		Bit 7	RESERVED	

Source: The Winn Rosch Hardware Bible (Brady), pages 459 through 462

See Also: 7.091. Hayes Modem Command Set
7.093. Hayes Modem Response Codes

7.093. HAYES MODEM RESPONSE CODES

Numeric Code	Verbose Code	Definition
0	OK	Command executed without error
1	CONNECT	Connection established at 300 bps
2	RING	Phone is ringing
3	NO CARRIER	Carrier was lost or never detected
4	ERROR	Error in command, or command too long
5	CONNECT 1200	Connection established at 1200 bps
6	NO DIALTONE	Dialtone not detected during the waiting period
7	BUSY	Modem detected a busy signal
8	NO ANSWER	No silence detected while waiting for quiet answer
10	CONNECT 2400	Connection established at 2400 bps

Source: The Winn Rosch Hardware Bible (Brady), page 463

See Also: 7.091. Hayes Modem Command Set
7.092. Hayes Modem S-Register Definitions

7.094. AT REAL TIME CLOCK RAM CONFIGURATION USAGE

Address	Function	Comments
0H	Seconds	
1H	Second alarm	
2H	Minutes	
3H	Minute alarm	
4H	Hours	
5H	Hour alarm	
6H	Day of week	
7H	Day of month	
8H	Month	
9H	Year	
0AH	Status register A	See 7.095. AT Real Time Clock Status Register A
0BH	Status register B	See 7.096. AT Real Time Clock Status Register B
0CH	Status register C	See 7.097. AT Real Time Clock Status Register C
0DH	Status register D	See 7.098. AT Real Time Clock Status Register D
0EH	Diagnostic status byte	See 7.099. AT CMOS RAM Configuration Diagnostic Status Byte
0FH	Shutdown status byte	Defined by power-on diagnostics
10H	Disk drive type byte	See 7.100. AT CMOS RAM Configuration Diskette Drive Type Byte
11H	RESERVED	
12H	Fixed drive type byte	See 7.101. AT CMOS RAM Configuration Fixed Drive Type Byte
13H	RESERVED	
14H	Equipment byte	See 7.102. AT CMOS RAM Configuration Equipment Byte
15H	Low-base memory byte	
16H	High-base memory byte	100H=256K, 200H=512K, 280H=512K-640K
17H	Low expansion memory byte	
18H	High expansion memory byte	200H=512K, 400H=1024K, 600-3C00H=1536K through 15360K
19H	Drive C extended byte	See 7.061. AT Fixed Disk Drive Types
1AH	Drive D extended byte	See 7.061. AT Fixed Disk Drive Types
1BH-2DH	RESERVED	
2EH-2FH	Checksum	Checksum based on 10-2DH addresses
30H	Low expansion memory byte	
31H	High expansion memory byte	200H=512K, 400H=1024K, 600-3C00H=1536K through 15360K
32H	Date century byte	BCD value for century
33H	Information flags	Bit 7 set = top 128K installed, bit 6 set = first user message
34H-3FH	RESERVED	

Source: IBM PC/AT Technical Reference, pages 1-56 through 1-68

See Also: 7.061. AT Fixed Disk Drive Types
7.095. AT Real Time Clock Status Register A
7.096. AT Real Time Clock Status Register B
7.097. AT Real Time Clock Status Register C
7.098. AT Real Time Clock Status Register D
7.099. AT CMOS RAM Configuration Diagnostic Status Byte
7.100. AT CMOS RAM Configuration Diskette Drive Type Byte
7.101. AT CMOS RAM Configuration Fixed Drive Type Byte
7.102. AT CMOS RAM Configuration Equipment Byte

7.095. AT REAL TIME CLOCK STATUS REGISTER A

Bit Number

7	6	5	4	3	2	1	0	Name	Function	Allowable Values
✓								Update in progress	Indicates update cycle in progress	0=date/time available, 1=date/time being updated
	✓	✓	✓					22-stage divider	Identifies time-base frequency used	default=010, 32.768KHz time base
				✓	✓	✓	✓	Rate selection	Identifies divider output frequency	default=0110, 1.024KHz frequency

Source: IBM PC/AT Technical Reference, pages 1-57 through 1-58

See Also: 7.096. AT Real Time Clock Status Register B
7.097. AT Real Time Clock Status Register C
7.098. AT Real Time Clock Status Register D

7.096. AT REAL TIME CLOCK STATUS REGISTER B

Bit Number

7	6	5	4	3	2	1	0	Name	Function	Allowable Values
✓								Set	Advances count (1 per second)	0=update normally, 1=abort update cycle
	✓							Periodic int enable	Allows interrupts at status reg A settings	0=disable int (default), 1=enable int
		✓						Alarm int enable	Sets alarm interrupt	0=disabled (default), 1=enabled
			✓					Update-ended int enable	Sets end-of-update interrupt	0=disabled (default), 1=enabled
				✓				Square wave enable	Sets frequency as per status reg A 0-3 bits	0=disabled (default), 1=enabled
					✓			Date mode	Sets binary or BCD updates	0=BCD (default), 1=binary
						✓		24/12 mode	Sets hours format in time	0=12-hour clock, 1=24-hour clock (default)
							✓	Daylight savings enable	Sets clock to recognize daylight savings	0=disabled (default), 1=enabled

Source: IBM PC/AT Technical Reference, pages 1-58 through 1-59

See Also: 7.095. AT Real Time Clock Status Register A
7.097. AT Real Time Clock Status Register C
7.098. AT Real Time Clock Status Register D

7.097. AT REAL TIME CLOCK STATUS REGISTER C

Bit Number

7	6	5	4	3	2	1	0	Name	Allowable Values
✓								IRQF flag	Read only
	✓							PF flag	Read only
		✓						AF flag	Read only
			✓					UF flag	Read only
				✓	✓	✓	✓	RESERVED	Should always be 0

Source: IBM PC/AT Technical Reference, page 1-59

See Also: 7.095. AT Real Time Clock Status Register A
7.096. AT Real Time Clock Status Register B
7.098. AT Real Time Clock Status Register D

7.098. AT REAL TIME CLOCK STATUS REGISTER D

Bit Number

7	6	5	4	3	2	1	0	Name	Function	Allowable Values
✓								Valid RAM bit	Status of power-sense pin (bat. level)	0=battery dead, RAM invalid, 1=battery good
	✓	✓	✓	✓	✓	✓	✓	RESERVED		Should always be 0

Source: IBM PC/AT Technical Reference, page 1-59

See Also: 7.095. AT Real Time Clock Status Register A
7.096. AT Real Time Clock Status Register B
7.097. AT Real Time Clock Status Register C

7.099. AT CMOS RAM CONFIGURATION DIAGNOSTIC STATUS BYTE

Bit Number

7	6	5	4	3	2	1	0	Function	Allowable Values
✔								Power status of RTC chip	0=chip hasn't lost power, 1=chip has lost power
	✔							Configuration record (checksum status)	0=checksum is good, 1=checksum bad
		✔						Incorrect configuration information	0=valid configuration, 1=invalid configuration
			✔					Memory size comparison	0=power-on check showed same memory size, 1=diff. size
				✔				Fixed disk status	0=proper function, 1=adapter or drive failed initialization
					✔			Time status indicator	0=time is valid, 1=time invalid
						✔	✔	RESERVED	

Source: IBM PC/AT Technical Reference, pages 1-59 through 1-60

See Also: 7.094. AT Real Time Clock RAM Configuration Usage

7.100. AT CMOS RAM CONFIGURATION DISKETTE DRIVE TYPE BYTE

Bit Number

7	6	5	4	3	2	1	0	Function	Allowable Values
✔	✔	✔	✔					Type of first diskette drive	0000=no drive, 0001=48TPI, 0010=96TPI
				✔	✔	✔	✔	Type of second diskette drive	0000=no drive, 0001=48TPI, 0010=96TPI

Source: IBM PC/AT Technical Reference, page 1-61

See Also: 7.094. AT Real Time Clock RAM Configuration Usage

7.101. AT CMOS RAM CONFIGURATION FIXED DRIVE TYPE BYTE

Bit Number

7	6	5	4	3	2	1	0	Function	Allowable Values
✔	✔	✔	✔					Type of first fixed drive	0000=no drive, otherwise see 7.061. AT Fixed Disk Drive Types
				✔	✔	✔	✔	Type of second fixed drive	0000=no drive, otherwise see 7.061. AT Fixed Disk Drive Types

Source: IBM PC/AT Technical Reference, page 1-62

See Also: 7.061. AT Fixed Disk Drive Types
7.094. AT Real Time Clock RAM Configuration Usage

7.102. AT CMOS RAM CONFIGURATION EQUIPMENT BYTE

Bit Number

7	6	5	4	3	2	1	0	Function	Allowable Values
✔	✔							Number of disk drives	00=1 drive, 01=2 drives, other values RESERVED
		✔	✔					Primary display type	00=display has own BIOS, 01=40 col CGA, 10=80 col CGA, 11=MDA
				✔	✔			NOT USED	
						✔		Math coprocessor	0=not installed, 1=math coprocessor available
							✔	Diskette drives available	0=no diskette drives available, 1=diskette drives available

Source: IBM PC/AT Technical Reference, pages 1-63 through 1-64

See Also: 7.094. AT Real Time Clock RAM Configuration Usage

7.103. 8086 FAMILY MEMORY ADDRESSING MODES

Mode	*Example*	*Explanation*
Direct register addressing	ADD AX,BX	Uses contents of registers for operation
Indirect memory addressing	ADD AX,[BX] ADD [BX],AX	Uses BX as a relative offset to point to memory
Immediate addressing	ADD AX,123	Uses immediate value (123)
Based addressing	MOV AX[BX+2] MOV AX,2[BX]	Uses the value 2 bytes past the offset contained in BX
Indexed addressing	MOV AX,[SI+2] MOV AX,2[SI]	Uses the value 2 bytes past the offset contained in SI

Based indexed addressing	MOV AX,[BP+SI+2]
	MOV AX,2[BP+SI]
	MOV AX,2[BP][SI]
		Uses the sum of BP and SI, plus two

String addressing	MOVSB	Copies the string from memory at DS:[SI] to ES:[DI]

Source: Programmer's Guide to the IBM PC and PS/2 (Microsoft Press), pages 34 through 35

7.104. 8086 FAMILY INSTRUCTION SET SUMMARY

Instruction	*Function*	*Bytes§*	*Flags Affected*	*Undefined Flags*	*88/86*	*286*	*386*	*486*
AAA	ASCII adjust AL after add	1	Aux, carry	Overflow, sign, zero, parity	✔	✔	✔	✔
AAD	ASCII adjust before divide	2	Sign, zero, parity	Overflow, aux, carry	✔	✔	✔	✔
AAM	ASCII adjust after multiply	1	Sign, zero, parity	Overflow, aux, carry	✔	✔	✔	✔
AAS	ASCII adjust after subtract	1	Aux, carry	Overflow, sign, zero, parity	✔	✔	✔	✔
ADC mem, imm	Add with carry	1 - 4	Overflow, sign, zero, aux, parity, carry	None	✔	✔	✔	✔
ADC mem, reg	Add with carry	1 - 4	Overflow, sign, zero, aux, parity, carry	None	✔	✔	✔	✔
ADC reg, imm	Add with carry	1 - 4	Overflow, sign, zero, aux, parity, carry	None	✔	✔	✔	✔
ADC reg, mem	Add with carry	1 - 4	Overflow, sign, zero, aux, parity, carry	None	✔	✔	✔	✔
ADC reg, reg	Add with carry	1 - 4	Overflow, sign, zero, aux, parity, carry	None	✔	✔	✔	✔
ADD mem, imm	Add integers	1 - 4	Overflow, sign, zero, aux, parity, carry	None	✔	✔	✔	✔
ADD mem, reg	Add integers	1 - 4	Overflow, sign, zero, aux, parity, carry	None	✔	✔	✔	✔
ADD reg, imm	Add integers	1 - 4	Overflow, sign, zero, aux, parity, carry	None	✔	✔	✔	✔
ADD reg, mem	Add integers	1 - 4	Overflow, sign, zero, aux, parity, carry	None	✔	✔	✔	✔
ADD reg, reg	Add integers	1 - 4	Overflow, sign, zero, aux, parity, carry	None	✔	✔	✔	✔
AND mem, imm	Logical AND	1 - 4	Overflow=0, sign, zero, parity, carry=0	Aux	✔	✔	✔	✔
AND mem, reg	Logical AND	1 - 4	Overflow=0, sign, zero, parity, carry=0	Aux	✔	✔	✔	✔
AND reg, imm	Logical AND	1 - 4	Overflow=0, sign, zero, parity, carry=0	Aux	✔	✔	✔	✔
AND reg, reg	Logical AND	1 - 4	Overflow=0, sign, zero, parity, carry=0	Aux	✔	✔	✔	✔
AND reg, mem	Logical AND	1 - 4	Overflow=0, sign, zero, parity, carry=0	Aux	✔	✔	✔	✔
ARPL reg, mem	Adjust requested privilege level	2	Zero	None		✔	✔	✔
ARPL mem, reg	Adjust requested privilege level	2	Zero	None		✔	✔	✔
BOUND reg,mem	Detect array index out of range	2 - 4	None	None		✔	✔	✔
BSF reg, mem	Bit scan forward	2 - 4	Zero	Overflow, sign, aux, parity, carry			✔	✔
BSF reg, reg	Bit scan forward	2 - 4	Zero	Overflow, sign, aux, parity, carry			✔	✔
BSR reg, mem	Bit scan reverse	2 - 4	Zero	Overflow, sign, aux, parity, carry			✔	✔
BSR reg, reg	Bit scan reverse	2 - 4	Zero	Overflow, sign, aux, parity, carry			✔	✔
BSWAP reg	Byte swap	4	None	None				✔
BT reg, imm	Test bit	2 - 4	Carry	Overflow, sign, zero, aux, parity			✔	✔
BT mem, imm	Test bit	2 - 4	Carry	Overflow, sign, zero, aux, parity			✔	✔
BT reg, reg	Test bit	2 - 4	Carry	Overflow, sign, zero, aux, parity			✔	✔
BT mem, reg	Test bit	2 - 4	Carry	Overflow, sign, zero, aux, parity			✔	✔
BTC reg, imm	Test bit and complement	2 - 4	Carry	Overflow, sign, zero, aux, parity			✔	✔
BTC mem, imm	Test bit and complement	2 - 4	Carry	Overflow, sign, zero, aux, parity			✔	✔

(Continued)

7.104. 8086 FAMILY INSTRUCTION SET SUMMARY (continued)

Instruction	Function	Bytes§	Flags Affected	Undefined Flags	88/86	286	386	486
BTC reg, reg	Test bit and complement	2 - 4	Carry	Overflow, sign, zero, aux, parity			✔	✔
BTC mem, reg	Test bit and complement	2 - 4	Carry	Overflow, sign, zero, aux, parity			✔	✔
BTR reg, imm	Test bit and reset	2 - 4	Carry	Overflow, sign, zero, aux, parity			✔	✔
BTR mem, imm	Test bit and reset	2 - 4	Carry	Overflow, sign, zero, aux, parity			✔	✔
BTR reg, reg	Test bit and reset	2 - 4	Carry	Overflow, sign, zero, aux, parity			✔	✔
BTR reg, imm	Test bit and reset	2 - 4	Carry	Overflow, sign, zero, aux, parity			✔	✔
BTS reg, imm	Test bit and set	2 - 4	Carry	Overflow, sign, zero, aux, parity			✔	✔
BTS mem, imm	Test bit and set	2 - 4	Carry	Overflow, sign, zero, aux, parity			✔	✔
BTS reg, reg	Test bit and set	2 - 4	Carry	Overflow, sign, zero, aux, parity			✔	✔
BTS reg, imm	Test bit and set	2 - 4	Carry	Overflow, sign, zero, aux, parity			✔	✔
CALL imm, CS:EIP <-- imm	Far procedure call	4 - 6	None	None	✔	✔	✔	✔
CALL mem, CS:EIP <-- mem	Far procedure call	4 - 6	None	None	✔	✔	✔	✔
CALL offset, EIP <-- EIP+offset	Near procedure call	2 - 4	None	None	✔	✔	✔	✔
CALL mem, EIP <-- mem	Near procedure call	2 - 4	None	None	✔	✔	✔	✔
CALL reg, EIP <-- reg	Near procedure call	2 - 4	None	None	✔	✔	✔	✔
CBW	Convert byte to word	1	None	None	✔	✔	✔	✔
CDQ	Convert double word to quad word	4	None	None			✔	✔
CLC	Clear carry flag	-	Carry=0	None	✔	✔	✔	✔
CLD	Clear direction flag	-	Direction=0	None	✔	✔	✔	✔
CLI	Clear interrupt flag	-	Interrupt=0	None	✔	✔	✔	✔
CLTS	Clear task switched bit	-	TS=0 in CR0 register	None		✔	✔	✔
CMC	Complement carry flag	-	Carry	None	✔	✔	✔	✔
CMP mem, imm	Compare integers	1 - 4	Overflow, sign, zero, aux, parity, carry	None	✔	✔	✔	✔
CMP mem,reg	Compare integers	1 - 4	Overflow, sign, zero, aux, parity, carry	None	✔	✔	✔	✔
CMP reg,imm	Compare integers	1 - 4	Overflow, sign, zero, aux, parity, carry	None	✔	✔	✔	✔
CMP reg,mem	Compare integers	1 - 4	Overflow, sign, zero, aux, parity, carry	None	✔	✔	✔	✔
CMP reg,reg	Compare integers	1 - 4	Overflow, sign, zero, aux, parity, carry	None	✔	✔	✔	✔
CMPSB	Compare string byte	1 - 4	Overflow, sign, zero, aux, parity, carry	None	✔	✔	✔	✔
CMPSD	Compare string double word	1 - 4	Overflow, sign, zero, aux, parity, carry	None	✔	✔	✔	✔
CMPSW	Compare string word	1 - 4	Overflow, sign, zero, aux, parity, carry	None	✔	✔	✔	✔
CMPXCHG reg, reg	Compare accumulator and exchange	1 - 4	Overflow, sign, zero, aux, parity, carry	None				✔
CMPXCHG mem, reg	Compare accumulator and exchange	1 - 4	Overflow, sign, zero, aux, parity, carry	None				✔
CWD	Convert word to double word	2	None	None	✔	✔	✔	✔
CWDE	Convert word to double word extended	2	None	None			✔	✔
DAA	Decimal adjust after add	1	Sign, zero, aux, parity, carry	Overflow	✔	✔	✔	✔
DAS	Decimal adjust after subtract	1	Sign, zero, aux, parity, carry	Overflow	✔	✔	✔	✔
DEC mem	Decrement	1 - 4	Overflow, sign, zero, aux, parity	None	✔	✔	✔	✔
DEC reg	Decrement	1 - 4	Overflow, sign, zero, aux, parity	None	✔	✔	✔	✔
DIV mem	Unsigned divide	1 - 4	None	Overflow, sign, zero, aux, parity, carry	✔	✔	✔	✔
DIV reg	Unsigned divide	1 - 4	None	Overflow, sign, zero, aux, parity, carry	✔	✔	✔	✔
ENTER imm, imm	Enter new stack frame	-	None	None		✔	✔	✔
HLT	Halt	-	None	None	✔	✔	✔	✔
IDIV mem	Signed integer divide	1 - 4	None	Overflow, sign, zero, aux, parity, carry	✔	✔	✔	✔
IDIV reg	Signed integer divide	1 - 4	None	Overflow, sign, zero, aux, parity, carry	✔	✔	✔	✔
IMUL reg	Signed integer multiply	1 - 4	Overflow, carry	Sign, zero, aux, parity	✔	✔	✔	✔
IMUL mem	Signed integer multiply	1 - 4	Overflow, carry	Sign, zero, aux, parity	✔	✔	✔	✔
IMUL reg, reg	Signed integer multiply	1 - 4	Overflow, carry	Sign, zero, aux, parity	✔	✔	✔	✔
IMUL reg, mem	Signed integer multiply	1 - 4	Overflow, carry	Sign, zero, aux, parity	✔	✔	✔	✔
IMUL reg, imm	Signed integer multiply	1 - 4	Overflow, carry	Sign, zero, aux, parity		✔	✔	✔
IMUL reg, reg, imm	Signed integer multiply	1 - 4	Overflow, carry	Sign, zero, aux, parity		✔	✔	✔
IMUL reg, mem, imm	Signed integer multiply	1 - 4	Overflow, carry	Sign, zero, aux, parity		✔	✔	✔

(Continued)

7.104. 8086 FAMILY INSTRUCTION SET SUMMARY (continued)

Instruction	*Function*	*Bytes§*	*Flags Affected*	*Undefined Flags*	*88/86*	*286*	*386*	*486*
IN accum, imm	Input from port	1 - 4	None	None	✔	✔	✔	✔
IN accum, DX	Input from DX port	1 - 4	None	None	✔	✔	✔	✔
INC mem	Increment	1 - 4	Overflow, sign, zero, aux, parity	None	✔	✔	✔	✔
INC reg	Increment	1 - 4	Overflow, sign, zero, aux, parity	None	✔	✔	✔	✔
INSB	Input string byte from port	1 - 4	None	None		✔	✔	✔
INSD	Input string double word from port	1 - 4	None	None		✔	✔	✔
INSW	Input string word from port	1 - 4	None	None		✔	✔	✔
INT imm	Interrupt	-	Interrupt, trap=0	None	✔	✔	✔	✔
INTO	Interrupt on overflow	-	Interrupt, trap=0	None	✔	✔	✔	✔
INVD	Invalidate cache	-	None	None				✔
INVLPG	Invalidate TLB Entry	4	None	None				✔
IRET	Interrupt return	-	All	All	✔	✔	✔	✔
JA offset	Jump above	-	Carry=0, zero=0	None	✔	✔	✔	✔
JAE offset	Jump above or equal	-	Carry=0	None	✔	✔	✔	✔
JB offset	Jump below	-	Carry=1	None	✔	✔	✔	✔
JBE offset	Jump below or equal	-	Carry=1, zero=1	None	✔	✔	✔	✔
JC offset	Jump if carry	-	Carry=1	None	✔	✔	✔	✔
JCXZ offset	Jump if CX=0	-	None	None	✔	✔	✔	✔
JE offset	Jump equal	-	Zero=1	None	✔	✔	✔	✔
JECXZ offset	Jump if ECX=0	-	None	None	✔	✔	✔	✔
JG offset	Jump greater	-	Sign=overflow, zero=o	None	✔	✔	✔	✔
JGE offset	Jump greater or equal	-	Sign=overflow	None	✔	✔	✔	✔
JL offset	Jump less	-	Sign≠overflow, zero=0	None	✔	✔	✔	✔
JLE offset	Jump less or equal	-	Sign≠overflow	None	✔	✔	✔	✔
JMP offset, EIP <-- EIP+offset	Near jump	-	None	None	✔	✔	✔	✔
JMP reg, EIP <-- reg	Near jump	-	None	None	✔	✔	✔	✔
JMP mem, EIP <-- mem	Near jump	-	None	None	✔	✔	✔	✔
JMP imm, CS:EIP <-- data	Far jump	-	None	None	✔	✔	✔	✔
JMP mem, CS:EIP <-- mem	Far jump	-	None	None	✔	✔	✔	✔
JNA offset	Jump not above (JBE)	-	Carry=1, zero=1	None	✔	✔	✔	✔
JNAE offset	Jump not above or equal (JB)	-	Carry=1	None	✔	✔	✔	✔
JNB offset	Jump not below (JAE)	-	Carry=0	None	✔	✔	✔	✔
JNBE offset	Jump not below or equal (JA)	-	Carry=0, zero=0	None	✔	✔	✔	✔
JNC offset	Jump no carry	-	Carry=0	None	✔	✔	✔	✔
JNE offset	Jump not equal	-	Zero=0	None	✔	✔	✔	✔
JNG offset	Jump not greater	-	Sign≠overflow, zero=1	None	✔	✔	✔	✔
JNGE offset	Jump not greater or equal (JL)	-	Sign≠overflow, zero=0	None	✔	✔	✔	✔
JNL offset	Jump not less (JGE)	-	Sign=overflow	None	✔	✔	✔	✔
JNLE offset	Jump not less or equal (JG)	-	Sign=overflow, zero=o	None	✔	✔	✔	✔
JNO offset	Jump no overflow	-	Overflow=0	None	✔	✔	✔	✔
JNP offset	Jump no parity	-	Parity=0	None	✔	✔	✔	✔
JNS offset	Jump no sign	-	Sign=0	None	✔	✔	✔	✔
JNZ offset	Jump not zero	-	Zero=0	None	✔	✔	✔	✔
JO offset	Jump if overflow	-	Overflow=1	None	✔	✔	✔	✔
JP offset	Jump if parity	-	Parity=1	None	✔	✔	✔	✔
JPE offset	Jump parity even	-	Parity=1	None	✔	✔	✔	✔
JPO offset	Jump parity odd	-	Parity=0	None	✔	✔	✔	✔
JS offset	Jump if sign	-	Sign=1	None	✔	✔	✔	✔
JZ offset	Jump if zero	-	Zero=1	None	✔	✔	✔	✔
LAHF	Load AH with flags (LO byte of flags)	1	None	None	✔	✔	✔	✔
LAR reg, reg	Load access rights byte	2 - 4	Zero	None		✔	✔	✔
LAR reg, mem	Load access rights byte	2 - 4	Zero	None		✔	✔	✔
LDS reg, mem	Load pointer to DS	2 - 4	None	None	✔	✔	✔	✔
LEA reg, mem	Load effective address to register	2 - 4	None	None	✔	✔	✔	✔
LEAVE	Leave procedure	-	None	None		✔	✔	✔
LES reg, mem	Load pointer to ES	2 - 4	None	None	✔	✔	✔	✔
LFS reg, mem	Load pointer to FS	2 - 4	None	None			✔	✔
LGDT mem	Load global descriptor table	-	None	None		✔	✔	✔
LGS reg, mem	Load pointer to GS	2 - 4	None	None			✔	✔
LIDT mem	Load interrupt descriptor table	-	None	None		✔	✔	✔
LLDT reg	Load local descriptor table	2	None	None		✔	✔	✔
LLDT mem	Load local descriptor table	2	None	None		✔	✔	✔
LMSW reg	Load machine status word	2	None	None		✔	✔	✔
LMSW mem	Load machine status word	2	None	None		✔	✔	✔

(Continued)

7.104. 8086 FAMILY INSTRUCTION SET SUMMARY (continued)

Instruction	Function	Bytes§	Flags Affected	Undefined Flags	88/86	286	386	486
LOCK	Bus lock prefix	-	None	None	✔	✔	✔	✔
LODSB	Load string byte	1 - 4	None	None	✔	✔	✔	✔
LODSD	Load string dword	1 - 4	None	None	✔	✔	✔	✔
LODSW	Load string word	1 - 4	None	None	✔	✔	✔	✔
LOOP offset	Loop	-	None	None	✔	✔	✔	✔
LOOPE offset	Loop	-	None	None	✔	✔	✔	✔
LOOPNE offset	Loop	-	None	None	✔	✔	✔	✔
LOOPNZ offset	Loop	-	None	None	✔	✔	✔	✔
LOOPZ offset	Loop	-	None	None	✔	✔	✔	✔
LSL reg, mem	Load segment limit	2 - 4	Zero flag	None		✔	✔	✔
LSL reg, reg	Load segment limit	2 - 4	Zero flag	None		✔	✔	✔
LSS reg, mem	Load pointer to SS	2 - 4	None	None			✔	✔
LTR reg	Load task register	2	None	None		✔	✔	✔
LTR mem	Load task register	2	None	None		✔	✔	✔
MOV reg, segreg	Move selector	2	None	None	✔	✔	✔	✔
MOV mem, imm	Move data	1 - 4	None	None	✔	✔	✔	✔
MOV mem, reg	Move data	1 - 4	None	None	✔	✔	✔	✔
MOV mem, segreg	Move selector	2	None	None	✔	✔	✔	✔
MOV reg, imm	Move data	1 - 4	None	None	✔	✔	✔	✔
MOV reg, mem	Move data	1 - 4	None	None	✔	✔	✔	✔
MOV reg, reg	Move data	1 - 4	None	None	✔	✔	✔	✔
MOV segreg, mem	Move selector	2	None	None	✔	✔	✔	✔
MOV segreg, reg	Move selector	2	None	None	✔	✔	✔	✔
MOV reg, reg	Move special	4	None	Overflow, sign, zero, aux, parity, carry			✔	✔
MOVSB	Move string byte	1 - 4	None	None	✔	✔	✔	✔
MOVSD	Move string double word	1 - 4	None	None	✔	✔	✔	✔
MOVSW	Move string word	1 - 4	None	None	✔	✔	✔	✔
MOVSX reg, reg	Move with sign extension	1 - 4	None	None			✔	✔
MOVSX reg, mem	Move with sign extension	1 - 4	None	None			✔	✔
MOVZX reg, reg	Move with zero extension	1 - 4	None	None			✔	✔
MOVZX reg, mem	Move with zero extension	1 - 4	None	None			✔	✔
MUL mem	Unsigned multiply	1 - 4	Overflow, carry	Sign, zero, aux, parity	✔	✔	✔	✔
MUL reg	Multiply	1 - 4	Overflow, carry	Sign, zero, aux, parity	✔	✔	✔	✔
NEG mem	Change sign	1 - 4	Overflow, sign, zero, aux, parity, carry	None	✔	✔	✔	✔
NEG reg	Change sign	1 - 4	Overflow, sign, zero, aux, parity, carry	None	✔	✔	✔	✔
NOP	No operation	-	None	None	✔	✔	✔	✔
NOT mem	Logical not	1 - 4	None	None	✔	✔	✔	✔
NOT reg	Logical not	1 - 4	None	None	✔	✔	✔	✔
OR mem, imm	Logical OR	1 - 4	Overflow=0, sign, zero, aux, parity, carry=0	None	✔	✔	✔	✔
OR mem, reg	Logical OR	1 - 4	Overflow=0, sign, zero, aux, parity, carry=0	None	✔	✔	✔	✔
OR reg, imm	Logical OR	1 - 4	Overflow=0, sign, zero, aux, parity, carry=0	None	✔	✔	✔	✔
OR reg, mem	Logical OR	1 - 4	Overflow=0, sign, zero, aux, parity, carry=0	None	✔	✔	✔	✔
OR reg, reg	Logical OR	1 - 4	Overflow=0, sign, zero, aux, parity, carry=0	None	✔	✔	✔	✔
OUT imm, accum	Output to port	1 - 4	None	None	✔	✔	✔	✔
OUT DX, accum	Output to DX port	1 - 4	None	None	✔	✔	✔	✔
OUTSB	Output string byte	1 - 4	None	None		✔	✔	✔
OUTSD	Output string double word	1 - 4	None	None		✔	✔	✔
OUTSW	Output string word	1 - 4	None	None		✔	✔	✔
POP mem	Restore from stack	2 - 4	None	None	✔	✔	✔	✔
POP reg	Restore from stack	2 - 4	None	None	✔	✔	✔	✔
POP segreg	Restore segment register	2	None	None	✔	✔	✔	✔
POPA	Restore all general registers from stack	2	None	None		✔	✔	✔
POPAD	Restore all 32-bit general registers from stack	4	None	None			✔	✔
POPF	Restore flags	2	All	None	✔	✔	✔	✔
POPFD	Pop stack into EFLAGS	4	All	None			✔	✔
PUSH imm	Save to stack	1 - 4	None	None	✔	✔	✔	✔
PUSH mem	Save to stack	1 - 4	None	None	✔	✔	✔	✔

(Continued)

7.104. 8086 FAMILY INSTRUCTION SET SUMMARY (continued)

Instruction	*Function*	*Bytes§*	*Flags Affected*	*Undefined Flags*	*88/86*	*286*	*386*	*486*
PUSH reg	Save to stack	1 - 4	None	None	✔	✔	✔	✔
PUSH segreg	Save to stack	1 - 4	None	None	✔	✔	✔	✔
PUSHA	Save 16-bit general registers	2	None	None		✔	✔	✔
PUSHAD	Save 32-bit general registers	4	None	None			✔	✔
PUSHF	Save 16-bit flags to stack	2	None	None	✔	✔	✔	✔
PUSHFD	Save EFLAGS register	4	None	None			✔	✔
RCL mem, imm	Rotate carry left	2 - 4	Overflow, carry	None	✔	✔	✔	✔
RCL reg, mem	Rotate carry left	2 - 4	Overflow, carry	None	✔	✔	✔	✔
RCL reg, CL	Rotate carry left	2 - 4	Overflow, carry	None	✔	✔	✔	✔
RCL mem, CL	Rotate carry left	2 - 4	Overflow, carry	None	✔	✔	✔	✔
RCR mem, imm	Rotate carry right	2 - 4	Overflow, carry	None	✔	✔	✔	✔
RCR reg, mem	Rotate carry right	2 - 4	Overflow, carry	None	✔	✔	✔	✔
RCR reg, CL	Rotate carry right	2 - 4	Overflow, carry	None	✔	✔	✔	✔
RCR mem, CL	Rotate carry right	2 - 4	Overflow, carry	None	✔	✔	✔	✔
REP	Repeat	-	None	None	✔	✔	✔	✔
REPE	Repeat equal	-	None	None	✔	✔	✔	✔
REPNE	Repeat not equal	-	None	None	✔	✔	✔	✔
REPNZ	Repeat not zero	-	None	None	✔	✔	✔	✔
REPZ	Repeat zero	-	None	None	✔	✔	✔	✔
RET	Near return	-	None	None	✔	✔	✔	✔
RET imm	Near return	-	None	None	✔	✔	✔	✔
RETF	Far return	-	None	None	✔	✔	✔	✔
RETF imm	Far return	-	None	None	✔	✔	✔	✔
ROL mem, imm	Rotate left	2 - 4	Overflow, carry	None	✔	✔	✔	✔
ROL reg, mem	Rotate left	2 - 4	Overflow, carry	None	✔	✔	✔	✔
ROL reg, CL	Rotate left	2 - 4	Overflow, carry	None	✔	✔	✔	✔
ROL mem, CL	Rotate left	2 - 4	Overflow, carry	None	✔	✔	✔	✔
ROR mem, imm	Rotate right	2 - 4	Overflow, carry	None	✔	✔	✔	✔
ROR reg, mem	Rotate right	2 - 4	Overflow, carry	None	✔	✔	✔	✔
ROR reg, CL	Rotate right	2 - 4	Overflow, carry	None	✔	✔	✔	✔
ROR mem, CL	Rotate right	2 - 4	Overflow, carry	None	✔	✔	✔	✔
SAHF	Store AH into flags	1	Sign, zero, aux, parity, carry	None	✔	✔	✔	✔
SAL reg, imm	Shift arithmetic left	1 - 4	Overflow, sign, zero, parity, carry	None	✔	✔	✔	✔
SAL mem, imm	Shift arithmetic left	1 - 4	Overflow, sign, zero, parity, carry	None	✔	✔	✔	✔
SAL reg, CL	Shift arithmetic left	1 - 4	Overflow, sign, zero, parity, carry	None	✔	✔	✔	✔
SAL mem, CL	Shift arithmetic left	1 - 4	Overflow, sign, zero, parity, carry	None	✔	✔	✔	✔
SAR reg, imm	Shift arithmetic right	1 - 4	Overflow, sign, zero, parity, carry	None		✔	✔	✔
SAR mem, imm	Shift arithmetic right	1 - 4	Overflow, sign, zero, parity, carry	None		✔	✔	✔
SAR reg, CL	Shift arithmetic right	1 - 4	Overflow, sign, zero, parity, carry	None		✔	✔	✔
SAR mem, CL	Shift arithmetic right	1 - 4	Overflow, sign, zero, parity, carry	None		✔	✔	✔
SBB mem, imm	Subtract with borrow	1 - 4	Overflow, sign, zero, aux, parity, carry	None	✔	✔	✔	✔
SBB mem, reg	Subtract with borrow	1 - 4	Overflow, sign, zero, aux, parity, carry	None	✔	✔	✔	✔
SBB reg, imm	Subtract with borrow	1 - 4	Overflow, sign, zero, aux, parity, carry	None	✔	✔	✔	✔
SBB reg, mem	Subtract with borrow	1 - 4	Overflow, sign, zero, aux, parity, carry	None	✔	✔	✔	✔
SBB reg, reg	Subtract with borrow	1 - 4	Overflow, sign, zero, aux, parity, carry	None	✔	✔	✔	✔
SCASB	Scan string byte	1 - 4	Overflow, sign, zero, aux, parity, carry	None	✔	✔	✔	✔
SCASD	Scan string double word	1 - 4	Overflow, sign, zero, aux, parity, carry	None	✔	✔	✔	✔
SCASW	Scan string word	1 - 4	Overflow, sign, zero, aux, parity, carry	None	✔	✔	✔	✔
SETA dest	Set if above	1	Carry=0, zero=0	None			✔	✔
SETAE dest	Set if above or equal	1	Carry=0	None			✔	✔
SETB dest	Set if below	1	Carry=1	None			✔	✔

(Continued)

7.104. 8086 FAMILY INSTRUCTION SET SUMMARY (continued)

Instruction	Function	Bytes§	Flags Affected	Undefined Flags	88/86	286	386	486
SETBE dest	Set if below or equal	1	Carry=1, zero=1	None			✔	✔
SETC dest	Set if if carry	1	Carry=1	None			✔	✔
SETE dest	Set if equal	1	Zero=1	None			✔	✔
SETG dest	Set if greater	1	Sign=overflow, zero=o	None			✔	✔
SETGE dest	Set if greater or equal	1	Sign=overflow	None			✔	✔
SETL dest	Set if less	1	Sign≠overflow	None			✔	✔
SETLE dest	Set if less or equal	1	Sign≠overflow, zero=1	None			✔	✔
SETNA dest	Set if not above (SETBE)	1	Carry=1, zero=1	None			✔	✔
SETNAE dest	Set if not above or equal (SETB)	1	Carry=1	None			✔	✔
SETNB dest	Set if not below (SETAE)	1	Carry=0	None			✔	✔
SETNBE dest	Set if not below or equal (SETA)	1	Carry=0, zero=0	None			✔	✔
SETNC dest	Set if no carry	1	Carry=0	None			✔	✔
SETNE dest	Set if not equal	1	Zero=0	None			✔	✔
SETNG dest	Set if not greater (SETLE)	1	Sign≠overflow, zero=1	None			✔	✔
SETNGE dest	Set if not greater or equal (SETL)	1	Sign≠overflow	None			✔	✔
SETNL dest	Set if not less (SETGE)	1	Sign=overflow	None			✔	✔
SETNLE dest	Set if not less or equal	1	Sign=overflow, zero=o	None			✔	✔
SETNO dest	Set if no overflow	1	Overflow=0	None			✔	✔
SETNP dest	Set if no parity	1	Parity=0	None			✔	✔
SETNS dest	Set if no sign	1	Sign=0	None			✔	✔
SETNZ dest	Set if not zero	1	Zero=0	None			✔	✔
SETO dest	Set if if overflow	1	Overflow=1	None			✔	✔
SETP dest	Set if if parity	1	Parity=1	None			✔	✔
SETPE dest	Set if parity even	1	Parity=1	None			✔	✔
SETPO dest	Set if parity odd	1	Parity=0	None			✔	✔
SETS dest	Set if if sign	1	Sign=1	None			✔	✔
SETZ dest	Set if if zero	1	Zero=1	None			✔	✔
SGDT	Store global descriptor table	-	None	None		✔	✔	✔
SHL reg, imm	Shift logical left	1 - 4	Overflow, sign, zero, parity, carry	None	✔	✔	✔	✔
SHL mem, imm	Shift logical left	1 - 4	Overflow, sign, zero, parity, carry	None	✔	✔	✔	✔
SHL reg, CL	Shift logical left	1 - 4	Overflow, sign, zero, parity, carry	None	✔	✔	✔	✔
SHL mem, CL	Shift logical left	1 - 4	Overflow, sign, zero, parity, carry	None	✔	✔	✔	✔
SHLD reg, reg, imm	Shift left double	2 - 4	Sign, zero, parity, carry	Overflow, aux			✔	✔
SHLD mem, reg, imm	Shift left double	2 - 4	Sign, zero, parity, carry	Overflow, aux			✔	✔
SHLD reg, reg, CL	Shift left double	2 - 4	Sign, zero, parity, carry	Overflow, aux			✔	✔
SHLD mem, reg, CL	Shift left double	2 - 4	Sign, zero, parity, carry	Overflow, aux			✔	✔
SHR reg, imm	Shift logical right	1 - 4	Overflow, sign, zero, parity, carry	None	✔	✔	✔	✔
SHR mem, imm	Shift logical right	1 - 4	Overflow, sign, zero, parity, carry	None	✔	✔	✔	✔
SHR reg, CL	Shift logical right	1 - 4	Overflow, sign, zero, parity, carry	None	✔	✔	✔	✔
SHR mem, CL	Shift logical right	1 - 4	Overflow, sign, zero, parity, carry	None	✔	✔	✔	✔
SHRD reg, reg, imm	Shift right double	2 - 4	Sign, zero, parity, carry	Overflow, aux			✔	✔
SHRD mem, reg, imm	Shift right double	2 - 4	Sign, zero, parity, carry	Overflow, aux			✔	✔
SHRD reg, reg, CL	Shift right double	2 - 4	Sign, zero, parity, carry	Overflow, aux			✔	✔
SHRD mem, reg, CL	Shift right double	2 - 4	Sign, zero, parity, carry	Overflow, aux			✔	✔
SIDT	Store interrupt descriptor table	-	None	None		✔	✔	✔
SLDT	Store local descriptor table	2	None	None		✔	✔	✔
SMSW	Store machine status word	2	None	None		✔	✔	✔
STC	Set carry flag	-	Carry=1	None	✔	✔	✔	✔
STD	Set direction flag	-	Direction	None	✔	✔	✔	✔
STI	Set interrupt flag	-	Interrupt	None	✔	✔	✔	✔
STOSB	Store string byte	1 - 4	None	None	✔	✔	✔	✔
STOSD	Store string double word	1 - 4	None	None	✔	✔	✔	✔
STOSW	Store string word	1 - 4	None	None	✔	✔	✔	✔
STR reg	Store task register	2	None	None		✔	✔	✔
STR mem	Store task register	2	None	None		✔	✔	✔
SUB mem, imm	Subtract	1 - 4	Overflow, sign, zero, aux, parity, carry	None	✔	✔	✔	✔
SUB mem, reg	Subtract	1 - 4	Overflow, sign, zero, aux, parity, carry	None	✔	✔	✔	✔
SUB reg, imm	Subtract	1 - 4	Overflow, sign, zero, aux, parity, carry	None	✔	✔	✔	✔
SUB reg, mem	Subtract	1 - 4	Overflow, sign, zero, aux, parity, carry	None	✔	✔	✔	✔
SUB reg, reg	Subtract	1 - 4	Overflow, sign, zero, aux, parity, carry	None	✔	✔	✔	✔
TEST mem, imm	AND function to flags	1 - 4	Overflow=0, sign, zero, parity, carry=0	Aux	✔	✔	✔	✔

(Continued)

7.104. 8086 FAMILY INSTRUCTION SET SUMMARY (continued)

Instruction	Function	Bytes§	Flags Affected	Undefined Flags	88/86	286	386	486
TEST reg, imm	AND function to flags	1 - 4	Overflow=0, sign, zero, parity, carry=0	Aux	✔	✔	✔	✔
TEST reg, mem	AND function to flags	1 - 4	Overflow=0, sign, zero, parity, carry=0	Aux	✔	✔	✔	✔
TEST reg, reg	AND function to flags	1 - 4	Overflow=0, sign, zero, parity, carry=0	Aux	✔	✔	✔	✔
TEST mem, reg	AND function to flags	1 - 4	Overflow=0, sign, zero, parity, carry=0	Aux	✔	✔	✔	✔
VERR reg	Verify read access	2	Zero	None		✔	✔	✔
VERR mem	Verify read access	2	Zero	None		✔	✔	✔
VERW	Verify write access	2	Zero	None		✔	✔	✔
WAIT	Wait until not busy	-	None	None	✔	✔	✔	✔
WBINVD	Write-back and invalidate cache	-	None	None				✔
XADD reg, reg	Exchange and add	1 - 4	Overflow, sign, zero, aux, parity, carry	None				✔
XADD mem, reg	Exchange and add	1 - 4	Overflow, sign, zero, aux, parity, carry	None				✔
XCHG mem, reg	Exchange	1 - 4	None	None	✔	✔	✔	✔
XCHG reg, reg	Exchange	1 - 4	None	None	✔	✔	✔	✔
XCHG reg, mem	Exchange	1 - 4	None	None	✔	✔	✔	✔
XLATB	Translate byte	-	None	None	✔	✔	✔	✔
XOR mem, imm	Exclusive OR	1 - 4	Overflow=0, sign, zero, parity, carry=0	Aux	✔	✔	✔	✔
XOR mem, reg	Exclusive OR	1 - 4	Overflow=0, sign, zero, parity, carry=0	Aux	✔	✔	✔	✔
XOR reg, imm	Exclusive OR	1 - 4	Overflow=0, sign, zero, parity, carry=0	Aux	✔	✔	✔	✔
XOR reg, mem	Exclusive OR	1 - 4	Overflow=0, sign, zero, parity, carry=0	Aux	✔	✔	✔	✔
XOR reg, reg	Exclusive OR	1 - 4	Overflow=0, sign, zero, parity, carry=0	Aux	✔	✔	✔	✔

§Number of bytes in instruction varies slightly depending on actual CPU used.

Flags: EFLAGS is a 32-bit register in the 80386.
FLAGS (LO word of EFLAGS) is a 16-bit register.

Legend: reg=register
mem=memory
accum=accumulator (AL, AX, EAX)
imm=immediate
segreg=segment register
offset=offset from current CS:IP

Note: Number preceding item indicates number of bit:

E Flags Register

Bit	Abbr.	Name
0	CF	Carry flag
1		RESERVED
2	PF	Parity flag
3		RESERVED
4	AF	Auxiliary carry flag
5		RESERVED
6	ZF	Zero flag
7	SF	Sign flag
8	TF	Trap flag
9	IF	Interrupt enable
10	DF	Direction flag
11	OF	Overflow
12-13	IOPL	I/O privilege level
14	NT	Nested tank flag
15		RESERVED
16	RF	Resume flag
17	VM	Virtual 8086 mode
18	AC	Alignment check
19-31		RESERVED

Source: Intel Microprocessors, Vol. 1, pages 2-26 through 2-30, 2-55 through 2-59, 2-85 through 2-89, 2-117 through 2-121, and 3-51 through 3-58
Intel Microprocessors, Vol. 2, pages 5-135 through 5-152
Intel 80386 Programmer's Reference, pages 17-18 through 17-174
i486 Microprocessor Programmer's Reference Manual, pages 26-1 through 26-289
Microsoft's 80386/80486 Programming Guide (Microsoft Press), pages 25 through 28 and 161 through 328

7.105. 8086 FAMILY REGISTER SUMMARY

For 8088/8086/80286:

< ---------------------- 16 bits ----------------------> ***Intel name for register***

	<------- 8 bits ----------	<------- 8 bits ---------->	
AX	AH	AL	Accumulator
BX	BH	BL	Base
CX	CH	CL	Count
DX	DH	DL	Data

Register	Intel name for register
SP	Stack Pointer
BP	Base Pointer
SI	Source Index
DI	Destination Index
IP	Instruction Pointer
CS	Status Flags ---->
DS	Code Segment
SS	Data Segment
ES	Stack Segment
	Extra Segment

Bit Number

15	14	13	12	11	10	9	8	7	6	5	4	3	2	1	0
-	NT	IOPL		OF	DF	I F	TF	SF	ZF	-	AF	-	PF	-	CF

NT=nested task	IF=interrupt flag	AF=auxiliary carry
IOPL=I/O privilege level	TF=trap flag	PF=parity flag
OF=overflow flag	SF=sign flag	CF=carry flag
DF=direction flag	ZF=zero flag	

For 80386/80486:

< ---------------------- 32 bits ----------------------> ***Intel name for register***

	<------- 16 bits --------	<------- 16 bits --------->	
EAX		AX	Extended Accumulator
EBX		BX	Extended Base
ECX		CX	Extended Count
EDX		DX	Extended Data
EDI		DI	Destination Index
ESI		SI	Source Index
EBP		BP	Base Pointer
ESP		SP	Stack Pointer
EIP		IP	Instruction Pointer
EFLAGS		FLAGS	Status Flags ---->

CS	Code Segment
SS	Stack Segment
DS	Extra Segment
ES	Data Segment (1)
FS	Data Segment (2)
GS	Data Segment (3)

Bit Number for 8086 compatible flags

15	14	13	12	11	10	9	8	7	6	5	4	3	2	1	0
-	NT	IOPL		OF	DF	I F	TF	SF	ZF	-	AF	-	PF	-	CF

NT=nested task	IF=interrupt flag	AF=auxiliary carry
IOPL=I/O privilege level	TF=trap flag	PF=parity flag
OF=overflow flag	SF=sign flag	CF=carry flag
DF=direction flag	ZF=zero flag	

Bit Number for extended 80386 flags

31	30	29	28	27	26	25	24	23	22	21	20	19	18	17	16
RESERVED FOR INTEL ONLY													AC	VM	RF

VM=virtual 8086 mode RF=resume flag AC=alignment check

CR0		Machine Control Register*
CR1	RESERVED	
CR2		Page Fault Linear Address†
CR3		Page Directory Base Address¥
GDT	(48 bits)	Global Descriptor Table
IDT	(48 bits)	Interrupt Descriptor Table
LDT		Local Descriptor Table
TSS		Task State Segment
DR0		Debug Register 0 (linear breakpoint address 0)
DR1		Debug Register 1 (linear breakpoint address 1)
DR2		Debug Register 2 (linear breakpoint address 2)
DR3		Debug Register 3 (linear breakpoint address 3)
DR4		Intel Reserved
DR5		Intel Reserved
DR6		Breakpoint Status
DR7		Breakpoint Control
TR3	(486 only)	Cache Test Data
TR4	(486 only)	Cache Test Status
TR5	(486 only)	Cache Test Control
TR6		TLB Test Control
TR7		TLB Test Status

*Bit 31=paging enable, bit 30=cache disable, bit 29=not write through, bit 18=alignment mask, bit 16=write protect, bit 5=numerics exception, bit 4=coprocessor extension type, bit 3=task switched, bit 2=emulate coprocessor, bit 1=monitor coprocessor, bit 0=protection enable
†Entire 32 bits used for address.
¥Bits 20-31 are page directory base register; remaining bits reserved.

Note: • 80286 also contains GDT, IDT, LDT, and TSS registers (see 80386 registers).
• 80486 also contains 80387 compatible registers.

Source: Intel Microprocessors, Vol. 1, pages 2-12, 2-44, 2-97, 3-5 through 3-6, and 5-14 through 5-30
i486 Microprocessor Programmer's Reference Manual, Chapter 2

7.106. 8086 FAMILY CPU CHIP VERSIONS

Chip	Clock Speed	Comments
8086	5Mhz	16-bit CPU in 40-pin CERDIP or plastic DIP package
8086-1	10Mhz	16-bit CPU in 40-pin CERDIP or plastic DIP package
8086-2	8Mhz	16-bit CPU in 40-pin CERDIP or plastic DIP package
80C86	5Mhz	16-bit CMOS CPU in 40-pin DIP or 44-pin PLCC package
80C86-2	8Mhz	16-bit CMOS CPU in 40-pin DIP
8088	5Mhz	8-bit CPU in 40-pin CERDIP package
8088-2	8Mhz	8-bit CPU in 40-pin CERDIP package
80C88	5Mhz	8-bit CMOS CPU in 40-pin DIP or 44-pin PLCC package
80C88-2	8Mhz	8-bit CMOS CPU in 40-pin DIP or 44-pin PLCC package
80286-6	6Mhz	16-bit Protection mode CPU in 68-pin LCC, PLCC, or PGA package
80286-8	8Mhz	16-bit Protection mode CPU in 68-pin LCC, PLCC, or PGA package
80286-10	10Mhz	16-bit Protection mode CPU in 68-pin LCC, PLCC, or PGA package
80286-12	12.5Mhz	16-bit Protection mode CPU in 68-pin LCC, PLCC, or PGA package
80386	16-33Mhz	32-bit Protection mode CPU in 132 PGA package
80386SX	16-20Mhz	100-pin quad flatpack package
486	25-33Mhz	168-pin PGA package

Note: Numbers are Intel numbers only. NEC makes compatible CPUs with numbers like V10, V20, etc.

Source: Intel Microprocessors, Vol. 1, pages 2-1, 2-31, 2-60, and 3-60
Intel Microprocessors, Vol. 2, pages 5-1, 5-287, and 5-864

See Also: 8.58. 8088 and 8086 Pinouts
8.59. 80286 Pinouts
8.60. 80386 Pinouts
8.61. 80386 SX Pinouts
8.62. i486 Pinouts

7.107. 8087 FAMILY INSTRUCTION SET SUMMARY

Instruction	Function	Exception Flags Affected	87	287	387
F2XM1	2^X - 1	Invalid, Denorm, Under, Prec, Stack	✔	✔	✔
FABS	Absolute value	Stack	✔	✔	✔
FADD	Add real and pop	Invalid, Denorm, Over, Under, Prec, Stack	✔	✔	✔
FADD mem32	Add real	Invalid, Denorm, Over, Under, Prec, Stack	✔	✔	✔
FADD mem64	Add real	Invalid, Denorm, Over, Under, Prec, Stack	✔	✔	✔
FADD ST(n)	Add real	Invalid, Denorm, Over, Under, Prec, Stack	✔	✔	✔
FADD ST(n), ST	Add real	Invalid, Denorm, Over, Under, Prec, Stack	✔	✔	✔
FADD ST, ST(n)	Add real	Invalid, Denorm, Over, Under, Prec, Stack	✔	✔	✔
FADDP ST(n), ST	Add real and pop	Invalid, Denorm, Over, Under, Prec, Stack	✔	✔	✔
FADDP ST, ST(n)	Add real and pop	Invalid, Denorm, Over, Under, Prec, Stack	✔	✔	✔
FBLD mem80	Packed decimal (BCD) load	Stack	✔	✔	✔
FBSTP mem80	Packed decimal (BCD) store and pop	Invalid, Stack	✔	✔	✔
FCHS	Change sign	Stack	✔	✔	✔
FCLEX	Clear exceptions	None	✔	✔	✔
FCOM	Compare real	Invalid, Denorm, Stack	✔	✔	✔
FCOM mem32	Compare real	Invalid, Denorm, Stack	✔	✔	✔
FCOM mem64	Compare real	Invalid, Denorm, Stack	✔	✔	✔
FCOM ST(n)	Compare real	Invalid, Denorm, Stack	✔	✔	✔
FCOMP mem32	Compare real and pop	Invalid, Denorm, Stack	✔	✔	✔
FCOMP mem64	Compare real and pop	Invalid, Denorm, Stack	✔	✔	✔
FCOMP ST(n)	Compare real and pop	Invalid, Denorm, Stack	✔	✔	✔
FCOMPP	Compare real and pop twice	Invalid, Denorm, Stack	✔	✔	✔
FCOS	Cosine	Invalid, Denorm, Stack, Prec, Under			✔
FDECSTP	Decrement stack pointer	None	✔	✔	✔
FDISI	Disable interrupts	None	✔		
FDIV	Divide real and pop	All	✔	✔	✔
FDIV mem32	Divide real	All	✔	✔	✔
FDIV mem64	Divide real	All	✔	✔	✔
FDIV ST(n)	Divide real	All	✔	✔	✔
FDIV ST(n), ST	Divide real	All	✔	✔	✔
FDIV ST, ST(n)	Divide real	All	✔	✔	✔
FDIVP ST(n), ST	Divide real and pop	All	✔	✔	✔
FDIVP ST, ST(n)	Divide real and pop	All	✔	✔	✔
FDIVR	Division reversed and pop	All	✔	✔	✔
FDIVR mem32	Division reversed	All	✔	✔	✔
FDIVR mem64	Division reversed	All	✔	✔	✔
FDIVR ST(n)	Division reversed	All	✔	✔	✔

(Continued)

7.107. 8087 FAMILY INSTRUCTION SET SUMMARY (continued)

Instruction	*Function*	*Exception Flags Affected*	*87*	*287*	*387*
FDIVR ST(n), ST	Division reversed	All	✔	✔	✔
FDIVR ST, ST(n)	Division reversed	All	✔	✔	✔
FDIVRP ST(n), ST	Division reversed and pop	All	✔	✔	✔
FDIVRP ST, ST(n)	Division reversed and pop	All	✔	✔	✔
FENI	Enable interrupts	None	✔		
FFREE ST(n)	Free register	None	✔	✔	✔
FIADD mem16	Integer add	Invalid, Denorm, Over, Prec, Under, Stack	✔	✔	✔
FIADD mem32	Integer add	Invalid, Denorm, Over, Prec, Under, Stack	✔	✔	✔
FICOM mem16	Integer compare	Invalid, Denorm, Stack	✔	✔	✔
FICOM mem32	Integer compare	Invalid, Denorm, Stack	✔	✔	✔
FICOMP mem16	Integer compare and pop	Invalid, Denorm, Stack	✔	✔	✔
FICOMP mem32	Integer compare and pop	Invalid, Denorm, Stack	✔	✔	✔
FIDIV mem16	Integer divide	All	✔	✔	✔
FIDIV mem32	Integer divide	All	✔	✔	✔
FIDIVR mem16	Integer divide reversed	All	✔	✔	✔
FIDIVR mem32	Integer divide reversed	All	✔	✔	✔
FILD mem16	Integer load	Stack	✔	✔	✔
FILD mem32	Integer load	Stack	✔	✔	✔
FILD mem64	Integer load	Stack	✔	✔	✔
FIMUL mem16	Integer multiply	Invalid, Denorm, Over, Prec, Under, Stack	✔	✔	✔
FIMUL mem32	Integer multiply	Invalid, Denorm, Over, Prec, Under, Stack	✔	✔	✔
FINCSTP	Increment stack pointer	None	✔	✔	✔
FINIT	Initialize processor	None	✔	✔	✔
FIST mem16	Integer store	Invalid, Prec, Stack	✔	✔	✔
FIST mem32	Integer store	Invalid, Prec, Stack	✔	✔	✔
FISTP dest	Integer store and pop	Invalid, Prec	✔	✔	✔
FISTP mem16	Integer store and pop	Invalid, Prec, Stack	✔	✔	✔
FISTP mem32	Integer store and pop	Invalid, Prec, Stack	✔	✔	✔
FISTP mem64	Integer store and pop	Invalid, Prec, Stack	✔	✔	✔
FISUB mem16	Integer subtract	Invalid, Denorm, Over, Prec, Under, Stack	✔	✔	✔
FISUB mem32	Integer subtract	Invalid, Denorm, Over, Prec, Under, Stack	✔	✔	✔
FISUBR mem32	Integer subtract reversed	Invalid, Denorm, Over, Prec, Under, Stack	✔	✔	✔
FISUBR mem16	Integer subtract reversed	Invalid, Denorm, Over, Prec, Under, Stack	✔	✔	✔
FLD mem32	Load real	Invalid, Denorm, Stack	✔	✔	✔
FLD mem64	Load real	Invalid, Denorm, Stack	✔	✔	✔
FLD mem80	Load real	Invalid, Denorm, Stack	✔	✔	✔
FLD ST(n)	Load real	Invalid, Denorm, Stack	✔	✔	✔
FLD1	Load constant	Stack	✔	✔	✔
FLDCW mem16	Load control word	All	✔	✔	✔
FLDENV memp	Load environment	All	✔	✔	✔
FLDL2E	Load log (2^e)	Stack	✔	✔	✔
FLDL2T	Load log (2^10)	Stack	✔	✔	✔
FLDLG2	Load log (10^2)	Stack	✔	✔	✔
FLDLN2	Load log (e^2)	Stack	✔	✔	✔
FLDPI	Load pi	Stack	✔	✔	✔
FLDZ	Load +0.0	Stack	✔	✔	✔
FMUL	Multiply real and pop	Invalid, Denorm, Over, Under, Prec, Stack	✔	✔	✔
FMUL mem32	Multiply real	Invalid, Denorm, Over, Under, Prec, Stack	✔	✔	✔
FMUL mem64	Multiply real	Invalid, Denorm, Over, Under, Prec, Stack	✔	✔	✔
FMUL ST(n)	Multiply real	Invalid, Denorm, Over, Under, Prec, Stack	✔	✔	✔
FMUL ST(n), ST	Multiply real	Invalid, Denorm, Over, Under, Prec, Stack	✔	✔	✔
FMUL ST(n), ST	Multiply real and pop	Invalid, Denorm, Over, Under, Prec, Stack	✔	✔	✔
FMUL ST, ST(n)	Multiply real	Invalid, Denorm, Over, Under, Prec, Stack	✔	✔	✔
FMULP ST, ST(n)	Multiply real and pop	Invalid, Denorm, Over, Under, Prec, Stack	✔	✔	✔
FNCLEX	Clear exceptions	None	✔	✔	✔
FNDISI	Disable interrupts	None	✔		
FNENI	Enable interrupts	None	✔		
FNINIT	Initialize processor	None	✔	✔	✔
FNOP	No operation	None	✔	✔	✔
FNSAVE memp	Save state	None	✔	✔	✔
FNSTCW mem16	Store control word	None	✔	✔	✔
FNSTENV memp	Store environment	None	✔	✔	✔
FNSTSW AX	Store status word	None	✔	✔	✔
FNSTSW mem16	Store status word	None	✔	✔	✔
FPATAN	Partial arctangent	Invalid, Denorm, Under, Prec, Stack	✔	✔	✔
FPREM	Partial remainder	None	✔	✔	✔
FPREM1	Partial remainder (IEEE)	Invalid, Denorm, Under, Stack			✔
FPTAN	Partial tangent	Invalid, Denorm, Under, Prec, Stack	✔	✔	✔
FRNDINT	Round to integer	Invalid, Denorm, Prec, Stack	✔	✔	✔

(Continued)

7.107. 8087 FAMILY INSTRUCTION SET SUMMARY (continued)

Instruction	*Function*	*Exception Flags Affected*	*87*	*287*	*387*
FRSTOR memp	Restore saved state	All	✔	✔	✔
FSAVE memp	Save state	None	✔	✔	✔
FSCALE	Scale	Invalid, Denorm, Over, Under, Prec, Stack	✔	✔	✔
FSETPM	Set protected mode	None		✔	✔
FSIN	Sine	Invalid, Denorm, Under, Prec, Stack			✔
FSINCOS	Sine and cosine	Invalid, Denorm, Under, Prec, Stack			✔
FSQRT	Square root	Invalid, Denorm, Under, Prec, Stack	✔	✔	✔
FST mem32	Store real	Invalid, Denorm, Over, Under, Prec, Stack	✔	✔	✔
FST mem64	Store real	Invalid, Denorm, Over, Under, Prec, Stack	✔	✔	✔
FST ST(n)	Store real	Invalid, Denorm, Over, Under, Prec, Stack	✔	✔	✔
FSTCW mem16	Store control word	None	✔	✔	✔
FSTENV memp	Store environment	None	✔	✔	✔
FSTP mem32	Store real and pop	Invalid, Denorm, Over, Under, Prec, Stack	✔	✔	✔
FSTP mem64	Store real and pop	Invalid, Denorm, Over, Under, Prec, Stack	✔	✔	✔
FSTP mem80	Store real and pop	Invalid, Denorm, Over, Under, Prec, Stack	✔	✔	✔
FSTP ST(n)	Store real and pop	Invalid, Denorm, Over, Under, Prec, Stack	✔	✔	✔
FSTSW AX	Store status word	None	✔	✔	✔
FSTSW mem16	Store status word	None	✔	✔	✔
FSUB	Subtract real and pop	Invalid, Denorm, Over, Under, Prec, Stack	✔	✔	✔
FSUB mem32	Subtract real	Invalid, Denorm, Over, Under, Prec, Stack	✔	✔	✔
FSUB mem64	Subtract real	Invalid, Denorm, Over, Under, Prec, Stack	✔	✔	✔
FSUB ST(n)	Subtract real	Invalid, Denorm, Over, Under, Prec, Stack	✔	✔	✔
FSUB ST(n), ST	Subtract real	Invalid, Denorm, Over, Under, Prec, Stack	✔	✔	✔
FSUB ST, ST(n)	Subtract real	Invalid, Denorm, Over, Under, Prec, Stack	✔	✔	✔
FSUBP ST(n), ST	Subtract real and pop	Invalid, Denorm, Over, Under, Prec, Stack	✔	✔	✔
FSUBP ST, ST(n)	Subtract real and pop	Invalid, Denorm, Over, Under, Prec, Stack	✔	✔	✔
FSUBR	Subtract real reversed and pop	Invalid, Denorm, Over, Under, Prec, Stack	✔	✔	✔
FSUBR mem32	Subtract real reversed	Invalid, Denorm, Over, Under, Prec, Stack	✔	✔	✔
FSUBR mem64	Subtract real reversed	Invalid, Denorm, Over, Under, Prec, Stack	✔	✔	✔
FSUBR ST(n)	Subtract real reversed	Invalid, Denorm, Over, Under, Prec, Stack	✔	✔	✔
FSUBR ST(n), ST	Subtract real reversed	Invalid, Denorm, Over, Under, Prec, Stack	✔	✔	✔
FSUBR ST, ST(n)	Subtract real reversed	Invalid, Denorm, Over, Under, Prec, Stack	✔	✔	✔
FSUBRP ST(n), ST	Subtract real reversed and pop	Invalid, Denorm, Over, Under, Prec, Stack	✔	✔	✔
FSUBRP ST, ST(n)	Subtract real reversed and pop	Invalid, Denorm, Over, Under, Prec, Stack	✔	✔	✔
FTST	Test stack top against +0.0	Invalid, Denorm, Stack	✔	✔	✔
FUCOM	Unordered compare	Invalid, Denorm, Stack			✔
FUCOM mem32	Unordered compare	Invalid, Denorm, Stack			✔
FUCOM mem64	Unordered compare	Invalid, Denorm, Stack			✔
FUCOM ST(n)	Unordered compare	Invalid, Denorm, Stack			✔
FUCOMP	Unordered compare and pop	Invalid, Denorm, Stack			✔
FUCOMP mem32	Unordered compare and pop	Invalid, Denorm, Stack			✔
FUCOMP mem64	Unordered compare and pop	Invalid, Denorm, Stack			✔
FUCOMP ST(n)	Unordered compare and pop	Invalid, Denorm, Stack			✔
FUCOMPP	Unordered compare and pop twice	Invalid, Denorm, Stack			✔
FWAIT	Wait until not busy	None	✔	✔	✔
FXAM	Examine stack top	None	✔	✔	✔
FXCH	Exchange registers	Stack	✔	✔	✔
FXCH ST(n)	Exchange registers	Stack	✔	✔	✔
FXTRACT	Extract exponent and significand	Invalid, Denorm, ZeroDiv, Stack	✔	✔	✔
FYL2X	Y * Log (2^X)	All	✔	✔	✔
FYL2XP1	Y * Log (2^X+1)	Invalid, Denorm, Under, Prec, Stack	✔	✔	✔

§N=number of times CPU examines TEST line while 8087 is busy

Legend:
EA=Effective address calculation
Denorm=Denormalized
Prec=Precision
Under=Underflow
Over=Overflow
ZeroDiv=ZeroDivide
Stack=Stack fault
memp=memory pointer

Note: There is no separate 80487 coprocessor. The floating point logic is incorporated in the 80486.

Source:
8087 Applications and Programming for the IBM PC (Brady), pages 244 through 258
Intel Microprocessors, Vol. 1, pages 2-140 through 2-143, and 3-145 through 3-147
Intel Microprocessors, Vol. 2, pages 5-148 through 5-149
i486 Microprocessor Programmer's Reference Manual, pages 26-1 through 26-289
Microsoft's 80386/80486 Programming Guide (Microsoft Press), pages 329 through 399

7.108. 8087 FAMILY REGISTER SUMMARY

< -- 80 bits --------------------------------------->

	<-- 1 bit -->	<------- 15 bits -------->	<--------------- 64 bits --------------->	<---- 2 bits ---->
R0	Sign	Exponent	Significand	Tag field
R1	Sign	Exponent	Significand	Tag field
R2	Sign	Exponent	Significand	Tag field
R3	Sign	Exponent	Significand	Tag field
R4	Sign	Exponent	Significand	Tag field
R5	Sign	Exponent	Significand	Tag field
R6	Sign	Exponent	Significand	Tag field
R7	Sign	Exponent	Significand	Tag field

<----------------- 16 bits --------------->
Control register
Status register
Tag word
Instruction Pointer*
Data Pointer*

*32 bits in 8087 and 80287; 48 bits in 80387

Source: Intel Microprocessors, Vol. 1, pages 2-125, 3-120, and 5-429

7.109. 8087 FAMILY CHIP VERSIONS

Chip	*Clock Speed*	*Comments*
8087	5Mhz	In 40-pin CERDIP
8087-1	10Mhz	In 40-pin CERDIP
8087-2	8Mhz	In 40-pin CERDIP
80287-3	3Mhz	In 40-pin DIP package
80287-6	6Mhz	In 40-pin DIP package
80287-8	8Mhz	In 40-pin DIP package
80287-10	10Mhz	In 40-pin DIP package
80387-16	16Mhz	In 68-pin PLCC package
80387-20	20Mhz	In 68-pin PLCC package
80486*	25-33Mhz	

*Includes equivalent to 80387 chip.

Note: Numbers are Intel numbers only.

Source: 8087/80287/80387 for the IBM PC and Compatibles (Brady), page 5

See Also:
8.63. 8087 (Coprocessor) Pinouts
8.64. 80287 (Coprocessor) Pinouts
8.65. 80387 (Coprocessor) Pinouts
8.66. 80387 SX (Coprocessor) Pinouts
8.67. WEITEK 3167 (Coprocessor) Pinouts

7.110. 8250 I/O PORT USAGE (REGISTERS)

I/O Port	*Register*	*Direction*	*Comments*
3F8H	Transmit data	Output	Only if line control register bit 7 is 0
	Receive data	Input	Only if line control register bit 7 is 0
	Baud rate divisor LO byte		Only if line control register bit 7 is 1
3F9H	Baud rate divisor HO byte		Only if line control register bit 7 is 1
	Interrupt enable		Only if line control register bit 7 is 0
3FAH	Interrupt ID		
3FBH	Line control		
3FCH	Modem control		
3FDH	Line status		
3FEH	Modem status		

Source: The IBM PC from the Inside Out (Addison Wesley), page 367

See Also: 4.080. INT 14H, Modem and Line Status Byte
4.081. INT 14H, COM Port Parameter Byte
7.076. Async Line Control Register
7.077. Async Divisor Latch Register
7.078. Async Line Status Register
7.079. Async Interrupt Identification Register
7.080. Async Interrupt Enable Register
7.081. Async Modem Control Register
7.082. Async Modem Status Register
7.111. 8253 I/O Port Usage (Registers)

7.111. 8253 I/O PORT USAGE (REGISTERS)

I/O Port	*Register*	*Direction*	*Comments*
40H	Timer 0	Output	
41H	Timer 1	Output	
42H	Timer 2	Output	
43H	Control word	Input	See 7.112. 8253 Control Word Byte

Source: The IBM PC from the Inside Out (Addison Wesley), pages 240 through 241

See Also: 7.112. 8253 Control Word Byte

7.112. 8253 CONTROL WORD BYTE

Bit Number

7	*6*	*5*	*4*	*3*	*2*	*1*	*0*	*Function*	*Allowable Values*
✔	✔							Timer number	00=timer 0, 01=timer 1, 10=timer 2
		✔	✔					Latch, read format	00=latch current count, 01=read low byte (no latching), 10=read high byte (no latching), 11=read low, then high byte
				✔	✔	✔		Mode number	000=interrupt on terminal count 001=programmable one-shot 010=rate generator 011=square wave generator 100=software triggered strobe 101=hardware triggered strobe
							✔	Count type	0=binary, 1=BCD

Source: The IBM PC from the Inside Out (Addison Wesley), pages 241 through 242

See Also: 7.111. 8253 I/O Port Usage (Registers)

7.113. 8253 COMMAND REGISTER BYTE

Bit Number 7	6	5	4	3	2	1	0	*Function*	*Comments*
✔	✔							Select counter	00=Counter 0, 01=Counter 1, 10=Counter 2, 11=Illegal
		✔	✔					Read/load	00=counter latch op, 01=read/load LSB, 10=read/load MSB, 11=reload/load LSB, then MSB
				✔	✔	✔		Mode	000=0, 001=1, X10=2, X11=3, 100=4, 101=5
							✔	BCD	0=binary counter, 1=BCD counter (4 decades)

Source: Intel Microprocessors, Vol. 2, page 2-17

See Also: 8.74. 8253 (Programmable Interval Controller) Pinouts

7.114. 6845 REGISTERS

Register	*Function*	*Unit*	*CGA 40x25*	*CGA 80x25*	*CGA Graphics*	*MDA 80x25*
R0	Horizontal total	Chars	38	71	38	61
R1	Horizontal displayed	Chars	28	50	28	50
R2	Horizontal sync position	Chars	2D	5A	2D	52
R3	Horizontal sync width	Chars	A	A	A	F
R4	Vertical total	Char rows	1F	1F	7F	19
R5	Vertical total adjust	Scan lines	6	6	6	6
R6	Vertical displayed	Char rows	19	19	64	19
R7	Vertical sync position	Char rows	1C	1C	70	19
R8	Interlace mode		2	2	2	2
R9	Max scan line address	Scan lines	7	7	1	D
R10	Cursor start	Scan lines	6	6	6	B
R11	Cursor end	Scan lines	7	7	7	C
R12	Start address high		0	0	0	0
R13	Start address low		0	0	0	0
R14	Cursor high					0
R15	Cursor low					0
R16	Light pen high					
R17	Light pen low					

Note: Except for register numbers, all values are in hex.

Source: IBM Options and Adapters Technical Reference, Vol. 2, pages Monochrome Adapter 5 and Color/Graphics Monitor Adapter 17

See Also: 7.115. 6845 Port and Select Factors
8.70. 6845 (Video Controller) Pinouts

7.115. 6845 PORT AND SELECT FACTORS

Bit Number

7	*6*	*5*	*4*	*3*	*2*	*1*	*0*	*Register*	*Function*	*Comments*
✔	✔							Color Select	Not used	
		✔						(CGA=3D9)	Active color set 320x200	00=set 1 (green/red/brown), 01=set 2 (cyan/magenta/white)
			✔						Intensity/background	Intensity in graphics, background color in alphanumeric mode
				✔					Intensity	Intense: border in 40x25, background in 320x200, foreground in 640x200
					✔				Red	Red: border in 40x25, background in 320x200, foreground in 640x200
						✔			Green	Green: border in 40x25, background in 320x200, foreground in 640x200
							✔		Blue	Blue: border in 40x25, background in 320x200, foreground in 640x200
		✔						Mode Cntrl	Blink	0=no blink, 1=blink (in text modes)
			✔					(CGA=3D8)	640x200	1=select 640x200 B/W graphics
				✔					Video enable/disable	0=disable video, 1=enable video
					✔				Color/mono	0=color mode, 1=monochrome mode
						✔			Mode	0=text mode, 1=320x200 graphics mode
							✔		Mode	0=40x25 text, 1=80x25 text
				✔				Status	Retrace	1=raster is in vertical retrace mode
					✔			(CGA=3DA)	Light pen	0=light pen switch on, 1=light pen switch off
						✔			Light pen	1=light pen trigger set
							✔		Regen-buffer	1=regen-buffer memory access can be made without interfering with display
				✔				Status	B/W video	
					✔			(MDA=3BA)	RESERVED	
						✔			RESERVED	
							✔		Horizontal drive	
✔	✔		✔		✔	✔		Control	NOT USED	
		✔						(MDA=3B8)	Enable blink	1=enabled
				✔					Enable video	1=enabled
							✔		High resolution mode	

Source: IBM Options and Adapters Technical Reference, Vol. 2, pages Monochrome Adapter 8 and Color/Graphics Monitor Adapter 18 through 21

See Also: 7.114. 6845 Registers
8.70. 6845 (Video Controller) Pinouts

7.116. DRAM CHIP FAMILIES

Size	Part Numbers
256Kx1	AM90C255 AM90C256 HM51256 HM51256L HY51256L HY51C256 KM41256A LH21256 M41256N M41256P MB81256 MCM6256B MN41256 MSM41256 MT1256 TMM41256
1Mx1	HM511000 HM511001MCM51102A HM511002 HY51C100 M5M4C1000 M5M4C1001 M5M4C1002 MCM511000A MCM511001A MSM41000 MSM41001 TC511000 TC511001 TC511002
64Kx4	HM50464 HY51464 HY51C464 LH2464 LH2465 M5M4464 MB81464 MCM41464 MT4064 TMM41464A
256Kx4	LH64256 LH64257 M441024K M441024P M5M44C256 M5M44C258 MCM514256A MCM514258A MSM41004 MSM41005

Source: Motorola Memory Data, page 1-5

See Also: 8.69. RAM Chip Pinouts Summary

Section 8

Connectors, Buses, and Pinouts

8.01. AT 9-PIN SERIAL PORT CONNECTOR

Pin Number	*Description*	*Signal*	*Direction**
1	Carrier detect	CD	
2	Receive data	RD	In
3	Transmit data	TD	Out
4	Data terminal ready	DTR	Out
5	Signal ground	SG	
6	Data set ready	DSR	In
7	Request to send	RTS	Out
8	Clear to send	CTS	In
9	Ring indicator	RI	In

*From computer

Note: • Pin numbers refer to a DB-9P connector.
• RI connection not required to operate.

Source: Communications and Networking for the IBM PC and Compatibles 3rd Edition (Brady), pages 93 through 95

See Also: 8.02. PC and AT 25-Pin Serial Port Connector
8.04. RS-232C Serial Port Connector (DTE Device)

8.02. PC AND XT 25-PIN SERIAL PORT CONNECTOR

Pin Number	*Description*	*Signal*	*Direction**
1	Chassis ground		
2	Transmit data	TD	Out
3	Receive data	RD	In
4	Request to send	RTS	Out
5	Clear to send	CTS	In
6	Data set ready	DSR	In
7	Signal ground	SG	
8	Carrier detect	DCD	In
9	Pos transmit current loop return†		Out
11	Neg transmit current loop data†		Out
18	Pos receive current loop data†		In
20	Data terminal ready	DTR	Out
22	Ring indicator	RI	In
25	Neg receive current loop return†		In

*From computer
†Used for current loop communications only

Note: • RI connection not required to operate.
• Pin numbers refer to a DB-25P connector.

Source: IBM Options and Adapters Technical Reference, Vol. 2, pages Async 23 through 24
Communications and Networking for the IBM PC and Compatibles 3rd Edition (Brady), pages 93 through 94

See Also: 8.01. AT 9-Pin Serial Port Connector
8.04. RS-232C Serial Port Connector (DTE Device)

8.03. PS/2 SERIAL PORT CONNECTOR

System End (DB25)

Pin Number	*Model 30*	*Model 50/60/80*	*Signal*	*Direction**
2	Transmit data	Transmit data	TD	Out
3	Receive data	Receive data	RD	In
4	Request to send	Request to send	RTS	Out
5	Clear to send	Clear to send	CTS	In
6	Data set ready	Data set ready	DSR	In
7	Signal ground	Signal ground	SG	
8	Data carrier detect	Data carrier detect	DCD	In
11	Connected to pin 20	Not connected		Out
20	Data terminal ready	Data terminal ready	DTR	Out
22	Ring indicator	Ring indicator	RI	In

*From computer

Note: Pin numbers refer to a standard D-Shell connector.

Source: IBM PS/2 Model 30 Technical Reference, page 1-22
IBM PS/2 Model 50 and 60 Technical Reference, page 4-171
IBM PS/2 Hardware Interface Technical Reference, pages Serial Port Controller 23 through 24

See Also: 8.01. AT 9-Pin Serial Port Connector
8.02. PC and AT 25-Pin Serial Port Connector
8.04. RS-232C Serial Port Connector (DTE Device)

8.04. RS-232C SERIAL PORT CONNECTOR (DTE DEVICE)

Pin Number	*Definition*	*Signal*	*Direction**
1	Protective ground (chassis ground)		
2	Transmitted data	TD	Out
3	Received data	RD	In
4	Request to send	RTS	Out
5	Clear to send	CTS	In
6	Data set ready	DSR	In
7	Signal ground	SG	
8	Received line signal detector	DCD	In
9	RESERVED		
10	RESERVED		
11	UNASSIGNED		
12	Secondary received line signal detector		In
13	Secondary clear to send		In
14	Secondary transmitted data		Out
15	Transmission signal element timing		In
16	Secondary received data		In
17	Receiver signal element timing		In
18	UNASSIGNED		
19	Secondary request to send		Out
20	Data terminal ready	DTR	Out
21	Signal quality detector		In
22	Ring indicator	RI	In
23	Data signal rate selector		
24	Transmit signal element timing		Out
25	UNASSIGNED		

*From computer

Note: Although not part of the standard, a DB-25P connector is often used at the DTE device. Its pinouts look like this:

```
1                        13
 o o o o o o o o o o o o o
  o o o o o o o o o o o o
  14                   25
```

Source: EIA Standard RS-232-C, August 1969, page 8
IBM PC/XT Technical Reference, page 1-211

See Also: 8.01. AT 9-Pin Serial Port Connector
8.02. PC and AT 25-Pin Serial Port Connector

8.05. MDA VIDEO CONNECTOR

Pin Number	*Description*	*Direction**
1	Ground	
2	Ground	
3	NOT USED	
4	NOT USED	
5	NOT USED	
6	+Intensity	Out
7	+Video	Out
8	+Horizontal	Out
9	-Vertical	Out

*From computer

Note:
- Pin numbers refer to a DB-9 connector.
- Signal voltages are 0.0 to 0.6Vdc (0 level) and +2.4 to 3.5Vdc (1 level).

Source: IBM Options and Adapters Technical Reference, Vol. 2, page Monochrome 9

See Also: 8.07. CGA Composite Video Connector
8.08. EGA RGB Connector
8.09. VGA RGB Connector
8.48. Parallel Printer Connector

8.06. CGA RGB CONNECTOR

Pin Number	*Description*	*Direction**
1	Ground	
2	Ground	
3	Red	Out
4	Green	Out
5	Blue	Out
6	+Intensity	Out
7	RESERVED	Out
8	+Horizontal drive	Out
9	-Vertical drive	Out

*From computer

Note: Pin numbers refer to a DB-9 connector.

Source: IBM Options and Adapters Technical Reference, Vol. 2, page Color/Graphics 24

See Also: 8.05. MDA Video Connector
8.07. CGA Composite Video Connector
8.08. EGA RGB Connector
8.09. VGA RGB Connector
8.12. CGA Light Pen Connector

8.07. CGA COMPOSITE VIDEO CONNECTOR

Pin Number	Description	Direction*
1	Peak to peak amplitude	Out
2	Ground	

*From computer

Note: Video signal is approximately 1.5Vdc.
Pin numbers refer to a composite phono jack (1=pin, 2=shell).

Source: IBM Options and Adapters Technical Reference, Vol. 2, page Color/Graphics 24

See Also: 8.05. MDA Video Connector
8.06. CGA RGB Connector
8.08. EGA RGB Connector

8.08. EGA RGB CONNECTOR

Pin Number	Description	Direction*
1	Ground	
2	S. red	Out
3	Red	Out
4	Green	Out
5	Blue	Out
6	Intensity/s. green	Out
7	Mono video/s. blue	Out
8	Horizontal drive	Out
9	Vertical drive	Out

*From computer

Note: Pin numbers refer to a DC-9 connector.

Source: Enhanced Graphics Adapter/Hercules, page 22

See Also: 8.05. MDA Video Connector
8.06. CGA RGB Connector
8.09. VGA RGB Connector

8.09. VGA RGB CONNECTOR

Pin Number	Function	Monochrome	Color	Direction*
1	Red		Red output	Out
2	Green	Mono output	Green output	Out
3	Blue		Blue output	Out
4	RESERVED			
5	Digital ground	Self test	Self test	
6	Red return (analog ground)	KEY	Red return	
7	Green return (analog ground)	Mono return	Green return	
8	Blue return (analog ground)		Blue return	
9	Plug			
10	Digital ground	Digital ground	Digital ground	
11	Monitor sensor 0		Digital ground	In
12	Monitor sensor 1	Digital ground		In
13	Horizontal drive	Horizontal drive	Horizontal drive	Out
14	Vertical drive	Vertical drive	Vertical drive	Out
15	RESERVED			

*From computer

Note: Pin numbers refer to a DC-15 connector.

Source: IBM PS/2 Model 50 and 60 Technical Reference, page 4-125
IBM PS/2 Hardware Interface Technical Reference, page Video Subsystem 99
IBM PS/2 Model 80 Technical Reference, page 4-125

See Also: 8.05. MDA Video Connector
8.06. CGA RGB Connector
8.08. EGA RGB Connector

8.10. PS/2 15-PIN VIDEO CONNECTOR

System End (DB 15)

Pin Number	*Monochrome*	*Color*	*Direction†*
1	NO PIN	Red	Out
2	Mono	Green	Out
3	NO PIN	Blue	Out
4	NO PIN	NO PIN	
5	Self test	Self test	
6	KEY	Red return*	
7	Mono return	Green return*	
8	NO PIN	Blue return*	
9	NO PIN	NO PIN	
10	Digital ground	Digital ground	
11	NO PIN	Digital ground	
12	Digital ground	NO PIN	
13	HSync	HSync	Out
14	VSync	VSync	Out
15	NO PIN	NO PIN	

*Analog grounds
†From computer

Note: Pin numbers refer to a DC-15 connector.

Source: IBM PS/2 Model 50 and 60 Technical Reference, page 4-125
IBM PS/2 Model 80 Technical Reference, page 4-125

See Also: 8.05. MDA Video Connector
8.06. CGA RGB Connector
8.08. EGA RGB Connector

8.11. EGA FEATURE CONNECTOR/VGA AUXILIARY CONNECTOR

EGA Feature Connector

Pin Number	*Signal*	*Direction**
1	GND	
2	-12Vdc	
3	+12Vdc	
4	J1	
5	J2	
6	G'OUT	Out
7	R'OUT	Out
8	B'OUT	Out
9	ATRS/L	
10	B OUT	Out
11	G OUT	Out
12	G	In
13	R'	In
14	B	In
15	R	In
16	R OUT	Out
17	FEAT 1	Out
18	BLANK	
19	FEAT 0	Out
20	FCI	In
21	FCO	In
22	G'/I	In
23	B'/V	In
24	HIN	In
25	VIN	In
26	14 MHz	
27	Internal	Out
28	EXT OSC	Out
29	V OUT	Out
30	H OUT	Out
31	GND	
32	+5Vdc	

VGA Auxillary Connector

Pin Number	*Signal*
1	PO
2	P1
3	P2
4	P3
5	P4
6	P5
7	P6
8	P7
9	BLANK
10	DCLK
11	HSYNC
12	VSYNC
13	ESYNC
14	EDCLK
15	EVIDEO
16	GROUND
17	GROUND
18	GROUND
19	GROUND
20	GROUND

*From computer

Note: Signals preceded by a minus sign are negative true.

Source: IBM PS/2 Hardware Interface Technical Reference, pages Video Subsystem 94 through 98

See Also: 8.08. EGA RGB Connector
8.10. PS/2 15-Pin Video Connector

8.12. CGA LIGHT PEN CONNECTOR

Pin Number	Description	Direction*
1	-Light pen input	In
2	KEY (NOT USED)	
3	-Light pen switch	In
4	Chassis ground	
5	+5Vdc	Out
6	+12Vdc	Out

*From computer

Note: Pin numbers refer to a 6-pin Berg Strip on CGA board (P2).

Source: IBM Options and Adapters Technical Reference, Vol. 2, page Color/Graphics 25

See Also: 8.05. MDA Video Connector
8.06. CGA RGB Connector
8.08. EGA RGB Connector
8.09. VGA RGB Connector

8.13. CGA RF MODULATOR CONNECTOR

Pin Number	Description	Direction*
1	+12Vdc	Out
2	KEY (NOT USED)	
3	Composite video output	Out
4	Logic ground	

*From computer

Note: Pin numbers refer to a 4-pin Berg Strip on CGA board (P1).

Source: IBM Options and Adapters Technical Reference, Vol. 2, page Color/Graphics 25

See Also: 8.05. MDA Video Connector
8.06. CGA RGB Connector
8.08. EGA RGB Connector
8.09. VGA RGB Connector
8.12. CGA Light Pen Connector

8.14. PC AND XT FLOPPY DISK CONTROLLER INTERNAL CONNECTOR

Pin Number	Signal	Direction
1	Ground	
2	UNUSED	
3	Ground	
4	UNUSED	
5	Ground	
6	UNUSED	
7	Ground	
8	Index	From drive
9	Ground	
10	Motor enable A	From controller
11	Ground	
12	Drive select B	From controller
13	Ground	
14	Drive select A	From controller
15	Ground	
16	Motor enable B	From controller
17	Ground	

Pin Number	Signal	Direction
18	Direction (stepper motor)	From controller
19	Ground	
20	Step pulse	From controller
21	Ground	
22	Write data	From controller
23	Ground	
24	Write enable	From controller
25	Ground	
26	Track 0	From drive
27	Ground	
28	Write protect	From drive
29	Ground	
30	Read data	From drive
31	Ground	
32	Select head 1	From controller
33	Ground	
34	UNUSED	

Note:
- All signals are at standard TTL levels.
- Connector is a 34-pin keyed edge connector (key between pins 6 and 8).
- Even numbers are on component side of board.

Source: IBM PC/XT Technical Reference, page 1-128

See Also: 8.15. PC and XT Floppy Disk Controller External Connector

8.15. PC AND XT FLOPPY DISK CONTROLLER EXTERNAL CONNECTOR

Pin Number	Signal	Direction	Pin Number	Signal	Direction
1	UNUSED		11	Direction (stepper motor)	From controller
2	UNUSED		12	Step pulse	From controller
3	UNUSED		13	Write data	From controller
4	UNUSED		14	Write enable	From controller
5	UNUSED		15	Track 0	From drive
6	Index	From drive	16	Write protect	From drive
7	Motor enable C	From controller	17	Read data	From drive
8	Drive select D	From controller	18	Select head 1	From controller
9	Drive select C	From controller	19	NOT USED	
10	Motor enable D	From controller	20-37	Ground	

Note:
- All signals are at standard TTL levels.
- Connector is a 37-pin D-Shell connector.

Source: IBM PC/XT Technical Reference, page 1-129

See Also: 8.14. PC and XT Floppy Disk Controller Internal Connector

8.16. XT FIXED DISK CONTROLLER CONNECTOR J1

Pin Number	Signal	Direction	Pin Number	Signal	Direction
1	Ground		18	-Head select 2^1	From controller
2	-Reduced write current	From controller	19	Ground	
3	Ground		20	-Index	From drive
4	RESERVED		21	Ground	
5	Ground		22	-Ready	From drive
6	-Write gate	From controller	23	Ground	
7	Ground		24	-Step	From controller
8	-Seek complete	From drive	25	Ground	
9	Ground		26	-Drive select 1	From controller
10	-Track 00	From drive	27	Ground	
11	Ground		28	-Drive select 2	From controller
12	-Write fault	From drive	29	Ground	
13	Ground		30	RESERVED	
14	-Head select 2^0	From controller	31	Ground	
15	Ground		32	RESERVED	
16	RESERVED		33	Ground	
17	Ground		34	-Direction in	From controller

Note:
- Signals preceded by a minus sign are negative true.
- Connector is a 34-pin double-row plug.

Source: IBM PC/XT Technical Reference, page 1-149

See Also:
8.14. PC and XT Floppy Disk Controller Internal Connector
8.15. PC and XT Floppy Disk Controller External Connector
8.17. XT Fixed Disk Controller Connectors J2 and J3

8.17. XT FIXED DISK CONTROLLER CONNECTORS J2 AND J3

Pin Number	Signal	Direction	Pin Number	Signal	Direction
1	Drive select	From drive	11	Ground	
2	Ground		12	Ground	
3	RESERVED		13	MFM write data	From controller
4	Ground		14	-MFM write data	From controller
5	KEY (no pin)		15	Ground	
6	Ground		16	Ground	
7	RESERVED		17	MFM read data	From drive
8	Ground		18	-MFM read data	From drive
9	UNUSED		19	Ground	
10	UNUSED		20	Ground	

Note:
- Signals preceded by a minus sign are negative true.
- Connector is a 20-pin double-row plug with key notch at pin 5.

Source: IBM PC/XT Technical Reference, page 1-149

See Also:
8.14. PC and XT Floppy Disk Controller Internal Connector
8.15. PC and XT Floppy Disk Controller External Connector
8.16. XT Fixed Disk Controller Connector J1

8.18. PS/2 MODEL 30 DISKETTE DRIVE CONNECTOR

Pin Number	*Signal*	*Direction**
1	Signal ground	
2	-High density select	Out
3	RESERVED	
4	RESERVED	
5	Signal ground	
6	RESERVED	
7	Signal ground	
8	-Index	In
9	Signal ground	
10	-Motor enable 1	Out
11	Signal ground	
12	-Drive select 0	Out
13	Signal ground	
14	-Drive select 1	Out
15	Signal ground	
16	-Motor enable 0	Out
17	Signal ground	
18	-Direction	Out
19	Signal ground	
20	-Step	Out

Pin Number	*Signal*	*Direction**
21	Signal ground	
22	-Write data	Out
23	Signal ground	
24	-Write enable	Out
25	Signal ground	
26	-Track 0	In
27	Signal ground	
28	-Write protect	In
29	Signal ground	
30	-Read data	In
31	Signal ground	
32	-Head 1 select	Out
33	Signal ground	
34	-Diskette change	In
35	Ground	
36	Ground	
37	Ground	
38	+5Vdc	Out
39	Ground	
40	+12Vdc	Out

*From controller

Note: Drive gets power via this connector.

Source: IBM PS/2 Model 30 Technical Reference, page 1-105

See Also: 8.20. PS/2 Model 50 Diskette Drive Connector

8.19. PS/2 MODEL 30 FIXED DRIVE CONNECTOR

Pin Number	*Signal*	*Direction**
1	RESET DRV	Out
2	-DISK installed	In
3	D0	In/Out
4	Ground	
5	D1	In/Out
6	Ground	
7	D2	In/Out
8	Ground	
9	D3	In/Out
10	Ground	
11	D4	In/Out
12	Ground	
13	D5	In/Out
14	Ground	
15	D6	In/Out
16	Ground	
17	D7	In/Out
18	Ground	
19	-IOR	Out
20	Ground	
21	-IOW	Out
22	Ground	

Pin Number	*Signal*	*Direction**
23	-DISK CS	Out
24	Ground	
25	A0	Out
26	Ground	
27	A1	Out
28	Ground	
29	A2	Out
30	+5Vdc	Out
31	RESERVED	
32	+5Vdc	Out
33	-DACK3	Out
34	Ground	
35	DRQ3	In
36	Ground	
37	IRQ5	In
38	Ground	
39	IO CH ready	In
40	+12Vdc	Out
41	Spare	
42	+12Vdc	Out
43	Spare	
44	+12Vdc	Out

*From controller

Note: Drive gets power via this connector.

Source: IBM PS/2 Model 30 Technical Reference, page 1-107

See Also: 8.16. XT Fixed Disk Controller Connector J1
8.17. XT Fixed Disk Controller Connectors J2 and J3

8.20. PS/2 MODEL 50 DISKETTE DRIVE CONNECTOR

50-Pin PC Edge Connecter

Pin Number	*Signal*	*Direction**
1	2nd drive installed	In
2	-High density select	Out
3	Ground	
4	Ground	
5	Ground	
6	RESERVED	
7	Signal ground	
8	-Index	In
9	Signal ground	
10	-Motor enable 0	Out
11	Signal ground	
12	-Drive select 1	Out
13	Ground	
14	-Drive select 0	Out
15	Signal ground	
16	-Motor enable 1	Out
17	Signal ground	
18	-Direction	Out
19	Signal ground	
20	-Step	Out
21	Signal ground	
22	-Write data	Out
23	Signal ground	
24	-Write enable	Out
25	Signal ground	

Pin Number	*Signal*	*Direction**
26	-Track 0	In
27	Signal ground	
28	-Write protect	In
29	Signal ground	
30	-Read data	In
31	Signal ground	
32	-Head 1 select	Out
33	Signal ground	
34	-Diskette change	In
35	Ground	
36	Ground	
37	Ground	
38	+5Vdc	
39	Ground	
40	+12Vdc	
41	RESERVED	
42	RESERVED	
43	RESERVED	
44	RESERVED	
45	RESERVED	
46	RESERVED	
47	RESERVED	
48	RESERVED	
49	RESERVED	
50	RESERVED	

*From controller

Source: IBM PS/2 Model 50 and 60 Technical Reference, page 4-153

See Also: 8.18. PS/2 Model 30 Diskette Drive Connector

8.21. PS/2 MODELS 60 AND 80 DISKETTE DRIVE CONNECTOR

2x20 Pin Connector (odd numbers on top)

Pin Number	*Signal*	*Direction**
1	-2nd Drive Installed	In
2	-High Density Selected	Out
3	Ground	
4	Ground	
5	Ground	
6	RESERVED	
7	Signal Ground	
8	-Index	In
9	Signal Ground	
10	-Motor Enable 0	Out
11	Signal Ground	
12	-Drive Select 1	Out
13	Ground	
14	-Drive Select 0	Out
15	Signal Ground	
16	-Motor Enable 1	Out
17	Signal Ground	
18	-Direction	Out
19	Signal Ground	
20	-Step	Out

Pin Number	*Signal*	*Direction**
21	Signal Ground	
22	-Write Data	Out
23	Signal Ground	
24	-Write Enable	Out
25	Signal Ground	
26	-Track 0	In
27	Signal Ground	
28	-Write Protect	In
29	Signal Ground	
30	-Read Data	In
31	Signal Ground	
32	-Head 1 Select	Out
33	Signal Ground	
34	-Diskette Change	In
35	Ground	
36	Ground	
37	Ground	
38	+5Vdc	
39	Ground	
40	+12Vdc	

*From controller

Source: IBM PS/2 Model 50 and 60 Technical Reference, page 4-154
IBM PS/2 Model 80 Technical Reference, page 4-153

See Also: 8.18. PS/2 Model 30 Diskette Drive Connector
8.20. PS/2 Model 50 Diskette Drive Connector
8.22. PS/2 Model 70 Diskette and Fixed Drive Bus Connector
8.24. PS/2 Model 70 Fixed Disk Drive Cable Connector
8.34. PS/2 Models 60 and 80 Power Supply Connector

8.22. PS/2 MODEL 70 DISKETTE AND FIXED DRIVE BUS CONNECTOR

56-Pin Edge Connector

Pin Number	*Signal*	*Direction**	*Pin Number*	*Signal*	*Direction**
B1	-High Density Select	Out	A1	-2nd Drive Installed	In
B2	+12Vdc	Out	A2	+12Vdc	Out
B3	+12Vdc	Out	A3	+12Vdc	Out
B4	+5Vdc	Out	A4	CD CHRDY	In
B5	-Index	In	A5	M/-IO	Out
B6	-Motor Enable 1	Out	A6	Ground	
B7	-Drive Select 0	Out	A7	-S1	Out
B8	Ground		A8	+V5dc	Out
B9	-Drive Select 1	Out	A9	-S0	Out
B10	-Motor Enable 0	Out	A10	Ground	
B11	-Direction In	Out	A11	RESERVED	
B12	Ground		A12	-TC	Out
B13	-Step	Out	A13	ARB/-GNT	Out
B14	-Write Data	Out	A14	Ground	
B15	-Write Enable	Out	A15	ARB 3	In/Out
B16	Frame Ground		A16	ARB 2	In/Out
B17	-Track 0	In	A17	ARB 1	In/Out
B18	-Write Protect	In	A18	Frame Ground	
B19	-Read Data	In	A19	RESERVED	
B20	-Head 1 Select	Out	A20	ARB 0	In/Out
B21	-Diskette Change	In	A21	-BURST	In
B22	-IRQ 14	In	A22	Ground	
B23	-CD DS 16	In	A23	-PREEMPT	In
B24	Ground		A24	+5Vdc	Out
B25	-SBHE	Out	A25	-ADL	Out
B26	D13	In/Out	A26	Ground	
B27	+12Vdc	Out	A27	+12Vdc	Out
B28	D11	In/Out	A28	A0	Out
B29	D10	In/Out	A29	A1	Out
B30	D7	In/Out	A30	Ground	
B31	D6	In/Out	A31	A2	Out
B32	Ground		A32	+5Vdc	Out
B33	D5	In/Out	A33	A3	Out
B34	D2	In/Out	A34	Ground	
B35	+12Vdc	Out	A35	+12Vdc	Out
B36	D0	In/Out	A36	A4	Out
B37	D15	In/Out	A37	A5	Out
B38	D14	In/Out	A38	Ground	
B39	D12	In/Out	A39	A6	Out
B40	Ground		A40	+5Vdc	Out
B41	D9	In/Out	A41	A7	Out
B42	D8	In/Out	A42	Ground	
B43	CHRESET	Out	A43	RESERVED	
B44	+5Vdc	Out	A44	RESERVED	
B45	D4	In/Out	A45	A8	Out
B46	Key		A46	Key	
B47	Key		A47	Key	
B48	Ground		A48	+5Vdc	Out
B49	D3	In/Out	A49	A9	Out
B50	D1	In/Out	A50	Ground	
B51	-CD SFDBK	In	A51	A10	Out
B52	Ground		A52	+5Vdc	Out
B53	-CMD	Out	A53	A11	Out
B54	A12	Out	A54	Ground	
B55	14.3 MHz Osc	Out	A55	A13	Out
B56	Ground		A56	+5Vdc	Out
B57	A14	Out	A57	-CD SETUP	Out
B58	A15	Out	A58	Ground	

*From controller

Source: IBM PS/2 Hardware Interface Technical Reference, pages Model 70 System Board 3-7 through 3-8

See Also: 8.18. PS/2 Model 30 Diskette Drive Connector
8.20. PS/2 Model 50 Diskette Drive Connector
8.23. PS/2 Model 70 Diskette Drive Cable Connector
8.24. PS/2 Model 70 Fixed Disk Drive Cable Connector

8.23. PS/2 MODEL 70 DISKETTE DRIVE CABLE CONNECTOR

2x20 Pin Connector (odd numbers on top)

Pin Number	*Signal*	*Direction**
1	-2nd Drive Installed	In
2	-High Density Selected	Out
3	RESERVED	
4	RESERVED	
5	Ground	
6	RESERVED	
7	Signal Ground	
8	-Index	In
9	Signal Ground	
10	RESERVED	
11	Signal Ground	
12	-Drive Select	Out
13	Ground	
14	RESERVED	
15	Signal Ground	
16	-Motor Enable	Out
17	Signal Ground	
18	-Direction In	Out
19	Signal Ground	
20	-Step	Out

Pin Number	*Signal*	*Direction**
21	Signal Ground	
22	-Write Data	Out
23	Signal Ground	
24	-Write Enable	Out
25	Signal Ground	
26	-Track 0	In
27	Signal Ground	
28	-Write Protect	In
29	Signal Ground	
30	-Read Data	In
31	Signal Ground	
32	-Head 1 Select	Out
33	Signal Ground	
34	-Diskette Change	In
35	Frame Ground	
36	Frame Ground	
37	Ground	
38	+5Vdc	Out
39	Ground	
40	+12Vdc	Out

*From controller

Source: IBM PS/2 Hardware Interface Technical Reference, page Model 70 System Board 3-9

See Also: 8.19. PS/2 Model 30 Diskette Drive Connector
8.20. PS/2 Model 50 Diskette Drive Connector
8.22. PS/2 Model 70 Diskette and Fixed Drive Bus Connector
8.24. PS/2 Model 70 Fixed Disk Drive Cable Connector

8.24. PS/2 MODEL 70 FIXED DISK DRIVE CABLE CONNECTOR

2x36 Pin Connector (Side A is top)

Pin Number	*Signal*	*Direction**	*Pin Number*	*Signal*	*Direction**
B1	A15	Out	A1	-CD SETUP	Out
B2	A14	Out	A2	A13	Out
B3	Ground		A3	Ground	
B4	14.3 MHz Osc	Out	A4	A11	Out
B5	Ground		A5	A10	Out
B6	A12	Out	A6	A9	Out
B7	-CMD	Out	A7	+5Vdc	Out
B8	-CD SFDBK	In	A8	A8	Out
B9	Ground		A9	A7	Out
B10	D1	In/Out	A10	A6	Out
B11	D3	In/Out	A11	Ground	
B12	D4	In/Out	A12	A5	Out
B13	Ground		A13	A4	Out
B14	CHRESET	Out	A14	A3	Out
B15	D8	In/Out	A15	+5Vdc	Out
B16	D9	In/Out	A16	A2	Out
B17	Ground		A17	A1	Out
B18	D12	In/Out	A18	A0	Out
B19	D14	In/Out	A19	+12Vdc	Out
B20	D15	In/Out	A20	-ADL	Out
B21	Ground		A21	-PREEMPT	In
B22	D0	In/Out	A22	-BURST	In
B23	D2	In/Out	A23	+5Vdc	Out
B24	D5	In/Out	A24	ARB 0	In
B25	Ground		A25	ARB 1	In
B26	D6	In/Out	A26	ARB 2	In
B27	D7	In/Out	A27	+12Vdc	
B28	D10	In/Out	A28	ARB 3	In
B29	Ground		A29	ARB/-GNT	Out
B30	D11	In/Out	A30	-TC	Out
B31	D13	In/Out	A31	+5Vdc	
B32	-SBHE	Out	A32	-S0	Out
B33	Ground		A33	-S1	Out
B34	-CD DS 16	In	A34	M/-IO	Out
B35	-IRQ 14	In	A35	Ground	
B36	Ground		A36	CD CHRDY	In

*From controller

(Continued)

8.24. PS/2 MODEL 70 FIXED DISK DRIVE CABLE CONNECTOR (continued)

Source: IBM PS/2 Hardware Interface Technical Reference, page Model 70 System Board 3-10

See Also: 8.19. PS/2 Model 30 Diskette Drive Connector
8.20. PS/2 Model 50 Diskette Drive Connector
8.22. PS/2 Model 70 Diskette and Fixed Drive Bus Connector
8.23. PS/2 Model 70 Diskette Drive Cable Connector

8.25. PS/2 MODELS 90 AND 95 DISKETTE DRIVE CONNECTORS

Pin Number	*Signal*
1	Ground
2	Data Rate Select 1
3	+5Vdc
4	Drive Type ID 1
5	Ground
6	+12Vdc
7	Ground
8	-Index
9	Drive Type ID 0
10	RESERVED
11	Ground
12	-Drive Select
13	Ground
14	RESERVED
15	Ground
16	-Motor Enable
17	Media Type ID 1

Pin Number	*Signal*
18	-Direction In
19	Ground
20	-Step
21	Ground
22	-Write Data
23	Ground
24	-Write Enable
25	Ground
26	-Track 0
27	Media Type ID 0
28	-Write Protect
29	Ground
30	-Read Data
31	Ground
32	-Head 1 Select 0
33	-Data Rate Select 0
34	-Diskette Change

Source: IBM PS/2 Hardware Interface Technical Reference, System Specific Information, pages Model 90 3-2 and Model 95 3-2

8.26. ESDI 34-PIN CONNECTOR

Pin Number	*Signal*	*Direction*
1	Ground	
2	Head Select 2 (3)	To disk
3	Ground	
4	Head Select 2 (2)	To disk
5	Ground	
6	Write Gate	To disk
7	Ground	
8	Config/Status Data	From disk
9	Ground	
10	Transfer Acknowledged	From disk
11	Ground	
12	Attention	From disk
13	Ground	
14	Head Select 2 (0)	To disk
15	Ground	
16	Sector/Address Mark Found	From disk
17	Ground	

Pin Number	*Signal*	*Direction*
18	Head Select 2 (1)	To disk
19	Ground	
20	Index	From disk
21	Ground	
22	Ready	From disk
23	Ground	
24	Transfer Request	To disk
25	Ground	
26	Drive Select 2 (0)	To disk
27	Ground	
28	Drive Select 2 (1)	To disk
29	Ground	
30	Drive Select 2 (2)	To disk
31	Ground	
32	Read Gate	To disk
33	Ground	
34	Command Data	To disk

Note: Connector is a 34-pin double-row plug.

Source: "The Evolution of ESDI," Byte, June 1990

See Also: 8.16. XT Fixed Disk Controller Connector J1
8.17. XT Fixed Disk Controller Connectors J2 and J3

8.27. ESDI 20-PIN CONNECTOR

Pin Number	*Signal*	*Direction*
1	Dirve Selected	From disk
2	Sector/Address Mark Found	From disk
3	Command Complete	From disk
4	Address Mark Enable	To disk
5	Ground	
6	Ground	
7	+Write Clock	To disk
8	-Write Clock	To disk
9	Ground	
10	+Read/Reference Clock	From disk

Pin Number	*Signal*	*Direction*
11	-Read/Reference Clock	From disk
12	Ground	
13	+Write Data	To disk
14	-Write Data	To disk
15	Ground	
16	Ground	
17	+Read Data	From disk
18	-Read Data	From disk
19	Ground	
20	Index	From disk

Note: • Signals preceded by a minus sign are negative true.
• Connector is a 20-pin double-row plug.

Source: "The Evolution of ESDI," Byte, June 1990

See Also: 8.26. ESDI 34-Pin Connector

8.28. SCSI DISK CONTROLLER CABLE CONNECTOR

Pin Number	*Signal (Single-Ended)*	*Signal (Differential)*
1	Ground	Shield Ground
2	-DB (0)	Ground
3	Ground	+DB (0)
4	-DB (1)	-DB (0)
5	Ground	+DB (1)
6	-DB (2)	-DB (1)
7	Ground	+DB (2)
8	-DB (3)	-DB (2)
9	Ground	+DB (3)
10	-DB (4)	-DB (3)
11	Ground	+DB (4)
12	-DB (5)	-DB (4)
13	Ground	+DB (5)
14	-DB (6)	-DB (5)
15	Ground	+DB (6)
16	-DB (7)	-DB (6)
17	Ground	+DB (7)
18	-DB (P)	-DB (7)
19	Ground	+DB (P)
20	Ground	-DB (P)
21	Ground	DIFFSENS
22	Ground	Ground
23	Ground	Ground
24	Ground	Ground
25	NOT CONNECTED	TERMPWR

Pin Number	*Signal (Single-Ended)*	*Signal (Differential)*
26	TERMPWR	TERMPWR
27	Ground	Ground
28	Ground	Ground
29	Ground	+ATN
30	Ground	-ATN
31	Ground	Ground
32	-ATN	Ground
33	Ground	+BSY
34	Ground	-BSY
35	Ground	+ACK
36	-BSY	-ACK
37	Ground	+RST
38	-ACK	-RST
39	Ground	+MSG
40	-RST	-MSG
41	Ground	+SEL
42	-MSG	-SEL
43	Ground	+C/D
44	-SEL	-C/D
45	Ground	+REQ
46	-C/D	-REQ
47	Ground	+I/O
48	-REQ	-I/O
49	Ground	Ground
50	-I/O	Ground

Note: • Signals preceded by a minus sign are negative true.
• Connector is a 50-pin Centronics-type connector.

Source: "The SCSI Bus," Byte, February 1990

8.29. PC AND XT POWER SUPPLY CONNECTORS

Connector	Pin Number	Signal
5.25 floppy drive	1	+12Vdc
	2	Ground
	3	Ground
	4	+5Vdc
Fixed disk drive (or 2nd floppy)	1	+12Vdc
	2	Ground
	3	Ground
	4	+5Vdc
System board 1	1	Ground
	2	Ground
	3	-5Vdc
	4	+5Vdc
	5	+5Vdc
	6	+5Vdc

Connector	Pin Number	Signal
System board 2	1	Power ground
	2	KEY
	3	+12Vdc
	4	-12Vdc
	5	Ground
	6	Ground

Note: Connectors are 4-pin molex connectors or 12-pin, 2-row plugs.

Source: IBM PC/XT Technical Reference, pages 1-21 through 1-24

8.30. AT BATTERY CONNECTOR J21

Pin Number	Signal
1	Ground
2	NOT USED
3	Key
4	6Vdc

Note: Connector is a 4-pin keyed Berg connector (keyed on pin 3).

Source: IBM PC/AT Technical Reference, page 1-72

See Also: 8.31. AT Power Supply Connectors PS8, PS9, PS10, PS11, and PS12

8.31. AT POWER SUPPLY CONNECTORS PS8, PS9, PS10, PS11, AND PS12

Connector	Pin Number	Signal
System board 1 PS8 Back of board	1	Power good
	2	+5Vdc
	3	+12Vdc
	4	-12Vdc
	5	Ground
	6	Ground
System board 2 PS9 Front of board	1	Ground
	2	Ground
	3	-5Vdc
	4	+5Vdc
	5	+5Vdc
	6	+5Vdc

Connector	Pin Number	Signal
PS10 1st floppy	1	+12Vdc
	2	Ground
	3	Ground
	4	+5Vdc
PS11 2nd floppy	1	+12Vdc
	2	Ground
	3	Ground
	4	+5Vdc
PS12 Fixed disk	1	+12Vdc
	2	Ground
	3	Ground
	4	+5Vdc

Note: Connectors are 4-pin molex connectors or 6-pin, 1-row plugs.

Source: IBM PC/AT Technical Reference, pages 1-71 and 3-7

See Also: 8.30. AT Battery Connector J21

8.32. PS/2 MODEL 30 POWER SUPPLY CONNECTORS

Connector	*Pin Number*	*Signal*
P3 Rear of system board	1	Power good
	2	Ground
	3	+12Vdc
	4	-12Vdc
	5	Ground
	6	Ground
P4 Front of system board	1	Ground
	2	Ground
	3	-5Vdc
	4	+5Vdc
	5	+5Vdc
	6	+5Vdc

Note: Connectors are 6-pin, 1-row plugs.

Source: IBM PS/2 Model 30 Technical Reference, page 3-6

8.33. PS/2 MODEL 50 POWER SUPPLY CONNECTOR

50-Pin PC Edge Connector

Pin Number	*Signal*
1	-12Vdc
2	Signal ground
3	+12Vdc
4	Signal ground
5	+12Vdc
6	Signal ground
7	+12Vdc
8	Signal ground
9	+12Vdc
10	Signal ground
11	+12Vdc
12	Signal ground
13	+12Vdc
14	Signal ground
15	+5Vdc
16	Signal ground
17	+5Vdc

Pin Number	*Signal*
18	Signal ground
19	+5Vdc
20	Signal ground
21	+5Vdc
22	Signal ground
23	+5Vdc
24	Signal ground
25	+5Vdc
26	Signal ground
27	+5Vdc
28	Signal ground
29	+5Vdc
30	Signal ground
31	+5Vdc
32	Signal ground
33	+5Vdc
34	Signal ground

Pin Number	*Signal*
35	+5Vdc
36	Signal ground
37	+5Vdc
38	Signal ground
39	+5Vdc
40	Signal ground
41	+5Vdc
42	Signal ground
43	+5Vdc
44	Signal ground
45	+5Vdc
46	Signal ground
47	+5Vdc
48	Signal ground
49	System status
50	Power good

Source: IBM PS/2 Model 50 and 60 Technical Reference, page 5-6

8.34. PS/2 MODELS 60 AND 80 POWER SUPPLY CONNECTOR

15-Pin Arranged as 3x5 Keyed Matrix

Pin Number	*Signal*
1	+5Vdc
2	Signal ground
3	+12Vdc
4	+5Vdc
5	Signal ground
6	Signal ground
7	+5Vdc
8	Signal ground
9	-12Vdc
10	+5Vdc
11	Signal ground
12	Power good
13	+5Vdc
14	Signal ground
15	System status

Source: IBM PS/2 Model 50 and 60 Technical Reference, page 5-7
IBM PS/2 Model 80 Technical Reference, page 5-6

8.35. PS/2 MODELS 60 AND 80 FIXED DISK POWER SUPPLY CONNECTOR

Pin Number	*Signal*
1	+12Vdc
2	Signal Ground
3	Signal Ground
4	+5Vdc

Source: IBM PS/2 Model 50 and 60 Technical Reference, page 5-8
IBM PS/2 Model 80 Technical Reference, page 5-7

8.36. PS/2 MODELS 90 AND 95 POWER SUPPLY CONNECTOR

Pin Number	*Signal*
1	+12Vdc
2	DC Return
3	DC Return
4	+5Vdc

Source: IBM PS/2 Hardware Interface Technical Reference, System Specific Information, pages Model 90 1-10 and Model 95 1-10

8.37. PC AND XT KEYBOARD CONNECTOR

Pin Number	*Signal*
1	+Keyboard clock (+5Vdc signal level)
2	+Keyboard data (+5Vdc signal level)
3	-Keyboard reset (not used by keyboard)
4	Ground
5	+5Vdc

Note: Connector is a 5-pin DIN connector.

Source: IBM PC/XT Technical Reference, page 1-29

See Also: 8.38. PS/2 Keyboard and Mouse Connector (at Computer)

8.38. PS/2 KEYBOARD AND MOUSE CONNECTOR (AT COMPUTER)

System End (6-Pin DIN)

Pin Number	*Signal*
1	+KBD DATA
2	RESERVED
3	Ground
4	+5Vdc
5	+KBD CLK
6	RESERVED

Source: IBM PS/2 Model 30 Technical Reference, page 4-41
IBM PS/2 Model 50 and 60 Technical Reference, page 4-18
IBM PS/2 Model 80 Technical Reference, page 4-18
IBM PS/2 Hardware Interface Technical Reference, page Keyboards (101 and 102 key) 50

See Also: 8.37. PC and XT Keyboard Connector
8.39. PS/2 Keyboard Connector (at Keyboard)

8.39. PS/2 KEYBOARD CONNECTOR (AT KEYBOARD)

Keyboard End (6-Pin Phone)

Pin Number	*Signal*
A	RESERVED
B	+KBD DATA
C	Ground
D	+KBD CLOCK
E	+5Vdc
F	RESERVED

Source: IBM PS/2 Model 30 Technical Reference, page 4-41
IBM PS/2 Hardware Interface Technical Reference, page Keyboard (101 and 102 key) 50
IBM PS/2 Model 50 and 60 Technical Reference, page 4-18
IBM PS/2 Model 80 Technical Reference, page 4-18

See Also: 8.37. PC and XT Keyboard Connector
8.38. PS/2 Keyboard and Mouse Connector (at Computer)

8.40. AT POWER LED AND KEYLOCK CONNECTOR J20

Pin Number	*Signal*
1	LED power
2	Key
3	Ground
4	Keyboard inhibit
5	Ground

Note: Connector is a 5-pin Berg strip.

Source: IBM PC/AT Technical Reference, page 1-72

8.41. PS/2 MODELS 50 AND 60 MEMORY CONNECTOR

30-Pin Connector

Pin Number	*Signal*	*Direction†*
1	+5Vdc	
2	-Column address strobe	In
3	D1	In/Out
4	A1	In
5	A2	In
6	D2	In/Out
7	A3	In
8	A4	In
9	Ground	
10	D3	In/Out
11	A5	In
12	A6	In
13	D4	In/Out
14	A7	In
15	A8	In

Pin Number	*Signal*	*Direction†*
16	D5	In/Out
17	A9	In
18	No connection	
19	RAS1*	In
20	D6	In/Out
21	-Write strobe	In
22	Ground	
23	D7	In/Out
24	Presence detect 1	Out
25	D8	In/Out
26	Presence detect 2	Out
27	Row address strobe	In
28	No connection	
29	D9 (parity)	In/Out
30	+5Vdc	

*Applicable only to 512K modules
†From memory card

Source: IBM PS/2 Model 50 and 60 Technical Reference, page 4-181

8.42. PS/2 MODEL 70 MEMORY CONNECTOR

72-Pin Connector

Pin Number	*Signal*	*Direction**
1	Ground	
2	Data 0	In/Out
3	Data 16	In/Out
4	Data 1	In/Out
5	Data 17	In/Out
6	Data 2	In/Out
7	Data 18	In/Out
8	Data 3	In/Out
9	Data 19	In/Out
10	+5Vdc	Out
11	-Column address strobe P	Out
12	Address 0	Out
13	Address 1	Out
14	Address 2	Out
15	Address 3	Out
16	Address 4	Out
17	Address 5	Out
18	Address 6	Out
19	RESERVED	
20	Data 4	In/Out
21	Data 20	In/Out
22	Data 5	In/Out
23	Data 21	In/Out
24	Data 6	In/Out
25	Data 22	In/Out
26	Data 7	In/Out
27	Data 23	In/Out
28	Address 7	Out
29	Block Select 0	Out
30	+5Vdc	Out
31	Address 8	Out
32	RESERVED	
33	Row address strobe 3	Out
34	Row address strobe 2	Out
35	Parity data 2	In/Out
36	Parity data 0	In/Out

Pin Number	*Signal*	*Direction**
37	Parity Data 1	In/Out
38	Parity Data 3	In/Out
39	Ground	
40	Column address stobe 0	Out
41	Column address strobe 2	Out
42	Column address strobe 3	Out
43	Column address strobe 1	Out
44	Row address strobe 0	Out
45	Row address strobe 1	Out
46	Block select 1	Out
47	Write enable	Out
48	RESERVED	
49	Data 8	In/Out
50	Data 24	In/Out
51	Data 9	In/Out
52	Data 25	In/Out
53	Data 10	In/Out
54	Data 26	In/Out
55	Data 11	In/Out
56	Data 27	In/Out
57	Data 12	In/Out
58	Data 28	In/Out
59	+5Vdc	Out
60	Data 29	In/Out
61	Data 13	In/Out
62	Data 30	In/Out
63	Data 14	In/Out
64	Data 31	In/Out
65	Data 15	In/Out
66	Block select 2	Out
67	Presence detect 0	In
68	Presence detect 1	In
69	Presence detect 2	In
70	Presence detect 3	In
71	Block select 3	Out
72	Ground	

*From memory card

Version: Applies to PS/2 Model 70 only.

Source: IBM PS/2 Hardware Interface Technical Reference, pages Model 70 3-22 through 3-23

8.43. PS/2 MODEL 80 MEMORY CONNECTOR

Pin Number	Signal	Direction*
A1	RESERVED	
A2	-Mem Write	In
A3	Address 0	In
A4	Address 1	In
A5	Address 2	In
A6	Address 3	In
A7	Address 4	In
A8	Address 5	In
A9	Address 6	In
A10	Address 7	In
A11	Address 8	In
A12	-Row Address Strobe 0	In
A13	-Row Address Strobe 1	In
A14	-Row Address Strobe 2	In
A15	-Row Address Strobe 3	In
A16	RESERVED	
A17	Presence Detector	Out
A18	RESERVED	
A19	-Column Address Strobe 0	In
A20	-Column Address Strobe 1	In
A21	-Column Address Strobe 2	In
A22	-Column Address Strobe 3	In
A23	Data Parity 0	In/Out
A24	Data Parity 1	In/Out
A25	Data Parity 2	In/Out
A26	Data Parity 3	In/Out
A27	-Byte Enable 0	In
A28	-Byte Enable 1	In
A29	-Byte Enable 2	In
A30	-Byte Enable 3	In
A31	-Column Address Strobe Parity	In
A32	Presence Detector	Out

Pin Number	Signal	Direction*
B1	Ground	NA
B2	+5Vdc	NA
B3	Ground	NA
B4	+5Vdc	NA
B5	Ground	NA
B6	+5Vdc	NA
B7	Ground	NA
B8	+5Vdc	NA
B9	Ground	NA
B10	+5Vdc	NA
B11	Ground	NA
B12	+5Vdc	NA
B13	Ground	NA
B14	+5Vdc	NA
B15	Ground	NA
B16	+5Vdc	NA
B17	Ground	NA
B18	+5Vdc	NA
B19	Ground	NA
B20	+5Vdc	NA
B21	Ground	NA
B22	+5Vdc	NA
B23	Ground	NA
B24	+5Vdc	NA
B25	Ground	NA
B26	+5Vdc	NA
B27	Ground	NA
B28	+5Vdc	NA
B29	Ground	NA
B30	+5Vdc	NA
B31	Ground	NA
B32	+5Vdc	NA

Pin Number	Signal	Direction*
C1	Data 0	In/Out
C2	Data 1	In/Out
C3	Data 2	In/Out
C4	Data 3	In/Out
C5	Data 4	In/Out
C6	Data 5	In/Out
C7	Data 6	In/Out
C8	Data 7	In/Out
C9	Data 8	In/Out
C10	Data 9	In/Out
C11	Data 10	In/Out
C12	Data 11	In/Out
C13	Data 12	In/Out
C14	Data 13	In/Out
C15	Data 14	In/Out
C16	Data 15	In/Out
C17	Data 16	In/Out
C18	Data 17	In/Out
C19	Data 18	In/Out
C20	Data 19	In/Out
C21	Data 20	In/Out
C22	Data 21	In/Out
C23	Data 22	In/Out
C24	Data 23	In/Out
C25	Data 24	In/Out
C26	Data 25	In/Out
C27	Data 26	In/Out
C28	Data 27	In/Out
C29	Data 28	In/Out
C30	Data 29	In/Out
C31	Data 30	In/Out
C32	Data 31	In/Out

*From memory card

Source: IBM PS/2 Model 80 Technical Reference, pages 4-181 through 4-182

8.44. PS/2 MODELS 90 AND 95 MEMORY CONNECTOR

72-Pin Connector

Pin Number	Signal
1	Ground
2	Data 0
3	Data 16
4	Data 1
5	Data 17
6	Data 2
7	Data 18
8	Data 3
9	Data 19
10	+5Vdc
11	-Column address strobe P
12	Address 0
13	Address 1
14	Address 2
15	Address 3
16	Address 4
17	Address 5
18	Address 6
19	RESERVED
20	Data 4
21	Data 20
22	Data 5
23	Data 21
24	Data 6
25	Data 22
26	Data 7
27	Data 23
28	Address 7
29	Block select 0
30	+5Vdc
31	Address 8
32	Address 9
33	Row address strobe 3
34	Row address strobe 2
35	Parity data 2
36	Parity data 0

Pin Number	Signal
37	Parity data 1
38	Parity data 3
39	Ground
40	Column address stobe 0
41	Column address strobe 2
42	Column address strobe 3
43	Column address strobe 1
44	Row address strobe 0
45	Row address strobe 1
46	Block select 1
47	Write enable
48	RESERVED
49	Data 8
50	Data 24
51	Data 9
52	Data 25
53	Data 10
54	Data 26
55	Data 11
56	Data 27
57	Data 12
58	Data 28
59	+5Vdc
60	Data 29
61	Data 13
62	Data 30
63	Data 14
64	Data 31
65	Data 15
66	Block select 2
67	Presence detect 0
68	Presence detect 1
69	Presence detect 2
70	Presence detect 3
71	Block select 3
72	Ground

Source: IBM PS/2 Hardware Interface Technical Reference, System Specific Information, pages Model 90 3-4 and Model 95 3-4

8.45. PS/2 PARALLEL PORT CONNECTOR

System End (DB25)

Pin Number	Signal	Direction*
1	-STROBE	In/Out
2	Data 0	In/Out
3	Data 1	In/Out
4	Data 2	In/Out
5	Data 3	In/Out
6	Data 4	In/Out
7	Data 5	In/Out
8	Data 6	In/Out
9	Data 7	In/Out
10	-ACK	In
11	BUSY	In
12	PE	In
13	SLCT	In

Pin Number	Signal	Direction*
14	-AUTO FEED XT	Out
15	-ERROR	In
16	-INIT	Out
17	-SLCT IN	Out
18	Ground	
19	Ground	
20	Ground	
21	Ground	
22	Ground	
23	Ground	
24	Ground	
25	Ground	

*From computer

Source: IBM PS/2 Model 30 Technical Reference, page 1-126
IBM PS/2 Model 50 and 60 Technical Reference, page 4-179
IBM PS/2 Model 80 Technical Reference, page 4-171

See Also: 8.46. Centronics Parallel Connector
8.48. Parallel Printer Connector

8.46. CENTRONICS PARALLEL CONNECTOR

Pin Number	*Definition*	*Direction**
1	-Strobe	In
2	Data 1	In
3	Data 2	In
4	Data 3	In
5	Data 4	In
6	Data 5	In
7	Data 6	In
8	Data 7	In
9	Data 8	In
10	-Acknowledge	Out
11	Busy	Out
12	Paper End	Out
13	Select	Out
14	-Auto Feed	In
15	NOT USED	
16	Logical Ground	
17	Chassis Ground	
18	NOT USED	
19	Ground Return for -Strobe	
20	Ground Return for Data 1	
21	Ground Return for Data 2	
22	Ground Return for Data 3	
23	Ground Return for Data 4	
24	Ground Return for Data 5	
25	Ground Return for Data 6	
26	Ground Return for Data 7	
27	Ground Return for Data 8	
28	Ground Return for -Acknowledge	
29	Ground Return for Busy	
30	Ground	
31	-Printer Init	In
32	Error	Out
33	Ground	
34	NOT USED	
35	Pulled up to +5Vdc through 4.7k-ohm resistor	
36	-Select In	In

*From computer

Note: Connector is an Amphenol 57-30360 or equivalent (Centronics parallel).

Source: IBM Options and Adapters Technical Reference, Vol. 1, pages Graphics Printer 29 through 31

See Also: 8.04. RS-232C Serial Port Connector (DTE Device)
8.45. PS/2 Parallel Port Connector
8.48. Parallel Printer Connector

8.47. GAME ADAPTER CONNECTOR

Pin Number	*Signal*	*Function*	*Direction**
1	+5Vdc		Out
2	Button 4	Paddle 1 button, joystick A button	In
3	Position 0	Paddle 1 position, joystick A x-coordinate	In
4	Ground		
5	Ground		
6	Position 1	Paddle 2 position, joystick A y-coordinate	In
7	Button 5	Paddle 2 button	In
8	+5Vdc		Out
9	+5Vdc		Out
10	Button 6	Paddle 3 button, joystick B button	In
11	Position 2	Paddle 3 position, joystick B x-coordinate	In
12	Ground		
13	Position 3	Paddle 4 position, joystick B y-coordinate	In
14	Button 7	Paddle 4 button	In
15	+5Vdc		Out

*From computer

Note: Connector is a female DB-15.

Source: IBM Options and Adapters Technical Reference, Vol. 2, pages Game Adapter 6 and 7

8.48. PARALLEL PRINTER CONNECTOR

Pin Number	Signal	Function	Direction*
1	-Strobe	Indicates valid data available	Out
2	Data bit 0	Least significant bit of data byte	Out
3	Data bit 1		Out
4	Data bit 2		Out
5	Data bit 3		Out
6	Data bit 4		Out
7	Data bit 5		Out
8	Data bit 6		Out
9	Data bit 7	Most significant bit of data byte	Out
10	-Acknowledge	Indicates data received and device is ready for more	In
11	Busy	Device cannot receive data	In
12	Paper End	Device is out of paper	In
13	Select	Device is in selected state	In
14	-Auto Feed	Device to perform line feed after each line sent	Out
15	-Error	Device unable to perform	In
16	-Initialize Printer	Reset device to initial state	Out
17	-Select Input	Device can accept input	In
18	Ground		
19	Ground		
20	Ground		
21	Ground		
22	Ground		
23	Ground		
24	Ground		
25	Ground		

*From computer

Note:
- Connector is a female DB-25.
- The original printer adapter and monochrome display adapter parallel ports are output-only; no provision for parallel input was made until introduction of the PS/2.

Source: IBM Options and Adapters Technical Reference, Vol. 2, page Printer Adapter 7

See Also: 8.45. PS/2 Parallel Port Connector
8.46. Centronics Parallel Connnector

8.49. PC AND XT SPEAKER CONNECTOR

Pin Number	Signal
1	Data
2	Key
3	Ground
4	+5Vdc

Note: Connector is a 4-pin keyed Berg connector (keyed on pin 2).

Source: IBM PC/XT Technical Reference, page 1-20

8.50. PC AND XT ADD-ON CARD SIZE

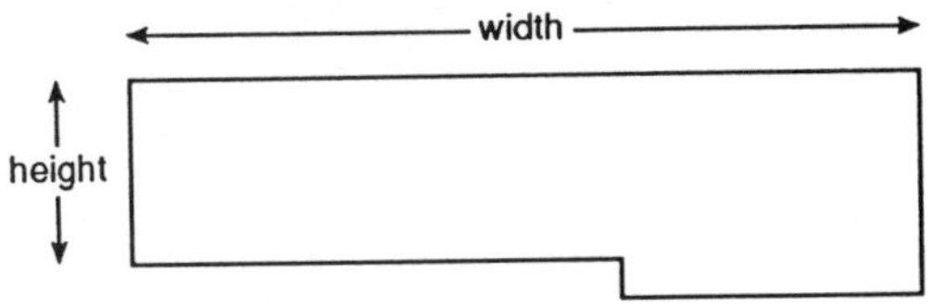
width
height

Height:	4.2 inches (106.68 mm)
Width:	13.15 inches (334.01 mm)
Pin layout:	62 pins with 100-mil card spacing

Source: IBM PC/XT Technical Reference, page E-4

See Also: 8.51. AT Add-On Card Size
8.52. Microchannel Card Size
8.54. PC and XT I/O Channel (System Bus) Pinouts

8.51. AT ADD-ON CARD SIZE

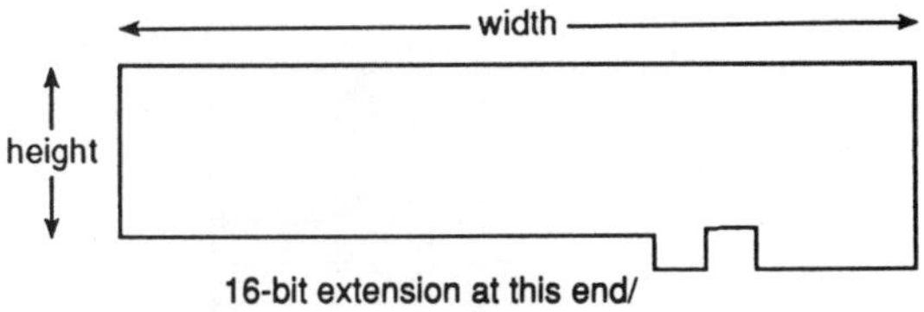
width
height
16-bit extension at this end/

Height:	4.5 inches (114 mm)
Width:	13.1 inches (333 mm)
Pin layout:	62 pins with 100-mil card spacing, plus 36-pin extension

Source: IBM Personal System/2: A Business Perspective (John Wiley), page 39

See Also: 8.50. PC and XT Add-On Card Size
8.52. Microchannel Card Size

8.52. MICROCHANNEL CARD SIZE

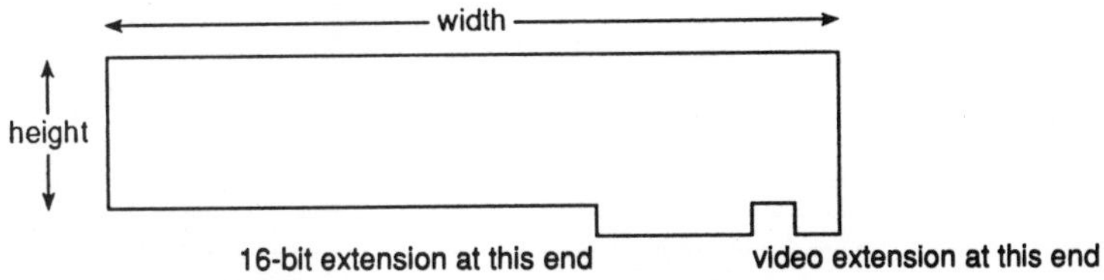
width
height
16-bit extension at this end
video extension at this end

Height:	3.475 inches (88.27mm)
Width:	11.50 inches (292.1mm)
Pin layout:	Dual 58-pin, 50-mil connector with 4 keyed positions Also allows for optional dual 10-pin video extension.

Version: Not applicable to Model 30

Source: IBM PS/2 Model 50 and 60 Technical Reference, pages 2-4 through 2-5 and 2-90 through 2-103
IBM PS/2 Model 80 Technical Reference, pages 2-6 through 2-7 and 2-114 through 2-12

See Also: 8.50. PC and XT Add-On Card Size
8.51. AT Add-On Card Size

8.53. EISA EXPANSION CARD SIZE

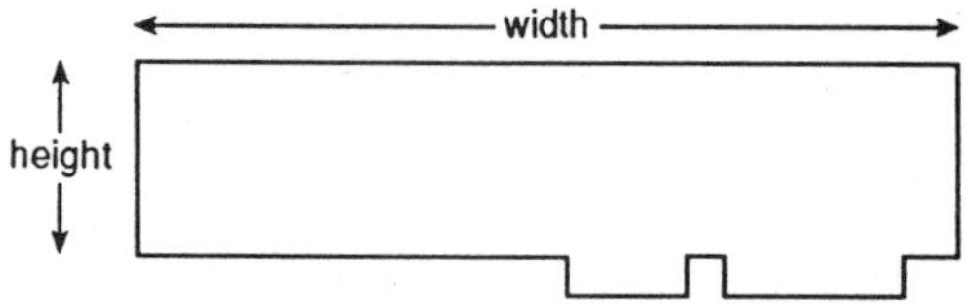
width
height

Height: 4.48 inches (113.8 mm)
Width: 13.38 inches (339.8 mm)
Pin layout: Two rows of dual pins:
-The upper row connects to the ISA contacts.
-The lower row connects to the EISA contacts.

Source: Inside the EISA Computer (Addison Wesley), pages 24 through 28 and 57 through 59

8.54. PC AND XT I/O CHANNEL (SYSTEM BUS) PINOUTS

Pin Number	*Signal*	*Description*	*Direction**
A1	-I/O CH CK	I/O channel check; active low=parity error	In
A2	+D7	Data bit 7	In/Out
A3	+D6	Data bit 6	In/Out
A4	+D5	Data bit 5	In/Out
A5	+D4	Data bit 4	In/Out
A6	+D3	Data bit 3	In/Out
A7	+D2	Data bit 2	In/Out
A8	+D1	Data bit 1	In/Out
A9	+D0	Data bit 0	In/Out
A10	+I/O CH RDY	I/O channel ready; pulled low to lengthen memory cycles	In
A11	+AEN	Address enable; active high when DMA controls bus	Out
A12	+A19	Address bit 19	Out
A13	+A18	Address bit 18	Out
A14	+A17	Address bit 17	Out
A15	+A16	Address bit 16	Out
A16	+A15	Address bit 15	Out
A17	+A14	Address bit 14	Out
A18	+A13	Address bit 13	Out
A19	+A12	Address bit 12	Out
A20	+A11	Address bit 11	Out
A21	+A10	Address bit 10	Out
A22	+A9	Address bit 9	Out
A23	+A8	Address bit 8	Out
A24	+A7	Address bit 7	Out
A25	+A6	Address bit 6	Out
A26	+A5	Address bit 5	Out
A27	+A4	Address bit 4	Out
A28	+A3	Address bit 3	Out
A29	+A2	Address bit 2	Out
A30	+A1	Address bit 1	Out
A31	+A0	Address bit 0	Out
B1	GROUND		
B2	+RESET DRV	Active high to reset or initialize system logic	Out
B3	+5Vdc		
B4	+IRQ2	Interrupt request 2	In
B5	-5Vdc		
B6	+DRQ2	DMA request 2	In
B7	-12Vdc		
B8	-CARD SLCTD	Card selected; activated by cards in XT's slot J8	In
B9	+12Vdc		
B10	GROUND		
B11	-MEMW	Memory write	Out
B12	-MEMR	Memory read	Out
B13	-IOW	I/O write	Out
B14	-IOR	I/O read	Out
B15	-DACK3	DMA acknowledge 3	Out
B16	+DRQ3	DMA request 3	In
B17	-DACK1	DMA acknowledge 1	Out
B18	+DRQ1	DMA request 1	In

(Continued)

8.54. PC AND XT I/O CHANNEL (SYSTEM BUS) PINOUTS (continued)

Pin Number	*Signal*	*Description*	*Direction**
B19	-DACK0	DMA acknowledge 0	Out
B20	CLOCK	System clock (210 ns, 4.77MHz); 33% duty cycle	Out
B21	+IRQ7	Interrupt request 7	In
B22	+IRQ6	Interrupt request 6	In
B23	+IRQ5	Interrupt request 5	In
B24	+IRQ4	Interrupt request 4	In
B25	+IRQ3	Interrupt request 3	In
B26	-DACK2	DMA acknowledge 2	Out
B27	+T/C	Terminal count; pulses high when DMA term. count reached	Out
B28	+ALE	Address latch enable	Out
B29	+5Vdc		
B30	+OSC	High-speed clock (70 ns,14.31818MHz), 50% duty cycle	Out
B31	GROUND		

*From system board

Note:
- All signals are at standard TTL levels.
- Connector is a 62-pin edge connector.
- A=component side of board; numbers start closest to rear panel of machine.

Source: IBM PC/XT Technical Reference, pages 1-15 through 1-19

See Also: 8.55. AT I/O Channel (System Bus) Pinouts
8.57. PS/2 Model 50/60/80 Microchannel Bus Pinouts

8.55. AT I/O CHANNEL (SYSTEM BUS) PINOUTS

Pin Number	*Signal*	*Description*	*Direction**
A1	-I/O CH CK	I/O channel check; active low=parity error	In
A2	SD7	Data bit 7	In/Out
A3	SD6	Data bit 6	In/Out
A4	SD5	Data bit 5	In/Out
A5	SD4	Data bit 4	In/Out
A6	SD3	Data bit 3	In/Out
A7	SD2	Data bit 2	In/Out
A8	SD1	Data bit 1	In/Out
A9	SD0	Data bit 0	In/Out
A10	-I/O CH RDY	I/O Channel ready; pulled low to lengthen memory cycles	In
A11	AEN	Address enable; active high when DMA controls bus	Out
A12	SA19	Address bit 19	Out
A13	SA18	Address bit 18	Out
A14	SA17	Address bit 17	Out
A15	SA16	Address bit 16	Out
A16	SA15	Address bit 15	Out
A17	SA14	Address bit 14	Out
A18	SA13	Address bit 13	Out
A19	SA12	Address bit 12	Out
A20	SA11	Address bit 11	Out
A21	SA10	Address bit 10	Out
A22	SA9	Address bit 9	Out
A23	SA8	Address bit 8	Out
A24	SA7	Address bit 7	Out
A25	SA6	Address bit 6	Out
A26	SA5	Address bit 5	Out
A27	SA4	Address bit 4	Out
A28	SA3	Address bit 3	Out
A29	SA2	Address bit 2	Out
A30	SA1	Address bit 1	Out
A31	SA0	Address bit 0	Out
B1	GROUND		
B2	RESET DRV	Active high to reset or initialize system logic	Out
B3	+5Vdc		
B4	IRQ9	Interrupt request 9	In
B5	-5Vdc		
B6	DRQ2	DMA request 2	In
B7	-12Vdc		
B8	-CARD SLCTD	Card selected; activated by cards in XT's slot J8	In
B9	+12Vdc		
B10	GROUND		

(Continued)

8.55. AT I/O CHANNEL (SYSTEM BUS) PINOUTS (continued)

Pin Number	Signal	Description	Direction*
B11	-MEMW	Memory write	Out
B12	-MEMR	Memory read	Out
B13	-IOW	I/O write	In/Out
B14	-IOR	I/O read	In/Out
B15	-DACK3	DMA acknowledge 3	Out
B16	DRQ3	DMA request 3	In
B17	-DACK1	DMA acknowledge 1	Out
B18	DRQ1	DMA request 1	In
B19	-REFRESH	Refresh	In/Out
B20	CLOCK	System clock (67 ns, 6 or 8MHz); 50% duty cycle	Out
B21	IRQ7	Interrupt request 7	In
B22	IRQ6	Interrupt request 6	In
B23	IRQ5	Interrupt request 5	In
B24	IRQ4	Interrupt request 4	In
B25	IRQ3	Interrupt request 3	In
B26	-DACK2	DMA acknowledge 2	Out
B27	T/C	Terminal count; pulses high when DMA term. count reached	Out
B28	ALE	Address latch enable	Out
B29	+5Vdc		
B30	OSC	High-speed clock (70 ns,14.31818MHz), 50% duty cycle	Out
B31	GROUND		
C1	SBHE	System bus high enable (data available on SD8-15)	In/Out
C2	LA23	Address bit 23 (unlatched)	In/Out
C3	LA22	Address bit 22 (unlatched)	In/Out
C4	LA21	Address bit 21 (unlatched)	In/Out
C5	LA20	Address bit 20 (unlatched)	In/Out
C6	LA19	Address bit 19 (unlatched)	In/Out
C7	LA18	Address bit 18 (unlatched)	In/Out
C8	LA17	Address bit 17 (unlatched)	In/Out
C9	-MEMR	Memory read (active on all memory read cycles)	In/Out
C10	-MEMW	Memory write (active on all memory write cycles)	In/Out
C11	SD08	Data bit 8	In/Out
C12	SD09	Data bit 9	In/Out
C13	SD10	Data bit 10	In/Out
C14	SD11	Data bit 11	In/Out
C15	SD12	Data bit 12	In/Out
C16	SD13	Data bit 13	In/Out
C17	SD14	Data bit 14	In/Out
C18	SD15	Data bit 15	In/Out
D1	-MEM CS16	Memory 16-bit chip select (1 wait, 16-bit memory cycle)	In
D2	-I/O CS16	I/O 16-bit chip select (1 wait, 16-bit I/O cycle)	In
D3	IRQ10	Interrupt request 10	In
D4	IRQ11	Interrupt request 11	In
D5	IRQ12	Interrupt request 12	In
D6	IRQ15	Interrupt request 15	In
D7	IRQ14	Interrupt request 14	In
D8	-DACK0	DMA acknowledge 0	Out
D9	DRQ0	DMA request 0	In
D10	-DACK5	DMA acknowledge 5	Out
D11	DRQ5	DMA request 5	In
D12	-DACK6	DMA acknowledge 6	Out
D13	DRQ6	DMA request 6	In
D14	-DACK7	DMA acknowledge 7	Out
D15	DRQ7	DMA request 7	In
D16	+5Vdc		
D17	-MASTER	Used with DRQ to gain control of system	In
D18	Ground		

*From system board

Note:
- All signals are at standard TTL levels.
- Connector is a 62-pin edge connector with a secondary 36-pin edge connector.
- A or C=component side of board; numbers start closest to rear panel of machine.

Source: IBM PC/AT Technical Reference, pages 1-25 through 1-37

See Also: 8.54. PC and XT I/O Channel (System Bus) Pinouts
8.57. PS/2 Model 50/60/80 Microchannel Bus Pinouts

8.56. EISA I/O CHANNEL (SYSTEM BUS) PINOUTS

Pin Number	*Signal*	*Description*
A1	-I/O CH CK	I/O channel check
A2	SD7	Data bit 7
A3	SD6	Data bit 6
A4	SD5	Data bit 5
A5	SD4	Data bit 4
A6	SD3	Data bit 3
A7	SD2	Data bit 2
A8	SD1	Data bit 1
A9	SD0	Data bit 0
A10	I/O CH RDY	I/O channel ready; pulled low to lengthen memory cycles
A11	AEN	Address enable; active high when DMA controls bus
A12	SA19	Address bit 19
A13	SA18	Address bit 18
A14	SA17	Address bit 17
A15	SA16	Address bit 16
A16	SA15	Address bit 15
A17	SA14	Address bit 14
A18	SA13	Address bit 13
A19	SA12	Address bit 12
A20	SA11	Address bit 11
A21	SA10	Address bit 10
A22	SA9	Address bit 9
A23	SA8	Address bit 8
A24	SA7	Address bit 7
A25	SA6	Address bit 6
A26	SA5	Address bit 5
A27	SA4	Address bit 4
A28	SA3	Address bit 3
A29	SA2	Address bit 2
A30	SA1	Address bit 1
A31	SA0	Address bit 0
B1	GROUND	
B2	RESET DRV	Active high to reset or initialize system logic
B3	+5Vdc	
B4	IRQ9	Interrupt request 9
B5	-5Vdc	
B6	DRQ2	DMA request 2
B7	-12Vdc	
B8	-NOWS	Indicates memory slave does not require remaining clock cycles
B9	+12Vdc	
B10	GROUND	
B11	-SMWTC	Indicates data on memory bus is valid and may be latched
B12	-SMRDC	Indicates memory slave should put data on memory bus
B13	-IOWC	I/O write
B14	-IORC	I/O read
B15	-DAK3	DMA acknowledge 3
B16	DRQ3	DMA request 3
B17	-DAK1	DMA acknowledge 1
B18	DRQ1	DMA request 1
B19	-REFRESH	
B20	8 CLK	System clock
B21	IRQ7	Interrupt request 7
B22	IRQ6	Interrupt request 6
B23	IRQ5	Interrupt request 5
B24	IRQ4	Interrupt request 4
B25	IRQ3	Interrupt request 3
B26	-DAK2	DMA acknowledge 2
B27	T/C	Terminal count; pulses high when DMA term. count reached
B28	BALE	Buffered address latch enable
B29	+5Vdc	
B30	+OSC	High-speed clock (70 ns,14.31818MHz); 50% duty cycle
B31	GROUND	
C1	-SBHE	System bus high enable (data available on SD8-15)
C2	LA23	Latchable address bit 23
C3	LA22	Latchable address bit 22
C4	LA21	Latchable address bit 21
C5	LA20	Latchable address bit 20
C6	LA19	Latchable address bit 19
C7	LA18	Latchable address bit 18
C8	LA17	Latchable address bit 17
C9	-MWTC	Indicates data on the memory bus is valid and may be latched
C10	-MRDC	Indicates memory slave should put its data on the memory bus
C11	D8	Data bit 8

(Continued)

8.56. EISA I/O CHANNEL (SYSTEM BUS) PINOUTS (continued)

Pin Number	Signal	Description
C12	D9	Data bit 9
C13	D10	Data bit 10
C14	D11	Data bit 11
C15	D12	Data bit 12
C16	D13	Data bit 13
C17	D14	Data bit 14
C18	D15	Data bit 15
D1	-MEM 16	Memory capable of 16-bit data transfer
D2	-I/O 16	I/O capable of 16-bit data transfer
D3	IRQ10	Interrupt request 10
D4	IRQ11	Interrupt request 11
D5	IRQ12	Interrupt request 12
D6	IRQ15	Interrupt request 15
D7	IRQ14	Interrupt request 14
D8	-DAK0	DMA acknowledge 0
D9	DRQ0	DMA request 0
D10	-DAK5	DMA acknowledge 5
D11	DRQ5	DMA request 5
D12	-DAK6	DMA acknowledge 6
D13	DRQ6	DMA request 6
D14	-DAK7	DMA acknowledge 7
D15	DRQ7	DMA request 7
D16	+5Vdc	
D17	-MASTER	Used with DRQ to gain control of system
D18	GROUND	
Upper A1	-CMD	Timing control for a command
Upper A2	-START	Timing control for the start of a cycle
Upper A3	EXRDY	Used by slave to request wait state timing
Upper A4	-EX32	Used by slave to indicate that it supports 32-bit transfers
Upper A5	GROUND	
Upper A6	KEY	
Upper A7	-EX16	Used by slave to indicate that it supports 16-bit transfers
Upper A8	-SLBURST	Used by bus slave to indicate it supports burst cycles
Upper A9	-MSBURST	Indicates to slave that bus master can provide burst cycles
Upper A10	W-R	Differentiates between write or read cycle
Upper A11	GROUND	
Upper A12	RESERVED	
Upper A13	RESERVED	
Upper A14	RESERVED	
Upper A15	GROUND	
Upper A16	KEY	
Upper A17	-BE1	Byte enable 1
Upper A18	LA31	Latchable address 31
Upper A19	GROUND	
Upper A20	LA30	Latchable address 30
Upper A21	LA28	Latchable address 28
Upper A22	LA27	Latchable address 27
Upper A23	LA25	Latchable address 25
Upper A24	GROUND	
Upper A25	KEY	
Upper A26	LA15	Latchable address 15
Upper A27	LA13	Latchable address 13
Upper A28	LA12	Latchable address 12
Upper A29	LA11	Latchable address 11
Upper A30	GROUND	
Upper A31	LA9	Latchable address 9
Upper B1	GROUND	
Upper B2	+5Vdc	
Upper B3	+5Vdc	
Upper B4	RESERVED	
Upper B5	RESERVED	
Upper B6	KEY	
Upper B7	RESERVED	
Upper B8	RESERVED	
Upper B9	+12Vdc	
Upper B10	M-IO	Used by bus master to identify memory or I/O cycle
Upper B11	-LOCK	Used by bus master to mandate exclusive access to memory
Upper B12	RESERVED	
Upper B13	GROUND	
Upper B14	RESERVED	
Upper B15	-BE3	Byte enable 3
Upper B16	KEY	
Upper B17	-BE2	Byte enable 2

(Continued)

8.56. EISA I/O CHANNEL (SYSTEM BUS) PINOUTS (continued)

Pin Number	*Signal*	*Description*
Upper B18	-BE0	Byte enable 0
Upper B19	GROUND	
Upper B20	+5Vdc	
Upper B21	LA29	Latchable address 29
Upper B22	GROUND	
Upper B23	LA26	Latchable address 26
Upper B24	LA24	Latchable address 24
Upper B25	KEY	
Upper B26	LA16	Latchable address 16
Upper B27	LA14	Latchable address 14
Upper B28	+5Vdc	
Upper B29	+5Vdc	
Upper B30	GROUND	
Upper B31	LA10	Latchable address 10
Upper C1	LA7	Latchable address 7
Upper C2	GROUND	
Upper C3	LA4	Latchable address 4
Upper C4	LA3	Latchable address 3
Upper C5	GROUND	
Upper C6	KEY	
Upper C7	SD17	Data bit 17
Upper C8	SD19	Data bit 19
Upper C9	SD20	Data bit 20
Upper C10	SD22	Data bit 22
Upper C11	GROUND	
Upper C12	SD25	Data bit 25
Upper C13	SD26	Data bit 26
Upper C14	SD28	Data bit 28
Upper C15	KEY	
Upper C16	GROUND	
Upper C17	SD30	Data bit 30
Upper C18	SD31	Data bit 31
Upper C19	-MREQx	Allows specific bus masters to request access to bus
Upper D1	LA8	Latchable address 8
Upper D2	LA6	Latchable address 6
Upper D3	LA5	Latchable address 5
Upper D4	+5Vdc	
Upper D5	LA2	Latchable address 2
Upper D6	KEY	
Upper D7	SD16	Data bit 16
Upper D8	SD18	Data bit 18
Upper D9	GROUND	
Upper D10	SD21	Data bit 21
Upper D11	SD23	Data bit 23
Upper D12	SD24	Data bit 24
Upper D13	GROUND	
Upper D14	SD27	Data bit 27
Upper D15	KEY	
Upper D16	SD29	Data bit 29
Upper D17	+5Vdc	
Upper D18	+5Vdc	
Upper D19	-MACK	Used by system board to grant bus access

Note:
- All signals are at standard TTL levels.
- Connector is a special two-tiered 62-pin edge connector with a secondary 36-pin edge connector.
- A or C=component side of board; numbers start closest to rear panel of machine.
- Upper refers to EISA extensions in upper tier of connector.

Source: Inside the EISA Computers (Addison-Wesley), pages 25 through 27 and 57 through 66

See Also: 8.54. PC and XT I/O Channel (System Bus) Pinouts
8.55. AT I/O Channel (System Bus) Pinouts
8.57. PS/2 Model 50/60/80 Microchannel Bus Pinouts

8.57. PS/2 MODEL 50/60/80 MICROCHANNEL BUS PINOUTS

58-Pin, 50-Mil Edge Connector

Pin Number	Signal	Description
A1	-CD SETUP	Card setup
A2	MADE 24	Memory address enable 24
A3	Ground	
A4	A11	Address bit 11
A5	A10	Address bit 10
A6	A09	Address bit 9
A7	+5Vdc	
A8	A08	Address bit 8
A9	A07	Address bit 7
A10	A06	Address bit 6
A11	+5Vdc	
A12	A05	Address bit 5
A13	A04	Address bit 4
A14	A03	Address bit 3
A15	+5Vdc	
A16	A02	Address bit 2
A17	A01	Address bit 1
A18	A00	Address bit 0
A19	+12Vdc	
A20	-ADL	Address decode latch
A21	-PREEMPT	Causes arbitration cycle to occur
A22	-BURST	Used to signal extended use of channel
A23	-12Vdc	
A24	ARB 00	Arbitration bus priority level bit 0
A25	ARB 01	Arbitration bus priority level bit 1
A26	ARB 02	Arbitration bus priority level bit 2
A27	-12Vdc	
A28	ARB 03	Arbitration bus priority level bit 3
A29	ARB/-GNT	High=arbitration in process, lo=channel awarded
A30	-TC	Terminal count
A31	+5Vdc	
A32	-SO	Status bit 0
A33	-S1	Status bit 1
A34	M/-IO	Memory/input output
A35	+12Vdc	
A36	CD CHRDY	Channel ready
A37	D00	Data bit 0
A38	D02	Data bit 2
A39	+5Vdc	
A40	D05	Data bit 5
A41	D06	Data bit 6
A42	D07	Data bit 7
A43	Ground	
A44	-DS 16 RTN	Data size 16 return
A45	-REFRESH	Memory refresh in progress when active
A46	KEY	
A47	KEY	
A48	+5Vdc	
A49	D10	Data bit 10
A50	D11	Data bit 11
A51	D13	Data bit 13
A52	+12Vdc	
A53	RESERVED	
A54	-SBHE	System byte high enable
A55	-CD DS 16	Card data size 16
A56	+5Vdc	
A57	-IRQ 14	Interrupt request 14
A58	-IRQ 15	Interrupt request 15
B1	AUDIO GND	
B2	AUDIO	Audio sum node (2.5v peak to peak)
B3	Ground	
B4	14.3 MHz Osc	Clock signal
B5	Ground	
B6	A23	Address bit 23
B7	A22	Address bit 22
B8	A21	Address bit 21
B9	Ground	
B10	A20	Address bit 20
B11	A19	Address bit 19
B12	A18	Address bit 18
B13	Ground	
B14	A17	Address bit 17
B15	A16	Address bit 16

(Continued)

8.57. PS/2 MODEL 50/60/80 MICROCHANNEL BUS PINOUTS (continued)

58-Pin, 50-Mil Edge Connector

Pin Number	*Signal*	*Description*
B16	A15	Address bit 15
B17	Ground	
B18	A14	Address bit 14
B19	A13	Address bit 13
B20	A12	Address bit 12
B21	Ground	
B22	-IRQ 9	Interrupt request 9
B23	-IRQ 3	Interrupt request 3
B24	-IRQ 4	Interrupt request 4
B25	Ground	
B26	-IRQ 5	Interrupt request 5
B27	-IRQ 6	Interrupt request 6
B28	-IRQ 7	Interrupt request 7
B29	Ground	
B30	RESERVED	
B31	RESERVED	
B32	-CHCK	Channel check
B33	Ground	
B34	-CMD	Command (data is valid on bus)
B35	CHRDYRTN	Channel ready return
B36	-CD SFDBK	Card selected feedback
B37	Ground	
B38	D1	Data bit 1
B39	D3	Data bit 3
B40	D4	Data bit 4
B41	Ground	
B42	CHRESET	Channel reset (init all adapters)
B43	RESERVED	
B44	RESERVED	
B45	Ground	
B46	Key	
B47	Key	
B48	D8	Data bit 8
B49	D9	Data bit 9
B50	Ground	
B51	D12	Data bit 12
B52	D14	Data bit 14
B53	D15	Data bit 15
B54	Ground	
B55	-IRQ 10	Interrupt request 10
B56	-IRQ 11	Interrupt request 11
B57	-IRQ 12	Interrupt request 12
B58	Ground	

Video Extension

Pin Number	*Signal*	*Description*
VA10	VSYNC	Vertical sync
VA9	HSYNC	Horizontal sync
VA8	BLANK	Blank input of video DAC
VA7	Ground	
VA6	P6	PEL input 6 to video DAC
VA5	EDCLK	Output enable for DCLK buffer
VA4	DCLK	Video PEL clock
VA3	Ground	
VA2	P7	PEL input 7 to video DAC
VA1	EVIDEO	Enable output (P0-P7)
KEY		
VB10	ESYNC	Enable VSYNC, HSYNC, BLANK
VB9	Ground	
VB8	P5	PEL input 5 to video DAC
VB7	P4	PEL input 4 to video DAC
VB6	P3	PEL input 3 to video DAC
VB5	Ground	
VB4	P2	PEL input 2 to video DAC
VB3	P1	PEL input 1 to video DAC
VB2	P0	PEL input 0 to video DAC
VB1	Ground	
KEY		

Note: Pin numbers Ax and VAx are on the component side; Bx and VBx are on the noncomponent side.

Source: IBM PS/2 Model 50 and 60 Technical Reference, pages 2-5 through 2-17
IBM PS/2 Model 80 Technical Reference, pages 2-6 through 2-25

See Also: 8.54. PC and XT I/O Channel (System Bus) Pinouts
8.55. AT I/O Channel (System Bus) Pinouts

8.58. 8088 AND 8086 PINOUTS

40-Pin DIP Packaging

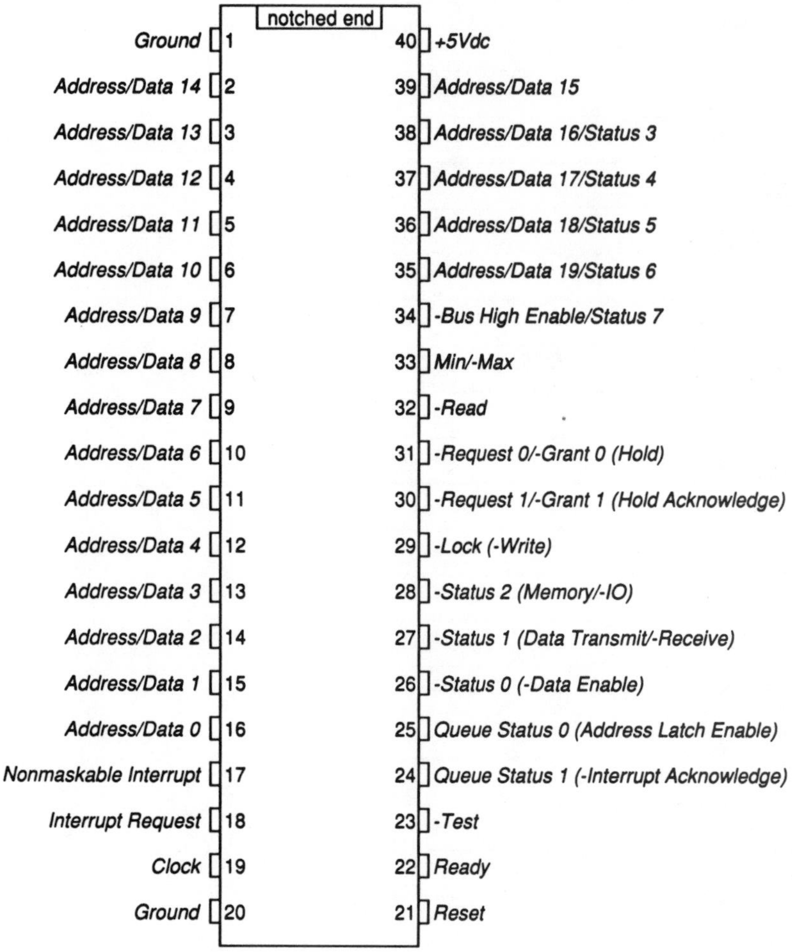
notched end
Ground 1
Address/Data 14 2
Address/Data 13 3
Address/Data 12 4
Address/Data 11 5
Address/Data 10 6
Address/Data 9 7
Address/Data 8 8
Address/Data 7 9
Address/Data 6 10
Address/Data 5 11
Address/Data 4 12
Address/Data 3 13
Address/Data 2 14
Address/Data 1 15
Address/Data 0 16
Nonmaskable Interrupt 17
Interrupt Request 18
Clock 19
Ground 20
40 +5Vdc
39 Address/Data 15
38 Address/Data 16/Status 3
37 Address/Data 17/Status 4
36 Address/Data 18/Status 5
35 Address/Data 19/Status 6
34 -Bus High Enable/Status 7
33 Min/-Max
32 -Read
31 -Request 0/-Grant 0 (Hold)
30 -Request 1/-Grant 1 (Hold Acknowledge)
29 -Lock (-Write)
28 -Status 2 (Memory/-IO)
27 -Status 1 (Data Transmit/-Receive)
26 -Status 0 (-Data Enable)
25 Queue Status 0 (Address Latch Enable)
24 Queue Status 1 (-Interrupt Acknowledge)
23 -Test
22 Ready
21 Reset

(Continued)

8.58. 8088 AND 8086 PINOUTS (continued)

80C86AL
44-Pin PLCC Packaging

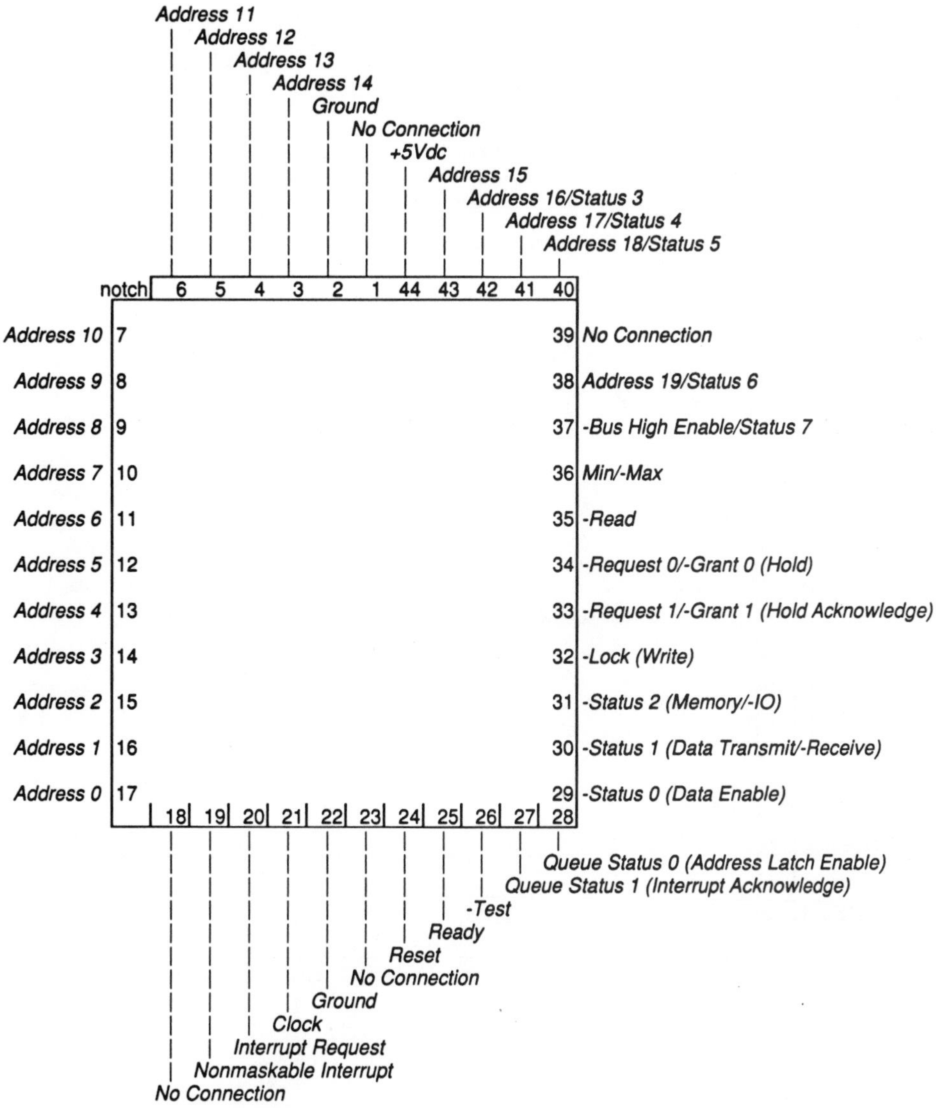
Address 11
Address 12
Address 13
Address 14
Ground
No Connection
+5Vdc
Address 15
Address 16/Status 3
Address 17/Status 4
Address 18/Status 5
notch
6 5 4 3 2 1 44 43 42 41 40
Address 10 7
Address 9 8
Address 8 9
Address 7 10
Address 6 11
Address 5 12
Address 4 13
Address 3 14
Address 2 15
Address 1 16
Address 0 17
39 No Connection
38 Address 19/Status 6
37 -Bus High Enable/Status 7
36 Min/-Max
35 -Read
34 -Request 0/-Grant 0 (Hold)
33 -Request 1/-Grant 1 (Hold Acknowledge)
32 -Lock (Write)
31 -Status 2 (Memory/-IO)
30 -Status 1 (Data Transmit/-Receive)
29 -Status 0 (Data Enable)
18 19 20 21 22 23 24 25 26 27 28
Queue Status 0 (Address Latch Enable)
Queue Status 1 (Interrupt Acknowledge)
-Test
Ready
Reset
No Connection
Ground
Clock
Interrupt Request
Nonmaskable Interrupt
No Connection

Version: 80C86AL information is included only in the 1989 edition of Intel Microprocessors (page 2-60).

Note: Items in parentheses refer to function when chip is in Minimum mode (pin 33 held high).

Source: Intel Microprocessors, Vol. 1, pages 2-1 through 2-5, 2-31, 2-60, and 2-90

See Also: 8.59. 80286 Pinouts
8.60. 80386 Pinouts

8.59. 80286 PINOUTS

68-Pin LCC Packaging

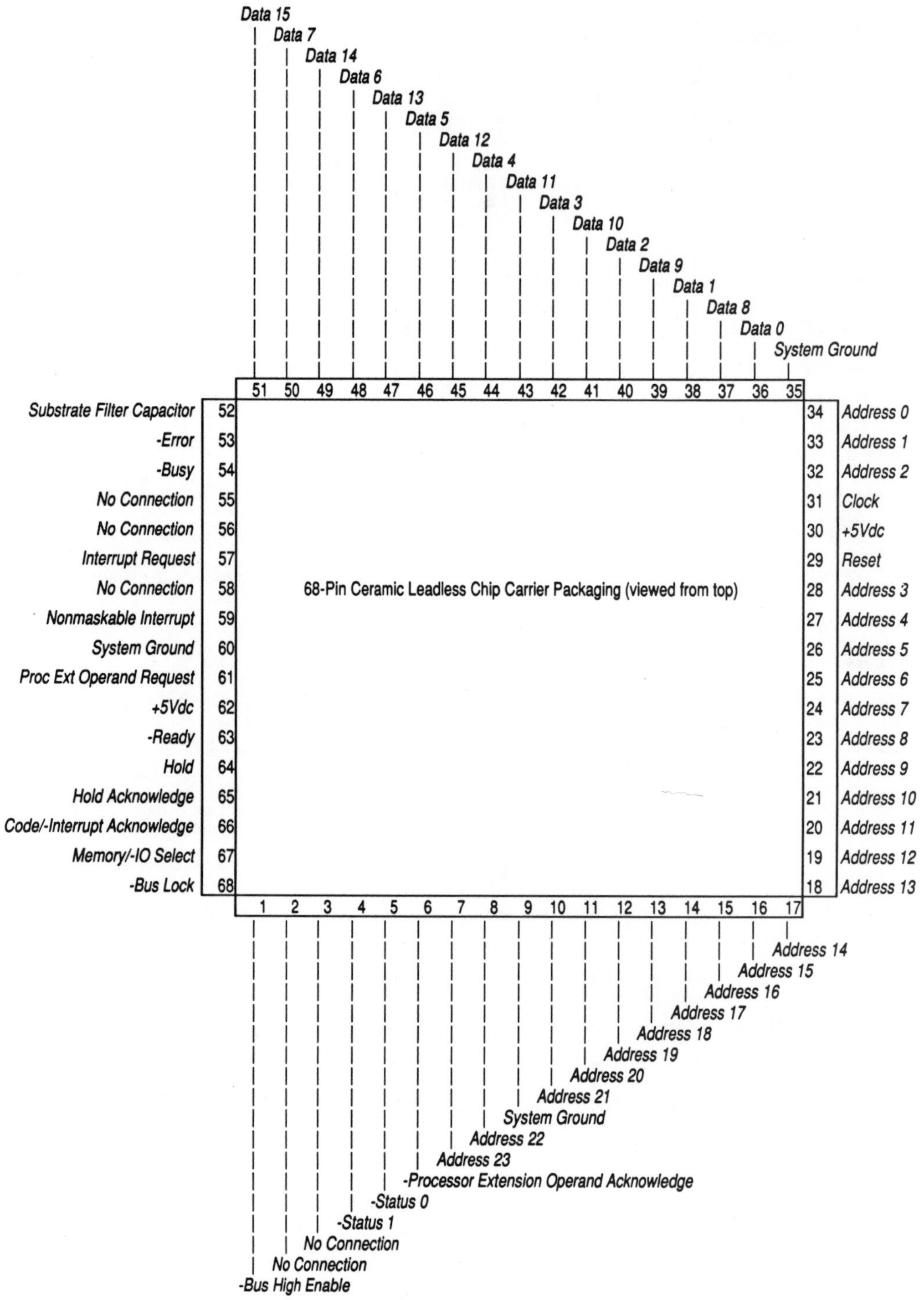
Data 15
Data 7
Data 14
Data 6
Data 13
Data 5
Data 12
Data 4
Data 11
Data 3
Data 10
Data 2
Data 9
Data 1
Data 8
Data 0
System Ground
51 50 49 48 47 46 45 44 43 42 41 40 39 38 37 36 35
Substrate Filter Capacitor 52
-Error 53
-Busy 54
No Connection 55
No Connection 56
Interrupt Request 57
No Connection 58
Nonmaskable Interrupt 59
System Ground 60
Proc Ext Operand Request 61
+5Vdc 62
-Ready 63
Hold 64
Hold Acknowledge 65
Code/-Interrupt Acknowledge 66
Memory/-IO Select 67
-Bus Lock 68
34 Address 0
33 Address 1
32 Address 2
31 Clock
30 +5Vdc
29 Reset
28 Address 3
27 Address 4
26 Address 5
25 Address 6
24 Address 7
23 Address 8
22 Address 9
21 Address 10
20 Address 11
19 Address 12
18 Address 13
68-Pin Ceramic Leadless Chip Carrier Packaging (viewed from top)
1 2 3 4 5 6 7 8 9 10 11 12 13 14 15 16 17
Address 14
Address 15
Address 16
Address 17
Address 18
Address 19
Address 20
Address 21
System Ground
Address 22
Address 23
-Processor Extension Operand Acknowledge
-Status 0
-Status 1
No Connection
No Connection
-Bus High Enable

(Continued)

8.59. 80286 PINOUTS (continued)

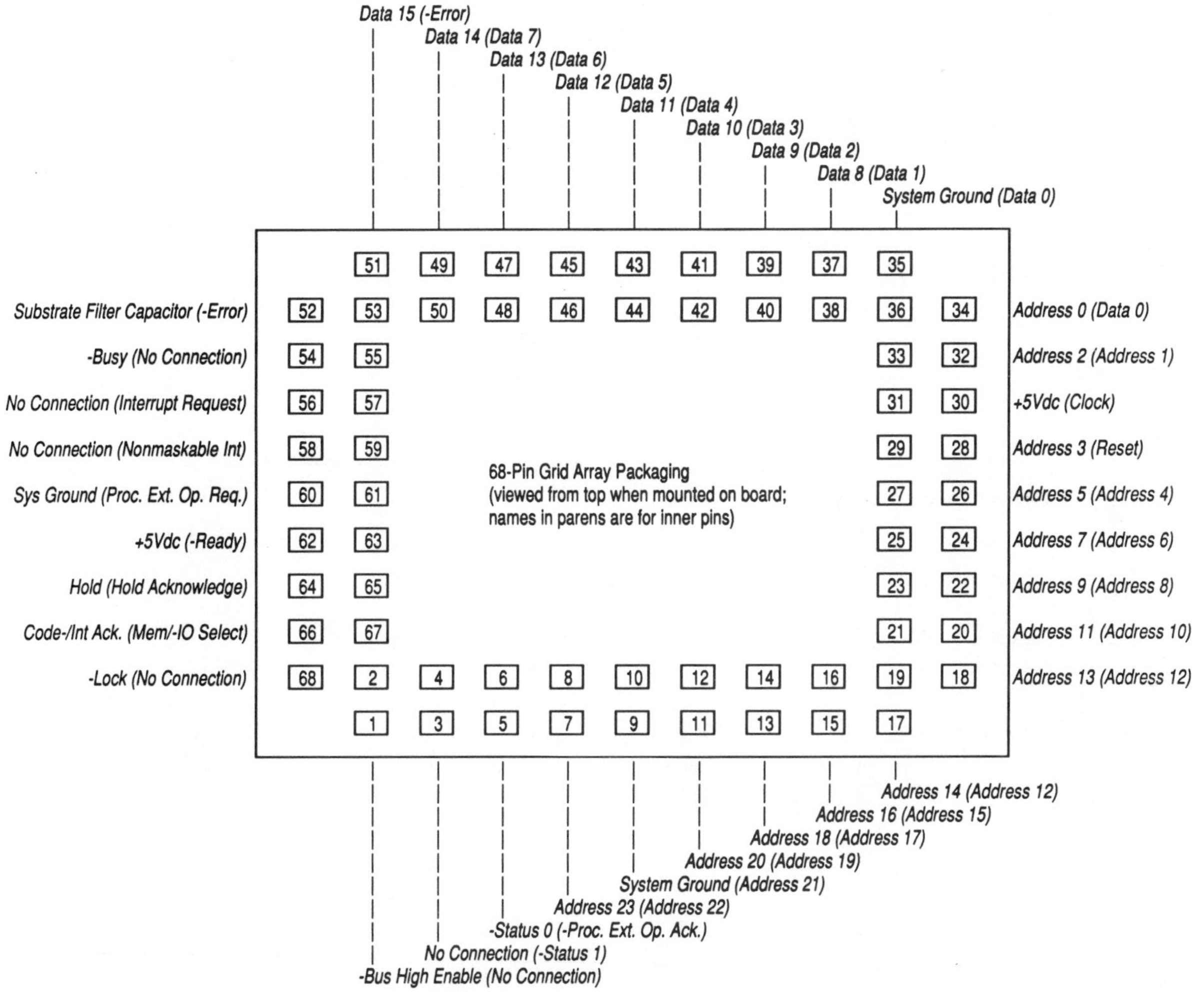
Data 15 (-Error)
Data 14 (Data 7)
Data 13 (Data 6)
Data 12 (Data 5)
Data 11 (Data 4)
Data 10 (Data 3)
Data 9 (Data 2)
Data 8 (Data 1)
System Ground (Data 0)
51 49 47 45 43 41 39 37 35
Substrate Filter Capacitor (-Error)
52 53 50 48 46 44 42 40 38 36 34
Address 0 (Data 0)
-Busy (No Connection)
54 55 33 32
Address 2 (Address 1)
No Connection (Interrupt Request)
56 57 31 30
+5Vdc (Clock)
No Connection (Nonmaskable Int)
58 59 29 28
Address 3 (Reset)
68-Pin Grid Array Packaging
(viewed from top when mounted on board;
names in parens are for inner pins)
Sys Ground (Proc. Ext. Op. Req.)
60 61 27 26
Address 5 (Address 4)
+5Vdc (-Ready)
62 63 25 24
Address 7 (Address 6)
Hold (Hold Acknowledge)
64 65 23 22
Address 9 (Address 8)
Code-/Int Ack. (Mem/-IO Select)
66 67 21 20
Address 11 (Address 10)
-Lock (No Connection)
68 2 4 6 8 10 12 14 16 19 18
Address 13 (Address 12)
1 3 5 7 9 11 13 15 17
Address 14 (Address 12)
Address 16 (Address 15)
Address 18 (Address 17)
Address 20 (Address 19)
System Ground (Address 21)
Address 23 (Address 22)
-Status 0 (-Proc. Ext. Op. Ack.)
No Connection (-Status 1)
-Bus High Enable (No Connection)

Note: Items in parentheses refer to inner pin connections on PGA packaging.

Source: Intel Microprocessors, Vol. 1, pages 3-2 through 3-4

See Also: 8.51. 8088 and 8086 Pinouts
8.53. 80386 Pinouts

8.60. 80386 PINOUTS

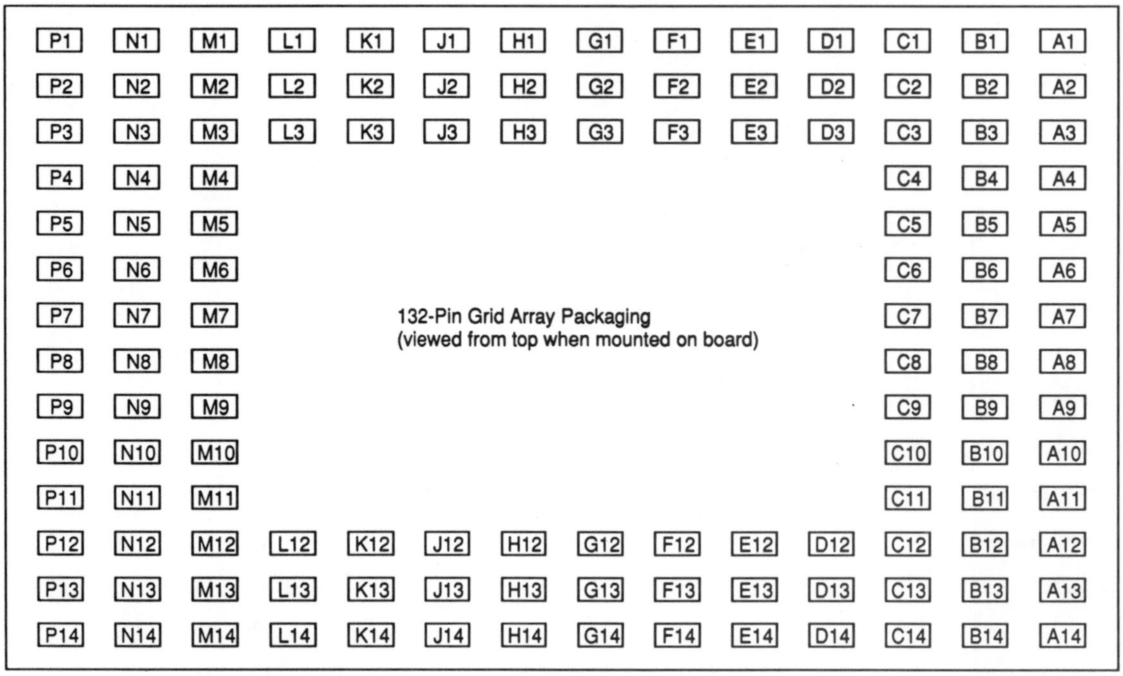
P1 N1 M1 L1 K1 J1 H1 G1 F1 E1 D1 C1 B1 A1
P2 N2 M2 L2 K2 J2 H2 G2 F2 E2 D2 C2 B2 A2
P3 N3 M3 L3 K3 J3 H3 G3 F3 E3 D3 C3 B3 A3
P4 N4 M4 C4 B4 A4
P5 N5 M5 C5 B5 A5
P6 N6 M6 C6 B6 A6
P7 N7 M7 C7 B7 A7
P8 N8 M8 C8 B8 A8
P9 N9 M9 C9 B9 A9
P10 N10 M10 C10 B10 A10
P11 N11 M11 C11 B11 A11
P12 N12 M12 L12 K12 J12 H12 G12 F12 E12 D12 C12 B12 A12
P13 N13 M13 L13 K13 J13 H13 G13 F13 E13 D13 C13 B13 A13
P14 N14 M14 L14 K14 J14 H14 G14 F14 E14 D14 C14 B14 A14
132-Pin Grid Array Packaging
(viewed from top when mounted on board)

Pin	*Signal*
A1	+5Vdc
A2	Ground
A3	Address 3
A4	No connection
A5	+5Vdc
A6	Ground
A7	+5Vdc
A8	-Error
A9	Ground
A10	+5Vdc
A11	Data/-Control
A12	Mem/-IO
A13	-Byte Enable 3
A14	+5Vdc

Pin	*Signal*
C1	Address 8
C2	Address 7
C3	Address 6
C4	Address 2
C5	+5Vdc
C6	No connection
C7	No connection
C8	Proc. Ext. Req.
C9	Reset
C10	-Lock
C11	Ground
C12	+5Vdc
C13	-Byte Enable 1
C14	-Bus Size 16

Pin	*Signal*
F1	Address 15
F2	Ground
F3	Ground
F12	Clock 2
F13	No connection
F14	Ground

Pin	*Signal*
G1	Address 16
G2	+5Vdc
G3	+5Vdc
G12	+5Vdc
G13	-Ready
G14	+5Vdc

Pin	*Signal*
K1	Address 21
K2	Address 22
K3	Address 25
K12	Data 7
K13	Data 5
K14	Data 4

Pin	*Signal*
L1	Address 23
L2	Address 24
L3	Address 28
L12	+5Vdc
L13	Data 8
L14	Data 6

Pin	*Signal*
N1	Address 27
N2	Address 31
N3	Ground
N4	+5Vdc
N5	Data 27
N6	Data 25
N7	+5Vdc
N8	Data 23
N9	Data 21
N10	Data 17
N11	Data 16
N12	Data 12
N13	Data 11
N14	Data 9

Pin	*Signal*
B1	Ground
B2	Address 5
B3	Address 4
B4	No connection
B5	Ground
B6	No connection
B7	Int. Request
B8	Nonmask. Int.
B9	-Busy
B10	Write/-Read
B11	Ground
B12	No connection
B13	-Byte Enable 2
B14	Ground

Pin	*Signal*
D1	Address 11
D2	Address 10
D3	Address 9
D12	+5Vdc
D13	-Next Address
D14	Hold

Pin	*Signal*
E1	Address 14
E2	Address 13
E3	Address 12
E12	-Byte Enable 0
E13	No connection
E14	-Address Status

Pin	*Signal*
H1	Address 17
H2	Address 18
H3	Address 19
H12	Data 0
H13	Data 1
H14	Data 2

Pin	*Signal*
J1	Address 20
J2	Ground
J3	Ground
J12	Ground
J13	Ground
J14	Data 3

Pin	*Signal*
M1	Address 26
M2	Address 29
M3	+5Vdc
M4	Ground
M5	Data 31
M6	Data 28
M7	+5Vdc
M8	Ground
M9	Data 20
M10	Ground
M11	Data 15
M12	Data 10
M13	+5Vdc
M14	Hold Ack.

Pin	*Signal*
P1	Address 30
P2	+5Vdc
P3	Data 30
P4	Data 29
P5	Data 26
P6	Ground
P7	Data 24
P8	+5Vdc
P9	Data 22
P10	Data 19
P11	Data 18
P12	Data 14
P13	Data 13
P14	Ground

Source: Intel Microprocessors, Vol. 2, pages 5-290 through 5-292

See Also: 8.58. 8088 and 8086 Pinouts
8.59. 80286 Pinouts

8.61. 80386 SX PINOUTS

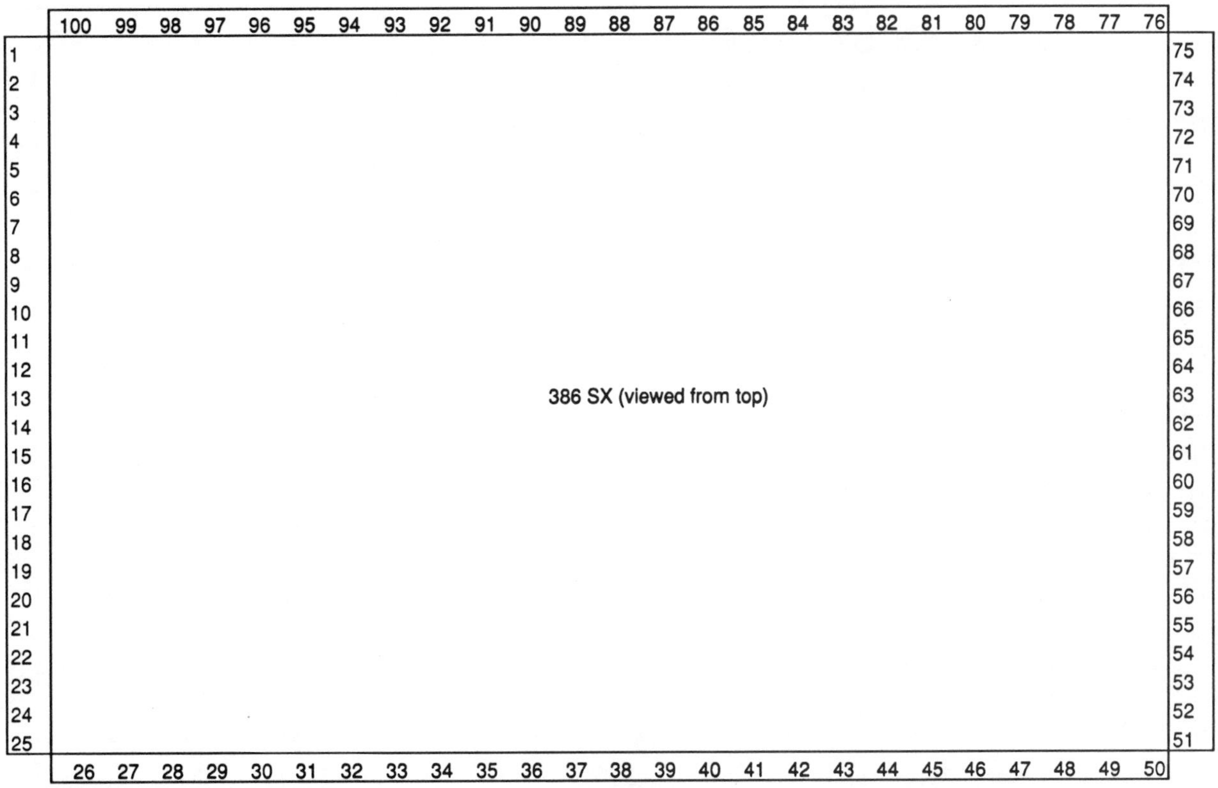
100 99 98 97 96 95 94 93 92 91 90 89 88 87 86 85 84 83 82 81 80 79 78 77 76
1 2 3 4 5 6 7 8 9 10 11 12 13 14 15 16 17 18 19 20 21 22 23 24 25
75 74 73 72 71 70 69 68 67 66 65 64 63 62 61 60 59 58 57 56 55 54 53 52 51
386 SX (viewed from top)
26 27 28 29 30 31 32 33 34 35 36 37 38 39 40 41 42 43 44 45 46 47 48 49 50

Pin	*Signal*	*Pin*	*Signal*	*Pin*	*Signal*	*Pin*	*Signal*
1	Data 0	26	Lock	51	Address 2	76	Address 21
2	Ground	27	No connection	52	Address 3	77	Ground
3	Hold ack.	28	-Float	53	Address 4	78	Ground
4	Hold req.	29	No connection	54	Address 5	79	Address 22
5	Ground	30	No connection	55	Address 6	80	Address 23
6	-Next address	31	No connection	56	Address 7	81	Data 15
7	-Bus ready	32	+5Vdc	57	+5Vdc	82	Data 14
8	+5Vdc	33	Reset	58	Address 8	83	Data 13
9	+5Vdc	34	-Busy	59	Address 9	84	+5Vdc
10	+5Vdc	35	Ground	60	Address 10	85	Ground
11	Ground	36	-Error	61	Address 11	86	Data 12
12	Ground	37	Proc. ext. req.	62	Address 12	87	Data 11
13	Ground	38	NMI req.	63	Ground	88	Data 10
14	Ground	39	+5Vdc	64	Address 13	89	Data 9
15	Clock 2	40	Interrupt req.	65	Address 14	90	Data 8
16	-Address status	41	Ground	66	Address 15	91	+5Vdc
17	-Byte enable	42	+5Vdc	67	Ground	92	Data 7
18	Address 1	43	No connection	68	Ground	93	Data 6
19	-Byte enable	44	No connection	69	+5Vdc	94	Data 5
20	No connection	45	No connection	70	Address 16	95	Data 4
21	+5Vdc	46	No connection	71	+5Vdc	96	Data 3
22	Ground	47	No connection	72	Address 17	97	+5Vdc
23	-Mem/IO	48	+5Vdc	73	Address 18	98	Ground
24	-Data/Control	49	Ground	74	Address 19	99	Data 2
25	-Write/Read	50	Ground	75	Address 20	100	Data 1

Source: Intel Microprocessors, Vol. 2, pages 5-866 through 5-868

8.62. i486 PINOUTS

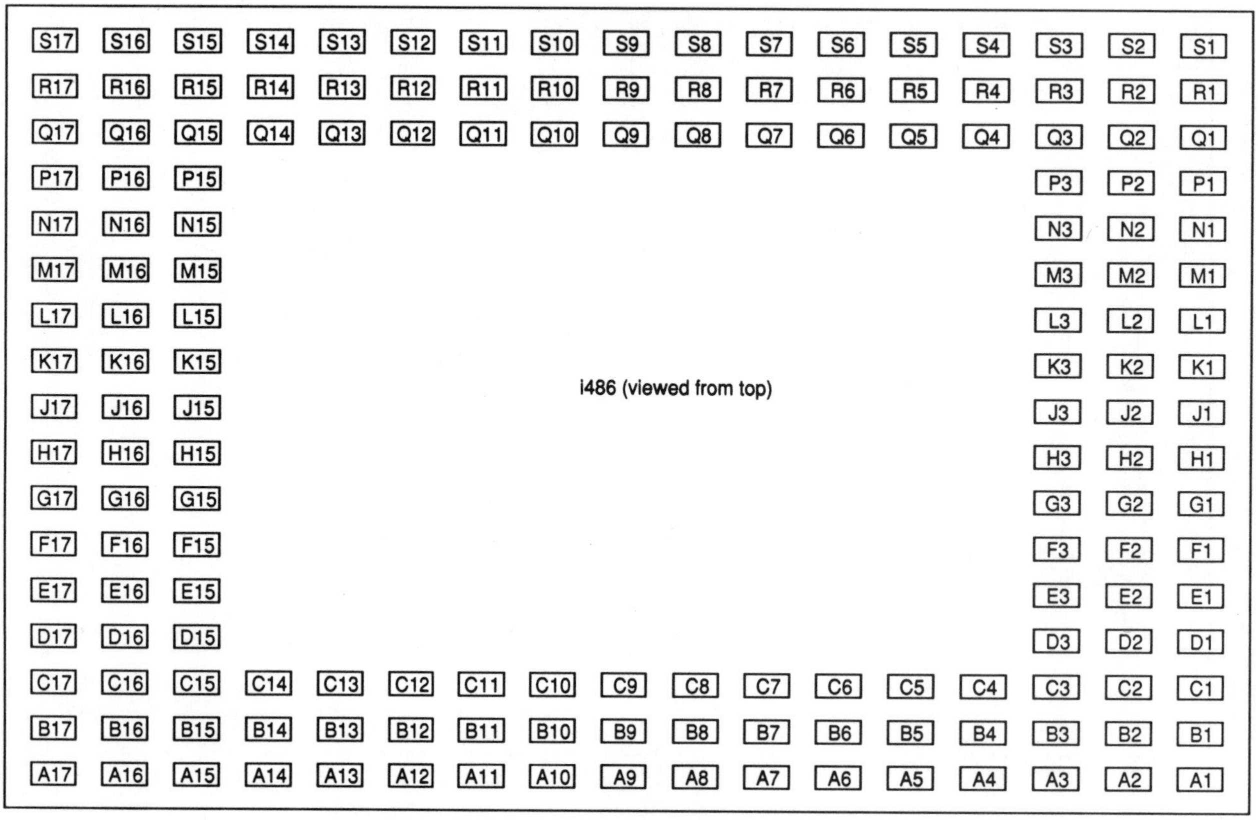
S17 S16 S15 S14 S13 S12 S11 S10 S9 S8 S7 S6 S5 S4 S3 S2 S1
R17 R16 R15 R14 R13 R12 R11 R10 R9 R8 R7 R6 R5 R4 R3 R2 R1
Q17 Q16 Q15 Q14 Q13 Q12 Q11 Q10 Q9 Q8 Q7 Q6 Q5 Q4 Q3 Q2 Q1
P17 P16 P15 P3 P2 P1
N17 N16 N15 N3 N2 N1
M17 M16 M15 M3 M2 M1
L17 L16 L15 L3 L2 L1
K17 K16 K15 K3 K2 K1
i486 (viewed from top)
J17 J16 J15 J3 J2 J1
H17 H16 H15 H3 H2 H1
G17 G16 G15 G3 G2 G1
F17 F16 F15 F3 F2 F1
E17 E16 E15 E3 E2 E1
D17 D16 D15 D3 D2 D1
C17 C16 C15 C14 C13 C12 C11 C10 C9 C8 C7 C6 C5 C4 C3 C2 C1
B17 B16 B15 B14 B13 B12 B11 B10 B9 B8 B7 B6 B5 B4 B3 B2 B1
A17 A16 A15 A14 A13 A12 A11 A10 A9 A8 A7 A6 A5 A4 A3 A2 A1

Pin	*Signal*
A1	Data 20
A2	Data 22
A3	No connection
A4	Data 23
A5	Data parity 3
A6	Data 24
A7	Ground
A8	Data 29
A9	Ground
A10	No connection
A11	Ground
A12	No connection
A13	No connection
A14	No connection
A15	-Ignore numeric error
A16	Interrupt
A17	Address hold

Pin	*Signal*
B1	Data 19
B2	Data 21
B3	Ground
B4	Ground
B5	Ground
B6	Data 25
B7	+5Vdc
B8	Data 31
B9	+5Vdc
B10	No connection
B11	+5Vdc
B12	No connection
B13	No connection
B14	No connection
B15	NMI
B16	No connection
B17	-External address

Pin	*Signal*
C1	Data 11
C2	Data 18
C3	Clock
C4	+5Vdc
C5	+5Vdc
C6	Data 27
C7	Data 26
C8	Data 28
C9	Data 30
C10	No connection
C11	No connection
C12	No connection
C13	No connection
C14	-Floating pt. error
C15	-Cache flush
C16	Reset
C17	-Bus Size 16

Pin	*Signal*
D1	Data 9
D2	Data 13
D3	Data 17
D15	-Address bit mask 20
D16	-Bus size 8
D17	-Back off

Pin	*Signal*
E1	Ground
E2	+5Vdc
E3	Data 10
E15	Bus hold request
E16	+5Vdc
E17	Ground

Pin	*Signal*
F1	Data parity 1
F2	Data 8
F3	Data 15
F15	-Cache enable
F16	-Nonburst ready
F17	-Byte enable 3

Pin	*Signal*
G1	Ground
G2	+5Vdc
G3	Data 12
G15	No connection
G16	+5Vdc
G17	Ground

Pin	*Signal*
H1	Ground
H2	Data 3
H3	Data parity 2
H15	-Bust ready
H16	+5Vdc
H17	Ground

Pin	*Signal*
J1	+5Vdc
J2	Data 5
J3	Data 6
J15	-Byte enable 2
J16	-Byte enable 1
J17	Page cache display

Pin	*Signal*
K1	Ground
K2	+5Vdc
K3	Data 14
K15	-Byte enable 0
K16	+5Vdc
K17	Ground

Pin	*Signal*
L1	Ground
L2	Data 6
L3	Data 7
L15	Page write through
L16	+5Vdc
L17	Ground

Pin	*Signal*
M1	Ground
M2	+5Vdc
M3	Data 4
M15	-Data/Control
M16	+5Vdc
M17	Ground

Pin	*Signal*
N1	Data 2
N2	Data 1
N3	Data parity 0
N15	-Bus lock
N16	-Mem/IO
N17	-Write/Read

(Continued)

8.62. I486 PINOUTS (continued)

Pin	*Signal*
P1	Data 0
P2	Address 29
P3	Address 30
P15	Hold ack.
P16	+5Vdc
P17	Ground

Pin	*Signal*
Q1	Address 31
Q2	Ground
Q3	Address 17
Q4	Address 19
Q5	Address 21
Q6	Address 24
Q7	Address 22
Q8	Address 20
Q9	Address 16
Q10	Address 13
Q11	Address 9
Q12	Address 5
Q13	Address 7
Q14	Address 2
Q15	Int. cycle pending
Q16	-Pseudo lock
Q17	-Parity status

Pin	*Signal*
R1	Address 28
R2	Address 25
R3	+5Vdc
R4	Ground
R5	Address 18
R6	+5Vdc
R7	Address 15
R8	+5Vdc
R9	+5Vdc
R10	+5Vdc
R11	+5Vdc
R12	Address 11
R13	Address 8
R14	+5Vdc
R15	Address 3
R16	-Burst last
R17	No connection

Pin	*Signal*
S1	Address 27
S2	Address 26
S3	Address 23
S4	No connection
S5	Address 14
S6	Ground
S7	Address 12
S8	Ground
S9	Ground
S10	Ground
S11	Ground
S12	Ground
S13	Address 10
S14	Ground
S15	Address 6
S16	Address 4
S17	-Address status

Source: Intel Microprocessors, Vol. 2, pages 5-7 through 5-30

8.63. 8087 (COPROCESSOR) PINOUTS

40-Pin DIP Packaging

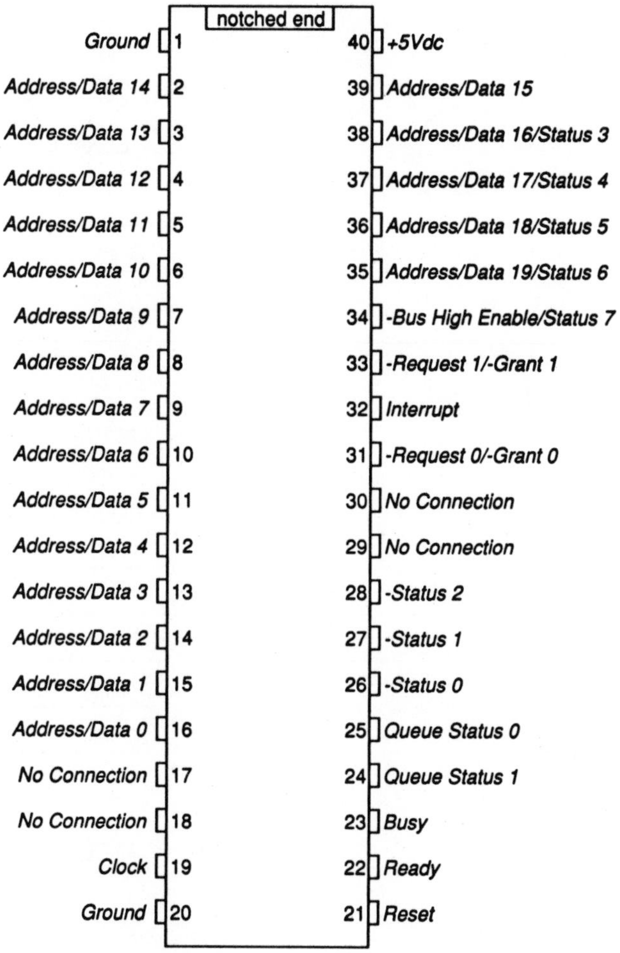
notched end
Ground 1
Address/Data 14 2
Address/Data 13 3
Address/Data 12 4
Address/Data 11 5
Address/Data 10 6
Address/Data 9 7
Address/Data 8 8
Address/Data 7 9
Address/Data 6 10
Address/Data 5 11
Address/Data 4 12
Address/Data 3 13
Address/Data 2 14
Address/Data 1 15
Address/Data 0 16
No Connection 17
No Connection 18
Clock 19
Ground 20
40 +5Vdc
39 Address/Data 15
38 Address/Data 16/Status 3
37 Address/Data 17/Status 4
36 Address/Data 18/Status 5
35 Address/Data 19/Status 6
34 -Bus High Enable/Status 7
33 -Request 1/-Grant 1
32 Interrupt
31 -Request 0/-Grant 0
30 No Connection
29 No Connection
28 -Status 2
27 -Status 1
26 -Status 0
25 Queue Status 0
24 Queue Status 1
23 Busy
22 Ready
21 Reset

Source: Intel Microprocessors, Vol. 1, pages 2-122 through 2-124

See Also: 8.64. 80287 (Coprocessor) Pinouts
8.65. 80387 (Coprocessor) Pinouts

8.64. 80287 (COPROCESSOR) PINOUTS

40-Pin DIP Packaging

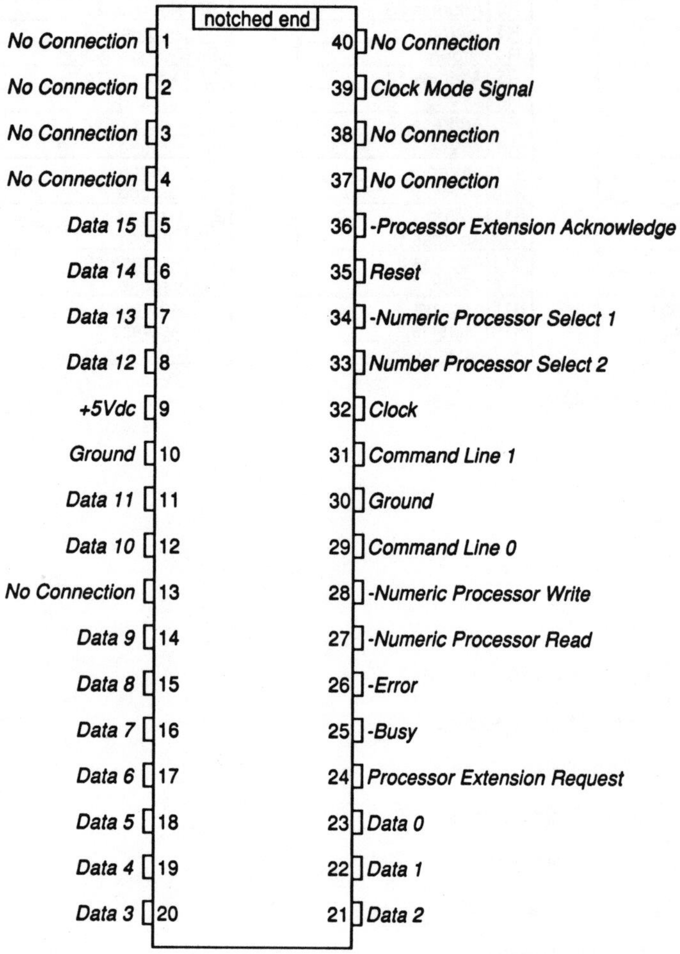
notched end
No Connection 1
No Connection 2
No Connection 3
No Connection 4
Data 15 5
Data 14 6
Data 13 7
Data 12 8
+5Vdc 9
Ground 10
Data 11 11
Data 10 12
No Connection 13
Data 9 14
Data 8 15
Data 7 16
Data 6 17
Data 5 18
Data 4 19
Data 3 20
40 No Connection
39 Clock Mode Signal
38 No Connection
37 No Connection
36 -Processor Extension Acknowledge
35 Reset
34 -Numeric Processor Select 1
33 Number Processor Select 2
32 Clock
31 Command Line 1
30 Ground
29 Command Line 0
28 -Numeric Processor Write
27 -Numeric Processor Read
26 -Error
25 -Busy
24 Processor Extension Request
23 Data 0
22 Data 1
21 Data 2

(Continued)

8.64. 80287 (COPROCESSOR) PINOUTS (continued)

44-Pin PLCC Packaging

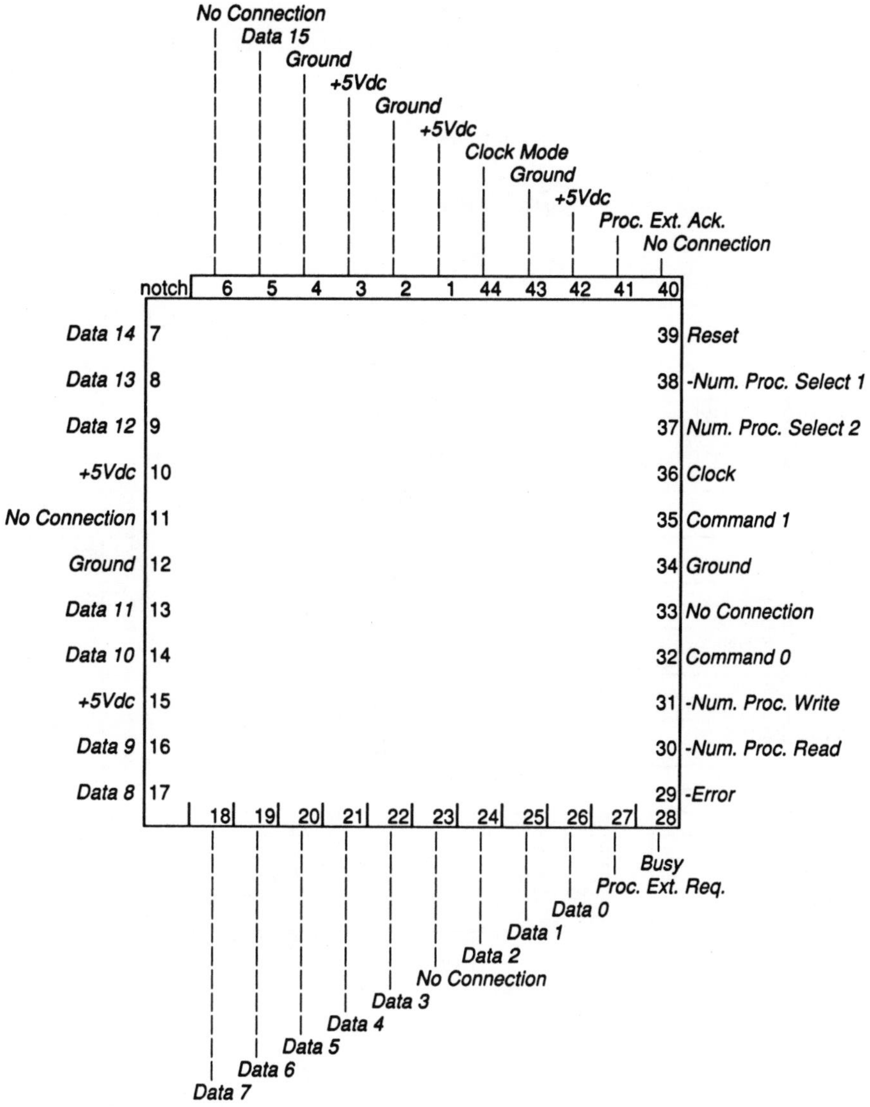
No Connection
Data 15
Ground
+5Vdc
Ground
+5Vdc
Clock Mode
Ground
+5Vdc
Proc. Ext. Ack.
No Connection
notch
6
5
4
3
2
1
44
43
42
41
40
Data 14 7
Data 13 8
Data 12 9
+5Vdc 10
No Connection 11
Ground 12
Data 11 13
Data 10 14
+5Vdc 15
Data 9 16
Data 8 17
39 Reset
38 -Num. Proc. Select 1
37 Num. Proc. Select 2
36 Clock
35 Command 1
34 Ground
33 No Connection
32 Command 0
31 -Num. Proc. Write
30 -Num. Proc. Read
29 -Error
18
19
20
21
22
23
24
25
26
27
28
Busy
Proc. Ext. Req.
Data 0
Data 1
Data 2
No Connection
Data 3
Data 4
Data 5
Data 6
Data 7

Source: Intel Microprocessors, Vol. 1, pages 3-130 through 3-131

See Also: 8.63. 8087 (Coprocessor) Pinouts
8.65. 80387 (Coprocessor) Pinouts

8.65. 80387 (COPROCESSOR) PINOUTS

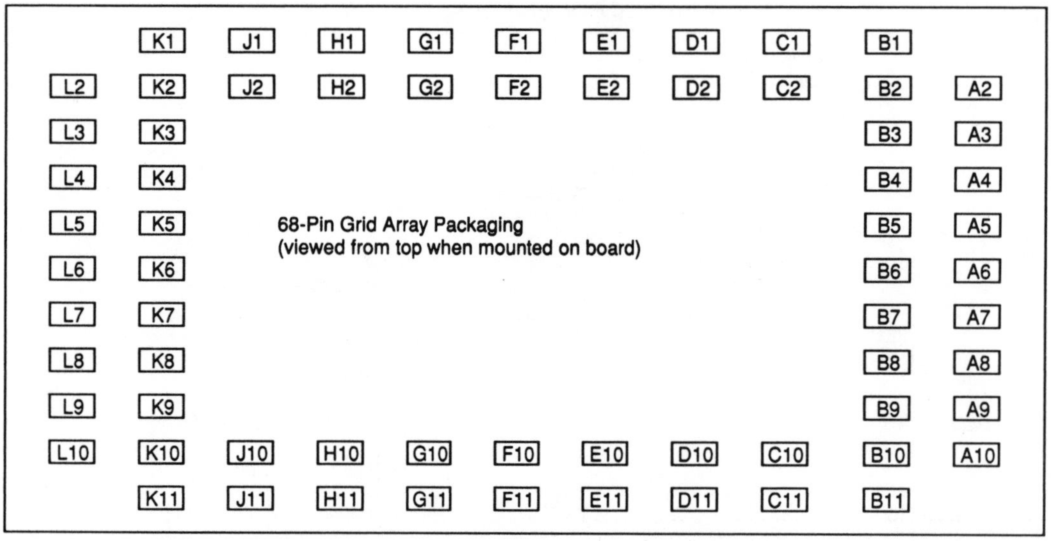
K1 J1 H1 G1 F1 E1 D1 C1 B1
L2 K2 J2 H2 G2 F2 E2 D2 C2 B2 A2
L3 K3 B3 A3
L4 K4 B4 A4
L5 K5 B5 A5
68-Pin Grid Array Packaging
(viewed from top when mounted on board)
L6 K6 B6 A6
L7 K7 B7 A7
L8 K8 B8 A8
L9 K9 B9 A9
L10 K10 J10 H10 G10 F10 E10 D10 C10 B10 A10
K11 J11 H11 G11 F11 E11 D11 C11 B11

Pin	*Signal*
A1	No Pin
A2	Data 9
A3	Data 11
A4	Data 12
A5	Data 14
A6	+5Vdc
A7	Data 16
A8	Data 18
A9	+5Vdc
A10	Data 21
A11	No Pin

Pin	*Signal*
B1	Data 8
B2	Ground
B3	Data 10
B4	+5Vdc
B5	Data 13
B6	Data 15
B7	Ground
B8	Data 17
B9	Data 19
B10	Data 20
B11	Data 22

Pin	*Signal*
C1	Data 7
C2	Data 6
C10	Data 23
C11	Ground

Pin	*Signal*
D1	Data 5
D2	Data 4
D10	Data 24
D11	Data 25

Pin	*Signal*
E1	+5Vdc
E2	Ground
E10	Data 26
E11	Data 27

Pin	*Signal*
F1	+5Vdc
F2	Ground
F10	+5Vdc
F11	Ground

Pin	*Signal*
G1	Data 3
G2	Data 2
G10	Data 28
G11	Data 29

Pin	*Signal*
H1	Data 1
H2	Data 0
H10	Data 30
H11	Data 31

Pin	*Signal*
J1	Ground
J2	+5Vdc
J10	Ground
J11	Clock Mode

Pin	*Signal*
K1	Proc. Ext. Req.
K2	-Busy
K3	TIE HIGH
K4	Write/Read
K5	+5Vdc
K6	NPS2
K7	-ADS
K8	-Ready
K9	No Connection
K10	386 Clock 2
K11	387 Clock 2

Pin	*Signal*
L1	No Pin
L2	-Error
L3	-Ready Out
L4	Status Enable
L5	Ground
L6	-NPS1
L7	+5Vdc
L8	-CMD0
L9	TIE HIGH
L10	Reset
L11	No Pin

Source: Intel Microprocessors, Vol. 2, pages 5-442 through 5-443

See Also: 8.63. 8087 (Coprocessor) Pinouts
8.64. 80287 (Coprocessor) Pinouts

8.66. 80387 SX (COPROCESSOR) PINOUTS

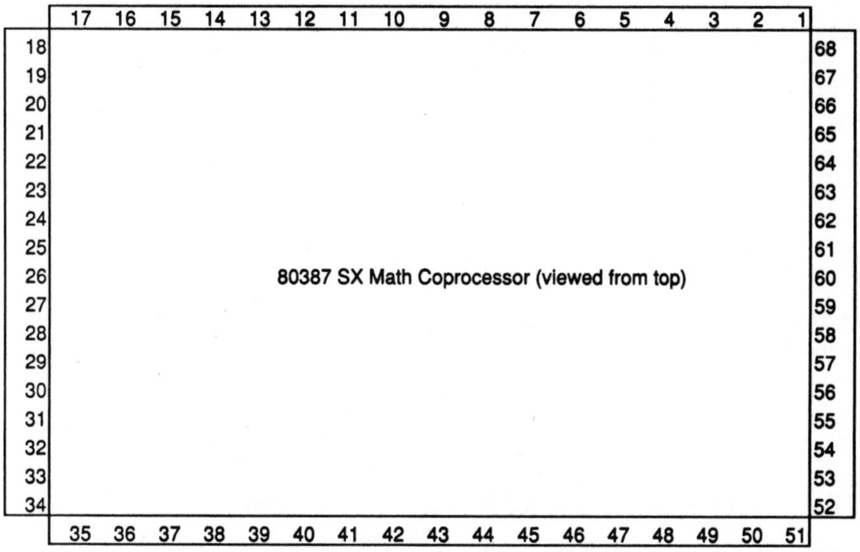
17 16 15 14 13 12 11 10 9 8 7 6 5 4 3 2 1
18 19 20 21 22 23 24 25 26 27 28 29 30 31 32 33 34
80387 SX Math Coprocessor (viewed from top)
68 67 66 65 64 63 62 61 60 59 58 57 56 55 54 53 52
35 36 37 38 39 40 41 42 43 44 45 46 47 48 49 50 51

Pin	*Signal*
1	No connection
2	Data 7
3	Data 6
4	+5Vdc
5	Ground
6	Data 5
7	Data 4
8	Data 3
9	+5Vdc
10	No connection
11	Data 15
12	Data 14
13	+5Vdc
14	Ground
15	Data 13
16	Data 12
17	No connection

Pin	*Signal*
18	No connection
19	Data 0
20	Data 1
21	Ground
22	+5Vdc
23	Data 2
24	Data 8
25	Ground
26	+5Vdc
27	Ground
28	Data 9
29	Data 10
30	Data 11
31	+5Vdc
32	Ground
33	+5Vdc
34	Ground

Pin	*Signal*
35	-Error
36	-Busy
37	+5Vdc
38	Ground
39	+5Vdc
40	Status enable
41	-Write/Read
42	Ground
43	+5Vdc
44	-NPX select 1
45	NPX select 2
46	+5Vdc
47	-Address strobe
48	-Command 0
49	-Bus ready
50	+5Vdc
51	Reset

Pin	*Signal*
52	No connection
53	387 SX clock 2
54	386 SX clock 2
55	Ground
56	Proc. ext. req.
57	-Ready output
58	+5Vdc
59	Clock mode
60	Ground
61	Ground
62	+5Vdc
63	Ground
64	+5Vdc
65	No connection
66	Ground
67	No connection
68	No connection

Source: Intel Microprocessors, Vol. 2, page 5-988

8.67. WEITEK 3167 (COPROCESSOR) PINOUTS

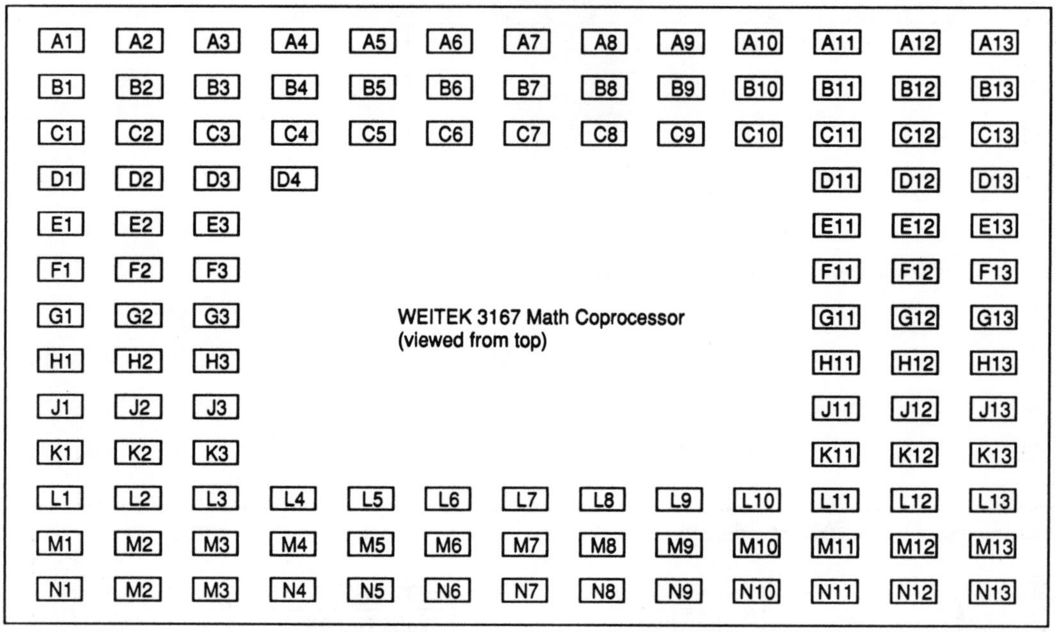
A1 A2 A3 A4 A5 A6 A7 A8 A9 A10 A11 A12 A13
B1 B2 B3 B4 B5 B6 B7 B8 B9 B10 B11 B12 B13
C1 C2 C3 C4 C5 C6 C7 C8 C9 C10 C11 C12 C13
D1 D2 D3 D4 D11 D12 D13
E1 E2 E3 E11 E12 E13
F1 F2 F3 F11 F12 F13
G1 G2 G3 G11 G12 G13
WEITEK 3167 Math Coprocessor
(viewed from top)
H1 H2 H3 H11 H12 H13
J1 J2 J3 J11 J12 J13
K1 K2 K3 K11 K12 K13
L1 L2 L3 L4 L5 L6 L7 L8 L9 L10 L11 L12 L13
M1 M2 M3 M4 M5 M6 M7 M8 M9 M10 M11 M12 M13
N1 M2 M3 N4 N5 N6 N7 N8 N9 N10 N11 N12 N13

Pin	*Signal*
A1	Ground
A2	Address 13
A3	Address 12
A4	Address 11
A5	Ground
A6	Address 10
A7	No connection
A8	Address 9
A9	Address 8
A10	Ground
A11	Address 7
A12	Address 6
A13	Address 5

Pin	*Signal*
B1	Address 15
B2	Address 14
B3	Data 9
B4	Data 11
B5	Data 12
B6	Data 14
B7	+5Vdc
B8	Data 16
B9	Data 18
B10	+5Vdc
B11	Data 21
B12	Address 4
B13	Address 3

Pin	*Signal*
C1	+5Vdc
C2	Data 8
C3	Ground
C4	Data 10
C5	+5Vdc
C6	Data 13
C7	Data 15
C8	Ground
C9	Data 17
C10	Data 19
C11	Data 20
C12	Data 22
C13	Address 2

Pin	*Signal*
D1	No connection
D2	Data 7
D3	Data 6
D4	No connection
D11	Data 23
D12	Ground
D13	+5Vdc

Pin	*Signal*
E1	No connection
E2	Data 5
E3	Data 4
E11	Data 24
E12	Data 25
E13	No connection

Pin	*Signal*
F1	Address 24
F2	+5Vdc
F3	Ground
F11	Data 26
F12	Data 27
F13	No connection

Pin	*Signal*
G1	Address 25
G2	+5Vdc
G3	Ground
G11	+5Vdc
G12	Ground
G13	-Byte enable 0

Pin	*Signal*
H1	Address 26
H2	Data 3
H3	Data 2
H11	Data 28
H12	Data 29
H13	-Byte enable 1

Pin	*Signal*
J1	Address 27
J2	Data 1
J3	Data 0
J11	Data 30
J12	Data 31
J13	-Byte enable 2

Pin	*Signal*
K1	+5Vdc
K2	Ground
K3	+5Vdc
K11	Ground
K12	Clocking mode
K13	No connection

Pin	*Signal*
L1	Address 28
L2	Proc. ext. req.
L3	-Busy
L4	Tie high
L5	-Write/Read
L6	+5Vdc
L7	Address 31
L8	-Address status
L9	-Ready input
L10	No connection
L11	Clock (WTL 3167)
L12	Clock (387)
L13	+5Vdc

Pin	*Signal*
M1	Address 29
M2	Interrupt
M3	-Error
M4	-Ready output
M5	Status enable
M6	Ground
M7	-Mem/IO
M8	+5Vdc
M9	-Command 0
M10	Tie high
M11	Reset
M12	WTL 3167 present
M13	No connection

Pin	*Signal*
N1	Address 30
N2	-AF32
N3	+5Vdc
N4	Ground
N5	-Ready input
N6	-Three cycle bus
N7	-Math copro. select
N8	Ground
N9	No connection
N10	+5Vdc
N11	No connection
N12	No connection
N13	Ground

Source: WEITEK 3167 Floating-Point Coprocessor, pages 4 through 7

8.68. WEITEK 4167 (COPROCESSOR) PINOUTS

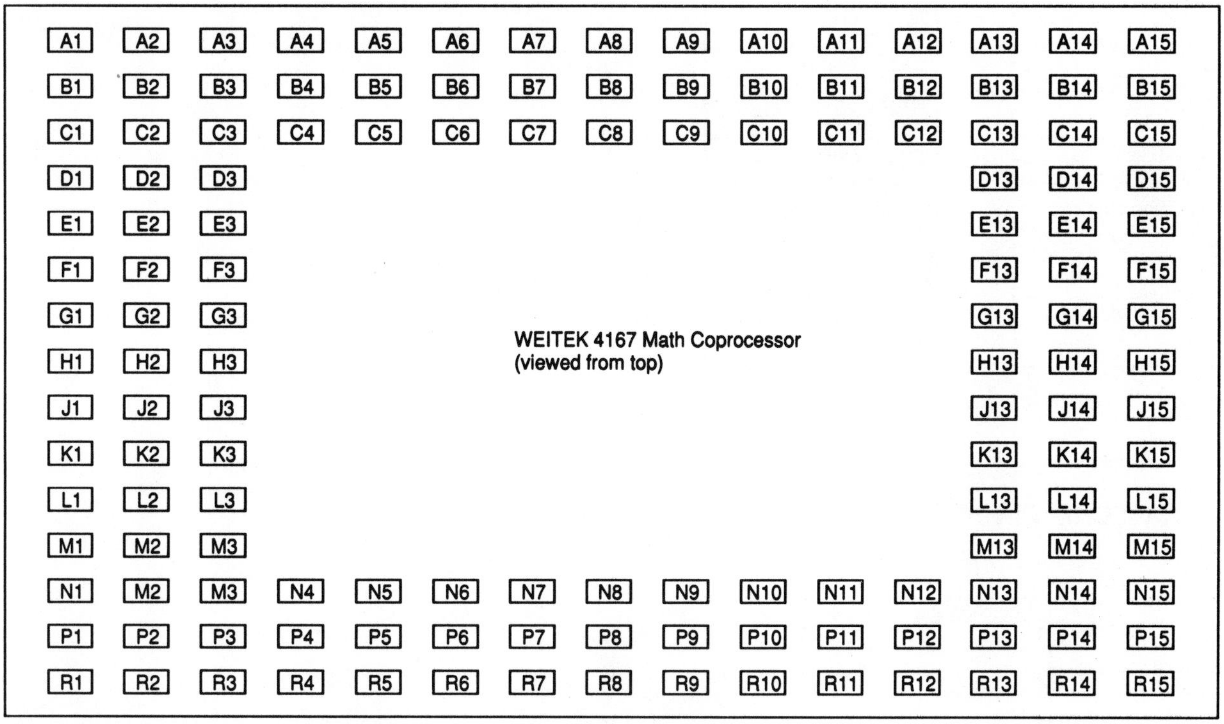
A1 A2 A3 A4 A5 A6 A7 A8 A9 A10 A11 A12 A13 A14 A15
B1 B2 B3 B4 B5 B6 B7 B8 B9 B10 B11 B12 B13 B14 B15
C1 C2 C3 C4 C5 C6 C7 C8 C9 C10 C11 C12 C13 C14 C15
D1 D2 D3 D13 D14 D15
E1 E2 E3 E13 E14 E15
F1 F2 F3 F13 F14 F15
G1 G2 G3 G13 G14 G15
WEITEK 4167 Math Coprocessor
(viewed from top)
H1 H2 H3 H13 H14 H15
J1 J2 J3 J13 J14 J15
K1 K2 K3 K13 K14 K15
L1 L2 L3 L13 L14 L15
M1 M2 M3 M13 M14 M15
N1 M2 M3 N4 N5 N6 N7 N8 N9 N10 N11 N12 N13 N14 N15
P1 P2 P3 P4 P5 P6 P7 P8 P9 P10 P11 P12 P13 P14 P15
R1 R2 R3 R4 R5 R6 R7 R8 R9 R10 R11 R12 R13 R14 R15

Pin	*Signal*
A1	No connection
A2	No connection
A3	+5Vdc
A4	Ground
A5	Ground
A6	+5Vdc
A7	Ground
A8	Ground
A9	+5Vdc
A10	Ground
A11	Ground
A12	+5Vdc
A13	Ground
A14	Data parity 1
A15	Data 7

Pin	*Signal*
B1	Data 22
B2	Data 23
B3	Data 21
B4	Data 19
B5	Ground
B6	Data 17
B7	Data parity 2
B8	Ground
B9	Data 14
B10	Data 12
B11	Ground
B12	Data 10
B13	Data 8
B14	+5Vdc
B15	Ground

Pin	*Signal*
C1	Data parity 3
C2	Ground
C3	+5Vdc
C4	Data 20
C5	+5Vdc
C6	Data 18
C7	Data 16
C8	+5Vdc
C9	Data 15
C10	Data 13
C11	+5Vdc
C12	Data 11
C13	Data 9
C14	Data 6
C15	Data 5

Pin	*Signal*
D1	Data 24
D2	Data 25
D3	Data 26
D11	+5Vdc
D12	Ground
D13	Ground

Pin	*Signal*
E1	Data 27
E2	Data 28
E3	Data 29
E11	Data 4
E12	Data 3
E13	+5Vdc

Pin	*Signal*
F1	Data 30
F2	Ground
F3	+5Vdc
F11	Data 2
F12	Data 1
F13	Ground

Pin	*Signal*
G1	Data 31
G2	Ground
G3	+5Vdc
G11	+5Vdc
G12	Ground
G13	Ground

Pin	*Signal*
H1	Ground
H2	Ground
H3	+5Vdc
H11	Data 0
H12	Data parity 0
H13	+5Vdc

Pin	*Signal*
J1	Reset
J2	-Parity check
J3	Clock
J11	No connection
J12	No connection
J13	Ground

Pin	*Signal*
K1	-Back off
K2	No connection
K3	+5Vdc
K11	+5Vdc
K12	Ground
K13	Ground

Pin	*Signal*
L1	Interrupt
L2	-Bus ready
L3	Ground
L4	No connection
L5	No connection
L6	No connection

Pin	*Signal*
M1	-Ready out
M2	Ground
M3	+5Vdc
M4	+5Vdc
M5	Ground
M6	No connection

Pin	*Signal*
N1	-Write/Read
N2	-Three cycle read
N3	-MCS
N4	Address 28
N5	+5Vdc
N6	Address 26
N7	Address 14
N8	+5Vdc
N9	Address 11
N10	Address 8
N11	+5Vdc
N12	Address 5
N13	Address 2
N14	-Byte enable 1
N15	-4167 copro. present

(Continued)

8.68. WEITEK 4167 (COPROCESSOR) PINOUTS (continued)

Pin	Signal
P1	No connection
P2	-Mem/IO
P3	Address 30
P4	Address 27
P5	Ground
P6	Address 25
P7	Address 13
P8	Ground
P9	Address 10
P10	Address 7
P11	Ground
P12	Address 4
P13	-Byte enable 2
P14	-Byte enable 0
P15	No connection

Pin	Signal
R1	-Address status
R2	Address 37
R3	Address 29
R4	No connection
R5	Ground
R6	Address 15
R7	Address 12
R8	Ground
R9	Address 9
R10	Address 6
R11	Ground
R12	Address 3
R13	No connection
R14	No connection
R15	Ground

Source: WEITEK 4167 Floating-Point Coprocessor, pages 4 through 7

8.69. RAM CHIP PINOUTS SUMMARY

4116 (16 KB x 1)

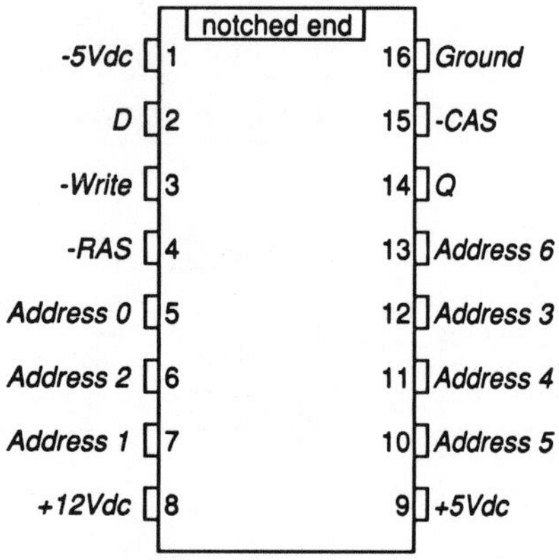
notched end
-5Vdc 1
D 2
-Write 3
-RAS 4
Address 0 5
Address 2 6
Address 1 7
+12Vdc 8
16 Ground
15 -CAS
14 Q
13 Address 6
12 Address 3
11 Address 4
10 Address 5
9 +5Vdc

(256 KB x 1)

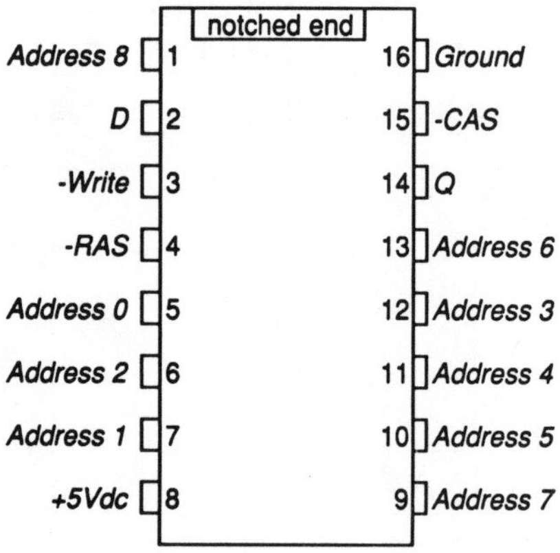
notched end
Address 8 1
D 2
-Write 3
-RAS 4
Address 0 5
Address 2 6
Address 1 7
+5Vdc 8
16 Ground
15 -CAS
14 Q
13 Address 6
12 Address 3
11 Address 4
10 Address 5
9 Address 7

4164 (64 KB x 1)

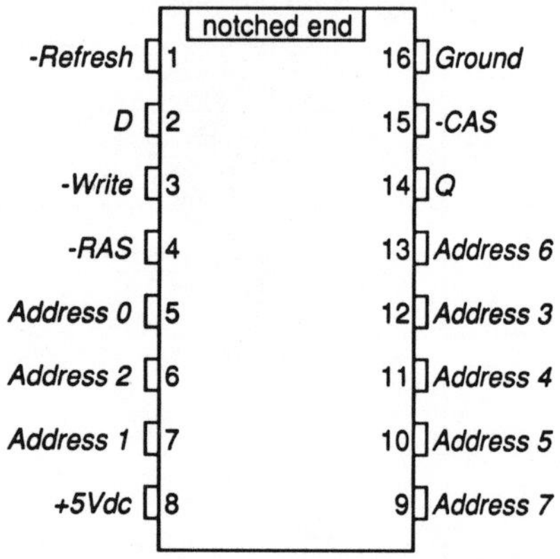
notched end
-Refresh 1
D 2
-Write 3
-RAS 4
Address 0 5
Address 2 6
Address 1 7
+5Vdc 8
16 Ground
15 -CAS
14 Q
13 Address 6
12 Address 3
11 Address 4
10 Address 5
9 Address 7

Source: The IBM PC from the Inside Out (Addison Wesley), page 227

See Also: 7.116. DRAM Chip Families

8.70. 6845 (VIDEO CONTROLLER) PINOUTS

40-Pin DIP Packaging

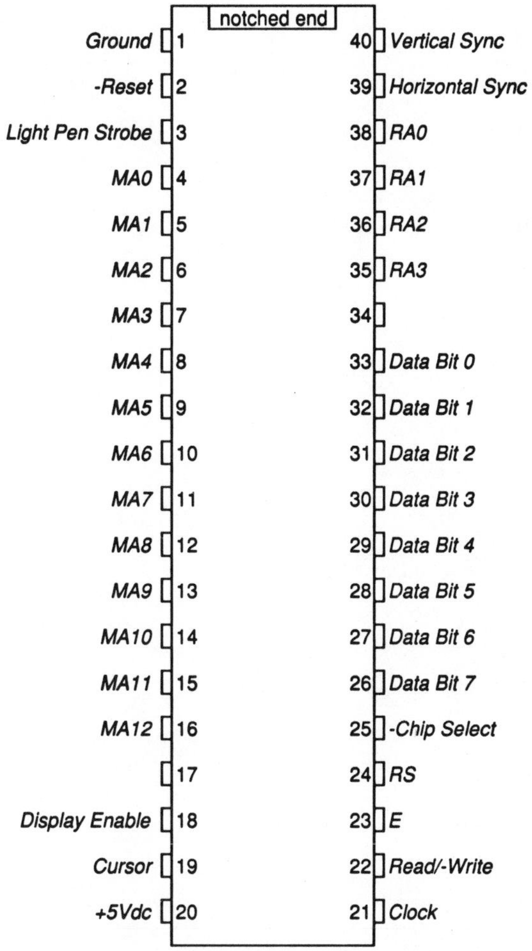
notched end
Ground 1
-Reset 2
Light Pen Strobe 3
MA0 4
MA1 5
MA2 6
MA3 7
MA4 8
MA5 9
MA6 10
MA7 11
MA8 12
MA9 13
MA10 14
MA11 15
MA12 16
17
Display Enable 18
Cursor 19
+5Vdc 20
40 Vertical Sync
39 Horizontal Sync
38 RA0
37 RA1
36 RA2
35 RA3
34
33 Data Bit 0
32 Data Bit 1
31 Data Bit 2
30 Data Bit 3
29 Data Bit 4
28 Data Bit 5
27 Data Bit 6
26 Data Bit 7
25 -Chip Select
24 RS
23 E
22 Read/-Write
21 Clock

Note: Only pins used in IBM monochrome and color adapters are shown.

Source: IBM PC/XT Technical Reference, pages D-27 and D-36

See Also: 7.114. 6845 Registers
7.115. 6845 Port and Select Factors

8.71. 82C284 (CLOCK GENERATOR) PINOUTS

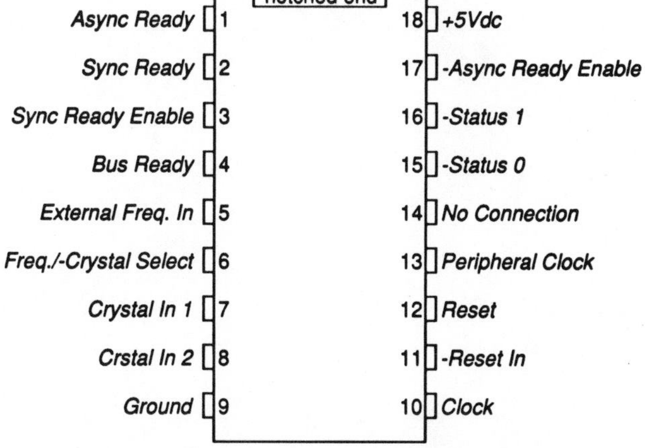
notched end
Async Ready 1
Sync Ready 2
Sync Ready Enable 3
Bus Ready 4
External Freq. In 5
Freq./-Crystal Select 6
Crystal In 1 7
Crstal In 2 8
Ground 9
18 +5Vdc
17 -Async Ready Enable
16 -Status 1
15 -Status 0
14 No Connection
13 Peripheral Clock
12 Reset
11 -Reset In
10 Clock

Source: Intel Microprocessor, Vol. 1, pages 3-169 through 3-172

8.72. 8237 (DMA CONTROLLER) PINOUTS

40-Pin DIP Packaging

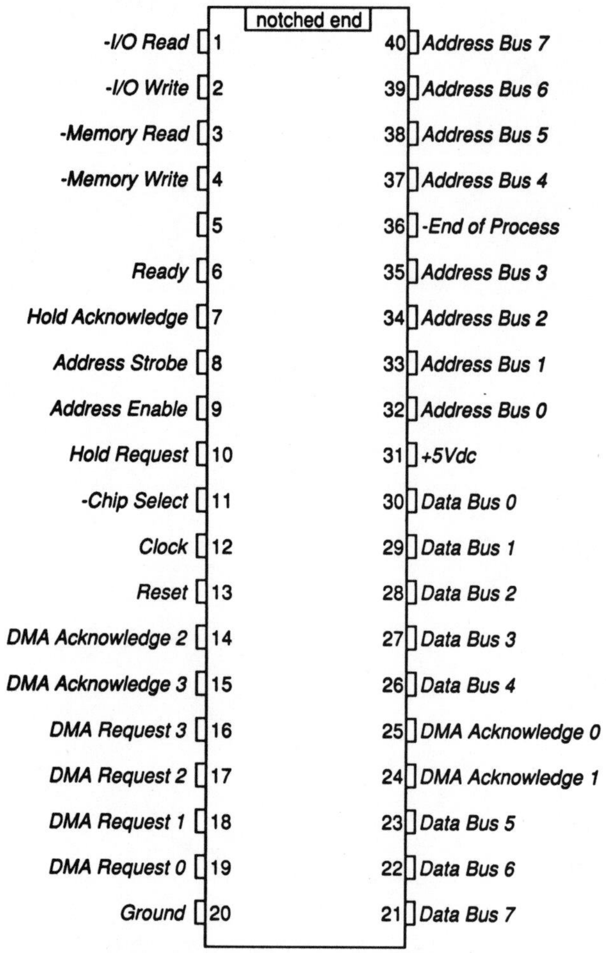
notched end
-I/O Read 1
-I/O Write 2
-Memory Read 3
-Memory Write 4
5
Ready 6
Hold Acknowledge 7
Address Strobe 8
Address Enable 9
Hold Request 10
-Chip Select 11
Clock 12
Reset 13
DMA Acknowledge 2 14
DMA Acknowledge 3 15
DMA Request 3 16
DMA Request 2 17
DMA Request 1 18
DMA Request 0 19
Ground 20
40 Address Bus 7
39 Address Bus 6
38 Address Bus 5
37 Address Bus 4
36 -End of Process
35 Address Bus 3
34 Address Bus 2
33 Address Bus 1
32 Address Bus 0
31 +5Vdc
30 Data Bus 0
29 Data Bus 1
28 Data Bus 2
27 Data Bus 3
26 Data Bus 4
25 DMA Acknowledge 0
24 DMA Acknowledge 1
23 Data Bus 5
22 Data Bus 6
21 Data Bus 7

Note: Available as 8237A (3MHz), 8237A-4 (4MHz), 8237A-5 (5MHz), and CHMOS 82C37A-5 (5MHz).

Source: Intel Peripheral Components, pages 3-33 through 3-36

See Also: 7.067. PS/2 Model 50/60/70/80 DMA I/O Address Map
7.068. PS/2 DMA Registers

8.73. 8250 (SERIAL INTERFACE CONTROLLER) PINOUTS

40-Pin DIP Packaging

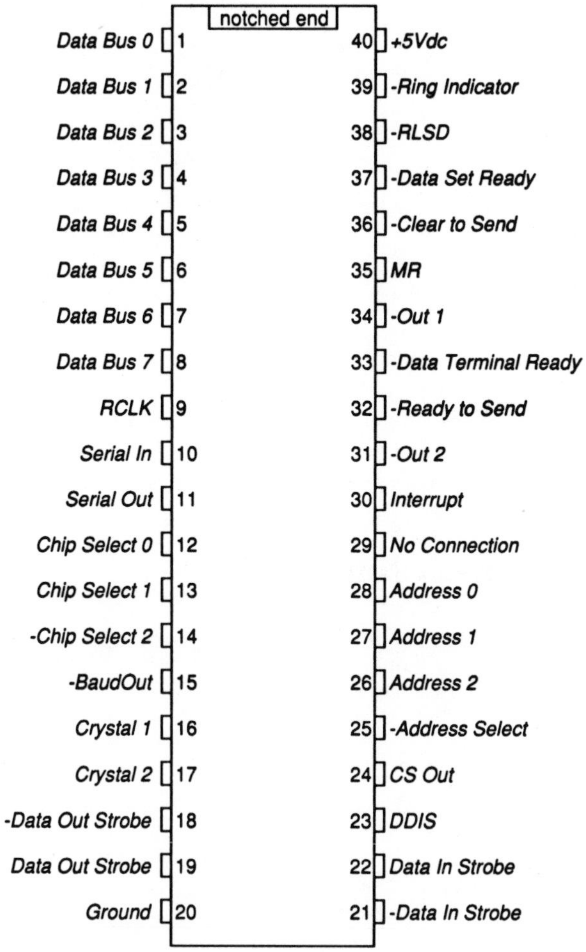
notched end
Data Bus 0 1
Data Bus 1 2
Data Bus 2 3
Data Bus 3 4
Data Bus 4 5
Data Bus 5 6
Data Bus 6 7
Data Bus 7 8
RCLK 9
Serial In 10
Serial Out 11
Chip Select 0 12
Chip Select 1 13
-Chip Select 2 14
-BaudOut 15
Crystal 1 16
Crystal 2 17
-Data Out Strobe 18
Data Out Strobe 19
Ground 20
40 +5Vdc
39 -Ring Indicator
38 -RLSD
37 -Data Set Ready
36 -Clear to Send
35 MR
34 -Out 1
33 -Data Terminal Ready
32 -Ready to Send
31 -Out 2
30 Interrupt
29 No Connection
28 Address 0
27 Address 1
26 Address 2
25 -Address Select
24 CS Out
23 DDIS
22 Data In Strobe
21 -Data In Strobe

Source: The IBM PC from the Inside Out (Addison Wesley), page 365

See Also: 7.110. 8250 I/O Port Usage (Registers)
7.111. 8253 I/O Port Usage (Registers)

8.74. 8253 (PROGRAMMABLE INTERVAL CONTROLLER) PINOUTS

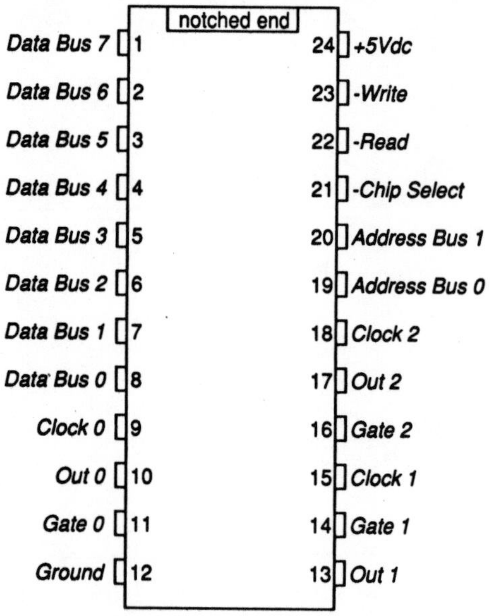
notched end
Data Bus 7 1
Data Bus 6 2
Data Bus 5 3
Data Bus 4 4
Data Bus 3 5
Data Bus 2 6
Data Bus 1 7
Data Bus 0 8
Clock 0 9
Out 0 10
Gate 0 11
Ground 12
24 +5Vdc
23 -Write
22 -Read
21 -Chip Select
20 Address Bus 1
19 Address Bus 0
18 Clock 2
17 Out 2
16 Gate 2
15 Clock 1
14 Gate 1
13 Out 1

Note: Available as 8253, 8253-5, 82C54 (8MHz), 8254-2 (10MHz), and 8254-5 (5Mhz).

Source: Intel Peripheral Components, pages 3-51 and 3-83

8.75. 8255 (PARALLEL INTERFACE CONTROLLER) PINOUTS

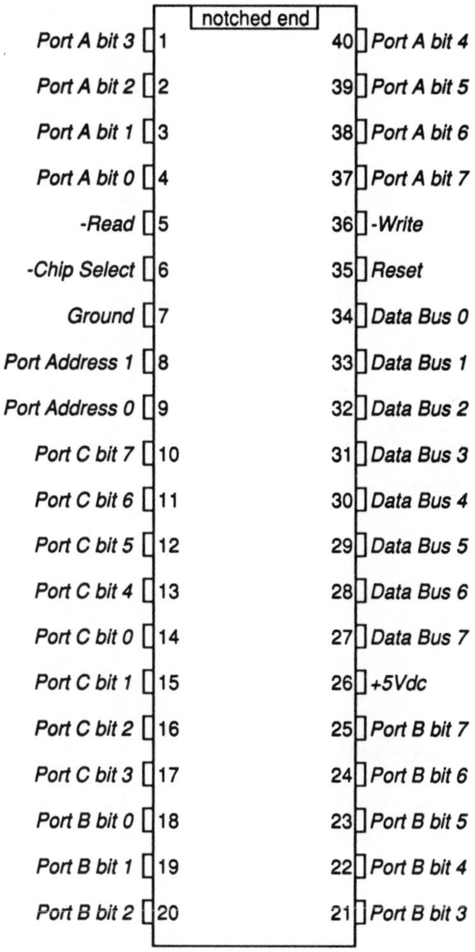
notched end
Port A bit 3 1
Port A bit 2 2
Port A bit 1 3
Port A bit 0 4
-Read 5
-Chip Select 6
Ground 7
Port Address 1 8
Port Address 0 9
Port C bit 7 10
Port C bit 6 11
Port C bit 5 12
Port C bit 4 13
Port C bit 0 14
Port C bit 1 15
Port C bit 2 16
Port C bit 3 17
Port B bit 0 18
Port B bit 1 19
Port B bit 2 20
40 Port A bit 4
39 Port A bit 5
38 Port A bit 6
37 Port A bit 7
36 -Write
35 Reset
34 Data Bus 0
33 Data Bus 1
32 Data Bus 2
31 Data Bus 3
30 Data Bus 4
29 Data Bus 5
28 Data Bus 6
27 Data Bus 7
26 +5Vdc
25 Port B bit 7
24 Port B bit 6
23 Port B bit 5
22 Port B bit 4
21 Port B bit 3

Note: Available as 8255A or CHMOS 82C55A.

Source: Intel Peripheral Components, pages 3-100 and 3-124

See Also: 7.112. 8253 Control Word Byte

8.76. 8259 (PROGRAMMABLE INTERRUPT CONTROLLER) PINOUTS

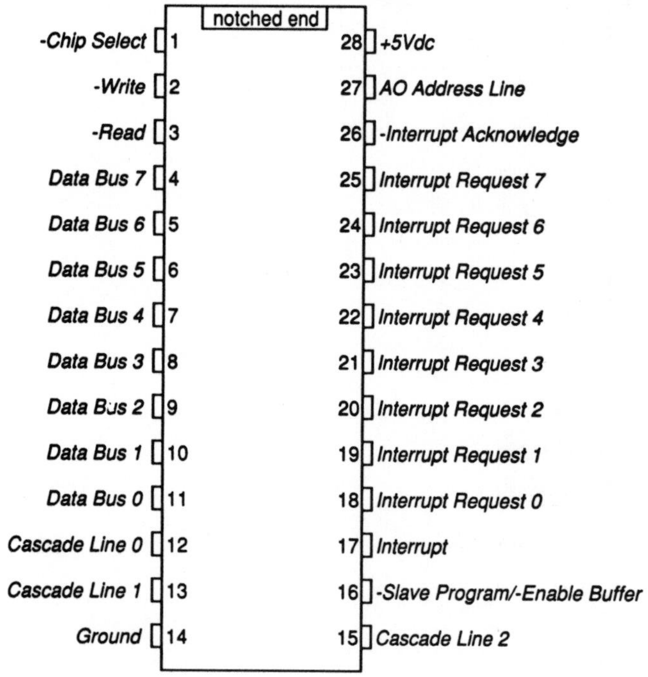
notched end
-Chip Select 1
-Write 2
-Read 3
Data Bus 7 4
Data Bus 6 5
Data Bus 5 6
Data Bus 4 7
Data Bus 3 8
Data Bus 2 9
Data Bus 1 10
Data Bus 0 11
Cascade Line 0 12
Cascade Line 1 13
Ground 14
28 +5Vdc
27 AO Address Line
26 -Interrupt Acknowledge
25 Interrupt Request 7
24 Interrupt Request 6
23 Interrupt Request 5
22 Interrupt Request 4
21 Interrupt Request 3
20 Interrupt Request 2
19 Interrupt Request 1
18 Interrupt Request 0
17 Interrupt
16 -Slave Program/-Enable Buffer
15 Cascade Line 2

Note: Available as 8259A, 8259A-2, and CHMOS 82C59A-2.

Source: Intel Peripheral Components, pages 3-171 through 3-172 and 3-195 through 3-196

See Also: 7.005. PC Interrupt Usage Summary

8.77. 82C288 (BUS CONTROLLER) PINOUTS

20-Pin DIP Packaging

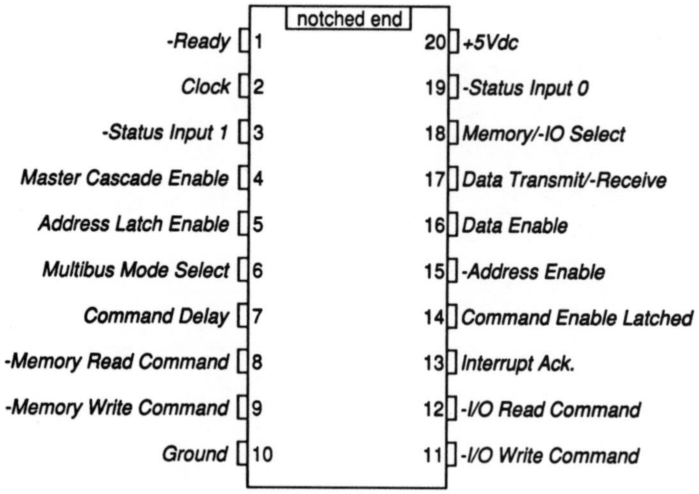
notched end
-Ready 1
Clock 2
-Status Input 1 3
Master Cascade Enable 4
Address Latch Enable 5
Multibus Mode Select 6
Command Delay 7
-Memory Read Command 8
-Memory Write Command 9
Ground 10
20 +5Vdc
19 -Status Input 0
18 Memory/-IO Select
17 Data Transmit/-Receive
16 Data Enable
15 -Address Enable
14 Command Enable Latched
13 Interrupt Ack.
12 -I/O Read Command
11 -I/O Write Command

Note: Available as 8288 and 82C88.

Source: Intel Microprocessors, Vol. 1, pages 3-149 through 3-152

8.78. MC146818 (AT CLOCK CONTROLLER) PINOUTS

24-Pin DIP Packaging

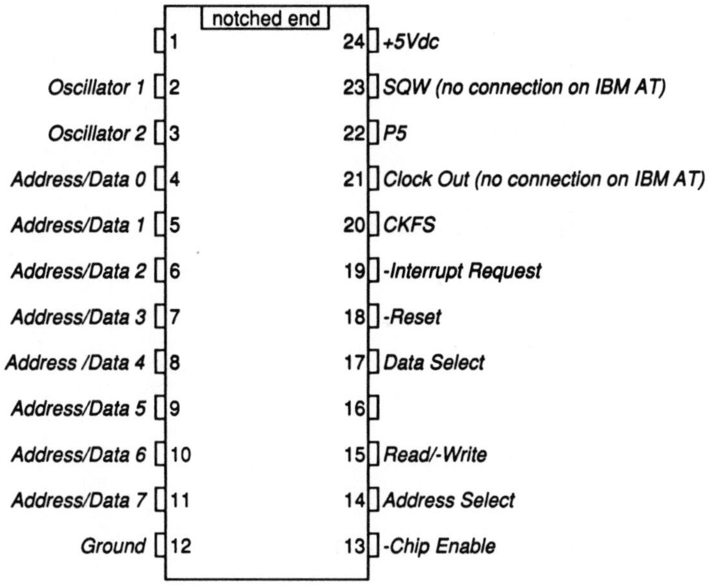
notched end
1
Oscillator 1 2
Oscillator 2 3
Address/Data 0 4
Address/Data 1 5
Address/Data 2 6
Address/Data 3 7
Address /Data 4 8
Address/Data 5 9
Address/Data 6 10
Address/Data 7 11
Ground 12
24 +5Vdc
23 SQW (no connection on IBM AT)
22 P5
21 Clock Out (no connection on IBM AT)
20 CKFS
19 -Interrupt Request
18 -Reset
17 Data Select
16
15 Read/-Write
14 Address Select
13 -Chip Enable

Note: Only pins used in IBM AT are shown.

Source: IBM PC/AT Technical Reference, page 1-93

See Also:
7.094. AT Real Time Clock RAM Configuration Usage
7.095. AT Real Time Clock Status Register A
7.096. AT Real Time Clock Status Register B
7.097. AT Real Time Clock Status Register C
7.098. AT Real Time Clock Status Register D
7.099. AT CMOS RAM Configuration Diagnostic Status Byte
7.100. AT CMOS RAM Configuration Diskette Drive Type Byte
7.101. AT CMOS RAM Configuration Fixed Drive Type Byte
7.102. AT CMOS RAM Configuration Equipment Byte

8.79. PD765 (FLOPPY DISK CONTROLLER) PINOUTS

40-Pin DIP Packaging

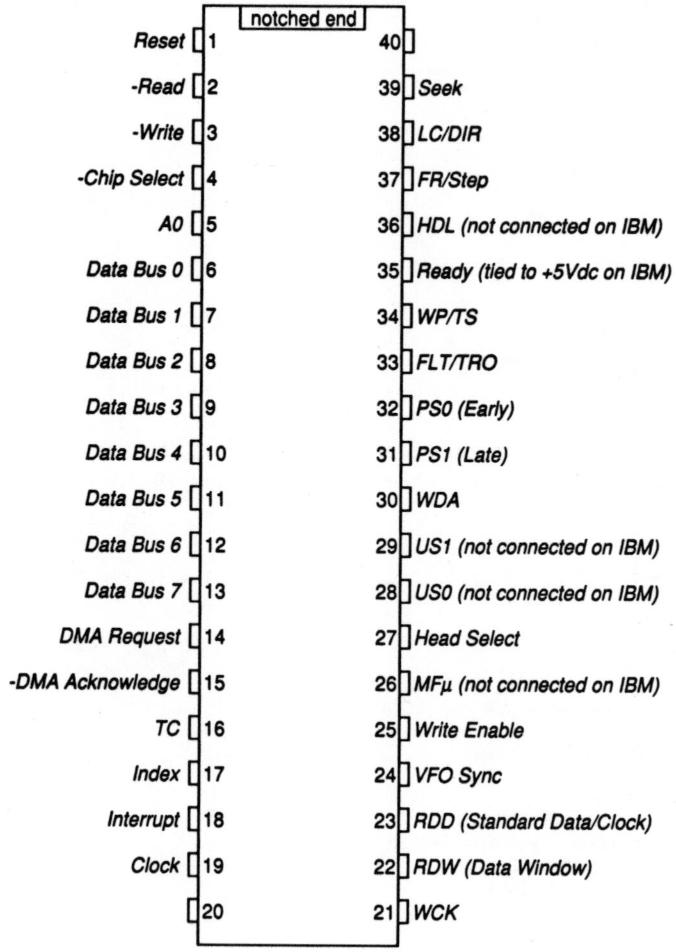
notched end
Reset 1
-Read 2
-Write 3
-Chip Select 4
A0 5
Data Bus 0 6
Data Bus 1 7
Data Bus 2 8
Data Bus 3 9
Data Bus 4 10
Data Bus 5 11
Data Bus 6 12
Data Bus 7 13
DMA Request 14
-DMA Acknowledge 15
TC 16
Index 17
Interrupt 18
Clock 19
20
40
39 Seek
38 LC/DIR
37 FR/Step
36 HDL (not connected on IBM)
35 Ready (tied to +5Vdc on IBM)
34 WP/TS
33 FLT/TRO
32 PS0 (Early)
31 PS1 (Late)
30 WDA
29 US1 (not connected on IBM)
28 US0 (not connected on IBM)
27 Head Select
26 MFμ (not connected on IBM)
25 Write Enable
24 VFO Sync
23 RDD (Standard Data/Clock)
22 RDW (Data Window)
21 WCK

Note: Only pins used in IBM floppy diskette adapters are shown.

Source: IBM PC/XT Technical Reference, pages D-46 through D-47

Appendix A

Select Bibliography

The following listing of works includes the primary or secondary sources of information used during the compilation of the second edition of this book. Where possible, complete bibliographic data has been provided, though for many sources it was difficult to ascertain the correct information from the documents themselves and so not all sources listed below include what is considered by traditional standards complete bibliographic information.

The first edition of *The Programmer's PC Sourcebook* included document or ISBN numbers for the books listed in its Bibliography. Since the first edition was published, however, many more primary and secondary source documents have been produced, both as updates to existing documents and completely new documents. Because document and ISBN numbers were difficult to ascertain for many of these sources, and because the constant change in these numbers by their manufacturers between editions (and sometimes even between printings) makes them of little value to readers to use as identifying factors, they are not included below.

The page numbers given for journal articles indicate either the page on which the article begins (when intervening material forces the reader to continue the article elsewhere in the journal), the range of pages (when no intervening material is present) which constitute the article, or the exact page on which the noteworthy information occurs.

Aldus Corporation and Microsoft Corporation. *Tag Image File Format Draft.* 22 October 1986.

Alford, Roger C. "The Evolution of ESDI." *Byte,* June 1990, 297.

Alford, Roger C. "The IDE Hard Disk Drive Interface." *Byte,* March 1991, 317.

Ansa Software. *Paradox User's Guide Release 2.0.* Belmont, Calif.: Ansa Software, 1987.

Bechtel, Brian. "The Ins and Outs of ISO 9660 and High Sierra." *Develop,* July 1990, 272.

Berger, Harvey. "Dynamic Data Exchange Enhances Application Connectivity." *Microsoft Systems Journal,* October 1986, 7-16.

Boling, Douglas, and Jeff Prosise. "Give Yourself a Smart DOS Command Line with ALIAS." *PC Magazine,* 26 December 1989, 253-268.

Borland International. *Paradox User's Guide Release 3.0.* Scotts Valley, Calif.: Borland International, 1988.

Dettmann, Terry. *DOS Programmer's Reference.* 2nd. ed. Carmel, Ind.: Que Corp., 1989.

Dowden, Tony. *Inside the EISA Computers.* Reading, Mass.: Addison-Wesley Publishing Co., 1990.

Duncan, Ray. *Advanced MS-DOS.* 1st ed. Redmond, Wash.: Microsoft Press, 1986.

Duncan, Ray. *Advanced MS-DOS Programming.* 2nd ed. Redmond, Wash.: Microsoft Press, 1988.

Duncan, Ray. *MS-DOS Extensions.* Redmond, Wash.: Microsoft Press, 1989.

Electronic Industries Association, Engineering Department. *EIA Standard RS-232-C.* August 1969 (Reaffirmed June 1981). Electronic Industries Assoc., 1981.

Glass, L. Brett. "Part 1: The SCSI Bus." *Byte,* February 1990, 267.

Hewlett-Packard Company. *LaserJet III Printer Technical Reference Manual.* 1st ed. (March 1990). Hewlett-Packard Co., 1990.

Hoskins, Jim. *IBM PS/2: A Business Perspective.* Rev. ed. New York: John Wiley & Sons, 1989.

IBM Corporation. *BIOS Interface Technical Reference for PS/1 Computer.* 1st ed. (April 1990). Lexington, Ky.: International Business Machines Corp., 1990.

IBM Corporation. *Disk Operating System 3.30 Technical Reference.* 1st ed. (April 1987). International Business Machines Corp., 1987.

IBM Corporation. *Disk Operating System Version 4.00 Technical Reference.* 1st ed. (July 1988). International Business Machines Corp., 1988.

IBM Corporation. *Getting Started with Disk Operating System Version 4.0.* 1st ed. (July 1988). International Business Machines Corp., 1988.

IBM Corporation. *Guide to Operations: Personal Computer AT Hardware Reference Library*. 1st ed. (March 1984). Boca Raton, Fla.: International Business Machines Corp., 1984.

IBM Corporation. *IBM Personal System/2 Hardware Interface Technical Reference*. (October 1990). International Business Machines Corp., 1990.

IBM Corporation. *IBM Personal System/2 Hardware Interface Technical Reference—System-Specific Information*. (1990). Includes information about PS/2 Models 50, 55, 60, 65, 70, 80, 90, and 95. International Business Machines Corp., 1990.

IBM Corporation. *IBM System/370 Principles of Operation*. Ver. 9 (January 1987). International Business Machines Corp., 1987.

IBM Corporation. *Personal System/2 Display Adapter 8514/A Technical Reference*. 1st ed. (April 1987). International Business Machines Corp., 1987.

IBM Corporation. *Personal System/2 Hardware Interface Technical Reference*. 1st ed. (May 1988). International Business Machines Corp., 1988.

IBM Corporation. *Personal System/2 Model 30 Technical Reference*. 1st ed. (January 1987). International Business Machines Corp., 1987.

IBM Corporation. *Personal System/2 Model 50 and 60 Technical Reference*. 1st ed. (April 1987). International Business Machines Corp., 1987.

IBM Corporation. *Personal System/2 Model 50 Technical Reference*. 3rd ed. (October 1990). International Business Machines Corp., 1990.

IBM Corporation. *Personal System/2 Model 80 Technical Reference*. 1st ed. (April 1987). International Business Machines Corp., 1987.

IBM Corporation. *Personal System/2 and Personal Computer BIOS Interface Technical Reference*. 2nd ed. (May 1988). International Business Machines Corp., 1988.

IBM Corporation. *Personal System/2 XGA Display Adapter/A Technical Reference*. 1st ed. (September 1990). International Business Machines Corp., 1990.

IBM Corporation. *Systems Application Architecture: Common User Access Advanced Interface Design Guide*. 1st ed. (June, 1989). International Business Machines Corp., 1989.

IBM Corporation. *Technical Reference: Options and Adapters*. Vol. 1. Rev. ed. (April 1984). Boca Raton, Fla.: International Business Machines Corp., 1984.

IBM Corporation. *Technical Reference: Options and Adapters*. Vol. 2. Rev. ed. (April 1984). Boca Raton, Fla.: International Business Machines Corp., 1984.

IBM Corporation. *Technical Reference: PC/XT and Portable Personal Computer Hardware Reference Library*. Rev. ed. (March 1986). Boca Raton, Fla: International Business Machines Corp., 1986.

IBM Corporation. *Technical Reference: Personal Computer AT*. 1st ed. (March 1984). Boca Raton, Fla.: International Business Machines Corp., 1984.

IBM Corporation. *Technical Reference: Personal Computer AT Hardware Reference Library*. Rev. ed. (March 1986). Boca Raton, Fla.: International Business Machines Corp., 1986.

IBM Corporation. *Technical Reference: Personal Computer XT*. 1st ed. (January 1983). Boca Raton, Fla.: International Business Machines Corp., 1983.

IBM Corporation. *Technical Reference: Personal Computer XT Hardware Reference Library*. Rev. ed. (March 1986). International Business Machines Corp., 1986.

IBM Corporation. *Technical Reference: Personal Computer XT and Portable Personal Computer*. Rev. ed. (March 1986). Boca Raton, Fla.: International Business Machines Corp., 1986.

IBM Corporation. *Using Disk Operating System Version 4.0*. 1st ed. (July 1988). International Business Machines Corp., 1988.

IBM Corporation. *XGA Video Subsystem Hardware Users Guide*. Preliminary Information (18 September 1990). Hants, England: International Business Machines Corp., 1990.

Intel Corporation. *80386 Programmer's Reference Manual*. Santa Clara, Calif.: Intel Corp., 1986.

Intel Corporation. *i486 Processor Programmer's Reference Manual*. Mt. Prospect, Ill.: Intel Corp., 1990.

Intel Corporation. Instruction booklet accompanying 8087 Math Coprocessor. Intel Corp., 1989.

Intel Corporation. *Microprocessors*. Vol. I. Mt. Prospect, Ill.: Intel Corp., 1991.

Intel Corporation. *Microprocessors*. Vol. II. Mt. Prospect, Ill.: Intel Corp., 1991.

Intel Corporation. *Peripheral Components*. Mt. Prospect, Ill.: Intel Corp., 1991.

International Organization for Standardization. *Information Processing—Volume and File Structure of CD-ROM for Information Interchange*. 1st ed. Irvine, Calif.: Global Engineering Documents, 1988.

Jordan, Larry and Bruce Churchill. *Communications and Networking for the IBM PC and Compatibles.* 3rd ed. New York: Brady Books, 1990.

Lotus Development Corporation, Intel Corporation, and Microsoft Corporation. *Lotus/Intel/Microsoft Expanded Memory Specification*. Ver. 4.0 (August 1987).

Lotus Development Corporation, Intel Corporation, Microsoft Corporation, and AST Research. *eXtended Memory Specification (XMS)*. Ver. 2.0. Redmond, Wash.: Microsoft Corp., 1988.

Microsoft Corporation. *Microsoft Mouse Programmer's Reference*. 1st ed. Redmond, Wash.: Microsoft Press, 1989.

Microsoft Corporation. *Microsoft Mouse Programmer's Reference*. 2nd ed. Redmond, Wash.: Microsoft Press, 1991.

Microsoft Corporation. *Microsoft MS-DOS CD-ROM Extensions Product Overview*. Ver. 2.20 (15 August 1990). Redmond, Wash.: Microsoft Corp., 1990.

Microsoft Corporation. *Microsoft MS-DOS: Getting Started*. Ver. 5.0. Redmond, Wash.: Microsoft Corp., 1991.

Microsoft Corporation. *Microsoft MS-DOS Programmer's Reference*. Ver. 5. Redmond, Wash.: Microsoft Press, 1991.

Microsoft Corporation. *Microsoft MS-DOS Shell User's Guide*. Redmond, Wash.: Microsoft Corp., 1988.

Microsoft Corporation. *Microsoft MS-DOS User's Guide: Operating System Version 3.3*. Redmond, Wash.: Microsoft Corp., 1987.

Microsoft Corporation. *Microsoft MS-DOS User's Guide: Operating System Version 4.0*. Redmond, Wash.: Microsoft Corp., 1988.

Microsoft Corporation. *Microsoft MS-DOS User's Guide and Reference for the MS-DOS Operating System Version 5.0*. Redmond, Wash.: Microsoft Corp., 1991.

Microsoft Corporation. *Microsoft MS-DOS Version 4.0 Programmer's Reference*. Redmond, Wash.: Microsoft Corp., 1988.

Microsoft Corporation. *Microsoft Windows Programmer's Reference*. Ver. 3. Redmond, Wash.: Microsoft Press, 1990.

Microsoft Corporation. *Microsoft Windows Programming Tools*. Ver. 3. Redmond, Wash.: Microsoft Press, 1990.

Microsoft Corporation. *Microsoft Windows Software Development Kit: Guide to Programming*. Ver. 3.0. Redmond, Wash.: Microsoft Corp., 1990.

Microsoft Corporation. *Microsoft Windows Software Development Kit: Reference Volume 1*. Ver. 3.0. Redmond, Wash.: Microsoft Corp., 1990.

Microsoft Corporation. *Microsoft Windows Software Development Kit: Tools*. Ver. 3.0. Redmond, Wash.: Microsoft Corp., 1990.

Microsoft Corporation. *Microsoft Windows User's Guide for the Windows Graphical Environment.* Ver. 3.0. Redmond, Wash.: Microsoft Corp., 1990.

Mueller, Scott. *Upgrading and Repairing PCs*. Carmel, Ind.: Que Corp., 1988.

Nelson, Ross P. *Microsoft's 80386/80486 Programming Guide*. Redmond, Wash.: Microsoft Press, 1991.

Norton, Peter, and Richard Wilton. *The New Peter Norton Programmer's Guide to the IBM PC & PS/2*. 1st ed. Redmond, Wash.: Microsoft Press, 1985.

Norton, Peter, and Richard Wilton. *The New Peter Norton Programmer's Guide to the IBM PC & PS/2*. 2nd ed. Redmond, Wash.: Microsoft Press, 1988.

Phoenix Technologies Ltd. *System BIOS for IBM PC/XT/AT Computers and Compatibles*. Reading, Mass.: Addison-Wesley Publishing Co., 1989.

Prosise, Jeff. "The DOS Partitioning Scheme." *PC Magazine*, 11 September 1990, 447.

Richter, Jake. "Harnessing the 8514/A." *MIPS*, January 1990, 88.

Rosch, Winn L. "IBM PS/2 Models 90 and 95: Upgradable 486 Architecture, XGA Graphics and SCSI Adapter." *PC Magazine*, 15 January 1991, 33.

Rosch, Winn L. "New IBM PS/2s Emphasize SCSI Mass Storage." *PC Magazine*, 29 May 1990, 33.

Rosch, Winn L. *The Winn Rosch Hardware Bible*. New York: Brady Books, 1989.

Ross, Matthew J. "IBM Unveils its 33-MHz 486 Portable." *PC Magazine*, 29 January 1991, 33.

Sanchez, Julio, and Maria P. Canton. *IBM Microcomputers: A Programmer's Handbook.* New York: McGraw-Hill, 1990.

Sargent, Murray III and Richard L. Shoemaker. *The IBM Personal Computer from the Inside Out.* Reading, Mass.: Addison-Wesley Publishing Co., 1984.

Startz, Richard. *8087/80287/80387 for the IBM PC & Compatibles: Applications and Programming with Intel's Math Coprocessors.* 3rd ed. New York: Brady Books, 1988.

Stinson, Craig, and Nancy Andrews. *Running Windows.* 2nd ed. Redmond, Wash.: Microsoft Press, 1990.

Virtual Control Program Interface. Version 1.0 (12 June 1989).

Weitek Corporation. *4167 Floating-point Coprocessor.* Advanced Data (July, 1989). Sunnyvale, Calif.: Weitek Corp., 1989.

Weitek Corporation. *WTL 3167 Floating-point Coprocessor.* (November, 1989). Sunnyvale, Calif.: Weitek Corp., 1989.

Welch, Kevin P. "Interprogram Communications Using Windows' Dynamic Data Exchange." *Microsoft Systems Journal*, November 1987, 13-38.

Woram, John. *PC Configuration Handbook.* 2nd ed. New York: Bantam Books, 1990.

Appendix B

Index

E

F

G

H

I

Q

R

T

The manuscript for this book was prepared and submitted to Microsoft Press in electronic form. Table files were processed and formatted using Microsoft Excel.

Pasteup and layout: Margarite Hargrave
Cover designer: Becky Geisler-Johnson
Cover color separator: Color Service Inc.

Table composition by Online Press in Helvetica and Helvetica Narrow with display type in Helvetica Bold, using Microsoft Excel 2.2. Text composition by Microsoft Press in Times Roman with display type in Times Roman Bold, using PageMaker 4.0. Final camera-ready copy produced by a NewGen laser printer.